Intermediate Accounting

University of Wisconsin Green Bay

Accounting

create.mheducation.com

ISBN-13: 9781265480790

ISBN-10: 1265480796

Contents

iv

About the Authors

DAVID SPICELAND

David Spiceland is Professor Emeritus in the School of Accountancy where he taught financial accounting at the undergraduate, master's, and doctoral levels for 36 years. He received his BS degree in finance from the University of Tennessee, his MBA from Southern Illinois University, and his PhD in accounting from the University of Arkansas.

Professor Spiceland has published articles in a variety of academic and professional journals including *The Accounting Review, Accounting and Business Research, Journal of Financial Research, Advances in Quantitative Analysis of Finance and Accounting,* and most accounting education journals: *Issues in Accounting Education, Journal of Accounting Education, Advances in Accounting Education, The Accounting Educators' Journal, Accounting Education, The Journal of Asynchronous Learning Networks,* and *Journal of Business Education.,* and is an author of McGraw-Hill's *Financial Accounting* with Wayne Thomas and Don Herrmann. Professor Spiceland has received university and college awards and recognition for his teaching, research, and technological innovations in the classroom.

MARK NELSON

Mark Nelson is the Anne and Elmer Lindseth Dean and Professor of Accounting at Cornell University's Samuel Curtis Johnson Graduate School of Management. He received his BBA degree from Iowa State University and his MA and PhD degrees from The Ohio State University. Professor Nelson has won ten teaching awards, including an inaugural Cook Prize from the American Accounting Association.

Professor Nelson's research focuses on decision making in financial accounting and auditing. His research has been published in the *Accounting Review;* the *Journal of Accounting Research; Contemporary Accounting Research; Accounting, Organizations and Society;* and several other journals. He has received the American Accounting Association's Notable Contribution to Accounting Literature Award, as well as the AAA's Wildman Medal for work judged to make a significant contribution to practice.

Professor Nelson served three terms as an area editor of *The Accounting Review* and is a member of the editorial boards of several journals. He also served for four years on the FASB's Financial Accounting Standards Advisory Council.

WAYNE THOMAS

Wayne Thomas is the W.K. Newton Chair and George Lynn Cross Research Professor of Accounting at the University of Oklahoma's Price College of Business. He received his BS degree from Southwestern Oklahoma State University and his MS and PhD from Oklahoma State University. He has received teaching awards at the university, college, and departmental levels, and has received the Outstanding Educator Award from the Oklahoma Society of CPAs. He is an author of McGraw-Hill's *Financial Accounting* with David Spiceland and Don Herrmann.

His research focuses on various financial reporting issues and has been published in *The Accounting Review, Journal of Accounting Research, Journal of Accounting and Economics, Contemporary Accounting Research, Review of Accounting Studies, Accounting Organizations and Society,* and others. He has served as an editor for *The Accounting Review* and has won the American Accounting Association's Competitive Manuscript Award and Outstanding International Accounting Dissertation.

Professor Thomas enjoys various activities such as tennis, basketball, golf, and crossword puzzles, and most of all, he enjoys spending time with his wife and kids.

Intermediate Accounting Tenth Edition:

Welcome to the new standard in intermediate accounting! Instructors recognize the "Spiceland advantage" in content that's intensive and thorough, as well as in writing that's fluid and precise—together, these combine to form a resource that's rigorous yet readable. By blending a comprehensive approach, clear conversational tone, current updates on key standards, and the market-leading technological innovations of Connect®, the Spiceland team delivers an unrivaled experience. As a result of Spiceland's rigorous yet readable learning system, students develop a deeper and more complete understanding of intermediate accounting topics.

> "The textbook is readable and easy to follow since the authors present basic concepts and then cover advanced issues. Conceptually-oriented and dependable as the authors are timely in updating new accounting standards."
>
> **—Hong Pak, California State Polytechnic University, Pomona**

The *Intermediate Accounting* learning system is built around four key attributes: current, comprehensive, clear, and Connect.

Current: Few disciplines see the rapid changes that accounting experiences. The Spiceland team is committed to keeping instructors' courses up to date. The tenth edition fully integrates the latest FASB updates, including:

- ASU No. 2018-02—Income Statement—Reporting Comprehensive Income (Topic 220)—Reclassification of Certain Tax Effects from Accumulated Other Comprehensive Income
- ASU No. 2016–013, Financial Instruments—Credit Losses (Topic 326) on "Current Expected Credit Loss" (CECL) model for accounting for credit losses, as well as current GAAP requirements for recognizing impairments of investments
- Comprehensive revision of Chapter 16, Accounting for Income Taxes, improving pedagogy as well as covering effects of the Tax Cuts and Jobs Act of 2017
- FASB ASC 842-10-15-42A: Leases-Overall-Scope and Scope Exceptions-Lessor
- FASB Accounting Standards Update, Compensation–Retirement Benefits (Topic 715): Improving the Presentation of Net Periodic Pension Cost and Net Periodic Postretirement Benefit Cost, FASB: December, 2016. SEC Amendment to Rule 15c6-1, Ex-Dividend Date, September 2017
- FASB Accounting Standards Update No. 2017-12, Derivatives and Hedging (Topic 815): Targeted Improvements to Accounting for Hedging Activities
- ASU No. 2017-04, Intangibles—Goodwill and Other (Topic 350): Simplifying the Test for Goodwill Impairment
- ASU No. 2015-05—Intangibles—Goodwill and Other—Internal-Use Software (Subtopic 350-40): Customer's Accounting for Fees Paid in a Cloud Computing Arrangement

The Spiceland team also ensures that Intermediate Accounting stays current with the latest pedagogy and digital tools. The authors have incorporated new Data Analytics cases featuring Tableau at the end of each chapter. These cases are auto-gradable in Connect and help students develop in-demand skills in analyzing and interpreting data, and effectively communicating findings.

Data Analytics   connect

The phrase *scientia est potentia* is a Latin aphorism meaning "knowledge is power!" In a business sense, this might be paraphrased as "Information is money!" Better information . . . better business decisions! This is the keystone of data analytics.

Data analytics is the process of examining data sets in order to draw conclusions about the information they contain. Data analytics is widely used in business to enable organizations to make better-informed business decisions. Increasingly, this is accomplished with the aid of specialized data visualization software such as Tableau.

The New Standard

Current events regularly focus public attention on the key role of accounting in providing information useful to financial decision makers. The CPA exam, too, has changed to emphasize the professional skills needed to critically evaluate accounting method alternatives. *Intermediate Accounting* provides a **decision makers' perspective,** highlighting the professional judgment and critical thinking skills required of accountants in today's business environment. New in the 10th edition, many of these cases have been translated to an auto-graded format in Connect.

"The use of real-world examples throughout the text helps bring accounting to life for students. For example, the use of Amazon Prime is excellent, illustrating the complexity of current business with an engaging example."

— Jennifer Winchel, University of Virginia

Comprehensive: The Spiceland team ensures comprehensive coverage and quality throughout the learning system by building content and assets with a unified methodology that meets rigorous standards. Students are challenged through diverse examples and carefully crafted problem sets which promote in-depth understanding and drive development of critical-thinking skills.

The author team is committed to providing a learning experience that fully prepares students for the future by solidifying core comprehension and enabling confident application of key concepts. Students can feel confident that the conceptual underpinnings and practical skills conveyed in the tenth edition will prepare them for a wide range of real world scenarios.

Clear: Reviewers, instructors, and students have all hailed *Intermediate Accounting's* ability to explain both simple and complex topics in language that is coherent and approachable. Difficult topics are structured to provide a solid conceptual foundation and unifying framework that is built upon with thorough coverage of more advanced topics. As examples, see chapters 6 (Revenue Recognition), 15 (Leases) and 16 (Income Taxes). The author team's highly acclaimed conversational writing style establishes a friendly dialogue—establishing the impression of a conversation with students, as opposed to lecturing at them.

This tone remains consistent throughout the learning system, as authors Spiceland, Nelson, and Thomas write not only the primary content, but also every major supplement: instructor's resource manual, solutions manual, and test bank. All end-of-chapter material, too, is written by the author team and tested in their classrooms. *Intermediate Accounting* is written to be the most complete, coherent, and student-oriented resource on the market.

Connect: Today's accounting students expect to learn in multiple modalities. As a result, the tenth edition of Spiceland's learning system features the following: Connect, SmartBook's adaptive learning and reading experience, **NEW** Concept Overview Videos, Guided Examples, **NEW** Excel® simulations, and General Ledger problems.

Quality assessment continues to be a focus of Connect, with over **2,500 questions** available for assignment, including more than 1,125 algorithmic questions.

McGraw-Hill Education is continually updating and improving our digital resources. To that end, our partnership with Roger CPA, provides multiple choice practice questions directly within our Connect banks, as well as assignable links to the Roger CPA site for complementary access to selected simulations.

Spiceland's Financial Accounting Series

Intermediate Accounting forms a complete learning system when paired with *Financial Accounting* by authors David Spiceland, Wayne Thomas, and Don Herrmann. Now in its fifth edition, *Financial Accounting* uses the same proven approach that has made *Intermediate Accounting* a success—a conversational writing style with real-world focus and author-prepared supplements, combined with Connect's market leading technology solutions and assessment.

What Keeps SPICELAND Users Coming Back?

Financial Reporting Cases

Each chapter opens with a Financial Reporting Case that places the student in the role of the decision maker, engaging the student in an interesting situation related to the accounting issues to come. Then, the cases pose questions for the student in the role of decision maker. Marginal notations throughout the chapter point out locations where each question is addressed. The case questions are answered at the end of the chapter.

Financial Reporting Case Solution

©goodluz/123RF

1. **What purpose do adjusting entries serve?** (p. 64)   Adjusting entries help ensure that all revenues are recognized in the period goods or services are transferred to customers, regardless of when cash is received. In this instance, for example, $13,000 cash has been received for services that haven't yet been performed. Also, adjusting entries enable a company to recognize all expenses incurred during a period, regardless of when cash is paid. Without depreciation, the friends' cost of using the equipment is not taken into account. Conversely, without adjustment, the cost of rent is overstated by $3,000 paid in advance for part of next year's rent.

With adjustments, we get an accrual income statement that provides a more complete measure of a company's operating performance and a better measure for predicting future operating cash flows. Similarly, the balance sheet provides a more...

Where We're Headed

These boxes describe the potential financial reporting effects of many of the FASB's proposed projects that have not yet been adopted, as well as joint proposed projects with the IASB. Where We're Headed boxes allow instructors to deal with ongoing projects to the extent they desire.

Where We're Headed

As part of its ongoing disclosure framework project, the FASB has proposed using the U.S. Supreme Court's description of materiality. Under that definition, which comes from court cases and interpretations, qualitative and quantitative disclosures are material if there is a substantial likelihood that omitting a disclosure would have been viewed by a reasonable user as having significantly altered the total mix of information made available in making a decision. This change is controversial because it could affect the amount of information that companies disclose. The FASB has committed to seek more input before moving forward with this proposal.

Additional Consideration Boxes

These are "on the spot" considerations of important, but incidental or infrequent, aspects of the primary topics to which they relate.

Additional Consideration

Solving for the unknown factor in either of these examples could just as easily be done using the future value tables. The number of years is the value of n that will provide a present value of $10,000 when $16,000 is the future amount and the interest rate is 10%.

$16,000 (future value) = $10,000 (present value) × ?*

*Future value of $1: $n = ?, i = 10\%$

Rearranging algebraically, the future value table factor is 1.6.

$16,000 (future value) ÷ $10,000 (present value) = 1.6*

*Future value of $1: $n = ?, i = 10\%$

When you consult the future value table, Table 1, you search the 10% column ($i = 10\%$) for this value and find 1.61051 in row five. So it would take approximately five years to accumulate $16,000 in the situation described.

Decision Makers' Perspective

These sections appear throughout the text to illustrate how accounting information is put to work in today's firms. With the CPA exam placing greater focus on application of skills in realistic work settings, these discussions help your students gain an edge that will remain with them as they enter the workplace.

Decision Makers' Perspective

Cash often is called a *nonearning* asset because it earns little or no interest. For this reason, managers invest idle cash in either cash equivalents or short-term investments, both of which provide a larger return than a checking account. Management's goal is to hold the minimum amount of cash necessary to conduct normal business operations, meet its obligations, and take advantage of opportunities. Too much cash reduces profits through lost returns, while too little cash increases risk. This trade-off between risk and return is an ongoing choice made by management (internal decision makers). Whether the choice made is appropriate is an ongoing assessment made by investors and creditors (external decision makers).

A company must have cash available for the compensating balances we discussed in the previous section as well as for planned disbursements related to normal operating, investing, and financing cash flows. However, because cash inflow and outflow can vary...

Companies hold cash to pay for planned and unplanned transactions

In talking with so many intermediate accounting faculty, we heard more than how to improve the book—there was much, much more that both users and nonusers insisted we not change. Here are some of the features that have made Spiceland such a phenomenal success.

> "Our students need to think about topics critically and broadly. Spiceland is superior in terms of presenting big picture cases and scenarios that help students understand how to think beyond simple journal entries and worksheet problems."
>
> **—James Brushwood, Colorado State University**

Decision Makers' Perspective

Apply your critical-thinking ability to the knowledge you've gained. These cases will provide you an opportunity to develop your research, analysis, judgment, and communication skills. You also will work with other students, integrate what you've learned, apply it in real-world situations, and consider its global and ethical ramifications. This practice will broaden your knowledge and further develop your decision-making abilities.

©ImageGap/Getty Images

Judgment Case 4–1
Earnings quality
● LO4–2, LO4–3

The financial community in the United States has become increasingly concerned with the quality of reported company earnings.

Required:
1. Define the term *earnings quality*.
2. Explain the distinction...

Decision Makers' Perspective Cases

Designed to further develop students' decision-making abilities, each chapter includes a robust set of powerful and effective cases, asking students to analyze, evaluate, and communicate findings, further building their critical thinking skills. Many of these cases are now auto-gradable in Connect.

Ethical Dilemma

You recently have been employed by a large retail chain that sells sporting goods. One of your tasks is to help prepare periodic financial statements for external distribution. The chain's largest creditor, National Savings & Loan, requires quarterly financial statements, and you are currently working on the statements for the three-month period ending June 30, 2021.

During the months of May and June, the company spent $1,200,000 on a hefty radio and TV advertising campaign. The $1,200,000 included the costs of producing the commercials as well as the radio and TV time purchased to air the commercials. All of the costs were charged to advertising expense. The company's chief financial officer (CFO) has asked you to prepare a June 30 adjusting entry to remove the costs from advertising expense and to set up an asset called *prepaid advertising* that will be expensed in July. The CFO explained that "This advertising campaign has led to significant sales in May and June and I think it

Ethical Dilemmas

Because ethical ramifications of business decisions impact so many individuals as well as the core of our economy, Ethical Dilemmas are incorporated within the context of accounting issues as they are discussed. These features lend themselves very well to impromptu class discussions and debates, and are complemented by Ethics Cases found in the Decision Makers' Perspective Case section at the end of each chapter.

Star Problems

P 15–25
Operating lease; uneven lease payments
● LO15–4, LO15–7

On January 1, 2021, Harlon Consulting entered into a three-year lease for new office space agreeing to lease payments of $5,000 in 2021, $6,000 in 2022, and $7,000 in 2023. Payments are due on December 31 of each year with the first payment being made on December 31, 2021. Harlon is aware that the lessor used a 5% interest rate when calculating lease payments.

Required:
1. Prepare the appropriate entries for Harlon Consulting on January 1, 2021, to record the lease.
2. Prepare all appropriate entries for Harlon Consulting on December 31, 2021, related to the lease.
3. Prepare all appropriate entries for Harlon Consulting on December 31, 2022, related to the lease.
4. Prepare all appropriate entries for Harlon Consulting on December 31, 2023, related to the lease.

In each chapter, particularly rigorous problems, designated by a ★, require students to combine multiple concepts or require significant use of judgment.

Students—study more efficiently, retain more and achieve better outcomes. Instructors—focus on what you love—teaching.

SUCCESSFUL SEMESTERS INCLUDE CONNECT

FOR INSTRUCTORS

You're in the driver's seat.

Want to build your own course? No problem. Prefer to use our turnkey, prebuilt course? Easy. Want to make changes throughout the semester? Sure. And you'll save time with Connect's auto-grading too.

65%
Less Time Grading

They'll thank you for it.

Adaptive study resources like SmartBook® help your students be better prepared in less time. You can transform your class time from dull definitions to dynamic debates. Hear from your peers about the benefits of Connect at **www.mheducation.com/highered/connect**

Make it simple, make it affordable.

Connect makes it easy with seamless integration using any of the major Learning Management Systems—Blackboard®, Canvas, and D2L, among others—to let you organize your course in one convenient location. Give your students access to digital materials at a discount with our inclusive access program. Ask your McGraw-Hill representative for more information.

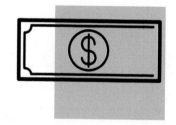

©Hill Street Studios/Tobin Rogers/Blend Images LLC

Solutions for your challenges.

A product isn't a solution. Real solutions are affordable, reliable, and come with training and ongoing support when you need it and how you want it. Our Customer Experience Group can also help you troubleshoot tech problems—although Connect's 99% uptime means you might not need to call them. See for yourself at **status.mheducation.com**

FOR STUDENTS

Effective, efficient studying.

Connect helps you be more productive with your study time and get better grades using tools like SmartBook, which highlights key concepts and creates a personalized study plan. Connect sets you up for success, so you walk into class with confidence and walk out with better grades.

©Shutterstock/wavebreakmedia

> " I really liked this app—it made it easy to study when you don't have your textbook in front of you. "
>
> - Jordan Cunningham, Eastern Washington University

Study anytime, anywhere.

Download the free ReadAnywhere app and access your online eBook when it's convenient, even if you're offline. And since the app automatically syncs with your eBook in Connect, all of your notes are available every time you open it. Find out more at **www.mheducation.com/readanywhere**

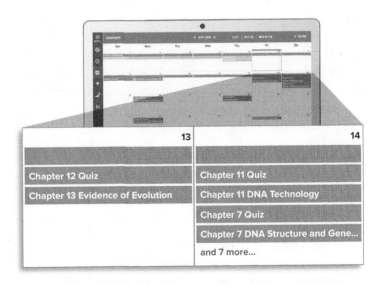

No surprises.

The Connect Calendar and Reports tools keep you on track with the work you need to get done and your assignment scores. Life gets busy; Connect tools help you keep learning through it all.

13	14
Chapter 12 Quiz	Chapter 11 Quiz
Chapter 13 Evidence of Evolution	Chapter 11 DNA Technology
	Chapter 7 Quiz
	Chapter 7 DNA Structure and Gene...
	and 7 more...

Learning for everyone.

McGraw-Hill works directly with Accessibility Services Departments and faculty to meet the learning needs of all students. Please contact your Accessibility Services office and ask them to email accessibility@mheducation.com, or visit **www.mheducation.com/accessibility** for more information.

THE NEW STANDARD:

Online Assignments

Connect helps students learn more efficiently by providing feedback and practice material when they need it, where they need it. Connect grades homework automatically and gives immediate feedback on any questions students may have missed. The extensive assignable, gradable end-of-chapter content includes a general journal application that looks and feels like what one would find in a general ledger software package. For this edition, numerous questions have been redesigned to test students' knowledge more fully. New to this edition, many Decision Makers' Perspective Cases have been incorporated as auto-gradable in Connect.

End-of-chapter questions in Connect include:
- Brief Exercises
- Exercises
- Problems
- New! Select Decision Makers' Perspective Cases, Target and Air France Cases, and Data Analytics Cases

> "The digital materials are an important learning resource for my students, and the constant updates between new editions are VERY useful."
>
> **—Pamela Trafford, University of Massachusetts, Amherst**

NEW! Data Analytics Cases

Data analytics is an enormously in-demand skill among employers. Students who can interpret data and effectively communicate their findings to help business makes better-informed decisions are in high-demand. New Data Analysis Cases featuring Tableau are now incorporated at the end of most chapters. These cases can easily be assigned in Connect and are auto-gradable for the instructor's convenience.

General Ledger Problems

General Ledger Problems allow students to see how transactions flow through the various financial statements. Students can audit their mistakes by easily linking back to their original journal entries. Many General Ledger Problems include an analysis tab that allows students to demonstrate their critical thinking skills and a deeper understanding of accounting concepts.

POWERFUL ONLINE TOOLS & ASSESSMENTS

Concept Overview Videos

Concept Overview Videos provide engaging narratives of key topics in an assignable and interactive online format. These videos follow the structure of the text and are available with all learning objectives within each chapter of *Intermediate Accounting*. The Concept Overview Videos provide additional explanation of material in the text, allowing students to learn at their own pace — and test their knowledge with assignable questions.

Excel Simulations

Simulated Excel Questions, assignable within Connect, allow students to practice their Excel skills—such as basic formulas and formatting—within the content of financial accounting. These questions feature animated, narrated Help and Show Me tutorials (when enabled), as well as automatic feedback and grading for both students and professors.

Guided Example/Hint Videos

The **Guided Examples** in Connect provide a narrated, animated, step-by-step walk-through of select exercises similar to those assigned, These short videos are presented to students as hints and provide reinforcement when students need it most. Instructors have the option of turning them on or off.

CPA SIMULATIONS

McGraw-Hill Education has partnered with Roger CPA Review, a global leader in CPA Exam preparation, to provide students a smooth transition from the accounting classroom to successful completion of the CPA Exam. While many aspiring accountants wait until they have completed their academic studies to begin preparing for the CPA Exam, research shows that those who become familiar with exam content earlier in the process have a stronger chance of successfully passing the CPA Exam. Accordingly, students using these McGraw-Hill materials will have access to sample CPA Exam Multiple-Choice questions and Task-based Simulations from Roger CPA Review, with expert-written explanations and solutions. All questions are either directly from the AICPA or are modeled on AICPA questions that appear in the exam. Task-based Simulations are delivered via the Roger CPA Review platform, which mirrors the look, feel and functionality of the actual exam. McGraw-Hill Education and Roger CPA Review are dedicated to supporting every accounting student along their journey, ultimately helping them achieve career success in the accounting profession. For more information about the full Roger CPA Review program, exam requirements and exam content, visit www.rogercpareview.com.

ALEKS®

ALEKS ACCOUNTING CYCLE

ALEKS Accounting Cycle is a web-based program that provides targeted coverage of prerequisite and introductory material necessary for student success in Intermediate Accounting. ALEKS uses artificial intelligence and adaptive questioning to assess precisely a student's preparedness and deliver personalized instruction on the exact topics the student is **most ready to learn.** Through comprehensive explanations, practice, and immediate feedback, ALEKS enables students to quickly fill individual knowledge gaps in order to build a strong foundation of critical accounting skills. Better prepared students save you valuable time at the beginning of your course!

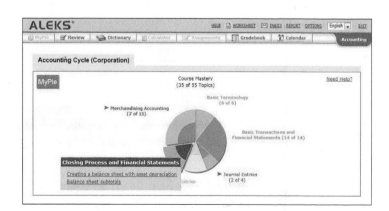

Use ALEKS Accounting Cycle as a pre-course assignment or during the first weeks of the term to see improved student confidence and performance, as well as fewer drops.

ALEKS Accounting Cycle Features:

- **Artificial Intelligence:** Targets Gaps in Prerequisite Knowledge
- **Individualized Learning and Assessment:** Ensure Student Preparedness
- **Open-Response Environment:** Avoids Multiple-Choice and Ensures Mastery
- **Dynamic, Automated Reports:** Easily Identify Struggling Students

For more information, please visit: www.aleks.com/highered/business.

Read ALEKS Success Stories: www.aleks.com/highered/business/success_stories.

The New Standard:

INSTRUCTOR LIBRARY

The Connect Instructor Library is a repository of additional resources to improve student engagement in and out of class. You can select and use any asset that enhances your lecture. The Connect Instructor Library includes:

In-Class Presentation Tools

PowerPoints   Three types of PowerPoint decks are available, each responding to a different instructional need:

- **Lecture PowerPoints with Concept Checks** allow instructors to intersperse short exercises that students can solve individually or do in groups before an answer is "revealed"

- **Lecture PowerPoints without Concept Checks**: No questions included, mirror presentation from book with key illustrations and notes

- **Accessible PowerPoints**: Allow slide content to be read by a screen reader and provide alternative text descriptions for any image files. Accessible PowerPoints are also designed with high-contrast color palettes and use texture instead of color whenever possible to denote different aspects of imagery.

Please note: All of our illustrations in the PowerPoint decks are fully editable so that you can change numbers, content, and easily customize our figures to your teaching. Teaching Tip: Use your students' names for company names in the Illustrations or Concept Checks!

Exercise Presentations   PowerPoint slides created from the Guided Example/Hint videos, these allow you to walk through a version of one of the book exercises in class without giving away the answers.

Digital Image Library   High-resolution images of all illustrations from the text.

Teaching Resources

New! Instructor's Edition   We know Intermediate Accounting is a daunting course not only for students, but also for instructors! This all-new digital guide to the Spiceland Intermediate learning program contains resources to help instructors think through effective course planning, including:

- Example syllabi

- Guides to Connect setup

- Course planning materials to help identify resources that align with your course goals

- Tips from the authors on key illustrations, teaching points, and end-of-chapter content they highlight and assign

- Bloom's rubrics for end-of-chapter content

Instructor's Manual   Specific to each chapter, contains learning outcomes, a full lecture outline, and suggestions for in-class activities including real world scenarios, group research activities, IFRS activities, and professional skills development activities. Assignment charts are also provided with topics and estimated completion times.

Solutions Manual   Created by the authors, includes solutions to end-of-chapter content.

Updates   Stop here for all the most recent updates from FASB. Our authors work tirelessly to keep you current — for instance, within a month of the 2017 Tax Reform bill, our authors had posted an updated PowerPoint deck, video walkthrough, and teaching tip material on how to address the new updates. We have your back!

Test Bank

Connect Test Bank   Multiple-choice, true/false and worksheet questions are all available to help assess students throughout all levels from understanding to evaluation. Create an effective test in 3 easy steps:

Flexible Instructor Resources

1. Tailor: Use Connect's robust filters to quickly identify the content you want based on difficulty, learning objective, Bloom's, AICPA and AACSB standards, and accessibility level.

2. Secure: Once you've identified the questions you want, Connect's policy setting help you create a secure test through features like question pooling, time limits, scrambling, feedback constraint, and Tegrity proctoring.

3. Report: Connect's rich reporting features allow you to quickly compile thorough reports that will wow your assessment committees. Teaching tip: Add your department learning objectives as tags in Connect for reporting completely aligned with your institution's objectives.

TestGen
TestGen is a complete, state-of-the-art test generator and editing application software that allows instructors to quickly and easily select test items from McGraw Hill's TestGen testbank content and to organize, edit and customize the questions and answers to rapidly generate paper tests. Questions can include stylized text, symbols, graphics, and equations that are inserted directly into questions using built-in mathematical templates. TestGen's random generator provides the option to display different text or calculated number values each time questions are used. With both quick-and-simple test creation and flexible and robust editing tools, TestGen is a test generator system for today's educators.

MCGRAW-HILL EDUCATION CUSTOMER EXPERIENCE GROUP CONTACT INFORMATION

At McGraw-Hill Education, we understand that getting the most from new technology can be challenging. That's why our services don't stop after you purchase our products. You can contact our Product Specialists 24 hours a day to get product training online. Or you can search the knowledge bank of Frequently Asked Questions on our support website. For Customer Support, call **800-331-5094,** or visit www.mhhe.com/support. One of our Technical Support Analysts will be able to assist you in a timely fashion.

ASSURANCE OF LEARNING

Many educational institutions today are focused on the notion of *assurance of learning,* an important element of some accreditation standards. *Intermediate Accounting* is designed specifically to support your assurance of learning initiatives with a simple, yet powerful solution.

Each test bank question for *Intermediate Accounting* maps to a specific chapter learning objective listed in the text. You can use Connect to easily query for learning outcomes/objectives that directly relate to the learning objectives for your course. You can then use the reporting features of Connect to aggregate student results in a similar fashion, making the collection and presentation of assurance of learning data simple and easy.

AACSB STATEMENT

McGraw-Hill Education is a proud corporate member of AACSB International. Understanding the importance and value of AACSB accreditation, *Intermediate Accounting* recognizes the curricula guidelines detailed in the AACSB standards for business accreditation by connecting selected questions in the test bank to the eight general knowledge and skill guidelines in the AACSB standards.

The statements contained in *Intermediate Accounting* are provided only as a guide for the users of this textbook. The AACSB leaves content coverage and assessment within the purview of individual schools, the mission of the school, and the faculty. While *Intermediate Accounting* and the teaching package make no claim of any specific AACSB qualification or evaluation, within the Test Bank to accompany *Intermediate Accounting* we have labeled selected questions according to the eight general knowledge and skill areas.

What's New in the Tenth Edition?

Spiceland is the new global standard for providing students the most accessible, comprehensive, and current Intermediate Accounting learning system. We take seriously the confidence the marketplace has accorded our text. Each revision carefully considers how the print and digital content work together to coordinate improvements in content and industry-leading technology to provide the most robust learning solution. The Spiceland team implements only those changes that constitute real improvements as identified through extensive research with users. The result is a learning system that enhances our reputation for providing the best preparation for passing the CPA exam and successful accounting careers.

Improvements in this edition include the following:

- **NEW! Updated content to reflect the latest GAAP and Accounting Standards Updates including:**
  - **Income taxes**
  - **Leases**
  - **Financial instruments**
  - **Revenue recognition**
- **NEW!** Most **Decision Makers' Perspective cases** are now *auto-gradable in Connect.*
- **NEW! Data Analytics Cases** providing students the opportunity to experience the power and efficacy of data analytics in the context of each chapter's topics, using Tableau as a tool, that are *auto-gradable in Connect.*
- Enhanced partnership with **Roger CPA Review,** with new CPA Exam Review multiple-choice questions that are *auto-gradable in Connect* and access to CPA Exam Review simulations.
- Updated and revised **real-world** illustrations, assignments, and discussions.
- Revised Continuing Cases featuring **Target Corporation** financial statements prepared using U.S. GAAP, now *auto-gradable in Connect.* A comprehensive version of the case is available in Appendix B.
- Revised Continuing Cases featuring **Air France–KLM** financial statements prepared using IFRS, now *auto-gradable in Connect.* A comprehensive version of the case is available in Appendix C.
- Incorporated the latest technology, including:
  - **NEW! Connect interface for students,** along with **Connect Insight for students**
  - an updated **SmartBook**
  - **General Ledger Problems** that auto-post from journal entries to T-accounts to trial balances (*auto-gradable in Connect*)
  - **Excel Simulations** that allow students to practice their Excel skills within the content of financial accounting with animated, narrated Help and Show Me tutorials (*auto-gradable in Connect*)
  - **NEW! Concept Overview Videos** that provide engaging narratives of key topics in an assignable and interactive online format (*assignable in Connect*)
  - **Guided Examples/Hint Videos** in Connect that provide a narrated, animated, step-by-step walk-through of select exercises that provide reinforcement when students need it most (can be turned on or off by instructors)
  - **NEW! Instructor's Edition** to help instructors to more easily design the course and organize chapter resources

Chapter 1

ENVIRONMENT AND THEORETICAL STRUCTURE OF FINANCIAL ACCOUNTING

- Provided more focused discussion of the convergence process.
- Revised discussion of FASB standard setting and ongoing projects (disclosure framework, materiality).
- Added or updated problems and cases relevant to The Gap.

Chapter 2

REVIEW OF THE ACCOUNTING PROCESS

- Revised and reorganized the presentation of the accounting processing cycle.
- Added the use of a Dividends account.
- Eliminated the use of Income Summary in the Closing Process.
- Added a Data Analytics case based on topics in the chapter, using Tableau as a tool (auto-gradable in Connect).

Chapter 3

THE BALANCE SHEET AND FINANCIAL DISCLOSURES

- Changed opening balance sheet to Nike.
- Clarified distinction between book value, market value, and fair value.
- Updated terminology in chapter and end-of-chapter material to reflect ASU 2016-01 for investments.
- Updated definition of long-term liability to include FASB's proposed definition.

- Discussed and provided an example of the new format for the auditor's report.
- Revised discussion of executive compensation to reflect the more prominent role of restricted stock compared to stock options.
- Added a Data Analytics case based on topics in the chapter, using Tableau as a tool (auto-gradable in Connect).

Chapter 4

THE INCOME STATEMENT, COMPREHENSIVE INCOME, AND THE STATEMENT OF CASH FLOWS

- Updated all illustrations and end-of-chapter assignments involving income taxes to a new overall rate of 25%.
- Revised definition and discussion of other comprehensive income.
- Added a Data Analytics case based on topics in the chapter, using Tableau as a tool (auto-gradable in Connect).

Chapter 5

TIME VALUE OF MONEY CONCEPTS

- Revised the Financial Reporting Case
- Added **LO5–5** Explain the role of present value techniques in the valuation of notes in the Preview of Accounting Applications of Present Value Techniques—Single Cash Amount section.
- Eliminated the Expected Cash Flow section in the Preview of Accounting Applications of Present Value Techniques—Single Cash Amount section.
- Added a Valuation of Long Term Notes section in the Preview of Accounting Applications of Present Value Techniques—Single Cash Amount section.
- Added a Valuation of Long Term Notes section in the Preview of Accounting Applications of Present Value Techniques—Annuities section

Chapter 6

REVENUE RECOGNITION

- Reordered chapters 5 and 6 to have time value of money (now 5) precede coverage of revenue recognition (now 6) and have revenue recognition immediately precede coverage of receivables (7).
- Expanded coverage of time value of money considerations, including numerical examples of significant financing components for prepayments and receivables, along with new end of chapter material in brief exercises and exercises.
- Added Microsoft real-world example to illustrate materiality of new treatment of licenses.

- Added new Trueblood cases.
- Added or updated problems and cases relevant to Expedia, Priceline, and Alphabet.
- Added a Data Analytics case based on topics in the chapter, using Tableau as a tool (auto-gradable in Connect).

Chapter 7

CASH AND RECEIVABLES

- In chapter, as well as Appendix 7B, enhanced coverage of ASU 2016–13's CECL model for accounting for credit losses.
- Modified coverage of IFRS to focus on IFRS No. 9.
- Enhanced end of chapter material with respect to credit losses and accounts receivable.
- Revised coverage on noninterest-bearing notes receivable.
- Added or updated problems and cases relevant to General Mills, Microsoft, Amdahl, Nike, Avon Products, Cisco, Sanofi-Aventis, Tyson Foods, and Pilgrim's Pride Corp.
- Added a Data Analytics case based on topics in the chapter, using Tableau as a tool (auto-gradable in Connect).

Chapter 8

INVENTORIES: MEASUREMENT

- Clarified discussion of consignment arrangements and related costs.
- Added details about calculation of cost of goods sold and ending inventory for specific identification.
- Clarified discussion of calculating of cost of goods sold and ending inventory using perpetual average cost.
- Clarified the use of LIFO calculations under periodic versus perpetual system in practice.
- Added discussion of the impact of technology and the use of the perpetual inventory system
- Modified the Concept Review Exercise on inventory cost flow to include LIFO reserve.
- Revised Illustration 8-5 to reflect entries under a perpetual inventory system.
- Revised discussion of purchase discounts under the gross versus net method
- Added BE 8-10 for LIFO reserve.
- Modified E 8-19 and P 8-1 to include LIFO reserve adjustment from perpetual FIFO to periodic LIFO.
- Modified E 8-16 to compare FIFO and LIFO when costs are increasing and when costs are decreasing.
- Added a Data Analytics case based on topics in the chapter, using Tableau as a tool (auto-gradable in Connect).

Chapter 9

INVENTORIES: ADDITIONAL ISSUES

- Modified Concept Review Exercise for lower of cost or net realizable value to include unit values.
- Clarified treatment of employee discounts in the conventional retail method and revised Illustration 9-13.
- Revised discussion of Dollar-Value LIFO Retail.
- Added a Data Analytics case based on topics in the chapter, using Tableau as a tool (auto-gradable in Connect).

Chapter 10

PROPERTY, PLANT, AND EQUIPMENT AND INTANGIBLE ASSETS: ACQUISITION

- Revised discussion of nonmonetary exchanges to include four steps, and added summary Illustration 10-16.
- Revised Illustration 10-14A to clarify recording of a nonmonetary exchange.
- Moved discussion and illustration of amortization of software development costs to chapter 11.
- Added discussion of accounting for cloud computing arrangements and related implementation costs.
- Added Brief Exercise 10-18 on accounting for software development costs for internal purposes.
- Added Brief Exercise 10-19 on accounting for software development costs in cloud computing arrangements.
- Added a Data Analytics case based on topics in the chapter, using Tableau as a tool (auto-gradable in Connect).

Chapter 11

PROPERTY, PLANT, AND EQUIPMENT AND INTANGIBLE ASSETS: UTILIZATION AND DISPOSITION

- Moved discussion and illustration of amortization of software development costs from chapter 10.
- Modified Illustration 11–7B to simplify and clarify calculation of partial year depreciation.
- Added discussion of amortization of software development costs for internal purposes and in cloud computing arrangements.
- Updated discussion of impairment for goodwill based on ASU No. 2017-04.
- Added Exercise 11-13 on reporting assets held for sale.

- Updated discussion of MACRS depreciation for changes enacted by the Tax Cuts and Jobs Act.
- Added a Data Analytics case based on topics in the chapter, using Tableau as a tool (auto-gradable in Connect).

Chapter 12
INVESTMENTS

- In chapter, as well as Appendix 12B, enhanced coverage of ASU 2016–13's CECL model for accounting for credit losses.
- Revised wording of account titles to provide more streamlined and cohesive presentation of accounting for HTM, TS, AFS, equity, and equity method investments.
- Provided new Decision Makers' Perspective cases for Intel, FCA and Merck.
- Added a Data Analytics case based on topics in the chapter, using Tableau as a tool (auto-gradable in Connect).

Chapter 13
CURRENT LIABILITIES AND CONTINGENCIES

- Updated General Mills example used in Illustration 13–1 and throughout the chapter.
- Updated contingent liability examples.
- Added a Data Analytics case based on topics in the chapter, using Tableau as a tool (auto-gradable in Connect).

Chapter 14
BONDS AND LONG-TERM NOTES

- Updated Real World Financials in Bonds section.
- Revised the journal entry in Illustration 14-A2 and added additional explanation.
- Replaced illustration of zero coupon securities in Ill. 14-7 with a newer real world example, Coca Cola.
- Added a Data Analytics case based on topics in the chapter, using Tableau as a tool (auto-gradable in Connect).

Chapter 15
LEASES

- Added discussion to the operating leases section *related* to our *recording* both interest and amortization even though, for an operating lease,

the *lessee* will *report* a single lease expense rather than the separate interest and amortization as with a finance lease.
- Added a *Why Lease?* section to Part A and added related EOC and TB questions.
- Added an *Is it a Lease?* section to Part C and added related EOC and TB questions.
- Added a paragraph at end of Nonlease Payments section in Part C to describe new ASU on simplification option for lessors.
- Added a Data Analytics case based on topics in the chapter, using Tableau as a tool (auto-gradable in Connect).

Chapter 16
ACCOUNTING FOR INCOME TAXES

- Reordered early coverage to provide more conceptual basis before walking through treatment of individual temporary differences.
- Revised illustrations to highlight the four-step process for calculating tax expense, using color-coded steps in all examples and solutions to end-of-chapter material.
- Revised coverage to walk through each combination of deferred tax assets and liabilities and revenue- and expense-related temporary differences.
- Modified all examples and end of chapter material to reflect new tax rates.
- Modified coverage of net operating loss carrybacks and carryforwards to reflect new tax act.
- Modified coverage of non-temporary differences to reflect new tax act, including Additional Consideration covering earning repatriation.
- Updated Real World "Shoe Carnival" case covering linkage between tax expense journal entry and changes in deferred tax assets, liabilities, and the valuation allowance.
- Added a Data Analytics case based on topics in the chapter, using Tableau as a tool (auto-gradable in Connect).

Chapter 17
PENSIONS AND OTHER POSTRETIREMENT BENEFIT PLANS

- Added Additional Consideration box to note the trend toward the "spot rate" method of determining the interest rate.
- Added Additional Consideration box to indicate that some companies are voluntarily choosing to

recognize pension gains and losses immediately rather than amortizing them.
- Most Decision Makers' Perspective cases are now auto-gradable in Connect.
- Added a Data Analytics case based on topics in the chapter, using Tableau as a tool (auto-gradable in Connect).

Chapter 18
SHAREHOLDERS' EQUITY

- Revised discussion and assignment material to reflect the SEC's revision of the ex-dividend date from two business days before the date of record to one.
- Replaced Alcoa Case with Nike Case.
- Added a Data Analytics case based on topics in the chapter, using Tableau as a tool (auto-gradable in Connect).

Chapter 19
SHARE-BASED COMPENSATION AND EARNINGS PER SHARE

- Modified all illustrations and end of chapter material to reflect new tax rates.
- Added a Data Analytics case based on topics in the chapter, using Tableau as a tool (auto-gradable in Connect).

Chapter 20
ACCOUNTING CHANGES AND ERROR CORRECTIONS

- Revised discussion of approaches to account for accounting changes to include the modified retrospective approach.
- Modified all illustrations and end of chapter material to reflect new tax rates.

Chapter 21
STATEMENT OF CASH FLOWS REVISITED

- Revised a CVS Caremark Corp illustration of presenting cash flows from operating activities by the direct method.
- Added an enhanced Additional Consideration box on reporting bad debt expense in the SCF.
- Added a real world illustration of presenting cash flows from operating activities by the indirect method.

- Modified all illustrations and end of chapter material to reflect new tax rates.
- Revised a Research Case related to FedEx's investing and financing activities.
- Added a Real World Case on Staples reporting of its SCF.
- Added a Data Analytics case based on topics in the chapter, using Tableau as a tool (auto-gradable in Connect).

Appendix A
DERIVATIVES

- Extensively revised all illustrations, discussions, and assignment material to reflect changes emanating from the new FASB Accounting Standards Update No. 2017-12, Derivatives and Hedging (Topic 815): Targeted Improvements to Accounting for Hedging Activities.

- Added new discussion, illustration and assignment material for a cash flow hedge, interest rate swap.
- Added new discussion, illustration and assignment material for an option contract,
- Added new discussion, illustration and assignment material for a nonfinancial forward contract
- Revised a Real World Case related to the Chicago Mercantile Exchange.
- Revised a Johnson & Johnson Real World Case on hedging transactions.

Acknowledgments

Intermediate Accounting is the work not just of its talented authors, but of the more than 750 faculty reviewers who shared their insights, experience, and insights with us. Our reviewers helped us to build *Intermediate Accounting* into the very best learning system available. A blend of Spiceland users and nonusers, these reviewers explained how they use texts and technology in their teaching, and many answered detailed questions about every one of Spiceland's 21 chapters. The work of improving *Intermediate Accounting* is ongoing—even now, we're scheduling new symposia and reviewers' conferences to collect even more opinions from faculty.

We would like to acknowledge and highlight the Special Reviewer role that Ilene Leopold Persoff of Long Island University (LIU Post) took on the tenth edition. Utilizing her accounting and reviewing expertise, Ilene verified the accuracy of the manuscript and promoted our efforts toward quality and consistency. Her deep subject-matter knowledge, keen eye for detail, and professional excellence in all aspects were instrumental in ensuring a current, comprehensive, and clear edition. Her contributions are deeply appreciated.

We are especially grateful for the contributions of Charlene Parnell Spiceland of Simmons University in developing the Data Analyitics Case sequence that is a key enhancement to the tenth edition of this textbook. Utilizing her expertise in Tableau, she ensured that these cases provide students the opportunity to glimpse the power and efficacy of data analytics. The cases encourage students to use Tableau to analyze data sets to make business decisions in the context of chapter topics as well as to appreciate the most effective and efficient ways to communicate their findings.

In addition, we want to recognize the valuable input of all those who helped guide our developmental decisions for the tenth edition.

H. Kyle Anderson, *Clemson University*

Matthew Anderson, *Michigan State University*

Avinash Arya, *William Paterson University*

Patricia Ball, *Massasoit Community College*

Michael Baker, *Southern New Hampshire University*

Brian Bratten, *University of Kentucky, Lexington*

Maureen Breen, *Drexel University*

Stephen Brown, *University of Maryland*

Esther Bunn, *Stephen F. Austin State University*

John Capka, *Cuyahoga Community College*

Kam Chan, *Pace University*

Chiaho Chang, *Montclair State University*

Carolyn Christesen, *SUNY Westchester Community College*

Simona Citron, *Northwestern University Southern New Hampshire University*

Mariah Dar, *John Tyler Community College*

Amy Donnelly, *Clemson University*

Jeffrey T. Doyle, *Utah State University*

Dov Fischer, *Brooklyn College*

Corinne Frad, *Eastern Iowa Community College*

Shari Fowler, *Indiana University East*

Dana Garner, *Virginia Tech*

Paul Goodchild, *University of Central Missouri*

Pamela J. Graybeal, *University of Central Florida Orlando*

Rick Johnston, *University of Alabama at Birmingham*

Beth Kane, *Columbia College of Missouri*

Gordon Klein, *University of California Los Angeles*

Melissa Larson, *Brigham Young University*

Ming Lu, *Santa Monica College*

Stephen McCarthy, *Kean University*

Dawn McKinley, *Harper College*

Jeanette Milius, *Nebraska Wesleyan University*

Anita Morgan. *Indiana University*

Ahmad (Sia) Nassiripour, *William Paterson University*

Anne Mary Nash-Haruna, *Bellevue College*

Sewon O, *Texas Southern University*

Hong S. Pak, *California State Polytechnic University, Pomona*

Debra Petrizzo-Wilkins, *Franklin University*

Kris Portz, *St. Cloud State University*

Linda Quick, *East Carolina University*

David Ravetch, *University of California Los Angeles*

Cecile Roberti, *Community College of Rhode Island*

Mark Ross, *Western Kentucky University*

Sheldon Smith, *Utah Valley University*

Larry G. Stephens, *Austin Community College District*

Vicki M Stewart, *Texas A & M University Commerce*

Peter Theuri, *Northern Kentucky University*

Geoffrey Tickell, *Indiana University of Pennsylvania*

Dick Williams, *Missouri State University*

Jennifer Winchel, *University of Virginia*

Lori Zaher, *Bucks County Community College*

We Are Grateful

We would like to acknowledge and thank the following individuals for their contributions in developing, reviewing and shaping the extensive ancillary package: Jeannie Folk, *College of DuPage;* Julie Hankins, User Euphoria; Patrick Lee, University of Connecticut; Beth Kobylarz of Accuracy Counts; Mark McCarthy, *East Carolina University;* Barbara Muller, *Arizona State University;* Patricia Plumb; Helen Roybark, *Radford University;* Jacob Shortt, *Virginia Tech*; Pamela Simmons, Cuyahoga Community College; Kevin Smith, *Utah Valley University;* Emily Vera, *University of Colorado–Denver;* Marcia Watson, University of North Carolina Charlotte; Jennifer Winchel, *University of Virginia* and Teri Zuccaro, *Clarke University,* who contributed new content and accuracy checks of Connect and LearnSmart. We greatly appreciate everyone's hard work on these products!

We are most grateful for the talented assistance and support from the many people at McGraw-Hill Education. We would particularly like to thank Tim Vertovec, managing director; Natalie King, marketing director; Rebecca Olson, executive brand manager; Christina Sanders and Danielle McLimore, senior product developers; Zach Rudin, marketing manager; Kevin Moran, director of digital content; Xin Lin, digital product analyst; Daryl Horrocks, program manager; Pat Frederickson, lead content project manager; Angela Norris, senior content project manager; Laura Fuller, buyer; Matt Diamond, senior designer; and Jacob Sullivan, content licensing specialists.

Finally, we extend our thanks to Roger CPA Review for their assistance developing simulations for inclusion in the end-of-chapter material, as well as Target and Air France–KLM for allowing us to use their Annual Reports throughout the text. We also acknowledge permission from the AICPA to adapt material from the Uniform CPA Examination, and the IMA for permission to adapt material from the CMA Examination.

David Spiceland   Mark Nelson   Wayne Thomas

Contents in Brief

Contents

1 | The Role of Accounting as an Information System

2 | Assets

12 CHAPTER
Investments 644

3 | Liabilities and Shareholders' Equity

13 CHAPTER
Current Liabilities and Contingencies 716

xxviii Contents

14 CHAPTER
Bonds and Long-Term Notes 772

15 CHAPTER
Leases 834

Contents   **xxix**

16 CHAPTER
Accounting for Income Taxes 908

17 CHAPTER
Pensions and Other Postretirement Benefits 976

18 CHAPTER
Shareholders' Equity 1046

4 | Additional Financial Reporting Issues

19 CHAPTER
Share-Based Compensation and Earnings Per Share 1104

CHAPTER

1

Environment and Theoretical Structure of Financial Accounting

OVERVIEW

The primary function of financial accounting is to provide useful financial information to users who are external to the business enterprise, particularly investors and creditors. These users make critical resource allocation decisions that affect the global economy. The primary means of conveying financial information to external users is through financial statements and related notes.

In this chapter you explore such important topics as the reason why financial accounting is useful, the process by which accounting standards are produced, and the conceptual framework that underlies financial accounting. The perspective you gain in this chapter serves as a foundation for more detailed study of financial accounting.

LEARNING OBJECTIVES

After studying this chapter, you should be able to:

- **LO1–1** Describe the function and primary focus of financial accounting. (p. 3)
- **LO1–2** Explain the difference between cash and accrual accounting. (p. 7)
- **LO1–3** Define generally accepted accounting principles (GAAP) and discuss the historical development of accounting standards, including convergence between U.S. and international standards. (p. 8)
- **LO1–4** Explain why establishing accounting standards is characterized as a political process. (p. 12)
- **LO1–5** Explain factors that encourage high-quality financial reporting. (p. 14)
- **LO1–6** Explain the purpose of the conceptual framework. (p. 18)
- **LO1–7** Identify the objective and qualitative characteristics of financial reporting information and the elements of financial statements. (p. 20)
- **LO1–8** Describe the four basic assumptions underlying GAAP. (p. 23)
- **LO1–9** Describe the recognition, measurement, and disclosure concepts that guide accounting practice. (p. 25)
- **LO1–10** Contrast a revenue/expense approach and an asset/liability approach to accounting standard setting. (p. 31)
- **LO1–11** Discuss the primary differences between U.S. GAAP and IFRS with respect to the development of accounting standards and the conceptual framework underlying accounting standards. (p. 11, 14 and 19)

©Rawpixel.com/Shutterstock

FINANCIAL REPORTING CASE

Misguided Marketing Major

During a class break in your investments class, a marketing major tells the following story to you and some friends:

The chief financial officer (CFO) of a large company is interviewing three candidates for the top accounting position with his firm. He asks each the same question:

CFO:	What is two plus two?
First candidate:	Four.
CFO:	What is two plus two?
Second candidate:	Four.
CFO:	What is two plus two?
Third candidate:	What would you like it to be?
CFO:	You're hired.

After you take some good-natured ribbing from the non-accounting majors, your friend says, "Seriously, though, there must be ways the accounting profession prevents that kind of behavior. Aren't there some laws, or rules, or something? Is accounting based on some sort of theory, or is it just arbitrary?"

By the time you finish this chapter, you should be able to respond appropriately to the questions posed in this case. Compare your response to the solution provided at the end of the chapter.

QUESTIONS

1. What should you tell your friend about the presence of accounting standards in the United States and the rest of the world? Who has the authority for standard setting? Who has the responsibility? (p. 8)

2. What is the economic and political environment in which standard setting occurs? (p. 12)

3. What is the relationship among management, auditors, investors, and creditors that tends to preclude the "What would you like it to be?" attitude? (p. 14)

4. In general, what is the conceptual framework that underlies accounting principles, and how does it encourage high-quality financial reporting? (p. 18)

Financial Accounting Environment

PART A

In 1902, George Dayton took ownership of the Dayton Dry Goods Company, the fourth largest department store in Minneapolis, Minnesota. Successive generations of Daytons were innovative managers, flying in inventory to prevent shortages (1920), committing to giving 5 percent of profits back to the community (1946), and creating the nation's first enclosed shopping mall (1956). In 1962, George's grandchildren transformed Dayton's, by then a regional department store chain, into the **Target Corporation**, promising "a quality store with quality merchandise at discount prices."[1] Today Target has grown to be the second largest general merchandise retailer in America, with over 1,800 stores, almost 350,000 employees, and **www.target.com** reaching the online market. However, Target still stands by its "Expect More, Pay Less" motto, and still donates 5 percent of profits back to the community (giving more than $4 million per week).

● LO1–1

[1]"Target Through the Years" at https://corporate.target.com/about/history/Target-through-the-years.

Many factors contributed to Target's success. The Daytons were visionary in their move into the upscale discount retail market. The company's commitment to quality products, customer service, and community support also played an important role. But the ability to raise money from investors and lenders at various times also was critical to Target's evolution. Target used proceeds from its 1967 initial public stock offering to expand nationally. Creditors (lenders) also supplied needed capital at various times. In fact, without access to capital, the Target Corporation we know today likely would not exist.

Investors and creditors use many different kinds of information before supplying capital to businesses like Target. They use the information to predict the future risk and potential return of their prospective investments or loans.[2] For example, information about the enterprise's products and its management is key to this assessment. Investors and creditors also rely on various kinds of accounting information.

Think of accounting as a special "language" that companies like Target use to communicate financial information to help people inside and outside of the business to make decisions. The Pathways Commission of the American Accounting Association developed an illustration to help visualize this important role of accounting.[3] As shown in Illustration 1–1, accounting provides useful information about economic activity to help produce good decisions and foster a prosperous society. Economic activity is complex, and decisions have real consequences, so critical thinking and many judgments are needed to produce the most useful accounting information possible.

The primary focus of financial accounting is on the information needs of investors and creditors.

This book focuses on **financial accounting**, which is chiefly concerned with providing financial information to various *external* users.[4] The chart in Illustration 1–2 lists a number of groups that provide financial information as well as several external user groups. For these groups, the primary focus of financial accounting is on the financial information

Illustration 1–1

Pathways Commission visualization: "THIS is accounting!"

---

[2]Risk refers to the variability of possible outcomes from an investment. Return is the amount received over and above the investment.
[3]Reprinted with permission from the American Accounting Association. This work is by The Pathways Commission and is licensed under a Creative Commons Attribution-NoDerivs 3.0 Unported License.
[4]In contrast, *managerial* accounting deals with the concepts and methods used to provide information to an organization's *internal users*, that is, its managers. You study managerial accounting elsewhere in your curriculum.

PROVIDERS OF FINANCIAL INFORMATION	USERS OF FINANCIAL INFORMATION
• Profit-oriented companies	• Investors
	• Creditors (banks, bondholders, other lenders)
	• Employees
	• Labor unions
• Not-for-profit entities (e.g., government entities, charitable organizations, schools)	• Customers
	• Suppliers
	• Government regulatory agencies (e.g., Internal Revenue Service, Securities and Exchange Commission)
• Households	• Financial intermediaries (e.g., financial analysts, stockbrokers, mutual fund managers, credit-rating organizations)

Illustration 1–2

Financial Information Providers and External User Groups

provided by *profit-oriented companies to their present and potential investors and creditors.* One external user group, often referred to as *financial intermediaries,* includes financial analysts, stockbrokers, mutual fund managers, and credit rating organizations. These users provide advice to investors and creditors and/or make investment-credit decisions on their behalf.

The primary means of conveying financial information to investors, creditors, and other external users is through financial statements and related disclosure notes. The financial statements most frequently provided are (1) the balance sheet, also called the statement of financial position, (2) the income statement, also called the statement of operations, (3) the statement of cash flows, and (4) the statement of shareholders' equity. Also, companies must either provide a statement of other comprehensive income immediately following the income statement or present a combined statement of comprehensive income that includes the information normally contained in both the income statement and the statement of other comprehensive income.[5] As you progress through this book, you will review and expand your knowledge of the information in these financial statements, the way the elements in these statements are measured, and the concepts underlying these measurements and related disclosures. We use the term financial reporting to refer to the process of providing this information to external users. Keep in mind, though, that external users receive important financial information in a variety of other formats as well, including news releases and management forecasts, prospectuses, and reports filed with regulatory agencies.

Target's financial statements for the fiscal year ended January 30, 2016, and related disclosure notes are provided in Connect. You also can access these statements and notes under the Investor Relations link at the company's website (Target.com). A Target case is included among the Real-Word Cases that accompany each chapter, so you can see how each chapter's topics relate to a single familiar company.

The Economic Environment and Financial Reporting

In the United States, we have a highly developed free-enterprise economy with the majority of productive resources privately owned rather than government owned. For the economy to operate efficiently, these resources should be allocated to private enterprises that will use

[5]FASB ASC 220-45: Comprehensive Income—Other Presentation Matters (originally "Presentation of Comprehensive Income," *Accounting Standards Update No. 2011-05* (Norwalk, CT: FASB, June 2011)).

them best to provide the goods and services desired by society and not to enterprises that will waste them. The mechanisms that foster this efficient allocation of resources are the capital markets. We can think of the capital markets simply as a composite of all investors and creditors.

The capital markets provide a mechanism to help our economy allocate resources efficiently.

Businesses go to the capital markets to get the cash necessary for them to function. The three primary forms of business organization are the sole proprietorship, the partnership, and the corporation. In the United States, sole proprietorships and partnerships outnumber corporations. However, the dominant form of business organization, in terms of the owner-ship of productive resources, is the corporation. Investors provide resources, usually cash, to a corporation in exchange for an ownership interest, that is, shares of stock. Creditors lend cash to the corporation, either by making individual loans or by purchasing publicly traded debt such as bonds.

Corporations acquire capital from investors in exchange for ownership interest and from creditors by borrowing.

What information do investors and creditors need when determining which companies will receive capital? We explore that question next.

The Investment-Credit Decision—A Cash Flow Perspective

While the decisions made by investors and by creditors are somewhat different, they are similar in at least one important way. Investors and creditors are willing to provide capital to a corporation (buy stocks or bonds) only if they expect to receive more cash in return at some time in the future. A corporation's shareholders will receive cash from their invest-ment through the ultimate sale of the ownership shares of stock. In addition, many corpora-tions distribute cash to their shareholders in the form of periodic dividends. For example, if an investor provides a company with $10,000 cash by purchasing stock at the end of 2020, receives $400 in dividends from the company during 2021, and sells the ownership interest (shares) at the end of 2021 for $10,600, the investment would have generated a rate of return of 10% for 2021, calculated as follows:

The expected rate of return and the uncertainty, or risk, of that return are key variables in the investment decision.

$$\frac{\$400 \text{ dividends} + \$600 \text{ share price appreciation}}{\$10,000 \text{ initial investment}} = 10\%$$

All else equal, investors and creditors would like to invest in stocks or bonds that provide the highest expected rate of return. However, there are many variables to consider before making an investment decision. For example, the *uncertainty,* or *risk,* of that expected return also is important. To illustrate, consider the following two investment options:

1. Invest $10,000 in a savings account insured by the U.S. government that will generate a 5% rate of return.
2. Invest $10,000 in a profit-oriented company.

A company will be able to provide a positive return to investors and creditors only if it can generate a profit from selling its products or services.

While the rate of return from option 1 is known with virtual certainty, the return from option 2 is uncertain. The amount and timing of the cash to be received in the future from option 2 are unknown. The company in option 2 will be able to provide investors with a return only if it can generate a profit. That is, it must be able to use the resources provided by investors and creditors to generate cash receipts from selling a product or service that exceed the cash disbursements necessary to provide that product or service. Therefore, potential investors require information about the company that will help them estimate the potential for future profits, as well as the return they can expect on their investment and the risk that is associated with it. If the potential return is high enough, investors will prefer to invest in the profit-oriented company, even if that return has more risk associated with it.

The objective of financial accounting is to provide investors and creditors with useful information for decision making.

In summary, the primary objective of financial accounting is to provide investors and cred-itors with information that will help them make investment and credit decisions. That informa-tion should help investors and creditors evaluate the *amounts, timing,* and *uncertainty* of the enterprise's future cash receipts and disbursements. The better this information is, the more efficient will be investor and creditor resource allocation decisions. But financial accounting doesn't only benefit companies and their investors and creditors. By providing key informa-tion to capital market participants, financial accounting plays a vital role that helps direct soci-ety's resources to the companies that will utilize those resources most effectively.

Cash versus Accrual Accounting

● LO1–2

Even though predicting future cash flows is the primary goal of many users of financial reporting, the model best able to achieve that goal is accrual accounting. A competing model is cash-basis accounting. Each model produces a periodic measure of performance that could be used by investors and creditors for predicting future cash flows.

CASH-BASIS ACCOUNTING Cash-basis accounting produces a measure called net operating cash flow. This measure is the difference between cash receipts and cash payments from transactions related to providing goods and services to customers during a reporting period.

Net operating cash flow is the difference between cash receipts and cash disbursements from providing goods and services.

Over the life of a company, net operating cash flow definitely is the measure of concern. However, over short periods of time, operating cash flows may not be indicative of the company's long-run cash-generating ability. Sometimes a company pays or receives cash in one period that relates to performance in multiple periods. For example, in one period a company receives cash that relates to prior period sales, or makes advance payments for costs related to future periods.

To see this more clearly, consider Carter Company's net operating cash flows during its first three years of operations, shown in Illustration 1–3. Carter's operations for these three years included the following:

1. Credit sales to customers were $100,000 each year ($300,000 total), while cash collections were $50,000, $125,000, and $125,000. Carter's customers owe Carter nothing at the end of year 3.
2. At the beginning of year 1, Carter prepaid $60,000 for three years' rent ($20,000 per year).
3. Employee salaries of $50,000 were paid in full each year.
4. Utilities cost was $10,000 each year, but $5,000 of the cost in year 1 was not paid until year 2.
5. In total, Carter generated positive net operating cash flow of $60,000.

Is the three-year pattern of net operating cash flows indicative of the company's year-by-year performance? No. Sales to customers and costs of operating the company (rent, salaries, and utilities) occurred evenly over the three years, but net operating cash flows occurred at an uneven rate. Net operating cash flows varied each year because Carter (a) didn't collect cash from customers in the same pattern that sales occurred and (b) didn't pay for rent and utilities in the same years in which those resources were actually consumed. This illustration also shows why operating cash flows may not predict the company's long-run cash-generating ability. Net operating cash flow in year 1 (negative $65,000)[6] is not an accurate predictor of Carter's future cash-generating ability in year 2 (positive $60,000) or year 3 (positive $65,000).

Over short periods of time, operating cash flow may not be an accurate predictor of future operating cash flows.

	Year 1	Year 2	Year 3	Total
Sales (on credit)	$100,000	$100,000	$100,000	$300,000
Net Operating Cash Flows				
Cash receipts from customers	$ 50,000	$125,000	$125,000	$300,000
Cash disbursements:				
Prepayment of three years' rent	(60,000)	–0–	–0–	(60,000)
Salaries to employees	(50,000)	(50,000)	(50,000)	(150,000)
Utilities	(5,000)	(15,000)	(10,000)	(30,000)
Net operating cash flow	$(65,000)	$ 60,000	$ 65,000	$ 60,000

Illustration 1–3

Cash-Basis Accounting

[6]If cash flow from operating the company is negative, the company can continue to operate by using cash obtained from investors or creditors to make up the difference.

Illustration 1–4

Accrual Accounting

CARTER COMPANY Income Statements				
	Year 1	**Year 2**	**Year 3**	**Total**
Revenues	$100,000	$100,000	$100,000	$300,000
Expenses:				
Rent	20,000	20,000	20,000	60,000
Salaries	50,000	50,000	50,000	150,000
Utilities	10,000	10,000	10,000	30,000
Total expenses	80,000	80,000	80,000	240,000
Net Income	$ 20,000	$ 20,000	$ 20,000	$ 60,000

Net income is the difference between *revenues* and *expenses*.

ACCRUAL ACCOUNTING   If we measure Carter's activities by the accrual accounting model, we get a more accurate prediction of future operating cash flows and a more reasonable portrayal of the periodic operating performance of the company. The accrual accounting model doesn't focus only on cash flows. Instead, it also reflects other resources provided and consumed by operations during a period. The accrual accounting model's measure of resources provided by business operations is called *revenues,* and the measure of resources sacrificed to produce revenues is called *expenses.* The difference between revenues and expenses is net income, or net loss if expenses are greater than revenues.[7]

Illustration 1–4 shows how we would measure revenues and expenses in this very simple situation.

Net income is considered a better indicator of future operating cash flows than is current net operating cash flow.

Revenue for year 1 is the $100,000 sales. Given that sales eventually are collected in cash, the year 1 revenue of $100,000 is a better measure of the inflow of resources from company operations than is the $50,000 cash collected from customers. Also, net income of $20,000 for year 1 appears to be a reasonable predictor of the company's cash-generating ability, as total net operating cash flow for the three-year period is a positive $60,000. Comparing the three-year pattern of net operating cash flows in Illustration 1–3 to the three-year pattern of net income in Illustration 1–4, the net income pattern is more representative of Carter Company's steady operating performance over the three-year period.[8]

While this example is somewhat simplistic, it allows us to see the motivation for using the accrual accounting model. Accrual income attempts to measure the resource inflows and outflows generated by operations during the reporting period, which may not correspond to cash inflows and outflows. Does this mean that information about cash flows from operating activities is not useful? No. Indeed, one of the basic financial statements—the statement of cash flows—reports information about cash flows from operating, investing, and financing activities, and provides important information to investors and creditors.[9] Focusing on accrual accounting as well as cash flows provides a more complete view of a company and its operations.

The Development of Financial Accounting and Reporting Standards

● LO1–3

FINANCIAL Reporting Case

Q1, p. 3

Accrual accounting is the financial reporting model used by the majority of profit-oriented companies and by many not-for-profit companies. The fact that companies use the same model is important to investors and creditors, allowing them to *compare* financial information among companies. To facilitate these comparisons, financial accounting employs a body of standards known as generally accepted accounting principles, often abbreviated as GAAP (and pronounced *gap*). GAAP is a dynamic set of both broad and specific guidelines that companies should follow when measuring and reporting the information in their

---

[7]Net income also includes gains and losses, which are discussed later in the chapter.

[8]Empirical evidence that accrual accounting provides a better measure of short-term performance than cash flows is provided by Patricia Dechow, "Accounting Earnings and Cash Flows as Measures of Firm Performance: The Role of Accrual Accounting," *Journal of Accounting and Economics* 18 (1994), pp. 3–42.

[9]The statement of cash flows is discussed in detail in Chapters 4 and 21.

financial statements and related notes. The more important concepts underlying GAAP are discussed in a subsequent section of this chapter and revisited throughout this book in the context of particular accounting topics.

Historical Perspective and Standards

Pressures on the accounting profession to establish uniform accounting standards began after the stock market crash of 1929. Some felt that insufficient and misleading financial statement information led to inflated stock prices and that this contributed to the stock market crash and the subsequent depression.

The 1933 Securities Act and the 1934 Securities Exchange Act were designed to restore investor confidence. The 1933 Act sets forth accounting and disclosure requirements for initial offerings of securities (stocks and bonds). The 1934 Act applies to secondary market transactions and mandates reporting requirements for companies whose securities are publicly traded on either organized stock exchanges or in over-the-counter markets.[10]

The 1934 Act also created the Securities and Exchange Commission (SEC). Congress gave the SEC the authority to set accounting and reporting standards for companies whose securities are publicly traded. However, the SEC, a government appointed body, has *delegated* the task of setting accounting standards to the private sector. It is important to understand that the power still lies with the SEC. If the SEC does not agree with a particular standard issued by the private sector, it can force a change in the standard. In fact, it has done so in the past.[11]

> The Securities and Exchange Commission (SEC) has the authority to set accounting standards for companies, but it relies on the private sector to do so.

EARLY U.S. STANDARD SETTING   The first private sector body to assume the task of setting accounting standards was the Committee on Accounting Procedure (CAP). The CAP was a committee of the American Institute of Accountants (AIA). The AIA was renamed the American Institute of Certified Public Accountants (AICPA) in 1957, which is the national professional organization for certified professional public accountants.

From 1938 to 1959, the CAP issued 51 *Accounting Research Bulletins (ARBs)* which dealt with specific accounting and reporting problems. No theoretical framework for financial accounting was established. This piecemeal approach of dealing with individual issues without a framework led to criticism.

In 1959 the Accounting Principles Board (APB) replaced the CAP. The APB operated from 1959 through 1973 and issued 31 *Accounting Principles Board Opinions (APBOs)*, various *Interpretations,* and four *Statements.* The *Opinions* also dealt with specific accounting and reporting problems. Many *ARBs* and *APBOs* still represent authoritative GAAP.

The APB suffered from a variety of problems. It was never able to establish a conceptual framework for financial accounting and reporting that was broadly accepted. Also, members served on the APB on a voluntary, part-time basis, so the APB was not able to act quickly enough to keep up with financial reporting issues as they developed. Perhaps the most important flaw of the APB was a perceived lack of independence. Because the APB was composed almost entirely of certified public accountants and supported by the AICPA, critics charged that the clients of the represented public accounting firms exerted self-interested pressure on the board and inappropriately influenced decisions. A related complaint was that other interest groups lacked an ability to provide input to the standard-setting process.

THE FASB   Criticism of the APB led to the creation in 1973 of the Financial Accounting Standards Board (FASB) and its supporting structure. There are seven full-time members of the FASB. FASB members represent various constituencies concerned with accounting standards, and have included representatives from the auditing profession, profit-oriented companies, accounting educators, financial analysts, and government. The FASB is supported by its parent organization, the Financial Accounting Foundation (FAF), which is

> The *FASB* was established to set U.S. accounting standards.

---

[10]Reporting requirements for SEC registrants include Form 10-K, the annual report form, and Form 10-Q, the report that must be filed for the first three quarters of each fiscal year.

[11]The SEC issues *Financial Reporting Releases (FRRs),* which regulate what information companies must report to it. The SEC staff also issues *Staff Accounting Bulletins* that provide the SEC's interpretation of standards previously issued by the private sector. To learn more about the SEC, consult its Internet site at www.sec.gov.

responsible for selecting the members of the FASB and its Financial Accounting Standards Advisory Council (FASAC), ensuring adequate funding of FASB activities and exercising general oversight of the FASB's activities.[12,13]

In 1984, the FASB's **Emerging Issues Task Force (EITF)** was formed to improve financial reporting by resolving narrowly defined financial accounting issues within the framework of existing GAAP. The EITF primarily addresses implementation issues, thereby speeding up the standard-setting process and allowing the FASB to focus on pervasive long-term problems. EITF rulings are ratified by the FASB and are considered part of GAAP.

Illustration 1–5 summarizes this discussion on accounting standards. The graphic shows the hierarchy of accounting standard setting in order of authority.

CODIFICATION   Present-day GAAP includes a huge amount of guidance. The FASB has developed a **conceptual framework** (discussed in Part B of this chapter) that is not authoritative GAAP but provides an underlying structure for the development of accounting standards. The FASB also has issued many accounting standards, currently called *Accounting Standards Updates* (*ASUs*) and previously called *Statements of Financial Accounting Standards* (*SFASs*), as well as numerous FASB *Interpretations, Staff Positions, Technical Bulletins,* and *EITF Issue Consensuses.* The SEC also has issued various important pronouncements. Determining the appropriate accounting treatment for a particular event or transaction might require an accountant to research several of these sources.

> The *FASB Accounting Standards Codification* is the only source of authoritative U.S. GAAP, other than rules and interpretive releases of the SEC.

To simplify the task of researching an accounting topic, in 2009 the FASB implemented its *FASB Accounting Standards Codification.* The Codification integrates and topically organizes all relevant accounting pronouncements comprising GAAP in a searchable, online database. It represents the single source of authoritative nongovernmental U.S. GAAP, and also includes portions of SEC accounting guidance that are relevant to financial reports filed with the SEC. When the FASB issues a new ASU, it becomes authoritative when it is entered into the Codification. The Codification is organized into nine main topics and approximately 90 subtopics. The main topics and related numbering system are presented in Illustration 1–6.[14] The Codification can be located at **www.fasb.org.**

Illustration 1–5

Accounting Standard Setting

HIERARCHY OF STANDARD-SETTING AUTHORITY

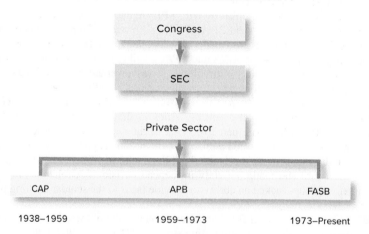

| Congress |
| SEC |
| Private Sector |

| CAP | APB | FASB |
| 1938–1959 | 1959–1973 | 1973–Present |

---

[12]The FAF's primary sources of funding are fees assessed against issuers of securities under the *Public Company Accounting Reform and Investor Protection Act of 2002,* commonly referred to as the *Sarbanes-Oxley Act.* The FAF is governed by trustees, the majority of whom are appointed from the membership of eight sponsoring organizations. These organizations represent important constituencies involved with the financial reporting process. For example, one of the founding organizations is the CFA Institute which represents financial information users, and another is the Financial Executives International which represents financial information preparers. The FAF also raises funds to support the activities of the Governmental Accounting Standards Board (GASB).

[13]The major responsibility of the FASAC is to advise the FASB on the priorities of its projects, including the suitability of new projects that might be added to its agenda. FASAC includes approximately 35 representatives from auditing firms, private companies, various user groups, and academia.

[14]FASB ASC 105–10: Generally Accepted Accounting Principles—Overall (previously "The FASB Accounting Standards Codification® and the Hierarchy of Generally Accepted Accounting Principles—a replacement of FASB Statement No. 162," *Statement of Financial Accounting Standards No. 168* (Norwalk, Conn.: FASB: 2009)).

FASB Accounting Standards Codification Topics	
Topic	**Numbered**
General Principles	100–199
Presentation	200–299
Assets	300–399
Liabilities	400–499
Equity	500–599
Revenues	600–699
Expenses	700–799
Broad Transactions	800–899
Industry	900–999

Illustration 1–6
FASB Accounting Standards Codification Topics

Additional Consideration

Accounting standards and the standard-setting process discussed above relate to profit-oriented organizations and nongovernmental not-for-profit entities. In 1984, the Governmental Accounting Standards Board (GASB) was created to develop accounting standards for governmental units such as states and cities. The FAF oversees and funds the GASB, and the Governmental Accounting Standards Advisory Council (GASAC) provides input to it.

Throughout this book, we use the Accounting Standards Codification System (ASC) in footnotes when referencing generally accepted accounting principles (FASB ASC followed by the appropriate number). Each footnote also includes a reference to the original accounting standard that is codified in the ASC.

INTERNATIONAL STANDARD SETTING   Most industrialized countries have organizations responsible for determining accounting and reporting standards. In some countries, the United Kingdom, for instance, the responsible organization is a private sector body similar to the FASB in the United States. In other countries, the organization is a governmental body. Historically, these different organizations often produced different accounting standards, which complicated accounting by multinational companies, reduced comparability between companies using different standards, and potentially made it harder for companies to raise capital in international markets.

● LO1–11

In response to these problems, the International Accounting Standards Committee (IASC) was formed in 1973 to develop global accounting standards. The IASC reorganized itself in 2001 and created a new standard-setting body called the International Accounting Standards Board (IASB). The IASB's main objective is to develop a single set of high-quality, understandable, and enforceable global accounting standards to help participants in the world's capital markets and other users make economic decisions.[15]

The *International Accounting Standards Board (IASB)* is dedicated to developing a single set of global accounting standards.

As shown in Illustration 1–7, the way international standard setting is structured is similar in many respects to the way standard setting is structured in the United States.

The IASC issued 41 International Accounting Standards (IASs), and the IASB endorsed these standards when it was formed in 2001. Since then, the IASB has revised many IASs and has issued new standards of its own, called International Financial Reporting Standards (IFRS). More and more countries are basing their national accounting standards on IFRS. By 2018, more than 120 jurisdictions, including Hong Kong, Egypt, Canada, Australia, and the countries in the European Union (EU), require or permit the use of IFRS or a local variant of IFRS.[16]

International Financial Reporting Standards are issued by the IASB.

---

[15] www.ifrs.org.
[16] See http://www.ifrs.com/ifrs_faqs.html.

Illustration 1–7
Comparison of Organizations of U.S. and International Standard Setters

	U.S. GAAP	**IFRS**
Regulatory oversight provided by:	Securities Exchange Commission (SEC)	Monitoring Board
Foundation providing oversight, appointing members, raising funds:	Financial Accounting Foundation (FAF): 14–18 trustees	IFRS Foundation: 22 trustees
Standard-setting board:	Financial Accounting Standards Board (FASB): 7 members	International Accounting Standards Board (IASB): 14 members
Advisory council providing input on agenda and projects:	Financial Accounting Standards Advisory Council (FASAC): 30–40 members	IFRS Advisory Council: approx. 50 members
Group to deal with emerging issues:	Emerging Issues Task Force (EITF): approx. 15 members	IFRS Interpretations Committee: 14 members

EFFORTS TO CONVERGE U.S. AND INTERNATIONAL STANDARDS Should the United States also adopt IFRS? Many argue that a single set of global standards would improve comparability of financial reporting and facilitate access to capital. In 2007, the SEC signaled its view that IFRS are of high quality by eliminating a requirement for foreign companies that issue stock in the United States to include in their financial statements a reconciliation of IFRS to U.S. GAAP. However, others argue that U.S. standards should remain customized to fit the stringent legal and regulatory requirements of the U.S. business environment. There also is concern that differences in implementation and enforcement from country to country make accounting under IFRS appear more uniform and comparable than actually is the case. Another argument is that competition between alternative standard-setting regimes is healthy and can lead to improved standards.[17]

The FASB and IASB have worked for many years to converge to one global set of accounting standards. Much progress has occurred, and in this book you will learn about already-converged standards that deal with such topics as revenue recognition, earnings per share, share-based compensation, nonmonetary exchanges, inventory costs, and the calculation of fair value. **Where We're Headed** boxes throughout the book describe additional projects that are ongoing.

However, at the time this book is being written, recent events suggest that full convergence will not be achieved in the foreseeable future. For example, as discussed further in Chapter 12, the FASB and IASB eventually concluded that full convergence was not possible with respect to accounting for financial instruments. While it appears likely that the FASB and IASB will continue to work together to converge where possible, some differences between IFRS and U.S. GAAP will remain.

Nonetheless, you should be aware of important differences that exist between U.S. GAAP and IFRS. Therefore, **International Financial Reporting Standards** boxes are included throughout the book to highlight circumstances in which IFRS differs from U.S. GAAP. Throughout this book, and also in the end-of-chapter questions, exercises, problems, and cases, IFRS-related material is marked with the globe icon that you see beside this paragraph. And, similar to the **Target** case, an **Air France–KLM (AF)** case is included among the Real-World Cases that accompany each chapter, so you can see how each chapter's IFRS material relates to a single, familiar company.

● LO1–4   ## The Standard-Setting Process

DUE PROCESS When developing accounting standards, a standard setter must understand the nuances of the economic transactions the standards address and the views of key constituents concerning how accounting would best capture that economic reality. Therefore, the FASB undertakes a series of elaborate information-gathering steps before issuing

FINANCIAL Reporting Case

Q2, p. 3

---

[17]For a comprehensive analysis of the pros and cons of U.S. adoption of IFRS, see L. Hail, C. Leuz and P. Wysocki, "Global Accounting Convergence and the Potential Adoption of IFRS in the US (Part 1): An Analysis of Economic and Policy Factors," *Accounting Horizons* 24 (No 3.), September 2010, pp. 355–394, and ". . . (Part 2): Political Factors and Future Scenarios for U.S. Accounting Standards," *Accounting Horizons* 24 (No. 4), December 2010, pp. 567–588.

Illustration 1–8
The FASB's Standard-Setting Process

The FASB undertakes a series of information-gathering steps before issuing an Accounting Standards Update.

Step	Explanation
1.	The Board identifies financial reporting issues based on requests/recommendations from stakeholders or through other means.
2.	The Board decides whether to add a project to the technical agenda based on a staff-prepared analysis of the issues.
3.	The Board deliberates at one or more public meetings the various issues identified and analyzed by the staff.
4.	The Board issues an Exposure Draft. (In some projects, a Discussion Paper may be issued to obtain input at an early stage that is used to develop an Exposure Draft.)
5.	The Board holds a public roundtable meeting on the Exposure Draft, if necessary.
6.	The staff analyzes comment letters, public roundtable discussion, and any other information. The Board redeliberates the proposed provisions at public meetings.
7.	The Board issues an Accounting Standards Update describing amendments to the Accounting Standards Codification.

an Accounting Standards Update. These steps include open hearings, deliberations, and requests for written comments from interested parties. Illustration 1–8 outlines the FASB's standard-setting process.[18]

These steps help the FASB acquire information to determine the preferred method of accounting. However, as a practical matter, this information gathering also exposes the FASB to much political pressure by various interest groups who want an accounting treatment that serves their economic best interest. As you will see later in this chapter, the FASB's concepts statements indicate that standards should present information in a neutral manner, rather than being designed to favor particular economic consequences, but sometimes politics intrudes on the standard-setting process.

POLITICS IN STANDARD SETTING A change in accounting standards can result in a substantial redistribution of wealth within our economy. Therefore, it is no surprise that the FASB has had to deal with intense political pressure over controversial accounting standards and sometimes has changed standards in response to that pressure.

One example of the effect of politics on standard setting occurred in the mid-1990s with respect to accounting for employee stock options. The accounting standards in place at that time typically did not recognize compensation expense if a company paid their employees with stock options rather than cash. Yet, the company was sacrificing something of value to compensate its employees. Therefore, the FASB proposed that companies recognize compensation expense in an amount equal to the fair value of the options, with some of the expense recognized in each of the periods in which the employee earned the options. Numerous companies (particularly in California's Silicon Valley, where high-tech companies had been compensating employees with stock options to a great extent) applied intense political pressure against this proposal, and eventually the FASB backed down and required only disclosure of options-related compensation expense in the notes to the financial statements. Nearly a decade later, this contentious issue resurfaced in a more amenable political climate, and the FASB issued a standard requiring expense recognition as originally proposed. This issue is discussed at greater length in Chapter 19.

Another example of the political process at work in standard setting is the controversy surrounding the implementation of the fair value accounting standard issued in 2007. Many financial assets and liabilities are reported at fair value in the balance sheet, and many types of fair value changes are included in net income. Some have argued that fair values were estimated in a manner that exacerbated the financial crisis of 2008–2009 by forcing financial institutions to take larger than necessary write-downs of financial assets in the illiquid markets that existed at that time. As discussed further in Chapter 12, pressure from lobbyists and politicians influenced the FASB to revise its guidance on recognizing investment losses in these situations, and ongoing pressure remains to reduce the extent to which fair value changes are included in the determination of net income.

---

[18]www.FASB.org.

14   SECTION 1   The Role of Accounting as an Information System

• LO1–11

International Financial Reporting Standards

> **Politics in International Standard Setting.** Political pressures on the IASB's standard-setting process are severe. Politicians from countries that use IFRS lobby for the standards they prefer. The European Union (EU) is a particularly important adopter of IFRS and utilizes a formal evaluation process for determining whether an IFRS standard will be endorsed for use in EU countries. Economic consequences for EU member nations are an important consideration in that process.
>
> For example, in 2008 the EU successfully pressured the IASB to suspend its due process and immediately allow reclassification of investments so that EU banks could avoid recognizing huge losses during a financial crisis.[19] Commenting on standards setting at that time, Charlie McCreevy, European Commissioner for Internal Markets and Service, stated that "Accounting is now far too important to be left to . . . accountants!"[20]

Additional Consideration

> **Private Company Council (PCC).** Are the complex, comprehensive standards that are necessary to reflect the activities of a huge multinational conglomerate like General Electric also appropriate for a private company that, say, just needs to provide financial statements to its bank to get a loan? Private companies might be able to avoid much of that complexity. They don't sell securities like stocks and bonds to the general public, and they usually can identify the information needs of the specific users who rely on their financial statements and provide direct access to management to answer questions. Private companies typically also have a smaller accounting staff than do public companies. For those reasons, private companies have long sought a version of GAAP that is less costly to apply and better meets the information needs of the users of their financial statements.
>
> In 2012, the Financial Accounting Foundation responded to this concern by establishing the Private Company Council (PCC). The ten-member PCC determines whether changes to existing GAAP are necessary to meet the needs of users of private company financial statements but a proposed exception or modification for private companies must be endorsed by the FASB before being issued as an Accounting Standards Update and added to the Codification. The PCC also advises the FASB about its current projects that affect private companies.

• LO1–5

Encouraging High-Quality Financial Reporting

FINANCIAL Reporting Case

Q3, p. 3

Auditors express an opinion on the compliance of financial statements with GAAP.

Numerous factors affect the quality of financial reporting. In this section, we discuss the role of the auditor, recent reforms in financial reporting, and the debate about whether accounting standards should emphasize rules or underlying principles.

The Role of the Auditor

It is the responsibility of management to apply GAAP appropriately. Another group, auditors, examine (audit) financial statements to express a professional, independent opinion about whether the statements fairly present the company's financial position, its results of operations, and its cash flows in compliance with GAAP. Audits add credibility to the financial statements, increasing the confidence of those who rely on the information. Auditors, therefore, play an important role in the capital markets.

---

[19]Sarah Deans and Dane Mott, "Lowering Standards," www.morganmarkets.com, 10/14/2008.
[20]Charlie McCreevy, Keynote Address, "Financial Reporting in a Changing World" Conference, Brussels, 5/7/2009.

Most companies receive what's called an unmodified audit report. For example, Apple Inc.'s 2017 audit report by Ernst & Young LLP states, "In our opinion, the financial statements referred to above present fairly, in all material respects, the consolidated financial position of Apple Inc. at September 30, 2017 and September 24, 2016, and the consolidated results of its operations and its cash flows for each of the three years in the period ended September 30, 2017, in conformity with U.S. generally accepted accounting principles." This is known as a clean opinion. Had there been any material departures from GAAP or other problems that caused the auditors to question the fairness of the statements, the report would have been modified to inform readers. Normally, companies correct any material misstatements that auditors identify in the course of an audit, so companies usually receive clean opinions. The audit report for public companies also provides the auditors' opinion on the effectiveness of the company's internal control over financial reporting.

In most states, only individuals licensed as certified public accountants (CPAs) can represent that the financial statements have been audited in accordance with generally accepted auditing standards. Requirements to be licensed as a CPA vary from state to state, but all states specify education, testing, and experience requirements. The testing requirement is to pass the Uniform CPA Examination.

Certified public accountants (CPAs) are licensed by states to provide audit services.

Financial Reporting Reform

The dramatic collapse of Enron in 2001 and the dismantling of the international public accounting firm of Arthur Andersen in 2002 severely shook U.S. capital markets. The credibility of the accounting profession itself as well as of corporate America was called into question. Public outrage over accounting scandals at high-profile companies like WorldCom, Xerox, Merck, Adelphia Communications, and others increased the pressure on lawmakers to pass measures that would restore credibility and investor confidence in the financial reporting process.

Driven by these pressures, Congress acted swiftly and passed the *Public Company Accounting Reform and Investor Protection Act of 2002,* commonly referred to as the *Sarbanes-Oxley Act*, or *SOX*, for the two congressmen who sponsored the bill. SOX applies to public securities-issuing entities. It provides for the regulation of auditors and the types of services they furnish to clients, increases accountability of corporate executives, addresses conflicts of interest for securities analysts, and provides for stiff criminal penalties for violators. Illustration 1–9 outlines key provisions of the Act.

Section 404 is perhaps the most controversial provision of SOX. It requires that company management document internal controls and report on their adequacy. Auditors also must express an opinion on whether the company has maintained effective control over financial reporting.

No one argues the importance of adequate internal controls, but many argued that the benefits of Section 404 did not justify the costs of complying with it. Research provides evidence that 404 reports affect investors' risk assessments and companies' stock prices, indicating these reports are seen as useful by investors.[21] Unfortunately, it is not possible to quantify the more important benefit of potentially avoiding business failures like Enron by focusing attention on the implementation and maintenance of adequate internal controls.

The costs of 404 compliance initially were quite steep. For example, one survey of Fortune 1,000 companies estimated that large companies spent, on average, approximately $8.5 million and $4.8 million (including internal costs and auditor fees) during the first two years of the act to comply with 404 reporting requirements.[22] As expected, the costs dropped significantly in the second year, and continued to drop as the efficiency of internal control audits increased. Many companies now perceive that the benefits of these internal control reports exceed their costs.[23]

We revisit Section 404 in Chapter 7 in the context of an introduction to internal controls.

---

[21]Hollis Ashbaugh Skaife, Daniel W. Collins, William R. Kinney, Jr., and Ryan LaFond, "The Effect of SOX Internal Control Deficiencies on Firm Risk and Cost of Equity," *Journal of Accounting Research* 47 (2009), pp. 1–43.

[22]"Sarbanes-Oxley 404 Costs and Implementation Issues: Spring 2006 Survey Update," CRA International (April 17, 2006).

[23]Protiviti, Inc., *2011 Sarbanes-Oxley Compliance Survey* (June, 2011).

Illustration 1–9

Public Company Accounting Reform and Investor Protection Act of 2002 (Sarbanes-Oxley)

Key Provisions of the Sarbanes-Oxley Act:

- **Oversight board.** The five-member (two accountants) Public Company Accounting Oversight Board has the authority to establish standards dealing with auditing, quality control, ethics, independence, and other activities relating to the preparation of audit reports, or can choose to delegate these responsibilities to the AICPA. Prior to the act, the AICPA set auditing standards. The SEC has oversight and enforcement authority.
- **Corporate executive accountability.** Corporate executives must personally certify the financial statements and company disclosures with severe financial penalties and the possibility of imprisonment for fraudulent misstatement.
- **Nonaudit services.** The law makes it unlawful for the auditors of public companies to perform a variety of nonaudit services for audit clients. Prohibited services include bookkeeping, internal audit outsourcing, appraisal or valuation services, and various other consulting services. Other nonaudit services, including tax services, require preapproval by the audit committee of the company being audited.
- **Retention of work papers.** Auditors of public companies must retain all audit or review work papers for seven years or face the threat of a prison term for willful violations.
- **Auditor rotation.** Lead audit partners are required to rotate every five years. Mandatory rotation of audit firms came under consideration.
- **Conflicts of interest.** Audit firms are not allowed to audit public companies whose chief executives worked for the audit firm and participated in that company's audit during the preceding year.
- **Hiring of auditor.** Audit firms are hired by the audit committee of the board of directors of the company, not by company management.
- **Internal control.** Section 404 of the act requires that company management document and assess the effectiveness of all internal control processes that could affect financial reporting. The PCAOB's *Auditing Standard No. 2* (since replaced by *AS 2201*) requires that the company auditors express an opinion on whether the company has maintained effective internal control over financial reporting.

A Move Away from Rules-Based Standards?

A *principles-based,* or *objectives-oriented,* approach to standard-setting stresses professional judgment, as opposed to following a list of rules.

The accounting scandals at Enron and other companies involved managers using elaborately structured transactions to try to circumvent specific rules in accounting standards. One consequence of those scandals was a rekindled debate over principles-based, or more recently termed objectives-oriented, versus rules-based accounting standards. In fact, a provision of the Sarbanes-Oxley Act required the SEC to study the issue and provide a report to Congress on its findings. That report, issued in July 2003, recommended that accounting standards be developed using an objectives-oriented approach.[24]

An objectives-oriented approach to standard setting emphasizes using professional judgment, as opposed to following a list of rules, when choosing how to account for a transaction. Proponents of an objectives-oriented approach argue that a focus on professional judgment means that there are few rules to sidestep and we are more likely to arrive at an appropriate accounting treatment. Detractors, on the other hand, argue that the absence of detailed rules opens the door to even more abuse, because management can use the latitude provided by objectives to justify their preferred accounting approach. Even in the absence of intentional misuse, reliance on professional judgment might result in different interpretations for similar transactions, raising concerns about comparability. Also, detailed rules help auditors withstand pressure from clients who want a more favorable accounting treatment and help companies ensure that they are complying with GAAP and avoid litigation or SEC

---

[24]"Study Pursuant to Section 108 (d) of the Sarbanes-Oxley Act of 2002 on the Adoption by the United States Financial Reporting System of a Principles-Based Accounting System," Securities and Exchange Commission (July 2003).

inquiry. For these reasons, it's challenging to avoid providing detailed rules in the U.S. reporting environment.

Regardless of whether accounting standards are based more on rules or on objectives, prior research highlights that there is some potential for abuse, either by structuring transactions around precise rules or opportunistically interpreting underlying principles.[25] The key is whether management is dedicated to high-quality financial reporting. It appears that poor ethical values on the part of management are at the heart of accounting abuses and scandals, so we now turn to a discussion of ethics in the accounting profession.

Ethics in Accounting

Ethics is a term that refers to a code or moral system that provides criteria for evaluating right and wrong. An ethical dilemma is a situation in which an individual or group is faced with a decision that tests this code. Many of these dilemmas are simple to recognize and resolve. For example, have you ever been tempted to call your professor and ask for an extension on the due date of an assignment by claiming a pretended illness? Temptation like this will test your personal ethics.

Ethics deals with the ability to distinguish right from wrong.

Accountants, like others in the business world, are faced with many ethical dilemmas, some of which are complex and difficult to resolve. For instance, the capital markets' focus on near-term profits may tempt a company's management to bend or even break accounting rules to inflate reported net income. In these situations, technical competence is not enough to resolve the dilemma.

ETHICS AND PROFESSIONALISM   One characteristic that distinguishes a profession from other occupations is the acceptance by its members of a responsibility for the interests of those it serves. Ethical behavior is expected of those engaged in a profession. That expectation often is articulated in a code of ethics. For example, law and medicine are professions that have their own codes of professional ethics. These codes provide guidance and rules to members in the performance of their professional responsibilities.

Public accounting has achieved widespread recognition as a profession. The AICPA, the national organization of certified public accountants, has its own Code of Professional Conduct that prescribes the ethical conduct members should strive to achieve. Similarly, the Institute of Management Accountants (IMA)—the primary national organization of accountants working in industry and government—has its own code of ethics, as does the Institute of Internal Auditors—the national organization of accountants providing internal auditing services for their own organizations.

ANALYTICAL MODEL FOR ETHICAL DECISIONS   Ethical codes are informative and helpful, but the motivation to behave ethically must come from within oneself and not just from the fear of penalties for violating professional codes. Presented below is a sequence of steps that provide a framework for analyzing ethical issues. These steps can help you apply your own sense of right and wrong to ethical dilemmas:[26]

Step 1.   Determine the facts of the situation. This involves determining the who, what, where, when, and how.

Step 2.   Identify the ethical issue and the stakeholders. Stakeholders may include shareholders, creditors, management, employees, and the community.

---

[25]Mark W. Nelson, John A. Elliott, and Robin L. Tarpley, "Evidence From Auditors About Manager' and Auditors Earnings Management Decisions," *The Accounting Review* 77 (2002), pp. 175–202.

[26]Adapted from Harold Q. Langenderfer and Joanne W. Rockness, "Integrating Ethics into the Accounting Curriculum: Issues, Problems, and Solutions," *Issues in Accounting Education* (Spring 1989). These steps are consistent with those provided by the American Accounting Association's Advisory Committee on Professionalism and Ethics in their publication *Ethics in the Accounting Curriculum: Cases and Readings, 1990.*

Ethical Dilemma

You recently have been employed by a large retail chain that sells sporting goods. One of your tasks is to help prepare periodic financial statements for external distribution. The chain's largest creditor, National Savings & Loan, requires quarterly financial statements, and you are currently working on the statements for the three-month period ending June 30, 2021.

During the months of May and June, the company spent $1,200,000 on a hefty radio and TV advertising campaign. The $1,200,000 included the costs of producing the commercials as well as the radio and TV time purchased to air the commercials. All of the costs were charged to advertising expense. The company's chief financial officer (CFO) has asked you to prepare a June 30 adjusting entry to remove the costs from advertising expense and to set up an asset called *prepaid advertising* that will be expensed in July. The CFO explained that "This advertising campaign has led to significant sales in May and June and I think it will continue to bring in customers through the month of July. By recording the ad costs as an asset, we can match the cost of the advertising with the additional July sales. Besides, if we expense the advertising in May and June, we will show an operating loss on our income statement for the quarter. The bank requires that we continue to show quarterly profits in order to maintain our loan in good standing."

Step 3. Identify the values related to the situation. For example, in some situations confidentiality may be an important value that might conflict with the right to know.

Step 4. Specify the alternative courses of action.

Step 5. Evaluate the courses of action specified in step 4 in terms of their consistency with the values identified in step 3. This step may or may not lead to a suggested course of action.

Step 6. Identify the consequences of each possible course of action. If step 5 does not provide a course of action, assess the consequences of each possible course of action for all of the stakeholders involved.

Step 7. Make your decision and take any indicated action.

Ethical dilemmas are presented throughout this book. The analytical steps outlined above provide a framework you can use to evaluate these situations.

PART B

● LO1–6

FINANCIAL Reporting Case

Q4, p. 3

The *conceptual framework* does not prescribe GAAP. It provides an underlying foundation for accounting standards.

The Conceptual Framework

Sturdy buildings are built on sound foundations. The U.S. Constitution is the foundation for the laws of our land. The conceptual framework has been described as an "Accounting Constitution" because it provides the underlying foundation for U.S. accounting standards. The conceptual framework provides structure and direction to financial accounting and reporting but does not directly prescribe GAAP. It is a coherent system of interrelated objectives and fundamentals that is intended to lead to consistent standards and that prescribes the nature, function, and limits of financial accounting and reporting. The fundamentals are the underlying concepts of accounting that guide the selection of events to be accounted for, the measurement of those events, and the means of summarizing and communicating them to interested parties.[27]

The FASB disseminates this framework through *Statements of Financial Accounting Concepts (SFACs). SFAC 8* discusses the objective of financial reporting and the qualitative characteristics of useful financial information. *SFAC 7* describes how cash flows and present values are used when making accounting measurements, *SFAC 6* defines the accounts and

---

[27]"Conceptual Framework for Financial Accounting and Reporting: Elements of Financial Statements and Their Measurement," *Discussion Memorandum* (Stamford, Conn.: FASB, 1976), p. 2.

Illustration 1–10

The Conceptual Framework

accrual accounting concepts that appear in financial statements, and *SFAC 5* discusses recognition and measurement concepts. Earlier *SFACs* either have been superseded or involve nonbusiness organizations that aren't considered in this book.

In the remainder of this section we discuss the components of the conceptual framework, as depicted in Illustration 1–10.

International Financial Reporting Standards

Role of the conceptual framework. The conceptual frameworks in U.S. GAAP and IFRS are very similar and are converging even more with ongoing efforts by the FASB and IASB. However, in U.S. GAAP, the conceptual framework primarily provides guidance to standard setters to help them develop high-quality standards. In IFRS, the conceptual framework guides standard setting, but in addition it provides a basis for practitioners to make accounting judgments when another IFRS standard does not apply. Also, IFRS emphasizes the overarching concept of the financial statements providing a "fair presentation" of the company. U.S. GAAP does not include a similar requirement, but U.S. auditing standards require this consideration.

● LO1–11

Objective of Financial Reporting

● LO1-7

As indicated in Part A of this chapter, the objective of general purpose financial reporting is to provide financial information about companies that is useful to capital providers in making decisions. For example, investors decide whether to buy, sell, or hold equity or debt securities, and creditors decide whether to provide or settle loans. Information that is useful to capital providers may also be useful to other users of financial reporting information, such as regulators or taxing authorities.

Investors and creditors are interested in the amount, timing, and uncertainty of a company's future cash flows. Information about a company's economic resources (assets) and claims against resources (liabilities) also is useful. Not only does this information about resources and claims provide insight into future cash flows, it also helps decision makers identify the company's financial strengths and weaknesses and assess liquidity and solvency.

Qualitative Characteristics of Financial Reporting Information

What characteristics should information have to best meet the objective of financial reporting? Illustration 1–11 indicates the desirable qualitative characteristics of financial reporting information, presented in the form of a hierarchy of their perceived importance. Notice that these characteristics are intended to enhance the decision usefulness of information.

Fundamental Qualitative Characteristics

Decision usefulness requires that information possess the qualities of relevance and faithful representation.

For financial information to be useful, it should possess the fundamental decision-specific qualities of relevance and faithful representation. Both are critical. Information is of little value if it's not relevant. And even if information is relevant, it is not as useful if it doesn't faithfully represent the economic phenomenon it purports to represent. Let's look closer at each of these two qualitative characteristics, including the components that make those characteristics desirable. We also consider other characteristics that enhance usefulness.

Illustration 1–11

Hierarchy of Qualitative Characteristics of Financial Information

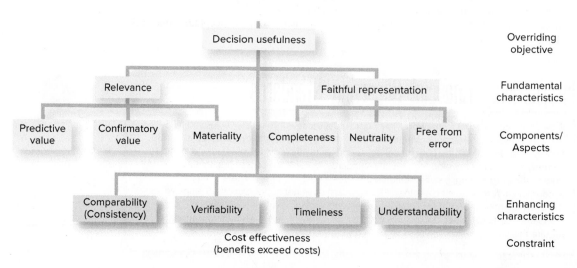

QUALITATIVE CHARACTERISTICS

RELEVANCE   Obviously, to make a difference in the decision process, information must be relevant to the decision. Relevance in the context of financial reporting means that information must possess predictive value and/or confirmatory value, typically both. For example, current-period net income has predictive value if it helps users predict a company's future cash flows, and it has confirmatory value if it helps investors confirm or change their prior assessments regarding a company's cash-flow generating ability. Predictive and confirmatory value are central to the concept of "earnings quality," the ability of reported earnings (income) to predict a company's future earnings.

Relevance requires that information have predictive and confirmatory value.

Financial information is material if it is probable that including or correcting the information would affect a user's judgment decisions. Materiality is an aspect of relevance that depends on a company's particular situation and is based on the nature or magnitude of the item that is being reported. Recall that Apple Inc.'s audit report discussed earlier only expressed an opinion about material items. If information is immaterial, it's not relevant.

Information is material if it could affect users' judgment.

The threshold for materiality often depends on the *relative* dollar amount of the transaction. For example, $10,000 in total anticipated bad debts for a multibillion dollar company would not be considered material. This same $10,000 amount, however, might easily be material for a neighborhood pizza parlor. Because of the context-specific nature of materiality, the FASB has been reluctant to establish any quantitative materiality guidelines. The threshold for materiality has been left to the subjective judgment of the company preparing the financial statements and its auditors.

Materiality often relates to the nature of the item as well. It has to be evaluated in light of surrounding circumstances, and it depends on qualitative as well as quantitative considerations. For example, an illegal payment of a $10,000 bribe to an official of a foreign government to secure a valuable contract probably would be considered material qualitatively even if the amount is small relative to the size of the company. Similarly, a small dollar amount that changes a net loss to a net income for the reporting period could be viewed as material to financial statement users for qualitative reasons.

Professional judgment determines what amount is material in each situation.

FAITHFUL REPRESENTATION   Faithful representation exists when there is agreement between a measure or description and the phenomenon it purports to represent. For example, the term *inventory* in the balance sheet of a retail company is understood by external users to represent items that are intended for sale in the ordinary course of business. If inventory includes, say, accounts receivable, it lacks faithful representation.

Faithful representation means agreement between a measure and a real-world phenomenon that the measure is supposed to represent.

To break it down further, faithful representation requires that information be *complete, neutral,* and *free from error.* A depiction of an economic phenomenon is complete if it includes all the information necessary for faithful representation of the economic phenomenon that it purports to represent. Omitting a portion of that information can cause it to be false or misleading.

A depiction is complete if it includes all information necessary for faithful representation.

A financial accounting standard, and the standard-setting process, is neutral if it is free from bias. You learned earlier that changes in accounting standards can lead to adverse economic consequences for certain companies and that political pressure is sometimes brought to bear on the standard-setting process in hopes of achieving particular outcomes. Accounting standards should be established with the goal of providing high-quality information, and should not try to achieve particular social outcomes or favor particular groups or companies. The FASB faces a difficult task in maintaining neutrality in the face of economic consequences and resulting political pressures.

Neutral implies freedom from bias.

Information is *free from error* if it contains no errors or omissions.

Representational faithfulness also is enhanced if information is free from error, meaning that there are no errors or omissions in the description of the amount or the process used to report the amount. Uncertainty is a fact of life when we measure many items of financial information included in financial statements. Estimates are common, and some inaccuracy is likely. An estimate is represented faithfully if it is described clearly and accurately as being an estimate, and financial statement users are given enough information to understand the potential for inaccuracy that exists.

Conservatism requires greater verification for good news than for bad news.

Many accountants have recommended that we deal with the potential for error by employing conservatism. Conservatism means that accountants require greater verification before recognizing good news than bad news. The result is that losses are reflected in net income more quickly than are gains, and net assets tend to be biased downwards.

SFAC 8 explicitly rejects conservatism as a desirable characteristic of accounting information, stating that conservatism undermines representational faithfulness by being inconsistent with neutrality. Nevertheless, some accounting practices appear to be generated by a desire to be conservative. For example, companies are required to recognize losses for declines in the value of inventory, buildings, and equipment, but aren't allowed to recognize gains for increases in those values. One justification for these practices is that investors and creditors who lose money on their investments are less likely to sue the company if bad news has been exaggerated and good news underestimated. Another justification is that conservative accounting can trigger debt covenants that allow creditors to protect themselves from bad management. So, despite the lack of support for conservatism in the conceptual framework, it is likely to persist as an important consideration in accounting practice and in the application of some accounting standards.

Enhancing Qualitative Characteristics

Illustration 1–11 identifies four *enhancing* qualitative characteristics: *comparability (*including *consistency), verifiability, timeliness,* and *understandability.*

Information is *comparable* if similar items are treated the same way and different items are treated differently.

Comparability helps users see similarities and differences between events and conditions. We already have discussed the importance of investors and creditors being able to compare information *among companies* to make their resource allocation decisions. Closely related to comparability is the notion that consistency of accounting practices over time permits valid comparisons *among different reporting periods.* The predictive and confirmatory value of information is enhanced if users can compare the performance of a company over time.[28] Companies typically include as Note 1 to the financial statements a summary of significant accounting policies and provide full disclosure of any changes in those policies to alert users to the potential for diminished consistency.

Information is *consistent* if it is measured and reported the same way in each time period.

Information is *verifiable* if different measurers would reach consensus about whether it is representationally faithful.

Verifiability implies that different knowledgeable and independent measurers would reach consensus regarding whether information is a faithful representation of what it is intended to depict. Direct verification involves observing the item being depicted. For example, the historical cost of a parcel of land to be reported in a company's balance sheet usually is highly verifiable. The cost can be traced to an exchange transaction, the purchase of the land. On the other hand, the fair value of that land is much more difficult to verify. Appraisers could differ in their assessment of fair value. Verification of their estimates would be indirect, involving examination of their valuation models and assessments of the reasonableness of model inputs. The term *objectivity* often is linked to verifiability. The historical cost of the land is objective and easy to verify, but the land's fair value is subjective, and may be influenced by the measurer's past experience and biases. A measurement that is subjective is more difficult to verify, which may make users doubt its representational faithfulness.

Information is *timely* if it is available to users before a decision is made.

Timeliness also is important for information to be useful. Information is timely when it's available to users early enough to allow them to use it in their decision process. To enhance

---

[28]Companies occasionally do change their accounting practices, which makes it difficult for users to make comparisons among different reporting periods. Chapter 4 and Chapter 20 describe the disclosures that a company makes in this situation to restore consistency among periods.

timeliness, the SEC requires its registrants to submit financial statement information on a quarterly as well as on an annual basis for each fiscal year.

Understandability means that users must be able to comprehend the information within the context of the decision being made. This is a user-specific quality because users will differ in their ability to comprehend any set of information. The overriding objective of financial reporting is to provide comprehensible information to those who have a *reasonable understanding* of business and economic activities and are diligent in studying the information.

> Information is *understandable* if users can comprehend it.

Key Constraint: Cost Effectiveness

Most of us learn early in life that we can't get everything we want. The latest electronic gadget may have all the qualitative characteristics that current technology can provide, but limited resources may lead us to buy a model with fewer bells and whistles. Cost effectiveness constrains the accounting choices we make. The benefits of endowing financial information with all the qualitative characteristics we've discussed must exceed the costs of doing so.

> Information is *cost effective* if the benefit of increased *decision usefulness* exceeds the costs of providing that information.

The costs of providing financial information include those of gathering, processing, and disseminating information. There also are costs to users when interpreting information. In addition, costs include possible adverse economic consequences of implementing accounting standards. For example, consider the requirement that companies having more than one operating segment must disclose certain disaggregated financial information.[29] In addition to the costs of information gathering, processing, and communicating that information, many companies feel that this reporting requirement imposes what could be called *competitive disadvantage costs*. These companies are concerned that their competitors will gain some advantage from having access to the disaggregated data.

> The costs of providing financial information include any possible adverse economic consequences of accounting standards.

The perceived benefit from this or any accounting standard is increased *decision usefulness* of the information provided, which, ideally, improves the resource allocation process. It is inherently impossible to quantify this benefit. The elaborate information-gathering process undertaken by the FASB in setting accounting standards is an attempt to assess both costs and benefits of a proposed accounting standard, even if in a subjective, nonquantifiable manner.

Elements of Financial Statements

SFAC 6 defines 10 elements of financial statements. These elements are "the building blocks with which financial statements are constructed—the classes of items that financial statements comprise."[30] They focus directly on items related to reporting financial position and measuring performance. The *accrual accounting* model is embodied in the element definitions. For now, we list and define the elements in Illustration 1–12. You will learn much more about these elements in subsequent chapters.

> The 10 elements of financial statements defined in *SFAC 6* describe financial position and periodic performance.

Underlying Assumptions

> ● LO1–8

Though not emphasized in the FASB's concepts statements, four basic assumptions underlie GAAP: (1) the economic entity assumption, (2) the going concern assumption, (3) the periodicity assumption, and (4) the monetary unit assumption. These assumptions identify the entity that is being reported on, the assumption that the entity will continue to exist, and the frequency and denomination in which reports occur.

Illustration 1–13 summarizes the four assumptions underlying GAAP.

Economic Entity Assumption

The economic entity assumption presumes that all economic events can be identified with a particular *economic entity*. Investors desire information about an economic entity that

> The *economic entity assumption* presumes that economic events can be identified with a particular economic entity.

---

[29]FASB ASC 280: Segment Reporting (previously "Disclosures about Segments of an Enterprise and Related Information," *Statement of Financial Accounting Standards No. 131* (Norwalk, Conn.: FASB, 1997)).

[30]"Elements of Financial Statements," *Statement of Financial Accounting Concepts No. 6* (Stamford, Conn.: FASB, 1985), par. 5.

Illustration 1–12

Elements of Financial Statements

	Elements of Financial Statements
Assets	Probable future economic benefits obtained or controlled by a particular entity as a result of past transactions or events.
Liabilities	Probable future sacrifices of economic benefits arising from present obligations of a particular entity to transfer assets or provide services to other entities in the future as a result of past transactions or events.
Equity (or net assets)	Called shareholders' equity or stockholders' equity for a corporation, it is the residual interest in the assets of an entity that remains after deducting its liabilities.
Investments by owners	Increases in equity of a particular business enterprise resulting from transfers to it from other entities of something of value to obtain or increase ownership interests in it.
Distributions to owners	Decreases in equity of a particular enterprise resulting from transfers to owners.
Comprehensive income	The change in equity of a business enterprise during a period from transactions and other events and circumstances from nonowner sources. It includes all changes in equity during a period except those resulting from investments by owners and distributions to owners.
Revenues	Inflows or other enhancements of assets of an entity or settlements of its liabilities during a period from delivering or producing goods, rendering services, or other activities that constitute the entity's ongoing major or central operations.
Expenses	Outflows or other using up of assets or incurrences of liabilities during a period from delivering or producing goods, rendering services, or other activities that constitute the entity's ongoing major or central operations.
Gains	Increases in equity from peripheral or incidental transactions of an entity.
Losses	Represent decreases in equity arising from peripheral or incidental transactions of an entity.

Illustration 1–13

Summary of Assumptions Underlying GAAP

Assumptions	Description
Economic entity	All economic events can be identified with a particular economic entity.
Going concern	In the absence of information to the contrary, it is anticipated that a business entity will continue to operate indefinitely.
Periodicity	The life of a company can be divided into artificial time periods to provide timely information to external users.
Monetary unit	In the United States, financial statement elements should be measured in terms of the U.S. dollar.

corresponds to their ownership interest. For example, if you were considering buying some ownership stock in **Alphabet** (the parent company of **Google**), you would want information on the various operating units that constitute Alphabet. You would need information not only about its United States operations but also about its European and other international operations. The financial information for the various companies (subsidiaries) in which Alphabet owns a controlling interest (greater than 50% ownership of voting stock) should be combined with that of Alphabet (the parent) to provide a complete picture. The parent and its subsidiaries are separate *legal* entities but one *accounting* entity.

Another key aspect of this assumption is the distinction between the economic activities of owners and those of the company. For example, the economic activities of a sole proprietorship, Uncle Jim's Restaurant, should be separated from the activities of its owner, Uncle Jim. Uncle Jim's personal residence, for instance, is not an asset of the business.

Going Concern Assumption

Another necessary assumption is that, in the absence of information to the contrary, we anticipate that a business entity will continue to operate indefinitely. Accountants realize that the going concern assumption does not always hold since there certainly are many business failures. However, this assumption is critical to many broad and specific accounting principles. For example, the assumption provides justification for measuring many assets based on their historical costs. If it were known that an enterprise would cease operations in the near future, assets and liabilities would be measured at their current liquidation values. Similarly, when we depreciate a building over an estimated life of 40 years, we assume the business will operate that long.

The *going concern* assumption presumes that a business will operate indefinitely.

Periodicity Assumption

The periodicity assumption relates to the qualitative characteristic of *timeliness*. External users need *periodic* information to make decisions. This need for periodic information requires that the economic life of a company (presumed to be indefinite) be divided into artificial time periods for financial reporting. Corporations whose securities are publicly traded are required to provide financial information to the SEC on a quarterly and annual basis.[31] Financial statements often are prepared on a monthly basis for banks and others that might need more timely information.

The *periodicity assumption* allows the life of a company to be divided into artificial time periods to provide timely information.

For many companies, the annual time period (the fiscal year) is the calendar year. However, other companies have chosen a fiscal year that does not correspond to the calendar year. The accounting profession and the SEC advocate that companies adopt a fiscal year that corresponds to their natural business year. A natural business year is the 12-month period that ends when the business activities of a company reach their lowest point in the annual cycle. For example, many retailers, such as Walmart, have adopted a fiscal year ending around January 31. Business activity in January generally is quite slow following the very busy Christmas period. The Campbell Soup Company's fiscal year ends in July; Clorox's in June; and Monsanto's in August.

Monetary Unit Assumption

The monetary unit assumption requires that financial statement elements be measured in nominal units of money, without any adjustment for changes in purchasing power. In the United States, the U.S. dollar is the monetary unit used in financial statements. In the European Union (EU), the euro is the monetary unit. Other countries use other currencies as their monetary units.

The *monetary unit assumption* states that financial statement elements should be measured in a particular monetary unit (in the United States, the U.S. dollar).

One problem with use of a monetary unit like the dollar or the euro is that it is presumed to be stable over time. That is, the value of the dollar, in terms of its ability to purchase certain goods and services, is assumed to be constant over time. This assumption obviously does not strictly hold. The U.S. economy has experienced periods of rapidly changing prices. To the extent that prices are unstable, and machines, trucks, and buildings were purchased at different times, the monetary unit used to measure them is not the same. The effect of changing prices on financial information generally is discussed elsewhere in your accounting curriculum, often in an advanced accounting course.

Recognition, Measurement, and Disclosure Concepts

● LO1–9

Now that we have identified the various elements and underlying assumptions of the financial statements, we discuss *when* the elements should be recognized (recorded) and how they should be *measured* and *disclosed*. For example, an asset was previously defined as a probable future economic benefit obtained or controlled by a company as a result of past transactions or events. But *when* should the asset be recorded, at *what* amount, and what other important information about the asset should be provided in the financial statements? *SFAC 5* addresses these issues. Recognition refers to the process of admitting information into the financial statements. Measurement is the process of associating numerical amounts with the elements. Disclosure refers to including pertinent information in the financial statements and accompanying notes.

---

[31]The report that must be filed for the first three quarters of each fiscal year is Form 10-Q and the annual report is Form 10-K.

Recognition

Recognition criteria determine whether items should be included in the financial statements.

GENERAL RECOGNITION CRITERIA   According to *SFAC 5,* an item should be recognized in the basic financial statements when it meets the following four criteria, subject to a cost effectiveness constraint and materiality threshold:

1. *Definition.* The item meets the definition of an element of financial statements.
2. *Measurability.* The item has a relevant attribute measurable with sufficient reliability.
3. *Relevance.* The information about it is capable of making a difference in user decisions.
4. *Reliability.* The information is representationally faithful, verifiable, and neutral.[32]

SFAC 5 provides further guidance with respect to revenue and expense recognition, and you will learn about more specific guidelines throughout this book.

Revenues are inflows of assets or settlements of liabilities as a result of providing goods or services to customers.

REVENUE RECOGNITION   Revenues are inflows of assets or settlements of liabilities resulting from providing a product or service to a customer. An income statement should report the results of these activities only for the time period specified in the financial statements. Therefore, the *timing* of revenue recognition is a key element of earnings measurement. Not adhering to revenue recognition criteria could result in overstating revenue and hence net income in one reporting period and, consequently, understating revenue and net income in another period.

Until recently, revenue recognition was guided by the *realization principle,* which requires that two criteria be satisfied before revenue can be recognized:

1. The earnings process is judged to be complete or virtually complete.
2. There is reasonable certainty as to the collectibility of the asset to be received (usually cash).

As discussed further in Chapter 6, *ASU No. 2014-09* changed how we determine the timing and measurement of revenue.[33] That standard requires that companies recognize revenue when goods or services are transferred to customers for the amount the company expects to be entitled to receive in exchange for those goods or services. Revenue is recognized at a point in time or over a period of time, depending on when goods or services are transferred to customers. For example, revenue for the sale of most goods is recognized upon delivery, but revenue for services like renting apartments or lending money is recognized over time as those services are provided. No revenue is recognized if it isn't probable that the seller will collect the amounts it's entitled to receive. While that standard doesn't rely on the realization principle, you can see that aspects of the realization principle remain—we still focus on the seller fulfilling its obligations to its customers, and before revenue can be recognized we still require a relatively high likelihood that the seller will be paid.

Notice that these criteria help implement the accrual accounting model. Revenue is recognized when the seller transfers goods or services to a customer, which isn't necessarily at the same time the seller is paid by the customer.

The timing of revenue recognition also affects the timing of asset recognition. When revenue is recognized by crediting a revenue account, the corresponding debit typically increases some asset, usually cash or an account receivable.

Expenses are outflows or other using up of assets or incurrences of liabilities from providing goods or services.

EXPENSE RECOGNITION   Expenses are outflows or other using up of assets or incurrences of liabilities from providing goods or services. When are expenses recognized? In practice, expense recognition often matches revenues and expenses that arise from the same

---

[32]"Recognition and Measurement in Financial Statements," *Statement of Financial Accounting Concepts No. 5* (Stamford, Conn.: FASB, 1984), par. 63. *SFAC 8* has replaced reliability with faithful representation as the second primary qualitative characteristic of financial information.

[33]"Revenue from Contracts with Customers (Topic 606)," *Accounting Standards Update 2014–09* (Norwalk, Conn: FASB, 2014).

transactions or other events.[34] There is a cause-and-effect relationship between revenue and expense recognition implicit in this approach. The net result is a measure—net income—that identifies the amount of profit or loss for the period provided by operations.

Although these concepts are straightforward, their implementation can be difficult, because many expenses are not incurred *directly* to produce a particular amount of revenue. Instead, the association between revenue and many expenses is indirect. Therefore, expense recognition is implemented by one of four different approaches, depending on the nature of the specific expense:[35]

- **Based on an exact cause-and-effect relationship.** This approach is appropriate for *cost of goods sold,* as one example. There is a definite cause-and-effect relationship between PetSmart's revenue from selling dog food and its costs to purchase that dog food from suppliers. Commissions paid to salespersons for obtaining revenues also is an example of an expense recognized based on this approach.

- **By associating an expense with the revenues recognized in a specific time period.** Many expenses can be related only to periods of time during which revenue is earned. For example, the monthly salary paid to an office worker is not directly related to any specific revenue event. Instead, the employee provides benefits to the company for that one month that *indirectly* relate to the revenue recognized in that same period.

- **By a systematic and rational allocation to specific time periods.** Some costs are incurred to acquire assets that provide benefits to the company for more than one reporting period, so we recognize expenses over those time periods. For example, straight-line depreciation is a "systematical and rational" way to allocate the cost of equipment to the periods in which that equipment is used to produce revenue.

- **In the period incurred, without regard to related revenues.** Sometimes costs are incurred, but it is impossible to determine in which period or periods, if any, related revenues will occur. For example, let's say Google spends $1 million for a series of television commercials. It's difficult to determine when, how much, or even whether additional revenues occur as a result of that particular series of ads. As a result, we recognize advertising expenditures as expenses in the period incurred.

The timing of expense recognition also affects the timing of asset and liability recognition and de-recognition. When we debit an expense, the corresponding credit usually either decreases an asset (for example, decreasing cash because it was used to pay an employee's salary) or increases a liability (for example, increasing salaries payable to accrue wages that will be paid at a later date).

Measurement

If an amount is to be recognized, it also must be measured. As indicated in *SFAC 5,* GAAP currently employs a "mixed attribute" measurement model. If you look at a balance sheet, for instance, you might see land measured at historical cost, inventory at net realizable value, a liability at the present value of future cash payments, and an investment at fair value. The attribute chosen to measure a particular item should be the one that maximizes the combination of relevance and representational faithfulness. *SFAC 5* lists five measurement attributes employed in GAAP:

1. Historical cost
2. Net realizable value
3. Current cost

---

[34]The term *matching principle* is sometimes used to refer to the practice of first recognizing revenue and then recognizing all expenses that were incurred to generate that revenue. However, the conceptual framework does not include that term. Rather, *SFACs 5* and 6 discuss matching as a result of recognizing expenses and revenues that arise from the same underlying transactions or events. Standard setters are reluctant to apply matching more broadly, because they are concerned that doing so could result in inappropriately recognizing as assets some amounts that do not provide "probable future economic benefits," and therefore don't meet the definition of an asset. We discuss this topic more in the "Evolving GAAP" section at the end of this chapter.

[35]"Elements of Financial Statements—a replacement of FASB Concepts Statement No. 3 (incorporating an amendment of FASB Concepts Statement No. 2)," *Statement of Financial Accounting Concepts No. 6* (Norwalk, Conn.: FASB, 1985).

4. Present (or discounted) value of future cash flows
5. Fair value

These different measurement attributes often indicate the same amount, particularly when the amount is initially recognized. However, sometimes they differ in important ways.

Historical cost bases measurements on the amount given or received in the original exchange transaction.

HISTORICAL COST   We often measure assets and liabilities based on their *original transaction value,* that is, their historical cost. Some accountants refer to this practice as applying the *historical cost principle.* For an asset, historical cost equals the value of what is given in exchange (usually cash) for the asset at its initial acquisition. For liabilities, it is the current cash equivalent received in exchange for assuming the liability. Historical cost for long-lived, revenue-producing assets such as equipment typically is adjusted subsequent to its initial measurement by recognizing depreciation or amortization.

Why base measurement on historical costs? First, historical cost provides important cash flow information as it represents the cash or cash equivalent paid for an asset or received in exchange for the assumption of a liability. Second, because historical cost valuation is the result of an exchange transaction between two independent parties, the agreed-upon exchange value is objective and highly verifiable.

Net realizable value bases measurements on the net amount of cash into which the asset or liability will be converted in the ordinary course of business.

NET REALIZABLE VALUE   Some assets are measured at their net realizable value, which is defined by the FASB as the estimated selling price in the ordinary course of business, less reasonably predictable costs of completion, disposal, and transportation. Intuitively, net realizable value is the net amount of cash into which an asset or liability is expected to be converted in the ordinary course of business. For example, if inventory could be sold for $10,000, and the company would incur additional costs of $2,000 to complete it and transport it to a customer, the inventory's net realizable value is $8,000. Departures from historical cost measurement such as this provide useful information to aid in the prediction of future cash flows.

Current cost is the cost that would be incurred to purchase or reproduce an asset.

CURRENT COST   Companies sometimes report current costs, particularly if they operate in inflationary economies. The current cost of an asset is the cost that would be incurred to purchase or reproduce the asset.

Present value bases measurement on future cash flows discounted for the time value of money.

PRESENT VALUE   Because of its importance to many accounting measurements, present value is the focus of a FASB concept statement, *SFAC 7,* which provides a framework for using future cash flows as the basis for accounting measurement and also indicates that the objective in valuing an asset or liability using present value is to approximate its fair value.[36] We explore the topic of present value in depth in Chapter 5 and the application of present value in accounting measurement in subsequent chapters.

Fair value bases measurements on the price that would be received to sell assets or transfer liabilities in an orderly market transaction.

FAIR VALUE   We measure many financial assets and liabilities at fair value (called *current market value* originally in *SFAC 5*). Also, we use fair values when determining whether the value of nonfinancial assets like property, plant, and equipment and intangible assets has been impaired. Given the complexity and growing importance of this measurement attribute, we discuss it in some detail.

Fair value is defined as the price that would be received to sell assets or paid to transfer a liability in an orderly transaction between market participants at the measurement date. A key aspect of this definition is its focus on the perspective of *market participants.* For instance, if a company buys a competitor's patent, not intending to use it but merely to keep the competitor from using it, the company still will have to assign a value to the asset because a market participant would find value in using the patent.

The FASB has provided a framework for measuring fair value whenever fair value is called for in applying generally accepted accounting principles.[37] The IASB uses the same

---

[36]"Using Cash Flow Information and Present Value in Accounting Measurements," *Statement of Financial Accounting Concepts No. 7* (Norwalk, Conn.: FASB, 2000).

[37]FASB ASC 820: Fair Value Measurements and Disclosures (previously "Fair Value Measurements," *Statement of Financial Accounting Standards No. 157* (Norwalk, Conn.: FASB, 2006)).

framework.[38] In the framework, three types of valuation techniques can be used to measure fair value. *Market approaches* base valuation on market information. For example, the value of a share of a company's stock that's not traded actively could be estimated by multiplying the earnings of that company by the P/E (price of shares/earnings) multiples of similar companies. *Income approaches* estimate fair value by first estimating future amounts (for example, earnings or cash flows) and then mathematically converting those amounts to a single present value. You will see how to apply such techniques in Chapter 5 when we discuss time value of money concepts. *Cost approaches* determine value by estimating the amount that would be required to buy or construct an asset of similar quality and condition. A firm can use one or more of these valuation approaches, depending on availability of information, and should try to use them consistently unless changes in circumstances require a change in approach.

> Fair value can be measured using:
> 1. Market approaches.
> 2. Income approaches.
> 3. Cost approaches.

To increase consistency and comparability in applying this definition, the framework provides a "hierarchy" that prioritizes the inputs companies should use when determining fair value. The priority is based on three broad preference levels. The higher the level (Level 1 is the highest), the more preferable the input. The framework encourages companies to strive to obtain the highest level input available for each situation. Illustration 1–14 describes the type of inputs and provides an example for each level.

Companies also must provide detailed disclosures about their use of fair value measurements. The disclosures include a description of the inputs used to measure fair value. For recurring fair value measurements that rely on significant *unobservable* inputs (within Level 3 of the fair value hierarchy), companies should disclose the effect of the measurements on earnings (or changes in net assets) for the period.

Illustration 1–14

Fair Value Hierarchy

Fair Value Hierarchy		
Level	**Inputs**	**Example**
1 **Most Desirable**	Quoted market prices in active markets for identical assets or liabilities.	In Chapter 12 you will learn that certain investments in marketable securities are reported at their *fair values*. Fair value in this case would be measured using the quoted market price from the NYSE, NASDAQ, or other exchange on which the security is traded.
2	Inputs other than quoted prices that are *observable* for the asset or liability. These inputs include quoted prices for *similar* assets or liabilities in active or inactive markets and inputs that are derived principally from or corroborated by observable related market data.	In Chapter 10 we discuss how companies sometimes acquire assets with consideration other than cash. In any noncash transaction, each element of the transaction is recorded at its *fair value*. If one of the assets in the exchange is a building, for instance, then quoted market prices for similar buildings recently sold could be used to value the building or, if there were no similar buildings recently exchanged from which to obtain a comparable market price, valuation could be based on the price per square foot derived from observable market data.
3 **Least Desirable**	*Unobservable* inputs that reflect the entity's own assumptions about the assumptions market participants would use in pricing the asset or liability developed based on the best information available in the circumstances.	Asset retirement obligations (AROs), discussed in Chapter 10, are measured at *fair value*. Neither Level 1 nor Level 2 inputs would be possible in most ARO valuation situations. Fair value would be estimated using Level 3 inputs to include the present value of expected cash flows estimated using the entity's own data if there is no information indicating that market participants would use different assumptions.

---

[38]"Fair Value Measurement," *International Financial Reporting Standard No. 13* (London, UK: IASCF, 2011).

The use of the fair value measurement attribute is increasing, both under U.S. GAAP and IFRS. This trend, though, is controversial. Proponents of fair value cite its relevance and are convinced that historical cost information may not be useful for many types of decisions. Opponents of fair value counter that estimates of fair value may lack representational faithfulness, particularly when based on inputs from Level 3 in the fair value hierarchy, and that managers might be tempted to exploit the unverifiability of such inputs to manipulate earnings. They argue that accounting should emphasize verifiability by recognizing only those gains and other increases in fair value that actually have been realized in transactions or are virtually certain to exist.

> The *fair value option* lets companies choose whether to value some financial assets and liabilities at fair value.

FAIR VALUE OPTION   Usually the measurement attribute we use for a particular financial statement item is not subject to choice. However, GAAP allows a fair value option in some circumstances which permits companies to choose whether to report specified *financial* assets and liabilities at fair value.[39] For example, in Chapter 14 you will learn that a company normally would report bonds payable at historical cost (adjusted for unamortized premium or discount), but the fair value option allows that company to choose instead to report the bonds payable at fair value. If a company chooses the fair value option, future changes in fair value are reported as gains and losses in the income statement.

Why allow the fair value option for financial assets and liabilities and not for, say, buildings or land? Financial assets and liabilities are cash and other assets and liabilities that convert directly into known amounts of cash. These include investments in stocks and bonds of other entities, notes receivable and payable, bonds payable, and derivative securities.[40] Some of these financial assets and liabilities currently are *required* under GAAP to be reported at fair value, and others are not, leading to some potential inconsistencies in how similar or related items are treated. The fair value option provides companies a way to reduce volatility in reported earnings without having to comply with complex hedge accounting standards. It also helps in the convergence with international accounting standards we discussed earlier in the chapter as the IASB also has adopted a fair value option for financial instruments.

Disclosure

> The *full-disclosure principle* requires that any information useful to decision makers be provided in the financial statements, subject to the cost effectiveness constraint.

Remember, the purpose of accounting is to provide information that is useful to decision makers. So, naturally, if there is accounting information not included in the primary financial statements that would benefit users, that information should be provided too. The full-disclosure principle means that the financial reports should include any information that could affect the decisions made by external users. Of course, the benefits of that information should exceed the costs of providing the information. Such information is disclosed in a variety of ways, including:

1. Parenthetical comments or modifying comments placed on the face of the financial statements.
2. Disclosure notes conveying additional insights about company operations, accounting principles, contractual agreements, and pending litigation.
3. Supplemental schedules and tables that report more detailed information than is shown in the primary financial statements.

We discuss and illustrate disclosure requirements as they relate to specific financial statement elements in later chapters as those elements are discussed.

Illustration 1–15 provides an overview of key recognition, measurement and disclosure concepts.

---

[39]FASB ASC 825–10–25–1: Financial Instruments—Overall—Recognition—Fair Value Option.
[40]The fair value option does not apply to certain specified financial instruments, including pension obligations and assets or liabilities arising from leases.

Concept	Description
Recognition	General criteria:
	1. Meets the definition of an element
	2. Has a measurement attribute
	3. Is relevant
	4. Is reliable (representationally faithful)
	Examples of recognition timing:
	1. Revenues
	2. Expenses
Measurement	Mixed attribute model in which the attribute used to measure an item is chosen to maximize relevance and representational faithfulness. These attributes include:
	1. Historical cost
	2. Net realizable value
	3. Current cost
	4. Present (or discounted) value of future cash flows
	5. Fair value
Disclosure	Financial reports should include all information that could affect the decisions made by external users.
	Examples of disclosures:
	1. Parenthetical amounts
	2. Notes to the financial statements
	3. Supplemental schedules and tables

Illustration 1–15

Summary of Recognition, Measurement, and Disclosure Concepts

Where We're Headed

"Disclosure overload" is a frequent complaint by companies and investors alike. The notes to the financial statements can be very useful, but they are costly for companies to prepare and difficult for many users to sift through and understand. In response to that concern, the FASB has been developing a framework intended to make disclosures more effective and less redundant. In August of 2018 the FASB issued an addition to Concepts Statement No. 8, titled *Chapter 8: Notes to Financial Statements,* which suggests a series of questions that the FASB and its staff should consider when determining what notes should be required by new standards.[41] A separate part of the project will develop further guidance to help companies apply judgment when meeting disclosure requirements.

Evolving GAAP

● LO1–10

U.S. and international GAAP have been evolving over time from an emphasis on revenues and expenses to an emphasis on assets and liabilities. Of course, you know from introductory accounting that the balance sheet and income statement are intertwined and must reconcile with each other. For example, the revenues reported in the income statement depict inflows of assets whose balances at a particular point in time are reported in the balance sheet. But which comes first, identifying revenues and expenses, or identifying assets and liabilities? That emphasis can affect accounting standards in important ways. To help you understand the changes taking place, we start by discussing the revenue/expense approach and then discuss the asset/liability approach.

---

[41]"Conceptual Framework for Financial Reporting—Chapter 8, *Notes to Financial Statements*" *Statement of Financial Accounting Concepts No. 8* (Norwalk, Conn.: FASB, 2018).

With the *revenue/expense approach,* recognition and measurement of revenues and expenses are emphasized.

Under the revenue/expense approach, we emphasize principles for recognizing revenues and expenses, with some assets and liabilities recognized as necessary to make the balance sheet reconcile with the income statement. For example, when accounting for sales revenue our focus would be on whether a good or service has been delivered, and if we determine that to be the case, we would record an asset (usually cash or accounts receivable) that is associated with that revenue.[42] We also would identify the expenses associated with delivering those goods and services, and then would adjust assets and liabilities accordingly.

With the *asset/liability approach,* recognition and measurement of assets and liabilities drives revenue and expense recognition.

Under the asset/liability approach, on the other hand, we first recognize and measure the assets and liabilities that exist at a balance sheet date and, secondly, recognize and measure the revenues, expenses, gains and losses needed to account for the changes in these assets and liabilities from the previous measurement date. Proponents of this approach point out that, since revenues and expenses are defined in terms of inflows and outflows of assets and liabilities, the fundamental concepts underlying accounting are assets and liabilities. Therefore, we should try to recognize and measure assets and liabilities appropriately, and as a result will also capture their inflows and outflows in a manner that provides relevant and representationally faithful information about revenues and expenses.

For example, when accounting for a sales transaction, our focus would be on whether a potential accounts receivable meets the definition of an asset (a probable future economic benefit). We would consider such factors as whether the receivable is supported by an enforceable contract and whether the seller has performed its obligations enough to be able to expect receipt of cash flows. The key would be determining if the seller has an asset and then recognizing whatever amount of revenue is implied by the inflow of that asset. Also, we would not attempt to match expenses to revenues. Rather, we would determine those net assets that had decreased as part of operations during the period, and recognize those decreases as expenses.

In subsequent chapters you will see that recent standards involving accounting for revenue, investments, and income taxes follow this asset/liability approach. These changes are controversial. It may seem like it shouldn't matter whether standard setters use the revenue/expense or asset/liability approach, given that both approaches affect both the income statement and balance sheet, and it is true that these approaches often will result in the same accounting outcomes. However, the particular approach used by a standard setter can affect recognition and measurement in important ways. In particular, the asset/liability approach encourages us to focus on accurately measuring assets and liabilities. It perhaps is not surprising, then, that a focus on assets and liabilities has led standard setters to lean more and more toward fair value measurement. The future changes to the conceptual framework discussed in the following Where We're Headed box are likely to continue this emphasis on the asset/liability approach.

Where We're Headed

Since 2010, the FASB and IASB worked separately on their conceptual frameworks. The FASB has worked on relatively narrow projects, such as the definition of materiality and a more general disclosure framework. The IASB, in contrast, has moved forward with a more comprehensive overhaul of its conceptual framework. The IASB's 2015 exposure draft of its concepts statement addressed a range of issues, including the objective and qualitative characteristics of financial reporting, the definitions of key financial-statement elements, when to recognize and de-recognize assets and liabilities, when to use various measurement approaches, the distinction between net income and other comprehensive income, and what constitutes a reporting entity. The IASB anticipates issuing a concepts statement sometime in 2018.

---

[42]Some assets and liabilities aren't related to revenue or expense. For example, issuance of shares of stock increases cash as well as shareholders' equity. The treatment of these sorts of transactions is not affected by whether GAAP emphasizes revenues and expenses or assets and liabilities.

Financial Reporting Case Solution

1. **What should you tell your friend about the presence of accounting standards in the United States and the rest of the world? Who has the authority for standard setting? Who has the responsibility?** *(p. 8)* In the United States we have a set of standards known as generally accepted accounting principles (GAAP). GAAP is a dynamic set of both broad and specific guidelines that companies should follow when measuring and reporting the information in their financial statements and related notes. The Securities and Exchange Commission has the authority to set accounting standards for companies whose securities are publicly traded but it relies on the private sector to accomplish that task. At present, the Financial Accounting Standards Board is the private sector body responsible for standard setting.

©Rawpixel.com/Shutterstock

2. **What is the economic and political environment in which standard setting occurs?** *(p. 12)* The setting of accounting and reporting standards often has been characterized as a *political process.* Standards, particularly changes in standards, can have significant differential effects on companies, investors and creditors, and other interest groups. A change in an accounting standard or the introduction of a new standard can result in a substantial redistribution of wealth within our economy. The FASB's due process is designed to obtain information from all interested parties to help determine the appropriate accounting approach, but standards are supposed to be neutral with respect to the interests of various parties. Nonetheless, both the FASB and IASB sometimes come under political pressure that sways the results of the standard-setting process.

3. **What is the relationship among management, auditors, investors, and creditors that tends to preclude the "What would you like it to be?" attitude?** *(p. 14)* It is the responsibility of management to apply accounting standards when communicating with investors and creditors through financial statements. Auditors serve as independent intermediaries to help ensure that the management-prepared statements are presented fairly in accordance with GAAP. In providing this assurance, the auditor precludes the "What would you like it to be?" attitude.

4. **In general, what is the conceptual framework that underlies accounting principles, and how does it encourage high-quality financial reporting?** *(p. 18)* The conceptual framework is a coherent system of interrelated objectives and fundamentals that improves financial reporting by encouraging consistent standards and by prescribing the nature, function, and limits of financial accounting and reporting. The fundamentals are the underlying concepts of accounting, concepts that guide the selection of events to be accounted for, the measurement of those events, and the means of summarizing and communicating them to interested parties. ●

The Bottom Line

- **LO1–1** Financial accounting is concerned with providing relevant financial information to various external users. However, the primary focus is on the financial information provided by profit-oriented companies to their present and potential investors and creditors. *(p. 3)*

- **LO1–2** Cash-basis accounting provides a measure of periodic performance called *net operating cash flow,* which is the difference between cash receipts and cash disbursements from transactions related to providing goods and services to customers. Accrual accounting provides a measure of performance called *net income,* which is the difference between revenues and expenses. Periodic net income is considered a better indicator of future operating cash flows than is current net operating cash flows. *(p. 7)*

- **LO1–3** Generally accepted accounting principles (GAAP) comprise a dynamic set of both broad and specific guidelines that companies follow when measuring and reporting the information in their financial statements and related notes. The Securities and Exchange Commission (SEC) has the authority to set accounting standards in the United States. However, the SEC has always delegated the task to a private sector body, at this time the Financial Accounting Standards Board (FASB). The International Accounting

Standards Board (IASB) sets global accounting standards and works with national accounting standard setters to achieve convergence in accounting standards around the world. (*p. 8*)

● **LO1–4**   Accounting standards can have significant differential effects on companies, investors, creditors, and other interest groups. Various interested parties sometimes lobby standard setters for their preferred outcomes. For this reason, the setting of accounting standards often has been characterized as a political process. (*p. 12*)

● **LO1–5**   Factors encouraging high-quality financial reporting include conceptually based financial accounting standards, external auditors, financial reporting reforms (such as the Sarbanes-Oxley Act), ethical management, and professional accounting organizations that prescribe ethical conduct and license practitioners. (*p. 14*)

● **LO1–6**   The FASB's conceptual framework is a set of cohesive objectives and fundamental concepts on which financial accounting and reporting standards can be based. (*p. 18*)

● **LO1–7**   The objective of financial reporting is to provide useful financial information to capital providers. The primary decision-specific qualities that make financial information useful are relevance and faithful representation. To be relevant, information must possess predictive value and/or confirmatory value, and all material information should be included. Completeness, neutrality, and freedom from error enhance faithful representation. The 10 elements of financial statements are assets, liabilities, equity, investments by owners, distributions to owners, revenues, expenses, gains, losses, and comprehensive income. (*p. 20*)

● **LO1–8**   The four basic assumptions underlying GAAP are (1) the economic entity assumption, (2) the going concern assumption, (3) the periodicity assumption, and (4) the monetary unit assumption. (*p. 23*)

● **LO1–9**   Recognition determines whether an item is reflected in the financial statements, and measurement determines the amount of the item. Measurement involves choice of a monetary unit and choice of a measurement attribute. In the United States, the monetary unit is the dollar. Various measurement attributes are used in GAAP, including historical cost, net realizable value, current cost, present value, and fair value. (*p. 25*)

● **LO1–10**   A revenue/expense approach to financial reporting emphasizes recognition and measurement of revenues and expenses, while an asset/liability approach emphasizes recognition and measurement of assets and liabilities. (*p. 31*)

● **LO1–11**   IFRS and U.S. GAAP are similar in the organizations that support standard setting and in the presence of ongoing political pressures on the standard-setting process. U.S. GAAP and IFRS also have similar conceptual frameworks, although the role of the conceptual framework in IFRS is to provide guidance to preparers as well as to standard setters, while the role of the conceptual framework in U.S. GAAP is more to provide guidance to standard setters. (*pp. 11, 14 and 19*) ●

Questions For Review of Key Topics

Q 1–1   What is the function and primary focus of financial accounting?

Q 1–2   What is meant by the phrase *efficient allocation of resources?* What mechanism fosters the efficient allocation of resources in the United States?

Q 1–3   Identify two important variables to be considered when making an investment decision.

Q 1–4   What must a company do in the long run to be able to provide a return to investors and creditors?

Q 1–5   What is the primary objective of financial accounting?

Q 1–6   Define net operating cash flows. Briefly explain why periodic net operating cash flows may not be a good indicator of future operating cash flows.

Q 1–7   What is meant by GAAP? Why should all companies follow GAAP in reporting to external users?

Q 1–8   Explain the roles of the SEC and the FASB in the setting of accounting standards.

Q 1–9   Explain the role of the auditor in the financial reporting process.

Q 1–10   List three key provisions of the Sarbanes-Oxley Act of 2002. Order your list from most important to least important in terms of the likely long-term impact on the accounting profession and financial reporting.

Q 1–11   Explain what is meant by *adverse economic consequences* of new or changed accounting standards.

Q 1–12   Why does the FASB undertake a series of elaborate information-gathering steps before issuing a substantive accounting standard?

Q 1–13   What is the purpose of the FASB's conceptual framework?

Q 1–14   Discuss the terms *relevance* and *faithful representation* as they relate to financial accounting information.

Q 1–15   What are the components of relevant information? What are the components of faithful representation?

Q 1–16   Explain what is meant by: The benefits of accounting information must exceed the costs.

Q 1–17   What is meant by the term *materiality* in financial reporting?

Q 1–18   Briefly define the financial accounting elements: (1) assets, (2) liabilities, (3) equity, (4) investments by owners, (5) distributions to owners, (6) revenues, (7) expenses, (8) gains, (9) losses, and (10) comprehensive income.

Q 1–19   What are the four basic assumptions underlying GAAP?

Q 1–20   What is the going concern assumption?

Q 1–21   Explain the periodicity assumption.

Q 1–22   What are four key accounting practices that often are referred to as principles in current GAAP?

Q 1–23   What are two advantages to basing the valuation of assets and liabilities on their historical cost?

Q 1–24   Describe how revenue recognition relates to transferring goods or services.

Q 1–25   What are the four different approaches to implementing expense recognition? Give an example of an expense that is recognized under each approach.

Q 1–26   In addition to the financial statement elements arrayed in the basic financial statements, what are some other ways to disclose financial information to external users?

Q 1–27   Briefly describe the inputs that companies should use when determining fair value. Organize your answer according to preference levels, from highest to lowest priority.

Q 1–28   What measurement attributes are commonly used in financial reporting?

Q 1–29   Distinguish between the revenue/expense and the asset/liability approaches to setting financial reporting standards.

IFRS   Q 1–30   What are the functions of the conceptual framework under IFRS?

IFRS   Q 1–31   What is the standard-setting body responsible for determining IFRS? How does it obtain its funding?

IFRS   Q 1–32   In its Final Staff Report (issued in 2012), what type of convergence between U.S. GAAP and IFRS did the SEC staff argue was not feasible? What reasons did the SEC staff give for that conclusion?

Brief Exercises

BE 1–1
Accrual accounting
● LO1–2

Cash flows during the first year of operations for the Harman-Kardon Consulting Company were as follows: Cash collected from customers, $340,000; Cash paid for rent, $40,000; Cash paid to employees for services rendered during the year, $120,000; Cash paid for utilities, $50,000.

In addition, you determine that customers owed the company $60,000 at the end of the year and no bad debts were anticipated. Also, the company owed the gas and electric company $2,000 at year-end, and the rent payment was for a two-year period. Calculate accrual net income for the year.

BE 1–2
Financial statement elements
● LO1–7

For each of the following items, identify the appropriate financial statement element or elements: (1) probable future sacrifices of economic benefits; (2) probable future economic benefits owned by the company; (3) inflows of assets from ongoing, major activities; (4) decrease in equity from peripheral or incidental transactions.

BE 1–3
Basic assumptions and principles
● LO1–7 through LO1–9

Listed below are several statements that relate to financial accounting and reporting. Identify the accounting concept that applies to each statement.
1. SiriusXM Radio Inc. files its annual and quarterly financial statements with the SEC.
2. The president of Applebee's International, Inc., travels on the corporate jet for business purposes only and does not use the jet for personal use.
3. Jackson Manufacturing does not recognize revenue for unshipped merchandise even though the merchandise has been manufactured according to customer specifications.
4. Lady Jane Cosmetics depreciates the cost of equipment over their useful lives.

BE 1–4
Basic assumptions and principles
● LO1–7 through LO1–9

Identify the accounting concept that was violated in each of the following situations.
1. Astro Turf Company recognizes an expense, cost of goods sold, in the period the product is manufactured.
2. McCloud Drug Company owns a patent that it purchased three years ago for $2 million. The controller recently revalued the patent to its approximate market value of $8 million.
3. Philips Company pays the monthly mortgage on the home of its president Larry Crosswhite and charges the expenditure to miscellaneous expense.

BE 1–5
Basic assumptions and principles
● **LO1–7 through LO1–9**

For each of the following situations, (1) indicate whether you agree or disagree with the financial reporting practice employed and (2) state the accounting concept that is applied (if you agree) or violated (if you disagree).
1. Winderl Corporation did not disclose that it was the defendant in a material lawsuit because the trial was still in progress.
2. Alliant Semiconductor Corporation files quarterly and annual financial statements with the SEC.
3. Reliant Pharmaceutical paid rent on its office building for the next two years and charged the entire expenditure to rent expense.
4. Rockville Engineering records revenue only after products have been shipped, even though customers pay Rockville 50% of the sales price in advance.

BE 1–6
IFRS
● **LO1–11**
⊗ **IFRS**

Indicate the organization related to IFRS that performs each of the following functions:
1. Obtains funding for the IFRS standard-setting process.
2. Determines IFRS.
3. Oversees the IFRS Foundation.
4. Provides input about the standard-setting agenda.
5. Provides implementation guidance about relatively narrow issues.

Exercises

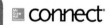

E 1–1
Accrual accounting
● **LO1–2**

Listed below are several transactions that took place during the first two years of operations for the law firm of Pete, Pete, and Roy.

	Year 1	Year 2
Amounts billed to clients for services rendered	$170,000	$220,000
Cash collected from clients	160,000	190,000
Cash disbursements		
Salaries paid to employees for services rendered during the year	90,000	100,000
Utilities	30,000	40,000
Purchase of insurance policy	60,000	–0–

In addition, you learn that the firm incurred utility costs of $35,000 in year 1, that there were no liabilities at the end of year 2, no anticipated bad debts on receivables, and that the insurance policy covers a three-year period.

Required:
1. Calculate the net operating cash flow for years 1 and 2.
2. Prepare an income statement for each year similar to Illustration 1–4 according to the accrual accounting model.
3. Determine the amount of receivables from clients that the firm would show in its year 1 and year 2 balance sheets prepared according to the accrual accounting model.

E 1–2
Accrual accounting
● **LO1–2**

Listed below are several transactions that took place during the second and third years of operations for the RPG Company.

	Year 2	Year 3
Amounts billed to customers for services rendered	$350,000	$450,000
Cash collected from credit customers	260,000	400,000
Cash disbursements:		
Payment of rent	80,000	–0–
Salaries paid to employees for services rendered during the year	140,000	160,000
Utilities	30,000	40,000
Advertising	15,000	35,000

In addition, you learn that the company incurred advertising costs of $25,000 in year 2, owed the advertising agency $5,000 at the end of year 1, and there were no liabilities at the end of year 3. Also, there were no anticipated bad debts on receivables, and the rent payment was for a two-year period, year 2 and year 3.

Required:
1. Calculate accrual net income for both years.
2. Determine the amount due the advertising agency that would be shown as a liability on RPG's balance sheet at the end of year 2.

E 1–3
FASB codification research
● LO1–3

C⊙DE

Access the *FASB Accounting Standards Codification* at the FASB website (www.fasb.org).

Required:
1. Identify the Codification topic number that provides guidance on fair value measurements.
2. What is the specific seven-digit Codification citation (XXX-XX-XX) that lists the disclosures required in the notes to the financial statements for each major category of assets and liabilities measured at fair value?

E 1–4
FASB codification research
● LO1–3

C⊙DE

Access the *FASB Accounting Standards Codification* at the FASB website (www.fasb.org). Determine the specific citation for each of the following items:
1. The topic number for business combinations
2. The topic number for related party disclosures
3. The specific seven-digit Codification citation (XXX-XX-XX) for the initial measurement of internal-use software
4. The specific seven-digit Codification citation (XXX-XX-XX) for the subsequent measurement of asset retirement obligations
5. The specific seven-digit Codification citation (XXX-XX-XX) for the recognition of stock compensation

E 1–5
Participants in establishing GAAP
● LO1–3

Three groups that participate in the process of establishing GAAP are users, preparers, and auditors. These groups are represented by various organizations. For each organization listed below, indicate which of these groups it primarily represents.
1. Securities and Exchange Commission
2. Financial Executives International
3. American Institute of Certified Public Accountants
4. Institute of Management Accountants
5. Association of Investment Management and Research

E 1–6
Financial statement elements
● LO1–7

For each of the items listed below, identify the appropriate financial statement element or elements.
1. Obligation to transfer cash or other resources as a result of a past transaction
2. Dividends paid by a corporation to its shareholders
3. Inflow of an asset from providing a good or service
4. The financial position of a company
5. Increase in equity during a period from nonowner transactions
6. Increase in equity from peripheral or incidental transaction
7. Sale of an asset used in the operations of a business for less than the asset's book value
8. The owners' residual interest in the assets of a company
9. An item owned by the company representing probable future benefits
10. Revenues plus gains less expenses and losses
11. An owner's contribution of cash to a corporation in exchange for ownership shares of stock
12. Outflow of an asset related to the production of revenue

E 1–7
Concepts; terminology; conceptual framework
● LO1–7

Listed below are several terms and phrases associated with the FASB's conceptual framework. Pair each item from List A (by letter) with the item from List B that is most appropriately associated with it.

List A	List B
_____ 1. Predictive value	a. Decreases in equity resulting from transfers to owners.
_____ 2. Relevance	b. Requires consideration of the costs and value of information.
_____ 3. Timeliness	c. Important for making interfirm comparisons.
_____ 4. Distribution to owners	d. Applying the same accounting practices over time.
_____ 5. Confirmatory value	e. Users understand the information in the context of the decision being made.
_____ 6. Understandability	f. Agreement between a measure and the phenomenon it purports to represent.
_____ 7. Gain	g. Information is available prior to the decision.
_____ 8. Faithful representation	h. Pertinent to the decision at hand.
_____ 9. Comprehensive income	i. Implies consensus among different measurers.
_____ 10. Materiality	j. Information confirms expectations.
_____ 11. Comparability	k. The change in equity from nonowner transactions.
_____ 12. Neutrality	l. The process of admitting information into financial statements.
_____ 13. Recognition	m. The absence of bias.
_____ 14. Consistency	n. Increases in equity from peripheral or incidental transactions of an entity.
_____ 15. Cost effectiveness	o. Information is useful in predicting the future.
_____ 16. Verifiability	p. Concerns the relative size of an item and its effect on decisions.

E 1–8
Qualitative characteristics
● LO1–7

The conceptual framework indicates the desired fundamental and enhancing qualitative characteristics of accounting information. Several constraints impede achieving these desired characteristics. Answer each of the following questions related to these characteristics and constraints.

1. Which component would allow a large company to record the purchase of a $120 printer as an expense rather than capitalizing the printer as an asset?

2. Donald Kirk, former chairman of the FASB, once noted that ". . . there must be public confidence that the standard-setting system is credible, that selection of board members is based on merit and not the influence of special interests . . ." Which characteristic is implicit in Mr. Kirk's statement?

3. Allied Appliances, Inc., changed its revenue recognition policies. Which characteristic is jeopardized by this change?

4. National Bancorp, a publicly traded company, files quarterly and annual financial statements with the SEC. Which characteristic is relevant to the timing of these periodic filings?

5. In general, relevant information possesses which qualities?

6. When there is agreement between a measure or description and the phenomenon it purports to represent, information possesses which characteristic?

7. Jeff Brown is evaluating two companies for future investment potential. Jeff's task is made easier because both companies use the same accounting methods when preparing their financial statements. Which characteristic does the information Jeff will be using possess?

8. A company should disclose information only if the perceived benefits of the disclosure exceed the costs of providing the information. Which constraint does this statement describe?

E 1–9
Basic assumptions, principles, and constraints
● LO1–7 through LO1–9

Listed below are several terms and phrases associated with the accounting concepts. Pair each item from List A (by letter) with the item from List B that is most appropriately associated with it.

List A	List B
_____ 1. Expense recognition	a. The enterprise is separate from its owners and other entities.
_____ 2. Periodicity assumption	b. A common denominator is the dollar.
_____ 3. Historical cost principle	c. The entity will continue indefinitely.
_____ 4. Materiality	d. Record expenses in the period the related revenue is recognized.
_____ 5. Revenue recognition	e. The original transaction value upon acquisition.
_____ 6. Going concern assumption	f. All information that could affect decisions should be reported.
_____ 7. Monetary unit assumption	g. The life of an enterprise can be divided into artificial time periods.
_____ 8. Economic entity assumption	h. Criteria usually satisfied for products at point of sale.
_____ 9. Full-disclosure principle	i. Concerns the relative size of an item and its effect on decisions.

E 1–10
Basic assumptions and principles
● LO1–7 through LO1–9

Listed below are several statements that relate to financial accounting and reporting. Identify the accounting concept that applies to each statement.

1. Jim Marley is the sole owner of Marley's Appliances. Jim borrowed $100,000 to buy a new home to be used as his personal residence. This liability was not recorded in the records of Marley's Appliances.

2. Apple Inc. distributes an annual report to its shareholders.

3. Hewlett-Packard Corporation depreciates machinery and equipment over their useful lives.

4. Crosby Company lists land on its balance sheet at $120,000, its original purchase price, even though the land has a current fair value of $200,000.

5. Honeywell International Inc. records revenue when products are delivered to customers, even though the cash has not yet been received.

6. Liquidation values are not normally reported in financial statements even though many companies do go out of business.

7. IBM Corporation, a multibillion dollar company, purchased some small tools at a cost of $800. Even though the tools will be used for a number of years, the company recorded the purchase as an expense.

E 1–11
Basic assumptions and principles
● LO1–8, LO1–9

Identify the accounting concept that was violated in each of the following situations.

1. Pastel Paint Company purchased land two years ago at a price of $250,000. Because the value of the land has appreciated to $400,000, the company has valued the land at $400,000 in its most recent balance sheet.

2. Atwell Corporation has not prepared financial statements for external users for over three years.

3. The Klingon Company sells farm machinery. Revenue from a large order of machinery from a new buyer was recorded the day the order was received.

4. Don Smith is the sole owner of a company called Hardware City. The company recently paid a $150 utility bill for Smith's personal residence and recorded a $150 expense.

5. Golden Book Company purchased a large printing machine for $1,000,000 (a material amount) and recorded the purchase as an expense.

6. Ace Appliance Company is involved in a major lawsuit involving injuries sustained by some of its employees in the manufacturing plant. The company is being sued for $2,000,000, a material amount, and is not insured. The suit was not disclosed in the most recent financial statements because no settlement had been reached.

E 1–12
Basic
assumptions and
principles
● LO1–7 through
LO1–9

For each of the following situations, indicate whether you agree or disagree with the financial reporting practice employed and state the accounting concept that is applied (if you agree) or violated (if you disagree).

1. Wagner Corporation adjusted the valuation of all assets and liabilities to reflect changes in the purchasing power of the dollar.

2. Spooner Oil Company changed its method of accounting for oil and gas exploration costs from successful efforts to full cost. No mention of the change was included in the financial statements. The change had a material effect on Spooner's financial statements.

3. Cypress Manufacturing Company purchased machinery having a five-year life. The cost of the machinery is being expensed over the life of the machinery.

4. Rudeen Corporation purchased equipment for $180,000 at a liquidation sale of a competitor. Because the equipment was worth $230,000, Rudeen valued the equipment in its subsequent balance sheet at $230,000.

5. Davis Bicycle Company received a large order for the sale of 1,000 bicycles at $100 each. The customer paid Davis the entire amount of $100,000 on March 15. However, Davis did not record any revenue until April 17, the date the bicycles were delivered to the customer.

6. Gigantic Corporation purchased two small calculators at a cost of $32.00. The cost of the calculators was expensed even though they had a three-year estimated useful life.

7. Esquire Company provides financial statements to external users every three years.

E 1–13
Basic
assumptions and
principles
● LO1–7 through
LO1–9

For each of the following situations, state whether you agree or disagree with the financial reporting practice employed, and briefly explain the reason for your answer.

1. The controller of the Dumars Corporation increased the carrying value of land from its original cost of $2 million to its recently appraised value of $3.5 million.

2. The president of Vosburgh Industries asked the company controller to charge miscellaneous expense for the purchase of an automobile to be used solely for personal use.

3. At the end of its 2020 fiscal year, Dower, Inc., received an order from a customer for $45,350. The merchandise will ship early in 2021. Because the sale was made to a long-time customer, the controller recorded the sale in 2020.

4. At the beginning of its 2020 fiscal year, Rossi Imports paid $48,000 for a two-year lease on warehouse space. Rossi recorded the expenditure as an asset to be expensed equally over the two-year period of the lease.

5. The Reliable Tire Company included a note in its financial statements that described a pending lawsuit against the company.

6. The Hughes Corporation, a company whose securities are publicly traded, prepares monthly, quarterly, and annual financial statements for internal use but disseminates to external users only the annual financial statements.

E 1–14
Basic
assumptions and
principles
● LO1–7 through
LO1–9

Listed below are accounting concepts discussed in this chapter.

a. Economic entity assumption

b. Going concern assumption

c. Periodicity assumption

d. Monetary unit assumption

e. Historical cost principle

f. Conservatism

g. Expense recognition

h. Full-disclosure principle

i. Cost effectiveness

j. Materiality

Identify by letter the accounting concept that relates to each statement or phrase below.

_____ 1. Inflation causes a violation of this assumption.

_____ 2. Information that could affect decision making should be reported.

_____ 3. Recognizing expenses in the period they were incurred to produce revenue.

40   SECTION 1   The Role of Accounting as an Information System

_____ 4. The basis for measurement of many assets and liabilities.

_____ 5. Relates to the qualitative characteristic of timeliness.

_____ 6. All economic events can be identified with a particular entity.

_____ 7. The benefits of providing accounting information should exceed the cost of doing so.

_____ 8. A consequence is that GAAP need not be followed in all situations.

_____ 9. Not a qualitative characteristic, but a practical justification for some accounting choices.

_____ 10. Assumes the entity will continue indefinitely.

E 1–15
Multiple choice;
concept
statements, basic
assumptions,
principles
● LO1–6 through
   LO1–9

Determine the response that best completes the following statements or questions.

1. The primary objective of financial reporting is to provide information
   a. About a firm's management team.
   b. Useful to capital providers.
   c. Concerning the changes in financial position resulting from the income-producing efforts of the entity.
   d. About a firm's financing and investing activities.

2. *Statements of Financial Accounting Concepts* issued by the FASB
   a. Represent GAAP.
   b. Have been superseded by *SFASs*.
   c. Are subject to approval of the SEC.
   d. Identify the conceptual framework within which accounting standards are developed.

3. In general, revenue is recognized when
   a. The sales price has been collected.
   b. A purchase order has been received.
   c. A good or service has been delivered to a customer.
   d. A contract has been signed.

4. In depreciating the cost of an asset, accountants are most concerned with
   a. Conservatism.
   b. Recognizing revenue in the appropriate period.
   c. Full disclosure.
   d. Recognizing expense in the appropriate period.

5. The primary objective of expense recognition is to
   a. Provide full disclosure.
   b. Record expenses in the period that related revenues are recognized.
   c. Provide timely information to decision makers.
   d. Promote comparability between financial statements of different periods.

6. The separate entity assumption states that, in the absence of contrary evidence, all entities will survive indefinitely.
   a. True
   b. False

Decision Makers' Perspective

©ImageGap/Getty Images

Apply your critical-thinking ability to the knowledge you've gained. These cases will provide you an opportunity to develop your research, analysis, judgment, and communication skills. You will also work with other students, integrate what you've learned, apply it in real-world situations, and consider its global and ethical ramifications. This practice will broaden your knowledge and further develop your decision-making abilities.

**Judgment
Case 1–1**
The development
of accounting
standards
● LO1–3

In 1934, Congress created the Securities and Exchange Commission (SEC).

Required:

1. Does the SEC have more authority or less authority than the FASB with respect to standard setting? Explain the relationship between the SEC and the FASB.

2. Can you think of any reasons why the SEC relies on private sector bodies to set accounting standards, rather than undertaking the task itself?

Research Case 1–2
Accessing SEC information through the Internet
● LO1–3

The purpose of this case is to introduce you to the information available on the website of the Securities and Exchange Commission (SEC) and its EDGAR database.

Required:
Access the SEC home page on the Internet. The web address is www.sec.gov. Answer the following questions:
1. Choose the subaddress "About the SEC." What are the two basic objectives of the 1933 Securities Act?
2. Return to the SEC home page and access EDGAR. Describe the contents of the database.

Research Case 1–3
Accessing FASB information through the Internet
● LO1–4

The purpose of this case is to introduce you to the information available on the website of the Financial Accounting Standards Board (FASB).

Required:
Access the FASB home page on the Internet. The web address is www.fasb.org. Answer the following questions:
1. The FASB has how many board members?
2. How many board members of the FASB have a background that is primarily drawn from accounting education?
3. Describe the mission of the FASB.
4. How are topics added to the FASB's technical agenda?

Research Case 1–4
Accessing IASB information through the Internet
● LO1–3

The purpose of this case is to introduce you to the information available on the website of the International Accounting Standards Board (IASB).

Required:
Access the IASB home page on the Internet. The web address is https://www.ifrs.org/groups/international-accounting-standards-board/. Answer the following questions.
1. The IASB has how many board members?
2. In what city is the IASB located?
3. Describe the mission of the IASB.

Communication Case 1–5
Relevance and representational faithfulness
● LO1–7

Some theorists contend that companies that create pollution should report the social cost of that pollution in income statements. They argue that such companies are indirectly subsidized as the cost of pollution is borne by society while only production costs (and perhaps minimal pollution fines) are shown in the income statement. Thus, the product sells for less than would be necessary if all costs were included.

Assume that the FASB is considering a standard to include the social costs of pollution in the income statement. The process would require considering both relevance and faithful representation of the information produced by the new standard. Your instructor will divide the class into two to six groups depending on the size of the class. The mission of your group is to explain how the concepts of relevance and faithful representation relate to this issue.

Required:
Each group member should consider the question independently and draft a tentative answer prior to the class session for which the case is assigned.

In class, each group will meet for 10 to 15 minutes in different areas of the classroom. During that meeting, group members will take turns sharing their suggestions for the purpose of arriving at a single group treatment.

After the allotted time, a spokesperson for each group (selected during the group meetings) will share the group's solution with the class. The goal of the class is to incorporate the views of each group into a consensus answer to the question.

Communication Case 1–6
Accounting standard setting
● LO1–4

One of your friends is a financial analyst for a major stock brokerage firm. Recently she indicated to you that she had read an article in a weekly business magazine that alluded to the political process of establishing accounting standards. She had always assumed that accounting standards were established by determining the approach that conceptually best reflected the economics of a transaction.

Required:
Write a one to two-page article for a business journal explaining what is meant by the political process for establishing accounting standards. Be sure to include in your article a discussion of the need for the FASB to balance accounting considerations and economic consequences.

Ethics Case 1–7
The auditors' responsibility
● LO1–4

Auditors often earn considerable fees from a company for examining (auditing) its financial statements. In addition, it's not uncommon for auditors to earn additional fees from the company by providing consulting, tax, and other advisory services.

Required:
1. Which party has primary responsibility—auditors or company executives—for properly applying accounting standards when communicating with investors and creditors through financial statements?
2. Are auditors considered employees of the company?

3. Does the fact that clients compensate auditors for providing audits and other consulting services have the potential to jeopardize an auditor's independence?

4. What pressures on a typical audit engagement might affect an auditor's independence?

Judgment Case 1–8
Qualitative characteristics
● LO1–7

A friend asks you about whether GAAP requires companies to disclose forecasts of financial variables to external users. She thinks that information could be very useful to investors.

Required:

1. What are the two primary qualitative characteristics of accounting information?

2. Does GAAP routinely require companies to disclose forecasts of financial variables to external users? Indicate yes or no and explain how your answer relates to the qualitative characteristics of accounting information.

Judgment Case 1–9
Cost effectiveness
● LO1–7

Assume that the FASB is considering revising an important accounting standard.

Required:

1. What constraint applies to the FASB's consideration of whether to require companies to provide new information?

2. In what Concepts Statement is that constraint discussed?

3. What are some of the possible costs that could result from a revision of an accounting standard?

4. What does the FASB do in order to assess possible benefits and costs of a proposed revision of an accounting standard?

Judgment Case 1–10
Revenue recognition
● LO1–9

A new client, the Wolf Company, asks your advice concerning the point in time that the company should recognize revenue from the rental of its office buildings under generally accepted accounting principles. Renters usually pay rent on a quarterly basis at the beginning of the quarter. The owners contend that the critical event that motivates revenue recognition should be the date the cash is received from renters. After all, the money is in hand and is very seldom returned.

Required:

Do you agree or disagree with the position of the owners of Wolf Company? State whether you agree or disagree, and support your answer by relating it to accrual accounting under GAAP.

Real World Case 1–11
Elements; disclosures; Gap Inc.
● LO1–7, LO1–9

Access the financial statements for the year ended January 28, 2017, for Gap Inc. by downloading them from www.gapinc.com, and use them to answer the following questions.

Required:

1. What amounts did Gap Inc. report for the following items for the fiscal year ended January 28, 2017?
   a. Total net revenues
   b. Total operating expenses
   c. Net income (earnings)
   d. Total assets
   e. Total stockholders' equity

2. How many shares of common stock had been issued by Gap Inc. as of January 28, 2017?

3. Does Gap Inc. report more than one year of data in its financial statements? Explain why or why not.

Case 1–12
Convergence
● LO1–11

IFRS

Consider the question of whether the United States should converge accounting standards with IFRS.

Required:

1. Make a list of arguments that favor convergence.

2. Make a list of arguments that favor nonconvergence.

3. Indicate your own conclusion regarding whether the United States should converge with IFRS, and indicate the primary considerations that determined your conclusion.

Data Analytics

The phrase *scientia est potentia* is a Latin aphorism meaning "knowledge is power!" In a business sense, this might be paraphrased as "Information is money!" Better information . . . better business decisions! This is the keystone of data analytics.

Data analytics is the process of examining data sets in order to draw conclusions about the information they contain. Data analytics is widely used in business to enable organizations to make better-informed business decisions. Increasingly, this is accomplished with the aid of specialized data visualization software such as Tableau.

In each chapter of this textbook, you will have the opportunity to experience the power and efficacy of data analytics in the context of that chapter's topics, using Tableau as a tool.

To prepare for this case—and those in subsequent chapters—using Tableau, you will need to download Tableau to your computer. Tableau provides free instructor and student licenses as well as free videos and support for utilizing and learning the software. You will receive further information on setting up Tableau from your instructor. Once you are set up with Tableau, watch the three "Getting Started" Tableau videos. Future cases will build off what you learn in these videos, and additional videos will be suggested. All short training videos can be found at **www.tableau.com/learn/training#getting-started**.

Data Analytics Case
Net Income and Cash Flows
● LO1–2

This case introduces you to data analysis in a very basic way by allowing you to quickly extract, visualize, and compare financial data over a span of ten years for two (hypothetical) publicly traded companies: Discount Goods and Big Store. For this case, assume you are an analyst conducting introductory research into the relative merits of investing in these companies. For this initial look, you want to visualize the pattern of net income and of net operating cash flows over the past ten years for the two companies.

Required:
Use Tableau to create charts depicting (a) the trend of net income and (b) the trend of net operating cash flows over the period 2012–2021 for each of the two companies. Based upon what you find, answer the following questions:
1. One of the companies reported a huge loss on its income statement related to a foreign expatriation of properties in one of the years. Which company, which year, and what was the amount of net income or net loss that resulted for that year?
2. What was the amount of net operating cash flow in the year of the loss for the company reporting the loss?
3. Which company reported the largest percentage change in net operating cash flows between 2012 and 2021, and what was the percentage change for that company (rounded to nearest whole percentage point)?
4. Which company reported the largest percentage change in net income between 2012 and 2021, and what was the percentage change for that company (rounded to nearest whole percentage point)?

Resources:
You have available to you an extensive data set that includes detailed financial data for Discount Goods and Big Store and for 2012–2021. The data set is in the form of an Excel file available to download from Connect, or under Student Resources within the Library tab. There are four Excel files available. The one for use in this chapter is named "Discount_Goods_Big_StoreCase1.xlsx." Download this file and save it to the computer on which you will be using Tableau.

After you view the training videos, follow these steps to create the charts you'll use for this case:
- Open Tableau and connect to the Excel spreadsheet you downloaded. You should see the data in the "canvas" area of Tableau.
- Click on the "Sheet 1" tab at the bottom of the canvas, to the right of the Data Source at the bottom of the screen.
- Move "Account name" into the Filters shelf. In the Filter dialog box that opens, if all accounts are selected, un-check all accounts by selecting the "None" button.
- Select only the account "Net cash flows from operating activities." Click OK. Note: the accounts are listed alphabetically.
- Drag "Store" and "Measure Names" into the "Columns" row at the top of the canvas.
- Drag "Measure Values" into "Rows".
- Remove "Number of Records" from "Measure Values" by clicking the pull-down menu arrow from the Measures Values dimension. Select "Edit Filter", unselect "Number of Records", and click "OK."
- On the "Show Me" menu in the upper right corner of the toolbar, select the side-by-side bars if they do not already appear in that chart format. Add labels to the bars by clicking on "Label" in the "Marks" card and clicking the box "Show mark label." In the same box, format the labels to Times New Roman, bold, black, 10-point by selecting those options using "Font".
- Change the title of the sheet to be "Operating Cash Flows: Discount Goods vs. Big Store" by right-clicking "Sheet 1" and selecting "Edit Title." Format the store names to Times New Roman, bold, black, and 15-point font. (We'll create the Net income/(loss) sheet next.)
- Change the colors of the bars by dragging "Measure Names" onto "Color" in the "Marks" card.
- Format the years by right-clicking on one year, selecting format in the Format Measures Name window (on the left)–Default Font dropdown box, select Times New Roman, bold, black, and 10-point options.
- To save time completing the next page, right-click the "Sheet 1" tab at the bottom of the canvas and select "Duplicate."
- Click on the "Sheet 2" tab. You should now see a duplicate of the "Sheet 1" canvas. Click on "Account name" on "Filter" in the "Marks" card. When the filter dialog box opens, un-check all accounts by selecting the "None" button. Note: The filter dialog box may open to the right of the canvas.
- Select only the account "Net income/(loss)." Change the title to "Net Income / (Loss): Discount Goods vs. Big Store" by editing the title as instructed above.
- Once complete, save the file as "DA1_Your initials.twbx."

Continuing Cases

Target Case

● LO1–9

Target Corporation prepares its financial statements according to U.S. GAAP. Target's financial statements and disclosure notes for the year ended February 3, 2018, are available in Connect. This material also is available under the Investor Relations link at the company's website (www.target.com).

Required:

1. What amounts did Target report for the following items for the year ended February 3, 2018?
    a. Total revenues
    b. Income from current operations
    c. Net income or net loss
    d. Total assets
    e. Total equity
2. What was Target's basic earnings per share for the year ended February 3, 2018?
3. What is Target's fiscal year-end? Why do you think Target chose that year-end?
4. Regarding Target's audit report:
    a. Who is Target's auditor?
    b. Did Target receive a "clean" (unmodified) audit opinion?

Air France–KLM Case

● LO1–11

 IFRS

Air France–KLM (AF), a Franco-Dutch company, prepares its financial statements according to International Financial Reporting Standards. AF's financial statements and disclosure notes for the year ended December 31, 2017, are available in Connect. This material is also available under the Finance link at the company's website (www.airfranceklm.com).

Required:

1. What amounts did AF report for the following items for the year ended December 31, 2017?
    a. Total revenues
    b. Income from current operations
    c. Net income or net loss (AF equity holders)
    d. Total assets
    e. Total equity
2. What was AF's basic earnings or loss per share for the year ended December 31, 2017?

CPA Exam Questions and Simulations

 ROGER
CPA Review

Sample CPA Exam questions from Roger CPA Review are available in Connect as support for the topics in this chapter. These multiple-choice questions and task-based simulations include expert-written explanations and solutions, and provide a starting point for students to become familiar with the content and functionality of the actual CPA Exam.

CHAPTER

2

Review of the Accounting Process

OVERVIEW

Chapter 1 explained that the primary means of conveying financial information to investors, creditors, and other external users is through financial statements and related notes. The purpose of this chapter is to review the fundamental accounting process used to produce the financial statements. This review establishes a framework for the study of the concepts covered in intermediate accounting.

Actual accounting systems differ significantly from company to company. This chapter focuses on the many features that tend to be common to any accounting system.

LEARNING OBJECTIVES

After studying this chapter, you should be able to:

● **LO2–1**   Understand routine economic events—transactions—and determine their effects on a company's financial position and on specific accounts. *(p. 48)*

● **LO2–2**   Describe the steps in the accounting processing cycle. *(p. 51)*

● **LO2–3**   Analyze and record transactions using journal entries. *(p. 55)*

● **LO2–4**   Post the effects of journal entries to general ledger accounts and prepare an unadjusted trial balance. *(p. 60)*

● **LO2–5**   Identify and describe the different types of adjusting journal entries. *(p. 63)*

● **LO2–6**   Record adjusting journal entries in general journal format, post entries, and prepare an adjusted trial balance. *(p. 64)*

● **LO2–7**   Describe the four basic financial statements. *(p. 72)*

● **LO2–8**   Explain the closing process. *(p. 76)*

● **LO2–9**   Convert from cash-basis net income to accrual-basis net income. *(p. 80)*

©goodluz/123RF

FINANCIAL REPORTING CASE

Engineering Profits

After graduating from college last year, two of your engineering-major friends started an Internet consulting practice. They began operations on July 1 and felt they did quite well during their first year. Now they would like to borrow $20,000 from a local bank to buy new computing equipment and office furniture. To support their loan application, the friends presented the bank with the following income statement for their first year of operations ending June 30:

Consulting revenue		$ 96,000
Operating expenses:		
Salaries	$32,000	
Rent	9,000	
Supplies	4,800	
Utilities	3,000	
Advertising	1,200	(50,000)
Net income		$ 46,000

The bank officer noticed that there was no depreciation expense in the income statement and has asked your friends to revise the statement after making year-end adjustments. After agreeing to help, you discover the following information:

a. The friends paid $80,000 for equipment when they began operations. They think the equipment will be useful for five years.

b. They pay $500 a month to rent office space. In January, they paid a full year's rent in advance. This is included in the $9,000 rent expense.

c. Included in consulting revenue is $13,000 they received from a customer in June as a deposit for work to be performed in August.

By the time you finish this chapter, you should be able to respond appropriately to the questions posed in this case. Compare your response to the solution provided at the end of the chapter.

QUESTIONS

1. What purpose do adjusting entries serve? (p. 64)

2. What year-end adjustments are needed to revise the income statement? Did your friends do as well their first year as they thought? (p. 64)

A solid foundation is vital to a sound understanding of intermediate accounting. So, we review the fundamental accounting process here to serve as a framework for the new concepts you will learn in this course.

Chapter 1 introduced the theoretical structure of financial accounting and the environment within which it operates. The primary function of financial accounting—to provide financial information to external users that possesses the fundamental decision-specific qualities of relevance and faithful representation—is accomplished by periodically disseminating financial statements and related notes. In this chapter we review the process used to identify, analyze, record, summarize, and then report the economic events affecting a company's financial position.

Keep in mind as you study this chapter that the accounting information systems businesses actually use are quite different from company to company. Larger companies generally use more complex systems than smaller companies use. The types of economic events affecting companies also cause differences in systems. We focus on the many features that tend to be common to all accounting systems.

It's important to understand that this chapter and its appendices are not intended to describe actual accounting systems. In most business enterprises, the sheer volume of data that must be processed precludes a manual accounting system. Fortunately, the computer provides a solution. *We describe and illustrate a manual accounting information system to provide an overview of the basic model that underlies the computer software programs actually used to process accounting information.*

Electronic data processing is fast, accurate, and affordable. Many large and medium-sized companies own or rent their own mainframe computers and company-specific data processing systems. Smaller companies can take advantage of technology with relatively inexpensive desktop and laptop computers and generalized data software packages such as QuickBooks and Peachtree Accounting Software. Enterprise Resource Planning (ERP) systems are now being installed in companies of all sizes. The objective of ERP is to create a customized software program that integrates all departments and functions across a company onto a single computer system that can serve the information needs of those different departments, including the accounting department.

> Computers are used to process accounting information. In this chapter we provide an overview of the basic model that underlies computer software programs.

● LO2–1

The Basic Model

> *Economic events* cause changes in the financial position of the company.

The first objective of any accounting system is to identify the economic events that can be expressed in financial terms by the system.[1] An economic event for accounting purposes is any event that *directly* affects the financial position of the company. Recall from Chapter 1 that financial position comprises assets, liabilities, and owners' equity. Broad and specific accounting principles determine which events should be recorded, when the events should be recorded, and the dollar amount at which they should be measured.

> *External events* involve an exchange between the company and another entity.

Economic events can be classified as either external events or internal events. External events involve an exchange between the company and a separate economic entity. Examples are transactions involving purchasing merchandise inventory for cash, borrowing cash from a bank, and paying salaries to employees. In each instance, the company receives something (merchandise, cash, and services) in exchange for something else (cash, assumption of a liability, or both).

> *Internal events* do not involve an exchange transaction but do affect the company's financial position.

On the other hand, internal events directly affect the financial position of the company but don't involve an exchange transaction with another entity. Examples are the depreciation of equipment and the use of supplies. As we will see later in the chapter, these events must be recorded to properly reflect a company's financial position and results of operations in accordance with the accrual accounting model.

The Accounting Equation

The accounting equation underlies the process used to capture the effect of economic events.

$$\text{Assets} = \text{Liabilities} + \text{Owners' Equity}$$

This general expression portrays the equality between the total economic resources of an entity (its assets)—shown on the left side of the equation—and the total claims against the entity (liabilities and equity)—shown on the right side. In other words, the resources of an enterprise are provided by creditors and owners. Look at that equation again, it's the key to all the discussion that follows.

---

[1]There are many economic events that affect a company *indirectly* and are not recorded. For example, when the Federal Reserve changes its discount rate, it is an important economic event that can affect the company in many ways, but it is not recorded by the company.

As discussed in Chapter 1, owners of a corporation are its shareholders, so owners' equity for a corporation is referred to as *shareholders'* equity. Shareholders' equity for a corporation arises primarily from two sources: (1) amounts *invested* by shareholders in the corporation and (2) amounts *earned* by the corporation (on behalf of its shareholders). These are reported as (1) paid-in capital and (2) retained earnings. Retained earnings equals net income less distributions to shareholders (primarily dividends) since the inception of the corporation. Illustration 2–1 shows the basic accounting equation for a corporation with shareholders' equity expanded to highlight its composition. We use the corporate format throughout the remainder of the chapter.

Owners' equity, for a corporation called shareholders' equity, is classified by source as either paid-in capital or retained earnings.

Illustration 2–1

Accounting Equation for a Corporation

The equation also implies that each economic event affecting this equation will have a dual effect because resources always must equal claims. For illustration, consider the events (we refer to these throughout the text as transactions) in Illustration 2–2. As we analyze each transaction to determine its effect on the equation, we also look at its effect on specific

Each event, or *transaction*, has a dual effect on the accounting equation.

Illustration 2–2

Transaction analysis

1. **An attorney invested $50,000 to open a law office.**
   An investment by the owner causes both assets and shareholders' (owners') equity to increase.

Assets	=	Liabilities	+	Shareholders' Equity
+$50,000 (cash)				+$50,000 (investment by owner)

2. **$40,000 was borrowed from a bank and a note payable was signed.**
   This transaction causes assets and liabilities to increase. A bank loan increases cash and creates an obligation to repay it.

Assets	=	Liabilities	+	Shareholders' Equity
+$40,000 (cash)		+$40,000 (note payable)		

3. **Supplies costing $3,000 were purchased on account.**
   Buying supplies on credit also increases both assets and liabilities.

Assets	=	Liabilities	+	Shareholders' Equity
+$3,000 (supplies)		+$3,000 (accounts payable)		

   Transactions 4, 5, and 6 are revenue and expense transactions. Revenues and expenses (and gains and losses) are events that cause shareholders' equity to change. Revenues and gains describe inflows of assets, causing shareholders' equity to increase. Expenses and losses describe outflows of assets (or increases in liabilities), causing shareholders' equity to decrease.

4. **Services were performed on account for $10,000.**

Assets	=	Liabilities	+	Shareholders' Equity
+$10,000 (accounts receivable)				+$10,000 (revenue)

5. **Salaries of $5,000 were paid to employees.**

Assets	=	Liabilities	+	Shareholders' Equity
−$5,000 (cash)				−$5,000 (expense)

6. **$500 of supplies were used.**

Assets	=	Liabilities	+	Shareholders' Equity
−$500 (supplies)				−$500 (expense)

7. **$1,000 was paid on account to the supplies vendor.**
   This transaction causes assets and liabilities to decrease.

Assets	=	Liabilities	+	Shareholders' Equity
−$1,000 (cash)		−$1,000 (accounts payable)		

financial elements, which we call accounts, that will be classified and reported to decision makers. To visualize these effects, we show the transactions in a columnar fashion within the equation layout.

Now let's see how these accounts are related.

Account Relationships

The double-entry system is used to process transactions.

All transactions could be recorded in columnar fashion as increases or decreases to elements of the accounting equation. However, even for a very small company with few transactions, this would become cumbersome. So, most companies use a process called the double-entry system. The term *double-entry* refers to the dual effect that each transaction has on the accounting equation.

A general ledger is a collection of storage areas, called accounts, used to keep track of increases, decreases, and balances in financial position elements.

Elements of the accounting equation are represented by accounts which are contained in a general ledger. Increases and decreases in each element of a company's financial position are recorded in these accounts allowing us to keep track of their balances. A separate account is maintained for individual assets and liabilities, retained earnings, and paid-in capital. Also, to accumulate information needed for the income statement, we use separate accounts to keep track of the changes in retained earnings caused by revenues, expenses, gains, and losses. The number of accounts depends on the complexity of the company's operations.

An account includes the account title, an account number to aid the processing task, and columns or fields for increases, decreases, the cumulative balance, and the date. For instructional purposes we use T-accounts instead of formal ledger accounts. A T-account has space at the top for the account title and two sides for recording increases and decreases.

Account Title

In the double-entry system, debit means left side of an account and credit means right side of an account.

For centuries, accountants have effectively used a system of debits and credits to increase and decrease account balances in the ledger. Debits merely represent the *left* side of the account and credits the *right* side, as shown below.

Account Title	
Debit side	Credit side

Asset increases are entered on the debit side of accounts and decreases are entered on the credit side. Liability and equity account increases are credits and decreases are debits.

Whether a debit or a credit represents an increase or a decrease depends on the type of account. Accounts on the left side of the accounting equation (assets) are *increased* (+) by *debit* entries and *decreased* (−) by *credit* entries. Accounts on the right side of the accounting equation (liabilities and shareholders' equity) are *increased* (+) by *credit* entries and *decreased* (−) by *debit* entries. This arbitrary, but effective, procedure ensures that for each transaction the net impact on the left sides of accounts always equals the net impact on the right sides of accounts.

For example, consider the bank loan in our earlier illustration. An asset, cash, increased by $40,000. Increases in assets are *debits*. Liabilities also increased by $40,000. Increases in liabilities are *credits*.

Assets		=	Liabilities		+	Shareholders' Equity
Cash			Note Payable			
Debit	Credit		Debit	Credit		
+ 40,000				40,000 +		

The debits equal the credits in every transaction (dual effect), so both before and after a transaction the accounting equation is in balance.

Prior exposure to the terms debit and credit probably comes from your experience with a bank account. For example, when a bank debits your checking account for service charges, it decreases your account balance. When you make a deposit, the bank credits your account, increasing your account balance. You must remember that from the bank's perspective, your bank account balance is a liability—it represents the amount that the bank owes you. Therefore, when the bank debits your account, it is decreasing its liability. When the bank credits your account, its liability increases.

Illustration 2–3 demonstrates the relationship among the accounting equation, debits and credits, and the increases and decreases in financial position elements.

Illustration 2–3
Accounting Equation, Debits and Credits, Increases and Decreases

Notice that increases and decreases in retained earnings are recorded *indirectly*. For example, an expense represents a decrease in retained earnings, which requires a debit. That debit, however, is recorded in an appropriate expense account rather than in retained earnings itself. This allows the company to maintain a separate record of expenses incurred during an accounting period. The debit to retained earnings for the expense is recorded in a closing entry (reviewed later) at the end of the period, only after the expense total is reflected in the income statement. Similarly, an increase in retained earnings due to revenue is recorded indirectly with a credit to a revenue account, which is later reflected as a credit to retained earnings.

The general ledger accounts serve as control accounts. Subsidiary accounts associated with a particular general ledger control account are maintained in separate subsidiary ledgers. For example, a subsidiary ledger for accounts receivable contains individual account receivable accounts for each of the company's credit customers and the total of all subsidiary accounts would equal the amount in the control account. Subsidiary ledgers are discussed in more detail in Appendix 2C.

Each general ledger account can be classified as either *permanent* or *temporary*. **Permanent accounts** represent assets, liabilities, and shareholders' equity at a point in time. **Temporary accounts** represent changes in the retained earnings component of shareholders' equity for a corporation caused by revenue, expense, gain, loss, and dividend transactions. It would be cumbersome to record each revenue/expense, gain/loss, and dividend transaction directly into the retained earnings account. The different types of events affecting retained earnings should be kept separate to facilitate the preparation of the financial statements. The balances in these temporary accounts are periodically, usually once a year, closed (zeroed out), and the net effect is recorded in the permanent retained earnings account. The temporary accounts need to be zeroed out to measure income on an annual basis. This closing process is discussed in a later section of this chapter.

Permanent accounts represent the basic financial position elements of the accounting equation.

Temporary accounts keep track of the changes in the retained earnings component of shareholders' equity.

The Accounting Processing Cycle

Now that we've reviewed the basics of the double-entry system, let's look closer at the process used to identify, analyze, record, and summarize transactions and prepare financial statements. This section deals only with *external transactions,* those that involve an exchange transaction with another entity and that change financial position when the event occurs. Internal transactions are discussed in a later section.

The 10 steps in the accounting processing cycle are listed in Illustration 2–4. Steps 1–4 occur during the accounting period while steps 5–8 are applied at the end of the accounting period. Steps 9 and 10 are needed only at the end of the year.

● LO2–2

Illustration 2–4

The Accounting Processing
Cycle

The Steps of the Accounting Processing Cycle

During the accounting period
- Step 1   Obtain information about external transactions from **source documents.**
- Step 2   **Analyze the transaction.**
- Step 3   Record the transaction in a **journal.**
- Step 4   **Post** from the journal to the general ledger accounts.

At the end of the accounting period
- Step 5   Prepare an **unadjusted trial balance.**
- Step 6   Record **adjusting entries** and post to the general ledger accounts.
- Step 7   Prepare an **adjusted trial balance.**
- Step 8   Prepare **financial statements.**

At the end of the year
- Step 9   **Close** the temporary accounts to retained earnings.
- Step 10   Prepare a **post-closing trial balance.**

Brief Overview of Accounting Processing Cycle

Now we will take a closer look at each of these steps. First, let's see a brief overview of each step, and then we will explore each one in more detail.

STEP 1

Obtain information about transactions from *source documents.*

The first step in the process is to *identify* external transactions affecting the accounting equation. An accountant usually does not directly witness business transactions. A mechanism is needed to relay the essential information about each transaction to the accountant. Source documents such as sales invoices, bills from suppliers, and cash register tapes serve this need.

STEP 2

Analyze the transaction.

These source documents usually identify the date and nature of each transaction, the participating parties, and the monetary terms. For example, a sales invoice identifies the date of sale, the customer, the specific goods sold, the dollar amount of the sale, and the payment terms. With this information, the second step in the processing cycle, transaction analysis, can proceed. Transaction analysis is the process of reviewing the source documents to determine the dual effect on the accounting equation and the specific elements (which we'll be calling accounts) that will be used to classify the item of analysis.

Let's revisit the seven transactions described previously in llustration 2–2 and expand that analysis to include their effects of specific account balances represented by T-accounts. We do this in Illustration 2–5. The item in each T-account is numbered to show the related transaction. We don't use dollar signs next to numbers in the accounting records (journal entries, journals, ledgers, trial balances)—only in the actual financial statements.

STEP 3

Record the transaction in a *journal.*

The third step in the process is to record the transaction in a journal. A journal provides a chronological record of all economic events affecting a firm. Each journal entry is expressed in terms of equal debits and credits to accounts affected by the transaction being recorded. Debits and credits represent increases or decreases to specific accounts, depending on the type of account, as explained earlier. For example, for credit sales, we record a debit to accounts receivable and a credit to sales revenue in a sales journal.

A sales journal is an example of a special journal used to record a repetitive type of transaction. In Appendix 2C we discuss the use of special journals in more depth. In this chapter and throughout the text, we use the general journal format to record all transactions.

Any type of transaction can be recorded in a general journal. It has a place for the date of the transaction, a place for account titles, account numbers, and supporting explanations, as well as a place for debit entries, and a place for credit entries. A simplified journal entry is used throughout the text that lists the account titles to be debited and credited and the dollar

Illustration 2–5 Transaction Analysis, the Accounting Equation, and Debits and Credits

Accounting Equation

Transaction	Transaction Analysis	Assets	=	Liabilities	+	Shareholders' Equity	Account Entry
1. An attorney invested $50,000 to open a law office.	Assets (cash) and shareholders' equity each increased by $50,000.	+50,000	=		+	+50,000	**Cash** 1. 50,000 **Shareholders' Equity** 50,000 1.
	Cumulative balances	50,000	=		+	50,000	
2. $40,000 was borrowed from a bank and a notes payable was signed.	Assets (cash) and liabilities (note payable) each increased by $40,000.	+40,000	=	+40,000	+		**Cash** 1. 50,000 / 2. 40,000 **Notes Payable** 40,000 2.
	Cumulative balances	90,000	=	40,000	+	50,000	
3. Supplies costing $3,000 were purchased on account.	Assets (supplies) and liabilities (accounts payable) each increased by $3,000.	+3,000	=	+3,000	+		**Supplies** 3. 3,000 **Accounts Payable** 3,000 3.
	Cumulative balances	93,000	=	43,000	+	50,000	
4. Services were performed on account for $10,000.	Assets (accounts receivable) and shareholders' equity (revenue) each increased by $10,000.	+10,000	=		+	+10,000	**Accounts Receivable** 4. 10,000 **Shareholders' Equity (Revenue)** 10,000 4.
	Cumulative balances	103,000	=	43,000	+	60,000	
5. Salaries of $5,000 were paid to employees.	Assets (cash) decreased and shareholders' equity decreased (salaries expense increased) by $5,000.	−5,000	=		+	−5,000	**Cash** 1. 50,000 / 2. 40,000 | 5,000 5. **Shareholders' Equity (Salaries Expense)** 5. 5,000
	Cumulative balances	98,000	=	43,000	+	55,000	
6. $500 of supplies were used.	Assets (supplies) decreased and shareholders' equity decreased (supplies expense increased) by $500.	−500	=		+	−500	**Supplies** 3. 3,000 | 500 6. **Shareholders' Equity (Supplies Expense)** 6. 500
	Cumulative balances	97,500	=	43,000	+	54,500	
7. $1,000 was paid on account to the supplies vendor.	Assets (cash) and liabilities (accounts payable) each decreased by $1,000.	−1,000	=	−1,000	+		**Cash** 1. 50,000 / 2. 40,000 | 5,000 5. / 1,000 7. **Accounts Payable** 7. 1,000 | 3,000 / 1,000 3.
	Cumulative balances	96,500	=	42,000	+	54,500	

amounts. A common convention is to list the debited accounts first, indent the credited accounts, and use the first of two columns for the debit amounts and the second column for the credit amounts. An explanation is entered for each journal entry (for ease in this example the explanation is located below the entry). For example, the journal entry for the bank loan in Illustration 2–1, which requires a debit to cash and a credit to notes payable, is recorded as follows:

Cash...	40,000	
Notes payable		40,000
To record the borrowing of cash and the signing of a note payable.		

STEP 4

Post from the journal to the general ledger accounts.

The fourth step is to periodically transfer or *post* the debit and credit information from the journal to individual ledger accounts. Recall that a ledger is simply a collection of all of the company's various accounts. Each account provides a summary of the effects of all events and transactions on that individual account. Posting involves transferring debits and credits recorded in individual journal entries to the specific accounts affected. As discussed earlier in the chapter, most accounting systems today are computerized. For these systems, the journal input information creates a stored journal and simultaneously posts each entry to the ledger accounts.

STEP 5

Prepare an unadjusted trial balance.

The fifth step is to prepare an unadjusted trial balance. The general ledger accounts provide the information needed. A trial balance is simply a list of general ledger accounts and their balances at a particular date. The unadjusted trial balance allows us to check for completeness, verify that the total of all debits is equal to the total of all credits, and detect some errors that may have occurred. We call it an *unadjusted* trial balance because, as we discuss later, we will prepare another trial balance after adjusting the accounts for items not yet reflected in the balances.

STEP 6

Record and post adjusting entries.

The sixth step is to record adjusting entries and post those to the general ledger accounts. Before we can prepare the financial statements, we need to bring our account balances up-to-date. We do this using adjusting entries at the end of the period. Adjusting entries are used to record changes in assets and liabilities (and their related revenues and expenses) that have occurred during the period but which we have not yet recorded.

STEP 7

Prepare an adjusted trial balance.

The seventh step is to prepare an adjusted trial balance. After posting the adjusting journal entries to the general ledger accounts, we prepare another trial balance, this time after all account balances are updated by the adjusting entries.

STEP 8

Prepare the financial statements.

The eigth step is to prepare the financial statements. In fact, the purpose of all the steps up to this point is so we have the information needed to do this. These statements:

- the income statement and statement of comprehensive income,
- the balance sheet,
- the statement of cash flows, and
- the statement of shareholders' equity

are the primary means of providing information to investors and other decision makers, which is the purpose of accounting. The adjusted trial balance supplies the necessary information to produce these statements.

STEP 9

Close the temporary accounts to retained earnings.

The ninth step is to record closing entries and post those to the general ledger accounts. Closing entries serve two purposes: (1) to transfer the balances of temporary accounts (revenues, expenses, gains, losses, and dividends) to the retained earnings account, and (2) to reduce the balances of these temporary accounts to zero to "wipe the slate clean" and ready them for measuring activity in the next period.

STEP 10

Prepare a post-closing trial balance.

The final step is to prepare a post-closing trial balance. After the temporary account balances (revenues, expenses, and dividends) are transferred to retained earnings and the closing entries are posted to the ledger accounts, we prepare another trial balance. This post-closing trial balance is comprised of final balances in permanent accounts that will be used to open (begin) the records in the next period.

Illustration of Accounting Processing Cycle

Now that we have looked at a brief overview of the ten steps of the accounting processing cycle, let's take a closer look at each one. We start by illustrating the first four steps in the processing cycle using the external transactions described in Illustration 2–6 that occurred during the month of July 2021, the first month of operations for Dress Right Clothing Corporation. The company operates a retail store that sells men's and women's clothing. Dress Right is organized as a corporation so owners' equity is classified by source as either paid-in capital or retained earnings.

Illustration 2–6

External Transactions for July 2021

July	1	Two individuals each invested $30,000 in the corporation. Each investor was issued 3,000 shares of common stock.
	1	Borrowed $40,000 from a local bank and signed two notes. The first note for $10,000 requires payment of principal and 10% interest in six months. The second note for $30,000 requires the payment of principal in two years. Interest at 10% is payable each year on July 1, 2022, and July 1, 2023.
	1	Paid $24,000 in advance for one year's rent on the store building.
	1	Purchased office equipment from eTronics for $12,000 cash.
	3	Purchased $60,000 of clothing inventory on account from the Birdwell Wholesale Clothing Company.
	6	Purchased $2,000 of supplies for cash.
	4–31	During the month, sold merchandise costing $20,000 for $35,000 cash.
	9	Sold clothing on account to Briarfield School for Girls for $3,500. The clothing cost $2,000.
	16	Subleased a portion of the building to a jewelry store. Received $1,000 in advance for the first two months' rent beginning on July 16.
	20	Paid Birdwell Wholesale Clothing $25,000 on account.
	20	Paid salaries to employees for the first half of the month, $5,000.
	25	Received $1,500 on account from Briarfield.
	30	The corporation paid its shareholders a cash dividend of $1,000.

The local bank requires that Dress Right furnish financial statements on a monthly basis. The transactions listed in the illustration are used to demonstrate the accounting processing cycle for the month of July, 2021.

Journal, Ledger, and Trial Balance

Now that we've overviewed the ten steps in the accounting processing cycle, we look closer at the process.

STEPS 1, 2, AND 3   Obtain information about transactions from *source documents.*
   Analyze the transaction.
   Record the transaction in a journal.
   For each transaction, a source document provides the necessary information to complete steps two and three in the processing cycle: transaction analysis and recording the appropriate journal entry. Each transaction described in Illustration 2–6 is analyzed below, preceded by the necessary journal entry.

JOURNAL ENTRIES

● LO2–3

To record the issuance of common stock.

July 1

Cash	60,000	
Common stock		60,000

This first transaction is an investment by owners that increases an asset, cash, and also increases shareholders' equity. Increases in assets are recorded as debits and increases in shareholders' equity are recorded as credits. We use the paid-in capital account called common stock because stock was issued in exchange for cash paid in.[2]

To record the borrowing of cash and the signing of a note payable.

July 1		
Cash..	40,000	
Notes payable		40,000

This transaction causes increases in both cash and the liability, notes payable. Increases in assets are debits and increases in liabilities are credits. The note requires payment of $40,000 in principal and $6,500[($10,000 \times 10\% \times \frac{6}{12} = \$500) + (\$30,000 \times 10\% \times 2$ years $= \$6,000)]$ in interest. However, at this point we are concerned only with the external transaction that occurs when the cash is borrowed and the note is signed. Later we discuss how the interest is recorded.

To record the payment of one year's rent in advance.

July 1		
Prepaid rent	24,000	
Cash		24,000

This transaction increased an asset called prepaid rent, which is debited, and decreased the asset cash (a credit). Dress Right acquired the right to use the building for one full year. This is an asset because it represents a future benefit to the company. As we will see later, this asset expires over the one-year rental period.

To record the purchase of office equipment.

July 1		
Office equipment...	12,000	
Cash		12,000

This transaction increases one asset, office equipment, and decreases another, cash.

To record the purchase of merchandise inventory.

July 3		
Inventory..	60,000	
Accounts payable..		60,000

This purchase of merchandise on account is recorded by a debit to inventory, an asset, and a credit to accounts payable, a liability. Increases in assets are debits. Increases in liabilities are credits.

The Dress Right Clothing Company uses the *perpetual inventory system* to keep track of its merchandise inventory. This system requires that the cost of merchandise purchased be recorded in inventory, an asset account. When inventory is sold, the inventory account is decreased by the cost of the item sold. An alternative method, the *periodic system,* is briefly discussed later in this chapter. We explore the topic of inventory in depth in Chapters 8 and 9.

To record the purchase of supplies.

July 6		
Supplies	2,000	
Cash		2,000

We record the acquisition of supplies as a debit to the asset account supplies (an increase) and as a credit to the asset cash (a decrease). Supplies are an asset because they represent future benefits.

---

[2]The different types of stock are discussed in Chapter 18.

July 4–31

Cash	35,000	
Sales revenue		35,000
Cost of goods sold (expense)	20,000	
Inventory		20,000

To record the month's cash sales and the cost of those sales.

During the month of July, cash sales to customers totaled $35,000. The company's assets (cash) increase by this amount as does shareholders' equity. This increase in equity is recorded by a credit to the temporary account sales revenue.

At the same time, an asset, inventory, decreases and retained earnings decreases. Recall that expenses are outflows or using up of assets from providing goods and services. Dress Right incurred an expense equal to the cost of the inventory sold. The temporary account cost of goods sold increases. However, this increase in an expense represents a *decrease* in shareholders' equity—retained earnings—and accordingly the account is debited. Both of these transactions are *summary* transactions. Normally each sale made during the month requires a separate and similar entry in a special journal, which we discuss in Appendix 2C.

July 9

Accounts receivable	3,500	
Sales revenue		3,500
Cost of goods sold	2,000	
Inventory		2,000

To record a credit sale and the cost of that sale.

This transaction is similar to the cash sale shown earlier. The only difference is that the asset acquired in exchange for merchandise is accounts receivable rather than cash.

Additional Consideration

Periodic Inventory System

The principal alternative to the perpetual inventory system is the periodic system. By this approach, we record the cost of merchandise purchased in a temporary account called *purchases*. When inventory is sold, the inventory account is not decreased and cost of goods sold is not recorded. Instead, we determine the balance in the inventory account only at the end of a reporting period (periodically), and then we can determine the cost of goods sold for the period.

For example, the purchase of $60,000 of merchandise on account by Dress Right Clothing is recorded as follows:

Purchases	60,000	
Accounts payable		60,000

No cost of goods sold entry is recorded when sales are made in the periodic system.

At the end of July, the amount of ending inventory is determined (either by means of a physical count of goods on hand or by estimation) to be $38,000 and cost of goods sold for the month is determined as follows:

Beginning inventory	$ –0–
Plus: Purchases	60,000
Less: Ending inventory	(38,000)
Cost of goods sold	$ 22,000

We record the cost of goods sold for the period and adjust the inventory account to the actual amount on hand (in this case from zero to $38,000) this way:

Cost of goods sold	22,000	
Inventory	38,000	
Purchases		60,000

We discuss inventory in depth in Chapters 8 and 9.

58 SECTION 1 The Role of Accounting as an Information System

To record the receipt of rent in advance.

July 16		
Cash..	1,000	
Deferred rent revenue (liability)..		1,000

Cash increases by $1,000 so we debit the cash account. At this point, Dress Right does not recognize revenue yet even though cash has been received. Instead, revenue is recorded only after Dress Right has provided the jewelry store with the use of facilities; that is, as the rental period expires. On receipt of the cash, a liability called *deferred rent revenue* increases and is credited. This liability represents Dress Right's obligation to provide the use of facilities to the jewelry store.

To record the payment of accounts payable.

July 20		
Accounts payable..	25,000	
Cash		25,000

This transaction decreases both an asset (cash) and a liability (accounts payable). A debit decreases the liability, and a credit decreases the asset.

To record the payment of salaries for the first half of the month.

July 20		
Salaries expense	5,000	
Cash		5,000

Employees were paid for services rendered during the first half of the month. The cash expenditure did not create an asset since no future benefits resulted. Cash decreases and is credited; shareholders' equity decreases and is debited. The reduction in shareholders' equity is recorded in the temporary account, salaries expense.

To record receipt of cash on account.

July 25		
Cash	1,500	
Accounts receivable		1,500

This transaction is an exchange of one asset, accounts receivable, for another asset, cash.

To record the payment of a cash dividend.

July 30		
Dividends..	1,000	
Cash		1,000

The payment of a cash dividend is a distribution to owners that reduces both cash and retained earnings. Dividends is a temporary account that later is closed (transferred) to retained earnings along with the other temporary accounts (revenues and expenses) at the end of the fiscal year. We discuss and illustrate the closing process later in the chapter.

Additional Consideration

An alternative method of recording a cash dividend is to debit retained earnings at the time the dividend is paid rather than reducing retained earnings during the closing process. The entry to record the dividend using this approach is as follows:

Retained earnings	1,000	
Cash		1,000

As an expedient, we apply this approach when discussing dividends in Chapter 18.

Illustration 2–7 summarizes each of the transactions we just discussed as they would appear in a general journal. In addition to the date, account titles, and debit and credit columns, the journal also has a column titled Post Ref. (Posting Reference). In this column we enter the number assigned to the general ledger account that is being debited or credited. For purposes of this illustration, all asset accounts have been assigned numbers in the 100s, all liabilities are 200s, permanent shareholders' equity accounts are 300s, revenues are 400s, expenses are 500s and dividends is 600.

Illustration 2–7
The General Journal

General Journal				Page 1
Date 2021	**Account Title and Explanation**	**Post Ref.**	**Debit**	**Credit**
July 1	Cash	100	60,000	
	Common stock	300		60,000
	To record the issuance of common stock.			
1	Cash	100	40,000	
	Notes payable	220		40,000
	To record the borrowing of cash and the signing of notes payable.			
1	Prepaid rent	130	24,000	
	Cash	100		24,000
	To record the payment of one year's rent in advance.			
1	Office equipment	150	12,000	
	Cash	100		12,000
	To record the purchase of office equipment.			
3	Inventory	140	60,000	
	Accounts payable	210		60,000
	To record the purchase of merchandise inventory.			
6	Supplies	125	2,000	
	Cash	100		2,000
	To record the purchase of supplies.			
4–31	Cash	100	35,000	
	Sales revenue	400		35,000
	To record cash sales for the month.			
4–31	Cost of goods sold	500	20,000	
	Inventory	140		20,000
	To record the cost of cash sales.			
9	Accounts receivable	110	3,500	
	Sales revenue	400		3,500
	To record credit sale.			
9	Cost of goods sold	500	2,000	
	Inventory	140		2,000
	To record the cost of a credit sale.			
16	Cash	100	1,000	
	Deferred rent revenue	230		1,000
	To record the receipt of rent in advance.			
20	Accounts payable	210	25,000	
	Cash	100		25,000
	To record the payment of accounts payable.			
20	Salaries expense	510	5,000	
	Cash	100		5,000
	To record the payment of salaries for the first half of the month.			
25	Cash	100	1,500	
	Accounts receivable	110		1,500
	To record the receipt of cash on account.			
30	Dividends	600	1,000	
	Cash	100		1,000
	To record the payment of a cash dividend.			

The ledger accounts also contain a posting reference, usually the page number of the journal in which the journal entry was recorded. This allows for easy cross-referencing between the journal and the ledger.

● LO2–4   **LEDGER ACCOUNTS**   Step 4 in the processing cycle is to transfer (post) the debit/credit information from the journal to the general ledger accounts. Illustration 2–8 contains the ledger accounts (in T-account form) for Dress Right *after* all the general journal transactions have been

Illustration 2–8

General Ledger Accounts

Balance Sheet Accounts

Cash			100
July 1 GJ1	60,000	24,000	July 1 GJ1
1 GJ1	40,000	12,000	1 GJ1
4-31 GJ1	35,000	2,000	6 GJ1
16 GJ1	1,000	25,000	20 GJ1
25 GJ1	1,500	5,000	20 GJ1
		1,000	30 GJ1
July 31 Bal.	**68,500**		

Prepaid Rent			130
July 1 GJ1	24,000		
July 31 Bal.	**24,000**		

Accounts Receivable			110
July 9 GJ1	3,500	1,500	July 25 GJ1
July 31 Bal.	**2,000**		

Inventory			140
July 3 GJ1	60,000	20,000	July 4–31
		2,000	9 GJ1
July 31 Bal.	**38,000**		

Supplies			125
July 6 GJ1	2,000		
July 31 Bal.	**2,000**		

Office equipment			150
July 1 GJ1	12,000		
July 31 Bal.	**12,000**		

Accounts Payable			210
July 20 GJ1	25,000	60,000	July 3 GJ1
		35,000	**July 31 Bal.**

Notes Payable			220
		40,000	July 1 GJ1
		40,000	**July 31 Bal.**

Deferred Rent Revenue			230
		1,000	July 16 GJ1
		1,000	**July 31 Bal.**

Common Stock			300
		60,000	July 1 GJ1
		60,000	**July 31 Bal.**

Retained Earnings			310
July 31 Bal.	**0**		

Income Statement Accounts

Sales Revenue			400
		35,000	July 4–31 GJ1
		3,500	9 GJ1
		38,500	**July 31 Bal.**

Cost of Goods Sold			500
July 4-31 GJ1	20,000		
9 GJ1	2,000		
July 31 Bal.	**22,000**		

Salaries Expense			510
July 20 GJ1	5,000		
July 31 Bal.	**5,000**		

Dividends

Dividends			600
July 30 GJ1	1,000		
July 31 Bal.	**1,000**		

posted. The reference GJ1 next to each of the posted amounts indicates that the source of the entry is page 1 of the general journal. An alternative is to number each of the entries in chronological order and reference them by number. Note that each account shows the balance that we call a *normal balance*—that is, the balance is the debit or credit side used to increase the account.

TRIAL BALANCE   Before preparing financial statements and adjusting entries (internal transactions) at the end of an accounting period, we prepare an unadjusted trial balance—step 5. A trial balance is simply a list of the general ledger accounts along with their balances at a particular date, listed in the order that they appear in the ledger. The purpose of the trial balance is to allow us to check for completeness and to verify that the sum of the accounts with debit balances equals the sum of the accounts with credit balances. The fact that the debits and credits are equal, though, does not necessarily ensure that the equal balances are correct. The trial balance could contain offsetting errors. As we will see later in the chapter, this trial balance also helps with preparing adjusting entries.

STEP 5

Prepare an *unadjusted trial balance.*

The unadjusted trial balance at July 31, 2021, for Dress Right appears in Illustration 2–9. Notice that dividends has a debit balance of $1,000. This reflects the payment of the cash dividend to shareholders. We record increases and decreases in retained earnings from revenue, expense, gain and loss transactions *indirectly* in temporary accounts. Before the start of the next year, we transfer these increases and decreases to the retained earnings account.

Illustration 2–9

Unadjusted Trial Balance

DRESS RIGHT CLOTHING CORPORATION
Unadjusted Trial Balance
July 31, 2021

Account Title	Debits	Credits
Cash	68,500	
Accounts receivable	2,000	
Supplies	2,000	
Prepaid rent	24,000	
Inventory	38,000	
Office equipment	12,000	
Accounts payable		35,000
Notes payable		40,000
Deferred rent revenue		1,000
Common stock		60,000
Retained earnings		0
Sales revenue		38,500
Cost of goods sold	22,000	
Salaries expense	5,000	
Dividends	1,000	
Totals	174,500	174,500

At any time, the total of all debit balances should equal the total of all credit balances.

Concept Review Exercise

The Wyndham Wholesale Company began operations on August 1, 2021. The following transactions occur during the month of August.

JOURNAL ENTRIES FOR EXTERNAL TRANSACTIONS

a. Owners invest $50,000 cash in the corporation in exchange for 5,000 shares of common stock.

b. Equipment is purchased for $20,000 cash.

c. On the first day of August, $6,000 rent on a building is paid for the months of August and September.

d. Merchandise inventory costing $38,000 is purchased on account. The company uses the perpetual inventory system.

e. $30,000 is borrowed from a local bank, and a note payable is signed.

f. Credit sales for the month are $40,000. The cost of merchandise sold is $22,000.

g. $15,000 is collected on account from customers.

h. $20,000 is paid on account to suppliers of merchandise.

i. Salaries of $7,000 are paid to employees for August.

j. A bill for $2,000 is received from the local utility company for the month of August.

k. $20,000 cash is loaned to another company, evidenced by a note receivable.

l. The corporation pays its shareholders a cash dividend of $1,000.

Required:

1. Prepare a journal entry for each transaction.
2. Prepare an unadjusted trial balance as of August 31, 2021.

Solution:

1. Prepare a journal entry for each transaction.

   a. The issuance of common stock for cash increases both cash and shareholders' equity (common stock).

Cash	50,000	
Common stock		50,000

   b. The purchase of equipment increases equipment and decreases cash.

Equipment	20,000	
Cash		20,000

   c. The payment of rent in advance increases prepaid rent and decreases cash.

Prepaid rent	6,000	
Cash		6,000

   d. The purchase of merchandise on account increases both inventory and accounts payable.

Inventory	38,000	
Accounts payable		38,000

   e. Borrowing cash and signing a note increases both cash and notes payable.

Cash	30,000	
Notes payable		30,000

   f. The sale of merchandise on account increases both accounts receivable and sales revenue. Also, cost of goods sold increases and inventory decreases.

Accounts receivable	40,000	
Sales revenue		40,000
Cost of goods sold	22,000	
Inventory		22,000

   g. The collection of cash on account increases cash and decreases accounts receivable.

Cash	15,000	
Accounts receivable		15,000

   h. The payment to suppliers on account decreases both accounts payable and cash.

Accounts payable	20,000	
Cash		20,000

i. The payment of salaries for the period increases salaries expense (decreases retained earnings) and decreases cash.

Salaries expense	7,000	
Cash		7,000

j. The receipt of a bill for services rendered increases both an expense (utilities expense) and accounts payable. The expense decreases retained earnings.

Utilities expense	2,000	
Accounts payable		2,000

k. The lending of cash to another entity and the signing of a note increases notes receivable and decreases cash.

Notes receivable	20,000	
Cash		20,000

l. Cash dividends paid to shareholders reduce both retained earnings and cash.

Dividends[3]	1,000	
Cash		1,000

2. Prepare an unadjusted trial balance as of August 31, 2021.

Account Title	Debits	Credits
Cash	21,000	
Accounts receivable	25,000	
Prepaid rent	6,000	
Inventory	16,000	
Notes receivable	20,000	
Equipment	20,000	
Accounts payable		20,000
Notes payable		30,000
Common stock		50,000
Retained earnings		0
Sales revenue		40,000
Cost of goods sold	22,000	
Salaries expense	7,000	
Utilities expense	2,000	
Dividends	1,000	
Totals	140,000	140,000

Adjusting Entries

● LO2–5

Step 6 in the processing cycle is to record in the general journal and post to the ledger accounts the effect of *internal events* on the accounting equation. These transactions do not involve an exchange transaction with another entity and, therefore, are not initiated by a source document. They are recorded *at the end of any period when financial statements are prepared*. These transactions are commonly referred to as adjusting entries.

    Even when all transactions and events are analyzed, corrected, journalized, and posted to appropriate ledger accounts, some account balances will require updating. Adjusting entries

STEP 6

Record *adjusting entries* and post to the ledger accounts.

---

[3]An alternative is to debit retained earnings at the time the dividend is distributed.

**FINANCIAL
Reporting Case**

Q1, p. 47

are required to implement the *accrual accounting model*. More specifically, these entries help ensure that all revenues are recognized in the period goods or services are transferred to customers, regardless of when the cash is received. Also, they enable a company to recognize all expenses incurred during a period, regardless of when cash payment is made. As a result, a period's income statement provides a more complete measure of a company's operating performance and a better measure for predicting future operating cash flows. The balance sheet also provides a more complete assessment of assets and liabilities as sources of future cash receipts and disbursements. You might think of adjusting entries as a method of bringing the company's financial information up-to-date before preparing the financial statements.

Adjusting entries are necessary for three situations:

**FINANCIAL
Reporting Case**

Q2, p. 47

1. **Prepayments**, sometimes referred to as *deferrals*
2. **Accruals**
3. **Estimates**

Prepayments

Prepayments are transactions in which the cash flow precedes expense or revenue recognition.

Prepayments occur when the cash flow *precedes* either expense or revenue recognition. For example, a company may buy supplies in one period but use them in a later period. The cash outflow creates an asset (supplies) which then must be expensed in a future period as the asset is used up. Similarly, a company may receive cash from a customer in one period but provide the customer with a good or service in a future period. For instance, magazine publishers usually receive cash in advance for magazine subscriptions. The cash inflow creates a liability (deferred revenue) that is recognized as revenue in a future period when the goods or services are transferred to customers.

Prepaid expenses represent assets recorded when a cash disbursement creates benefits beyond the current reporting period.

PREPAID EXPENSES   Prepaid expenses are the costs of assets acquired in one period and expensed in a future period. Whenever cash is paid, and it is not to (1) satisfy a liability or (2) pay a dividend or return capital to owners, it must be determined whether or not the payment creates future benefits or whether the payment benefits only the current period. The purchase of buildings, equipment, or supplies or the payment of rent in advance are examples of payments that create future benefits and should be recorded as assets. The benefits provided by these assets expire in future periods and their cost is expensed in future periods as related revenues are recognized.

The adjusting entry required for a prepaid expense is a debit to an expense and a credit to an asset.

To illustrate this concept, assume that a company paid a radio station $2,000 in July for advertising. If that $2,000 were for advertising provided by the radio station during the month of July, the entire $2,000 would be expensed in the same period as the cash disbursement. If, however, the $2,000 was a payment for advertising to be provided in a future period, say the month of August, then the cash disbursement creates an asset called *prepaid advertising*. Then, an adjusting entry is required at the end of August to increase advertising expense (decrease shareholders' equity) and to decrease the asset, prepaid advertising, by $2,000. So, the adjusting entry for a prepaid expense is a *debit to an expense* and a *credit to an asset*.

● **LO2–6**

The unadjusted trial balance can provide a starting point for determining which adjusting entries are required for a period, particularly for prepayments. Review the July 31, 2021, unadjusted trial balance for the Dress Right Clothing Corporation in Illustration 2–9 and try to anticipate the required adjusting entries for prepaid expenses.

Supplies		
Beg. bal. 0		
2,000	800	
End bal. 1,200		

Supplies Expense		
Beg. bal. 0		
800		
End. bal. 800		

The first asset that requires adjustment is supplies, $2,000 of which were purchased during July. This transaction created an asset as the supplies will be used in future periods. The company could either track the supplies used or simply count the supplies at the end of the period and determine the dollar amount of supplies remaining. Assume that Dress Right determines that at the end of July, $1,200 of supplies remain. The following adjusting journal entry is required.

To record the cost of supplies used during the month of July.

July 31		
Supplies expense...	800	
Supplies...		800

The next prepaid expense requiring adjustment is rent. Recall that at the beginning of July, the company paid $24,000 to its landlord representing one year's rent in advance. As it is reasonable to assume that the rent services provided each period are equal, the monthly rent is $2,000. At the end of July 2021, one month's prepaid rent has expired and must be recognized as expense.

July 31		
Rent expense ($24,000 ÷ 12)..	2,000	
Prepaid rent		2,000

To record the cost of expired rent for the month of July.

After this entry is recorded and posted to the ledger accounts, the prepaid rent account will have a debit balance of $22,000, representing 11 remaining months at $2,000 per month, and the rent expense account will have a $2,000 debit balance.

The final prepayment involves the asset represented by office equipment that was purchased for $12,000. This asset has a long life but nevertheless will expire over time. For the previous two adjusting entries, it was fairly straightforward to determine the amount of the asset that expired during the period.

However, it is difficult, if not impossible, to determine how much of the benefits from using the office equipment expired during any particular period. Recall from Chapter 1 that one approach is to recognize an expense "by a systematic and rational allocation to specific time periods."

Assume that the office equipment has a useful life of five years (60 months) and will be worthless at the end of that period, and that we choose to allocate the cost equally over the period of use. The amount of monthly expense, called *depreciation expense,* is $200 ($12,000 ÷ 60 months = $200), and the following adjusting entry is recorded.

Rent Expense

Beg. bal.	0	
	2,000	
End bal.	2,000	

Prepaid Rent

Beg. bal.	0	
	24,000	2,000
End. bal.	22,000	

July 31		
Depreciation expense...	200	
Accumulated depreciation..		200

To record depreciation of office equipment for the month of July.

The entry reduces an asset, office equipment, by $200. However, the asset account is not reduced directly. Instead, the credit is to an account called *accumulated depreciation.* This is a contra account to office equipment. The normal balance in a contra asset account will be a credit, that is, "contra," or opposite, to the normal debit balance in an asset account. The purpose of the contra account is to keep the original cost of the asset intact while reducing it indirectly. In the balance sheet, office equipment is reported net of accumulated depreciation. When we have multiple depreciable assets, it's helpful to differentiate accumulated depreciation accounts, like accumulated depreciation—office equipment, accumulated depreciation—buildings, etc. This topic is covered in depth in Chapter 11.

After this entry is recorded and posted to the ledger accounts, the accumulated depreciation account will have a credit balance of $200 and the depreciation expense account will have a $200 debit balance. If a required adjusting entry for a prepaid expense is not recorded, net income, assets, and shareholders' equity (retained earnings) will be overstated.

DEFERRED REVENUES Deferred revenues are created when a company receives cash from a customer in one period for goods or services that are to be provided in a future period. The cash receipt, an external transaction, is recorded as a debit to cash and a credit to a liability. This liability reflects the company's obligation to provide goods or services in the future.

Deferred revenues represent liabilities recorded when cash is received from customers in advance of providing a good or service.

To illustrate a deferred revenue transaction, assume that during the month of June a magazine publisher received $24 in cash for a 24-month subscription to a monthly magazine. The subscription begins in July. On receipt of the cash, the publisher records a liability, deferred subscription revenue, of $24. Subsequently, revenue of $1 is recognized as each

The adjusting entry required when deferred revenues are recognized is a debit to a liability and a credit to revenue.

monthly magazine is published and mailed to the customer. An adjusting entry is required each month to increase shareholders' equity (revenue) to recognize the $1 in revenue and to decrease the liability. Assuming that the cash receipt entry included a credit to a liability, the adjusting entry for deferred revenues, therefore, is a *debit to a liability,* in this case deferred subscription revenue, and a *credit to revenue.*

Once again, the unadjusted trial balance provides information concerning deferred revenues. For Dress Right Clothing Corporation, the only deferred revenue in the trial balance is deferred rent revenue. Recall that the company subleased a portion of its building to a jewelry store for $500 per month. On July 16, the jewelry store paid Dress Right $1,000 in advance for the first two months' rent. The transaction was recorded as a debit to cash and a credit to deferred rent revenue.

At the end of July, how much of the $1,000 must be recognized? Approximately one-half of one month's rent service has been provided, or $250, requiring the following adjusting entry.

To record previously deferred rent revenue recognized during July.

July 31		
Deferred rent revenue	250	
Rent revenue		250

Deferred Rent Revenue

	0	Beg. bal.
250	1,000	
	750	End bal.

Rent Revenue

	0	Beg. bal.
	250	
	250	End bal.

After this entry is recorded and posted to the ledger accounts, the deferred rent revenue account is reduced to a credit balance of $750 for the remaining one and one-half months' rent, and the rent revenue account will have a $250 credit balance. If this entry is not recorded, net income and shareholders' equity (retained earnings) will be understated, and liabilities will be overstated.

ALTERNATIVE APPROACH TO RECORD PREPAYMENTS   The same end result can be achieved for prepayments by recording the external transaction directly into an expense or revenue account. In fact, many companies prefer this approach. For simplicity, bookkeeping instructions might require all cash payments for expenses to be debited to the appropriate expense accounts and all cash payments for revenues to be credited to the appropriate revenue accounts. In the adjusting entry, then, the *unexpired* prepaid expense (asset) or *deferred* revenue (liability) as of the end of the period are recorded.

For example, on July 1, 2021, Dress Right paid $24,000 in cash for one year's rent on its building. The entry included a debit to prepaid rent. The company could have debited rent expense instead of prepaid rent.

Rent Expense

Beg. bal.	0		
	24,000	22,000	
End bal.	2,000		

Alternative Approach		
July 1		
Rent expense...	24,000	
Cash		24,000

The adjusting entry then records the amount of prepaid rent as of the end of July, $22,000, and reduces rent expense to $2,000, the cost of rent for the month of July.

Prepaid Rent

Beg. bal.	0	
	22,000	
End bal.	22,000	

Alternative Approach		
July 31		
Prepaid rent	22,000	
Rent expense...		22,000

The net effect of handling the transactions in this manner is the same as the previous treatment. Either way, the prepaid rent account will have a debit balance at the end of July of $22,000 to represent 11 months remaining prepaid rent, and the rent expense account will have a debit balance of $2,000 to represent the one month of rent used in the period of this income statement being prepared. What's important is that an adjusting entry is recorded to ensure the appropriate amounts are reflected in both the expense and asset *before financial statements are prepared.*

Similarly, the July 16 cash receipt from the jewelry store representing an advance for two months' rent initially could have been recorded by Dress Right as a credit to rent revenue instead of deferred rent revenue (a liability).

Alternative Approach		
July 16		
Cash...	1,000	
Rent revenue		1,000

Rent Revenue		
		0 Beg. bal.
	750	1,000
		250 End bal.

If Dress Right records the entire $1,000 as rent revenue in this way, it would then use the adjusting entry to record the amount of deferred revenue as of the end of July, $750 to represent the one and one-half month of rent revenue remaining as collected in advance, and the rent revenue account will have a credit balance of $250, which is for the one-half month of July that has passed in the current period.

Alternative Approach		
July 31		
Rent revenue	750	
Deferred rent revenue		750

Deferred Rent Revenue		
		0 Beg. bal.
		750
		750 End bal.

Accruals

Accruals occur when the cash flow comes *after* either expense or revenue recognition. For example, a company often uses the services of another entity in one period and pays for them in a subsequent period. An expense must be recognized in the period incurred and an accrued liability recorded. Also, goods and services often are provided to customers on credit. In such instances, a revenue is recognized in the period goods or services are transferred to customers and an asset, a receivable, is recorded.

Accruals involve transactions where the cash outflow or inflow takes place in a period subsequent to expense or revenue recognition.

Many accruals involve external transactions that automatically are recorded from a source document. For example, a sales invoice for a credit sale provides all the information necessary to record the debit to accounts receivable and the credit to sales revenue. However, there are some accruals that involve internal transactions and thus require adjusting entries. Because accruals involve recognition of expense or revenue before cash flow, the unadjusted trial balance will not be as helpful in identifying required adjusting entries as with prepayments.

ACCRUED LIABILITIES For accrued liabilities, we are concerned with expenses incurred but not yet paid. Dress Right Clothing Corporation requires two adjusting entries for accrued liabilities at July 31, 2021.

Accrued liabilities represent liabilities recorded when an expense has been incurred prior to cash payment.

The first entry is for employee salaries for the second half of July. Recall that on July 20 the company paid employees $5,000 for salaries for the first half of the month. Salaries for the second half of July probably will be paid in early August. Nevertheless, an expense is incurred in July for services rendered to the company by its employees. The accrual income statement for July must reflect these services for the entire month regardless of when the cash payment is made.

Therefore, an obligation exists at the end of July to pay the salaries earned by employees for the last half of that month. An adjusting entry is required to increase salaries expense (decrease shareholders' equity) and to increase liabilities for the salaries payable. The adjusting entry for an accrued liability always includes a *debit to an expense,* and a *credit to a liability.* Assuming that salaries for the second half of July are $5,500, the following adjusting entry is recorded.

The adjusting entry required to record an accrued liability is a *debit to an expense* and a *credit to a liability.*

July 31		
Salaries expense..	5,500	
Salaries payable...		5,500

Salaries Payable		
		0 Beg. bal.
		5,500
		5,500 End bal.

Salaries Expense		
Beg. bal.	0	
July 20	5,000	
	5,500	
End bal.	10,500	

After this entry is recorded and posted to the general ledger, the salaries expense account will have a debit balance of $10,500 ($5,000 + 5,500), and the salaries payable account will have a credit balance of $5,500.

The unadjusted trial balance does provide information about the second required accrued liability entry. In the trial balance we can see a balance in the notes payable account of $40,000. The company borrowed this amount on July 1, 2021, evidenced by two notes, each requiring the payment of 10% interest. Whenever the trial balance reveals interest-bearing debt, and interest is not paid on the last day of the period, an adjusting entry is required for the amount of interest that has built up (accrued) since the last payment date or the last date interest was accrued. In this case, we calculate interest as follows:

$$\text{Principal} \times \text{Interest rate} \times \text{Time} = \text{Interest}$$
$$\$40{,}000 \times 10\% \times \tfrac{1}{12} = \$333 \text{ (rounded)}$$

Interest rates always are stated as the annual rate. Therefore, the above calculation uses this annual rate multiplied by the principal amount multiplied by the amount of time outstanding, in this case one month or one-twelfth of a year.

To accrue interest expense for July on notes payable.

July 31		
Interest expense...	333	
Interest payable		333

After this entry is recorded and posted to the ledger accounts, the interest expense account will have a debit balance of $333, and the interest payable account will have a credit balance of $333. Failure to record a required adjusting entry for an accrued liability will cause net income and shareholders' equity (retained earnings) to be overstated and liabilities to be understated.[4]

It's important to note that we differentiate accrued liabilities like salaries payable and interest payable from accounts payable accounts. Accounts payable is the account we use for purchases of merchandise that will be resold in the ordinary course of business and for property, plant, and equipment that will be not paid for with notes payable or other types of financing.

Also, sometimes we use an account titled "accrued liabilities" instead of specific payable accounts. This is particularly useful when grouping several relatively small liabilities that aren't large enough to warrant separate reporting.

ACCRUED RECEIVABLES   Accrued receivables involve the recognition of revenue for goods or services transferred to customers *before* cash is received. An example of an internal accrued revenue event is the recognition of interest earned on a loan to another entity. For example, assume that Dress Right loaned another corporation $30,000 at the beginning of August, evidenced by a note receivable. Terms of the note call for the payment of principal, $30,000, and interest at 8% in three months. An external transaction records the cash disbursement—a debit to note receivable and a credit to cash of $30,000.

Accrued receivables involve situations when the revenue is recognized in a period prior to the cash receipt.

What adjusting entry would be required at the end of August? Dress Right needs to record the interest revenue earned but not yet received along with the corresponding receivable. Interest receivable increases and interest revenue (shareholders' equity) also increases. The adjusting entry for accrued receivables always includes a *debit to an asset,* a receivable, and a *credit to revenue.* In this case, at the end of August Dress Right recognizes $200 in interest revenue ($30,000 × 8% × 1/12) and makes the following adjusting entry. If this entry is not recorded, net income, assets, and shareholders' equity (retained earnings) will be understated.

The adjusting entry required to record an accrued revenue is a debit to an asset, a receivable, and a credit to revenue.

To accrue interest revenue earned in August on a note receivable.

August 31		
Interest receivable	200	
Interest revenue...		200

There are no accrued revenue adjusting entries required for Dress Right at the end of July.

The required adjusting entries for prepayments and accruals are recapped with the aid of T-accounts in Illustration 2–10. In each case an expense or revenue is recognized in a period that differs from the period in which cash was paid or received. These adjusting

---

[4]Dress Right Clothing is a corporation. Corporations are income-tax-paying entities. Income taxes—federal, state, and local—are assessed on an annual basis and payments are made throughout the year. An additional adjusting entry would be required for Dress Right to accrue the amount of estimated income taxes payable that are applicable to the month of July. Accounting for income taxes is introduced in Chapter 4 and covered in depth in Chapter 16.

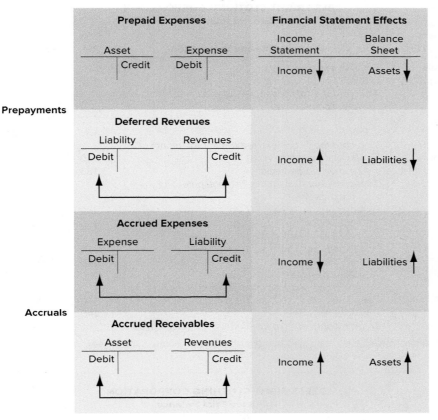

Illustration 2–10

Adjusting Entries

entries are necessary to properly measure operating performance and financial position on an accrual basis.

Estimates

A third classification of adjusting entries is estimates. Accountants often must make estimates of future events to comply with the accrual accounting model. For example, the calculation of depreciation expense requires an estimate of expected useful life of the asset being depreciated as well as its expected residual value. We discussed the adjusting entries for depreciation expense in the context of its being a prepayment, but it also could be thought of as an estimate.

One adjusting-entry situation involving an estimate that does not fit neatly into either the prepayment or accrual classification is bad debts. Accounting for bad debts requires a company to estimate the amount of accounts receivable that ultimately will prove to be uncollectible and to reduce accounts receivable by that estimated amount. This is neither a prepayment nor an accrual because it does not involve the payment of cash either before or after income is reduced. We explore accounts receivable and bad debts in depth in Chapter 7.

Illustration 2–11 recaps the July 31, 2021, adjusting entries for Dress Right Clothing Corporation as they would appear in a general journal. The journal entries are numbered (1) to (6) corresponding to the numbers used in the worksheet illustrated in Appendix 2A.

After the adjusting entries are posted to the general ledger accounts, the next step—step 7—in the processing cycle is to prepare an adjusted trial balance. The term adjusted refers to the fact that adjusting entries have now been posted to the accounts. Recall that the column titled Post. Ref. (Posting Reference) is the number assigned to the general ledger account that is being debited or credited. Illustration 2–12 shows the July 31, 2021, adjusted trial balance for Dress Right Clothing Corporation.

Accountants often must make *estimates* in order to comply with the accrual accounting model.

Illustration 2–11

The General Journal—
Adjusting Entries

DRESS RIGHT CLOTHING CORPORATION
General Journal   **Page 2**

Date 2021		Account Title and Explanation	Post. Ref.	Debit	Credit
July (1)	31	Supplies expense	520	800	
		Supplies	125		800
		To record the cost of supplies used during the month of July.			
(2)	31	Rent expense	530	2,000	
		Prepaid rent	130		2,000
		To record the cost of expired rent for the month of July.			
(3)	31	Depreciation expense	540	200	
		Accumulated depreciation	155		200
		To record depreciation of office equipment for the month of July.			
(4)	31	Deferred rent revenue	230	250	
		Rent revenue	410		250
		To record previously deferred rent revenue recognized during July.			
(5)	31	Salaries expense	510	5,500	
		Salaries payable	230		5,500
		To record accrued salaries at the end of July.			
(6)	31	Interest expense	550	333	
		Interest payable	240		333
		To accrue interest expense for July on notes payable.			

Illustration 2–12

Adjusted Trial Balance

STEP 7

Prepare an *adjusted trial balance*.

DRESS RIGHT CLOTHING CORPORATION
Adjusted Trial Balance
July 31, 2021

Account Title	Debits	Credits
Cash	68,500	
Accounts receivable	2,000	
Supplies	1,200	
Prepaid rent	22,000	
Inventory	38,000	
Office equipment	12,000	
Accumulated depreciation		200
Accounts payable		35,000
Notes payable		40,000
Deferred rent revenue		750
Salaries payable		5,500
Interest payable		333
Common stock		60,000
Retained earnings		0
Sales revenue		38,500
Rent revenue		250
Cost of goods sold	22,000	
Salaries expense	10,500	
Supplies expense	800	
Rent expense	2,000	
Depreciation expense	200	
Interest expense	333	
Dividends	1,000	
Totals	180,533	180,533

Concept Review Exercise

The Wyndham Wholesale Company needs to prepare financial statements at the end of   **ADJUSTING ENTRIES**
August 2021 for presentation to its bank. An unadjusted trial balance as of August 31, 2021,
was presented in a previous Concept Review Exercise.

The following information also is available:

a. The notes payable account contains one note. The note requires the entire $30,000
in principal plus interest at 10% to be paid on July 31, 2022. The date of the note is
August 1, 2021.

b. Depreciation on the equipment for the month of August is $500.

c. The notes receivable account contains one note. It is dated August 16, 2021. The note
requires the entire $20,000 in principal plus interest at 12% to be repaid in four months
(the loan was outstanding for one-half month during August).

d. The prepaid rent of $6,000 represents rent for the months of August and September.

Required:

1. Prepare any necessary adjusting entries at August 31, 2021.

2. Prepare an adjusted trial balance as of August 31, 2021.

3. What is the total net effect on income (overstated or understated) if the adjusting entries
are not recorded?

Solution:

1. Prepare any necessary adjusting entries at August 31, 2021.

   a. An adjusting entry is required to accrue the interest expense on the note payable for
the month of August. Accrued interest is calculated as follows:

$$\$30,000 \times 10\% \times \tfrac{1}{12} = \$250$$

Interest expense...	250	
Interest payable		250

   b. Depreciation expense on the equipment must be recorded.

Depreciation expense...	500	
Accumulated depreciation...		500

   c. An adjusting entry is required for the one-half month of accrued interest revenue
earned on the note receivable. Accrued interest is calculated as follows:

$$\$20,000 \times 12\% \times \tfrac{1}{12} \times \tfrac{1}{2} = \$100$$

Interest receivable	100	
Interest revenue..		100

   d. An adjusting entry is required to recognize the amount of prepaid rent that expired
during August.

Rent expense...	3,000	
Prepaid rent		3,000

2. Prepare an adjusted trial balance as of August 31, 2021.

Account Title	Debits	Credits
Cash	21,000	
Accounts receivable	25,000	
Prepaid rent	3,000	
Inventory	16,000	
Interest receivable	100	
Notes receivable	20,000	
Equipment	20,000	
Accumulated depreciation		500
Accounts payable		20,000
Interest payable		250
Notes payable		30,000
Common stock		50,000
Retained earnings		0
Sales revenue		40,000
Interest revenue		100
Cost of goods sold	22,000	
Salaries expense	7,000	
Utilities expense	2,000	
Interest expense	250	
Depreciation expense	500	
Rent expense	3,000	
Dividends	1,000	
Totals	140,850	140,850

3. What is the effect on income (overstated or understated), if the adjusting entries are not recorded?

Adjusting Entry	Income overstated (understated)
Interest expense	$ 250
Depreciation expense	500
Interest revenue	(100)
Rent expense	3,000
Net effect, income overstated by	$3,650

We now turn our attention to the preparation of financial statements.

Preparing the Financial Statements

● LO2–7

STEP 8

Preparation of *financial statements*.

The purpose of each of the steps in the processing cycle to this point is to provide information for step 8—preparation of the financial statements. The adjusted trial balance contains the necessary information. After all, the financial statements are the primary means of communicating financial information to external parties.

The Income Statement and the Statement of Comprehensive Income

The *income statement* is a *change* statement that summarizes the profit-generating transactions that caused shareholders' equity (retained earnings) to change during the period.

The purpose of the income statement is to summarize the profit-generating activities of a company that occurred during a particular period of time. It is a *change* statement in that it reports the changes in shareholders' equity (retained earnings) that occurred during the period as a result of revenues, expenses, gains, and losses. Illustration 2–13 shows the income statement for Dress Right Clothing Corporation for the month of July 2021.

The income statement indicates a profit for the month of July of $2,917. During the month, the company was able to increase its net assets (equity) from activities related to selling its product. Dress Right is a corporation and subject to the payment of income tax on its profits. We ignore this required accrual here and address income taxes in a later chapter.

The components of the income statement usually are classified, that is, grouped according to common characteristics. A common classification scheme is to separate operating items from nonoperating items, as we do in Dress Right's income statement. Operating items

DRESS RIGHT CLOTHING CORPORATION
Income Statement
For the Month of July 2021

Sales revenue		$38,500
Cost of goods sold		22,000
Gross profit		16,500
Operating expenses:		
Salaries expense	$10,500	
Supplies expense	800	
Rent expense	2,000	
Depreciation expense	200	
Total operating expenses		13,500
Operating income		3,000
Other income (expense):		
Rent revenue	250	
Interest expense	(333)	(83)
Net income		$ 2,917

Illustration 2–13
Income Statement

include revenues and expenses directly related to the principal revenue-generating activities of the company. For example, operating items for a manufacturing company include sales revenues from the sale of products and all expenses related to this activity. Companies that sell products like Dress Right often report a subtotal within operating income, sales less cost of goods sold, called *gross profit*. Nonoperating items include certain gains and losses and revenues and expenses from peripheral activities. For Dress Right Clothing, rent revenue and interest expense are nonoperating items because they do not relate to the principal revenue-generating activity of the company, selling clothes. In Chapter 4 we discuss the format and content of the income statement in more depth.

The *statement of comprehensive income* extends the income statement by reporting all changes in shareholders' equity during the period that were not a result of transactions with owners. A few types of gains and losses, called other comprehensive income (OCI) or loss items, are excluded from the determination of net income and the income statement, but are included in the broader concept of comprehensive income. Comprehensive income can be reported in one of two ways: (1) in a single, continuous statement of comprehensive income, or (2) in two separate, but consecutive statements.[5]

In the single statement approach, net income is a subtotal within the statement followed by these OCI items, culminating in a final total of comprehensive income. In the two statement approach, a company presents an income statement immediately followed by a statement of comprehensive income. The statement of comprehensive income begins with net income as the first component followed by OCI items to arrive at comprehensive income. Obviously, the approaches are quite similar; in the separate statement approach, we separate the continuous statement into two parts, but the content is the same.

Dress Right Clothing has no OCI items so the company presents only an income statement in Illustration 2–13. An entity that has no OCI items is not required to report OCI or comprehensive income. We discuss comprehensive income and the alternative approaches to its presentation in more depth in Chapter 4.

The Balance Sheet

The purpose of the balance sheet is to present the financial position of the company on a particular date. Unlike the income statement, which is a change statement reporting events that occurred *during a period of time,* the balance sheet is a statement that

The *balance sheet* presents an organized list of assets, liabilities, and equity at a particular point in time.

[5]FASB ASC 220–10–45–1: Comprehensive Income—Overall—Other Presentation Matters (*Accounting Standards Update No. 2011–05* (Norwalk, Conn.: FASB, June 2011)).

presents an organized list of assets, liabilities, and shareholders' equity *at a point in time.* To provide a quick overview, Illustration 2–14 shows the balance sheet for Dress Right at July 31, 2021.

Illustration 2–14

Balance Sheet

DRESS RIGHT CLOTHING CORPORATION		
Balance Sheet		
At July 31, 2021		
Assets		
Current assets:		
Cash		$ 68,500
Accounts receivable		2,000
Supplies		1,200
Inventory		38,000
Prepaid rent		22,000
Total current assets		131,700
Property and equipment:		
Office equipment	$12,000	
Less: Accumulated depreciation	200	11,800
Total assets		$ 143,500
Liabilities and Shareholders' Equity		
Current liabilities:		
Accounts payable		$ 35,000
Salaries payable		5,500
Deferred rent revenue		750
Interest payable		333
Notes payable		10,000
Total current liabilities		51,583
Long-term liabilities:		
Notes payable		30,000
Shareholders' equity:		
Common stock (6,000 shares issued and outstanding)	$60,000	
Retained earnings	1,917*	
Total shareholders' equity		61,917
Total liabilities and shareholders' equity		$ 143,500

*Beginning retained earnings + Net income − Dividends
  $0   +   2,917   −   1,000   = $1,917

Balance sheet items usually are classified (grouped) according to common characteristics.

As we do in the income statement, we group the balance sheet elements into meaningful categories. For example, most balance sheets include the classifications of current assets and current liabilities. Current assets are those assets that are cash, will be converted into cash, or will be used up within one year from the balance sheet date (or operating cycle, if longer). Current liabilities are those liabilities that will be satisfied within one year from the balance sheet date (or operating cycle, if longer). For a manufacturing company, the operating cycle refers to the period of time necessary to convert cash to raw materials, raw materials to a finished product, the finished product to receivables, and then finally receivables back to cash. For most companies, this period is less than a year.

Examples of assets not classified as current include property and equipment and long-term receivables and investments. The only noncurrent asset that Dress Right has at July 31, 2021, is office equipment, which is classified under the property and equipment category.

All liabilities not classified as current are listed as long term. Dress Right's liabilities at July 31, 2021, include the $30,000 note payable due to be paid in 23 months. This liability is classified as long term.

Shareholders' equity lists the *paid-in capital* portion of equity—common stock—and *retained earnings*. Notice that the income statement we looked at in Illustration 2–13 ties in to the balance sheet through retained earnings. Specifically, the revenue, expense, gain, and loss transactions that make up net income in the income statement ($2,917) become the major components of retained earnings. Later in the chapter we discuss the closing process we use to transfer, or close, these *temporary* income statement accounts along with the temporary account, dividends. to the *permanent* retained earnings account.

During the month, retained earnings, which increased by the amount of net income, also decreased by the amount of the cash dividend paid to shareholders, $1,000. The net effect of these two changes is an increase in retained earnings from zero at the beginning of the period to $1,917 ($2,917 − $1,000) at the end of the period and also is reported in the statement of shareholders' equity in Illustration 2–16.

The Statement of Cash Flows

Similar to the income statement, the statement of cash flows also is a change statement. The purpose of the statement is to report the events that caused cash to change during the period. The statement classifies all transactions affecting cash into one of three categories: (1) operating activities, (2) investing activities, and (3) financing activities. Operating activities are inflows and outflows of cash related to transactions entering into the determination of net income. Investing activities involve the acquisition and sale of (1) long-term assets used in the business and (2) nonoperating investment assets. Financing activities involve cash inflows and outflows from transactions with creditors and owners.

> The purpose of the *statement of cash flows* is to report the events that caused cash to change during the period.

The statement of cash flows for Dress Right for the month of July 2021 is shown in Illustration 2–15. As this is the first period of operations for Dress Right, the cash balance at the beginning of the period is zero. The net increase in cash of $68,500, therefore, equals the ending balance of cash disclosed in the balance sheet.

Illustration 2–15
Statement of Cash Flows

DRESS RIGHT CLOTHING CORPORATION
Statement of Cash Flows
For the Month of July 2021

Cash Flows from Operating Activities		
Cash inflows:		
From customers	$36,500	
From rent	1,000	
Cash outflows:		
For rent	(24,000)	
For supplies	(2,000)	
To suppliers of merchandise	(25,000)	
To employees	(5,000)	
Net cash flows from operating activities		$(18,500)
Cash Flows from Investing Activities		
Purchase of office equipment		(12,000)
Cash Flows from Financing Activities		
Issue of common stock	$60,000	
Increase in notes payable	40,000	
Payment of cash dividend	(1,000)	
Net cash flows from financing activities		99,000
Net increase in cash		$ 68,500

There are two generally accepted formats that can be used to report operating activities, the direct method and the indirect method. In Illustration 2–15 we use the direct method. These two methods are discussed and illustrated in subsequent chapters.

The Statement of Shareholders' Equity

The *statement of shareholders' equity* discloses the sources of changes in the permanent shareholders' equity accounts.

The final statement, the statement of shareholders' equity, also is a change statement. Its purpose is to disclose the sources of the changes in the various permanent shareholders' equity accounts that occurred during the period from investments by owners, distributions to owners, net income, and other comprehensive income. Illustration 2–16 shows the statement of shareholders' equity for Dress Right for the month of July 2021.[6]

Illustration 2–16

Statement of Shareholders' Equity

DRESS RIGHT CLOTHING CORPORATION
Statement of Shareholders' Equity
For the Month of July 2021

	Common Stock	Retained Earnings	Total Shareholders' Equity
Balance at July 1, 2021	$ –0–	$ –0–	$ –0–
Issue of common stock	60,000		60,000
Net income for July 2021		2,917	2,917
Less: Dividends		(1,000)	(1,000)
Balance at July 31, 2021	$ 60,000	$ 1,917	$ 61,917

The individual profit-generating transactions causing retained earnings to change are summarized in the income statement. Therefore, the statement of shareholders' equity only shows the net effect of these transactions on retained earnings, in this case an increase of $2,917. In addition, the company paid its shareholders a cash dividend that reduced retained earnings.

The Closing Process

STEP 9

Close the temporary accounts to retained earnings (at year-end only).

● LO2–8

At the end of any interim reporting period, the accounting processing cycle is now complete. An interim reporting period is any period when financial statements are produced other than at the end of the fiscal year. However, at the end of the fiscal year, two final steps are necessary, closing the temporary accounts—step 9—and preparing a post-closing trial balance—step 10.

The closing process serves a *dual purpose:* (1) the temporary accounts (revenues, expenses, gains and losses, and dividends) are reduced to *zero balances,* ready to measure activity in the upcoming accounting period, and (2) these temporary account balances are *closed (transferred) to retained earnings* to reflect the changes that have occurred in that account during the period.

To illustrate the closing process, assume that the fiscal year-end for Dress Right Clothing Corporation is July 31. Using the adjusted trial balance in Illustration 2–12, we can prepare the following closing entries.

To close the revenue accounts to retained earnings.

July 31

Sales revenue	38,500	
Rent revenue	250	
Retained earnings		38,750

The first closing entry transfers the revenue account balances to retained earnings. Because revenue accounts have credit balances, we debit each one to bring their balances to zero. After this entry is posted to the accounts, both revenue accounts have a zero balance.

---

[6]Some companies choose to disclose the changes in the retained earnings component of shareholders' equity in a separate statement or in a combined statement of income and retained earnings.

July 31		
Retained earnings	35,833	
Cost of goods sold		22,000
Salaries expense		10,500
Supplies expense		800
Rent expense		2,000
Depreciation expense		200
Interest expense		333

To close the expense accounts to retained earnings.

The second closing entry transfers the expense account balances to retained earnings. Because expense accounts have debit balances, we credit them to bring their balances to zero. After this entry is posted to the accounts, the expense accounts have a zero balance. Also, because retained earnings in this example began the reporting period with a zero balance, after we add (credit) revenues to the account and subtract (debit) expenses, the retained earnings account has a credit balance equal to net income for the period, in this case $2,917.

Retained Earnings

Expenses	35,833	38,750	Revenues
		2,917	Net income

Additional Consideration

> A company can choose to prepare closing entries by closing revenues and expenses to a temporary account called income summary. If so, the income summary account is then closed to retained earnings. This alternative set of closing entries provides the same effect of closing revenues and expenses directly to the retained earnings account as in our illustration. Most companies, though, have computerized accounting systems that perform the closing process automatically without the income summary account.

In the third entry we close the dividends account to retained earnings. Like expenses, dividends reduce retained earnings.

July 31		
Retained earnings	1,000	
Dividends		1,000

To close the dividends account to retained earnings.

After this entry is posted to the accounts, the temporary accounts have zero balances and retained earnings has increased by the amount of the net income and decreased by dividends distributed from that net income. It's important to remember that the temporary accounts are closed only at year-end and not at the end of any interim period. Closing the temporary accounts during the year would make it difficult to prepare the annual income statement.

STEP 10

Prepare a *post-closing trial balance* (at year-end only).

Additional Consideration

> A previous additional consideration indicated that an alternative method of recording a cash dividend is to debit retained earnings when the dividends are declared. If this approach is used, this third closing entry to close the dividends account to retained earnings isn't needed.
>
> The net result of a cash dividend is the same—a reduction in retained earnings and a reduction in cash.

After the closing entries are posted to the ledger accounts, a post-closing trial balance is prepared. The purpose of this trial balance is to verify that the closing entries were prepared and posted correctly and that the accounts are now ready for next year's transactions. Illustration 2–17 shows the post-closing trial balance for Dress Right at July 31, 2021, assuming a July 31 fiscal year-end.

Illustration 2–17

Post-Closing Trial Balance

DRESS RIGHT CLOTHING CORPORATION
Post-Closing Trial Balance
July 31, 2021

Account Title	Debits	Credits
Cash	68,500	
Accounts receivable	2,000	
Supplies	1,200	
Prepaid rent	22,000	
Inventory	38,000	
Office equipment	12,000	
Accumulated depreciation—office equipment		200
Accounts payable		35,000
Notes payable		40,000
Deferred rent revenue		750
Salaries payable		5,500
Interest payable		333
Common stock		60,000
Retained earnings		1,917
Totals	143,700	143,700

Concept Review Exercise

FINANCIAL STATEMENT PREPARATION AND CLOSING

Refer to the August 31, 2021, adjusted trial balance of the Wyndham Wholesale Company presented in the previous Concept Review Exercise.

Required:

1. Prepare an income statement and a statement of shareholders' equity for the month ended August 31, 2021, and a classified balance sheet as of August 31, 2021.

2. Assume that August 31 is the company's fiscal year-end. Prepare the necessary closing entries and a post-closing trial balance.

Solution:

1. Prepare an income statement and a statement of shareholders' equity for the month ended August 31, 2021, and a classified balance sheet as of August 31, 2021.

WYNDHAM WHOLESALE COMPANY
Income Statement
For the Month of August 2021

Sales revenue		$40,000
Cost of goods sold		22,000
Gross profit		18,000
Operating expenses:		
Salaries	$7,000	
Utilities	2,000	
Depreciation	500	
Rent	3,000	
Total operating expenses		12,500
Operating income		5,500
Other income (expense):		
Interest revenue	100	
Interest expense	(250)	(150)
Net income		$ 5,350

WYNDHAM WHOLESALE COMPANY
Statement of Shareholders' Equity
For the Month of August 2021

	Common Stock	Retained Earnings	Total Shareholders' Equity
Balance at August 1, 2021	$ —0—	$ —0—	$ —0—
Issue of common stock	50,000		50,000
Net income for August 2021		5,350	5,350
Less: Dividends		(1,000)	(1,000)
Balance at August 31, 2021	$50,000	$4,350	$54,350

WYNDHAM WHOLESALE COMPANY
Balance Sheet
At August 31, 2021
Assets

Current assets:		
Cash		$ 21,000
Accounts receivable		25,000
Inventory		16,000
Interest receivable		100
Notes receivable		20,000
Prepaid rent		3,000
Total current assets		85,100
Property and equipment:		
Equipment	$20,000	
Less: Accumulated depreciation	500	19,500
Total assets		$104,600

Liabilities and Shareholders' Equity

Current liabilities:		
Accounts payable		$ 20,000
Interest payable		250
Notes payable		30,000
Total current liabilities		50,250
Shareholders' equity:		
Common stock, 5,000 shares issued and outstanding	$50,000	
Retained earnings	4,350	
Total shareholders' equity		54,350
Total liabilities and shareholders' equity		$104,600

2. Assume that August 31 is the company's fiscal year-end. Prepare the necessary closing entries and a post-closing trial balance.

August 31			To close the revenue accounts to retained earnings.
Sales revenue	40,000		
Interest revenue	100		
Retained earnings		40,100	
August 31			To close the expense accounts to retained earnings.
Retained earnings	34,750		
Cost of goods sold		22,000	
Salaries expense		7,000	
Utilities expense		2,000	
Depreciation expense		500	
Rent expense		3,000	
Interest expense		250	
August 31			To close the dividends account to retained earnings.
Retained earnings	1,000		
Dividends		1,000	

Post-Closing Trial Balance

Account Title	Debits	Credits
Cash	21,000	
Accounts receivable	25,000	
Prepaid rent	3,000	
Inventory	16,000	
Interest receivable	100	
Notes receivable	20,000	
Equipment	20,000	
Accumulated depreciation—equipment		500
Accounts payable		20,000
Interest payable		250
Notes payable		30,000
Common stock		50,000
Retained earnings		4,350
Totals	105,100	105,100

Conversion from Cash Basis to Accrual Basis

● LO2–9   In Chapter 1, we discussed and illustrated the differences between cash and accrual accounting. Cash-basis accounting produces a measure called *net operating cash flow*. This measure is the difference between cash receipts and cash disbursements during a reporting period from transactions related to providing goods and services to customers. On the other hand, the accrual-accounting model measures an entity's accomplishments and resource sacrifices during the period, regardless of when cash is received or paid. At this point, you might wish to review the material in Chapter 1 to reinforce your understanding of the motivation for using the accrual-accounting model.

Adjusting entries, for the most part, are conversions from cash basis to accrual basis. Prepayments and accruals occur when cash flow precedes or follows expense or revenue recognition.

Accountants sometimes are called upon to convert cash-basis financial statements to accrual-basis financial statements, particularly for small businesses. You now have all of the tools you need to make this conversion. For example, if a company paid $20,000 cash for insurance during the fiscal year and you determine that there was $5,000 in prepaid insurance at the beginning of the year and $3,000 at the end of the year, then you can determine (accrual basis) *insurance expense* for the year. Prepaid insurance decreased by $2,000 during the year, so insurance expense must be $22,000 ($20,000 in cash paid *plus* the decrease in prepaid insurance). You can visualize as follows:

	Prepaid Insurance
Balance, beginning of year	$ 5,000
Plus: Cash paid	20,000
Less: Insurance expense	?
Balance, end of year	$ 3,000

Insurance expense of $22,000 completes the explanation of the change in the balance of prepaid insurance. Prepaid insurance of $3,000 is reported as an asset in an accrual-basis balance sheet.

Suppose a company paid $150,000 for salaries to employees during the year and you determine that there were $12,000 and $18,000 in salaries payable at the beginning and end of the year, respectively. What was salaries expense for the year?

Salaries Payable

Balance, beginning of year	$ 12,000
Plus: Salaries expense	?
Less: Cash paid	(150,000)
Balance, end of year	$ 18,000

Salaries payable increased by $6,000 during the year, so *salaries expense* must be $156,000 ($150,000 in cash paid *plus* the increase in salaries payable). Salaries payable of $18,000 is reported as a liability in an accrual-basis balance sheet.

Using T-accounts is a convenient approach for converting from cash to accrual accounting.

Salaries Payable			**Salaries Expense**	
	12,000 Beg. balance			
Cash paid 150,000			?	
	? Salaries expense			
	18,000 End. balance			

The debit to salaries expense and credit to salaries payable must have been $156,000 to balance the salaries payable account.

For another example using T-accounts, assume that the amount of cash collected from customers during the year was $220,000, and you know that accounts receivable at the beginning of the year was $45,000 and $33,000 at the end of the year. You can use T-accounts to determine that *sales revenue* for the year must have been $208,000, the necessary debit to accounts receivable and credit to sales revenue to balance the accounts receivable account.

Accounts Receivable			**Sales Revenue**	
Beg. balance 45,000				
Credit sales ?			? Credit sales	
	220,000 Cash collections			
End. balance 33,000				

Now suppose that, on occasion, customers pay in advance of receiving a product or service. Recall from our previous discussion of adjusting entries that this event creates a liability called deferred revenue. Assume the same facts in the previous example except you also determine that deferred revenues were $10,000 and $7,000 at the beginning and end of the year, respectively. A $3,000 decrease in deferred revenues means that the company recognized an additional $3,000 in sales revenue for which the cash had been collected in a previous year. So, *sales revenue* for the year must have been $211,000, the $208,000 determined in the previous example *plus* the $3,000 decrease in deferred revenue.

Illustration 2–18 provides another example of converting from cash-basis net income to accrual-basis net income.

Notice a pattern in the adjustments to cash-basis net income. When converting from cash-basis to accrual-basis income, we add increases and deduct decreases in assets. For example, an increase in accounts receivable means that the company recognized more revenue than cash collected, requiring the addition to cash-basis income. Conversely, we add decreases and deduct increases in accrued liabilities. For example, a decrease in interest payable means that the company incurred less interest expense than the cash interest it paid, requiring the addition to cash-basis income. These adjustments are summarized in Illustration 2–19.

Most companies keep their books on an accrual basis.[7] A more important conversion for these companies is from the accrual basis to the cash basis. This conversion, essential for the preparation of the statement of cash flows, is discussed and illustrated in Chapters 4

Most companies must convert from an accrual basis to a cash basis when preparing the statement of cash flows.

---

[7]Generally accepted accounting principles require the use of the accrual basis. Some small, nonpublic companies might use the cash basis in preparing their financial statements as an other basis of accounting.

Illustration 2–18

Cash to Accrual

The Krinard Cleaning Services Company maintains its records on the cash basis, with one exception. The company reports equipment as an asset and records depreciation expense on the equipment. During 2021, Krinard collected $165,000 from customers, paid $92,000 in operating expenses, and recorded $10,000 in depreciation expense, resulting in net income of $63,000. The owner has asked you to convert this $63,000 in net income to full accrual net income. You are able to determine the following information about accounts receivable, prepaid expenses, accrued liabilities, and deferred revenues:

	January 1, 2021	December 31, 2021
Accounts receivable	$16,000	$25,000
Prepaid expenses	7,000	4,000
Accrued liabilities	2,100	1,400
(for operating expenses)		
Deferred revenues	3,000	4,200

Accrual net income is $68,500, determined as follows:

Cash-basis net income	$63,000
Add: Increase in accounts receivable	9,000
Deduct: Decrease in prepaid expenses	(3,000)
Add: Decrease in accrued liabilities	700
Deduct: Increase in deferred revenues	(1,200)
Accrual-basis net income	$ 68,500

Illustration 2–19

Converting Cash-Basis to Accrual-Basis Income

Converting Cash-Basis Income to Accrual-Basis Income		
	Increases	Decreases
Assets	Add	Deduct
Liabilities	Deduct	Add

and 21. The lessons learned here, though, will help you with that conversion. For example, if sales revenue for the period is $120,000 and beginning and ending accounts receivable are $20,000 and $24,000, respectively, how much cash did the company collect from its customers during the period? The answer is $116,000. An increase in accounts receivable of $4,000 means that the company collected $4,000 less from customers than accrual sales revenue, and cash-basis income is $4,000 less than accrual-basis income.

Financial Reporting Case Solution

©goodluz/123RF

1. **What purpose do adjusting entries serve?** (p. 64)   Adjusting entries help ensure that all revenues are recognized in the period goods or services are transferred to customers, regardless of when cash is received. In this instance, for example, $13,000 cash has been received for services that haven't yet been performed. Also, adjusting entries enable a company to recognize all expenses incurred during a period, regardless of when cash is paid. Without depreciation, the friends' cost of using the equipment is not taken into account. Conversely, without adjustment, the cost of rent is overstated by $3,000 paid in advance for part of next year's rent.

   With adjustments, we get an accrual income statement that provides a more complete measure of a company's operating performance and a better measure for predicting future operating cash flows. Similarly, the balance sheet provides a more complete assessment of assets and liabilities as sources of future cash receipts and disbursements.

2. **What year-end adjustments are needed to revise the income statement? Did your friends do as well their first year as they thought?** *(p. 64)*   Three year-end adjusting entries are needed:

1. Depreciation expense ($80,000 ÷ 5 years)	16,000	
Accumulated depreciation		16,000
2. Prepaid rent [$500 × 6 months (July–Dec.)]	3,000	
Rent expense		3,000
3. Consulting revenue	13,000	
Deferred consulting revenue		13,000

No, your friends did not fare as well as their cash-based statement would have indicated. With appropriate adjustments, their net income is actually only $20,000:

Consulting revenue ($96,000 − $13,000)		$83,000
Operating expenses:		
Salaries expense	$32,000	
Rent expense ($9,000 − $3,000)	6,000	
Supplies expense	4,800	
Utilities expense	3,000	
Advertising expense	1,200	
Depreciation expense	16,000	63,000
Net income		$20,000

The Bottom Line

LO2–1   The accounting equation underlies the process used to capture the effect of economic events. The equation (Assets = Liabilities + Owners' Equity) implies an equality between the total economic resources of an entity (its assets) and the total claims against the entity (liabilities and equity). It also implies that each economic event affecting this equation will have a dual effect because resources always must equal claims. (*p. 48*)

LO2–2   The accounting processing cycle is the process used to identify, analyze, record, and summarize transactions and prepare financial statements. (*p. 51*)

LO2–3   After determining the dual effect of external events on the accounting equation, the transaction is recorded in a journal. A journal is a chronological list of transactions in debit/credit form. (*p. 55*)

LO2–4   The next step in the processing cycle is to periodically transfer, or *post,* the debit and credit information from the journal to individual general ledger accounts. A general ledger is simply a collection of all of the company's various accounts. Each account provides a summary of the effects of all events and transactions on that individual account. The process of entering items from the journal to the general ledger is called *posting.* An unadjusted trial balance is then prepared. (*p. 60*)

LO2–5   The next step in the processing cycle is to record the effect of *internal events* on the accounting equation. These transactions are commonly referred to as *adjusting entries.* Adjusting entries can be classified into three types: (1) prepayments, (2) accruals, and (3) estimates. Prepayments are transactions in which the cash flow *precedes* expense or revenue recognition. Accruals involve transactions where the cash outflow or inflow takes place in a period *subsequent* to expense or revenue recognition. Estimates for items such as future bad debts on receivables often are required to comply with the accrual accounting model. (*p. 63*)

LO2–6   Adjusting entries are recorded in the general journal and posted to the ledger accounts at the end of any period when financial statements must be prepared for external use. After these entries are posted to the general ledger accounts, an adjusted trial balance is prepared. (*p. 64*)

LO2–7   The adjusted trial balance is used to prepare the financial statements. The basic financial statements are: (1) the income statement, (2) the statement of comprehensive income, (3) the balance sheet, (4) the statement of cash flows, and (5) the statement of shareholders' equity. The purpose of the income statement is to summarize the profit-generating activities of the company that occurred during a particular period of time. A company also must report its other comprehensive income (OCI) or loss items either in a single, continuous statement or in a separate statement of comprehensive income. In the single-statement approach, net income is a subtotal within the statement followed by these OCI items, culminating in a

84   SECTION 1   The Role of Accounting as an Information System

final total of comprehensive income. In the two-statement approach, a company presents an income statement immediately followed by a statement of comprehensive income. The statement of comprehensive income begins with net income as the first component followed by OCI items to arrive at comprehensive income. The balance sheet presents the financial position of the company on a particular date. The statement of cash flows discloses the events that caused cash to change during the reporting period. The statement of shareholders' equity discloses the sources of the changes in the various permanent shareholders' equity accounts that occurred during the period. (*p. 72*)

● **LO2–8**   At the end of the fiscal year, a final step in the accounting processing cycle, closing, is required. The closing process serves a *dual purpose:* (1) the temporary accounts (revenues, expenses. and dividends) are reduced to *zero balances,* ready to measure activity in the upcoming accounting period, and (2) these temporary account balances are *closed (transferred) to retained earnings* to reflect the changes that have occurred in that account during the period. After the entries are posted to the general ledger accounts, a post-closing trial balance is prepared. (*p. 76*)

● **LO2–9**   Cash-basis accounting produces a measure called *net operating cash flow.* This measure is the difference between cash receipts and cash disbursements during a reporting period from transactions related to providing goods and services to customers. On the other hand, the accrual-accounting model measures an entity's accomplishments and resource sacrifices during the period, regardless of when cash is received or paid. Accountants sometimes are called upon to convert cash-basis financial statements to accrual-basis financial statements, particularly for small businesses. (*p. 80*) ●

APPENDIX 2A   Using a Worksheet

A *worksheet* can be used as a tool to facilitate the preparation of adjusting and closing entries and the financial statements.

A **worksheet** often is used to organize the accounting information needed to prepare adjusting and closing entries and the financial statements. It is an informal tool only and is not part of the accounting system. There are many different ways to design and use worksheets. We will illustrate a representative method using the financial information for the Dress Right Clothing Corporation presented in the chapter. Software such Excel facilitates the use of worksheets.

Illustration 2A–1 presents the completed worksheet. The worksheet is utilized in conjunction with Step 5 in the processing cycle, preparation of an unadjusted trial balance.

Illustration 2A–1   Worksheet, Dress Right Clothing Corporation, July 31, 2021
Source: Microsoft Excel 2007

Account Titles	Unadjusted Trial Balance Dr.	Unadjusted Trial Balance Cr.	Adjusting Entries Dr.	Adjusting Entries Cr.	Adjusted Trial Balance Dr.	Adjusted Trial Balance Cr.	Income Statement Dr.	Income Statement Cr.	Balance Sheet Dr.	Balance Sheet Cr.
Cash	68,500				68,500				68,500	
Accounts receivable	2,000				2,000				2,000	
Supplies	2,000			(1) 800	1,200				1,200	
Prepaid Rent	24,000			(2) 2,000	22,000				22,000	
Inventory	38,000				38,000				38,000	
Office equipment	12,000				12,000				12,000	
Accumulated depreciation		0		(3) 200		200				200
Accounts payable		35,000				35,000				35,000
Notes payable		40,000				40,000				40,000
Deferred rent revenue		1,000	(4) 250			750				750
Salaries payable		0		(5) 5,500		5,500				5,500
Interest payable		0		(6) 333		333				333
Common stock		60,000				60,000				60,000
Retained earnings		0				0		0		0
Sales revenue		38,500				38,500		38,500		
Rent revenue		0		(4) 250		250		250		
Cost of goods sold	22,000				22,000		22,000			
Salaries expense	5,000		(5) 5,500		10,500		10,500			
Supplies expense	0		(1) 800		800		800			
Rent expense	0		(2) 2,000		2,000		2,000			
Depreciation expense	0		(3) 200		200		200			
Interest expense	0		(6) 333		333		333			
Dividends	1,000				1,000				1,000	
Totals:	174,500	174,500	9,083	9,083	180,533	180,533				
Net income							2,917			2,917
Totals							38,750	38,750	144,700	144,700

Sheet1

Step 1. The account titles as they appear in the general ledger are entered in column A and the balances of these accounts are copied onto columns B and C, titled Unadjusted Trial Balance. The accounts are copied in the same order as they appear in the general ledger, which usually is assets, liabilities, shareholders' equity permanent accounts, revenues, and expenses. The debit and credit columns are totaled to make sure that they balance. This procedure is repeated for each set of columns in the worksheet to check for accuracy.

The first step is to enter account titles in column A and the unadjusted account balances in columns B and C.

Step 2. The end-of-period adjusting entries are determined and entered directly on the worksheet in columns D and E, titled Adjusting Entries. The adjusting entries for Dress Right Clothing Corporation were discussed in detail in the chapter and exhibited in general journal form in Illustration 2–11. You should refer back to this illustration and trace each of the entries to the worksheet. For worksheet purposes, the entries have been numbered from (1) to (6) for easy referencing.

The second step is to determine end-of-period adjusting entries and enter them in columns D and E.

For example, entry (1) records the cost of supplies used during the month of July with a debit to supplies expense and a credit to supplies for $800. A (1) is placed next to the $800 in the debit column in the supplies expense row as well as next to the $800 in the credit column in the supplies row. This allows us to more easily reconstruct the entry for general journal purposes and locate errors if the debit and credit columns do not balance.

Step 3. The effects of the adjusting entries are added to or deducted from the account balances listed in the Unadjusted Trial Balance columns and copied across to columns F and G, titled Adjusted Trial Balance. For example, supplies had an unadjusted balance of $2,000. Adjusting entry (1) credited this account by $800, reducing the balance to $1,200.

The third step adds or deducts the effects of the adjusting entries on the account balances.

Step 4. The balances in the temporary retained earnings accounts, revenues and expenses, are transferred to columns H and I, titled Income Statement. The difference between the total debits and credits in these columns is equal to net income or net loss. In this case, because credits (revenues) exceed debits (expenses), a net income of $2,917 results. To balance the debits and credits in this set of columns, a $2,917 debit entry is made in the line labeled Net income.

The fourth step is to transfer the temporary retained earnings account balances to columns H and I.

Step 5. The balances in the permanent accounts are transferred to columns J and K, titled Balance Sheet. To keep the debits and credits equal in the worksheet, a $2,917 credit must be entered to offset the $2,917 debit entered in step 4 and labeled as net income. This credit represents the fact that when the temporary revenue and expense accounts are closed out to retained earnings, a $2,917 credit to retained earnings will result. The credit in column K, therefore, represents an increase in retained earnings for the period, that is, net income. The balance in the temporary account, dividends, is also transferred to column J, titled Balance Sheet. This debit represents the fact that when the dividends account is closed to retained earnings, the $2,917 balance in that account resulting from net income will be reduced by the $1,000 of net income distributed to shareholders as a dividend.

The fifth step is to transfer the balances in the permanent accounts to columns J and K.

After the worksheet is completed, the financial statements can be prepared directly from columns H–K. The financial statements for Dress Right Clothing Corporation are shown in Illustrations 2–13 through 2–16 . The accountant must remember to then record the adjusting entries and the closing entries in the general journal and post them to the general ledger accounts. An adjusted trial balance should then be prepared identical to the one in the worksheet, which is used to prepare the financial statements. At fiscal year-end, the income statement columns can then be used to prepare closing entries. After that, a post-closing trial balance is prepared to wipe the slate clean for the next reporting period. ●

Reversing Entries

APPENDIX 2B

Accountants sometimes use reversing entries at the beginning of a reporting period. These optional entries remove the effects of some of the adjusting entries recorded at the end of the previous reporting period for the sole purpose of simplifying journal entries recorded during the new period. If the accountant does use reversing entries, these entries are recorded in the general journal and posted to the general ledger accounts on the first day of the new period.

Reversing entries are used most often with accruals. For example, the following adjusting entry for accrued salaries was recorded at the end of July 2021 for the Dress Right Clothing Corporation in the chapter:

To record accrued salaries at the end of July.

July 31		
Salaries expense	5,500	
Salaries payable		5,500

If reversing entries are not used, when the salaries actually are paid in August, the accountant needs to remember to debit salaries payable and not salaries expense.

The account balances before and after salary payment can be seen below with the use of T-accounts.

Salaries Expense				Salaries Payable		
Bal. July 31	10,500				5,500	Bal. July 31
			Cash payment	5,500		
					–0–	Balance

If the accountant for Dress Right employs reversing entries, the following entry is recorded on August 1, 2021:

To reverse accrued salaries expense recorded at the end of July.

August 1		
Salaries payable	5,500	
Salaries expense		5,500

This entry reduces the salaries payable account to zero and reduces the salary expense account by $5,500. When salaries actually are paid in August, the debit is to salaries expense, thus increasing the account by $5,500.

Salaries Expense				Salaries Payable		
Bal. July 31	10,500				5,500	Bal. July 31
		5,500	(Reversing entry)	5,500		
Cash payment	5,500					
Balance	10,500				–0–	Balance

We can see that balances in the accounts after cash payment is made are identical. The use of reversing entries for accruals, which is optional, simply allows cash payments or cash receipts to be entered directly into the temporary expense or revenue accounts without regard to the accruals recorded at the end of the previous period.

Reversing entries also can be used with prepayments and deferred revenues. For example, earlier in the chapter Dress Right Clothing Corporation used the following entry to record the purchase of supplies on July 6:

To record the purchase of supplies.

July 6		
Supplies	2,000	
Cash		2,000

If reversing entries are not used, an adjusting entry is needed at the end of July to record the amount of supplies consumed during the period. In the illustration, Dress Right recorded this adjusting entry at the end of July:

To record the cost of supplies used during the month of July.

July 31		
Supplies expense	800	
Supplies		800

T-accounts help us visualize the account balances before and after the adjusting entry.

	Supplies				**Supplies Expense**	
(Cash payment)	2,000					
		800	(Adjusting entry)		800	
Bal. July 31	1,200			Bal. July 31	800	

If the accountant for Dress Right employs *reversing entries*, the purchase of supplies is recorded as follows:

July 6		
Supplies expense...	2,000	
Cash		2,000

To record the purchase of supplies.

The adjusting entry then is used to establish the balance in the supplies account at $1,200 (amount of supplies still on hand at the end of the month) and reduce the supplies expense account from the amount purchased to the amount used.

July 31		
Supplies (balance on hand)...	1,200	
Supplies expense ($2,000 – $800)...		1,200

To record the cost of supplies on hand at the end of July.

T-accounts make the process easier to see before and after the adjusting entry.

	Supplies				**Supplies Expense**	
			Cash payment	2,000		
	1,200		(Adjusting entry)		1,200	
Bal. July 31	1,200		Bal. July 31	800		

Notice that the ending balances in both accounts are the same as when reversing entries are not used. Up to this point, this approach is the alternate approach to recording prepayments discussed in a previous section of this chapter. The next step is an optional expediency.

On August 1, the following reversing entry can be recorded:

August 1		
Supplies expense...	1,200	
Supplies..		1,200

To reverse the July adjusting entry for supplies on hand.

This entry reduces the supplies account to zero and increases the supplies expense account to $2,000. Subsequent purchases would then be entered into the supplies expense account and future adjusting entries would record the amount of supplies still on hand at the end of the period. At the end of the fiscal year, the supplies expense account, along with all other temporary accounts, is closed to retained earnings.

Using reversing entries for prepayments, which is optional, simply allows cash payments to be entered directly into the temporary expense accounts without regard to whether only the current, or both the current and future periods, are benefitted by the expenditure. Adjustments are then recorded at the end of the period to reflect the amount of the unexpired benefit (asset). ●

APPENDIX 2C

Subsidiary Ledgers and Special Journals

Subsidiary Ledgers

The general ledger contains what are referred to as *control accounts*. In addition to the general ledger, a subsidiary ledger contains a group of subsidiary accounts associated with a particular general ledger control account. For example, there will be a subsidiary ledger for accounts receivable that keeps track of the increases and decreases in the account receivable

Accounting systems employ a *subsidiary ledger*, which contains a group of subsidiary accounts associated with particular general ledger control accounts.

balance for each of the company's customers purchasing goods or services on credit. After all of the postings are made from the appropriate journals, the balance in the accounts receivable control account should equal the sum of the balances in the accounts receivable subsidiary ledger accounts. Subsidiary ledgers also are used for accounts payable, property and equipment, investments, and other accounts.

Special Journals

For most external transactions, *special journals* are used to capture the dual effect of the transaction in debit/ credit form.

An actual accounting system employs many different types of journals. The purpose of each journal is to record, in chronological order, the dual effect of a transaction in debit/credit form. The chapter used the general journal format to record each transaction. However, even for small companies with relatively few transactions, the general journal is used to record only a few types of transactions.[8]

The majority of transactions are recorded in special journals. These journals capture the dual effect of *repetitive* types of transactions. For example, cash receipts are recorded in a cash receipts journal, cash disbursements in a cash disbursements journal, credit sales in a sales journal, and the purchase of merchandise on account in a purchases journal.

Special journals simplify the recording process in the following ways:

1. Journalizing the effects of a particular transaction is made more efficient through the use of specifically designed formats.
2. Individual transactions are not posted to the general ledger accounts but are accumulated in the special journals and a summary posting is made on a periodic basis.
3. The responsibility for recording journal entries for the repetitive types of transactions is placed on individuals who have specialized training in handling them.

The concepts of subsidiary ledgers and special journals are illustrated using the *sales journal* and the *cash receipts journal*.

Sales Journal

All credit sales are recorded in the *sales journal*.

The purpose of the sales journal is to record all credit sales. Cash sales are recorded in the cash receipts journal. Every entry in the sales journal has exactly the same effect on the accounts; the sales revenue account is credited and the accounts receivable control account is debited. Therefore, there is only one column needed to record the debit/credit effect of these transactions. Other columns are needed to capture information for updating the accounts receivable subsidiary ledger. Illustration 2C–1 presents the sales journal for Dress Right Clothing Corporation for the month of August 2021.

Illustration 2C–1

Sales Journal, Dress Right Clothing Corporation, August 2021

				Page 1
Date	Accounts Receivable Subsidiary Account No.	Customer Name	Sales Invoice No.	Cr. Sales Revenue (400) Dr. Accounts Receivable (110)
2021				
Aug. 5	801	Leland High School	10-221	1,500
9	812	Mr. John Smith	10-222	200
18	813	Greystone School	10-223	825
22	803	Ms. Barbara Jones	10-224	120
29	805	Hart Middle School	10-225	650
				3,295

[8] For example, end-of-period adjusting entries would be recorded in the general journal.

During the month of August, the company made five credit sales, totaling $3,295. This amount is posted as a debit to the accounts receivable control account, account number 110, and a credit to the sales revenue account, account number 400. The T-accounts for accounts receivable and sales revenue appear below. The reference SJ1 refers to page 1 of the sales journal.

General Ledger

Accounts Receivable	110		Sales Revenue	400
July 31 Balance 2,000				
Aug. 31 SJ1 3,295			3,295 Aug. 31 SJ1	

In a computerized accounting system, as each transaction is recorded in the sales journal, the subsidiary ledger accounts for the customer involved will automatically be updated. For example, the first credit sale of the month is to Leland High School for $1,500. The sales invoice number for this sale is 10-221 and the customer's subsidiary account number is 801. As this transaction is entered, the subsidiary account 801 for Leland High School is debited for $1,500

Accounts Receivable Subsidiary Ledger

Leland High School	801
August 5 SJ1 1,500	

As cash is collected from this customer, the cash receipts journal records the transaction with a credit to the accounts receivable control account and a debit to cash. At the same time, the accounts receivable subsidiary ledger account number 801 also is credited. After the postings are made from the special journals, the balance in the accounts receivable control account should equal the sum of the balances in the accounts receivable subsidiary ledger accounts.

Cash Receipts Journal

The purpose of the cash receipts journal is to record all cash receipts, regardless of the source. Every transaction recorded in this journal produces a debit entry to the cash account with the credit to various other accounts. Illustration 2C–2 shows a cash receipts journal using transactions of the Dress Right Clothing Corporation for the month of August 2021.

All cash receipts are recorded in the cash receipts journal.

Illustration 2C–2

Cash Receipts Journal, Dress Right Clothing Corporation, August 2021

Page 1

Date	Explanation or Account Name	Dr. Cash (100)	Cr. Accounts Receivable (110)	Cr. Sales Revenue (400)	Cr. Other	Other Accounts
2021						
Aug. 7	Cash sale	500		500		
11	Borrowed cash	10,000			10,000	Notes payable (220)
17	Leland High School	750	750			
20	Cash sale	300		300		
25	Mr. John Smith	200	200			
		11,750	950	800	10,000	

Because every transaction results in a debit to the cash account, No. 100, a column is provided for that account. At the end of August, an $11,750 debit is posted to the general ledger cash account with the source labeled CR1, cash receipts journal, page 1.

Because cash and credit sales are common, separate columns are provided for these accounts. At the end of August, a $950 credit is posted to the accounts receivable general ledger account, No. 110, and an $800 credit is posted to the sales revenue account, No. 400. Two additional credit columns are provided for uncommon cash receipt transactions, one for the credit amount and one for the account being credited. We can see that in August, Dress Right borrowed $10,000 requiring a credit to the notes payable account, No. 220.

In addition to the postings to the general ledger control accounts, each time an entry is recorded in the accounts receivable column, a credit is posted to the accounts receivable subsidiary ledger account for the customer making the payment. For example, on August 17, Leland High School paid $750 on account. The subsidiary ledger account for Leland High School is credited for $750.

Accounts Receivable Subsidiary Ledger

Leland High School		801
August 5 SJ1	1,500	
	750	August 17 CR1

Questions For Review of Key Topics

Q 2–1   Explain the difference between external events and internal events. Give an example of each type of event.

Q 2–2   Each economic event or transaction will have a dual effect on financial position. Explain what is meant by this dual effect.

Q 2–3   What is the purpose of a journal? What is the purpose of a general ledger?

Q 2–4   Explain the difference between permanent accounts and temporary accounts. Why does an accounting system include both types of accounts?

Q 2–5   Describe how debits and credits affect assets, liabilities, and permanent owners' equity accounts.

Q 2–6   Describe how debits and credits affect temporary owners' equity accounts.

Q 2–7   What is the first step in the accounting processing cycle? What role do source documents fulfill in this step?

Q 2–8   Describe what is meant by transaction analysis.

Q 2–9   Describe what is meant by posting, the fourth step in the processing cycle.

Q 2–10 Describe the events that correspond to the following two journal entries:

1. Inventory	20,000	
Accounts payable		20,000
2. Accounts receivable	30,000	
Sales revenue		30,000
Cost of goods sold	18,000	
Inventory		18,000

Q 2–11 What is an unadjusted trial balance? An adjusted trial balance?

Q 2–12 Define adjusting entries and discuss their purpose.

Q 2–13 Define closing entries and their purpose.

Q 2–14 Define prepaid expenses and provide at least two examples.

Q 2–15 Deferred revenues represent liabilities recorded when cash is received from customers in advance of providing a good or service. What adjusting journal entry is required at the end of a period to recognize the amount of deferred revenues that were recognized during the period?

Q 2–16 Define accrued liabilities. What adjusting journal entry is required to record accrued liabilities?

Q 2–17 Describe the purpose of each of the five primary financial statements.

Q 2–18 [Based on Appendix A] What is the purpose of a worksheet? In a columnar worksheet similar to Illustration 2A–1, what would be the result of incorrectly transferring the balance in a liability account to column I, the credit column under Income Statement?

Q 2–19 [Based on Appendix B] Define reversing entries and discuss their purpose.

Q 2–20 [Based on Appendix C] What is the purpose of special journals? In what ways do they simplify the recording process?

Q 2–21 [Based on Appendix C] Explain the difference between the general ledger and a subsidiary ledger.

Brief Exercises

BE 2–1
Transaction analysis
● LO2–1

The Marchetti Soup Company entered into the following transactions during the month of June: (1) purchased inventory on account for $165,000 (assume Marchetti uses a perpetual inventory system); (2) paid $40,000 in salaries to employees for work performed during the month; (3) sold merchandise that cost $120,000 to credit customers for $200,000; (4) collected $180,000 in cash from credit customers; and (5) paid suppliers of inventory $145,000. Analyze each transaction and show the effect of each on the accounting equation for a corporation.

BE 2–2
Journal entries
● LO2–3

Prepare journal entries for each of the transactions listed in BE 2–1.

BE 2–3
T-accounts
● LO2–4

Post the journal entries prepared in BE 2–2 to T-accounts. Assume that the opening balances in each of the accounts is zero except for cash, accounts receivable, and accounts payable that had opening balances of $65,000, $43,000, and $22,000, respectively.

BE 2–4
Journal entries
● LO2–3

Prepare journal entries for each of the following transactions for a company that has a fiscal year-end of December 31: (1) on October 1, $12,000 was paid for a one-year fire insurance policy; (2) on June 30 the company advanced its chief financial officer $10,000; principal and interest at 6% on the note are due in one year; and (3) equipment costing $60,000 was purchased at the beginning of the year for cash.

BE 2–5
Adjusting entries
● LO2–6

Prepare the necessary adjusting entries at December 31 for each of the items listed in BE 2–4. Depreciation on the equipment is $12,000 per year.

BE 2–6
Adjusting entries; income determination
● LO2–5, LO2–6

If the adjusting entries prepared in BE 2–5 were not recorded, would net income be higher or lower and by how much?

BE 2–7
Adjusting entries
● LO2–6

Prepare the necessary adjusting entries at its year-end of December 31, 2021, for the Jamesway Corporation for each of the following situations. No adjusting entries were recorded during the year.
1. On December 10, 2021, Jamesway received a $4,000 payment from a customer for services begun on that date and which were completed by December 31, 2021. Deferred service revenue was credited.
2. On December 1, 2021, the company paid a local radio station $2,000 for 40 radio ads that were to be aired, 20 per month, throughout December and January. Prepaid advertising was debited.
3. Employee salaries for the month of December totaling $16,000 will be paid on January 7, 2022.
4. On August 31, 2021, Jamesway borrowed $60,000 from a local bank. A note was signed with principal and 8% interest to be paid on August 31, 2022.

BE 2–8
Income determination
● LO2–5

If none of the adjusting journal entries prepared in BE 2–7 were recorded, would assets, liabilities, and shareholders' equity on the 12/31/2021 balance sheet be higher or lower and by how much?

BE 2–9
Adjusting entries
● LO2–6

Prepare the necessary adjusting entries for Johnstone Controls at the end of its December 31, 2021, fiscal year-end for each of the following situations. No adjusting entries were recorded during the year.
1. On March 31, 2021, the company lent $50,000 to another company. A note was signed with principal and interest at 6% payable on March 31, 2022.
2. On September 30, 2021, the company paid its landlord $12,000 representing rent for the period September 30, 2021, to September 30, 2022. Johnstone debited prepaid rent.
3. Supplies on hand at the end of 2020 totaled $3,000. Additional supplies costing $5,000 were purchased during 2021 and debited to the supplies account. At the end of 2021, supplies costing $4,200 remain on hand.
4. Vacation pay of $6,000 for the year that had been earned by employees was not paid or recorded. The company records vacation pay as salaries expense.

BE 2–10
Financial statements
● LO2–7

The following account balances were taken from the 2021 adjusted trial balance of the Bowler Corporation: sales revenue, $325,000; cost of goods sold, $168,000; salaries expense, $45,000; rent expense, $20,000; depreciation expense, $30,000; and miscellaneous expense, $12,000. Prepare an income statement for 2021.

BE 2–11
Financial statements
● LO2–7

The following account balances were taken from the 2021 post-closing trial balance of the Bowler Corporation: cash, $5,000; accounts receivable, $10,000; inventory, $16,000; equipment, $100,000; accumulated depreciation, $40,000; accounts payable, $20,000; salaries payable, $12,000; retained earnings, $9,000; and common stock, $50,000. Prepare a 12/31/2021 balance sheet.

BE 2–12
Closing entries
● LO2–8

The year-end adjusted trial balance of the Timmons Tool and Die Corporation included the following account balances: retained earnings, $220,000; dividends, $12,000; sales revenue, $850,000; cost of goods sold, $580,000; salaries expense, $180,000; rent expense, $40,000; and interest expense, $15,000. Prepare the necessary closing entries.

BE 2–13
Cash versus accrual accounting
● LO2–9

Newman Consulting Company maintains its records on a cash basis. During 2021 the following cash flows were recorded: cash received for services rendered to clients, $420,000; and cash paid for salaries, utilities, and advertising, $240,000, $35,000, and $12,000, respectively. You also determine that customers owed the company $52,000 and $60,000 at the beginning and end of the year, respectively, and that the company owed the utility company $6,000 and $4,000 at the beginning and end of the year, respectively. Determine accrual net income for the year.

Exercises

E 2–1
Transaction analysis
● LO2–1

The following transactions occurred during March 2021 for the Wainwright Corporation. The company owns and operates a wholesale warehouse.
1. Issued 30,000 shares of no-par common stock in exchange for $300,000 in cash.
2. Purchased equipment at a cost of $40,000. $10,000 cash was paid and a note payable to the seller was signed for the balance owed.
3. Purchased inventory on account at a cost of $90,000. The company uses the perpetual inventory system.
4. Credit sales for the month totaled $120,000. The cost of the goods sold was $70,000.
5. Paid $5,000 in rent on the warehouse building for the month of March.
6. Paid $6,000 to an insurance company for fire and liability insurance for a one-year period beginning April 1, 2021.
7. Paid $70,000 on account for the merchandise purchased in 3.
8. Collected $55,000 from customers on account.
9. Recorded depreciation expense of $1,000 for the month on the equipment.

Required:
Analyze each transaction and show the effect of each on the accounting equation for a corporation.
Example:

Assets   = Liabilities + Paid-In Capital + Retained Earnings
1. +300,000 (cash)   + 300,000 (common stock)

E 2–2
Journal entries
● LO2–3

Prepare journal entries to record each of the transactions listed in E 2–1.

E 2–3
T-accounts and trial balance
● LO2–4

Post the journal entries prepared in E 2–2 to T-accounts. Assume that the opening balances in each of the accounts is zero. Prepare a trial balance from the ending account balances.

E 2–4
Journal entries
● LO2–3

The following transactions occurred during the month of June 2021 for the Stridewell Corporation. The company owns and operates a retail shoe store.
1. Issued 100,000 shares of common stock in exchange for $500,000 cash.
2. Purchased office equipment at a cost of $100,000. $40,000 was paid in cash and a note payable was signed for the balance owed.
3. Purchased inventory on account at a cost of $200,000. The company uses the perpetual inventory system.
4. Credit sales for the month totaled $280,000. The cost of the goods sold was $140,000.
5. Paid $6,000 in rent on the store building for the month of June.

6. Paid $3,000 to an insurance company for fire and liability insurance for a one-year period beginning June 1, 2021.

7. Paid $120,000 on account for the merchandise purchased in 3.

8. Collected $55,000 from customers on account.

9. Paid shareholders a cash dividend of $5,000.

10. Recorded depreciation expense of $2,000 for the month on the office equipment.

11. Recorded the amount of prepaid insurance that expired for the month.

Required:
Prepare journal entries to record each of the transactions and events listed above.

E 2–5
The accounting processing cycle
● LO2–2

Listed below are several terms and phrases associated with the accounting processing cycle. Pair each item from List A (by letter) with the item from List B that is most appropriately associated with it.

List A	List B
_____ 1. Source documents	a. Record of the dual effect of a transaction in debit/credit form.
_____ 2. Transaction analysis	b. Internal events recorded at the end of a reporting period.
_____ 3. Journal	c. Primary means of disseminating information to external decision makers.
_____ 4. Posting	d. To zero out the temporary accounts.
_____ 5. Unadjusted trial balance	e. Determine the dual effect on the accounting equation.
_____ 6. Adjusting entries	f. List of accounts and their balances before recording adjusting entries.
_____ 7. Adjusted trial balance	g. List of accounts and their balances after recording closing entries.
_____ 8. Financial statements	h. List of accounts and their balances after recording adjusting entries.
_____ 9. Closing entries	i. A means of organizing information: not part of the formal accounting system.
_____ 10. Post-closing trial balance	j. Transferring balances from the journal to the ledger.
_____ 11. Worksheet	k. Used to identify and process external transactions.

E 2–6
Debits and credits
● LO2–1

Indicate whether a *debit* will increase (I) or decrease (D) each of the following accounts listed in items 1 through 15.

Increase (I) or Decrease (D)	Account
1. _____	Inventory
2. _____	Depreciation expense
3. _____	Accounts payable
4. _____	Prepaid rent
5. _____	Sales revenue
6. _____	Common stock
7. _____	Salaries payable
8. _____	Cost of goods sold
9. _____	Utilities expense
10. _____	Equipment
11. _____	Accounts receivable
12. _____	Utilities payable
13. _____	Rent expense
14. _____	Interest expense
15. _____	Interest revenue

E 2–7
Journal entries; debits and credits
● LO2–3

Some of the ledger accounts for the Sanderson Hardware Company are numbered and listed below. For each of the October 2021 transactions numbered 1 through 10 below, indicate by account number which accounts should be debited and which should be credited when preparing journal entries. The company uses the perpetual inventory system.

(1) Accounts payable   (2) Equipment   (3) Inventory
(4) Accounts receivable   (5) Cash   (6) Supplies
(7) Supplies expense   (8) Prepaid rent   (9) Sales revenue
(10) Retained earnings   (11) Notes payable   (12) Common stock
(13) Deferred sales revenue (14) Rent expense   (15) Salaries payable
(16) Cost of goods sold   (17) Salaries expense   (18) Interest expense
(19) Dividends

	Account(s) Debited	Account(s) Credited
Example: Purchased inventory for cash	3	5

1. Paid a cash dividend.
2. Paid rent for the next three months.
3. Sold goods to customers on account.
4. Purchased inventory on account.
5. Purchased supplies for cash.
6. Issued common stock in exchange for cash.
7. Collected cash from customers for goods sold in 3.
8. Borrowed cash from a bank and signed a note.
9. At the end of October, recorded the amount of supplies that had been used during the month.
10. Received cash for advance payment from customer.

E 2–8
Adjusting entries
● **LO2–6**

Prepare the necessary adjusting entries at December 31, 2021, for the Falwell Company for each of the following situations. Assume that no financial statements were prepared during the year and no adjusting entries were recorded.

1. A three-year fire insurance policy was purchased on July 1, 2021, for $12,000. The company debited insurance expense for the entire amount.
2. Depreciation on equipment totaled $15,000 for the year.
3. Employee salaries of $18,000 for the month of December will be paid in early January 2022.
4. On November 1, 2021, the company borrowed $200,000 from a bank. The note requires principal and interest at 12% to be paid on April 30, 2022.
5. On December 1, 2021, the company received $3,000 in cash from another company that is renting office space in Falwell's building. The payment, representing rent for December, January, and February was credited to deferred rent revenue.
6. In the previous transaction, suppose the company credited rent revenue rather than deferred rent revenue for $3,000 on December 1, 2021. What would be the appropriate adjusting entry at December 31, 2021?

E 2–9
Adjusting entries
● **LO2–6**

Prepare the necessary adjusting entries at December 31, 2021, for the Microchip Company for each of the following situations. Assume that no financial statements were prepared during the year and no adjusting entries were recorded.

1. On October 1, 2021, Microchip lent $90,000 to another company. A note was signed with principal and 8% interest to be paid on September 30, 2022.
2. On November 1, 2021, the company paid its landlord $6,000 representing rent for the months of November through January. Prepaid rent was debited.
3. On August 1, 2021, collected $12,000 in advance rent from another company that is renting a portion of Microchip's factory. The $12,000 represents one year's rent and the entire amount was credited to deferred rent revenue.
4. Depreciation on office equipment is $4,500 for the year.
5. Vacation pay for the year that had been earned by employees but not paid to them or recorded is $8,000. The company records vacation pay as salaries expense.
6. Microchip began the year with $2,000 in its asset account, supplies. During the year, $6,500 in supplies were purchased and debited to supplies. At year-end, supplies costing $3,250 remain on hand.

E 2–10
Adjusting entries;
solving for
unknowns
● **LO2–5, LO2–6**

The Eldorado Corporation's controller prepares adjusting entries only at the end of the reporting year. The following adjusting entries were prepared on December 31, 2021:

	Debit	Credit
Interest expense	7,200	
Interest payable		7,200
Rent expense	35,000	
Prepaid rent		35,000
Interest receivable	500	
Interest revenue		500

Additional information:

1. The company borrowed $120,000 on March 31, 2021. Principal and interest are due on March 31, 2022. This note is the company's only interest-bearing debt.
2. Rent for the year on the company's office space is $60,000. The rent is paid in advance.
3. On October 31, 2021, Eldorado lent money to a customer. The customer signed a note with principal and interest at 6% due in one year.

Required:

Determine the following:

1. What is the interest rate on the company's note payable?
2. The 2021 rent payment was made at the beginning of which month?
3. How much did Eldorado lend its customer on October 31?

E 2–11
Adjusting entries; fiscal year
● LO2–6

The Mazzanti Wholesale Food Company's fiscal year-end is June 30. The company issues quarterly financial statements requiring the company to prepare adjusting entries at the end of each quarter. Assuming all quarterly adjusting entries were properly recorded, prepare the necessary year-end adjusting entries at the end of June 30, 2021, for the following situations.

1. On December 1, 2020, the company paid its annual fire insurance premium of $6,000 for the year beginning December 1 and debited prepaid insurance.
2. On August 31, 2020, the company borrowed $80,000 from a local bank. The note requires principal and interest at 8% to be paid on August 31, 2021.
3. Mazzanti owns a warehouse that it rents to another company. On January 1, 2021, Mazzanti collected $24,000 representing rent for the 2021 calendar year and credited deferred rent revenue.
4. Depreciation on the office building is $20,000 for the fiscal year.
5. Employee salaries for the month of June 2021 of $16,000 will be paid on July 20, 2021.

E 2–12
Financial statements and closing entries
● LO2–7, LO2–8

The December 31, 2021, adjusted trial balance for the Blueboy Cheese Corporation is presented below.

Account Title	Debits	Credits
Cash	21,000	
Accounts receivable	300,000	
Prepaid rent	10,000	
Inventory	50,000	
Office equipment	600,000	
Accumulated depreciation		250,000
Accounts payable		60,000
Notes payable (due in six months)		60,000
Salaries payable		8,000
Interest payable		2,000
Common stock		400,000
Retained earnings		100,000
Sales revenue		800,000
Cost of goods sold	480,000	
Salaries expense	120,000	
Rent expense	30,000	
Depreciation expense	60,000	
Interest expense	4,000	
Advertising expense	5,000	
Totals	1,680,000	1,680,000

Required:

1. Prepare an income statement for the year ended December 31, 2021, and a classified balance sheet as of December 31, 2021.
2. Prepare the necessary closing entries at December 31, 2021.

E 2–13
Closing entries
● LO2–8

American Chip Corporation's reporting year-end is December 31. The following is a partial adjusted trial balance as of December 31, 2021.

Account Title	Debits	Credits
Retained earnings		80,000
Sales revenue		750,000
Interest revenue		3,000
Cost of goods sold	420,000	
Salaries expense	100,000	
Rent expense	15,000	
Depreciation expense	30,000	
Interest expense	5,000	
Insurance expense	6,000	

Required:

Prepare the necessary closing entries at December 31, 2021.

E 2–14
Closing entries
● LO2–8

Presented below is income statement information of the Schefter Corporation for the year ended December 31, 2021.

Sales revenue	$492,000	Cost of goods sold	284,000
Salaries expense	80,000	Insurance expense	12,000
Interest revenue	6,000	Interest expense	4,000
Advertising expense	10,000	Income tax expense	30,000
Gain on sale of investments	8,000	Depreciation expense	20,000

Required:
Prepare the necessary closing entries at December 31, 2021.

E 2–15
Cash versus
accrual
accounting;
adjusting entries
● LO2–5, LO2–6,
LO2–9

The Righter Shoe Store Company prepares monthly financial statements for its bank. The November 30 and December 31, 2021, trial balances contained the following account information:

	Nov. 30		Dec. 31	
	Dr.	Cr.	Dr.	Cr.
Supplies	1,500		3,000	
Prepaid insurance	6,000		4,500	
Salaries payable		10,000		15,000
Deferred rent revenue		2,000		1,000

The following information also is known:
a. The December income statement reported $2,000 in supplies expense.
b. No insurance payments were made in December.
c. $10,000 was paid to employees during December for salaries.
d. On November 1, 2021, a tenant paid Righter $3,000 in advance rent for the period November through January. Deferred rent revenue was credited.

Required:
1. What was the cost of supplies purchased during December?
2. What was the adjusting entry recorded at the end of December for prepaid insurance?
3. What was the adjusting entry recorded at the end of December for accrued salaries?
4. What was the amount of rent revenue recognized in December? What adjusting entry was recorded at the end of December for deferred rent revenue?

E 2–16
External
transactions and
adjusting entries
● LO2–3, LO2–6

The following transactions occurred during 2021 for the Beehive Honey Corporation:

Feb. 1	Borrowed $12,000 from a bank and signed a note. Principal and interest at 10% will be paid on January 31, 2022.
Apr. 1	Paid $3,600 to an insurance company for a two-year fire insurance policy.
July 17	Purchased supplies costing $2,800 on account. The company records supplies purchased in an asset account. At the year-end on December 31, 2021, supplies costing $1,250 remained on hand.
Nov. 1	A customer borrowed $6,000 and signed a note requiring the customer to pay principal and 8% interest on April 30, 2022.

Required:
1. Record each transaction in general journal form. Omit explanations.
2. Prepare any necessary adjusting entries at the year-end on December 31, 2021. No adjusting entries were recorded during the year for any item.

E 2–17
Accrual
accounting
income
determination
● LO2–5, LO2–9

During the course of your examination of the financial statements of the Hales Corporation for the year ended December 31, 2021, you discover the following:
a. An insurance policy covering three years was purchased on January 1, 2021, for $6,000. The entire amount was debited to insurance expense and no adjusting entry was recorded for this item.
b. During 2021, the company received a $1,000 cash advance from a customer for merchandise to be manufactured and shipped in 2022. The $1,000 was credited to sales revenue. No entry was recorded for the cost of merchandise.
c. There were no supplies listed in the balance sheet under assets. However, you discover that supplies costing $750 were on hand at December 31.
d. Hales borrowed $20,000 from a local bank on October 1, 2021. Principal and interest at 12% will be paid on September 30, 2022. No accrual was recorded for interest.
e. Net income reported in the 2021 income statement is $30,000 before reflecting any of the above items.

Required:
Determine the proper amount of net income for 2021.

E 2–18
Cash versus accrual accounting
● LO2–9

Stanley and Jones Lawn Service Company (S&J) maintains its books on a cash basis. However, the company recently borrowed $100,000 from a local bank, and the bank requires S&J to provide annual financial statements prepared on an accrual basis. During 2021, the following cash flows were recorded:

Cash collected for: Services to customers		$320,000
Cash paid for:		
Salaries	$180,000	
Supplies	25,000	
Rent	12,000	
Insurance	6,000	
Miscellaneous	20,000	243,000
Net operating cash flow		$ 77,000

You are able to determine the following information about accounts receivable, prepaid expenses, and accrued liabilities:

	January 1, 2021	December 31, 2021
Accounts receivable	$32,000	$27,000
Prepaid insurance	–0–	2,000
Supplies	1,000	1,500
Accrued liabilities	2,400	3,400
(for miscellaneous expenses)		

In addition, you learn that the bank loan was dated September 30, 2021, with principal and interest at 6% due in one year. Depreciation on the company's equipment is $10,000 for the year.

Required:
Prepare an accrual basis income statement for 2021. (Ignore income taxes.)

E 2–19
Cash versus accrual accounting
● LO2–9

Haskins and Jones, Attorneys-at-Law, maintains its books on a cash basis. During 2021, the law firm collected $545,000 for services rendered to its clients and paid out $412,000 in expenses. You are able to determine the following information about accounts receivable, prepaid expenses, deferred service revenue, and accrued liabilities:

	January 1, 2021	December 31, 2021
Accounts receivable	$62,000	$55,000
Prepaid insurance	4,500	6,000
Prepaid rent	9,200	8,200
Deferred service revenue	9,200	11,000
Accrued liabilities	12,200	15,600
(for various expenses)		

In addition, 2021 depreciation expense on office equipment is $22,000.

Required:
Determine accrual basis net income for 2021.

E 2–20
Worksheet
● Appendix 2A

The December 31, 2021, unadjusted trial balance for the Wolkstein Drug Company is presented below. December 31 is the company's year-end reporting date.

Account Title	Debits	Credits
Cash	20,000	
Accounts receivable	35,000	
Prepaid rent	5,000	
Inventory	50,000	
Equipment	100,000	
Accumulated depreciation		30,000
Accounts payable		25,000
Salaries payable		–0–
Common stock		100,000
Retained earnings		29,000
Sales revenue		323,000
Cost of goods sold	180,000	
Salaries expense	71,000	
Rent expense	30,000	
Depreciation expense	–0–	
Utilities expense	12,000	
Advertising expense	4,000	
Totals	507,000	507,000

The following year-end adjusting entries are required:

a. Depreciation expense for the year on the equipment is $10,000.

b. Salaries at year-end should be accrued in the amount of $4,000.

Required:

1. Prepare and complete a worksheet similar to Illustration 2A–1.

2. Prepare an income statement for 2021 and a balance sheet as of December 31, 2021.

E 2–21
Reversing entries
● Appendix 2B

The employees of Xitrex, Inc., are paid each Friday. The company's fiscal year-end is June 30, which falls on a Wednesday for the current year. Salaries are earned evenly throughout the five-day work week, and $10,000 will be paid on Friday, July 2.

Required:

1. Prepare an adjusting entry to record the accrued salaries as of June 30, a reversing entry on July 1, and an entry to record the payment of salaries on July 2.

2. Prepare journal entries to record the accrued salaries as of June 30 and the payment of salaries on July 2 assuming a reversing entry is not recorded.

E 2–22
Reversing entries
● Appendix 2B

Refer to E 2–9 and respond to the following requirements.

Required:

1. If Microchip's accountant employed reversing entries for accruals, which adjusting entries would she likely reverse at the beginning of the following year?

2. Prepare the adjusting entries at the end of 2021 for the adjustments you identified in requirement 1.

3. Prepare the appropriate reversing entries at the beginning of 2022.

E 2–23
Special journals
● Appendix 2C

The White Company's accounting system consists of a general journal (GJ), a cash receipts journal (CR), a cash disbursements journal (CD), a sales journal (SJ), and a purchases journal (PJ). For each of the following, indicate which journal should be used to record the transaction.

Transaction	Journal
1. Purchased merchandise on account.	_____
2. Collected an account receivable.	_____
3. Borrowed $20,000 and signed a note.	_____
4. Recorded depreciation expense.	_____
5. Purchased equipment for cash.	_____
6. Sold merchandise for cash (the sale only, not the cost of the merchandise).	_____
7. Sold merchandise on credit (the sale only, not the cost of the merchandise).	_____
8. Recorded accrued salaries payable.	_____
9. Paid employee salaries.	_____
10. Sold equipment for cash.	_____
11. Sold equipment on credit.	_____
12. Paid a cash dividend to shareholders.	_____
13. Issued common stock in exchange for cash.	_____
14. Paid accounts payable.	_____

E 2–24
Special journals
● Appendix 2C

The accounting system of K and M Manufacturing consists of a general journal (GJ), a cash receipts journal (CR), a cash disbursements journal (CD), a sales journal (SJ), and a purchases journal (PJ). For each of the following, indicate which journal should be used to record the transaction.

Transaction	Journal
1. Paid interest on a loan.	_____
2. Recorded depreciation expense.	_____
3. Purchased office equipment for cash.	_____
4. Purchased merchandise on account.	_____
5. Sold merchandise on credit (the sale only, not the cost of the merchandise).	_____
6. Sold merchandise for cash (the sale only, not the cost of the merchandise).	_____
7. Paid rent.	_____
8. Recorded accrued interest payable.	_____
9. Paid advertising bill.	_____
10. Sold a factory building in exchange for a note receivable.	_____
11. Collected cash from customers on account.	_____
12. Paid employee salaries.	_____
13. Collected interest on the note receivable.	_____

Problems

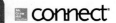

P 2–1
Accounting
cycle through
unadjusted trial
balance

● LO2–3, LO2–4

Halogen Laminated Products Company began business on January 1, 2021. During January, the following transactions occurred:

Jan. 1   Issued common stock in exchange for $100,000 cash.

   2   Purchased inventory on account for $35,000 (the perpetual inventory system is used).

   4   Paid an insurance company $2,400 for a one-year insurance policy. Prepaid insurance was debited for the entire amount.

   10   Sold merchandise on account for $12,000. The cost of the merchandise was $7,000.

   15   Borrowed $30,000 from a local bank and signed a note. Principal and interest at 10% is to be repaid in six months.

   20   Paid employees $6,000 salaries for the first half of the month.

   22   Sold merchandise for $10,000 cash. The cost of the merchandise was $6,000.

   24   Paid $15,000 to suppliers for the merchandise purchased on January 2.

   26   Collected $6,000 on account from customers.

   28   Paid $1,000 to the local utility company for January gas and electricity.

   30   Paid $4,000 rent for the building. $2,000 was for January rent, and $2,000 for February rent. Prepaid rent and rent expense were debited for their appropriate amounts.

Required:

1. Prepare general journal entries to record each transaction. Omit explanations.

2. Post the entries to T-accounts.

3. Prepare an unadjusted trial balance as of January 30, 2021.

P 2–2
Accounting
cycle through
unadjusted trial
balance

● LO2–3, LO2–4

The following is the post-closing trial balance for the Whitlow Manufacturing Corporation as of December 31, 2020.

Account Title	Debits	Credits
Cash	5,000	
Accounts receivable	2,000	
Inventory	5,000	
Equipment	11,000	
Accumulated depreciation		3,500
Accounts payable		3,000
Accrued liabilities		–0–
Common stock		10,000
Retained earnings		6,500
Sales revenue		–0–
Cost of goods sold	–0–	
Salaries expense	–0–	
Rent expense	–0–	
Advertising expense	–0–	
Totals	23,000	23,000

The following transactions occurred during January 2021:

Jan. 1   Sold merchandise for cash, $3,500. The cost of the merchandise was $2,000. The company uses the perpetual inventory system.

   2   Purchased equipment on account for $5,500 from the Strong Company.

   4   Received a $150 invoice from the local newspaper requesting payment for an advertisement that Whitlow placed in the paper on January 2.

   8   Sold merchandise on account for $5,000. The cost of the merchandise was $2,800.

   10   Purchased merchandise on account for $9,500.

   13   Purchased equipment for cash, $800.

   16   Paid the entire amount due to the Strong Company.

   18   Received $4,000 from customers on account.

   20   Paid $800 to the owner of the building for January's rent.

   30   Paid employees $3,000 for salaries for the month of January.

   31   Paid a cash dividend of $1,000 to shareholders.

Required:

1. Set up T-accounts and enter the beginning balances as of January 1, 2021.

2. Prepare general journal entries to record each transaction. Omit explanations.

3. Post the entries to T-accounts.

4. Prepare an unadjusted trial balance as of January 31, 2021.

100   SECTION 1   The Role of Accounting as an Information System

P 2–3
Adjusting entries
● LO2–6

Pastina Company sells various types of pasta to grocery chains as private label brands. The company's reporting year-end is December 31. The unadjusted trial balance as of December 31, 2021, appears below.

Account Title	Debits	Credits
Cash	30,000	
Accounts receivable	40,000	
Supplies	1,500	
Inventory	60,000	
Notes receivable	20,000	
Interest receivable	–0–	
Prepaid rent	2,000	
Prepaid insurance	6,000	
Office equipment	80,000	
Accumulated depreciation		30,000
Accounts payable		31,000
Salaries payable		–0–
Notes payable		50,000
Interest payable		–0–
Deferred sales revenue		2,000
Common stock		60,000
Retained earnings		28,500
Dividends	4,000	
Sales revenue		146,000
Interest revenue		–0–
Cost of goods sold	70,000	
Salaries expense	18,900	
Rent expense	11,000	
Depreciation expense	–0–	
Interest expense	–0–	
Supplies expense	1,100	
Insurance expense	–0–	
Advertising expense	3,000	
Totals	347,500	347,500

Information necessary to prepare the year-end adjusting entries appears below.

1. Depreciation on the office equipment for the year is $10,000.

2. Employee salaries are paid twice a month, on the 22nd for salaries earned from the 1st through the 15th, and on the 7th of the following month for salaries earned from the 16th through the end of the month. Salaries earned from December 16 through December 31, 2021, were $1,500.

3. On October 1, 2021, Pastina borrowed $50,000 from a local bank and signed a note. The note requires interest to be paid annually on September 30 at 12%. The principal is due in 10 years.

4. On March 1, 2021, the company lent a supplier $20,000, and a note was signed requiring principal and interest at 8% to be paid on February 28, 2022.

5. On April 1, 2021, the company paid an insurance company $6,000 for a two-year fire insurance policy. The entire $6,000 was debited to prepaid insurance.

6. $800 of supplies remained on hand at December 31, 2021.

7. A customer paid Pastina $2,000 in December for 1,500 pounds of spaghetti to be delivered in January 2022. Pastina credited deferred sales revenue.

8. On December 1, 2021, $2,000 rent was paid to the owner of the building. The payment represented rent for December 2021 and January 2022 at $1,000 per month. The entire amount was debited to prepaid rent.

Required:
Prepare the necessary December 31, 2021, adjusting journal entries.

P 2–4
Accounting cycle;
adjusting entries
through post-
closing trial balance

● LO2–4, LO2–6
through LO2–8

Refer to P 2–3 and complete the following steps:

1. Enter the unadjusted balances from the trial balance into T-accounts.

2. Post the adjusting entries prepared in P 2–3 to the accounts.

3. Prepare an adjusted trial balance.

4. Prepare an income statement and a statement of shareholders' equity for the year ended December 31, 2021, and a classified balance sheet as of December 31, 2021. Assume that no common stock was issued during the year and that $4,000 in cash dividends were paid to shareholders during the year.

5. Prepare closing entries and post to the accounts.

6. Prepare a post-closing trial balance.

P 2–5
Adjusting entries
● LO2–6

Howarth Company's reporting year-end is December 31. Below are the unadjusted and adjusted trial balances for December 31, 2021.

Account Title	Unadjusted Debits	Unadjusted Credits	Adjusted Debits	Adjusted Credits
Cash	50,000		50,000	
Accounts receivable	35,000		35,000	
Prepaid rent	2,000		1,200	
Supplies	1,500		800	
Inventory	60,000		60,000	
Notes receivable	30,000		30,000	
Interest receivable	–0–		1,500	
Office equipment	45,000		45,000	
Accumulated depreciation		15,000		21,500
Accounts payable		34,000		34,000
Salaries payable		–0–		6,200
Notes payable		50,000		50,000
Interest payable		–0–		2,500
Deferred rent revenue		2,000		–0–
Common stock		46,000		46,000
Retained earnings		20,000		20,000
Sales revenue		244,000		244,000
Rent revenue		4,000		6,000
Interest revenue		–0–		1,500
Cost of goods sold	126,000		126,000	
Salaries and wages expense	45,000		51,200	
Rent expense	11,000		11,800	
Depreciation expense	–0–		6,500	
Supplies expense	1,100		1,800	
Interest expense	5,400		7,900	
Advertising expense	3,000		3,000	
Totals	415,000	415,000	431,700	431,700

Required:
Prepare the adjusting journal entries that were recorded at December 31, 2021.

P 2–6
Accounting cycle
● LO2–3 through
LO2–8

The general ledger of the Karlin Company, a consulting company, at January 1, 2021, contained the following account balances:

Account Title	Debits	Credits
Cash	30,000	
Accounts receivable	15,000	
Equipment	20,000	
Accumulated depreciation		6,000
Salaries payable		9,000
Common stock		40,500
Retained earnings		9,500
Total	65,000	65,000

The following is a summary of the transactions for the year:
a. Service revenue, $100,000, of which $30,000 was on account and the balance was received in cash.
b. Collected on accounts receivable, $27,300.
c. Issued shares of common stock in exchange for $10,000 in cash.
d. Paid salaries, $50,000 (of which $9,000 was for salaries payable at the end of the prior year).
e. Paid miscellaneous expense for various items, $24,000.
f. Purchased equipment for $15,000 in cash.
g. Paid $2,500 in cash dividends to shareholders.

Required:
1. Set up the necessary T-accounts and enter the beginning balances from the trial balance.
2. Prepare a general journal entry for each of the summary transactions listed above.

3. Post the journal entries to the accounts.

4. Prepare an unadjusted trial balance.

5. Prepare and post adjusting journal entries. Accrued salaries at year-end amounted to $1,000. Depreciation for the year on the equipment is $2,000.

6. Prepare an adjusted trial balance.

7. Prepare an income statement for 2021 and a balance sheet as of December 31, 2021.

8. Prepare and post-closing entries.

9. Prepare a post-closing trial balance.

P 2–7

Adjusting entries and income effects

● LO2–5, LO2–6

The information necessary for preparing the December 31, 2021 year-end adjusting entries for Vito's Pizza Parlor appears below.

a. On July 1, 2021, purchased $10,000 of IBM Corporation bonds at face value. The bonds pay interest twice a year on January 1 and July 1. The annual interest rate is 12%.

b. Vito's depreciable equipment has a cost of $30,000, a five-year life, and no salvage value. The equipment was purchased in 2019. The straight-line depreciation method is used.

c. On November 1, 2021, the bar area was leased to Jack Donaldson for one year. Vito's received $6,000 representing the first six months' rent and credited deferred rent revenue.

d. On April 1, 2021, the company paid $2,400 for a two-year fire and liability insurance policy and debited insurance expense.

e. On October 1, 2021, the company borrowed $20,000 from a local bank and signed a note. Principal and interest at 12% will be paid on September 30, 2022.

f. At year-end, there is a $1,800 debit balance in the supplies (asset) account. Only $700 of supplies remain on hand.

Required:

1. Prepare the necessary adjusting journal entries at December 31, 2021.

2. Determine the amount by which net income would be misstated if Vito's failed to record these adjusting entries. (Ignore income tax expense.)

P 2–8

Adjusting entries

● LO2–6

Excalibur Corporation sells video games for personal computers. The unadjusted trial balance as of December 31, 2021, appears below. December 31 is the company's reporting year-end. The company uses the perpetual inventory system.

Account Title	Debits	Credits
Cash	23,300	
Accounts receivable	32,500	
Supplies	–0–	
Prepaid rent	–0–	
Inventory	65,000	
Office equipment	75,000	
Accumulated depreciation		10,000
Accounts payable		26,100
Salaries payable		3,000
Notes payable		30,000
Common stock		80,000
Retained earnings		22,050
Dividends	6,000	
Sales revenue		180,000
Cost of goods sold	95,000	
Interest expense	–0–	
Salaries expense	32,350	
Rent expense	14,000	
Supplies expense	2,000	
Utilities expense	6,000	
Totals	351,150	351,150

Information necessary to prepare the year-end adjusting entries appears below.

1. The office equipment was purchased in 2019 and is being depreciated using the straight-line method over a ten-year useful life with no salvage value.

2. Accrued salaries at year-end should be $4,500.

3. The company borrowed $30,000 on September 1, 2021. The principal is due to be repaid in 10 years. Interest is payable twice a year on each August 31 and February 28 at an annual rate of 10%.

4. The company debits supplies expense when supplies are purchased. Supplies on hand at year-end cost $500.

5. Prepaid rent at year-end should be $1,000.

Required:
Prepare the necessary December 31, 2021, adjusting entries.

P 2–9
Accounting cycle;
unadjusted trial
balance through
closing
● LO2–4, LO2–6,
LO2–8

The unadjusted trial balance as of December 31, 2021, for the Bagley Consulting Company appears below. December 31 is the company's reporting year-end.

Account Title	Debits	Credits
Cash	8,000	
Accounts receivable	9,000	
Prepaid insurance	3,000	
Land	200,000	
Buildings	50,000	
Accumulated depreciation—buildings		20,000
Office equipment	100,000	
Accumulated depreciation—office equipment		40,000
Accounts payable		35,050
Salaries payable		–0–
Deferred rent revenue		–0–
Common stock		200,000
Retained earnings		56,450
Service revenue		90,000
Interest revenue		3,000
Rent revenue		7,500
Salaries expense	37,000	
Depreciation expense	–0–	
Insurance expense	–0–	
Utilities expense	30,000	
Maintenance expense	15,000	
Totals	452,000	452,000

Required:

1. Enter the account balances in T-accounts.

2. From the trial balance and information given, prepare adjusting entries and post to the accounts.

    a. The buildings have an estimated useful life of 50 years with no salvage value. The company uses the straight-line depreciation method.

    b. The office equipment is depreciated at 10 percent of original cost per year.

    c. Prepaid insurance expired during the year, $1,000.

    d. Accrued salaries at year-end, $1,500.

    e. Deferred rent revenue at year-end should be $1,200.

3. Prepare an adjusted trial balance.

4. Prepare closing entries.

5. Prepare a post-closing trial balance.

P 2–10
Accrual
accounting;
financial
statements
● LO2–5, LO2–7,
LO2–9

McGuire Corporation began operations in 2021. The company purchases computer equipment from manufacturers and then sells to retail stores. During 2021, the bookkeeper used a check register to record all cash receipts and cash disbursements. No other journals were used. The following is a recap of the cash receipts and disbursements made during the year.

Cash receipts:	
Issue of common stock	$ 50,000
Collections from customers	320,000
Borrowed from local bank on April 1, note signed requiring principal and interest at 12% to be paid on March 31, 2022	40,000
Total cash receipts	$410,000

(continued)

104 SECTION 1 The Role of Accounting as an Information System

(concluded)

Cash disbursements:

Purchase of merchandise	$220,000
Payment of salaries	80,000
Purchase of office equipment	30,000
Payment of rent on building	14,000
Miscellaneous expense	10,000
Total cash disbursements	$354,000

You are called in to prepare financial statements at December 31, 2021. The following additional information was provided to you:

1. Customers owed the company $22,000 at year-end.

2. At year-end, $30,000 was still due to suppliers of merchandise purchased on credit.

3. At year-end, merchandise inventory costing $50,000 still remained on hand.

4. Salaries owed to employees at year-end amounted to $5,000.

5. On December 1, $3,000 in rent was paid to the owner of the building used by McGuire. This represented rent for the months of December through February.

6. The office equipment, which has a 10-year life and no salvage value, was purchased on January 1, 2021. Straight-line depreciation is used.

Required:
Prepare an income statement for 2021 and a balance sheet as of December 31, 2021.

P 2–11
Cash versus accrual accounting
● LO2–9

Selected balance sheet information for the Wolf Company at November 30, and December 31, 2021, is presented below. The company uses the perpetual inventory system and all sales to customers are made on credit.

	Nov. 30		Dec. 31	
	Debits	**Credits**	**Debits**	**Credits**
Accounts receivable	10,000		3,000	
Prepaid insurance	5,000		7,500	
Inventory	7,000		6,000	
Accounts payable		12,000		15,000
Salaries payable		5,000		3,000

The following cash flow information also is available:

a. Cash collected from credit customers, $80,000

b. Cash paid for insurance, $5,000

c. Cash paid to suppliers of inventory, $60,000 (the entire accounts payable amounts relate to inventory purchases)

d. Cash paid to employees for salaries, $10,000

Required:

1. Determine the following for the month of December:

    a. Sales revenue

    b. Cost of goods sold

    c. Insurance expense

    d. Salaries expense

2. Prepare summary journal entries to record the month's sales and cost of those sales.

P 2–12
Cash versus accrual accounting
● LO2–9

Zambrano Wholesale Corporation maintains its records on a cash basis. At the end of each year the company's accountant obtains the necessary information to prepare accrual basis financial statements. The following cash flows occurred during the year ended December 31, 2021:

Cash receipts:

From customers	$675,000
Interest on note	4,000
Loan from a local bank	100,000
Total cash receipts	$779,000
Cash disbursements:	
Purchase of merchandise	$390,000
Annual insurance payment	6,000
Payment of salaries	210,000
Dividends paid to shareholders	10,000
Annual rent payment	24,000
Total cash disbursements	$640,000

Selected balance sheet information:

	12/31/2020	12/31/2021
Cash	$ 25,000	$ 164,000
Accounts receivable	62,000	92,000
Inventory	80,000	62,000
Prepaid insurance	2,500	?
Prepaid rent	11,000	?
Interest receivable	3,000	?
Notes receivable	50,000	50,000
Equipment	100,000	100,000
Accumulated depreciation	(40,000)	(50,000)
Accounts payable (for merchandise)	110,000	122,000
Salaries payable	20,000	24,000
Notes payable	–0–	100,000
Interest payable	–0–	?

Additional information:

1. On March 31, 2020, Zambrano lent a customer $50,000. Interest at 8% is payable annually on each March 31. Principal is due in 2024.

2. The annual insurance payment is paid in advance on April 30. The policy period begins on May 1.

3. On October 31, 2021, Zambrano borrowed $100,000 from a local bank and signed a note promising repayment. Principal and interest at 6% are due on October 31, 2022.

4. Annual rent on the company's facilities is paid in advance on June 30. The rental period begins on July 1.

Required:

1. Prepare an accrual basis income statement for 2021 (ignore income taxes).

2. Determine the following balance sheet amounts on December 31, 2021:

   a. Prepaid insurance

   b. Prepaid rent

   c. Interest receivable

   d. Interest payable

P 2–13
Worksheet
● Appendix 2A

Using the information from P 2–8, prepare and complete a worksheet similar to Illustration 2A–1. Use the information in the worksheet to prepare an income statement and a statement of shareholders' equity for 2021 and a balance sheet as of December 31, 2021. Cash dividends paid to shareholders during the year amounted to $6,000. Also prepare the necessary closing entries assuming that adjusting entries have been correctly posted to the accounts.

Decision Makers' Perspective

©ImageGap/Getty Images

Apply your critical-thinking ability to the knowledge you've gained. These cases will provide you an opportunity to develop your research, analysis, judgment, and communication skills. You also will work with other students, integrate what you've learned, apply it in real-world situations, and consider its global and ethical ramifications. This practice will broaden your knowledge and further develop your decision-making abilities.

**Discussion
Case 2–1**
Cash versus
accrual
accounting;
adjusting entries;
Chapters 1 and 2
● LO2–5, LO2–9

You have recently been hired by Davis & Company, a small public accounting firm. One of the firm's partners, Alice Davis, has asked you to deal with a disgruntled client, Mr. Sean Pitt, owner of the city's largest hardware store. Mr. Pitt is applying to a local bank for a substantial loan to remodel his store. The bank requires accrual-based financial statements, but Mr. Pitt has always kept the company's records on a cash basis. He doesn't see the purpose of accrual-based statements. His most recent outburst went something like this: "After all, I collect cash from customers, pay my bills in cash, and I am going to pay the bank loan with cash. And, I already show my building and equipment as assets and depreciate them. I just don't understand the problem."

Required:

Draft a memo to Mr. Pitt providing an explanation of why the bank requests accrual-based financial statements for loan requests such as his. Include in the memo.

- An explanation of the difference between a cash basis and an accrual basis measure of performance.

- Why, in most cases, that accrual-basis net income provides a better measure of performance than net operating cash flow.

- The purpose of adjusting entries as they relate to the difference between cash and accrual accounting.

Judgment Case 2–2
Cash versus accrual accounting
● LO2–9

Refer to Case 2–1 above. Mr. Pitt has relented and agrees to provide you with the information necessary to convert his cash basis financial statements to accrual basis statements. He provides you with the following transaction information for the fiscal year ending December 31, 2021:

1. A new comprehensive insurance policy requires an annual payment of $12,000 for the upcoming year. Coverage began on September 1, 2021, at which time the first payment was made.

2. Mr. Pitt allows customers to pay using a credit card. At the end of the current year, various credit card companies owed Mr. Pitt $6,500. At the end of last year, customer credit card charges outstanding were $5,000.

3. Employees are paid once a month, on the 10th of the month following the work period. Cash disbursements to employees were $8,200 and $7,200 for January 10, 2022, and January 10, 2021, respectively.

4. Utility bills outstanding totaled $1,200 at the end of 2021 and $900 at the end of 2020.

5. A physical count of inventory is always taken at the end of the fiscal year. The merchandise on hand at the end of 2021 cost $35,000. At the end of 2020, inventory on hand cost $32,000.

6. At the end of 2020, Mr. Pitt did not have any bills outstanding to suppliers of merchandise. However, at the end of 2021, he owed suppliers $4,000.

Required:

1. Mr. Pitt's 2021 cash basis net income (after one adjustment for depreciation expense) is $26,000. Determine net income applying the accrual accounting model.

2. Explain the effect on Mr. Pitt's balance sheet of converting from cash to accrual. That is, would assets, liabilities, and owner's equity be higher or lower and by what amounts?

Communication Case 2–3
Adjusting entries
● LO2–5

"I don't understand," complained Chris, who responded to your bulletin board posting for tutoring in introductory accounting. The complaint was in response to your statements that recording adjusting entries is a critical step in the accounting processing cycle, and the two major classifications of adjusting entries are prepayments and accruals.

Required:
Respond to Chris.

1. When do prepayments occur? Accruals?

2. Describe the appropriate adjusting entry for prepaid expenses and for deferred revenues. What is the effect on net income, assets, liabilities, and shareholders' equity of not recording a required adjusting entry for prepayments?

3. Describe the required adjusting entry for accrued liabilities and for accrued receivables. What is the effect on net income, assets, liabilities, and shareholders' equity of not recording a required adjusting entry for accruals?

Data Analytics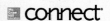

Data analytics is the process of examining data sets in order to draw conclusions about the information they contain. Data analytics is widely used in business to enable organizations to make better-informed business decisions. Increasingly, this is accomplished with the aid of specialized software such as Tableau. In each chapter of our textbook, you will have the opportunity to glimpse the power and efficacy of data analytics in the context of that chapter's topics, using Tableau as a tool.

To prepare for this case—and those in subsequent chapters—using Tableau, you will need to download Tableau to your computer. Tableau provides free instructor and student licenses as well as free videos and support for utilizing and learning the software. You will receive further information on setting up Tableau from your instructor. Once you are set up with Tableau, watch the first few training videos on the Tableau website. If you completed the first Data Analytics Case, you already have watched the three "Getting Started" videos. Now to prepare for this case you should view the "Ways to Filter," "Using the Filter Shelf," and "The Formatting Pane" videos listed under "Visual Analytics." Future cases will build off of your knowledge gained from these, and additional videos will be suggested. All short training videos can be found at www.tableau.com/learn/training#getting-started.

Data Analytics Case
Composition of the Balance Sheet
● LO2–7

In the Chapter 1 Data Analytics Case, you applied Tableau to examine a data set and create bar charts to compare ten-year trends in operating cash flows and net income for our two (hypothetical) publicly traded companies: Discount Goods and Big Store. In this case you continue in your role as an analyst conducting introductory research into the relative merits of investing in one or both of these companies, this time comparing the proportional composition of the assets, liabilities, and stockholders' equity of the two companies. You want to create pie charts to visualize the relative size of the components of the balance sheets for each of the two companies to garner some initial insights.

Required:

Total assets are equal to Total liabilities plus Total shareholders' equity. This equation is based on the fact that a company's assets come from these two sources: (1) amounts borrowed and (2) amounts provided by owners ([a] amounts *invested* by shareholders in the corporation, reported as paid-in capital and [b] amounts *earned* by the corporation on behalf of its shareholders, reported as retained earnings). The relative proportion of assets provided by liabilities can be an indication of the riskiness of an investment, making these relationships valuable when analyzing a company's financial position. Use Tableau to create pie charts depicting the relative size of the assets, liabilities, and stockholders' equity for each of the two companies in 2021. Based upon what you find, answer the following questions:

1. For Discount Goods, do liabilities or shareholders' equity provide the greater proportion of the company's total assets?
2. For Big Store, do liabilities or shareholders' equity provide the greater proportion of the company's total assets?
3. Which of the two companies has the highest ratio of current liabilities to total liabilities? What is the ratio for that company (rounded to nearest whole percentage point)?
4. Which of the two companies has the highest ratio of current assets to current liabilities? What is the ratio for that company (rounded to nearest whole percentage point)?

Resources:

You have available to you an extensive data set that includes detailed financial data for Discount Goods and Big Store and for 2012 - 2021. The data set is in the form of an Excel file available to download from Connect, or under Student Resources within the Library tab. There are four Excel files available. The one for use in this chapter is named "Discount_Goods_Big_StoreCase1.xlsx." Download this file and save it to the computer on which you will be using Tableau.

For this case, you will need to review the raw data in the Excel file for both companies before beginning. Review the questions above to determine which account classifications, like "Total current assets," to include in your pie charts. These will be the items you include in what's called "Account name." Notice that the two companies have somewhat different names for their accounts, but the major groups are the same.

After you view the training videos, follow these steps to create the charts you'll use for this case:

- Open Tableau and connect to the Excel spreadsheet you downloaded. Starting on the "Sheet 1" tab, at the bottom of the canvas to the right of the data source at the bottom of the screen, double click on "2021" under "Measures" to add it to the canvas.
- Click the pull-down menu arrow on "Store" under "Dimensions" and click "Show Filter." The filter box will appear on the right side. Un-click the "(All)" button and click only Discount Goods.
- Move "Account name" into the Filter shelf. In the Filter dialog box that opens, click all Discount Goods' account classifications you've identified as needed for the case. You can determine this information by checking the raw data as instructed above. Hint: You should have selected a total of 5 account classifications.
- Drag "Account name" to "Color" in the "Marks" card to add more colors to the chart. On the "Show me" tab in the upper right corner of the toolbar, select the pie chart.
- Enlarge the pie chart by holding down the shift-control-and-clicking the "B" key several times until your pie chart fills most of the screen (at least 25 times).
- Add "Labels" to the pie sections by clicking on "Label" in the "Marks" card and clicking the box "Show mark label."
- Format the label amounts to Times New Roman, bold, black, 12-point font by selecting the label, right-clicking, and clicking on "Format."
- Change the title of the sheet to be "Discount Goods 2021 Balance Sheet" by right-clicking and selecting "Edit title." Format the title to Times New Roman, bold, black and 15-point font.
- To save time completing the next page, right-click the "Sheet 1" tab at the bottom of the canvas and select "Duplicate."
- Click on the "Sheet 2" tab. You should now see a duplicate of the "Sheet 1" canvas. In the filter box on the right-hand side, click only the Big Store button.
- Change the title of the sheet to be "Big Store 2021 Balance Sheet" by right-clicking and selecting "Edit title." Format the title to Times New Roman, bold, black and 15-point font.
- Once complete, save the file as "*DA2_Your initials*.twbx."

Continuing Cases

Target Case

● LO2–4, LO2–8

Target Corporation prepares its financial statements according to U.S. GAAP. Target's financial statements and disclosure notes for the year ended February 3, 2018, are available in Connect. This material also is available under the Investor Relations link at the company's website (www.target.com).

Required:

1. Refer to Target's balance sheet for the years ended February 3, 2018, and January 28, 2017. Based on the amounts reported for accumulated depreciation, and assuming no depreciable assets were sold during the year, prepare an adjusting entry to record Target's depreciation for the year.

108   SECTION 1   The Role of Accounting as an Information System

2. Refer to Target's statement of cash flows for the year ended February 3, 2018. Assuming your answer to requirement 1 includes all depreciation expense recognized during the year, how much amortization expense was recognized during the year?

3. Note 13 provides information on Target's current assets. Assume all prepaid expenses are for prepaid insurance and that insurance expense comprises $50 million of the $14,248 million of selling, general, and administrative expenses reported in the income statement for the year ended February 3, 2018. How much cash did Target pay for insurance coverage during the year? Prepare the adjusting entry Target would make to record all insurance expense for the year. What would be the effect on the income statement and balance sheet if Target didn't record an adjusting entry for prepaid expenses?

Air France–KLM Case

● LO2–4

Air France-KLM (AF), a Franco-Dutch company, prepares its financial statements according to International Financial Reporting Standards. AF's financial statements and disclosure notes for the year ended December 31, 2017, are provided in Connect. This material also is available under the Finance link at the company's website (www.airfranceklm.com).

Required:

1. Refer to AF's balance sheet and compare it to the balance sheet presentation in Illustration 2–14. What differences do you see in the format of the two balance sheets?

2. What differences do you see in the terminology used in the two balance sheets?

CPA Exam Questions and Simulations

Sample CPA Exam questions from Roger CPA Review are available in Connect as support for the topics in this chapter. These multiple-choice questions and task-based aimulations include expert-written explanations and solutions, and provide a starting point for students to become familiar with the content and functionality of the actual CPA Exam.

CHAPTER

The Balance Sheet and Financial Disclosures

OVERVIEW ———●— Chapter 1 stressed the importance of the financial statements to investors and creditors, and Chapter 2 reviewed the preparation of those financial statements. In this chapter, we'll take a closer look at the balance sheet, along with accompanying disclosures. The balance sheet provides relevant information useful in helping investors and creditors not only to predict future cash flows, but also to make the related assessments of liquidity and long-term solvency. In Chapter 4 we'll continue our conversation about the financial statements with discussion of the income statement, statement of comprehensive income, and statement of cash flows.

LEARNING ———●— **After studying this chapter, you should be able to:**
OBJECTIVES

● **LO3–1**   Describe the purpose of the balance sheet and understand its usefulness and limitations. (*p. 112*)

● **LO3–2**   Identify and describe the various asset classifications. (*p. 114*)

● **LO3–3**   Identify and describe the various liability and shareholders' equity classifications. (*p. 118*)

● **LO3–4**   Explain the purpose of financial statement disclosures. (*p. 122*)

● **LO3–5**   Describe disclosures related to management's discussion and analysis, responsibilities, and compensation. (*p. 125*)

● **LO3–6**   Explain the purpose of an audit and describe the content of the audit report. (*p. 128*)

● **LO3–7**   Describe the techniques used by financial analysts to transform financial information into forms more useful for analysis. (*p. 130*)

● **LO3–8**   Identify and calculate the common liquidity and solvency ratios used to assess risk. (*p. 131*)

● **LO3–9**   Discuss the primary differences between U.S. GAAP and IFRS with respect to the balance sheet, financial disclosures, and segment reporting. (*pp. 120* and *139*)

©TY Lim/Shutterstock

FINANCIAL REPORTING CASE

What's It Worth?

"I can't believe it. Why don't you accountants prepare financial statements that are relevant?" Your friend Jerry is a finance major and is constantly badgering you about what he perceives to be a lack of relevance of financial statements prepared according to generally accepted accounting principles. "For example, take a look at this balance sheet for Nike that I just downloaded off the Internet. The equity (or book value) of the company according to the 2017 balance sheet was about $12.4 billion. But if you multiply the number of outstanding shares by the stock price per share at the same point in time, the company's market value was nearly $88 billion. I thought equity was supposed to represent the value of the company, but those two numbers aren't close." You decide to look at the company's balance sheet and try to set Jerry straight.

By the time you finish this chapter, you should be able to respond appropriately to the questions posed in this case. Compare your response to the solution provided at the end of the chapter.

QUESTIONS

1. Respond to Jerry's criticism that shareholders' equity does not represent the market value of the company. What information does the balance sheet provide? (*p. 113*)

2. The usefulness of the balance sheet is enhanced by classifying assets and liabilities according to common characteristics. What are the classifications used in the balance sheet and what elements do those categories include? (*p. 113*)

Most companies provide their financial statements and accompanying disclosures on their website in an "Investor Relations" link, but this information also can be found at the SEC's website (www.sec.gov) through its electronic filing system known as EDGAR (Electronic Data Gathering, Analysis, and Retrieval system). Companies are required to file their financial information in a timely manner using the EDGAR system. As stated by the SEC, "Its (EDGAR system's) primary purpose is to increase the efficiency and fairness of the securities market for the benefit of investors, corporations, and the economy by accelerating the receipt, acceptance, dissemination, and analysis of time-sensitive corporate information filed with the agency."

The first part of this chapter begins our discussion of the financial statements by providing an overview of the balance sheet. The balance sheet reports a company's assets, liabilities, and shareholders' equity. You can see an example of Nike's balance sheet on the next page.

In the second part of this chapter, we discuss additional disclosures that companies are required to provide beyond the basic financial statements. These disclosures are critical to understanding the financial statements and to evaluating a firm's performance and financial health.

In the third part of this chapter, we discuss how information in the financial statements can be used by decision makers to assess business risk (liquidity and long-term solvency).

The SEC's EDGAR system improves the efficiency with which company information is collected and disseminated.

Real World Financials

NIKE, INC.
Consolidated Balance Sheet
May 31, 2017
($ in millions)

Assets

Current assets:

Cash and equivalents	$3,808	
Short-term investments	2,371	
Accounts receivable (net)	3,677	
Inventories	5,055	
Prepaid expenses and other current assets	1,150	
Total current assets		$16,061
Property, plant and equipment (net)	3,989	
Identifiable intangible assets (net)	283	
Goodwill	139	
Deferred income taxes and other assets	2,787	
Total long-term assets		7,198
Total assets		$23,259

Liabilities and Shareholders' Equity

Current liabilities:

Current portion of long-term debt	$ 6	
Notes payable	325	
Accounts payable	2,048	
Accrued liabilities	3,011	
Income taxes payable	84	
Total current liabilities		$ 5,474
Long-term debt	3,471	
Deferred income taxes and other liabilities	1,907	
Total long-term liabilities		5,378
Total liabilities		$10,852
Shareholders' equity:		
Common stock	3	
Additional paid-in capital	8,638	
Retained earnings	3,979	
Accumulated other comprehensive loss	(213)	
Total shareholders' equity		12,407
Total liabilities and shareholders' equity		$23,259

PART A

• LO3–1

The Balance Sheet

The balance sheet, sometimes referred to as the **statement of financial position**, presents an organized list of assets, liabilities, and equity *at a point in time*. It is a freeze frame or snapshot of a company's financial position at the end of a particular day marking the end of an accounting period.

Usefulness

The balance sheet
provides information
useful for assessing future
cash flows, liquidity, and
long-term solvency.

The balance sheet provides a list of assets and liabilities that are classified (grouped) according to common characteristics. These classifications, which we explore in the next section, along with related disclosure notes, help the balance sheet to provide useful information about liquidity and long-term solvency. Liquidity most often refers to the ability of a company to convert its assets to cash to pay its *current* liabilities. Long-term solvency refers to an assessment of whether a company will be able to pay all its liabilities, which includes *long-term* liabilities as well. Other things being equal, the risk that a company will not be able to pay its debt increases as its liabilities, relative to equity, increases.

Solvency also provides information about *financial flexibility*—the ability of a company to alter cash flows in order to take advantage of unexpected investment opportunities and needs.

For example, the higher the percentage of a company's liabilities to its equity, the more difficult it typically will be to borrow additional funds either to take advantage of a promising investment opportunity or to meet obligations. In general, the less financial flexibility, the more risk there is that an enterprise will fail. In Part C of this chapter, we introduce some common ratios used to assess liquidity and long-term solvency.[1]

Limitations

Despite its usefulness, the balance sheet has limitations. One important limitation is that a company's book value, its reported assets minus liabilities as shown in the balance sheet, usually *will not directly measure the company's market value.* Market value represents the price at which something could be sold in a given market. In the case of a public corporation, market value is represented by the trading price of a share of the corporation's stock. We can get an idea of the corporation's overall market value by multiplying the share price times the number of shares outstanding.

The two primary reasons that a company's book value in the balance sheet does not equal its market value are:

1. Many assets, like land and buildings, are measured at their historical costs rather than amounts for which the assets could be sold (often referred to as the assets' fair values). For example, suppose a company owns land and the amount for which the land could be sold increases. The increase in the land's fair value is not reported in the balance sheet, so it has no effect on the company's book value. However, to the extent the increase in the land's fair value is known by investors, that increase will be reflected in the company's overall market value.

2. Many aspects of a company may represent valuable resources (such as trained employees, experienced management team, loyal customer relationships, and product knowledge). These items, however, are not recorded as assets in the balance sheet and therefore have zero book value. Investors understand the ability of these resources to generate future profits and therefore these resources will be reflected in a company's overall market value.

As an example of the second item, in 2017, Facebook spent nearly $8 billion on research and development to design new products and improve existing services. While these costs likely improve the company's ability to generate future profits (and therefore increase the market value of the company to shareholders), these items are not reported in the balance sheet as an asset. They typically are expensed in the year incurred. As a result of this and other items, Facebook's ratio of market value to book value at the end of 2017 was 7.2. In comparison, the average ratio of market value to book value for companies in the S&P 500 index was about 3.0.

Another limitation of the balance sheet is that many items in the balance sheet are heavily reliant on *estimates and judgments rather than determinable amounts.* For example, companies estimate (a) the amount of receivables they will be able to actually collect, (b) the amount of warranty costs they will eventually incur for products already sold, (c) the residual values and useful lives of their long-term assets, and (d) amounts used to calculate employee pension obligations. Each of these estimates affects amounts reported in the balance sheet.

In summary, even though the balance sheet *does not directly measure* the market value of the entity, it provides valuable information that can be used to *help judge* market value.

Classification of Elements

The usefulness of the balance sheet is enhanced when assets and liabilities are grouped according to common characteristics. *The broad distinction made in the balance sheet is the current versus long-term (noncurrent) classification of both assets and liabilities.* The remainder of Part A provides an overview of the balance sheet. We discuss each of the three primary elements of the balance sheet (assets, liabilities, and shareholders' equity) in the

FINANCIAL Reporting Case

Q1, p. 111

Assets minus liabilities, measured according to GAAP, is not likely to be representative of the market value of the entity.

FINANCIAL Reporting Case

Q2, p. 111

The key classification of assets and liabilities in the balance sheet is the current versus long-term distinction.

---

[1]Another way the balance sheet is useful is in combination with income statement items. We explore some of these relationships in Chapter 4.

order they are reported in the statement as well as the classifications typically made within the elements. The balance sheet elements were defined in Chapter 1 as follows:

Assets are probable future economic benefits obtained or controlled by a particular entity as a result of past transactions or events. Simply, these are the economic resources of a company.

Liabilities are probable future sacrifices of economic benefits arising from present obligations of a particular entity to transfer assets or provide services to other entities in the future as a result of past transactions or events. Simply, these are the obligations of a company.

Equity (or net assets), called **shareholders' equity** or **stockholders' equity** for a corporation, is the residual interest in the assets of an entity that remains after deducting liabilities. Stated another way, equity equals total assets minus total liabilities.

Illustration 3–1 shows the relationship among assets, liabilities, and shareholders' equity, often referred to as the accounting equation. Included in the illustration are the subclassifications of each element. We will discuss each of these subclassifications next.

Illustration 3–1

Classification of Elements within a Balance Sheet

Assets	=	**Liabilities**	+	**Shareholders' Equity**
1. Current assets		1. Current liabilities		1. Paid-in capital
2. Long-term assets		2. Long-term liabilities		2. Retained earnings

Assets

● LO3–2

Current assets include cash and all other assets expected to become cash or be consumed within one year from the balance sheet date (or *operating cycle,* if longer).

CURRENT ASSETS   Current assets include cash and other assets that are reasonably expected to be converted to cash or consumed within one year from the balance sheet date, or within the normal operating cycle of the business if that's longer than one year. The operating cycle for a typical merchandising or manufacturing company refers to the period of time from the initial outlay of cash for the purchase of inventory until the time the company collects cash from a customer from the sale of inventory.

For a merchandising company, the initial purchase of inventory often is for a finished good, although some preparation may be necessary to get the inventory ready for sale (such as packaging or distribution). *For a manufacturing company,* the initial outlay of cash often involves the purchase of raw materials, which are then converted into a finished product through the manufacturing process. The concept of an operating cycle is shown in Illustration 3–2.

In some businesses, such as shipbuilding or distilleries, the operating cycle extends far beyond one year. For example, if it takes two years to build an oil-carrying supertanker, then the shipbuilder will classify as current those assets that will be converted to cash or consumed within two years from the balance sheet date. But for most businesses, the operating cycle will be shorter than one year. In these situations, the one-year convention is used to classify both assets and liabilities. Where a company has no clearly defined operating cycle, the one-year convention is used.

Illustration 3–3 presents the current assets section of Nike's balance sheet for the years ended May 31, 2017, and May 31, 2016. In keeping with common practice, the individual current assets are listed in the order of their liquidity (the ability to convert the asset to cash).

Cash and Cash Equivalents.   The most liquid asset, cash, is listed first. Cash includes cash on hand and in banks that is available for use in the operations of the business and such items as bank drafts, cashier's checks, and money orders. Cash equivalents are defined as short-term investments that have a maturity date no longer than three months *from the date of purchase.* Examples include certain negotiable items such as

Illustration 3–2

Operating Cycle of a Typical Merchandising or Manufacturing Company

1. Use cash to acquire inventory

2. Prepare inventory for sale to customers

3. Deliver inventory to customer

4. Collect cash from customer

($ in millions)	May 31, 2017	May 31, 2016
Current assets:		
Cash and equivalents	$ 3,808	$ 3,138
Short-term investments	2,371	2,319
Accounts receivable (net)	3,677	3,241
Inventory	5,055	4,838
Prepaid expenses and other current assets	1,150	1,489
Total current assets	$16,061	$15,025

Source: Nike, Inc.

Illustration 3–3

Current Assets—Nike, Inc.

Real World Financials

commercial paper, money market funds, and U.S. treasury bills. These items are listed as cash equivalents because they are highly liquid investments that can be quickly converted into cash with little risk of loss. Nike's policy for classifying items as cash equivalents is stated in its disclosure note on summary of significant accounting policies, as shown in Illustration 3–4.

Cash and equivalents represent cash and short-term, highly liquid investments, including commercial paper, U.S. Treasury, U.S. Agency, money market funds, time deposits, and corporate debt securities with maturities of 90 days or less at the date of purchase.

Source: Nike, Inc.

Illustration 3–4

Disclosure of Cash Equivalents—Nike, Inc.

Real World Financials

Cash that is restricted for a special purpose and not available for current operations should not be included in the primary balance of cash and cash equivalents. These restrictions could include future plans to repay debt, purchase equipment, or make investments. Restricted cash is classified as a current asset if it is expected to be used within one year from the balance sheet date. Otherwise, restricted cash is classified as a long-term asset.

Short-Term Investments.   Investments not classified as cash equivalents that the company has the ability and intent to sell within one year (or operating cycle, if longer) are reported as short-term investments. These investments include items such as equity investments in the common stock of other corporations, as well as debt investments in commercial paper and U.S. Treasury securities. We discuss accounting for equity and debt investments in Chapter 12.

Accounts Receivable.   Accounts receivable result from the sale of goods or services on account (discussed in Chapter 7). Accounts receivable often are referred to as *trade receivables* because they arise in the course of a company's normal trade. *Nontrade receivables* result from loans or advances by the company to individuals and other entities. When receivables are supported by a formal agreement or note that specifies payment terms they are called notes receivable.

Accounts receivable usually are due in 30 to 60 days, depending on the terms offered to customers and are, therefore, classified as current assets. Any receivable, regardless of the source, not expected to be collected within one year (or operating cycle, if longer) is classified as a long-term investment. In addition, receivables are typically reported at the net amount expected to be collected. The net amount is calculated as total receivables less an allowance for the estimate of uncollectible accounts. Nike reported net accounts receivable of $3,677 million in the 2017 balance sheet. In a disclosure note, the company indicated that total accounts receivable were $3,704 million, indicating an allowance for uncollectible accounts of $27 million.

Inventory.   Inventory for a wholesale or retail company consists of finished goods for sale to customers. For example, you buy finished goods such as shoes and athletic wear from Nike, potato chips at Costco, school supplies at Staples, and a new shirt at Gap. However, the inventory of a manufacturer will include not only finished goods but also goods in the

Inventory consists of assets that a retail or wholesale company acquires for resale or goods that manufacturers produce for sale.

course of production (work in process) and goods to be consumed directly or indirectly in production (raw materials). Manufacturers typically report all three types of inventory either directly in the balance sheet or in a disclosure note. Illustration 3–5 demonstrates how Intel Corp., a semiconductor chip manufacturer, discloses its components of inventory.

Illustration 3–5

Inventory Disclosure—Intel Corp.

Real World Financials

($ in millions)	December 30, 2017	December 31, 2016
Raw materials	$1,098	$ 695
Work in process	3,893	3,190
Finished goods	1,992	1,668
Total inventory	$6,983	$5,553

Source: Intel Corp.

Inventory is reported as a current asset because it normally is sold within the operating cycle.

Prepaid Expenses. Recall from Chapter 2 that a prepaid expense arises when a company incurs a cost of acquiring an asset in one period that won't be expensed until a future period. Examples are supplies, prepaid rent, and prepaid insurance. These assets are not converted to cash, like receivables collected and inventory sold, but they instead are consumed in the future. Supplies are used, prepaid rent expires over the rental period, and prepaid insurance expires over the period of insurance coverage.

Whether a prepaid expense is current or noncurrent depends on the period in which the item is consumed. For example, if rent on an office building were prepaid for one year, then the prepayment is classified as a current asset. However, if rent were prepaid for a period extending beyond the coming year, that portion of the prepayment is classified as a long-term asset.[2] Nike includes prepaid expenses with other current assets. Other current assets could include assets such as nontrade receivables that, because their amounts are not material, do not warrant separate disclosure.

LONG-TERM ASSETS When assets are expected to be converted to cash or consumed in more than one year (or operating cycle, if longer), they are reported as *long-term* (or *noncurrent) assets*. Typical classifications of long-term assets are as follows:

1. Investments
2. Property, plant, and equipment
3. Intangible assets
4. Other long-term assets

Next, we'll discuss each of these categories of long-term assets.

Investments are assets not used directly in operations.

Investments. Most companies occasionally acquire assets that are not used directly in the operations of the business. These assets include investments in debt and equity securities of other corporations, land held for speculation, long-term receivables, and cash set aside for special purposes (such as for future plant expansion). These assets are classified as long-term because management does not intend to convert the assets into cash in the next year (or operating cycle, if longer).

Tangible, long-lived assets used in the operations of the business are classified as *property, plant, and equipment.*

Property, Plant, and Equipment. Virtually all companies own assets classified as property, plant, and equipment. The common characteristics these assets share are that they are *tangible, long-lived,* and *used in the operations of the business.* Property, plant, and equipment often are the primary revenue-generating assets of the business.

---

[2]Companies often include prepayments for benefits extending beyond one year in the other assets category. When amounts are not material, some companies simply report all prepayments as current assets.

Property, plant, and equipment include land, buildings, equipment, machinery, furniture, and vehicles, as well as natural resources, such as mineral mines, timber tracts, and oil wells. These various assets often are reported in the balance sheet by showing their original cost on one line and their accumulated depreciation (or depletion for natural resources) to date on the next line. The difference between original cost and accumulated depreciation is the net amount of property, plant, and equipment. Sometimes, companies combine the original cost and accumulated depreciation for all property, plant, and equipment and report a single net amount in the balance sheet. In this case, a separate disclosure note provides details of the original cost and accumulated depreciation for each major asset category included in property, plant, and equipment. Land is included as part of property, plant, and equipment, but it has an unlimited useful life and therefore is not depreciated.

Illustration 3–6 shows the long-term asset section of Nike's balance sheets, including its property, plant, and equipment, net of accumulated depreciation.

Illustration 3–6

Long-term Assets—Nike, Inc.

Real World Financials

($ in millions)	May 31, 2017	May 31, 2016
Long-term assets:		
Property, plant and equipment (net)	$3,989	$3,520
Identifiable intangible assets (net)	283	281
Goodwill	139	131
Deferred income taxes and other assets	2,787	2,422
Total long-term assets	$7,198	$6,354

Source: Nike, Inc.

Intangible Assets.　Some assets used in the operations of a business have no physical substance. These assets are appropriately called intangible assets. Many intangible assets grant an exclusive right to a company to provide a product or service. This right can be a valuable resource in generating future revenues. Patents, copyrights, franchises, and trademarks are examples.

Intangible assets generally represent exclusive rights that a company can use to generate future revenues.

Many intangible assets are reported in the balance sheet at their purchase price less accumulated *amortization*. The calculation is similar to how we report property, plant, and equipment at their purchase price less accumulated *depreciation*. Companies most often combine the purchase price and accumulated amortization to report a single net amount for intangible assets. A disclosure note is used to detail amounts for individual types of intangible assets. In 2017, Nike reported identifiable intangible assets, net of their amortization, of $283 million. These consist primarily of acquired trade names and trademarks.

Another common type of intangible asset, also reported by Nike, is *goodwill*. Goodwill isn't associated with any specific identifiable right, but instead arises when one company acquires another company. The amount reported for goodwill equals the acquisition price above the fair value of the identifiable net assets acquired. We'll discuss goodwill and other intangible assets in more detail in Chapter 10.

Not all intangible assets are purchased; some are developed internally. For example, instead of purchasing a patent granting the exclusive right to manufacture a certain drug, a pharmaceutical company may spend significant amounts in research and development to discover the drug and obtain a patent on its own. For internally developed intangibles, none of the research and development costs incurred in developing the intangible asset are included in reported cost. Instead, research and development costs are expensed as incurred. Pfizer, one of the world's largest pharmaceutical companies, typically spends $7 to $8 billion each year on researching and developing new medicines, vaccines, medical devices, and other health care products. These costs may help to generate future profits, but none of them were reported as an asset. Similarly, Nike spends large amounts on advertising and marketing to create brand recognition and help maintain its long-term competitiveness, but these costs are expensed in the period incurred (rather than reported as an intangible asset).

Other Long-Term Assets.　This category of long-term assets (reported by most companies) represents a catchall classification of long-term assets that were not reported separately in one of the other long-term classifications. This amount most often includes long-term prepaid expenses, called *deferred charges*. For instance, Nike includes promotional expenditures related to long-term endorsement contracts and long-term advertising in this category. Nike also includes deferred charges related to income taxes.

This category might also include any long-term investments that are not material in amount and that were not reported separately in the long-term investments category discussed earlier. In the disclosure notes to its financial statements, Nike revealed that it did have a small amount of long-term investments as well as long-term receivables that were combined with deferred charges and reported in this category (instead of being reported separately in a long-term investments category).

> **Asset classification is affected by management intent.**

A key to understanding which category an asset is reported is *management intent*. For example, in which category will land be reported? It depends on management intent. Management may intend to use land for long-term operating purposes (property, plant, and equipment), hold it for future resale (investment), or sell it in its ordinary course of business (inventory for a real estate company).

Liabilities

● LO3–3

Liabilities represent obligations to other entities. The information value of reporting these amounts is enhanced by classifying them as current liabilities and long-term liabilities. Illustration 3–7 shows the liability section of Nike's balance sheets.

Illustration 3–7

Liabilities—Nike, Inc.

Real World Financials

($ in millions)	May 31, 2017	May 31, 2016
Current liabilities:		
Current portion of long-term debt	$ 6	$ 44
Notes payable	325	1
Accounts payable	2,048	2,191
Accrued liabilities	3,011	3,037
Income taxes payable	84	85
Total current liabilities	5,474	5,358
Long-term debt	3,471	1,993
Deferred income taxes and other liabilities	1,907	1,770
Total liabilities	$10,852	$9,121

Source: Nike, Inc.

> **Current liabilities are expected to be satisfied within one year from the balance sheet date (or operating cycle, if longer).**

CURRENT LIABILITIES Current liabilities are those obligations that are expected to be satisfied through the use of current assets or the creation of other current liabilities. So, this classification includes all liabilities that are expected to be satisfied within one year from the balance sheet date (or within the operating cycle if that's longer than one year). As of May 31, 2017, Nike had current liabilities of $5,474 million that it planned to pay in the next 12 months.

The most common current liabilities are accounts payable, notes payable (short-term borrowings), deferred revenues, accrued liabilities, and the currently maturing portion of long-term debt.

Accounts payable are obligations to suppliers of merchandise or of services purchased on account, with payment usually due in 30 to 60 days.

Notes payable are written promises to pay cash at some future date (I.O.U.s). Unlike accounts payable, notes usually require the payment of explicit interest in addition to the original obligation amount.

Deferred revenues, sometimes called *unearned revenues,* represent cash received from a customer for goods or services to be provided in a future period. For example, a company records deferred revenue when it sells gift cards. Revenue is not recorded until those gift cards are redeemed by the customer for merchandise or expire without being used.

Accrued liabilities represent obligations created when expenses have been incurred but amounts owed will not be paid until a subsequent reporting period. For example, a company might owe salaries at the end of the fiscal year to be paid some time in the following year. In this case, the company would report *salaries payable* as an accrued liability in the current year's balance sheet (as well as the related salaries expense in the income statement). Other common examples of accrued liabilities include interest payable, taxes payable, utilities payable, and legal fees payable. In most financial statements, these items are reported in the balance sheet for a single amount as total accrued liabilities, and the individual account balances may be found listed in the disclosure notes.

Current maturities of long-term debt refer to the portion of long-term notes, loans, mortgages, and bonds payable that is payable within the next year (or operating cycle, if longer).[3] For example, a $1,000,000 note payable requiring $100,000 in principal payments to be made in each of the next 10 years is classified as a $100,000 current liability and a $900,000 long-term liability. Nike classifies the current portion of its long-term debt as a current liability.

An exception for the current liability classification is a liability that management intends to refinance on a long-term basis. For example, if management intends to refinance a six-month note payable by substituting a two-year note payable and has the ability to do so, then the six-month note payable would not be classified as current even though it's due within the coming year. This exception and issues related to current liabilities are discussed in more detail in Chapter 13.

LONG-TERM LIABILITIES   Long-term liabilities are obligations that are (a) due to be settled or (b) have a contractual right by the borrowing company to be settled in more than one year (or operating cycle, if longer) after the balance sheet date. Examples are long-term notes, bonds, pension obligations, and lease obligations.

> Noncurrent, or long-term liabilities, usually are those payable beyond one year from the balance sheet date (or operating cycle, if longer).

But simply classifying a liability as long-term doesn't provide complete information to external users. For instance, long-term could mean anything from 2 to 20, 30, or 40 years. Payment terms, interest rates, and other details needed to assess the impact of these obligations on future cash flows and long-term solvency are reported in a disclosure note. Nike reports long-term liabilities related to corporate bonds and promissory notes.

Shareholders' Equity

Owners' equity is simply total assets minus total liabilities. For that reason, it's sometimes referred to as the *net assets* or *book value* of a company. Because owners of a corporation are its shareholders, owners' equity for a corporation typically is referred to as *shareholders' equity* or *stockholders' equity*. Here's a simple way to think of equity. If someone buys a house for $200,000 by making an initial $50,000 payment and borrowing the remaining $150,000, then the house's owner has an asset of $200,000, a liability of $150,000, and equity of $50,000.

Shareholders' equity for a corporation arises primarily from

1. Paid-in capital.
2. Retained earnings.

Paid-in capital is the amount that shareholders have invested in the company. It most often arises when the company issues stock. As shown in Illustration 3–8, the shareholders' equity section of Nike's balance sheets reports the full amount of paid-in capital in two accounts—common stock and additional paid-in capital. Information about the number of shares the company has authorized and how many shares have been issued and are outstanding also must be disclosed either directly in the balance sheet or in a note.

($ in millions)	May 31, 2017	May 31, 2016
Shareholders' equity:		
Common stock (1,643 and 1,682 shares outstanding)	$ 3	$ 3
Additional paid-in capital	8,638	7,786
Retained earnings	3,979	4,151
Accumulated other comprehensive (loss) income	(213)	318
Total shareholders' equity	$12,407	$12,258
Source: Nike, Inc.		

Illustration 3–8

Shareholders' Equity—Nike, Inc.

Real World Financials

---

[3]Payment can be with current assets or the creation of other current liabilities.

Retained earnings represents the accumulated net income reported by a company since its inception minus all dividends distributed to shareholders. In other words, it's the accumulated lifetime profits a company has earned for its shareholders but has not yet distributed to those shareholders. The fact that a company does not distribute all of its profits each year as dividends is not necessarily a bad thing from the shareholders' perspective. Instead of paying additional cash dividends, Nike's management can put those undistributed profits to productive use, such as buying additional inventory or equipment or paying liabilities as they come due. Nike has been quite profitable over its lifetime (since 1964) and has distributed some of those profits as dividends to investors and retained the remaining portion of $3,979 million (that's almost $4 billion). Some other companies have not been as profitable. Companies that report net losses could end up with a negative balance in the retained earnings account. When this occurs, the retained earnings account often is referred to as the *accumulated deficit* account.

Nike also reports a *third component of stockholders' equity*—**accumulated other comprehensive income (AOCI)**. Other comprehensive income refers to changes in stockholders' equity other than transactions with owners and other than transactions that affect net income. We accumulate items of other comprehensive income in the *accumulated other comprehensive (loss) income* account, just like we accumulate each year's net income (that hasn't been distributed as dividends) in the *retained earnings* account. The AOCI account is discussed in detail in Chapter 4.

While accumulated other comprehensive income typically is not a large portion of total shareholders' equity, companies are required to report this amount separately. We will discuss specific examples of items included in other comprehensive income in Chapters 4, 12, and 18.

We also will discuss other transactions affecting equity, such as a company's purchase of its own stock that is not retired (*treasury stock*) in Chapter 18. Purchased shares are essentially the same as shares that never were issued at all. A company may decide to resell those shares in the future, but until then, they are reported as negative (or contra) shareholders' equity. Nike does not report any treasury stock but many companies do.

International Financial Reporting Standards

● LO3–9

Balance Sheet Presentation. There are more similarities than differences in balance sheets prepared according to U.S. GAAP and those prepared applying IFRS. Some of the differences are

- International standards specify a minimum list of items to be presented in the balance sheet. U.S. GAAP has no minimum requirements.
- *IAS No. 1, revised,*[4] changed the title of the balance sheet to *statement of financial position,* although companies are not required to use that title. Some U.S. companies use the statement of financial position title as well.
- Under U.S. GAAP, we present current assets and liabilities before noncurrent assets and liabilities. IAS No. 1 doesn't prescribe the format of the balance sheet, but balance sheets prepared using IFRS often report noncurrent items first. A recent survey of large companies that prepare their financial statements according to IFRS reports that 73% of the surveyed companies list noncurrent items first.[5] For example, H&M, a Swedish-based clothing company, reported assets, liabilities, and shareholders' equity in its balance sheet in the following order:

	(SEK in millions)
Noncurrrent assets (including property, plant, and equipment)	47,916
Current assets	50,663
Total assets	98,579
Shareholders' equity	61,236
Long-term liabilities	5,638
Current liabilities	31,705
Total liabilities and equity	98,579

---

[4]"Financial Statement Presentation," *International Accounting Standard No. 1* (IASCF), as amended effective January 1, 2018.
[5]*IFRS Accounting Trends and Techniques—2011* (New York, AICPA, 2011), p.133.

Concept Review Exercise

The following is a post-closing trial balance for the Sepia Paint Corporation at December 31, 2021, the end of the company's fiscal year:

BALANCE SHEET CLASSIFICATION

Account Title	Debits	Credits
Cash	$ 80,000	
Accounts receivable	200,000	
Allowance for uncollectible accounts		$ 20,000
Inventory	300,000	
Prepaid expenses	30,000	
Notes receivable (due in one month)	60,000	
Investment in equity securities	50,000	
Land	120,000	
Buildings	550,000	
Machinery	500,000	
Accumulated depreciation—buildings		200,000
Accumulated depreciation—machinery		250,000
Patent (net of amortization)	50,000	
Accounts payable		170,000
Salaries payable		40,000
Interest payable		10,000
Notes payable		100,000
Bonds payable (due in 10 years)		500,000
Common stock (no par)		400,000
Retained earnings		250,000
Totals	$1,940,000	$1,940,000

The company intends to hold the $50,000 investment in equity securities of other corporations for at least three years. The $100,000 note payable is an installment loan. $10,000 of the principal, plus interest, is due on each July 1 for the next 10 years. At the end of the year, 100,000 shares of common stock were issued and outstanding. The company has 500,000 shares of common stock authorized.

Required:
Prepare a classified balance sheet for the Sepia Paint Corporation at December 31, 2021.

Solution:

SEPIA PAINT CORPORATION
Balance Sheet
At December 31, 2021
Assets

Current assets:		
Cash		$ 80,000
Accounts receivable	$ 200,000	
Less: Allowance for uncollectible accounts	(20,000)	180,000
Notes receivable		60,000
Inventory		300,000
Prepaid expenses		30,000
Total current assets		650,000
Investments:		
Investment in equity securities		50,000
Property, plant, and equipment:		
Land	120,000	
Buildings	550,000	
Machinery	500,000	
	1,170,000	
Less: Accumulated depreciation—buildings	(200,000)	
Less: Accumulated depreciation—machinery	(250,000)	
Net property, plant, and equipment		720,000
Intangible assets:		
Patent (net)		50,000
Total assets		$1,470,000

(continued)

(concluded)

Liabilities and Shareholders' Equity

Current liabilities:		
Accounts payable		$ 170,000
Salaries payable		40,000
Interest payable		10,000
Current maturities of long-term debt		10,000
Total current liabilities		230,000
Long-term liabilities:		
Notes payable	$ 90,000	
Bonds payable	500,000	
Total long-term liabilities		590,000
Total liabilities		820,000
Shareholders' equity:		
Common stock (no par, 500,000 shares authorized,		
100,000 shares issued and outstanding)	400,000	
Retained earnings	250,000	
Total shareholders' equity		650,000
Total liabilities and shareholders' equity		$1,470,000

The usefulness of the balance sheet, as well as the other financial statements, is significantly enhanced by financial statement disclosures. We now turn our attention to these disclosures.

PART B

Annual Report Disclosures

At the end of each fiscal year, companies with public securities are required to provide shareholders with an *annual report*. The annual report includes financial statements such as the balance sheet. Financial statements, though, are only part of the information provided in the annual report. Critical to understanding the financial statements and to evaluating a company's performance and financial health are additional disclosures included as part of the financial statements and also as part of the annual reporting requirements to the SEC.

The amount of information provided by annual report disclosures can be significant. For example, Nike's 2017 annual report filed with the SEC (known as the Form 10-K) included five pages of financial statements followed by 19 pages of related disclosure notes. There were another 50 pages of disclosures related to business conditions, risk factors, legal proceedings, the company's stock performance, management's discussion and analysis, and internal control procedures. We will discuss some of the annual report disclosures in the next section.

Disclosure Notes

● LO3–4

The full-disclosure principle requires that financial statements provide all material relevant information concerning the reporting entity.

Some financial statement disclosures are provided by including additional information, often parenthetically, on the face of the statement. Common examples of disclosures included on the face of the balance sheet are the allowance for uncollectible accounts and information about common stock. Other disclosures include supporting discussion, calculations, and schedules in notes following the financial statements. These notes are the most common means of providing additional disclosure. For instance, the fair values of financial instruments and "off-balance-sheet" risk associated with financial instruments are disclosed in notes. Information providing details of many financial statement items is provided using disclosure notes. Some examples include

- Pension plans.
- Leases.
- Long-term debt.
- Investments.

- Income taxes.
- Property, plant, and equipment.
- Employee benefit plans.

Disclosure notes must include certain specific notes such as a summary of significant accounting policies, descriptions of subsequent events, and related third-party transactions, but many notes are fashioned to suit the disclosure needs of the particular reporting enterprise. Actually, any explanation that contributes to investors' and creditors' understanding of the results of operations, financial position, and cash flows of the company should be included. Let's take a look at just a few disclosure notes.

Summary of Significant Accounting Policies

There are many areas where management chooses from among equally acceptable alternative accounting methods. For example, management chooses whether to use accelerated or straight-line depreciation, whether to use FIFO, LIFO, or average cost to measure inventories, and whether to measure certain financial investments at fair value or cost. The company also defines which securities it considers to be cash equivalents and its policies regarding the timing of recognizing revenues and the estimated useful lives of its depreciable assets. Typically, the first disclosure note consists of a summary of significant accounting policies that discloses the choices the company makes.[6] Illustration 3–9 shows a portion of a typical summary note from a recent annual report of the **Starbucks Corporation**.

The summary of significant accounting policies conveys valuable information about the company's choices from among various alternative accounting methods.

Illustration 3–9   Summary of Significant Accounting Policies—Starbucks Corporation   Real World Financials

Note 1: Summary of Accounting Policies (in part)

Principles of Consolidation
The consolidated financial statements reflect the financial position and operating results of Starbucks, including wholly owned subsidiaries and investees that we control.

Cash and Cash Equivalents
We consider all highly liquid instruments with a maturity of three months or less at the time of purchase to be cash equivalents.

Inventories
Inventories are stated at the lower of cost (primarily moving average cost) or market. We record inventory reserves for obsolete and slow-moving inventory and for estimated shrinkage between physical inventory counts.

Property, Plant, and Equipment
Property, plant, and equipment are carried at cost less accumulated depreciation. Cost includes all direct costs

necessary to acquire and prepare assets for use, including internal labor and overhead in some cases. Depreciation of property, plant, and equipment, which includes assets under capital leases, is provided on the straight-line method over estimated useful lives, generally ranging from 2 to 15 years for equipment and 30 to 40 years for buildings. Leasehold improvements are amortized over the shorter of their estimated useful lives or the related lease life, generally 10 years.

Revenue Recognition
Consolidated revenues are presented net of intercompany eliminations for wholly-owned subsidiaries and investees controlled by us and for product sales to and royalty and other fees from licensees accounted for under the equity method. Additionally, consolidated revenues are recognized net of any discounts, returns, allowances, and sales incentives, including coupon redemptions and rebates.

Source: Starbucks

Studying this note is an essential step in analyzing financial statements. Obviously, knowing which methods were used to derive certain accounting numbers is critical to assessing the adequacy of those amounts.

Subsequent Events

When an event that has a material effect on the company's financial position occurs after the fiscal year-end but before the financial statements are issued or "available to be issued," the

---

[6]FASB ASC 235–10–50: Notes to Financial Statements—Overall—Disclosure (previously "Disclosure of Accounting Policies," *Accounting Principles Board Opinion No. 22* (New York: AICPA, 1972)).

124 SECTION 1 The Role of Accounting as an Information System

A *subsequent event* is a significant development that occurs after a company's fiscal year-end but before the financial statements are issued or available to be issued.

event is described in a subsequent event disclosure note.[7] Examples include the issuance of debt or equity securities, a business combination or the sale of a business, the sale of assets, an event that sheds light on the outcome of a loss contingency, or any other event having a material effect on operations. Illustration 3–10 illustrates an event that Target Corporation disclosed in its annual report for the year ending January 31, 2015, but before the release of those financial statements. We cover subsequent events in more depth in Chapter 13.

Illustration 3–10

Subsequent Event—Target Corp.

Real World Financials

---

29. Subsequent Events

In March 2015, we announced a headquarters workforce reduction. As a result, we expect to record approximately $100 million of severance and other benefits-related charges within SG&A in the first quarter of 2015, the vast majority of which are expected to require cash expenditures.

Source: Target Corp.

Noteworthy Events and Transactions

Some transactions and events occur only occasionally but, when they do occur, they are potentially important to evaluating a company's financial statements. In this category are related-party transactions, errors and fraud, and illegal acts. The most frequent of these is related-party transactions.

The economic substance of *related-party* transactions should be disclosed, including dollar amounts involved.

Sometimes a company will engage in transactions with owners, management, families of owners or management, affiliated companies, and other parties that can significantly influence or be influenced by the company. The potential problem with related-party transactions is that their economic substance may differ from their legal form. For instance, borrowing or lending money at an interest rate that differs significantly from the market interest rate is an example of a transaction that could result from a related-party involvement. As a result of the potential for misrepresentation, financial statement users are particularly interested in more details about these transactions.

When related-party transactions occur, companies must disclose the nature of the relationship, provide a description of the transactions, and report the dollar amounts of transactions and any amounts due from or to related parties.[8] Illustration 3–11 shows a disclosure

Illustration 3–11

Related-Party Transactions Disclosure—Champions Oncology, Inc.

Real World Financials

Note 4. Related-Party Transactions

Related-party transactions include transactions between the Company and its shareholders, management, or affiliates. The following transactions were in the normal course of operations and were measured and recorded at the exchange amount, which is the amount of consideration established and agreed to by the parties.

Consulting Services

For both years ended April 30, 2017 and 2016, the Company paid a member of its Board of Directors $72,000 for consulting services unrelated to his duties as board member. During the years ended April 30, 2017 and 2016, the Company paid a board member's company $0 and $8,800, respectively, for consulting services unrelated to his duties as a board member. During the year ended April 30, 2017, the Company paid a board member $48,214 and granted 45,000 options that vest annually over a three-year period and have a fair value of $94,192 for consulting services unrelated to his duties as a board member. All of the amounts paid to these related parties have been recognized in expense in the period the services were performed.

Source: Champions Oncology, Inc.

---

[7]Financial statements are viewed as issued if they have been widely distributed to financial statement users in a format consistent with GAAP. Some entities (for example, private companies) don't widely distribute their financial statements to users. For those entities, the key date for subsequent events is not the date of issuance but rather the date upon which the financial statements are "available to be issued," which occurs when the financial statements are complete, in a format consistent with GAAP, and have obtained the necessary approvals for issuance. Companies must disclose the date through which subsequent events have been evaluated. FASB ASC 855: Subsequent Events (previously "Subsequent Events," *Statement of Financial Accounting Standards No. 165* (Stamford, Conn.: FASB, 2009)).
[8]FASB ASC 850–10–50: Related Party Disclosures—Overall—Disclosure (previously "Related Party Disclosures," *Statement of Financial Accounting Standards No. 57* (Stamford, Conn.: FASB, 1982)).

note from a recent annual report of Champions Oncology, Inc. The note describes payments for consulting services to a member of its Board of Directors.

Less frequent events are errors and fraud. The distinction between these two terms is that *errors are unintentional* while *fraud is intentional* misappropriation of assets or incorrect financial reporting.[9] Errors and fraud may require disclosure (e.g., of assets lost through either errors or fraud). Obviously, the existence of fraud involving management might cause a user to approach financial analysis from an entirely different and more cautious viewpoint.

Closely related to fraud are illegal acts such as bribes, kickbacks, illegal contributions to political candidates, and other violations of the law. Accounting for illegal practices has been influenced by the Foreign Corrupt Practices Act passed by Congress in 1977. The Act is intended to discourage illegal business practices through tighter controls and also encourage better disclosure of those practices when encountered. The nature of such disclosures should be influenced by the materiality of the impact of illegal acts on amounts disclosed in the financial statements.[10] However, the SEC issued guidance expressing its view that exclusive reliance on quantitative benchmarks to assess materiality in preparing financial statements is inappropriate.[11] A number of other factors, including whether the item in question involves an unlawful transaction, should also be considered when determining materiality.

As you might expect, any disclosures of related-party transactions, fraud, and illegal acts can be quite sensitive. Although auditors must be considerate of the privacy of the parties involved, that consideration cannot be subordinate to users' needs for full disclosure.

We've discussed only a few of the disclosure notes most frequently included as an integral part of the financial statements. Other common disclosures include details concerning earnings per share calculations, income taxes, property and equipment, contingencies, long-term debt, leases, pensions, stock compensation, changes in accounting methods, fair values of financial instruments, and exposure to market risk and credit risk. We discuss and illustrate these in later chapters in the context of related financial statement elements.

> Disclosure notes for some financial statement elements are required. Others are provided when required by specific situations in the interest of full disclosure.

Management's Discussion and Analysis

> ● LO3–5

In addition to the financial statements and accompanying disclosure notes, each annual report of a public company requires a fairly lengthy discussion and analysis provided by the company's management. In this section, which precedes the financial statements and the auditor's report, management provides its views on significant events, trends, and uncertainties pertaining to the company's (a) operations, (b) liquidity, and (c) capital resources. Although the management's discussion and analysis (MD&A) section may embody management's biased perspective, it can offer an informed insight that might not be available elsewhere. As an example, Illustration 3–12 contains a portion of GameStop Corporation's MD&A regarding liquidity and capital resources that is in its annual report.

> Management's discussion and analysis provides a biased but informed perspective of a company's (a) operations, (b) liquidity, and (c) capital resources.

Management's Responsibilities

Management prepares and is responsible for the financial statements and other information in the annual report. To enhance the awareness of the users of financial statements concerning the relative roles of management and the auditor, annual reports of public companies include a management's responsibilities section that asserts the responsibility of management for the information contained in the annual report as well as an assessment of the company's internal control procedures.

> Management acknowledges responsibility and certifies accuracy of financial statements.

[9]"Consideration of Fraud in a Financial Statement Audit," *AICPA Professional Standards AU 240* (New York: AICPA, 2012).
[10]"Consideration of Laws and Regulations in an Audit of Financial Statements," *AICPA Professional Standards AU 250* (New York: AICPA, 2012).
[11]FASB ASC 250–10–S99–1, SAB Topic 1.M: Assessing Materiality (originally "Materiality," *Staff Accounting Bulletin No. 99* (Washington, D.C.: SEC, August 1999)).

Illustration 3–12

Management's Discussion and Analysis—GameStop Corp.

Real World Financials

Management's Discussion and Analysis of Financial Condition and Results of Operations
(In part: Liquidity and Capital Resources)

Overview

Based on our current operating plans, we believe that available cash balances, cash generated from our operating activities and funds available under our $400.0 million asset-based revolving credit facility (the "Revolver") together will provide sufficient liquidity to fund our operations, store openings and remodeling activities and corporate capital allocation programs, including acquisitions, share repurchases and the payment of dividends declared by the Board of Directors, for at least the next 12 months.

Cash Flow

During fiscal 2016, cash provided by operations was $537.1 million, compared to cash provided by operations of $656.8 million in fiscal 2015. The decrease in cash provided by operations of $119.7 million from fiscal 2015 to fiscal 2016 was primarily due to the decrease in net income combined with a decrease in cash provided by changes in operating assets and liabilities of $99.6 million, due primarily to the timing of payments for income taxes and accounts payable.

Acquisitions and Capital Expenditures

We opened or acquired 583 Technology Brands stores and opened 73 Video Game Brands stores in fiscal 2016. We expect to open approximately 35 stand-alone collectibles stores and approximately 65 stores in our Technology Brands segment in fiscal 2017.

In fiscal 2016, in connection with the continued expansion of our Technology Brands segment, Spring Mobile completed the acquisition of 507 AT&T authorized retailer stores for an aggregate of $440.3 million in cash (net of cash acquired), which includes working capital adjustments, and future contingent consideration, which we estimate will range from $40.0 million to $50.0 million. The majority of the store acquisitions were funded by our 2021 Senior Notes. The contingent consideration will be paid in two installments. The first installment of $20 million is contingent on the relocation of certain stores and is due the latter of August 2017 or when relocations are completed. The second installment, which we expect to range from $20.0 million to $30.0 million, is contingent on sales performance of certain stores and is due in March 2018.

Source: GameStop Corp.

Illustration 3–13 contains Management's Report on Internal Control over Financial Reporting for Nike, included with the company's financial statements for the year ended May 31, 2017. Recall from our discussion of financial reporting reform in Chapter 1, that the *Sarbanes-Oxley Act of 2002* requires corporate executives to personally certify the financial statements. Submission of false statements carries a penalty of up to 20 years in jail. Mark G. Parker, Nike's president and chief executive officer, and Donald W. Blair, the chief financial officer, signed the required certifications.

Compensation of Directors and Top Executives

The compensation large U.S. corporations pay their top executives is an issue of considerable public debate and controversy. Shareholders, employees, politicians, and the public in general sometimes question the huge pay packages received by company officials at the same time that more and more rank-and-file employees are being laid off as a result of company cutbacks. Contributing to the debate is the realization that the compensation gap between executives and lower-level employees is much wider in the United States than in most other industrialized countries.

A substantial portion of executive pay often is in the form of stock options or restricted stock awards. Executive stock options give their holders the right to buy the company's

Management's Responsibility for Financial Statements (in part)

Management of NIKE, Inc. is responsible for the information and representations contained in this report. The financial statements have been prepared in conformity with accounting principles generally accepted in the United States of America ("U.S. GAAP") and include certain amounts based on our best estimates and judgments. Other financial information in this report is consistent with these financial statements.

The Audit Committee is responsible for the appointment of the independent registered public accounting firm and reviews, with the independent registered public accounting firm, management and the internal audit staff, the scope and the results of the annual audit, the effectiveness of the accounting control system and other matters relating to the financial affairs of NIKE as the Audit Committee deems appropriate. The independent registered public accounting firm and the internal auditors have full access to the Audit Committee, with and without the presence of management, to discuss any appropriate matters.

Management's Report on Internal Control over Financial Reporting (in part)

Management is responsible for establishing and maintaining adequate internal control over financial reporting, as such term is defined in Rule 13(a)-15(f) and Rule 15(d)-15(f) of the Securities Exchange Act of 1934, as amended. Internal control over financial reporting is a process designed to provide reasonable assurance regarding the reliability of financial reporting and the preparation of the financial statements for external purposes in accordance with generally accepted accounting principles in the United States of America.

While "reasonable assurance" is a high level of assurance, it does not mean absolute assurance. Because of its inherent limitations, internal control over financial reporting may not prevent or detect every misstatement and instance of fraud. Controls are susceptible to manipulation, especially in instances of fraud caused by the collusion of two or more people, including our senior management.

Under the supervision and with the participation of our Chief Executive Officer and Chief Financial Officer, our management conducted an evaluation of the effectiveness of our internal control over financial reporting based upon the framework in Internal Control — Integrated Framework (2013) issued by the Committee of Sponsoring Organizations of the Treadway Commission (COSO). Based on the results of our evaluation, our management concluded that our internal control over financial reporting was effective as of May 31, 2017.

Mark G. Parker   Donald W. Blair
President & Chief Executive Officer   Chief Financial Officer

Source: Nike, Inc.

Illustration 3–13

Management's Responsibilities and Certification—Nike, Inc.

Real World Financials

stock at a set price, regardless of how high the stock price rises. Restricted stock is a unit of stock given to an employee, but that unit of stock is not fully transferable until certain conditions are met (such as length of employment or attainment of performance goals). In recent years, restricted stock as a form of compensation has become more popular than stock options. Both forms of stock compensation are discussed in depth in Chapter 19.

To help shareholders and others sort out the content of executive pay packages and better understand the commitments of the company in this regard, SEC requirements provide for disclosures on compensation to directors and executives. A proxy statement is provided each year and includes compensation information for directors and top executives. The statement also invites shareholders to the annual meeting to elect board members and to vote on issues before the shareholders or to vote by proxy. Illustration 3–14 shows a portion of Best Buy's summary compensation table included in a recent proxy statement.

The proxy statement contains disclosures on compensation to directors and executives.

Illustration 3–14   Summary Compensation Table—Best Buy Co., Inc.   Real World Financials

Summary Compensation Table (in part)

Name and Principal Position	Salary	Stock Awards	Option Awards	Short-Term Incentive Plan Payout	All Other Compensation	Total
Hubert July Chairman and Chief Executive Officer	$1,175,000	$7,689,879	$1,800,076	$2,878,750	$494,275	$14,037,980
Corie S. Barry Chief Financial Officer	713,462	1,689,495		1,184,167	14,893	3,602,017
Shari L. Ballard President, Multi-Channel Retail and Operations	800,000	1,930,865		1,470,000	62,737	4,263,602
R. Michael Mohan Chief Merchandising and Marketing Officer	833,654	2,895,073		1,531,251	55,284	5,315,262
Keith Nelsen General Counsel and Secretary	650,000	1,592,960		796,250	68,761	3,107,971

Source: Best Buy Co., Inc.

Auditor's Report

● LO3–6

Auditors examine financial statements and the internal control procedures designed to support the content of those statements. Their role is to attest to the fairness of the financial statements based on that examination. The auditor's attest function for public business entities results in an opinion stated in the auditor's report.

There are four basic types of auditor's reports, as follows:

1. Unqualified
2. Unqualified with an explanatory or emphasis paragraph
3. Qualified
4. Adverse or disclaimer

An auditor issues an *unqualified* (or "clean") opinion when the auditor has undertaken professional care to ensure that the financial statements are presented in conformity with generally accepted accounting principles (GAAP). Professional care would include sufficient planning of the audit, understanding the company's internal control procedures, and gathering evidence to attest to the accuracy of the amounts reported in the financial statements.

The unqualified auditor's report prepared by Ernst & Young (EY) for the financial statements of Facebook is shown in Illustration 3–15.

In most cases, including the report for Facebook, the auditors will be satisfied that the financial statements "present fairly" the financial position, results of operations, and cash flows and are "in conformity with U.S. generally accepted accounting principles." These situations prompt an unqualified opinion. Notice that the report also references the auditor's opinion on the effectiveness of the company's internal control over financial reporting.[12]

---

[12]The auditors' reports of public companies must be in compliance with the specifications of the PCAOB as specified in AS 2201: An Audit of Internal Control over Financial Reporting That Is Integrated with An Audit of Financial Statements.

Report of Independent Registered Public Accounting Firm (in part)

To the Stockholders and Board of Directors of Facebook, Inc.

Opinion on the Financial Statements

We have audited the accompanying consolidated balance sheets of Facebook, Inc. (the Company) as of December 31, 2017 and 2016, and the related consolidated statements of income, comprehensive income, stockholders' equity and cash flows for each of the three years in the period ended December 31, 2017, and the related notes (collectively referred to as the "financial statements"). In our opinion, the financial statements present fairly, in all material respects, the consolidated financial position of the Company at December 31, 2017 and 2016, and the consolidated results of its operations and its cash flows for each of the three years in the period ended December 31, 2017, in conformity with U.S. generally accepted accounting principles.

We also have audited, in accordance with the standards of the Public Company Accounting Oversight Board (United States) (PCAOB), the Company's internal control over financial reporting as of December 31, 2017, based on criteria established in Internal Control—Integrated Framework issued by the Committee of Sponsoring Organizations of the Treadway Commission (2013 framework) and our report dated February 1, 2018 expressed an unqualified opinion thereon.

Basis for Opinion

These financial statements are the responsibility of the Company's management. Our responsibility is to express an opinion on the Company's financial statements based on our audits. We are a public accounting firm registered with the PCAOB and are required to be independent with respect to the Company in accordance with the U.S. federal securities laws and the applicable rules and regulations of the Securities and Exchange Commission and the PCAOB.

We conducted our audits in accordance with the standards of the PCAOB. Those standards require that we plan and perform the audit to obtain reasonable assurance about whether the financial statements are free of material misstatement, whether due to error or fraud. Our audits included performing procedures to assess the risks of material misstatement of the financial statements, whether due to error or fraud, and performing procedures that respond to those risks. Such procedures included examining, on a test basis, evidence regarding the amounts and disclosures in the financial statements. Our audits also included evaluating the accounting principles used and significant estimates made by management, as well as evaluating the overall presentation of the financial statements. We believe that our audits provide a reasonable basis for our opinion.

/s/ Ernst & Young LLP

We have served as the Company's auditor since 2007.
San Francisco, California
February 1, 2018

Source: Facebook

Illustration 3–15

Auditor's Report—
Facebook, Inc.

Real World Financials

Sometimes circumstances cause the auditor to issue an opinion that is *unqualified with an explanatory paragraph.* In these circumstances, the auditor believes the financial statements are in conformity with GAAP (unqualified), but the auditor feels that other important information needs to be emphasized to financial statement users. Most notably, these situations include the following:

- *Lack of consistency* due to a change in accounting principle such that comparability is affected even though the auditor concurs with the desirability of the change.
- *Going concern* when the auditor determines there is significant doubt as to whether the company will be able to pay its debts as they come due. Indicators of a going concern include significant operating losses, loss of a major customer, or legal proceedings that might jeopardize the company's ability to continue operations.[13]
- *Material misstatement* in previously issued financial statements has been corrected.

---

[13]"The Auditor's Consideration of an Entity's Ability to Continue as a Going Concern (Redrafted)," *Statement on Auditing Standards No. 126, AICPA Professional Standards AU 570* (New York: AICPA, 2012). Management is also required to assess the company's ability to continue as a going concern and provide certain disclosures when substantial doubt exists (ASC 205-40).

An audit opinion may also include a paragraph on *emphasis of a matter*. This discussion would include items such as significant transactions with related parties, important events subsequent to the balance sheet date, or uncertainty relating to the future outcome of significant litigation or regulatory actions.

An example of a going concern paragraph in the 2016 auditor's report of Timberline Resources is shown in Illustration 3–16.

Illustration 3–16

Going Concern Paragraph—Timberline Resources Corp.

Real World Financials

> The accompanying consolidated financial statements have been prepared assuming that the Company will continue as a going concern. As discussed in Note 2 to the financial statements, the Company has accumulated losses since inception and has negative working capital. These factors raise substantial doubt about its ability to continue as a going concern. Management's plans in regard to these matters are also described in Note 2. The financial statements do not include any adjustments that might result from the outcome of this uncertainty.
>
> Source: Timberline Resources Corp.

The auditor's report calls attention to problems that might exist in the financial statements.

Some audits result in the need to issue other than an unqualified opinion due to exceptions such as (a) nonconformity with generally accepted accounting principles, (b) inadequate disclosures, and (c) a limitation or restriction of the scope of the examination. In these situations the auditor will issue one of the following:

- *Qualified opinion* when either the audit process has been limited (scope limitation) or there has been a departure from GAAP, but neither is of sufficient seriousness to invalidate the financial statements as a whole.
- *Adverse opinion* when the auditor has specific knowledge that financial statements or disclosures are seriously misstated or misleading. Adverse opinions are rare because auditors usually are able to persuade management to rectify problems to avoid this undesirable report.
- *Disclaimer* when the auditor is not able to gather sufficient information that financial statements are in conformity with GAAP.

Obviously, the auditor's report is most informative when any of these deviations from the standard unqualified opinion are present. These departures from the norm should raise a red flag to a financial analyst and prompt additional search for information.

PART C

Risk Analysis
Using Financial Statement Information

● LO3–7

Investors and others use information that companies provide in corporate financial reports to make decisions. Although the financial reports focus primarily on the past performance and the present financial condition of the reporting company, users are most interested in information about the future. Investors want to know a company's default risk. This is the risk that a company won't be able to pay its obligations when they come due. Another aspect of risk is operational risk, which relates more to how adept a company is at withstanding various events and circumstances that might impair its ability to earn profits.

Trying to gain a glimpse of the future from past and present data entails using various tools and techniques to formulate predictions. This is the goal of financial statement analysis. Common methods for analyzing financial statements include the following:

1. Comparative financial statements. Financial statements that are accompanied by the corresponding financial statement of the preceding year, and often the previous two years.
2. Horizontal analysis. Each item in a financial statement is expressed as a percentage of that same item in the financial statements of another year (base amount). For example,

comparing inventory this year to inventory last year would provide the percentage change in inventory.

3. Vertical analysis. Each item in the financial statements is expressed as a percentage of an appropriate corresponding total, or base amount, but within the same year. For example, cash, receivables, and inventory in the current year can be restated as a percentage of total assets in the current year.

4. Ratio analysis. Financial statement items are converted to ratios for evaluating the performance and risk of a company.

As an example, we presented the current asset section of Nike's comparative balance sheets in Illustration 3–3. From this, we could easily calculate the current year's percentage change in cash (horizontal analysis) or cash as a percentage of total current assets (vertical analysis). Understanding Nike's cash position, either relative to the previous year or relative to other current assets, provides some information for assessing the cash available to pay debt or to respond to other operating concerns.

However, the most common way to analyze financial statements is ratio analysis. Next, we'll analyze Nike's risk by using ratio analysis to investigate liquidity and long-term solvency. In Chapter 4, we introduce ratios related to profitability analysis. You will also employ ratios in Decision Makers' Perspective sections of many of the chapters in this text. Analysis cases that benefit from ratio analysis are included in many of these chapters as well.

We use ratios every day. Batting averages indicate how well our favorite baseball players are performing. We evaluate basketball players by field goal percentage and rebounds per game. Speedometers measure the speed of our cars in terms of miles per hour. We compare grocery costs on the basis of price per pound or ounce. In each of these cases, the ratio is more meaningful than a single number by itself. Do 45 hits indicate satisfactory performance? It depends on the number of at-bats. Is $2 a good price for cheese? It depends on how many ounces the $2 buys. Ratios make these measurements meaningful.

Likewise, we can use ratios to help evaluate a firm's performance and financial position. Is net income of $4 million a cause for shareholders to celebrate? Probably not if shareholders' equity is $10 billion. But if shareholders equity is $10 million, that's a return on equity of 40% (net income divided by shareholders' equity)! Although ratios provide more meaningful information than absolute numbers alone, the ratios are most useful when analyzed relative to some standard of comparison. That standard of comparison may be previous performance of the same company, the performance of a competitor company, or an industry average for the particular ratio. Such comparisons are useful to investors and analysts in evaluating the company's performance, to management for planning and control purposes, and to auditors in assessing the reasonableness of amounts in financial statements.

Evaluating information in ratio form allows analysts to control for size differences over time and among firms.

Liquidity Ratios

Liquidity most often refers to the ability of a company to convert its assets to cash to pay its *current* obligations. By examining a company's liquidity, we can obtain a general idea of the firm's ability to pay its short-term debts as they come due.

● LO3–8

Current assets usually are thought of as the most liquid of a company's assets, because these assets are easier to convert to cash than are long-term assets. Obviously, though, some current assets are more liquid than others, so it's important also to evaluate the specific makeup of current assets.

Two common measures of liquidity are (1) the current ratio and (2) the acid-test ratio (or quick ratio) calculated as follows:

$$\text{Current ratio} = \frac{\text{Current assets}}{\text{Current liabilities}}$$

$$\text{Acid-test (or quick ratio)} = \frac{\text{Quick assets}}{\text{Current liabilities}}$$

CURRENT RATIO Implicit in the definition of a current liability is the relationship between current assets and current liabilities. The difference between current assets and current liabilities is called working capital. By comparing a company's obligations that will

Working capital, the difference between current assets and current liabilities, is a popular measure of a company's ability to satisfy its short-term obligations.

shortly become due with the company's cash and other assets that, by definition, will shortly be converted to cash or used to generate cash, the analysis offers some indication of an ability to pay current debts. This ratio is particularly useful to lenders considering whether to offer short-term credit. Nike's working capital (in millions) at the end of its May 31, 2017, fiscal year is $10,587. This amount is computed as Nike's current assets of $16,061 (Illustration 3–3) minus its current liabilities of $5,474 (Illustration 3–7).

$$\text{Working capital} = \$16,061 - \$5,474 = \$10,587$$

The current ratio equals current assets divided by current liabilities. Nike's current ratio indicates the company has $2.93 of current assets for each $1 of current liabilities.

$$\text{Current ratio} = \frac{\$16,061}{\$5,474} = 2.93$$

Care should be taken, however, in assessing liquidity based solely on the current ratio. Liabilities usually are paid with cash, not other types of current assets. A company could have difficulty paying its liabilities even with a current ratio significantly greater than 1.0. For example, if a significant portion of current assets consisted of inventories, and inventories usually are not converted to cash for several months, there could be a problem in paying accounts payable due in 30 days. On the other hand, a current ratio of less than 1.0 doesn't necessarily mean the company will have difficulty meeting its current obligations. A line of credit, for instance, which the company can use to borrow funds, provides financial flexibility. That also must be considered in assessing liquidity.

ACID-TEST RATIO (OR QUICK RATIO).   Some analysts like to modify the current ratio to consider only current assets that are readily available to pay current liabilities. One such variation in common use is the acid-test ratio. This ratio excludes inventories, prepaid items, and restricted cash from current assets before dividing by current liabilities. The numerator, then, consists of (unrestricted) cash, short-term investments, and accounts receivable, which are referred to as the "quick assets." By eliminating current assets that are less readily convertible into cash, the acid-test ratio provides a more rigorous indication of liquidity than does the current ratio.

> The *acid-test ratio* provides a more stringent indication of a company's ability to pay its current obligations.

Illustration 3–3 shows that Nike's quick assets (in millions) total $9,856 ($3,808 + $2,371 + $3,677). The acid-test ratio can be computed as follows:

$$\text{Acid-test ratio} = \frac{\$9,856}{\$5,474} = 1.80$$

Are these liquidity ratios adequate? It's generally difficult to say without some point of comparison. As indicated previously, common standards for such comparisons are industry averages for similar ratios or ratios of the same company in prior years. Industry averages for the above two ratios are as follows:

Industry Average
Current ratio = 1.43
Acid-test ratio = 1.15

Nike's ratios are higher than the industry average, so Nike's liquidity appears to be in good shape. What if the ratios were lower? Would that indicate a liquidity problem? Not necessarily, but it would raise a red flag that calls for caution in analyzing other areas. Remember that each ratio is but one piece of the entire puzzle. For instance, profitability is perhaps the best indication of liquidity in the long run. We discuss ratios that measure profitability in Chapter 4.

> Liquidity ratios should be assessed in the context of both profitability and efficiency of managing assets.

Also, management may be very efficient in managing current assets so that, let's say, receivables are collected faster than normal or inventory is sold faster than normal, making those assets more liquid than they otherwise would be. Higher turnover ratios, relative to those of a competitor or the industry, generally indicate a more liquid position for a given level of the current ratio. We discuss these turnover ratios in Chapter 4.

Ethical Dilemma

The Raintree Cosmetic Company has several loans outstanding with a local bank. The debt agreements all contain a covenant stipulating that Raintree must maintain a current ratio of at least 0.9. Jackson Phillips, company controller, estimates that the 2021 year-end current assets and current liabilities will be $2,100,000 and $2,400,000, respectively. These estimates provide a current ratio of only 0.875. Violation of the debt agreement will increase Raintree's borrowing costs as the loans are renegotiated at higher rates.

Jackson proposes to the company president that Raintree purchase inventory of $600,000 on credit before year-end. This will cause both current assets and current liabilities to increase by the same amount, but the current ratio will increase to 0.9. The extra $600,000 in inventory will be used over the later part of 2022. However, the purchase will cause warehousing costs and financing costs to increase.

Jackson is concerned about the ethics of his proposal. What do you think?

Solvency Ratios

Investors and creditors, particularly long-term creditors, are vitally interested in long-term solvency, a company's ability to pay its long-term debts. Two common solvency ratios are (1) the debt to equity ratio and (2) the times interest earned ratio:

$$\text{Debt to equity ratio} = \frac{\text{Total liabilities}}{\text{Shareholders' equity}}$$

$$\text{Times interest earned ratio} = \frac{\text{Net income} + \text{Interest expense} + \text{Income taxes}}{\text{Interest expense}}$$

DEBT TO EQUITY RATIO   The debt to equity ratio compares resources provided by creditors with resources provided by owners. It is calculated by dividing total liabilities (current and long-term) by total shareholders' equity (including retained earnings). The mixture of liabilities and shareholders' equity in a company refers to its capital structure.[14]

The *debt to equity ratio* indicates the extent of reliance on creditors, rather than owners, in providing resources.

Other things being equal, the higher the ratio, the higher the company's risk. The higher the ratio, the greater the creditor claims on assets, so the higher the likelihood an individual creditor would not be paid in full if the company is unable to meet its obligations.

Nike's liabilities (in millions) are $10,852 (Illustration 3–7), and stockholders' equity is $12,407 (Illustration 3–8). The debt to equity ratio can be computed as follows:

$$\text{Debt to equity ratio} = \frac{\$10,852}{\$12,407} = 0.87$$

As with all ratios, the debt to equity ratio is more meaningful if compared to some standard such as an industry average or a competitor. For example, an industry average debt to equity ratio of 0.95 would indicate that Nike has a lower portion of liabilities in its capital structure than does the average firm in its industry. Does this mean that Nike's default risk is lower? Other things equal—yes. Is that good? Not necessarily. As discussed in the next section, it may be that debt is being underutilized by Nike. More debt might increase the potential for return to shareholders, but with higher debt comes higher risk. This is a fundamental trade-off faced by virtually all firms when trying to settle on the optimal amount of debt versus equity in its capital structure.

The makeup of liabilities also is important. For example, liabilities could include deferred revenues. Recall that deferred revenues are liabilities recorded when cash is received from customers in advance of providing a good or service. Companies satisfy these liabilities not by paying cash, but by providing the good or service to their customers.

---

[14]A commonly used variation of the debt to equity ratio is found by dividing total liabilities by *total assets*, rather than by shareholders' equity only. Of course, in this configuration the ratio measures precisely the same attribute of the firm's capital structure but can be interpreted as the percentage of a company's total assets provided by funds from creditors, rather than by owners.

TIMES INTEREST EARNED RATIO   A ratio that is commonly used in conjunction with the debt to equity ratio is the times interest earned ratio. This ratio is calculated as income before subtracting interest expense and income taxes, divided by interest expense. To remain solvent or to take on more debt if needed, a company needs to have funds available in the current year to pay interest charges. The ability of a company to "cover" its interest charges commonly is measured by the extent to which income exceeds interest charges in the current period.

> The *times interest earned ratio* indicates the margin of safety provided to creditors.

If income is many times greater than interest expense, creditors' interests are more protected than if income just barely covers this expense. For this purpose, income should be the amount available to pay interest, which is income before subtracting interest and income taxes, calculated by adding back to net income the interest and income taxes that were deducted.

As an example, Nike reports the following:

	($ in millions)
Net income	$4,240
Interest expense	+ 59
Income taxes	+ 646
Income before interest and taxes	$4,945

The times interest earned ratio can be computed as follows:

$$\text{Times interest earned ratio} = \frac{\$4,945}{\$59} = 83.81$$

The ratio of 83.81 indicates a considerable margin of safety for creditors. Income could decrease many times and the company would still be able to meet its interest payment obligations.[15] Nike is a highly profitable company with little interest-bearing debt. In comparison, the average times interest earned ratio for its industry is approximately 36.4 times.

Relationship Between Risk and Profitability.   Now that we've assessed a company's liquidity and solvency, let's look at why a company might want to borrow money. While there are default risks associated with borrowing, a company can use those borrowed funds to provide greater returns to its shareholders. This is referred to as favorable financial leverage and is a very common (but risky) business activity.

To see how financial leverage works, consider a newly formed corporation attempting to determine the appropriate mix of debt and equity. The initial capitalization goal is $50 million. The capitalization mix alternatives have been narrowed to two: (1) $10 million in debt and $40 million in equity and (2) $30 million in debt and $20 million in equity.

Also assume that regardless of the capitalization mix chosen, the corporation will be able to generate a 16% annual return, *before payment of interest and income taxes,* on the $50 million in assets acquired. In other words, income before interest and taxes will be $8 million (16% × $50 million). If the interest rate on debt is 8% and the income tax rate is 25%, comparative net income for the first year of operations for the two capitalization alternatives can be calculated as follows:

	Alternative 1 Debt = $10 million Equity = $40 million	Alternative 2 Debt = $30 million Equity = $20 million
Income before interest and income taxes	$ 8,000,000	$ 8,000,000
Less: Interest expense	(800,000)*	(2,400,000)†
Income before income taxes	7,200,000	5,600,000
Less: Income tax expense (25%)	(1,800,000)	(1,400,000)
Net income	$5,400,000	$4,200,000

*8% × $10,000,000
†8% × $30,000,000

---

[15]Of course, interest is paid with cash, not with "income." The times interest earned ratio often is calculated by using cash flow from operations before subtracting either interest payments or tax payments as the numerator and interest payments as the denominator.

Would shareholders be in favor of alternative 1? Probably not. Although alternative 1 provides a higher net income, the return on the shareholders' equity (net income divided by shareholders' equity) is higher for alternative 2. Under alternative 1, shareholders had to invest $40 million to earn $5.4 million. Under alternative 2, shareholders had to invest only $20 million to earn $4.2 million.

Favorable financial leverage means earning a return on borrowed funds that exceeds the cost of borrowing the funds.

	Alternative 1	**Alternative 2**
Return on equity[16] $=$	$\dfrac{\$5,400,000}{\$40,000,000}$	$\dfrac{\$4,200,000}{\$20,000,000}$
$=$	13.5%	21.0%

Alternative 2 generated a higher return for each dollar invested by shareholders. This is because the company leveraged its $20 million equity investment with additional debt. *Any time the cost of the additional debt (8%) is less than the return on assets invested (16%), the return to shareholders is higher with borrowing.* This is the essence of favorable financial leverage.

Be aware, though, leverage is risky and not always favorable; the cost of borrowing the funds might exceed the returns they provide. If the return on assets invested turned out to be less than expected, the additional debt could result in a lower return on equity for alternative 2. If, for example, the return on assets invested (before interest and income taxes) had been 6% of $50,000,000 (or $3,000,000), rather than 16%, alternative 1 would have provided the better return on equity:

	Alternative 1 **Debt = $10 million** **Equity = $40 million**	**Alternative 2** **Debt = $30 million** **Equity = $20 million**
Income before interest and income taxes	$ 3,000,000	$ 3,000,000
Less: Interest expense	(800,000)*	(2,400,000)†
Income before income taxes	2,200,000	600,000
Less: Income tax expense (25%)	(550,000)	(150,000)
Net income	$1,650,000	$ 450,000

*8% × $10,000,000
†8% × $30,000,000

	Alternative 1	**Alternative 2**
Return on equity[17] $=$	$\dfrac{\$1,650,000}{\$40,000,000}$	$\dfrac{\$450,000}{\$20,000,000}$
$=$	4.125%	2.250%

If the return on assets are too low and the company has become too leveraged, it faces the risk of not being able to make its interest and debt payments. So, shareholders typically are faced with a trade-off between the risk that high debt denotes and the potential for a higher return from having the higher debt. Liquidity and solvency ratios can help with that decision.

---

[16] If return is calculated on *average* shareholders' equity, we're technically assuming that all income is paid to shareholders in cash dividends, so that beginning, ending, and average shareholders' equity are the same. If we assume *no* dividends are paid, rates of return would be

	Alternative 1	**Alternative 2**
Return on equity $=$	$\dfrac{\$5,400,000}{(\$40,000,000 + \$45,400,000)/2}$	$\dfrac{\$4,200,000}{(\$20,000,000 + \$24,200,000)/2}$
$=$	12.65%	19.00%

In any case, our conclusions are the same.

[17] If we assume *no* dividends are paid, rates of return would be

	Alternative 1	**Alternative 2**
Return on equity $=$	$\dfrac{\$1,650,000}{(\$40,000,000 + \$41,650,000)/2}$	$\dfrac{\$450,000}{(\$20,000,000 + \$20,450,000)/2}$
$=$	4.04%	2.23%

In any case, our conclusions are the same.

Financial Reporting Case Solution

©TY Lim/Shutterstock

1. **Respond to Jerry's criticism that shareholders' equity does not represent the market value of the company. What information does the balance sheet provide?** *(p. 113)* Jerry is correct. The financial statements are supposed to help investors and creditors value a company. However, the balance sheet is not intended to portray the market value of the company. The assets of a company minus its liabilities as shown in the balance sheet (shareholders' equity) usually will not equal the company's market value for several reasons. For example, many assets are measured at their historical costs rather than their fair values. Also, many company resources, including its trained employees, its experienced management team, and its reputation are not recorded as assets at all. The balance sheet must be used in conjunction with other financial statements, disclosure notes, and other publicly available information.

   The balance sheet does, however, provide valuable information that can be used by investors and creditors to help determine market value. After all, it is the balance sheet that describes many of the resources a company has available for generating future cash flows. The balance sheet also provides important information about liquidity and long-term solvency.

2. **The usefulness of the balance sheet is enhanced by classifying assets and liabilities according to common characteristics. What are the classifications used in the balance sheet and what elements do those categories include?** *(p. 113)* Nike's balance sheet contains the following classifications:

Assets:

- *Current assets* include cash and several other assets that are reasonably expected to be converted to cash or consumed within the coming year or within the normal operating cycle of the business if that's longer than one year.
- *Property, plant and equipment* are the tangible long-lived assets used in the operations of the business. This category includes land, buildings, equipment, machinery, and furniture, as well as natural resources.
- *Intangible assets* are assets that represent exclusive rights to something such as a product, a process, or a name. Patents, copyrights, and franchises are examples.
- *Goodwill* is a unique intangible asset in that its cost can't be directly associated with any specifically identifiable right and is not separable from the company as a whole. It represents the unique value of the company as a whole over and above all identifiable tangible and intangible assets.
- *Deferred income taxes* result from temporary differences between taxable income and accounting income.
- *Other long-term assets* is a "catchall" classification of long-term (noncurrent) assets and could include long-term prepaid expenses and any long-term asset not included in one of the other categories.

Liabilities:

- *Current liabilities* are those obligations that are expected to be satisfied through the use of current assets or the creation of other current liabilities. Usually, this means liabilities that are expected to be paid within one year from the balance sheet date (or within the operating cycle if that's longer than one year).
- *Long-term liabilities* are obligations that will *not* be satisfied in the next year or operating cycle, whichever is longer. Examples are long-term notes, bonds, pension obligations, and lease obligations.

Shareholders' equity:

- *Common stock* and *additional paid-in capital* collectively equal the amounts invested by shareholders in the corporation.

- *Retained earnings* represents the accumulated net income or net loss reported since inception of the corporation less dividends distributed to shareholders. If this amount is negative, it is called *accumulated deficit*.
- *Accumulated other comprehensive income/loss* is the cumulative amount of other comprehensive income/loss items. This topic is addressed in subsequent chapters. ●

The Bottom Line

● **LO3–1**   The balance sheet is a position statement that presents an organized list of assets, liabilities, and equity at a point in time. The statement does not portray the market value of the entity. However, the information in the statement can be useful in assessing market value, as well as in providing important information about liquidity and long-term solvency. (*p. 112*)

● **LO3–2**   Current assets include cash and other assets that are reasonably expected to be converted to cash or consumed within one year from the balance sheet date, or within the normal operating cycle of the business if that's longer than one year. All other assets are classified as various types of noncurrent assets. In addition to cash and cash equivalents, current assets include short-term investments, accounts receivable, inventory, and prepaid expenses. Long-term asset classifications include investments; property, plant, and equipment; intangible assets; and other assets. (*p. 114*)

● **LO3–3**   Current liabilities are those obligations that are expected to be satisfied through the use of current assets or the creation of other current liabilities. All other liabilities are classified as long term. Current liabilities include notes and accounts payable, deferred revenues, accrued liabilities, and the current maturities of long-term debt. Long-term liabilities include long-term notes, loans, mortgages, bonds, pension and lease obligations, as well as deferred income taxes. Shareholders' equity for a corporation arises primarily from two sources: (1) paid-in capital—amounts invested by shareholders in the corporation, and (2) retained earnings—accumulated net income reported by a company since its inception minus all dividends distributed to shareholders. (*p. 118*)

● **LO3–4**   Financial statement disclosures are used to convey additional information about the account balances in the basic financial statements as well as to provide supplemental information. This information is disclosed, often parenthetically in the basic financial statements, or in disclosure notes that often include supporting schedules. (*p. 122*)

● **LO3–5**   Annual reports of public companies will include management's discussion and analysis of key aspects of the company's business. The purpose of this disclosure is to provide external parties with management's insight into certain transactions, events, and circumstances that affect the enterprise, including their financial impact. (*p. 125*)

● **LO3–6**   The purpose of an audit is to provide a professional, independent opinion as to whether or not the financial statements are prepared in conformity with generally accepted accounting principles. The standard audit report of a public company identifies the financial statements and their dates, issues an opinion on whether those financial statements are presented fairly, explains the basis for that opinion, and states that the financial statements are the responsibility of management. Explanatory language and emphasis of matters might be included. (*p. 128*)

● **LO3–7**   Financial analysts use various techniques to transform financial information into forms more useful for analysis. Horizontal analysis provides a useful way of analyzing year-to-year changes, while vertical analysis allows individual items to be expressed as a percentage of some base amount within the same year. Ratio analysis allows analysts to control for size differences over time and among firms while investigating important relationships among financial variables. (*p. 130*)

● **LO3–8**   The balance sheet provides information that can be useful in assessing risk. A key element of risk analysis is investigating a company's ability to pay its obligations when they come due. Liquidity ratios and solvency ratios provide information about a company's ability to pay its obligations. (*p. 131*)

● **LO3–9**   There are more similarities than differences in balance sheets and financial disclosures prepared according to U.S. GAAP and those prepared applying IFRS. Balance sheet presentation is one important difference. Under U.S. GAAP, we present current assets and liabilities before long-term assets and liabilities. IFRS doesn't prescribe the format of the balance sheet, but balance sheets prepared using IFRS often report long-term items first. Reportable segment disclosures also are similar. However, IFRS requires an additional disclosure, the amount of segment liabilities (Appendix 3). (*pp. 120* and *139*) ●

APPENDIX 3 | Reporting Segment Information

Many companies operate in several business segments as a strategy to achieve growth and to reduce operating risk through diversification.

Financial analysis of diversified companies is especially difficult. Consider, for example, a company that operates in several distinct business segments including computer peripherals, home health care systems, textiles, and consumer food products. The results of these distinctly different activities will be aggregated into a single set of financial statements, making difficult an informed projection of future performance. It may well be that the five-year outlook differs greatly among the areas of the economy represented by the different segments. To make matters worse for an analyst, the integrated financial statements do not reveal the relative investments in each of the business segments nor the success the company has had within each area. Given the fact that so many companies these days have chosen to balance their operating risks through diversification, aggregated financial statements pose a widespread problem for analysts, lending and credit officers, and other financial forecasters.

Reporting by Operating Segment

Segment reporting facilitates the financial statement analysis of diversified companies.

To address the problem, the accounting profession requires public business entities to provide supplemental information concerning individual operating segments. The supplemental disaggregated data do not include complete financial statements for each reportable segment, only certain specified items.

WHAT IS A REPORTABLE OPERATING SEGMENT? According to U.S. GAAP guidelines, a *management approach* is used in determining which segments of a company are reportable. This approach is based on the way that management organizes the segments within the company for making operating decisions and assessing performance. The segments are, therefore, evident from the structure of the company's internal organization.

More formally, the following characteristics define an operating segment[18] as a component of a public business entity:

- That engages in business activities from which it may recognize revenues and incur expenses (including revenues and expenses relating to transactions with other components of the same entity).
- Whose operating results are regularly reviewed by the entity's chief operating decision maker to make decisions about resources to be allocated to the segment and assess its performance.
- For which discrete financial information is available.

The FASB hopes that this approach provides insights into the risk and opportunities management sees in the various areas of company operations. Also, reporting information based on a company's internal organization should reduce the incremental cost to companies of providing the data. In addition, there are quantitative thresholds for the definition of an operating segment to limit the number of reportable segments. Only segments of material size (10% or more of total company revenues, assets, or net income) must be disclosed. However, a company must account for at least 75% of consolidated revenue through segment disclosures.

WHAT AMOUNTS ARE REPORTED BY AN OPERATING SEGMENT? For areas determined to be reportable operating segments, the following disclosures are required:

a. General information about the operating segment.
b. Information about reported segment profit or loss, including certain revenues and expenses included in reported segment profit or loss, segment assets, and the basis of measurement.
c. Reconciliations of the totals of segment revenues, reported profit or loss, assets, and other significant items to corresponding entity amounts.
d. Interim period information.[19]

---

[18]FASB ASC 280–10–50–1: Segment Reporting—Overall—Disclosure (previously "Disclosures about Segments of an Enterprise and Related Information," *Statement of Financial Accounting Standards No. 131* (Norwalk, Conn.: FASB, 1997), par. 10).
[19]FASB ASC 280–10–50–20 through 26 and 280–10–50–32: Segment Reporting—Overall—Disclosure (previously "Disclosures about Segments of an Enterprise and Related Information," *Statement of Financial Accounting Standards No. 131* (Norwalk, Conn.: FASB, 1997), par. 25).

Illustration 3A–1 shows the business segment information reported by Abbott Laboratories, in its 2017 annual report.

Business Segment Information
($ in millions)

Segments	Net Sales	Operating Earnings	Total Assets	Depr. and Amort.	Capital Expenditures
Established Pharmaceuticals	$ 4,287	$ 848	$ 2,728	$ 90	$ 181
Nutritionals	6,925	1,589	3,160	164	147
Diagnostics	5,616	1,468	4,226	300	374
Cardiovascular	8,911	2,720	5,074	298	206
Other	1,651	—	—	194	227
Total	$27,390	$6,625	$15,188	$1,046	$1,135

Source: Abbott Laboratories, Inc.

Illustration 3A–1

Business Segment Information Disclosure—Abbott Laboratories, Inc.

Real World Financials

International Financial Reporting Standards

Segment Reporting. U.S. GAAP requires companies to report information about reported segment profit or loss, including certain revenues and expenses included in reported segment profit or loss, segment assets, and the basis of measurement. The international standard on segment reporting, *IFRS No. 8*,[20] requires that companies also disclose total *liabilities* of its reportable segments.

● LO3–9

REPORTING BY GEOGRAPHIC AREA   In today's global economy it is sometimes difficult to distinguish domestic and foreign companies. Most large U.S. firms conduct significant operations in other countries in addition to having substantial export sales from this country. Differing political and economic environments from country to country means risks and associated rewards sometimes vary greatly among the various operations of a single company. For instance, manufacturing facilities in a South American country embroiled in political unrest pose different risks from having a plant in Vermont, or even Canada. Without disaggregated financial information, these differences cause problems for analysts.

U.S. GAAP requires a public business entity to report certain geographic information unless it is impracticable to do so. This information includes the following:

a. Revenues from external customers (1) attributed to the entity's country of domicile and (2) attributed to all foreign countries in total from which the entity derives revenues, and

b. Long-lived assets other than financial instruments, long-term customer relationships of a financial institution, mortgage and other servicing rights, deferred policy acquisition costs, and deferred tax assets (1) located in the entity's country of domicile and (2) located in all foreign countries in total in which the entity holds material assets.[21]

Abbott Laboratories reports its geographic sales by separate countries in 2017, as shown in Illustration 3A–2. Notice that both the business segment (Illustration 3A–1) and geographic information disclosures include a reconciliation to company totals. In both illustrations, net sales of both the business segments and the geographic areas are reconciled to the company's total net sales of $27,390 million.

[20]"Operating Segments," *International Financial Reporting Standard No. 8* (IASCF), as amended effective January 1, 2018.
[21]FASB ASC 280–10–50–41: Segment Reporting—Overall—Disclosure (previously "Disclosures about Segments of an Enterprise and Related Information," *Statement of Financial Accounting Standards No. 131* (Norwalk, Conn.: FASB, 1997), par. 38).

Illustration 3A–2

Geographic Area Sales
Disclosure—Abbott
Laboratories, Inc.

Real World Financials

Geographic Areas

($ in millions)

Net Sales

U.S.	$9,673	France	628
China	2,146	Brazil	541
Germany	1,366	Italy	507
Japan	1,255	United Kingdom	498
India	1,237	Columbia	494
Netherlands	929	Canada	443
Switzerland	841	Vietnam	427
Russia	664	All Others	5,741
		Total	$27,390

Source: Abbott Laboratories, Inc.

Revenues from major
customers must be
disclosed.

INFORMATION ABOUT MAJOR CUSTOMERS   Financial analysts are extremely interested in information concerning the extent to which a company's prosperity depends on one or more major customers. For this reason, if 10% or more of the revenue of an entity is derived from transactions with a single customer, the entity must disclose that fact, the total amount of revenue from each such customer, and the identity of the operating segment or segments reporting the revenue. The identity of the major customer or customers need not be disclosed, although companies routinely provide that information. In its 2017 annual report, Abbott Laboratories did not report any major customer information.

Lockheed Martin Corporation reported a major customer in its 2017 segment disclosures. The company reported that the U.S. government accounts for 69% of its revenues. Many companies in the defense industry derive substantial portions of their revenues from contracts with the Defense Department. When cutbacks occur in national defense or in specific defense systems, the impact on a company's operations can be considerable. ●

Questions For Review of Key Topics

Q 3–1   Describe the purpose of the balance sheet.

Q 3–2   Explain why the balance sheet does not portray the market value of the entity.

Q 3–3   Define current assets and list the typical asset categories included in this classification.

Q 3–4   Define current liabilities and list the typical liability categories included in this classification.

Q 3–5   Describe what is meant by an operating cycle for a typical manufacturing company.

Q 3–6   Explain the difference(s) between investments in equity securities classified as current assets versus those classified as long-term (noncurrent) assets.

Q 3–7   Describe the common characteristics of assets classified as property, plant, and equipment and identify some assets included in this classification.

Q 3–8   Distinguish between property, plant, and equipment and intangible assets.

Q 3–9   Explain how each of the following liabilities would be classified in the balance sheet:

- A note payable of $100,000 due in five years
- A note payable of $100,000 payable in annual installments of $20,000 each, with the first installment due next year

Q 3–10   Define the terms *paid-in capital* and *retained earnings*.

Q 3–11   Disclosure notes are an integral part of the information provided in financial statements. In what ways are the notes critical to understanding the financial statements and to evaluating the firm's performance and financial health?

Q 3–12   A summary of the company's significant accounting policies is a required disclosure. Why is this disclosure important to external financial statement users?

Q 3–13   Define a subsequent event.

Q 3–14   Every annual report of a public company includes an extensive discussion and analysis provided by the company's management. Specifically, which aspects of the company must this discussion address? Isn't management's perspective too biased to be of use to investors and creditors?

Q 3–15 What is a proxy statement? What information does it provide?

Q 3–16 The auditor's report provides the analyst with an independent and professional opinion about the fairness of the representations in the financial statements. What are the four main types of opinion an auditor of a public company might issue? Describe each.

Q 3–17 Define the terms *working capital, current ratio,* and *acid-test ratio* (or *quick ratio*).

Q 3–18 Show the calculation of the following solvency ratios: (1) the debt to equity ratio, and (2) the times interest earned ratio.

IFRS Q 3–19 Where can we find authoritative guidance for balance sheet presentation under IFRS?

IFRS Q 3–20 Describe at least two differences between U.S. GAAP and IFRS in balance sheet presentation.

Q 3–21 (Based on Appendix 3) Segment reporting facilitates the financial statement analysis of diversified companies. What determines whether an operating segment is a reportable segment for this purpose?

Q 3–22 (Based on Appendix 3) For segment reporting purposes, what amounts are reported by each operating segment?

IFRS Q 3–23 (Based on Appendix 3) Describe any differences in segment disclosure requirements between U.S. GAAP and IFRS.

Brief Exercises

BE 3–1
Current versus long-term classification
● LO3–2, LO3–3

Indicate whether each of the following assets and liabilities typically should be classified as current or long-term: (a) accounts receivable; (b) prepaid rent for the next six months; (c) notes receivable due in two years; (d) notes payable due in 90 days; (e) notes payable due in five years; and (f) patent.

BE 3–2
Balance sheet classification
● LO3–2, LO3–3

The trial balance for K and J Nursery, Inc., listed the following account balances at December 31, 2021, the end of its fiscal year: cash, $16,000; accounts receivable, $11,000; inventory, $25,000; equipment (net), $80,000; accounts payable, $14,000; salaries payable, $9,000; interest payable, $1,000; notes payable (due in 18 months), $30,000; common stock, $50,000. Calculate total current assets and total current liabilities that would appear in the company's year-end balance sheet.

BE 3–3
Balance sheet classification
● LO3–2, LO3–3

Refer to the situation described in BE 3–2. Determine the year-end balance in retained earnings for K and J Nursery, Inc.

BE 3–4
Balance sheet classification
● LO3–2, LO3–3

Refer to the situation described in BE 3–2. Prepare a classified balance sheet for K and J Nursery, Inc. The equipment originally cost $140,000.

BE 3–5
Balance sheet classification
● LO3–2, LO3–3

The following is a December 31, 2021, post-closing trial balance for Culver City Lighting, Inc. Prepare a classified balance sheet for the company.

Account Title	Debits	Credits
Cash	$ 55,000	
Accounts receivable	39,000	
Inventory	45,000	
Prepaid insurance	15,000	
Equipment	100,000	
Accumulated depreciation		$ 34,000
Patent (net)	40,000	
Accounts payable		12,000
Interest payable		2,000
Notes payable (due in 10 years)		100,000
Common stock		70,000
Retained earnings		76,000
Totals	$294,000	$294,000

BE 3–6
Balance sheet classification
● LO3–2, LO3–3

You have been asked to review the December 31, 2021, balance sheet for Champion Cleaning. After completing your review, you list the following three items for discussion with your superior:
1. An investment of $30,000 is included in current assets. Management has indicated that it has no intention of liquidating the investment in 2022.
2. A $100,000 note payable is listed as a long-term liability, but you have determined that the note is due in 10 equal annual installments with the first installment due on March 31, 2022.
3. Deferred revenue of $60,000 is included as a current liability even though only two-thirds will be recognized as revenue in 2022, and the other one-third in 2023.

Determine the appropriate classification of each of these items.

BE 3–7
Balance sheet preparation; missing elements
● LO3–2, LO3–3

Use the following information from the balance sheet of Raineer Plumbing to determine the missing amounts.

Cash and cash equivalents	$40,000	Accounts payable	$32,000
Retained earnings	?	Accounts receivable	120,000
Inventory	?	Notes payable (due in 2 years)	50,000
Common stock	100,000	Property, plant and equipment (net)	?
Total current assets	235,000	Total assets	400,000

BE 3–8
Financial statement disclosures
● LO3–4

For each of the following note disclosures, indicate whether the disclosure would likely appear in (A) the summary of significant accounts policies or (B) a separate note: (1) depreciation method; (2) contingency information; (3) significant issuance of common stock after the fiscal year-end; (4) cash equivalent designation; (5) long-term debt information; and (6) inventory costing method.

BE 3–9
Calculating ratios
● LO3–8

Refer to the trial balance information in BE 3–5. Calculate the (a) current ratio, (b) acid-test ratio, and (c) debt to equity ratio.

BE 3–10
Effect of decisions on ratios
● LO3–8

At the end of 2021, Barker Corporation's preliminary trial balance indicated a current ratio of 1.2. Management is contemplating paying some of its accounts payable balance before the end of the fiscal year. Determine whether the effect this transaction would increase or decrease the current ratio. Would your answer be the same if the preliminary trial balance indicated a current ratio of 0.8?

BE 3–11
Calculating ratios; solving for unknowns
● LO3–8

The current asset section of Stibbe Pharmaceutical Company's balance sheet included cash of $20,000 and accounts receivable of $40,000. The only other current asset is inventory. The company's current ratio is 2.0 and its acid-test ratio is 1.5. Determine the ending balance in inventory and total current liabilities.

Exercises

E 3–1
Balance sheet; missing elements
● LO3–2, LO3–3, LO3–8

The following December 31, 2021, fiscal year-end account balance information is available for the Stonebridge Corporation:

Cash and cash equivalents	$ 5,000
Accounts receivable (net)	20,000
Inventory	60,000
Property, plant, and equipment (net)	120,000
Accounts payable	44,000
Salaries payable	15,000
Paid-in capital	100,000

The only asset not listed is short-term investments. The only liabilities not listed are $30,000 notes payable due in two years and related accrued interest of $1,000 due in four months. The current ratio at year-end is 1.5:1.

Required:
Determine the following at December 31, 2021:
1. Total current assets
2. Short-term investments
3. Retained earnings

E 3–2

Balance sheet classification

● LO3–2, LO3–3

The following are the typical classifications used in a balance sheet:

a. Current assets
b. Investments
c. Property, plant, and equipment
d. Intangible assets
e. Other assets

f. Current liabilities
g. Long-term liabilities
h. Paid-in capital
i. Retained earnings

Required:

For each of the following balance sheet items, use the letters above to indicate the appropriate classification category. If the item is a contra account, place a minus sign before the chosen letter.

1. _____ Equipment
2. _____ Accounts payable
3. _____ Allowance for uncollectible accounts
4. _____ Land (held for investment)
5. _____ Notes payable (due in 5 years)
6. _____ Deferred revenue (for the next 12 months)
7. _____ Notes payable (due in 6 months)
8. _____ Accumulated amount of net income less dividends
9. _____ Investment in XYZ Corp. (long-term)

10. _____ Inventory
11. _____ Patent
12. _____ Land (used in operations)
13. _____ Accrued liabilities (due in 6 months)
14. _____ Prepaid rent (for the next 9 months)
15. _____ Common stock
16. _____ Building (used in operations)
17. _____ Cash
18. _____ Income taxes payable

E 3–3

Balance sheet classification

● LO3–2, LO3–3

The following are the typical classifications used in a balance sheet:

a. Current assets
b. Investments
c. Property, plant, and equipment
d. Intangible assets
e. Other assets

f. Current liabilities
g. Long-term liabilities
h. Paid-in capital
i. Retained earnings

Required:

For each of the following 2021 balance sheet items, use the letters above to indicate the appropriate classification category. If the item is a contra account, place a minus sign before the chosen letter.

1. _____ Interest payable (due in 3 months)
2. _____ Franchise
3. _____ Accumulated depreciation
4. _____ Prepaid insurance (for 2022)
5. _____ Bonds payable (due in 10 years)
6. _____ Current maturities of long-term debt
7. _____ Notes payable (due in 3 months)
8. _____ Long-term receivables
9. _____ Restricted cash (will be used to retire bonds in 10 years)

10. _____ Supplies
11. _____ Machinery
12. _____ Land (used in operations)
13. _____ Deferred revenue (for 2022)
14. _____ Copyrights
15. _____ Common stock
16. _____ Land (held for speculation)
17. _____ Cash equivalents
18. _____ Salaries payable

E 3–4

Balance sheet preparation

● LO3–2, LO3–3

The following is a December 31, 2021, post-closing trial balance for the Jackson Corporation.

Account Title	Debits	Credits
Cash	$ 40,000	
Accounts receivable	34,000	
Inventory	75,000	
Prepaid rent (for the next 8 months)	16,000	
Investment in equity securities (short term)	10,000	
Machinery	145,000	
Accumulated depreciation		$ 11,000
Patent (net)	83,000	
Accounts payable		8,000
Salaries payable		4,000
Income taxes payable		32,000
Bonds payable (due in 10 years)		200,000
Common stock		100,000
Retained earnings		48,000
Totals	$403,000	$403,000

Required:

Prepare a classified balance sheet for Jackson Corporation at December 31, 2021, by properly classifying each of the accounts.

E 3–5
Balance sheet preparation
● LO3–2, LO3–3

The following are the ending balances of accounts at December 31, 2021, for the Valley Pump Corporation.

Account Title	Debits	Credits
Cash	$ 25,000	
Accounts receivable	56,000	
Inventory	81,000	
Interest payable		$ 10,000
Investment in equity securities	44,000	
Land	120,000	
Buildings	300,000	
Accumulated depreciation—buildings		100,000
Equipment	75,000	
Accumulated depreciation—equipment		25,000
Copyright (net)	12,000	
Prepaid expenses (next 12 months)	32,000	
Accounts payable		65,000
Deferred revenue (next 12 months)		20,000
Notes payable		250,000
Allowance for uncollectible accounts		5,000
Common stock		200,000
Retained earnings		70,000
Totals	$745,000	$745,000

Additional Information:
1. The $120,000 balance in the land account consists of $100,000 for the cost of land where the plant and office buildings are located. The remaining $20,000 represents the cost of land being held for speculation.
2. The $44,000 balance in the investment in equity securities account represents an investment in the common stock of another corporation. Valley intends to sell one-half of the stock within the next year.
3. The notes payable account consists of a $100,000 note due in six months and a $150,000 note due in three annual installments of $50,000 each, with the first payment due in August of 2022.

Required:

Prepare a classified balance sheet for the Valley Pump Corporation at December 31, 2021. Use the additional information to help determine appropriate classifications and account balances.

E 3–6
Balance sheet;
Current versus
long-term
classification
● LO3–2, LO3–3

Presented next are the ending balances of accounts for the Kansas Instruments Corporation at December 31, 2021.

Account Title	Debits	Credits
Cash	$ 20,000	
Accounts receivable	130,000	
Raw materials	24,000	
Notes receivable	100,000	
Interest receivable	3,000	
Interest payable		$ 5,000
Investment in debt securities	32,000	
Land	50,000	
Buildings	1,300,000	
Accumulated depreciation—buildings		620,000
Work in process	42,000	
Finished goods	89,000	
Equipment	300,000	
Accumulated depreciation—equipment		130,000
Patent (net)	120,000	
Prepaid rent (for the next two years)	60,000	
Deferred revenue		36,000
Accounts payable		180,000
Notes payable		400,000
Restricted cash (for payment of notes payable)	80,000	
Allowance for uncollectible accounts		13,000
Sales revenue		800,000
Cost of goods sold	450,000	
Rent expense	28,000	

Additional Information:
1. The notes receivable, along with any accrued interest, are due on November 22, 2022.
2. The notes payable are due in 2025. Interest is payable annually.
3. The investment in debt securities consist of treasury bills, all of which mature next year.
4. Deferred revenue will be recognized as revenue equally over the next two years.

Required:
Determine the company's working capital (current assets minus current liabilities) at December 31, 2021.

E 3–7
Balance sheet preparation; errors
● LO3–2, LO3–3

The following balance sheet for the Los Gatos Corporation was prepared by a recently hired accountant. In reviewing the statement you notice several errors.

LOS GATOS CORPORATION
Balance Sheet
At December 31, 2021
Assets

Cash	$ 40,000
Accounts receivable	80,000
Inventory	55,000
Machinery (net)	120,000
Franchise (net)	30,000
Total assets	$325,000

Liabilities and Shareholders' Equity

Accounts payable	$ 50,000
Allowance for uncollectible accounts	5,000
Notes payable	55,000
Bonds payable	110,000
Shareholders' equity	105,000
Total liabilities and shareholders' equity	$325,000

Additional Information:
1. Cash includes a $20,000 restricted amount to be used for repayment of the bonds payable in 2025.
2. The cost of the machinery is $190,000.
3. Accounts receivable includes a $20,000 note receivable from a customer due in 2024.
4. The notes payable balance includes accrued interest of $5,000. Principal and interest are both due on February 1, 2022.
5. The company began operations in 2016. Net income less dividends since inception of the company totals $35,000.
6. 50,000 shares of no par common stock were issued in 2016. 100,000 shares are authorized.

Required:
Prepare a corrected, classified balance sheet. Use the additional information to help determine appropriate classifications and account balances. The cost of machinery and its accumulated depreciation are shown separately.

E 3–8
Balance sheet; current versus long-term classification
● LO3–2, LO3–3

Cone Corporation is in the process of preparing its December 31, 2021, balance sheet. There are some questions as to the proper classification of the following items:
a. $50,000 in cash restricted in a savings account to pay bonds payable. The bonds mature in 2025.
b. Prepaid rent of $24,000, covering the period January 1, 2022, through December 31, 2023.
c. Notes payable of $200,000. The notes are payable in annual installments of $20,000 each, with the first installment payable on March 1, 2022.
d. Accrued interest payable of $12,000 related to the notes payable.
e. Investment in equity securities of other corporations, $80,000. Cone intends to sell one-half of the securities in 2022.

Required:
Prepare the asset and liability sections of a classified balance sheet to show how each of the above items should be reported.

146   SECTION 1   The Role of Accounting as an Information System

E 3–9
Balance sheet
preparation
● LO3–2, LO3–3

The following is the balance sheet of Korver Supply Company at December 31, 2020 (prior year).

KORVER SUPPLY COMPANY
Balance Sheet
At December 31, 2020
Assets

Cash	$120,000
Accounts receivable	300,000
Inventory	200,000
Furniture and fixtures (net)	150,000
Total assets	$770,000

Liabilities and Shareholders' Equity

Accounts payable (for merchandise)	$190,000
Notes payable	200,000
Interest payable	6,000
Common stock	100,000
Retained earnings	274,000
Total liabilities and shareholders' equity	$770,000

Transactions during 2021 (current year) were as follows:

1. Sales to customers on account	$800,000
2. Cash collected from customers	780,000
3. Purchase of merchandise on account	550,000
4. Cash payment to suppliers	560,000
5. Cost of merchandise sold	500,000
6. Cash paid for operating expenses	160,000
7. Cash paid for interest on notes	12,000

Additional Information:
The notes payable are dated June 30, 2020, and are due on June 30, 2022. Interest at 6% is payable annually on June 30. Depreciation on the furniture and fixtures for 2021 is $20,000. The furniture and fixtures originally cost $300,000.

Required:
Prepare a classified balance sheet at December 31, 2021, by updating ending balances from 2020 for transactions during 2021 and the additional information. The cost of furniture and fixtures and their accumulated depreciation are shown separately.

E 3–10
Financial
statement
disclosures
● LO3–4

The following are typical disclosures that would appear in the notes accompanying financial statements. For each of the items listed, indicate where the disclosure would likely appear—either in (A) the significant accounting policies note or (B) a separate note.

1. Inventory costing method	A
2. Information on related party transactions	___
3. Composition of property, plant, and equipment	___
4. Depreciation method	___
5. Subsequent event information	___
6. Measurement basis for certain financial instruments	___
7. Important merger occurring after year-end	___
8. Composition of receivables	___

E 3–11
Disclosure notes
● LO3–4

Hallergan Company produces car and truck batteries that it sells primarily to auto manufacturers. Dorothy Hawkins, the company's controller, is preparing the financial statements for the year ended December 31, 2021. Hawkins asks for your advice concerning the following information that has not yet been included in the statements. The statements will be issued on February 28, 2022.

1. Hallergan leases its facilities from the brother of the chief executive officer.

2. On January 8, 2022, Hallergan entered into an agreement to sell a tract of land that it had been holding as an investment. The sale, which resulted in a material gain, was completed on February 2, 2022.

3. Hallergan uses the straight-line method to determine depreciation on all of the company's depreciable assets.

4. On February 8, 2022, Hallergan completed negotiations with its bank for a $10,000,000 line of credit.

5. Hallergan uses the first-in, first-out (FIFO) method to value inventory.

Required:
For each of the above items, discuss any additional disclosures that Hawkins should include in Hallergan's financial statements.

E 3–12
Financial statement disclosures
● LO3–4

Parkman Sporting Goods is preparing its annual report for its 2021 fiscal year. The company's controller has asked for your help in determining how best to disclose information about the following items:
1. A related-party transaction.
2. Depreciation method.
3. Allowance for uncollectible accounts.
4. Composition of investments.
5. Composition of long-term debt.
6. Inventory costing method.
7. Number of shares of common stock authorized, issued, and outstanding.
8. Employee benefit plans.

Required:
Indicate whether the above items should be disclosed (A) in the summary of significant accounting policies note, (B) in a separate disclosure note, or (C) on the face of the balance sheet.

E 3–13
FASB codification research
● LO3–4

CODE

Access the *FASB Accounting Standards Codification* at the FASB website (www.fasb.org). Determine each of the following:
1. The topic number (Topic XXX) that provides guidance on information contained in the notes to the financial statements.
2. The specific seven-digit Codification citation (XXX-XX-XX) that requires a company to identify and describe in the notes to the financial statements the accounting principles and methods used to prepare the financial statements.
3. Describe the disclosure requirements.

E 3–14
FASB codification research
● LO3–2, LO3–4

CODE

Access the *FASB Accounting Standards Codification* at the FASB website (www.fasb.org). Determine the specific eight-digit Codification citation (XXX-XX-XX-X) for each of the following:
1. The balance sheet classification for a note payable due in six months that was used to purchase a building.
2. The assets that may be excluded from current assets.
3. Whether a note receivable from a related party would be included in the balance sheet with notes receivable or accounts receivable from customers.
4. The items that are nonrecognized subsequent events that require a disclosure in the notes to the financial statements.

E 3–15
Concepts; terminology
● LO3–2 through LO3–4, LO3–6

Listed below are several terms and phrases associated with the balance sheet and financial disclosures. Pair each item from List A (by letter) with the item from List B that is most appropriately associated with it.

List A	List B
_____ 1. Balance sheet	a. Will be satisfied through the use of current assets.
_____ 2. Liquidity	b. Items expected to be converted to cash or consumed within one year or the operating cycle, whichever is longer.
_____ 3. Current assets	c. The statements are presented fairly in conformity with GAAP.
_____ 4. Operating cycle	d. An organized array of assets, liabilities, and equity.
_____ 5. Current liabilities	e. Important to a user in comparing financial information across companies.
_____ 6. Cash equivalent	f. Scope limitation or a departure from GAAP.
_____ 7. Intangible asset	g. Recorded when an expense is incurred but not yet paid.
_____ 8. Working capital	h. Refers to the ability of a company to convert its assets to cash to pay its current obligations.
_____ 9. Accrued liabilities	i. Occurs after the fiscal year-end but before the statements are issued.
_____ 10. Summary of significant accounting policies	j. Period of time from payment of cash to collection of cash.
_____ 11. Subsequent events	k. One-month U.S. Treasury bill.
_____ 12. Unqualified opinion	l. Current assets minus current liabilities.
_____ 13. Qualified opinion	m. Lacks physical substance.

148   SECTION 1   The Role of Accounting as an Information System

E 3–16
Calculating ratios
● LO3–8

The 2021 balance sheet for Hallbrook Industries, Inc., is shown below.

HALLBROOK INDUSTRIES, INC.
Balance Sheet
December 31, 2021
($ in thousands)
Assets

Cash	$ 200
Short-term investments	150
Accounts receivable	200
Inventory	350
Property, plant, and equipment (net)	1,000
Total assets	$1,900

Liabilities and Shareholders' Equity

Current liabilities	$ 400
Long-term liabilities	350
Paid-in capital	750
Retained earnings	400
Total liabilities and shareholders' equity	$1,900

The company's 2021 income statement reported the following amounts ($ in thousands):

Net sales	$4,600
Interest expense	40
Income tax expense	100
Net income	160

Required:
Determine the following ratios for 2021:
1. Current ratio
2. Acid-test ratio
3. Debt to equity ratio
4. Times interest earned ratio

E 3–17
Calculating ratios;
Best Buy
● LO3–8

Real World Financials

Best Buy Co, Inc., is a leading retailer specializing in consumer electronics. A condensed income statement and balance sheet for the fiscal year ended January 28, 2017, are shown next.

Best Buy Co., Inc.
Balance Sheet
At January 28, 2017
($ in millions)
Assets

Current assets:	
Cash and cash equivalents	$ 2,240
Short-term investments	1,681
Accounts receivable (net)	1,347
Inventory	4,864
Other current assets	384
Total current assets	10,516
Long-term assets	3,340
Total assets	$13,856

Liabilities and Shareholders' Equity

Current liabilities:	
Accounts payable	$ 4,984
Other current liabilities	2,138
Total current liabilities	7,122
Long-term liabilities	2,025
Shareholders' equity	4,709
Total liabilities and shareholders' equity	$13,856

Best Buy Co., Inc.
Income Statement
For the Year Ended January 28, 2017
($ in millions)

Revenues	$39,403
Costs and expenses	37,549
Operating income	1,854
Other income (expense)*	(38)
Income before income taxes	1,816
Income tax expense	609
Net income	$ 1,207

*Includes $72 of interest expense.

Liquidity and solvency ratios for the industry are as follows:

	Industry Average
Current ratio	1.43
Acid-test ratio	1.15
Debt to equity	0.68
Times interest earned	8.25 times

Required:
1. Determine the following ratios for Best Buy for its fiscal year ended January 28, 2017.
   a. Current ratio
   b. Acid-test ratio
   c. Debt to equity ratio
   d. Times interest earned ratio

2. Using the ratios from requirement 1, assess Best Buy's liquidity and solvency relative to its industry.

E 3–18
Calculating
ratios; solve for
unknowns
● LO3–8

The current asset section of the Excalibur Tire Company's balance sheet consists of cash, marketable securities, accounts receivable, and inventory. The December 31, 2021, balance sheet revealed the following:

Inventory	$ 840,000
Total assets	$2,800,000
Current ratio	2.25
Acid-test ratio	1.2
Debt to equity ratio	1.8

Required:
Determine the following 2021 balance sheet items:
1. Current assets
2. Shareholders' equity
3. Long-term assets
4. Long-term liabilities

E 3–19
Calculating
ratios; solve for
unknowns
● LO3–8

The current asset section of Guardian Consultant's balance sheet consists of cash, accounts receivable, and pre-paid expenses. The 2021 balance sheet reported the following: cash, $1,300,000; prepaid expenses, $360,000; long-term assets, $2,400,000; and shareholders' equity, $2,500,000. The current ratio at the end of the year was 2.0 and the debt to equity ratio was 1.4.

Required:
Determine the following 2021 amounts and ratios:
1. Current liabilities
2. Long-term liabilities
3. Accounts receivable
4. The acid-test ratio

E 3–20
Effect of
management
decisions on ratios
● LO3–8

Most decisions made by management impact the ratios analysts use to evaluate performance. Indicate (by letter) whether each of the actions listed below will immediately increase (I), decrease (D), or have no effect (N) on the ratios shown. Assume each ratio is less than 1.0 before the action is taken.

Action	Current Ratio	Acid-Test Ratio	Debt to Equity Ratio
1. Issuance of long-term bonds	___	___	___
2. Issuance of short-term notes	___	___	___
3. Payment of accounts payable	___	___	___
4. Purchase of inventory on account	___	___	___
5. Purchase of inventory for cash	___	___	___
6. Purchase of equipment with a 4-year note	___	___	___
7. Repayment of long-term notes payable	___	___	___
8. Issuance of common stock	___	___	___
9. Payment for advertising expense	___	___	___
10. Purchase of short-term investment for cash	___	___	___
11. Reclassification of long-term notes payable to current notes payable	___	___	___

E 3–21
Segment reporting
● Appendix 3

The Canton Corporation operates in four distinct business segments. The segments, along with 2021 information on revenues, assets, and net income, are listed below ($ in thousands):

Segment	Revenues	Assets	Net Income
Pharmaceuticals	$2,000	$1,000	$200
Plastics	3,000	1,500	270
Farm equipment	2,500	1,250	320
Electronics	500	250	40
Total company	$8,000	$4,000	$830

Required:
1. For which segments must Canton report supplementary information according to U.S. GAAP?
2. What amounts must be reported for the segments you identified in requirement 1?

E 3–22
Segment reporting
● Appendix 3
LO3–9

 IFRS

Refer to E 3–21.

Required:
How might your answers differ if Canton Corporation prepares its segment disclosure according to International Financial Reporting Standards?

Problems

connect

P 3–1
Balance sheet preparation
● LO3–2, LO3–3

Presented below is a list of balance sheet accounts.

Accounts payable
Accounts receivable
Accumulated depreciation—buildings
Accumulated depreciation—equipment
Allowance for uncollectible accounts
Restricted cash (to be used in 10 years)
Bonds payable (due in 10 years)
Buildings
Notes payable (due in 6 months)
Notes receivable (due in 2 years)
Patent (net)
Additional paid-in capital
Prepaid expenses

Cash
Common stock
Copyright (net)
Equipment
Interest receivable (due in three months)
Inventory
Land (in use)
Long-term investments
Interest payable (current)
Retained earnings
Short-term investments
Income taxes payable
Salaries payable

Required:
Prepare a classified balance sheet ignoring monetary amounts. Include headings for each classification, as well as titles for each classification's subtotal. An example of a classified balance sheet can be found in the Concept Review Exercise at the end of Part A of this chapter.

P 3–2
Balance sheet preparation; missing elements
● LO3–2, LO3–3

The data listed below are taken from a balance sheet of Trident Corporation at December 31, 2021. Some amounts, indicated by question marks, have been intentionally omitted.

	($ in thousands)
Cash and cash equivalents	$ 239,186
Short-term investments	353,700
Accounts receivable	504,944
Inventory	?
Prepaid expenses (current)	83,259
Total current assets	1,594,927
Long-term receivables	110,800
Equipment (net)	?
Total assets	?
Notes payable (current)	31,116
Accounts payable	?
Accrued liabilities	421,772
Other current liabilities	181,604
Total current liabilities	693,564
Long-term debt	?
Total liabilities	956,140
Common stock	370,627
Retained earnings	1,000,000

Required:
1. Determine the missing amounts.
2. Prepare Trident's classified balance sheet. Include headings for each classification, as well as titles for each classification's subtotal. An example of a classified balance sheet can be found in the Concept Review Exercise at the end of Part A of this chapter.

P 3–3
Balance sheet preparation
● LO3–2, LO3–3

The following is a December 31, 2021, post-closing trial balance for Almway Corporation.

Account Title	Debits	Credits
Cash	$ 45,000	
Investment in equity securities	110,000	
Accounts receivable	60,000	
Inventory	200,000	
Prepaid insurance (for the next 9 months)	9,000	
Land	90,000	
Buildings	420,000	
Accumulated depreciation—buildings		$ 100,000
Equipment	110,000	
Accumulated depreciation—equipment		60,000
Patent (net)	10,000	
Accounts payable		75,000
Notes payable		130,000
Interest payable		20,000
Bonds payable		240,000
Common stock		300,000
Retained earnings		129,000
Totals	$1,054,000	$1,054,000

Additional Information:
1. The investment in equity securities account includes an investment in common stock of another corporation of $30,000 which management intends to hold for at least three years. The balance of these investments is intended to be sold in the coming year.
2. The land account includes land which cost $25,000 that the company has not used and is currently listed for sale.
3. The cash account includes $15,000 restricted in a fund to pay bonds payable that mature in 2024 and $23,000 restricted in a three-month Treasury bill.
4. The notes payable account consists of the following:
   a. a $30,000 note due in six months.
   b. a $50,000 note due in six years.
   c. a $50,000 note due in five annual installments of $10,000 each, with the next installment due February 15, 2022.

5. The $60,000 balance in accounts receivable is net of an allowance for uncollectible accounts of $8,000.

6. The common stock account represents 100,000 shares of no par value common stock issued and outstanding. The corporation has 500,000 shares authorized.

Required:

Prepare a classified balance sheet for the Almway Corporation at December 31, 2021. Include headings for each classification, as well as titles for each classification's subtotal. An example of a classified balance sheet can be found in the Concept Review Exercise at the end of Part A of this chapter.

P 3–4

Balance sheet preparation

● LO3–2, LO3–3

The following is the ending balances of accounts at December 31, 2021, for the Weismuller Publishing Company.

Account Title	Debits	Credits
Cash	$ 65,000	
Accounts receivable	160,000	
Inventory	285,000	
Prepaid expenses	148,000	
Equipment	320,000	
Accumulated depreciation		$ 110,000
Investments	140,000	
Accounts payable		60,000
Interest payable		20,000
Deferred revenue		80,000
Income taxes payable		30,000
Notes payable		200,000
Allowance for uncollectible accounts		16,000
Common stock		400,000
Retained earnings		202,000
Totals	$1,118,000	$1,118,000

Additional Information:

1. Prepaid expenses include $120,000 paid on December 31, 2021, for a two-year lease on the building that houses both the administrative offices and the manufacturing facility.

2. Investments include $30,000 in Treasury bills purchased on November 30, 2021. The bills mature on January 30, 2022. The remaining $110,000 is an investment in equity securities that the company intends to sell in the next year.

3. Deferred revenue represents customer prepayments for magazine subscriptions. Subscriptions are for periods of one year or less.

4. The notes payable account consists of the following:

    a. a $40,000 note due in six months.

    b. a $100,000 note due in six years.

    c. a $60,000 note due in three annual installments of $20,000 each, with the next installment due August 31, 2022.

5. The common stock account represents 400,000 shares of no par value common stock issued and outstanding. The corporation has 800,000 shares authorized.

Required:

Prepare a classified balanced sheet for the Weismuller Publishing Company at December 31, 2021. Include headings for each classification, as well as titles for each classification's subtotal. An example of a classified balance sheet can be found in the Concept Review Exercise at the end of Part A of this chapter.

P 3–5

Balance sheet preparation

● LO3–2, LO3–3

The following is the ending balances of accounts at June 30, 2021, for Excell Company.

Account Title	Debits	Credits
Cash	$ 83,000	
Short-term investments	65,000	
Accounts receivable (net)	280,000	
Prepaid expenses (for the next 12 months)	32,000	
Land	75,000	
Buildings	320,000	
Accumulated depreciation—buildings		$ 160,000
Equipment	265,000	
Accumulated depreciation—equipment		120,000
Accounts payable		173,000

(continued)

(concluded)

Account Title	Debits	Credits
Accrued liabilities		45,000
Notes payable		100,000
Mortgage payable		250,000
Common stock		100,000
Retained earnings		172,000
Totals	$1,120,000	$1,120,000

Additional Information:
1. The short-term investments account includes $18,000 in U.S. treasury bills purchased in May. The bills mature in July, 2021.
2. The accounts receivable account consists of the following:

a. Amounts owed by customers	$225,000
b. Allowance for uncollectible accounts—trade customers	(15,000)
c. Nontrade notes receivable (due in three years)	65,000
d. Interest receivable on notes (due in four months)	5,000
Total	$280,000

3. The notes payable account consists of two notes of $50,000 each. One note is due on September 30, 2021, and the other is due on November 30, 2022.
4. The mortgage payable is a loan payable to the bank in *semiannual* installments of $5,000 each plus interest. The next payment is due on October 31, 2021. Interest has been properly accrued and is included in accrued expenses.
5. Five hundred thousand shares of no par common stock are authorized, of which 200,000 shares have been issued and are outstanding.
6. The land account includes $50,000 representing the cost of the land on which the company's office building resides. The remaining $25,000 is the cost of land that the company is holding for investment purposes.

Required:
Prepare a classified balance sheet for the Excell Company at June 30, 2021. Include headings for each classification, as well as titles for each classification's subtotal. An example of a classified balance sheet can be found in the Concept Review Exercise at the end of Part A of this chapter.

P 3–6
Balance sheet preparation; disclosures
● LO3–2 through LO3–4

The following is the ending balances of accounts at December 31, 2021, for the Vosburgh Electronics Corporation.

Account Title	Debits	Credits
Cash	$ 67,000	
Short-term investments	182,000	
Accounts receivable	123,000	
Long-term investments	35,000	
Inventory	215,000	
Receivables from employees	40,000	
Prepaid expenses (for 2022)	16,000	
Land	280,000	
Building	1,550,000	
Equipment	637,000	
Patent (net)	152,000	
Franchise (net)	40,000	
Notes receivable	250,000	
Interest receivable	12,000	
Accumulated depreciation—building		$ 620,000
Accumulated depreciation—equipment		210,000
Accounts payable		189,000
Dividends payable (payable on 1/16/2022)		10,000
Interest payable		16,000
Income taxes payable		40,000
Deferred revenue		60,000
Notes payable		300,000
Allowance for uncollectible accounts		8,000
Common stock		2,000,000
Retained earnings		146,000
Totals	$3,599,000	$3,599,000

Additional Information:

1. The common stock represents 1 million shares of no par stock authorized, 500,000 shares issued and outstanding.

2. The receivables from employees are due on June 30, 2022.

3. The notes receivable are due in installments of $50,000, payable on each September 30. Interest is payable annually.

4. Short-term investments consist of securities that the company plans to sell in 2022 and $50,000 in treasury bills purchased on December 15 of the current year that mature on February 15, 2022. Long-term investments consist of securities that the company does not plan to sell in the next year.

5. Deferred revenue represents payments from customer for extended service contracts. Eighty percent of these contracts expire in 2022, the remainder in 2023.

6. Notes payable consists of two notes, one for $100,000 due on January 15, 2023, and another for $200,000 due on June 30, 2024.

Required:

1. Prepare a classified balance sheet for Vosburgh at December 31, 2021. Include headings for each classification, as well as titles for each classification's subtotal. An example of a classified balance sheet can be found in the Concept Review Exercise at the end of Part A of this chapter.

2. Identify the items that would require additional disclosure, either on the face of the balance sheet or in a disclosure note.

P 3–7
Balance sheet
preparation;
errors
● LO3–2, LO3–3

The following balance sheet for the Hubbard Corporation was prepared by the company:

HUBBARD CORPORATION
Balance Sheet
At December 31, 2021
Assets

Buildings	$ 750,000
Land	250,000
Cash	60,000
Accounts receivable (net)	120,000
Inventory	240,000
Machinery	280,000
Patent (net)	100,000
Investment in equity securities	60,000
Total assets	$1,860,000

Liabilities and Shareholders' Equity

Accounts payable	$ 215,000
Accumulated depreciation	255,000
Notes payable	500,000
Appreciation of inventory	80,000
Common stock (authorized and issued 100,000 shares of no par stock)	430,000
Retained earnings	380,000
Total liabilities and shareholders' equity	$1,860,000

Additional Information:

1. The buildings, land, and machinery are all stated at cost except for a parcel of land that the company is holding for future sale. The land originally cost $50,000 but, due to a significant increase in market value, is listed at $120,000. The increase in the land account was credited to retained earnings.

2. The investment in equity securities account consists of stocks of other corporations and are recorded at cost, $20,000 of which will be sold in the coming year. The remainder will be held indefinitely.

3. Notes payable are all long term. However, a $100,000 note requires an installment payment of $25,000 due in the coming year.

4. Inventory is recorded at current resale value. The original cost of the inventory is $160,000.

Required:

Prepare a corrected classified balance sheet for the Hubbard Corporation at December 31, 2021. Include headings for each classification, as well as titles for each classification's subtotal. An example of a classified balance sheet can be found in the Concept Review Exercise at the end of Part A of this chapter.

P 3–8
Balance sheet;
errors; missing
amounts
● LO3–2, LO3–3

The following incomplete balance sheet for the Sanderson Manufacturing Company was prepared by the company's controller. As accounting manager for Sanderson, you are attempting to reconstruct and revise the balance sheet.

Sanderson Manufacturing Company
Balance Sheet
At December 31, 2021
($ in thousands)
Assets

Current assets:		
Cash		$ 1,250
Accounts receivable		3,500
Allowance for uncollectible accounts		(400)
Finished goods inventory		6,000
Prepaid expenses		1,200
Total current assets		11,550
Long-term assets:		
Investments		3,000
Raw materials and work in process inventory		2,250
Equipment		15,000
Accumulated depreciation		(4,200)
Patent (net)		?
Total assets		$?

Liabilities and Shareholders' Equity

Current liabilities:		
Accounts payable		$ 5,200
Notes payable		4,000
Interest payable (on notes)		100
Deferred revenue		3,000
Total current liabilities		12,300
Long-term liabilities:		
Bonds payable		5,500
Interest payable (on bonds)		200
Shareholders' equity:		
Common stock	$?	
Retained earnings	?	?
Total liabilities and shareholders' equity		?

Additional Information ($ in thousands):

1. Certain records that included the account balances for the patent and shareholders' equity items were lost. However, the controller told you that a complete, preliminary balance sheet prepared before the records were lost showed a debt to equity ratio of 1.2. That is, total liabilities are 120% of total shareholders' equity. Retained earnings at the beginning of the year was $4,000. Net income for 2021 was $1,560 and $560 in cash dividends were declared and paid to shareholders.

2. Management intends to sell the investments in the next six months.

3. Interest on both the notes and the bonds is payable annually.

4. The notes payable are due in annual installments of $1,000 each.

5. Deferred revenue will be recognized as revenue equally over the next two fiscal years.

6. The common stock represents 400,000 shares of no par stock authorized, 250,000 shares issued and outstanding.

Required:
Prepare a complete, corrected, classified balance sheet. Include headings for each classification, as well as titles for each classification's subtotal. An example of a classified balance sheet can be found in the Concept Review Exercise at the end of Part A of this chapter.

P 3–9
Balance sheet
preparation
● LO3–2, LO3–3

Presented below is the balance sheet for HHD, Inc., at December 31, 2021.

Current assets	$ 600,000	Current liabilities	$ 400,000
Investments	500,000	Long-term liabilities	1,100,000
Property, plant, and equipment	2,000,000	Shareholders' equity	1,800,000
Intangible assets	200,000		
Total assets	$3,300,000	Total liabilities and shareholders' equity	$3,300,000

The captions shown in the summarized statement above include the following:

a. Current assets: cash, $150,000; accounts receivable (net), $200,000; inventory, $225,000; and prepaid insurance, $25,000.

b. Investments: investment in equity securities, short term, $90,000, and long term, $160,000; and restricted cash, long term, $250,000.

c. Property, plant, and equipment: buildings, $1,500,000 less accumulated depreciation, $600,000; equipment, $500,000 less accumulated depreciation, $200,000; and land, $800,000.

d. Intangible assets net of amortization: patent, $110,000; and copyright, $90,000.

e. Current liabilities: accounts payable, $100,000; notes payable, short term, $150,000, and long term, $90,000; and income taxes payable, $60,000.

f. Long-term liabilities: bonds payable due 2023.

g. Shareholders' equity: common stock, $1,000,000; retained earnings, $800,000. Five hundred thousand shares of no par common stock are authorized, of which 200,000 shares were issued and are outstanding.

Required:

Prepare a corrected classified balance sheet for HHD, Inc., at December 31, 2021. Include headings for each classification, as well as titles for each classification's subtotal. An example of a classified balance sheet can be found in the Concept Review Exercise at the end of Part A of this chapter.

P 3–10
Balance sheet
preparation
● LO3–2. LO3–3

Melody Lane Music Company was started by John Ross early in 2021. Initial capital was acquired by issuing shares of common stock to various investors and by obtaining a bank loan. The company operates a retail store that sells records, tapes, and compact discs. Business was so good during the first year of operations that John is considering opening a second store on the other side of town. The funds necessary for expansion will come from a new bank loan. In order to approve the loan, the bank requires financial statements.

John asks for your help in preparing the balance sheet and presents you with the following information for the year ending December 31, 2021:

a. Cash receipts consisted of the following:

From customers	$360,000
From issue of common stock	100,000
From bank loan	100,000

b. Cash disbursements were as follows:

Purchase of inventory	$300,000
Rent	15,000
Salaries	30,000
Utilities	5,000
Insurance	3,000
Purchase of equipment	40,000

c. The bank loan was made on March 31, 2021. A note was signed requiring payment of interest and principal on March 31, 2022. The interest rate is 12%.

d. The equipment was purchased on January 3, 2021, and has an estimated useful life of 10 years with no anticipated salvage value. Depreciation per year is $4,000.

e. Inventory on hand at the end of the year cost $100,000.

f. Amounts owed at December 31, 2021, were as follows:

To suppliers of inventory	$20,000
To the utility company	1,000

g. Rent on the store building is $1,000 per month. On December 1, 2021, four months' rent was paid in advance.

h. Net income for the year was $76,000. Assume that the company is not subject to federal, state, or local income tax.

i. One hundred thousand shares of no par common stock are authorized, of which 20,000 shares were issued and are outstanding.

Required:

Prepare a balance sheet at December 31, 2021. Include headings for each classification, as well as titles for each classification's subtotal. An example of a classified balance sheet can be found in the Concept Review Exercise at the end of Part A of this chapter.

Decision Makers' Perspective

©ImageGap/Getty Images

Apply your critical-thinking ability to the knowledge you've gained. These cases will provide you an opportunity to develop your research, analysis, judgment, and communication skills. You also will work with other students, integrate what you've learned, apply it in real-world situations, and consider its global and ethical ramifications. This practice will broaden your knowledge and further develop your decision-making abilities.

Communication Case 3–1
Current versus long-term classification
● LO3–2

A first-year accounting student is confused by a statement made in a recent class. Her instructor stated that the assets listed in the balance sheet of the IBM Corporation include computers that are classified as current assets as well as computers that are classified as long-term (noncurrent) assets. In addition, the instructor stated that investments in equity securities of other corporations could be classified in the balance sheet as either current or long-term assets.

Required:
Explain to the student the distinction between current and long-term assets pertaining to the IBM computers and the investments in equity securities.

Analysis Case 3–2
Current versus long-term classification
● LO3–2, LO3–3

The usefulness of the balance sheet is enhanced when assets and liabilities are grouped according to common characteristics. The broad distinction made in the balance sheet is the current versus long-term classification of both assets and liabilities.

Required:
1. Discuss the factors that determine whether an asset or liability should be classified as current or long term in a balance sheet.
2. Identify six items that under different circumstances could be classified as either current or long term. Indicate the factors that would determine the correct classification.

Communication Case 3–3
FASB codification research; inventory or property, plant, and equipment
● LO3–2

The Red Hen Company produces, processes, and sells fresh eggs. The company is in the process of preparing financial statements at the end of its first year of operations and has asked for your help in determining the appropriate treatment of the cost of its egg-laying flock. The estimated life of a laying hen is approximately two years, after which they are sold to soup companies.

The controller considers the company's operating cycle to be two years and wants to present the cost of the egg-producing flock as inventory in the current asset section of the balance sheet. He feels that the hens are "goods awaiting sale." The chief financial officer does not agree with this treatment. He thinks that the cost of the flock should be classified as property, plant, and equipment because the hens are used in the production of product—the eggs.

The focus of this case is the balance sheet presentation of the cost of the egg-producing flock. Your instructor will divide the class into two to six groups depending on the size of the class. The mission of your group is to reach consensus on the appropriate presentation.

Required:
1. Each group member should deliberate the situation independently and draft a tentative argument prior to the class session for which the case is assigned.
2. In class, each group will meet for 10 to 15 minutes in different areas of the classroom. During that meeting, group members will take turns sharing their suggestions for the purpose of arriving at a single group treatment.
3. After the allotted time, a spokesperson for each group (selected during the group meetings) will share the group's solution with the class. The goal of the class is to incorporate the views of each group into a consensus approach to the situation.

IFRS Case 3–4
Balance sheet presentation; Vodafone Group, Plc.
● LO3–2, LO3–3, LO3–9

IFRS

Vodafone Group, Plc., a U.K. company, is the largest mobile telecommunications network company in the world. The company prepares its financial statements in accordance with International Financial Reporting Standards. Below are partial company balance sheets (statements of financial position) included in a recent annual report:

Vodafone Group, Plc. Consolidated Statements of Financial Position At March 31		
	2017	2016
	£m	£m
Long-term assets:		
Goodwill	26,808	28,238
Other intangible assets	19,412	30,326
Property, plant, and equipment	30,204	35,515
		(continued)

(concluded)

	2017	2016
	£m	£m
Investments in associates and joint ventures	3,138	479
Other investments	3,459	4,631
Deferred tax assets	24,300	28,306
Post employment benefits	57	224
Trade and other receivables	4,569	5,793
	111,947	133,512
Current assets:		
Inventory	576	716
Taxation recoverable	150	1,402
Trade and other receivables	9,861	11,561
Other investments	6,120	5,337
Cash and cash equivalents	8,835	12,922
Assets held for sale	17,195	3,657
	42,737	35,595
Total assets	154,684	169,107
Equity (details provided in complete statements)	73,719	85,136
Long-term liabilities:		
Long-term borrowings	34,523	37,089
Deferred tax liabilities	535	564
Post employment benefits	651	565
Provisions	1,130	1,619
Trade and other payables	1,737	1,899
	38,576	41,736
Current liabilities:		
Short-term borrowings	12,051	20,260
Taxation liabilities	661	683
Provisions	1,049	958
Trade and other payables	16,834	19,896
Liabilities held for sale	11,794	438
	42,389	42,235
Total equity and liabilities	154,684	169,107

Required:

1. Describe the differences between Vodafone's balance sheets and a typical U.S. company balance sheet.
2. What type of liabilities do you think are included in the *provisions* category in Vodafone's balance sheets?

Judgment Case 3–5
Balance sheet; errors
● LO3–2 through LO3–4

You recently joined the internal auditing department of Marcus Clothing Corporation. As one of your first assignments, you are examining a balance sheet prepared by a staff accountant.

MARCUS CLOTHING CORPORATION
Balance Sheet
At December 31, 2021
Assets

Current assets:		
Cash		$ 137,000
Accounts receivable (net)		80,000
Notes receivable		53,000
Inventory		240,000
Investments		66,000
Total current assets		576,000
Other assets:		
Land	$ 200,000	
Equipment (net)	320,000	
Prepaid expenses (for the next 12 months)	27,000	
Patent (net)	22,000	
Total other assets		569,000
Total assets		$1,145,000

(continued)

(concluded)	**Liabilities and Shareholders' Equity**		
Current liabilities:			
Accounts payable			$ 125,000
Salaries payable			32,000
Total current liabilities			157,000
Long-term liabilities:			
Notes payable		$ 100,000	
Bonds payable (due in 5 years)		300,000	
Interest payable		20,000	
Total long-term liabilities			420,000
Shareholders' equity:			
Common stock		500,000	
Retained earnings		68,000	
Total shareholders' equity			568,000
Total liabilities and shareholders' equity			$1,145,000

In the course of your examination you uncover the following information pertaining to the balance sheet:

1. The company rents its facilities. The land that appears in the statement is being held for future sale.
2. The notes receivable account contains one note that is due in 2023. The balance of $53,000 includes $3,000 of accrued interest. The next interest payment is due in July 2022.
3. The notes payable account contains one note that is due in installments of $20,000 per year. All interest is payable annually.
4. The company's investments consist of marketable equity securities of other corporations. Management does not intend to liquidate any investments in the coming year.

Required:

Identify and explain the deficiencies in the statement prepared by the company's accountant. Include in your answer items that require additional disclosure, either on the face of the statement or in a note.

Judgment Case 3–6
Financial disclosures
● LO3–4

You recently joined the auditing staff of Best, Best, and Krug, CPAs. You have been assigned to the audit of Clearview, Inc., and have been asked by the audit senior to examine the balance sheet prepared by Clearview's accountant.

CLEARVIEW, INC.
Balance Sheet
At December 31, 2021
($ in millions)
Assets

Current assets:		
Cash		$ 10.5
Accounts receivable		112.1
Inventory		220.6
Prepaid expenses		5.5
Total current assets		348.7
Investments		22.0
Property, plant, and equipment (net)		486.9
Total assets		$857.6
Liabilities and Shareholders' Equity		
Current liabilities:		
Accounts payable		$ 83.5
Accrued taxes and interest		25.5
Current maturities of long-term debt		20.0
Total current liabilities		129.0
Long-term liabilities:		420.0
Total liabilities		549.0
Shareholders' equity:		
Common stock	$100.0	
Retained earnings	208.6	
Total shareholders' equity		308.6
Total liabilities and shareholders' equity		$857.6

Required:

Identify the items in the statement that most likely would require further disclosure either on the face of the statement or in a note. Further identify those items that would require disclosure in the significant accounting policies note.

Real World Case 3–7
Balance sheet and significant accounting policies disclosure; Walmart

● LO3–2 through LO3–4, LO3–8

Real World Financials

The balance sheet and disclosure of significant accounting policies taken from the 2017 annual report of Walmart Stores Inc. appear below. Use this information to answer the following questions:

1. Does Walmart separately report current assets versus long-term assets, and current liabilities versus long-term liabilities (yes/no)?

2. What amounts did Walmart report for the following items for 2017:
   a. Total assets   d. Total equity
   b. Current assets   e. Retained earnings
   c. Current liabilities   f. Inventory

3. What is Walmart's largest current asset? What is its largest current liability?

4. Compute Walmart's current ratio for 2017.

5. Identify the following items from the summary of significant accounting policies:
   a. Does the company have any securities classified as cash equivalents (yes/no)?
   b. What cost method does the company use for its U.S. inventory?
   c. When does the company recognize revenue from service transactions?

WAL-MART STORES, INC.
Consolidated Balance Sheets
($ in millions except per share data)

	As of January 31,	
	2017	2016
Assets		
Current assets:		
Cash and cash equivalents	$ 6,867	$ 8,705
Receivables (net)	5,835	5,624
Inventories	43,046	44,469
Prepaid expenses and other	1,941	1,441
Total current assets	57,689	60,239
Property and equipment:		
Property and equipment	179,492	176,958
Less accumulated depreciation	(71,782)	(66,787)
Property and equipment (net)	107,710	110,171
Property under capital leases:		
Property under capital lease and financing obligations	11,637	11,096
Less accumulated amortization	(5,169)	(4,751)
Property under capital leases and financing obligations (net)	6,468	6,345
Goodwill	17,037	16,695
Other assets and deferred charges	9,921	6,131
Total assets	$198,825	$199,581
Liabilities, Redeemable Noncontrolling Interest and Equity		
Current liabilities:		
Short-term borrowings	$ 1,099	$ 2,708
Accounts payable	41,433	38,487
Accrued liabilities	20,654	19,607
Accrued income taxes	921	521
Long-term debt due within one year	2,256	2,745
Capital lease and financing obligations due within one year	565	551
Total current liabilities	66,928	64,619
Long-term debt	36,015	38,214
Long-term capital lease and financing obligations	6,003	5,816
Deferred income taxes and other	9,344	7,321
Commitments and contingencies Equity:		
Common stock	305	317
Capital in excess of par value	2,371	1,805
Retained earnings	89,354	90,021
Accumulated other comprehensive income (loss)	(14,232)	(11,597)
Total Walmart shareholders' equity	77,798	80,546
Nonredeemable noncontrolling interest	2,737	3,065
Total equity	80,535	83,611
Total liabilities, redeemable noncontrolling interest and equity	$198,825	$199,581

Source: Wal-Mart

> **NOTES TO CONSOLIDATED FINANCIAL STATEMENTS**
> **WAL-MART STORES, INC.**
> **1 Summary of Significant Accounting Policies (in part)**
>
> *Cash and Cash Equivalents*
> The Company considers investments with a maturity when purchased of three months or less to be cash equivalents.
>
> *Inventories*
> The Company values inventories at the lower of cost or market as determined primarily by the retail inventory method of accounting, using the last-in, first-out ("LIFO") method for substantially all of the Walmart U.S. segment's inventories. The inventory at the Walmart International segment is valued primarily by the retail inventory method of accounting, using the first-in, first-out ("FIFO") method. At January 31, 2017 and January 31, 2016, the Company's inventories valued at LIFO approximated those inventories as if they were valued at FIFO.
>
> *Revenue Recognition*
> The Company recognizes sales revenue, net of sales taxes and estimated sales returns, at the time it sells merchandise to the customer. Digital retail sales include shipping revenue and are recorded upon delivery to the customer. Customer purchases of shopping cards, to be utilized in our stores or on our e-commerce websites, are not recognized as revenue until the card is redeemed and the customer purchases merchandise using the shopping card. The Company recognizes revenue from service transactions at the time the service is performed. Generally, revenue from services is classified as a component of net sales in the Company's Consolidated Statements of Income.
>
> Source: Wal-Mart

Judgment Case 3–8
Post fiscal year-end events
● LO3–4

The fiscal year-end for the Northwest Distribution Corporation is December 31. The company's 2021 financial statements were issued on March 15, 2022. The following events occurred between December 31, 2021, and March 15, 2022.

1. On January 22, 2022, the company negotiated a major merger with Blandon Industries. The merger will be completed by the middle of 2022.

2. On February 3, 2022, Northwest negotiated a $10 million long-term note with the Credit Bank of Ohio. The amount of the note is material.

3. On February 25, 2022, a flood destroyed one of the company's manufacturing plants causing $600,000 of uninsured damage.

Required:
Determine whether each of these events should be disclosed with the 2021 financial statements of Northwest Distribution Corporation.

Research Case 3–9
FASB codification; locate and extract relevant information and cite authoritative support for a financial reporting issue; related-party disclosures; Enron Corporation
● LO3–4

Real World Financials

Real World Case 3–10
Disclosures; proxy statement; Coca-Cola
● LO3–4, LO3–5

Real World Financials

Enron Corporation was a darling in the energy-provider arena, and in January 2001 its stock price rose above $100 per share. A collapse of investor confidence in 2001 and revelations of accounting fraud led to one of the largest bankruptcies in U.S. history. By the end of the year, Enron's stock price had plummeted to less than $1 per share. Investigations and lawsuits followed. One problem area concerned transactions with related parties that were not adequately disclosed in the company's financial statements. Critics stated that the lack of information about these transactions made it difficult for analysts following Enron to identify problems the company was experiencing.

Access the *FASB Accounting Standards Codification* at the FASB website (www.fasb.org). Determine each of the following:

1. The specific eight-digit Codification citation (XXX-XX-XX-X) that outlines the required information on related-party disclosures that must be included in the notes to the financial statements?

2. Describe the disclosures required for related-party transactions.

3. Use EDGAR (www.gov.sec) or another method to locate the December 31, 2000, financial statements of Enron. Search for the related-party disclosure. Briefly describe the relationship central to the various transactions described.

4. Why is it important that companies disclose related-party transactions? Use the Enron disclosure of the sale of dark fiber inventory in your answer.

EDGAR, the Electronic Data Gathering, Analysis, and Retrieval system, performs automated collection, validation, indexing, and forwarding of submissions by companies and others who are required by law to file forms with the SEC. All publicly traded domestic companies use EDGAR to make the majority of their filings. (Some foreign companies file voluntarily.) Form 10-K, which includes the annual report, is required to be filed on EDGAR. The SEC makes this information available on the Internet.

Required:

1. Access EDGAR on the Internet. The web address is www.sec.gov.

2. Search for The Coca-Cola Company. Access the 10-K for the year ended December 31, 2016. Search or scroll to find the disclosure notes and audit report.

3. Answer the following questions:

   a. Describe the subsequent events disclosed by the company.

   b. Which firm is the company's auditor? What type of audit opinion did the auditor render?

4. Access the proxy statement filed with the SEC on March 9, 2017 (the proxy statement designation is Def 14A), locate the executive officers summary compensation table and answer the following questions:

   a. What is the principal position of Muhtar Kent?

   b. What was the salary paid to Mr. Kent during the year ended December 31, 2016?

Judgment Case 3–11
Debt versus equity
● LO3–7

A common problem facing any business entity is the debt versus equity decision. When funds are required to obtain assets, should debt or equity financing be used? This decision also is faced when a company is initially formed. What will be the mix of debt versus equity in the initial capital structure? The characteristics of debt are very different from those of equity as are the financial implications of using one method of financing as opposed to the other.

Cherokee Plastics Corporation is formed by a group of investors to manufacture household plastic products. Their initial capitalization goal is $50,000,000. That is, the incorporators have decided to raise $50,000,000 to acquire the initial assets of the company. They have narrowed down the financing mix alternatives to two:

1. All equity financing

2. $20,000,000 in debt financing and $30,000,000 in equity financing

No matter which financing alternative is chosen, the corporation expects to be able to generate a 10% annual return, before payment of interest and income taxes, on the $50,000,000 in assets acquired. The interest rate on debt would be 8%. The effective income tax rate will be approximately 25%.

Alternative 2 will require specified interest and principal payments to be made to the creditors at specific dates. The interest portion of these payments (interest expense) will reduce the taxable income of the corporation and hence the amount of income tax the corporation will pay. The all-equity alternative requires no specified payments to be made to suppliers of capital. The corporation is not legally liable to make distributions to its owners. If the board of directors does decide to make a distribution, it is not an expense of the corporation and does not reduce taxable income and hence the taxes the corporation pays.

Required:

1. Prepare abbreviated income statements that compare first-year profitability for each of the two alternatives.

2. Which alternative would be expected to achieve the highest first-year profits? Why?

3. Which alternative would provide the highest rate of return on equity? Why?

4. Which alternative is considered to be riskier, all else equal?

Analysis Case 3–12
Obtain and critically evaluate an actual annual report
● LO3–4, LO3–6 through LO3–8

Real World Financials

Financial reports are the primary means by which corporations report their performance and financial condition. Financial statements are one component of the annual report mailed to their shareholders and to interested others.

Required:

Obtain an annual report from a corporation with which you are familiar. Using techniques you learned in this chapter and any analysis you consider useful, respond to the following questions:

1. Do the firm's auditors provide a clean opinion on the financial statements?

2. Has the company made changes in any accounting methods it uses?

3. Have there been any subsequent events, errors and fraud, illegal acts, or related-party transactions that have a material effect on the company's financial position?

4. What are two trends in the company's operations or capital resources that management considers significant to the company's future?

5. Is the company engaged in more than one significant line of business? If so, compare the relative profitability of the different segments.

6. How stable are the company's operations?

7. Has the company's situation deteriorated or improved with respect to liquidity, solvency, asset management, and profitability?

Note: You can obtain a copy of an annual report from a local company, from a friend who is a shareholder, from the investor relations department of the corporation, from a friendly stockbroker, or from EDGAR (Electronic Data Gathering, Analysis, and Retrieval) on the Internet (www.sec.gov).

Analysis Case 3–13
Obtain and compare annual reports from companies in the same industry
● LO3–4, LO3–7, LO3–8

Real World Financials

Insight concerning the performance and financial condition of a company often comes from evaluating its financial data in comparison with other firms in the same industry.

Required:

Obtain annual reports from three corporations in the same primary industry. Using techniques you learned in this chapter and any analysis you consider useful, respond to the following questions:

1. Are there differences in accounting methods that should be taken into account when making comparisons?
2. How do earnings trends compare in terms of both the direction and stability of income?
3. Which of the three firms had the greatest earnings relative to resources available?
4. Which corporation has made most effective use of financial leverage?
5. Of the three firms, which seems riskiest in terms of its ability to pay short-term obligations? Long-term obligations?

   Note: You can obtain copies of annual reports from friends who are shareholders, from the investor relations department of the corporations, from a friendly stockbroker, or from EDGAR (Electronic Data Gathering, Analysis, and Retrieval) on the Internet (www.sec.gov).

Analysis Case 3–14
Balance sheet information
● LO3–2 through LO3–4

Real World Financials

Target Corporation prepares its financial statements according to U.S. GAAP. Target's financial statements and disclosure notes for the year ended February 3, 2018, are available in the Connect library. This material also is available under the Investor Relations link at the company's website (www.target.com).

Required:

1. Does the company separately report current assets and long-term assets, as well as current liabilities and long-term liabilities?
2. Are any investments shown as a current asset? Why?
3. In which liability account would the company report the balance of its gift card liability?
4. What method does the company use to depreciate its property and equipment?
5. What purpose do the disclosure notes serve?

Analysis Case 3–15
Segment reporting concepts
● Appendix 3, LO3–9

 IFRS

Levens Co. operates in several distinct business segments. The company does not have any reportable foreign operations or major customers.

Required:

1. What is the purpose of operating segment disclosures?
2. Define an operating segment.
3. List the amounts to be reported by operating segment.
4. How would your answer to requirement 3 differ if Levens Co. prepares its segment disclosure according to International Financial Reporting Standards?

Ethics Case 3–16
Segment reporting
● Appendix 3

You are in your third year as an accountant with McCarver-Lynn Industries, a multidivisional company involved in the manufacturing, marketing, and sales of surgical prosthetic devices. After the fiscal year-end, you are working with the controller of the firm to prepare geographic area disclosures. Yesterday you presented her with the following summary information:

	Domestic	Libya	Egypt	France	Cayman Islands	Total
				($ in millions)		
Revenues	$ 845	$222	$265	$343	$2,311	$3,986
Operating income	145	76	88	21	642	972
Assets	1,005	301	290	38	285	1,919

Upon returning to your office after lunch, you find the following memo:
Nice work. Let's combine the data this way:

	Domestic	Africa	Europe and Other Foreign	Total
			($ in millions)	
Revenues	$ 845	$487	$2,654	$3,986
Capital expenditures	145	164	663	972
Assets	1,005	591	323	1,919

Because of political instability in North Africa, let's not disclose specific countries. In addition, we restructured most of our French sales and some of our U.S. sales to occur through our offices in the Cayman Islands. This allows us to avoid paying higher taxes in those countries. The Cayman Islands has a 0% corporate income tax rate. We don't want to highlight our ability to shift profits to avoid taxes.

Required:

**Data Analytics
Case 3–17**

Do you perceive an ethical dilemma? What would be the likely impact of following the controller's suggestions? Who would benefit? Who would be injured?

Data Analytics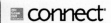

Data analytics is the process of examining data sets in order to draw conclusions about the information they contain. To prepare for this case, you will need to download Tableau to your computer. If you have not completed any of the prior data analytics cases, follow the instructions listed in the Chapter 1 Data Analytics case to get set up. You will need to watch the videos referred to in both the Chapter 1 and Chapter 2 Data Analytics cases. To prepare for this video, you should watch "Getting Started with Calculations" and "Calculation Syntax" videos listed under "Calculations." Future cases will build off of your knowledge gained from these, and additional videos will be suggested. All short training videos can be found here: www.tableau.com/learn/training#getting-started.

**Data Analytics
Case
Liquidity
● LO3–7**

In the Chapter 1 and Chapter 2 Data Analytics Cases, you applied Tableau to examine a data set and create charts to compare our two (hypothetical) publicly traded companies: Discount Goods and Big Store. In this case, you continue in your role as an analyst conducting introductory research into the relative merits of investing in one or both of these companies. This time you assess the companies' liquidity: i.e., their ability to pay short-term debts as they come due. You do so by comparing liquidity ratios in a line chart.

Required:

Use Tableau to calculate the liquidity ratios for each of the two companies in each year from 2012 to 2021. Based upon what you find, answer the following questions:

1. Analyzing the liquidity ratios over the ten-year period, is Discount Goods current ratio (a) generally increasing, (b) roughly the same, or (c) generally decreasing from year to year?

2. Analyzing the liquidity ratios over the ten-year period, is Big Store's current ratio (a) generally increasing, (b) roughly the same, or (c) generally decreasing from year to year?

3. What is the current ratio in 2021 for Discount Goods? For Big Store?

4. What is the acid-test (or quick) ratio in 2021 for Discount Goods? For Big Store?

5. Which company has more favorable liquidity ratios in 2021?

Note: As you assess the liquidity aspect of the companies, keep in mind that liquidity ratios should be evaluated in the context of both profitability and efficiency of managing assets.

Resources:

You have available to you an extensive data set that includes detailed financial data for Discount Goods and Big Store and for 2012 - 2021. The data set is in the form of an Excel file available to download from Connect, or under Student Resources within the Library tab. There are four Excel files available. The one for use in this chapter is named "Discount_Goods_Big_Store_Financials.xlsx" Download this file and save it to the computer on which you will be using Tableau. Open Tableau and connect to the Excel spreadsheet you downloaded.

For this case, you will create several calculations to produce a line chart of liquidity ratios to allow you to compare and contrast the two companies. You also will need to change data from *continuous* to *discrete*. Continuous data are data that is identified as a range of numeric values. A bar chart uses continuous data. "Measures" are usually identified by Tableau as continuous data and produce a range of data when dragged to the row shelf. If you want only one number, you must change the data to be discrete data. The *pill* that represents the data on the shelves will be blue if it is discrete and green if it is continuous.

After you view the training videos, follow these steps to create the charts you'll use for this case:

● Open Tableau and connect to the Excel spreadsheet you downloaded.

● Click on the "Sheet 1" tab at the bottom of the canvas, to the right of the Data Source at the bottom of the screen. Drag "Company" under "Dimensions" to the Columns shelf.

● Drag the "Year" under "Dimensions" to the Columns shelf. If the "Year" pill is green, Tableau has identified it as continuous data. Select the drop-down menu box on the "Year" pill and click "Discrete" instead of "Continuous." Note the pill is now blue.

● Drag "Total current assets" under "Measures" to the Rows shelf. Change to "Discrete" data following the same instructions above. Note: You must drag accounts into the Rows shelf if you are going to use them in calculated fields and need an *aggregated* sum. If this is not done first, your answer will not match the solutions.

- Drag "Total current liabilities" under Measures to the Rows shelf. Follow the same instructions above for "Total current assets."
- Create a calculated field by clicking the "Analysis" tab from the Toolbar at the top of the screen and selecting "Create Calculated field." A calculation box will pop up. Name the calculation "Quick Assets." Drag "Cash and cash equivalents" under "Measures" into the calculation box. Add a plus sign and drag "Receivables, net" into the calculation box. Make sure the box says that the calculation is valid and click OK. The new field "Quick Assets" will now appear under "Measures."
- Create another calculated field named "Current Ratio" by dragging "Total current assets" into the calculation box, typing a division sign, then dragging "Total current liabilities" beside it. Make sure the box says that the calculation is valid and click OK. The new field "Current Ratio" will now appear under Measures. Drag "Current Ratio" to the Rows shelf. Click on the dropdown from the "Current Ratio" pill, click 'Format', set the formatting options. From the 'Font' dropdown select Times New Roman, 10-point font, Bold, Black. From the 'Numbers' dropdown select 'Number (custom) "3" decimal places.
- Create a calculated field "Quick Ratio" following the same process. Drag the newly created "Quick Assets" under "Measures" into the calculation box. Type a division sign, then drag Total current liabilities" under "Measures" beside it. Make sure the box says that the calculation is valid and click OK. Drag "Quick Ratio" to the Rows shelf. Click on the dropdown from the "Quick Ratio" pill, set Formats as noted above.
- Drag "Sum: Total current assets" and "Sum: Total current liabilities" from the "Rows" shelf back under "Measures." This will remove them from the canvas.
- In the "Marks" card, select the drop-down menu for presentation type and select "Line" (it defaults to "Automatic"). In the "Label" box, select "Show mark labels." Format to Times New Roman, bold, and 10-point font.
- Change the title of the sheet to be "Liquidity" by right-clicking and selecting "Edit title." Format the title to Times New Roman, bold, black and 20-point font. Change the title of "Sheet 1" to match the sheet title by right-clicking, selecting "Rename" and typing in the new title.
- Once complete, save the file as "DA3_Your initials.twbx."

Continuing Cases

Target Case

● LO3–2, LO3–3, LO3–8

Target Corporation prepares its financial statements according to U.S. GAAP. Target's financial statements and disclosure notes for the year ended February 3, 2018, are available in Connect. This material is also available under the Investor Relations link at the company's website (www.target.com).

Required:

1. By what name does Target label its balance sheet?
2. What amounts did Target report for the following items on February 3, 2018?
   a. Current assets
   b. Long-term assets
   c. Total assets
   d. Current liabilities
   e. Long-term liabilities
   f. Total liabilities
   g. Total shareholders' equity
3. What was Target's largest current asset? What was its largest current liability?
4. Compute Target's current ratio and debt to equity ratio in 2018?
5. Assuming Target's industry had an average current ratio of 1.0 and an average debt to equity ratio of 2.5, comment on Target's liquidity and long-term solvency.

Air France–KLM Case

● LO3–9

 IFRS

Air France–KLM (AF), a Franco-Dutch company, prepares its financial statements according to International Financial Reporting Standards. AF's financial statements and disclosure notes for the year ended December 31, 2017, are provided in Connect. This material is also available under the Finance link at the company's website (www.airfranceklm.com).

Required:

Describe the apparent differences in the order of presentation of the components of the balance sheet between IFRS as applied by Air France–KLM (AF) and a typical balance sheet prepared in accordance with U.S. GAAP.

CPA Exam Questions and Simulations

 ROGER CPA Review

Sample CPA Exam questions from Roger CPA Review are available in Connect as support for the topics in this chapter. These multiple-choice questions and task-based simulations include expert-written explanations and solutions, and provide a starting point for students to become familiar with the content and functionality of the actual CPA Exam.

CHAPTER

4

The Income Statement, Comprehensive Income, and the Statement of Cash Flows

This chapter has three purposes: (1) to consider important issues dealing with the content, presentation, and disclosure of net income and other components of comprehensive income; (2) to provide an *overview* of the statement of cash flows, which is covered in depth in Chapter 21; and (3) to examine common ratios used in profitability analysis.

The income statement summarizes the profit-generating activities that occurred during a particular reporting period. Comprehensive income includes net income as well as other gains and losses that are not part of net income.

The statement of cash flows provides information about the cash receipts and cash disbursements of an enterprise's operating, investing, and financing activities that occurred during the period.

Profitability ratios measure how well a company manages its operations and utilizes resources to generate a profit. Profitability is a key metric in understanding the company's ability to generate cash in the future.

LEARNING OBJECTIVES

After studying this chapter, you should be able to:

- **LO4–1** Discuss the importance of income from continuing operations and describe its components. (*p. 168*)
- **LO4–2** Describe earnings quality and how it is impacted by management practices to alter reported earnings. (*p. 173*)
- **LO4–3** Discuss the components of operating and nonoperating income and their relationship to earnings quality. (*p. 173*)
- **LO4–4** Define what constitutes discontinued operations and describe the appropriate income statement presentation for these transactions. (*p. 177*)
- **LO4–5** Discuss additional reporting issues related to accounting changes, error corrections, and earnings per share (EPS). (*p. 182*)
- **LO4–6** Explain the difference between net income and comprehensive income and how we report components of the difference. (*p. 185*)
- **LO4–7** Describe the purpose of the statement of cash flows. (*p. 189*)
- **LO4–8** Identify and describe the various classifications of cash flows presented in a statement of cash flows. (*p. 190*)
- **LO4–9** Discuss the primary differences between U.S. GAAP and IFRS with respect to the income statement, statement of comprehensive income, and statement of cash flows. (*pp. 172, 186, and 195*)
- **LO4–10** Identify and calculate the common ratios used to assess profitability. (*p. 197*)

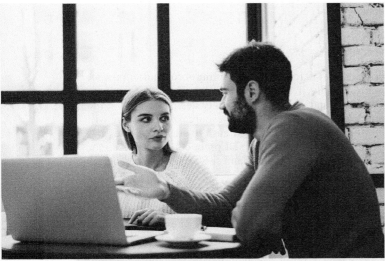

©GaudiLab/Shutterstock

FINANCIAL REPORTING CASE

Abbott Laboratories

Your friend, Becky Morgan, just received a generous gift from her grandfather. Accompanying a warm letter were 200 shares of stock of Abbott Laboratories, a global health care company, along with the most recent annual financial statements of the company. Becky knows that you are an accounting major and pleads with you to explain some items in the company's income statement. "I remember studying the income statement in my introductory accounting course," says Becky, "but I am still confused. What is this item *discontinued operations?* I also read in the annual report the company has *restructuring costs?* These don't sound good. Are they something I should worry about? We studied earnings per share briefly, but what does *earnings per common share—diluted* mean?" You agree to try to help.

ABBOTT LABORATORIES AND SUBSIDIARY COMPANIES
Statements of Earnings For the Year Ended December 31
($ in millions, except per share data)

	2016	2015
Net sales	$ 20,853	$20,405
Costs and expenses:		
Cost of products sold	9,024	8,747
Amortization of intangible assets	550	601
Research and development expenses	1,422	1,405
Selling, general and administrative	6,672	6,785
Operating income	3,185	2,867
Other income (deductions)	(1,776)	316
Income from continuing operations before income taxes	1,413	3,183
Provision for taxes on income	350	577
Income from continuing operations	1,063	2,606
Income from discontinued operations, net of tax	337	1,817
Net income	$ 1,400	$ 4,423
Earnings per common share—basic:		
Continuing operations	$ 0.71	$ 1.73
Discontinued operations	0.23	1.21
Net income	$ 0.94	$ 2.94
Earnings per common share—diluted:		
Continuing operations	$ 0.71	$ 1.72
Discontinued operations	0.23	1.20
Net income	$ 0.94	$ 2.92

Source: Abbott Laboratories, Inc.

By the time you finish this chapter, you should be able to respond appropriately to the questions posed in this case. Compare your response to the solution provided at the end of the chapter.

QUESTIONS

1. How would you explain restructuring costs to Becky? Are restructuring costs something Becky should worry about?

2. Explain to Becky what is meant by discontinued operations and describe to her how that item is reported in an income statement.

3. Describe to Becky the difference between basic and diluted earnings per share.

In Chapter 1, we discussed the critical role of financial accounting information in allocating resources within our economy. Ideally, resources should be allocated to private enterprises that will (1) provide the goods and services our society desires and (2) at the same time provide a fair rate of return to those who supply the resources. A company will be able to achieve these goals only if it can generate enough cash to stay in business. A company's ability to generate cash relates to its ability to sell products and services for amounts greater than the costs of providing those products and services (that is, generate a profit).

Two financial statements that are critical for understanding the company's ability to earn profits and generate cash in the future are as follows:

1. **Income statement** (also called *statement of operations* or *statement of earnings*).
2. **Statement of cash flows.**

The income statement reports a company's profit during a particular reporting period. Profit equals revenues and gains minus expenses and losses. A few types of gains and losses are excluded from the income statement but are included in the broader concept of comprehensive income. We refer to these other gains and losses as other comprehensive income (OCI).

The statement of cash flows provides information about the cash receipts and cash payments of a company during a particular reporting period. The difference between cash receipts and cash payments represents the change in cash for the period. To help investors and creditors better understand the sources and uses of cash during the period, the statement of cash flows distinguishes among operating, investing, and financing activities.

PART A   The Income Statement and Comprehensive Income

Before we discuss the specific components of an income statement in much depth, let's take a quick look at the general makeup of the statement. Illustration 4–1 offers an income statement for McAllister's Manufacturing, a hypothetical company, that you can refer to as we proceed through the chapter. At this point, our objective is only to gain a general perspective on the items reported and classifications contained in corporate income statements. In addition, each income statement should include in the heading the name of the company, the title of the statement, and the date or time period. McAllister's income statement is for the year ended December 31. This means that amounts in the income statement are the result of transactions from January 1 to December 31 of that year. In reality, many companies have reporting periods (often referred to as *fiscal years*) that end in months other than December, as you'll see demonstrated later in this chapter. Illustration 4–1 shows comparative income statements for two consecutive years.

Let's first look closer at the components of net income. At the end of Part A, we'll see how net income fits within the concept of comprehensive income and how comprehensive income is reported.

Income from Continuing Operations

Revenues, Expenses, Gains, and Losses

● LO4–1   Unlike the balance sheet, which is a position statement *at a point in time,* the income statement measures activity *over a period of time.* The income statement reports the revenues, expenses, gains, and losses that have occurred during the reporting period. For example, if a company reports revenues of $100 million in its income statement for the year ended December 31, 2021, this means that the company had revenue transactions from January 1, 2021, to December 31, 2021, equal to $100 million.

Revenues are inflows of resources resulting from providing goods or services to customers. For merchandising companies like Walmart, the main source of revenue is sales revenue derived from selling merchandise. Service companies such as FedEx and State Farm Insurance generate revenue by providing services.

Illustration 4–1

Income Statement

McAllister's Manufacturing
Income Statement
($ in millions, except per share data)

	Year Ended December 31	
	2021	**2020**
Sales revenue	$1,450.6	$1,380.0
Cost of goods sold	832.6	800.4
Gross profit	618.0	579.6
Operating expenses:		
Selling expense	123.5	110.5
General and administrative expense	147.8	139.1
Research and development expense	55.0	65.0
Restructuring costs	125.0	—
Total operating expenses	451.3	314.6
Operating income	166.7	265.0
Other income (expense):		
Interest revenue	12.4	11.1
Interest expense	(25.9)	(24.8)
Gain on sale of investments	18.0	19.0
Income from continuing operations before income taxes	171.2	270.3
Income tax expense	59.9	94.6
Income from continuing operations	111.3	175.7
Discontinued operations:		
Loss from operations of discontinued component (including gain on disposal in 2021 of $47)	(7.6)	(45.7)
Income tax benefit	2.0	13.0
Loss on discontinued operations	(5.6)	(32.7)
Net income	$ 105.7	$ 143.0
Earnings per common share—basic:		
Income from continuing operations	$ 2.14	$ 3.38
Discontinued operations	(0.11)	(0.63)
Net income	$ 2.03	$ 2.75
Earnings per common share—diluted:		
Income from continuing operations	$ 2.06	$ 3.25
Discontinued operations	(0.10)	(0.61)
Net income	$ 1.96	$ 2.64

Income from Continuing Operations — bracketed label on left
Discontinued Operations — bracketed label on left
Earnings per Share — bracketed label on left

Expenses are outflows of resources incurred while generating revenue. They represent the costs of providing goods and services. When recognizing expenses, we attempt to establish a causal relationship between revenues and expenses. If causality can be determined, expenses are reported in the same period that the related revenue is recognized. If a causal relationship cannot be established, we relate the expense to a particular period, allocate it over several periods, or expense it as incurred.

Gains and **losses** are increases or decreases in equity from peripheral or incidental transactions of an entity. In general, these gains and losses do not reflect normal operating activities of the company, but they nevertheless represent transactions that affect a company's financial position. For example, gains and losses can arise when a company sells investments or property, plant, and equipment for an amount that differs from their recorded amount. Losses can occur on inventory due to obsolescence, on assets for impaired values, and on litigation claims. We will discuss many types of gains and losses throughout this book.

To understand a company's ability to generate cash in the future, investors and creditors assess which components of net income are likely to continue into the future. **Income from continuing operations** includes revenues, expenses (including income taxes), gains, and

Income from continuing operations includes the revenues, expenses, gains and losses from operations that are more likely to continue into the future.

losses arising from operations that are more likely to continue. In contrast, income from *discontinued operations* will not continue into the future.[1]

The three major components of income from continuing operations include the following:

1. Operating income
2. Nonoperating income
3. Income tax expense

Operating Income versus Nonoperating Income

Operating income includes revenues, expenses, gains, and losses directly related to the *primary revenue-generating activities* of the company. For a manufacturing company, operating income includes sales revenue from selling the products it manufactures minus cost of goods sold and operating expenses related to its primary activities.[2] As shown in Illustration 4–1, operating income is often presented as gross profit (sales revenue minus cost of goods sold) minus operating expenses. In practice, many companies include *net sales* on the first line of the income statement to represent total sales revenue less sales discounts, returns, and allowances, which we discuss in depth in chapters 6 and 7. For a service company, operating income would include service revenue minus operating expenses (and no cost of goods sold).

Nonoperating income includes revenues, expenses, gains, and losses related to *peripheral or incidental activities* of the company. For example, a manufacturer would include interest revenue, gains and losses from selling investments, and interest expense in nonoperating income. These items are not directly related to the primary revenue-generating activities of a manufacturing company. On the other hand, a financial institution like a bank would consider those items to be a part of operating income because they relate to the primary revenue-generating activities for that type of business. As shown in Illustration 4–1, nonoperating items often are included in the income statement under the heading *Other income (expense)*.

Income Tax Expense

Income taxes are levied on taxpayers in proportion to the amount of taxable income that is reported to taxing authorities. Like individuals, corporations are income-tax-paying entities.[3] Because of the importance and size of income tax expense (sometimes called *provision for income taxes*), it always is reported in a separate line in corporate income statements. In addition, as we'll discuss in more detail later in this chapter, companies are required to report income tax expense associated with operations that are *continuing* separately from income tax expense associated with operations that are being *discontinued*. Separately reporting income tax expense in this way is known as *intraperiod tax allocation*.

Income tax expense is reported in a separate line in the income statement.

When tax rules and GAAP differ regarding the timing of revenue or expense recognition, the actual payment of taxes may occur in a period different from when income tax expense is reported in the income statement. We discuss this and other issues related to accounting for income taxes in Chapter 16. At this point, simply consider income tax expense to be a percentage of income before taxes.

Illustration 4–2 presents the 2017 income statement for The Home Depot, Inc., a retail company specializing in home improvement products. Notice that Home Depot distinguishes between operating income, nonoperating income, and income tax expense. Operating income includes revenues and expenses from primary business activities related to merchandise sales. After operating income is determined, nonoperating items are added or subtracted. For a retail company like Home Depot, activities related to interest and investments are not primary operations and therefore are listed as nonoperating items. Finally, income tax expense is subtracted to arrive at net income.

Now let's consider the format used to report the components of net income.

---

[1]Discontinued operations are addressed in a subsequent section.

[2]In certain situations, operating income might also include gains and losses from selling equipment and other assets used in the manufacturing process. FASB ASC 360-10-45-5: Property, plant, and equipment—Overall—Other Presentation Matters (previously "Accounting for the Impairment of Long-Lived Assets and for Long-Lived Assets to Be Disposed Of," *Statement of Financial Accounting Standards No. 144* (Norwalk, Conn.: FASB, 2001)).

[3]Partnerships are not tax-paying entities. Their taxable income or loss is included in the taxable income of the individual partners.

Consolidated Statement of Earnings
($ in millions)

	Year ended January 29, 2017
Net sales	$94,595
Cost of goods sold	62,282
Gross profit	32,313
Selling, general, and administrative expenses	17,132
Depreciation and amortization	1,754
Operating income	13,427
Interest and investment income	36
Interest expense	(972)
Income before income taxes	12,491
Income tax expense	4,534
Net income	$ 7,957

Source: Home Depot, Inc.

Illustration 4–2

Income Statement—The Home Depot, Inc.

Real World Financials

Income Statement Formats

No specific standards dictate how income from continuing operations must be displayed, so companies have considerable latitude in how they present the components of income from continuing operations. This flexibility has resulted in a variety of income statement presentations. However, we can identify two general approaches, the single-step and the multiple-step formats, that might be considered the two extremes, with the income statements of most companies falling somewhere in between.

The **single-step** format first lists all the revenues and gains included in income from continuing operations. Then, expenses and losses are grouped, subtotaled, and subtracted—in a single step—from revenues and gains to derive income from continuing operations. In a departure from that, though, companies usually report income tax expense in a separate line in the statement. In a single-step income statement, operating and nonoperating items are not separately classified. Illustration 4–3 shows an example of a single-step income statement for a hypothetical manufacturing company, Maxwell Gear Corporation.

A *single-step* income statement format groups all revenues and gains together and all expenses and losses together.

MAXWELL GEAR CORPORATION
Income Statement
For the Year Ended December 31, 2021

Revenues and gains:		
Sales revenue	$573,522	
Interest revenue	5,500	
Gain on sale of investments	26,400	
Total revenues and gains		$605,422
Expenses and losses:		
Cost of goods sold	302,371	
Selling expense	47,341	
General and administrative expense	24,888	
Research and development expense	16,300	
Interest expense	14,522	
Total expenses and losses		405,422
Income before income taxes		200,000
Income tax expense		50,000
Net income		$150,000

Illustration 4–3

Single-Step Income Statement

172 SECTION 1 The Role of Accounting as an Information System

A *multiple-step* income statement format includes a number of intermediate subtotals before arriving at income from continuing operations.

Illustration 4–4
Multiple-Step
Income Statement

The **multiple-step** format reports a series of intermediate subtotals such as gross profit, operating income, and income before taxes. Most of the real-world income statements are in this format. Illustration 4–4 presents a multiple-step income statement for the Maxwell Gear Corporation.

MAXWELL GEAR CORPORATION Income Statement For the Year Ended December 31, 2021		
Sales revenue		$573,522
Cost of goods sold		302,371
Gross profit		271,151
Operating expenses:		
Selling expense	$47,341	
General and administrative expense	24,888	
Research and development expense	16,300	
Total operating expenses		88,529
Operating income		182,622
Other income (expense):		
Interest revenue	5,500	
Gain on sale of investments	26,400	
Interest expense	(14,522)	
Total other income, net		17,378
Income before income taxes		200,000
Income tax expense		50,000
Net income		$150,000

A primary advantage of the multiple-step format is that, by separately classifying operating and nonoperating items, it provides information that might be useful in analyzing trends. Similarly, the classification of expenses by function also provides useful information. For example, reporting *gross profit* for merchandising companies highlights the important relationship between sales revenue and cost of goods sold. *Operating income* provides a measure of profitability for core (or normal) operations, a key performance measure for predicting the future profit-generating ability of the company. *Income before taxes* could be useful for comparing the performance of companies in different tax jurisdictions or comparing corporations (tax-paying entities) with sole proprietorships or partnerships (typically non-tax-paying entities).

It is important to note that the difference between the single-step and multiple-step income statement is one of presentation. The bottom line, *net income,* is the same regardless of the format used. Most companies use the multiple-step format. We use the multiple-step format for illustration purposes throughout the remainder of this chapter.

International Financial Reporting Standards

● LO4–9

Income Statement Presentation. There are more similarities than differences between income statements prepared according to U.S. GAAP and those prepared applying international standards. Some of the differences are as follows:

- International standards require certain minimum information to be reported on the face of the income statement. U.S. GAAP has no minimum requirements.
- International standards allow expenses to be classified either by function (e.g., cost of goods sold, general and administrative, etc.), or by natural description (e.g., salaries, rent, etc.). SEC regulations require that expenses be classified by function.
- In the United States, the "bottom line" of the income statement usually is called either *net income* or *net loss.* The descriptive term for the bottom line of the income statement prepared according to international standards is either *profit* or *loss.*

Earnings Quality

Investors, creditors, and financial analysts are concerned with more than just the bottom line of the income statement—net income. The presentation of the components of net income and the related supplemental disclosures provide clues to the user of the statement in an assessment of *earnings quality*. Earnings quality is used as a framework for more in-depth discussions of operating and nonoperating income.

● LO4–2

One meaning of earnings quality is the ability of reported earnings (income) to predict a company's future earnings. The relevance of any historical-based financial statement hinges on its predictive value. To enhance predictive value, analysts try to separate a company's *temporary earnings* from its *permanent earnings*. Temporary earnings arise from transactions or events that are not likely to occur again in the foreseeable future or that are likely to have a different impact on earnings in the future. In contrast, permanent earnings arise from operations that are expected to generate similar profits in the future. Analysts begin their assessment of permanent earnings with income before discontinued operations, that is, income from continuing operations. Later in the chapter we address discontinued operations that, because of their nature, are required to be reported separately at the bottom of the income statement.

Earnings quality refers to the ability of reported earnings (income) to predict a company's future earnings.

It would be a mistake, though, to assume that all items included in income from continuing operations reflect permanent earnings. Some income items that fall under this category may be temporary. In a sense, the label *continuing* may be misleading.

Income Smoothing and Classification Shifting

An often-debated contention is that, within GAAP, managers have the power to change reported income by altering assumptions and estimates. And these alternatives are not always in the direction of higher income. Survey evidence suggests that managers often alter income upwards in one year but downward in other years.[4] For example, in a year when income is high, managers may create reserves by overestimating certain expenses (such as future bad debts or warranties). These reserves reduce reported income in the current year. Then, in later years, they can use those reserves by underestimating expenses, which will increase reported income. By shifting income in this manner, managers effectively smooth the pattern in reported income over time, portraying a steadier income stream to investors, creditors, and other financial statement users.[5]

Management's *income smoothing* behavior is controversial. While some believe that a smoother income pattern helps investors and creditors to better predict future performance, others believe that managers are doing this to hide the true risk (volatility) of operations. By hiding this underlying volatility through manipulation of the income pattern over time, managers may be "fooling" investors and creditors into believing that the company's operations are lower-risk than they really are.

Income smoothing may help investors to predict future performance but it could also hide underlying risk.

Another way that managers affect reported income is through *classification shifting* in the income statement.[6] The most common example of this involves misclassifying operating expenses as nonoperating expenses. By shifting operating expenses to a nonoperating expense classification (often referred to as "special charges" or "special items"), managers report fewer operating expenses and therefore higher operating income. This type of manipulation creates the appearance of stronger performance for core operations. While bottom-line net income remains unaffected, investors and creditors may believe the core business is stronger than it really is.

Classification shifting inflates core performance.

Operating Income and Earnings Quality

Should all items of revenue and expense included in operating income be considered indicative of a company's permanent earnings? No, not necessarily. Sometimes a company will

● LO4–3

---

[4]See, for example, I. Dichev, J. Graham, H. Campbell, and S. Rajgopal, "Earnings Quality: Evidence from the Field," *Journal of Accounting and Economics* 56 (2013), pp. 1–33.

[5]J. Graham, H. Campbell, and S. Rajgopal, "The Economic Implications of Corporate Financial Reporting," *Journal of Accounting and Economics* 40 (2005), pp. 3–73.

[6] S. McVay, "Earnings Management Using Classification Shifting: An Examination of Core Earnings and Special Items," *The Accounting Review* 81 (2006), pp. 501–31.

174 SECTION 1 The Role of Accounting as an Information System

have an unusual or infrequent event. Even though these events may be unlikely to occur again in the near future, we report them as part of operating income because they are so closely related to the company's core business.[7]

What kind of items might be included in this category? Look closely at the partial income statements of The Hershey Company, the largest producer of chocolate in North America, presented in Illustration 4–5. Which items appear unusual? Certainly not net sales, cost of sales, or selling, marketing and administrative expenses. But what about "Goodwill and other intangible asset impairment charges" and "Business realignment charges"? Let's consider both.

Illustration 4–5

Partial Income Statement—
The Hershey Company

Real World Financials

Income Statements (in part)
($ in thousands)

	Year Ended	
	December 31, 2016	December 31, 2015
Net sales	$7,440,181	$7,386,626
Cost of sales	4,282,290	4,003,951
Selling, marketing and administrative expenses	1,915,378	1,969,308
Goodwill and other intangible asset impairment charges	4,204	280,802
Business realignment charges	32,526	94,806
Operating profit	$1,205,783	$1,037,759

Source: The Hershey Company

FINANCIAL Reporting Case

Q1, p. 167

Restructuring costs include costs associated with shutdown or relocation of facilities or downsizing of operations.

GAAP requires that restructuring costs be recognized only in the period incurred.

RESTRUCTURING COSTS It's not unusual for a company to reorganize its operations to attain greater efficiency. When this happens, the company often incurs significant restructuring costs (sometimes referred to as *reorganization costs* or *realignment costs*). Restructuring costs are associated with management's plans to materially change the scope of business operations or the manner in which they are conducted.[8] For example, facility closings and related employee layoffs translate into costs incurred for severance pay and relocation costs. The Hershey Company had restructuring costs related to reorganization of operations in Brazil to enhance distribution of the company's products, as well as employee severance costs related to eliminating several positions as part of the company's Productivity Initiative.

Restructuring costs are recognized in the period the exit or disposal cost obligation actually is incurred. Suppose, as part of a restructuring plan, employees to be terminated are offered various benefits but only if they complete a certain period of work for the company. In that case, a liability for termination benefits, and corresponding expense, should be accrued in the required period(s) of work. On the other hand, if future work by the employee is not required to receive the termination benefits, the liability and corresponding expense for benefits are recognized at the time the company communicates the arrangement to employees. Similarly, costs associated with closing facilities and relocating employees are recognized when goods or services associated with those activities are received.

Because it usually takes considerable time to sell or terminate a line of business, or to close a location or facility, many restructuring costs represent long-term liabilities. GAAP requires initial measurement of these liabilities to be at fair value, which often is determined as the present value of future estimated cash outflows. Companies also are required to provide many disclosures in the notes, including the years over which the restructuring is expected to take place.

Should restructuring costs be considered part of a company's permanent earnings stream?

Now that we understand the nature of restructuring costs, we can address the important question: Should financial statement users attempting to forecast future earnings consider these costs to be part of a company's permanent earnings stream, or are they unlikely to occur again? There is no easy answer. For example, Hershey has reported some amount of restructuring costs in each year from 2005–2016. However, the amount reported in 2016

---

[7]GAAP previously required events that were both unusual and infrequent to be classified as "extraordinary items" and reported net of tax after income from continuing operations. As part of the FASB's Simplification Initiative, Accounting Standards Update No. 2015-01 eliminated the extraordinary classification. International accounting standards also do not recognize the extraordinary classification.
[8]FASB ASC 420-10-20: Exit or Disposal Cost Obligations—Overall—Glossary (previously "Accounting for Costs Associated with Exit or Disposal Activities," *Statement of Financial Accounting Standards No. 146* (Norwalk, Conn.: FASB, 2002)).

was substantially less than the amount in 2015. Will the company incur these costs again in the near future? Probably. A recent survey reports that of the 500 companies surveyed, 40% included restructuring costs in their income statements.[9] The inference: A financial statement user must interpret restructuring charges in light of a company's past history and financial statement note disclosures that outline the plan and the period over which it will take place. In general, the more frequently these sorts of unusual charges occur, the more appropriate it is that financial statement users include them in their estimation of the company's permanent earnings stream.[10]

OTHER UNUSUAL ITEMS   Two other expenses in Hershey's income statements that warrant additional scrutiny are *goodwill impairments* and *asset impairments.* Any long-lived asset, whether tangible or intangible, should have its balance reduced if there has been a significant impairment of value. We explore property, plant, and equipment and intangible assets in Chapters 10 and 11. After discussing this topic in more depth in those chapters, we revisit the concept of earnings quality as it relates to asset impairment.

These aren't the only components of operating expenses that call into question this issue of earnings quality. For example, in Chapter 9 we discuss the write-down of inventory that can occur with obsolete or damaged inventory. Other possibilities include losses from natural disasters such as earthquakes and floods and gains and losses from litigation settlements. Earnings quality also is influenced by the way a company records income from investments (Chapter 12) and accounts for its pension plans (Chapter 17).

> Unusual items included in operating income require investigation to determine their permanent or temporary nature.

Earnings quality is affected by revenue issues as well. As an example, suppose that toward the end of its fiscal year, a company loses a major customer that can't be replaced. That would mean the current year's revenue number includes a component that will not occur again next year. Of course, in addition to its effect on revenues, losing the customer would have implications for certain related expenses and net income.

Another issue affecting earnings quality is the intentional misstatement of revenue. In 2016, the Securities and Exchange Commission (SEC) charged Lime Energy with reporting nonexistent revenues. The allegations include executives faking "pipeline" revenue that didn't really exist. Executives were alleged to have recognized revenue on contract proposals that had been presented to customers, but those customers hadn't yet agreed to or signed the contract. We explore additional issues of revenue recognition in Chapter 6. Now, though, let's discuss earnings quality issues related to *nonoperating* items.

Nonoperating Income and Earnings Quality

Most of the components of earnings in an income statement relate directly to the ordinary, continuing operations of the company. Some, though, such as interest or the gains and losses on the sale of investments relate only tangentially to normal operations. We refer to these as nonoperating items. How should these items be interpreted in terms of their relationship to future earnings? Are these expenses likely to occur again next year? Investors need to understand that some of these items may recur, such as interest expense, while others are less likely to recur, such as gains and losses on investments.

> Gains and losses from the sale of investments typically relate only tangentially to normal operations.

Home Depot's partial income statement is shown in Illustration 4–6. There are two non-operating amounts reported after operating income. The first one is "Interest and investment income" that primarily includes gains on the sale of investments in another company's stock. Because Home Depot's primary business includes selling home improvement products, sales of investments are not considered normal operations. Therefore, Home Depot reports these amounts as nonoperating items. Home Depot disclosed in the notes of its 2016 report that gains on the sale of investments were $144 million. Once these investments were sold, their gains were not expected to continue into future profitability, so investors would not consider these gains to be a permanent component of profit. In 2017, we see that there were no gains on the sale of investments, consistent with this source of income not continuing. The remaining relatively minor amount in this nonoperating category in 2017 comes from interest income.

---

[9]*U.S. GAAP Financial Statements—Best Practices in Presentation and Disclosure*—2013 (New York: AICPA, 2013).
[10]Arthur Levitt, Jr. "The Numbers Game," *The CPA Journal,* December 1998, p. 16.

Illustration 4–6

Income Statements (in part)—The Home Depot, Inc.

Real World Financials

Income Statements (in part)
($ in millions)

	Year Ended	
	January 29, 2017	**January 31, 2016**
Operating income	$13,427	$11,774
Interest and investment income	36	166
Interest expense	(972)	(919)
Income before taxes	$12,491	$11,021

Source: Home Depot, Inc.

Another large nonoperating item reported by most companies is interest expense. In its 2017 report, Home Depot reported $972 million in interest expense. The company also reported long-term debt of nearly $22 billion in the balance sheet. Because this long-term debt will not be repaid for several years, the company will have to pay interest for several years. Therefore, interest expense represents a type of nonoperating item that is expected by investors to be a more permanent component of future profitability.

Non-GAAP Earnings

Companies are required to report earnings based on Generally Accepted Accounting Principles (GAAP). This number includes *all revenues and expenses.* Most companies, however, also voluntarily provide non-GAAP earnings when they announce annual or quarterly earnings. Non-GAAP earnings *exclude certain expenses* and sometimes certain revenues. Common expenses excluded are restructuring costs, acquisition costs, write-downs of impaired assets, and stock-based compensation. Supposedly, non-GAAP earnings are management's view of "permanent earnings," in the sense of being a better long-run measure of its company's performance.

> Many companies voluntarily provide *non-GAAP earnings*— management's assessment of permanent earnings.

Nearly all major companies report non-GAAP earnings. For example, **Yelp** regularly reports non-GAAP earnings, defined as net income excluding stock-based compensation expense, amortization of intangibles, gains (losses) on the disposal of business units, restructuring and integration costs, and certain tax effects. For its year ended 2016, the effect of these exclusions was to increase reported performance from a GAAP loss of nearly $5 million to a non-GAAP profit of $60 million. **Microsoft** reported GAAP earnings in 2017 of $21.2 billion. At the same time, the company announced that its non-GAAP earnings for the year were $25.9 billion (22% higher than GAAP earnings). The company stated that the difference in earnings numbers related primarily to management adjusting for Windows 10 revenue deferrals.

> Non-GAAP earnings are controversial.

Non-GAAP earnings are controversial because determining which expenses to exclude is at the discretion of management. By removing certain expenses from reported GAAP earnings, management has the potential to report misleadingly higher profits. In 2015, companies in the S&P 500 reported non-GAAP earnings that were 33% *higher* than GAAP earnings.[11] Some companies that reported non-GAAP profits actually had GAAP losses. The issue is: Do non-GAAP earnings represent management's true belief of core, long-term performance (so excluding certain temporary expenses is helpful to investors), or do non-GAAP earnings represent management's attempt to mislead investors into believing the company is more profitable than it actually is (and therefore harming investors)? Many are concerned that the latter is more likely.

> The Sarbanes-Oxley Act requires reconciliation between non-GAAP earnings and earnings determined according to GAAP.

The Sarbanes-Oxley Act addressed non-GAAP earnings in its Section 401. One of the act's important provisions requires that if non-GAAP earnings are included in any periodic or other report filed with the SEC or in any public disclosure or press release, the company also must provide a reconciliation with earnings determined according to GAAP.[12]

We now turn our attention to discontinued operations, an item that is not part of a company's permanent earnings and, appropriately, is excluded from continuing operations.

---

[11]"S&P 500 Earnings: Far Worse Than Advertised," *The Wall Street Journal* (February 24, 2016).
[12]The Congress of the United States of America, *The Sarbanes-Oxley Act of 2002,* Section 401 (b) (2), Washington, D.C., 2004.

Discontinued Operations

Companies sometimes decide to sell or dispose of a component of their business. The operations of that business component are known as discontinued operations. For example, as we discussed in the introduction, Abbott Laboratories decided to sell its businesses related to developed markets branded generic pharmaceuticals and animal health. Obviously, profits from these discontinued operations *will not continue.* Because discontinued operations represent a material[13] component of the company, the results from discontinued operations are reported separately in the income statement to allow financial statement users to more clearly understand results from continuing operations.

● LO4–4

For example, suppose a company has total pretax profits for the year of $1,200. This includes $1,000 from operations that are continuing, and $200 from operations that are discontinued by the end of the year. Assuming a 25% tax rate, the presentation of discontinued operations is mandated as follows:[14]

Income from continuing operations before income taxes	$ 1,000
Income tax expense (25%)	250
Income from continuing operations	750
Income from discontinued operations ($200 net of $50 tax expense)	150
Net income	$ 900

FINANCIAL Reporting Case

Q2, p. 167

The objective of this format is to inform financial statements users of which components of net income are continuing. We do this by separately reporting income from continuing operations ($750) and income from discontinued operations ($150). All else the same, investors should not expect next year's net income to be $900, because only $750 of profits from this year are part of continuing operations.

Separate reporting includes taxes as well. The income tax expense associated with continuing operations is reported separately from the income tax of discontinued operations. Also, in the case that there is a loss from discontinued operations, there would be an *income tax benefit* (instead of income tax expense); losses from discontinued operations are tax deductible and would reduce overall taxes owed, thereby providing a benefit. The process of associating income tax effects with the income statement components that create those effects is referred to as *intraperiod tax allocation,* something we discuss in depth in Chapter 16.

Income from discontinued operations (and its tax effect) are reported separately.

What are some examples of discontinued operations? In recent years, General Electric sold its financial services businesses. Campbell Soup Company sold its European simple meals business to Soppa Investments. Google sold its Motorola Mobility smartphone subsidiary to Lenovo. Procter & Gamble sold its batteries division. These are all examples of discontinued operations.

What Constitutes a Discontinued Operation?

Discontinued operations are reported when

1. A *component of an entity* or group of components has been sold or disposed of, or is considered held for sale,
2. If the disposal represents a *strategic shift* that has, or will have, a major effect on a company's operations and financial results.[15]

For the first item, a *component of an entity* includes activities and cash flows that can be clearly distinguished, operationally and for financial reporting purposes, from the rest of the

---

[13]We discussed the concept of materiality in Chapter 1.

[14]The presentation of discontinued operations is the same for single-step and multiple-step income statement formats. The single-step versus multiple-step distinction applies to items included in income from continuing operations.

[15]A discontinued operation is also defined as business or nonprofit activity that is considered held for sale *when acquired* (FASB ASC 205-20-15-2). A business is a set of activities and assets that is managed for purposes of providing economic benefits to the company. A nonprofit activity is similar to a business but is not intended to provide goods and services to customers at a profit.

company. A component could include an operating segment, a reporting unit, a subsidiary, or an asset group.[16]

For the second item, whether the disposal represents a *strategic shift* requires the judgment of company management. Examples of possible strategic shifts include the disposal of operations in a major geographical area, a major line of business, a major equity method investment,[17] or other major parts of the company.

As part of the continuing process to converge U.S. GAAP and international standards, the FASB and IASB have developed a common definition and a common set of disclosures for discontinued operations.[18]

Reporting Discontinued Operations

By definition, the income or loss stream from a discontinued operation no longer will continue. A financial statement user is more interested in the results of a company's operations that will continue. It is informative, then, for companies to separate the effects of the discontinued operations from the results of operations that will continue. For this reason, the revenues, expenses, gains, losses, and income tax related to a *discontinued* operation must be removed from *continuing* operations and reported separately *for all years presented.*

For example, even though Abbott Laboratories did not sell its generic pharmaceuticals and animal health businesses until 2015, it's important for comparative purposes to separate the effects for any prior years presented. This allows an apples-to-apples comparison of income from *continuing* operations. So, in its 2015 three-year comparative income statements, the 2014 and 2013 income statements reclassified income from generic pharmaceuticals and animal health businesses to income from discontinued operations. In addition, there was a disclosure note to inform readers that prior years were reclassified.[19] Furthermore, you can see in the introduction to this chapter how the results of those discontinued operations didn't continue into 2016. The amount reported in 2016 reflected the remaining income tax benefit of a prior discontinued operation in 2013 (AbbVie).

Sometimes a discontinued component actually has been sold by the end of a reporting period. Often, though, the disposal transaction has not yet been completed as of the end of the reporting period. We consider these two possibilities next.

WHEN THE COMPONENT HAS BEEN SOLD   When the discontinued component is sold before the end of the reporting period, the reported income effects of a discontinued operation will include two elements.

1. Income or loss from operations (revenues, expenses, gains, and losses) of the component from the beginning of the reporting period *to the disposal date*
2. Gain or loss on disposal of the component's assets

The first element would consist primarily of income from daily operations of this discontinued component of the company. This would include typical revenues from sales to customers and ordinary expenses such as cost of goods sold, salaries, rent, and insurance. The second element includes gains and losses on the sale of assets, such as selling a building or office equipment of this discontinued component.

These two elements can be combined or reported separately, net of their tax effects. If combined, the gain or loss component must be indicated. In our illustrations to follow, we combine the income effects. Illustration 4–7 describes a situation in which the discontinued component is sold before the end of the reporting period.

Notice that an *income tax benefit* occurs because a *loss* reduces taxable income, saving the company $500,000 in taxes.

On the other hand, suppose Duluth's discontinued division had a pretax loss from operations of only $1,000,000 (and still had a gain on disposal of $3,000,000). In this case,

---

[16]FASB ASC 205-20-20 : Presentation of Financial Statements—Discontinued Operations—Glossary.

[17]Equity method investments are discussed in Chapter 12.

[18]"Noncurrent Assets Held for Sale and Discontinued Operations," *International Financial Reporting Standard No. 5* (IASCF), as amended effective January 1, 2016.

[19]The presentation of discontinued operations in comparative income statements enhances the qualitative characteristics of comparability and consistency. We discussed the concepts of comparability and consistency in Chapter 1.

In October 2021, management of Duluth Holding Company decided to sell one of its divisions that qualifies as a separate component according to generally accepted accounting principles. On December 18, 2021, **the division was sold**. Consider the following facts related to the division:

1. From January 1 through disposal, the division had a pretax loss from operations of $5,000,000.
2. The assets of the division had a net selling price of $15,000,000 and book value of $12,000,000.

Duluth's income statement for 2021, beginning with after-tax income from continuing operations of $20,000,000, would be reported as follows (assuming a 25% tax rate):

Income from continuing operations		$20,000,000
Discontinued operations:		
Loss from operations of discontinued component		
(including gain on disposal of $3,000,000*)	$(2,000,000)†	
Income tax benefit	500,000‡	
Loss on discontinued operations		**(1,500,000)**
Net income		$18,500,000

*Net selling price of $15 million less book value of $12 million
†Loss from operations of $5 million less gain on disposal of $3 million
‡$2,000,000 × 25%

Illustration 4–7
Discontinued Operations
Sold—Loss

the combined amount of $2,000,000 represents *income* from operations of the discontinued component, and the company would have an additional *income tax expense* of $500,000, as demonstrated below.

Income from continuing operations		$20,000,000
Discontinued operations:		
Income from operations of discontinued component		
(including gain on disposal of $3,000,000*)	$2,000,000†	
Income tax expense	(500,000)‡	
Income on discontinued operations		1,500,000
Net income		$21,500,000

*Net selling price of $15 million less book value of $12 million
†Loss from operations of $1 million plus gain on disposal of $3 million
‡$2,000,000 × 25%

Additional Consideration

For reporting discontinued operations in the income statement, some companies separate the income/loss from operations and the gain/loss on disposal. For example, in Illustration 4–7, Duluth Holding Company could have reported the $5,000,000 loss from operations separately from the $3,000,000 gain on disposal, with each shown net of their tax effects (25%).

Income from continuing operations		$ 20,000,000
Discontinued operations:		
Loss from operations (net of tax benefit)	$(3,750,000)†	
Gain on disposal (net of tax expense)	2,250,000‡	
Loss on discontinued operations		(1,500,000)
Net income		$ 18,500,000

†$5,000,000 − ($5,000,000 × 25%)
‡$15,000,000 − $12,000,000 = $3,000,000; $3,000,000 − ($3,000,000 × 25%) = $2,250,000

(continued)

(concluded)

The amount of the loss on discontinued operations of $1,500,000 is the same with either presentation. In practice, most companies report on the face of the income statement a single net amount for discontinued operations, with a note disclosure providing details of the calculation.

Income from continuing operations	$20,000,000
Loss on discontinued operations (net of tax)	(1,500,000)
Net income	$18,500,000

If a component to be discontinued has not yet been sold, its income effects, including any impairment loss, usually still are reported separately as discontinued operations.

WHEN THE COMPONENT IS CONSIDERED HELD FOR SALE   What if a company has decided to discontinue a component but, when the reporting period ends, the component has not yet been sold? If the situation indicates that the component is likely to be sold within a year, the component is considered "held for sale."[20] In that case, the income effects of the discontinued operation still are reported, but the two components of the reported amount are modified as follows:

1. Income or loss from operations (revenues, expenses, gains and losses) of the component from the beginning of the reporting period *to the end of the reporting period.*
2. An impairment loss if the book value (sometimes called carrying value or carrying amount) of the assets of the component is more than fair value minus cost to sell.

The two income elements can be combined or reported separately, net of their tax effects. In addition, if the amounts are combined and there is an impairment loss, the loss must be disclosed, either parenthetically on the face of the statement or in a disclosure note. Consider the example in Illustration 4–8.

Illustration 4–8

Discontinued Operations Held for Sale—Impairment Loss

In October 2021, management of Duluth Holding Company decided to sell one of its divisions that qualifies as a separate component according to generally accepted accounting principles. On December 31, 2021, the end of the company's fiscal year, **the division had not yet been sold.** Consider the following facts related to the division:

1. For the year, the division reported a pretax loss from operations of $5,000,000.
2. On December 31, assets of the division had a book value of $12,000,000 and a fair value, minus anticipated cost to sell, of $9,000,000.

Duluth's income statement for 2021, beginning with after-tax income from continuing operations of $20,000,000, would be reported as follows (assuming a 25% tax rate):

Income from continuing operations		$20,000,000
Discontinued operations:		
Loss from operations of discontinued component		
(including impairment loss of $3,000,000*)	$(8,000,000)'	
Income tax benefit	2,000,000'	
Loss on discontinued operations		(6,000,000)
Net income		$14,000,000

*Book value of $12 million less fair value net of cost to sell of $9 million
'Loss from operations of $5 million plus impairment loss of $3 million
'$8,000,000 × 25%

Also, the net-of-tax income or loss from operations of the component being discontinued is reported separately from continuing operations for any prior year that is presented for comparison purposes along with the 2021 income statement. Then, in the year of actual

---

[20]Six criteria are used to determine whether the component is likely to be sold and therefore considered "held for sale." You can find these criteria in FASB ASC 360-10-45-9: Property, Plant, and Equipment—Overall—Other Presentation Matters—Long-Lived Assets Classified as Held for Sale (previously "Accounting for the Impairment or Disposal of Long-Lived Assets," *Statement of Financial Accounting Standards No. 144* (Norwalk, Conn.: FASB, 2001), par. 30).

disposal, the discontinued operations section of the income statement will include the final gain or loss on the sale of the discontinued segment's assets. The gain or loss is determined relative to the revised book values of the assets after the impairment write-down.

Important information about discontinued operations, whether sold or held for sale, is reported in a disclosure note. The note provides additional details about the discontinued component, including its identity, its major classes of assets and liabilities, the major revenues and expenses constituting pretax income or loss from operations, the reason for the discontinuance, and the expected manner of disposition if held for sale.[21]

In Illustration 4–8, if the fair value of the division's assets minus cost to sell exceeded the book value of $12,000,000, there is no impairment loss and the income effects of the discontinued operation would include only the loss from operations of $5,000,000, less the income tax benefit.

The balance sheet is affected, too. The assets and liabilities of the component considered held for sale are reported at the lower of their book value or fair value minus cost to sell. And, because it's not in use, an asset classified as held for sale is no longer reported as part of property, plant, and equipment or intangible assets and is not depreciated or amortized.[22]

For example, in 2016, Abbott Laboratories decided to sell its businesses related to vision care. The 2016 year-end balance sheet reported $513 million in "Current assets held for disposition," and $245 million in "Current liabilities held for disposition." Information about the discontinued operations was included in the disclosure note shown in Illustration 4–9.

Illustration 4–9

Discontinued Operations Disclosure—Abbott Laboratories.

Real World Financials

NOTE 3—DISCONTINUED OPERATIONS (in part)

The following is a summary of the assets and liabilities held for disposition:

($ in millions)	December 31, 2016
Trade receivables, net	$ 222
Total inventories	240
Prepaid expenses and other current assets	51
Current assets held for disposition	$513
Trade accounts payable	$ 71
Salaries, wages, commissions and other accrued liabilities	174
Current liabilities held for disposition	$245

Source: Abbott Laboratories.

Notice that the assets and liabilities held for sale are classified as *current* because the company expects to complete the transfer of these assets and liabilities in the next fiscal year.

INTERIM REPORTING   Remember that companies whose ownership shares are publicly traded in the United States must file quarterly reports with the Securities and Exchange Commission. If a component of an entity is considered held for sale at the end of a quarter, the income effects of the discontinued component must be separately reported in the quarterly income statement. These effects would include the income or loss from operations for the quarter as well as an impairment loss if the component's assets have a book value more than fair value minus cost to sell. If the assets are impaired and written down, any gain or loss on disposal in a subsequent quarter is determined relative to the new, written-down book value.

---

[21]For a complete list of disclosure requirements, see FASB ASC 205-20-50: Presentation of Financial Statements—Discontinued Operations—Disclosure.

[22]The assets and liabilities held for sale are not offset and presented as a single net amount, but instead are listed separately (ASC 205-20-45-10).

Accounting Changes

● LO4–5   Accounting changes fall into one of three categories: (1) a change in an accounting principle, (2) a change in estimate, or (3) a change in reporting entity. The correction of an error is another adjustment that is accounted for in the same way as certain accounting changes. A brief overview of a change in accounting principle, a change in estimate, and correction of errors is provided here. We cover accounting changes, including changes in reporting entities, and accounting errors in detail in subsequent chapters, principally in Chapter 20.

Change in Accounting Principle

A change in accounting principle refers to a change from one acceptable accounting method to another. There are many situations that allow alternative treatments for similar transactions. Common examples of these situations include the choice among FIFO, LIFO, and average cost for the measurement of inventory and among alternative revenue recognition methods. New accounting standard updates issued by the FASB also may require companies to change their accounting methods.

MANDATED CHANGES IN ACCOUNTING PRINCIPLES Sometimes the FASB requires a change in accounting principle. These changes in accounting principles potentially hamper the ability of external users to compare financial information among reporting periods because information lacks consistency. The board considers factors such as this, as well as the cost and complexity of adopting new standards, and chooses among various approaches to require implementation by companies.

1. **Retrospective approach.** The new standard is applied to all periods presented in the financial statements. That is, we restate prior period financial statements as if the new accounting method had been used in those prior periods. We revise the balance of each account affected to make those statements appear as if the newly adopted accounting method had been applied all along.
2. **Modified retrospective approach.** The new standard is applied to the adoption period only. Prior period financial statements are not restated. The cumulative effect of the change on prior periods' net income is shown as an adjustment to the beginning balance of retained earnings in the adoption period.
3. **Prospective approach.** This approach requires neither a modification of prior period financial statements nor an adjustment to account balances. Instead, the change is simply implemented in the current period and all future periods.

VOLUNTARY CHANGES IN ACCOUNTING PRINCIPLES   Occasionally, without being required by the FASB, a company will change from one generally accepted accounting principle to another. For example, a company may decide to change its inventory method from LIFO to FIFO. When this occurs, inventory and cost of goods sold are measured in one reporting period using LIFO, but then are measured using FIFO in a subsequent period. Inventory and cost of goods sold, and hence net income, for the two periods are not comparable. To improve comparability and consistency, GAAP typically requires that voluntary accounting changes be accounted for retrospectively.[23],[24]

We will see these aspects of accounting for the change in accounting principle demonstrated in Chapter 9 in the context of our discussion of inventory methods. We'll also discuss changes in accounting principles in depth in Chapter 20.

---

[23]FASB ASC 250-10-45-5: Accounting Changes and Error Corrections—Overall—Other Presentation Matters (previously "Accounting Changes and Error Corrections—a replacement of APB Opinion No. 20 and FASB Statement No. 3," *Statement of Financial Accounting Standard No. 154* (Norwalk, Conn.: FASB, 2005)).

[24]Sometimes a lack of information makes it impracticable to report a change retrospectively so the new method is simply applied prospectively, that is, we simply use the new method from now on. Also, if a new standard specifically requires prospective accounting, that requirement is followed.

Change in Depreciation, Amortization, or Depletion Method

A change in depreciation, amortization, or depletion method is considered to be a change in accounting estimate that is achieved by a change in accounting principle. We account for this change prospectively, almost exactly as we would any other change in estimate. One difference is that most changes in estimate don't require a company to justify the change. However, this change in estimate is a result of changing an accounting principle and therefore requires a clear justification as to why the new method is preferable. Chapter 11 provides an illustration of a change in depreciation method.

Changes in depreciation, amortization, or depletion methods are accounted for the same way as a change in an accounting estimate.

Change in Accounting Estimate

Estimates are a necessary aspect of accounting. A few of the more common accounting estimates are the amount of future bad debts on existing accounts receivable, the useful life and residual value of a depreciable asset, and future warranty expenses.

A *change in accounting estimate* is reflected in the financial statements of the current period and future periods.

Because estimates require the prediction of future events, it's not unusual for them to turn out to be wrong. When an estimate is modified as new information comes to light, accounting for the change in estimate is quite straightforward. We do not revise prior years' financial statements to reflect the new estimate. Instead, we merely incorporate the new estimate in any related accounting determinations from that point on; that is, we account for a change in accounting estimate prospectively.[25] If the effect of the change is material, a disclosure note is needed to describe the change and its effect on both net income and earnings per share. Chapters 11 and 20 provide illustrations of changes in accounting estimates.

Correction of Accounting Errors

Errors occur when transactions are either recorded incorrectly or not recorded at all. We briefly discuss the correction of errors here as an overview and in later chapters in the context of the effect of errors on specific chapter topics. In addition, Chapter 20 provides comprehensive coverage of the correction of errors.

Accountants employ various control mechanisms to ensure that transactions are accounted for correctly. In spite of this, errors occur. When errors do occur, they can affect any one or several of the financial statement elements on any of the financial statements a company prepares. In fact, many kinds of errors simultaneously affect more than one financial statement. When errors are discovered, they should be corrected.

Most errors are discovered in the same year that they are made. These errors are simple to correct. The original erroneous journal entry is reversed and the appropriate entry is recorded. If an error is discovered in a year subsequent to the year the error is made, the accounting treatment depends on whether or not the error is material with respect to its effect on the financial statements. In practice, the vast majority of errors are not material and are, therefore, simply corrected in the year discovered. However, material errors that are discovered in subsequent periods require a prior period adjustment.

Prior Period Adjustments

Assume that after its financial statements are published and distributed to shareholders, Roush Distribution Company discovers a material error in the statements. What does it do? Roush must make a prior period adjustment.[26] Roush would record a journal entry that adjusts any balance sheet accounts to their appropriate levels and would account for the income effects of the error by increasing or decreasing the beginning retained earnings balance in a statement of shareholders' equity. Remember, net income in prior periods was closed to retained earnings so, by adjusting retained earnings, the prior period adjustment accounts for the error's effect on prior periods' net income.

---

[25] If the original estimate had been based on erroneous information or calculations or had not been made in good faith, the revision of that estimate would constitute the correction of an error (discussed in the next section).

[26] FASB ASC 250-10-45-23: Accounting Changes and Error Corrections-Overall-Other Presentation Matters (previously "Prior Period Adjustments," *Statement of Financial Accounting Standards No. 16* (Norwalk, Conn.: FASB, 1977)).

Simply reporting a corrected retained earnings amount might cause a misunderstanding for someone familiar with the previously reported amount. Explicitly reporting a prior period adjustment in the statement of shareholders' equity (or statement of retained earnings if that's presented instead) highlights the adjustment and avoids this confusion.

In addition to reporting the prior period adjustment to retained earnings, previous years' financial statements that are incorrect as a result of the error are retrospectively restated to reflect the correction. Also, a disclosure note communicates the impact of the error on prior periods' net income.

Earnings per Share

We've discussed that the income statement reports a company's net income for the period. Net income is reported in total dollars (total dollars of revenues minus total dollars of expenses) and represents the total profits that the company has generated for *all shareholders* during the period. However, for individual decision making, investors want to know how much profit has been generated for *each shareholder*. To know this, we calculate earnings per share (EPS) to relate the amount of net income a company generates to the number of common shares outstanding.

EPS provides a convenient way for investors to link the company's profitability to the value of an individual share of ownership. The ratio of stock price per share to earnings per share (the PE ratio) is one of the most widely used financial metrics in the investment world. EPS also makes it easier to compare the performance of the company over time or with other companies. Larger companies may naturally have larger dollar amounts of net income, but they do not always generate more profit for each shareholder.

All corporations whose common stock is publicly traded must disclose EPS.

U.S. GAAP requires that public companies report two specific calculations of EPS: (1) basic EPS and (2) diluted EPS. Basic EPS equals total net income (less any dividends to preferred shareholders) divided by the weighted-average number of common shares outstanding. Dividends to preferred shareholders are subtracted from net income in the numerator because those dividends are distributions of the company not available to common shareholders. The denominator is the weighted-average number of common shares outstanding, rather than the number of shares outstanding at the beginning or end of the period, because the goal is to relate performance for the period to the shares that were in place throughout that period. The number of common shares may change over the year from additional issuances or company buybacks, so a weighted average better reflects the number of shares outstanding for the period. The resulting EPS provides a measure of net income generated for each share of common stock during the period.

FINANCIAL Reporting Case

Q3, p. 167

For example, suppose the Fetzer Corporation reported net income of $600,000 for its fiscal year ended December 31, 2021. Preferred stock dividends of $75,000 were declared during the year. Fetzer had 1,000,000 shares of common stock outstanding at the beginning of the year and issued an additional 1,000,000 shares on March 31, 2021. Basic EPS of $0.30 per share for 2021 is computed as follows:

$$\frac{\$600,000 - \$75,000}{\underbrace{1,000,000}_{\substack{\text{Shares} \\ \text{at Jan. 1}}} + \underbrace{1,000,000}_{\substack{\text{New} \\ \text{shares}}} (9/12)} = \frac{\$525,000}{1,750,000} = \$0.30$$

Diluted EPS incorporates the dilutive effect of all *potential* common shares in the calculation of EPS. Dilution refers to the reduction in EPS that occurs as the number of common shares outstanding increases. Companies may have certain securities outstanding that could be converted into common shares, or they could have stock options outstanding that create additional common shares if the options were exercised. Because these items could cause the number of shares in the denominator to increase, they potentially decrease EPS. We devote a substantial portion of Chapter 19 to understanding these two measures of EPS. Here, we provide only an overview.

When the income statement includes discontinued operations, we report per-share amounts for both income (loss) from continuing operations and for net income (loss), as well as for the discontinued operations. We see this demonstrated for Abbott Laboratories in Illustration 4–10.

Abbott Laboratories **Statements of Earnings For the Year Ended December 31 (in part)**		
($ in millions, except per share amounts)	**2016**	**2015**
Income from continuing operations	$1,063	$2,606
Income from discontinued operations, net of tax	337	1,817
Net income	$1,400	$4,423
Earnings per common share—basic:		
Continuing operations	$ 0.71	$ 1.73
Discontinued operations	0.23	1.21
Net income	$ 0.94	$ 2.94
Earnings per common share—diluted:		
Continuing operations	$ 0.71	$ 1.72
Discontinued operations	0.23	1.20
Net income	$ 0.94	$ 2.92
Source: Abbott Laboratories.		

Illustration 4–10

EPS Disclosures—Abbott Laboratories.

Real World Financials

Comprehensive Income

● LO4–6

Changes in shareholders' equity arise from two sources—transactions with owners (shareholders) and transactions with nonowners. Transactions with owners include events such as increasing equity by issuing stock to shareholders or decreasing equity by purchasing stock from shareholders and paying dividends. All other changes in equity during the period arise from nonowner sources and represent comprehensive income.

Comprehensive income is the total change in equity for a reporting period other than from transactions with owners.

The transactions and events that lead to changes in equity from nonowner sources are recorded as revenues, expenses, gains, and losses for the period. You are already familiar with many of these items; they are reported in the income statement and are used to calculate net income. However, there are a few gains and losses that are not reported in the income statement but nevertheless affect equity. These other gains and losses are reported as other comprehensive income (OCI). Therefore, the broader concept of comprehensive income includes net income plus *other* changes in shareholders' equity from nonowner sources:

Comprehensive income = Net income + Other comprehensive income

Accounting professionals have engaged in an ongoing debate concerning whether certain gains and losses should be included as components of net income or as part of other comprehensive income. For example, in Chapter 12 you will learn that investments in certain securities are reported in the balance sheet at their fair values. The gains and losses from adjusting investments to their fair values are considered to be unrealized because the securities have not been sold. For many debt and equity securities, these unrealized gains and losses are included in net income. However, for certain investments in debt securities (known as *available-for-sale debt securities*), unrealized gains and losses are reported as other comprehensive income in shareholders' equity.

Currently, the FASB has established *no conceptual basis* for determining which gains and losses qualify for net income versus other comprehensive income. To help avoid confusion about which amounts are included in net income versus other comprehensive income, companies are required to provide a reconciliation from net income to comprehensive income.[27] The reconciliation simply extends net income from the income statement to include other comprehensive income items, reported net of tax, as shown in Illustration 4–11.

Reporting comprehensive income can be accomplished with a single, continuous statement or in two separate, but consecutive statements.

Flexibility in Reporting

The information in the income statement and other comprehensive income items shown in Illustration 4–11 can be presented either (1) in a single, continuous statement of

---

[27] FASB ASC 220-10-45-1A and 1B: Comprehensive Income-Overall-Other Presentation Matters (previously "Reporting Comprehensive Income," *Statement of Financial Accounting Standards No. 130* (Norwalk, Conn.: FASB, 1997)).

Illustration 4–11

Comprehensive Income

Net income		$xxx
Other comprehensive income, net of tax:		
Gain (loss) on debt securities*	$ x	
Gain (loss) on projected benefit obligation†	(x)	
Gain (loss) on derivatives‡	(x)	
Foreign currency translation adjustment§	x	
Total other comprehensive income (loss)		xx
Comprehensive income		$xxx

*Changes in the fair value of investments in debt securities (described in Chapter 12)
†Gain or loss due to revising assumptions of the employee pension plan (described in Chapter 17).
‡When a derivative designated as a cash flow hedge is adjusted to fair value, the gain or loss is deferred as a component of comprehensive income and included in earnings later, at the same time as earnings are affected by the hedged transaction (described in the Derivatives Appendix to the text).
§The amount could be an addition to or reduction in shareholders' equity. (This item is discussed elsewhere in your accounting curriculum.)

comprehensive income or (2) in two separate, but consecutive statements, an income statement and a statement of comprehensive income. Each component of other comprehensive income can be displayed net of tax, as in Illustration 4–11, or alternatively, before tax with one amount shown for the aggregate income tax expense (or benefit).[28]

AstroNova, Inc., a manufacturer of a broad range of specialty technology products, chose to report a separate statement of comprehensive income, as shown in Illustration 4–12.

Illustration 4–12

Comprehensive Income Presented as a Separate Statement—AstroNova, Inc.

Real World Financials

ASTRONOVA, INC.		
Consolidated Statements of Comprehensive Income		
For the Years Ended January 31		
($ in thousands)	**2017**	**2016**
Net income	$4,228	$4,525
Other comprehensive income, net of taxes:		
Foreign currency translation adjustments	(65)	(269)
Unrealized gain (loss) on securities available for sale	(16)	(7)
Other comprehensive income	(81)	(276)
Comprehensive income	$ 4,147	$4,249

Source: AstroNova, Inc.

International Financial Reporting Standards

● LO4–9

Comprehensive Income. Both U.S. GAAP and IFRS allow companies to report comprehensive income in either a single statement of comprehensive income or in two separate statements.

Other comprehensive income items are similar under the two sets of standards. However, an additional OCI item, *changes in revaluation surplus,* is possible under IFRS. In Chapter 11 you will learn that *IAS No. 16*[29] permits companies to value property, plant, and equipment at (1) cost less accumulated depreciation or (2) fair value (revaluation). *IAS No. 38*[30] provides a similar option for the valuation of intangible assets. U.S. GAAP prohibits revaluation.

If the revaluation option is chosen and fair value is higher than book value, the difference, changes in revaluation surplus, is reported as *other comprehensive income* and then accumulates in a revaluation surplus account in equity.

---

[28]GAAP does not require the reporting of comprehensive earnings per share.
[29]"Property, Plant and Equipment," *International Accounting Standard No. 16* (IASCF), as amended effective January 1, 2018.
[30]"Intangible Assets," *International Accounting Standard No. 38* (IASCF), as amended effective January 1, 2018.

Accumulated Other Comprehensive Income

In addition to reporting OCI that occurs in the current reporting period, we must also report these amounts on a cumulative basis in the balance sheet. This is consistent with the way we report net income for the period in the income statement and also report accumulated net income (that hasn't been distributed as dividends) in the balance sheet as retained earnings. Similarly, we report OCI for the period in the statement of comprehensive income and also report accumulated other comprehensive income (AOCI) in the balance sheet as a component of shareholders' equity. This is demonstrated in Illustration 4–13 for AstroNova, Inc.

> The cumulative total of OCI (or comprehensive loss) is reported as accumulated other comprehensive income (AOCI), an additional component of shareholders' equity that is displayed separately.

Illustration 4–13

Shareholders' Equity—AstroNova, Inc.

Real World Financials

ASTRONOVA, INC.
Consolidated Balance Sheets (in part)
As of January 31

($ in thousands)	2017	2016
Shareholders' equity:		
Common stock	492	483
Additional paid-in capital	47,524	45,675
Retained earnings	44,358	42,212
Treasury stock, at cost	(20,781)	(20,022)
Accumulated other comprehensive income	(1,056)	(975)
Total shareholders' equity	$70,537	$67,373

Supplementing information in Illustration 4–13 with numbers reported in Illustration 4–12 along with dividends declared by AstroNova, we can reconcile the changes in both retained earnings and AOCI:

($ in thousands)	Retained Earnings	Accumulated Other Comprehensive Income
Balance, 1/31/2016	$42,212	$ (975)
Add: Net income	4,228	
Deduct: Dividends	(2,082)	
Other comprehensive income		(81)
Balance, 1/31/2017	$44,358	$(1,056)

To further understand the relationship between net income and other comprehensive income, consider the following example. Philips Corporation began the year with retained earnings of $700 million and accumulated other comprehensive income of $30 million. Let's also assume that net income for the year, before considering the gain discussed below, is $100 million, of which $40 million was distributed to shareholders as dividends. Now assume that Philips had a $10 million net-of-tax gain that was also reported in one of two ways:

1. As a gain in net income, or
2. As a gain in other comprehensive income.

Under the first alternative, the gain will be included in shareholders' equity through retained earnings.

($ in millions)	Retained Earnings	Accumulated Other Comprehensive Income
Beginning Balance	$700	$30
Net income ($100 + 10)	110	
Dividends	(40)	
Other comprehensive income		–0–
Ending Balance	$770	$30

$800

Under the second alternative, the net-of-tax gain of $10 million is reported as a component of *other comprehensive income (loss)*. The gain will be included in shareholders' equity through *accumulated other comprehensive income (loss),* rather than retained earnings, as demonstrated below. The total of retained earnings and accumulated other comprehensive income is $800 million either way.

($ in millions)	Retained Earnings	Accumulated Other Comprehensive Income
Beginning Balance	$700	$30
Net income	100	
Dividends	(40)	
Other comprehensive income		10
Ending Balance	$760	$40

$800

Net income and comprehensive income are identical for an enterprise that has no other comprehensive income items. When this occurs for all years presented, a statement of comprehensive income is not required. Components of other comprehensive income are described in subsequent chapters.

Concept Review Exercise

INCOME STATEMENT PRESENTATION; COMPREHENSIVE INCOME

The Barrington Company sells clothing and furniture. On September 30, 2021, the company decided to sell the entire furniture business for $40 million. The sale was completed on December 15, 2021. Income statement information for 2021 is provided below for the two components of the company.

	($ in millions)	
	Clothing Component	Furniture Component
Sales revenue	$650	$425
Cost of goods sold	200	225
Gross profit	450	200
Operating expenses	226	210
Operating income	224	(10)
Other income (loss)*	16	(30)
Income (loss) before income taxes	240	(40)
Income tax expense (benefit)†	60	(10)
Net income (loss)	$180	$ (30)

*For the furniture component, the entire Other income (loss) amount represents the loss on sale of assets of the component for $40 million when their book value was $70 million.
†A 25% tax rate applies to all items of income or loss.

In addition, in 2021 the company had a pretax net unrealized gain on debt securities of $6 million and a positive foreign currency translation adjustment of $2 million.

Required:

1. Prepare a single, continuous 2021 statement of comprehensive income for the Barrington Company including EPS disclosures. There were 100 million shares of common stock outstanding throughout 2021. The company had no potentially dilutive securities outstanding or stock options that could cause additional common shares. Use the multiple-step approach for the income statement portion of the statement.

2. Prepare a separate 2021 statement of comprehensive income.

Solution:

1. Prepare a single, continuous 2021 statement of comprehensive income.

BARRINGTON COMPANY
Statement of Comprehensive Income
For the Year Ended December 31, 2021
($ in millions, except per share amounts)

Sales revenue		$ 650
Cost of goods sold		200
Gross profit		450
Operating expenses		226
Operating income		224
Other income		16
Income from continuing operations before income taxes		240
Income tax expense		60
Income from continuing operations		180
Discontinued operations:		
Loss from operations of discontinued furniture component		
(including loss on disposal of $30)	$(40)	
Income tax benefit	10	
Loss on discontinued operations		(30)
Net income		150
Other comprehensive income, net of tax:		
Gain on debt securities	4.5	
Foreign currency translation adjustment	1.5	
Total other comprehensive income		6
Comprehensive income		$ 156
Earnings per share:		
Income from continuing operations		$1.80
Discontinued operations		(0.30)
Net income		$1.50

2. Prepare a separate 2021 statement of comprehensive income.

BARRINGTON COMPANY
Statement of Comprehensive Income
For the Year Ended December 31, 2021
($ in millions)

Net income		$150
Other comprehensive income, net of tax:		
Gain on debt securities	$4.5	
Foreign currency translation adjustment	1.5	
Total other comprehensive income		6
Comprehensive income		$156

Now that we have discussed the presentation and content of the income statement, we turn our attention to the statement of cash flows.

The Statement of Cash Flows

PART B

When a balance sheet and an income statement are presented, a statement of cash flows (SCF) is required for each income statement period.[31] The purpose of the SCF is to provide information about the cash receipts and cash disbursements of an enterprise. Similar to the income statement, it is a *change* statement, summarizing the transactions that affected cash during the period. The term *cash* in the statement of cash flows refers to the total of cash,

● LO4–7

A *statement of cash flows* is presented for each period for which an income statement is provided.

---

[31]FASB ASC 230-10-45: Statement of Cash Flows-Overall-Other Presentation Matters (previously "Statement of Cash Flows," *Statement of Financial Accounting Standards No. 95* (Norwalk, Conn.: FASB, 1987)).

cash equivalents, and restricted cash. Cash equivalents, discussed in Chapter 3, include highly liquid (easily converted to cash) investments such as Treasury bills. Chapter 21 is devoted exclusively to the SCF. A brief overview is provided here.

Usefulness of the Statement of Cash Flows

We discussed the difference between cash and accrual accounting in Chapter 1. It was pointed out and illustrated that over short periods of time, operating cash flows may not be indicative of the company's long-run cash-generating ability, and that accrual-based net income provides a more accurate prediction of future operating cash flows. Nevertheless, information about cash flows from operating activities, when combined with information about cash flows from other activities, can provide information helpful in assessing future profitability, liquidity, and long-term solvency. After all, a company must pay its debts with cash, not with income.

Of particular importance is the amount of cash generated from operating activities. In the long run, a company must be able to generate positive cash flow from activities related to selling its product or service. These activities must provide the necessary cash to pay debts, provide dividends to shareholders, and provide for future growth.

Classifying Cash Flows

● LO4–8

A list of cash flows is more meaningful to investors and creditors if they can determine the type of transaction that gave rise to each cash flow. Toward this end, the statement of cash flows classifies all transactions affecting cash into one of three categories: (1) operating activities, (2) investing activities, and (3) financing activities.

Operating Activities

Operating activities are inflows and outflows of cash related to the transactions entering into the determination of net operating income.

The inflows and outflows of cash that result from activities reported in the income statement are classified as cash flows from operating activities. In other words, this classification of cash flows includes the elements of net income reported on a cash basis rather than an accrual basis.[32]

Cash inflows include cash received from the following:

1. Customers from the sale of goods or services.
2. Interest and dividends from investments.

These amounts may differ from sales revenue and investment income reported in the income statement. For example, sales revenue measured on the accrual basis reflects revenue recognized during the period, not necessarily the cash actually collected. Revenue will not equal cash collected from customers if receivables from customers or deferred revenue changed during the period.

Cash outflows include cash paid for the following:

1. The purchase of inventory.
2. Salaries, wages, and other operating expenses.
3. Interest on debt.
4. Income taxes.

Likewise, these amounts may differ from the corresponding accrual expenses reported in the income statement. Expenses are reported when incurred, not necessarily when cash is actually paid for those expenses. Also, some revenues and expenses, like depreciation expense, don't affect cash at all and aren't included as cash outflows from operating activities.

The difference between the inflows and outflows is called *net cash flows from operating activities*. This is equivalent to net income if the income statement had been prepared on a cash basis rather than an accrual basis.

---

[32]Cash flows related to gains and losses from the sale of assets shown in the income statement are reported as investing activities in the SCF.

DIRECT AND INDIRECT METHODS OF REPORTING   Two generally accepted formats can be used to report operating activities, the direct method and the indirect method. Under the direct method, the cash effect of each operating activity is reported directly in the statement. For example, *cash received from customers* is reported as the cash effect of sales activities. Income statement transactions that have no cash flow effect, such as depreciation, are simply not reported.

By the indirect method, on the other hand, we arrive at net cash flow from operating activities indirectly by starting with reported net income and working backwards to convert that amount to a cash basis. Two types of adjustments to net income are needed.

1. Components of net income that do not affect operating cash are reversed. That means that noncash revenues and gains are subtracted, while noncash expenses and losses are added. For example, depreciation expense does not reduce cash, but it is subtracted in the income statement. To reverse this, then, we add back depreciation expense to net income to arrive at the amount that we would have had if depreciation had not been subtracted in the first place.

2. Net income is adjusted for changes in operating assets and liabilities during the period. These changes represent amounts that are included as components of net income but that are not cash flows. For instance, suppose accounts receivable increase during the period because revenue from credit sales is greater than cash collected from customers. This increase in accounts receivable would then be subtracted from net income to arrive at *cash flow from operating activities*. In the indirect method, positive adjustments to net income are made for decreases in related assets and increases in related liabilities, while negative adjustments are made for increases in those assets and decreases in those liabilities.

To contrast the direct and indirect methods further, consider the income statement and balance sheet for Arlington Lawn Care (ALC) in Illustration 4–14. We'll use these to construct the operating activities section of the statement of cash flows.

DIRECT METHOD   Let's begin with the direct method of presentation. We illustrated this method previously in Chapter 2. In that chapter, specific cash transactions were provided and we simply included them in the appropriate cash flow category in the SCF. Here, we start with account balances, so the direct method requires a bit more reasoning.

From the income statement, we see that ALC's net income has four components. Three of those—service revenue, general and administrative expense, and income tax expense—affect cash flows, but not by the accrual amounts reported in the income statement. One component—depreciation—reduces net income but not cash; it's simply an allocation over time of a prior year's expenditure for a depreciable asset. So, to report these operating activities on a cash basis, rather than an accrual basis, we take the three items that affect cash and adjust the amounts to reflect cash inflow rather than revenue recognized, and cash outflows rather than expenses incurred. Let's start with service revenue.

Service revenue is $100,000, but ALC did not collect that much cash from its customers. We know that because accounts receivable increased from $0 to $12,000. ALC must have collected to date only $88,000.

Similarly, general and administrative expense of $32,000 was incurred, but $7,000 of that hasn't yet been paid. We know that because accrued liabilities increased by $7,000. Also, prepaid insurance increased by $4,000 so ALC must have paid $4,000 more cash for insurance coverage than the amount that expired and was reported as insurance expense. That means cash paid thus far for general and administrative expense was only $29,000 ($32,000 less the $7,000 increase in accrued liabilities plus the $4,000 increase in prepaid insurance). The other expense, income tax, was $15,000, but the increase in income taxes payable indicates that $5,000 hasn't yet been paid. This means the amount paid must have been only $10,000.

We can report ALC's cash flows from operating activities using the direct method as shown in Illustration 4–14A.

INDIRECT METHOD   To report operating cash flows using the indirect method, we take a different approach. We start with ALC's net income but realize that the $45,000 includes both cash and noncash components. We need to adjust net income, then, to eliminate the

---

By the direct method, the cash effect of each operating activity is reported directly in the SCF.

By the indirect method, cash flow from operating activities is derived indirectly by starting with reported net income and adding or subtracting items to convert that amount to a cash basis.

Accounts receivable			
Beg. bal.	0		
Revenue	100		
		88	Cash
End. bal.	12		

Illustration 4–14

Contrasting the Direct and Indirect Methods of Presenting Cash Flows from Operating Activities

Net income is $45,000, but cash flow from these same activities is not necessarily the same

Arlington Lawn Care (ALC) began operations at the beginning of 2021. ALC's 2021 income statement and its year-end balance sheet are shown below ($ in thousands).

ARLINGTON LAWN CARE
Income Statement
For the Year Ended December 31, 2021

Service revenue		$100
Operating expenses:		
General and administrative expense	$32*	
Depreciation expense	8	
Total operating expenses		40
Income before income taxes		60
Income tax expense		15
Net income		$ 45

*Includes $6 in insurance expense

ARLINGTON LAWN CARE
Balance Sheet
At December 31, 2021

Assets			Liabilities and Shareholders' Equity		
Current assets:			Current liabilities:		
Cash	$ 54		Accrued liabilities**	$ 7	
Accounts receivable	12		Income taxes payable	5	
Prepaid insurance	4		Total current liabilities	12	
Total current assets	70		Shareholders' equity:		
Equipment	40		Common stock	50	
Less: Accumulated depreciation	(8)		Retained earnings	40†	
Total assets	$102		Total liabilities and shareholders' equity	$102	

**For various items of general and administrative expense
†Net income of $45 less $5 in cash dividends paid

Changes in assets and liabilities can indicate that cash inflows are different from revenues and cash outflows are different from expenses.

Illustration 4–14A

Direct Method of Presenting Cash Flows from Operating Activities

By the direct method, we report the components of net income on a cash basis.

ARLINGTON LAWN CARE
Statement of Cash Flows
For the Year Ended December 31, 2021

	($ in thousands)
Cash Flows from Operating Activities	
Cash received from customers*	$ 88
Cash paid for general and administrative expense**	(29)
Cash paid for income taxes***	(10)
Net cash flows from operating activities	$ 49

*Service revenue of $100 thousand, less increase of $12 thousand in accounts receivable.
**General and administrative expense of $32 thousand, less increase of $7 thousand in accrued liabilities, plus increase of $4 thousand in prepaid insurance.
***Income tax expense of $15 thousand, less increase of $5 thousand in income taxes payable.

Depreciation expense does not reduce cash, but is subtracted in the income statement. So, we add back depreciation expense to net income to eliminate it.

noncash effects so that we're left with only the cash flows. We start by eliminating the only noncash component of net income in our illustration—depreciation expense. As shown in Illustration 4-14B, depreciation of $8,000 was subtracted in the income statement, so to eliminate its negative effect on net income, we simply add it back.

That leaves us with three components of net income that do affect cash but not necessarily by the amounts reported—service revenue, general and administrative expense, and income tax expense. For those, we need to make adjustments to net income to cause it to reflect cash flows rather than accrual amounts. For instance, we saw earlier that even though

$100,000 in service revenue is reflected in net income, only $88,000 cash was received from customers. That means we need to include an adjustment to reduce net income by $12,000, the increase in accounts receivable.

In a similar manner, we include adjustments for the changes in prepaid insurance, accrued liabilities, and income taxes payable to adjust net income to reflect cash payments rather than expenses incurred. For prepaid insurance, because insurance expense in the income statement was less than cash paid for insurance, we need to subtract the difference, which equals the increase in prepaid insurance. If this asset had decreased, we would have added, rather than subtracted, the change. For accrued liabilities and income taxes payable, because the related expense in the income statement was more than cash paid for those expenses, we need to add back the differences. If these liabilities had decreased, we would have subtracted, rather than added, the changes.

Cash flows from operating activities using the indirect method are shown in Illustration 4–14B.

> We make adjustments for changes in assets and liabilities that indicate that components of net income are not the same as cash flows.

ARLINGTON LAWN CARE
Statement of Cash Flows
For the Year Ended December 31, 2021

($ in thousands)

Cash Flows from Operating Activities		
Net income		$45
Adjustments for noncash effects:		
Depreciation expense	$ 8	
Changes in operating assets and liabilities:		
Increase in accounts receivable	(12)	
Increase in prepaid insurance	(4)	
Increase in accrued liabilities	7	
Increase in income taxes payable	5	4
Net cash flows from operating activities		$49

Illustration 4–14B

Indirect Method of Presenting Cash Flows from Operating Activities

By the indirect method, we start with net income and work backwards to convert that amount to a cash basis.

Both the direct and the indirect methods produce the same net cash flows from operating activities ($49,000 in our illustration); they are merely alternative approaches to reporting the cash flows. The FASB, in promulgating GAAP for the statement of cash flows, stated its preference for the direct method. However, nearly all U.S. companies use the indirect method.

The choice of presentation method for cash flow from operating activities has no effect on how investing activities and financing activities are reported. We now look at how cash flows are classified into those two categories.

Investing Activities

Cash flows from investing activities include inflows and outflows of cash related to the acquisition and disposition of long-lived assets used in the operations of the business (such as property, plant, and equipment) and investment assets (except those classified as cash equivalents and trading securities). The purchase and sale of inventory are not considered investing activities. Inventory is purchased for the purpose of being sold as part of the company's operations, so the purchase and sale are included with operating activities rather than investing activities.

Cash outflows from investing activities include cash paid for the following:

> *Investing activities* involve the acquisition and sale of (1) long-term assets used in the business and (2) nonoperating investment assets.

1. The purchase of long-lived assets used in the business.
2. The purchase of investment securities like stocks and bonds of other entities (other than those classified as cash equivalents and trading securities).
3. Loans to other entities.

Later, when the assets are disposed of, cash inflow from the sale of the assets (or collection of loans and notes) also is reported as cash flows from investing activities.

As a result, cash inflows from these transactions are considered investing activities as follows:

1. The sale of long-lived assets used in the business.
2. The sale of investment securities (other than cash equivalents and trading securities).
3. The collection of a nontrade receivable (excluding the collection of interest, which is an operating activity).

Net cash flows from investing activities equal the difference between the inflows and outflows. The only investing activity indicated in Illustration 4–14 is ALC's investment of $40,000 cash for equipment. We know $40,000 was paid to buy equipment because that balance sheet account increased from $0 to $40,000.

Financing Activities

Financing activities involve cash inflows and outflows from transactions with creditors (excluding trade payables) and owners.

Financing activities relate to the external financing of the company. Cash inflows occur when cash is borrowed from creditors or invested by owners. Cash outflows occur when cash is paid back to creditors or distributed to owners. The payment of interest to a creditor, however, is classified as an operating activity.

Financing cash inflows include cash received from the following:

1. Owners when shares are sold to them.
2. Creditors when cash is borrowed through notes, loans, mortgages, and bonds.

Financing cash outflows include cash paid to the following:

1. Owners in the form of dividends or other distributions.
2. Owners for the reacquisition of shares previously sold.
3. Creditors as repayment of the principal amounts of debt (excluding trade payables that relate to operating activities).

Net cash flows from financing activities equal the difference between the inflows and outflows. The only financing activities indicated in Illustration 4–14 are ALC's receipt of $50,000 cash from issuing common stock and the payment of $5,000 in cash dividends. Because common stock increased from $0 to $50,000, we know that common stock was issued for that amount. For dividends, we know the balance of retained earnings increases by the amount of net income minus dividends. This means that the increase in retained earnings of $40,000 represents net income of $45,000 minus dividends of $5,000.

The 2021 statement of cash flows for ALC, beginning with net cash flows from operating activities, is shown in Illustration 4–15.

Illustration 4–15

Statement of Cash Flows (beginning with net cash flows from operating activities)

ARLINGTON LAWN CARE
Statement of Cash Flows (in part)
For the Year Ended December 31, 2021

		($ in thousands)
Net cash flows from operating activities (from Illustration 4–14A or 4–14B)		$49
Cash flows from investing activities:		
Purchase of equipment		(40)
Cash flows from financing activities:		
Issuance of common stock	$50	
Dividends paid to shareholders	(5)	
Net cash flows from financing activities		45
Net increase in cash		54
Cash balance, January 1		0
Cash balance, December 31		$54

International Financial Reporting Standards

Classification of Cash Flows. Like U.S. GAAP, international standards also require a statement of cash flows. Consistent with U.S. GAAP, cash flows are classified as operating, investing, or financing. However, the U.S. standard designates cash outflows for interest payments and cash inflows from interest and dividends received as operating cash flows. Dividends paid to shareholders are classified as financing cash flows.

● LO4–9

IAS No. 7,[33] on the other hand, allows more flexibility. Companies can report interest and dividends paid as either operating or financing cash flows and interest and dividends received as either operating or investing cash flows. Interest and dividend payments usually are reported as financing activities. Interest and dividends received normally are classified as investing activities.

Typical Classification of Cash Flows from Interest and Dividends

U.S. GAAP	IFRS
Operating Activities	*Operating Activities*
Dividends received	
Interest received	
Interest paid	
Investing Activities	*Investing Activities*
	Dividends received
	Interest received
Financing Activities	*Financing Activities*
Dividends paid	Dividends paid
	Interest paid

Siemens AG, a German company, prepares its financial statements according to IFRS. In its statement of cash flows for 2017, the company reported interest and dividends received as operating cash flows, as would a U.S. company. However, Siemens classified interest paid as a financing cash flow.

SIEMENS AG
Statement of Cash Flows (partial)
For the Year Ended September 30, 2017

	(€ in millions)
Cash flows from financing activities:	
Transactions with owners	191
Issuance of long-term debt	6,958
Repayment of long-term debt	(4,868)
Change in short-term debt and other financing activities	260
Interest paid	(1,000)
Dividends paid	(3,101)
Cash flows from financing activities	(1,560)

Noncash Investing and Financing Activities

As we just discussed, the statement of cash flows provides useful information about the investing and financing activities in which a company is engaged. Even though these primarily result in cash inflows and cash outflows, there may be significant investing and financing activities occurring during the period that do not involve cash flows at all. In order to provide complete information about these activities, any significant noncash investing and financing activities (that is, noncash exchanges) are reported either on the face of the SCF or in a disclosure note. An example of a significant noncash investing and financing activity is the acquisition of equipment (an investing activity) by simultaneously issuing either a long-term note payable or equity securities (a financing activity) to the seller of the equipment.

---

[33]"Statement of Cash Flows," *International Accounting Standard No. 7* (IASCF), as amended effective January 1, 2016.

Concept Review Exercise

STATEMENT OF CASH FLOWS

Dublin Enterprises, Inc. (DEI), owns a chain of retail electronics stores located in shopping malls. The following are the company's 2021 income statement and comparative balance sheets ($ in millions):

Income Statement
For the Year Ended December 31, 2021

Sales revenue		$2,100
Cost of goods sold		1,400
Gross profit		700
Operating expenses:		
Selling and administrative expense	$ 355	
Depreciation expense	85	
Total operating expenses		440
Income before income taxes		260
Income tax expense		65
Net income		$ 195

Comparative Balance Sheets	12/31/2021	12/31/2020
Assets:		
Cash	$ 300	$ 220
Accounts receivable	227	240
Inventory	160	120
Property, plant, and equipment	960	800
Less: Accumulated depreciation	(405)	(320)
Total assets	$1,242	$1,060
Liabilities and shareholders' equity:		
Accounts payable	$ 145	$ 130
Accrued liabilities (for selling and admin. expense)	147	170
Income taxes payable	82	50
Long-term debt	–0–	100
Common stock	463	400
Retained earnings	405	210
Total liabilities and shareholders' equity	$1,242	$1,060

Required:

1. Prepare DEI's 2021 statement of cash flows using the direct method.
2. Prepare the cash flows from operating activities section of DEI's 2021 statement of cash flows using the indirect method.

Solution:

1. Prepare DEI's 2021 statement of cash flows using the direct method.

DUBLIN ENTERPRISES, INC.
Statement of Cash Flows
For the Year Ended December 31, 2021
($ in millions)

Cash Flows from Operating Activities		
Cash received from customers*	$2,113	
Cash paid for inventory**	(1,425)	
Cash paid for selling and administrative expense†	(378)	
Cash paid for income taxes‡	(33)	
Net cash flows from operating activities		$277
Cash Flows from Investing Activities		
Purchase of property, plant, and equipment		(160)
Cash Flows from Financing Activities		
Issuance of common stock	63	
Payment on long-term debt	(100)	

(continued)

(concluded)

Net cash flows from financing activities	(37)
Net increase in cash	80
Cash, January 1	220
Cash, December 31	$300

*Sales revenue of $2,100 million, plus $13 million decrease in accounts receivable.
**Cost of goods sold of $1,400 million, plus $40 million increase in inventory, less $15 million increase in accounts payable.
†Selling and administrative expense of $355 million, plus $23 million decrease in accrued liabilities.
‡Income tax expense of $65 million, less $32 million increase in income taxes payable.

2. Prepare the cash flows from operating activities section of DEI's 2021 statement of cash flows using the indirect method.

DUBLIN ENTERPRISES, INC.
Statement of Cash Flows
For the Year Ended December 31, 2021
($ in millions)

Cash Flows from Operating Activities	
Net Income	$195
Adjustments for noncash effects:	
Depreciation expense	85
Changes in operating assets and liabilities:	
Decrease in accounts receivable	13
Increase in inventory	(40)
Increase in accounts payable	15
Increase in income taxes payable	32
Decrease in accrued liabilities	(23)
Net cash flows from operating activities	$277

Profitability Analysis

Chapter 3 provided an overview of financial statement analysis and introduced some of the common ratios used in risk analysis to investigate a company's liquidity and long-term solvency. We now look at ratios related to profitability analysis.

Activity Ratios

One key to profitability is how well a company manages and utilizes its assets. Some ratios are designed to evaluate a company's effectiveness in managing assets. Of particular interest are the activity, or turnover ratios, of certain assets. The greater the number of times an asset turns over, the fewer assets that are required to maintain a given level of activity (revenue). Therefore, high turnover ratios usually are preferred.

Activity ratios measure a company's efficiency in managing its assets.

Although, in concept, the activity or turnover can be measured for any asset, activity ratios are most frequently calculated for total assets, accounts receivable, and inventory. These ratios are calculated as follows:

$$\text{Asset turnover ratio} = \frac{\text{Net sales}}{\text{Average total assets}}$$

$$\text{Receivables turnover ratio} = \frac{\text{Net sales}}{\text{Average accounts receivable (net)}}$$

$$\text{Inventory turnover ratio} = \frac{\text{Cost of goods sold}}{\text{Average inventory}}$$

ASSET TURNOVER   A broad measure of asset efficiency is the asset turnover ratio. The ratio is computed by dividing a company's net sales by the average total assets available for use during a period. The denominator, average assets, is determined by adding beginning and ending total assets and dividing by two. The asset turnover ratio provides an indication of how efficiently a company utilizes all of its assets to generate revenue.

The asset turnover ratio measures a company's efficiency in using assets to generate revenue.

The receivables turnover ratio offers an indication of how quickly a company is able to collect its accounts receivable.

RECEIVABLES TURNOVER   The receivables turnover ratio is calculated by dividing a period's net credit sales by the average net accounts receivable. Because income statements seldom distinguish between cash sales and credit sales, this ratio usually is computed using total net sales as the numerator. The denominator, average accounts receivable, is determined by adding beginning and ending net accounts receivable (gross accounts receivable less allowance for uncollectible accounts) and dividing by two.[34]

The receivables turnover ratio provides an indication of a company's efficiency in collecting cash from customers. The ratio shows the number of times during a period that the average accounts receivable balance is collected. The higher the ratio, the shorter the average time between sales and cash collection.

A convenient extension is the average collection period. This measure is computed by dividing 365 days by the receivables turnover ratio. The result is an approximation of the number of days the average accounts receivable balance is outstanding.

$$\text{Average collection period} = \frac{365}{\text{Receivables turnover ratio}}$$

The average collection period indicates the average age of accounts receivable.

Monitoring the receivables turnover ratio (and average collection period) over time can provide useful information about a company's future prospects. For example, a decline in the receivables turnover ratio (an increase in the average collection period) could be an indication that sales are declining because of customer dissatisfaction with the company's products. Another possible explanation is that the company has changed its credit policy and is granting extended credit terms in order to maintain customers. Either explanation could signal a future increase in bad debts. Ratio analysis does not explain what is wrong. It does provide information that highlights areas for further investigation. We cover additional details of the receivables turnover ratio and average collection period in Chapter 7.

INVENTORY TURNOVER   An important activity measure for a merchandising company (a retail, wholesale, or manufacturing company) is the inventory turnover ratio. The ratio shows the number of times the average inventory balance is sold during a reporting period. It indicates how quickly inventory is sold. The more frequently a business is able to sell, or turn over, its inventory, the lower its investment in inventory must be for a given level of sales. The ratio is computed by dividing the period's cost of goods sold by the average inventory balance. The denominator, average inventory, is determined by adding beginning and ending inventory and dividing by two.[35]

The inventory turnover ratio measures a company's efficiency in managing its investment in inventory.

A relatively high ratio, say compared to a competitor, usually is desirable. A high ratio indicates comparative strength, perhaps caused by a company's superior sales force or maybe a successful advertising campaign. However, it might also be caused by a relatively low inventory level, which could mean either very efficient inventory management or stock-outs and lost sales in the future.

On the other hand, a relatively low ratio, or a decrease in the ratio over time, usually is perceived to be unfavorable. Too much capital may be tied up in inventory. A relatively low ratio may result from overstocking, the presence of obsolete items, or poor marketing and sales efforts.

Similar to the receivables turnover, we can divide the inventory turnover ratio into 365 days to compute the average days in inventory. This measure indicates the number of days it normally takes to sell inventory.

$$\text{Average days in inventory} = \frac{365}{\text{Inventory turnover ratio}}$$

---

[34]Although net accounts receivable typically is used in practice for the denominator of receivables turnover, some prefer to use gross accounts receivable. Why? As the allowance for bad debts increases, net accounts receivable decreases, so if net accounts receivable is in the denominator, more bad debts have the effect of decreasing the denominator and therefore increasing receivables turnover. All else equal, an analyst would rather see receivables turnover improve because of more sales or less gross receivables, and not because of an increase in the allowance for bad debts.

[35] Notice the consistency in the measure used for the numerator and denominator of the two turnover ratios. For the receivables turnover ratio, both numerator and denominator are based on sales dollars, whereas they are both based on cost for the inventory turnover ratio.

Profitability Ratios

A fundamental element of an analyst's task is to develop an understanding of a firm's profitability. Profitability ratios attempt to measure a company's ability to earn an adequate return relative to sales or resources devoted to operations. Resources devoted to operations can be defined as total assets or only those assets provided by owners, depending on the evaluation objective.

> Profitability ratios assist in evaluating various aspects of a company's profit-making activities.

Three common profitability measures are (1) the profit margin on sales, (2) the return on assets, and (3) the return on equity. These ratios are calculated as follows:

$$\text{Profit margin on sales} = \frac{\text{Net income}}{\text{Net sales}}$$

$$\text{Return on assets} = \frac{\text{Net income}}{\text{Average total assets}}$$

$$\text{Return on equity} = \frac{\text{Net income}}{\text{Average shareholders' equity}}$$

Notice that for all of the profitability ratios, our numerator is net income. Recall our discussion earlier in this chapter on earnings quality. The relevance of any historical-based financial statement hinges on its predictive value. To enhance predictive value, analysts often adjust net income in these ratios to separate a company's *temporary earnings* from its *permanent earnings*. Analysts begin their assessment of permanent earnings with income from continuing operations. Then, adjustments are made for any unusual, one-time gains or losses included in income from continuing operations. It is this adjusted number that they use as the numerator in these ratios.

> When calculating profitability ratios, analysts often adjust net income for any temporary income effects.

PROFIT MARGIN ON SALES   The profit margin on sales is simply net income divided by net sales. The ratio measures an important dimension of a company's profitability. It indicates the portion of each dollar of revenue that is available after all expenses have been covered. It offers a measure of the company's ability to withstand either higher expenses or lower revenues.

> The *profit margin on sales* measures the amount of net income achieved per sales dollar.

What is considered to be a desirable profit margin is highly sensitive to the nature of the business activity. For instance, you would expect a specialty shop to have a higher profit margin than, say, Walmart. A low profit margin can be compensated for by a high asset turnover rate, and vice versa, which brings us to considering the trade-offs inherent in generating return on assets.

RETURN ON ASSETS   The return on assets (ROA) ratio expresses income as a percentage of the average total assets available to generate that income. Because total assets are partially financed with debt and partially by equity funds, this is an inclusive way of measuring earning power that ignores specific sources of financing.

A company's return on assets is related to both profit margin and asset turnover. Specifically, profitability can be achieved by either a high profit margin, high asset turnover, or a combination of the two. In fact, the return on assets can be calculated by multiplying the profit margin and the asset turnover.

> Profit margin and asset turnover combine to yield *return on assets*, which measures the return generated by a company's assets.

$$\text{Return on assets} = \text{Profit margin} \times \text{Asset turnover}$$
$$\frac{\text{Net income}}{\text{Average total assets}} = \frac{\text{Net income}}{\text{Net sales}} \times \frac{\text{Net sales}}{\text{Average total assets}}$$

Industry standards are particularly important when evaluating asset turnover and profit margin. Some industries are characterized by low turnover but typically make up for it with higher profit margins. Others have low profit margins but compensate with high turnover. Grocery stores typically have relatively low profit margins but relatively high asset turnover. In comparison, a manufacturer of specialized equipment will have a higher profit margin but a lower asset turnover ratio.

Additional Consideration

The return on assets ratio often is computed as follows:

$$\text{Return on assets} = \frac{\text{Net income} + \text{Interest expense (1 - Tax rate)}}{\text{Average total assets}}$$

The reason for adding back interest expense (net of tax) is that interest represents a return to suppliers of debt capital and should not be deducted in the computation of net income when computing the return on assets. In other words, the numerator is the total amount of income available to both debt and equity capital.

Return on equity measures the return to suppliers of equity capital.

RETURN ON SHAREHOLDERS' EQUITY Shareholders are concerned with how well management uses their equity to generate a profit. A closely watched measure that captures this concern is return on equity (ROE), calculated as net income divided by average shareholders' equity.

The DuPont framework shows that return on equity depends on profitability, activity, and financial leverage.

In addition to monitoring return on equity, investors want to understand how that return can be improved. The DuPont framework provides a convenient basis for analysis that breaks return on equity into three key components:[36]

- **Profitability,** measured by the profit margin (Net income ÷ Sales). As discussed already, a higher profit margin indicates that a company generates more profit from each dollar of sales.

- **Activity,** measured by asset turnover (Sales ÷ Average total assets). As discussed already, higher asset turnover indicates that a company uses its assets efficiently to generate more sales from each dollar of assets.

- **Financial Leverage,** measured by the equity multiplier (Average total assets ÷ Average total equity). A high equity multiplier indicates that relatively more of the company's assets have been financed with debt; that is, the company is more leveraged. As discussed in Chapter 3, leverage can provide additional return to the company's equity holders.

In equation form, the DuPont framework looks like this:

Return on equity = Profit margin × Asset turnover × Equity multiplier

$$\frac{\text{Net income}}{\text{Avg. total equity}} = \frac{\text{Net income}}{\text{Net sales}} \times \frac{\text{Net sales}}{\text{Avg. total assets}} \times \frac{\text{Avg. total assets}}{\text{Avg. total equity}}$$

Notice that net sales and average total assets appear in the numerator of one ratio and the denominator of another, so they cancel to yield net income ÷ average total equity, or ROE.

We have already seen that ROA is determined by profit margin and asset turnover, so another way to compute ROE is by multiplying ROA by the equity multiplier:

Return on equity = Return on assets × Equity multiplier

$$\frac{\text{Net income}}{\text{Avg. total equity}} = \frac{\text{Net income}}{\text{Avg. total assets}} \times \frac{\text{Avg. total assets}}{\text{Avg. total equity}}$$

We can see from this equation that an equity multiplier of greater than 1 will produce a return on equity that is higher than the return on assets. However, as with all ratio analysis, there are trade-offs. If leverage is too high, creditors become concerned about the potential for default on the company's debt and require higher interest rates. Because interest is recognized as an expense, net income is reduced, so at some point the benefits of a higher equity multiplier are offset by a lower profit margin. Part of the challenge of managing a

---

[36]DuPont analysis is so named because the basic model was developed by F. Donaldson Brown, an electrical engineer who worked for DuPont in the early part of the twentieth century.

Additional Consideration

Sometimes when return on equity is calculated, shareholders' equity is viewed more narrowly to include only common shareholders. In that case, preferred stock is excluded from the denominator, and preferred dividends are deducted from net income in the numerator. The resulting rate of return on equity focuses on profits generated on resources provided by common shareholders.

company is to identify the combination of profitability, activity, and leverage that produces the highest return for equity holders.

Illustration 4–16 provides a recap of the ratios we have discussed.

Activity ratios

$$\text{Asset turnover} = \frac{\text{Net sales}}{\text{Average total assets}}$$

$$\text{Receivables turnover} = \frac{\text{Net sales}}{\text{Average accounts receivable (net)}}$$

$$\text{Average collection period} = \frac{365}{\text{Receivables turnover ratio}}$$

$$\text{Inventory turnover} = \frac{\text{Cost of goods sold}}{\text{Average inventory}}$$

$$\text{Average days in inventory} = \frac{365}{\text{Inventory turnover ratio}}$$

Profitability ratios

$$\text{Profit margin on sales} = \frac{\text{Net income}}{\text{Net sales}}$$

$$\text{Return on assets} = \frac{\text{Net income}}{\text{Average total assets}}$$

$$\text{Return on equity} = \frac{\text{Net income}}{\text{Average shareholders' equity}}$$

Leverage ratio

$$\text{Equity multiplier} = \frac{\text{Average total assets}}{\text{Average total equity}}$$

Illustration 4–16
Summary of Profitability Analysis Ratios

Profitability Analysis—An Illustration

To illustrate the application of the DuPont framework and the computation of the activity and profitability ratios, we analyze the 2017 financial statements of two well-known retailers, **Costco Wholesale Corporation** and **Walmart Stores Inc.**[37] The operations of these two companies are similar in their focus on operating large general merchandising and food discount stores. Illustration 4–17 presents selected financial statement information for the two companies (all numbers are in millions of dollars).

In absolute dollars, it appears that Walmart is far more profitable than Costco. As shown at the bottom of Illustration 4–17, Walmart's 2017 net income was $14,293 million, compared to Costco's $2,679 million. But that's not the whole story. Even though both are very large companies, Walmart is more than five times the size of Costco in terms of total assets, so how can they be compared? Focusing on financial ratios helps adjust for size differences, and the DuPont framework helps identify the determinants of profitability from the perspective of shareholders.

Illustration 4–18 includes the DuPont analysis for Walmart and Costco, as well as some additional activity ratios we've discussed. The first item to notice is that Walmart's profit

[37]Walmart's financial statements are for the fiscal year ended January 31, 2017. Walmart refers to this as its 2017 fiscal year. Costco's financial statements are for the fiscal year ended August 30, 2017.

202 SECTION 1 The Role of Accounting as an Information System

Illustration 4–17 Selected Financial Information for Costco Wholesale Corporation and Walmart Stores Inc. Real World Financials

	Costco		Walmart	
	2017	**2016**	**2017**	**2016**
($ in millions)				
Balance Sheet—2017				
Accounts receivable (net)	$ 1,432	$ 1,252	$ 5,835	$ 5,624
Inventories	9,834	8,969	43,046	44,469
Total assets	36,347	33,163	198,825	199,581
Total liabilities	25,268	20,831	118,290	115,970
Total shareholders' equity	10,778	12,079	80,535	83,611
Average for 2017:				
Accounts receivable (net)		$ 1,342.0		$ 5,729.5
Inventories		9,401.5		43,757.5
Total assets		34,755.0		199,203.0
Total shareholders' equity		11,428.5		82,073.0
Income Statement—2017				
Net sales		126,172		481,317
Cost of goods sold		111,882		361,256
Net Income		2,679		14,293

Source: Costco; Walmart

Illustration 4–18 DuPont Framework and Activity Ratios—Costco Wholesale Corporation and Walmart Stores Inc. Real World Financials

DuPont analysis	Costco	Walmart	Industry Average*
Profit margin on sales	$= \dfrac{\$2,679}{\$126,172} = 2.12\%$	$\dfrac{\$14,293}{\$481,317} = 2.97\%$	4.38%
×	×	×	
Asset turnover	$= \dfrac{\$126,172}{\$34,755} = 3.63$	$\dfrac{\$481,317}{\$199,203} = 2.42$	1.82
=	=	=	
Return on assets	$= \dfrac{\$2,679}{\$34,755} = 7.71\%$	$\dfrac{\$14,293}{\$199,203} = 7.18\%$	9.10%
×	×	×	
Equity Multiplier	$= \dfrac{\$34,755}{\$11,428.5} = 3.04$	$\dfrac{\$199,203}{\$82,073} = 2.43$	2.08
=	=	=	
Return on equity	$= \dfrac{\$2,679}{\$11,428.5} = 23.44\%$	$\dfrac{\$14,293}{\$82,073} = 17.41\%$	18.95%
Other activity ratios			
Receivables turnover	$= \dfrac{\$126,172}{\$1,342} = 94.02$	$\dfrac{\$481,317}{\$5,729.5} = 84.01$	80.24
Average collection period	$= \dfrac{365}{94.02} = 3.88$ days	$\dfrac{365}{84.01} = 4.34$ days	4.55 days
Inventory turnover	$= \dfrac{\$111,882}{\$9,401.5} = 11.90$	$\dfrac{\$361,256}{\$43,757.5} = 8.26$	6.96
Average days in inventory	$= \dfrac{365}{11.90} = 30.67$ days	$\dfrac{365}{8.26} = 44.19$ days	52.44 days

*www.reuters.com.

Source: www.reuters.com

margin is higher than Costco's (2.97% for Walmart compared to 2.12% for Costco). This means that Walmart generates more profit for each $1 of sales. However, by looking at the asset turnover ratio, we see that Costco is better able to use its assets to generate sales. Costco's asset turnover ratio of 3.63 is noticeably higher than Walmart's ratio of only 2.42. Then, we see from the equity multiplier of each company that Costco's strategy is to use more debt (or conversely, less equity) to finance the purchase of its assets. This strategy has paid off for its shareholders. By using financial leverage to purchase more productive assets, Costco is able to generate a higher return on equity (ROE) for its shareholders (23.44% for Costco versus only 17.41% for Walmart). The DuPont analysis helps us understand how this occurs.

Other activity ratios further reveal Costco's greater operating efficiency. Two components of asset turnover are inventory turnover and receivables turnover. Based on the inventory turnover ratio, we see that inventory sells much more quickly at Costco. Inventory takes only 31 days on average before being sold at Costco, compared with 44 days at Walmart. Costco also turns over its accounts receivable slightly faster than Walmart does. While accounts receivable are relatively small for both companies, the difference in the receivables turnover could provide investors with another signal of Costco management's greater overall operating efficiency.

The essential point of our discussion here, and in Part C of Chapter 3, is that raw accounting numbers alone mean little to decision makers. The numbers gain value when viewed in relation to other numbers. Similarly, the financial ratios formed by those relationships provide even greater perspective when compared with similar ratios of other companies, or with averages for several companies in the same industry. Accounting information is useful in making decisions. Financial analysis that includes comparisons of financial ratios enhances the value of that information.

Financial Reporting Case Solution

1. **How would you explain restructuring costs to Becky? Are restructuring costs something Becky should worry about?** *(p. 174)*   Restructuring costs include employee severance and termination benefits plus other costs associated with the shutdown or relocation of facilities or downsizing of operations. Restructuring costs are not necessarily bad. In fact, the objective is to make operations more efficient. The costs are incurred now in hopes of better earnings later.

©GaudiLab/Shutterstock

2. **Explain to Becky what is meant by discontinued operations and describe to her how that item is reported in an income statement.** *(p. 177)*   Separate reporting as a discontinued operation is required when the disposal of a component represents a strategic shift that has, or will have, a major effect on a company's operations and financial results. The net-of-tax effect of discontinued operations is separately reported below income from continuing operations. If the component has been disposed of by the end of the reporting period, the income effects include: (1) income or loss from operations of the discontinued component from the beginning of the reporting period through the disposal date and (2) gain or loss on disposal of the component's assets. If the component has not been disposed of by the end of the reporting period, the income effects include: (1) income or loss from operations of the discontinued component from the beginning of the reporting period through the end of the reporting period, and (2) an impairment loss if the fair value minus cost to sell of the component's assets is less than their book value.

3. **Describe to Becky the difference between basic and diluted earnings per share.** *(p 184)*   Basic earnings per share is computed by dividing net income available to common shareholders (net income less any preferred stock dividends) by the weighted-average number of common shares outstanding for the period. Diluted earnings per share reflects the potential dilution that could occur for companies that have certain securities outstanding that are convertible into common shares or stock options that could create additional common shares if the options were exercised. These items could cause earnings per share to decrease (become diluted). Because of the complexity of the calculation and the importance of earnings per share to investors, the text devotes a substantial portion of Chapter 19 to this topic. ●

The Bottom Line

● **LO4–1** The components of income from continuing operations are revenues, expenses (including income taxes), gains, and losses, excluding those related to discontinued operations. Companies often distinguish between operating and nonoperating income within continuing operations. (*p. 168*)

● **LO4–2** The term *earnings quality* refers to the ability of reported earnings (income) to predict a company's future earnings. The relevance of any historical-based financial statement hinges on its predictive value. To enhance predictive value, analysts try to separate a company's *temporary earnings* from its *permanent earnings*. Many believe that manipulating income reduces earnings quality because it can mask permanent earnings. Two major methods used by managers to manipulate earnings are (1) income shifting and (2) income statement classification. (*p. 173*)

● **LO4–3** Analysts begin their assessment of permanent earnings with income from continuing operations. It would be a mistake to assume income from continuing operations reflects permanent earnings entirely. In other words, there may be temporary earnings effects included in both operating and nonoperating income. (*p. 173*)

● **LO4–4** A discontinued operation refers to the disposal or planned disposal of a component of the entity. The net-of-tax effect of discontinued operations is separately reported below income from continuing operations. (*p. 177*)

● **LO4–5** Accounting changes include changes in principle, changes in estimate, or changes in reporting entity. Their effects on the current period and prior period financial statements are reported using various approaches—retrospective, modified retrospective, and prospective. Error corrections are made by restating prior period financial statements. Any correction to retained earnings is made with an adjustment to the beginning balance in the current period. Earnings per share (EPS) is the amount of income achieved during a period expressed per share of common stock outstanding. EPS must be disclosed for income from continuing operations and for discontinued operations. (*p. 182*)

● **LO4–6** The FASB's Concept Statement 6 defines the term *comprehensive income* as the change in equity from nonowner transactions. The calculation of net income, however, excludes certain transactions that are included in comprehensive income. To convey the relationship between the two measures, companies must report both net income and comprehensive income and reconcile the difference between the two. The presentation can be (1) in a single, continuous statement of comprehensive income, or (2) in two separate, but consecutive statements—an income statement and a statement of comprehensive income. (*p. 185*)

● **LO4–7** When a company provides a balance sheet and income statement, a statement of cash flows also is provided. The purpose of the statement of cash flows is to provide information about the cash receipts and cash disbursements that occurred during the period. (*p. 189*)

● **LO4–8** To enhance the usefulness of the information, the statement of cash flows classifies all transactions affecting cash into one of three categories: (1) operating activities, (2) investing activities, or (3) financing activities. (*p. 190*)

● **LO4–9** There are more similarities than differences between income statements and statements of cash flows prepared according to U.S. GAAP and those prepared applying international standards. In a statement of cash flows, some differences are possible in the classifications of interest and divided revenue, interest expense, and dividends paid. (*pp. 172, 186, and 195*)

● **LO4–10** Activity and profitability ratios provide information about a company's profitability. Activity ratios include the receivables turnover ratio, the inventory turnover ratio, and the asset turnover ratio. Profitability ratios include the profit margin on sales, the return on assets, and the return on equity. DuPont analysis explains return on equity as determined by profit margin, asset turnover, and the extent to which assets are financed with equity versus debt. (*p. 197*) ●

APPENDIX 4 | Interim Reporting

Interim reports are issued for periods of less than a year, typically as quarterly financial statements.

Financial statements covering periods of less than a year are called *interim reports*. Companies registered with the SEC, which includes most public companies, must submit quarterly reports, and you will see excerpts from these reports throughout this book.[38] Though there is no requirement to do so, most also provide quarterly reports to their shareholders

---

[38] Quarterly reports are filed with the SEC on Form 10-Q. Annual reports to the SEC are on Form 10-K.

and typically include abbreviated, unaudited interim reports as supplemental information within their annual reports. For instance, Illustration 4A–1 shows the quarterly information disclosed in the annual report of **The Home Depot, Inc.**, for the fiscal year ended January 29, 2017. Amounts for each of the four quarters sum to the reported amount for the full year. Compare these numbers to the annual income statement in Illustration 4–2.

NOTE 16 – SUMMARY OF QUARTERLY RESULTS OF OPERATIONS (UNAUDITED)

Year Ended January 29, 2017	1st Quarter	2nd Quarter	3rd Quarter	4th Quarter	Full Year
($ in millions, except per share data)					
Net sales	$22,762	$26,472	$23,154	$22,207	$ 94,595
Gross profit	7,791	8,927	8,042	7,553	32,313
Net income	1,803	2,441	1,969	1,744	7,957
Basic	$ 1.45	$ 1.98	$ 1.61	$ 1.45	$ 6.47*
Diluted	$ 1.44	$ 1.97	$ 1.60	$ 1.44	$ 6.45

*Rounding error of $0.02
Source: Home Depot, Inc.

Illustration 4A–1

Interim Data in Annual Report—The Home Depot, Inc.

Real World Financials

For accounting information to be useful to decision makers, it must be available on a timely basis. One of the objectives of interim reporting is to enhance the timeliness of financial information. In addition, quarterly reports provide investors and creditors with additional insight on the seasonality of business operations that might otherwise get lost in annual reports. Why are sales and net income higher in the 2nd and 3rd quarters (compared to the 1st and 4th quarters) for Home Depot? Most home improvement projects occur in the warmer months. These months occur in the 2nd and 3rd quarters, so it is expected that sales would be higher in these quarters. Because the company sells home products for a profit, profitability is also higher in quarters with greater sales.

However, the downside to interim reporting is that the amounts often are less reliable. With a shorter reporting period, questions associated with estimation and allocation are magnified. For example, certain expenses often benefit an entire year's operations and yet are incurred primarily within a single interim period. Similarly, should smaller companies use lower tax rates in the earlier quarters and higher rates in later quarters as higher tax brackets are reached? Another result of shorter reporting periods is the intensified effect of unusual events such as material gains and losses. A second quarter casualty loss, for instance, that would reduce annual profits by 10% might reduce second quarter profits by 40% or more. Is it more realistic to allocate such a loss over the entire year? These and similar questions tend to hinge on the way we view an interim period in relation to the fiscal year. More specifically, should each interim period be viewed as a *discrete* reporting period or as an *integral part* of the annual period?

The fundamental debate regarding interim reporting centers on the choice between the *discrete* and *integral part* approaches.

Reporting Revenues and Expenses

Existing practice and current reporting requirements for interim reporting generally follow the viewpoint that interim reports are an integral part of annual statements, although the discrete approach is applied to some items. Most revenues and expenses are recognized using the same accounting principles applicable to annual reporting. Some modifications are necessary to help cause interim statements to relate better to annual statements. This is most evident in the way costs and expenses are recognized. Most are recognized in interim periods as incurred. But when an expenditure clearly benefits more than just the period in which it is incurred, the expense should be allocated among the periods benefited on an allocation basis consistent with the company's annual allocation procedures. For example, annual repair expenses, property tax expense, and advertising expenses incurred in the first quarter that clearly benefit later quarters are assigned to each quarter through the use of accruals and deferrals. Costs and expenses subject to year-end adjustments, such as depreciation expense, are estimated and allocated to interim periods in a systematic way. Similarly, income tax expense at each interim date should be based on estimates of the effective tax

With only a few exceptions, the same accounting principles applicable to annual reporting are used for interim reporting.

rate for the whole year. This would mean, for example, that if the estimated effective rate has changed since the previous interim period(s), the tax expense in the current period would be determined as the new rate times the cumulative pretax income to date, less the total tax expense reported in previous interim periods.

Reporting Unusual Items

Discontinued operations and unusual items are reported entirely within the interim period in which they occur.

On the other hand, major events such as discontinued operations should be reported separately in the interim period in which they occur. That is, these amounts should not be allocated among individual quarters within the fiscal year. The same is true for items that are unusual. Treatment of these items is more consistent with the discrete view than the integral part view.

International Financial Reporting Standards

● LO4–9

Interim Reporting. *IAS No. 34* requires that a company apply the same accounting policies in its interim financial statements as it applies in its annual financial statements. Therefore, IFRS takes much more of a discrete-period approach than does U.S. GAAP. For example, costs for repairs, property taxes, and advertising that do not meet the definition of an asset at the end of an interim period are expensed entirely in the period in which they occur under IFRS, but are accrued or deferred and then charged to each of the periods they benefit under U.S. GAAP. This difference would tend to make interim period income more volatile under IFRS than under U.S. GAAP. However, as in U.S. GAAP, income taxes are accounted for based on an estimate of the tax rate expected to apply for the entire year.[39]

Earnings Per Share

Quarterly EPS calculations follow the same procedures as annual calculations.

A second item that is treated in a manner consistent with the discrete view is earnings per share. EPS calculations for interim reports follow the same procedures as annual calculations that you will study in Chapter 19. The calculations are based on conditions actually existing during the particular interim period rather than on conditions estimated to exist at the end of the fiscal year.

Reporting Accounting Changes

Accounting changes made in an interim period are reported by retrospectively applying the changes to prior financial statements.

Recall that we account for a change in accounting principle retrospectively, meaning we recast prior years' financial statements when we report those statements again in comparative form. In other words, we make those statements appear as if the newly adopted accounting method had been used in those prior years. It's the same with interim reporting. We retrospectively report a change made during an interim period in similar fashion. Then in financial reports of subsequent interim periods of the same fiscal year, we disclose how that change affected (a) income from continuing operations, (b) net income, and (c) related per share amounts for the postchange interim period.

Minimum Disclosures

Complete financial statements are not required for interim period reporting, but certain minimum disclosures are required as follows:[40]

- Sales, income taxes, and net income.
- Earnings per share.
- Seasonal revenues, costs, and expenses.
- Significant changes in estimates for income taxes.
- Discontinued operations and unusual items.

---

[39]"Interim Financial Reporting," *International Accounting Standard No. 34* (IASCF), as amended effective January 1, 2016, par. 28–30.
[40]FASB ASC 270-10-50: Interim Reporting—Overall—Disclosure (previously "Interim Financial Reporting," *Accounting Principles Board Opinion No 28* (New York: AICPA, 1973)).

- Contingencies.
- Changes in accounting principles or estimates.
- Information about fair value of financial instruments and the methods and assumptions used to estimate fair values.
- Significant changes in financial position.

When fourth quarter results are not separately reported, material fourth quarter events, including year-end adjustments, should be reported in disclosure notes to annual statements.

Questions For Review of Key Topics

Q 4–1 The income statement is a change statement. Explain what is meant by this.

Q 4–2 What transactions are included in income from continuing operations? Briefly explain why it is important to segregate income from continuing operations from other transactions affecting net income.

Q 4–3 Distinguish between operating and nonoperating income in relation to the income statement.

Q 4–4 Briefly explain the difference between the single-step and multiple-step income statement formats.

Q 4–5 Explain what is meant by the term *earnings quality*.

Q 4–6 What are restructuring costs and where are they reported in the income statement?

Q 4–7 Define intraperiod tax allocation. Why is the process necessary?

Q 4–8 How are discontinued operations reported in the income statement?

Q 4–9 What is meant by a change in accounting principle? Describe the possible accounting treatments for a mandated change in accounting principle.

Q 4–10 Accountants very often are required to make estimates, and very often those estimates prove incorrect. In what period(s) is the effect of a change in an accounting estimate reported?

Q 4–11 The correction of a material error discovered in a year subsequent to the year the error was made is considered a prior period adjustment. Briefly describe the accounting treatment for prior period adjustments.

Q 4–12 Define earnings per share (EPS). For which income statement items must EPS be disclosed?

Q 4–13 Define comprehensive income. What are the two ways companies can present comprehensive income?

Q 4–14 Describe the purpose of the statement of cash flows.

Q 4–15 Identify and briefly describe the three categories of cash flows reported in the statement of cash flows.

Q 4–16 Explain what is meant by noncash investing and financing activities pertaining to the statement of cash flows. Give an example of one of these activities.

Q 4–17 Distinguish between the direct method and the indirect method for reporting the results of operating activities in the statement of cash flows.

IFRS Q 4–18 Describe the potential statement of cash flows classification differences between U.S. GAAP and IFRS.

Q 4–19 Show the calculation of the following activity ratios: (1) the receivables turnover ratio, (2) the inventory turnover ratio, and (3) the asset turnover ratio. What information about a company do these ratios offer?

Q 4–20 Show the calculation of the following profitability ratios: (1) the profit margin on sales, (2) the return on assets, and (3) the return on equity. What information about a company do these ratios offer?

Q 4–21 Show the DuPont framework's calculation of the three components of return on equity. What information about a company do these ratios offer?

Q 4–22 Interim reports are issued for periods of less than a year, typically as quarterly financial statements. Should these interim periods be viewed as separate periods or integral parts of the annual period?

IFRS Q 4–23 [Based on Appendix 4] What is the primary difference between interim reports under IFRS and U.S. GAAP?

Brief Exercises

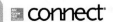

BE 4–1
Single-step
income statement
● LO4–1

The adjusted trial balance of Pacific Scientific Corporation on December 31, 2021, the end of the company's fiscal year, contained the following income statement items ($ in millions): sales revenue, $2,106; cost of goods sold, $1,240; selling expense, $126; general and administrative expense, $105; interest expense, $40; and gain on sale of investments, $45. Income tax expense has not yet been recorded. The income tax rate is 25%.

Using the account balances, prepare a single-step income statement for 2021. An example of a single-step income statement can be found in Illustration 4–3 of this chapter.

BE 4–2
Multiple-step
income statement
● LO4–1, LO4–3

Refer to the situation described in BE 4–1. If the company's accountant prepared a multiple-step income statement, what amount would appear in that statement for (a) operating income and (b) nonoperating income?

BE 4–3
Multiple-step
income statement
● LO4–1, LO4–3

Refer to the situation described in BE 4–1. Using the account balances, prepare a multiple-step income statement for 2021. An example of a multiple-step income statement can be found in Illustration 4–4 of this chapter.

BE 4–4
Multiple-step
income statement
● LO4–1, LO4–3

The following is a partial year-end adjusted trial balance.

Account Title	Debits	Credits
Sales revenue		$300,000
Loss on sale of investments	$ 22,000	
Interest revenue		4,000
Cost of goods sold	160,000	
General and administrative expense	40,000	
Restructuring costs	50,000	
Selling expense	25,000	
Income tax expense	?	

Income tax expense has not yet been recorded. The income tax rate is 25%. Determine the following: (a) operating income (loss), (b) income (loss) before income taxes, and (c) net income (loss).

BE 4–5
Income from
continuing
operations
● LO4–3, LO4–5

The following are partial income statement account balances taken from the December 31, 2021, year-end trial balance of White and Sons, Inc.: restructuring costs, $300,000; interest revenue, $40,000; before-tax loss on discontinued operations, $400,000; and loss on sale of investments, $50,000. Income tax expense has not yet been recorded. The income tax rate is 25%.

Prepare the lower portion of the 2021 income statement beginning with $800,000 income from continuing operations before income taxes. Include appropriate EPS disclosures. The company had 100,000 shares of common stock outstanding throughout the year.

BE 4–6
Discontinued
operations
● LO4–4

On December 31, 2021, the end of the fiscal year, Revolutionary Industries completed the sale of its robotics business for $9 million. The robotics business segment qualifies as a component of the entity according to GAAP. The book value of the assets of the segment was $7 million. The income from operations of the segment during 2021 was $4 million. Pretax income from continuing operations for the year totaled $12 million. The income tax rate is 25%. Prepare the lower portion of the 2021 income statement beginning with income from continuing operations before income taxes. Ignore EPS disclosures.

BE 4–7
Discontinued
operations
● LO4–4

On December 31, 2021, the end of the fiscal year, California Microtech Corporation completed the sale of its semiconductor business for $10 million. The semiconductor business segment qualifies as a component of the entity according to GAAP. The book value of the assets of the segment was $8 million. The loss from operations of the segment during 2021 was $3.6 million. Pretax income from continuing operations for the year totaled $5.8 million. The income tax rate is 25%. Prepare the lower portion of the 2021 income statement beginning with income from continuing operations before income taxes. Ignore EPS disclosures.

BE 4–8
Discontinued
operations
● LO4–4

Refer to the situation described in BE 4–7. Assume that the semiconductor segment was not sold during 2021 but was held for sale at year-end. The estimated fair value of the segment's assets, less costs to sell, on December 31 was $10 million. Prepare the lower portion of the 2021 income statement beginning with income from continuing operations before income taxes. Ignore EPS disclosures.

BE 4–9
Discontinued
operations
● LO4–4

Refer to the situation described in BE 4–8. Assume instead that the estimated fair value of the segment's assets, less costs to sell, on December 31 was $7 million rather than $10 million. Prepare the lower portion of the 2021 income statement beginning with income from continuing operations before income taxes. Ignore EPS disclosures.

BE 4–10
Comprehensive income
● LO4–6

O'Reilly Beverage Company reported net income of $650,000 for 2021. In addition, the company deferred a $60,000 pretax loss on derivatives and had pretax net unrealized gains on debt securities of $40,000. Prepare a separate statement of comprehensive income for 2021. The company's income tax rate is 25%.

BE 4–11
Statement of cash flows; direct method
● LO4–8

The following are summary cash transactions that occurred during the year for Hilliard Healthcare Co. (HHC):

Cash received from:	
Customers	$660,000
Interest on notes receivable	12,000
Collection of notes receivable	100,000
Sale of land	40,000
Issuance of common stock	200,000
Cash paid for:	
Interest on notes payable	18,000
Purchase of equipment	120,000
Operating expenses	440,000
Dividends to shareholders	30,000

Prepare the cash flows from operating activities section of HHC's statement of cash flows using the direct method.

BE 4–12
Statement of cash flows; investing and financing activities
● LO4–8

Refer to the situation described in BE 4–11. Prepare the cash flows from investing and financing activities sections of HHC's statement of cash flows.

BE 4–13
Statement of cash flows; indirect method
● LO4–8

Net income of Mansfield Company was $45,000. The accounting records reveal depreciation expense of $80,000 as well as increases in prepaid rent, salaries payable, and income taxes payable of $60,000, $15,000, and $12,000, respectively. Prepare the cash flows from operating activities section of Mansfield's statement of cash flows using the indirect method.

BE 4–14
IFRS; Statement of cash flows
● LO4–8, LO4–9

 IFRS

Refer to the situation described in BE 4–11 and BE 4–12. How might your solution to those brief exercises differ if Hilliard Healthcare Co. prepares its statement of cash flows according to International Financial Reporting Standards?

BE 4–15
Receivables and inventory turnover ratios
● LO4–10

Universal Calendar Company began the year with accounts receivable (net) and inventory balances of $100,000 and $80,000, respectively. Year-end balances for these accounts were $120,000 and $60,000, respectively. Sales for the year of $600,000 generated a gross profit of $200,000. Calculate the receivables and inventory turnover ratios for the year.

BE 4–16
Profitability ratios
● LO4–10

The 2021 income statement for Anderson TV and Appliance reported net sales of $420,000 and net income of $65,000. Average total assets for 2021 was $800,000. Shareholders' equity at the beginning of the year was $500,000, and $20,000 was paid to shareholders as dividends. There were no other shareholders' equity transactions that occurred during the year. Calculate the profit margin on sales, return on assets, and return on equity for 2021.

BE 4–17
Profitability ratios
● LO4–10

Refer to the facts described in BE 4–16. Show the DuPont framework's calculation of the three components of the 2021 return on equity for Anderson TV and Appliance.

BE 4–18
Inventory turnover ratio
● LO4–10

During 2021, Rogue Corporation reported net sales of $600,000. Inventory at both the beginning and end of the year totaled $75,000. The inventory turnover ratio for the year was 6.0. What amount of gross profit did the company report in its 2021 income statement?

Exercises

E 4–1
Operating versus nonoperating Income
● LO4–1

Pandora Corporation operates several factories in the Midwest that manufacture consumer electronics. The December 31, 2021, year-end trial balance contained the following income statement items:

Account Title	Debits	Credits
Sales revenue		$12,500,000
Interest revenue		50,000
Loss on sale of investments	$ 100,000	
Cost of goods sold	6,200,000	
Selling expense	620,000	
General and administrative expense	1,520,000	
Interest expense	40,000	
Research and development expense	1,200,000	
Income tax expense	900,000	

Required:
Calculate the company's operating income for the year.

E 4–2
Income statement format; single step and multiple step
● LO4–1, LO4–5

The following is a partial trial balance for the Green Star Corporation as of December 31, 2021:

Account Title	Debits	Credits
Sales revenue		$1,300,000
Interest revenue		30,000
Gain on sale of investments		50,000
Cost of goods sold	$720,000	
Selling expense	160,000	
General and administrative expense	75,000	
Interest expense	40,000	
Income tax expense	130,000	

There were 100,000 shares of common stock outstanding throughout 2021.

Required:
1. Prepare a single-step income statement for 2021, including EPS disclosures, by inserting the amounts above into the appropriate section.
2. Prepare a multiple-step income statement for 2021, including EPS disclosures, by inserting the amounts above into the appropriate section.

E 4–3
Income statement format; single step and multiple step
● LO4–1, LO4–3, LO4–5

The following is a partial trial balance for General Lighting Corporation as of December 31, 2021:

Account Title	Debits	Credits
Sales revenue		$2,350,000
Interest revenue		80,000
Loss on sale of investments	$ 22,500	
Cost of goods sold	1,200,300	
Loss on inventory write-down (obsolescence)	200,000	
Selling expense	300,000	
General and administrative expense	150,000	
Interest expense	90,000	

There were 160,000 shares of common stock outstanding throughout 2021. Income tax expense has not yet been recorded. The income tax rate is 25%.

Required:
1. Prepare a single-step income statement for 2021, including EPS disclosures. Be sure to include appropriate headings and subtotal titles. An example of a single-step income statement can be found in Illustration 4–3 of this chapter.

2. Prepare a multiple-step income statement for 2021, including EPS disclosures. Be sure to include appropriate headings and subtotal titles. An example of a multiple-step income statement can be found in Illustration 4–4 of this chapter.

E 4–4
Multiple-step continuous statement of comprehensive income
● LO4–1, LO4–5, LO4–6

The trial balance for Lindor Corporation, a manufacturing company, for the year ended December 31, 2021, included the following accounts:

Account Title	Debits	Credits
Sales revenue		$2,300,000
Cost of goods sold	$1,400,000	
Selling and administrative expense	420,000	
Interest expense	40,000	
Gain on debt securities		80,000

The gain on debt securities is unrealized and classified as other comprehensive income. The trial balance does not include the accrual for income taxes. Lindor's income tax rate is 25%. There were 1,000,000 shares of common stock outstanding throughout 2021.

Required:
Prepare a single, continuous multiple-step statement of comprehensive income for 2021, including appropriate EPS disclosures.

E 4–5
Income statement presentation
● LO4–1, LO4–5

The following *incorrect* income statement was prepared by the accountant of the Axel Corporation:

AXEL CORPORATION
Income Statement
For the Year Ended December 31, 2021

Revenues and gains:		
Sales revenue		$592,000
Interest revenue		32,000
Gain on sale of investments		86,000
Total revenues and gains		710,000
Expenses and losses:		
Cost of goods sold	$325,000	
Selling expense	67,000	
Administrative expense	87,000	
Interest expense	16,000	
Restructuring costs	55,000	
Income tax expense	40,000	
Total expenses and losses		590,000
Net Income		$120,000
Earnings per share		$ 1.20

Required:
Prepare a multiple-step income statement for 2021 applying generally accepted accounting principles. The income tax rate is 25%. Be sure to include appropriate headings and subtotal titles. An example of a multiple-step income statement can be found in Illustration 4–4 of this chapters.

E 4–6
Discontinued operations
● LO4–4, LO4–5

Chance Company had two operating divisions, one manufacturing farm equipment and the other office supplies. Both divisions are considered separate components as defined by generally accepted accounting principles. The farm equipment component had been unprofitable, and on September 1, 2021, the company adopted a plan to sell the assets of the division. The actual sale was completed on December 15, 2021, at a price of $600,000. The book value of the division's assets was $1,000,000, resulting in a before-tax loss of $400,000 on the sale.

The division incurred a before-tax operating loss from operations of $120,000 from the beginning of the year through December 15. The income tax rate is 25%. Chance's after-tax income from its continuing operations is $550,000.

Required:
Prepare an income statement for 2021 beginning with income from continuing operations. Include appropriate EPS disclosures assuming that 100,000 shares of common stock were outstanding throughout the year.

E 4–7
Income statement presentation; discontinued operations; restructuring costs
● LO4–1, LO4–3, LO4–4

Esquire Comic Book Company had income before tax of $1,000,000 in 2021 *before* considering the following material items:

1. Esquire sold one of its operating divisions, which qualified as a separate component according to generally accepted accounting principles. The before-tax loss on disposal was $340,000. The division generated before-tax income from operations from the beginning of the year through disposal of $500,000.

2. The company incurred restructuring costs of $80,000 during the year.

Required:
Prepare a 2021 income statement for Esquire beginning with income from continuing operations. Assume an income tax rate of 25%. Ignore EPS disclosures.

E 4–8
Discontinued operations; disposal in subsequent year
● LO4–4

Kandon Enterprises, Inc., has two operating divisions; one manufactures machinery and the other breeds and sells horses. Both divisions are considered separate components as defined by generally accepted accounting principles. The horse division has been unprofitable, and, on November 15, 2021, Kandon adopted a formal plan to sell the division. The sale was completed on April 30, 2022. At December 31, 2021, the component was considered held for sale.

On December 31, 2021, the company's fiscal year-end, the book value of the assets of the horse division was $240,000. On that date, the fair value of the assets, less costs to sell, was $200,000. The before-tax loss from operations of the division for the year was $140,000. The company's effective tax rate is 25%. The after-tax income from continuing operations for 2021 was $400,000.

Required:
1. Prepare a partial income statement for 2021 beginning with income from continuing operations. Ignore EPS disclosures.

2. Repeat requirement 1 assuming that the estimated net fair value of the horse division's assets was $400,000, instead of $200,000.

E 4–9
Discontinued operations; disposal in subsequent year; solving for unknown
● LO4–4

On September 17, 2021, Ziltech, Inc., entered into an agreement to sell one of its divisions that qualifies as a component of the entity according to generally accepted accounting principles. By December 31, 2021, the company's fiscal year-end, the division had not yet been sold, but was considered held for sale. The net fair value (fair value minus costs to sell) of the division's assets at the end of the year was $11 million. The pretax income from operations of the division during 2021 was $4 million. Pretax income from continuing operations for the year totaled $14 million. The income tax rate is 25%. Ziltech reported net income for the year of $7.2 million.

Required:
Determine the book value of the division's assets on December 31, 2021.

E 4–10
Earnings per share
● LO4–5

The Esposito Import Company had 1 million shares of common stock outstanding during 2021. Its income statement reported the following items: income from continuing operations, $5 million; loss from discontinued operations, $1.6 million. All of these amounts are net of tax.

Required:
Prepare the 2021 EPS presentation for the Esposito Import Company.

E 4–11
Comprehensive income
● LO4–6

The Massoud Consulting Group reported net income of $1,354,000 for its fiscal year ended December 31, 2021. In addition, during the year the company experienced a positive foreign currency translation adjustment of $240,000 and an unrealized loss on debt securities of $80,000. The company's effective tax rate on all items affecting comprehensive income is 25%. Each component of other comprehensive income is displayed net of tax.

Required:
Prepare a separate statement of comprehensive income for 2021.

E 4–12
Statement of cash flows; classifications
● LO4–8

The statement of cash flows classifies all cash inflows and outflows into one of the three categories shown below and lettered from a through c. In addition, certain transactions that do not involve cash are reported in the statement as noncash investing and financing activities, labeled d.

a. Operating activities

b. Investing activities

c. Financing activities

d. Noncash investing and financing activities

Required:
For each of the following transactions, use the letters above to indicate the appropriate classification category.

1._____ Purchase of equipment for cash.

2._____ Payment of employee salaries.

3._____ Collection of cash from customers.

4._____ Cash proceeds from notes payable.

5._____ Purchase of common stock of another corporation for cash.

6._____ Issuance of common stock for cash.

7._____ Sale of equipment for cash.

8._____ Payment of interest on notes payable.

9._____ Issuance of bonds payable in exchange for land and building.

10._____ Payment of cash dividends to shareholders.

11._____ Payment of principal on notes payable

E 4–13
Statement of cash flows preparation; direct method
● LO4–8

The following summary transactions occurred during 2021 for Bluebonnet Bakers:

Cash Received from:	
Collections from customers	$380,000
Interest on notes receivable	6,000
Collection of notes receivable	50,000
Sale of investments	30,000
Issuance of notes payable	100,000
Cash Paid for:	
Purchase of inventory	160,000
Interest on notes payable	5,000
Purchase of equipment	85,000
Salaries to employees	90,000
Payment of notes payable	25,000
Dividends to shareholders	20,000

The balance of cash and cash equivalents at the beginning of 2021 was $17,000.

Required:
Prepare a statement of cash flows for 2021 for Bluebonnet Bakers. Use the direct method for reporting operating activities.

E 4–14
IFRS; statement of cash flows
● LO4–8, LO4–9
 IFRS

Refer to the situation described in E 4–13.

Required:
Prepare the statement of cash flows assuming that Bluebonnet prepares its financial statements according to International Financial Reporting Standards. Where IFRS allows flexibility, use the classification used most often in IFRS financial statements.

E 4–15
Indirect method; reconciliation of net income to net cash flows from operating activities
● LO4–8

The accounting records of Hampton Company provided the data below ($ in thousands).

Net income	$17,300
Depreciation expense	7,800
Increase in accounts receivable	4,000
Decrease in inventory	5,500
Decrease in prepaid insurance	1,200
Decrease in salaries payable	2,700
Increase in interest payable	800

Required:
Prepare a reconciliation of net income to net cash flows from operating activities.

E 4–16
Statement of cash flows; directly from transactions
● LO4–8

The following transactions occurred during March 2021 for the Wainwright Corporation. The company owns and operates a wholesale warehouse. [These are the same transactions analyzed in Exercise 2–1, when we determined their effect on elements of the accounting equation.]

1. Issued 30,000 shares of common stock in exchange for $300,000 in cash.

2. Purchased equipment at a cost of $40,000. $10,000 cash was paid and a note payable to the seller was signed for the balance owed.
3. Purchased inventory on account at a cost of $90,000. The company uses the perpetual inventory system.
4. Credit sales for the month totaled $120,000. The cost of the goods sold was $70,000.
5. Paid $5,000 in rent on the warehouse building for the month of March.
6. Paid $6,000 to an insurance company for fire and liability insurance for a one-year period beginning April 1, 2021.
7. Paid $70,000 on account for the merchandise purchased in 3.
8. Collected $55,000 from customers on account.
9. Recorded depreciation expense of $1,000 for the month on the equipment.

Required:
1. Analyze each transaction and classify each as a financing, investing, and/or operating activity (a transaction can represent more than one type of activity). In doing so, also indicate the cash effect of each, if any. If there is no cash effect, simply place a check mark (√) in the appropriate column(s).
   Example:

	Operating	Investing	Financing
1.			$300,000

2. Prepare a statement of cash flows, using the direct method to present cash flows from operating activities. Assume the cash balance at the beginning of the month was $40,000.

E 4–17
Statement of cash flows; indirect method
● LO4–8

Cemptex Corporation prepares its statement of cash flows using the indirect method to report operating activities. Net income for the 2021 fiscal year was $624,000. Depreciation and amortization expense of $87,000 was included with operating expenses in the income statement. The following information describes the changes in current assets and liabilities other than cash:

Decrease in accounts receivable	$22,000
Increase in inventory	9,200
Increase prepaid expenses	8,500
Increase in salaries payable	10,000
Decrease in income taxes payable	14,000

Required:
Prepare the operating activities section of the 2021 statement of cash flows.

E 4–18
Statement of cash flows; indirect method
● LO4–8

Chew Corporation prepares its statement of cash flows using the indirect method of reporting operating activities. Net income for the 2021 fiscal year was $1,250,000. Depreciation expense of $140,000 was included with operating expenses in the income statement. The following information describes the changes in current assets and liabilities other than cash:

Increase in accounts receivable	$152,000
Decrease in inventory	108,000
Decrease prepaid expenses	62,000
Decrease in salaries payable	30,000
Increase in income taxes payable	44,000

Required:
Calculate cash flows from operating activities for 2021.

E 4–19
IFRS; statement of cash flows
● LO4–8, LO4–9
● IFRS

The statement of cash flows for the year ended December 31, 2021, for Bronco Metals is presented below.

BRONCO METALS
Statement of Cash Flows
For the Year Ended December 31, 2021

Cash flows from operating activities:	
Collections from customers	$353,000
Interest on notes receivable	4,000
Dividends received from investments	2,400
Purchase of inventory	(186,000)
Payment of operating expenses	(67,000)

(continued)

(concluded)

Payment of interest on notes payable	(8,000)	
Net cash flows from operating activities		$ 98,400
Cash flows from investing activities:		
Collection of notes receivable	100,000	
Purchase of equipment	(154,000)	
Net cash flows from investing activities		(54,000)
Cash flows from financing activities:		
Proceeds from issuance of common stock	200,000	
Dividends paid to shareholders	(40,000)	
Net cash flows from financing activities		160,000
Net increase in cash		204,400
Cash and cash equivalents, January 1		28,600
Cash and cash equivalents, December 31		$233,000

Required:

Prepare the statement of cash flows assuming that Bronco prepares its financial statements according to International Financial Reporting Standards. Where IFRS allows flexibility, use the classification used most often in IFRS financial statements.

E 4–20
Statement of cash flows; indirect method
● LO4–8

Presented below is the 2021 income statement and comparative balance sheet information for Tiger Enterprises.

TIGER ENTERPRISES
Income Statement
For the Year Ended December 31, 2021

($ in thousands)		
Sales revenue		$7,000
Operating expenses:		
Cost of goods sold	$3,360	
Depreciation expense	240	
Insurance expense	100	
General and administrative expense	1,800	
Total operating expenses		5,500
Income before income taxes		1,500
Income tax expense		(600)
Net income		$ 900

Balance Sheet Information ($ in thousands)	Dec. 31, 2021	Dec. 31, 2020
Assets:		
Cash	$ 300	$ 200
Accounts receivable	750	830
Inventory	640	600
Prepaid insurance	50	20
Equipment	2,100	1,800
Less: Accumulated depreciation	(840)	(600)
Total assets	$3,000	$2,850
Liabilities and Shareholders' Equity:		
Accounts payable	$ 300	$ 360
Accrued liabilities (for general & admin. expense)	300	400
Income taxes payable	200	150
Notes payable (due 12/31/2022)	800	600
Common stock	900	800
Retained earnings	500	540
Total liabilities and shareholders' equity	$3,000	$2,850

Required:

Prepare Tiger's statement of cash flows, using the indirect method to present cash flows from operating activities. (*Hint:* You will have to calculate dividend payments).

E 4–21
Statement of cash flows; direct method
● LO4–8

Refer to the situation described in E 4–20.

Required:

Prepare the cash flows from operating activities section of Tiger's 2021 statement of cash flows using the direct method. Assume that all purchases and sales of inventory are on account, and that there are no anticipated bad

216   SECTION 1   The Role of Accounting as an Information System

debts for accounts receivable. (*Hint:* Use the Concept Review Exercise at the end of Part B as a guide to help determine your answers).

E 4–22
FASB codification research
● **LO4–5**

Access the *FASB Accounting Standards Codification* at the FASB website (**www.fasb.org**). Determine each of the following:

1. The topic number (Topic XXX) that provides the accounting for earnings per share.
2. The specific eight-digit Codification citation (XXX-XX-XX-X) that describes the additional information for earnings per share that must be included in the notes to the financial statements.
3. The specific eight-digit Codification citation (XXX-XX-XX-X) that requires disclosure of transactions affecting the number of common shares outstanding that occur after the most recent reporting period but before the financial statements are issued.

E 4–23
FASB codification research
● **LO4–5, LO4–6, LO4–8**

Access the *FASB Accounting Standards Codification* at the FASB website (**www.fasb.org**). Determine the specific eight-digit Codification citation (XXX-XX-XX-X) for each of the following:

1. The calculation of the weighted average number of shares for basic earnings per share purposes.
2. The alternative formats permissible for reporting comprehensive income.
3. The classifications of cash flows required in the statement of cash flows.

E 4–24
Concepts; terminology
● **LO4–1, LO4–2, LO4–3, LO4–4, LO4–5, LO4–6, LO4–7, LO4–8**

Listed below are several terms and phrases associated with income statement presentation and the statement of cash flows. Pair each item from List A (by letter) with the item from List B that is most appropriately associated with it.

List A	List B
_____ 1. Intraperiod tax allocation	a. An other comprehensive income item.
_____ 2. Comprehensive income	b. Starts with net income and works backwards to convert to cash.
_____ 3. Unrealized gain on debt securities	c. Reports the cash effects of each operating activity directly on the statement.
_____ 4. Operating income	d. Correction of a material error of a prior period.
_____ 5. A discontinued operation	e. Related to the external financing of the company.
_____ 6. Earnings per share	f. Associates tax with income statement item.
_____ 7. Prior period adjustment	g. Total nonowner change in equity.
_____ 8. Financing activities	h. Related to the transactions entering into the determination of net income.
_____ 9. Operating activities (SCF)	i. Related to the acquisition and disposition of long-term assets.
_____ 10. Investing activities	j. Required disclosure for publicly traded corporation.
_____ 11. Direct method	k. A component of an entity.
_____ 12. Indirect method	l. Directly related to principal revenue-generating activities.

E 4–25
Inventory turnover; calculation and evaluation
● **LO4–10**

The following is a portion of the condensed income statement for Rowan, Inc., a manufacturer of plastic containers:

Net sales		$2,460,000
Less: Cost of goods sold:		
Inventory, January 1	$ 630,000	
Net purchases	1,900,000	
Inventory, December 31	(690,000)	1,840,000
Gross profit		$ 620,000

Required:
1. Determine Rowan's inventory turnover.
2. What information does this ratio provide?

E 4–26
Evaluating efficiency of asset management
● **LO4–10**

The 2021 income statement of Anderson Medical Supply Company reported net sales of $8 million, cost of goods sold of $4.8 million, and net income of $800,000. The following table shows the company's comparative balance sheets for 2021 and 2020:

CHAPTER 4   The Income Statement, Comprehensive Income, and the Statement of Cash Flows   **217**

	($ in thousands)	
	2021	**2020**
Assets		
Cash	$ 300	$ 380
Accounts receivable	700	500
Inventory	900	700
Property, plant, and equipment (net)	2,400	2,120
Total assets	$4,300	$3,700
Liabilities and Shareholders' Equity		
Current liabilities	$ 960	$ 830
Bonds payable	1,200	1,200
Common stock	1,000	1,000
Retained earnings	1,140	670
Total liabilities and shareholders' equity	$4,300	$3,700

Some industry averages for Anderson's line of business are

Inventory turnover	5 times
Average collection period	25 days
Asset turnover	1.8 times

Required:
1. Determine the following ratios for 2021:
   a. Inventory turnover
   b. Receivables turnover
   c. Average collection period
   d. Asset turnover
2. Assess Anderson's asset management relative to its industry.

E 4–27
Profitability ratios
● **LO4–10**

The following condensed information was reported by Peabody Toys, Inc., for 2021 and 2020:

	($ in thousands)	
	2021	**2020**
Income statement information		
Net sales	$5,200	$4,200
Net income	180	124
Balance sheet information		
Current assets	$ 800	$ 750
Property, plant, and equipment (net)	1,100	950
Total assets	$1,900	$1,700
Current liabilities	$ 600	$ 450
Long-term liabilities	750	750
Common stock	400	400
Retained earnings	150	100
Liabilities and shareholders' equity	$1,900	$1,700

Required:
1. Determine the following ratios for 2021:
   a. Profit margin on sales
   b. Return on assets
   c. Return on equity
2. Determine the amount of dividends paid to shareholders during 2021.

E 4–28
DuPont analysis
● **LO4–10**

This exercise is based on the Peabody Toys, Inc., data from E 4–27.
Required:
1. Determine the following components of the DuPont framework for 2021:
   a. Profit margin on sales

    b. Asset turnover

    c. Equity multiplier

    d. Return on equity

2. Write an equation that relates these components in calculating ROE. Use the Peabody Toys data to show that the equation is correct.

E 4–29
Interim financial statements; income tax expense
● Appendix 4

Joplin Laminating Corporation reported income before income taxes during the first three quarters, and management's estimates of the annual effective tax rate at the end of each quarter as shown below:

	Quarter		
	First	**Second**	**Third**
Income before income taxes	$50,000	$40,000	$100,000
Estimated annual effective tax rate	22%	25%	24%

Required:
Determine the income tax expense to be reported in the income statement in each of the three quarterly reports.

E 4–30
Interim reporting; recognizing expenses
● Appendix 4

Security-Rand Corporation determines executive incentive compensation at the end of its fiscal year. At the end of the first quarter, management estimated that the amount will be $300 million. Depreciation expense for the year is expected to be $60 million. Also during the quarter, the company realized a gain of $23 million from selling two of its manufacturing plants.

Required:
What amounts for these items should be reported in the first quarter's income statement?

E 4–31
Interim financial statements; reporting expenses
● Appendix 4

Shields Company is preparing its interim report for the second quarter ending June 30. The following payments were made during the first two quarters:

Required:

Expenditure	Date	Amount
Annual advertising	January	$800,000
Property tax for the fiscal year	February	350,000
Annual equipment repairs	March	260,000
One-time research and development fee to consultant	May	96,000

    For each expenditure, indicate the amount that would be reported in the quarterly income statements for the periods ending March 31, June 30, September 30, and December 31.

E 4–32
Interim financial statements
● Appendix 4

IFRS

Assume the same facts as in E 4–31, but that Shields Company reports under IFRS. For each expenditure, indicate the amount that would be reported in the quarterly income statements for the periods ending March 31, June 30, September 30, and December 31.

Problems

P 4–1
Comparative income statements; multiple-step format
● LO4–1, LO4–3,
  LO4–4, LO4–5

Selected information about income statement accounts for the Reed Company is presented below (the company's fiscal year ends on December 31).

	2021	2020
Sales revenue	$4,400,000	$3,500,000
Cost of goods sold	2,860,000	2,000,000
Administrative expense	800,000	675,000
Selling expense	360,000	302,000
Interest revenue	150,000	140,000
Interest expense	200,000	200,000
Loss on sale of assets of discontinued component	48,000	—

On July 1, 2021, the company adopted a plan to discontinue a division that qualifies as a component of an entity as defined by GAAP. The assets of the component were sold on September 30, 2021, for $48,000 less than their book value. Results of operations for the component (*included* in the above account balances) were as follows:

	1/1/2021–9/30/2021	2020
Sales revenue	$400,000	$500,000
Cost of goods sold	(290,000)	(320,000)
Administrative expense	(50,000)	(40,000)
Selling expense	(20,000)	(20,000)
Operating income before taxes	$ 40,000	$120,000

In addition to the account balances above, several events occurred during 2021 that have *not* yet been reflected in the above accounts:

1. A fire caused $50,000 in uninsured damages to the main office building. The fire was considered to be an unusual event.

2. Inventory that had cost $40,000 had become obsolete because a competitor introduced a better product. The inventory was written down to its scrap value of $5,000.

3. Income taxes have not yet been recorded.

Required:
Prepare a multiple-step income statement for the Reed Company for 2021, showing 2020 information in comparative format, including income taxes computed at 25% and EPS disclosures assuming 300,000 shares of outstanding common stock.

P 4–2
Discontinued operations
● LO4–4

The following condensed income statements of the Jackson Holding Company are presented for the two years ended December 31, 2021 and 2020:

	2021	2020
Sales revenue	$15,000,000	$9,600,000
Cost of goods sold	9,200,000	6,000,000
Gross profit	5,800,000	3,600,000
Operating expenses	3,200,000	2,600,000
Operating income	2,600,000	1,000,000
Gain on sale of division	600,000	—
	3,200,000	1,000,000
Income tax expense	800,000	250,000
Net income	$ 2,400,000	$ 750,000

On October 15, 2021, Jackson entered into a tentative agreement to sell the assets of one of its divisions. The division qualifies as a component of an entity as defined by GAAP. The division was sold on December 31, 2021, for $5,000,000. Book value of the division's assets was $4,400,000. The division's contribution to Jackson's operating income before-tax for each year was as follows:

2021	$400,000
2020	$300,000

Assume an income tax rate of 25%.

Required:

1. Prepare revised income statements according to generally accepted accounting principles, beginning with income from continuing operations before income taxes. Ignore EPS disclosures.

2. Assume that by December 31, 2021, the division had not yet been sold but was considered held for sale. The fair value of the division's assets on December 31 was $5,000,000. What would be the amount presented for discontinued operations?

3. Assume that by December 31, 2021, the division had not yet been sold but was considered held for sale. The fair value of the division's assets on December 31 was $3,900,000. What would be the amount presented for discontinued operations?

P 4–3
Income statement presentation; discontinued operations; accounting error
● LO4–4, LO4–5

For the year ending December 31, 2021, Olivo Corporation had income from continuing operations before taxes of $1,200,000 before considering the following transactions and events. All of the items described below are before taxes and the amounts should be considered material.

1. In November 2021, Olivo sold its PizzaPasta restaurant chain that qualified as a component of an entity. The company had adopted a plan to sell the chain in May 2021. The income from operations of the chain from January 1, 2021, through November was $160,000 and the loss on sale of the chain's assets was $300,000.

2. In 2021, Olivo sold one of its six factories for $1,200,000. At the time of the sale, the factory had a book value of $1,100,000. The factory was not considered a component of the entity.

3. In 2019, Olivo's accountant omitted the annual adjustment for patent amortization expense of $120,000. The error was not discovered until December 2021.

Required:

Prepare Olivo's income statement, beginning with income from continuing operations before taxes, for the year ended December 31, 2021. Assume an income tax rate of 25%. Ignore EPS disclosures.

P 4–4
Restructuring costs; discontinued operations; accounting error
● LO4–3, LO4–4, LO4–5

The preliminary 2021 income statement of Alexian Systems, Inc., is presented below:

ALEXIAN SYSTEMS, INC.
Income Statement
For the Year Ended December 31, 2021
($ in millions, except earnings per share)

Revenues and gains:	
Sales revenue	$ 425
Interest revenue	4
Other income	126
Total revenues and gains	555
Expenses:	
Cost of goods sold	245
Selling and administrative expense	154
Income tax expense	39
Total expenses	438
Net Income	$ 117
Earnings per share	$5.85

Additional Information:

1. Selling and administrative expense includes $26 million in restructuring costs.

2. Included in other income is $120 million in income from a discontinued operation. This consists of $90 million in operating income and a $30 million gain on disposal. The remaining $6 million is from the gain on sale of investments.

3. Cost of goods sold was increased by $40 million to correct an error in the calculation of 2020's ending inventory. The amount is material.

Required:

For each of the three additional facts listed in the additional information, discuss the appropriate presentation of the item described. Do not prepare a revised statement.

P 4–5
Income statement presentation; restructuring costs; discontinued operations; accounting error
● LO4–1, LO4–3, LO4–4, LO4–5

[This is a variation of the previous problem focusing on income statement presentation.]

Required:

Refer to the information presented in P 4–4. Prepare a revised income statement for 2021 reflecting the additional facts. Use a multiple-step format similar to Illustration 4–4 of this chapter to prepare income from continuing operations, and then add to this the discontinued operations portion of the income statement. Assume that an income tax rate of 25% applies to all income statement items, and that 20 million shares of common stock were outstanding throughout the year.

P 4–6
Income statement presentation; discontinued operations; EPS
● LO4–1, LO4–3, LO4–4, LO4–5

Rembrandt Paint Company had the following income statement items for the year ended December 31, 2021 ($ in thousands):

Sales revenue	$18,000
Interest revenue	100
Interest expense	300
Cost of goods sold	10,500
Selling and administrative expense	2,500
Restructuring costs	800

In addition, during the year, the company completed the disposal of its plastics business and incurred a loss from operations of $1.6 million and a gain on disposal of the component's assets of $2 million. There were 500,000 shares of common stock outstanding throughout 2021. Income tax expense has not yet been recorded. The income tax rate is 25% on all items of income (loss).

Required:
Prepare a multiple-step income statement for 2021, including EPS disclosures. Use a multiple-step format similar to Illustration 4–4 of this chapter to prepare income from continuing operations, and then add to this the discontinued operations portion of the income statement.

P 4–7
Income statement presentation; statement of comprehensive income; unusual items

● LO4–1, LO4–3 through LO4–6

The following income statement items appeared on the adjusted trial balance of Schembri Manufacturing Corporation for the year ended December 31, 2021 ($ in thousands): sales revenue, $15,300; cost of goods sold, $6,200; selling expenses, $1,300; general and administrative expenses, $800; interest revenue, $40; interest expense, $180. Income taxes have not yet been recorded. The company's income tax rate is 25% on all items of income or loss. These revenue and expense items appear in the company's income statement every year. The company's controller, however, has asked for your help in determining the appropriate treatment of the following nonrecurring transactions that also occurred during 2021 ($ in thousands). All transactions are material in amount.

1. Investments were sold during the year at a loss of $220. Schembri also had an unrealized gain of $320 for the year on investments in debt securities that qualify as components of comprehensive income.

2. One of the company's factories was closed during the year. Restructuring costs incurred were $1,200.

3. During the year, Schembri completed the sale of one of its operating divisions that qualifies as a component of the entity according to GAAP. The division had incurred a loss from operations of $560 in 2021 prior to the sale, and its assets were sold at a gain of $1,400.

4. In 2021, the company's accountant discovered that depreciation expense in 2020 for the office building was understated by $200.

5. Negative foreign currency translation adjustment for the year totaled $240.

Required:
1. Prepare Schembri's single, continuous multiple-step statement of comprehensive income for 2021, including earnings per share disclosures. There were 1,000,000 shares of common stock outstanding at the beginning of the year and an additional 400,000 shares were issued on July 1, 2021. Use a multiple-step format similar to the one in the Concept Review Exercise at the end of Part A of this chapter.

2. Prepare a separate statement of comprehensive income for 2021.

P 4–8
Multiple-step statement of income and comprehensive income

● LO4–1, LO4–3, LO4–5, LO4–6

Duke Company's records show the following account balances at December 31, 2021:

Sales revenue	$15,000,000
Cost of goods sold	9,000,000
General and administrative expense	1,000,000
Selling expense	500,000
Interest expense	700,000

Income tax expense has not yet been determined. The following events also occurred during 2021. All transactions are material in amount.

1. $300,000 in restructuring costs were incurred in connection with plant closings.

2. Inventory costing $400,000 was written off as obsolete. Material losses of this type are considered to be unusual.

3. It was discovered that depreciation expense for 2020 was understated by $50,000 due to a mathematical error.

4. The company experienced a negative foreign currency translation adjustment of $200,000 and had an unrealized gain on debt securities of $180,000.

Required:
Prepare a single, continuous multiple-step statement of comprehensive income for 2021. The company's effective tax rate on all items affecting comprehensive income is 25%. Each component of other comprehensive income should be displayed net of tax. Ignore EPS disclosures. Use a multiple-step format similar to the one in the Concept Review Exercise at the end of Part A of this chapter (excluding discontinued operations shown there).

P 4–9
Statement of cash flows

● LO4–8

The Diversified Portfolio Corporation provides investment advice to customers. A condensed income statement for the year ended December 31, 2021, appears below:

Service revenue	$900,000
Operating expenses	700,000
Income before income taxes	200,000
Income tax expense	50,000
Net income	$150,000

The following balance sheet information also is available:

	12/31/2021	12/31/2020
Cash	$305,000	$ 70,000
Accounts receivable	120,000	100,000
Accrued liabilities (for operating expenses)	70,000	60,000
Income taxes payable	10,000	15,000

In addition, the following transactions took place during the year:

1. Common stock was issued for $100,000 in cash.
2. Long-term investments were sold for $50,000 in cash. The original cost of the investments also was $50,000.
3. $80,000 in cash dividends was paid to shareholders.
4. The company has no outstanding debt, other than those payables listed above.
5. Operating expenses include $30,000 in depreciation expense.

Required:

1. Prepare a statement of cash flows for 2021 for the Diversified Portfolio Corporation. Use the direct method for reporting operating activities. Use a format similar to the one in the Concept Review Exercise at the end of Part B of this chapter.

2. Prepare the cash flows from operating activities section of Diversified's 2021 statement of cash flows using the indirect method. Use a format similar to the one in the Concept Review Exercise at the end of Part B of this chapter.

P 4–10
Integration of financial statements; Chapters 3 and 4
● LO4–8

The chief accountant for Grandview Corporation provides you with the company's 2021 statement of cash flows and income statement. The accountant has asked for your help with some missing figures in the company's comparative balance sheets. These financial statements are shown next ($ in millions).

GRANDVIEW CORPORATION
Statement of Cash Flows
For the Year Ended December 31, 2021

Cash Flows from Operating Activities:		
Collections from customers	$71	
Payment to suppliers	(30)	
Payment of general & administrative expense	(18)	
Payment of income taxes	(9)	
Net cash flows from operating activities		$14
Cash Flows from Investing Activities:		
Sale of investments		65
Cash Flows from Financing Activities:		
Issuance of common stock	10	
Payment of dividends	(3)	
Net cash flows from financing activities		7
Net increase in cash		$86

GRANDVIEW CORPORATION
Income Statement
For the Year Ended December 31, 2021

Sales revenue		$80
Cost of goods sold		32
Gross profit		48
Operating expenses:		
General and administrative expense	$18	
Depreciation expense	10	
Total operating expenses		28
Operating income		20
Other income:		
Gain on sale of investments		15
Income before income taxes		35
Income tax expense		7
Net income		$28

(continued)

(concluded)

GRANDVIEW CORPORATION
Balance Sheets
At December 31

	2021	2020
Assets:		
Cash	$ 145	$?
Accounts receivable	?	84
Investments	—	50
Inventory	60	?
Property, plant & equipment	150	150
Less: Accumulated depreciation	(65)	?
Total assets	?	?
Liabilities and Shareholders' Equity:		
Accounts payable	$ 40	$ 30
Accrued liabilities (for selling & admin. expense)	9	9
Income taxes payable	22	?
Common stock	240	230
Retained earnings	?	47
Total liabilities and shareholders' equity	?	?

Required:
1. Calculate the missing amounts.
2. Prepare the operating activities section of Grandview's 2021 statement of cash flows using the indirect method. Use a format similar to the one in the Concept Review Exercise at the end of Part B of this chapter.

P 4–11
Statement of cash flows; indirect method
● LO4–8

Presented below are the 2021 income statement and comparative balance sheets for Santana Industries.

SANTANA INDUSTRIES
Income Statement
For the Year Ended December 31, 2021
($ in thousands)

Sales revenue	$14,250	
Service revenue	3,400	
Total revenue		$17,650
Operating expenses:		
Cost of goods sold	7,200	
Selling expense	2,400	
General and administrative expense	1,500	
Total operating expenses		11,100
Operating income		6,550
Interest expense		150
Income before income taxes		6,400
Income tax expense		1,600
Net income		$ 4,800

Balance Sheet Information ($ in thousands)	Dec. 31, 2021	Dec. 31, 2020
Assets:		
Cash	$ 8,300	$ 2,200
Accounts receivable	2,500	2,200
Inventory	4,000	3,000
Prepaid rent	150	300
Equipment	14,500	12,000
Less: Accumulated depreciation	(5,100)	(4,500)
Total assets	$24,350	$15,200
Liabilities and shareholders' equity:		
Accounts payable	$ 1,400	$ 1,100
Interest payable	100	0
Deferred revenue	800	600
Income taxes payable	550	800
Notes payable (due 12/31/2023)	5,000	0
Common stock	10,000	10,000
Retained earnings	6,500	2,700
Total liabilities and shareholders' equity	$24,350	$15,200

Additional information for the 2021 fiscal year ($ in thousands):

1. Cash dividends of $1,000 were declared and paid.

2. Equipment costing $4,000 was purchased with cash.

3. Equipment with a book value of $500 (cost of $1,500 less accumulated depreciation of $1,000) was sold for $500.

4. Depreciation of $1,600 is included in operating expenses.

Required:

Prepare Santana Industries' 2021 statement of cash flows, using the indirect method to present cash flows from operating activities. Use a format similar to the one in the Concept Review Exercise at the end of Part B of this chapter.

P 4–12
Calculating
activity and
profitability ratios
● LO4–10

Financial statements for Askew Industries for 2021 are shown below (in thousands):

2021 Income Statement

Net sales	$9,000
Cost of goods sold	(6,300)
Gross profit	2,700
Operating expenses	(2,100)
Interest expense	(200)
Income tax expense	(100)
Net income	$ 300

Comparative Balance Sheets

	Dec. 31	
	2021	**2020**
Assets		
Cash	$ 600	$ 500
Accounts receivable	600	400
Inventory	800	600
Property, plant, and equipment (net)	2,000	2,100
	$4,000	$3,600
Liabilities and Shareholders' Equity		
Current liabilities	$1,100	$ 850
Bonds payable	1,400	1,400
Common stock	600	600
Retained earnings	900	750
	$4,000	$3,600

Required:

Calculate the following ratios for 2021.

1. Inventory turnover ratio

2. Average days in inventory

3. Receivables turnover ratio

4. Average collection period

5. Asset turnover ratio

6. Profit margin on sales

7. Return on assets

8. Return on equity

9. Equity multiplier

10. Return on equity (using the DuPont framework)

P 4–13
Use of ratios to
compare two
companies in the
same industry
● LO4–10

Presented below are condensed financial statements adapted from those of two actual companies competing in the pharmaceutical industry—Johnson and Johnson (J&J) and Pfizer, Inc. ($ in millions, except per share amounts).

Required:

Evaluate and compare the two companies by responding to the following questions. *Note:* Because two-year comparative statements are not provided, you should use year-end balances in place of average balances as appropriate.

1. Which of the two companies appears more efficient in collecting its accounts receivable and managing its inventory?
2. Which of the two firms had greater earnings relative to resources available?
3. Have the two companies achieved their respective rates of return on assets with similar combinations of profit margin and turnover?
4. From the perspective of a common shareholder, which of the two firms provided a greater rate of return?
5. From the perspective of a common shareholder, which of the two firms appears to be using leverage more effectively to provide a return to shareholders above the rate of return on assets?

Balance Sheets
($ in millions, except per share data)

	J&J	Pfizer
Assets:		
Cash	$ 5,377	$ 1,520
Short-term investments	4,146	10,432
Accounts receivable (net)	6,574	8,775
Inventory	3,588	5,837
Other current assets	3,310	3,177
Current assets	22,995	29,741
Property, plant, and equipment (net)	9,846	18,287
Intangibles and other assets	15,422	68,747
Total assets	$48,263	$116,775
Liabilities and Shareholders' Equity:		
Accounts payable	$ 4,966	$2,601
Short-term notes	1,139	8,818
Other current liabilities	7,343	12,238
Current liabilities	13,448	23,657
Long-term debt	2,955	5,755
Other long-term liabilities	4,991	21,986
Total liabilities	21,394	51,398
Common stock (par and additional paid-in capital)	3,120	67,050
Retained earnings	30,503	29,382
Accumulated other comprehensive income (loss)	(590)	195
Less: Treasury stock and other equity adjustments	(6,164)	(31,250)
Total shareholders' equity	26,869	65,377
Total liabilities and shareholders' equity	$48,263	$116,775
Income Statements		
Net sales	$41,862	$45,188
Cost of goods sold	12,176	9,832
Gross profit	29,686	35,356
Operating expenses	19,763	28,486
Other (income) expense—net	(385)	3,610
Income before taxes	10,308	3,260
Income tax expense	3,111	1,621
Net income	$ 7,197	$ 1,639*
Basic net income per share	$ 2.42	$ 0.22

*This is before income from discontinued operations.

P 4–14
Creating a balance sheet from ratios;
Chapters 3 and 4
● LO4–10

Cadux Candy Company's income statement for the year ended December 31, 2021, reported interest expense of $2 million and income tax expense of $12 million. Current assets listed in its balance sheet include cash, accounts receivable, and inventory. Property, plant, and equipment is the company's only noncurrent asset. Financial ratios for 2021 are listed below. Profitability and turnover ratios with balance sheet items in the denominator were calculated using year-end balances rather than averages.

Debt to equity ratio	1.0
Current ratio	2.0
Acid-test ratio	1.0
Times interest earned ratio	17 times
Return on assets	10%
Return on equity	20%

(continued)

(concluded)

Profit margin on sales	5%
Gross profit margin	40%
(gross profit divided by net sales)	
Inventory turnover	8 times
Receivables turnover	20 times

Required:

Prepare a December 31, 2021, balance sheet for the Cadux Candy Company.

P 4–15

Compare two companies in the same industry; Chapters 3 and 4

● LO4–10

Presented below are condensed financial statements adapted from those of two actual companies competing as the primary players in a specialty area of the food manufacturing and distribution industry ($ in millions, except per share amounts).

	BalanceSheets	
	Metropolitan	**Republic**
Assets:		
Cash	$ 179.3	$ 37.1
Accounts receivable (net)	422.7	325.0
Short-term investments	—	4.7
Inventory	466.4	635.2
Prepaid expenses and other current assets	134.6	476.7
Current assets	1,203.0	1,478.7
Property, plant, and equipment (net)	2,608.2	2,064.6
Intangibles and other assets	210.3	464.7
Total assets	$4,021.5	$4,008.0
Liabilities and Shareholders' Equity		
Accounts payable	$ 467.9	$ 691.2
Short-term notes	227.1	557.4
Accruals and other current liabilities	585.2	538.5
Current liabilities	1,280.2	1,787.1
Long-term debt	535.6	542.3
Deferred tax liability	384.6	610.7
Other long-term liabilities	104.0	95.1
Total liabilities	2,304.4	3,035.2
Common stock (par and additional paid-in capital)	144.9	335.0
Retained earnings	2,476.9	1,601.9
Less: Treasury stock	(904.7)	(964.1)
Total liabilities and shareholders' equity	$4,021.5	$4,008.0
Income Statements		
Net sales	$5,698.0	$7,768.2
Cost of goods sold	(2,909.0)	(4,481.7)
Gross profit	2,789.0	3,286.5
Operating expenses	(1,743.7)	(2,539.2)
Interest expense	(56.8)	(46.6)
Income before taxes	988.5	700.7
Income tax expense	(394.7)	(276.1)
Net income	$ 593.8	$ 424.6
Net income per share	$ 2.40	$ 6.50

Required:

Evaluate and compare the two companies by responding to the following questions.

Note: Because comparative statements are not provided you should use year-end balances in place of average balances as appropriate.

1. Which of the two firms had greater earnings relative to resources available?
2. Have the two companies achieved their respective rates of return on assets with similar combinations of profit margin and turnover?
3. From the perspective of a common shareholder, which of the two firms provided a greater rate of return?
4. Which company is most highly leveraged and which has made most effective use of financial leverage?
5. Of the two companies, which appears riskier in terms of its ability to pay short-term obligations?
6. How efficiently are current assets managed?

7. From the perspective of a creditor, which company offers the most comfortable margin of safety in terms of its ability to pay fixed interest charges?

P 4–16
Interim financial reporting
● Appendix 4

Branson Electronics Company is a small, publicly traded company preparing its first quarter interim report to be mailed to shareholders. The following information for the quarter has been compiled:

Sales revenue		$180,000
Cost of goods sold		35,000
Operating expenses:		
Fixed	$59,000	
Variable	48,000	107,000

Fixed operating expenses include payments of $50,000 to an advertising firm to promote Branson through various media throughout the year. The income tax rate for Branson's level of operations in the first quarter is 20%, but management estimates the effective rate for the entire year will be 25%.

Required:
Prepare the income statement to be included in Branson's first quarter interim report.

Decision Makers' Perspective

©ImageGap/Getty Images

Apply your critical-thinking ability to the knowledge you've gained. These cases will provide you an opportunity to develop your research, analysis, judgment, and communication skills. You also will work with other students, integrate what you've learned, apply it in real-world situations, and consider its global and ethical ramifications. This practice will broaden your knowledge and further develop your decision-making abilities.

**Judgment
Case 4–1**
Earnings quality
● LO4–2, LO4–3

The financial community in the United States has become increasingly concerned with the quality of reported company earnings.

Required:
1. Define the term *earnings quality*.
2. Explain the distinction between permanent and temporary earnings as it relates to the concept of earnings quality.
3. How do earnings management practices affect the quality of earnings?
4. Assume that a manufacturing company's annual income statement included a large gain from the sale of investment securities. What factors would you consider in determining whether or not this gain should be included in an assessment of the company's permanent earnings?

**Judgment
Case 4–2**
Restructuring costs
● LO4–3

The appearance of restructuring costs in corporate income statements increased significantly in the 1980s and 1990s and continues to be relevant today.

Required:
1. What types of costs are included in restructuring costs?
2. When are restructuring costs recognized?
3. How would you classify restructuring costs in a multi-step income statement?
4. What factors would you consider in determining whether or not restructuring costs should be included in an assessment of a company's permanent earnings?

**Judgment
Case 4–3**
Earnings management
● LO4–2, LO4–3

Companies often are under pressure to meet or beat Wall Street earnings projections in order to increase stock prices and also to increase the value of stock options. Some resort to earnings management practices to artificially create desired results.

Required:
Is *earnings management* always intended to produce higher income? Explain.

**Real World
Case 4–4**
Earnings quality and non-GAAP earnings
● LO4–3

Companies often voluntarily provide non-GAAP earnings when they announce annual or quarterly earnings.

Required:
1. What is meant by the term *non-GAAP earnings* in this context?
2. How do non-GAAP earnings relate to the concept of earnings quality?

228   SECTION 1   The Role of Accounting as an Information System

Research Case 4–5

FASB codification; locate and extract relevant information and cite authoritative support for a financial reporting issue; restructuring costs; exit or disposal cost obligations

● LO4–2, LO4–3

Access the *FASB Accounting Standards Codification* at the FASB website (www.fasb.org). Determine each of the following:

1. The topic number (Topic XXX) that addresses exit or disposal cost obligations.
2. The specific eight-digit Codification citation (XXX-XX-XX-X) that addresses the initial measurement of these obligations.
3. The amount for which these obligations and related costs are measured.
4. The specific eight-digit Codification citation (XXX-XX-XX-X) that describes the disclosure requirements in the notes to the financial statements for exit or disposal obligations.
5. List the required disclosures.

Judgment Case 4–6

Income statement presentation

● LO4–3, LO4–4, LO4–5

Each of the following situations occurred during 2021 for one of your audit clients:

1. An inventory write-down due to obsolescence.
2. Discovery that depreciation expenses were omitted by accident from 2020's income statement.
3. The useful lives of all machinery were changed from eight to five years.
4. The depreciation method used for all equipment was changed from the declining-balance to the straight-line method.
5. Restructuring costs were incurred.
6. The Stridewell Company, a manufacturer of shoes, sold all of its retail outlets. It will continue to manufacture and sell its shoes to other retailers. A loss was incurred in the disposition of the retail stores. The retail stores are considered a component of the entity.
7. The inventory costing method was changed from FIFO to average cost.

Required:

1. For each situation, identify the appropriate reporting treatment from the list below (consider each event to be material):
   a. As an unusual gain or loss
   b. As a prior period adjustment
   c. As a change in accounting principle
   d. As a discontinued operation
   e. As a change in accounting estimate
   f. As a change in accounting estimate achieved by a change in accounting principle
2. Indicate whether each situation would be included in the income statement in continuing operations (CO) or below continuing operations (BC), or if it would appear as an adjustment to retained earnings (RE). Use the format shown below to answer requirements 1 and 2.

Situation	Treatment (a–f)	Financial Statement Presentation (CO, BC, or RE)
1.		
2.		
3.		
4.		
5.		
6.		
7.		

Judgment Case 4–7

Income statement presentation

● LO4–3, LO4–4, LO4–5

The following events occurred during 2021 for various audit clients of your firm. Consider each event to be independent and the effect of each event to be material.

1. A manufacturing company recognized a loss on the sale of investments.

2. An automobile manufacturer sold all of the assets related to its financing component. The operations of the financing business is considered a component of the entity.

3. A company changed its depreciation method from the double-declining-balance method to the straight-line method.

4. Due to obsolescence, a company engaged in the manufacture of high-technology products incurred a loss on inventory write-down.

5. One of your clients discovered that 2020's depreciation expense was overstated. The error occurred because of a miscalculation of depreciation for the office building.

6. A cosmetics company decided to discontinue the manufacture of a line of women's lipstick. Other cosmetic lines will be continued. A loss was incurred on the sale of assets related to the lipstick product line. The operations of the discontinued line is not considered a component of the entity.

Required:
Determine whether each of the above events would be reported as income from continuing operations, income from discontinued operations, or not reported in the current year's income statement.

IFRS Case 4–8
Statement of cash flows; GlaxoSmithKline Plc.

● LO4–8, LO4–9

Real World Financials

GlaxoSmithKline Plc. (GSK) is a global pharmaceutical and consumer health-related products company located in the United Kingdom. The company prepares its financial statements in accordance with International Financial Reporting Standards. Below is a portion of the company's statements of cash flows included in recent financial statements:

GLAXOSMITHKLINE PLC.
Consolidated Cash Flow Statement
For the Year Ended 31 December

	£m
Cash flow from operating activities	
Profit after taxation for the year	5,628
Adjustments reconciling profit after tax to operating cash flows	2,871
Cash generated from operations	8,499
Taxation paid	(1,277)
Net cash inflow from operating activities	7,222
Cash flow from investing activities	
Purchase of property, plant and equipment	(1,188)
Proceeds from sale of property, plant and equipment	46
Purchase of intangible assets	(513)
Proceeds from sale of intangible assets	136
Purchase of equity investments	(133)
Proceeds from sale of equity investments	59
Purchase of businesses, net of cash acquired	(247)
Disposal of businesses	1,851
Investments in associates and joint ventures	(8)
Proceeds from disposal of subsidiary and interest in associate	429
Decrease in liquid investments	15
Interest received	59
Dividends from associates and joint ventures	18
Net cash inflow/(outflow) from investing activities	524
Cash flow from financing activities	
Proceeds from own shares for employee share options	—
Shares acquired by ESOP Trusts	(45)
Issue of share capital	585
Purchase of own shares for cancellation or to be held as Treasury shares	(1,504)
Purchase of non-controlling interests	(588)
Increase in long-term loans	1,913
Increase in short-term loans	—
Repayment of short-term loans	(1,872)
Net repayment of obligations under finance leases	(31)
Interest paid	(749)
Dividends paid to shareholders	(3,680)
Distributions to non-controlling interests	(238)
Other financing cash flows	(64)

(continued)

(concluded)

Net cash outflow from financing activities	(6,273)
Increase/(decrease) in cash and bank overdrafts	1,473
Cash and bank overdrafts at beginning of year	3,906
Exchange adjustments	(148)
Increase/(decrease) in cash and bank overdrafts	1,473
Cash and bank overdrafts at end of year	5,231
Cash and bank overdrafts at end of year comprise:	
Cash and cash equivalents	5,534
Overdrafts	(303)
	5,231

Required:
Identify the items in the above statement that would be reported differently if GlaxoSmithKline prepared its financial statements according to U.S. GAAP rather than IFRS.

Judgment Case 4–9
Income statement presentation; unusual items; comprehensive income
● LO4–3, LO4–4, LO4–5, LO4–6

Norse Manufacturing Inc. prepares an annual single, continuous statement of income and comprehensive income. The following situations occurred during the company's 2021 fiscal year:
1. Restructuring costs were incurred due to the closing of a factory.
2. Investments were sold, and a loss was recognized.
3. A positive foreign currency translation adjustment was recognized.
4. Interest expense was incurred.
5. A division was sold that qualifies as a separate component of the entity according to GAAP.
6. Obsolete inventory was written off.
7. The controller discovered an error in the calculation of 2020's patent amortization expense.

Required:
1. For each situation, identify the appropriate reporting treatment from the list below (consider each event to be material):
    a. As a component of operating income
    b. As a nonoperating income item (other income or expense)
    c. As a discontinued operation
    d. As an other comprehensive income item
    e. As an adjustment to retained earnings
2. Identify the situations that would be reported net-of-tax.

Judgment Case 4–10
Management incentives for change
● LO4–2

It has been suggested that not all accounting choices are made by management in the best interest of fair and consistent financial reporting.

Required:
What motivations can you think of for management's choice of accounting methods?

Research Case 4–11
Non-GAAP earnings
● LO4–3

Companies often voluntarily provide non-GAAP earnings when they announce annual or quarterly earnings. These numbers are controversial as they represent management's view of permanent earnings. The Sarbanes-Oxley Act (SOX), issued in 2002, requires that if non-GAAP earnings are included in any periodic or other report filed with the SEC or in any public disclosure or press release, the company also must provide a reconciliation with earnings determined according to GAAP.

Professors Entwistle, Feltham, and Mbagwu, in "Financial Reporting Regulation and the Reporting of Pro Forma Earnings," examine whether firms changed their reporting practice in response to the regulations included in SOX.

Required:
1. In your library or from some other source, locate the indicated article in *Accounting Horizons,* March 2006.
2. What sample of firms did the authors use in their examination?
3. What percent of firms reported non-GAAP earnings (referred to as *pro forma earnings* by the authors) in 2001? In 2003?
4. What percent of firms had non-GAAP earnings greater than GAAP earnings in 2001? In 2003?

5. What was the most frequently reported adjusting item in 2001? In 2003?

6. What are the authors' main conclusions of the impact of SOX on non-GAAP reporting?

Integrating Case 4–12
Balance sheet and income statement; Chapters 3 and 4
● LO4–3

Rice Corporation is negotiating a loan for expansion purposes and the bank requires financial statements. Before closing the accounting records for the year ended December 31, 2021, Rice's controller prepared the following financial statements:

RICE CORPORATION
Balance Sheet At December 31, 2021
($ in thousands)

Assets	
Cash	$ 275
Investments	78
Accounts receivable	487
Inventory	425
Allowance for uncollectible accounts	(50)
Property and equipment (net)	160
Total assets	$1,375
Liabilities and Shareholders' Equity	
Accounts payable and accrued liabilities	$ 420
Notes payable	200
Common stock	260
Retained earnings	495
Total liabilities and shareholders' equity	$1,375

RICE CORPORATION
Income Statement
For the Year Ended December 31, 2021
($ in thousands)

Sales revenue		$1,580
Expenses:		
Cost of goods sold	$755	
Selling and administrative expense	385	
Miscellaneous expense	129	
Income tax expense	100	
Total expenses		1,369
Net income		$ 211

Additional Information:

1. The company's common stock is traded on an organized stock exchange.

2. The investment portfolio consists of short-term investments valued at $57,000. The remaining investments will not be sold until the year 2023.

3. Notes payable consist of two notes: Note 1: $80,000 face value dated September 30, 2021. Principal and interest at 10% are due on September 30, 2022.

   Note 2: $120,000 face value dated April 30, 2021. Principal is due in two equal installments of $60,000 plus interest on the unpaid balance. The two payments are scheduled for April 30, 2022, and April 30, 2023.

   Interest on both loans has been correctly accrued and is included in accrued liabilities on the balance sheet and selling and administrative expense in the income statement.

4. Selling and administrative expense includes $90,000 representing costs incurred by the company in restructuring some of its operations. The amount is material.

Required:

Identify and explain the deficiencies in the presentation of the statements prepared by the company's controller. Do not prepare corrected statements. Include in your answer a list of items that require additional disclosure, either on the face of the statement or in a note.

Analysis Case 4–13
Income statement information
● LO4–1

Refer to the income statement of The Home Depot, Inc., in Illustration 4–2 of this chapter.

Required:

1. Is this income statement presented in the single-step or multiple-step format?

2. What is the company's approximate income tax rate?

3. What is the percentage of net income relative to net sales?

232 SECTION 1 The Role of Accounting as an Information System

Real World Case 4–14
Income statement information

● LO4–1, LO4–3, LO4–4

Real World Financials

EDGAR, the Electronic Data Gathering, Analysis, and Retrieval system, performs automated collection, validation, indexing, and forwarding of submissions by companies and others who are required by law to file forms with the U.S. Securities and Exchange Commission (SEC). All publicly traded domestic companies use EDGAR to make the majority of their filings. (Some foreign companies file voluntarily.) Form 10-K, which includes the annual report, is required to be filed on EDGAR. The SEC makes this information available on the Internet.

Required:
1. Access EDGAR on the Internet. The web address is www.sec.gov.
2. Search for a public company with which you are familiar. Access the most recent 10-K filing. Search or scroll to find the financial statements and related notes.
3. Answer the following questions related to the company's income statement:
   a. Does the company use the single-step or multiple-step format, or a variation?
   b. Does the income statement contain any income or loss on discontinued operations? If it does, describe the component of the company that was discontinued. (*Hint:* there should be a related disclosure note.)
   c. Describe the trend in net income over the years presented.
4. Repeat requirements 2 and 3 for two additional companies.

Real World Case 4–15
Income statement format; restructuring costs; earnings per share; comprehensive income; statement of cash flows; Ralph Lauren

● LO4–1, LO4–3, LO4–5, LO4–6, LO4–8

Real World Financials

Ralph Lauren Corporation is a global leader in the design, marketing, and distribution of premium lifestyle products, including men's, women's and children's apparel. Below are selected financial statements taken from a recent 10-K filing.

Required:
Use the information in the financial statements to answer the following questions.
1. Does the company use the single-step or multiple-step format to present its income statements?
2. Does the company report restructuring costs (yes/no)? What are restructuring costs?
3. Does the company report asset impairments (yes/no)? What are asset impairments?
4. Does the company chose to report comprehensive income in two consecutive statements or a combined statement?
5. What "other comprehensive items (OCI)" did the company report?
6. What method does the company use to report net cash provided by operating activities? What other method(s) could the company have used?
7. What is the largest cash outflow from investing activities?

RALPH LAUREN CORPORATION
CONSOLIDATED STATEMENTS OF OPERATIONS

($ in millions, except per share data)	Fiscal Year Ended April 1, 2017
Net sales	$ 6,652.8
Cost of goods sold	(3,001.7)
Gross profit	3,651.1
Other costs and expenses:	
Selling, general, and administrative expenses	(3,149.4)
Amortization of intangible assets	(24.1)
Impairments of assets	(253.8)
Restructuring and other costs	(318.6)
Total other costs and expenses, net	(3,745.9)
Operating loss	(94.8)
Foreign currency losses	(1.1)
Interest expense	(12.4)
Interest and other income, net	8.7
Equity in losses of equity-method investees	(5.3)
Loss before provision for income taxes	(104.9)
Provision for income taxes	(5.6)
Net loss	$ (99.3)
Net loss per common share:	
Basic	$ (1.20)
Diluted	$ (1.20)

(continued)

(concluded)

RALPH LAUREN CORPORATION
CONSOLIDATED STATEMENTS OF COMPREHENSIVE INCOME

	Fiscal Year Ended April 1, 2017
Net loss	$ (99.3)
Other comprehensive loss, net of tax:	
Foreign currency translation loss	(48.6)
Net gains on cash flow hedges	26.6
Net gains on defined benefit plans	5.1
Other comprehensive loss	(16.9)
Total comprehensive loss	$(116.2)

RALPH LAUREN CORPORATION
CONSOLIDATED STATEMENTS OF CASH FLOWS

	Fiscal Year Ended April 1, 2017
Cash flows from operating activities:	
Net loss	$ (99.3)
Adjustments to reconcile net loss to net cash provided by operating activities:	
Depreciation and amortization expense	307.5
Deferred income tax expense (benefit)	(38.9)
Equity in losses of equity-method investees	5.2
Non-cash stock-based compensation expense	63.6
Non-cash impairment of assets	253.8
Non-cash inventory charges	197.9
Other non-cash charges, net	29.2
Excess tax benefits from stock-based compensation arrangements	(0.3)
Changes in operating assets and liabilities:	
Accounts receivable	54.1
Inventories	120.4
Prepaid expenses and other current assets	(27.8)
Accounts payable and accrued liabilities	112.9
Income tax receivables and payables	(34.0)
Deferred income	(20.7)
Other balance sheet changes, net	28.7
Net cash provided by operating activities	952.3
Cash flows from investing activities:	
Capital expenditures	(284.0)
Purchases of investments	(860.4)
Proceeds from sales and maturities of investments	942.4
Acquisitions and ventures, net of cash acquired	(6.1)
Change in restricted cash deposits	0.3
Net cash used in investing activities	(207.8)
Cash flows from financing activities:	
Proceeds from issuance of debt	3,735.2
Repayment of debt	(3,851.3)
Payments of capital lease obligations	(27.3)
Payments of dividends	(164.8)
Repurchases of common stock, including shares surrendered for tax withholdings	(215.2)
Proceeds from exercise of stock options	5.0
Excess tax benefits from stock-based compensation arrangements	0.3
Other financing activities	—
Net cash used in financing activities	(518.1)
Effect of exchange rate changes on cash and cash equivalents	(14.4)
Net increase (decrease) in cash and cash equivalents	212.0
Cash and cash equivalents at beginning of period	456.3
Cash and cash equivalents at end of period	$ 668.3

Analysis Case 4–16
Evaluating profitability and asset management; obtain and compare annual reports from companies in the same industry
● LO4–10

Performance and profitability of a company often are evaluated using the financial information provided by a firm's annual report in comparison with other firms in the same industry. Ratios are useful in this assessment.

Required:

Obtain annual reports from two corporations in the same primary industry. Using techniques you learned in this chapter and any analysis you consider useful, respond to the following questions:

1. How do earnings trends compare in terms of both the direction and stability of income?
2. Which of the two firms had greater earnings relative to resources available?
3. How efficiently are current assets managed?
4. Has each of the companies achieved its respective rate of return on assets with similar combinations of profit margin and turnover?
5. Are there differences in accounting methods that should be taken into account when making comparisons?

Note: You can obtain copies of annual reports from friends who are shareholders, the investor relations department of the corporations, from a friendly stockbroker, or from EDGAR (Electronic Data Gathering, Analysis, and Retrieval) on the Internet (www.sec.gov).

Analysis Case 4–17
Relationships among ratios; Chapters 3 and 4
● LO4–10

You are a part-time financial advisor. A client is considering an investment in common stock of a waste recycling firm. One motivation is a rumor the client heard that the company made huge investments in a new fuel creation process. Unable to confirm the rumor, your client asks you to determine whether the firm's assets had recently increased significantly.

Because the firm is small, information is sparse. Last quarter's interim report showed total assets of $324 million, approximately the same as last year's annual report. The only information more current than that is a press release last week in which the company's management reported "record net income for the year of $21 million, representing a 14.0% return on equity. Performance was enhanced by the Company's judicious use of financial leverage on a debt/equity ratio of 2 to 1."

Required:

Use the information available to calculate total assets, total liabilities, and total shareholders' equity.

Integrating Case 4–18
Using ratios to test reasonableness of data; Chapters 3 and 4
● LO4–10

You are a new staff accountant with a large regional CPA firm, participating in your first audit. You recall from your auditing class that CPAs often use ratios to test the reasonableness of accounting numbers provided by the client. Since ratios reflect the relationships among various account balances, if it is assumed that prior relationships still hold, prior years' ratios can be used to estimate what current balances should approximate. However, you never actually performed this kind of analysis until now. The CPA in charge of the audit of Covington Pike Corporation brings you the list of ratios shown below and tells you these reflect the relationships maintained by Covington Pike in recent years.

Profit margin on sales = 5%

Return on assets = 7.5%

Gross profit margin = 40%

Inventory turnover ratio = 6 times

Receivables turnover ratio = 25 times

Acid-test ratio = 0.9 to one

Current ratio = 2 to 1

Return on equity = 10%

Debt to equity ratio = 1/3

Times interest earned ratio = 12 times

Jotted in the margins are the following notes:

- Net income $15,000.
- Only one short-term note ($5,000); all other current liabilities are trade accounts.
- Property, plant, and equipment are the only noncurrent assets.
- Bonds payable are the only noncurrent liabilities.
- The effective interest rate on short-term notes and bonds is 8%.
- No investment securities.
- Cash balance totals $15,000.

Required:

You are requested to approximate the current year's balances in the form of a balance sheet and income statement, to the extent the information allows. Accompany those financial statements with the calculations you use to estimate each amount reported.

Data Analytics

Data Analytics Case

Profitability Ratios

● LO4-10

Data analytics is the process of examining data sets in order to draw conclusions about the information they contain. To prepare for this case, you will need to download Tableau to your computer. If you have not completed any of the prior data analytics cases, follow the instructions listed in the Chapter 1 Data Analytics case to get set up. You will need to watch the videos referred to in the Chapter 1, Chapter 2, and Chapter 3 Data Analytics cases. No additional videos are required for this case. Future cases will build off of your knowledge gained from these, and additional videos will be suggested. All short training videos can be found here: **www.tableau.com/learn/training#getting-started**.

In the Chapter 3 Data Analytics Case, you applied Tableau to examine a data set and create calculations to compare two companies' liquidity. In this case, you continue in your role as an analyst conducting introductory research into the relative merits of investing in one or both of these companies. This time assess the companies' return on assets and how that return is related to both profit margin and asset turnover.

Required:

Use Tableau to calculate (a) profit margin on sales, (b) asset turnover, and (c) return on assets for each of the two companies in each year from 2012 to 2021. Based upon what you find, answer the following questions:

1. What is the return on assets for Big Store (a) in 2012 and (b) in 2021?

2. What is the return on assets for Discount Goods (a) in 2012 and (b) in 2021?

To help determine why the relative profitability of the two companies has shifted over the ten-year period and to get a better company-to-company comparison, drag the second "pill": (**Year** Dimension) to the left of the "pill": (**Company** Dimension in the text chart).

3. The return on assets is a result of the profit margin and the asset turnover. Demonstrate this for Big Store in 2021 by showing that the profit margin times the asset turnover equals return on assets.

4. Analyzing the asset turnover ratios over the ten-year period, is Big Store's asset turnover (a) generally increasing, (b) roughly the same, or (c) generally decreasing from year to year?

5. Analyzing the asset turnover ratios over the ten-year period, is Discount Goods' turnover (a) generally increasing, (b) roughly the same, or (c) generally decreasing from year to year?

6. As of 2021, which company reports a more favorable return on assets and is this primarily attributable to its asset turnover or profit margin?

Note: As you assess the profitability aspect of the companies, keep in mind that profitability should be evaluated in the context of both risk and efficiency of managing assets.

Resources:

You have available to you an extensive data set that includes detailed financial data for Discount Goods and Big Store and for 2012-2021. The data set is in the form of an Excel file available to download from Connect, under Student Resources within the Library tab. There are four Excel files available. The one for use in this chapter is named "Discount_Goods_Big_Store_Financials.xlsx." Download this file and save it to the computer on which you will be using Tableau.

For this case, you will create several calculations to produce a text chart of profitability ratios to allow you to compare and contrast the two companies. You also will need to change data from continuous to discrete (see Chapter 3 Data Analytics case for more information on this).

After you view the training videos, follow these steps to create the charts you'll use for this case:

- Open Tableau and connect to the Excel spreadsheet you downloaded.
- Click on the "Sheet 1" tab at the bottom of the canvas, to the right of the Data Source at the bottom of the screen.
- Drag "Year" and "Company" under "Dimensions" to the Rows shelf. Change "Year" to discrete by right-clicking and selecting "Discrete."
- Drag the "Net income/(loss)," "Net sales," and "Average total assets" under "Measures" to the Rows shelf. Change each to *discrete*, following the process above.
- Create a calculated field by clicking the "Analysis" tab at the top of the screen and selecting "Create Calculated field." A calculation box will pop up. Name the calculation "Return on Assets." In the calculation box, from the Rows shelf, drag "Net income/(loss)," type a division sign, then drag "Average total assets" beside it. Make sure the box says that the calculation is valid and click OK.
- Repeat the process by creating a calculated field named "Profit Margin on Sales" that consists of "Net income/(loss)," divided by "Net sales."
- Repeat the process one more time by creating a calculated field "Asset Turnover" that consists of "Net sales" divided by "Average total assets."
- Drag the newly created "Return on Assets" to add it to the Rows shelf. Format it to Discrete, Times New Roman, 10-point font, black, center alignment, and percentage.
- Drag the newly created "Profit Margin on Sales" and "Asset Turnover" to the Rows shelf. Format them both to Discrete, Times New Roman, 10-point font, black, center alignment, and percentage.

- Right click the "Net income / (loss)," "Net sales," and "Average total assets" on the Rows shelf and un-click "Show header." This will hide these items from view but still allow them to be used in the formulas.
- Change the title of the sheet to be "Profitability Ratios" by right-clicking and selecting "Edit title." Format the title to Times New Roman, bold, black and 15-point font. Change the title of "Sheet 1" to match the sheet title by right-clicking, selecting "Rename" and typing in the new title.
- Click on the New Worksheet tab on the lower left ("Sheet 2" should open). Drag "Year" to the Columns shelf and "Return on Assets," "Profit Margin on Sales" and "Asset Turnover" to the Rows shelf.
- Drag "Company" under "Dimensions" to "Color" on the "Marks" card. You should see two lines in the three graphs.
- Format the labels on the left of the sheet ("Return on Assets," "Profit Margin on Sales," and "Asset Turnover") to Times New Roman, 10-point font, bold, and black.
- Change the title of the sheet to be "Graph of Profitability Ratios" by right-clicking and selecting "Edit title." Format the title to Times New Roman, bold, black and 15-point font. Change the title of "Sheet 2" to match the sheet title by right-clicking, selecting "Rename" and typing in the new title.
- Once complete, save the file as "DA4_Your initials.twbx."

Continuing Cases

Target Case

● LO4–3, LO4–4, LO4–6, LO4–8

Target Corporation prepares its financial statements according to U.S. GAAP. Target's financial statements and disclosure notes for the year ended February 3, 2018, are available in Connect. This material is also available under the Investor Relations link at the company's website (www.target.com).

Required:

1. By what name does Target label its income statement?
2. What amounts did Target report for the following items for the year ended February 3, 2018?
   a. Sales
   b. Gross margin
   c. Earnings from continuing operations before income taxes
   d. Net earnings from continuing operations
   e. Net earnings
3. Does Target report any items as part of its comprehensive income? If so, what are they.
4. Does Target prepare the statement of cash flows using the direct method or the indirect method?
5. Which is higher, net earnings or operating cash flows? Which line item is the biggest reason for this difference? Explain why.
6. What is the largest investing cash flow and the largest financing cash flow reported by the company for the year ended February 3, 2018?

Air France–KLM Case

● LO4–9

 IFRS

Air France–KLM (AF), a Franco-Dutch company, prepares its financial statements according to International Financial Reporting Standards. AF's financial statements and disclosure notes for the year ended December 31, 2017, are provided in Connect. This material is also available under the Finance link at the company's website (www.airfranceklm.com).

Required:

1. How does AF classify operating expenses in its income statement? How are these expenses typically classified in a U.S. company income statement?
2. How does AF classify interest paid, interest received, and dividends received in its statement of cash flows? What other alternatives, if any, does the company have for the classification of these items? How are these items classified under U.S. GAAP?

CPA Exam Questions and Simulations

 ROGER CPA Review

Sample CPA Exam questions from Roger CPA Review are available in Connect as support for the topics in this chapter. These multiple-choice questions and task-based simulations include expert-written explanations and solutions, and provide a starting point for students to become familiar with the content and functionality of the actual CPA Exam.

5

Time Value of Money Concepts

OVERVIEW ——————— Time value of money concepts, specifically future value and present value, are essential in a variety of accounting situations. These concepts and the related computational procedures are the subjects of this chapter. Present values and future values of *single amounts* and present values and future values of *annuities* (series of equal periodic payments) are described separately but shown to be interrelated.

LEARNING OBJECTIVES ——————— After studying this chapter, you should be able to:

- **LO5–1**   Explain the difference between simple and compound interest. (*p. 240*)
- **LO5–2**   Compute the future value of a single amount. (*p. 241*)
- **LO5–3**   Compute the present value of a single amount. (*p. 242*)
- **LO5–4**   Solve for either the interest rate or the number of compounding periods when present value and future value of a single amount are known. (*p. 243*)
- **LO5–5**   Apply present value techniques in the valuation of notes. (*p. 246*)
- **LO5–6**   Explain the difference between an ordinary annuity and an annuity due situation. (*p. 248*)
- **LO5–7**   Compute the future value of both an ordinary annuity and an annuity due. (*p. 248*)
- **LO5–8**   Compute the present value of an ordinary annuity, an annuity due, and a deferred annuity. (*p. 250*)
- **LO5–9**   Solve for unknown values in annuity situations involving present value. (*p. 255*)
- **LO5–10**   Briefly describe how the concept of the time value of money is incorporated into the valuation of bonds, long-term leases, installment notes, and pension obligations. (*p. 259*)

©Gabriel Petrescu/Shutterstock

FINANCIAL REPORTING CASE

The Winning Ticket

"I was just there to buy it for luck. It was just chance, a chance I had to take," she said. On August 23, 2017, Mavis Wanczyk, 53, of Chicopee, MA, blissfully discovered she had purchased the winning $758.7 million Powerball ticket, the largest jackpot in U.S. history. Imagine her surprise, though, when she was told that, having chosen a lump-sum payout rather than 30-year installment payments, she would get a check for "only" $336 million. Sure, federal tax was withheld at a 25% rate and Massachusetts added another 5%, but this difference was far more than the amount of the tax.

By the time you finish this chapter, you should be able to respond appropriately to the questions posed in this case. Compare your response to the solution provided at the end of the chapter.

QUESTIONS

1. Why was Mavis to receive $336 million rather than the $758.7 million lottery prize? (*p. 251*)

2. What interest (discount) rate did the state of Massachusetts use to calculate the $336 million lump-sum payment? (*p. 256*)

3. What are some of the accounting applications that incorporate the time value of money into valuation? (*p. 259*)

Basic Concepts

Time Value of Money

PART A

The key to solving the problem described in the financial reporting case is an understanding of the concept commonly referred to as the time value of money. This concept means that money invested today will grow to a larger dollar amount in the future. For example, $100 invested in a savings account at your local bank yielding 6% annually will grow to $106 in one year. The difference between the $100 invested now—the present value of the investment—and its $106 future value represents the time value of money.

> The *time value of money* means that money can be invested today to earn interest and grow to a larger dollar amount in the future.

This concept has nothing to do with the worth or buying power of those dollars. Prices in our economy can change. If the inflation rate were higher than 6%, then the $106 you would have in the savings account actually would be worth less than the $100 you had a year earlier. The time value of money concept concerns only the growth in the dollar amounts of money, ignoring inflation.

The concepts you learn in this chapter are useful in solving business decisions such as determining the lottery award presented in the financial reporting case. More important, the concepts are necessary when valuing assets and liabilities for financial reporting purposes. Most accounting applications that incorporate the time value of money involve the concept of present value. The valuation of leases, bonds, pension obligations, and certain notes receivable and payable are a few prominent examples. It's important that you master the concepts and tools we review here because they are essential for the remainder of your accounting education.

> Time value of money concepts are useful in valuing several assets and liabilities as well as some revenues and expenses.

Simple versus Compound Interest

● LO5–1

Interest is the amount of money paid or received in excess of the amount borrowed or lent.

Interest is the "rent" paid for the use of money for some period of time. In dollar terms, it is the amount of money paid or received in excess of the amount of money borrowed or lent. If you lend someone $100 today and "receive" $106 a year from now, your interest would be $6. Interest also can be expressed as a rate at which money will grow. In this case, that rate is 6%. It is this interest that gives money its time value.

Simple interest is computed by multiplying an initial investment times both the applicable interest rate and the period of time for which the money is used. For example, simple interest earned each year on a $1,000 investment paying 10% is $100 ($1,000 × 10%).

Compound interest includes interest not only on the initial investment but also on the accumulated interest in previous periods.

Compound interest occurs when money remains invested for multiple periods. It results in increasingly larger interest amounts for each period of the investment. The reason is that interest is then being generated not only on the initial investment amount but also on the accumulated interest earned in previous periods.

For example, Cindy Johnson invested $1,000 in a savings account paying 10% interest *compounded* annually. How much interest will she earn each year, and what will be her investment balance after three years?

Date	Interest (Interest rate × Outstanding balance = Interest)	Balance
Initial deposit		$1,000
End of year 1	10% × $1,000 = $100	$1,100
End of year 2	10% × $1,100 = $110	$1,210
End of year 3	10% × $1,210 = $121	$1,331

With compound interest at 10% annually, the $1,000 investment would grow to $1,331 at the end of the three-year period. If Cindy withdrew the interest earned each year, she would earn only $100 in interest each year (the amount of simple interest). If the investment period had been 20 years, 20 calculations would be needed. However, calculators, Excel, and compound interest tables, like those in an appendix to this textbook, make these calculations easier.

Interest rates are typically stated as annual rates.

Most banks compound interest more frequently than once a year. Daily compounding is common for savings accounts. More rapid compounding has the effect of increasing the actual rate, which is called the **effective rate**, at which money grows per year. It is important to note that interest is typically stated as an annual rate regardless of the length of the compounding period involved. In situations when the compounding period is less than a year, the interest rate per compounding period is determined by dividing the annual rate by the number of periods. Assuming an annual rate of 12%:

Compounded	Interest Rate Per Compounding Period
Semiannually	12% ÷ 2 = 6%
Quarterly	12% ÷ 4 = 3%
Monthly	12% ÷ 12 = 1%

As an example, now let's assume Cindy Johnson invested $1,000 in a savings account paying 10% interest *compounded* twice a year. There are two six-month periods paying interest at 5% (the annual rate divided by two periods). How much interest will she earn the first year, and what will be her investment balance at the end of the year?

Date	Interest (Interest rate × Outstanding balance = Interest)	Balance
Initial deposit		$ 1,000.00
After six months	5% × $1,000 = $50.00	$ 1,050.00
End of year 1	5% × $1,050 = $52.50	$1,102.50

The *effective interest rate* is the rate at which money actually will grow during a full year.

The $1,000 would grow by $102.50, the interest earned, to $1,102.50, $2.50 more than if interest were compounded only once a year. The effective annual interest rate, often referred to as the annual *yield,* is 10.25% ($102.50 ÷ $1,000).

Future Value of a Single Amount

In the first Cindy example, in which $1,000 was invested for three years at 10% compounded annually, the $1,331 is referred to as the future value (FV). A time diagram is a useful way to visualize this relationship, with 0 indicating the date of the initial investment.

● LO5–2

$$n = 3, i = 10\%$$

The future value after one year can be calculated as $1,000 × 1.10 (1.00 + .10) = $1,100. After three years, the future value is $1,000 × 1.10 × 1.10 × 1.10 = $1,331. In fact, the future value of any invested amount can be determined as follows:

$$FV = I(1 + i)^n$$

where: FV = Future value of the invested amount
          I = Amount invested at the beginning of the period
          i = Interest rate
          n = Number of compounding periods

The *future value* of a single amount is the amount of money that a dollar will grow to at some point in the future.

The future value can be determined by using Table 1, Future Value of $1, located at the end of this textbook. The table contains the future value of $1 invested for various periods of time, *n*, and at various rates, *i*.

Use this table to determine the future value of any invested amount simply by multiplying that invested amount by the table value at the *intersection* of the column for the desired rate and the row for the number of compounding periods. Illustration 5–1 provides an excerpt from Table 1.

	Interest Rates (*i*)					
Periods (*n*)	**7%**	**8%**	**9%**	**10%**	**11%**	**12%**
1	1.07000	1.08000	1.09000	1.10000	1.11000	1.12000
2	1.14490	1.16640	1.18810	1.21000	1.23210	1.25440
3	1.22504	1.25971	1.29503	1.33100	1.36763	1.40493
4	1.31080	1.36049	1.41158	1.46410	1.51807	1.57352
5	1.40255	1.46933	1.53862	1.61051	1.68506	1.76234

Illustration 5–1

Future Value of $1 (excerpt from Table 1 located at the end of this book)

The table shows various values of $(1 + i)^n$ for different combinations of *i* and *n*. From the table you can find the future value factor (table value) for three periods at 10% to be 1.331. This means that $1 invested at 10% compounded annually will grow to approximately $1.33 in three years. So, the future value of $1,000 invested for three years at 10% is $1,331:

$$FV = I \times FV \text{ factor}$$
$$FV = \$1,000 \times 1.331^* = \$1,331$$
*Future value of $1; $n = 3, i = 10\%$

The future value function in financial calculators or in an Excel spreadsheet calculates future values in the same way. Determining future values (and present values) electronically avoids the need for tables such as those in the appendix. But, we use the tables extensively in the book to make it easier for you to visualize how the amounts are actually determined. It's important to remember that the *n* in the future value formula refers to the number of compounding periods, not necessarily the number of years. For example, suppose you wanted to know the future value *two* years from today of $1,000 invested at 12% with *quarterly* compounding. The number of periods is therefore eight, and the compounding rate is 3% (12% annual rate divided by four, the number of quarters in a year). The future value factor from Table 1 is 1.26677, so the future value is $1,266.77 ($1,000 × 1.26677).[1]

Present Value of a Single Amount

● LO5–3

The present value of a single amount is today's equivalent to a particular amount in the future.

The example used to illustrate future value reveals that $1,000 invested today is equivalent to $1,100 received after one year, $1,210 after two years, or $1,331 after three years, assuming 10% interest compounded annually. Thus, the **$1,000** investment (I) is the **present value (PV)** of the single sum of $1,331 to be received at the end of three years. It is also the present value of $1,210 to be received in two years or $1,100 in one year.

Remember that the future value of a present amount is the present amount *times* $(1 + i)^n$. Logically, then, that computation can be reversed to find the *present value* of a future amount to be the future amount *divided* by $(1 + i)^n$. We substitute PV for I (invested amount) in the future value formula above.

$$FV = PV(1 + i)^n$$
$$PV = \frac{FV}{(1 + i)^n}$$

In our example,

$$PV = \frac{\$1,331}{(1 + .10)^3} = \frac{\$1,331}{1.331} = \$1,000$$

Of course, dividing by $(1 + i)^n$ is the same as multiplying by its reciprocal, $1/(1 + i)^n$.

$$PV = \$1,331 \times \frac{1}{(1 + .10)^3} = \$1,331 \times 0.75131 = \$1,000$$

So, for instance, the future value amount $1,331 times the PV factor of 0.75131 gives us a present value of $1,000, and the present value amount of $1,000 times the FV factor of 1.331 gives us the future value of $1,331 three years from now.

As with future value, these computations are simplified by using calculators, Excel, or present value tables. Table 2, Present Value of $1, provides the solutions of $1/(1 + i)^n$ for various interest rates (*i*) and compounding periods (*n*). These amounts represent the present value of $1 to be received at the *end* of the different periods. The table can be used to find the present value of any single amount to be received in the future by *multiplying* that future amount by the value in the table that lies at the *intersection* of the column for the appropriate rate and the row for the number of compounding periods.[2] Illustration 5–2 provides an excerpt from Table 2.

Illustration 5–2

Present Value of $1
(excerpt from Table 2)

Periods (*n*)	Interest Rates (*i*)					
	7%	**8%**	**9%**	**10%**	**11%**	**12%**
1	0.93458	0.92593	0.91743	0.90909	0.90090	0.89286
2	0.87344	0.85734	0.84168	0.82645	0.81162	0.79719
3	0.81630	0.79383	0.77218	0.75131	0.73119	0.71178
4	0.76290	0.73503	0.70843	0.68301	0.65873	0.63552
5	0.71299	0.68058	0.64993	0.62092	0.59345	0.56743

We can see a couple of interesting patterns in this table. First, look at any of the *rows*. Notice that the present value factors get smaller and smaller as the interest rates increase.

---

[1]When interest is compounded more frequently than once a year, the effective annual interest rate, or yield, can be determined using the following equation:

$$Yield = (1 + \frac{i}{p})^p - 1$$

with *i* being the annual interest rate and *p* the number of compounding periods per year. In this example, the annual yield would be 12.55%, calculated as follows:

$$Yield = (1 + \frac{12}{4})^4 - 1 = 1.1255 - 1 = .1255$$

Determining the yield is useful when comparing returns on investment instruments with different compounding period length.

[2]The factors in Table 2 are the reciprocals of those in Table 1. For example, the future value factor for 10%, three periods is 1.331, while the present value factor is .75131. $1 ÷ 1.331 = $.75131, and $1 ÷ 0.75131 = $1.331.

That demonstrates that the higher the time value of money, the lower is the present value of a future amount. That's logical. The higher the return you can get from putting to use money you have now (higher time value of money), the less desirable it is to wait to get the money (lower present value of the future amount).

Now, look at any of the *columns*. Notice that the further into the future the $1 is to be received, the less valuable it is now. That demonstrates that the longer you have to wait for your money, the more you give up in terms of return you could be getting if you could put the money to work now, and the lower is the present value of the future amount.

This is the essence of the concept of the time value of money. Given a choice between $1,000 now and $1,000 three years from now, you would choose to have the money now. If you have it now, you could put it to use. But the choice between, say, $740 now and $1,000 three years from now would depend on your time value of money. If your time value of money is 10%, you would choose the $1,000 in three years, because the $740 invested at 10% for three years would grow to only $984.94 [$740 × 1.331 (FV of $1, $i = 10\%$, $n = 3$)]. On the other hand, if your time value of money is 11% or higher, you would prefer the $740 now.[3] Presumably, you would invest the $740 now and have it grow to $1,012.05 ($740 × 1.36763) in three years. So, if your time value of money is 11%, you should be indifferent with respect to receiving $740 now or $1,012.05 three years from now.

Using the present value table in Illustration 5–2, the present value of $1,000 to be received in three years assuming a time value of money of 10% is $751.31 [$1,000 × 0.75131 (PV of $1, $i = 10\%$ and $n = 3$)]. Because the present value of the future amount, $1,000, is higher than $740 we could have today, we again determine that with a time value of money of 10%, the $1,000 in three years is preferred to the $740 now.

In our earlier example, $1,000 now is equivalent to $1,331 in three years, assuming the time value of money is 10%. Graphically, the relation between the present value and the future value can be viewed this way:

	End of year 1	End of year 2	End of year 3
0			
$100	$110	$121	

$1,000 ——————————————————————— $1,331
PV   FV

While the calculation of *future value* of a single sum invested today requires the *inclusion* of compound interest, *present value* problems require the *removal* of compound interest. The process of computing present value *removes* the $331 of interest earned over the three-year period from the future value of *$1,331*, just as the process of computing future value *adds* $331 of interest to the present value of *$1,000* to arrive at the future value of *$1,331*.

As we demonstrate later in this chapter and in subsequent chapters, present value calculations are incorporated into accounting valuation much more frequently than future value.

> The calculation of future value requires the addition of interest, while the calculation of present value requires the removal of interest.
>
> Accountants use PV calculations much more frequently than FV.

Solving for Other Values When FV and PV are Known

There are four variables in the process of adjusting single cash flow amounts for the time value of money: the present value (PV), the future value (FV), the number of compounding periods (n), and the interest rate (i). If you know any three of these, the fourth can be determined. Illustration 5–3 solves for an unknown interest rate and Illustration 5–4 determines an unknown number of periods.

● LO5–4

DETERMINING THE UNKNOWN INTEREST RATE

Suppose a friend asks to borrow $500 today and promises to repay you $605 two years from now. What is the annual interest rate you would be agreeing to?

Illustration 5–3

Determining i When PV, FV, and n are Known

---
[3]The interest rate used to find the present value sometimes is called the *discount rate*, and finding the present value is sometimes called "discounting" a future amount to its present value.

244   SECTION 1   The Role of Accounting as an Information System

The following time diagram illustrates the situation:

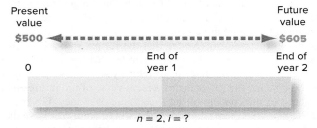

The interest rate is the rate that will provide a present value of $500 when determining the present value of the $605 to be received in two years:

$$\$500 \text{ (present value)} = \$605 \text{ (future value)} \times ?^*$$
*Present value of $1: $n = 2$, $i = ?$

Rearranging algebraically, we find that the present value table factor is 0.82645.

> **The unknown variable is the interest rate.**

$$\$500 \text{ (present value)} \div \$605 \text{ (future value)} = 0.82645^*$$
*Present value of $1: $n = 2$, $i = ?$

When you consult the present value table, Table 2, you search row two ($n = 2$) for this value and find it in the 10% column. So the effective interest rate is 10%. Notice that the computed factor value exactly equals the table factor value.[4]

DETERMINING THE UNKNOWN NUMBER OF PERIODS

Illustration 5–4

Determining *n* When PV, FV, and *i* are Known

> You want to invest $10,000 today to accumulate $16,000 for graduate school. If you can invest at an interest rate of 10% compounded annually, how many years will it take to accumulate the required amount?

The following time diagram illustrates the situation:

The years it will take is the value of *n* that will provide a present value of $10,000 when finding the present value of $16,000 at a rate of 10%:

$$\$10,000 \text{ (present value)} = \$16,000 \text{ (future value)} \times ?^*$$
*Present value of $1; $n = ?$, $i = 10\%$

> **The unknown variable is *n*, the number of periods.**

Rearranging algebraically, we find that the present value table factor is 0.625.

$$\$10,000 \text{ (present value)} \div \$16,000 \text{ (future value)} = 0.625^*$$
*Present value of $1: $n = ?$, $i = 10\%$

When you consult the present value table, Table 2, you search the 10% column ($i = 10\%$) for this value and find 0.62092 in row five. So it would take approximately five years to accumulate $16,000 in the situation described.

---

[4]If the calculated factor lies between two table factors, interpolation is useful in finding the unknown value. For example, if the future value in our example is $600, instead of $605, the calculated PV factor is 0.83333 ($500 ÷ $600). This factor lies between the 9% factor of 0.84168 and the 10% factor of 0.82645. The total difference between these factors is 0.01523 (0.84168 − 0.82645). The difference between the calculated factor of 0.83333 and the 10% factor of 0.82645 is 0.00688. This is 45% of the difference between the 9% and 10% factors:

$$\frac{0.00688}{0.01523} = 0.45$$

Therefore, the interpolated interest rate is 9.55% (10 − 0.45).

Additional Consideration

Solving for the unknown factor in either of these examples could just as easily be done using the future value tables. The number of years is the value of n that will provide a present value of $10,000 when $16,000 is the future amount and the interest rate is 10%.

$$\$16,000 \text{ (future value)} = \$10,000 \text{ (present value)} \times ?^*$$

*Future value of $1: $n = ?$, $i = 10\%$

Rearranging algebraically, the future value table factor is 1.6.

$$\$16,000 \text{ (future value)} \div \$10,000 \text{ (present value)} = 1.6^*$$

*Future value of $1: $n = ?$, $i = 10\%$

When you consult the future value table, Table 1, you search the 10% column ($i = 10\%$) for this value and find 1.61051 in row five. So it would take approximately five years to accumulate $16,000 in the situation described.

Concept Review Exercise

Using the appropriate table, answer each of the following independent questions.

VALUING A SINGLE CASH FLOW AMOUNT

1. What is the future value of $5,000 at the end of six periods at 8% compound interest?
2. What is the present value of $8,000 to be received eight periods from today assuming a compound interest rate of 12%?
3. What is the present value of $10,000 to be received two *years* from today assuming an annual interest rate of 24% and *monthly* compounding?
4. If an investment of $2,000 grew to $2,520 in three periods, what is the interest rate at which the investment grew? Solve using both present and future value tables.
5. Approximately how many years would it take for an investment of $5,250 to accumulate to $15,000, assuming interest is compounded at 10% annually? Solve using both present and future value tables.

Solution:

1. FV = $5,000 × 1.58687* = $7,934

   *Future value of $1: $n = 6$, $i = 8\%$ (from Table 1)

2. PV = $8,000 × 0.40388* = $3,231

   *Present value of $1: $n = 8$, $i = 12\%$ (from Table 2)

3. PV = $10,000 × 0.62172* = $6,217

   *Present value of $1: $n = 24$, $i = 2\%$ (from Table 2)

4. Using present value table,

   $$\frac{\$2,000}{\$2,520} = 0.7937^*$$

   *Present value of $1: $n = 3$, $i = ?$ (from Table 2, i approximately **8%**)

   Using future value table,

   $$\frac{\$2,520}{\$2,000} = 1.260^*$$

   *Future value of $1: $n = 3$, $i = ?$ (from Table 1, i approximately **8%**)

5. Using present value table,

   $$\frac{\$5,250}{\$15,000} = 0.35^*$$

   *Present value of $1: $n = ?$, $i = 10\%$ (from Table 2, n approximately **11 years**)

   Using future value table,

   $$\frac{\$15,000}{\$5,250} = 2.857^*$$

   *Future value of $1: $n = ?$, $i = 10\%$ (from Table 1, n approximately **11 years**)

Preview of Accounting Applications of Present Value Techniques—Single Cash Amount

Doug Smith switched off his television set immediately after watching the Super Bowl game and swore to himself that this would be the last year he would watch the game on his 10-year-old 24-inch TV. "Next year, a big screen 4K LED," he promised himself. Soon after, he saw an advertisement in the local newspaper from Slim Jim's TV and Appliance offering a Samsung 78-inch television on sale for $1,800. And the best part of the deal was that Doug could take delivery immediately but would not have to pay the $1,800 for one whole year! "In a year, I can easily save the $1,800," he thought.

In the above scenario, the seller, Slim Jim's TV and Appliance, records a sale when the TV is delivered to Doug. How should the company value its receivable and corresponding sales revenue? We provide a solution to this question at the end of this section. The following discussion will help you to understand that solution.

> Most *monetary assets* and *monetary liabilities* are valued at the present value of future cash flows.

Many assets and most liabilities are monetary in nature. Monetary assets include money and claims to receive money, the amount of which is fixed or determinable. Examples include cash and most receivables. Monetary liabilities are obligations to pay amounts of cash, the amount of which is fixed or determinable. Most liabilities are monetary. For example, if you borrow money from a bank and sign a note payable, the amount of cash to be repaid to the bank is fixed. Monetary receivables and payables are valued based on the fixed amount of cash to be received or paid in the future taking into account the time value of money. In other words, we value most receivables and payables at the present value of future cash flows, reflecting an appropriate time value of money.[5]

● LO5–5

The example in Illustration 5–5 demonstrates the application of present value techniques in valuing a note receivable and note payable for which the time period is one year and the interest rate is known.

> **Illustration 5–5**
>
> Valuing a Note: One Payment, Explicit Interest

Explicit Interest

The Stridewell Wholesale Shoe Company manufactures athletic shoes for sale to retailers. The company recently sold a large order of shoes to Harmon Sporting Goods for $50,000. Stridewell agreed to accept a note in payment for the shoes requiring payment of $50,000 in one year plus interest at 10%.

How should Stridewell value the note receivable and corresponding sales revenue? How should Harmon value the note payable and corresponding inventory purchased? As long as the interest rate explicitly stated in the agreement properly reflects the time value of money, the answer is $50,000, the face value of the note. It's important to realize that this amount also equals the present value of future cash flows at 10%. Future cash flows equal $55,000, the $50,000 note itself plus $5,000 interest ($50,000 × 10%). Here's a time diagram:

In equation form, we can solve for present value as follows:

$$\$55,000 \text{ (future value)} \times 0.90909^* = \$50,000 \text{ (present value)}$$

*Present value of $1: $n = 1$, $i = 10\%$

---

[5]FASB ASC 835–30: Interest—Imputation of Interest (previously "Interest on Receivables and Payables," *Accounting Principles Board Opinion No. 21* (New York: AICPA, 1971)). As you will learn in Chapter 7, we value normal trade accounts receivable and accounts payable at the amounts expected to be received or paid, not the present value of those amounts. The difference between the amounts expected to be received or paid and present values often is immaterial.

By calculating the present value of $55,000 to be received in one year, the interest of $5,000 is removed from the future value, resulting in the appropriate note receivable/sales revenue value of $50,000 for Stridewell and a $50,000 note payable/inventory value for Harmon.

While most notes, loans, and mortgages explicitly state an interest rate that will properly reflect the time value of money, there can be exceptions. Consider the example in Illustration 5–6 which uses present value techniques to value a note due in two years and for which the interest rate is not known.

No Explicit Interest

The Stridewell Wholesale Shoe Company recently sold a large order of shoes to Harmon Sporting Goods. Terms of the sale require Harmon to sign a noninterest-bearing note of $60,500 with payment due in two years.

Illustration 5–6

Valuing a Note: One Payment, No Explicit Interest

How should Stridewell and Harmon value the note receivable/payable and corresponding sales revenue/inventory? Even though the agreement states a noninterest-bearing note, the $60,500 does, in fact, include interest for the two-year period of the loan. We need to remove the interest portion of the $60,500 to determine the portion that represents the sales price of the shoes. We do this by calculating the present value. The following time diagram illustrates the situation assuming that a rate of 10% reflects the appropriate interest rate for a loan of this type:

Present value		Future value
?	◄■■■■■■■■■■■■■■■	**$60,500**
0	End of year 1	End of year 2

$n = 2, i = 10\%$

Again, using the present value of $1 table,

$60,500 (future value) × 0.82645* = $50,000 (present value)

*Present value of $1: $n = 2, i = 10\%$

Both the note receivable for Stridewell and the note payable for Harmon initially will be valued at $50,000. The difference of $10,500 ($60,500 − $50,000) represents interest revenue/expense to be recognized over the life of the note. The appropriate journal entries are illustrated in later chapters.

Now can you answer the question posed in the scenario at the beginning of this section? Assuming that a rate of 10% reflects the appropriate interest rate in this situation, Slim Jim's TV and Appliance records a receivable and sales revenue of $1,636, which is the present value of the $1,800 to be received from Doug Smith one year from the date of sale.

$1,800 (future value) × 0.90909* = $1,636 (present value)

*Present value of $1: $n = 1, i = 10\%$ (from Table 2)

Additional Consideration

In Illustration 5–5, if Harmon Sporting Goods had prepaid Stridewell for delivery of the shoes in two years, rather than buying now and paying later, Harmon would be viewed as providing a two-year loan to Stridewell. Assuming that Harmon pays Stridewell $41,323, the present value of $50,000 for two-periods at 10%, Stridewell would record interest expense and Harmon would record interest revenue of $8,677 ($50,000 − $41,323) over the two-year period. When delivery occurs in two years, Stridewell records sales revenue of $50,000 and Harmon values the inventory acquired at $50,000.

| **PART B** | # Basic Annuities |

● LO5–6

The previous examples involved the receipt or payment of a single future amount. Financial instruments frequently involve multiple receipts or payments of cash. If the same amount is to be received or paid each period, the series of cash flows is referred to as an annuity. A common annuity encountered in practice is a loan on which periodic interest is paid in equal amounts. For example, bonds typically pay interest semiannually in an amount determined by multiplying a stated rate by a fixed principal amount. Some loans and most leases are paid in equal installments during a specified period of time.

In an ordinary annuity, cash flows occur at the end of each period.

An agreement that creates an annuity can produce either an *ordinary annuity* or an *annuity due* (sometimes referred to as an annuity in advance) situation. The first cash flow (receipt or payment) of an ordinary annuity is made one compounding period *after* the date on which the agreement begins. The final cash flow takes place on the *last* day covered by the agreement. For example, an installment note payable dated December 31, 2021, might require the debtor to make three equal annual payments, with the first payment due on December 31, 2022, and the last one on December 31, 2024. The following time diagram illustrates an ordinary annuity:

	12/31/21	12/31/22	12/23/23	12/31/24
Ordinary annuity		1st payment	2nd payment	3rd payment

In an annuity due, cash flows occur at the beginning of each period.

The first payment of an annuity due is made on the *first* day of the agreement, and the last payment is made one period *before* the end of the agreement. For example, a three-year lease of a building that begins on December 31, 2021, and ends on December 31, 2024, may require the first year's lease payment in advance on December 31, 2021. The third and last payment would take place on December 31, 2023, the beginning of the third year of the lease. The following time diagram illustrates this situation:

	12/31/21	12/31/22	12/23/23	12/31/24
Annuity due	1st payment	2nd payment	3rd payment	

Future Value of an Annuity

Future Value of an Ordinary Annuity

● LO5–7

Let's first consider the future value of an ordinary annuity in Illustration 5–7.

Illustration 5–7
Future Value of an Ordinary Annuity

Rita Grant wants to accumulate a sum of money to pay for graduate school. Rather than investing a single amount today that will grow to a future value, she decides to invest $10,000 a year over the next three years in a savings account paying 10% interest compounded annually. She decides to make the first payment to the bank one year from today.

The following time diagram illustrates this ordinary annuity situation. Time 0 is the start of the first period.

	End of year 1	End of year 2	Future value ? End of year 3
0			
	$10,000	$10,000	$10,000

$n = 3, i = 10\%$

Using the FV of $1 factors from Table 1, we can calculate the future value of this annuity by calculating the future value of each of the individual payments as follows:

	Payment		FV of $1 $i = 10\%$		Future Value (at the end of year 3)	n
First payment	$10,000	×	1.21	=	$ 12,100	2
Second payment	10,000	×	1.10	=	11,000	1
Third payment	10,000	×	1.00	=	10,000	0
Total			3.31		$33,100	

From the time diagram, we can see that the first payment has two compounding periods to earn interest. The factor used, 1.21, is the FV of $1 invested for two periods at 10%. The second payment has one compounding period, and the last payment does not earn any interest because it is invested on the last day of the three-year annuity period. Therefore, the factor used is 1.00.

This illustration shows that it's possible to calculate the future value of the annuity by separately calculating the FV of each payment and then adding these amounts together. Fortunately, that's not necessary. Table 3, Future Value of an Ordinary Annuity of $1, simplifies the computation by summing the individual FV of $1 factors for various factors of n and i. Illustration 5–8 contains an excerpt from Table 3.

In an ordinary annuity, the last cash payment will not include any interest.

	Interest Rates (i)					
Periods (n)	7%	8%	9%	10%	11%	12%
1	1.0000	1.0000	1.0000	1.0000	1.0000	1.0000
2	2.0700	2.0800	2.0900	2.1000	2.1100	2.1200
3	3.2149	3.2464	3.2781	3.3100	3.3421	3.3744
4	4.4399	4.5061	4.5731	4.6410	4.7097	4.7793
5	5.7507	5.8666	5.9847	6.1051	6.2278	6.3528

Illustration 5–8

Future Value of an Ordinary Annuity of $1 (excerpt from Table 3)

The future value of $1 at the end of each of three periods invested at 10% is shown in Table 3 to be $3.31. We can simply multiply this factor by $10,000 to derive the FV of our ordinary annuity (FVA):

$$\text{FVA} = \$10,000 \text{ (annuity amount)} \times 3.31^* = \$33,100$$

*Future value of an ordinary annuity of $1: n = 3, i = 10%

Future Value of an Annuity Due

Let's modify the previous illustration to create an annuity due in Illustration 5–9.

Illustration 5–9

Future Value of an
Annuity Due

> Rita Grant wants to accumulate a sum of money to pay for graduate school. Rather than investing a single amount today that will grow to a future value, she decides to invest $10,000 a year over the next three years in a savings account paying 10% interest compounded annually. She decides to make the first payment to the bank immediately. How much will Rita have available in her account at the end of three years?

The following time diagram depicts the situation. Again, note that 0 is the start of the first period.

$$n = 3, i = 10\%$$

The future value can be found by separately calculating the FV of each of the three payments and then summing those individual future values:

In an annuity due, the last
cash payment will include
interest.

	Payment		FV of $1 $i = 10\%$		Future Value (at the end of year 3)	n
First payment	$10,000	×	1.331	=	$13,310	3
Second payment	10,000	×	1.210	=	12,100	2
Third payment	10,000	×	1.100	=	11,000	1
Total			3.641		$36,410	

And, again, this same future value can be found by using the future value of an annuity due (FVAD) factor from Table 5, Future Value of an Annuity Due of $1 as follows:

$$\text{FVAD} = \$10,000 \text{ (annuity amount)} \times 3.641^* = \$36,410$$

*Future value of an annuity due of $1: $n = 3, i = 10\%$

Of course, if *unequal* amounts are invested each year, we can't solve the problem by using the annuity tables. The future value of each payment would have to be calculated separately using the Future Value of $1 for each individual period and adding them together.

Present Value of an Annuity

Present Value of an Ordinary Annuity

● LO5–8   You will learn in later chapters that liabilities and receivables, with the exception of certain trade receivables and payables, are reported in financial statements at their present values. Most of these financial instruments specify equal periodic interest payments or installment payments (which represent a combination of interest and principal). As a result, the most common accounting applications of the time value of money involve determining the present value of annuities. As in the future value applications we discussed above, an annuity can be either an ordinary annuity or an annuity due. Let's look at an ordinary annuity first.

In Illustration 5–7, we determined that Rita Grant could accumulate $33,100 for graduate school by investing $10,000 at the end of each of three years at 10%. The $33,100 is the future value of the ordinary annuity described. Another alternative is to invest one single amount at the beginning of the three-year period. (See Illustration 5–10.) This single amount will equal the present value at the beginning of the three-year period of the $33,100 future value. It will also equal the present value of the $10,000 three-year annuity.

FINANCIAL Reporting Case

Q1, p. 239

Rita Grant wants to accumulate a sum of money to pay for graduate school. She wants to invest a single amount today in a savings account earning 10% interest compounded annually that is equivalent to investing $10,000 at the end of each of the next three years.

Illustration 5–10

Present Value of an Ordinary Annuity

The present value can be found by separately calculating the PV of each of the three payments and then summing those individual present values as follows:

	Payment		PV of $1 $i = 10\%$		Present Value (at the beginning of year 1)	n
First payment	$10,000	×	0.90909	=	$ 9,091	1
Second payment	10,000	×	0.82645	=	8,264	2
Third payment	10,000	×	0.75131	=	7,513	3
Total			2.48685		$24,868	

A more efficient method of calculating present value is to use Table 4, Present Value of an Ordinary Annuity of $1. Illustration 5–11 contains an excerpt from Table 4.

	Interest Rates (i)					
Periods (n)	7%	8%	9%	10%	11%	12%
1	0.93458	0.92593	0.91743	0.90909	0.90090	0.89286
2	1.80802	1.78326	1.75911	1.73554	1.71252	1.69005
3	2.62432	2.57710	2.53129	2.48685	2.44371	2.40183
4	3.38721	3.31213	3.23972	3.16987	3.10245	3.03735
5	4.10020	3.99271	3.88965	3.79079	3.69590	3.60478

Illustration 5–11

Present Value of an Ordinary Annuity of $1 (excerpt from Table 4)

Using Table 4, we calculate the PV of the ordinary annuity (PVA) as follows:

$$\text{PVA} = \$10,000 \text{ (annuity amount)} \times 2.48685^* = \$24,868$$

*Present value of an ordinary annuity of $1: $n = 3$, $i = 10\%$

The relationship between the present value and the future value of the annuity can be depicted graphically as follows:

Present value $24,868		End of year 1		End of year 2		Future value $33,100 End of year 3
0		$10,000		$10,000		$10,000

$n = 3$, $i = 10\%$

This can be interpreted in several ways.

1. $10,000 invested at 10% at the end of each of the next three years will accumulate to $33,100 at the end of the third year.
2. $24,868 invested at 10% now will grow to $33,100 after three years.
3. Someone whose time value of money is 10% would be willing to pay $24,868 now to receive $10,000 at the end of each of the next three years.
4. If your time value of money is 10%, you should be indifferent with respect to paying/receiving (a) $24,868 now, (b) $33,100 three years from now, or (c) $10,000 at the end of each of the next three years. In other words, at the end of the third year you would have the same $33,100, regardless of the option chosen to get there.

Additional Consideration

We also can verify that these are the present value and future value of the same annuity by calculating the present value of a single cash amount of $33,100 three years hence:

PV = $33,100 (future value) × 0.75131* = $24,868

*Present value of $1: $n = 3, i = 10\%$

Present Value of an Annuity Due

Illustration 5–12

Present Value of an Annuity Due

In the previous illustration, suppose that the three equal payments of $10,000 are to be made at the *beginning* of each of the three years. Recall from Illustration 5–9 that the future value of this annuity is $36,410. What is the present value?

The following time diagram depicts this situation:

Present value ?

| 0 | End of year 1 | End of year 2 | End of year 3 |

$10,000 $10,000 $10,000

$n = 3, i = 10\%$

Once again, using individual PV factors of $1 from Table 2, the PV of the annuity due can be calculated as follows:

	Payment		PV of $1 $i = 10\%$		Present Value (at the beginning of year 1)	n
First payment	$10,000	×	1.00000	=	$ 10,000	0
Second payment	10,000	×	0.90909	=	9,091	1
Third payment	10,000	×	0.82645	=	8,264	2
Total			2.73554		$27,355	

In an annuity due, the first cash payment won't include interest.

The first payment does not contain any interest since it is made on the first day of the three-year annuity period. Therefore, the factor used is 1.00. The second payment has one compounding period and the factor used of 0.90909 is the PV factor of $1 for one period and

10%, and we need to remove two compounding periods of interest from the third payment. The factor used of 0.82645 is the PV factor of $1 for two periods and 10%.

The relationship between the present value and the future value of the annuity can be depicted graphically as follows:

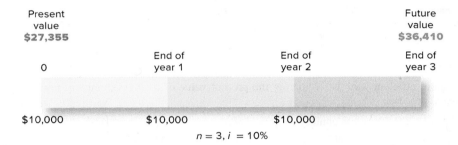

Present
value
$27,355

| | End of year 1 | End of year 2 | Future value **$36,410** End of year 3 |

| | | | |

$10,000 $10,000 $10,000

$n = 3, i = 10\%$

Using Table 6, Present Value of an Annuity Due, we can more efficiently calculate the PV of the annuity due (PVAD):

$$PVAD = \$10,000 \text{ (annuity amount)} \times 2.73554^* = \$27,355$$

*Present value of an annuity due of $1: $n = 3, i = 10\%$

To better understand the relationship between Tables 4 and 6, notice that the PVAD factor for three periods, 10%, from Table 6 is 2.73554. This is simply the PVA factor for two periods, 10%, of 1.73554, plus 1.0. The addition of 1.0 reflects the fact that the first payment occurs immediately and thus includes no interest.

Of course, if payment amounts are *not the same* each year, we don't have an annuity and can't find a solution by using the annuity tables. In that case, we'd need to find the present value of each payment separately using the Present Value of $1 for each individual period and add them together.

Present Value of a Deferred Annuity

Accounting valuations often involve the present value of annuities in which the first cash flow is expected to occur more than one time period after the date of the agreement. As the inception of the annuity is deferred beyond a single period, this type of annuity is referred to as a **deferred annuity**.[6]

> A *deferred annuity* exists when the first cash flow occurs more than one period after the date the agreement begins.

Illustration 5–13
Deferred Annuity

> At January 1, 2021, you are considering acquiring an investment that will provide three equal payments of $10,000 each to be received at the end of three consecutive years. However, the first payment is not expected until *December 31, 2023*. The time value of money is 10%. How much would you be willing to pay for this investment?

The following time diagram depicts this situation:

Present
value
?

| 1/1/21 | 12/31/21 | 12/31/22 | 12/31/23 | $i = 10\%$ 12/31/24 | 12/31/25 |

$10,000 $10,000 $10,000

$n = 2$ $n = 3$

---

[6]The future value of a deferred annuity is the same as the future amount of an annuity not deferred. That's because there are no interest compounding periods prior to the beginning of the annuity period.

The present value of the deferred annuity can be calculated by summing the present values of the three individual cash flows, as of today.

	Payment		PV of $1 $i = 10\%$		Present Value	n
First payment	$10,000	×	0.75131	=	$ 7,513	3
Second payment	10,000	×	0.68301	=	6,830	4
Third payment	10,000	×	0.62092	=	6,209	5
					$20,552	

A more efficient way of calculating the present value of a deferred annuity involves a two-step process.

1. Calculate the PV of the annuity *as of the beginning of the annuity period.*
2. Reduce the single amount calculated in (1) to its present value *as of today.*

In this case, we compute the present value of the annuity as of December 31, 2022, by multiplying the annuity amount by the three-period ordinary annuity factor:

$$PVA = \$10,000 \text{ (annuity amount)} \times 2.48685^* = \$24,868$$

*Present value of an ordinary annuity of $1: $n = 3$, $i = 10\%$

This is the present value as of December 31, 2022. This single amount is then reduced to present value as of January 1, 2021, by making the following calculation:

$$PV = \$24,868 \text{ (future amount)} \times 0.82645^* = \$20,552$$

*Present value of $1: $n = 2$, $i = 10\%$

The following time diagram illustrates this two-step process:

Present value		Present value (at beginning of the annuity period)		$i = 10\%$	
$20,552		**$24,868**			
1/1/21	12/31/21	12/31/22	12/31/23	12/31/24	12/31/25
			$10,000	$10,000	$10,000
	$n = 2$			$n = 3$	

If you recall the concepts you learned in this chapter, you might think of other ways the present value of a deferred annuity can be determined. Among them:

1. Calculate the PV of an annuity due, rather than an ordinary annuity, and then reduce that amount **three** periods rather than two:

$$PVAD = \$10,000 \text{ (annuity amount)} \times 2.73554^* = \$27,355$$

*Present value of an annuity due of $1: $n = 3$, $i = 10\%$

This is the present value as of December 31, 2023. This single amount is then reduced to present value as of January 1, 2021 by making the following calculation:

$$PV = \$27,355 \times 0.75131^* = \$20,552$$

*Present value of $1: $n = 3$, $i = 10\%$

2. From Table 4, subtract the two-period PVA factor (1.73554) from the five-period PVA factor (3.79079) and multiply the difference (2.05525) by $10,000 to get $20,552.

Financial Calculators and Excel

As previously mentioned, financial calculators can be used to solve future and present value problems. For example, a Texas Instruments model BA-35 has the following pertinent keys:

$\boxed{\text{N}}$ $\boxed{\%\text{I}}$ $\boxed{\text{PV}}$ $\boxed{\text{FV}}$ $\boxed{\text{PMT}}$ $\boxed{\text{CPT}}$

These keys are defined as follows:

N = number of periods
%I = interest rate
PV = present value
FV = future value
PMT = annuity payments
CPT = compute button

To illustrate its use, assume that you need to determine the present value of a 10-period ordinary annuity of $200 using a 10% interest rate. You would enter $\boxed{\text{N}}$ 10, $\boxed{\%\text{I}}$ 10, $\boxed{\text{PMT}}$ –200, then press $\boxed{\text{CPT}}$ and $\boxed{\text{PV}}$ to obtain the answer of $1,229.

Many professionals choose to use spreadsheet software, such as Excel, to solve time value of money problems. These spreadsheets can be used in a variety of ways. A template can be created using the formulas shown in Illustration 5–22. An alternative is to use the software's built-in financial functions. For example, Excel has a function called PV that calculates the present value of an ordinary annuity. To use the function, you would select the pull-down menu for "Insert," click on "Function" and choose the category called "Financial." Scroll down to PV and double-click. You will then be asked to input the necessary variables—interest rate, the number of periods, and the payment amount.

In subsequent chapters we illustrate the use of both a calculator and Excel in addition to present value tables to solve present value calculations for selected examples and illustrations.

Using a calculator:
enter: $\boxed{\text{N}}$ 10 $\boxed{\text{I}}$ 10
$\boxed{\text{PMT}}$ –200
Output: $\boxed{\text{PV}}$ 1,229

Using Excel,
enter: PV(.10,10,–200)
Output: 1,229

Solving for Unknown Values in Present Value Situations

In present value problems involving annuities, there are four variables: (1) present value of an ordinary annuity (PVA) or present value of an annuity due (PVAD), (2) the amount of each annuity payment, (3) the number of periods, *n*, and (4) the interest rate, *i*. If you know any three of these, the fourth can be determined.

● LO5–9

Assume that you borrow $700 from a friend and intend to repay the amount in four equal annual installments beginning one year from today. Your friend wishes to be reimbursed for the time value of money at an 8% annual rate. What is the required annual payment that must be made (the annuity amount), to repay the loan in four years?

Illustration 5–14
Determining the Annuity Amount When Other Variables Are Known

The following time diagram illustrates the situation:

Present
value

$700	End of	End of	End of	End of
0	year 1	year 2	year 3	year 4

?   ?   ?   ?

$n = 4, i = 8\%$

The required payment is the annuity amount that will provide a present value of $700 when using an interest rate of 8%.

$$\$700 \text{ (present value)} = 3.31213^* \times \text{annuity amount}$$

*Present value of an ordinary annuity of $1: $n = 4$, $i = 8\%$

Rearranging algebraically, we find that the annuity amount is $211.34.

$$\$700 \text{ (present value)} \div 3.31213^* = \$211.34 \text{ (annuity amount)}$$

*Present value of an ordinary annuity of $1: $n = 4$, $i = 8\%$

You would have to make four annual payments of $211.34 to repay the loan. Total payments of $845.36 (4 × $211.34) would include $145.36 in interest ($845.36 − $700.00).

The unknown variable is the annuity amount.

Illustration 5–15
Determining *n* When Other Variables Are Known

> Assume that you borrow $700 from a friend and intend to repay the amount in equal installments of $100 per year over a period of years. The payments will be made at the end of each year beginning one year from now. Your friend wishes to be reimbursed for the time value of money at a 7% annual rate. How many years would it take before you repaid the loan?

Once again, this is an ordinary annuity situation because the first payment takes place one year from now. The following time diagram illustrates the situation:

Present value

| $700 | End of | End of | End of | End of |
| 0 | year 1 | year 2 | year $n-1$ | year n |

$n = ?, i = 7\%$

The number of years is the value of n that will provide a present value of $700 when finding the present value of $100 payments using an interest rate of 7%:

$$\$700 \text{ (present value)} = \$100 \text{ (annuity amount)} \times ?^*$$

*Present value of an ordinary annuity of $1: $n = ?$, $i = 7\%$

The unknown variable is the number of periods.

Rearranging algebraically, we find that the PVA table factor is 7.0.

$$\$700 \text{ (present value)} \div \$100 \text{ (annuity amount)} = 7.0^*$$

*Present value of an ordinary annuity of $1: $n = ?$, $i = 7\%$

When you consult the PVA table, Table 4, you search the 7% column ($i = 7\%$) for this value and find 7.02358 in row 10. So it would take approximately 10 years to repay the loan in the situation described.

Illustration 5–16
Determining *i* When Other Variables Are Known

FINANCIAL Reporting Case

Q2, p. 239

> Suppose that a friend asked to borrow $331 today (present value) and promised to repay you $100 (the annuity amount) at the end of each of the next four years. What is the annual interest rate implicit in this agreement?

First of all, we are dealing with an ordinary annuity situation as the payments are at the end of each period. The following time diagram illustrates the situation:

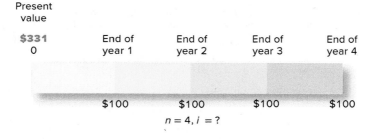

Present value

$331	End of	End of	End of	End of
0	year 1	year 2	year 3	year 4
	$100	$100	$100	$100

$n = 4, i = ?$

The interest rate is the rate that will provide a present value of $331 when finding the present value of the $100 four-year ordinary annuity.

$$\$331 \text{ (present value)} = \$100 \text{ (annuity amount)} \times ?^*$$

*Present value of an ordinary annuity of $1: $n = 4$, $i = ?$

The unknown variable is the interest rate.

Rearranging algebraically, we find that the PVA table factor is 3.31.

$$\$331 \text{ (present value)} \div \$100 \text{ (annuity amount)} = 3.31^*$$

*Present value of an ordinary annuity of $1: $n = 4$, $i = ?$

When you consult the PVA table, Table 4, you search row four ($n = 4$) for this value and find it in the 8% column. So the effective interest rate is 8%.

Suppose that you borrowed $400 from a friend and promised to repay the loan by making three annual payments of $100 at the end of each of the next three years plus a final payment of $200 at the end of year four. What is the interest rate implicit in this agreement?

Illustration 5–17

Determining *i* When Other Variables Are Known— Unequal Cash Flows

---

The following time diagram illustrates the situation:

Present value

$400	End of	End of	End of	End of
0	year 1	year 2	year 3	year 4

| | $100 | $100 | $100 | $200 |

$100 annuity has $n = 3$, $i = ?$
$200 single payment has $n = 4$, $i = ?$

The interest rate is the rate that will provide a present value of $400 when finding the present value of the $100 three-year ordinary annuity plus the $200 to be received in four years:

$$\$400 \text{ (present value)} = \$100 \text{ (annuity amount)} \times ?^* + \$200 \text{ (single payment)} \times ?^\dagger$$

*Present value of an ordinary annuity of $1: $n = 3$, $i = ?$
†Present value of $1: $n = 4$, $i = ?$

The unknown variable is the interest rate.

This equation involves two unknowns and is not as easily solved as the two previous examples. One way to solve the problem is to trial-and-error the answer. For example, if we assumed *i* to be 9%, the total PV of the payments would be calculated as follows:

$$PV = \$100 \ (2.53129^*) + \$200 \ (0.70843^\dagger) = \$395$$

*Present value of an ordinary annuity of $1: $n = 3$, $i = 9\%$
†Present value of $1: $n = 4$, $i = 9\%$

Because the present value computed is less than the $400 borrowed, using 9% removes too much interest. Recalculating PV with $i = 8\%$ results in a PV of $405. This indicates that the interest rate implicit in the agreement is between 8% and 9%.

Concept Review Exercise

Using the appropriate table, answer each of the following independent questions.   **ANNUITIES**

1. What is the future value of an annuity of $2,000 invested at the *end* of each of the next six periods at 8% interest?
2. What is the future value of an annuity of $2,000 invested at the *beginning* of each of the next six periods at 8% interest?

3. What is the present value of an annuity of $6,000 to be received at the *end* of each of the next eight periods assuming an interest rate of 10%?

4. What is the present value of an annuity of $6,000 to be received at the *beginning* of each of the next eight periods assuming an interest rate of 10%?

5. Jane bought a $3,000 audio system and agreed to pay for the purchase in 10 equal annual installments of $408 beginning one year from today. What is the interest rate implicit in this agreement?

6. Jane bought a $3,000 audio system and agreed to pay for the purchase in 10 equal annual installments beginning one year from today. The interest rate is 12%. What is the amount of the annual installment?

7. Jane bought a $3,000 audio system and agreed to pay for the purchase by making nine equal annual installments beginning one year from today plus a lump-sum payment of $1,000 at the end of 10 periods. The interest rate is 10%. What is the required annual installment?

8. Jane bought an audio system and agreed to pay for the purchase by making four equal annual installments of $800 beginning one year from today plus a lump-sum payment of $1,000 at the end of five years. The interest rate is 12%. What was the cost of the audio system? (*Hint:* What is the present value of the cash payments?)

9. Jane bought an audio system and agreed to pay for the purchase by making five equal annual installments of $1,100 beginning four years from today. The interest rate is 12%. What was the cost of the audio system? (*Hint:* What is the present value of the cash payments?)

Solution:

1. $FVA = \$2,000 \times 7.3359^* = \$14,672$

   *Future value of an ordinary annuity of $1: $n = 6$, $i = 8\%$ (from Table 3)

2. $FVAD = \$2,000 \times 7.9228^* = \$15,846$

   *Future value of an annuity due of $1: $n = 6$, $i = 8\%$ (from Table 5)

3. $PVA = \$6,000 \times 5.33493^* = \$32,010$

   *Present value of ordinary annuity of $1: $n = 8$, $i = 10\%$ (from Table 4)

4. $PVAD = \$6,000 \times 5.86842^* = \$35,211$

   *Present value of an annuity due of $1: $n = 8$, $i = 10\%$ (from Table 6)

5. $\dfrac{\$3,000}{\$408} = 7.35^*$

   *Present value of an ordinary annuity of $1: $n = 10$, $i = ?$ (from Table 4, i approximately 6%)

6. Each annuity payment $= \dfrac{\$3,000}{5.65022^*} = \$531$

   *Present value of an ordinary annuity of $1: $n = 10$, $i = 12\%$ (from Table 4)

7. Each annuity payment $= \dfrac{\$3,000 - [\text{PV of } \$1,000\ (n = 10, i = 10\%)]}{5.75902^*}$

   Each annuity payment $= \dfrac{\$3,000 - (\$1,000 \times .38554^\dagger)}{5.75902^*}$

   Each annuity payment $= \dfrac{\$2,614}{5.75902^*} = \$454$

   *Present value of an ordinary annuity of $1: $n = 9$, $i = 10\%$ (from Table 4)
   †Present value of $1: $n = 10$, $i = 10\%$ (from Table 2)

8. $PV = \$800 \times 3.03735^* + \$1,000 \times 0.56743^\dagger = \$2,997$

   *Present value of an ordinary annuity of $1: $n = 4$, $i = 12\%$ (from Table 4)
   †Present value of $1: $n = 5$, $i = 12\%$ (from Table 2)

9. $PVA = \$1,100 \times 3.60478^* = \$3,965$

   *Present value of an ordinary annuity of $1: $n = 5$, $i = 12\%$ (from Table 4)

This is the present value three years from today (the beginning of the five-year ordinary annuity). This single amount is then reduced to present value as of today by making the following calculation:

$$PV = \$3,965 \times 0.71178^\dagger = \$2,822$$

†Present value of \$1: $n = 3$, $i = 12\%$, (from Table 2)

Preview of Accounting Applications of Present Value Techniques—Annuities

● LO5–10

The time value of money has many applications in accounting. Most of these applications involve the concept of present value. Because financial instruments typically specify equal periodic payments, these applications quite often involve annuity situations. For example, let's consider one accounting situation using both an ordinary annuity and the present value of a single amount (long-term bonds), two using an annuity due (long-term leases and installment notes), and a fourth using a deferred annuity (pension obligations).

**FINANCIAL
Reporting Case**

Q3, p. 239

Valuation of Long-Term Bonds

You will learn in Chapter 14 that a long-term bond usually requires the issuing (borrowing) company to repay a specified amount at maturity and make periodic stated interest payments over the life of the bond. The *stated* interest payments are equal to the contractual stated rate multiplied by the face value of the bonds. At the date the bonds are issued (sold), the marketplace will determine the price of the bonds based on the *market* rate of interest for investments with similar characteristics. The market rate at date of issuance may not equal the bonds' stated rate in which case the price of the bonds (the amount the issuing company actually is borrowing) will not equal the bonds' face value. Bonds issued at more than face value are said to be issued at a premium, while bonds issued at less than face value are said to be issued at a discount. Consider the example in Illustration 5–18.

On June 30, 2021, Fumatsu Electric issued 10% stated rate bonds with a face amount of \$200 million. The bonds mature on June 30, 2041 (20 years). The market rate of interest for similar issues was 12%. Interest is paid semiannually (5%) on June 30 and December 31, beginning December 31, 2021. The interest payment is \$10 million (5% × \$200 million). What was the price of the bond issue? What amount of interest expense will Fumatsu record for the bonds in 2021?

Illustration 5–18

Valuing a Long-Term Bond Liability

To determine the price of the bonds, we calculate the present value of the 40-period annuity (40 semiannual interest payments of \$10 million) and the lump-sum (single amount) payment of \$200 million paid at maturity using the semiannual market rate of interest of 6%. In equation form,

$$PVA = \$10 \text{ million (annuity amount)} \times 15.04630^* = \$150,463,000$$
$$PV = \$200 \text{ million (lump-sum)} \times 0.09722^\dagger = \underline{19,444,000}$$
$$\text{Price of the bond issue} = \underline{\underline{\$169,907,000}}$$

*Present value of an ordinary annuity of \$1: $n = 40$, $i = 6\%$
†Present value of \$1: $n = 40$, $i = 6\%$

The bonds will sell for \$169,907,000, which represents a discount of \$30,093,000 (\$200,000,000 − \$169,907,000). The discount results from the difference between the semiannual stated rate of 5% and the market rate of 6%. Fumatsu records a \$169,907,000 increase in cash and a corresponding liability for bonds payable.

Interest expense for the first six months is determined by multiplying the carrying value (book value) of the bonds (\$169,907,000) by the semiannual effective rate (6%) as follows:

$$\$169,907,000 \times 6\% = \$10,194,420$$

The difference between interest expense ($10,194,420) and interest paid ($10,000,000) increases the carrying value of the bond liability. Interest for the second six months of the bonds' life is determined by multiplying the new carrying value by the 6% semiannual effective rate.[7]

We discuss the specific accounts used to record these transactions in Chapters 12 and 14.

Valuation of Long-Term Leases

Companies frequently acquire the use of assets by leasing rather than purchasing them. Leases usually require the payment of fixed amounts at regular intervals over the life of the lease. You will learn in Chapter 15 that certain leases are treated in a manner similar to an installment purchase by the lessee. In other words, the lessee records an asset and corresponding lease liability at the present value of the lease payments. Consider the example in Illustration 5–19.

Illustration 5–19

Valuing a Long-Term Lease Liability

On January 1, 2021, the Stridewell Wholesale Shoe Company signed a 25-year lease agreement for an office building. Terms of the lease call for Stridewell to make annual lease payments of $10,000 at the beginning of each year, with the first payment due on January 1, 2021. Assuming an interest rate of 10% properly reflects the time value of money in this situation, how should Stridewell value the asset acquired and the corresponding lease liability?

Leases require the recording of an asset and corresponding liability at the present value of future lease payments.

Once again, by computing the present value of the lease payments, we remove the portion of the payments that represents interest, leaving the portion that represents payment for the asset itself. Because the first payment is due immediately, as is common for leases, this is an annuity due situation. In equation form:

$$PVAD = \$10,000 \text{ (annuity amount)} \times 9.98474^* = \$99,847$$

*Present value of an annuity due of $1: $n = 25$, $i = 10\%$

Stridewell initially will value the leased asset and corresponding lease liability at $99,847.

Journal entry at the beginning of the lease.

Right-of-use asset	99,847	
Lease payable..		99,847

The difference between this amount and total future cash payments of $250,000 ($10,000 × 25) represents the interest that is implicit in this agreement. That difference is recorded as interest over the life of the lease.

Valuation of Installment Notes

If you have purchased a car, or maybe a house, unless you paid cash, you signed a note promising to pay a portion of the purchase price over, say, five years for the car or 30 years for the house. Such notes usually call for payment in monthly installments rather than by a single amount at maturity. Corporations also often borrow using installment notes. Usually, installment payments are equal amounts each period so they constitute an annuity. Each payment includes both an amount that represents interest and an amount that represents a reduction of the outstanding balance (principal reduction). The periodic reduction of the balance is sufficient that, at maturity, the note is completely paid. If we know the amount of the periodic installment payments, we can calculate the amount at which to record the note in precisely the same way as we did in the previous illustration for a lease. But, suppose instead that we know the amount of the loan and want to calculate the amount of the installment payments. In that case, rather than multiplying the payment by the appropriate present value of an annuity factor to get the present value, we would invert the calculation and divide the amount of the loan by that present value factor. For instance, consider the example in Illustration 5–20.

[7]In Chapters 12 and 14, we refer to the process of determining interest as the effective interest rate times the loan balance as the *effective interest method.*

Illustration 5–20

Calculating Installment
Note Payments

On January 1, 2021, the Stridewell Wholesale Shoe Company purchased a $35,000 machine, with a $5,000 down payment and a 5-year installment note for the remaining $30,000. Terms of the note call for Stridewell to make annual installment payments at the beginning, with the first payment due on January 1, 2021, and at each December 31 thereafter. Assuming an interest rate of 4%, what is the amount of the annual installment payments?

The annual installment payment amount that would pay a $30,000 loan over 5 years at a 4% interest rate is:

$$\$30,000 \div 4.62990^* = \$6,480$$
*present value of an annuity due of $1: $n = 5, i = 4\%$

Stridewell initially will record the machine at its $35,000 cost with credits to cash and notes payable.

Machine	35,000	
Cash		5,000
Notes payable		30,000

Stridewell will record the first installment payment at the date of purchase:

Notes payable	6,480	
Cash		6,480

No interest is needed for the first installment payment because no time had yet passed, so no interest had accrued. With the second payment, though, the payment represents part interest and part reduction of the loan:

Interest expense*	941	
Notes payable	5,539	
Cash		6,480

*Interest expense is 4% times the amount owed initially reduced by the first payment a year earlier, or 4% × ($30,000 − $6,480) = $941.

Valuation of Pension Obligations

Pension plans are important compensation vehicles used by many U.S. companies. These plans are essentially forms of deferred compensation as the pension benefits are paid to employees after they retire. You will learn in Chapter 17 that some pension plans create obligations during employees' service periods that must be paid during their retirement periods. These obligations are funded during the employment period. This means companies contribute cash to pension funds annually with the intention of accumulating sufficient funds to pay employees the retirement benefits they have earned. The amounts contributed are determined using estimates of retirement benefits. The actual amounts paid to employees during retirement depend on many factors including future compensation levels and length of life. Consider Illustration 5–21.

Illustration 5–21

Valuing a Pension
Obligation

On January 1, 2021, the Stridewell Wholesale Shoe Company hired Terry Elliott. Terry is expected to work for 25 years before retirement on December 31, 2045. Annual retirement payments will be paid at the end of each year during his retirement period, expected to be 20 years. The first payment will be on December 31, 2046. During 2021 Terry earned an annual retirement benefit estimated to be $2,000 per year. The company plans to contribute cash to a pension fund that will accumulate to an amount sufficient to pay Terry this benefit. Assuming that Stridewell anticipates earning 6% on all funds invested in the pension plan, how much would the company have to contribute at the end of 2021 to pay for pension benefits earned in 2021?

To determine the required contribution, we calculate the present value on December 31, 2021, of the deferred annuity of $2,000 that begins on December 31, 2046, and is expected to end on December 31, 2065.

The following time diagram depicts this situation:

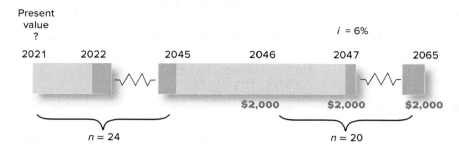

We can calculate the present value of the annuity using a two-step process. The first step computes the present value of the annuity as of December 31, 2045, by multiplying the annuity amount by the 20-period ordinary annuity factor.

$$\text{PVA} = \$2,000 \text{ (annuity amount)} \times 11.46992^* = \$22,940$$
*Present value of an ordinary annuity of $1: $n = 20$, $i = 6\%$

This is the present value as of December 31, 2045. This single amount is then reduced to present value as of December 31, 2021, by a second calculation.

$$\text{PV} = \$22,940 \text{ (future amount)} \times 0.24698^* = \$5,666$$
*Present value of $1: $n = 24$, $i = 6\%$

Stridewell would have to contribute $5,666 at the end of 2021 to fund the estimated pension benefits earned by its employee in 2021. Viewed in reverse, $5,666 invested now at 6% will accumulate a fund balance of $22,940 at December 31, 2045. If the fund balance remains invested at 6%, $2,000 can be withdrawn each year for 20 years before the fund is depleted.

Among the other situations you'll encounter using present value techniques are valuing notes (Chapters 10 and 14) and other postretirement benefits (Chapter 17).

Summary of Time Value of Money Concepts

Illustration 5–22 summarizes the time value of money concepts discussed in this chapter.

Illustration 5–22

Summary of Time Value of Money Concepts

Concept	Summary	Formula	Table
Future value (FV) of $1	The amount of money that a dollar will grow to at some point in the future.	$FV = \$1(1 + i)^n$	1
Present value (PV) of $1	The amount of money today that is equivalent to a given amount to be received or paid in the future.	$PV = \dfrac{\$1}{(1 + i)^n}$	2
Future value of an ordinary annuity (FVA) of $1	The future value of a series of equal-sized cash flows with the first payment taking place at the end of the first compounding period.	$FVA = \dfrac{(1 + i)^n - 1}{i}$	3

(continued)

(concluded)

Concept	Summary	Formula	Table
Present value of an ordinary annuity (PVA) of $1	The present value of a series of equal-sized cash flows with the first payment taking place at the end of the first compounding period.	$PVA = \dfrac{1 - \dfrac{1}{(1 + i)^n}}{i}$	4
Future value of an annuity due (FVAD) of $1	The future value of a series of equal-sized cash flows with the first payment taking place at the beginning of the annuity period.	$FVAD = \left[\dfrac{(1 + i)^n - 1}{i}\right] \times (1 + i)$	5
Present value of an annuity due (PVAD) of $1	The present value of a series of equal-sized cash flows with the first payment taking place at the beginning of the annuity period.	$PVAD = \left[\dfrac{1 - \dfrac{1}{(1 + i)^n}}{i}\right] \times (1 + i)$	6

Financial Reporting Case Solution

1. **Why was Mavis to receive $336 million rather than the $758.7 million lottery prize?** *(p 251)*
   Mavis chose to receive her lottery winnings in one lump-sum payment immediately rather than in 30 installment payments. The state calculates the present value of the payments, withholds the necessary federal and state income tax, and pays Mavis the remainder.

©Gabriel Petrescu/Shutterstock

2. **What interest (discount) rate did the state of Massachusetts use to calculate the $336 million lump-sum payment** *(p. 256)* Assuming equal annual installment payments beginning immediately, the amount of the payments is determined by dividing $758.7 million by 30 periods:

$758.7 million ÷ 30 =	$25,290,000
Less: 30% income tax	(7,587,000)
Net-of-tax payment	$17,703,000

   Because the first payment is made immediately, this is an annuity due situation. We must find the interest rate that provides a present value of $336 million. $336,000,000 ÷ $17,703,000 is 18.98, the present value factor that equates the payments and their present value. Searching for that factor in row 30 of Table 6, we find the factor closest to 18.98 in the 3.5% column. So, the discount rate used by the state was approximately 3.5%.

3. **What are some of the accounting applications that incorporate the time value of money into valuation?** *(p. 259)* Accounting applications that incorporate the time value of money techniques into valuation include the valuation of long-term notes receivable and various long-term liabilities that include bonds, notes, leases, pension obligations, and other postretirement benefits. We study these in detail in later chapters. ●

The Bottom Line

● **LO5–1** Compound interest includes interest not only on the initial investment but also on the accumulated interest in previous periods. *(p. 240)*

● **LO5–2** The future value of a single amount is the amount of money that a dollar will grow to at some point in the future. It is computed by *multiplying* the single amount by $(1 + i)^n$, where i is the interest rate and n the number of compounding periods. The Future Value of $1 table allows for the calculation of future value for any single amount by providing the factors for various combinations of i and n. (p. 241)

● LO5–3   The present value of a single amount is the amount of money today that is equivalent to a given amount to be received or paid in the future. It is computed by *dividing* the future amount by $(1 + i)^n$. The Present Value of $1 table simplifies the calculation of the present value of any future amount. (p. 242)

● LO5–4   There are four variables in the process of adjusting single cash flow amounts for the time value of money: present value (PV), future value (FV), i and n. If we know any three of these, the fourth can be computed easily. (p. 243)

● LO5–5   We value most notes receivable and notes payable at the present value of future cash flows they call for, reflecting an appropriate time value of money. (p. 246)

● LO5–6   An annuity is a series of equal-sized cash flows occurring over equal intervals of time. An ordinary annuity exists when the cash flows occur at the end of each period. An annuity due exists when the cash flows occur at the beginning of each period. (p. 248)

● LO5–7   The future value of an ordinary annuity (FVA) is the future value of a series of equal-sized cash flows with the first payment taking place at the end of the first compounding period. The last payment will not earn any interest since it is made at the end of the annuity period. The future value of an annuity due (FVAD) is the future value of a series of equal-sized cash flows with the first payment taking place at the beginning of the annuity period (the beginning of the first compounding period). (p. 248)

● LO5–8   The present value of an ordinary annuity (PVA) is the present value of a series of equal-sized cash flows with the first payment taking place at the end of the first compounding period. The present value of an annuity due (PVAD) is the present value of a series of equal-sized cash flows with the first payment taking place at the beginning of the annuity period. The present value of a deferred annuity is the present value of a series of equal-sized cash flows with the first payment taking place more than one time period after the date of the agreement. (p. 250)

● LO5–9   In present value problems involving annuities, there are four variables: PVA or PVAD, the annuity amount, the number of compounding periods (n) and the interest rate (i). If you know any three of these, you can determine the fourth. (p. 255)

● LO5–10   Most accounting applications of the time value of money involve the present values of annuities. The initial valuation of long-term bonds is determined by calculating the present value of the periodic stated interest payments and the present value of the lump-sum payment made at maturity. Certain leases require the lessee to compute the present value of future lease payments to value the leased asset and corresponding lease obligation. Similarly, installment notes sometimes require us to calculate the present value of installment payments as the amount at which to record the note. Also, pension plans require the payment of deferred annuities to retirees. (p. 259) ●

Questions For Review of Key Topics

Q 5–1   Define interest.

Q 5–2   Explain compound interest.

Q 5–3   What would cause the annual interest rate to be different from the annual effective rate or yield?

Q 5–4   Identify the three items of information necessary to calculate the future value of a single amount.

Q 5–5   Define the present value of a single amount.

Q 5–6   Explain the difference between monetary and nonmonetary assets and liabilities.

Q 5–7   What is an annuity?

Q 5–8   Explain the difference between an ordinary annuity and an annuity due.

Q 5–9   Explain the relationship between Table 2, Present Value of $1, and Table 4, Present Value of an Ordinary Annuity of $1.

Q 5–10 Prepare a time diagram for the present value of a four-year ordinary annuity of $200. Assume an interest rate of 10% per year.

Q 5–11 Prepare a time diagram for the present value of a four-year annuity due of $200. Assume an interest rate of 10% per year.

Q 5–12   What is a deferred annuity?

Q 5–13   Assume that you borrowed $500 from a friend and promised to repay the loan in five equal annual installments beginning one year from today. Your friend wants to be reimbursed for the time value of money at an 8% annual rate. Explain how you would compute the required annual payment.

Q 5–14   Compute the required annual payment in Question 5–13.

Q 5–15   Explain how the time value of money concept is incorporated into the valuation of certain leases.

Brief Exercises

BE 5–1
Simple versus compound interest
● LO5–1

Fran Smith has two investment opportunities. The interest rate for both investments is 8%. Interest on the first investment will compound annually while interest on the second will compound quarterly. Which investment opportunity should Fran choose? Why?

BE 5–2
Future value; single amount
● LO5–2

Bill O'Brien would like to take his wife, Mary, on a trip three years from now to Europe to celebrate their 40th anniversary. He has just received a $20,000 inheritance from an uncle and intends to invest it for the trip. Bill estimates the trip will cost $23,500 and he believes he can earn 5% interest, compounded annually, on his investment. Will he be able to pay for the trip with the accumulated investment amount?

BE 5–3
Future value; solving for unknown; single amount
● LO5–4

Refer to the situation described in BE 5–2. Assume that the trip will cost $26,600. What interest rate, compounded annually, must Bill earn to accumulate enough to pay for the trip?

BE 5–4
Present value; single amount
● LO5–3

John has an investment opportunity that promises to pay him $16,000 in four years. He could earn a 6% annual return investing his money elsewhere. What is the maximum amount he would be willing to invest in this opportunity?

BE 5–5
Present value; solving for unknown; single amount
● LO5–4

Refer to the situation described in BE 5–4. Suppose the opportunity requires John to invest $13,200 today. What is the interest rate John would earn on this investment?

BE 5–6
Future value; ordinary annuity
● LO5–7

Leslie McCormack is in the spring quarter of her freshman year of college. She and her friends already are planning a trip to Europe after graduation in a little over three years. Leslie would like to contribute to a savings account over the next three years in order to accumulate enough money to take the trip. Assuming an interest rate of 4%, compounded quarterly, how much will she accumulate in three years by depositing $500 at the *end* of each of the next 12 quarters, beginning three months from now?

BE 5–7
Future value; annuity due
● LO5–7

Refer to the situation described in BE 5–6. How much will Leslie accumulate in three years by depositing $500 at the *beginning* of each of the next 12 quarters?

BE 5–8
Present value; ordinary annuity; installment notes
● LO5–8, LO5–10

Canliss Mining Company borrowed money from a local bank. The note the company signed requires five annual installment payments of $10,000 beginning one year from today. The interest rate on the note is 7%. What amount did Canliss borrow?

BE 5–9
Present value; annuity due; installment notes
● LO5–8, LO5–10

Refer to the situation described in BE 5–8. What amount did Canliss borrow assuming that the first $10,000 payment was due immediately?

BE 5–10
Deferred annuity
● LO5–8, LO5–10

Refer to the situation described in BE 5–8. What amount did Canliss borrow assuming that the first of the five annual $10,000 payments was not due for three years?

BE 5–11
Solve for unknown; annuity
● LO5–9

Kingsley Toyota borrowed $100,000 from a local bank. The loan requires Kingsley to pay 10 equal annual installments beginning one year from today. Assuming an interest rate of 8%, what is the amount of each annual installment payment?

BE 5–12
Price of a bond
● LO5–10

On December 31, 2021, Interlink Communications issued 6% stated rate bonds with a face amount of $100 million. The bonds mature on December 31, 2051. Interest is payable annually on each December 31, beginning in 2022. Determine the price of the bonds on December 31, 2021, assuming that the market rate of interest for similar bonds was 7%.

BE 5–13
Lease payment
● LO5–10

On September 30, 2021, Ferguson Imports leased a warehouse. Terms of the lease require Ferguson to make 10 annual lease payments of $55,000 with the first payment due immediately. Accounting standards require the company to record a lease liability when recording this type of lease. Assuming an 8% interest rate, at what amount should Ferguson record the lease liability on September 30, 2021, before the first payment is made?

Exercises

E 5–1
Future value; single amount
● LO5–2

Determine the future value of the following single amounts:

	Invested Amount	Interest Rate	No. of Periods
1.	$15,000	6%	12
2.	20,000	8	10
3.	30,000	12	20
4.	50,000	4	12

E 5–2
Future value; single amounts
● LO5–2

Determine the future value of $10,000 under each of the following sets of assumptions:

	Annual Rate	Period Invested	Interest Compounded
1.	10%	10 years	Semiannually
2.	12	5 years	Quarterly
3.	24	30 months	Monthly

E 5–3
Present value; single amounts
● LO5–3

Determine the present value of the following single amounts:

	Future Amount	Interest Rate	No. of Periods
1.	$20,000	7%	10
2.	14,000	8	12
3.	25,000	12	20
4.	40,000	10	8

E 5–4
Present value; multiple, unequal amounts
● LO5–3

Determine the combined present value as of December 31, 2021, of the following four payments to be received at the end of each of the designated years, assuming an annual interest rate of 8%.

Payment	Year Received
$5,000	2022
6,000	2023
8,000	2025
9,000	2027

E 5–5
Solving for unknowns; single amounts
● LO5–4

For each of the following situations involving single amounts, solve for the unknown (?). Assume that interest is compounded annually. (i = interest rate, and n = number of years)

	Present Value	Future Value	i	n
1.	?	$ 40,000	10%	5
2.	$36,289	65,000	?	10
3.	15,884	40,000	8	?
4.	46,651	100,000	?	8
5.	15,376	?	7	20

E 5–6
Noninterest-bearing note; single payment
● LO5–5

The Field Detergent Company sold merchandise to the Abel Company on June 30, 2021. Payment was made in the form of a noninterest-bearing note requiring Abel to pay $85,000 on June 30, 2023. Assume that a 10% interest rate properly reflects the time value of money in this situation.

Required:
Calculate the amount at which Field should record the note receivable and corresponding sales revenue on June 30, 2021.

E 5–7
Concepts; terminology
● LO5–1 through LO5–3, LO5–6

Listed below are several terms and phrases associated with concepts discussed in the chapter. Pair each item from List A with the item from List B (by letter) that is most appropriately associated with it.

List A	List B
_____ 1. Interest	a. First cash flow occurs one period after agreement begins
_____ 2. Monetary asset	b. The rate at which money will actually grow during a year
_____ 3. Compound interest	c. First cash flow occurs on the first day of the agreement
_____ 4. Simple interest	d. The amount of money that a dollar will grow to
_____ 5. Annuity	e. Amount of money paid/received in excess of amount borrowed/lent
_____ 6. Present value of a single amount	f. Obligation to pay a sum of cash, the amount of which is fixed
_____ 7. Annuity due	g. Money can be invested today and grow to a larger amount
_____ 8. Future value of a single amount	h. No fixed dollar amount attached
_____ 9. Ordinary annuity	i. Computed by multiplying an invested amount by the interest rate
_____ 10. Effective rate or yield	j. Interest calculated on invested amount plus accumulated interest
_____ 11. Nonmonetary asset	k. A series of equal-sized cash flows
_____ 12. Time value of money	l. Amount of money required today that is equivalent to a given future amount
_____ 13. Monetary liability	m. Claim to receive a fixed amount of money

E 5–8
Future value; compound interest
● LO5–7

Wiseman Video plans to make four annual deposits of $2,000 each to a special building fund. The fund's assets will be invested in mortgage instruments expected to pay interest at 12% on the fund's balance. Using the appropriate time-value of money table, determine how much will be accumulated in the fund on December 31, 2024, under each of the following situations:

1. The first $2,000 deposit is made on December 31, 2021, and interest is compounded annually.
2. The first $2,000 deposit is made on December 31, 2020, and interest is compounded annually.
3. The first $2,000 deposit is made on December 31, 2020, and interest is compounded quarterly.
4. The first $2,000 deposit is made on December 31, 2020, interest is compounded annually, *and* interest earned is withdrawn at the end of each year.

E 5–9
Present value; annuities
● LO5–8

Using the appropriate present value table and assuming a 12% annual interest rate, determine the present value on December 31, 2021, of a five-period annual annuity of $5,000 under each of the following situations:

1. The first payment is received on December 31, 2022, and interest is compounded annually.
2. The first payment is received on December 31, 2021, and interest is compounded annually.
3. The first payment is received on December 31, 2022, and interest is compounded quarterly.

E 5–10
Future and present value
● LO5–3, LO5–7, LO5–8

Answer each of the following independent questions.

1. Alex Meir recently won a lottery and has the option of receiving one of the following three prizes: (1) $64,000 cash immediately, (2) $20,000 cash immediately and a six-period annuity of $8,000 beginning one year from today, or (3) a six-period annuity of $13,000 beginning one year from today. Assuming an interest rate of 6%, which option should Alex choose?
2. The Weimer Corporation wants to accumulate a sum of money to repay certain debts due on December 31, 2030. Weimer will make annual deposits of $100,000 into a special bank account at the end of each of 10 years beginning December 31, 2021. Assuming that the bank account pays 7% interest compounded annually, what will be the fund balance after the last payment is made on December 31, 2030?

E 5–11
Deferred annuities
● LO5–8

Lincoln Company purchased merchandise from Grandville Corp. on September 30, 2021. Payment was made in the form of a noninterest-bearing note requiring Lincoln to make six annual payments of $5,000 on each September 30, beginning on September 30, 2024.

Required:
Calculate the amount at which Lincoln should record the note payable and corresponding purchases on September 30, 2021, assuming that an interest rate of 10% properly reflects the time value of money in this situation.

E 5–12
Future value;
solving for
annuities and
single amount
● LO5–4, LO5–9

John Rider wants to accumulate $100,000 to be used for his daughter's college education. He would like to have the amount available on December 31, 2026. Assume that the funds will accumulate in a certificate of deposit paying 8% interest compounded annually.

Required:
Answer each of the following independent questions.

1. If John were to deposit a single amount, how much would he have to invest on December 31, 2021?
2. If John were to make five equal deposits on each December 31, beginning on December 31, 2022, what is the required amount of each deposit?
3. If John were to make five equal deposits on each December 31, beginning on December 31, 2021, what is the required amount of each deposit?

E 5–13
Solving for
unknowns;
annuities
● LO5–9

For each of the following situations involving annuities, solve for the unknown (?). Assume that interest is compounded annually and that all annuity amounts are received at the *end* of each period. (*i* = interest rate, and *n* = number of years)

	Present Value	Annuity Amount	*i*	*n*
1.	?	$ 3,000	8%	5
2.	$242,980	75,000	?	4
3.	161,214	20,000	9	?
4.	500,000	80,518	?	8
5.	250,000	?	10	4

E 5–14
Solving for
unknown annuity
amount
● LO5–9

Sandy Kupchack just graduated from State University with a bachelor's degree in history. During her four years at the university, Sandy accumulated $12,000 in student loans. She asks for your help in determining the amount of the *quarterly* loan payment. She tells you that the loan must be paid back in five years and that the annual interest rate is 8%. Payments begin in three months.

Required:
Determine Sandy's quarterly loan payment.

E 5–15
Deferred
annuities; solving
for annuity
amount
● LO5–8, LO5–9

On April 1, 2021, John Vaughn purchased appliances from the Acme Appliance Company for $1,200. In order to increase sales, Acme allows customers to pay in installments and will defer any payments for six months. John will make 18 equal monthly payments, beginning October 1, 2021. The annual interest rate implicit in this agreement is 24%.

Required:
Calculate the monthly payment necessary for John to pay for his purchases.

E 5–16
Price of a bond
● LO5–9, LO5–10

On September 30, 2021, the San Fillipo Corporation issued 8% stated rate bonds with a face amount of $300 million. The bonds mature on September 30, 2041 (20 years). The market rate of interest for similar bonds was 10%. Interest is paid semiannually on March 31 and September 30.

Required:
Determine the price of the bonds on September 30, 2021.

E 5–17
Price of a bond;
interest expense
● LO5–9, LO5–10

On June 30, 2021, Singleton Computers issued 6% stated rate bonds with a face amount of $200 million. The bonds mature on June 30, 2036 (15 years). The market rate of interest for similar bond issues was 5% (2.5% semiannual rate). Interest is paid semiannually (3%) on June 30 and December 31, beginning on December 31, 2021.

Required:
1. Determine the price of the bonds on June 30, 2021.
2. Calculate the interest expense Singleton reports in 2021 for these bonds.

E 5–18
Solving for
unknown annuity
payment;
installment notes
● LO5–9, LO5–10

Don James purchased a new automobile for $20,000. Don made a cash down payment of $5,000 and agreed to pay the remaining balance in 30 monthly installments, beginning one month from the date of purchase. Financing is available at a 24% *annual* interest rate.

Required:
Calculate the amount of the required monthly payment.

E 5–19
Solving for
unknown interest
rate; installment
notes
● LO5–9, LO5–10

Lang Warehouses borrowed $100,000 from a bank and signed a note requiring 20 annual payments of $13,388 beginning one year from the date of the agreement.

Required:
Determine the interest rate implicit in this agreement.

E 5–20
Lease payments
● **LO5–9, LO5–10**

On June 30, 2021, Fly-By-Night Airlines leased a jumbo jet from Boeing Corporation. The terms of the lease require Fly-By-Night to make 20 annual payments of $400,000 on each June 30. Generally accepted accounting principles require this lease to be recorded as a liability for the present value of scheduled payments. Assume that a 7% interest rate properly reflects the time value of money in this situation.

Required:
1. At what amount should Fly-By-Night record the lease liability on June 30, 2021, assuming that the first payment will be made on June 30, 2022?
2. At what amount should Fly-By-Night record the lease liability on June 30, 2021, *before* any payments are made, assuming that the first payment will be made on June 30, 2021?

E 5–21
Lease payments; solve for unknown interest rate
● **LO5–9, LO5–10**

On March 31, 2021, Southwest Gas leased equipment from a supplier and agreed to pay $200,000 annually for 20 years beginning March 31, 2022. Generally accepted accounting principles require that a liability be recorded for this lease agreement for the present value of scheduled payments. Accordingly, at inception of the lease, Southwest recorded a $2,293,984 lease liability.

Required:
Determine the interest rate implicit in the lease agreement.

Problems

P 5–1
Analysis of alternatives
● **LO5–3, LO5–8**

Esquire Company needs to acquire a molding machine to be used in its manufacturing process. Two types of machines that would be appropriate are presently on the market. The company has determined the following:

Machine A could be purchased for $48,000. It will last 10 years with annual maintenance costs of $1,000 per year. After 10 years the machine can be sold for $5,000.

Machine B could be purchased for $40,000. It also will last 10 years and will require maintenance costs of $4,000 in year three, $5,000 in year six, and $6,000 in year eight. After 10 years, the machine will have no salvage value.

Required:
Determine which machine Esquire should purchase. Assume an interest rate of 8% properly reflects the time value of money in this situation and that maintenance costs are paid at the end of each year. Ignore income tax considerations.

P 5–2
Present and future value
● **LO5–7, LO5–8, LO5–10**

Johnstone Company is facing several decisions regarding investing and financing activities. Address each decision independently.
1. On June 30, 2021, the Johnstone Company purchased equipment from Genovese Corp. Johnstone agreed to pay Genovese $10,000 on the purchase date and the balance in five annual installments of $8,000 on each June 30 beginning June 30, 2022. Assuming that an interest rate of 10% properly reflects the time value of money in this situation, at what amount should Johnstone value the equipment?
2. Johnstone needs to accumulate sufficient funds to pay a $400,000 debt that comes due on December 31, 2026. The company will accumulate the funds by making five equal annual deposits to an account paying 6% interest compounded annually. Determine the required annual deposit if the first deposit is made on December 31, 2021.
3. On January 1, 2021, Johnstone leased an office building. Terms of the lease require Johnstone to make 20 annual lease payments of $120,000 beginning on January 1, 2021. A 10% interest rate is implicit in the lease agreement. At what amount should Johnstone record the lease liability on January 1, 2021, *before* any lease payments are made?

P 5–3
Analysis of alternatives
● **LO5–3, LO5–8**

Harding Company is in the process of purchasing several large pieces of equipment from Danning Machine Corporation. Several financing alternatives have been offered by Danning:
1. Pay $1,000,000 in cash immediately.
2. Pay $420,000 immediately and the remainder in 10 annual installments of $80,000, with the first installment due in one year.
3. Make 10 annual installments of $135,000 with the first payment due immediately.
4. Make one lump-sum payment of $1,500,000 five years from date of purchase.

Required:
Determine the best alternative for Harding, assuming that Harding can borrow funds at an 8% interest rate.

P 5–4
Investment
analysis; uneven
cash flows
● LO5–3, LO5–8

John Wiggins is considering the purchase of a small restaurant. The purchase price listed by the seller is $800,000. John has used past financial information to estimate that the net cash flows (cash inflows less cash outflows) generated by the restaurant would be as follows:

Years	Amount
1–6	$80,000
7	70,000
8	60,000
9	50,000
10	40,000

If purchased, the restaurant would be held for 10 years and then sold for an estimated $700,000.

Required:
Assuming that John desires a 10% rate of return on this investment, should the restaurant be purchased? (Assume that all cash flows occur at the end of the year.)

P 5–5
Investment
decision; varying
rates
● LO5–3, LO5–8

John and Sally Claussen are considering the purchase of a hardware store from John Duggan. The Claussens anticipate that the store will generate cash flows of $70,000 per year for 20 years. At the end of 20 years, they intend to sell the store for an estimated $400,000. The Claussens will finance the investment with a variable rate mortgage. Interest rates will increase twice during the 20-year life of the mortgage. Accordingly, the Claussens' desired rate of return on this investment varies as follows:

Years 1–5	8%
Years 6–10	10%
Years 11–20	12%

Required:
What is the maximum amount the Claussens should pay John Duggan for the hardware store? (Assume that all cash flows occur at the end of the year.)

P 5–6
Solving for
unknowns
● LO5–3. LO5–9

The following situations should be considered independently.

1. John Jamison wants to accumulate $60,000 for a down payment on a small business. He will invest $30,000 today in a bank account paying 8% interest compounded annually. Approximately how long will it take John to reach his goal?

2. The Jasmine Tea Company purchased merchandise from a supplier for $28,700. Payment was a noninterest-bearing note requiring Jasmine to make five annual payments of $7,000 beginning one year from the date of purchase. What is the interest rate implicit in this agreement?

3. Sam Robinson borrowed $10,000 from a friend and promised to pay the loan in 10 equal annual installments beginning one year from the date of the loan. Sam's friend would like to be reimbursed for the time value of money at a 9% annual rate. What is the annual payment Sam must make to pay back his friend?

P 5–7
Deferred
annuities
● LO5–8

On January 1, 2021, the Montgomery Company agreed to purchase a building by making six payments. The first three are to be $25,000 each, and will be paid on December 31, 2021, 2022, and 2023. The last three are to be $40,000 each and will be paid on December 31, 2024, 2025, and 2026. Montgomery borrowed other money at a 10% annual rate.

Required:
1. At what amount should Montgomery record the note payable and corresponding cost of the building on January 1, 2021?
2. How much interest expense on this note will Montgomery recognize in 2021?

P 5–8
Deferred
annuities
● LO5–8

John Roberts is 55 years old and has been asked to accept early retirement from his company. The company has offered John three alternative compensation packages to induce John to retire.
1. $180,000 cash payment to be paid immediately
2. A 20-year annuity of $16,000 beginning immediately
3. A 10-year annuity of $50,000 beginning at age 65

Required:
Which alternative should John choose assuming that he is able to invest funds at a 7% rate?

P 5–9
Noninterest-bearing note; annuity and lump-sum payment
● LO5–3, LO5–8

On January 1, 2021, The Barrett Company purchased merchandise from a supplier. Payment was a noninterest-bearing note requiring five annual payments of $20,000 on each December 31 beginning on December 31, 2021, and a lump-sum payment of $100,000 on December 31, 2025. A 10% interest rate properly reflects the time value of money in this situation.

Required:
Calculate the amount at which Barrett should record the note payable and corresponding merchandise purchased on January 1, 2021.

P 5–10
Solving for unknowns; installment notes
● LO5–9

Lowlife Company defaulted on a $250,000 loan that was due on December 31, 2021. The bank has agreed to allow Lowlife to repay the $250,000 by making a series of equal annual payments beginning on December 31, 2022.

Required:
Calculate the amount at which Barrett should record the note payable and corresponding merchandise purchased on January 1, 2021.
1. Calculate the required annual payment if the bank's interest rate is 10% and four payments are to be made.
2. Calculate the required annual payment if the bank's interest rate is 8% and five payments are to be made.
3. If the bank's interest rate is 10%, how many annual payments of $51,351 would be required to repay the debt?
4. If three payments of $104,087 are to be made, what interest rate is the bank charging Lowlife?

P 5–11
Solving for unknown lease payment
● LO5–9, LO5–10

Benning Manufacturing Company is negotiating with a customer for the lease of a large machine manufactured by Benning. The machine has a cash price of $800,000. Benning wants to be reimbursed for financing the machine at an 8% annual interest rate.

Required:
1. Determine the required lease payment if the lease agreement calls for 10 equal annual payments beginning immediately.
2. Determine the required lease payment if the first of 10 annual payments will be made one year from the date of the agreement.
3. Determine the required lease payment if the first of 10 annual payments will be made immediately and Benning will be able to sell the machine to another customer for $50,000 at the end of the 10-year lease.

P 5–12
Solving for unknown lease payment; compounding periods of varying length
● LO5–9, LO5–10

[This is a variation of P 5–11 focusing on compounding periods of varying length.]
    Benning Manufacturing Company is negotiating with a customer for the lease of a large machine manufactured by Benning. The machine has a cash price of $800,000. Benning wants to be reimbursed for financing the machine at a 12% annual interest rate over the five-year lease term.

Required:
1. Determine the required lease payment if the lease agreement calls for 10 equal semiannual payments beginning six months from the date of the agreement.
2. Determine the required lease payment if the lease agreement calls for 20 equal quarterly payments beginning immediately.
3. Determine the required lease payment if the lease agreement calls for 60 equal monthly payments beginning one month from the date of the agreement. The present value of an ordinary annuity factor for $n = 60$ and $i = 1\%$ is 44.9550.

P 5–13
Lease vs. buy alternatives
● LO5–3, LO5–8, LO5–10

Kiddy Toy Corporation needs to acquire the use of a machine to be used in its manufacturing process. The machine needed is manufactured by Lollie Corp. The machine can be used for 10 years and then sold for $10,000 at the end of its useful life. Lollie has presented Kiddy with the following options:
1. *Buy machine.* The machine could be purchased for $160,000 in cash. All insurance costs, which approximate $5,000 per year, would be paid by Kiddy.
2. *Lease machine.* The machine could be leased for a 10-year period for an annual lease payment of $25,000 with the first payment due immediately. All insurance costs will be paid for by the Lollie Corp. and the machine will revert back to Lollie at the end of the 10-year period.

Required:
Assuming that a 12% interest rate properly reflects the time value of money in this situation and that all maintenance and insurance costs are paid at the end of each year, determine which option Kiddy should choose. Ignore income tax considerations.

P 5–14
Deferred annuities;
pension obligation
● LO5–8, LO5–10

Three employees of the Horizon Distributing Company will receive annual pension payments from the company when they retire. The employees will receive their annual payments for as long as they live. Life expectancy for each employee is 15 years beyond retirement. Their names, the amount of their annual pension payments, and the date they will receive their first payment are shown below:

Employee	Annual Payment	Date of First Payment
Tinkers	$20,000	12/31/24
Evers	25,000	12/31/25
Chance	30,000	12/31/26

Required:

1. Compute the present value of the pension obligation to these three employees as of December 31, 2021. Assume an 11% interest rate.

2. The company wants to have enough cash invested at December 31, 2024, to provide for all three employees. To accumulate enough cash, they will make three equal annual contributions to a fund that will earn 11% interest compounded annually. The first contribution will be made on December 31, 2021. Compute the amount of this required annual contribution.

P 5–15
Bonds and leases;
deferred annuities
● LO5–3, LO5–8,
LO5–10

On the last day of its fiscal year ending December 31, 2021, the Sedgwick & Reams (S&R) Glass Company completed two financing arrangements. The funds provided by these initiatives will allow the company to expand its operations.

1. S&R issued 8% stated rate bonds with a face amount of $100 million. The bonds mature on December 31, 2041 (20 years). The market rate of interest for similar bond issues was 9% (4.5% semiannual rate). Interest is paid semiannually (4%) on June 30 and December 31, beginning on June 30, 2022.

2. The company leased two manufacturing facilities. Lease A requires 20 annual lease payments of $200,000 beginning on January 1, 2022. Lease B also is for 20 years, beginning January 1, 2022. Terms of the lease require 17 annual lease payments of $220,000 beginning on January 1, 2025. Generally accepted accounting principles require both leases to be recorded as liabilities for the present value of the scheduled payments. Assume that a 10% interest rate properly reflects the time value of money for the lease obligations.

Required:
What amounts will appear in S&R's December 31, 2021, balance sheet for the bonds and for the leases?

Decision Makers' Perspective

©ImageGap/Getty Images

Apply your critical-thinking ability to the knowledge you've gained. These cases will provide you an opportunity to develop your research, analysis, judgment, and communication skills. You also will work with other students, integrate what you've learned, apply it in real-world situations, and consider its global and ethical ramifications. This practice will broaden your knowledge and further develop your decision-making abilities.

Ethics Case 5–1
Rate of return
● LO5–1

The Damon Investment Company manages a mutual fund composed mostly of speculative stocks. You recently saw an ad claiming that investments in the funds have been earning a rate of return of 21%. This rate seemed quite high so you called a friend who works for one of Damon's competitors. The friend told you that the 21% return figure was determined by dividing the two-year appreciation on investments in the fund by the average investment. In other words, $100 invested in the fund two years ago would have grown to $121 ($21 ÷ $100 = 21%).

Required:
Discuss the ethics of the 21% return claim made by the Damon Investment Company.

Analysis Case 5–2
Bonus alternatives;
present value analysis
● LO5–3, LO5–8

Sally Hamilton has performed well as the chief financial officer of the Maxtech Computer Company and has earned a bonus. She has a choice among the following three bonus plans:

1. A $50,000 cash bonus paid now.

2. A $10,000 annual cash bonus to be paid each year over the next six years, with the first $10,000 paid now.

3. A three-year $22,000 annual cash bonus with the first payment due three years from now.

Required:
Evaluate the three alternative bonus plans. Sally can earn a 6% annual return on her investments.
1. What is the present value of the first alternative?
2. What is the present value of the second alternative?
3. What is the present value of the third alternative?

Communication Case 5–3
Present value of annuities
● LO5–8

Harvey Alexander, an all-league professional football player, has just declared free agency. Two teams, the San Francisco 49ers and the Dallas Cowboys, have made Harvey the following offers to obtain his services:

> 49ers: $1 million signing bonus payable immediately and an annual salary of $1.5 million for the five-year term of the contract.
>
> Cowboys: $2.5 million signing bonus payable immediately and an annual salary of $1 million for the five-year term of the contract.

With both contracts, the annual salary will be paid in one lump sum at the end of the football season.

Required:
You have been hired as a consultant to Harvey's agent, Phil Marks, to evaluate the two contracts. Write a short letter to Phil with your recommendation including the method you used to reach your conclusion. Assume that Harvey has no preference between the two teams and that the decision will be based entirely on monetary considerations. Also assume that Harvey can invest his money and earn an 8% annual return.

Communication Case 5–4
Present value of an annuity
● LO5–8

On a rainy afternoon two years ago, John Smiley left work early to attend a family birthday party. Eleven minutes later, a careening truck slammed into his SUV on the freeway causing John to spend two months in a coma. Now he can't hold a job or make everyday decisions and is in need of constant care. Last week, the 40-year-old Smiley won an out-of-court settlement from the truck driver's company. He was awarded payment for all medical costs and attorney fees, plus a lump-sum settlement of $2,330,716. At the time of the accident, John was president of his family's business and earned approximately $200,000 per year. He had anticipated working 25 more years before retirement.[8]

John's sister, Sara, an acquaintance of yours from college, has asked you to explain to her how the attorneys came up with the settlement amount. "They said it was based on his lost future income and a 7% rate of some kind," she explained. "But it was all 'legal-speak' to me."

Required:
Construct the text of an e-mail to Sara describing how the amount of the lump-sum settlement was determined. Include a calculation that might help Sara and John understand.

Judgment Case 5–5
Replacement decision
● LO5–3, LO5–8

Hughes Corporation is considering replacing a machine used in the manufacturing process with a new, more efficient model. The purchase price of the new machine is $150,000 and the old machine can be sold for $100,000. Output for the two machines is identical; they will both be used to produce the same amount of product for five years. However, the annual operating costs of the old machine are $18,000 compared to $10,000 for the new machine. Also, the new machine has a salvage value of $25,000, but the old machine will be worthless at the end of the five years.

You are deciding whether the company should sell the old machine and purchase the new model. You have determined that an 8% rate properly reflects the time value of money in this situation and that all operating costs are paid at the end of the year. For this initial comparison you ignore the effect of the decision on income taxes.

Required:
1. What is the incremental cash outflow required to acquire the new machine?
2. What is the present value of the benefits of acquiring the new machine?

Real World Case 5–6
Zero-coupon bonds; Johnson & Johnson
● LO5–3, LO5–10

Real World Financials

Johnson & Johnson is one of the world's largest manufacturers of health care products. The company's July 2, 2017, financial statements included the following information in the long-term debt disclosure note:

	($ in millions) July 2, 2017
Zero-coupon convertible subordinated debentures, due 2020	$69

The bonds were issued at the beginning of 2000. The disclosure note stated that the effective interest rate for these bonds is 3% annually. Some of the original convertible bonds have been converted into Johnson & Johnson shares of stock. The $69 million is the present value of the bonds not converted and thus reported in the financial statements. Each individual bond has a maturity value (face amount) of $1,000. The maturity value indicates the amount that Johnson & Johnson will pay bondholders at the beginning of 2020. Zero-coupon bonds pay no cash interest during the term to maturity. The company is "accreting" (gradually increasing) the issue price to maturity value using the bonds' effective interest rate computed on a semiannual basis.

---

[8]This case is based on actual events.

Required:

1. Determine to the nearest million dollars the maturity value of the zero-coupon bonds that Johnson & Johnson will pay bondholders at the beginning of 2020.

2. Determine to the nearest dollar the issue price at the beginning of 2000 of a single, $1,000 maturity-value bond.

Real World Case 5–7
Leases; Southwest Airlines
● LO5–3, LO5–10

Real World Financials

Southwest Airlines provides scheduled air transportation services in the United States. Like many airlines, Southwest leases many of its planes from Boeing Company. In its long-term debt disclosure note included in the financial statements for the year ended December 31, 2017, the company listed $885 million in lease obligations. The existing leases had an approximate ten-year remaining life and future lease payments average approximately $100 million per year.

Required:

1. Determine (to the nearest one-half percent) the effective interest rate the company used to determine the lease liability assuming that lease payments are made at the end of each fiscal year.

2. Repeat requirement 1 assuming that lease payments are made at the beginning of each fiscal year.

Continuing Cases

Target Case
● LO5–3, LO5–8
LO5–10

Target Corporation prepares its financial statements according to U.S. GAAP. Target's financial statements and disclosure notes for the year ended February 3, 2018, are available in Connect. This material is also available under the Investor Relations link at the company's website (www.target.com). Target leases most of its facilities.

Required:

1. Refer to disclosure note 22 following Target's financial statements. What is the amount reported for "capital" leases (shown as the present value of minimum lease payments)? What is the total of those lease payments? What accounts for the difference between the two amounts?

2. What is the total of the operating lease payments?

3. New lease accounting guidance (discussed in Chapter 15) will require companies to report a liability for operating leases at present value as well as for capital leases (now called finance leases). If Target had used the new lease accounting guidance in its fiscal 2017 financial statements, what would be the amount reported as a liability for operating leases? *Hint:* Assume the payments "after 2022" are to be paid evenly over a 16 years period and all payments are at the end of years indicated. Target indicates elsewhere in its financial statements that 6% is an appropriate discount rate for its leases.

Air France–KLM Case
● LO5–10

 IFRS

Air France–KLM (AF), a Franco-Dutch company, prepares its financial statements according to International Financial Reporting Standards. AF's financial statements and disclosure notes for the year ended December 31, 2017, are available in Connect. This material is also available under the Finance link at the company's website (www.airfranceklm.com.) The presentation of financial statements often differs between U.S. GAAP and IFRS, particularly with respect to the balance sheet.

Using IFRS, companies discount their pension obligations using an interest rate approximating the average interest rate on high-quality corporate bonds. U.S. GAAP allows much more flexibility in the choice of a discount rate. By both sets of standards, the rate used is reported in the disclosure note related to pensions.

Required:

Refer to AF's Note 30.2 "Description of the actuarial assumptions and related sensitivities."

1. What are the average discount rates used to measure AF's (a) 10–15 year and (b) 15 year and more pension obligations in the "euro" geographic zone in 2017?

2. If the rate used had been 1% (100 basis points) higher, what change would have occurred in the pension obligation in 2017? What if the rate had been 1% lower?

CPA Exam Questions and Simulations

 ROGER CPA Review

Sample CPA Exam questions from Roger CPA Review are available in Connect as support for the topics in this chapter. These multiple-choice questions and task-based simulations include expert-written explanations and solutions, and provide a starting point for students to become familiar with the content and functionality of the actual CPA Exam.

CHAPTER

7

Cash and Receivables

OVERVIEW ——————————•— We begin our study of assets by looking at cash and receivables—the two assets typically listed first in a balance sheet. For cash, the key issues are internal control and classification in the balance sheet. For receivables, the key issues are valuation and the related income statement effects of transactions involving accounts receivable and notes receivable.

LEARNING ——————————•— **After studying this chapter, you should be able to:**
OBJECTIVES

● **LO7–1**   Define what is meant by internal control and describe some key elements of an internal control system for cash receipts and disbursements. (p. 340)

● **LO7–2**   Explain the possible restrictions on cash and their implications for classification in the balance sheet. (p. 341)

● **LO7–3**   Distinguish between the gross and net methods of accounting for cash discounts. (p. 344)

● **LO7–4**   Describe the accounting treatment for merchandise returns. (p. 346)

● **LO7–5**   Describe the accounting treatment of anticipated uncollectible accounts receivable. (p. 350)

● **LO7–6**   Describe how to estimate the allowance for uncollectible accounts and introduce the CECL model. (p. 352)

● **LO7–7**   Describe the accounting treatment of notes receivable. (p. 356)

● **LO7–8**   Differentiate between the use of receivables in financing arrangements accounted for as a secured borrowing and those accounted for as a sale. (p. 362)

● **LO7–9**   Describe the variables that influence a company's investment in receivables and calculate the key ratios used by analysts to monitor that investment. (p. 370)

● **LO7–10** Discuss the primary differences between U.S. GAAP and IFRS with respect to cash and receivables. (pp. 342, 361, and 369)

©PhotosIndia.com/Glow Images

FINANCIAL REPORTING CASE

Bad Debt Trouble

Your roommate, Karen Buckley, was searching for some information about her future employer, Community Health Systems. Karen, a nursing major, noticed an article online titled "CHS Missed Big in Q4." "This doesn't look good," Karen said. "This article says my new employer's provision for bad debts is $200 million. Does that mean those patients haven't paid? What is CHS doing for cash—I want my paycheck to clear!" You look over the article and start to explain. "First of all, the term *provision* just means expense. The company uses what is called the allowance method to account for bad debts. It looks like CHS recorded more in expense and increased the allowance for uncollectible accounts. That doesn't necessarily mean they have a cash flow problem." Karen was not happy with your answer. "So, it isn't that the patients haven't paid, it's that they aren't going to pay? How does CHS know what they are going to do? And here is another article saying that CHS is securitizing its receivables to get more cash. Does that mean they are making the receivables more secure?" "Okay," you offer, "let's start at the beginning."

By the time you finish this chapter, you should be able to respond appropriately to the questions posed in this case. Compare your response to the solution provided at the end of the chapter.

QUESTIONS

1. Explain the allowance method of accounting for bad debts. (*p. 350*)

2. What approaches might CHS have used to arrive at the $200 million bad debt provision? (*p. 351*)

3. Are there any alternatives to the allowance method? (*p. 354*)

4. What does it mean for CHS to securitize its receivables? (*p. 364*)

In the earlier chapters of this text, we studied the underlying measurement and reporting concepts for the basic financial statements presented to external decision makers. Now we turn our attention to the elements of those financial statements. Specifically, we further explore the elements of the balance sheet, and also consider the income statement effects of transactions involving these elements. We first address assets, then liabilities, and finally shareholders' equity. This chapter focuses on the current assets cash and cash equivalents and receivables.

Cash and Cash Equivalents

PART A

Cash includes currency and coins, balances in checking accounts, and items acceptable for deposit in these accounts, such as checks and money orders received from customers. These forms of cash represent amounts readily available to pay off debt or to use in operations, without any legal or contractual restriction.

Managers typically invest temporarily idle cash to earn interest on those funds rather than keep an unnecessarily large checking account. These amounts are essentially equivalent to cash because they can quickly become available for use as cash. So, short-term, highly liquid investments that can be readily converted to cash with little risk of loss are viewed as cash equivalents. For financial reporting, we make no distinction between cash in the form of currency or bank account balances and amounts held in cash-equivalent investments.

A company's policy concerning which short-term, highly liquid investments it classifies as *cash equivalents* should be described in a disclosure note.

Cash equivalents include money market funds, treasury bills, and commercial paper. To be classified as cash equivalents, these investments must have a maturity date no longer than three months *from the date of purchase.* Companies are permitted flexibility in designating cash equivalents and must establish individual policies regarding which short-term, highly liquid investments are classified as cash equivalents. A company's policy should be consistent with the usual motivation for acquiring these investments. The policy should be disclosed in the notes to the financial statements.

Illustration 7–1 shows a note from the 2017 annual report of **Walgreens Boots Alliance, Inc.**, which operates the second largest drugstore chain in the United States.

Illustration 7–1

Disclosure of Cash Equivalents—Walgreens Boots Alliance, Inc.

Real World Financials

> **Note 2: Summary of Major Accounting Policies (in part) Cash and Cash Equivalents**
>
> Cash and cash equivalents include cash on hand and all highly liquid investments with an original maturity of three months or less. Credit and debit card receivables from banks, which generally settle within two to seven business days, of $98 million and $114 million were included in cash and cash equivalents at August 31, 2017 and 2016, respectively.
>
> Source: Walgreens Boots Alliance, Inc.

Credit and debit card receivables often are included in cash equivalents.

The measurement and reporting of cash and cash equivalents are largely straightforward because cash generally presents no measurement problems. It is the standard medium of exchange and the basis for measuring assets and liabilities. Cash and cash equivalents usually are combined and reported as a single amount in the balance sheet. However, cash that is not available for use in current operations because it is restricted for a special purpose usually is classified in one of the noncurrent asset categories. Restricted cash is discussed later in this chapter.

All assets must be safeguarded against possible misuse. However, cash is the most liquid asset and the asset most easily stolen. As a result, a system of internal control of cash is a key accounting issue.

Internal Control

The success of any business enterprise depends on an effective system of internal control. Internal control refers to a company's plan to (a) encourage adherence to company policies and procedures, (b) promote operational efficiency, (c) minimize errors and theft, and (d) enhance the reliability and accuracy of accounting data. From a financial accounting perspective, the focus is on controls intended to improve the accuracy and reliability of accounting information and to safeguard the company's assets.

● LO7–1

Recall from our discussion in Chapter 1 that Section 404 of the *Sarbanes-Oxley Act of 2002* requires that companies document their internal controls and assess their adequacy. The Public Company Accounting Oversight Board AS 2201 further requires the auditor to express its own opinion on whether the company has maintained effective internal control over financial reporting.

The Sarbanes-Oxley Act requires a company to document and assess its internal controls. Auditors express an opinion on management's assessment.

Many companies have incurred significant costs in an effort to comply with the requirements of Section 404.[1] A framework for designing an internal control system is provided by the *Committee of Sponsoring Organizations (COSO)* of the Treadway Commission.[2] Formed in 1985, the organization is dedicated to improving the quality of financial reporting through, among other things, effective internal controls.

COSO defines internal control as a process, undertaken by an entity's board of directors, management, and other personnel, designed to provide reasonable assurance regarding the achievement of objectives in the following categories:

- Effectiveness and efficiency of operations.
- Reliability of financial reporting.
- Compliance with applicable laws and regulations.[3]

---

[1]PCAOB AS 2201 emphasizes audit efficiency with a focused, risk-based testing approach that is intended to reduce the total costs of 404 compliance.

[2]The sponsoring organizations include the AICPA, the Financial Executives International, the Institute of Internal Auditors, the American Accounting Association, and the Institute of Management Accountants.

[3]www.coso.org.

Internal Control Procedures—Cash Receipts

As cash is the most liquid of all assets, a well-designed and functioning system of internal control must surround all cash transactions. Separation of duties is critical. Individuals that have physical responsibility for assets should not also have access to accounting records. So, employees who handle cash should not be involved in or have access to accounting records nor be involved in the reconciliation of cash book balances to bank balances.

Consider the cash receipts process. Most nonretail businesses receive payment for goods by checks received through the mail. An approach to internal control over cash receipts that utilizes separation of duties might include the following steps:

1. Employee A opens the mail each day and prepares a multicopy listing of all checks including the amount and payor's name.
2. Employee B takes the checks, along with one copy of the listing, to the person responsible for depositing the checks in the company's bank account.
3. A second copy of the check listing is sent to the accounting department, where Employee C enters receipts into the accounting records.

Good internal control helps ensure accuracy as well as safeguard against theft. The bank-generated deposit slip can be compared with the check listing to verify that the amounts received were also deposited. And, because the person opening the mail is not the person who maintains the accounting records, it's impossible for one person to steal checks and alter accounting records to cover up their theft.

> Employees involved in recordkeeping should not also have physical access to the assets.

Internal Control Procedures—Cash Disbursements

Proper controls for cash disbursements should be designed to prevent any unauthorized payments and ensure that disbursements are recorded in the proper accounts. Important elements of a cash disbursement control system include the following:

1. All disbursements, other than very small disbursements from petty cash, should be made by check. This provides a permanent record of all disbursements.
2. All expenditures should be *authorized* before a check is prepared. For example, a vendor invoice for the purchase of inventory should be compared with the purchase order and receiving report to ensure the accuracy of quantity, price, part numbers, and so on. This process should include verification of the proper ledger accounts to be debited.
3. Checks should be signed only by authorized individuals.

Once again, separation of duties is important. Responsibilities for check signing, check writing, check mailing, cash disbursement documentation, and recordkeeping should be separated whenever possible. That way, a single person can't write checks to himself and disguise that theft as a payment to an approved vendor.

An important part of any system of internal control of cash is the periodic reconciliation of book balances and bank balances to the correct balance. In addition, a petty cash system is employed by many business enterprises. We cover these two topics in Appendix 7A.

Restricted Cash and Compensating Balances

We discussed the classification of assets and liabilities in Chapter 3. You should recall that only cash available for current operations or to satisfy current liabilities is classified as a current asset. Cash that is restricted in some way and not available for current use usually is reported as a noncurrent asset such as *investments* or *other assets*.

● LO7–2

Restrictions on cash can be informal, arising from management's intent to use a certain amount of cash for a specific purpose. For example, a company may set aside funds for future plant expansion. This cash, if material, should be classified as investments or other assets. Sometimes restrictions are contractually imposed. Debt instruments, for instance, frequently require the borrower to set aside funds (often referred to as a sinking fund) for the future payment of a debt. In these instances, the restricted cash is classified as noncurrent investments or other assets if the debt is classified as noncurrent. On the other hand, if the liability is current, the restricted cash also is classified as current. Disclosure notes should describe any material restrictions of cash and indicate the amounts and line items in which

342   SECTION 2   Assets

restricted cash appears in the balance sheet. Also, on the statement of cash flows, restricted cash and cash equivalents should be included with cash and cash equivalents when reconciling the beginning-of-period and end-of-period cash balances.

Banks frequently require cash restrictions in connection with loans or loan commitments (lines of credit). Typically, the borrower is asked to maintain a specified balance in a low interest or noninterest-bearing account at the bank (creditor). The required balance usually is some percentage of the committed amount (say 2% to 5%). These are known as **compensating balances** because they compensate the bank for granting the loan or extending the line of credit.

A compensating balance results in the borrower's paying an effective interest rate higher than the stated rate on the debt. For example, suppose that a company borrows $10,000,000 from a bank at an interest rate of 12%. If the bank requires a compensating balance of $2,000,000 to be held in a noninterest-bearing checking account, the company really is borrowing only $8,000,000 (the loan less the compensating balance). This means an effective interest rate of 15% ($1,200,000 interest divided by $8,000,000 cash available for use).

The classification and disclosure of a compensating balance depends on the nature of the restriction and the classification of the related debt.[4] If the restriction is legally binding, the cash is classified as either current or noncurrent (investments or other assets) depending on the classification of the related debt. In either case, note disclosure is appropriate.

If the compensating balance arrangement is informal with no contractual agreement that restricts the use of cash, the compensating balance can be reported as part of cash and cash equivalents, with note disclosure of the arrangement.

Illustration 7–2 provides an example of a note disclosure from Walgreens' annual report.

Illustration 7–2

Disclosure of Restricted Cash—Walgreens Boots Alliance, Inc.

Real World Financials

Note 2: Summary of Major Accounting Policies (in part) Restricted Cash

The Company is required to maintain cash deposits with certain banks which consist of deposits restricted under contractual agency agreements and cash restricted by law and other obligations. As of August 31, 2017 and 2016, the amount of such restricted cash was $202 million and $185 million, respectively, and is reported in other current assets on the Consolidated Balance Sheets.

Source: Walgreens Boots Alliance, Inc.

International Financial Reporting Standards

● LO7–10

Cash and Cash Equivalents. In general, cash and cash equivalents are treated similarly under IFRS and U.S. GAAP. One difference relates to bank overdrafts, which occur when withdrawals from a bank account exceed the available balance. U.S. GAAP requires that overdrafts typically be treated as liabilities. In contrast, *IAS No. 7* allows bank overdrafts to be offset against other cash accounts when overdrafts are payable on demand and fluctuate between positive and negative amounts as part of the normal cash management program that a company uses to minimize its cash balance.[5] For example, LaDonia Company has two cash accounts with the following balances as of December 31, 2021:

| National Bank | $300,000 |
| Central Bank | (15,000) |

Under U.S. GAAP, LaDonia's 12/31/21 balance sheet would report a cash asset of $300,000 and an overdraft current liability of $15,000. Under IFRS, LaDonia would report a cash asset of $285,000.

---

[4]FASB ASC 210–10–S99–2: SAB Topic 6.H–Balance Sheet—Overall—SEC Materials, *Accounting Series Release 148*.
[5]"Statement of Cash Flows," *International Accounting Standard No. 7* (IASCF), as amended effective January 1, 2018, par. 8.

Decision Makers' Perspective

Cash often is called a *nonearning* asset because it earns little or no interest. For this reason, managers invest idle cash in either cash equivalents or short-term investments, both of which provide a larger return than a checking account. Management's goal is to hold the minimum amount of cash necessary to conduct normal business operations, meet its obligations, and take advantage of opportunities. Too much cash reduces profits through lost returns, while too little cash increases risk. This trade-off between risk and return is an ongoing choice made by management (internal decision makers). Whether the choice made is appropriate is an ongoing assessment made by investors and creditors (external decision makers).

A company must have cash available for the compensating balances we discussed in the previous section as well as for planned disbursements related to normal operating, invest-ing, and financing cash flows. However, because cash inflows and outflows can vary from planned amounts, a company needs an additional cash cushion as a precaution against unex-pected events. The size of the cushion depends on the company's ability to convert cash equivalents and short-term investments into cash quickly, along with its short-term borrow-ing capacity.

> Companies hold cash to pay for planned and unplanned transactions and to satisfy compensating balance requirements.

Liquidity is a measure of a company's cash position and overall ability to obtain cash in the normal course of business to pay liabilities as they come due. A company is assumed to be liquid if it has sufficient cash or is capable of converting its other assets to cash in a relatively short period of time so that current needs can be met. Frequently, liquidity is measured with respect to the ability to pay currently maturing debt. The current ratio is one of the most common ways of measuring liquidity and is calculated by dividing current assets by current liabilities. By comparing liabilities that must be satisfied in the near term with assets that either are cash or will be converted to cash in the near term we have a base measure of a company's liquidity. We can refine the measure by adjusting for the implicit assumption of the current ratio that all current assets are equally liquid. In the acid-test or quick ratio, the numerator consists of "quick assets," which include only cash and cash equivalents, short-term investments, and accounts receivable. By eliminating inventories and prepaid expenses, the current assets that are less readily convertible into cash, we get a more precise indication of a company's short-term liquidity than with the current ratio. We discussed and illustrated these liquidity ratios in Chapter 3.

We should evaluate the adequacy of any ratio in the context of the industry in which the company operates and other specific circumstances. Bear in mind, though, that industry aver-ages are only one indication of acceptability and any ratio is but one indication of liquidity. Profitability, for instance, is perhaps the best long-run indication of liquidity. And a company may be very efficient in managing its current assets so that, say, receivables are more liquid than they otherwise would be. The receivables turnover ratio we discuss in Part B of this chapter offers a measure of management's efficiency in this regard.

There are many techniques that a company can use to manage cash balances. A discus-sion of these techniques is beyond the scope of this text. However, it is sufficient here to understand that management must make important decisions related to cash that have a direct impact on a company's profitability and risk. Because the lack of prudent cash management can lead to the failure of an otherwise sound company, it is essential that managers, as well as outside investors and creditors, maintain close vigil over this facet of a company's health. ●

> A manager should actively monitor the company's cash position.

Current Receivables

PART B

Receivables represent a company's claims to the future collection of cash, other assets, or services. Receivables resulting from the sale of goods or services on account (also called *credit sales*) are called accounts receivable and often are referred to as *trade receivables*. *Nontrade receivables* are those other than trade receivables and include tax refund claims, interest receivable, and advances to employees. When a receivable, trade or nontrade, is accompanied by a formal promissory note, it is referred to as a *note receivable*. We consider notes receivable after first discussing accounts receivable.

An account receivable and an account payable reflect opposite sides of the same transaction.

As you study receivables, realize that one company's claim to the future collection of cash corresponds to another company's (or individual's) obligation to pay cash. For example, one company's account receivable will be the mirror image of another company's account payable. Chapter 13 addresses accounts payable and other current liabilities.

Accounts Receivable

Typically, revenue and related accounts receivable are recognized at the point of delivery of the product or service.

Accounts receivable are created when sellers recognize revenue associated with a credit sale. Recall from Chapter 6 that revenue is recognized when a seller satisfies a performance obligation. For most products or services, the performance obligation is satisfied at the point of delivery of the product or service, so revenue and the related receivable are recognized at that time.

Accounts receivable are current assets because their normal collection period falls within one year (or the company's operating cycle, if longer).

Most businesses provide credit to their customers, either because it's not practical to require immediate cash payment or to encourage customers to purchase the company's product or service. Accounts receivable are *informal* credit arrangements supported by an invoice and normally are due in 30 to 60 days after the sale. They almost always are classified as current assets because their normal collection period falls within one year (or the company's operating cycle, if longer).

Initial Valuation of Accounts Receivable

You learned in Chapter 6 that sellers recognize an amount of revenue equal to the amount they are entitled to receive in exchange for satisfying a performance obligation. Sellers allocate the transaction price to the various performance obligations in a contract and then recognize revenue (and the corresponding receivable for credit sales) when performance obligations are satisfied. Clearly, revenue recognition and accounts receivable recognition are closely related. That means that some of the complexities that affect revenue recognition also affect accounts receivable.

Accounts receivable typically are not shown at present value.

One potential complexity relates to time value of money. Because credit sales allow a customer to get goods or services now but pay for them in the future, you can view a credit sale as providing a loan in addition to whatever goods or services are included in a contract. However, as you learned in Chapter 6, sellers can ignore this "financing component" when it is not significant, which typically is the case when receivables are due in less than one year. Therefore, sellers usually record relatively short-term accounts receivable at the entire amount the seller expects to receive, rather than at the present value of that amount.[6] For long-term receivables, the financing component is more significant and sellers have to account for it, as you will see when we cover notes receivable later in this section.

Another type of complexity relates to variable consideration. As you learned in Chapter 6, contracts can include some aspect of variable consideration that must be estimated when determining the transaction price, and therefore the amount of the receivable. In particular, contracts can allow cash discounts as well as sales returns and allowances. Let's discuss each of those complexities in turn.

Trade discounts allow a customer to pay an amount that is below the list price.

DISCOUNTS   There are two types of discounts that companies commonly offer, trade discounts and cash discounts. Companies frequently offer trade discounts to customers, usually a percentage reduction from the list price. For example, a manufacturer might list a machine part at $2,500 but sell it to an important customer at a 10% discount. That discount of $250 is reflected by recording the sale at the agreed-upon price of $2,250.

Trade discounts are not variable consideration.

Trade discounts are not variable consideration, because the amount the company is entitled to receive from the customer doesn't depend on the outcome of a *future* event. Trade discounts are simply a way to specify the current transaction price and thus affect reported revenue at that time. Many companies use trade discounts to offer reduced prices to certain customers (such as college students at the nearby pizza restaurant or senior citizens at the

● LO7–3

---

[6]FASB ASC 606-10-32-15: Revenue from Contracts with Customers—Overall—Measurement—The Existence of a Significant Financing Component (previously "Revenue from Contracts with Customers (Topic 606)" *Accounting Standards Update 2014-09* (Norwalk, Conn: FASB, 2014)).

local ballgame), to give quantity discounts to large customers, or perhaps to disguise real prices from competitors.

Sales discounts, often called *cash discounts*, represent reductions in the amount to be received by the company from a customer that makes payment within a specified period of time. A sales discount provides an incentive for quick payment. The amount of a sales discount and the time period within which it's available usually are conveyed by terms like 2/10, n/30 (meaning a 2% discount if paid within 10 days, otherwise full payment within 30 days).

Sales discounts reduce the amount to be received from the customer if payment occurs within a specified short period of time.

Sales discounts are variable consideration, because the amount to be received by the company depends on a future event—whether cash is received from the customer within the discount period. However, it is usually difficult for a seller to estimate the amount of discount that will be taken with every sale. Therefore, sellers use two methods in practice that simplify the process of recording sales discounts: the *gross method* and the *net method*. To see how these methods work, consider the example in Illustration 7–3.

Sales discounts are variable consideration.

Illustration 7–3

Sales Discounts Using the Gross Method versus Net Method

The Hawthorne Manufacturing Company offers credit customers a 2% sales discount if the sales price is paid within 10 days. Any amounts not paid within 10 days are due in 30 days. These payment terms are stated as 2/10, n/30. The following events occurred:

1. On October 5, 2021, Hawthorne sold merchandise at a price of $20,000.
2. The customer paid $13,720 ($14,000 less the 2% cash discount) on October 14.
3. The customer paid the remaining balance of $6,000 on November 4.

The appropriate journal entries to record the sale and cash collection, comparing the gross and net methods are as follows:

Gross Method			Net Method		
October 5, 2021			**October 5, 2021**		
Accounts receivable........	20,000		Accounts receivable.............	19,600	
Sales revenue		20,000	Sales revenue		19,600
October 14, 2021			**October 14, 2021**		
Cash..................................	13,720		Cash..	13,720	
Sales discounts................	280		Accounts receivable.........		13,720
Accounts receivable....		14,000			
November 4, 2021			**November 4, 2021**		
Cash..................................	6,000		Cash..	6,000	
Accounts receivable....		6,000	Accounts receivable.........		5,880
			Sales discounts forfeited....		120

Using the **gross method**, we initially record the revenue and related receivable at the full **$20,000** price. Using the **net method**, we record revenue and the related accounts receivable at the agreed-upon price *less* the 2% discount offered, yielding **$19,600** of revenue at the time of sale. Subsequent accounting under both methods depends on whether payment occurs within the discount period.

Payment within the discount period. On October 14, Hawthorne receives payment for $14,000 of the $20,000 merchandise sold. Because payment is within the 10-day discount period, the company allows a discount of **$280** ($14,000 × 2%) and receives only $13,720 ($14,000 − $280). Under the gross method, we record the discount as a debit to an account called *sales discounts*. This is a contra account to sales revenue and is deducted from sales revenue to derive the net sales revenue reported in the income statement. Under the net method, we simply debit cash and credit accounts receivable for $13,720, because the discount was recorded at the time of the sale.

The *gross method* assumes customers won't take sales discounts and then reduces revenue for any discounts taken.

Payment *not* within the discount period. On November 4, Hawthorne receives final payment for the remaining $6,000 of merchandise sold. This payment is after the 10-day discount period, and the customer forfeits the possible discount of **$120** ($6,000 × 2%).

The *net method* assumes customers will take sales discounts and then increases revenue for discounts forfeited.

Under the gross method, we simply record the collection on account for $6,000, the gross amount of receivable originally recorded. Under the net method, we reduce the receivable by $5,880 and record the $120 discount not taken by the customer as a credit to an account called *sales discounts forfeited.* This account is added to sales revenue to calculate net sales revenue.[7]

With both methods, net sales revenue ends up being reduced by only those discounts that are actually taken. Therefore, both methods get us to the same place from the perspective of net sales revenue and total net income recognized, as shown in the table below.

Revenue comparison of the gross method and the net method.

	Gross Method	**Net Method**
Sales revenue	$20,000	$19,600
Less: Sales discounts	(280)	–0–
Add: Discounts forfeited	0	120
Net sales revenue	$ 19,720	$ 19,720

The net method is more correct conceptually.

Which method is correct? Remember from Chapter 6 that sales revenue and the corresponding accounts receivable should be stated at the amount of consideration the seller expects to be entitled to receive. The net method typically better reflects that amount, because the discount is a savings that prudent customers are unwilling to forgo. To appreciate the size of that savings, consider a 2/10, n/30 discount offer on a $100 sale. In order to save $2 (equal to $100 × 2%), the customer must pay $98 twenty days earlier than otherwise due, effectively "investing" $98 to "earn" $2. That equals a rate of return of 2.04% ($2/$98) for a 20-day period. To convert this 20-day rate to an annual rate, we multiply by 365/20:

$$2.04\% \times 365/20 = 37.23\% \text{ effective rate}$$

Wouldn't you like to earn a sure return of over 37%? You can see why customers try to take the discount if at all possible. That's why recording the receivable net of the discount more accurately reflects the amount the seller expects to be entitled to receive. Still, even though the net method is more correct conceptually, both methods are used in practice, because many sellers prefer to record receivables at gross and then make downward adjustments at the time the receivable is collected. The dollar value of the difference between methods usually is viewed as immaterial.

SALES RETURNS Customers frequently are given the right to return merchandise they purchase. When practical, a customer might be given a special price reduction as an incentive to keep the merchandise they want to return.[8] We use the term sales returns to refer to these returns and other adjustments. Sales returns are common in industries such as food products, publishing, and retailing.

● LO7–4

Sales returns are variable consideration.

As we discussed in Chapter 6, sales returns are a form of variable consideration. Because products might be returned or prices adjusted, there is uncertainty as to the final amount the seller will be entitled to receive (the transaction price). Recognizing returns only at the time they happen might cause revenue and profit to be overstated in the period the sale is made and understated in the return period. For example, assume merchandise is sold to a customer for $10,000 in December 2021, the last month in the selling company's fiscal year, and that the merchandise cost $6,000. The company would recognize gross profit of $4,000 in 2021 ($10,000 – $6,000). If all of the merchandise is returned in 2022, after financial statements for 2021 are issued, gross profit will be overstated in 2021 and understated in 2022 by $4,000. The 2021 balance sheet also is affected, with a refund liability understated by $10,000 and inventory understated by $6,000.

[7]Conceptually, sales discounts forfeited is similar to interest revenue, since it is extra revenue received because a receivable is outstanding for a longer period of time. In fact, prior to the effective date of *ASU 2014-09* (which specified how variable consideration should be treated in revenue recognition), sales discounts forfeited were often disclosed as interest revenue or other revenue in the income statement.
[8]Price reductions sometimes are referred to as *sales allowances* and are distinguished from situations when the products actually are returned for a refund or credit (sales returns).

To avoid overstating revenue and net assets in 2021, the seller should reduce revenue for all returns of current-period sales, including those that occur in the current period as well as those the seller estimates will occur eventually. We accomplish this by debiting a contra revenue account, sales returns, which reduces sales revenue indirectly. This way, the income statement will report net sales revenue (sales revenue minus actual and estimated sales returns).

When should estimated returns be recognized? Technically, the seller should estimate returns each time a sale is made and adjust the transaction price accordingly at that time. However, as we noted in Chapter 6, it is impractical for most sellers to estimate returns every time they make a sale. For that reason, sellers typically account for any returns during the reporting period when the returns actually occur, and then use an adjusting entry at the end of the reporting period to recognize additional future returns expected to occur as a result of the current period's sales transactions. In that adjusting entry, the seller debits sales returns and credits a refund liability for the amount the seller estimates will be refunded to customers who make returns. We see that approach in Illustration 7–4.

As shown in Illustration 7–4, Hawthorne initially sells merchandise to customers for $2,000,000. The company records the cash collected and sales revenue. At the same time, the company also records cost of goods sold and a decrease in inventory of $1,200,000.

> Sellers should reduce revenue for estimated future *sales returns*.
>
> A contra revenue account used to reduce revenue for actual and estimated sales returns.
>
> | | |
> |---|---|
> | Sales revenue | |
> | Less: Sales returns | |
> | Net sales revenue | |
>
> A *refund liability* reflects the amount the seller estimates will be refunded to customers who make returns.

Illustration 7–4
Accounting for Sales Returns

During 2021, its first year of operations, the Hawthorne Manufacturing Company sold merchandise for $2,000,000 cash. This merchandise cost Hawthorne $1,200,000 (60% of the selling price). Industry experience indicates that 10% of all sales will be returned, which equals $200,000 ($2,000,000 × 10%) in this case. Customers returned $130,000 of sales during 2021. Hawthorne uses a perpetual inventory system.

Sales of $2,000,000 occurred in 2021, with cost of goods sold of $1,200,000.	Cash...	2,000,000	
	Sales revenue		2,000,000
	Cost of goods sold..	1,200,000	
	Inventory..		1,200,000
Sales returns of $130,000 occurred during 2021. The cost of returned inventory is $78,000 ($130,000 × 60%).	Sales returns...	130,000	
	Cash..		130,000
	Inventory...	78,000	
	Cost of goods sold......................................		78,000
At the end of 2021, an additional $70,000 of sales returns are expected. The cost of the inventory expected to be returned is $42,000 ($70,000 × 60%).	Sales returns...	70,000	
	Refund liability..		70,000
	Inventory—est. returns................................	42,000	
	Cost of goods sold......................................		42,000
Sales returns of $70,000 occurred during 2022. The cost of returned inventory is $42,000.	Refund liability	70,000	
	Cash..		70,000
	Inventory...	42,000	
	Inventory—est. returns.............................		42,000

Actual Returns.   During the period, as actual returns occur, the company needs to reduce the sales revenue previously recognized. This is done by debiting sales returns, a contra revenue account. The credit to cash represents the amount of the refund. If the sales initially had been made on credit, Hawthorne would have debited accounts receivable rather than cash at the time of sale. Then, if the receivable was still outstanding at the time the return occurred, Hawthorne would credit accounts receivable to show that the receivable is no longer outstanding.

Hawthorne also must adjust inventory to account for the returned merchandise. In a perpetual inventory system we record increases (debits) and decreases (credits) in the inventory account as events occur. So, when actual returns occur, Hawthorne increases inventory to include the $78,000 cost of returned items. The return also means that the previous amount for cost of goods sold should be reduced.

Estimated Returns.   At the end of the period, Hawthorne estimates that another $70,000 of sales will be returned. One common way of making this estimate would be to base it on the difference between an estimate of the total amount of returns of current year sales ($200,000) and the amount already returned during the year ($130,000). To account for this estimate of $70,000 of future returns, we reduce revenue in the current period by debiting sales returns and recognizing a refund liability. The refund liability represents an estimate of additional cash that will be refunded when customers return products in the future. Even if the initial sale was for credit and cash had not yet been received, Hawthorne still would recognize a refund liability for estimated future returns.[9] The $42,000 of inventory *expected* to be returned in 2022 is included as an asset, *Inventory—estimated returns,* which reflects Hawthorne's right to any inventory that is returned. That asset is shown in Hawthorne's 2021 balance sheet, separate from Hawthorne's normal inventory.

Be sure to notice that this accounting approach reports Hawthorne's 2021 income net of *actual* and *estimated* returns. Hawthorne's 2021 income statement reports net sales revenue of $1,800,000, which is gross sales revenue of $2,000,000 reduced by actual and estimated returns of $200,000 ($130,000 + $70,000). Hawthorne's 2021 cost of goods sold equals $1,080,000, which is $1,200,000 reduced by the cost of actual and estimated returns of $120,000 ($78,000 + $42,000).[10]

Sometimes a customer will return damaged or defective merchandise. This possibility is included in a company's estimate of returns. As we will see in Chapter 9, the amount recorded in inventory for damaged or defective merchandise reflects a value less than its original cost.

What happens if Hawthorne's estimate of future returns is wrong, such that returns end up being more or less than $70,000? Hawthorne won't revise prior years' financial statements to reflect the new estimate. Instead, as you learned in Chapter 6, Hawthorne must adjust the accounts to reflect the change in estimated returns, with any effect on income recognized in the period in which the adjustment is made. For example, suppose in our illustration that only $60,000 of 2021 sales were returned in 2022, instead of the $70,000 that Hawthorne anticipated, and that Hawthorne estimates that no more returns will occur. In that case, the refund liability still has a pre-adjustment balance of **$10,000** remaining from 2021 sales. Likewise, the inventory—estimated returns account still has a pre-adjustment balance of **$6,000** (60% × $10,000) remaining from 2021 sales.

Changes in estimated returns are recorded in whatever period the estimate changes.

---

[9]ASC 606-10-32-10 requires that sellers recognize a refund liability even if the seller has not yet been paid and has a receivable outstanding. That may seem odd, as the seller is showing a liability to refund cash it has not yet received. Depending on the specifics of the sales contract, some sellers may conclude that offsetting the refund liability against the receivable is appropriate, such that accounts receivable are shown net of refund liabilities in the balance sheet.

[10]As indicated in Chapter 6, companies technically should estimate all variable consideration, including sales returns, at the time a sale is made. The financial statement outcomes of that approach are the same as those shown in Illustration 7–4, but the journal entries that get us there are somewhat different. To adapt our example to account for estimated returns at the time of sale, look at the journal entries that Hawthorne makes at the end of 2021 to account for estimated future returns. Hawthorne would record the same journal entries at the time of sale, but for the full amount of estimated sales returns ($200,000) and estimated inventory to be returned ($200,000 × 60% = $120,000). After recording the estimated returns at the time of the sale, all *actual* returns would be accounted for as shown in our example for actual returns occurring in 2022, debiting the refund liability and crediting cash as individual returns occur.

Refund liability			Inventory—estimated returns		
1/1/2022		70,000	1/1/2022	42,000	
2022 returns	60,000		2022 returns		36,000
Pre-adjustment balance		**10,000**	Pre-adjustment balance	**6,000**	
Change in estimate	10,000		Change in estimate		6,000
12/31/2022		-0-	12/31/2022		-0-

In 2022, Hawthorne would record its change in estimated returns of 2021 sales as follows:

Refund liability...	10,000	
Sales returns ($70,000 – $60,000)		10,000
Cost of goods sold (60% × $10,000)...	6,000	
Inventory—estimated returns..		6,000

These adjustments remove the remaining 2021 balance from the refund liability and inventory—estimated returns. They also increase net sales revenue (by reducing sales returns) and cost of goods sold in 2022, the period in which the change in estimate occurs.

How do companies estimate returns? They rely on past history, but they also consider any changes that might affect future experience. For example, changes in customer base, payment terms offered to customers, and overall economic conditions might suggest that future returns will differ from past returns. The task of estimating returns is made easier for many large retail companies whose fiscal year-end is the end of January. Since retail companies generate a large portion of their annual sales during the Christmas season, most returns from these sales already have been accounted for by the end of January. In fact, that's an important motivation for those companies to choose to end their fiscal years at the end of January.

AVX Corporation is a leading manufacturer of electronic components. Illustration 7–5, drawn from AVX's 2017 annual report, describes the company's approach to estimating returns.

Experience guides firms when estimating returns.

Revenue Recognition and Accounts Receivable (in part): Returns

Sales revenue and cost of sales reported in the statement of operations are reduced to reflect estimated returns. We record an estimated sales allowance for returns at the time of sale based on historical trends, current pricing and volume information, other market specific information, and input from sales, marketing, and other key management personnel. The amount accrued reflects the return of value of the customer's inventory. These procedures require the exercise of significant judgments. We believe that these procedures enable us to make reliable estimates of future returns. Our actual results have historically approximated our estimates. When the product is returned and verified, the customer is given credit against their accounts receivable.

Source: AVX Corporation

Illustration 7–5

Disclosure of Sales Returns Policy—AVX Corporation

Real World Financials

In some industries, returns typically are small and infrequent. Companies in these industries usually don't bother to estimate returns and simply record returns in the period they occur, because the effect on income measurement and asset valuation is immaterial. Also, companies sometimes lack sufficient information to make a good estimate of returns. As you learned in Chapter 6, companies must recognize only the amount of revenue that is probable to not require reversal in the future. That way, sales are less likely to be overstated in the period of the transfer of goods or services. Difficulty estimating returns requires a larger estimate of returns (and therefore a smaller amount of net sales revenue recognized) than would be the case if a more precise estimate was possible.

Subsequent Valuation of Accounts Receivable

● LO7–5

You learned in Chapter 6 that revenue and a corresponding receivable are recognized for the amount the seller is *entitled* to receive for satisfying a performance obligation. However, being entitled to receive payment doesn't necessarily mean that the seller *will* be paid. In fact, credit losses (bad debts) are an inherent cost of granting credit. How should we account for the fact that not every account receivable is likely to be collected?

DIRECT WRITE-OFF METHOD (NOT GAAP)   A simple approach to recognizing bad debts that is *not* allowed by GAAP is to wait until a particular account is deemed uncollectible and write it off at that time. This approach is called the direct write-off method. For example, if a customer goes bankrupt and it becomes clear that a $15,000 account receivable will not be collected, the company would reduce net income for the amount of the bad debt, and eliminate the receivable from total assets, because the account is no longer expected to be collected:

Bad debt expense...	15,000	
Accounts receivable...		15,000

The two shortcomings of the direct write-off method are that it:

1. Overstates the balance in accounts receivable in the periods prior to the write-off, because it fails to anticipate that some accounts receivable will prove uncollectible.
2. Distorts net income by postponing recognition of any bad debt expense until the period in which the customer actually fails to pay, even though some bad debt expense was predictable before that time.

FINANCIAL Reporting Case

Q1, p. 339

The carrying value of accounts receivable is reduced by the allowance for uncollectible accounts.

These conceptual problems are why the direct write-off method isn't allowed for financial reporting purposes unless the amount of bad debt is not material. However, the direct write-off method is required for income tax purposes for most companies.

ALLOWANCE METHOD (GAAP)   GAAP requires use of the allowance method whenever the amount of bad debts is material. Under the allowance method, companies use a contra-asset account, the allowance for uncollectible accounts, to reduce the carrying value of accounts receivable to the amount of cash they expect to collect.[11] Both the carrying value and the amount of the allowance typically are shown on the face of the balance sheet. For example, Illustration 7–6 shows how Johnson & Johnson, the large pharmaceutical company, reported accounts receivable in its comparative balance sheets for 2017 and 2016.

Illustration 7–6

Disclosure of Accounts Receivable—Johnson & Johnson

Real World Financials

	($ in millions)	
	2017	**2016**
Accounts receivable trade, less allowances for doubtful accounts $291 (2016, $252)...	13,490	11,699
Source: Johnson & Johnson		

Johnson & Johnson's balance sheet communicates that, as of year-end 2017, it had net accounts receivable of $13,490 and an allowance for doubtful accounts of $291, which implies a gross accounts receivable of $13,490 + $291 = $13,781.

The allowance method recognizes bad debt expense when the allowance is adjusted for estimated bad debts, not when specific accounts are written off.

Under the allowance method, bad debt expense is *not* recognized when specific accounts are written off. Rather, bad debt expense is recognized earlier, when accounts are *estimated* to be uncollectible and the allowance is created. Later, when a specific account receivable is deemed *actually* uncollectible, both the allowance and the specific account receivable are reduced to write off the receivable.

---

[11]You may see this carrying value referred to as "net realizable value". However, as you will learn in Chapter 9, that term has a very specific definition in GAAP that should not be misused.

An example will clarify how the allowance method works. Assume the Hawthorne Manufacturing Company started operations in 2021. It had sales of $1,200,000 and collections of $895,000, leaving a balance of **$305,000** in accounts receivable as of December 31, 2021.

Accounts Receivable		
1/1/2021	-0-	
Sales	1,200,000	
Collections		895,000
12/31/2021	**305,000**	

Recognizing allowance for uncollectible accounts (end of first year). Hawthorne's analysis indicates it expects to collect $280,000 of its accounts receivable, so it must establish an allowance for uncollectible accounts of $25,000 ($305,000 – $280,000). (Later we'll talk about how Hawthorne would estimate the allowance. For now let's assume that number.) Hawthorne establishes the necessary allowance with the following journal entry:

Allowance for Uncollectible Accounts		
1/1/2021		-0-
Bad debt expense		25,000
12/31/2021		25,000

Bad debt expense	25,000	
Allowance for uncollectible accounts		25,000

The balances in accounts receivable (**$305,000**) and the contra asset allowance for uncollectible accounts ($25,000) offset to carry receivables at a net amount of $280,000 on the balance sheet.

Of course, at this point Hawthorne doesn't know which particular accounts receivable will prove uncollectible. (If it could predict that perfectly, it wouldn't have made those sales to begin with!) Hawthorne only can record an estimate of the amount of uncollectible accounts for its outstanding receivables. That estimate both reduces net income (through bad debt expense) and reduces the carrying value of Hawthorne's accounts receivable.

When accounts are deemed uncollectible. On April 24, 2022, Hawthorne concludes that it will not collect a $15,000 account receivable from a customer that recently has gone bankrupt. Hawthorne would make the following journal entry:

Allowance for uncollectible accounts	15,000	
Accounts receivable		15,000

Accounts Receivable			Allowance for Uncollectible Accounts		
1/1/2022	305,000		1/1/2022		25,000
Specific write-off		15,000	Specific write-off	15,000	
	290,000				10,000

Note that the journal entry didn't affect net income, and that accounts receivable still are carried at a net amount of $280,000 (**$290,000** – $10,000) on the balance sheet.

When previously written-off accounts are reinstated. Occasionally, a receivable that has been written off is later reinstated because the company gets new information and now believes the receivable will be collected in part or in full. When this happens, the entry to write off the account is reversed. For example, assume Hawthorne learns on May 30 that the financial situation of its customer has improved and it will collect $1,200 of the receivable that previously was written off. Hawthorne reinstates that amount of the receivable with the following journal entry:

The write-off of an account receivable reduces both gross receivables and the allowance, thus having no effect on net income or financial position.

FINANCIAL Reporting Case

Q2, p. 339

Accounts receivable	1,200	
Allowance for uncollectible accounts		1,200

Accounts Receivable			Allowance for Uncollectible Accounts	
	290,000			10,000
Reinstatement	1,200		Reinstatement	1,200
	291,200			11,200

Reinstating a previously written-off accounts receivable increases both gross receivables and the allowance, thus having no effect on net income or financial position.

Note that, once again, the journal entry didn't affect net income and that accounts receivable still are carried at a net amount of $280,000 (**$291,200** – $11,200) on the balance sheet. Just as the carrying value of accounts receivable was not affected by writing off a specific receivable, it also is not affected by reversing the write-off of a specific receivable.

Once the receivable is reinstated, collection is recorded the same way it would be if the receivable had never been written off, debiting cash and crediting accounts receivable.

ESTIMATING THE ALLOWANCE FOR UNCOLLECTIBLE ACCOUNTS   Basing bad debt expense on the appropriate carrying value of accounts receivable is very much a *balance sheet approach*. The company estimates what the ending balance of the allowance for uncollectible accounts should be to have the carrying value of accounts receivable reflect the net amount expected to be collected. The company then records whatever amount of bad debt expense that's necessary to adjust the allowance to that desired balance.

● LO7–6

Companies estimate the necessary balance in the allowance for uncollectible accounts using the CECL ("Current Expected Credit Loss") model.[12] That model does not specify a particular method for estimating bad debts ("credit losses"). Rather, it allows a company to apply any method that reasonably captures its expectation of credit losses, so that the resulting carrying value of net accounts receivable reflects the cash the company expects to collect. That estimate should consider all receivables and be based on all relevant information, including historical experience, current conditions, and reasonable and supportable forecasts. Estimation could be done by analyzing each customer account, by applying an estimate of the percentage of bad debts to the entire outstanding receivable balance, or by applying different percentages to accounts receivable balances depending on the length of time outstanding. This latter approach employs an accounts receivable aging schedule and is very common in practice. For example, Illustration 7–7 shows the aging schedule for Hawthorne's December 31, 2021 accounts receivable balance of $305,000.

Illustration 7–7

Accounts Receivable Aging Schedule

Customer	Accounts Receivable 12/31/2021	0–60 Days	61–90 Days	91–120 Days	Over 120 Days
Axel Manufacturing Co.	$ 20,000	$ 14,000	$ 6,000		
Banner Corporation	33,000		20,000	$10,000	$ 3,000
Dando Company	60,000	50,000	10,000		
~~	~~	~~	~~	~~	~~
~~	~~	~~	~~	~~	~~
Xicon Company	18,000	10,000	4,000	3,000	1,000
Totals	$305,000	$220,000	$50,000	$25,000	$10,000

Summary

Age Group	Amount	Estimated Percent Uncollectible	Estimated Allowance
0–60 days	$220,000	5%	$11,000
61–90 days	50,000	10%	5,000
91–120 days	25,000	20%	5,000
Over 120 days	10,000	40%	4,000
Allowance for uncollectible accounts			$25,000

[12]"Financial Instruments—Credit Losses (Topic 326)" *Accounting Standards Update 2016-13* (Norwalk, Conn: FASB, 2016).

The schedule classifies the year-end receivable balances according to their length of time outstanding. Typically, the longer an account has been outstanding, the more likely it will prove uncollectible. Therefore, the schedule applies higher estimated default percentages to groups of older receivables. Because the schedule calculates a necessary balance in the allowance of $25,000, Hawthorn would adjust the balance of the allowance to that amount, as shown previously in this section.

Recognizing allowance for uncollectible accounts (end of second year). At the end of the second year of operations (and each year thereafter), Hawthorne must once again estimate what the carrying value of its accounts receivable should be, and adjust the allowance as necessary to produce that carrying value. Let's suppose that at the end of 2022 Hawthorne has a gross accounts receivable balance of **$400,000** but believes it only will collect $360,000. That implies that Hawthorne needs an allowance of $40,000 (**$400,000** − $360,000). Unlike the first year, the balance of the allowance for uncollectible accounts in later years may not be zero at the time Hawthorne makes the adjustment. In our example, the pre-adjustment balance is $11,200. What adjustment is needed to update the allowance account from $11,200 to the new estimate of $40,000? The adjusting entry is a "plug" of $28,800.

Allowance for Uncollectible Accounts

(Pre-adjustment balance)	11,200
Bad debt expense	28,800
(Post-adjustment balance)	40,000

Bad debt expense	28,800	
Allowance for uncollectible accounts		28,800

Be sure to understand that the amount of bad debt expense recognized in this journal entry is purely a plug that is determined by the difference between the pre-adjustment balance and the necessary post-adjustment balance in the allowance. For example, if Hawthorne had written off so many accounts receivable during 2022 that the adjustment account had a pre-adjustment balance that was a *debit* of $2,000, Hawthorne would have to *credit* the allowance for $42,000 (and debit bad debt expense for the same amount) to reach the necessary $40,000 post-adjustment balance.

Allowance for Uncollectible Accounts

Pre-adjustment balance	2,000		
		42,000	Bad debt expense
		40,000	Post-Adjustment Balance

On the other hand, if the pre-adjustment balance in the allowance was a *credit* of $11,200 and the quality of Hawthorne's receivables improved so much that Hawthorne believed the post-adjustment balance in the allowance should be only $5,000, Hawthorne would need to *debit* the allowance for $6,200.

Allowance for Uncollectible Accounts

		11,200	Pre-adjustment balance
Bad debt expense	6,200		
		5,000	Post-adjustment balance

A debit to the allowance requires a credit to bad debt expense. While crediting an expense looks weird, think of it as driven by a change in an estimate. The allowance was increased by too much in a prior period, so Hawthorne has to reduce it this period. As with changes in other estimates, we don't restate prior year financial statements, but instead show the effect of the change in estimate in current-period net income.

FINANCIAL
Reporting Case

Q3, p. 339

Income statement approach. An alternative to the balance sheet approach is to estimate bad debt expense directly as a percentage of each period's net credit sales. This percentage usually is determined by reviewing the company's recent history of the relationship between credit sales and actual bad debts. For a relatively new company, this percentage may be estimated by referring to other sources such as industry averages. For example, if Hawthorne had sales of $1,200,000 in 2021, and estimated that 2% of those sales would prove uncollectible, it would debit bad debt expense and credit the allowance for uncollectible accounts for $24,000 (= $1,200,000 × 2%).

It's important to notice that this income statement approach focuses on the current year's credit sales, so the effect on the balance sheet—the allowance for uncollectible accounts and hence net accounts receivable—is an incidental result of estimating the expense. An income statement approach should be used only if it doesn't provide a distorted estimate of the net amount of cash that is expected to be collected from accounts receivable.

Combined approaches. Some companies use a combination of approaches when estimating bad debts. For example, Hawthorne might decide it's more convenient to estimate bad debts on a quarterly basis using the income statement approach and then refine the estimate by employing the balance sheet approach at the end of the year based on an aging of receivables. In our example, Hawthorne recognized $24,000 in the allowance and the bad debt expense accounts during the year under the income statement approach. If at the end of the year Hawthorne's aging schedule indicated that a total of $25,000 was needed in the allowance, Hawthorne would recognize an additional $1,000 of allowance and bad debt expense to adjust the total to the necessary balance.

**Allowance for
Uncollectible
Accounts**

	24,000
	1,000
	25,000

Bad debt expense..	1,000	
Allowance for uncollectible accounts...		1,000

Ethical Dilemma

The management of the Auto Parts Division of the Santana Corporation receives a bonus if the division's income achieves a specific target. For 2021 the target will be achieved by a wide margin. Mary Beth Williams, the controller of the division, has been asked by Philip Stanton, the head of the division's management team, to try to reduce this year's income and "bank" some of the profits for future years. Mary Beth suggests that the division's bad debt expense as a percentage of the gross accounts receivable balance for 2021 be increased from 3% to 5%. She believes that 3% is the more accurate estimate but knows that both the corporation's internal auditors as well as the external auditors allow some flexibility when estimates are involved. Does Mary Beth's proposal present an ethical dilemma?

Illustration 7–8 summarizes the key issues involving measuring and reporting accounts receivable.

Illustration 7–8

Measuring and Reporting
Accounts Receivable

Recognition	Depends on revenue recognition; for most credit sales, revenue and the related receivables are recognized at the point of delivery.
Initial valuation	Initially recorded at the amount of consideration the seller is entitled to receive. Affected by cash discounts and variable consideration such as sales discounts and sales returns.
Subsequent valuation	Initial valuation reduced by allowance for uncollectible accounts, so accounts receivable are shown at the amount of cash the seller expects to receive.
Classification	Almost always classified as a current asset.

Additional Consideration

Guidance in this area has changed. Companies are required to use the CECL ("Current Expected Credit Loss") model starting in 2020, and companies can choose to use that approach starting in 2019.[13] We emphasize the CECL model because it will be in effect during your career.

GAAP in place prior to the CECL model accounted for bad debts as loss contingencies, because the amount of loss depends on some future event, like a customer's failure to pay. As discussed further in Chapter 13, an allowance and corresponding expense is only recognized for a contingent loss if the loss is both probable to occur and can be reasonably estimated, based on events that have occurred to date. The CECL model was developed after the global financial crisis of 2008/2009 because of a concern that this preexisting approach could understate bad debt expense. The "probable" threshold for identifying bad debts means that sellers don't record an estimate of bad debts that they view as only possible. Also, basing estimates only on events that already have occurred could ignore forecasts of future economic conditions that suggest impending problems. Given these differences, it is likely that bad debts accruals will be larger under the CECL model than under preexisting GAAP.

Concept Review Exercise

The Crowe Company offers 30 days of credit to its customers. At the end of the year, bad debts expense is estimated and the allowance for uncollectible accounts is adjusted based on an aging of accounts receivable. The company began 2022 with the following balances in its accounts:

UNCOLLECTIBLE ACCOUNTS RECEIVABLE

Accounts receivable	$350,000
Allowance for uncollectible accounts	(30,000)
Net accounts receivable	$320,000

During 2022, sales on credit were $1,300,000, cash collections from customers were $1,253,000, and actual write-offs of accounts were $25,000.

Crowe Company Accounts Receivable Aging
December 31, 2022

	Summary	
Age Group	Amount	Estimated Percent Uncollectible
0–60 days	$250,000	6%
61–90 days	80,000	15%
91–120 days	32,000	25%
Over 121 days	10,000	50%
Total	$372,000	

Required:

1. Determine the balances in accounts receivable and allowance for uncollectible accounts at the end of 2022.
2. Determine bad debt expense for 2022.
3. Prepare journal entries to write off receivables and to recognize bad debt expense for 2022.

---

[13]"Financial Instruments—Credit Losses (Topic 326)" *Accounting Standards Update 2016-13* (Norwalk, Conn: FASB, 2016).

Solution:

1. Determine the balances in accounts receivable and allowance for uncollectible accounts at the end of 2022.

Accounts Receivable

12/31/2021	350,000		
Sales	1,300,000		
		1,253,000	Collections
		25,000	Write-offs
12/31/2022	**372,000**		

Crowe Company Accounts Receivable
Aging December 31, 2022

Summary

Age Group	Amount	Estimated Percent Uncollectible	Estimated Allowance
0–60 days	$ 250,000	6%	$15,000
61–90 days	80,000	15%	12,000
91–120 days	32,000	25%	8,000
Over 121 days	10,000	50%	5,000
Total	$372,000		$40,000

Allowance for Uncollectible Accounts

		30,000	12/31/2021
Write-offs	25,000		
		35,000	Bad debt expense
		40,000	12/31/2022

As shown in the T-account, the ending balance in accounts receivable is **$372,000**. As shown in the calculation within the aging of accounts receivable, the ending balance in the allowance for uncollectible accounts is $40,000.

2. Determine bad debt expense for 2022.

As shown in the T-account above, the plug necessary to reach the required ending balance in the allowance for uncollectible accounts is $35,000, so that is bad debt expense for 2022.

3. Prepare journal entries to write off receivables and to recognize bad debt expense for 2022.

Allowance for uncollectible accounts...	25,000	
Accounts receivable..		25,000
Write-off of accounts receivable as they are determined uncollectible.		
Bad debt expense...	35,000	
Allowance for uncollectible accounts..		35,000
Year-end adjusting entry for bad debts.		

Notes Receivable

● LO7–7

Notes receivable are formal credit arrangements between a creditor (lender) and a debtor (borrower) that specify payment terms. Notes arise from loans made to people and companies who need cash, including stockholders and employees, as well as from the sale of merchandise, other assets, or services under relatively long-term payment arrangements. Notes receivable are classified as either current or noncurrent depending on the expected collection date(s).

When the term of a note is less than a year, it is reported as a short-term note. We start by discussing short-term notes, and then discuss long-term notes.

Short-Term Interest-Bearing Notes

The typical interest-bearing note receivable involves collection of a specified face amount, also called principal, at a specified maturity date or dates. In addition, interest is received at a stated percentage of the face amount. Interest on notes is calculated as

Face amount × Annual rate × Fraction of the annual period

For an example, consider Illustration 7–9.

Illustration 7–9
Interest-Bearing Notes Receivable

The Stridewell Wholesale Shoe Company manufactures athletic shoes that it sells to retailers. On May 1, 2021, the company sold shoes to Harmon Sporting Goods. Stridewell agreed to accept a $700,000, 6-month, 12% note in payment for the shoes. Interest is receivable at maturity. Assume that an interest rate of 12% is appropriate for a note of this type. Stridewell would account for the note as follows:*

May 1, 2021

Notes receivable	700,000	
Sales revenue		700,000
To record the sale of goods in exchange for a note receivable.		

November 1, 2021

Cash ($700,000 + $42,000)...	742,000	
Interest revenue ($700,000 × 12% × 6/12)		42,000
Notes receivable		700,000
To record the collection of the note at maturity.		

*To focus on recording the note we intentionally omit the entry required for the cost of the goods sold if the perpetual inventory system is used.

If the sale in the illustration instead occurred on August 1, 2021, and the company's fiscal year-end is December 31, a year-end adjusting entry accrues interest earned.

December 31, 2021

Interest receivable	35,000	
Interest revenue ($700,000 × 12% × 5/12)		35,000

The February 1 collection is then recorded as follows:

February 1, 2022

Cash ($700,000 + [$700,000 × 12% × 6/12])..	742,000	
Interest revenue ($700,000 × 12% × 1/12)		7,000
Interest receivable (accrued at December 31, 2021).........................		35,000
Notes receivable		700,000

Short-Term Noninterest-Bearing Notes

Sometimes a receivable assumes the form of a so-called noninterest-bearing note. The name is a misnomer, though. Noninterest-bearing notes actually do bear interest, but the interest is deducted (or *discounted*) from the face amount to determine the cash proceeds made available to the borrower at the outset. For example, what if Stridewell accepted a six-month, $700,000 noninterest-bearing note in exchange for delivering goods that have a cash sales price of $658,000?

You learned in Chapter 6 that, as a practical matter, a seller can assume the time value of money is not significant if the period between delivery and payment is less than a year. If Stridewell views the financing component of the note to be insignificant, it would ignore the interest rate and simply record sales revenue and an account receivable for $700,000. However, Stridewell could view the financing component of the contract to be significant. In that case, $42,000 (= $700,000 − $658,000) interest would be discounted at the outset rather than explicitly stated, and sales revenue of $658,000 recognized upon delivery. Stridewell still receives total revenue of $700,000, but that total revenue is recognized as sales revenue of $658,000 and interest revenue of $42,000. Assuming a May 1, 2021 sale, the transaction is recorded as follows:[14]

May 1, 2021		
Notes receivable (face amount)...	700,000	
Discount on notes receivable (to balance)............................		42,000
Sales revenue		658,000
November 1, 2021		
Discount on notes receivable	42,000	
Interest revenue		42,000
Cash...	700,000	
Notes receivable (face amount)		700,000

The discount on notes receivable is a contra account to the notes receivable account. That is, the notes receivable would be reported in the balance sheet net (less) any remaining discount. The discount represents future interest revenue that will be recognized as it is earned over time. We can calculate the effective interest rate as follows.

	$ 42,000	Interest for 6 months
÷	$658,000	Sales price
=	6.383%	Rate for 6 months
×	2*	To annualize the rate
=	12.766%	Effective interest rate

*Two 6-month periods

Using a calculator,
enter: N 1 I .06383
PMT − 700000
Output: PV 658,000

Using Excel, enter:
= PV (.06383,1,700000)
Output: 658,000

This note should be valued at the present value of future cash receipts. The present value of $700,000 to be received in six months using an effective interest rate of 6.383% is $658,000 (= $700,000 ÷ 1.06383 = $658,000). The use of present value techniques for valuation purposes was introduced in Chapter 5, and we'll use these techniques extensively in subsequent chapters to value various long-term notes receivable, investments, and liabilities.

In the illustration, if the sale occurs on August 1, the December 31, 2021, adjusting entry and the entry to record the cash collection on February 1, 2022, are recorded as follows:

December 31, 2021		
Discount on notes receivable	35,000	
Interest revenue ($42,000 × ⅚)*..		35,000
February 1, 2022		
Discount on notes receivable	7,000	
Interest revenue ($42,000 × ⅙)		7,000
Cash...	700,000	
Notes receivable (face amount)		700,000

*We also can calculate interest revenue by multiplying the net notes receivable balance by the effective interest rate ($658,000 × 12.766% × 5/12 = $35,000).

[14] The entries shown assume the note is recorded by the gross method. By the net method, the interest component is netted against the face amount of the note as follows:

May 1, 2016

Notes receivable...	658,000	
Sales revenue...		658,000

November 1, 2016

Cash...	700,000	
Notes receivable		658,000
Interest revenue ($700,000 × 12% × ⁶/₁₂)		42,000

In the December 31, 2021 balance sheet, the note receivable is shown at $693,000: the face amount ($700,000) less remaining discount ($7,000).

Long-Term Notes Receivable

We account for long-term notes receivable the same way we account for short-term notes receivable, but the time value of money has a larger effect. Therefore, if long-term notes are received in exchange for goods and services, the financing component of the transaction typically is viewed as significant for revenue recognition purposes. To provide an example, Illustration 7–10 modifies the facts in Illustration 7–9 to have Stridewell agree on January 1, 2021, to accept a two-year noninterest-bearing note.

Illustration 7–10
Long-Term Noninterest-Bearing Notes Receivable

The Stridewell Wholesale Shoe Company manufactures athletic shoes that it sells to retailers. On January 1, 2021, the company sold shoes to Harmon Sporting Goods. Stridewell agreed to accept a $700,000, two-year note in payment for the shoes. Assuming a 12% effective interest rate, Stridewell would account for the note as follows:*

January 1, 2021

Notes receivable	700,000	
Discount on notes receivable		141,964
Sales revenue†		558,036

    To record the sale of goods in exchange for a two-year note receivable.

December 31, 2021

Discount on notes receivable	66,964	
Interest revenue ($558,036 × 12%)		66,964

    To record interest revenue in 2021.

December 31, 2022

Cash	700,000	
Discount on notes receivable	75,000	
Interest revenue [($558,036 + $66,964) × 12%]		75,000
Notes receivable		700,000

    To record interest revenue in 2022 and collection of the note.

*To focus on recording the note we intentionally omit the entry required for the cost of the goods sold if the perpetual inventory system is used.
†$700,000 × Present value of $1; n = 2, i = 12%

Using a calculator,
enter: N 2 I .12
FV – 700000
Output: PV 558,036

Using Excel, enter:
= PV(0.12,2,0,−700000)
Output: 558,036

It's useful to consider a couple of aspects of Illustration 7–10. First, notice that the sales revenue in 2021 is not recorded for the full $700,000. Instead, sales revenue is calculated as ($558,036), the *present value* of the amount ($700,000) to be received in two years. The net amount of the note receivable equals its present value ($558,036), which is the notes receivable of $700,000 less the discount on notes receivable of $141,964. Recall from Chapter 6 that sellers need to recognize the financing component of a contract when the time value of money is significant. That is what Stridewell is doing. It earns sales revenue of $558,036 from selling shoes, and interest revenue totaling $141,964 (= $66,964 + $75,000) for financing the transaction.

Second, interest revenue each period is calculated based on the *net* notes receivable as of the beginning of that period. As a consequence, interest revenue differs between periods because the net notes receivable increases over time. In our example, Stridewell's 2021 interest revenue of $66,964 is calculated based on the initial net notes receivable balance ($558,036 × 12%). We reduce the discount on notes receivable for 2021 interest revenue, which increases the net notes receivable balance to $625,000 (= $558,036 + $66,964). So, Stridewell's 2022 interest revenue of $75,000 is calculated based on that higher net notes receivable balance ($625,000 × 12%), reducing the discount on notes receivable to zero by the end of 2022. At that point, the book value of the note, sometimes called the carrying value, carrying amount, or amortized cost basis, is $700,000, and that is the amount of cash that is collected. The effective interest rate stays the same over time, but interest revenue increases as that rate is multiplied by a receivable balance that increases over time. This is an application of the **effective interest method**, by which we calculate interest revenue or interest expense by multiplying the outstanding balance of a long-term receivable or

In the *effective interest method*, interest is determined by multiplying the outstanding balance by the effective interest rate.

360   SECTION 2   Assets

liability by the effective interest rate. As you will see in later chapters, that method is used for all long-term receivables and liabilities.

We discuss long-term notes receivable in greater detail in Chapter 14 at the same time we discuss accounting for long-term notes payable. That discussion provides more examples of accounting for long-term noninterest-bearing notes, as well as long-term interest-bearing notes, and also considers accounting for notes receivable that are collected in equal installment payments.

Marriott International accepts both interest-bearing and noninterest-bearing notes from developers and franchisees of new hotels. The 2016 disclosure note shown in Illustration 7–11 describes the company's accounting policy for these notes.

Illustration 7–11

Disclosure of Notes Receivable—Marriott International

Real World Financials

Summary of Significant Accounting Policies (in part)	
We may make senior, mezzanine, and other loans to owners of hotels that we operate or franchise, generally to facilitate the development of a hotel and sometimes to facilitate brand programs or initiatives. We expect the owners to repay the loans in accordance with the loan agreements, or earlier as the hotels mature and capital markets permit.	
Note 9: Notes Receivable (in part)	
Notes Receivable Principal Payments (net of reserves and unamortized discounts) and Interest Rates ($ in millions)	**Amount**
Balance at year-end 2016	$248
Range of stated interest rates at year-end 2016	0 to 18%

When a noninterest-bearing note is received solely in exchange for cash, the amount of cash exchanged is the basis for valuing the note.

NOTES RECEIVED SOLELY FOR CASH   If a note with an unrealistic interest rate—even a noninterest-bearing note—is received *solely* in exchange for cash, the cash paid to the issuer is considered to be the note's present value.[15] Even if this means recording interest at a ridiculously low or zero rate, the amount of cash exchanged is the basis for valuing the note. If the noninterest-bearing note in the previous example had been received solely in exchange for $700,000 cash, the transaction would be recorded as follows:

Notes receivable (face amount)...	700,000	
Cash (given)...		700,000

Subsequent Valuation of Notes Receivable

Similar to accounts receivable, companies are required to estimate bad debts (also called credit losses) on notes receivable, and use an allowance account to reduce the receivable to the appropriate carrying value. The process of recording bad debt expense is the same as with accounts receivable.

Under the CECL model, companies consider all relevant information when assessing credit losses, including reasonable and supportable forecasts about the future. Companies can use a variety of approaches to estimate uncollectible notes receivable, including the aging method illustrated for accounts receivable. They often use discounted cash flow techniques, estimating the amount of necessary allowance by comparing the balance in notes receivable to the present value of the cash flows expected to be received, discounted at the interest rate that was effective when each note was initially recognized. An example of that approach is included in Appendix 7B.

One of the more difficult measurement problems facing banks and other lending institutions is the estimation of bad debts on their long-term notes (loans). It's difficult to predict uncollectible accounts for these arrangements. As an example, **Wells Fargo & Company,** a large bank holding company, reported the following in the asset section of its December 31, 2016, balance sheet:

---

[15]This assumes that no other present or future considerations are included in the agreement. For example, a noninterest-bearing note might be given to a vendor in exchange for cash *and* a promise to provide future inventories at prices lower than anticipated market prices. The issuer values the note at the present value of cash payments using a realistic interest rate, and the difference between present value and cash payments is recognized as interest revenue over the life of the note. This difference also increases future inventory purchases to realistic market prices.

($ in millions)	December 31, 2017	December 31, 2016
Loans	$956,770	$967,604
Allowance for loan losses	(11,004)	(11,419)
Net loans	$945,766	$956,185

A disclosure note, reproduced in Illustration 7–12, describes Wells Fargo's loan loss policy.

Illustration 7–12

Disclosure of Allowance for Loan Losses—Wells Fargo & Company

Real World Financials

> **Allowance for Credit Losses (ACL) (in part)**
>
> The allowance for credit losses is management's estimate of credit losses inherent in the loan portfolio, including unfunded credit commitments, at the balance sheet date. We have an established process to determine the appropriateness of the allowance for credit losses that assesses the losses inherent in our portfolio and related unfunded credit commitments. We develop and document our allowance methodology at the portfolio segment level—commercial loan portfolio and consumer loan portfolio. While we attribute portions of the allowance to our respective commercial and consumer portfolio segments, the entire allowance is available to absorb credit losses inherent in the total loan portfolio and unfunded credit commitments.
>
> Source: Wells Fargo & Company

Sometimes a company grants a concession to a borrower because the borrower faces financial difficulties. In the case of such a *troubled debt restructuring,* the creditor modifies the terms of the receivable and no longer expects to collect all amounts that were due to it originally. Accounting for troubled debt restructurings is discussed in Appendix 7B.

GAAP requires that companies disclose the fair value of their notes receivable in the disclosure notes (they don't have to disclose the fair value of accounts receivable when the book value of the receivables approximates fair value).[16] Also, companies can choose to carry receivables at fair value in their balance sheets, with changes in fair value recognized as gains or losses in the income statements.[17] This "fair value option" is discussed in Chapter 12.

International Financial Reporting Standards

● LO7–10

> **Accounts and Notes Receivable.** *IFRS No. 9* governs treatment of accounts and notes receivable. Its requirements are similar to U.S. GAAP with respect to trade and cash discounts, sales returns, recognition of interest on notes receivable, and use of an allowance for uncollectible accounts (which typically is called a "provision for bad debts" under IFRS).[18] A few key differences remain. IFRS and U.S. GAAP both allow a "fair value option" for accounting for receivables, but the IFRS standard restricts the circumstances in which that option is allowed (we discuss this more in Chapter 12). Also, U.S. GAAP allows "available for sale" accounting for investments in debt securities, but *IFRS No. 9* does not allow that approach (we also discuss that approach further in Chapter 12). Also, U.S. GAAP requires more disaggregation of accounts and notes receivable in the balance sheet or notes to the financial statements. For example, companies need to separately disclose accounts receivable from customers, from related parties, and from others. IFRS recommends but does not require separate disclosure.
>
> A final important difference relates to estimating bad debts. IFRS uses the ECL ("Expected Credit Loss") model. For most receivables, the ECL model reports a "12-month ECL," which bases expected credit losses only on defaults that could occur within the next twelve months. Only if a receivable's credit quality has deteriorated significantly does the creditor instead report the "lifetime ECL," which also includes credit losses expected to occur from defaults after twelve months, as is done for all receivables under the CECL model used in U.S. GAAP. As a result of this lack of convergence, it is likely that accruals for credit losses under IFRS will be lower, and occur later, than under U.S. GAAP.

---

[16]FASB ASC 825–10–50–10: Financial Instruments—Overall—Disclosure—Fair Value of Financial Instruments.

[17]FASB ASC 825–10–25: Financial Instruments—Overall—Recognition Fair Value Option.

[18]Source: "Financial Instruments," *International Financial Reporting Standard No. 9* (IASCF), as amended effective January 1, 2018.

Financing with Receivables

● LO7–8

Financial institutions have developed a wide variety of ways for companies to use their receivables to obtain immediate cash. Companies can find this attractive because it shortens their operating cycles by providing cash immediately rather than having to wait until credit customers pay the amounts due. Also, many companies avoid the difficulties of servicing (billing and collecting) receivables by having financial institutions take on that role. Of course, financial institutions require compensation for providing these services, usually interest and/or a finance charge.

The various approaches used to finance with receivables differ with respect to which rights and risks are retained by the *transferor* (the company who was the original holder of the receivables) and which are passed on to the *transferee* (the new holder, the financial institution). Despite this diversity, any of these approaches can be described as either

1. A *secured borrowing*. Under this approach, the transferor (borrower) simply acts like it borrowed money from the transferee (lender), with the receivables remaining in the transferor's balance sheet and serving as collateral for the loan. On the other side of the transaction, the transferee recognizes a note receivable.
2. A *sale of receivables*. Under this approach, the transferor (seller) "derecognizes" (removes) the receivables from its balance sheet, acting like it sold them to the transferee (buyer). On the other side of the transaction, the transferee recognizes the receivables as assets in its balance sheet and measures them at their fair value.

As you will see in the examples that follow, the transferor (borrower) debits cash regardless of whether the transaction is treated as a secured borrowing or a sale of receivables. What differs is whether the borrower credits a liability (for a secured borrowing) or credits the receivable asset (for a sale of receivables). Let's discuss each of these approaches in more detail as they apply to accounts receivable and notes receivable. Then we'll discuss the circumstances under which GAAP requires each approach.

Secured Borrowing

> When companies *pledge* accounts receivable as collateral for debt, a disclosure note describes the arrangement.

Sometimes companies pledge accounts receivable as collateral for a loan. Assets that serve as collateral are forfeited if the borrower defaults on the loan. No particular receivables are associated with the loan. Rather, the entire receivables balance serves as collateral. The responsibility for collection of the receivables remains solely with the company. No special accounting treatment is needed for pledged receivables, but the arrangement should be described in a disclosure note. For example, Illustration 7–13 shows a portion of the long-term debt disclosure note included in the 2016 annual report of Virco Mfg. Corporation, a manufacturer of office furniture.

Illustration 7–13

Disclosure of Receivables Used as Collateral—Virco Mfg. Corporation

Real World Financials

Liquidity and Capital Resources (in part)

The Revolving Credit Facility is an asset-based line of credit that is subject to a borrowing base limitation and generally provides for advances of up to 85% of eligible accounts receivable . . .

Source: Virco Mfg. Corporation

Alternatively, financing arrangements can require that companies assign particular receivables to serve as collateral for loans. You already may be familiar with the concept of assigning an asset as collateral if you or someone you know has a mortgage on a home. The bank or other financial institution holding the mortgage will require that, if the homeowner defaults on the mortgage payments, the home be sold and the proceeds used to pay off the mortgage debt. Similarly, in the case of an assignment of receivables, nonpayment of a debt will require the proceeds from collecting the assigned receivables to go directly toward repayment of the debt.

In these arrangements, the lender typically lends an amount of money that is less than the amount of receivables assigned by the borrower. The difference provides some protection for the lender to allow for possible uncollectible accounts. Also, the lender (sometimes called an *assignee*) usually charges the borrower (sometimes called an *assignor*) an upfront finance charge in addition to stated interest on the loan. The receivables might be collected either by the lender or the borrower, depending on the details of the arrangement. Illustration 7–14 provides an example.

On December 1, 2021, the Santa Teresa Glass Company borrowed $500,000 from Finance Bank and signed a promissory note. Interest at 12% is payable monthly. The company assigned $620,000 of its receivables as collateral for the loan. Finance Bank charges a finance fee equal to 1.5% of the accounts receivable assigned.

Santa Teresa Glass records the borrowing as follows:

Cash (difference)	490,700	
Finance charge expense* (1.5% × $620,000)...	9,300	
Liability—financing arrangement..		500,000

*In theory, this fee should be allocated over the entire period of the loan rather than recorded as an expense in the initial period. However, amounts usually are small and the loan period usually is short. For expediency, then, we expense the entire fee immediately.

Santa Teresa will continue to collect the receivables, and will record any discounts, sales returns, and bad debt write-offs, but will remit the cash to Finance Bank, usually on a monthly basis. If $400,000 of the receivables assigned are collected in December, Santa Teresa Glass records the following entries:

Cash...	400,000	
Accounts receivable...		400,000
Interest expense ($500,000 × 12% × ¹⁄₁₂)...	5,000	
Liability—financing arrangement..	400,000	
Cash..		405,000

Illustration 7–14

Assignment of Accounts Receivable

Accounts Receivable

620,000	
	400,000
220,000	

Liability—Financing Arrangement

	500,000
400,000	
	100,000

In Santa Teresa's financial statements, the arrangement is described in a disclosure note.

Sale of Receivables

Accounts and notes receivable, like any other assets, can be sold at a gain or a loss. The basic accounting treatment for the sale of receivables is similar to accounting for the sale of other assets. The seller (transferor) (a) removes from the accounts the receivables (and any allowance for bad debts associated with them), (b) recognizes at fair value any assets acquired or liabilities assumed by the seller in the transaction, and (c) records the difference as a gain or loss.

The sale of accounts receivable is a popular method of financing. A technique once used by companies in a few industries or with poor credit ratings, the sale of receivables is now a common occurrence for many different types of companies. For example, General Motors, Deere & Co., and Bank of America all sell receivables. The two most common types of selling arrangements are **factoring** and **securitization**. We'll now discuss each type.

In a factoring arrangement, the company sells its accounts receivable to a financial institution. The financial institution typically buys receivables for cash, handles the billing and collection of the receivables, and charges a fee for this service. Actually, credit cards like VISA and Mastercard are forms of factoring arrangements. The seller relinquishes all rights to the future cash receipts in exchange for cash from the buyer (the *factor*).

Two popular arrangements used for the sale of receivables are factoring and securitization.

As an example, Illustration 7–15 shows an excerpt from the website of BusinessCash. Com, a financial institution that offers factoring as one of its services.

Accounts Receivable Factoring

0.79-1.99% 30-Day Rates!   Funding in 24–48 hours!

Accounts Receivable Financing is the sale of a company's receivables at a discount in exchange for immediate cash. The percentage of working capital a company can receive upfront ranges from 70%–92%. AR financing can be a perfect solution for many industries, including to textiles, to wine distributors, and to start-ups.

Illustration 7–15

Advertisement of Factoring BusinessCash.Com

Real World Financials

Notice that the factor, BusinessCash.com, advances only between 70%–92% of the factored receivables. The remaining balance is retained as security until all of the receivables are collected and then remitted to the transferor, net of the factor's fee. The interest rate charged by this factor might seem low, but realize it is a 30-day rate. Multiply it by 12, and you will see a range of annual interest rates from 9.5% to almost 24%. The specific rate charged depends on, among other things, the quality of the receivables and the length of time before payment is required.

Another popular arrangement used to sell receivables is securitization. In a typical accounts receivable securitization, the company creates a "special purpose entity" (SPE), usually a trust or a subsidiary. The SPE buys a pool of trade receivables, credit card receivables, or loans from the company, and then sells related securities, typically debt such as bonds or commercial paper, that are backed (collateralized) by the receivables. Securitizing receivables using an SPE can provide significant economic advantages, allowing companies to reach a large pool of investors and to obtain more favorable financing terms.[19]

As an example of a securitization, Illustration 7–16 shows a portion of the disclosure note included in the 2017 annual report of **Flextronics International Limited,** a worldwide leader in design, manufacturing, and logistics services, describing the securitization of its trade accounts receivable.

FINANCIAL Reporting Case

Q4, p. 339

Illustration 7–16

Description of Securitization Program— Flextronics International Limited

Real World Financials

> **Note 10: Trade Receivables Securitization**
>
> The Company continuously sells designated pools of trade receivables . . . to affiliated special purpose entities, each of which in turn sells 100% of the receivables to unaffiliated financial institutions . . . . The company services, administers and collects the receivables on behalf of the special purpose entities and receives a servicing fee of 0.1% to 0.5% of serviced receivables per annum.
>
> Source: Flextronics International Limited

The specifics of sale accounting vary depending on the particular arrangement between the seller and buyer (transferee).[20] One key feature is whether the receivables are transferred without recourse or with recourse.

The buyer assumes the risk of uncollectibility when accounts receivable are sold *without recourse.*

SALE WITHOUT RECOURSE   If a factoring arrangement is made without recourse, the buyer can't ask the seller for more money if the receivables prove to be uncollectible. Therefore, the buyer assumes the risk of bad debts. Illustration 7–17 provides an example of receivables factored without recourse.

Note that in Illustration 7–17 the fair value ($50,000) of the last 10% of the receivables to be collected is less than 10% of the total book value of the receivables (10% × $600,000 = $60,000). That's common, because the last receivables to be collected are likely to be reduced by sales returns and allowances, and therefore have a lower fair value.

The seller retains the risk of uncollectibility when accounts receivable are sold *with recourse.*

SALE WITH RECOURSE   When a company sells accounts receivable with recourse, the seller retains all of the risk of bad debts. In effect, the seller guarantees that the buyer will be paid even if some receivables prove to be uncollectible. To compensate the seller for retaining the risk of bad debts, the buyer usually charges a lower factoring fee when receivables are sold with recourse.

In Illustration 7–17, even if the receivables were sold with recourse, Santa Teresa Glass still could account for the transfer as a sale so long as the conditions for sale treatment are met. The only difference is the additional requirement that Santa Teresa record the estimated

---

[19] Although SPEs usually aren't viewed as separate entities for accounting purposes, they typically are separate entities for legal purposes. As a consequence, an SPE typically is viewed as "bankruptcy remote," meaning that the transferor's creditors can't access the receivables if the transferor goes bankrupt. This increases the safety of the SPE's assets and typically allows it to obtain more favorable financing terms than could the transferor.

[20] FASB ASC 860: Transfers and Servicing.

Illustration 7–17
Accounts Receivable
Factored without Recourse

In December 2021, the Santa Teresa Glass Company entered into the following factoring arrangement with Factor Bank:

- Santa Teresa transfered accounts receivable that had a book value of $600,000.
- The transfer was made without recourse.
- Factor immediately remitted to Santa Teresa cash equal to 90% of the factored amount (90% × $600,000 = $540,000).
- Factor retains the remaining 10% to cover its factoring fee (equal to 4% of the total factored amount; 4% × $600,000 = $24,000) and to provide a cushion against potential sales returns and allowances.
- After Factor has collected cash equal to the amount advanced to Santa Teresa plus the factoring fee, Factor will remit the excess to Santa Teresa. Therefore, Santa Teresa has a "beneficial interest" in the transferred receivables equal to the fair value of the last 10% of the receivables to be collected (which management estimates to equal $50,000), less the 4% factoring fee.*

Santa Teresa Glass records the transfer as follows:

Cash (90% × $600,000)	540,000	
Loss on sale of receivables (to balance)	34,000	
Receivable from factor ($50,000 – $24,000 fee)	26,000	
Accounts receivable (book value sold)		600,000

*Illustration 7–17 depicts an arrangement in which the factor's fee is paid out of the 10% of receivables retained by the factor. Alternatively, a factoring arrangement could be structured to have the factor's fee withheld from the cash advanced to the company at the start of the arrangement. In that case, in Illustration 7–17 the journal entry recorded by Santa Teresa would be

Cash ([90% × $600,000] – $24,000 fee)	516,000	
Loss on sale of receivables (to balance)	34,000	
Receivable from factor	50,000	
Accounts receivable (book value sold)		600,000

fair value of its recourse obligation as a liability. The recourse obligation is the estimated amount that Santa Teresa will have to pay Factor Bank as a reimbursement for uncollectible receivables. Illustration 7–18 provides an example of receivables factored with recourse.

Illustration 7–18
Accounts Receivable
Factored with Recourse

Assume the same facts as in Illustration 7–17, except that Santa Teresa sold the receivables to Factor Bank *with recourse* and estimates the fair value of the recourse obligation to be $5,000. Santa Teresa records the transfer as follows:

Cash (90% × $600,000)	540,000	
Loss on sale of receivables (to balance)	39,000	
Receivable from factor ($50,000 – $24,000 fee)	26,000	
Recourse liability		5,000
Accounts receivable (book value sold)		600,000

When comparing Illustration 7–17 and 7–18, notice that the estimated recourse liability of $5,000 increases the loss on sale by $5,000. If the factor eventually collects all of the receivables, Santa Teresa eliminates the recourse liability and recognizes a gain.

Transfers of Notes Receivable

We handle transfers of notes receivable in the same manner as transfers of accounts receivable. A note receivable can be used to obtain immediate cash from a financial institution either by pledging the note as collateral for a loan or by selling the note. Notes also can be securitized.

The transfer of a note to a financial institution is referred to as discounting. The financial institution accepts the note and gives the seller cash equal to the maturity value of the note reduced by a discount. The discount is computed by applying a discount rate to the maturity value and represents the financing fee the financial institution charges for the transaction. Illustration 7–19 provides an example of the calculation of the proceeds received by the transferor.

The transfer of a note receivable to a financial institution is called *discounting*.

Illustration 7–19

Discounting a Note Receivable

On December 31, 2021, the Stridewell Wholesale Shoe Company sold land in exchange for a nine-month, 10% note. The note requires the payment of $200,000 plus interest on September 30, 2022. The company's fiscal year-end is December 31. The 10% rate properly reflects the time value of money for this type of note. On March 31, 2022, Stridewell discounted the note at the Bank of the East. The bank's discount rate is 12%.

Because the note had been outstanding for three months before it was discounted at the bank, Stridewell first records the interest that has accrued prior to being discounted:

March 31, 2022

STEP 1: Accrue interest earned on the note receivable prior to its being discounted.

Interest receivable	5,000	
Interest revenue ($200,000 × 10% × 3/12)		5,000

Next, the value of the note if held to maturity is calculated. Then the discount for the time remaining to maturity is deducted to determine the cash proceeds from discounting the note:

STEP 2: Add interest to maturity to calculate maturity value.

STEP 3: Deduct discount to calculate cash proceeds.

$ 200,000	Face amount
15,000	Interest to maturity ($200,000 × 10% × 9/12)
215,000	Maturity value
(12,900)	Discount ($215,000 × 12% × 6/12)
$202,100	Cash proceeds

Similar to accounts receivable, Stridewell potentially could account for the transfer as a sale or a secured borrowing. For example, Illustration 7–20 shows the appropriate journal entry to account for the transfer as a sale without recourse.

Illustration 7–20

Discounted Note Treated as a Sale

Cash (proceeds determined above)...	202,100	
Loss on sale of notes receivable (to balance)...	2,900	
Notes receivable (face amount)...		200,000
Interest receivable (accrued interest determined above)...................		5,000

Deciding Whether to Account for a Transfer as a Sale or a Secured Borrowing

Transferors usually prefer to use the sale approach rather than the secured borrowing approach to account for the transfer of a receivable because the sale approach makes the transferor seem less leveraged, more liquid, and perhaps more profitable than does the secured borrowing approach. Illustration 7–21 explains why by describing particular effects on key accounting metrics.

Illustration 7–21

Why Do Transferors of Receivables Generally Want to Account for the Transfer as a Sale?

Does the Accounting Approach	Sale	Secured Borrowing	Why Sales Approach is Preferred by the Transferor
Derecognize A/R, reducing assets?	Yes	No	Sale approach produces lower total assets and higher return on assets (ROA).
Recognize liability for cash received?	No	Yes	Sale approach produces lower liabilities and less leverage (debt/equity).
Where is cash received shown in the statement of cash flows?	May be in operating or financing sections	Always in financing section	Sale approach can produce higher cash flow from operations at time of transfer.
Recognize gain on transfer?	More likely	Less likely	Sale approach can produce higher income at time of transfer.

So when is a company allowed to account for the transfer of receivables as a sale? The most critical element is the extent to which the company (the transferor) *surrenders control over the assets transferred.* For some arrangements, surrender of control is clear (e.g., when a receivable is sold without recourse and without any other involvement by the transferor). However, for other arrangements this distinction is not obvious. Indeed, some companies appear to structure transactions in ways that qualify for sale treatment but retain enough involvement to have control. This led the FASB to provide guidelines designed to constrain inappropriate use of the sale approach. Specifically, the transferor (defined to include the company, its consolidated affiliates, and people acting on behalf of the company) is determined to have surrendered control over the receivables if and only if all of the following conditions are met:[21]

a. The transferred assets have been isolated from the transferor—beyond the reach of the transferor and its creditors.

b. Each transferee has the right to pledge or exchange the assets it received.

c. The transferor does not maintain *effective control* over the transferred assets, for example, by structuring the transfer such that the assets are likely to end up returned to the transferor.

> If the transferor is deemed to have surrendered control over the transferred receivables, the arrangement is accounted for as a sale; otherwise as a secured borrowing.

If *all* of these conditions are met, the transferor accounts for the transfer as a sale. If *any* of the conditions are not met, the transferor treats the transaction as a secured borrowing.

It is not surprising that some companies have aggressively tried to circumvent these conditions by creating elaborate transactions to qualify for sale treatment. The most famous recent case was Lehman Brothers' use of "Repo 105" transactions, discussed in Illustration 7–22.

Lehman Brothers' bankruptcy in 2008 was the largest ever to occur in the United States. One factor that likely contributed to investor losses was Lehman's use of "Repo 105" transactions that concealed how overburdened with liabilities the company had become. Here is how a Repo 105 transaction worked. Near the end of each quarter, Lehman would transfer financial assets like receivables to a bank or other financial institution in exchange for cash, and would account for that transfer as a sale of the financial assets. Lehman would use the cash obtained from the transfer to pay down liabilities, so the net effect of the transaction was to reduce assets, reduce liabilities, and therefore make Lehman appear less leveraged and less risky. Lehman also agreed to repurchase ("repo") the assets in the next quarter for an amount of cash that exceeded the amount it initially received.

In substance, this transaction is a loan, since Lehman ended up retaining the financial assets and paying amounts equivalent to principal and interest. However, Lehman argued that the assets were beyond its *effective control,* because the cash it received for transferring the assets was insufficient to enable Lehman to repurchase those assets (the "105" in "Repo 105" refers to the assets being worth at least 105% of the cash Lehman was getting for them). Although Lehman's interpretation was supported by the GAAP in effect at the time, these transactions were very poorly disclosed, and when they eventually came to light, the financial markets and investing public reacted very negatively. In response to the Lehman debacle, the FASB has taken steps to close the loophole that allowed Repo 105 transactions to be accounted for as sales.*

*FASB ASC 860–10–55: Transfers and Servicing—Overall—Implementation Guidance and Illustrations.

Source: Lehman Brothers

Illustration 7–22

Repo 105 Transactions—
Lehman Brothers

Real World Financials

Illustration 7–23 summarizes the decision process that is used to determine whether a transfer of a receivable is accounted for as a secured borrowing or a sale.

Disclosures

Much disclosure is required when the transferor has continuing involvement in the transferred assets but accounts for the transfer as a sale. Why? Those are the circumstances under

---

[21] FASB ASC 860–10–40: Transfers and Servicing–Overall–Derecognition (previously "Accounting for Transfers and Servicing of Financial Assets and Extinguishments of Liabilities," *Statement of Financial Accounting Standards No. 140* (Norwalk, Conn.: FASB, 2000), as amended by *SFAS No. 166*).

368   SECTION 2   Assets

Illustration 7–23   Accounting for the Financing of Receivables

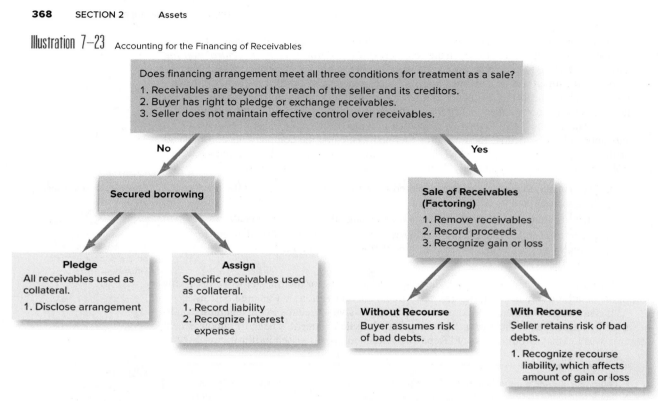

which it's most likely that the transferor may still bear significant risk associated with the arrangement, so those are the arrangements that analysts often view instead as a secured borrowing. As a result, transferors must provide enough information about the transfer to allow financial statement users to fully understand (a) the transfer, (b) any continuing involvement with the transferred assets, and (c) any ongoing risks to the transferor.

The company also has to provide information about the quality of the transferred assets. For example, for transferred receivables, the company needs to disclose the amount of receivables that are past due and any credit losses occurring during the period. Among the other information the company must disclose are these:

- How fair values were estimated when recording the transaction.
- Any cash flows occurring between the transferor and the transferee.
- How any continuing involvement in the transferred assets will be accounted for on an ongoing basis.[22]

Additional Consideration

Participating Interests. What if, rather than transferring all of a particular receivable, a company transfers only part of it? For example, what if a company transfers the right to receive future interest payments on a note, but retains the right to receive the loan principal? U.S. GAAP requires that a partial transfer be treated as a secured borrowing unless the amount transferred qualifies as a "participating interest" as well as meeting the "surrender of control" requirements described above. Participating interests are defined as having a proportionate ownership interest in the receivable and sharing proportionally in the cash flows of the receivable. Many common securitization arrangements do not qualify as participating interests, so this change in GAAP makes it harder for partial transfers to qualify for the sale approach.

---

[22]FASB ASC 860–10–40: Transfers and Servicing—Overall—Derecognition (previously "Accounting for Transfers of Financial Assets, an amendment of FASB Statement No. 140," *Statement of Financial Accounting Standards No. 166* (Norwalk, Conn.: FASB, 2009), par. 17).

International Financial Reporting Standards

● LO7–10

> **Transfers of Receivables.** *IFRS No. 9* and *FASB ASC 860* cover financing with receivables under IFRS and U.S. GAAP, respectively.[23,24] The international and U.S. guidance often lead to similar accounting treatments. Both seek to determine whether an arrangement should be treated as a secured borrowing or a sale, and, having concluded which approach is appropriate, both account for the approaches in a similar fashion.
>
> Where IFRS and U.S. GAAP most differ is in the conceptual basis for their choice of accounting approaches and in the decision process they require to determine which approach to use. As you have seen in this chapter, U.S. GAAP focuses on whether control of assets has shifted from the transferor to the transferee. In contrast, IFRS requires a more complex decision process. The company has to have transferred the rights to receive the cash flows from the receivable and then considers whether the company has transferred "substantially all of the risks and rewards of ownership," as well as whether the company has transferred control. Under IFRS,
>
> 1. If the company *transfers* substantially all of the risks and rewards of ownership, the transfer is treated as a sale.
>
> 2. If the company *retains* substantially all of the risks and rewards of ownership, the transfer is treated as a secured borrowing.
>
> 3. If neither conditions 1 or 2 hold, the company accounts for the transaction as a sale if it has transferred control, and as a secured borrowing if it has retained control.
>
> Whether risks and rewards have been transferred is evaluated by comparing how variability in the amounts and timing of the cash flows of the transferred asset affect the company before and after the transfer.
>
> This is a broad overview of the IFRS guidance. Application of the detailed rules is complex, and, depending on the specifics of an arrangement, a company could have different accounting under IFRS and U.S. GAAP.
>
> Source: International Financial Reporting Standards

Concept Review Exercise

FINANCING WITH RECEIVABLES

The Hollywood Lumber Company obtains financing from the Midwest Finance Company by factoring (or discounting) its receivables. During June 2021, the company factored $1,000,000 of accounts receivable to Midwest. The transfer was made *without* recourse. The factor, Midwest Finance, remits 80% of the factored receivables and retains 20%. When the receivables are collected by Midwest, the retained amount, less a 3% fee (3% of the total factored amount), will be remitted to Hollywood Lumber. Hollywood estimates that the fair value of the amount retained by Midwest is $180,000.

In addition, on June 30, 2021, Hollywood discounted a note receivable without recourse. The note, which originated on March 31, 2021, requires the payment of $150,000 *plus* interest at 8% on March 31, 2022. Midwest's discount rate is 10%. The company's fiscal year-end is December 31.

Required:
Prepare journal entries for Hollywood Lumber for the factoring of accounts receivable and the note receivable discounted on June 30. Assume that the required criteria are met and the transfers are accounted for as sales.

---

[23] "Financial Instruments," *International Financial Reporting Standard No. 9* (IASCF), as amended effective January 1, 2018.
[24] FASB ASC 860: Transfers and Servicing.

Solution:

The Factoring of Receivables

Cash ($1,000,000 × 80%)...	800,000	
Loss on sale of receivables (to balance)	50,000	
Receivable from factor ($180,000 – $30,000 fee)..	150,000	
Accounts receivable (balance sold)		1,000,000

The Note Receivable Discounted

Interest receivable	3,000	
Interest revenue ($150,000 × 8% × 3/12)...		3,000
Cash (proceeds determined below)...	149,850	
Loss on sale of notes receivable (difference)	3,150	
Notes receivable (face amount)...		150,000
Interest receivable (accrued interest determined above).....................		3,000

$150,000	Face amount
12,000	Interest to maturity ($150,000 × 8%)
162,000	Maturity value
(12,150)	Discount ($162,000 × 10% × 9/12)
$149,850	Cash proceeds

Decision Makers' Perspective

RECEIVABLES MANAGEMENT   A company's investment in receivables is influenced by several variables, including the level of sales, the nature of the product or service sold, and credit and collection policies. These variables are, of course, related. For example, a change in credit policies could affect sales. In fact, more liberal credit policies—allowing customers a longer time to pay or offering cash discounts for early payment—often are initiated with the specific objective of increasing sales volume.

● LO7–9

Management must evaluate the costs and benefits of any change in credit and collection policies.

Management's choice of credit and collection policies often involves trade-offs. For example, offering cash discounts may increase sales volume, accelerate customer payment, and reduce bad debts. These benefits are not without cost. The cash discounts reduce the amount of cash collected from customers who take advantage of the discounts. Extending payment terms also may increase sales volume. However, this creates an increase in the required investment in receivables and may increase bad debts.

The ability to use receivables as a method of financing also offers management alternatives. Assigning, factoring, and discounting receivables are alternative methods of financing operations that must be evaluated relative to other financing methods such as lines of credit or other types of short-term borrowing.

Investors, creditors, and financial analysts can gain important insights by monitoring a company's investment in receivables. Chapter 4 introduced the receivables turnover ratio and the related average collection period, ratios designed to monitor receivables. Recall that these ratios are calculated as follows:

$$\text{Receivables turnover ratio} = \frac{\text{Net sales}}{\text{Average accounts receivable (net)}}$$

$$\text{Average collection period} = \frac{365 \text{ days}}{\text{Receivables turnover ratio}}$$

The turnover ratio shows the number of times during a period that the average accounts receivable balance is collected, and the average collection period is an approximation of the number of days the average accounts receivable balance is outstanding.

As a company's sales grow, receivables also will increase. If the percentage increase in receivables is greater than the percentage increase in sales, the receivables turnover ratio will decline (the average collection period will increase). This could indicate customer dissatisfaction with the product or that the company has extended too generous payment terms in order to attract new customers, which, in turn, could increase sales returns and bad debts.

These ratios also can be used to compare the relative effectiveness of companies in managing the investment in receivables. Of course, it would be meaningless to compare the receivables turnover ratio of a computer products company such as IBM with that of, say, a food products company like Hershey. A company selling high-priced, low-volume products like mainframe computers generally will grant customers longer payment terms than a company selling lower-priced, higher-volume food products. Illustration 7–24 lists the 2017 receivables turnover ratio for some well-known companies. The differences are as expected, given the nature of the companies' products and operations. In particular, companies designing expensive products for medical and business applications turn over their receivables less frequently than do consumer-goods manufacturers and wholesalers.

Company	2017 Receivables Turnover Ratio
Medtronic (medical technology)	5.33
Autodesk (design software)	3.67
General Mills (wholesale consumer foods)	11.19

Illustration 7–24

Receivables Turnover Ratios

To illustrate receivables analysis in more detail, let's compute the 2017 receivables turnover ratio and the average collection period for two companies in the software industry, Symantec Corp. and CA, Inc.

	($ in millions)			
	Symantec Corp.		**CA, Inc.**	
	2017	**2016**	**2017**	**2016**
Accounts receivable (net)	$649	$556	$764	$625
Two-year averages	$ 603		$ 695	
Net sales—2017	$4,019		$4,036	

	Symantec Corp.	**CA, Inc.**	**Industry Average**
Receivables Turnover	$= \dfrac{\$4,019}{\$603} = 6.67$ times	$\dfrac{\$4,036}{\$695} = 5.81$ times	8.38 times
Average Collection Period	$= \dfrac{365}{6.67} = 54.72$ days	$\dfrac{365}{5.81} = 62.82$ days	43.56 days

On average, Symantec collects its receivables 8 days sooner than does CA, but 11 days slower than the industry average. A major portion of Symantec's sales of products like Norton antivirus software are made directly to consumers online who pay immediately with credit cards, significantly accelerating payment. CA, on the other hand, sells primarily to businesses, which take longer to pay.

EARNINGS QUALITY   Recall our discussion in Chapter 4 concerning earnings quality. We learned that managers have the ability, to a limited degree, to manipulate reported income and that many observers believe this practice diminishes earnings quality because it can mask "permanent" earnings. Former SEC Chairman Arthur Levitt listed discretionary accruals, which he called "Miscellaneous Cookie Jar Reserves," as one of the most popular methods companies use to manipulate income.

Sometimes financial statement users can examine accounts receivable, the allowance for bad debts, and other accounts to detect low earnings quality. For example, in an analysis that eventually led to an important SEC fraud case, PaineWebber Inc. downgraded its

Bad debt expense is one of a variety of discretionary accruals that provide management with the opportunity to manipulate income.

stock recommendation for Sunbeam, Inc., after noticing unusually high accounts receivable and unexpected increases in sales of certain products. Also, Sunbeam's allowance for uncollectible accounts had shown large increases in prior periods. It eventually came to light that Sunbeam had been manipulating its income by using a "bill and hold" strategy with retail buyers. This involved selling products at large discounts to retailers before they normally would buy and then holding the products in third-party warehouses, with delivery at a later date. More generally, research indicates that companies sometimes manage earnings by building up large allowances for bad debts in good periods and then reducing those allowances to increase earnings in bad periods.[25]

Another area for accounting-quality concern is the sale method used to account for transfers of receivables. Research suggests that some companies manage earnings by distorting the fair value estimates that are made as part of recording securitizations.[26] Also, some firms classify cash flows associated with selling their accounts receivable in the operating section of the statement of cash flows, such that changes in the extent to which accounts receivable are sold can be used to manipulate cash flow from operations. In fact, evidence suggests that sophisticated investors and bond-rating agencies undo sales accounting to treat transfers of receivables as secured borrowings before assessing the riskiness of a company's debt.[27] Still, Wall Street is very good at identifying clever ways to structure transactions around accounting standards, so it is important to be vigilant regarding the accounting for these transactions. ●

Financial Reporting Case Solution

©PhotosIndia.com/Glow Images

1. **Explain the allowance method of accounting for bad debts.** *(p. 350)*   The allowance method is used to report the carrying value of accounts receivable at the net amount expected to be collected. In an adjusting entry, we record bad debt expense and reduce accounts receivable indirectly by crediting a contra account to accounts receivable for an estimate of the amount that eventually will prove uncollectible.

2. **What approaches might CHS have used to arrive at the $200 million bad debt provision?** *(p. 351)*   CHS would determine the balance in the allowance for uncollectible accounts that is necessary to show net accounts receivable at the appropriate carrying value and then would record whatever adjustment and corresponding bad debt expense resulted in that balance. It likely would use an aging of accounts receivable to calculate the appropriate balance. It might also use a percentage of net sales to estimate bad debt expense, particularly on an interim basis, but that approach would only be allowed if it produced a similar carrying value as the balance sheet approach.

3. **Are there any alternatives to the allowance method?** *(p. 354)*   An alternative to the allowance method is the direct write-off method. Using this method, adjusting entries are not recorded and any bad debt that does arise simply is written off as bad debt expense. The direct write-off method is not permitted by GAAP except in limited circumstances.

4. **What does it mean for CHS to securitize its receivables?** *(p. 364)*   Securitization is a method used to sell accounts receivable. In a typical securitization, a company creates a "special purpose entity" that buys receivables from the company and issues securities that are collateralized by the receivables. Securitization allows CHS to obtain cash for its receivables sooner than it could otherwise, and to reach a large pool of investors at favorable financing rates. ●

---

[25]S. B. Jackson and X. Liu, "The Allowance for Uncollectible Accounts, Conservatism, and Earnings Management," *Journal of Accounting Research* 48, No. 3 (2010). pp. 565–601.

[26]P. M. Dechow, L. A. Myers, and C. Shakespeare, "Fair Value Accounting and Gains from Asset Securitizations: A Convenient Earnings Management Tool with Compensation Side-Benefits," *Journal of Accounting and Economics* 49, No. 2 (2010), pp. 2–25.

[27]Other recent research provides evidence that investors treat securitizations as loans rather than asset sales, suggesting that they are unconvinced that a sale has truly taken place. For example, see W. R. Landsman, K. Peasnell, and C. Shakespeare, "Are Asset Securitizations Sales or Loans?" *The Accounting Review* 83, No. 5 (2008), pp. 1251–72.

The Bottom Line

● **LO7–1**   Internal control refers to the plan designed to encourage adherence to company policies and procedures; promote operational efficiency; minimize errors, thefts, or fraud; and maximize the reliability and accuracy of accounting data. Key elements of an internal control system for cash receipts and disbursements include separation of record keeping from control of cash duties and the periodic preparation of a bank reconciliation. (*p. 340*)

● **LO7–2**   Cash can be informally restricted by management for a particular purpose. Restrictions also can be contractually imposed. If restricted cash is available for current operations or to pay current liabilities, it's classified as a current asset; otherwise, it's classified as investments and funds or other assets. (*p. 341*)

● **LO7–3**   The gross method of accounting for cash discounts considers a discount not taken as part of sales revenue. The net method considers a discount not taken as sales discount forfeited. (*p. 344*)

● **LO7–4**   When merchandise returns are anticipated, a refund liability should be recorded, and sales revenue should be reduced by anticipated sales returns. (*p. 346*)

● **LO7–5**   At the end of each period, the company estimates the necessary balance in the allowance for uncollectible accounts and then records whatever adjustment to the allowance and corresponding bad debt expense is necessary to reach that balance. (*p. 350*)

● **LO7–6**   The balance sheet approach determines bad debt expense by estimating the appropriate carrying value of accounts receivable to be reported in the balance sheet and then adjusting the allowance for uncollectible accounts as necessary to reach that carrying value. The income statement approach estimates bad debt expense based on the notion that a certain percentage of each period's credit sales will prove to be uncollectible. (*p. 352*)

● **LO7–7**   Notes receivable are formal credit arrangements between a creditor (lender) and a debtor (borrower). The typical note receivable requires the payment of a specified face amount, also called principal, at a specified maturity date or dates. In addition, interest is paid at a stated percentage of the face amount. Interest on notes is calculated by multiplying the face amount by the annual rate by the fraction of the annual period. (*p. 356*)

● **LO7–8**   A wide variety of methods exists for companies to use their receivables to obtain immediate cash. These methods can be described as either a secured borrowing or a sale of receivables. If three conditions indicating surrender of control are met, the transferor accounts for the transfer of receivables as a sale; otherwise as a secured borrowing. (*p. 362*)

● **LO7–9**   A company's investment in receivables is influenced by several related variables, to include the level of sales, the nature of the product or service, and credit and collection policies. Investors, creditors, and financial analysts can gain important insights by monitoring a company's investment in receivables. The receivables turnover and average collection period ratios are designed to monitor receivables. (*p. 370*)

● **LO7–10**   Accounting for cash and accounts receivable are similar under U.S. GAAP and IFRS. Other than some differences in terminology and balance sheet classifications, the most important differences involve accounting for transfers of receivables. Both IFRS and U.S. GAAP seek to distinguish between determining whether a sales treatment or secured borrowing treatment is appropriate, but they use different conceptual frameworks to guide that choice. U.S. GAAP focuses on whether control of the receivables is transferred, while IFRS uses a more complex decision process that also considers whether substantially all of the risks and rewards of ownership have been transferred. (*p. 342, 361, and 369*) ●

Cash Controls   APPENDIX 7A

Bank Reconciliation

One of the most important tools used in the control of cash is the bank reconciliation. Since all cash receipts are deposited into the bank account and cash disbursements are made by check, the bank account provides a separate record of cash. It's desirable to periodically compare the bank balance with the balance in the company's own records and reconcile any differences.

You probably know from your own personal experience that the ending balance in your checking account reported on your monthly bank statement rarely equals the balance you have recorded in your checkbook. Differences arise from two types of items: timing differences and errors.

Timing differences occur when the company and the bank record transactions at different times. At any point in time the company may have adjusted the cash balance for items of which the bank is not yet aware. Likewise, the bank may have adjusted its record of that balance by items of which the company is not yet aware. For example, checks written and cash deposits are not all processed by the bank in the same month that they are recorded by the company. Also, the bank may adjust the company's account for items such as service charges that the company is not aware of until the bank statement is received.

Errors can be made either by the company or the bank. For example, a check might be written for $210 but recorded on the company's books as a $120 disbursement; a deposit of $500 might be processed incorrectly by the bank as a $50 deposit. In addition to serving as a safeguard of cash, the bank reconciliation also uncovers errors such as these and helps ensure that the proper cash balance is reported in the balance sheet.

Bank reconciliations include adjustments to the balance per bank for timing differences involving transactions already reflected in the company's accounting records that have not yet been processed by the bank. These adjustments usually include *checks outstanding* and *deposits outstanding* (also called *deposits in transit*). In addition, the balance per bank would be adjusted for any bank errors discovered. These adjustments produce an adjusted bank balance that represents the corrected cash balance.

The balance per books is similarly adjusted for timing differences involving transactions already reflected by the bank of which the company is unaware until the bank statement is received. These would include service charges, charges for NSF (nonsufficient funds) checks, and collections made by the bank on the company's behalf. In addition, the balance per books is adjusted for any company errors discovered, resulting in an adjusted book balance that will also represent the corrected cash balance. *Each of these adjustments requires a journal entry to correct the book balance.* Only adjustments to the book balance require journal entries. Illustration 7A–1 recaps these reconciling items.

Differences between the cash book and bank balance occur due to differences in the timing of recognition of certain transactions and errors.

STEP 1: Adjust the bank balance to the corrected cash balance.

STEP 2: Adjust the book balance to the corrected cash balance.

Illustration 7A–1

Bank Reconciliation—
Reconciling Items

Balance per Bank
+ Deposits outstanding
− Checks outstanding
± Errors
———————————
Corrected balance
———————————

Balance per Book
+ Collections by bank
− Service charges
− NSF checks
± Errors
———————————
Corrected balance
———————————

The two corrected balances must equal.

Step 1: Adjustments to Bank Balance

1. *Add deposits outstanding.* These represent cash amounts received by the company and debited to cash that have not been deposited in the bank by the bank statement cutoff date and cash receipts deposited in the bank near the end of the period that are not recorded by the bank until after the cutoff date.

2. *Deduct checks outstanding.* These represent checks written and recorded by the company as credits to cash that have not yet been processed by the bank before the cutoff date.

3. *Bank errors.* These will either be increases or decreases depending on the nature of the error.

Step 2: Adjustments to Book Balance

1. *Add collections made by the bank* on the company's behalf and other increases in cash that the company is unaware of until the bank statement is received.

2. *Deduct service and other charges* made by the bank that the company is unaware of until the bank statement is received.

3. *Deduct NSF (nonsufficient funds) checks.* These are checks previously deposited for which the payors do not have sufficient funds in their accounts to cover the amount of the checks. The checks are returned to the company whose responsibility it is to seek payment from payors.

4. *Company errors.* These will either be increases or decreases depending on the nature of the error.

To demonstrate the bank reconciliation process, consider Illustration 7A–2.

The Hawthorne Manufacturing Company maintains a general checking account at the First Pacific Bank. First Pacific provides a bank statement and canceled checks once a month. The cutoff date is the last day of the month. The bank statement for the month of May is summarized as follows:

Illustration 7A–2
Bank Reconciliation

Balance, May 1, 2021	$ 32,120
Deposits	82,140
Checks processed	(78,433)
Service charges	(80)
NSF checks	(2,187)
Note payment collected by bank (includes $120 interest)	1,120
Balance, May 31, 2021	$34,680

The company's general ledger cash account has a balance of $35,276 at the end of May. A review of the company records and the bank statement reveals the following:

1. Cash receipts not yet deposited totaled $2,965.

2. A deposit of $1,020 was made on May 31 that was not credited to the company's account until June.

3. All checks written in April have been processed by the bank. Checks written in May that had not been processed by the bank total $5,536.

4. A check written for $1,790 was incorrectly recorded by the company as a $790 disbursement. The check was for payment to a supplier of raw materials.

The bank reconciliation prepared by the company appears as follows:

Step 1: Bank Balance to Corrected Balance	
Balance per bank statement	$34,680
Add: Deposits outstanding	3,985*
Deduct: Checks outstanding	(5,536)
Corrected cash balance	$ 33,129

Step 2: Book Balance to Corrected Balance	
Balance per books	$35,276
Add: Note collected by bank	1,120
Deduct:	
Service charges	(80)
NSF checks	(2,187)
Error—understatement of check	(1,000)
Corrected cash balance	$ 33,129

*$2,965 + 1,020 = $3,985

The next step is to prepare adjusting journal entries to reflect each of the adjustments to the balance per books. These represent amounts the company was not previously aware of until receipt of the bank statement. No adjusting entries are needed for the adjustments to the balance per bank because the company has already recorded these items. However, the bank needs to be notified of any errors discovered.

To record the receipt of principal and interest on note collected directly by the bank		
Cash..	1,120	
Notes receivable...		1,000
Interest revenue...		120

(continued)

(concluded)

To record credits to cash revealed by the bank reconciliation		
Miscellaneous expense (bank service charges)	80	
Accounts receivable (NSF checks)	2,187	
Accounts payable (error in check to supplier)	1,000	
Cash		3,267

After these entries are posted, the general ledger cash account will equal the corrected balance of $33,129.

Petty Cash

Most companies keep a small amount of cash on hand to pay for low-cost items such as postage, office supplies, delivery charges, and entertainment expenses. It would be inconvenient, time-consuming, and costly to process a check each time these small payments are made. A petty cash fund provides a more efficient way to handle these payments.

> The petty cash fund always should have cash and receipts that together equal the amount of the fund.

A petty cash fund is established by transferring a specified amount of cash from the company's general checking account to an employee designated as the petty cash custodian. The amount of the fund should approximate the expenditures made from the fund during a relatively short period of time (say a week or a month). The custodian disburses cash from the fund when the appropriate documentation is presented, such as a receipt for the purchase of office supplies. At any point in time, the custodian should be in possession of cash and appropriate receipts that sum to the amount of the fund. The receipts serve as the basis for recording appropriate expenses each time the fund is replenished. Consider the example in Illustration 7A–3.

Illustration 7A–3

Petty Cash Fund

On May 1, 2021, the Hawthorne Manufacturing Company established a $200 petty cash fund. John Ringo is designated as the petty cash custodian. The fund will be replenished at the end of each month. On May 1, 2021, a check is written for $200 made out to John Ringo, petty cash custodian. During the month of May, John paid bills totaling $160 summarized as follows:

Postage	$ 40
Office supplies	35
Delivery charges	55
Entertainment	30
Total	$160

In journal entry form, the transaction to establish the fund would be recorded as follows:

May 1, 2021

Petty Cash	200	
Cash (checking account)		200

> A petty cash fund is established by writing a check to the custodian.

No entries are recorded at the time the actual expenditures are made from the fund. The expenditures are recorded when reimbursement is requested at the end of the month. At that time, a check is written to John Ringo, petty cash custodian, for the total of the fund receipts, $160 in this case. John cashes the check and replenishes the fund to $200. In journal entry form, replenishing the fund would be recorded as follows:

May 31, 2021

Postage expense	40	
Office supplies expense	35	
Delivery expense	55	
Entertainment expense	30	
Cash (checking account)		160

The petty cash account is not debited when replenishing the fund. If, however, the size of the fund is increased at time of replenishment, the account is debited for the increase. Similarly, petty cash would be credited if the size of the fund is decreased.

To maintain the control objective of separation of duties, the petty cash custodian should not be involved in the process of writing or approving checks, nor in recordkeeping. In addition, management should arrange for surprise counts of the fund.

> The appropriate expense accounts are debited when the petty cash fund is reimbursed.

Accounting for a Troubled Debt Restructuring[28]

APPENDIX 7B

> A *troubled debt restructuring* occurs when the creditor makes concessions to the debtor in response to the debtor's financial difficulties.

Sometimes a creditor changes the original terms of a debt agreement in response to the debtor's financial difficulties. The creditor makes concessions to the debtor that make it easier for the debtor to pay, with the goal of maximizing the amount of cash that the creditor can collect. In that case, the new arrangement is referred to as a troubled debt restructuring. Because identifying an arrangement as a troubled debt restructuring requires recognizing any loss associated with the arrangement, creditors might be reluctant to conclude that a troubled debt restructuring has occurred, so the FASB provides guidance to help ensure that all troubled debt restructurings are properly identified.[29]

WHEN THE RECEIVABLE IS CONTINUED, BUT WITH MODIFIED TERMS   In a troubled debt restructuring, it's likely that the creditor allows the receivable to continue but with the terms of the debt agreement modified to make it easier for the debtor to comply. The creditor might agree to reduce or delay the scheduled interest payments. Or, it may agree to reduce or delay the maturity amount. Often a troubled debt restructuring will call for some combination of these concessions.

The CECL approach used to account for credit losses also applies to accounting for troubled debt restructurings. The creditor uses its normal methodology to calculate credit losses. Often that methodology involves calculating discounted cash flows, so that is what we illustrate in Illustration 7B–1.

Note that the interest rate used in the illustration is the original rate (10%) included in the original credit agreement. That is because a troubled debt restructuring does not result in a new loan, but rather is part of the creditor's ongoing efforts to collect the original loan.

As First Prudent receives the reduced interest payments and principal, it will record receipt of cash and reduce the allowance for uncollectible accounts for the difference between the amount of interest it was supposed to receive originally and the amount it receives under the troubled debt restructuring:

December 31, 2021		
Cash (per agreement)	2,000,000	
Allowance for uncollectible accounts (to balance)	413,233	
Interest revenue (($30,000,000 − $5,867,670) × 10%)		2,413,233

Reducing the allowance increases the carrying value of the note receivable, so under the effective interest method the interest revenue associated with the receivable is higher in the next period:

December 31, 2022		
Cash (per agreement)...	2,000,000	
Allowance for uncollectible accounts (to balance).................................	454,556	
Interest revenue (($30,000,000 − ($5,867,670 − 413,233)) × 10%)........		2,454,556

---

[28]When a receivable has been securitized, or when a company has elected to account for a receivable under the fair value option, the receivable is viewed as an investment and different GAAP applies, as described in Appendix 12B.

[29]These terms have been clarified (ASC 310–40–15: Receivables—Troubled Debt Restructurings by Creditors—Scope and Scope Exceptions). A debtor is viewed as experiencing *financial difficulties* if it is probable that the debtor will default on any of its liabilities unless the creditor restructures the debt. A *concession* has occurred if, as a result of the restructuring, the creditor does not expect to collect all amounts due, including accrued interest. A concession also can occur if the creditor restructures the terms of the debt in a way that provides the debtor with funds at a better rate of interest than the debtor could receive if the debtor tried to obtain new debt with similar terms (for example, a similar payment schedule, collateral, and guarantees) as the restructured debt. But, not all changes are concessions. For example, a restructuring that results in an insignificant delay of payment is not a concession.

378   SECTION 2   Assets

Illustration 7B–1

Troubled Debt Restructuring with Modified Terms

The date is January 1, 2021. Brillard Properties owes First Prudent Bank $30 million under a 10% note with two years remaining to maturity. Due to Brillard's financial difficulties, the previous year's interest ($3 million) was not paid. First Prudent and Brillard renegotiated Brillard's debt as follows:

- forgive the interest accrued from last year,
- reduce the two remaining interest payments from $3 million each to $2 million each, and
- reduce the face amount from $30 million to $25 million

How would First Prudent account for this troubled debt restructuring?

Analysis

Previous Value		
Accrued interest (10% × $30,000,000)	$ 3,000,000	
Principal	30,000,000	
Book value of the receivable		$33,000,000

The discounted present value of the cash flows prior to the loss is the same as the receivable's book value.

The discounted present value of the cash flows after the loss is less than book value.

New Value (based on estimated cash flows to be received)		
Present value of accrued interest	= $ 0	
Present value of future interest	$ 2 million × 1.73554* = 3,471,080	
Present value of estimated principal	$25 million × 0.82645† = 20,661,250	
Present value of the receivable		(24,132,330)
Loss		$ 8,867,670

*Present value of an ordinary annuity of $1: $n = 2, i = 10\%$
†Present value of $1: $n = 2, i = 10\%$

The difference is a credit loss, debited to bad debt expense.

Journal Entry on January 1, 2021

Bad debt expense (to balance)#	8,867,670	
Interest receivable		3,000,000
Allowance for uncollectible accounts@		
($30,000,000 − $24,132,330)		5,867,670

#Rather than debiting bad debt expense, First Prudent might debit Loss on troubled debt restructuring or some similar title.
@This account might also be called Allowance for loan losses, Allowance for credit losses, or some similar title.

When the note matures, First Prudent records receipt of cash and reduces the note receivable and related allowance for uncollectible accounts to zero.

WHEN THE RECEIVABLE IS SETTLED OUTRIGHT   Sometimes a receivable in a troubled debt restructuring is actually settled at the time of the restructuring by the debtor making a payment of cash, some other noncash assets, or even shares of the debtor's stock. In that case, the creditor records a loss for the difference between the carrying amount of the receivable and the fair value of the asset(s) or equity securities received. Illustration 7B–2 provides an example.

Illustration 7B–2

Debt Settled at the Time of a Restructuring

First Prudent Bank is owed $30 million by Brillard Properties under a 10% note with two years remaining to maturity. Due to Brillard's financial difficulties, the previous year's interest ($3 million) was not received. The bank agrees to settle the receivable (and not receive the accrued interest receivable) in exchange for property having a fair value of $20 million. Assume that $2 million of bad debt expense has previously been accrued for this loan, resulting in a balance of $2 million in the allowance for uncollectible accounts. First Prudent, the creditor, would record the following journal entry:

	($ in millions)
Land (fair value)	20
Allowance for uncollectible accounts@	2
Bad debt expense (to balance)*	11
Interest receivable (10% × $30 million)	3
Notes receivable (account balance)	30

@This account might also be called Allowance for loan losses, Allowance for credit losses, or some similar title.
*Rather than debiting bad debt expense, First Prudent might debit Loss on troubled debt restructuring or some similar title.

You may be wondering whether recognizing a loss on a troubled debt restructuring leads to a double counting of bad debt expense. After all, the receivable first was included in a group of receivables for which bad debt expense was estimated, and then was singled out for recognition of a loss. Creditors avoid this problem by separately estimating bad debt expense for the restructured troubled debt receivable and for the rest of the receivables. That way there is no double counting.

In this appendix we have focused on creditors' accounting for troubled debt restructurings. We discuss those topics from the standpoint of the debtor in Chapter 14, Appendix B.

Questions For Review of Key Topics

Q 7–1 Define cash equivalents.

Q 7–2 Explain the primary functions of internal controls procedures in the accounting area. What is meant by separation of duties?

Q 7–3 What are the responsibilities of management described in Section 404 of the Sarbanes-Oxley Act? What are the responsibilities of the company's auditor?

Q 7–4 Is restricted cash included in the reconciliation of cash balances on a statement of cash flows? Explain.

Q 7–5 Define a compensating balance. How are compensating balances reported in financial statements?

IFRS Q 7–6 Do U.S. GAAP and IFRS differ in how bank overdrafts are treated? Explain.

Q 7–7 Explain the difference between a trade discount and a cash discount.

Q 7–8 Distinguish between the gross and net methods of accounting for cash discounts.

Q 7–9 Briefly explain the accounting treatment for sales returns.

Q 7–10 Explain the typical way companies account for uncollectible accounts receivable (bad debts). When is it permissible to record bad debt expense only at the time when receivables actually prove uncollectible?

Q 7–11 Define the CECL model for accounts receivable. On what does it base the estimate of the allowance for uncollectible accounts?

IFRS Q 7–12 Define the ECL model for accounts receivable. How does it differ from the CECL model?

Q 7–13 Briefly explain the difference between the income statement approach and the balance sheet approach to estimating bad debts.

IFRS Q 7–14 If a company has accounts receivable from ordinary customers and from related parties, can they combine those receivables in their financial statements under U.S. GAAP? Under IFRS?

Q 7–15 Is any special accounting treatment required for the assigning of accounts receivable in general as collateral for debt?

Q 7–16 Explain any possible differences between accounting for an account receivable factored with recourse compared with one factored without recourse.

IFRS Q 7–17 Do U.S. GAAP and IFRS differ in the criteria they use to determine whether a transfer of receivables is treated as a sale? Explain.

Q 7–18 What is meant by the discounting of a note receivable? Describe the four-step process used to account for discounted notes.

Q 7–19 What are the key variables that influence a company's investment in receivables? Describe the two ratios used by financial analysts to monitor a company's investment in receivables.

Q 7–20 (Based on Appendix 7A) In a two-step bank reconciliation, identify the items that might be necessary to adjust the bank balance to the corrected cash balance. Identify the items that might be necessary to adjust the book balance to the corrected cash balance.

Q 7–21 (Based on Appendix 7A) How is a petty cash fund established? How is the fund replenished?

Q 7–22 (Based on Appendix 7B) Marshall Companies, Inc., holds a note receivable from a former subsidiary. Due to financial difficulties, the former subsidiary has been unable to pay the previous year's interest on the note. Marshall agreed to restructure the debt by both delaying and reducing remaining cash payments. The concessions result in a credit loss on the creditor's investment in the receivable. How is the credit loss on the troubled debt restructuring calculated?

Brief Exercises

🔲 connect

BE 7–1
Internal control
● LO7–1

Janice Dodds opens the mail for the Ajax Plumbing Company. She lists all customer checks on a spreadsheet that includes the name of the customer and the check amount. The checks, along with the spreadsheet, are then sent to Jim Seymour in the accounting department who records the checks and deposits them daily in the company's checking account. How could the company improve its internal control procedure for the handling of its cash receipts?

380   SECTION 2   Assets

BE 7–2
Bank overdrafts
● LO7–2, LO7–10

 IFRS

Cutler Company has a cash account with a balance of $250,000 with Wright Bank and a cash account with an overdraft of $5,000 at Lowe Bank. What would the current assets section of Cutler's balance sheet include for "cash" under IFRS? Under U.S. GAAP?

BE 7–3
Cash and cash equivalents
● LO7–2

The following items appeared on the year-end trial balance of Consolidated Freight Corporation: cash in a checking account, U.S. Treasury bills that mature in six months, undeposited customer checks, cash in a savings account, and currency and coins. Which of these items would be included in the company's balance sheet as cash and cash equivalents?

BE 7–4
Cash discounts; gross method
● LO7–3

On December 28, 2021, Tristar Communications sold 10 units of its new satellite uplink system to various customers for $25,000 each. The terms of each sale were 1/10, n/30. Tristar uses the gross method to account for sales discounts. In what year will income before tax be affected by discounts, assuming that all customers paid the net-of-discount amount on January 6, 2022? By how much?

BE 7–5
Cash discounts; net method
● LO7–3

Refer to the situation described in BE 7–4. Answer the questions assuming that Tristar uses the net method to account for sales discounts.

BE 7–6
Sales returns
● LO7–4

During 2021, its first year of operations, Hollis Industries recorded sales of $10,600,000 and experienced returns of $720,000. Cost of goods sold totaled $6,360,000 (60% of sales). The company estimates that 8% of all sales will be returned. Prepare the year-end adjusting journal entries to account for anticipated sales returns under the assumption that all sales are made for cash (no accounts receivable are outstanding).

BE 7–7
Sales returns
● LO7–4

Refer to the situation described in BE 7–6. Prepare the year-end adjusting journal entries to account for anticipated sales returns, assuming that all sales are made on credit and all accounts receivable are outstanding.

BE 7–8
Accounts receivable classification
● LO7–5, LO7–10

 IFRS

Singletary Associates has accounts receivable due from normal credit customers and also has an account receivable due from a director of the company. Singletary would like to combine both of those receivables on one line in the current assets section of their balance sheet and in the disclosure notes. Is that permissible under U.S. GAAP? Under IFRS? Explain.

BE 7–9
Uncollectible accounts; establishing an allowance
● LO7–5, LO7–6

At the end of the first year of operations, Gaur Manufacturing had gross accounts receivable of $300,000. Gaur's management estimates that 6% of the accounts will prove uncollectible. What journal entry should Gaur record to establish an allowance for uncollectible accounts?

BE 7–10
Uncollectible accounts; adjusting the allowance, credit balance
● LO7–5, LO7–6

At the end of the year, Breyer Associates had a *credit* balance in its allowance for uncollectible accounts of $12,000 before adjustment. The balance in Breyer's gross accounts receivable is $600,000. Breyer's management estimates that 10% of its accounts receivable balance will not be collected. What journal entry should Breyer record to adjust its allowance for uncollectible accounts?

BE 7–11
Uncollectible accounts; adjusting the allowance, debit balance
● LO7–5, LO7–6

At the end of the year, Syer Associates had a *debit* balance in its allowance for uncollectible accounts of $12,000 before adjustment. The balance in Syer's gross accounts receivable is $600,000. Syer's management estimates that 10% of its accounts receivable balance will not be collected. What journal entry should Syer record to adjust its allowance for uncollectible accounts?

BE 7–12
Calculate
uncollectible
accounts using
the aging method
● LO7–5, LO7–6

Crell Computers categorizes its accounts receivable into four age groups for purposes of estimating its allowance for uncollectible accounts.
1. Accounts not yet due = $60,000; estimated uncollectible = 5%.
2. Accounts 1–30 days past due = $15,000; estimated uncollectible = 10%.
3. Accounts 31–60 days past due = $10,000; estimated uncollectible = 20%.
4. Accounts more than 60 days past due = $5,000; estimated uncollectible = 30%.

What should be the balance in Crell's allowance for uncollectible accounts?

BE 7–13
Uncollectible
accounts; income
statement
approach
● LO7–5, LO7–6

The following information relates to a company's accounts receivable: gross accounts receivable balance at the beginning of the year, $300,000; allowance for uncollectible accounts at the beginning of the year, $25,000 (credit balance); credit sales during the year, $1,500,000; accounts receivable written off during the year, $16,000; cash collections from customers, $1,450,000. Assuming the company estimates bad debts at an amount equal to 2% of credit sales, calculate (1) bad debt expense for the year and (2) the year-end balance in the allowance for uncollectible accounts.

BE 7–14
Uncollectible
accounts; balance
sheet approach
● LO7–5, LO7–6

Refer to the situation described in BE 7–13. Answer the two questions assuming the company estimates that future bad debts will equal 10% of the year-end balance in accounts receivable.

BE 7–15
Uncollectible
accounts; solving
for unknown
● LO7–5, LO7–6

A company's year-end balance in accounts receivable is $2,000,000. The allowance for uncollectible accounts had a beginning-of-year credit balance of $30,000. An aging of accounts receivable at the end of the year indicates a required allowance of $38,000. If bad debt expense for the year was $40,000, what was the amount of bad debts written off during the year?

BE 7–16
Uncollectible
accounts; solving
for unknown
● LO7–5, LO7–6

Refer to the situation described in BE 7–15. If credit sales for the year were $8,200,000 and $7,950,000 was collected from credit customers, what was the beginning-of-year balance in accounts receivable?

BE 7–17
Note receivable
● LO7–7

On December 1, 2021, Davenport Company sold merchandise to a customer for $20,000. In payment for the merchandise, the customer signed a 6% note requiring the payment of interest and principal on March 1, 2022. How much interest revenue will the company recognize during 2021? In 2022?

BE 7–18
Long-term notes
receivable
● LO7–7

On April 19, 2021, Millipede Machinery sold a tractor to Thomas Hartwood, accepting a note promising payment of $120,000 in five years. The applicable effective interest rate is 7%. What amount of sales revenue would Millipede recognize on April 19, 2021, for the Hartwood transaction?

BE 7–19
Factoring
of accounts
receivable
● LO7–8

Logitech Corporation transferred $100,000 of accounts receivable to a local bank. The transfer was made without recourse. The local bank remits 85% of the factored amount to Logitech and retains the remaining 15%. When the bank collects the receivables, it will remit to Logitech the retained amount less a fee equal to 3% of the total amount factored. Logitech estimates a fair value of its 15% interest in the receivables of $11,000 (not including the 3% fee). What is the effect of this transaction on the company's assets, liabilities, and income before income taxes?

BE 7–20
Factoring
of accounts
receivable
● LO7–8

Refer to the situation described in BE 7–19. Assuming that the sale criteria are not met, describe how Logitech would account for the transfer.

BE 7–21
Transfers
of accounts
receivable
● LO7–8, LO7–10
 IFRS

Huling Associates plans to transfer $300,000 of accounts receivable to Mitchell Inc. in exchange for cash. Huling has structured the arrangement so that it retains substantially all the risks and rewards of ownership but shifts control over the receivables to Mitchell. Assuming all other criteria are met for recognizing the transfer as a sale, how would Huling account for this transaction under IFRS? Under U.S. GAAP?

382   SECTION 2   Assets

BE 7–22
Discounting a note
● LO7–8

On March 31, Dower Publishing discounted a $30,000 note at a local bank. The note was dated February 28 and required the payment of the principal amount and interest at 6% on May 31. The bank's discount rate is 8%. How much cash will Dower receive from the bank on March 31?

BE 7–23
Receivables turnover
● LO7–9

Camden Hardware's credit sales for the year were $320,000. Accounts receivable at the beginning and end of the year were $50,000 and $70,000, respectively. Calculate the accounts receivable turnover ratio and the average collection period for the year.

BE 7–24
Bank reconciliation
● Appendix 7A

Marin Company's general ledger indicates a cash balance of $22,340 as of September 30, 2021. Early in October Marin received a bank statement indicating that during September Marin had an NSF check of $1,500 returned to a customer and incurred service charges of $45. Marin also learned it had incorrectly recorded a check received from a customer on September 15 as $500 when in fact the check was for $550. Calculate Marin's correct September 30, 2021, cash balance.

BE 7–25
Bank reconciliation
● Appendix 7A

Shan Enterprises received a bank statement listing its May 31, 2021, bank balance as $47,582. Shan determined that as of May 31 it had cash receipts of $2,500 that were not yet deposited and checks outstanding of $7,224. Calculate Shan's correct May 31, 2021, cash balance.

BE 7–26
Troubled debt restructuring
● Appendix 7B

Thaler Inc. holds a $1 million receivable ($800,000 principal, $200,000 accrued interest) from Einhorn Industries, and agrees to settle the receivable outright for $900,000 given Einhorn's difficult financial situation. How much gain or loss should Thaler recognize on this troubled debt restructuring?

Exercises   connect

E 7–1
Cash and cash equivalents; restricted cash
● LO7–2

The controller of the Red Wing Corporation is in the process of preparing the company's 2021 financial statements. She is trying to determine the correct balance of cash and cash equivalents to be reported as a current asset in the balance sheet. The following items are being considered:

a. Balances in the company's accounts at the First National Bank; checking $13,500, savings $22,100.

b. Undeposited customer checks of $5,200.

c. Currency and coins on hand of $580.

d. Savings account at the East Bay Bank with a balance of $400,000. This account is being used to accumulate cash for future plant expansion (in 2023).

e. $20,000 in a checking account at the East Bay Bank. The balance in the account represents a 20% compensating balance for a $100,000 loan with the bank. Red Wing may not withdraw the funds until the loan is due in 2024.

f. U.S. Treasury bills; 2-month maturity bills totaling $15,000, and 7-month bills totaling $20,000.

Required:

1. Determine the correct balance of cash and cash equivalents to be reported in the current asset section of the 2021 balance sheet.

2. For each of the items not included in your answer to requirement 1, explain the correct classification of the item.

E 7–2
Cash and cash equivalents
● LO7–2

Delta Automotive Corporation has the following assets listed in its 12/31/2021 trial balance:

Cash in bank—checking account	$22,500
U.S. Treasury bills (mature in 60 days)*	5,000
Cash on hand (currency and coins)	1,350
U.S. Treasury bills (mature in six months)*	10,000
Undeposited customer checks	1,840

*Purchased on 11/30/2021

Required:

1. Determine the correct balance of cash and cash equivalents to be reported in the current asset section of the 2021 balance sheet.

2. For each of the items not included in your answer to requirement 1, explain the correct classification of the item.

E 7–3
FASB codification research
● LO7–2, LO7–6, LO7–7

Access the *FASB Accounting Standards Codification* at the FASB website (www.fasb.org).

Required:
Indicate the specific seven-digit Codification citation (XXX-XX-XX) for each of the following items:
1. Accounts receivables from related parties should be shown separately from trade receivables
2. The definition of cash equivalents (Hint: see Statement of Cash Flows.)
3. The requirement to value notes exchanged for cash at the cash proceeds
4. The two conditions that must be met to accrue a loss on an accounts receivable

E 7–4
Bank overdrafts
● LO7–2, LO7–10

 IFRS

Parker Inc. has the following cash balances:

First Bank	$150,000
Second Bank	(10,000)
Third Bank	25,000
Fourth Bank	(5,000)

Required:
1. Prepare the current assets and current liabilities section of Parker's 2021 balance sheet, assuming Parker reports under U.S. GAAP.
2. Prepare the current assets and current liabilities section of Parker's 2021 balance sheet, assuming Parker reports under IFRS.

E 7–5
Trade and cash discounts; the gross method and the net method compared
● LO7–3

Tracy Company, a manufacturer of air conditioners, sold 100 units to Thomas Company on November 17, 2021. The units have a list price of $600 each, but Thomas was given a 30% trade discount. The terms of the sale were 2/10, n/30.

Required:
1. Prepare the journal entries to record the sale on November 17 (ignore cost of goods) and collection on November 26, 2021, assuming that the gross method of accounting for cash discounts is used.
2. Prepare the journal entries to record the sale on November 17 (ignore cost of goods) and collection on December 15, 2021, assuming that the gross method of accounting for cash discounts is used.
3. Repeat requirements 1 and 2 assuming that the net method of accounting for cash discounts is used.

E 7–6
Cash discounts; the gross method
● LO7–3

Harwell Company manufactures automobile tires. On July 15, 2021, the company sold 1,000 tires to the Nixon Car Company for $50 each. The terms of the sale were 2/10, n/30. Harwell uses the gross method of accounting for cash discounts.

Required:
1. Prepare the journal entries to record the sale on July 15 (ignore cost of goods) and collection on July 23, 2021.
2. Prepare the journal entries to record the sale on July 15 (ignore cost of goods) and collection on August 15, 2021.

E 7–7
Cash discounts; the net method
● LO7–3

[This is a variation of E 7–6 modified to focus on the net method of accounting for cash discounts.]
    Harwell Company manufactures automobile tires. On July 15, 2021, the company sold 1,000 tires to the Nixon Car Company for $50 each. The terms of the sale were 2/10, n/30. Harwell uses the net method of accounting for cash discounts.

Required:
1. Prepare the journal entries to record the sale on July 15 (ignore cost of goods) and payment on July 23, 2021.
2. Prepare the journal entries to record the sale on July 15 (ignore cost of goods) and payment on August 15, 2021.

E 7–8
Sales returns
● LO7–4

Halifax Manufacturing allows its customers to return merchandise for any reason up to 90 days after delivery and receive a credit to their accounts. All of Halifax's sales are for credit (no cash is collected at the time of sale). The company began 2021 with a refund liability of $300,000. During 2021, Halifax sold merchandise on account for $11,500,000. Halifax's merchandise costs are 65% of merchandise selling price. Also during the year, customers returned $450,000 in sales for credit, with $250,000 of those being returns of merchandise sold prior to 2021, and the rest being merchandise sold during 2021. Sales returns, estimated to be 4% of sales, are recorded as an adjusting entry at the end of the year.

Required:
1. Prepare entries to (a) record actual returns in 2021 of merchandise that was sold *prior to* 2021; (b) record actual returns in 2021 of merchandise that was sold *during* 2021; and (c) adjust the refund liability to its appropriate balance at year end.
2. What is the amount of the year-end refund liability after the adjusting entry is recorded?

384   SECTION 2   Assets

E 7–9
FASB codification research
● LO7–5

The *FASB Accounting Standards Codification* represents the single source of authoritative U.S. generally accepted accounting principles.

Required:
1. Obtain the relevant authoritative literature on accounting for accounts receivable using the FASB's Codification Research System at the FASB website (www.fasb.org). What is the specific eight-digit Codification citation (XXX-XX-XX-X) that describes the information about loans and trade receivables that is to be disclosed in the summary of significant accounting policies?
2. List the disclosure requirements.

E 7–10
Establish an allowance and account for bad debts
● LO7–5, LO7–6

Pincus Associates uses the allowance method to account for bad debts. During 2021, its first year of operations, Pincus provided a total of $250,000 of services on account. In 2021, the company wrote off uncollectible accounts of $10,000. By the end of 2021, cash collections on accounts receivable totaled $210,000. Pincus estimates that 20% of the accounts receivable balance at 12/31/2021 will prove uncollectible.

Required:
1. What journal entry did Pincus record to write off uncollectible accounts during 2021?
2. What journal entry should Pincus record to recognize bad debt expense for 2021?

E 7–11
Uncollectible accounts; allowance method vs. direct write-off method
● LO7–5, LO7–6

Johnson Company calculates its allowance for uncollectible accounts as 10% of its ending balance in gross accounts receivable. The allowance for uncollectible accounts had a credit balance of $30,000 at the beginning of 2021. No previously written-off accounts receivable were reinstated during 2021. At 12/31/2021, gross accounts receivable totaled $500,000, and prior to recording the adjusting entry to recognize bad debts expense for 2021, the allowance for uncollectible accounts had a debit balance of 55,000.

Required:
1. What was the balance in gross accounts receivable as of 12/31/2020?
2. What journal entry should Johnson record to recognize bad debt expense for 2021?
3. Assume Johnson made no other adjustment of the allowance for uncollectible accounts during 2021. Determine the amount of accounts receivable written off during 2021.
4. If Johnson instead used the direct write-off method, what would bad debt expense be for 2021?

E 7–12
Uncollectible accounts; allowance method estimating bad debts as percentage of net sales vs. direct write-off method
● LO7–5, LO7–6

Ervin Company uses the allowance method to account for uncollectible accounts receivable. Bad debt expense is established as a percentage of credit sales. For 2021, net credit sales totaled $4,500,000, and the estimated bad debt percentage is 1.5%. No previously written-off accounts receivable were reinstated during 2021. The allowance for uncollectible accounts had a credit balance of $42,000 at the beginning of 2021 and $40,000, after adjusting entries, at the end of 2021.

Required:
1. What is bad debt expense for 2021 as a percent of net credit sales?
2. Assume Ervin makes no other adjustment of bad debt expense during 2021. Determine the amount of accounts receivable written off during 2021.
3. If the company uses the direct write-off method, what would bad debt expense be for 2021?

E 7–13
Calculate uncollectible accounts using the aging method; record adjustment
● LO7–5, LO7–6

Dhaliwal Digital categorizes its accounts receivable into three age groups for purposes of estimating its allowance for uncollectible accounts.
1. Accounts not yet due = $180,000; estimated uncollectible = 10%.
2. Accounts 1–45 days past due = $25,000; estimated uncollectible = 20%.
3. Accounts more than 45 days past due = $10,000; estimated uncollectible = 30%.

Before recording any adjustments, Dhaliwal has a debit balance of $45,000 in its allowance for uncollectible accounts.

Required:
1. Estimate the appropriate 12/31/2021 balance for Dhaliwal's allowance for uncollectible accounts.
2. What journal entry should Dhaliwal record to adjust its allowance for uncollectible accounts?

E 7–14
Calculate uncollectible accounts using the aging method; record adjustments
● LO7–5, LO7–6

Zuo Software categorizes its accounts receivable into four age groups for purposes of estimating its allowance for uncollectible accounts.
1. Accounts not yet due = $400,000; estimated uncollectible = 8%.
2. Accounts 1–30 days past due = $50,000; estimated uncollectible = 15%.
3. Accounts 31–90 days past due = $40,000; estimated uncollectible = 30%
4. Accounts more than 90 days past due = $30,000; estimated uncollectible = 50%.

At 12/31/2021, before recording any adjustments, Zuo has a credit balance of $22,000 in its allowance for uncollectible accounts.

Required:
1. Estimate the appropriate 12/31/2021 balance for Zuo's allowance for uncollectible accounts.
2. What journal entry should Zuo record to adjust its allowance for uncollectible accounts?
3. Calculate Zuo's 12/31/2021 net accounts receivable balance.

E 7–15
Uncollectible accounts; allowance method; balance sheet approach
● LO7–5, LO7–6

Colorado Rocky Cookie Company offers credit terms to its customers. At the end of 2021, accounts receivable totaled $625,000. The allowance method is used to account for uncollectible accounts. The allowance for uncollectible accounts had a credit balance of $32,000 at the beginning of 2021 and $21,000 in receivables were written off during the year as uncollectible. Also, $1,200 in cash was received in December from a customer whose account previously had been written off. The company estimates bad debts by applying a percentage of 10% to accounts receivable at the end of the year.

Required:
1. Prepare journal entries to record the write-off of receivables, the collection of $1,200 for previously written off receivables, and the year-end adjusting entry for bad debt expense.
2. How would accounts receivable be shown in the 2021 year-end balance sheet?

E 7–16
Uncollectible accounts; allowance method and direct write-off method compared; solving for unknown
● LO7–6

Castle Company provides estimates for its uncollectible accounts. The allowance for uncollectible accounts had a credit balance of $17,280 at the beginning of 2021 and a $22,410 credit balance at the end of 2021 (after adjusting entries). If the direct write-off method had been used to account for uncollectible accounts (bad debt expense equals actual write-offs), the income statement for 2021 would have included bad debt expense of $17,100 and revenue of $2,200 from the collection of previously written off bad debts.

Required:
Determine bad debt expense for 2021 according to the allowance method.

E 7–17
Uncollectible accounts; allowance method; solving for unknowns; General Mills
● LO7–5, LO7–6
Real World Financials

General Mills reported the following information in its 2017 financial statements ($ in millions):

	2017	**2016**
Balance Sheet:		
Accounts receivable, net	$ 1,430.1	$1,360.8
Income statement:		
Sales revenue	$15,619.8	

A note disclosed that the allowance for uncollectible accounts had a balance of $24.3 million and $29.6 million at the end of 2017 and 2016, respectively. Bad debt expense for 2017 was $16.6 million.

Required:
Determine the amount of cash collected from customers during 2017.

E 7–18
Notes receivable
● LO7–7

On June 30, 2021, the Esquire Company sold some merchandise to a customer for $30,000. In payment, Esquire agreed to accept a 6% note requiring the payment of interest and principal on March 31, 2022. The 6% rate is appropriate in this situation.

Required:
1. Prepare journal entries to record the sale of merchandise (omit any entry that might be required for the cost of the goods sold), the December 31, 2021 interest accrual, and the March 31, 2022 collection.
2. If the December 31 adjusting entry for the interest accrual is not prepared, by how much will income before income taxes be over- or understated in 2021 and 2022?

E 7–19
Noninterest-bearing notes receivable
● LO7–7

[This is a variation of E 7–18 modified to focus on a noninterest-bearing note.]
    On June 30, 2021, the Esquire Company sold merchandise to a customer and accepted a noninterest-bearing note in exchange. The note requires payment of $30,000 on March 31, 2022. The fair value of the merchandise exchanged is $28,200. Esquire views the financing component of this contract as significant.

Required:
1. Prepare journal entries to record the sale of merchandise (omit any entry that might be required for the cost of the goods sold), any December 31, 2021 interest accrual, and the March 31, 2022 collection.
2. What is the *effective* interest rate on the note?

E 7–20
Long-term notes receivable
● LO7–7

On January 1, 2021, Wright Transport sold four school buses to the Elmira School District. In exchange for the buses, Wright received a note requiring payment of $515,000 by Elmira on December 31, 2023. The effective interest rate is 8%.

386   SECTION 2   Assets

Required:
1. How much sales revenue would Wright recognize on January 1, 2021, for this transaction?
2. Prepare journal entries to record the sale of merchandise on January 1, 2021 (omit any entry that might be required for the cost of the goods sold), the December 31, 2021, interest accrual, the December 31, 2022, interest accrual, and receipt of payment of the note on December 31, 2023.

E 7–21
Interest-bearing
notes receivable;
solving for
unknown rate
● LO7–7

On January 1, 2021, the Apex Company exchanged some shares of common stock it had been holding as an investment for a note receivable. The note principal plus interest is due on January 1, 2022. The 2021 income statement reported $2,200 in interest revenue from this note and a $6,000 gain on sale of investment in stock. The stock's book value was $16,000. The company's fiscal year ends on December 31.

Required:
1. What is the note's effective interest rate?
2. Reconstruct the journal entries to record the sale of the stock on January 1, 2021, and the adjusting entry to record interest revenue at the end of 2021. The company records adjusting entries only at year-end.

E 7–22
Assigning of
specific accounts
receivable
● LO7–8

On June 30, 2021, the High Five Surfboard Company had outstanding accounts receivable of $600,000. On July 1, 2021, the company borrowed $450,000 from the Equitable Finance Corporation and signed a promissory note. Interest at 10% is payable monthly. The company assigned specific receivables totaling $600,000 as collateral for the loan. Equitable Finance charges a finance fee equal to 1.8% of the accounts receivable assigned.

Required:
Prepare the journal entry to record the borrowing on the books of High Five Surfboard.

E 7–23
Factoring
of accounts
receivable
without recourse
● LO7–8

Mountain High Ice Cream Company transferred $60,000 of accounts receivable to the Prudential Bank. The transfer was made *without recourse*. Prudential remits 90% of the factored amount to Mountain High and retains 10%. When the bank collects the receivables, it will remit to Mountain High the retained amount (which Mountain estimates has a fair value of $5,000) less a 2% fee (2% of the total factored amount).

Required:
Prepare the journal entry to record the transfer on the books of Mountain High assuming that the sale criteria are met.

E 7–24
Factoring
of accounts
receivable with
recourse
● LO7–8

[This is a variation of E 7–23 modified to focus on factoring with recourse.]
    Mountain High Ice Cream Company transferred $60,000 of accounts receivable to the Prudential Bank. The transfer was made *with recourse*. Prudential remits 90% of the factored amount to Mountain High and retains 10% to cover sales returns and allowances. When the bank collects the receivables, it will remit to Mountain High the retained amount (which Mountain estimates has a fair value of $5,000). Mountain High anticipates a $3,000 recourse obligation. The bank charges a 2% fee (2% of $60,000), and requires that amount to be paid at the start of the factoring arrangement.

Required:
Prepare the journal entry to record the transfer on the books of Mountain High assuming that the sale criteria are met.

E 7–25
Factoring
of accounts
receivable with
recourse under
IFRS
● LO7–8, LO7–10

 IFRS

[This is a variation of E 7–24 modified to focus on factoring with recourse under IFRS.]
    Mountain High Ice Cream Company reports under IFRS. Mountain High transferred $60,000 of accounts receivable to the Prudential Bank. The transfer was made *with recourse*. Prudential remits 90% of the factored amount to Mountain High and retains 10% to cover sales returns and allowances. When the bank collects the receivables, it will remit to Mountain High the retained amount (which Mountain estimates has a fair value of $5,000). Mountain High anticipates a $3,000 recourse obligation. The bank charges a 2% fee (2% of $60,000), and requires that amount to be paid at the start of the factoring arrangement. Mountain High has transferred control over the receivables, but determines that it still retains substantially all risks and rewards associated with them.

Required:
Prepare the journal entry to record the transfer on the books of Mountain High, considering whether the sale criteria under IFRS have been met.

E 7–26
Discounting a
note receivable
● LO7–8

Selkirk Company obtained a $15,000 note receivable from a customer on January 1, 2021. The note, along with interest at 10%, is due on July 1, 2021. On February 28, 2020, Selkirk discounted the note at Unionville Bank. The bank's discount rate is 12%.

Required:
Prepare the journal entries required on February 28, 2021, to accrue interest and to record the discounting (round all calculations to the nearest dollar) for Selkirk. Assume that the discounting is accounted for as a sale.

E 7–27
Concepts;
terminology
● LO7–1 through
LO7–8

Listed below are several terms and phrases associated with cash and receivables. Pair each item from List A (by letter) with the item from List B that is most appropriately associated with it.

List A	List B
_____ 1. Internal control	a. Restriction on cash.
_____ 2. Trade discount	b. Cash discount not taken is sales revenue.
_____ 3. Cash equivalents	c. Includes separation of duties.
_____ 4. Allowance for uncollectibles	d. Bad debt expense a % of credit sales.
_____ 5. Cash discount	e. Recognizes bad debts as they occur.
_____ 6. Balance sheet approach	f. Sale of receivables to a financial institution.
_____ 7. Income statement approach	g. Include highly liquid investments.
_____ 8. Net method	h. Estimate of bad debts.
_____ 9. Compensating balance	i. Reduction in amount paid by credit customer.
_____ 10. Discounting	j. Reduction below list price.
_____ 11. Gross method	k. Cash discount not taken is sales discount forfeited.
_____ 12. Direct write-off method	l. Bad debt expense determined by estimating amount of accounts receivable expected to be received.
_____ 13. Factoring	m. Sale of note receivable to a financial institution.

E 7–28
Receivables;
transaction
analysis
● LO7–3, LO7–5
through LO7–8

Weldon Corporation's fiscal year ends December 31. The following is a list of transactions involving receivables that occurred during 2021:

Mar. 17 — Accounts receivable of $1,700 were written off as uncollectible. The company uses the allowance method.

30 — Loaned an officer of the company $20,000 and received a note requiring principal and interest at 7% to be paid on March 30, 2022.

May 30 — Discounted the $20,000 note at a local bank. The bank's discount rate is 8%. The note was discounted without recourse and the sale criteria are met.

June 30 — Sold merchandise to the Blankenship Company for $12,000. Terms of the sale are 2/10, n/30. Weldon uses the gross method to account for cash discounts.

July 8 — The Blankenship Company paid its account in full.

Aug. 31 — Sold stock in a nonpublic company with a book value of $5,000 and accepted a $6,000 noninterest-bearing note with a discount rate of 8%. The $6,000 payment is due on February 28, 2022. The stock has no ready market value.

Dec. 31 — Weldon estimates that the allowance for uncollectible accounts should have a balance in it at year-end equal to 2% of the gross accounts receivable balance of $700,000. The allowance had a balance of $12,000 at the start of 2021.

Required:
1. Prepare journal entries for each of the above transactions (round all calculations to the nearest dollar).
2. Prepare any additional year-end adjusting entries indicated.

E 7–29
Ratio analysis;
Microsoft
● LO7–9
Real World Financials

Microsoft Corporation reported the following information in its financial statements for three successive quarters ($ in millions):

	Three Months Ended		
	9/30/2017 (Q1)	6/30/2017 (Q4)	3/31/2017 (Q3)
Balance sheets:			
Accounts receivable, net	$14,561	$19,792	$12,882
Income statements:			
Sales revenue	$24,538	$23,317	$22,090

Required:
Compute the receivables turnover ratio and the average collection period for Q1 and Q4. Assume that each quarter consists of 91 days.

E 7–30
Ratio analysis
● LO7–9

The current asset section of the Moorcroft Outboard Motor Company's balance sheet reported the following amounts:

	12/31/2021	12/31/2020
Accounts receivable, net	$400,000	$300,000

The average collection period for 2021 is 50 days.

Required:
Determine net sales for 2021.

388   SECTION 2   Assets

E 7–31
Petty cash
● **Appendix 7A**

Loucks Company established a $200 petty cash fund on October 2, 2021. The fund is replenished at the end of each month. At the end of October 2021, the fund contained $37 in cash and the following receipts:

Office supplies	$76
Advertising	48
Postage	20
Miscellaneous	19

Required:
Prepare the necessary general journal entries to establish the petty cash fund on October 2 and to replenish the fund on October 31.

E 7–32
Petty cash
● **Appendix 7A**

The petty cash fund of Ricco's Automotive contained the following items at the end of September 2021:

Currency and coins		$ 58
Receipts for the following expenditures:		
Delivery charges	$16	
Printer paper	11	
Paper clips and rubber bands	8	35
Lent money to an employee		25
Postage		32
Total		$150

The petty cash fund was established at the beginning of September with a transfer of $150 from cash to the petty cash account.

Required:
Prepare the journal entry to replenish the fund at the end of September.

E 7–33
Bank reconciliation
● **Appendix 7A**

Jansen Company's general ledger showed a checking account balance of $23,820 at the end of May 2021. The May 31 cash receipts of $2,340, included in the general ledger balance, were placed in the night depository at the bank on May 31 and were processed by the bank on June 1. The bank statement dated May 31, 2021, showed bank service charges of $38. All checks written by the company had been processed by the bank by May 31 and were listed on the bank statement except for checks totaling $1,890.

Required:
Prepare a bank reconciliation as of May 31, 2021. [*Hint:* You will need to compute the balance that would appear on the bank statement.]

E 7–34
Bank reconciliation and adjusting entries
● **Appendix 7A**

Harrison Company maintains a checking account at the First National City Bank. The bank provides a bank statement along with canceled checks on the last day of each month. The July 2021 bank statement included the following information:

Balance, July 1, 2021	$ 55,678
Deposits	179,500
Checks processed	(192,610)
Service charges	(30)
NSF checks	(1,200)
Monthly payment on note, deducted directly by bank from account (includes $320 in interest)	(3,320)
Balance, July 31, 2021	$ 38,018

The company's general ledger account had a balance of $38,918 at the end of July. Deposits outstanding totaled $6,300 and all checks written by the company were processed by the bank except for those totaling $8,420. In addition, a $2,000 July deposit from a credit customer was recorded as a $200 debit to cash and credit to accounts receivable, and a check correctly recorded by the company as a $30 disbursement was incorrectly processed by the bank as a $300 disbursement.

Required:
1. Prepare a bank reconciliation for the month of July.
2. Prepare the necessary journal entries at the end of July to adjust the general ledger cash account.

E 7–35
Troubled debt
restructuring
● Appendix 7B

At January 1, 2021, Clayton Hoists Inc. owed Third BancCorp $12 million, under a 10% note due December 31, 2022. Interest was paid last on December 31, 2019. Clayton was experiencing severe financial difficulties and asked Third BancCorp to modify the terms of the debt agreement. After negotiation Third BancCorp agreed to do the following:

- Forgive the interest accrued for the year just ended.
- Reduce the remaining two years' interest payments to $1 million each.
- Reduce the principal amount to $11 million.

Required:
Prepare the journal entries by Third BancCorp necessitated by the restructuring of the debt at
1. January 1, 2021.
2. December 31, 2021.
3. December 31, 2022.

E 7–36
General Ledger
Exercise
● LO7–5, LO7–6,
LO7–7, LO7–9

On January 1, 2021, the general ledger of 3D Family Fireworks includes the following account balances:

Accounts	Debit	Credit
Cash	$ 23,900	
Accounts Receivable	13,600	
Allowance for Uncollectible Accounts		$ 1,400
Supplies	2,500	
Notes Receivable (6%, due in 2 years)	20,000	
Land	77,000	
Accounts Payable		7,200
Common Stock		96,000
Retained Earnings		32,400
Totals	$137,000	$137,000

During January 2021, the following transactions occur:

1. January 2	Provide services to customers for cash, $35,100.
2. January 6	Provide services to customers on account, $72,400.
3. January 15	Write off accounts receivable as uncollectible, $1,000.
4. January 20	Pay cash for salaries, $31,400.
5. January 22	Receive cash on accounts receivable, $70,000.
6. January 25	Pay cash on accounts payable, $5,500.
7. January 30	Pay cash for utilities during January, $13,700.

The following information is available on January 31, 2021.
1. At the end of January, $5,000 of accounts receivable are past due, and the company estimates that 20% of these accounts will not be collected. Of the remaining accounts receivable, the company estimates that 5% will not be collected. The note receivable of $20,000 is considered fully collectible and therefore is not included in the estimate of uncollectible accounts.
2. Supplies at the end of January total $700.
3. Accrued interest revenue on notes receivable for January. Interest is expected to be received each December 31.
4. Unpaid salaries at the end of January are $33,500.

Required:
1. Record each of the transactions listed above in the 'General Journal' tab (these are shown as items 1–7). Review the 'General Ledger' and the 'Trial Balance' tabs to see the effect of the transactions on the account balances.
2. Record adjusting entries on January 31. in the 'General Journal' tab (these are shown as items 8-11).
3. Review the adjusted 'Trial Balance' as of January 31, 2021, in the 'Trial Balance' tab.
4. Prepare an income statement for the period ended January 31, 2021, in the 'Income Statement' tab).
5. Prepare a classified balance sheet as of January 31, 2021, in the 'Balance Sheet' tab.
6. Record closing entries in the 'General Journal' tab (these are shown as items 12 and 13).
7. Using the information from the requirements above, complete the 'Analysis' tab.

390   SECTION 2   Assets

Problems   ▣ connect

P 7–1
Uncollectible
accounts;
allowance
method; income
statement and
balance sheet
approach

● LO7–5, LO7–6

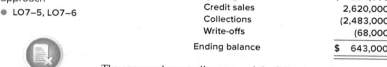

Swathmore Clothing Corporation grants its customers 30 days' credit. The company uses the allowance method for its uncollectible accounts receivable. During the year, a monthly bad debt accrual is made by multiplying 3% times the amount of credit sales for the month. At the fiscal year-end of December 31, an aging of accounts receivable schedule is prepared and the allowance for uncollectible accounts is adjusted accordingly.

At the end of 2020, accounts receivable were $574,000 and the allowance account had a credit balance of $54,000. Accounts receivable activity for 2021 was as follows:

Beginning balance	$ 574,000
Credit sales	2,620,000
Collections	(2,483,000)
Write-offs	(68,000)
Ending balance	$ 643,000

The company's controller prepared the following aging summary of year-end accounts receivable:

	Summary	
Age Group	Amount	Percent Uncollectible
0–60 days	$430,000	4%
61–90 days	98,000	15
91–120 days	60,000	25
Over 120 days	55,000	40
Total	$643,000	

Required:
1. Prepare a summary journal entry to record the monthly bad debt accrual and the write-offs during the year.
2. Prepare the necessary year-end adjusting entry for bad debt expense.
3. What is total bad debt expense for 2021? How would accounts receivable appear in the 2021 balance sheet?

P 7–2
Uncollectible
accounts; EMC
Corporation

● LO7–5

Real World Financials

★

EMC Corporation manufactures large-scale, high-performance computer systems. In a recent annual report, the balance sheet included the following information ($ in millions):

	2015	2014
Current assets:		
Receivables, less allowances of $90 in 2015 and $72 in 2014	$3,977	$4,413

In addition, the income statement reported sales revenue of $24,704 ($ in millions) for the current year. All sales are made on a credit basis. The statement of cash flows indicates that cash collected from customers during the current year was $25,737 ($ in millions). Note that there could have been significant recoveries of accounts receivable previously written off.

Required:
1. Compute the following ($ in millions):
   a. The net amount of bad debts written off or reinstated by EMC during 2015.
   b. The amount of bad debt expense or reduction of bad debt expense that EMC included in its income statement for 2015.
2. Suppose that EMC had used the direct write-off method to account for bad debts. Compute the following ($ in millions):
   a. The accounts receivable information that would be included in the 2015 year-end balance sheet.
   b. The amount of bad debt expense or reduction of bad debt expense that EMC included in its 2015 income statement.

P 7–3
Bad debts; Nike,
Inc.

● LO7–5

Real World Financials

Nike, Inc., is a leading manufacturer of sports apparel, shoes, and equipment. The company's 2017 financial statements contain the following information ($ in millions):

	2017	2016
Balance sheets:		
Accounts receivable, net	$ 3,677	$ 3,241
Income statements:		
Sales revenue	$34,350	$32,376

A note disclosed that the allowance for uncollectible accounts had a balance of $19 million and $43 million at the end of 2017 and 2016, respectively. Bad debt expense for 2017 was $40 million. Assume that all sales are made on a credit basis.

Required:
1. What is the amount of gross (total) accounts receivable due from customers at the end of 2017 and 2016?
2. What is the amount of bad debt write-offs during 2017?
3. Analyze changes in the gross accounts receivable account to calculate the amount of cash received from customers during 2017.
4. Analyze changes in net accounts receivable to calculate the amount of cash received from customers during 2017.

P 7–4
Uncollectible accounts
● LO7–5, LO7–6

Raintree Cosmetic Company sells its products to customers on a credit basis. An adjusting entry for bad debt expense is recorded only at December 31, the company's fiscal year-end. The 2020 balance sheet disclosed the following:

> Current assets:
> Receivables, net of allowance for uncollectible accounts of $30,000 $432,000

During 2021, credit sales were $1,750,000, cash collections from customers $1,830,000, and $35,000 in accounts receivable were written off. In addition, $3,000 was collected from a customer whose account was written off in 2020. An aging of accounts receivable at December 31, 2021, reveals the following:

Age Group	Percentage of Year-End Receivables in Group	Percent Uncollectible
0–60 days	65%	4%
61–90 days	20	15
91–120 days	10	25
Over 120 days	5	40

Required:
1. Prepare summary journal entries to account for the 2021 write-offs and the collection of the receivable previously written off.
2. Prepare the year-end adjusting entry for bad debts according to each of the following situations:
   a. Bad debt expense is estimated to be 3% of credit sales for the year.
   b. Bad debt expense is estimated by adjusting the allowance for uncollectible accounts to the balance that reduces the carrying value of accounts receivable to the amount of cash expected to be collected. The allowance for uncollectible accounts is estimated to be 10% of the year-end balance in accounts receivable.
   c. Bad debt expense is estimated by adjusting the allowance for uncollectible accounts to the balance that reduces the carrying value of accounts receivable to the amount of cash expected to be collected. The allowance for uncollectible accounts is determined by an aging of accounts receivable.
3. For situations (a)–(c) in requirement 2 above, what would be the net amount of accounts receivable reported in the 2021 balance sheet?

P 7–5
Receivables; bad debts and returns; Avon Products, Inc.
● LO7–4, LO7–5
Real World Financials

Avon Products, Inc., located in New York City, is one of the world's largest producers of beauty and related products. The company's consolidated balance sheets for the 2016 and 2015 fiscal years included the following ($ in thousands):

	2016	2015
Current assets:		
Receivables, less allowances of $131,100 in 2016 and $86,700 in 2015	$458,900	$440,000

A disclosure note accompanying the financial statements reported the following ($ in thousands):

	Year Ended	
	2016	2015
Calculation of account receivables, net:		
Receivables	$ 590,000	$ 526,700
Less: allowance for doubtful accounts	(122,900)	(77,600)
Less: reserve for product returns	(8,200)	(9,100)
Trade accounts receivable, net	$ 458,900	$ 440,000

Assume that the company reported bad debt expense in 2016 of $191,000 and had products returned for credit totaling $187,000 (sales price). Net sales for 2016 were $5,578,800 ($ in thousands).

Required:
1. What is the amount of accounts receivable due from customers at the end of 2016 and 2015?
2. What amount of accounts receivable did Avon write off during 2016?
3. What is the amount of Avon's gross sales for the 2016 fiscal year?
4. Assuming that all sales are made on a credit basis, what is the amount of cash Avon collected from customers during the 2016 fiscal year?

P 7–6
Notes receivable; solving for unknowns
● LO7–7

Cypress Oil Company's December 31, 2021, balance sheet listed $645,000 of notes receivable and $16,000 of interest receivable included in current assets. The following notes make up the notes receivable balance:

Note 1	Dated 8/31/2021, principal of $300,000 and interest at 10% due on 2/28/2022.
Note 2	Dated 6/30/2021, principal of $150,000 and interest due 3/31/2022.
Note 3	$200,000 face value noninterest-bearing note dated 9/30/2021, due 3/31/2022. Note was issued in exchange for merchandise.

The company records adjusting entries only at year-end. There were no other notes receivable outstanding during 2021.

Required:
1. Determine the rate used to discount the noninterest-bearing note.
2. Determine the explicit interest rate on Note 2.
3. What is the amount of interest revenue that appears in the company's 2021 income statement related to these notes?

P 7–7
Factoring versus assigning of accounts receivable
● LO7–8

Lonergan Company occasionally uses its accounts receivable to obtain immediate cash. At the end of June 2021, the company had accounts receivable of $780,000. Lonergan needs approximately $500,000 to capitalize on a unique investment opportunity. On July 1, 2021, a local bank offers Lonergan the following two alternatives:
a. Borrow $500,000, sign a note payable, and assign the entire receivable balance as collateral. At the end of each month, a remittance will be made to the bank that equals the amount of receivables collected plus 12% interest on the unpaid balance of the note at the beginning of the period.
b. Transfer $550,000 of specific receivables to the bank without recourse. The bank will charge a 2% factoring fee on the amount of receivables transferred. The bank will collect the receivables directly from customers. The sale criteria are met.

Required:
1. Prepare the journal entries that would be recorded on July 1 for each of the alternatives.
2. Assuming that 80% of all June 30 receivables are collected during July, prepare the necessary journal entries to record the collection and the remittance to the bank.
3. For each alternative, explain any required note disclosures that would be included in the July 31, 2021, financial statements.

P 7–8
Factoring of accounts receivable; without recourse
● LO7–8

Samson Wholesale Beverage Company regularly factors its accounts receivable with the Milpitas Finance Company. On April 30, 2021, the company transferred $800,000 of accounts receivable to Milpitas. The transfer was made without recourse. Milpitas remits 90% of the factored amount and retains 10%. When Milpitas collects the receivables, it remits to Samson the retained amount less a 4% fee (4% of the total factored amount). Samson estimates the fair value of the last 10% of its receivables to be $60,000.

Required:
Prepare the journal entry for Samson Wholesale Beverage for the transfer of accounts receivable on April 30, assuming the sale criteria are met.

P 7–9
Cash and accounts receivable under IFRS
● LO7–2, LO7–5, LO7–8, LO7–10
🌐 **IFRS**

The following facts apply to Walken Company during December 2021:
a. Walken began December with an accounts receivable balance (net of bad debts) of €25,000.
b. Walken had credit sales of €85,000.
c. Walken had cash collections of €30,000.
d. Walken factored €20,000 of net accounts receivable with Reliable Factor Company, transferring all risks and rewards associated with the receivable, and otherwise meeting all criteria necessary to qualify for treating the transfer of receivables as a sale.

e. Walken factored €15,000 of net accounts receivable with Dependable Factor Company, retaining all risks and rewards associated with the receivable, and otherwise meeting all criteria necessary to qualify for treating the transfer of receivables as a sale.

f. Walken did not recognize any additional bad debts expense, and had no write-offs of bad debts during the month.

g. At December 31, 2021, Walken had a balance of €40,000 of cash at M&V Bank and an overdraft of (€5,000) at First National Bank. (That cash balance includes any effects on cash of the other transactions described in this problem.)

Required:
Prepare the cash and accounts receivable lines of the current assets section of Walken's balance sheet, as of December 31, 2021.

P 7–10
Miscellaneous receivable transactions

● LO7–3, LO7–4, LO7–7, LO7–8

Evergreen Company sells lawn and garden products to wholesalers. The company's fiscal year-end is December 31. During 2021, the following transactions related to receivables occurred:

Feb. 28	Sold merchandise to Lennox, Inc., for **$10,000** and accepted a 10%, 7-month note. 10% is an appropriate rate for this type of note.	
Mar. 31	Sold merchandise to Maddox Co. that had a fair value of **$7,200**, and accepted a noninterest-bearing note for which **$8,000** payment is due on March 31, 2022.	
Apr. 3	Sold merchandise to Carr Co. for **$7,000** with terms 2/10, n/30. Evergreen uses the gross method to account for cash discounts.	
11	Collected the entire amount due from Carr Co.	
17	A customer returned merchandise costing **$3,200**. Evergreen reduced the customer's receivable balance by **$5,000**, the sales price of the merchandise. Sales returns are recorded by the company as they occur.	
30	Transferred receivables of **$50,000** to a factor without recourse. The factor charged Evergreen a 1% finance charge on the receivables transferred. The sale criteria are met.	
June 30	Discounted the Lennox, Inc., note at the bank. The bank's discount rate is 12%. The note was discounted without recourse.	
Sep. 30	Lennox, Inc., paid the note amount plus interest to the bank.	

Required:
1. Prepare the necessary journal entries for Evergreen for each of the above dates. For transactions involving the sale of merchandise, ignore the entry for the cost of goods sold (round all calculations to the nearest dollar).

2. Prepare any necessary adjusting entries at December 31, 2021. Adjusting entries are only recorded at year-end (round all calculations to the nearest dollar).

3. Prepare a schedule showing the effect of the journal entries in requirements 1 and 2 on 2021 income before taxes.

P 7–11
Discounting a note receivable

● LO7–7

Descriptors are provided below for six situations involving notes receivable being discounted at a bank. In each case, the maturity date of the note is December 31, 2021, and the principal and interest are due at maturity. For each, determine the proceeds received from the bank on discounting the note.

Note	Note Face Value	Date of Note	Interest Rate	Date Discounted	Discount Rate
1	$50,000	3/31/2021	8%	6/30/2021	10%
2	50,000	3/31/2021	8	9/30/2021	10
3	50,000	3/31/2021	8	9/30/2021	12
4	80,000	6/30/2021	6	10/31/2021	10
5	80,000	6/30/2021	6	10/31/2021	12
6	80,000	6/30/2021	6	11/30/2021	10

P 7–12
Accounts and notes receivable; discounting a note receivable; receivables turnover ratio

● LO7–5, LO7–6, LO7–7, LO7–8, LO7–9

Chamberlain Enterprises Inc. reported the following receivables in its December 31, 2021, year-end balance sheet:

Current assets:	
Accounts receivable, net of $24,000 in allowance for uncollectible accounts	$218,000
Interest receivable	6,800
Notes receivable	260,000

Additional Information:
1. The notes receivable account consists of two notes, a $60,000 note and a $200,000 note. The $60,000 note is dated October 31, 2021, with principal and interest payable on October 31, 2022. The $200,000 note is dated June 30, 2021, with principal and 6% interest payable on June 30, 2022.

394 SECTION 2 Assets

2. During 2022, sales revenue totaled $1,340,000, $1,280,000 cash was collected from customers, and $22,000 in accounts receivable were written off. All sales are made on a credit basis. Bad debt expense is recorded at year-end by adjusting the allowance account to an amount equal to 10% of year-end accounts receivable.

3. On March 31, 2022, the $200,000 note receivable was discounted at the Bank of Commerce. The bank's discount rate is 8%. Chamberlain accounts for the discounting as a sale.

Required:

1. In addition to sales revenue, what revenue and expense amounts related to receivables will appear in Chamberlain's 2022 income statement?

2. What amounts will appear in the 2022 year-end balance sheet for accounts receivable?

3. Calculate the receivables turnover ratio for 2022.

P 7–13
Bank reconciliation and adjusting entries; cash and cash equivalents
● Appendix 7A

The bank statement for the checking account of Management Systems Inc. (MSI) showed a December 31, 2021, balance of $14,632.12. Information that might be useful in preparing a bank reconciliation is as follows:

a. Outstanding checks were $1,320.25.

b. The December 31, 2021, cash receipts of $575 were not deposited in the bank until January 2, 2022.

c. One check written in payment of rent for $246 was correctly recorded by the bank but was recorded by MSI as a $264 disbursement.

d. In accordance with prior authorization, the bank withdrew $450 directly from the checking account as payment on a note payable. The interest portion of that payment was $350. MSI has made no entry to record the automatic payment.

e. Bank service charges of $14 were listed on the bank statement.

f. A deposit of $875 was recorded by the bank on December 13, but it did not belong to MSI. The deposit should have been made to the checking account of MIS, Inc.

g. The bank statement included a charge of $85 for an NSF check. The check was returned with the bank statement and the company will seek payment from the customer.

h. MSI maintains a $200 petty cash fund that was appropriately reimbursed at the end of December.

i. According to instructions from MSI on December 30, the bank withdrew $10,000 from the account and purchased U.S. Treasury bills for MSI. MSI recorded the transaction in its books on December 31 when it received notice from the bank. Half of the Treasury bills mature in two months and the other half in six months.

Required:

1. Prepare a bank reconciliation for the MSI checking account at December 31, 2021. You will have to compute the balance per books.

2. Prepare any necessary adjusting journal entries indicated.

3. What amount would MSI report as cash and cash equivalents in the current asset section of the December 31, 2021, balance sheet?

P 7–14
Bank reconciliation and adjusting entries
● Appendix 7A

El Gato Painting Company maintains a checking account at American Bank. Bank statements are prepared at the end of each month. The November 30, 2021, reconciliation of the bank balance is as follows:

Balance per bank, November 30		$3,231
Add: Deposits outstanding		1,200
Less: Checks outstanding		
#363	$123	
#365	201	
#380	56	
#381	86	
#382	340	(806)
Adjusted balance per bank, November 30		$3,625

The company's general ledger checking account showed the following for December:

Balance, December 1	$ 3,625
Receipts	42,650
Disbursements	(41,853)
Balance, December 31	$ 4,422

The December bank statement contained the following information:

Balance, December 1	$ 3,231
Deposits	43,000
Checks processed	(41,918)
Service charges	(22)
NSF checks	(440)
Balance, December 31	$ 3,851

The checks that were processed by the bank in December include all of the outstanding checks at the end of November except for check #365. In addition, there are some December checks that had not been processed by the bank by the end of the month. Also, you discover that check #411 for $320 was correctly recorded by the bank but was incorrectly recorded on the books as a $230 disbursement for advertising expense. Included in the bank's deposits is a $1,300 deposit incorrectly credited to the company's account. The deposit should have been posted to the credit of the Los Gatos Company. The NSF checks have not been redeposited and the company will seek payment from the customers involved.

Required:

1. Prepare a bank reconciliation for the El Gato checking account at December 31, 2021.
2. Prepare any necessary adjusting journal entries indicated.

P 7–15
Troubled debt
restructuring
● Appendix 7B

Rothschild Chair Company, Inc., was indebted to First Lincoln Bank under a $20 million, 10% unsecured note. The note was signed January 1, 2011, and was due December 31, 2024. Annual interest was last paid on December 31, 2019. At January 1, 2021, Rothschild Chair Company was experiencing severe financial difficulties and negotiated a restructuring of the terms of the debt agreement.

Required:
Prepare all journal entries by First Lincoln Bank to record the restructuring and any remaining transactions, for current and future years, relating to the debt under each of the independent circumstances below:

1. First Lincoln Bank agreed to settle the debt in exchange for land having a fair value of $16 million but carried on Rothschild Chair Company's books at $13 million.
2. First Lincoln Bank agreed to (a) forgive the interest accrued from last year, (b) reduce the remaining four interest payments to $1 million each, and (c) reduce the principal to $15 million.

Decision Makers' Perspective

©ImageGap/Getty Images

Apply your critical-thinking ability to the knowledge you've gained. These cases will provide you an opportunity to develop your research, analysis, judgment, and communication skills. You also will work with other students, integrate what you've learned, apply it in real-world situations, and consider its global and ethical ramifications. This practice will broaden your knowledge and further develop your decision-making abilities.

**Communication
Case 7–1**
Uncollectible
accounts
● LO7–5

You have been hired as a consultant by a parts manufacturing firm to provide advice as to the proper accounting methods the company should use in some key areas. In the area of receivables, the company president does not understand your recommendation to use the allowance method for uncollectible accounts. She stated, "Financial statements should be based on objective data rather than the guesswork required for the allowance method. Besides, since my uncollectibles are fairly constant from period to period, with significant variations occurring infrequently, the direct write-off method is just as good as the allowance method."

Required:
Draft a one-page response in the form of a memo to the president in support of your recommendation for the company to use the allowance method.

**Judgment
Case 7–2**
Accounts
receivable
● LO7–3, LO7–7,
LO7–8

Hogan Company uses the net method of accounting for sales discounts. Hogan offers trade discounts to various groups of buyers.

On August 1, 2021, Hogan factored some accounts receivable on a without recourse basis. Hogan incurred a finance charge.

Hogan also has some notes receivable bearing an appropriate rate of interest. The principal and total interest are due at maturity. The notes were received on October 1, 2021, and mature on September 30, 2022. Hogan's operating cycle is less than one year.

Required:

1. a. Using the net method, do sales discounts affect the amount recorded as sales revenue and accounts receivable at the time of sale? What is the rationale for the amount recorded as sales under the net method?

   b. Using the net method, is there an effect on Hogan's sales revenues and net income when customers do not take the sales discounts?

2. Do trade discounts affect the amount recorded as sales revenue and accounts receivable? Why?

3. Should Hogan decrease accounts receivable to account for the receivables factored on August 1, 2021? Why?

4. Would Hogan classify the interest-bearing notes receivable as current or non-current in its December 31, 2021, balance sheet? Why?

(AICPA adapted)

Real World Case 7–3
Sales returns; Green Mountain Coffee Roasters
● LO7–4

Real World Financials

The following is an excerpt from Sam Antar, "Is Green Mountain Coffee Roasters Shuffling the Beans to Beat Earnings Expectations?" (*Phil's Stock World delivered by Newstex,* May 9, 2011.)

On May 3, 2011, Green Mountain Coffee Roasters (NASDAQ: GMCR) beat analysts' earnings estimates by $0.10 per share for the thirteen-week period ended March 26, 2011. The next day, the stock price had risen to $11.91 per share to close at $75.98 per share, a staggering 18.5% increase over the previous day's closing stock price. CNBC Senior Stocks Commentator Herb Greenberg raised questions about the quality of Green Mountain Coffees earnings because its provision for sales returns dropped $22 million in the thirteen-week period. He wanted to know if there was a certain adjustment to reserves ("a reversal") that helped Green Mountain Coffee beat analysts' earnings estimates. . . .

During the thirteen-week period ended March 26, 2011, it was calculated that Green Mountain Coffee had a negative $22.259 million provision for sales returns. In its latest 10-Q report, Green Mountain Coffee disclosed that its provision for sales returns was $5.262 million for the twenty-six week period ending March 26, 2011, but the company did not disclose amounts for the thirteen-week period ended March 26, 2011. In its previous 10-Q report for the thirteen-week period ended December 25, 2010, Green Mountain Coffee disclosed that its provision for sales returns was $27.521 million. Therefore, the provision for sales returns for the thirteen-week period ended March 26, 2011 was a negative $22.259 million ($5.262 million minus $27.521 million).

Required:

1. Access EDGAR on the Internet. The web address is www.sec.gov.

2. Search for Green Mountain Coffee Roasters, Inc.'s 10-K for the fiscal year ended September 25, 2010 (filed December 9, 2010). (*Note:* the company now is named Keurig Green Mountain, Inc.) Answer the following questions related to the company's 2010 accounting for sales returns:

   a. Note: in 2010, companies could reduce the carrying value of accounts receivable for estimated returns, rather than recognizing a refund liability. What type of an account (for example, asset, contra liability) is Sales Returns Reserve? Explain.

   b. Prepare a T-account for fiscal 2010's sales returns account. Include entries for the beginning and ending balance, acquisitions, amounts charged to cost and expense, and deductions.

   c. Prepare journal entries for amounts charged to cost and expense and for deductions. Provide a brief explanation of what each of those journal entries represents.

   d. For any of the amounts included in your journal entries that appear in Green Mountain's operations section of its statement of cash flows on page F-8, indicate whether the amount appears as an increase or decrease to cash flows and explain why it appears as an increase or decrease.

3. Now consider the information provided by Antar in the excerpt at the beginning of this case.

   a. Prepare a T-account for the first quarter of fiscal 2011's sales returns reserve. Assume amounts associated with acquisitions and deductions are zero, such that the only entry affecting the account during the first quarter of fiscal 2011 is to record amounts charged or recovered from cost and expense. Compute the ending balance of the account.

   b. Prepare a T-account for the second quarter of fiscal 2011's sales returns reserve. Assume amounts associated with acquisitions and deductions are zero, such that the only entry affecting the account during the first quarter of fiscal 2011 is to record amounts charged or recovered from cost and expense. Compute the ending balance of the account.

   c. Assume that actual returns were zero during the second quarter of fiscal 2011. Prepare a journal entry to record amounts charged or recovered from cost and expense during the second quarter of fiscal 2011. How would that journal entry affect 2011 net income?

   d. Speculate as to what might have caused the activity in Green Mountain's sales returns account during the second quarter of fiscal 2011. Consider how this result could occur unintentionally, or why it might occur intentionally as a way to manage earnings.

Ethics Case 7–4
Uncollectible
accounts
● LO7–5

You have recently been hired as the assistant controller for Stanton Industries, a large, publicly held manufacturing company. Your immediate superior is the controller who, in turn, is responsible to the vice president of finance.

The controller has assigned you the task of preparing the year-end adjusting entries. In the receivables area, you have prepared an aging of accounts receivable and have applied historical percentages to the balances of each of the age categories. The analysis indicates that an appropriate balance for the allowance for uncollectible accounts is $180,000. The existing balance in the allowance account prior to any adjusting entry is a $20,000 credit balance.

After showing your analysis to the controller, he tells you to change the aging category of a large account from over 120 days to current status and to prepare a new invoice to the customer with a revised date that agrees with the new aging category. This will change the required allowance for uncollectible accounts from $180,000 to $135,000. Tactfully, you ask the controller for an explanation for the change and he tells you "We need the extra income; the bottom line is too low."

Required:
1. What is the effect on income before taxes of the change requested by the controller?
2. Discuss the ethical dilemma you face. Consider your options and responsibilities along with the possible consequences of any action you might take.

Judgment Case 7–5
Internal control
● LO7–1

For each of the following independent situations, indicate whether there is an apparent internal control weakness, and, if one exists, suggest alternative procedures to eliminate the weakness.
1. John Smith is the petty cash custodian. John approves all requests for payment out of the $200 fund, which is replenished at the end of each month. At the end of each month, John submits to his supervisor a list of all accounts and amounts to be charged, along with supporting documentation. Once the supervisor indicates approval, a check is written to replenish the fund for the total amount. John's supervisor performs surprise counts of the fund to ensure that the cash and/or receipts equal $200 at all times.
2. All of the company's cash disbursements are made by check. Each check must be supported by an approved voucher, which is in turn supported by the appropriate invoice and, for purchases, a receiving document. The vouchers are approved by Dean Leiser, the chief accountant, after reviewing the supporting documentation. Betty Hanson prepares the checks for Leiser's signature. Leiser also maintains the company's check register (the cash disbursements journal) and reconciles the bank account at the end of each month.
3. Fran Jones opens the company's mail and makes a listing of all checks and cash received from customers. A copy of the list is sent to Jerry McDonald who maintains the general ledger accounts. Fran prepares and makes the daily deposit at the bank. Fran also maintains the subsidiary ledger for accounts receivable, which is used to generate monthly statements to customers.

Real World Case 7–6
Receivables;
bad debts; Cisco
Systems, Inc.
● LO7–5

Real World Financials

EDGAR, the Electronic Data Gathering, Analysis, and Retrieval system, performs automated collection, validation, indexing, and forwarding of submissions by companies and others who are required by law to file forms with the U.S. Securities and Exchange Commission (SEC). All publicly traded domestic companies use EDGAR to make the majority of their filings. (Some foreign companies file voluntarily). Form 10-K or 10-KSB, which include the annual report, is required to be filed on EDGAR. The SEC makes this information available on the Internet.

Required:
1. Access EDGAR on the Internet. The web address is www.sec.gov.
2. Search for Cisco Systems, Inc. Access the 10-K filing for the fiscal year ended July 29, 2017. Search or scroll to find the financial statements.
3. Answer the following questions related to the company's accounts receivable and bad debts:
   a. What is the amount of gross trade accounts receivable at the end of the year?
   b. What is the amount of bad debt expense for the year? (*Hint:* check the statement of cash flows).
   c. Determine the amount of actual bad debt write-offs made during the year. Assume that all bad debts relate only to trade accounts receivable.
   d. Using only information from the balance sheets, income statements, and your answer to requirement 3(c), determine the amount of cash collected from customers during the year. Assume that all sales are made on a credit basis, that the company provides no allowances for sales returns, that no previously written-off receivables were collected, and that all sales relate to trade accounts receivable.

Integrating Case 7–7
Change in
estimate of bad
debts
● LO7–5

McLaughlin Corporation uses the allowance method to account for bad debts. At the end of the company's fiscal year, accounts receivable are analyzed and the allowance for uncollectible accounts is adjusted. At the end of 2021, the company reported the following amounts:

Accounts receivable	$10,850,000
Less: Allowance for uncollectible accounts	(450,000)
Accounts receivable, net	$10,400,000

In 2022, it was determined that $1,825,000 of year-end 2021 receivables had to be written off as uncollectible. This was due in part to the fact that Hughes Corporation, a long-standing customer that had always paid its bills, unexpectedly declared bankruptcy in 2022. Hughes owed McLaughlin $1,400,000. At the end of 2021, none of the Hughes receivable was considered uncollectible.

Required:

Should McLaughlin's underestimation of bad debts be treated as an error correction (requiring retroactive restatement) or a change in estimate (and accounted for prospectively)? Describe the appropriate accounting treatment and required disclosures in the financial statements issued for the 2021 fiscal year.

Real World Case 7–8
Financing with receivables; Sanofi-Aventis
● LO7–5, LO7–8, LO7–10
🌐 IFRS

Search on the Internet for the 2016 annual report for Sanofi-Aventis. Find the accounts receivable disclosure note.

Required:

1. Has Sanofi-Aventis factored or securitized accounts receivable? How do you know?

2. Assume that Sanofi-Aventis decided to increase the extent to which it securitizes its accounts receivable, changing to a policy of securitizing accounts receivable immediately upon making a sale and treating the securitization as a sale of accounts receivable. Indicate the likely effect of that change in policy on
   a. Accounts receivable in the period of the change (reduce, increase, or no change from prior period)
   b. Cash flow from operations in the period of the change (reduce, increase, or no change from prior period)
   c. Accounts receivable in subsequent periods (stabilize at higher, lower or same level as in periods prior to the change)
   d. Cash flow from operations in subsequent periods (stabilize at higher, lower or same level as in periods prior to the change)

3. Given your answers to requirement 2, could a company change the extent to which it factors or securitizes receivables to create one-time changes in its cash flow? Answer yes or no, and explain.

Research Case 7–9
Locate and extract relevant information and authoritative support for a financial reporting issue; financing with receivables
● LO7–8

You are spending the summer working for a local wholesale furniture company, Samson Furniture, Inc. The company is considering a proposal from a local financial institution, Old Reliant Financial, to factor Samson's receivables. The company controller is unfamiliar with the prevailing GAAP that deals with accounting for the transfer of financial assets and has asked you to do some research. The controller wants to make sure the arrangement with the financial institution is structured in such a way as to allow the factoring to be accounted for as a sale.

Old Reliant has offered to factor all of the company's receivables on a "without recourse" basis. Old Reliant will remit to Samson 90% of the factored amount, collect the receivables from Samson's customers, and retain the remaining 10% until all of the receivables have been collected. When Old Reliant collects all of the receivables, it will remit to Samson the retained amount, less a 4% fee (4% of the total factored amount).

Required:

1. Access the relevant authoritative literature on accounting for the transfer of financial assets using the *FASB Accounting Standards Codification*. You might gain access at the FASB website (www.fasb.org), from your school library, or some other source. What conditions must be met for a transfer of receivables to be accounted for as a sale (or in accounting terms, "derecognized")? What is the specific seven-digit Codification citation (XXX-XX-XX) that Samson would rely on in applying that accounting treatment?

2. Assuming that the conditions for treatment as a sale are met, prepare Samson's journal entry to record the factoring of $400,000 of receivables. Assume that the fair value of the last 10% of Samson's receivables is equal to $25,000.

3. An agreement that both entitles and obligates the transferor, Samson, to repurchase or redeem transferred assets from the transferee, Old Reliant, maintains the transferor's effective control over those assets and the transfer is accounted for as a secured borrowing, not a sale, if and only if what conditions are met?

Analysis Case 7–10
Compare receivables management using ratios; Tyson Foods Inc. and Pilgrim's Pride Corp.
● LO7–9

The table below contains selected financial information included in the 2016 financial statements of Tyson Foods Inc. and Pilgrim's Pride Corp.

	($ in millions)			
	Tyson		**Pilgrim's Pride**	
	2016	**2015**	**2016**	**2015**
Balance sheets:				
Accounts receivable, net	$ 1,542	$ 1,620	$ 317	$ 349
Income statements:				
Net sales	$36,881	$41,373	$7,931	$8,180

Required:

1. Calculate the 2016 receivables turnover ratio and average collection period for both companies. Evaluate the management of each company's investment in receivables.

2. Obtain annual reports from three corporations in the same primary industry and compare the management of each company's investment in receivables.

   Note: You can obtain copies of annual reports from your library, from the investor relations department of the corporations, or from EDGAR (Electronic Data Gathering, Analysis, and Retrieval) on the Internet (www.sec.gov).

Data Analytics

Data analytics is the process of examining data sets in order to draw conclusions about the information they contain. If you have not completed any of the prior data analytics cases, follow the instructions listed in the Chapter 1 Data Analytics case to get set up. You will need to watch the videos referred to in the Chapters 1 - 3 Data Analytics cases. No additional videos are required for this case. All short training videos can be found here: https://www.tableau.com/learn/training#getting-started.

Data Analytics Case
Receivables Management
● LO7–9

In prior chapters, you applied Tableau to examine a data set and create calculations to compare two companies' financial information. In this case, you continue in your role as an analyst conducting introductory research into the relative merits of investing in one or both of these companies. This time you assess the companies' receivables management and how effective the companies are in managing the investment in receivables.

Required:

Use Tableau to calculate (a) receivables turnover ratios, and (b) average collection periods for each of the two companies in each year from 2012 to 2021. Based upon what you find, answer the following questions:

1. What is the receivables turnover ratio for Big Store (a) in 2012 and (b) in 2021?

2. What is the receivables turnover ratio for Discount Goods (a) in 2012 and (b) in 2021?

3. Which company exhibited more favorable receivables management, as measured by average collection period, in *2020,* Big Store or Discount Goods? What was that company's average collection period, and is it longer or shorter than the industry average in 2020?

   The average collection period for the retail industry sector is 4.0 in 2020 and 5.1 in 2021.

4. Which company exhibited more favorable receivables management, as measured by average collection period, in *2021,* Big Store or Discount Goods? What was that company's average collection period, and is it longer or shorter than the industry average in 2021?

Resources:

You have available to you an extensive data set that includes detailed financial data for 2012-2021 for both Discount Goods and Big Store. The data set is in the form of four Excel files available to download from Connect, or under Student Resources within the Library tab. Download the file "Discount_Goods_Big_Store_Financials. xlsx" to the computer, save it, and open it in Tableau.

For this case, you will create several calculations to produce a text and line chart of the receivables analysis to allow you to compare and contrast the two companies' receivables management.

After you view the training videos and review instructions in Chapters 1-3, follow these steps to create the charts you'll use for this case:

- Click on the "Sheet 1" tab at the bottom of the canvas, to the right of the Data Source at the bottom of the screen.

- Drag "Year" and "Company" under "Dimensions" to the Rows shelf. Change "Year" to discrete data type by right-clicking and selecting "Discrete."

- Drag the "Net sales" and "Average accounts receivable net" under Measures to the Rows shelf. Change each to discrete. Format each to Times New Roman, 10-point font, black, center alignment, and Currency (custom), 0 decimal places by right-clicking each and selecting "Format." Format selections will open to the left of the canvas.

- Create a calculated field by clicking the "Analysis" tab from the Toolbar at the top of the screen and selecting "Create Calculated field." A calculation box will pop up. Name the calculation "Receivables Turnover." In the Calculation Editor window, from the Rows shelf, drag "Net sales" to the window, type a division sign, then drag "Average accounts receivable net" beside it. Make sure the window says that the calculation is valid and click OK.

400   SECTION 2   Assets

- Repeat the process one more time by creating a calculated field "Average Collection Period" that consists of the number 365 divided by the newly created "Receivables Turnover."
- Drag the "Receivables Turnover" and "Average Collection Period" to the Rows shelf. Change both to discrete data type. Format both to Times New Roman, 10-point font, black, center alignment, and Number (Custom), 2 decimal places.
- Change the title of the sheet to be "Receivables Management" by right-clicking and selecting "Edit title." Format the title to Times New Roman, bold, black and 15-point font. Change the title of "Sheet 1" to match the sheet title by right-clicking, selecting "Rename" and typing in the new title.
- Click on the "Sheet 2" tab and drag "Year" to the Columns shelf and "Receivables Turnover" and "Average Collection Period" to the Rows shelf.
- Drag "Company" under "Dimensions" to the Color in the Marks card. You should now see two colored lines in the two graphs.
- Format all the labels on the sheet ("Receivables Turnover," "Average Collection Period," and "Year") to Times New Roman, 10-point font, and black.
- Change the title of the sheet to be "Graph of Receivables Management" by right-clicking and selecting "Edit title." Format the title to Times New Roman, bold, black and 15-point font. Change the title of "Sheet 2" to match the sheet title by right-clicking, selecting "Rename" and typing in the new title.
- Once complete, save the file as "DA7_Your initials.twbx."

Continuing Cases

Target Case

● LO7–2, LO7–5

Target Corporation prepares its financial statements according to U.S. GAAP. Target's financial statements and disclosure notes for the year ended February 3, 2018, are available in Connect. This material also is available under the Investor Relations link at the company's website (www.target.com).

Required:

1. What is Target's policy for designating investments as cash equivalents?
2. What is Target's balance of cash equivalents for the fiscal year ended February 3, 2018?
3. What is Target's policy with respect to accounting for merchandise returns?
4. Does Target have accounts receivable? Speculate as to why it has the balance that it has. (*Hint:* See Disclosure Notes 9, 11, and 13).

Air France–KLM Case

● LO7–8

 IFRS

Air France–KLM (AF), a Franco-Dutch company, prepares its financial statements according to International Financial Reporting Standards. AF's financial statements and disclosure notes for the year ended December 31, 2017, are available in Connect. This material is also available under the Finance link at the company's website (www.airfranceklm.com).

Required:

1. In note 4.11, AF describes how it values trade receivables. How does the approach used by AF compare to U.S. GAAP?
2. In note 25, AF reconciles the beginning and ending balances of its valuation allowances for trade accounts receivable. Prepare a T-account for the valuation allowance and include entries for the beginning and ending balances as well as any reconciling items that affected the account during 2017.
3. Examine note 27. Does AF have any bank overdrafts? If so, are the overdrafts shown in the balance sheet the same way they would be shown under U.S. GAAP?

CPA Exam Questions and Simulations

 ROGER CPA Review

Sample CPA Exam questions from Roger CPA Review are available in Connect as support for the topics in this chapter. These multiple-choice questions and task-based simulations include expert-written explanations and solutions, and provide a starting point for students to become familiar with the content and functionality of the actual CPA Exam.

CHAPTER

8

Inventories: Measurement

OVERVIEW — The next two chapters continue our study of assets by investigating the measurement and reporting issues involving inventories and the related expense—cost of goods sold. Inventory refers to the assets a company (1) intends to sell in the normal course of business, (2) has in production for future sale, or (3) uses currently in the production of goods to be sold.

LEARNING OBJECTIVES — After studying this chapter, you should be able to:

- **LO8–1** Explain the types of inventory and the differences between a perpetual inventory system and a periodic inventory system. (p. 404)

- **LO8–2** Explain which physical units of goods should be included in inventory. (p. 408)

- **LO8–3** Account for transactions that affect net purchases and prepare a cost of goods sold schedule. (p. 409)

- **LO8–4** Differentiate between the specific identification, FIFO, LIFO, and average cost methods used to determine the cost of ending inventory and cost of goods sold. (p. 412)

- **LO8–5** Discuss the factors affecting a company's choice of inventory method. (p. 420)

- **LO8–6** Understand supplemental disclosures of LIFO reserves and the effect of LIFO liquidations on net income. (p. 422)

- **LO8–7** Calculate the key ratios used by analysts to monitor a company's investment in inventories. (p. 427)

- **LO8–8** Determine ending inventory using the dollar-value LIFO inventory method. (p. 431)

- **LO8–9** Discuss the primary difference between U.S. GAAP and IFRS with respect to determining the cost of inventory. (p. 420)

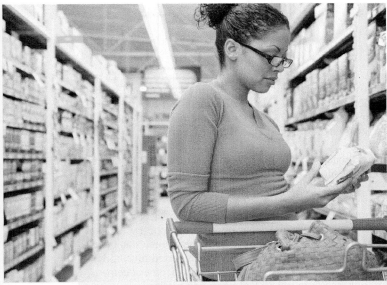

© Blend Images/Dave and Les Jacobs/Getty Images

FINANCIAL REPORTING CASE

Inventory Measurement at Kroger Company

As you were reading the annual report of Kroger Company, one of the world's largest grocery retailers, you notice the company accounts for nearly all of its grocery inventory based on a LIFO method (last-in, first-out). This means the company reports its most recent inventory purchases as sold *first*. However, you understand that most grocery inventory consists of perishable food items, meaning that the company in reality almost certainly sells its most recent purchases *last*. Otherwise, there would be considerable inventory spoilage. You decide to look a little deeper and notice the following discussion in the company's annual report:

Inventories (in part)

Inventories are stated at the lower of cost (principally on a last-in, first-out "LIFO" basis) or market. In total, approximately 93% of inventories in 2017 and 89% of inventories in 2016 were valued using the LIFO method. Replacement cost was higher than the carrying amount by $1,248 at February 3, 2018, and $1,291 at January 28, 2017.

($ in millions)	2018	2017
FIFO Inventory	$ 7,781	$7,852
LIFO reserve	(1,248)	(1,291)
Reported inventories	$ 6,533	$ 6,561

After seeing this information, you are further confused because you don't understand why Kroger would choose to report inventory for more than $1 billion below its replacement cost. Doesn't that make the company's inventory look less valuable and therefore the company less profitable?

You do some more research and find that other retail companies, as well as companies in industries such as automobiles, consumer products, energy, manufacturing, and mining, also use the LIFO method. Each of these companies most likely sells its actual inventory on a first-in, first-out (FIFO) basis, so why are they assuming the opposite?

By the time you finish this chapter, you should be able to respond appropriately to the questions posed in this case. Compare your response to the solution provided at the end of the chapter.

QUESTIONS

1. How is the LIFO method used to calculate inventories? Is this permissible according to GAAP? (*p. 419*)

2. What is the purpose of disclosing the difference between the reported LIFO inventory amounts and replacement cost, assuming that replacement cost is equivalent to a FIFO basis? (*p. 422*)

3. Are you correct that, by using LIFO, Kroger reports lower inventory and lower profits? Why would Kroger do that? (*p. 427*)

Recording and Measuring Inventory

PART A

Inventory refers to the assets a company (1) intends to sell in the normal course of business, (2) has in production for future sale (work in process), or (3) uses currently in the production of goods to be sold (raw materials). The computers produced by **Hewlett-Packard (HP)** that are intended for sale to customers are inventory, as are partially completed components,

404   SECTION 2   Assets

the computer chips, and memory modules that will go into computers produced later. The computers *used* by HP's employees to maintain its accounting system and other company operations, however, are not available for sale to customers and therefore are classified and accounted for as equipment. Similarly, the stocks and bonds a securities dealer holds for sale are inventory, whereas HP would classify the securities it holds as investments.

Cost of goods sold is the expense related to inventory. The inventory amount in the balance sheet represents the cost of the inventory still on hand (not yet sold) at the end of the period, while cost of goods sold in the income statement represents the cost of the inventory sold during the period.

Inventory usually is one of the most valuable assets listed in the balance sheet for manufacturing, wholesale, and retail companies (enterprises that produce revenue by selling goods). Similarly, cost of goods sold typically is the largest expense in the income statement of these companies. For example, a recent balance sheet for Best Buy reported inventories of $5.2 billion, which represented 53% of current assets. The company's income statement reported cost of goods sold of $32 billion, representing 80% of operating expenses.

As we'll see in this and the next chapter, it's usually difficult to measure inventory and cost of goods sold at the exact cost of the actual physical quantities on hand and sold. Fortunately, accountants can use one of several techniques to approximate the desired result and satisfy our measurement objectives.

Types of Inventory

Merchandising Inventory

● LO8–1

Wholesale and retail companies purchase goods that are primarily in finished form. These companies are intermediaries in the process of moving goods from the manufacturer to the end-user. They often are referred to as merchandising companies and their inventory as merchandise inventory. *The cost of merchandise inventory includes the purchase price plus any other costs necessary to get the goods in condition and location for sale.* We discuss the concept of condition and location and the types of costs that typically constitute inventory later in this chapter.

Manufacturing Inventories

Unlike merchandising companies, manufacturing companies actually produce the goods they sell to wholesalers, retailers, other manufacturers, or consumers. Inventory for a manufacturer consists of (1) raw materials, (2) work in process, and (3) finished goods.

Raw materials represent the cost of components purchased from suppliers that will become part of the finished product. For example, Hewlett-Packard's raw materials inventory includes semiconductors, circuit boards, plastic, and glass that go into the production of personal computers.

Work-in-process inventory refers to the products that are not yet complete in the manufacturing process. The cost of work in process includes the cost of raw materials used in production, the cost of labor that can be directly traced to the goods in process, and an allocated portion of other manufacturing costs, called *manufacturing overhead*. Overhead costs include electricity and other utility costs to operate the manufacturing facility, depreciation of manufacturing equipment, and many other manufacturing costs that cannot be directly linked to the production of specific goods.

Finished goods are goods that have been completed in the manufacturing process but have not yet been sold. They have reached their final stage and now await sale to a customer. Their cost includes the cost of all raw materials and work in process used in production.

Manufacturing companies generally disclose, either in a note or directly in the balance sheet, the dollar amount of each inventory category. For example, Intel, one of the world's largest semiconductor chip manufacturers, reports inventory as shown in Illustration 8–1.

	($ in millions)	
	December 30, 2017	**December 31, 2016**
Raw materials	$ 1,098	$ 695
Work in process	3,893	3,190
Finished goods	1,992	1,668
Total Inventories	$6,983	$5,553

Source: Intel Corporation

Illustration 8–1

Inventories Disclosure—
Intel Corporation

Real World Financials

The inventory accounts and the cost flows for a typical manufacturing company are shown using T-accounts in Illustration 8–2. The costs of raw materials used, direct labor applied, and manufacturing overhead applied flow into work in process and then to finished goods. When the goods are sold, the cost of those goods flows to cost of goods sold.

Illustration 8–2

Inventory Components
and Cost Flow for a
Manufacturing Company

The costs of inventory
units follow their physical
movement from one stage
of activity to another.

① Raw materials purchased

② Direct labor incurred

③ Manufacturing overhead incurred

④ Raw materials used

⑤ Direct labor applied

⑥ Manufacturing overhead applied

⑦ Work in process transferred to finished goods

⑧ Finished goods sold

We focus in this text primarily on merchandising companies (wholesalers and retailers). Still, most of the accounting principles and procedures discussed here also apply to manufacturing companies. The unique problems involved with accumulating the direct costs of raw materials and labor and with allocating manufacturing overhead are addressed in managerial and cost accounting textbooks.

Types of Inventory Systems

Perpetual Inventory System

Two accounting systems are used to record transactions involving inventory: the **perpetual inventory system** and the **periodic inventory system**. The perpetual system was introduced in Chapter 2. The system is aptly termed perpetual because the *inventory* account is continually adjusted for each change in inventory, whether it's caused by a purchase, a sale, or a return of inventory (a *purchase return* for the buyer, a *sales return* for the seller).[1] In addition, the *cost of goods sold* account is adjusted each time goods are sold or are

---

[1]We discussed accounting for sales returns in Chapter 7.

returned by a customer. The perpetual inventory system is applied to the Lothridge Whole-sale Beverage Company for which inventory information is provided in Illustration 8–3. This hypothetical company also will be used in the next several illustrations.

Illustration 8–3

Perpetual Inventory System

The Lothridge Wholesale Beverage Company purchases soft drinks from producers and then sells them to retailers. The company begins 2021 with inventory of $120,000 on hand. The following information relates to inventory transactions during 2021:

1. Additional soft drink inventory is purchased on account at a cost of $600,000.
2. Sales for the year, all on account, totaled $820,000.
3. The cost of the soft drink inventory sold is $540,000.

Lothridge uses the **perpetual inventory system** to keep track of both inventory quantities and inventory costs. The system indicates that the cost of inventory on hand at the end of the year is $180,000.

The following summary journal entries record the inventory transactions for the Lothridge Company:

During 2021

Inventory..	600,000	
Accounts payable		600,000
To record the purchase of inventory.		

During 2021

Accounts receivable...	820,000	
Sales revenue		820,000
To record sales on account.		
Cost of goods sold..	540,000	
Inventory		540,000
To record the cost of sales.		

An important feature of a perpetual system is that it is designed to track inventory quantities from their acquisition to their sale. If the system is accurate, it allows management to determine how many goods are on hand on any date without having to take a physical count. However, physical counts of inventory usually are made anyway, either at the end of the fiscal year or on a sample basis throughout the year, to verify that the perpetual system is correctly tracking quantities. Differences between the quantity of inventory determined by the physical count and the quantity of inventory according to the perpetual system could be caused by system errors, theft, breakage, or spoilage. In addition to keeping up with inventory purchases, a perpetual system also directly determines how many items are sold during a period.

When a company uses a perpetual inventory system to record inventory and cost of goods sold transactions, merchandise cost data also is included in the system. That way, when merchandise is purchased/sold, the system records not only the addition/reduction in inventory *quantity* but also the addition/reduction in inventory *cost*.

A perpetual inventory system continuously tracks both inventory quantities and inventory costs.

Nearly all major companies use a perpetual inventory system to maintain a record of inventory transactions.

Technology and inventory accounting.   You're familiar with the barcode scanning mechanisms used at grocery stores and other checkout counters. Scanners, such as these, are linked to a company's accounting records to allow for continuous tracking of inventory. Each time inventory is purchased or sold, employees scan barcodes attached to merchandise. This provides management with real-time information about inventory levels and cost. In addition to barcode scanning, companies have developed techniques to further automate their management and recording of inventory. For example, some companies use inventory software linked to radio frequency identification (RFID) tags, allowing inventory to be recorded automatically as it moves in and out of a company. Companies are developing "smart" systems to use with "big data" to monitor customer trends and automatically initiate orders in real time as those trends change. These types of technological advances help to reduce the burden of physical inventory counts and manual record keeping, and make the use of a perpetual inventory system easier and more efficient. *That's why nearly all major companies use a perpetual inventory system, and that's why we focus on the use of the perpetual system in this chapter.* Nevertheless, even with the advances in technology to improve the automation of inventory accounting, many companies still must physically count the inventory on hand at the end of the period to verify the accuracy of the accounting records and to account for inventory damaged or stolen.

Periodic Inventory System

A periodic inventory system does not maintain a continual record of inventory quantity or cost during the period. Instead, the quantity of inventory is determined only at the end of the period based on a physical count. The balance of the inventory account is updated for purchases and sales that occurred during the year using a year-end adjusting entry. A periodic system also does not maintain a record of the cost of goods sold with each sale. The balance is established in the year-end adjusting entry for an amount that equals beginning inventory plus net purchases during the year (total purchases plus freight-in less purchase returns and discounts) minus ending inventory:

> Beginning inventory + Net purchases − Ending inventory = Cost of goods sold

A periodic inventory system adjusts inventory and records cost of goods sold only at the end of each reporting period.

Cost of goods sold equation

Implied in the calculation of cost of goods sold is that any beginning inventory or net purchases that are not included in ending inventory must have been sold. This may not be the case if inventory items were either damaged or stolen. If damaged and stolen inventory are identified, they may be removed from beginning inventory or purchases before calculating cost of goods sold and then classified as a separate expense item.

Illustration 8–4 looks at the periodic system using the Lothridge Wholesale Beverage Company example.

Illustration 8–4

Periodic Inventory System

The Lothridge Wholesale Beverage Company purchases soft drinks from producers and then sells them to retailers. The company begins 2021 with inventory of $120,000 on hand. The following information relates to inventory transactions during 2021:

1. Additional soft drink inventory is purchased on account at a cost of $600,000.

2. Sales for the year, all on account, totaled $820,000.

Lothridge uses the **periodic inventory system.** After a physical count of inventory at the end of the year, the cost of ending inventory is determined to be $180,000.

The following summary journal entries record the inventory transactions for the Lothridge Company:

During 2021

Purchases..	600,000	
Accounts payable		600,000

To record the purchase of inventory.

During 2021

Accounts receivable..	820,000	
Sales revenue		820,000

To record sales on account.

No entry is recorded for the cost of inventory sold.

Because cost of goods sold isn't determined continually by the periodic system, it must be determined indirectly after a physical inventory count at the end of the year. Cost of goods sold for 2021 is determined as follows:

Beginning inventory	$ 120,000
Plus: Purchases	600,000
Cost of goods available for sale	720,000
Less: Ending inventory (per physical count)	(180,000)
Cost of goods sold	$540,000

We then make the following entry to update the balance in the inventory account and combine the components of cost of goods sold into a single expense account:

December 31, 2021

Cost of goods sold...	540,000	
Inventory (ending)	180,000	
Inventory (beginning)..		120,000
Purchases		600,000

To adjust inventory, close the purchases account, and record cost of goods sold.

This entry adjusts the inventory account to the correct period-end amount, closes the temporary purchases account, and records cost of goods sold. Now let's compare the two inventory accounting systems.

A Comparison of the Perpetual and Periodic Inventory Systems

Beginning inventory plus net purchases during the period is the *cost of goods available for sale*. The main difference between a perpetual and a periodic system is that the periodic system allocates cost of goods available for sale between ending inventory and cost of goods sold *only at the end of the period* (periodically). In contrast, the perpetual system updates the balance of inventory and cost of goods sold *each time goods are sold* (perpetually).

The impact on the financial statements of choosing one system over the other generally is not significant. The choice between the two approaches usually is motivated by management control considerations as well as the comparative costs of implementation. Perpetual systems can provide more information about the dollar amounts of inventory levels on a continuous basis. They also facilitate the preparation of interim (for example, quarterly) financial statements by providing fairly accurate information without the necessity of a physical count of inventory. Periodic systems require a physical count of inventory, complicating preparation of interim financial statements unless an inventory estimation technique is used.[2]

On the other hand, a perpetual system may be more expensive to implement than a periodic system. This is particularly true for inventories consisting of large numbers of low-cost items. Perpetual systems are more workable with inventories of high-cost items such as construction equipment or automobiles. However, with the help of computers and electronic sales devices such as cash register systems with barcode scanners or RFID tags, the perpetual inventory system now is available to many small businesses that previously could not afford them and is economically feasible for a broader range of inventory items than before.

> A perpetual system provides more timely information but generally is more costly.

What is Included in Inventory?

Physical units Included in Inventory

> LO8-2

Regardless of the system used, the measurement of inventory and cost of goods sold starts with determining the physical units of goods. Typically, determining the physical units that should be included in inventory is a simple matter because it consists of items in the possession of the company. However, in some situations the identification of items that should be included in inventory is more difficult. Consider, for example, goods in transit, goods on consignment, and sales returns.

GOODS IN TRANSIT   At the end of a reporting period, it's important to ensure a proper inventory cutoff. This means ownership must be determined for goods that are in transit between the company and its customers as well as between the company and its suppliers.

For example, in December 2021, the Lothridge Wholesale Beverage Company sold goods to the Jabbar Company.

1. The goods were shipped from Lothridge on December 29, 2021, but
2. The goods didn't arrive at Jabbar until January 3, 2022.

---

[2]In Chapter 9 we discuss inventory estimation techniques that avoid the necessity of a physical count to determine ending inventory and cost of goods sold.

If both companies have December 31 fiscal year ends, whose inventory is it on December 31, 2021? In other words, which company will report these goods in ending inventory in the balance sheet as of December 31, 2021? The answer depends on who owns the goods on December 31. Ownership depends on the terms of the agreement between the two companies.

If the goods are shipped **f.o.b. (free on board) shipping point**, then legal title to the goods passes from the seller to the buyer at the *point of shipment* (when the seller hands over the goods to the delivery company, such as **FedEx**). In this case, the buyer is responsible for shipping costs and transit insurance. Lothridge records the sale of inventory on December 29, 2021, and Jabbar records the purchase of inventory on that same day. Jabbar will include these goods in its 2021 ending inventory even though the company is not in physical possession of the goods on the last day of the fiscal year.

On the other hand, if the goods are shipped **f.o.b. destination**, then legal title to the goods does not pass from the seller to the buyer until the goods arrive at their *destination* (the customer's location). In this case, the seller is responsible for shipping costs and transit insurance. In our example, if the goods are shipped f.o.b. destination, Lothridge waits to record the sale until January 3, 2022, and Jabbar records the purchase of inventory on that same day. Lothridge includes the goods in its 2021 ending inventory even though the inventory has already been shipped as of the last day of the financial statement reporting period.

> Inventory shipped *f.o.b. shipping point* is included in the purchaser's inventory as soon as the merchandise is shipped.

> Inventory shipped *f.o.b. destination* is included in the purchaser's inventory only after it reaches the purchaser's destination.

GOODS ON CONSIGNMENT Sometimes a company arranges for another company to sell its product under **consignment**. The goods are physically transferred to the other company (the consignee), but the transferor (consignor) retains legal title. If the consignee can't find a buyer, the goods are returned to the consignor. If a buyer is found, the consignee remits the selling price (less commission and approved expenses) to the consignor.

> Goods held on *consignment* are included in the inventory of the consignor until sold by the consignee.

For example, suppose Pratt Clothing (consignor) ships merchandise to Regal Outlets (consignee). The arrangement specifies that Regal will attempt to sell the merchandise, and in return, Pratt will pay to Regal a 10% sales commission on any merchandise sold. Any inventory not sold within six months will be returned to Pratt. In this arrangement, Regal obtains physical possession of the inventory and has responsibility to sell to customers, but Pratt retains legal title to the inventory and risk of ownership and therefore keeps this inventory in its own records until the merchandise is sold to a customer. We discussed this issue in Chapter 6. The sale is not complete (revenue is not recognized) until an eventual sale to a third party occurs. In addition, any costs paid by Pratt to ship the inventory to Regal would be included in Pratt's cost of inventory at the time the cost was incurred. However, other costs incurred by Pratt, such as advertising or sales commissions to Regal, would be expensed as incurred and not included in the cost of inventory.

SALES RETURNS Recall from our discussions in Chapters 6 and 7 that when the right of return exists, a seller must be able to estimate those returns before revenue can be recognized. The adjusting entry for estimated sales returns includes a debit to sales returns and a credit to refund liability. At the same time, cost of goods sold is reduced and an estimate of inventory to be returned is made (see Illustration 7–4). As a result, a company includes in ending inventory the cost of merchandise sold that it anticipates will be returned.

Now that we've considered which goods are part of inventory, let's examine the types of costs associated with those inventory units.

Transactions Affecting Net Purchases

As mentioned earlier, the cost of inventory includes all necessary expenditures to acquire the inventory and bring it to its desired *condition* and *location* for sale or for use in the manufacturing process. Obviously, the cost includes the purchase price of the goods. But usually the cost of acquiring inventory also includes freight charges on incoming goods borne by the buyer; insurance costs incurred by the buyer while the goods are in transit (if shipped f.o.b. shipping point); and the costs of unloading, unpacking, and preparing merchandise

> ● LO8–3

410   SECTION 2   Assets

Expenditures necessary
to bring inventory to its
condition and *location* for
sale or use are included in
its cost.

inventory for sale or raw materials inventory for use.[3] The costs included in inventory are called **product costs**. They are associated with products and *expensed as cost of goods sold only when the related products are sold.*[4]

FREIGHT-IN ON PURCHASES   Freight-in on purchases is commonly included in the cost of inventory. These costs clearly are necessary to get the inventory in location for sale or use and can generally be associated with particular goods. Freight costs are added to the *inventory* account in a perpetual system.

The cost of *freight-in* paid
by the purchaser generally
is part of the cost of
inventory.

In a periodic system, freight costs generally are recorded in a temporary account called **freight-in** or **transportation-in**, which is added to total purchases in determining net purchases for inclusion in cost of goods sold. (See also the cost of goods sold schedule in Illustration 8–6 later in this section.) From a control perspective, by recording freight-in as a separate item, management can more easily track its freight costs. The same perspectives pertain to purchase returns and purchase discounts, which are discussed in the next sections.

Shipping charges on
outgoing goods are
reported either as part of
cost of goods sold or as an
operating expense, usually
among selling expenses.

Shipping charges on outgoing goods (freight-out) are not included in the cost of inventory. They are reported in the income statement either as part of cost of goods sold or as an operating expense, usually among selling expenses. If a company adopts a policy of not including shipping charges in cost of goods sold, both the amounts incurred during the period as well as the income statement classification of the expense must be disclosed.[5]

PURCHASE RETURNS   In Chapter 7 we discussed merchandise returns from the perspective of the selling company. At the time a customer returns merchandise, the seller records a sales return (a contra revenue account). We now address returns from the buyer's point of view. When merchandise is returned, the buyer records a **purchase return**. In a perpetual inventory system, the purchase return is recorded directly as a reduction to the *inventory* account. In a periodic system, we use a *purchase returns* account to temporarily accumulate these amounts. Recall our earlier discussion of the cost of goods sold calculation (Beginning inventory + *Net purchases* − Ending inventory = Cost of goods sold). Purchase returns are subtracted from total purchases to calculate net purchases. (See also the cost of goods sold schedule in Illustration 8–6 later in this section.)

Purchase discounts
represent reductions in
the amount to be paid if
remittance is made within
a designated period of
time.

PURCHASE DISCOUNTS   Cash discounts were discussed from the seller's perspective in Chapter 7. Here, we discuss them from the buyer's perspective. Discounts offer incentives to the buyer to make quick payment. The amount of the discount and the time period within which it's available are conveyed by terms like 2/10, n/30 (meaning a 2% discount if paid within 10 days, otherwise full payment within 30 days). As with the seller, the purchaser can record these **purchase discounts** using either the **gross method** or the **net method**.

Consider Illustration 8–5. On October 5, Lothridge purchases $20,000 of inventory and is offered a discount of 2% for any amount paid within 10 days. The full invoice is due within 30 days. Under the *gross method,* we record the purchase for the full (or gross) amount of the inventory's cost. Under the *net method,* we record the purchase of inventory for its $20,000 cost minus the possible discount of $400 ($20,000 × 2%), resulting in a net purchase amount of $19,600.

Payment within the discount period.   On October 14, Lothridge decides to make payment for $14,000 of the $20,000 purchase. Because payment is within the 10-day discount period, the company receives a discount of $280 ($14,000 × 2%) and must pay only $13,720

---

[3]Generally accepted accounting principles require that abnormal amounts of certain costs be recognized as current period expenses rather than being included in the cost of inventory, specifically idle facility costs, freight, handling costs, and waste materials (spoilage). FASB ASC 330–10–30: Inventory—Overall—Initial Measurement.

[4]For practical reasons, though, some of these expenditures often are not included in inventory cost and are treated as **period costs.** They often are immaterial or it is impractical to associate the expenditures with particular units of inventory (for example, unloading and unpacking costs). Period costs are not associated with products and are expensed in the *period* incurred.

[5]FASB ASC 605–45–50–2: Revenue Recognition—Principal Agent Considerations—Disclosure—Shipping and Handling Fees and Costs.

Illustration 8–5

Purchase Discounts Using the Gross Method versus Net Method—Perpetual System

Consider the following transactions for the Lothridge Wholesale Beverage Company that uses a perpetual inventory system:

1. October 5—Purchased merchandise with a cost of $20,000. The payment terms are stated as 2/10, n/30.
2. October 14—Paid $13,720 ($14,000 of the invoice less a 2% cash discount on that amount).
3. November 4—Paid the remaining $6,000 balance of the invoice.

Gross Method			Net Method		
October 5			**October 5**		
Inventory*.............................	20,000		Inventory*...............................	19,600	
Accounts payable		20,000	Accounts payable		19,600
October 14			**October 14**		
Accounts payable................	14,000		Accounts payable.................	13,720	
Inventory**.........................		280	Cash.....................................		13,720
Cash...................................		13,720			
November 4			**November 4**		
Accounts payable................	6,000		Accounts payable.................	5,880	
Cash...................................		6,000	Purchase discounts lost........	120	
			Cash.....................................		6,000

*The purchases account is used in a periodic inventory system.
**The purchase discounts account is used in a periodic inventory system.

($14,000 − $280). The discount effectively reduces the cost of inventory. Under the gross method, we record the discount by decreasing the inventory account. Under the net method, the discount was recorded at the time of the purchase, so no further reduction to the inventory account is needed at the time of payment.

Payment *not* within the discount period. On November 4, Lothridge makes final payment for the remaining $6,000 of inventory. This payment is after the 10-day discount period. Lothridge loses the possible discount of $120 ($6,000 × 2%). Under the gross method, we simply record the payment on account. Under the net method, we record the purchase discount lost. Most companies that use the net method expect to pay within the discount period. In practice, purchase discounts lost are generally immaterial.[6]

RECORDING TRANSACTIONS IN A PERPETUAL AND PERIODIC SYSTEM Illustration 8–6 compares the perpetual and periodic inventory systems, using the gross method. A schedule to demonstrate the calculation of cost of goods sold is provided at the end.

Illustration 8–6

Inventory Transactions Using the Gross Method—Perpetual and Periodic Systems

The Lothridge Wholesale Beverage Company purchases soft drinks from producers and then sells them to retailers. The company began the year with merchandise inventory of $120,000 on hand. During the year, additional inventory transactions include:

- Purchases of merchandise on account totaled $620,000, with terms 2/10, n/30.
- Freight charges paid by Lothridge were $16,000.
- Merchandise with a cost of $20,000 was returned to suppliers for credit.
- All purchases on account were paid within the discount period.
- Sales on account totaled $830,000. The cost of soft drinks sold was $550,000.
- Inventory remaining on hand at the end of the year totaled $174,000.

The above transactions are recorded in summary form according to both the perpetual and periodic inventory systems using the gross method:

(continued)

---

[6]There is variation in practice of how the purchase discounts lost account is classified. Many companies report this account as part of other expenses, similar to the treatment of interest expense. Other companies include the discount lost as part of goods sold, either at the time of payment or once those goods are sold.

412   SECTION 2   Assets

(concluded)

($ in thousands)

Perpetual System		Periodic System		
Purchases				
Inventory 620		Purchases 620		
Accounts payable	620	Accounts payable		620
Freight				
Inventory 16		Freight-in 16		
Cash....................................	16	Cash		16
Returns				
Accounts payable 20		Accounts payable 20		
Inventory	20	Purchase returns		20
Discounts				
Accounts Payable 600		Accounts Payable 600		
Inventory ($600 × 2%)	12	Purchase discounts ($600 × 2%)		12
Cash	588	Cash		588
Sales				
Accounts receivable 830		Accounts receivable 830		
Sales revenue	830	Sales revenue		830
Cost of goods sold 550		No entry		
Inventory	550			
		End of period		
No entry		Cost of goods sold (below)..................... 550		
		Inventory (ending) 174		
		Purchase returns 20		
		Purchase discounts.................................. 12		
		Inventory (beginning)		120
		Purchases..		620
		Freight-in		16
		Supporting Schedule		
		Cost of goods sold:		
		Beginning Inventory...................................		$120
		Net purchases:		
		Purchases $620		
		Plus: Freight-in.................................... 16		
		Less: Returns.. (20)		
		Less: Discounts.................................... (12)	604	
		Cost of good available	724	
		Less: Ending inventory......................	(174)	
		Cost of goods sold ·································	$550	

Inventory Cost Flow Assumptions

● LO8–4

Regardless of whether the perpetual or periodic system is used, it's necessary to assign dollar amounts to the physical quantities of goods sold and goods remaining in ending inventory. Unless each item of inventory is specifically identified and traced through the system, assigning dollars is accomplished by making an assumption regarding how units of goods (and their associated costs) flow through the system. We examine the common cost flow assumptions next. In previous illustrations, dollar amounts of the cost of goods sold and the cost of ending inventory were assumed known. However, if various portions of inventory are acquired at different costs, we need a way to decide which units were sold and which remain in inventory. Illustration 8–7 will help explain.

Illustration 8–7

Inventory Information

Goods available for sale include beginning inventory plus purchases.

The Browning Company has the following inventory information for 2021:

Beginning Inventory and Purchases During 2021

Date	Units	Unit Cost*	Total Cost
Jan. 1 (Beginning Inventory)	4,000	$5.50	$22,000
Purchases:			
Jan. 17	1,000	6.00	6,000
Mar. 22	3,000	7.00	21,000
Oct. 15	3,000	7.50	22,500
Goods available for sale	11,000		$71,500

Sales

Date of Sale	Units
Jan. 10	2,000
Apr. 15	1,500
Nov. 20	3,000
Total sales	6,500

*Includes purchase price and cost of freight.

Browning began the year with 4,000 units and purchased another 7,000 units, so there were 11,000 units available for sale. Of this amount, 6,500 units were sold. This means 4,500 units remain in ending inventory. This allocation of units is depicted in Illustration 8–7A.

Illustration 8–7A

Allocation of Units Available for Sale

But what is the *cost* of the 6,500 units sold? What is the *cost* of the 4,500 units remaining on hand at the end of the year? To answer this, let's first consider that the total cost of the 11,000 goods available for sale (beginning inventory plus purchases during the year) is $71,500. This total amount will be allocated to ending inventory and cost of goods sold. The allocation decision is depicted in Illustration 8–7B.

Illustration 8–7B

Allocation of Cost of Goods Available for Sale

The allocation of the total cost of goods available for sale to ending inventory and cost of goods sold is also depicted in the schedule below. We'll use this schedule in the following sections.

Beginning inventory (4,000 units @ $5.50)	$ 22,000
Plus: Purchases (7,000 units @ various prices)	49,500
Cost of goods available for sale (11,000 units)	$71,500
Less: Ending inventory (4,500 units @ ?)	?
Cost of goods sold (6,500 units @ ?)	?

Let's turn our attention now to the various inventory costing methods that can be used to achieve the allocation between ending inventory and cost of goods sold.

Specific Identification

It's sometimes possible for each unit sold during the period or each unit on hand at the end of the period to be matched with its actual cost. Actual costs can be determined by reference to the invoice representing the purchase of the item. The specific identification method is used frequently by companies selling unique, expensive products with low sales volume which makes it relatively easy and economically feasible to associate each item with its actual cost. For example, automobiles have unique serial numbers that can be used to match a specific auto with the invoice identifying the actual purchase price.

In our example for Browning Company, we might have been able to track each of the 6,500 units sold. Suppose the *actual* units sold include 4,000 units of beginning inventory, 800 units of the January 17 purchase, 1,400 units from the March 22 purchase, and 300 units of the October 15 purchase. The cost of those 6,500 units would be reported as cost of goods sold. The cost of the 4,500 units remaining (consisting of 200 from the January 17 purchase, 1,600 from the March 22 purchase, and 2,700 units from the October 15 purchase) would be reported as ending inventory.

However, keeping track of each unit of inventory typically is not practicable for most companies. Consider the inventory at The Home Depot, Inc. or Macy's: large stores and numerous items, many of which are relatively inexpensive. Specific identification would be very difficult for such merchandisers. Although bar codes and RFID tags now make it possible to instantly track purchases and sales of specific types of inventory, it may be too costly to know the specific unit cost for each individual sale. For that reason, the specific identification method is used primarily by companies with unique, expensive products with low sales volume.

Most companies instead use one of the three inventory cost flow assumptions—average cost, FIFO, or LIFO. Note the use of the word *assumptions*. FIFO, LIFO, and weighted-average cost *assume* a particular pattern of inventory cost flows. However, the *actual* flow of inventory does not need to match the *assumed* cost flow in order for the company to use a particular method. That's okay. Companies are allowed to report inventory costs by *assuming* which units of inventory are sold and not sold, even if this does not match the *actual* flow. This is another example of using estimates in financial accounting.

Average Cost

The average cost method assumes that cost of goods sold and ending inventory consist of a mixture of all the goods available for sale. The average unit cost applied to goods sold or to ending inventory is an average unit cost *weighted* by the number of units acquired at the various unit costs. The average is not simply an average of the various unit costs of purchases during the period.

PERIODIC AVERAGE COST   In a periodic inventory system, this weighted average is calculated only at the end of the period as follows:

$$\text{Weighted-average unit cost} = \frac{\text{Cost of goods available for sale}}{\text{Quantity available for sale}}$$

The specific identification method records actual units sold.

FIFO, LIFO, and weighted-average assume which units are sold.

The average cost method assumes that items sold and items in ending inventory come from a mixture of all the goods available for sale.

In a periodic inventory system, the average cost is computed only at the end of the period.

The calculation of average cost is demonstrated in Illustration 8–7C using data from Illustration 8–7.

Beginning inventory (4,000 units @ $5.50)	$ 22,000
Plus: Purchases (7,000 units @ various prices)	49,500
Cost of goods available for sale (11,000 units)	71,500
Less: Ending inventory* (determined below)	(29,250)
Cost of goods sold (6,500 units)	$42,250

*Cost of Ending Inventory:

$$\text{Weighted-average unit cost} = \frac{\$71,500}{11,000 \text{ units}} = \$6.50$$

4,500 units × $6.50 = $29,250

Illustration 8–7C

Average Cost—Periodic Inventory System

Cost of goods sold also could be determined directly by multiplying the weighted-average unit cost of $6.50 by the number of units sold ($6.50 × 6,500 units = $42,250).

PERPETUAL AVERAGE COST   The weighted-average unit cost in a perpetual inventory system becomes a moving-average unit cost. *A new weighted-average unit cost is calculated each time additional units are purchased.* The new average is determined after each purchase by (1) summing the cost of the previous inventory balance and the cost of the new purchase, and (2) dividing this new total cost (cost of goods available for sale) by the number of units on hand (the inventory units that are available for sale). This average is then used to cost any units sold before the next purchase is made. The moving-average concept is applied in Illustration 8–7D.

In a perpetual inventory system, the average cost method is applied by computing a moving-average unit cost each time additional inventory is purchased.

Illustration 8–7D   Average Cost—Perpetual Inventory System

Date	Purchased	Sold	Balance
Beginning inventory	4,000 @ $5.50 = $22,000		4,000 @ $5.50 = $22,000
Jan. 10		2,000 @ $5.50 = $ 11,000	2,000 @ $5.50 = $11,000
Jan. 17	1,000 @ $6.00 = $6,000		$11,000 + $6,000 = $17,000
Average cost per unit →	$\left[\frac{\$17,000}{3,000 \text{ units}}\right]$ = **$5.667**/unit		2,000 + 1,000 = 3,000 units
Mar. 22	3,000 @ $7.00 = $21,000		$17,000 + $21,000 = $38,000
Average cost per unit →	$\left[\frac{\$38,000}{6,000 \text{ units}}\right]$ = $6.333/unit		3,000 + 3,000 = 6,000 units
Apr. 15		1,500 @ $6.333 = $9,500	4,500 @ $6.333 = $28,500
Oct. 15	3,000 @ $7.50 = $22,500		$28,500 + $22,500 = $51,000
Average cost per unit →	$\left[\frac{\$51,000}{7,500 \text{ units}}\right]$ = $6.80/unit		4,500 + 3,000 = 7,500 units
Nov. 20		3,000 @ $6.80 = $ 20,400	4,500 @ $6.80 = **$30,600**
	Total cost of goods sold	= **$40,900**	

On January 17 the new average of **$5.667** (rounded) is calculated by dividing the $17,000 cost of goods available ($11,000 from beginning inventory + $6,000 purchased on January 17) by the 3,000 units available (2,000 units from beginning inventory + 1,000 units acquired on January 17). The average is updated to $6.333 (rounded) with the March 22 purchase. The 1,500 units sold on April 15 are then costed at the average cost of $6.333.

416   SECTION 2   Assets

The average is updated once again to $6.80 with the October 15 purchase, and 3,000 units are costed at that unit cost on November 20.

Cost of goods sold for the year equals the assumed cost of inventory sold for all sales, which equals **$40,900** in this example. Ending inventory equals the number of units in ending inventory times the most recently computed average inventory cost. That amount is **$30,600.** Periodic average cost and perpetual average cost generally produce different allocations to cost of goods sold and ending inventory.

First-In, First-Out (FIFO)

Ending inventory applying FIFO consists of the most recently acquired items.

The first-in, first-out (FIFO) method assumes that the first units purchased are the first ones sold. Beginning inventory is sold first, followed by purchases during the period in the chronological order of their acquisition. Using the example in Illustration 8–7, 6,500 units were sold during 2021. Applying FIFO, these would be the 4,000 units in beginning inventory, the 1,000 units purchased on January 17, and 1,500 of the 3,000 units purchased on March 22.

Ending inventory consists of the remaining units assumed not to be sold. In this case, the 4,500 units in ending inventory consist of 1,500 of the 3,000 units purchased on March 22 and all of the 3,000 units purchased on October 15. Graphically, the flow is as follows:

Units Available

Beg. inv.	4,000	
Jan. 17	1,000	6,500 units sold
Mar. 22	1,500	
Mar. 22	1,500	
Oct. 15	3,000	4,500 units in ending inventory
Total	11,000	

PERIODIC FIFO   Recall that we determine physical quantities on hand in a periodic inventory system by taking a physical count. Costing the 4,500 units in ending inventory this way automatically gives us the cost of goods sold as well. Using the numbers from our illustration, we determine cost of goods sold to be $38,500 by subtracting the $33,000 ending inventory from $71,500 cost of goods available for sale as shown in Illustration 8–7E.

Illustration 8–7E

FIFO—Periodic Inventory System

Beginning inventory (4,000 units @ $5.50)	$22,000
Plus: Purchases (7,000 units @ various prices)	49,500
Cost of goods available for sale (11,000 units)	71,500
Less: Ending inventory* (determined below)	(33,000)
Cost of goods sold (6,500 units)	$38,500

***Cost of Ending Inventory:**

Date of Purchase	Units	Unit Cost	Total Cost
Mar. 22	1,500	$7.00	$ 10,500
Oct. 15	3,000	7.50	22,500
Total ending inventory	4,500		$33,000

Of course, the 6,500 units sold could be costed directly as follows:

Date of Purchase	Units	Unit Cost	Total Cost
Jan. 1 (Beginning inventory)	4,000	$5.50	$22,000
Jan. 17	1,000	6.00	6,000
Mar. 22	1,500	7.00	10,500
Total goods sold	6,500		$38,500

PERPETUAL FIFO   *The ending inventory and cost of goods sold will have the same amounts in a perpetual inventory system as in a periodic inventory system when FIFO is used.* This is because the same units and costs are first in and first out whether cost of goods sold is determined as each sale is made or at the end of the period as a residual amount. The application of FIFO in a perpetual system is shown in Illustration 8–7F.

Perpetual FIFO results in cost of goods sold and ending inventory amounts that are the same as those obtained using periodic FIFO.

Illustration 8–7F

FIFO—Perpetual Inventory System

Date	Purchased	Sold	Balance
Beginning inventory	4,000 @ $5.50 = $22,000		4,000 @ $5.50 = $22,000
Jan. 10		2,000 @ $5.50 = $ 11,000	2,000 @ $5.50 = $11,000
Jan. 17	1,000 @ $6.00 = $ 6,000		2,000 @ $5.50 ⎱ $17,000 1,000 @ $6.00 ⎰
Mar. 22	3,000 @ $7.00 = $21,000		2,000 @ $5.50 ⎫ 1,000 @ $6.00 ⎬ $38,000 3,000 @ $7.00 ⎭
Apr. 15		1,500 @ $5.50 = $ 8,250	500 @ $5.50 ⎫ 1,000 @ $6.00 ⎬ $29,750 3,000 @ $7.00 ⎭
Oct. 15	3,000 @ $7.50 = $22,500		500 @ $5.50 ⎫ 1,000 @ $6.00 ⎬ $52,250 3,000 @ $7.00 ⎪ 3,000 @ $7.50 ⎭
Nov. 20		500 @ $5.50 + 1,000 @ $6.00 + 1,500 @ $7.00 = $ 19,250	1,500 @ $7.00 ⎱ $33,000 3,000 @ $7.50 ⎰
	Total cost of goods sold	= $38,500	

Last-In, First-Out (LIFO)

The **last-in, first-out (LIFO) method** assumes that the last units purchased are the first ones sold. This is opposite the assumption of FIFO. In reality, virtually no company actually sells its inventory on a LIFO basis, but companies are allowed to assume LIFO for reporting purposes.

PERIODIC LIFO   Let's use the information in Illustration 8–7 to determine LIFO amounts under a periodic inventory system. The 6,500 units sold for the year are assumed to consist of the 6,500 units most recently purchased *from the end of the year.* This includes the 3,000 units purchased on October 15, the 3,000 units purchased on March 22, and 500 of the 1,000 units purchased on January 17. Ending inventory, then, consists of the remaining units assumed not sold; in this case, 500 of the 1,000 units purchased on January 17 and all of the 4,000 units from beginning inventory. Graphically, the flow is as follows:

Ending inventory applying LIFO consists of the items acquired first.

Units Available

Beg. inv.	4,000 ⎱	4,500 units in ending inventory
Jan. 17	500 ⎰	
Jan. 17	500 ⎱	
Mar. 22	3,000 ⎬	6,500 units sold
Oct. 15	3,000 ⎭	
Total	11,000	

As shown in Illustration 8–7G, the cost of the 4,500 units assumed in ending inventory is $25,000. We subtract this amount from the cost of goods available for sale to calculate cost of goods sold of $46,500.

Illustration 8–7G

LIFO—Periodic Inventory System

Beginning inventory (4,000 units @ $5.50)		$ 22,000
Plus: Purchases (7,000 units @ various prices)		49,500
Cost of goods available for sale (11,000 units)		71,500
Less: Ending inventory* (determined below)		(25,000)
Cost of goods sold (6,500 units)		$46,500

*Cost of Ending Inventory:

Date of Purchase	Units	Unit Cost	Total Cost
Jan. 1 (Beginning inventory)	4,000	$5.50	$22,000
Jan. 17	500	6.00	3,000
Total ending inventory	4,500		$25,000

Cost of goods sold could be calculated directly as follows:

Date of Purchase	Units	Unit Cost	Total Cost
Jan. 17	500	$6.00	$ 3,000
Mar. 22	3,000	7.00	21,000
Oct. 15	3,000	7.50	22,500
Total goods sold	6,500		$46,500

PERPETUAL LIFO In contrast to the periodic system, a perpetual system using LIFO assumes that units are sold based on the last units purchased *at the time of the sale*. However, for reasons we discuss later, *companies rarely, if ever, actually use a perpetual inventory system when reporting on a LIFO basis*. In practice, companies using LIFO report inventory and cost of goods sold based on calculations similar to the periodic system presented previously in Illustration 8–7G. We demonstrate the perpetual system here to emphasize the differences between periodic and perpetual amounts.

The application of LIFO in a perpetual system is shown in Illustration 8–7H. The 2,000 units sold on January 10 are assumed to include the units most recently purchased—beginning inventory. However, as we saw previously when using the periodic system, those 2,000 units sold on January 10 were assumed to come from the last purchase of the year—the November 20 purchase.

Additional purchases of 1,000 units on January 17 and 3,000 units on March 22 add to inventory. Then the sale of 1,500 units on April 15 is assumed to include the units most recently purchased—those purchased on March 22. This process continues with each purchase and sale throughout the year.

Illustration 8–7H

LIFO—Perpetual Inventory System

Date	Purchased	Sold	Balance	
Beginning inventory	4,000 @ $5.50 = $22,000		4,000 @ $5.50 =	$22,000
Jan. 10		2,000 @ $5.50 = $11,000	2,000 @ $5.50 =	$11,000
Jan. 17	1,000 @ $6.00 = $6,000		2,000 @ $5.50 ⎱ 1,000 @ $6.00 ⎰	$17,000
Mar. 22	3,000 @ $7.00 = $21,000		2,000 @ $5.50 ⎱ 1,000 @ $6.00 ⎰ 3,000 @ $7.00	$38,000

(continued)

(concluded)

Date	Purchased	Sold	Balance	
Apr. 15		1,500 @ $7.00 = $ 10,500	2,000 @ $5.50 1,000 @ $6.00 1,500 @ $7.00	$27,500
Oct. 15	3,000 @ $7.50 = $22,500		2,000 @ $5.50 1,000 @ $6.00 1,500 @ $7.00 3,000 @ $7.50	$50,000
Nov. 20		3,000 @ $7.50 = $22,500	2,000 @ $5.50 1,000 @ $6.00 1,500 @ $7.00	$27,500
	Total cost of goods sold	= $44,000		

Notice that the total cost of goods available for sale is allocated $44,000 to cost of goods sold and $27,500 to ending inventory (the balance after the last transaction), which is different from the periodic LIFO result of $46,500 and $25,000. *If inventory costs are rising throughout the year, periodic LIFO will generally result in lower cost of ending inventory and higher cost of goods sold than when applying perpetual LIFO.*

> Perpetual LIFO generally results in cost of goods sold and inventory amounts that are different from those obtained by applying periodic LIFO.

Comparison of Cost Flow Methods

The three cost flow methods are compared below assuming a periodic inventory system.

	Average	FIFO	LIFO
Cost of goods sold	$42,250	$38,500	$46,500
Ending inventory	29,250	33,000	25,000
Goods available for sale	$71,500	$71,500	$71,500

Notice that the average cost method in this example produces amounts that fall between the FIFO and LIFO amounts for both cost of goods sold and ending inventory. This will usually be the case. Whether it will be FIFO or LIFO that produces the highest or lowest value of cost of goods sold depends on the pattern of the actual unit cost changes during the period.

During periods of rising costs, as in our example, FIFO results in a lower cost of goods sold because the lower costs of the earliest purchases are assumed sold. LIFO cost of goods sold will include the more recent higher cost purchases. On the other hand, FIFO ending inventory includes the most recent higher cost purchases, which results in a higher ending inventory. LIFO ending inventory includes the lower costs of the earliest purchases. Conversely, if costs are declining, then FIFO will result in a higher cost of goods sold and lower ending inventory.[7]

> If unit costs are increasing, LIFO will result in a higher cost of goods sold and lower ending inventory.

All three methods are permissible according to generally accepted accounting principles and are frequently used in practice. Also, a company need not use the same method for its entire inventory. For example, International Paper Company uses LIFO for its raw materials and finished pulp and paper products, and both the FIFO and average cost methods for other inventories. Because of the importance of inventories and the possible differential effects of different methods on the financial statements, a company must identify in a disclosure note the method(s) it uses. The chapter's opening case included an example of this disclosure for Kroger, and you will encounter additional examples later in the chapter.

> **FINANCIAL Reporting Case**
>
> Q1, p. 403
>
> A company must disclose the inventory method(s) it uses.

Illustration 8–8 shows the results of a survey of inventory methods used by 500 large public companies.[8] FIFO is the most popular method, but both LIFO and average cost are used

---

[7]The differences between the various methods also hold when a perpetual inventory system is used.

[8]*U.S. GAAP Financial Statements—Best Practices in Presentation and Disclosure—2013* (New York, New York: AICPA, 2013).

420   SECTION 2   Assets

by many companies. Notice that the column total for the number of companies is greater than 500, indicating that many companies included in this sample do use multiple methods.

Illustration 8–8

Inventory Cost Flow Methods Used in Practice

Real World Financials

	# of Companies	% of Companies
FIFO	312	47%
LIFO	163	24
Average	133	20
Other* and not disclosed	61	9
Total	669	100%

*"Other" includes the specific identification method and miscellaneous less popular methods.

● **LO8–9**

Real World Financials

International Financial Reporting Standards

Inventory Cost Flow Assumptions. *IAS No. 2* does not permit the use of LIFO.[9] Because of this restriction, many U.S. multinational companies use LIFO only for their domestic inventories and FIFO or average cost for their foreign subsidiaries. A disclosure note included in a recent annual report of General Mills provides an example:

Inventories (in part)

All inventories in the United States other than grain are valued at the lower of cost, using the last-in, first-out (LIFO) method, or market. Inventories outside of the United States generally are valued at the lower of cost, using the first-in, first-out (FIFO) method, or net realizable value.

This difference could prove to be a significant impediment to U.S. convergence to international standards. Unless the U.S. Congress repeals the LIFO conformity rule, convergence would cause many corporations to lose a valuable tax shelter, the use of LIFO for tax purposes. If these companies were immediately taxed on the difference between LIFO inventories and inventories valued using another method, it would cost companies billions of dollars. Some industries would be particularly hard hit. Most oil companies and auto manufacturers, for instance, use LIFO. The government estimates that the repeal of the LIFO method would increase federal tax revenues by $76 billion over a ten-year period.[10] The companies affected most certainly will lobby heavily to retain the use of LIFO for tax purposes.

Factors Influencing Method Choice

● **LO8–5**   What factors motivate companies to choose one method over another? What factors have caused the increased popularity of LIFO? Choosing among alternative accounting methods is a complex issue. Often such choices are not made in isolation but in such a way that the combination of inventory cost flow assumptions, depreciation methods, pension assumptions, and other choices meet a particular objective. Also, many believe managers sometimes make these choices to maximize their own personal benefits rather than those of the company or its external constituents. But regardless of the motive, the impact on reported numbers is an important consideration in each choice of method. The inventory choice determines (a) how closely reported costs reflect the actual physical flow of inventory, (b) the timing of reported income and income tax expense, and (c) how well costs are matched with associated revenues.

PHYSICAL FLOW   If a company wanted to choose a method that most closely approximates specific identification, then the actual physical flow of inventory in and out of the company would motivate the choice of method.

---

[9]"Inventories," *International Accounting Standard No. 2* (IASCF), as amended effective January 1, 2018.
[10]Andrew Lundeen, "Proposed Tax Changes in President Obama's Fiscal Year 2016 Budget," (taxfoundation.org).

For example, companies often attempt to sell the oldest goods in inventory first for some of their products. This certainly is the case with perishable goods such as many grocery items. The FIFO method best mirrors the physical flow in these situations. The average cost method might be used for liquids such as chemicals where items sold are taken from a mixture of inventory acquired at different times and different prices. There are very few inventories that actually flow in a LIFO manner. It is important for you to understand that there is no requirement that companies choose an inventory method that approximates actual physical flow and few companies make the choice on this basis. In fact, as we discuss next, the effect of inventory method on income and income taxes is the primary motivation that influences method choice.

> A company is not required to choose an inventory method that approximates actual physical flow.

INCOME TAXES AND NET INCOME If the unit cost of inventory changes during a period, the inventory method chosen can have a significant effect on the amount of income reported by the company to external parties and also on the amount of income taxes paid to the Internal Revenue Service (IRS) and state and local taxing authorities. Over the entire life of a company, cost of goods sold for all years will equal actual costs of items sold regardless of the inventory method used. However, as we have discussed, different inventory methods can produce significantly different results in each particular year.

When inventory costs rise and inventory quantities are not decreasing, LIFO produces a higher cost of goods sold and therefore lower net income than the other methods. The company's income tax returns will report a lower taxable income using LIFO and lower taxes will be paid currently. Taxes are not reduced permanently, only deferred. The reduced amount will be paid to the taxing authorities when either the unit cost of inventory or the quantity of inventory subsequently declines. However, we know from our discussion of the time value of money that it is advantageous to save a dollar today even if it must be paid back in the future. In the past, high inflation (increasing prices) periods motivated many companies to switch to LIFO in order to gain this tax benefit. This is also why companies using LIFO calculate cost of goods sold using a periodic system instead of a perpetual system. As inventory costs rise throughout the year, companies are able to reduce taxes by a greater amount by assuming the last purchase of the year (highest cost units) are the first ones sold.

> Many companies choose LIFO in order to reduce income taxes in periods when prices are rising.

A corporation's taxable income comprises revenues, expenses (including cost of goods sold), gains, and losses measured according to the regulations of the appropriate taxing authority. Income before tax as reported in the income statement does not always equal taxable income. In some cases, differences are caused by the use of different measurement methods.[11] However, IRS regulations, which determine federal taxable income, require that if a company uses LIFO to measure taxable income, the company also must use LIFO for external financial reporting. This is known as the LIFO conformity rule with respect to inventory methods.

> If a company uses LIFO to measure its taxable income, IRS regulations require that LIFO also be used to measure income reported to investors and creditors (the *LIFO conformity rule*).

Because of the LIFO conformity rule, to obtain the tax advantages of using LIFO in periods of rising prices, lower net income is reported to shareholders, creditors, and other external parties. The income tax motivation for using LIFO may be offset by a desire to report higher net income. Reported net income could have an effect on a corporation's share price,[12] on bonuses paid to management, or on debt agreements with lenders. For example, research has indicated that the managers of companies with bonus plans tied to income measures are more likely to choose accounting methods that maximize their bonuses (often those that increase net income).[13]

---

[11]For example, a corporation can take advantage of incentives offered by Congress by deducting more depreciation in the early years of an asset's life in its federal income tax return than it reports in its income statement.

[12]The concept of capital market efficiency has been debated for many years. In an efficient capital market, the market is not fooled by differences in accounting method choice that do not translate into real cash flow differences. The only apparent cash flow difference caused by different inventory methods is the amount of income taxes paid currently. In an efficient market, we would expect the share price of a company that switched its method to LIFO and saved tax dollars to increase even though it reported lower net income than if LIFO had not been adopted. Research on this issue is mixed. For example, see William E. Ricks, "Market's Response to the 1974 LIFO Adoptions," *Journal of Accounting Research* (Autumn 1982); and Robert Moren Brown, "Short-Range Market Reaction to Changes to LIFO Using Preliminary Earnings Announcement Dates," *Journal of Accounting Research* (Spring 1980).

[13]For example, see P. M. Healy, "The Effect of Bonus Schemes on Accounting Decisions," *Journal of Accounting and Economics* (April 1985); and D. Dhaliwal, G. Salamon, and E. Smith, "The Effect of Owner Versus Management Control on the Choice of Accounting Methods," *Journal of Accounting and Economics* (July 1982).

422   **SECTION 2**   Assets

FINANCIAL Reporting Case

Q2, p. 403

Illustration 8–9

Inventories Disclosures—Dollar General Corporation

Real World Financials

The LIFO conformity rule permits LIFO users to report non-LIFO inventory valuations in a disclosure note, but not on the face of the income statement. For example, Illustration 8–9 shows the notes provided in a recent annual report of Dollar General Corporation, a large variety store chain, disclosing its use of LIFO to value its inventories.

Inventories

Inventories are stated at the lower of cost or market with cost determined using the retail last-in, first-out ("LIFO") method as this method results in a better matching of costs and revenues.

    The excess of current cost over LIFO cost was approximately $78.5 million and $80.7 million at February 2, 2018, and February 3, 2017, respectively. Current cost is determined using the RIM on a first-in, first-out basis.

Source: Dollar General Corporation

LIFO Reserves and LIFO Liquidation

● LO8–6   **LIFO RESERVES** Many companies maintain their internal records throughout the reporting period using FIFO or average cost but use LIFO for external reporting and income tax purposes at the end of the reporting period. There are many reasons that companies choose not to maintain internal records on a LIFO basis, including: (1) the high record-keeping costs for LIFO, (2) contractual agreements such as bonus or profit sharing plans that calculate net income with a method other than LIFO, and (3) using FIFO or average cost information for pricing decisions.

Generally, the conversion to LIFO from the internal records occurs at the end of the reporting period without actually entering the adjustment into the company's records. Some companies, though, enter the conversion adjustment—the difference between the internal method and LIFO—directly into the records as a "contra account" to inventory. This contra account is called the LIFO reserve or the *LIFO allowance*.

For illustration, let's say that the Doubletree Corporation uses perpetual FIFO throughout the year to maintain internal records but at the end of the year adjusts these amounts to LIFO for financial reporting purposes. Assume the company began 2021 with a balance of $475,000 in its LIFO reserve account. This balance means that at the beginning of the year, the inventory balance reported under LIFO was $475,000 lower than it would be under FIFO. By the end of 2021, assume the difference between LIFO and FIFO inventory balances increased to $535,000. The LIFO reserve needs to be adjusted to reflect the increase in the reserve during the year. The LIFO reserve (a contra asset) has a normal credit balance, so the entry to increase its balance is recorded as follows:

Cost of goods sold...	60,000	
LIFO reserve ($535,000 − $475,000)		60,000

An increase in the LIFO reserve reduces reported profits.

A decrease in the LIFO reserve increases reported profits.

The entry to increase the LIFO reserve also involves an increase to cost of goods sold. The debit to cost of goods sold increases total expenses and therefore lowers reported profitability.

If the difference between inventory valued internally using FIFO and inventory valued using LIFO had *decreased* over the year, the LIFO reserve would need to be decreased with a debit. The corresponding credit would be to cost of goods sold. In this situation, when cost of goods sold is decreased, profits will increase. This situation demonstrates that even though reported inventory is lower under LIFO than FIFO, LIFO profits might be larger than FIFO profits when the LIFO reserve decreases during the year.

As an example of the disclosure of the LIFO reserve, Illustration 8–10 provides a disclosure note of McKesson Corporation, an American company distributing pharmaceuticals at a retail sale level and providing health information technology, medical supplies, and care management tools. The note shows the company's inventories valued at FIFO (the internal method), less the LIFO reserve, to arrive at the LIFO amount reported in the company's balance sheet.

Illustration 8–10

Inventories Disclosure—
McKesson Corporation

Real World Financials

Inventories (in part)		
($ in millions)	**2017**	**2016**
Inventories (at FIFO)	$16,283	$16,347
Less: LIFO reserve	(1,005)	(1,012)
Net inventories (at LIFO)	$15,278	$15,335
Source: McKesson Corporation		

Under LIFO, inventory is reported in the 2017 balance sheet at a lower amount, which indicates the need for a LIFO reserve of $1,005 million. The LIFO reserve at the beginning of 2017 was $1,012 million, so its balance needs to be decreased by $7 million ($1,012 − $1,005). The decrease is recorded with a debit to the LIFO reserve. At the same time, we decrease (or credit) cost of goods sold, thereby increasing reported profit.

LIFO LIQUIDATIONS   Earlier in the text, we demonstrated the importance of matching revenues and expenses in creating an income statement that is useful in predicting future cash flows. Under LIFO, sales reflect the most recent selling prices, and cost of goods sold includes the costs of the most recent purchases.

Proponents of LIFO argue that it results in a better match of revenues and expenses.

For the same reason, though, inventory costs in the balance sheet with LIFO generally are out of date because they reflect old purchase transactions. It is not uncommon for a company's LIFO inventory balance to be based on unit costs actually incurred several years earlier.

This distortion sometimes carries over to the income statement as well. When inventory quantities decline during a period, then these out-of-date inventory layers are liquidated and cost of goods sold will partially match noncurrent costs with current selling prices. This occurrence is known as a LIFO liquidation. If costs have been increasing (decreasing), LIFO liquidations produce higher (lower) net income than would have resulted if the liquidated inventory were included in cost of goods sold at current costs. The paper profits (losses) caused by including out-of-date, low (high) costs in cost of goods sold is referred to as the effect on income of liquidations of LIFO inventory.

To illustrate this problem, consider the example in Illustration 8–11.

Illustration 8–11

LIFO Liquidation

National Distributors, Inc., uses the LIFO inventory method. The company began the year with inventory of 20,000 units that cost $16 per unit. During the year, 30,000 units were purchased for $20 each. The cost of goods available for sale is determined as:

Beginning inventory	20,000 units @ $16 per unit =	$320,000
Purchases during the year	30,000 units @ $20 per unit =	600,000
Goods available for sale	50,000 units	$920,000

By the end of the year, 45,000 units were sold. Under the LIFO assumption, cost of goods sold is determined as:

From beginning inventory	15,000 units @ $16 per unit =	$240,000
From purchases	30,000 units @ $20 per unit =	600,000
Cost of goods sold	45,000 units	$840,000

Ending inventory equals $80,000 (= 5,000 units of beginning inventory @ $16 per unit).

Under the LIFO assumption, the 45,000 units sold include the 30,000 units purchased during the year and 15,000 units of beginning inventory. If the company had purchased at least 45,000 units, no liquidation in beginning inventory would have occurred. Then cost of goods sold would have been $900,000 (45,000 units × $20 per unit) instead of $840,000. The difference between these two cost of goods sold figures is $60,000 ($900,000 − $840,000). This is the before-tax income effect of the LIFO liquidation. We also can determine the $60,000 before-tax LIFO liquidation profit by multiplying the 15,000 beginning units liquidated by the difference between the $20 *current cost* per unit and the $16 *acquisition cost* per unit we included in cost of goods sold (15,000 units × [$20 − $16] = $60,000).

The after-tax LIFO liquidation effect (assuming a 25% income tax rate) is an increase to net income of $45,000 [$60,000 × (1 − 0.25)]. The lower the costs of the units liquidated, the more severe the effect on cost of goods sold and net income. National Distributors must disclose that the LIFO liquidation increased net income by $45,000 in 2021, assuming that this effect is considered material.

Illustration 8–12 shows the disclosure note included with recent financial statements of **Genuine Parts Company**, a distributor of automotive replacement parts, industrial replacement parts, office products, and electrical parts.

Illustration 8–12

LIFO Liquidation
Disclosure—Genuine Parts
Company

Real World Financials

> **Summary of Significant Accounting Policies (in part)**
>
> **Merchandise Inventories**
>
> During 2017 and 2016, reductions in industrial parts inventories resulted in liquidations of LIFO inventory layers. The effect of the LIFO liquidations in 2017 and 2016 reduced cost of goods sold by approximately $2,000,000 and $6,000,000, respectively. There were no LIFO liquidations in 2015.
>
> Source: Genuine Parts Company

We've discussed several factors that influence companies in their choice of inventory method. A company could be influenced by the actual physical flow of its inventory, by the effect of inventory method on reported net income and the amount of income taxes payable currently, or by a desire to provide a better match of expenses with revenues. You've seen that the direction of the change in unit costs determines the effect of using different methods on net income and income taxes. While the United States has experienced persistent inflation for many years (increases in the general price-level), the prices of many goods and services have experienced periods of declining prices (for example, personal computers).

Concept Review Exercise

INVENTORY COST FLOW METHODS

Inventory information for the Rogers Company for the first six months of the year is as follows:

Date	Transaction
Jan. 1	Beginning inventory of 10 million units at a cost of $5 each.
Feb. 15	Purchased, on account, 5 million units at a cost of $6 each.
Mar. 20	Sold, on account, 12 million units at a selling price of $12 each.
Apr. 30	Purchased, on account, 5 million units at a cost of $7 each.

On June 30, units on hand were 8 million.

Required:

1. Record the inventory purchases and sales during the year, assuming the company uses a perpetual FIFO system to maintain internal records of inventory transactions.
2. Calculate the balance of ending inventory using perpetual FIFO.

3. Assume the company uses periodic LIFO for financial reporting purposes.
   a. Calculate the amounts to be reported for cost of goods sold and ending inventory.
   b. Record the adjusting entry for the LIFO reserve on June 30, assuming the balance of the reserve at the beginning of the year was $9 million.
4. Calculate the amounts to be reported for cost of goods sold and ending inventory assuming the company instead uses
   a. A perpetual average cost system.
   b. A periodic average cost system.

Solution:

1. Record the inventory purchases and sales during the year, assuming the company uses a perpetual FIFO system to maintain internal records of inventory transactions.

	($ in millions)	
February 15		
Inventory (5 million × $6)..	30	
Accounts payable...		30
To record the purchase of inventory.		
March 20		
Accounts receivable (12 million × $12)..	144	
Sales revenue...		144
To record sales on account.		
Cost of goods sold (determined below)...	62	
Inventory...		62
To record cost of goods sold.		
April 30		
Inventory (5 million × $7)..	35	
Accounts payable...		35
To record the purchase of inventory.		

Cost of goods sold assuming FIFO:

Units Sold	Cost of Units Sold	Total Cost
10 million (from Beg. inv.)	$5	$50
2 million (from Feb. 15 purchase)	6	12
12 million		$62

2. Calculate the balance of ending inventory using perpetual FIFO.

Units in Ending Inventory	Cost of Units	Total Cost
3 million (from Feb. 15 purchase)	$6	$18
5 million (from Apr. 30 purchase)	7	35
8 million		$53

3. Assume the company uses periodic LIFO for financial reporting purposes.
   a. Calculate the amounts to be reported for cost of goods sold and ending inventory.
   Cost of goods sold:

Units Sold	Cost of Units Sold	Total Cost
5 million (from Apr. 30 purchase)	$7	$35
5 million (from Feb. 15 purchase)	6	30
2 million (from Beg. inv.)	5	10
12 million		$75

Cost of ending inventory:

Units in Ending Inventory	Cost of Units	Total Cost
8 million (from Beg. inv.)	$5	$40

b. Record the adjusting entry for the LIFO reserve on June 30, assuming the balance of the reserve at the beginning of the year was $9 million.

June 30		($ in millions)
Cost of goods sold...	4	
LIFO reserve (determined below)		4
To record the LIFO reserve adjustment.		

Ending inventory under FIFO (above)	$ 53
Less: Ending inventory under LIFO (above)	(40)
Ending LIFO reserve	$13
Less: Beginning LIFO reserve	(9)
LIFO reserve adjustment needed	$ 4

4. Calculate the amounts to be reported for cost of goods sold and ending inventory assuming the company instead uses:

   a. A perpetual average cost system.

   Cost of goods sold:

Date	Purchased	Sold	Balance
Beg. inv.	10 million @ $5 = $50		$50
Feb. 15	5 million @ $6 = $30		$50 + $30 = $80
	$\dfrac{\$80}{15 \text{ million units}} = \$5.33/\text{unit}$		
Mar. 20		12 million @ $5.33 = $64	

   Cost of ending inventory:

Units in Ending Inventory	Cost of Units	Total Cost
3 million (from Beg. inv. and Feb. 15 purchase)	$5.33	$16
5 million (from Apr. 30 purchase)	7.00	35
8 million		$51

   b. A periodic average cost system.

Date	Units	Unit Cost	Total Cost
Beg. inv.	10 million	$5	$ 50
Feb. 15	5 million	6	30
April 30	5 million	7	35
Goods available for sale	20 million		$115

$$\text{Weighted-average unit cost} = \frac{\$115}{20 \text{ million units}} = \$5.75$$

Cost of good sold: 12 million × $5.75 (above) = $69
Cost of ending inventory: 8 million × $5.75 (above) = $46

Decision Makers' Perspective— Inventory management

Managers closely monitor inventory levels to (1) ensure that the inventories needed to sustain operations are available and to (2) hold the cost of ordering and carrying inventories to the lowest possible level.[14] Unfortunately, these objectives often conflict with one another. Companies must maintain sufficient quantities of inventory to meet customer demand. However, maintaining inventory is costly. Fortunately, a variety of tools are available, including computerized inventory control systems and the outsourcing of inventory component production, to help balance these conflicting objectives.[15]

A just-in-time (JIT) system is another valuable technique that many companies have adopted to assist them with inventory management. JIT is a system used by a manufacturer to coordinate production with suppliers so that raw materials or components arrive just as they are needed in the production process. Harley-Davidson is a company known for its custom-ordered motorcycles, and the company's JIT inventory system in an important part of the company's success. This system enables Harley-Davidson to maintain relatively low inventory balances. At the same time, the company's efficient production techniques, along with its excellent relationships with suppliers ensuring prompt delivery of components, enables it to quickly meet customer demand. For the year ended December 31, 2017, Harley-Davidson reported sales of motorcycles and related parts of $4,915.0 million and cost of goods sold of only $3,261.7 million. That's a gross profit of $1,653.3 (or 33.6% of sales).

As we discussed in Chapter 4, one factor financial analysts use to evaluate management's success is how well the company utilizes its assets. This evaluation, which often is based on the calculation of certain ratios, is influenced by the company's inventory method choice. The different inventory methods affect reported amounts, requiring analysts to make adjustments when comparing companies that use different methods. For companies that use LIFO, supplemental disclosures help to convert inventory amounts to those that would have been reported using FIFO, allowing a better comparison to a company that reports using FIFO.

For example, Harley-Davidson uses the LIFO method. Additional inventory information from the company's recent financial statements is provided below.

● LO8-7

> A company should maintain sufficient inventory quantities to meet customer demand while at the same time minimizing inventory ordering and carrying costs.

FINANCIAL Reporting Case

Q3, p. 403

	For the Year Ended	
($ in millions)	**December 31, 2017**	**December 31, 2016**
Balance sheets:		
Inventories	$ 538.2	$ 499.9
Income statements:		
Net sales	$ 4,915.0	$ 5,271.4
Cost of goods sold	3,261.7	3,419.7

Real World Financials

Suppose an analyst wanted to compare Harley-Davidson with a competitor that used all FIFO, or that used both LIFO and FIFO but with different percentages of LIFO and FIFO. To compare apples with apples, we can convert Harley-Davidson's inventories and cost of goods sold (and the competitor's if necessary) to a 100% FIFO basis before comparing the two companies. The information necessary for this conversion is provided as a supplemental disclosure by-Harley Davidson:

> Supplemental LIFO disclosures can be used to convert LIFO inventories and cost of goods sold amounts.

	2017	**2016**
Inventories (LIFO)	$538.2	$499.9
Add: conversion to FIFO	52.4	48.3
Inventories (100% FIFO)	$590.6	$548.2

[14]The cost of carrying inventory includes the possible loss from the write-down of obsolete inventory. We discuss inventory write-downs in Chapter 9. There are analytical models available to determine the appropriate amount of inventory a company should maintain. A discussion of these models is beyond the scope of this text.

[15]Eugene Brigham and Joel Houston, *Fundamentals of Financial Management,* 12th ed. (Florence, Kentucky: South-Western, 2010).

If Harley-Davidson had used FIFO instead of LIFO, ending inventory in 2017 would have been $52.4 million higher. The large difference in reported inventory can have a material effect on financial ratios (as demonstrated below).

The use of FIFO versus LIFO also affects the calculation of cost of goods sold and therefore gross profit and net income. For Harley-Davidson, the *difference* between FIFO and LIFO inventory increased by $4.1 million during 2017 (from $48.3 to $52.4 million). This means the company would have recorded an increase of $4.1 million in the LIFO reserve in 2017, along with an increase in cost of goods sold (see earlier discussion of the LIFO reserve adjustment). The increase in cost of goods sold indicates that reported profits under LIFO were lower than if FIFO had been used. If the LIFO reserve had decreased during the year, profits would have been higher under LIFO than FIFO.

One useful profitability indicator that involves cost of goods sold is the gross profit ratio. The ratio is computed as follows:

$$\text{Gross profit ratio} = \frac{\text{Gross profit}}{\text{Net sales}} \text{ or } \frac{\text{Net sales} - \text{Cost of goods sold}}{\text{Net sales}}$$

The *gross profit ratio* provides a measure of how much of each sales dollar is available to pay for expenses other than cost of goods.

This ratio provides a measure of how much of each sales dollar is available to pay for expenses other than cost of goods. For example, inventory that costs $100 and sells for $125 provides a gross profit of $25 ($125 − $100) and a gross profit ratio of 20% ($25 ÷ $125). This means that each $1 of sales generates $0.20 that can be used to help pay for expenses other than cost of goods sold or remain as profit. If that same inventory can be sold for $150, gross profit increases to $50 and the gross profit ratio increases to 33% ($50 ÷ $150).

As we discussed previously, the 2017 gross profit for Harley-Davidson's motorcycle sales is $1,653.3 million (equal to sales of $4,915.0 million minus cost of goods sold of $3,261.7 million). That's a gross profit ratio of 33.6%. The industry average is 20.0%. Harley-Davidson is able to sell its products at significantly higher markups. If the LIFO reserve adjustment that increased cost of goods sold in 2017 had not been made, cost of goods sold on a FIFO basis would have been $4.1 million lower and gross profit would have been even higher than reported for the year.

Monitoring the gross profit ratio over time can provide valuable insights. For example, a declining ratio might indicate that the company is unable to offset rising costs with corresponding increases in selling price, or perhaps that sales prices are declining without a commensurate reduction in costs. In either case, the decline in the ratio has important implications for future profitability.

In Chapter 4 we were introduced to an important ratio, the inventory turnover ratio, which is designed to evaluate a company's effectiveness in managing its investment in inventory. The ratio shows the number of times the average inventory balance is sold during a reporting period. The more frequently a business is able to sell or turn over its inventory, the lower its investment in inventory must be for a given level of sales. Monitoring the inventory turnover ratio over time can highlight potential problems. A declining ratio generally is unfavorable and could be caused by the presence of obsolete or slow-moving products, or poor marketing and sales efforts.

Recall that the ratio is computed as follows:

$$\text{Inventory turnover ratio} = \frac{\text{Cost of goods sold}}{\text{Average inventory}}$$

If the analysis is prepared for the fiscal year reporting period, we can divide the inventory turnover ratio into 365 days to calculate the average days in inventory, which indicates the average number of days it normally takes the company to sell its inventory. In 2017, Harley-Davidson's inventory turnover ratio using reported LIFO amounts is 6.28 {$3,261.7 ÷ [($538.2 + $499.9) ÷ 2]} and the average days in inventory is 58.1 days (365 ÷ 6.28).

Alternatively, if we convert amounts to those under FIFO, we see that Harley-Davidson's inventory turnover ratio would have been only 5.72 {$3,257.6 ÷ [($590.6 + $548.2) ÷ 2]} and the average days in inventory would have been 63.8 days (365 ÷ 5.72). The difference in inventory turnover ratios between LIFO and FIFO is caused primarily by lower average inventory under LIFO and demonstrates the noticeable effect that the choice of inventory method can have on financial ratios.

EARNINGS QUALITY.   Changes in the ratios we discussed above often provide information about the quality of a company's current period earnings. For example, a slowing turnover ratio combined with higher than normal inventory levels may indicate the potential for decreased production, obsolete inventory, or a need to decrease prices to sell inventory (which will then decrease gross profit ratios and net income). This proposition was tested in an important academic research study. Professors Lev and Thiagarajan empirically demonstrated the importance of a set of 12 fundamental variables in valuing companies' common stock. The set of variables included inventory (change in inventory minus change in sales). The inventory variable was found to be a significant indicator of returns on investments in common stock, particularly during high and medium inflation years.[16]

The choice of which inventory method to use also affects earnings quality, particularly in times of rapidly changing prices. Earlier in this chapter we discussed the effect of a LIFO liquidation on company profits. A LIFO liquidation profit (or loss) reduces the quality of current period earnings. Fortunately for analysts, companies must disclose these profits or losses, if material. In addition, LIFO cost of goods sold determined using a periodic inventory system is more susceptible to manipulation than is FIFO. Year-end purchases can have a dramatic effect on LIFO cost of goods sold in rapid cost-change environments. Recall again our discussion in Chapter 4 concerning earnings quality. Many believe that manipulating income reduces earnings quality because it can mask permanent earnings. Inventory write-downs and changes in inventory method are two additional inventory-related techniques a company could use to manipulate earnings. We discuss these issues in the next chapter. ●

Methods of Simplifying LIFO

PART B

The LIFO method described and illustrated to this point is called *unit LIFO*[17] because the last-in, first-out concept is applied to individual units of inventory. One problem with unit LIFO is that it can be very costly to implement. It requires records of each unit of inventory. The costs of maintaining these records can be significant, particularly when a company has numerous individual units of inventory and when unit costs change often during a period.

The recordkeeping costs of unit LIFO can be significant.

In the previous section, a second disadvantage of unit LIFO was identified—the possibility that LIFO layers will be liquidated if the quantity of a particular inventory unit declines below its beginning balance. Even if a company's total inventory quantity is stable or increasing, if the quantity of any particular inventory unit declines, unit LIFO will liquidate all or a portion of a LIFO layer of inventory. When inventory quantity declines in a period of rising costs, noncurrent lower costs will be included in cost of goods sold and matched with current selling prices, resulting in LIFO liquidation profit.

Another disadvantage of unit LIFO is the possibility of LIFO liquidation.

This part of the chapter discusses techniques that can be used to significantly reduce the record-keeping costs of LIFO and to minimize the probability of LIFO inventory layers being liquidated. Specifically, we discuss the use of inventory pools and the dollar-value LIFO method.

LIFO Inventory Pools

The objectives of using LIFO inventory pools are to simplify record-keeping by grouping inventory units into pools based on physical similarities of the individual units and to reduce the risk of LIFO layer liquidation. For example, a glass company might group its various grades of window glass into a single window pool. Other pools might be auto glass and sliding-door glass. A lumber company might pool its inventory into hardwood, framing lumber, paneling, and so on.

A pool consists of inventory units grouped according to natural physical similarities.

This allows a company to account for a few inventory pools rather than every specific type of inventory separately. Within pools, all purchases during a period are considered to

The average cost for all of the pool purchases during the period is applied to the current year's LIFO layer.

---

[16]B. Lev and S. R. Thiagarajan, "Fundamental Information Analysis," *Journal of Accounting Research* (Autumn 1993). The main conclusion of the study was that fundamental variables, not just earnings, are useful in firm valuation, particularly when examined in the context of macroeconomic conditions such as inflation.

[17]Unit LIFO sometimes is called *specific goods LIFO.*

have been made at the same time and at the same cost. Individual unit costs are converted to an average cost for the pool. If the quantity of ending inventory for the pool increases, then ending inventory will consist of the beginning inventory plus a single layer added during the period at the average acquisition cost for that pool.

Here's an example. Let's say Diamond Lumber Company has a rough-cut lumber inventory pool that includes three types: pine, oak, and maple. The beginning inventory consisted of the following:

	Quantity (Board Feet)	Cost (Per Foot)	Total Cost
Pine	16,000	$2.20	$35,200
Oak	10,000	3.00	30,000
Maple	14,000	2.40	33,600
	40,000		$98,800

The average cost for this pool is $2.47 per board foot ($98,800 ÷ 40,000 board feet). Now assume that during the next reporting period Diamond purchased 50,000 board feet of lumber as follows:

	Quantity (Board Feet)	Cost (Per Foot)	Total Cost
Pine	20,000	$2.25	$ 45,000
Oak	14,000	3.00	42,000
Maple	16,000	2.50	40,000
	50,000		$127,000

The average cost for this pool is $2.54 per board foot ($127,000 ÷ 50,000 board feet). Assuming that Diamond sold 46,000 board feet during this period, the quantity of inventory for the pool increased by 4,000 board feet (50,000 purchased less 46,000 sold). Ending inventory includes the beginning 40,000 feet of inventory and a new LIFO layer consisting of the 4,000 board feet purchased this period. We would add this LIFO layer at the average cost of purchases made during the period, $2.54. The ending inventory of $108,960 now consists of two layers:

	Quantity (Board Feet)	Cost (Per Foot)	Total Cost
Beginning inventory	40,000	$2.47	$ 98,800
LIFO layer added	4,000	2.54	10,160
Ending inventory	44,000		$108,960

Despite the advantages of LIFO inventory pools, it's easy to imagine situations in which its benefits are not achieved. Suppose, for instance, that a company discontinues a certain product included in one of its pools. The old costs that existed in prior layers of inventory would be recognized as cost of goods sold and produce LIFO liquidation profit. Even if the product is replaced with another product, the replacement may not be similar enough to be included in the same inventory pool. In fact, the process itself of having to periodically redefine pools as changes in product mix occur can be expensive and time-consuming. Next we discuss the dollar-value LIFO approach which helps overcome these problems.

Dollar-Value LIFO

A DVL pool is made up of items that are likely to face the same cost change pressures.

Many companies that report inventory using LIFO actually use a method called dollar-value LIFO (DVL). DVL extends the concept of inventory pools by allowing a company to combine a large variety of goods into one pool. Pools are not based on physical units. Instead, an inventory pool is viewed as comprising layers of dollar value from different periods. Specifically, a pool should consist of those goods that are likely to be subject to the same cost change pressures.

● **LO8–8**

Cost Indexes

In either the unit LIFO approach or the pooled LIFO approach, we determine whether a new LIFO layer was added by comparing the ending quantity with the beginning quantity. The focus is on *units* of inventory. Under DVL, we determine whether a new LIFO layer was added by comparing the ending dollar amount with the beginning dollar amount. The focus is on inventory *value,* not units. However, if the price level has changed, we need a way to determine whether an observed increase is a real increase (an increase in the quantity of inventory) or one caused by an increase in prices. *So before we compare the beginning and ending inventory amounts, we need to deflate inventory dollar amounts by any increase in prices so that both the beginning and ending amounts are measured in terms of the same price level.* We accomplish this by using cost indexes. A cost index for a particular layer year is determined as follows:

$$\text{Cost index in layer year} = \frac{\text{Cost in layer year}}{\text{Cost in base year}}$$

The base year is the year in which the DVL method is adopted and the layer year is any subsequent year in which an inventory layer is created. The cost index for the base year is set at 1.00. Subsequent years' indexes reflect cost changes relative to the base year. For example, if a "basket" of inventory items cost $120 at the end of the current year, and $100 at the end of the base year, the cost index for the current year would be: $120 ÷ $100 = 120%, or 1.20. This index simply tells us that costs in the layer year are 120% of what they were in the base year (i.e., costs increased by 20%).

The cost index for the base year (the year DVL is initially adopted) is set at 1.00.

There are several techniques that can be used to determine an index for a DVL pool. An external index like the Consumer Price Index (CPI) or the Producer Price Index (PPI) can be used. For example, assume that a company adopted the DVL method on January 1, 2021, when the CPI was 200. This amount is set equivalent to 1.00, the base year index. Then, the index in the layer year, say the end of 2021, would be determined relative to 200. So, if the CPI is 210 at the end of 2021, the 2021 index for DVL purposes would be 1.05 (210 ÷ 200).

However, in most cases these indexes would not properly reflect cost changes for any individual DVL pool. Instead, most companies use an internally generated index. These indexes can be calculated using one of several techniques such as the *double-extension method* or the *link-chain method.* A discussion of these methods is beyond the scope of this text. In our examples and illustrations, we assume cost indexes are given.

The DVL Inventory Estimation Technique

To see the calculation of ending inventory using DVL, consider the following example. Assume that Hanes Company adopted DVL on January 1, 2021, when the inventory cost was $400,000. On December 31, 2021, Hanes determines the year-end cost of inventory is $462,000. This amount is obtained by taking the physical units of inventory on hand at the end of the year and multiplying by year-end costs. It's not necessary for Hanes to track the item-by-item cost of purchases during the year.

Assuming a cost index for 2021 of 1.05 (105%), we'll use three steps to calculate the amount to report for ending inventory using dollar-value LIFO.

STEP 1: Convert ending inventory to base year cost. Notice inventory increased from $400,000 at the beginning of the year to $462,000 at the end of the year. Does this $62,000 increase in inventory represent an increase in the *quantity* and/or an increase in the *cost* of inventory? To determine this, the first step is to convert the ending inventory from year-end costs to base year costs. We do this by dividing ending inventory by the year's cost index.

$$\text{Ending inventory at } base\ year \text{ cost} = \frac{\$462,000}{1.05} = \$440,000$$

432   SECTION 2   Assets

STEP 2: Identify the layers of ending inventory created each year. The 2021 ending inventory deflated to base year cost is $440,000. From this, we can determine that the $62,000 increase in the cost of total inventory for the year consists of a $40,000 increase due to quantity (new inventory layer added in 2021) plus $22,000 due to an increase in the cost index of inventory (= $440,000 × 5%).

The calculation above is important for identifying the two layers of inventory *quantity* for applying the LIFO concept: (1) beginning inventory layer of $400,000 and (2) $40,000 layer added in 2021. These are the costs as if each layer was acquired at base year prices. The increase in inventory due to rising costs ($22,000) does not represent more units purchased.

$400,000	(beginning inventory cost in 2021; beginning layer)
+ 40,000	(increase in *quantity* in 2021; new layer)
+ 22,000	(increase in *cost* = $440,000 × 5%)
$462,000	(ending inventory cost in 2021)

STEP 3: Restate each layer using the cost index in the year acquired. Once the layers are identified, each is restated to prices existing when the layers were acquired. This is done by multiplying each layer by the cost index for the year it was acquired. The $400,000 layer was acquired when prices were 1.00, and the $40,000 layer was acquired when prices were 1.05. All layers are added, and ending inventory under DVL would be reported at $442,000.[18]

Date	Ending Inventory at Base Year Cost	×	Cost Index	=	Ending Inventory at DVL Cost
1/1/2021	$400,000		1.00		$400,000
2021 layer	40,000		1.05		42,000
Totals	$440,000				$442,000

In cases where the quantity of inventory *decreases,* no layer would be added in the current year. In our example, if inventory at the end of 2021 had a base year cost of only $380,000 rather than $440,000, then no layer would have been added in 2021. Instead, the existing layer at the beginning of the year is reduced by $20,000. If more than one layer existed at the beginning of the year, then layers are reduced in LIFO order. The remaining layers are multiplied by the cost index that existed in the year those layers were added. Then, any future increases in inventory quantity (in 2022 or after) would add new layers beyond the $380,000 at the cost index relating to the year of the additional layer.

The identification of inventory layers is demonstrated further in the Concept Review Exercise below. In years when there is an increase in inventory at base year cost (2022 and 2024), a new inventory layer is added. In years when there is a decrease in inventory at base year cost (2023), we use LIFO and assume the inventory sold was from the last layer added.

Concept Review Exercise

DOLLAR-VALUE LIFO

On January 1, 2021, the Johnson Company adopted the dollar-value LIFO method. The inventory value on this date was $500,000. Inventory data for 2021 through 2024 are as follows:

Date	Ending Inventory at Year-End Costs	Cost Index
12/31/2021	$556,500	1.05
12/31/2022	596,200	1.10
12/31/2023	615,250	1.15
12/31/2024	720,000	1.25

[18]It is important to note that the costs of the year's layer are only an approximation of actual acquisition cost. DVL assumes that all inventory quantities added during a particular year were acquired at a single cost.

Required:

Calculate Johnson's ending inventory for the years 2021 through 2024.

Solution:

JOHNSON COMPANY

Date	Ending Inventory at Year-End Cost	Step 1 Ending Inventory at Base Year Cost	Step 2 Inventory Layers at Base Year Cost	Step 3 Inventory Layers Converted to Acquisition Year Cost	Ending Inventory at DVL Cost
1/1/2021	$500,000 (base year)	$\frac{\$500,000}{1.00} = \$500,000$	$500,000 (base)	$500,000 × 1.00 = $500,000	$500,000
12/31/2021	556,500	$\frac{\$556,500}{1.05} = \$530,000$	$500,000 (base) 30,000 (2021)	$500,000 × 1.00 = $500,000 30,000 × 1.05 = 31,500	531,500
12/31/2022	596,200	$\frac{\$596,200}{1.10} = \$542,000$	$500,000 (base) 30,000 (2021) 12,000 (2022)	$500,000 × 1.00 = $500,000 30,000 × 1.05 = 31,500 12,000 × 1.10 = 13,200	544,700
12/31/2023	615,250	$\frac{\$615,250}{1.15} = \$535,000*$	$500,000 (base) 30,000 (2021) 5,000 (2022)	$500,000 × 1.00 = $500,000 30,000 × 1.05 = 31,500 5,000 × 1.10 = 5,500	537,000
12/31/2024	720,000	$\frac{\$720,000}{1.25} = \$576,000$	$500,000 (base) 30,000 (2021) 5,000 (2022) 41,000 (2024)	$500,000 × 1.00 = $500,000 30,000 × 1.05 = 31,500 5,000 × 1.10 = 5,500 41,000 × 1.25 = 51,250	588,250

*Since inventory declined during 2023 (from $542,000 to $535,000 at base year costs), no new layer is added. Instead the most recently acquired layer, 2022, is reduced by $7,000 (from $12,000 to $5,000).

Advantages of DVL

The DVL method has important advantages. First, it simplifies the record-keeping procedures compared to unit LIFO because no information is needed about unit flows. Second, it minimizes the probability of the liquidation of LIFO inventory layers, even more so than the use of pools alone, through the aggregation of many types of inventory into larger pools. In addition, the method can be used by firms that do not replace units sold with new units of the same kind. For firms whose products are subject to annual model changes, for example, the items in one year's inventory are not the same as those of the prior year. Under pooled LIFO, however, the new replacement items must be substantially identical to previous models to be included in the same pool. Under DVL, no distinction is drawn between the old and new merchandise on the basis of their physical characteristics, so a much broader range of goods can be included in the pool. That is, the acquisition of the new items is viewed as replacement of the dollar value of the old items. Because the old layers are maintained, this approach retains the benefits of LIFO by matching the most recent acquisition cost of goods with sales measured at current selling prices.

Financial Reporting Case Solution

1. **How is the LIFO method used to calculate inventories? Is this permissible according to GAAP?** *(p. 419)*   The LIFO method uses the assumption that the most recent inventory purchased is sold first. Yes, this method is permissible according to generally accepted accounting principles. A company need not use the same method that represents its actual inventory flow.

2. **What is the purpose of disclosing the difference between the reported LIFO inventory amounts and replacement cost, assuming that replacement cost is equivalent to a FIFO basis?** *(p. 422)* The LIFO conformity rule requires that if a company uses LIFO to measure taxable income, it also must use LIFO for external financial reporting. The choice of using LIFO instead of FIFO for financial reporting, however, will affect amounts reported for inventory and cost of goods sold. This difference makes it harder to compare companies using LIFO to companies using FIFO. To make this comparison easier, companies using LIFO can disclose the amount of inventory they would have reported under FIFO. Kroger's disclosure note offers this additional information.

3. **Are you correct that, by using LIFO, Kroger reports lower inventory and lower profits? Why would Kroger do that?** *(p. 427)* Because Kroger uses LIFO instead of FIFO, reported inventory in the balance sheet is lower. For the year ended February 3, 2018, Kroger reported LIFO inventory of only $6,533 million, compared to $7,781 million that it would have reported under FIFO. This is a difference of $1,248 million. In the previous year, the difference between LIFO and FIFO was $1,291 million. This means the LIFO effect (or LIFO reserve) has decreased by $43 million (from $1,291 million to $1,248 million). A decrease in the LIFO reserve is recorded as a reduction of cost of goods sold, increasing profits. However, if the LIFO reserve had increased in the current year, cost of goods sold would be increased and profits would have been lower. ●

The Bottom Line

● **LO8–1** Inventory for a manufacturing company includes raw materials, work in process, and finished goods. Inventory for a merchandising company includes goods primarily in finished form ready for sale. In a perpetual inventory system, inventory is continually adjusted for each change in inventory. Cost of goods sold is adjusted each time goods are sold or returned by a customer. A periodic inventory system adjusts inventory and records cost of goods sold only at the end of a reporting period. *(p. 404)*

● **LO8–2** Generally, determining the physical quantity that should be included in inventory is a simple matter because it consists of items in the possession of the company. However, at the end of a reporting period it's important to determine the ownership of goods that are in transit between the company and its customers as well as between the company and its suppliers. Also, goods on consignment should be included in inventory of the consignor even though the company doesn't have physical possession of the goods. In addition, a company anticipating sales returns includes in inventory the cost of merchandise it estimates will be returned. *(p. 408)*

● **LO8–3** The cost of inventory includes all expenditures necessary to acquire the inventory and bring it to its desired condition and location for sale or use. Generally, these expenditures include the purchase price of the goods reduced by any returns and purchase discounts, plus freight-in charges. *(p. 409)*

● **LO8–4** Once costs are determined, the cost of goods available for sale must be allocated between cost of goods sold and ending inventory. Unless each item is specifically identified and traced through the system, the allocation requires an assumption regarding the flow of costs. First-in, first-out (FIFO) assumes that units sold are the first units acquired. Last-in, first-out (LIFO) assumes that the units sold are the most recent units purchased. The average cost method assumes that cost of goods sold and ending inventory consist of a mixture of all the goods available for sale. *(p. 412)*

● **LO8–5** A company's choice of inventory method will be influenced by (a) how closely cost flow reflects the actual physical flow of its inventory, (b) the timing of income tax expenses, and (c) how costs are matched with revenues. *(p. 420)*

● **LO8–6** The LIFO conformity rule requires that if a company uses LIFO to measure taxable income, it also must use LIFO for external financial reporting. LIFO users often provide a disclosure note describing the effect on inventories of using another method for inventory valuation rather than LIFO. If a company uses LIFO and inventory quantities decline during a period, then out-of-date inventory layers are liquidated and the cost of goods sold will partially match noncurrent costs with current selling prices. If costs have been increasing (decreasing), LIFO liquidations produce higher (lower) net income than would have resulted if the liquidated inventory were included in cost of goods sold at current costs. The paper profits (losses) caused by including out-of-date, low (high) costs in cost of goods sold is referred to as the effect on income of liquidations of LIFO inventory. (*p. 422*)

● **LO8–7** Investors, creditors, and financial analysts can gain important insights by monitoring a company's investment in inventories. The gross profit ratio, inventory turnover ratio, and average days in inventory are designed to monitor inventories. (*p. 427*)

● **LO8–8** The dollar-value LIFO method converts ending inventory at year-end cost to base year cost using a cost index. After identifying the layers in ending inventory with the years they were created, each year's base year cost measurement is converted to layer year cost measurement using the layer year's cost index. The layers are then summed to obtain total ending inventory at cost. (*p. 431*)

● **LO8–9** The primary difference between U.S. GAAP and IFRS with respect to determining the cost of inventory is that IFRS does not allow the use of the LIFO method to value inventory. (*p. 420*) ●

Questions For Review of Key Topics

Q 8–1 Describe the three types of inventory of a manufacturing company.

Q 8–2 What is the main difference between a perpetual inventory system and a periodic inventory system? Which system is used more often by major companies?

Q 8–3 The Cloud Company employs a perpetual inventory system and the McKenzie Corporation uses a periodic system. Describe the differences between the two systems in accounting for the following events: (1) purchase of merchandise, (2) sale of merchandise, (3) return of merchandise to supplier, and (4) payment of freight charge on merchandise purchased. Indicate which inventory-related accounts would be debited or credited for each event.

Q 8–4 The Bockner Company shipped merchandise to Laetner Corporation on December 28, 2021. Laetner received the shipment on January 3, 2022. December 31 is the fiscal year-end for both companies. The merchandise was shipped f.o.b. shipping point. Explain the difference in the accounting treatment of the merchandise if the shipment had instead been designated f.o.b. destination.

Q 8–5 What is a consignment arrangement? Explain the accounting treatment of goods held on consignment.

Q 8–6 Distinguish between the gross and net methods of accounting for purchase discounts.

Q 8–7 The Esquire Company employs a periodic inventory system. Indicate the effect (increase or decrease) of the following items on cost of goods sold:

1. Beginning inventory
2. Purchases
3. Ending inventory
4. Purchase returns
5. Freight-in

Q 8–8 Identify four inventory costing methods for assigning cost to ending inventory and cost of goods sold and briefly explain the difference in the methods.

Q 8–9 It's common in the electronics industry for unit costs of raw materials inventories to decline over time. In this environment, explain the difference between LIFO and FIFO in terms of the effect on cost of goods sold and ending inventory. Assume that inventory quantities remain the same for the period.

Q 8–10 Explain why proponents of LIFO argue that it provides a better match of revenue and expenses. In what situation would it not provide a better match?

Q 8–11 Explain what is meant by the Internal Revenue Service conformity rule with respect to the inventory method choice.

Q 8–12 Describe the ratios used by financial analysts to monitor a company's investment in inventories.

Q 8–13 What is a LIFO inventory pool? How is the cost of ending inventory determined when pools are used?

Q 8–14 Identify two advantages of dollar-value LIFO compared with unit LIFO.

Q 8–15 The Austin Company uses the dollar-value LIFO inventory method with internally developed price indexes. Assume that ending inventory at year-end cost has been determined. Outline the remaining steps used in the dollar-value LIFO computations.

IFRS Q 8–16 Identify any differences between U.S. GAAP and International Financial Reporting Standards in the methods allowed to value inventory.

436   SECTION 2   Assets

Brief Exercises

BE 8–1
Determining ending inventory
● LO8–1

A company began its fiscal year with inventory of $186,000. Purchases and cost of goods sold for the year were $945,000 and $982,000, respectively. What was the amount of ending inventory?

BE 8–2
Perpetual system; journal entries
● LO8–1

Litton Industries uses a perpetual inventory system. The company began its fiscal year with inventory of $267,000. Purchases of merchandise on account during the year totaled $845,000. Merchandise costing $902,000 was sold on account for $1,420,000. Prepare the journal entries to record these transactions.

BE 8–3
Goods in transit
● LO8–2

Kelly Corporation shipped goods to a customer f.o.b. destination on December 29, 2021. The goods arrived at the customer's location in January. In addition, one of Kelly's major suppliers shipped goods to Kelly f.o.b. shipping point on December 30. The merchandise arrived at Kelly's location in January. Which shipments should be included in Kelly's December 31 inventory?

BE 8–4
Purchase discounts; gross method
● LO8–3

On December 28, 2021, Videotech Corporation (VTC) purchased 10 units of a new satellite uplink system from Tristar Communications for $25,000 each. The terms of each sale were 1/10, n/30. VTC uses the gross method to account for purchase discounts and a perpetual inventory system. VTC paid the net-of-discount amount on January 6, 2022. Prepare the journal entries on December 28 and January 6 to record the purchase and payment.

BE 8–5
Purchase discounts; net method
● LO8–3

Refer to the situation described in BE 8–4. Prepare the necessary journal entries assuming that VTC uses the net method to account for purchase discounts.

BE 8–6
Inventory cost flow methods; perpetual system
● LO8–4

Samuelson and Messenger (SAM) began 2021 with 200 units of its one product. These units were purchased near the end of 2020 for $25 each. During the month of January, 100 units were purchased on January 8 for $28 each and another 200 units were purchased on January 19 for $30 each. Sales of 125 units and 100 units were made on January 10 and January 25, respectively. There were 275 units on hand at the end of the month. SAM uses a *perpetual* inventory system. Calculate ending inventory and cost of goods sold for January using (1) FIFO and (2) average cost.

BE 8–7
Inventory cost flow methods; periodic system
● LO8–4

Refer to the situation described in BE 8–6. SAM uses a *periodic* inventory system. Calculate ending inventory and cost of goods sold for January using (1) FIFO and (2) average cost.

BE 8–8
LIFO method
● LO8–4

Esquire Inc. uses the LIFO method to report its inventory. Inventory at January 1, 2021, was $500,000 (20,000 units at $25 each). During 2021, 80,000 units were purchased, all at the same price of $30 per unit. 85,000 units were sold during 2021. Calculate the December 31, 2021, ending inventory and cost of goods sold for 2021 based on a periodic inventory system.

BE 8–9
LIFO method
● LO8–4

AAA Hardware uses the LIFO method to report its inventory. Inventory at the beginning of the year consisted of 10,000 units of the company's one product. These units cost $15 each. During the year, 60,000 units were purchased at a cost of $18 each and 64,000 units were sold. Near the end of the fiscal year, management is considering the purchase of an additional 5,000 units at $18. What would be the effect of this purchase on income before income taxes? Would your answer be the same if the company used FIFO instead of LIFO?

BE 8–10
LIFO liquidation
● LO8–6

Refer to the situation described in BE 8–8. Assuming an income tax rate of 25%, what is LIFO liquidation profit or loss that the company would report in a disclosure note accompanying its financial statements?

BE 8–11
LIFO Reserve
● LO8–6

King Supply maintains its internal inventory records using perpetual FIFO, but for financial reporting purposes, reports ending inventory and cost of goods sold using periodic LIFO. At the beginning of the year, the company had a balance of $60,000 in its LIFO reserve account. By the end of the year, internal records reveal that FIFO ending inventory is $75,000 greater than LIFO ending inventory. Record the year-end adjusting entry for the LIFO reserve.

BE 8–12
Supplemental
LIFO reserve
disclosures;
Walgreens
● LO8–6
Real World Financials

Walgreens Boots Alliance, Inc., reported inventories of $8,899 million and $8,956 million in its August 31, 2017, and August 31, 2016, balance sheets, respectively. Cost of goods sold for the year ended August 31, 2017, was $89,052 million. The company uses primarily the LIFO inventory method. A disclosure note reported that if FIFO had been used instead of LIFO, inventory would have been higher by $3,000 million and $2,800 million at the end of the August 31, 2017, and August 31, 2016, periods, respectively. Calculate cost of goods sold for the year ended August 31, 2017, assuming Walgreens used FIFO instead of LIFO.

BE 8–13
Ratio analysis
● LO8–7

Selected financial statement data for Schmitzer Inc. is shown below:

	2021	**2020**
Balancesheet:		
Inventories	$60,000	$48,000
Ratios:		
Gross profit ratio for 2021	40%	
Inventory turnover ratio for 2021	5	

What was the amount of net sales for 2021?

BE 8–14
Dollar-value LIFO
● LO8–8

At the beginning of 2021, a company adopts the dollar-value LIFO inventory method for its one inventory pool. The pool's value on that date was $1,400,000. The 2021 ending inventory valued at year-end costs was $1,664,000 and the year-end cost index was 1.04. Calculate the inventory value at the end of 2021 using the dollar-value LIFO method.

Exercises

 connect

E 8–1
Perpetual
inventory system;
journal entries
● LO8–1

John's Specialty Store uses a perpetual inventory system. The following are some inventory transactions for the month of May:
1. John's purchased merchandise on account for $5,000. Freight charges of $300 were paid in cash.
2. John's returned some of the merchandise purchased in (1). The cost of the merchandise was $600 and John's account was credited by the supplier.
3. Merchandise costing $2,800 was sold for $5,200 in cash.

Required:
Prepare the necessary journal entries to record these transactions.

E 8–2
Periodic inventory
system; journal
entries
● LO8–1

[This is a variation of E 8–1 modified to focus on the periodic inventory system.]
    John's Specialty Store uses a periodic inventory system. The following are some inventory transactions for the month of May:
1. John's purchased merchandise on account for $5,000. Freight charges of $300 were paid in cash.
2. John's returned some of the merchandise purchased in (1). The cost of the merchandise was $600 and John's account was credited by the supplier.
3. Merchandise costing $2,800 was sold for $5,200 in cash.

Required:
Prepare the necessary journal entries to record these transactions.

E 8–3
Determining cost
of goods sold
● LO8–1

The June 30, 2021, year-end trial balance for Askew Company contained the following information:

Account	Debit	Credit
Inventory, 7/1/2020	32,000	
Sales revenue		380,000
Sales returns	12,000	
Purchases	240,000	
Purchase discounts		6,000
Purchase returns		10,000
Freight-in	17,000	

In addition, you determine that the June 30, 2021, inventory balance is $40,000.

438   SECTION 2   Assets

Required:

Calculate the cost of goods sold for the Askew Company for the year ending June 30, 2021.

E 8–4
Perpetual
and periodic
inventory systems
compared
● LO8–1

The following information is available for the Johnson Corporation:

Beginning inventory	$ 25,000
Inventory purchases (on account)	155,000
Freight charges on purchases (paid in cash)	10,000
Inventory returned to suppliers (for credit)	12,000
Ending inventory	30,000
Sales (on account)	250,000
Cost of inventory sold	148,000

Required:

Applying both a perpetual and a periodic inventory system, prepare the journal entries that summarize the transactions that created these balances. Include all end-of-period adjusting entries indicated.

E 8–5
Inventory
transactions;
missing data
● LO8–1

The Playa Company has the following information in its records. Certain data have been intentionally omitted ($ in thousands).

	2021	2022	2023
Beginning inventory	?	?	225
Cost of goods sold	627	621	?
Ending inventory	?	225	216
Cost of goods available for sale	876	?	800
Purchases (gross)	630	?	585
Purchase discounts	18	15	?
Purchase returns	24	30	14
Freight-in	13	32	16

Required:

Determine the missing numbers. Show computations where appropriate.

E 8–6
Goods in transit
● LO8–2

The Kwok Company's inventory balance on December 31, 2021, was $165,000 (based on a 12/31/2021 physical count) *before* considering the following transactions:

1. Goods shipped to Kwok f.o.b. destination on December 20, 2021, were received on January 4, 2022. The invoice cost was $30,000.
2. Goods shipped to Kwok f.o.b. shipping point on December 28, 2021, were received on January 5, 2022. The invoice cost was $17,000.
3. Goods shipped from Kwok to a customer f.o.b. destination on December 27, 2021, were received by the customer on January 3, 2022. The sales price was $40,000 and the merchandise cost $22,000.
4. Goods shipped from Kwok to a customer f.o.b. destination on December 26, 2021, were received by the customer on December 30, 2021. The sales price was $20,000 and the merchandise cost $13,000.
5. Goods shipped from Kwok to a customer f.o.b. shipping point on December 28, 2021, were received by the customer on January 4, 2022. The sales price was $25,000 and the merchandise cost $12,000.

Required:

Determine the correct inventory amount to be reported in Kwok's 2021 balance sheet.

E 8–7
Goods in transit;
consignment
● LO8–2

The December 31, 2021, year-end inventory balance of the Raymond Corporation is $210,000. You have been asked to review the following transactions to determine if they have been correctly recorded.

1. Goods shipped to Raymond f.o.b. destination on December 26, 2021, were received on January 2, 2022. The invoice cost of $30,000 *is* included in the preliminary inventory balance.
2. At year-end, Raymond held $14,000 of merchandise on consignment from the Harrison Company. This merchandise *is* included in the preliminary inventory balance.
3. On December 29, merchandise costing $6,000 was shipped to a customer f.o.b. shipping point and arrived at the customer's location on January 3, 2022. The merchandise is *not* included in the preliminary inventory balance.
4. At year-end, Raymond had merchandise costing $15,000 on consignment with the Joclyn Corporation. The merchandise is *not* included in the preliminary inventory balance.

Required:
Determine the correct inventory amount to be reported in Raymond's 2021 balance sheet.

E 8–8
Physical quantities and costs included in inventory
● LO8–2

The Phoenix Corporation's fiscal year ends on December 31. Phoenix determines inventory quantity by a physical count of inventory on hand at the close of business on December 31. The company's controller has asked for your help in deciding if the following items should be included in the year-end inventory count.

1. Merchandise held on consignment for Trout Creek Clothing.
2. Goods shipped f.o.b. destination on December 28 that arrived at the customer's location on January 4.
3. Goods purchased from a vendor shipped f.o.b. shipping point on December 26 that arrived on January 3.
4. Goods shipped f.o.b. shipping point on December 28 that arrived at the customer's location on January 5.
5. Phoenix had merchandise on consignment at Lisa's Markets, Inc.
6. Goods purchased from a vendor shipped f.o.b. destination on December 27 that arrived on January 3.
7. Freight charges on goods purchased in 3.

Required:
Determine if each of the items above should be included or excluded from the company's year-end inventory.

E 8–9
Purchase discounts; the gross method
● LO8–3

On July 15, 2021, the Nixon Car Company purchased 1,000 tires from the Harwell Company for $50 each. The terms of the sale were 2/10, n/30. Nixon uses a perpetual inventory system and the *gross* method of accounting for purchase discounts.

Required:
1. Prepare the journal entries to record the (a) purchase on July 15 and (b) payment on July 23, 2021.
2. Prepare the journal entry for the payment, assuming instead that it was made on August 15, 2021.
3. If Nixon instead uses a periodic inventory system, explain any changes to the journal entries created in requirements 1 and 2.

E 8–10
Purchase discounts; the net method
● LO8–3

[This is a variation of E 8-9 modified to focus on the net method of accounting for purchase discounts.]
On July 15, 2021, the Nixon Car Company purchased 1,000 tires from the Harwell Company for $50 each. The terms of the sale were 2/10, n/30. Nixon uses a perpetual inventory system and the *net* method of accounting for purchase discounts.

Required:
1. Prepare the journal entries to record the (a) purchase on July 15 and (b) payment on July 23, 2021.
2. Prepare the journal entry for the payment, assuming instead that it was made on August 15, 2021.
3. If Nixon instead uses a periodic inventory system, explain any changes to the journal entries created in requirements 1 and 2.

E 8–11
Trade and purchase discounts; the gross method and the net method compared
● LO8–3

Tracy Company, a manufacturer of air conditioners, sold 100 units to Thomas Company on November 17, 2021. The units have a list price of $500 each, but Thomas was given a 30% trade discount. The terms of the sale were 2/10, n/30. Thomas uses a perpetual inventory system.

Required:
1. Prepare the journal entries to record the (a) purchase by Thomas on November 17 and (b) payment on November 26, 2021. Thomas uses the gross method of accounting for purchase discounts.
2. Prepare the journal entry for the payment, assuming instead that it was made on December 15, 2021.
3. Repeat requirements 1 and 2 using the net method of accounting for purchase discounts.

E 8–12
FASB codification research
● LO8–2, LO8–3

Access the *FASB Accounting Standards Codification* at the FASB website (www.fasb.org). Determine each of the following:

1. The specific eight-digit Codification citation (XXX-XX-XX-X) that describes the meaning of cost as it applies to the initial measurement of inventory.
2. The specific nine-digit Codification citation (XXX-XXX-XX-X) that describes the circumstances when it is appropriate to initially measure agricultural inventory at fair value.
3. The specific eight-digit Codification citation (XXX-XX-XX-X) that describes the major objective of accounting for inventory.
4. The specific eight-digit Codification citation (XXX-XX-XX-X) that describes the abnormal freight charges included in the cost of inventory.

440   SECTION 2   Assets

E 8–13
Inventory cost
flow methods;
periodic system
● LO8–1, LO8–4

Altira Corporation provides the following information related to its merchandise inventory during the month of August 2021:

Aug. 1	Inventory on hand—2,000 units; cost $5.30 each.
8	Purchased 8,000 units for $5.50 each.
14	Sold 6,000 units for $12.00 each.
18	Purchased 6,000 units for $5.60 each.
25	Sold 7,000 units for $11.00 each.
28	Purchased 4,000 units for $5.80 each.
31	Inventory on hand—7,000 units.

Required:
Using calculations based on a periodic inventory system, determine the inventory balance Altira would report in its August 31, 2021, balance sheet and the cost of goods sold it would report in its August 2021 income statement using each of the following cost flow methods:
1. First-in, first-out (FIFO)
2. Last-in, first-out (LIFO)
3. Average cost

E 8–14
Inventory cost
flow methods;
perpetual system
● LO8–1, LO8–4

[This is a variation of E 8–13 modified to focus on the perpetual inventory system and alternative cost flow methods.]
  Altira Corporation provides the following information related to its merchandise inventory during the month of August 2021:

Aug. 1	Inventory on hand—2,000 units; cost $5.30 each.
8	Purchased 8,000 units for $5.50 each.
14	Sold 6,000 units for $12.00 each.
18	Purchased 6,000 units for $5.60 each.
25	Sold 7,000 units for $11.00 each.
28	Purchased 4,000 units for $5.80 each.
31	Inventory on hand—7,000 units.

Required:
Using calculations based on a perpetual inventory system, determine the inventory balance Altira would report in its August 31, 2021, balance sheet and the cost of goods sold it would report in its August 2021 income statement using each of the following cost flow methods:
1. First-in, first-out (FIFO)
2. Average cost

E 8–15
LIFO; perpetual
system
● LO8–1, LO8–4

[This is a variation of E 8–14 modified to focus on LIFO in a perpetual inventory system.]
  Altira Corporation provides the following information related to its merchandise inventory during the month of August 2021:

Aug. 1	Inventory on hand—2,000 units; cost $5.30 each.
8	Purchased 8,000 units for $5.50 each.
14	Sold 6,000 units for $12.00 each.
18	Purchased 6,000 units for $5.60 each.
25	Sold 7,000 units for $11.00 each.
28	Purchased 4,000 units for $5.80 each.
31	Inventory on hand—7,000 units.

Required:
Using calculations based on a perpetual inventory system, determine the inventory balance Altira would report in its August 31, 2021, balance sheet and the cost of goods sold it would report in its August 2021 income statement using last-in, first-out (LIFO).

E 8–16
Comparison of
FIFO and LIFO;
periodic system
● LO8–1, LO8–4

Alta Ski Company's inventory records contained the following information regarding its latest ski model. The company uses a periodic inventory system.

Beginning inventory, January 1, 2021	600 units @ $80 each
Purchases:	
January 15	1,000 units @ $95 each
January 21	800 units @ $100 each
Sales:	
January 5	400 units @ $120 each
January 22	800 units @ $130 each
January 29	400 units @ $135 each
Ending inventory, January 31, 2021	800 units

Required:

1. Which method, FIFO or LIFO, will result in the highest cost of goods sold figure for January 2021? Why? Which method will result in the highest ending inventory balance? Why?

2. Compute cost of goods sold for January and the ending inventory using both the FIFO and LIFO methods.

3. Now assume that inventory costs were *declining* during January. The inventory purchased on January 15 had a unit cost of $70, and the inventory purchased on January 21 had a unit cost of $65. All other information is the same. Repeat requirements 1 and 2.

E 8–17
Average cost method; periodic and perpetual systems
● LO8–1, LO8–4

The following information is taken from the inventory records of the CNB Company for the month of September:

Beginning inventory, 9/1/2021	5,000 units @ $10.00
Purchases:	
9/7	3,000 units @ $10.40
9/25	8,000 units @ $10.75
Sales:	
9/10	4,000 units
9/29	5,000 units
7,000 units were on hand at the end of September.	

Required:

1. Assuming that CNB uses a periodic inventory system and employs the average cost method, determine cost of goods sold for September and September's ending inventory.

2. Repeat requirement 1 assuming that the company uses a perpetual inventory system.

E 8–18
FIFO, LIFO, and average cost methods
● LO8–1, LO8–4

Causwell Company began 2021 with 10,000 units of inventory on hand. The cost of each unit was $5.00. During 2021, an additional 30,000 units were purchased at a single unit cost, and 20,000 units remained on hand at the end of 2021 (20,000 units therefore were sold during 2021). Causwell uses a periodic inventory system. Cost of goods sold for 2021, applying the average cost method, is $115,000. The company is interested in determining what cost of goods sold would have been if the FIFO or LIFO methods were used.

Required:

1. Determine the cost of goods sold for 2021 using the FIFO method. [*Hint:* Determine the cost per unit of 2021 purchases.]

2. Determine the cost of goods sold for 2021 using the LIFO method.

E 8–19
Perpetual FIFO adjusted to periodic LIFO; LIFO reserve
● LO8–1, LO8–4, LO8–6

To more efficiently manage its inventory, Treynor Corporation maintains its internal inventory records using first-in, first-out (FIFO) under a perpetual inventory system. The following information relates to its merchandise inventory during the year:

Jan. 1	Inventory on hand—20,000 units; cost $12.20 each.
Feb. 12	Purchased 70,000 units for $12.50 each.
Apr. 30	Sold 50,000 units for $20.00 each.
Jul. 22	Purchased 50,000 units for $12.80 each.
Sep. 9	Sold 70,000 units for $20.00 each.
Nov. 17	Purchased 40,000 units for $13.20 each.
Dec. 31	Inventory on hand—60,000 units.

Required:

1. Determine the amount Treynor would calculate internally for ending inventory and cost of goods sold using first-in, first-out (FIFO) under a perpetual inventory system.

2. Determine the amount Treynor would report externally for ending inventory and cost of goods sold using last-in, first-out (LIFO) under a periodic inventory system.

3. Determine the amount Treynor would report for its LIFO reserve at the end of the year.

4. Record the year-end adjusting entry for the LIFO reserve, assuming the balance at the beginning of the year was $10,000.

E 8–20
Perpetual average cost adjusted to periodic LIFO; LIFO reserve
● LO8–1, LO8–4, LO8–6

Tipton Processing maintains its internal inventory records using average cost under a perpetual inventory system. The following information relates to its inventory during the year:

Jan. 1	Inventory on hand—80,000 units; cost $4.25 each.
Feb. 14	Purchased 120,000 units for $4.50 each.
Mar. 5	Sold 150,000 units for $14.00 each.
Aug. 27	Purchased 50,000 units for $4.80 each.
Sep. 12	Sold 60,000 units for $14.00 each.
Dec. 31	Inventory on hand—40,000 units.

442 SECTION 2 Assets

Required:

1. Determine the amount Tipton would calculate internally for ending inventory and cost of goods sold using average cost under a perpetual inventory system.

2. Determine the amount Tipton would report externally for ending inventory and cost of goods sold using last-in, first-out (LIFO) under a periodic inventory system.

3. Determine the amount Tipton would report for its LIFO reserve at the end of the year.

4. Record the year-end adjusting entry for the LIFO reserve, assuming the balance at the beginning of the year was $8,000.

E 8–21
Supplemental
LIFO disclosures;
LIFO reserve;
AmerisourceBergen
● LO8–6
Real World Financials

AmerisourceBergen is an American drug wholesale company. The company uses the LIFO inventory method for external reporting but maintains its internal records using FIFO. The following disclosure note was included in a recent quarterly report:

5. Inventories (in part)

Inventories are comprised of the following ($ in millions):

	September 30, 2017	September 30, 2016
Inventories (under FIFO)	$12,928	$12,349
Less: LIFO reserve	(1,467)	(1,625)
Inventories (under LIFO)	$11,461	$10,724

The company's income statements reported cost of goods sold of $148,598 million for the quarter ended September 30, 2017.

Required:

1. Assume that AmerisourceBergen adjusts the LIFO reserve at the end of its quarter. Prepare the September 30, 2017, adjusting entry to record the cost of goods sold adjustment.

2. If AmerisourceBergen had used FIFO to report its inventories, what would cost of goods sold have been for the quarter ended September 30, 2017?

E 8–22
LIFO liquidation
● LO8–1, LO8–4,
LO8–6

The Reuschel Company began 2021 with inventory of 10,000 units at a cost of $7 per unit. During 2021, 50,000 units were purchased for $8.50 each. Sales for the year totaled 54,000 units leaving 6,000 units on hand at the end of 2021. Reuschel uses a periodic inventory system and the LIFO inventory cost method.

Required:

1. Calculate cost of goods sold for 2021.

2. From a financial reporting perspective, what problem is created by the use of LIFO in this situation? Describe the disclosure required to report the effects of this problem.

E 8–23
LIFO liquidation
● LO8–4, LO8–6

The Churchill Corporation uses a periodic inventory system and the LIFO inventory cost method for its one product. Beginning inventory of 20,000 units consisted of the following, listed in chronological order of acquisition:

12,000 units at a cost of $8.00 per unit = $96,000
8,000 units at a cost of $9.00 per unit = 72,000

During 2021, inventory quantity declined by 10,000 units. All units purchased during 2021 cost $12.00 per unit.

Required:

Calculate the before-tax LIFO liquidation profit or loss that the company would report in a disclosure note, assuming the amount determined is material.

E 8–24
FASB codification
research
● LO8–6

Access the *FASB Accounting Standards Codification* at the FASB website (www.fasb.org). Determine each of the following:

1. The specific nine-digit Codification citation (XXX-XX-XXX-X) that describes the disclosure requirements that must be made by publicly traded companies for a LIFO liquidation. (Hint: Look in the SEC Materials section.)

2. Describe the disclosure requirements.

E 8–25
Ratio analysis;
Home Depot and
Lowe's
● LO8–7

Real World Financials

The table below contains selected information from recent financial statements of The Home Depot, Inc., and Lowe's Companies, Inc., two companies in the home improvement retail industry ($ in millions):

	Home Depot		Lowe's	
	1/28/2018	**1/29/2017**	**2/2/2018**	**2/3/2017**
Net sales	$100,904	$94,595	$68,619	$65,017
Cost of goods sold	66,548	62,282	45,210	42,553
Year-end inventory	12,748	12,549	11,393	10,458
Industry averages:				
Gross profit ratio	27.25%			
Inventory turnover ratio	3.63 times			
Average days in inventory	101 days			

Required:
Calculate the gross profit ratio, the inventory turnover ratio, and the average days in inventory for the two companies for their fiscal years ending in 2018. Compare your calculations for the two companies, taking into account the industry averages.

E 8–26
Dollar-value LIFO
● LO8–8

On January 1, 2021, the Haskins Company adopted the dollar-value LIFO method for its one inventory pool. The pool's value on this date was $660,000. The 2021 and 2022 ending inventory valued at year-end costs were $690,000 and $760,000, respectively. The appropriate cost indexes are 1.04 for 2021 and 1.08 for 2022.

Required:
Calculate the inventory value at the end of 2021 and 2022 using the dollar-value LIFO method.

E 8–27
Dollar-value LIFO
● LO8–8

Mercury Company has only one inventory pool. On December 31, 2021, Mercury adopted the dollar-value LIFO inventory method. The inventory on that date using the dollar-value LIFO method was $200,000. Inventory data are as follows:

Year	Ending Inventory at Year-End Costs	Ending Inventory at Base Year Costs
2022	$231,000	$220,000
2023	299,000	260,000
2024	300,000	250,000

Required:
Compute the inventory at December 31, 2022, 2023, and 2024, using the dollar-value LIFO method.

(AICPA adapted)

E 8–28
Dollar-value LIFO
● LO8–8

Carswell Electronics adopted the dollar-value LIFO method on January 1, 2021, when the inventory value of its one inventory pool was $720,000. The company decided to use an external index, the Consumer Price Index (CPI), to adjust for changes in the cost level. On January 1, 2021, the CPI was 240. On December 31, 2021, inventory valued at year-end cost was $880,000 and the CPI was 264.

Required:
Calculate the inventory value at the end of 2021 using the dollar-value LIFO method.

E 8–29
Concepts;
terminology
● LO8–1 through
LO8–5

Listed below are several terms and phrases associated with inventory measurement. Pair each item from List A with the item from List B (by letter) that is most appropriately associated with it.

List A	List B
_____ 1. Perpetual inventory system	a. Legal title passes when goods are delivered to common carrier.
_____ 2. Periodic inventory system	b. Goods are transferred to another company but title remains with transferor.
_____ 3. F.o.b. shipping point	c. Purchases are recorded for the full cost of inventory.
_____ 4. Gross method	d. If LIFO is used for taxes, it must be used for financial reporting.
_____ 5. Net method	e. Assumes items sold are those acquired first.
_____ 6. Cost index	f. Assumes items sold are those acquired last.
_____ 7. F.o.b. destination	g. Purchase discounts are recorded for the full cost of inventory less any possible discount.
_____ 8. FIFO	h. Used to convert ending inventory at year-end cost to base year cost.
_____ 9. LIFO	i. Continuously records changes in inventory.
_____ 10. Consignment	j. Assumes items sold come from a mixture of goods acquired during the period.
_____ 11. Average cost	k. Legal title passes when goods arrive at location.
_____ 12. IRS conformity rule	l. Adjusts inventory at the end of the period.

444   SECTION 2   Assets

E 8–30
General ledger exercise; inventory transactions
● LO8–1 through LO8–8

On January 1, 2021, Displays Incorporated had the following account balances:

Account Title	Debits	Credits
Cash	$ 22,000	
Accounts receivable	19,000	
Supplies	25,000	
Inventory	60,000	
Land	227,000	
Accounts payable		$ 18,000
Notes payable (5%, due next year)		20,000
Common stock		186,000
Retained earnings		129,000
Totals	$353,000	$353,000

From January 1 to December 31, the following summary transactions occurred:

a. Purchased inventory on account for $330,000.

b. Sold inventory on account for $570,000. The cost of the inventory sold was $310,000.

c. Received $540,000 from customers on accounts receivable.

d. Paid freight on inventory received, $24,000.

e. Paid $320,000 to inventory suppliers on accounts payable of $325,000. The difference reflects purchase discounts of $5,000.

f. Paid rent for the current year, $42,000. The payment was recorded to Rent Expense.

g. Paid salaries for the current year, $150,000. The payment was recorded to Salaries Expense.

Required:

1. Record each of the transactions listed above in the 'General Journal' tab (these are shown as items 1-8) assuming a perpetual inventory system. Review the 'General Ledger' and the 'Trial Balance' tabs to see the effect of the transactions on the account balances.

2. Record adjusting entries on December 31 in the 'General Journal' tab (these are shown as items 9-11).

   a. Supplies on hand at the end of the year are $8,000.

   b. Accrued interest expense on notes payable for the year.

   c. Accrued income taxes at the end of December are $18,000.

3. Review the adjusted 'Trial Balance' as of December 31, 2018, in the 'Trial Balance' tab.

4. Prepare a multiple-step income statement for the period ended December 31, 2021, in the 'Income Statement' tab.

5. Prepare a classified balance sheet as of December 31, 2021, in the 'Balance Sheet' tab.

6. Record the closing entries in the 'General Journal' tab (these are shown as items 12-13).

7. Using the information from the requirements above, complete the 'Analysis' tab.

   a. Suppose Displays Incorporated decided to maintain its internal records using FIFO but to use LIFO for external reporting. Assuming the ending balance of inventory under LIFO would have been $85,000, calculate the LIFO reserve.

   b. Assume Displays Incorporated $60,000 beginning balance of inventory comes from the base year with a cost index of 1.00. The cost index at the end of 2021 of 1.10. Calculate the amount the company would report for inventory using dollar-value LIFO.

   c. Indicate whether each of the following amounts below would be *higher* or *lower* when reporting inventory using LIFO (or dollar-value LIFO) instead of FIFO in periods of rising inventory costs and stable inventory quantities: Inventory turnover ratio, average days in inventory, gross profit ratio.

E 8–31
General ledger exercise; receivable and inventory transactions
● LO8–1, LO8–3, LO8–5

On January 1, 2021, the general ledger of Tripley Company included the following account balances:

Account Title	Debits	Credits
Cash	$ 70,000	
Accounts receivable	40,000	
Allowance for uncollectible accounts		$ 5,000
Inventory	30,000	
Building	70,000	

Account Title	Debits	Credits
Accumulated depreciation		10,000
Land	200,000	
Accounts payable		20,000
Notes payable (8%, due in 3 years)		36,000
Common stock		100,000
Retained earnings		239,000
Totals	$410,000	$410,000

The $30,000 beginning balance of inventory consists of 300 units, each costing $100. During January 2021, the company had the following transactions:

Jan. 2 Lent $20,000 to an employee by accepting a 6% note due in six months.

5 Purchased 3,500 units of inventory on account for $385,000 ($110 each) with terms 1/10, n/30.

8 Returned 100 defective units of inventory purchased on January 5.

15 Sold 3,300 units of inventory on account for $429,000 ($130 each) with terms 2/10, n/30.

17 Customers returned 200 units sold on January 15. These units were initially purchased by the company on January 5. The units are placed in inventory to be sold in the future.

20 Received cash from customers on accounts receivable. This amount includes $36,000 from 2020 plus amount receivable on sale of 2,700 units sold on January 15.

21 Wrote off remaining accounts receivable from 2020.

24 Paid on accounts payable. The amount includes the amount owed at the beginning of the period plus the amount owed from purchase of 3,100 units on January 5.

28 Paid cash for salaries during January, $28,000.

29 Paid cash for utilities during January, $10,000.

30 Paid dividends, $3,000.

Required:

1. Record each of the transactions listed above in the 'General Journal' tab (these are shown as items 1-10) assuming a perpetual FIFO inventory system. Purchases and sales of inventory are recorded using the gross method for cash discounts. Review the 'General Ledger' and the 'Trial Balance' tabs to see the effect of the transactions on the account balances.

2. Record adjusting entries on January 31 in the 'General Journal' tab (these are shown as items 11-14):

   a. Of the remaining accounts receivable, the company estimates that 10% will not be collected.

   b. Accrued interest revenue on notes receivable for January.

   c. Accrued interest expense on notes payable for January.

   d. Accrued income taxes at the end of January for $5,000.

   e. Depreciation on the building, $2,000

3. Review the adjusted 'Trial Balance' as of January 31, 2021, in the 'Trial Balance' tab.

4. Prepare a multiple-step income statement for the period ended January 31, 2021, in the 'Income Statement' tab.

5. Prepare a classified balance sheet as of January 31, 2021, in the 'Balance Sheet' tab.

6. Record closing entries in the 'General Journal' tab (these are shown as items 15-16).

7. Using the information from the requirements above, complete the 'Analysis' tab.

   a. Calculate the inventory turnover ratio for the month of January. If the industry average of the inventory turnover ratio for the month of January is 4.5 times, is the company selling its inventory *more* or *less* quickly than other companies in the same industry?

   b. Calculate the gross profit ratio for the month of January. If the industry average gross profit ratio is 33%, is the company *more* or *less* profitable per dollar of sales than other companies in the same industry?

   c. Used together, what might the inventory turnover ratio and gross profit ratio suggest about the company's business strategy? Is the company's strategy to sell a *higher volume of less expensive* items or does the company appear to be selling a *lower volume of more expensive* items?

Problems

P 8–1
Various inventory transactions; journal entries
● LO8–1 through LO8–3

James Company began the month of October with inventory of $15,000. The following inventory transactions occurred during the month:

a. The company purchased merchandise on account for $22,000 on October 12. Terms of the purchase were 2/10, n/30. James uses the net method to record purchases. The merchandise was shipped f.o.b. shipping point and freight charges of $500 were paid in cash.

b. On October 31, James paid for the merchandise purchased on October 12.

c. During October merchandise costing $18,000 was sold on account for $28,000.

d. It was determined that inventory on hand at the end of October cost $19,060.

Required:

1. Assuming that the James Company uses a perpetual inventory system, prepare journal entries for the above transactions.

2. Assuming that the James Company uses a periodic inventory system, prepare journal entries for the above transactions including the adjusting entry at the end of October to record cost of goods sold. James considers purchase discounts lost as part of interest expense.

P 8–2
Items to be included in inventory
● LO8–2

The following inventory transactions took place near December 31, 2021, the end of the Rasul Company's fiscal year-end:

1. On December 27, 2021, merchandise costing $2,000 was shipped to the Myers Company on consignment. The shipment arrived at Myers's location on December 29, but none of the merchandise was sold by the end of the year. The merchandise was *not* included in the 2021 ending inventory.

2. On January 5, 2022, merchandise costing $8,000 was received from a supplier and recorded as a purchase on that date and *not* included in the 2021 ending inventory. The invoice revealed that the shipment was made f.o.b. shipping point on December 28, 2021.

3. On December 29, 2021, the company shipped merchandise costing $12,000 to a customer f.o.b. destination. The goods, which arrived at the customer's location on January 4, 2022, were *not* included in Rasul's 2021 ending inventory. The sale was recorded in 2021.

4. Merchandise costing $4,000 was received on December 28, 2021, on consignment from the Aborn Company. A purchase was *not* recorded and the merchandise was *not* included in 2021 ending inventory.

5. Merchandise costing $6,000 was received and recorded as a purchase on January 8, 2022. The invoice revealed that the merchandise was shipped from the supplier on December 28, 2021, f.o.b. destination. The merchandise was *not* included in 2021 ending inventory.

Required:

State whether Rasul correctly accounted for each of the above transactions. Give the reason for your answer.

P 8–3
Costs included in inventory
● LO8–2, LO8–3

Reagan Corporation is a wholesale distributor of truck replacement parts. Initial amounts taken from Reagan's records are as follows:

Inventory at December 31 (based on a physical count of goods in Reagan's warehouse on December 31)			$1,250,000
Accounts payable at December 31:			

Vendor	Terms	Amount
Baker Company	2%, 10 days, net 30	$ 265,000
Charlie Company	Net 30	210,000
Dolly Company	Net 30	300,000
Eagler Company	Net 30	225,000
Full Company	Net 30	—
Greg Company	Net 30	—
Accounts payable, December 31		$1,000,000
Sales for the year		$9,000,000

Additional Information:

1. Parts held by Reagan on consignment from Charlie, amounting to $155,000, were included in the physical count of goods in Reagan's warehouse and in accounts payable at December 31.

2. Parts totaling $22,000, which were purchased from Full and paid for in December, were sold in the last week of the year and *appropriately* recorded as sales of $28,000. The parts were included in the physical count of goods in Reagan's warehouse on December 31 because the parts were on the loading dock waiting to be picked up by customers.

3. Parts in transit on December 31 to customers, shipped f.o.b. shipping point on December 28, amounted to $34,000. The customers received the parts on January 6 of the following year. Sales of $40,000 to the customers for the parts were recorded by Reagan on January 2.

4. Retailers were holding goods on consignment from Reagan, which had a cost of $210,000 and a retail value of $250,000.

5. Goods were in transit from Greg to Reagan on December 31. The cost of the goods was $25,000, and they were shipped f.o.b. shipping point on December 29.

6. A freight bill in the amount of $2,000 specifically relating to merchandise purchased in December, all of which was still in the inventory at December 31, was received on January 3. The freight bill was not included in either the inventory or in accounts payable at December 31.

7. All the purchases from Baker occurred during the last seven days of the year. These items have been recorded in accounts payable and accounted for in the physical inventory at cost before discount. Reagan's policy is to pay invoices in time to take advantage of all discounts, adjust inventory accordingly, and record accounts payable net of discounts.

Required:

Prepare a schedule of adjustments to the initial amounts using the format shown below. Show the effect, if any, of each of the transactions separately and if the transactions would have no effect on the amount shown, state *none*.

	Inventory	Accounts Payable	Sales
Initial amounts	$1,250,000	$ 1,000,000	$9,000,000
Adjustments—increase (decrease):			
1.			
2.			
3.			
4.			
5.			
6.			
7.			
Total adjustments			
Adjusted amounts	$	$	$

(AICPA adapted)

P 8–4

Various inventory transactions; determining inventory and cost of goods; LIFO reserve

● LO8–1 through LO8–4, LO8–6

Johnson Corporation began the year with inventory of 10,000 units of its only product. The units cost $8 each. The company uses a perpetual inventory system and the FIFO cost method. The following transactions occurred during the year:

a. Purchased 50,000 additional units at a cost of $10 per unit. Terms of the purchases were 2/10, n/30, and 100% of the purchases were paid for within the 10-day discount period. The company uses the gross method to record purchase discounts. The merchandise was purchased f.o.b. shipping point and freight charges of $0.50 per unit were paid by Johnson.

b. 1,000 units purchased during the year were returned to suppliers for credit. Johnson was also given credit for the freight charges of $0.50 per unit it had paid on the original purchase. The units were defective and were returned two days after they were received.

c. Sales for the year totaled 45,000 units at $18 per unit.

d. On December 28, Johnson purchased 5,000 additional units at $10 each. The goods were shipped f.o.b. destination and arrived at Johnson's warehouse on January 4 of the following year.

e. 14,000 units were on hand at the end of the year.

Required:

1. Determine ending inventory and cost of goods sold at the end of the year.

2. Assuming that operating expenses other than those indicated in the above transactions amounted to $150,000, determine income before income taxes for the year.

3. For financial reporting purposes, the company uses LIFO (amounts based on a periodic inventory system). Record the year-end adjusting entry for the LIFO reserve, assuming the balance in the LIFO reserve at the beginning of the year is $15,000.

4. Determine the amount the company would report as income before taxes for the year under LIFO. Operating expenses other than those indicated in the above transactions amounted to $150,000.

448   SECTION 2   Assets

P 8–5
Various inventory
costing methods
● LO8–1, LO8–4

Ferris Company began January with 6,000 units of its principal product. The cost of each unit is $8. Merchandise transactions for the month of January are as follows:

	Purchases		
Date of Purchase	Units	Unit Cost*	Total Cost
Jan. 10	5,000	$ 9	$ 45,000
Jan. 18	6,000	10	60,000
Total purchases	11,000		$ 105,000

*Includes purchase price and cost of freight.

Sales	
Date of Sale	Units
Jan. 5	3,000
Jan. 12	2,000
Jan. 20	4,000
Total sales	9,000

8,000 units were on hand at the end of the month.

Required:
Calculate January's ending inventory and cost of goods sold for the month using each of the following alternatives:
1. FIFO, periodic system
2. LIFO, periodic system
3. FIFO, perpetual system
4. Average cost, periodic system
5. Average cost, perpetual system

P 8–6
Various inventory
costing methods;
gross profit ratio
● LO8–1, LO8–4,
LO8–7

Topanga Group began operations early in 2021. Inventory purchase information for the quarter ended March 31, 2021, for Topanga's only product is provided below. The unit costs include the cost of freight. The company uses a periodic inventory system to report inventory and cost of goods sold.

Date of Purchase	Units	Unit Cost	Total Cost
Jan. 7	5,000	$4.00	$ 20,000
Feb. 16	12,000	4.50	54,000
March 22	17,000	5.00	85,000
Total purchases	34,000		$159,000

Sales for the quarter, all at $7.00 per unit, totaled 20,000 units leaving 14,000 units on hand at the end of the quarter.

Required:
1. Calculate Topanga's gross profit ratio for the first quarter using:
   a. FIFO
   b. LIFO
   c. Average cost
2. Comment on the relative effect of each of the three inventory methods on the gross profit ratio.

P 8–7
Various inventory
costing methods
● LO8–1, LO8–4

Carlson Auto Dealers Inc. sells a handmade automobile as its only product. Each automobile is identical; however, they can be distinguished by their unique ID number. At the beginning of 2021, Carlson had three cars in inventory, as follows:

Car ID	Cost
203	$60,000
207	60,000
210	63,000

During 2021, each of the three autos sold for $90,000. Additional purchases (listed in chronological order) and sales for the year were as follows:

Car ID	Cost	Selling Price
211	$63,000	$ 90,000
212	63,000	93,000
213	64,500	not sold
214	66,000	96,000
215	69,000	100,500
216	70,500	not sold
217	72,000	105,000
218	72,300	106,500
219	75,000	not sold

Required:

1. Calculate 2021 ending inventory and cost of goods sold assuming the company uses the specific identification inventory method.
2. Calculate ending inventory and cost of goods sold assuming FIFO and a periodic inventory system.
3. Calculate ending inventory and cost of goods sold assuming LIFO and a periodic inventory system.
4. Calculate ending inventory and cost of goods sold assuming the average cost method and a periodic inventory system.

P 8–8
Supplemental
LIFO disclosures;
Caterpillar
● LO8–4, LO8–6
Real World Financials

Caterpillar, Inc., is one of the world's largest manufacturers of construction, mining, and forestry machinery. The following disclosure note is included in the company's 2017 financial statements:

> **D. Inventories ($ in millions)**
> Inventories are stated at the lower of cost or net realizable value. Cost is principally determined using the last-in, first-out (LIFO) method. The value of inventories on the LIFO basis represented about 65 percent and 60 percent of total inventories at December 31, 2017 and 2016. If the FIFO (first-in, first-out) method had been in use, inventories would have been $1,934 million and $2,139 million higher than reported at December 31, 2017 and 2016, respectively.

Required:

1. The company reported LIFO cost of goods sold of $31,049 million. Calculate the amount that would be reported for cost of goods sold had Caterpillar used the FIFO inventory method for all of its inventory during 2017.
2. How does the amount in requirement 1 affect income before taxes?
3. Why might the information contained in the disclosure note be useful to a financial analyst?

P 8–9
LIFO liquidation
● LO8–4, LO8–6

Taylor Corporation reports inventory and cost of goods sold based on calculations from a LIFO periodic inventory system. The company's records under this system reveal the following inventory layers at the beginning of 2021 (listed in chronological order of acquisition):

10,000 units @ $15	$150,000
15,000 units @ $20	300,000
Beginning inventory	$450,000

During 2021, 30,000 units were purchased for $25 per unit. Due to unexpected demand for the company's product, 2021 sales totaled 40,000 units at various prices, leaving 15,000 units in ending inventory.

Required:

1. Calculate the amount to report for cost of goods sold for 2021.
2. Determine the amount of LIFO liquidation profit that the company must report in a disclosure note to its 2021 financial statements. Assume an income tax rate of 25%.
3. If the company decided to purchase an additional 10,000 units at $25 per unit at the end of the year, how much income tax currently payable would be saved?

450   SECTION 2   Assets

P 8–10
LIFO liquidation
● LO8–4, LO8–6

Cansela Corporation reports inventory and cost of goods sold based on calculations from a LIFO periodic inventory system. The company began 2021 with inventory of 4,500 units of its only product. The beginning inventory balance of $64,000 consisted of the following layers:

2,000 units at $12 per unit	=	$24,000
2,500 units at $16 per unit	=	40,000
Beginning inventory		$64,000

During the three years 2021–2023 the cost of inventory remained constant at $18 per unit. Unit purchases and sales during these years were as follows:

	Purchases	Sales
2021	10,000	11,000
2022	13,000	14,500
2023	12,000	13,000

Required:
1. Calculate cost of goods sold for 2021, 2022, and 2023.
2. Disregarding income tax, determine the LIFO liquidation profit or loss, if any, for each of the three years.
3. Prepare the company's LIFO liquidation disclosure note that would be included in the 2023 financial statements to report the effects of any liquidation on cost of goods sold and net income. Assume any liquidation effects are material and that Cansela's effective income tax rate is 25%. Cansela's 2023 financial statements include income statements for two prior years for comparative purposes.

P 8–11
Inventory cost
flow methods:
LIFO liquidation;
ratios
● LO8–4, LO8–6,
LO8–7

Cast Iron Grills, Inc., manufactures premium gas barbecue grills. The company reports inventory and cost of goods sold based on calculations from a LIFO periodic inventory system. Cast Iron's December 31, 2021, fiscal year-end inventory consisted of the following (listed in chronological order of acquisition):

Units	Unit Cost
5,000	$700
4,000	800
6,000	900

The replacement cost of the grills throughout 2022 was $1,000. Cast Iron sold 27,000 grills during 2022. The company's selling price is set at 200% of the current replacement cost.

Required:
1. Compute the gross profit (sales minus cost of goods sold) and the gross profit ratio for 2022 assuming that Cast Iron purchased 28,000 units during the year.
2. Repeat requirement 1 assuming that Cast Iron purchased only 15,000 units.
3. Why does the number of units purchased affect your answers to the above requirements?
4. Repeat requirements 1 and 2 assuming that Cast Iron reports the FIFO inventory cost method rather than the LIFO method.
5. Why does the number of units purchased have no effect on your answers to requirements 1 and 2 when the FIFO method is used for reporting purposes?

P 8–12
Integrating
problem;
inventories
and accounts
receivable;
Chapters 7 and 8
● LO8–4, LO8–6,
LO8–7

Inverness Steel Corporation is a producer of flat-rolled carbon, stainless and electrical steels, and tubular products. The company's income statement for the 2021 fiscal year reported the following information ($ in millions):

Sales	$6,255
Cost of goods sold	5,190

The company's balance sheets for 2021 and 2020 included the following information ($ in millions):

	2021	2020
Current assets:		
Accounts receivable, net	$703	$583
Inventories	880	808

The statement of cash flows reported bad debt expense for 2021 of $8 million. The summary of significant accounting policies included the following notes ($ in millions):

Accounts Receivable (in part)

The allowance for uncollectible accounts was $10 and $7 at December 31, 2021 and 2020, respectively. All sales are on credit.

Inventories

Inventories are valued at the lower of cost or market. The cost of the majority of inventories is measured using the last-in, first-out (LIFO) method. Other inventories are measured principally at average cost and consist mostly of foreign inventories and certain raw materials. If the entire inventory had been valued on an average cost basis, inventory would have been higher by $480 and $350 at the end of 2021 and 2020, respectively.

During 2021, 2020, and 2019, liquidation of LIFO layers generated income of $6, $7, and $25, respectively.

Required:
Using the information provided:
1. Determine the amount of accounts receivable Inverness wrote off during 2021.
2. Calculate the amount of cash collected from customers during 2021.
3. Calculate what cost of goods sold would have been for 2021 if the company had used average cost to value its entire inventory.
4. Calculate the following ratios for 2021:
    a. Receivables turnover ratio
    b. Inventory turnover ratio
    c. Gross profit ratio
5. Explain briefly what caused the income generated by the liquidation of LIFO layers. Assuming an income tax rate of 25%, what was the effect of the liquidation of LIFO layers on cost of goods sold in 2021?

P 8–13
Dollar-value LIFO
● LO8–8

On January 1, 2021, the Taylor Company adopted the dollar-value LIFO method. The inventory value for its one inventory pool on this date was $400,000. Inventory data for 2021 through 2023 are as follows:

Date	Ending Inventory at Year-End Costs	Cost Index
12/31/2021	$441,000	1.05
12/31/2022	487,200	1.12
12/31/2023	510,000	1.20

Required:
Calculate Taylor's ending inventory for 2021, 2022, and 2023.

P 8–14
Dollar-value LIFO
● LO8–8

Kingston Company uses the dollar-value LIFO method of computing inventory. An external price index is used to convert ending inventory to base year. The company began operations on January 1, 2021, with an inventory of $150,000. Year-end inventories at year-end costs and cost indexes for its one inventory pool were as follows:

Year Ended December 31	Ending Inventory at Year-End Costs	Cost Index (Relative to Base Year)
2021	$200,000	1.08
2022	245,700	1.17
2023	235,980	1.14
2024	228,800	1.10

Required:
Calculate inventory amounts at the end of each year.

P 8–15
Dollar-value LIFO
● LO8–8

On January 1, 2021, Avondale Lumber adopted the dollar-value LIFO inventory method. The inventory value for its one inventory pool on this date was $260,000. An internally generated cost index is used to convert ending

452   SECTION 2   Assets

inventory to base year. Year-end inventories at year-end costs and cost indexes for its one inventory pool were as follows:

Year Ended December 31	Inventory Year-End Costs	Cost Index (Relative to Base Year)
2021	$340,000	1.02
2022	350,000	1.06
2023	400,000	1.07
2024	430,000	1.10

Required:
Calculate inventory amounts at the end of each year.

P 8–16
Dollar-value
LIFO; solving for
unknowns
● LO8–8

At the beginning of 2021, Quentin and Kopps (Q&K) adopted the dollar-value LIFO (DVL) inventory method. On that date the value of its one inventory pool was $84,000. The company uses an internally generated cost index to convert ending inventory to base year. Inventory data for 2021 through 2024 are as follows:

Year Ended December 31	Ending Inventory at Year-End Costs	Ending Inventory at Base Year Costs	Cost Index	Ending Inventory at DVL cost
2021	$100,800	$ 96,000	1.05	?
2022	136,800	?	1.14	?
2023	150,000	125,000	?	?
2024	?	?	1.25	$133,710

Required:
Determine the missing amounts.

Decision Makers' Perspective

©ImageGap/Getty Images

**Judgment
Case 8–1**
Riding the
Merry-Go-Round
● LO8–7

Real World Financials

Apply your critical-thinking ability to the knowledge you've gained. These cases will provide you an opportunity to develop your research, analysis, judgment, and communication skills. You also will work with other students, integrate what you've learned, apply it in real-world situations, and consider its global and ethical ramifications. This practice will broaden your knowledge and further develop your decision-making abilities.

Merry-Go-Round Enterprises, the clothing retailer for dedicated followers of young men's and women's fashion, was looking natty as a company. It was March 1993, and the Joppa, Maryland-based outfit had just announced the acquisition of Chess King, a rival clothing chain, a move that would give it the biggest share of the young men's clothing market. Merry-Go-Round told brokerage firm analysts that the purchase would add $13 million, or 15 cents a share, to profits for the year. So some Wall Street analysts raised their earnings estimates for Merry-Go-Round. The company's stock rose $2.25, or 15%, to $17 on the day of the Chess King news. Merry-Go-Round was hot—$100 of its stock in January 1988 was worth $804 five years later. In 1993, the chain owned 1,460 stores in 44 states, mostly under the Cignal, Chess King, and Merry-Go-Round names.

Merry-Go-Round's annual report for the fiscal year ended January 30, 1993, reported a 15% sales growth, to $877.5 million from $761.2 million. A portion of the company's balance sheet is reproduced below:

	Jan. 30, 1993	Feb. 1, 1992
Assets		
Cash and cash equivalents	$40,115,000	$29,781,000
Marketable securities	—	9,703
Receivables	6,466,000	6,195
Merchandise inventories	82,197,000	59,971,000

But Merry-Go-Round spun out. The company lost $544,000 in the first six months of 1993, compared with earnings of $13.5 million in the first half of 1992. In the fall of 1992, Leonard "Boogie" Weinglass, Merry-Go-Round's flamboyant founder and chairman who had started the company in 1968, boarded up his Merry-Go-Ranch in Aspen, Colorado, and returned to management after a 12-year hiatus. But the pony-tailed, shirtsleeved entrepreneur—the inspiration for the character Boogie in the movie *Diner*—couldn't save his company from bankruptcy. In January 1994, the company filed for Chapter 11 protection in Baltimore. Shares crumbled below $3.

Required:

In retrospect, can you identify any advance warning at the date of the financial statements of the company's impending bankruptcy?

[Adapted from Jonathan Burton, "Due Diligence," *Worth*, June 1994, pp. 89–96.]

Real World Case 8–2
Physical quantities and costs included in inventory; Dick's Sporting Goods
● LO8–2

Real World Financials

Determining the physical quantity that should be included in inventory normally is a simple matter because that amount consists of items in the possession of the company. The cost of inventory includes all necessary expenditures to acquire the inventory and bring it to its desired *condition* and *location* for sale or for use in the manufacturing process.

Required:

1. Identify and describe the situations in which physical quantity included in inventory is more difficult than simply determining items in the possession of the company.

2. In addition to the direct acquisition costs such as the price paid and transportation costs to obtain inventory, what other expenditures might be necessary to bring the inventory to its desired condition and location?

3. Access EDGAR on the Internet. The web address is www.sec.gov. Search for Dick's Sporting Goods, a leading omni-channel sporting goods retailer. Access the 10-K filing for the most recent fiscal year. Search or scroll to find the disclosure notes (footnotes). What types of costs does the company include in its inventory?

Judgment Case 8–3
The specific identification inventory method; inventoriable costs
● LO8–3, LO8–4

Happlia Co. imports household appliances. Each model has many variations and each unit has an identification number. Happlia pays all costs for getting the goods from the port to its central warehouse in Des Moines. After repackaging, the goods are consigned to retailers. A retailer makes a sale, simultaneously buys the appliance from Happlia, and pays the balance due within one week.

To alleviate the overstocking of refrigerators at a Minneapolis retailer, some were reshipped to a Kansas City retailer where they were still held in inventory at December 31, 2021. Happlia paid the costs of this reshipment. Happlia uses the specific identification inventory costing method.

Required:

1. In regard to the specific identification inventory costing method:

   a. Describe its key elements.

   b. Discuss why it is appropriate for Happlia to use this method.

2. a. What general criteria should Happlia use to determine inventory carrying amounts at December 31, 2021?

   b. Give four examples of costs included in these inventory carrying amounts.

3. What costs should be reported in Happlia's 2021 income statement?

(AICPA adapted)

Communication Case 8–4
LIFO versus FIFO
● LO8–4, LO8–5

You have just been hired as a consultant to Tangier Industries, a newly formed company. The company president, John Meeks, is seeking your advice as to the appropriate inventory method Tangier should use to value its inventory and cost of goods sold. Mr. Meeks has narrowed the choice to LIFO and FIFO. He has heard that LIFO might be better for tax purposes, but FIFO has certain advantages for financial reporting to investors and creditors. You have been told that the company will be profitable in its first year and for the foreseeable future.

Required:

Prepare a report for the president describing the factors that should be considered by Tangier in choosing between LIFO and FIFO.

Communication Case 8–5
LIFO versus FIFO
● LO8–4, LO8–5

An accounting intern for a local CPA firm was reviewing the financial statements of a client in the electronics industry. The intern noticed that the client used the FIFO method of determining ending inventory and cost of goods sold. When she asked a colleague why the firm used FIFO instead of LIFO, she was told that the client used FIFO to minimize its income tax liability. This response puzzled the intern because she thought that LIFO would minimize income tax liability.

Required:

What would you tell the intern to resolve the confusion?

Judgment Case 8–6
Goods in transit
● LO8–2

At the end of 2021, the Biggie Company performed its annual physical inventory count. John Lawrence, the manager in charge of the physical count, was told that an additional $22,000 in inventory that had been sold and was in transit to the customer should be included in the ending inventory balance. John was of the opinion that the merchandise shipped should be excluded from the ending inventory since Biggie was not in physical possession of the merchandise.

Required:

Discuss the situation and indicate why John's opinion might be incorrect.

454   SECTION 2   Assets

Ethics Case 8–7
Profit
manipulation
● LO8–4

In 2020, the Moncrief Company purchased from Jim Lester the right to be the sole distributor in the western states of a product called Zelenex. In payment, Moncrief agreed to pay Lester 20% of the gross profit recognized from the sale of Zelenex in 2021.

Moncrief reports inventory using the periodic LIFO assumption. Late in 2021, the following information is available concerning the inventory of Zelenex:

Beginning inventory, 1/1/2021 (10,000 units @ $30)	$ 300,000
Purchases (40,000 units @ $30)	1,200,000
Sales (35,000 units @ $60)	2,100,000

By the end of the year, the purchase price of Zelenex had risen to $40 per unit. On December 28, 2021, three days before year-end, Moncrief is in a position to purchase 20,000 additional units of Zelenex at the $40 per unit price. Due to the increase in purchase price, Moncrief will increase the selling price in 2022 to $80 per unit. Inventory on hand before the purchase, 15,000 units, is sufficient to meet the next six months' sales and the company does not anticipate any significant changes in purchase price during 2022.

Required:

1. Determine the effect of the purchase of the additional 20,000 units on the 2021 gross profit from the sale of Zelenex and the payment due to Jim Lester.
2. Discuss the ethical dilemma Moncrief faces in determining whether or not the additional units should be purchased.

**Real World
Case 8–8**
Effects of
inventory
valuation
methods;
supplemental
LIFO disclosures;
Wolverine World
Wide, Inc.
● LO8–4, LO8–6

Real World Financials

Income statement and balance sheet information abstracted from a recent annual report of Wolverine World Wide, Inc., appears below:

Balance Sheets
($ in millions)

	December 30, 2017	December 31, 2016
Current assets:		
Inventories	$276.7	$348.7

Income Statements
($ in millions)

	For the Year Ended	
	December 30, 2017	December 31, 2016
Net sales	$2,350.0	$2,494.6
Cost of goods sold	1,426.6	1,526.4
Gross profit	$ 923.4	$ 968.2

The significant accounting policies note disclosure contained the following:

Inventories

The Company used the LIFO method to value inventories of $53.2 million at December 30, 2017 and $66.2 million at December 31, 2016. During fiscal 2017, a reduction in inventory quantities resulted in a liquidation of applicable LIFO inventory quantities carried at lower costs in prior years. This LIFO liquidation decreased cost of goods sold by $6.0 million. If the FIFO method had been used, inventories would have been $16.4 million and $22.4 million higher than reported at December 30, 2017 and December 31, 2016, respectively.

Required:

1. Why is Wolverine disclosing the FIFO cost of its LIFO inventory?
2. Calculate what beginning inventory and ending inventory would have been for the year ended December 30, 2017, if Wolverine had used FIFO for all of its inventories.
3. Calculate what cost of goods sold and gross profit would have been for the year ended December 30, 2017, if Wolverine had used FIFO for all of its inventories.
4. In 2017, Wolverine reported a LIFO liquidation. Why do companies separately disclose LIFO liquidations due to declines in the quantity of ending inventory?

**Real World
Case 8–9**
Effects of
inventory
valuation
methods; Whole
Foods Market

● LO8–4, LO8–5,
LO8–7

Real World Financials

EDGAR, the Electronic Data Gathering, Analysis, and Retrieval system, performs automated collection, validation, indexing, and forwarding of submission by companies and others who are required by law to file forms with the U.S. Securities and Exchange Commission (SEC). All publicly traded domestic companies use EDGAR to make the majority of their filings. (Some foreign companies file voluntarily.) Form 10-K, which includes the annual report, is required to be filed on EDGAR. The SEC makes this information available on the Internet.

Required:

1. Access EDGAR on the Internet. The web address is www.sec.gov.

2. Search for Whole Foods Market, Inc. Access the 10-K filing for the year ended September 24, 2017. Search or scroll to find the financial statements and related notes.

3. Answer the following questions related to the company's inventories:

    a. What method(s) does the company use to value its inventories?

    b. Calculate what cost of sales would have been for the year if the company had used FIFO to value its inventories.

    c. Calculate inventory turnover for the year using the reported numbers.

**Communication
Case 8–10**
Dollar-value LIFO
method

● LO8–8

Maxi Corporation uses the unit LIFO inventory method. The costs of the company's products have been steadily rising since the company began operations in 2008 and cost increases are expected to continue. The chief financial officer of the company would like to continue using LIFO because of its tax advantages. However, the controller, Sally Hamel, would like to reduce the record-keeping costs of LIFO that have steadily increased over the years as new products have been added to the company's product line. Sally suggested the use of the dollar-value LIFO method. The chief financial officer has asked Sally to describe the dollar-value LIFO procedure.

Required:

Describe the dollar-value LIFO procedure.

**Research
Case 8–11**
FASB codification;
locate and
extract relevant
information and
authoritative
support for
a financial
reporting issue;
product financing
arrangement

● LO8–2, LO8–3

You were recently hired to work in the controller's office of the Balboa Lumber Company. Your boss, Alfred Eagleton, took you to lunch during your first week and asked a favor. "Things have been a little slow lately, and we need to borrow a little cash to tide us over. Our inventory has been building up and the CFO wants to pledge the inventory as collateral for a short-term loan. But I have a better idea." Mr. Eagleton went on to describe his plan. "On July 1, 2021, the first day of the company's third quarter, we will sell $100,000 of inventory to the Harbaugh Corporation for $160,000. Harbaugh will pay us immediately and then we will agree to repurchase the merchandise in two months for $164,000. The $4,000 is Harbaugh's fee for holding the inventory and for providing financing. I already checked with Harbaugh's controller and he has agreed to the arrangement. Not only will we obtain the financing we need, but the third quarter's before-tax profits will be increased by $56,000, the gross profit on the sale less the $4,000 fee. Go research the issue and make sure we would not be violating any specific accounting standards related to product financing arrangements."

Required:

1. Access the *FASB Accounting Standards Codification* at the FASB website (www.fasb.org). Determine the specific eight-digit Codification citation (XXX-XX-XX-X) that provides guidance for determining whether an arrangement involving the sale of inventory is "in substance" a financing arrangement?

2. Determine the specific eight-digit Codification citation (XXX-XX-XX-X) that addresses the recognition of a product financing arrangement?

3. Determine the appropriate treatment of product financing arrangements like the one proposed by Mr. Eagleton.

4. Prepare the journal entry for Balboa Lumber to record the "sale" of the inventory and subsequent repurchase.

**Analysis
Case 8–12**
Compare
inventory
management
using ratios;
Kohl's and Dillards

● LO8–7

Real World Financials

The table below contains selected financial information included in the 2017 financial statements of Kohl's Corporation and Dillards, Inc., two companies in the department store industry.

	($ in millions)			
	Kohl's Corp.		**Dillards, Inc.**	
	2017	**2016**	**2017**	**2016**
Balance sheet:				
Inventories	$ 3,542	$3,795	$1,464	$1,406
Income statement—2017:				
Net sales	$19,095		$6,261	
Cost of goods sold	12,176		4,200	

456   SECTION 2   Assets

Required:

1. Calculate the 2017 gross profit ratio, inventory turnover ratio, and average days in inventory for both companies. Evaluate the management of each company's investment in inventory.

2. Obtain annual reports from three corporations in an industry other than department stores and compare the management of each company's investment in inventory.

Note: You can obtain copies of annual reports from your library, from friends who are shareholders, from the investor relations department of the corporations, from a friendly stockbroker, or from EDGAR (Electronic Data Gathering, Analysis, and Retrieval) on the Internet (www.gov.sec).

Data Analytics

Data analytics is the process of examining data sets in order to draw conclusions about the information they contain. If you have not completed any of the prior data analytics cases, follow the instructions listed in the Chapter 1 Data Analytics case to get set up. You will need to watch the videos referred to in the Chapters 1 - 3 Data Analytics cases. No additional videos are required for this case. All short training videos can be found here: https://www.tableau.com/learn/training#getting-started.

Data Analytics Case
Gross Profit and Gross Profit Ratio
● **LO8–7**

In prior chapters, you used Tableau to examine a data set and create calculations to compare two companies' financial information. In this case you are seeking to gain insight into the relative profitability of a company in various regions of the country and various states in which it sells. Your focus is on assessing the company's ability to generate gross profit on the sale of its inventory. Gross profit represents a company's ability to cover expenses other than cost of goods sold.

Required:

Use Tableau to calculate (a) gross profit and (b) gross profit ratios for the company in each of the five regions of the country designated in the company's data base and each of the states in which the company sells products. Based upon what you find, answer the following questions:

1. Which of the five regions' operations has the highest gross profit?

2. Which of the five regions' operations has the lowest gross profit?

To help determine the relative profitability of each state's sales, get a better state-by-state comparison by analyzing the "map" chart. Once the chart is created, move your cursor to hover above various circles within states in the chart. Notice that an information box appears to reveal the pertinent gross profit and gross profit ratios for that state.

3. Which state's operations provides the highest gross profit ratio?

4. Which state's operations provides the lowest gross profit ratio?

Resources:

You have available to you an extensive data set that includes detailed financial data for the company's inventory sales. The data set is in the form of an Excel file available to download from Connect, or under Student Resources within the Library tab. There are four Excel files available. The one for use in this case is named "Inventory.xlsx." Download this file to the computer, save it, and open it in Tableau.

For this case, you will create several calculations to produce a bar chart and a map of the gross profit to allow you to compare and contrast a company's inventory measurement.

After you view the training videos and review instructions in Chapters 1-3, follow these steps to create the charts you'll use for this case:

· Click on the "Sheet 1" tab, at the bottom of the canvas, to the right of the Data Source at the bottom of the screen. Drag "Region" under Dimensions to the Columns shelf.

· Drag "Status" under Dimensions to the Filter's card. When the Filter window opens, click the "S" so only the sold items will be viewed. Click OK.

· Click on the "Analysis" tab from the Toolbar at the top of the screen and select "Create Calculated Field." A calculation box will pop up. Name the calculation "Total Sales." Drag "Number" to the Calculation Editor window, type an asterisk sign for multiplication, and then drag "Selling Price" beside it. Make sure the window says that the calculation is valid and click OK.

· Repeat the process by creating a calculated field for "Cost of Goods Sold" that consists of "Number" times "Cost."

· Repeat the process by creating a calculated field for "Gross Profit" that consists of "Total Sales" minus "Cost of Goods Sold."

· From the "Measures" section on the middle left side of the canvas, drag "Total Sales," "Cost of Goods Sold," and "Gross Profit" to the Rows shelf.

· Click the "Show Me" box on right side of the toolbar and select the "side-by-side bars."

- Show the labels by clicking on the Label box on the "Marks" card and checking "Show mark labels." Format the labels to Times New Roman, bold, black and 9-point font.
- Change the title of the sheet to be "Total Sales, COGS, and Gross Profit by Region" by right-clicking and selecting "Edit title." Format the title to Times New Roman, bold, black and 15-point font. Change the title of "Sheet 1" to match the sheet title by right-clicking, selecting "Rename" and typing in the new title.
- Format all the labels on the sheet to Times New Roman, 10-point font, and black.
- Click on the New Worksheet tab on the lower left ("Sheet 2" should open).
- Drag "State" from Dimensions to the Columns shelf.
- Drag "Gross Profit" and "Total Sales" to the Rows shelf.
- Create a calculated field "Gross Profit Ratio by State" by dragging "Sum(Gross Profit)" from the Rows shelf and then dividing by "Sum(Total Sales)" from the Rows shelf to calculate an "aggregated" measure for each state.
- Remove "Sum(Total Sales)" from the Rows shelf by dragging it back over to Dimensions.
- In the "Show Me" box on right side of the toolbar, select the "symbol map" and you should see circles appear in states with data. Drag "Gross Profit Ratio by State" from "Measures" to the bottom of the "Marks" card. Click on the circle symbol beside the "Gross Profit Ratio by State" and select "Color." The dots should now vary in size and color based on the size of the gross profit ratio and gross profit. Enlarge the dots by clicking "Size" on the "Marks" card and adjusting the slide. You can also change the color variation by clicking "Color" on the "Marks" card and editing the color.
- Change the title of the sheet to be "Gross Profit Ratio by State" by right-clicking and selecting "Edit title." Format the title to Times New Roman, bold, black and 15-point font. Change the title of "Sheet 2" to match the sheet title by right-clicking, selecting "Rename" and typing in the new title.
- Once complete, save the file as "*DA8_Your initials*.twbx."

Continuing Cases

Target Case

 LO8–1, LO8–4, LO8–7

Target Corporation prepares its financial statements according to U.S. GAAP. Target's financial statements and disclosure notes for the year ended February 3, 2018, are available in Connect. This material is also available under the Investor Relations link at the company's website (www.target.com).

Required:

1. Does Target use average cost, FIFO, or LIFO as its inventory cost flow assumption?
2. In addition to the purchase price, what additional expenditures does the company include in the initial cost of merchandise?
3. Calculate the gross profit ratio and the inventory turnover ratio for the fiscal year ended February 3, 2018. Compare Target's ratios with the industry averages of 24.5% and 7.1 times. Determine whether Target's ratios indicate the company is more/less profitable and sells its inventory more/less frequently compared to the industry average.

Air France–KLM Case

LO8–9

IFRS

Air France–KLM (AF), a Franco-Dutch company, prepares its financial statements according to International Financial Reporting Standards. AF's financial statements and disclosure notes for the year ended December 31, 2017, are available in Connect. This material is also available under the Finance link at the company's website (www.airfranceklm.com).

Required:

What method does the company use to value its inventory? What other alternatives are available under IFRS? Under U.S. GAAP?

CPA Exam Questions and Simulations

Sample CPA Exam questions from Roger CPA Review are available in Connect as support for the topics in this chapter. These multiple-choice questions and task-based simulations include expert-written explanations and solutions, and provide a starting point for students to become familiar with the content and functionality of the actual CPA Exam.

CHAPTER

9

Inventories: Additional Issues

OVERVIEW ———— We covered most of the principal measurement and reporting issues involving the asset inventory and the corresponding expense cost of goods sold in the previous chapter. In this chapter, we complete our discussion of inventory measurement by explaining how inventories are measured at the end of the period. In addition, we investigate inventory estimation techniques, methods of simplifying LIFO, changes in inventory method, and inventory errors.

LEARNING ————
OBJECTIVES

After studying this chapter, you should be able to:

- **LO9–1**   Understand and apply rules for measurement of inventory at the end of the reporting period. (p. 459)

- **LO9–2**   Estimate ending inventory and cost of goods sold using the gross profit method. (p. 467)

- **LO9–3**   Estimate ending inventory and cost of goods sold using the retail inventory method, applying the various cost flow methods. (p. 469)

- **LO9–4**   Explain how the retail inventory method can be made to approximate the lower of cost or market rule. (p. 472)

- **LO9–5**   Determine ending inventory using the dollar-value LIFO retail inventory method. (p. 477)

- **LO9–6**   Explain the appropriate accounting treatment required when a change in inventory method is made. (p. 480)

- **LO9–7**   Explain the appropriate accounting treatment required when an inventory error is discovered. (p. 482)

- **LO9–8**   Discuss the primary differences between U.S. GAAP and IFRS with respect to the lower of cost or net realizable value rule for valuing inventory. (p. 463)

©QualityHD/Shutterstock.com

FINANCIAL REPORTING CASE

Does It Count?

Today you drove over to Dollar General to pick up a few items. You recall from class yesterday that your accounting professor had discussed inventory measurement issues and the different methods (FIFO, LIFO, and average) used by companies to determine ending inventory and cost of goods sold. As of March 2, 2018, Dollar General had 14,609 store locations. You can't imagine actually counting the inventory in all of the stores around the country. You consider that there must be some way Dollar General can avoid counting all of that inventory every time they want to produce financial statements. When you get home, you check their financial statements on the Internet to see what kind of inventory method they use. You find the following in the summary of significant accounting policies included in Dollar General's most recent financial statements:

Merchandise Inventories:

Inventories are stated at the lower of cost or market ("LCM") with cost determined using the retail last-in, first-out ("LIFO") method as this method results in a better matching of costs and revenues. Under the Company's retail inventory method ("RIM"), the calculation of gross profit and the resulting valuation of inventories at cost are computed by applying a calculated cost-to-retail inventory ratio to the retail value of sales at a department level. The use of the RIM will result in valuing inventories at LCM if markdowns are currently taken as a reduction of the retail value of inventories. Costs directly associated with warehousing and distribution are capitalized into inventory.

The excess of current cost over LIFO cost was approximately $78.5 million and $80.7 million at February 2, 2018, and February 3, 2017, respectively. Current cost is determined using the RIM on a first-in, first-out basis. Under the LIFO inventory method, the impacts of rising or falling market price changes increase or decrease cost of sales (the LIFO provision or benefit). The Company recorded a LIFO provision (benefit) of $(2.2) million in 2017, $(12.2) million in 2016, and $(2.3) million in 2015, which is included in cost of goods sold in the consolidated statements of income.

By the time you finish this chapter, you should be able to respond appropriately to the questions posed in this case. Compare your response to the solution provided at the end of the chapter.

QUESTIONS

1. How does Dollar General avoid counting all its inventory every time it produces financial statements? (*p. 477*)

2. What is the index formulation used for? (*p. 477*)

Subsequent Measurement of Inventory

PART A

● LO9–1

As you would expect, companies hope to sell their inventory for more than its cost. Yet, this doesn't always happen. Sometimes circumstances arise after (or *subsequent* to) the purchase or production of inventory that indicate the company will have to sell its inventory for less than its cost. This might happen because of inventory damage, physical deterioration, obsolescence, changes in price levels, or any situation that lessens demand for the inventory. Consider, for example, the value of unsold electronics inventory when the next generation comes out, or the leftover clothing inventory at the end of the selling season. Usually, the only way these items can be sold is at deeply discounted prices (well-below their purchase cost).

GAAP requires that companies evaluate their unsold inventory at the end of each reporting period (for reasons mentioned above). When the expected benefit of unsold inventory is estimated to have fallen below its cost, companies must depart from the cost basis of reporting ending inventory; an adjusting entry is needed to reduce the reported amount of inventory and to reduce net income for the period. This end-of-period adjusting entry is known as an *inventory write-down*.

An inventory write-down has the effect of reducing inventory and reducing net income.

The two measurement approaches for recording an inventory write-down are listed in Illustration 9–1. The approach chosen by a company depends on which inventory costing method the company uses.[1] For companies that use a cost method other than LIFO or the retail inventory method, we report inventory at the *lower of cost or net realizable value.* For companies that use LIFO or the retail inventory method (discussed later in this chapter), we report inventory at the *lower of cost or market.*

Illustration 9–1

Subsequent Inventory Measurement

Measurement Approach	For Companies that Use	Financial Statement Effects of Inventory Write-Downs
1. **Lower of cost or net realizable values (LCNRV)**	FIFO, average cost, or any other method besides LIFO or the retail inventory method	a. Reduce reported inventory b. Reduce net income
2. **Lower of cost or market (LCM)**	LIFO or retail inventory method	a. Reduce reported inventory b. Reduce net income

For both measurement approaches, the financial statement effects of an inventory write-down are the same: (a) reduce reported inventory and (b) reduce net income. Both approaches have the same conceptual purpose of reporting inventory conservatively at the lower of two amounts. The difference between the two approaches is the measurement of the *amount* of the inventory write-down. We discuss those measurements next.[2]

Lower of Cost or Net Realizable Value (LCNRV)

Net realizable value (NRV) is the estimated selling price reduced by any costs of completion, disposal, and transportation.

Companies that use FIFO, average cost, or any other method besides LIFO or the retail inventory method report inventory using the lower of cost or net realizable value (LCNRV) approach. To do this, a company compares the inventory's cost to the inventory's net realizable value (NRV). NRV is the estimated selling price of the inventory in the ordinary course of business reduced by reasonably predictable costs of completion, disposal, and transportation (such as sales commissions and shipping costs).

Another way to think about NRV is that it's the *net* amount a company expects to *realize* (or collect in cash) from the sale of the inventory. Companies often estimate the "costs to sell" by applying a predetermined percentage to the selling price. For example, if the selling price of Product A is $10 per unit, and the company estimates that sales commissions and shipping costs average approximately 10% of selling price, NRV would be $9 [$10 – ($10 × 10%)].

After comparing cost and NRV, a company reports inventory at the lower of the two amounts.

When NRV is lower than cost, an inventory write-down is recorded.

1. If NRV is lower than cost, we need an adjusting entry to reduce inventory from its already recorded purchase cost to the lower NRV. NRV then becomes the new carrying value of inventory reported in the balance sheet.

2. If cost is lower than NRV, no adjusting entry is needed. Inventory already is recorded at cost at the time it was purchased, and this cost is lower than total NRV at the end of the period.

The LCNRV approach avoids reporting inventory at an amount greater than the cash it can provide to the company. Reporting inventories this way causes income to be reduced in the period the value of inventory declines below its cost rather than in the period in which the goods ultimately are sold.[3]

---

[1]FASB ASC 330-10-35-1A through 35-1C: Inventory—Overall—Subsequent Measurement.

[2]Interestingly, the two approaches to subsequent measurement of inventory arose out of *Accounting Standards Update (ASU) No. 2015–11,* which was part of the FASB's Simplification Initiative aimed at *reducing* reporting complexity. However, *ASU 2015–11 increases* the number of subsequent measurement approaches. Prior to *ASU 2015 – 11,* all companies reported inventory using a single approach—the lower of cost or market. Some may argue that the introduction of a second approach increases reporting complexity. Some companies use multiple inventory methods and may need to use both approaches, and financial statement users must be aware of different methods when comparing companies.

[3]In other words, if the inventory was not written down to NRV (and instead remained at cost) at the end of the current period, the full cost amount would become cost of goods sold and thus reduce net income when the inventory is sold in a subsequent period.

Applying Lower of Cost or Net Realizable Value

For financial reporting purposes, LCNRV can be applied (a) to individual inventory items, (b) to major categories of inventory, or (c) to the entire inventory.[4] Illustration 9–2 demonstrates the LCNRV approach with each of the three possible applications.

> The LCNRV rule can be applied to individual inventory items, major inventory categories, or the entire inventory.

Illustration 9–2
Lower of Cost or Net Realizable Value—Application at Different Levels of Aggregation

The Collins Company has five inventory items on hand at the end of the year. The year-end cost (determined by applying the FIFO cost method) and net realizable value (current selling prices less costs of completion, disposal, and transportation) for each of the items are presented below.

Items A and B are a collection of similar items, and items C, D, and E are another collection of similar items. Each collection can be considered a category of inventory.

| | | | Lower of Cost or NRV | | |
| | | | By Individual Items | By Category | By Total Inventory |
Item	Cost	NRV			
A	$ 50,000	$ 85,000	$ 50,000		
B	100,000	90,000	90,000		
Total A and B	$150,000	$175,000		$ 150,000	
C	$ 80,000	$ 75,000	75,000		
D	90,000	85,000	85,000		
E	95,000	96,000	95,000		
Total C, D, and E	$265,000	$256,000		256,000	
Total	$415,000	$431,000	$395,000	$406,000	$415,000

If we first consider LCNRV *by individual items,* we see that cost is lower than NRV for items A and E (see "By Individual Items" column). These inventory items were initially recorded at cost at the time of purchase. So, under the LCNRV approach, they are currently recorded at their proper amounts. No adjustment is needed. However, for items B, C, and D, we see that NRV is below cost. Therefore, we need to adjust the carrying value of these items downward from cost to NRV to report them at NRV in the balance sheet. After determining the lower of cost or NRV for each individual item, the total amount to report for inventory is $395,000.

Now let's see what happens if we apply the LCNRV approach *by inventory category* (see "By Category" column). The first category of inventory (items A and B) has a combined cost of $150,000 and a combined NRV of $175,000, so we report this second inventory group at its cost of $150,000. For the second category (items C, D, and E), the combined NRV ($256,000) is lower than the combined cost ($265,000), so we report this second inventory group at its NRV of $256,000. We report inventory at $406,000 ($150,000 + $256,000).

Finally, if we apply the LCNRV approach *by total inventory,* we see that inventory's total cost ($415,000) is lower than its total NRV ($431,000). Inventory would be reported at its cost of $415,000.

As shown in this illustration, applying the LCNRV rule to groups of inventory items will cause a higher inventory valuation than if applied on an item-by-item basis. The reason is that group application permits increases in the net realizable value of some items to offset decreases in others. Each approach is acceptable but should be applied consistently from one period to another.

---

[4]FASB ASC 330–10–35–8: Inventory—Overall—Subsequent Measurement. In addition, for income tax purposes, the rule must be applied on an individual item basis.

462   SECTION 2   Assets

Ethical Dilemma

The Hartley Company, owned and operated by Bill Hartley, manufactures and sells high-end ergonomic office chairs and custom bookshelves. The company has reported profits in the majority of years since the company's inception in 1975 and is projecting a profit in 2021 of $65,000, down from $96,000 in 2020.

Near the end of 2021, the company is in the process of applying for a bank loan. The loan proceeds will be used to replace manufacturing equipment to modernize the manufacturing operation. In preparing the financial statements for the year, the chief accountant, Don Davis, mentioned to Bill Hartley that net realizable value (NRV) of the bookshelf inventory is below its cost by $40,000 and should be written down in 2021. However, no write-down is necessary for office chairs because their NRV is $50,000 above cost.

Bill is worried that the write-down would lower 2021 net income to a level that might cause the bank to refuse the loan. Without the loan, it would be difficult for the company to compete. This could decrease future business, and employees might have to be laid off. Bill suggests to Don that the company combine the office chairs and bookshelves into a single inventory category (office furniture) for reporting purposes, so that the combined NRV is above the combined cost. In this case, no inventory write-down would be needed. The company has not previously combined these inventory items and has no stated policy on the matter. Don is contemplating his responsibilities in this situation.

Adjusting Cost to Net Realizable Value

When NRV is below cost, companies are required to write down inventory to the lower NRV. These write-downs usually are included as part of cost of goods sold because they are a natural consequence of holding inventory and therefore part of the inventory's normal cost. However, when a write-down is substantial and unusual, the write-down should be recorded in a separate loss account instead. That loss must be expressly disclosed. This could be accomplished with a disclosure note alone or also by reporting the loss as a separate line in the income statement, usually among operating expenses.

Referring back to Illustration 9–2, assume that we report inventory using the LCNRV approach by individual items. The recorded cost of inventory ($415,000) needs to be written down to its NRV ($395,000) at the end of the period. The amount of the reduction is $20,000. The period-end adjusting entry for the typical occurrence of decline to net realizable value would be the following:

Inventory	
415,000	
	20,000
395,000	

Cost of goods sold*	20,000	
Inventory		20,000

*In situations when a write-down is substantial and unusual, the write-down should be recorded in a loss on inventory write-down account.

After the adjustment from original cost to net realizable value, the reduced inventory amount becomes the new cost basis for subsequent reporting. If the inventory value later increases prior to its sale, we do not write it back up.[5]

---

[5]The SEC, in *Staff Accounting Bulletin No. 100,* "Restructuring and Impairment Charges" (Washington, D.C.: SEC, November, 1999), paragraph B.B., (FASB ASC 330–10–S35–1: SAB Topic 5.BB), reaffirmed the provisions of GAAP literature on this issue. For interim reporting purposes, however, recoveries of losses on the same inventory in subsequent interim periods of the same fiscal year through market price recoveries should be recognized as gains in the later interim period, not to exceed the previously recognized losses.

International Financial Reporting Standards

Lower of cost or net realizable value. You just learned that in the United States some companies report inventory at the *lower of cost or net realizable value*. This is the same approach used under IFRS. However, there are some differences between U.S. GAAP and IFRS in the application of lower of cost or net realizable value.

● LO9–8

First, *IAS No. 2* specifies that if circumstances indicate that an inventory write-down is no longer appropriate, it must be reversed.[6] Reversals are not permitted under U.S. GAAP.

Second, under U.S. GAAP, the lower of cost or net realizable value rule can be applied to individual items, inventory categories, or the entire inventory. Under the international standard, the assessment usually is applied to individual items, although using inventory categories is allowed under certain circumstances.

Siemens AG, a German electronics and electrical engineering company, prepares its financial statements according to IFRS. The following disclosure note illustrates the valuation of inventory at the lower of cost or net realizable value.

Inventories (in part)
Inventory is valued at the lower of acquisition or production cost and net realizable value, cost being generally determined on the basis of an average or first-in, first-out method.

Concept Review Exercise

LOWER OF COST OR NET REALIZABLE VALUE

The Strand Company sells four products that can be grouped into two major categories and employs the FIFO cost method. Information needed to apply the lower of cost or NRV (LCNRV) rule on December 31, 2021 (end of the period), for each of the four products is presented below. Sales commissions and transportation costs average 10% of selling price. Inventory write-downs are a normal occurrence for Strand.

Product	Quantity	Unit Cost	Unit Selling Price	Total Cost	Total Selling Price
101	4,000	$30	$40	$120,000	$160,000
102	5,000	35	36	175,000	180,000
201	3,200	50	50	160,000	160,000
202	15,000	3	4	45,000	60,000

Products 101 and 102 are in category A, and products 201 and 202 are in category B.

Required:
Determine the reported amount of ending inventory and record any necessary year-end adjusting entry to write down inventory, applying the LCNRV approach to the following:
1. Individual items
2. Major categories
3. Total inventory

Solution:
Determine the reported amount of ending inventory and record any necessary year-end adjusting entry to write down inventory, applying the LCNRV approach.

---

[6]"Inventories," *International Accounting Standard No. 2* (IASCF), as amended effective January 1, 2018.

			Lower of Cost or NRV		
Product	Cost	NRV*	By Individual Products	By Category	By Total Inventory
101	$120,000	$144,000	$120,000		
102	175,000	162,000	162,000		
Total 101 + 102	$295,000	$306,000		$295,000	
201	$160,000	$144,000	144,000		
202	45,000	54,000	45,000		
Total 201 + 202	$205,000	$198,000		198,000	
Total	$500,000	$504,000	$471,000	$493,000	$500,000

*NRV = Selling price less costs to sell. For product 101, $160,000 − ($160,000 × 10%) = $ 144, 000..

The NRV for both the individual product and category applications are lower than cost so inventory write-downs are needed. On the other hand, cost is lower than NRV at the total inventory level, so no adjustment would be needed.

1. Individual items

Reported ending inventory = $471,000 (NRV)

December 31, 2021		
Cost of goods sold†	29,000*	
Inventory		29,000
*$500,000 (recorded cost) − $471,000 (NRV)		

2. Major categories

Reported ending inventory = $493,000 (NRV)

December 31, 2021		
Cost of goods sold†	7,000*	
Inventory		7,000
†$500,000 (recorded cost) − $493,000 (NRV)		

†For the two entries above, we record the adjustment to the cost of goods sold account because the inventory write-down is considered usual. If the write-down had been substantial and unusual, we record the adjustment to a loss on inventory write-down account.

3. Total inventory

Reported ending inventory = $500,000 (Cost)
Because inventory already is recorded at cost as of December 31, 2021, and because total cost is lower than total NRV ($504,000), no year-end adjustment is needed.

Additional Consideration

Critics of reporting inventory lower than its cost contend that this causes losses to be recognized that haven't actually occurred. Others maintain that it introduces needless inconsistency in order to be conservative, because decreases in value are recognized as they occur, but not increases. As you learned in Chapter 1, conservatism is not part of the conceptual framework. So, why not record increases as well? Recall the revenue recognition guidance we discussed in Chapter 6. Recognizing increases in the value of inventory prior to sale would, in most cases, result in premature revenue recognition, because the seller would be acting as if it had satisfied a performance obligation (selling inventory) before that actually occurred. For example, let's say that merchandise costing $100 now has a net realizable value of $150. Recognizing a gain for the increase in value would increase pretax income by $50. This is equivalent to recognizing revenue of $150, cost of goods sold of $100, and gross profit of $50. The effect is to increase pretax income in a period prior to sale of the product. That's not allowed.

Lower of Cost or Market (LCM)

Companies that use LIFO or the retail inventory method report inventory using the lower of cost or market (LCM) approach. You might interpret the term *market* to mean the amount that could be realized if the inventory were sold. This would be similar to the concept of *net realizable value* discussed above. However, market is defined differently.

Market is the inventory's current replacement cost (by purchase or reproduction) except that:

1. Market should not be greater than the net realizable value (this forms a "ceiling" on market), and
2. Market should not be less than net realizable value reduced by an allowance for an approximately normal profit margin (this forms a "floor" on market).

In effect, we have a ceiling and a floor between which market (that is, replacement cost) must fall. If replacement cost is between the ceiling and the floor, it represents market; if replacement cost is above the ceiling or below the floor, the ceiling or the floor becomes market. The designated market amount is compared with cost, and the lower of the two is used to value inventory.

To see an example, let's look at Illustration 9–3. In the top part of the illustration, we calculate the ceiling and the floor. In the bottom part, we calculate LCM.

Market is current replacement cost, but not above the ceiling or below the floor.

Illustration 9–3

Lower of Cost or Market (LCM)

The Collins Company has five inventory items on hand at the end of the year. The year-end selling prices, and estimated costs of completion, disposal, and transportation (selling costs) for each of the items are given below. The normal profit for each of the products is 20% of selling price. These amounts are used to calculate the ceiling and floor as follows:

Item	Selling Price	Estimated Selling Costs	NRV [Ceiling]*	Normal Profit Margin (20% of Selling Price)	NRV – NPM [Floor]†
A	$100,000	$15,000	$85,000	$20,000	$65,000
B	120,000	30,000	90,000	24,000	66,000
C	90,000	15,000	75,000	18,000	57,000
D	100,000	15,000	85,000	20,000	65,000
E	110,000	14,000	96,000	22,000	74,000

Additional information related to year-end inventory cost (determined by applying the LIFO cost method) and replacement cost are given in the first two columns. Determination of LCM is a two-step process: (1) calculate the market amount using replacement cost, subject to a ceiling and floor, and (2) select the lower of cost or market.

	(1)	(2)	(3)	(4)	(5)	
			Market			
Item	Cost	Replacement Cost	NRV [Ceiling]	NRV – NPM [Floor]	Market [Middle of (2), (3), (4)]	LCM [Lower of (1) or (5)]
A	$ 50,000	$55,000	$85,000	$65,000	$65,000	$ 50,000
B	100,000	97,000	90,000	66,000	90,000	90,000
C	80,000	70,000	75,000	57,000	70,000	70,000
D	90,000	95,000	85,000	65,000	85,000	85,000
E	95,000	92,000	96,000	74,000	92,000	92,000
Total	$415,000					$387,000

*NRV = Estimated selling price less estimated selling costs. For item A, $100,000 − $15,000 = $85,000.
†NRV − NPM = NRV less a normal profit margin. For item A, $85,000 − ($100,000 selling price × 20%) = $65,000.

Notice the market amount for each inventory item is simply the middle value among replacement cost, NRV (ceiling), and NRV – NPM (floor). When replacement cost is

a. *Below the floor* (item A), we select the floor as the market.
b. *Above the ceiling* (items B and D), we select the ceiling as the market.
c. *Between the ceiling and the floor* (items C and E), we select replacement cost as the market.

We then compare each item's designated market amount to its cost and choose the lower of the two. After doing this, ending inventory under LCM is $387,000. This means that the recorded cost of $415,000 needs to be reduced by $28,000 ($415,000 – $387,000). We record that adjustment to cost of goods sold if the decrease to market is considered normal for this company.

Inventory	
415,000	
	28,000
387,000	

Cost of goods sold*	28,000	
Inventory..		28,000

*In situations when a write-down is substantial and unusual, the write-down should be recorded in a loss on inventory write-down account.

The example in Illustration 9–3 calculates LCM on an individual items basis. The LCM method also can be applied to major categories of inventory or to the entire inventory, just like we saw in Illustration 9–2 under the LCNRV approach. As shown in Illustration 9–3A, inventory using the LCM approach applied *by category* would be reported as $397,000. If we calculate LCM *by total inventory,* the amount to report for ending inventory would be $402,000.

Illustration 9–3A

Lower of Cost or Market—Application at Different Levels of Aggregation

From the information in Illustration 9–3, also assume items A and B are a collection of similar items, and items C, D, and E are another collection of similar items. Each collection can be considered a category of inventory.

			Lower of Cost or Market		
Item	Cost	Market	By Individual Items	By Category	By Total Inventory
A	$ 50,000	$ 65,000	$ 50,000		
B	100,000	90,000	90,000		
Total A and B	$150,000	$155,000		$ 150,000	
C	$ 80,000	$ 70,000	70,000		
D	90,000	85,000	85,000		
E	95,000	92,000	92,000		
Total C, D, and E	$265,000	$247,000		247,000	
Total	$415,000	$402,000	$387,000	$397,000	$402,000

PART B

Inventory Estimation Techniques

For some companies or in certain situations, it becomes difficult or impossible to physically count each unit of inventory. For example, consider a large retail company that has locations over the entire nation and sells many different items. Trying to track the cost of each item would be nearly impossible. In these situations, companies have developed methods for estimating inventory. We'll study those methods next.

The Gross Profit Method

The gross profit method, also known as the gross margin method, is useful in situations where estimates of inventory are desirable. The technique is valuable in a variety of situations, including the following:

○ LO9–2

1. In determining the cost of inventory that has been lost, destroyed, or stolen.
2. In estimating inventory and cost of goods sold for interim reports, avoiding the expense of a physical inventory count.
3. In auditors' testing of the overall reasonableness of inventory amounts reported by clients.
4. In budgeting and forecasting.

The technique relies on a relationship you learned in the previous chapter—ending inventory and cost of goods sold always equal the cost of goods available for sale. Even when inventory is unknown, we can estimate it because accounting records usually indicate the cost of goods available for sale (beginning inventory plus net purchases), and the cost of goods sold can be estimated from available information. So by subtracting the cost of goods sold estimate from the cost of goods available for sale, we obtain an estimate of ending inventory. Let's compare that with the way inventory and cost of goods sold normally are determined.

Usually, in a periodic inventory system, ending inventory is known from a physical count and cost of goods sold is *derived* as follows:

Beginning inventory	(from the accounting records)
Plus: Net purchases	(from the accounting records)
Goods available for sale	
Less: Ending inventory	(from a physical count)
Cost of goods sold	

However, when using the gross profit method, the ending inventory is *not* known. Instead, the amount of sales is known—from which we can estimate the cost of goods sold—and ending inventory is the amount calculated.

Beginning inventory	(from the accounting records)
Plus: Net purchases	(from the accounting records)
Goods available for sale	
Less: Cost of goods sold	(estimated)
Ending inventory	(estimated)

So, a first step in estimating inventory is to estimate cost of goods sold. This estimate relies on the historical relationship among (a) net sales, (b) cost of goods sold, and (c) gross profit. Gross profit, you will recall, is simply net sales minus cost of goods sold. So, if we know what net sales are, and if we know what percentage of net sales the gross profit is, we can fairly accurately estimate cost of goods sold. Companies often sell products that have similar gross profit ratios. As a result, accounting records usually provide the information necessary to estimate the cost of ending inventory, even when a physical count is impractical.

Suppose a company began 2021 with inventory of $600,000, and on March 17 a warehouse fire destroyed the entire inventory. Company records indicate net purchases of $1,500,000 and net sales of $2,000,000 prior to the fire. The gross profit ratio in each of the previous three years has been very close to 40%. Illustration 9–4 shows how the company can estimate the cost of the inventory destroyed for its insurance claim.

A Word of Caution

The gross profit method provides only an estimate. The key to obtaining good estimates is the reliability of the gross profit ratio. The ratio usually is estimated from relationships between sales and cost of goods sold. However, the current relationship may differ from the past. In that case, all available information should be used to make necessary adjustments. For example, the company may have made changes in the markup percentage of some of its

The key to obtaining good estimates is the reliability of the gross profit ratio.

Illustration 9–4

Gross Profit Method

Beginning inventory (from records)		$ 600,000
Plus: Net purchases (from records)		1,500,000
Goods available for sale		2,100,000
Less: Cost of goods sold:		
Net sales	$2,000,000	
Less: Estimated gross profit of 40%	(800,000)	
Estimated cost of goods sold*		(1,200,000)
Estimated ending inventory		$ 900,000

*Alternatively, cost of goods sold can be calculated as $2,000,000 × (1 − 0.40) = $1,200,000.

products. Very often different products have different markups. In these situations, a blanket ratio should not be applied across the board. The accuracy of the estimate can be improved by grouping inventory into pools of products that have similar gross profit relationships rather than using one gross profit ratio for the entire inventory.

The company's cost flow assumption should be implicitly considered when estimating the gross profit ratio. For example, if LIFO is used and the relationship between cost and selling price has changed for recent acquisitions, this would suggest a ratio different from one where the average cost method was used.

Another difficulty with the gross profit method is that it does not explicitly consider possible theft or spoilage of inventory. The method assumes that if the inventory was not sold, then it must be on hand at the end of the period. Suspected theft or spoilage would require an adjustment to estimates obtained using the gross profit method.

The gross profit method is not acceptable for the preparation of annual financial statements.

Because of these deficiencies, the gross profit method is not allowed under generally accepted accounting principles for annual financial statements. The method can be used for interim reports.

Additional Consideration

The gross profit ratio is, by definition, a percentage of sales. Sometimes, though, the gross profit is stated as a percentage of cost instead. In that case, it is referred to as the markup on cost. For instance, a 66⅔% markup on cost is equivalent to a gross profit ratio of 40%. Here's why:

A gross profit ratio of 40% can be formulated as follows:

$$\text{Sales} = \text{Cost} + \text{Gross profit}$$
$$100\% = 60\% + 40\%$$

Now, expressing gross profit as a percentage of cost we get the following:

$$\text{Gross profit \%} \div \text{Cost\%} = \text{Gross profit as a \% of cost}$$
$$40\% \div 60\% = 66\tfrac{2}{3}\%$$

Conversely, gross profit as a percentage of cost can be converted to gross profit as a percentage of sales (the gross profit ratio) as follows:

$$\text{Gross profit as a \% of sales} = \frac{\text{Gross profit as a \% of cost}}{1 + \text{Gross profit as a \% of cost}}$$

$$\frac{66\tfrac{2}{3}\%}{1 + 66\tfrac{2}{3}\%} = 40\%$$

Be careful to note which way the percentage is being stated. If stated as a markup on cost, it can be converted to the gross profit ratio, and the gross profit method can be applied the usual way.

The Retail Inventory Method

As the name implies, the retail inventory method is used by many retail companies such as Target, Walmart, Sears Holding Corporation, J.C. Penney, and Macy's. Certain retailers like auto dealers and jewelry stores, whose inventory consists of few, high-priced items, can economically use the specific identification inventory method. However, high-volume retailers selling many different items at low unit prices find the retail inventory method ideal. Its principal benefit is that a physical count of inventory is not required to estimate ending inventory and cost of goods sold.[7]

● LO9–3

The retail inventory method is used to estimate ending inventory and cost of goods sold.

In its simplest form, the retail inventory method first estimates the amount of ending inventory (at retail) by subtracting sales (at retail) from goods available for sale (at retail). *Retail* amounts refer to current selling prices. Ending inventory (at retail) is then multiplied by the current cost-to-retail percentage to estimate ending inventory (at cost). The cost-to-retail percentage is found by dividing goods available for sale at *cost* by goods available for sale at *current selling price*.

Illustration 9–5 provides an example of the retail inventory method. It shows how Home Improvement Stores, Inc., can use the relation between its inventory's cost and retail to estimate ending inventory and cost of goods sold for the month of June.

Illustration 9–5

Retail Inventory Method—Estimating ending inventory and cost of goods sold

Home Improvement Stores, Inc., uses a periodic inventory system and the retail inventory method to estimate ending inventory and cost of goods sold. The following data are available from the company's records for the month of June:

	Cost	Retail
Beginning inventory	$ 60,000	$ 100,000
Plus: Net purchases	287,200	460,000
Goods available for sale	347,200	560,000
Cost-to-retail percentage: $\frac{\$347,200}{\$560,000} = 62\%$		
Less: Net sales		(400,000)
Estimated ending inventory at retail		$160,000
Estimated ending inventory at cost ($160,000 × 62%)	**(99,200)**	
Estimated cost of goods sold	**$248,000***	

*Goods available for sale (at cost) minus ending inventory (at cost).

Home Improvement Stores first estimates ending inventory at retail ($160,000) by subtracting net sales from goods available for sale (at retail). Ending inventory at retail is multiplied by the cost-to-retail percentage (62%), which is found by dividing goods available for sale at *cost* by goods available for sale at *current selling price*. This multiplication leads to an estimate of ending inventory of $99,200. This amount is subtracted from the cost of goods available for sale to estimate cost of goods sold of $248,000.

The retail inventory method tends to provide a more accurate estimate than the gross profit method because it's based on the current relation between cost and selling prices rather than the historical gross profit ratio. This is one reason the retail inventory method is allowed for financial reporting purposes.

Another advantage of the retail inventory method is that different cost flow methods can be explicitly incorporated into the estimation technique. In other words, we can modify the application of the method to estimate ending inventory and cost of goods sold using FIFO, LIFO, or average cost.

As shown in Illustration 9–6, American Eagle Outfitters uses the retail inventory method with average cost to value its inventory.

---

[7]The retail inventory method is acceptable for external financial reporting if the results of applying the method are sufficiently close to what would have been achieved using a more rigorous determination of the cost of ending inventory. Also, it's allowed by the Internal Revenue Service as a method that can be used to determine cost of goods sold for income tax purposes.

Illustration 9–6

Inventory Method
Disclosure—American
Eagle Outfitters

Real World Financials

> **Summary of Significant Accounting Policies (in part)**
>
> *Merchandise Inventory*
>
> Merchandise inventory is valued at the lower of average cost or market, utilizing the retail method.
>
> Source: American Eagle Outfitters

Later in the chapter we illustrate average cost and LIFO with the retail inventory method. We do not illustrate the FIFO method with the retail inventory method because it is used infrequently in practice.

Like the gross profit method, the retail inventory method also can be used to estimate the cost of inventory lost, stolen, or destroyed; for testing the overall reasonableness of physical counts; in budgeting and forecasting as well as in generating information for interim financial statements. Even though the retail method provides fairly accurate estimates, a physical count of inventory usually is performed at least once a year to verify accuracy and detect spoilage, theft, and other irregularities.[8]

Retail Terminology

Changes in the selling prices must be included in the determination of ending inventory at retail.

Our example above is simplified in that we implicitly assumed that the selling prices of beginning inventory and of merchandise purchased did not change from date of acquisition to the end of the period. This frequently is an unrealistic assumption. After the initial markup of inventory but before it has been sold, companies sometimes increase the selling price further (additional markup) or reduce the selling price (markdown). For applying the retail inventory method, we need to track the movement in the selling price until it is sold. The terms in Illustration 9–7 are associated with changing retail prices of merchandise inventory.

Illustration 9–7

Terminology Used in
Applying the Retail Method

Initial markup	Original amount of markup from cost to selling price.
Additional markup	Increase in selling price subsequent to initial markup.
Markup cancellation	Elimination of an additional markup.
Markdown	Reduction in selling price below the original selling price.
Markdown cancellation	Elimination of a markdown.

To illustrate, assume that a product purchased for $6 is initially listed with a selling price of $10 (that is, there is a $4 initial markup). If the selling price is subsequently increased to $12, the additional markup is $2. If the selling price is then subsequently decreased to $10.50, the markup cancellation is $1.50. A markup cancellation reduces an additional markup but not below the original selling price. We refer to the net effect of additional markups and markup cancellations ($2.00 – $1.50 = $0.50) as the net markup. Illustration 9–8A depicts these events.

Now, let's say the selling price of the product, purchased for $6 and initially marked up to $10, is reduced to $7. The markdown is $3. If the selling price is later increased to $8, the markdown cancellation is $1. A markdown cancellation reduces a markdown but not above the original selling price. We refer to the net effect of markdowns and markdown cancellations ($3 – $1 = $2) as the net markdown. Illustration 9–8B depicts this possibility.

Net markups and net markdowns are included in the retail column to determine ending inventory at retail.

When applying the retail inventory method, *net markups and net markdowns must be included in the determination of ending inventory at retail.* We now continue our illustration of the retail inventory method, but expand it to incorporate markups and markdowns as well as to approximate cost by each of the alternative inventory cost flow methods.

---

[8]The retail inventory method also is allowable under IFRS. *"Inventories," International Accounting Standard No. 2 (IASCF),* as amended effective January 1, 2018, par. 22.

Illustration 9–8A

Retail Inventory Method
Terminology

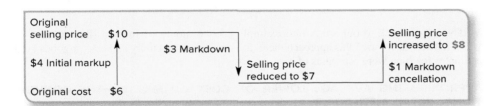

Illustration 9–8B

Retail Inventory Method
Terminology

Cost Flow Methods

Let's continue our example of Home Improvement Stores, Inc., from Illustration 9–5. We'll use the data in Illustration 9–9 to see how the retail inventory method can be used to approximate different cost flow assumptions.

Home Improvement Stores, Inc., uses a periodic inventory system and the retail inventory method to estimate ending inventory and cost of goods sold. The following data are available from the company's records for the month of July:

	Cost	Retail
Beginning inventory	$ 99,200	$ 160,000
Net purchases	305,280*	470,000**
Net markups		10,000
Net markdowns		8,000
Net sales		434,000†

*Purchases at cost less returns, plus freight-in.
**Original selling price of purchased goods less returns at retail.
†Gross sales less returns.

Illustration 9–9

The Retail Inventory
Method—Various Cost Flow
Methods

APPROXIMATING AVERAGE COST Recall that the average cost method assumes that cost of goods sold and ending inventory each consist of a *mixture* of all the goods available for sale. So when we use the retail method to approximate average cost, the cost-to-retail percentage should be based on the weighted averages of the costs and retail amounts for *all* goods available for sale. This is achieved by calculating the cost-to-retail percentage by dividing the total cost of goods available for sale by total goods available for sale at retail. When this average percentage is applied to ending inventory at retail, we get an estimate of ending inventory at average cost.

We demonstrate the retail inventory method approximating average costs for July in Illustration 9–10. Notice that both markups and markdowns are included in the determination of goods available for sale at retail.

To approximate average cost, the cost-to-retail percentage is determined for all goods available for sale.

472   SECTION 2   Assets

Illustration 9–10

Retail Inventory Method—
Average Cost

	Cost	Retail
Beginning inventory	$ 99,200	$ 160,000
Plus: Net purchases	305,280	470,000
Net markups		10,000
Less: Net markdowns		(8,000)
Goods available for sale	404,480	632,000
Cost-to-retail percentage: $\frac{\$404,480}{\$632,000} = 64\%$		
Less: Net sales		(434,000)
Estimated ending inventory at retail		$198,000
Estimated ending inventory at cost ($198,000 × 64%)	**(126,720)**	
Estimated cost of goods sold	**$ 277,760**	

If you look back to our simplified example for the month of June in Illustration 9–5, you'll notice that we used this approach there. So, our ending inventory and cost-of-goods-sold estimates for June were estimates of average cost.[9]

● LO9–4   **APPROXIMATING AVERAGE LOWER OF COST OR MARKET—THE CONVEN-TIONAL RETAIL METHOD**   Recall from our discussion earlier in the chapter that companies using the retail inventory method report inventory in the balance sheet at the lower of cost or market. Fortunately, we can apply the retail inventory method in such a way that the lower of average cost or market is approximated. This method often is referred to as the **conventional retail method**. We apply the method by *excluding markdowns from the calculation of the cost-to-retail percentage*. Markdowns still are subtracted in the retail column but only after the percentage is calculated. To approximate lower of average cost or market, the retail method is modified as shown in Illustration 9–11.

To approximate the lower of average cost or market, markdowns are not included in the calculation of the cost-to-retail percentage.

Illustration 9–11

Retail Inventory
Method—Conventional

	Cost	Retail
Beginning inventory	$ 99,200	$ 160,000
Plus: Net purchases	305,280	470,000
Net markups		10,000
Goods available for sale (excluding net markdowns)	404,480	640,000
Cost-to-retail percentage: $\frac{\$404,480}{\$640,000} = 63.2\%$		
Less: Net markdowns		(8,000)
Goods available for sale (including net markdowns)		632,000
Less: Net sales		(434,000)
Estimated ending inventory at retail		$198,000
Estimated ending inventory at cost ($198,000 × 63.2%)	**(125,136)**	
Estimated cost of goods sold	**$ 279,344**	

Notice that by not subtracting net markdowns from the denominator, the cost-to-retail percentage is lower than it was previously (63.2% versus 64%). This always will be the case when markdowns exist. As a result, the cost approximation of ending inventory always will be less when markdowns exist.

The logic for using this approximation is that a markdown is evidence of a reduction in the utility of inventory.

To understand why this lower amount approximates the lower of average cost or market, we need to realize that markdowns usually occur when obsolescence, spoilage, overstocking, price declines, or competition has lessened the utility of the merchandise. To recognize this decline in utility in the period it occurs, we exclude net markdowns from the calculation

---

[9]We also implicitly assumed no net markups or markdowns in Illustration 9–5.

of the cost-to-retail percentage. It should be emphasized that this approach provides only an *approximation* of what ending inventory might be as opposed to applying the lower of cost or market rule in the more exact way described earlier in the chapter.

Also notice that the ending inventory at retail is the same using both approaches ($198,000). This will be the case regardless of the cost flow method used because in all approaches this amount reflects the ending inventory at current retail prices.

The conventional retail variation generally is not used in combination with LIFO. This does not mean that a company using LIFO ignores the lower of cost or market rule. Any obsolete or slow-moving inventory that has not been marked down by year-end can be written down to market after the estimation of inventory using the retail method. This usually is not a significant problem. If prices are rising, LIFO ending inventory includes old lower-priced items whose costs are likely to be lower than current market. The conventional retail variation could be applied to the FIFO method.

THE LIFO RETAIL METHOD   The last-in, first-out (LIFO) method assumes that units sold are those most recently acquired. When there's a net increase in inventory quantity during a period, the use of LIFO results in ending inventory that includes the beginning inventory as well as one or more additional layers added during the period. When there's a net decrease in inventory quantity, LIFO layer(s) are liquidated. In applying LIFO to the retail method in the simplest way, we assume that the retail prices of goods remained stable during the period. This assumption, which is relaxed later in the chapter, allows us to look at the beginning and ending inventory in dollars to determine if inventory quantity has increased or decreased.

We'll use the numbers from our previous example to illustrate using the retail method to approximate LIFO so we can compare the results with those of the conventional retail method. Recall that beginning inventory at retail is $160,000 and ending inventory at retail is $198,000. If we assume stable retail prices, inventory quantity must have increased during the year. This means ending inventory includes the beginning inventory layer of $160,000 ($99,200 at cost) as well as some additional merchandise purchased during the period. To estimate total ending inventory at LIFO cost, we also need to determine the inventory layer added during the period. When using the LIFO retail method, we assume no more than one inventory layer is added per period if inventory increases.[10] Each layer will carry its own cost-to-retail percentage.

If inventory at retail increases during the year, a new layer is added.

Illustration 9–12 shows how Home Improvement Stores would estimate total ending inventory and cost of goods sold for the period using the LIFO retail method. The beginning inventory layer carries a cost-to-retail percentage of 62% ($99,200 ÷ $160,000). The layer of inventory added during the period is $38,000 at retail, which is determined by subtracting beginning inventory at retail from ending inventory at retail ($198,000 – $160,000). This layer will be converted to cost by multiplying it by its own cost-to-retail percentage reflecting the *current* period's ratio of cost to retail amounts, in this case 64.68%.

The next period's (August's) beginning inventory will include the two distinct layers (June and July), each of which carries its own unique cost-to-retail percentage. Notice in the illustration that both net markups and net markdowns are included in the calculation of the current period's cost-to-retail percentage.

Other Issues Pertaining to the Retail Method

To focus on the key elements of the retail method, we've so far ignored some of the details of the retail process. Fundamental elements such as returns and allowances, discounts, freight, spoilage, and shortages can complicate the retail method.

For calculating the cost-to-retail percentage, we use the cost of net purchases in the cost amount (numerator). Recall that net purchases is found by adding freight-in to purchases and subtracting both purchase returns and purchase discounts. This means that freight-in adds to the cost amount, while purchase returns and purchase discounts reduce the cost amount. For the retail amount (denominator), we calculate net purchases as total purchases (at retail) minus purchase returns (at retail). We subtract purchase returns for the simple reason that these items are no longer available for sale. We do not include freight-in and

---

[10]Of course, any number of layers at different costs can actually be added through the years. When using the regular LIFO method, rather than LIFO retail, we would keep track of each of those layers.

Illustration 9–12
LIFO Retail Method

	Cost	Retail
Beginning inventory	$ 99,200	$160,000
Plus: Net purchases	305,280	470,000
Net markups		10,000
Less: Net markdowns		(8,000)
Goods available for sale (excluding beginning inventory)	305,280	472,000
Goods available for sale (including beginning inventory)	404,480	632,000

Beginning inventory cost-to-retail percentage: $\dfrac{\$99,200}{\$160,000} = 62.00\%$

July cost-to-retail percentage: $\dfrac{\$305,280}{\$472,000} = 64.68\%$

Less: Net sales		(434,000)
Estimated ending inventory at retail		$198,000
Estimated ending inventory at cost (calculated below)	(123,778)	
Estimated cost of goods sold	$280,702	

Calculation of ending inventory at cost:

	Retail		Cost
Beginning inventory	$160,000 × 62.00%	=	$ 99,200
Current period's layer	38,000 × 64.68%	=	24,578
Estimated ending Inventory	$198,000		**$123,778**

Each layer has its own cost-to-retail percentage.

purchase discounts in the calculation of net purchases for the retail amount because these are not items to be sold and therefore have no corresponding retail amounts.

After calculating the cost-to-retail percentage, we deduct net sales from goods available for sale (at retail). Net sales, for purposes of applying the retail inventory method, include *sales returns* but exclude *sales discounts* and *employee discounts*.

Net sales, for purposes of applying the retail inventory method, include sales returns but exclude sales discounts and employee discounts.

- Sales returns are subtracted from total sales because they represent inventory that has not been sold and therefore should not be included in the sales (or retail) amount.

- Sales discounts are not subtracted in calculating net sales because they do not represent an adjustment in selling prices but instead represent a financial incentive for customers to pay early. If sales initially were recorded net of sales discounts, those discounts are added back in calculating net sales.

- Employee discounts are not included in calculating net sales. The reason is that the cost-to-retail percentage did not include employee discounts, so the retail amount of ending inventory also should not be affected by employee discounts in estimating its cost. If sales to employees initially were recorded net of the employee-discounts, those discounts are added back in calculating net sales.

We also need to consider spoilage, breakage, and theft. So far we've assumed that by subtracting goods sold from goods available for sale, we find ending inventory. It's possible, though, that some of the goods available for sale were lost to such shortages and therefore do not remain in ending inventory.

Normal shortages are deducted in the retail column after the calculation of the cost-to-retail percentage.

Abnormal shortages are deducted in both the cost and retail columns before the calculation of the cost-to-retail percentage.

To take these shortages into account when using the retail method, we deduct the retail value of inventory lost due to spoilage, breakage, or theft in the retail column. These losses are expected for most retail ventures so they are referred to as *normal shortages* (spoilage, breakage, etc.), and are deducted from goods available for sale (at retail). Because these losses are anticipated, they are included implicitly in the determination of selling prices. Including normal spoilage in the calculation of the percentage would distort the normal relationship between cost and retail. In contrast, *abnormal shortages* are deducted from both the cost and retail amounts used to calculate the cost-to-retail percentage. These losses are not anticipated and are not included in the determination of selling prices.

We recap the treatment of special elements in the application of the retail method in Illustration 9–13 and illustrate the use of some of them in the concept review exercise that follows.

Illustration 9–13 Recap of Other Retail Method Elements

Element	Treatment
For calculating the cost-to-retail percentage:	
Freight-in	*Added* to the cost amount.
Purchase returns	*Deducted* from both the cost and retail amounts.
Purchase discounts taken (if gross method used to record purchases)	*Deducted* from the cost amount.
Abnormal shortages (spoilage, breakage, theft)	*Deducted* from both the cost and retail amounts.
After calculating the cost-to-retail percentage:	
Net sales (Total sales less sales returns)*	*Deducted* from goods available for sale (at retail).
Normal shortages (spoilage, breakage, theft)	*Deducted* from goods available for sale (at retail).

*The calculation of net sales for the retail inventory method does not include sales discounts or employee discounts.

Concept Review Exercise

The Henderson Company uses the retail inventory method to estimate ending inventory and cost of goods sold. The following data are available in Henderson's accounting records:

RETAIL INVENTORY METHOD

	Cost	Retail
Beginning inventory	$ 8,000	$12,000
Purchases	68,000	98,000
Freight-in	3,200	
Purchase returns	3,000	4,200
Net markups		6,000
Net markdowns		2,400
Normal spoilage		1,800
Sales		97,000
Sales returns		5,000
Employee discounts		2,300

Sales of $97,000 include a reduction for employee discounts of $2,300.

Required:

1. Estimate Henderson's ending inventory and cost of goods sold for the year using the average cost retail method.
2. Estimate Henderson's ending inventory and cost of goods sold for the year using the conventional retail method.
3. Estimate Henderson's ending inventory and cost of goods sold for the year using the LIFO retail method.

Solution:

1. Estimate Henderson's ending inventory and cost of goods sold for the year using the average cost retail method.

	Cost	Retail
Beginning inventory	$ 8,000	$ 12,000
Plus: Purchases	68,000	98,000
Freight-in	3,200	
Less: Purchase returns	(3,000)	(4,200)
Plus: Net markups		6,000
Less: Net markdowns		(2,400)
Goods available for sale	76,200	109,400

Cost-to-retail percentage: $\dfrac{\$76,200}{\$109,400} = 69.65\%$

(continued)

	Cost	Retail
Less: Normal spoilage		(1,800)
Less: Net sales		
Sales	$97,000	
Employee discounts	2,300	
Sales returns	(5,000)	(94,300)
Estimated ending inventory at retail		$ 13,300
Estimated ending inventory at cost (69.65% × $13,300)	(9,263)	
Estimated cost of goods sold	$66,937	

2. Estimate Henderson's ending inventory and cost of goods sold for the year using the conventional retail method.

	Cost	Retail
Beginning inventory	$ 8,000	$ 12,000
Plus: Purchases	68,000	98,000
Freight-in	3,200	
Less: Purchase returns	(3,000)	(4,200)
Plus: Net markups		6,000
		111,800

Cost-to-retail percentage: $\frac{\$76,200}{\$111,800} = 68.16\%$

	Cost	Retail
Less: Net markdowns		(2,400)
Goods available for sale	76,200	109,400
Less: Normal spoilage		(1,800)
Less: Net sales:		
Sales	$97,000	
Employee discounts	2,300	
Sales returns	(5,000)	(94,300)
Estimated ending inventory at retail		$ 13,300
Estimated ending inventory at cost (68.16% × $13,300)	(9,065)	
Estimated cost of goods sold	$67,135	

3. Estimate Henderson's ending inventory and cost of goods sold for the year using the LIFO retail method.

	Cost	Retail
Beginning inventory	$ 8,000	$ 12,000
Plus: Purchases	68,000	98,000
Freight-in	3,200	
Less: Purchase returns	(3,000)	(4,200)
Plus: Net markups		6,000
Less: Net markdowns		(2,400)
Goods available for sale (excluding beginning inventory)	68,200	97,400
Goods available for sale (including beginning inventory)	76,200	109,400

Cost-to-retail percentage: $\frac{\$68,200}{\$97,400} = 70.02\%$

	Cost	Retail
Less: Normal spoilage		(1,800)
Less: Net sales:		
Sales	$97,000	
Employee discounts	2,300	
Sales returns	(5,000)	(94,300)
Estimated ending inventory at retail		$ 13,300
Estimated ending inventory at cost (see below)	(8,910)	
Estimated cost of goods sold	$67,290	

	Retail	Cost
Beginning inventory	$12,000 × 66.67%* =	$8,000
Current period's layer	1,300 × 70.02% =	910
Estimated Ending Inventory	$13,300	$8,910

*$8,000 ÷ $12,000 = 66.67%

Dollar-Value LIFO Retail

PART C

● LO9–5

In our earlier discussion of the LIFO retail method, we assumed that the retail prices of the inventory remained stable during the period. If you recall from Illustration 9–12, we compared the ending inventory (at retail) with the beginning inventory (at retail) to see if inventory had increased. If the dollar amount of ending inventory exceeded the beginning amount, we assumed a new LIFO layer had been added. But this isn't necessarily true. It may be that the dollar amount of ending inventory exceeded the beginning amount simply because retail prices increased, without an actual change in the quantity of goods. So, to see if there's been a "real" increase in quantity, we need a way to eliminate the effect of any price changes before we compare the ending inventory with the beginning inventory. Fortunately, we can accomplish this by combining two methods we've already discussed—the LIFO retail method (Part B of this chapter) and dollar-value LIFO (previous chapter). The combination is called the dollar-value LIFO retail method.

FINANCIAL Reporting Case

Q1, p. 459

Allow for retail prices to change during the period.

Using the retail method to approximate LIFO is referred to as the *dollar-value LIFO retail method.*

To illustrate, we return to the Home Improvement Stores situation (Illustration 9–12) in which we applied LIFO retail. We keep the same inventory data, but change the illustration from the month of July to the fiscal year 2021. This allows us to build into Illustration 9–14 a significant change in retail prices over the year of 10% (an increase in the retail price index from 1.00 to 1.10). We follow the LIFO retail procedure up to the point of comparing the ending inventory with the beginning inventory. However, because prices have risen, the apparent increase in inventory is only partly due to an additional layer of inventory and partly due to the increase in retail prices. The real increase is found by deflating the ending inventory amount to beginning of the year prices before comparing beginning and ending amounts. We did this with the dollar-value LIFO technique discussed in the previous chapter.[11]

FINANCIAL Reporting Case

Q2, p. 459

Illustration 9–14
The Dollar-Value LIFO Retail Method

	Cost	Retail
Beginning inventory	$ 99,200	$160,000
Plus: Net purchases	305,280	470,000
Net markups		10,000
Less: Net markdowns		(8,000)
Goods available for sale (excluding beginning inventory)	305,280	472,000
Goods available for sale (including beginning inventory)	404,480	632,000
Base layer cost-to-retail percentage: $\frac{\$99,200}{\$160,000} = 62\%$		
2021 layer cost-to-retail percentage: $\frac{\$305,280}{\$472,000} = 64.68\%$		
Less: Net sales		(434,000)
Ending inventory at current year retail prices		$198,000
Estimated ending inventory at cost (calculated below)	(113,430)	
Estimated cost of goods sold	$ 291,050	

Calculation of ending inventory at cost:

Ending Inventory at Year-End Retail Prices	Step 1 Ending Inventory at Base Year Retail Prices	Step 2 Inventory Layers at Base Year Retail Prices	Step 3 Inventory Layers Converted to LIFO Cost
$198,000 (assumed) →	$\frac{\$198,000}{1.10}$ = $180,000 →	$180,000	
		160,000 (base) × 1.00 × 0.62	= $ 99,200
		20,000 (2021) × 1.10 × 0.6468 =	14,230
Total ending inventory at dollar-value LIFO retail cost			$113,430

[11]The index used here is analogous to the cost index used in regular DVL except that it reflects the change in retail prices rather than in acquisition costs.

Each layer year carries its unique retail price index and its unique cost-to-retail percentage.

In this illustration, the ending inventory (at retail) of $198,000 is restated to base year prices ($180,000). Comparing this restated amount to beginning inventory layer of $160,000 reveals that a layer of $20,000 has been added in 2021. Multiplying each layer by its retail price index and by its cost-to-retail percentage converts it from retail to cost. The two layers are added to derive ending inventory at dollar-value LIFO retail cost.

When additional layers are added in subsequent years, their LIFO amounts are determined the same way. For illustration, let's assume ending inventory in 2022 is $226,200 at current retail prices and the price level has risen to 1.16. Also assume that the cost-to-retail percentage for 2022 net purchases is 63%. In Illustration 9–14A, the ending inventory converted to base year retail prices equals $195,000 (step 1). This amount represents the base year layer of $160,000 plus the layer of $20,000 added in 2021 plus a new layer of $15,000 added in 2022 (step 2). Each of these layers is multiplied by its retail price index and by its cost-to-retail percentage to calculate ending inventory of $124,392 (step 3).

Illustration 9–14A

The Dollar-Value LIFO Retail Inventory Method—Layer Added in Subsequent Year

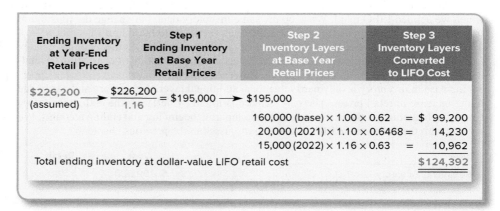

Now, let's assume that ending inventory in 2022 is $204,160 at current retail prices (instead of $226,200 as in the previous example) and the price level has risen to 1.16. Also assume that the cost-to-retail percentage for 2022 net purchases is 63%. As shown in step 1 of Illustration 9–14B, we convert ending inventory to a base year price of $176,000 ($204,160 ÷ 1.16).

When inventory decreases, no new layer is added and a previous layer is (partially) removed.

Next, we determine the layers of inventory (step 2). To do that, let's first recall from Illustration 9–14 that inventory layers at the end of 2021 consist of $160,000 from the base year and $20,000 added in 2021. Those layers totaled $180,000. In 2022, total inventory at base year prices has *declined* to $176,000. The decline means that no layer was added in 2022, and $4,000 of the $20,000 layer in 2021 has been sold, reducing the previous 2021 layer to a remainder of $16,000. Each layer is multiplied by its retail price index and by its cost-to-retail percentage to calculate ending inventory of $110,584 (step 3).

Illustration 9–14B

The Dollar-Value LIFO Retail Inventory Method—No Layer Added in Subsequent Year

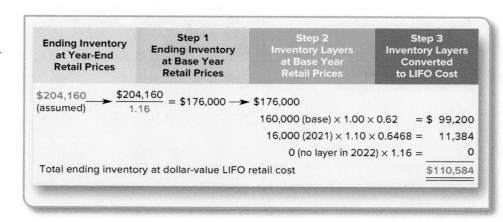

As we mentioned earlier in this section, many high-volume retailers selling many different items use the retail method. Costco Wholesale Corporation, for example, uses the dollar-value LIFO variation of the retail method. Illustration 9–15 shows the inventory disclosure note included in the company's recent financial statements.

> **Merchandise Inventories (in part)**
>
> Merchandise inventories are stated at the lower of cost or market. U.S. merchandise inventories are valued by the cost method of accounting, using the last-in, first-out (LIFO) basis. The Company believes the LIFO method more fairly presents the results of operations by more closely matching current costs with current revenues. The Company records an adjustment each quarter, if necessary, for the projected annual effect of inflation or deflation, and these estimates are adjusted to actual results determined at year-end, after actual inflation or deflation rates and inventory levels for the year have been determined.
>
> Source: Costco Wholesale Corporation

Illustration 9–15

Disclosure of Inventory Method—Costco Wholesale Corporation

Real World Financials

Concept Review Exercise

On January 1, 2021, the Nicholson Department Store adopted the dollar-value LIFO retail inventory method. Inventory transactions at both cost and retail and cost indexes for 2021 and 2022 are as follows:

DOLLAR-VALUE LIFO RETAIL METHOD

	2021		2022	
	Cost	Retail	Cost	Retail
Beginning inventory	$16,000	$24,000		
Net purchases	42,000	58,500	$45,000	$58,700
Net markups		3,000		2,400
Net markdowns		1,500		1,100
Net sales		56,000		57,000
Price index:				
January 1, 2021	1.00			
December 31, 2021	1.08			
December 31, 2022	1.15			

Required:

Estimate the 2021 and 2022 ending inventory and cost of goods sold using the dollar-value LIFO retail inventory method.

Solution:

	2021		2022	
	Cost	Retail	Cost	Retail
Beginning inventory	$ 16,000	$ 24,000	$ 17,456	$ 28,000
Plus: Net purchases	42,000	58,500	45,000	58,700
Net markups		3,000		2,400
Less: Net markdowns		(1,500)		(1,100)
Goods available for sale (excluding beg. inv.)	42,000	60,000	45,000	60,000
Goods available for sale (including beg. inv.)	58,000	84,000	62,456	88,000

Base layer
Cost-to-retail percentage: $\frac{\$16,000}{\$24,000} = 66.67\%$

2021
Cost-to-retail percentage: $\frac{\$42,000}{\$60,000} = 70.00\%$

2022
Cost-to-retail percentage: $\frac{\$45,000}{\$60,000} = 75.00\%$

	Cost	Retail	Cost	Retail
Less: Net sales		(56,000)		(57,000)
Estimated ending inv. at current year retail prices		$ 28,000		$ 31,000
Less: Estimated ending inventory at cost (below)	(17,456)		(18,345)	
Estimated cost of goods sold	$ 40,544		$ 44,111	

480   SECTION 2   Assets

		2021	
Ending Inventory at Year-End Retail Prices	**Step 1 Ending Inventory at Base Year Retail Prices**	**Step 2 Inventory Layers at Base Year Retail Prices**	**Step 3 Inventory Layers Converted to Cost**
$28,000 (above)	$\dfrac{\$28,000}{1.08} = \$25,926$	$24,000 (base) × 1.00 × 66.67% =	$16,000
		1,926 (2021) × 1.08 × 70.00% =	1,456
Total ending inventory at dollar-value LIFO retail cost			$17,456

		2022	
Ending Inventory at Year-End Retail Prices	**Step 1 Ending Inventory at Base Year Retail Prices**	**Step 2 Inventory Layers at Base Year Retail Prices**	**Step 3 Inventory Layers Converted to Cost**
$31,000 (above)	$\dfrac{\$31,000}{1.15} = \$26,957$	$24,000 (base) × 1.00 × 66.67% =	$16,000
		1,926 (2021) × 1.08 × 70.00% =	1,456
		1,031 (2022) × 1.15 × 75.00% =	889
Total ending inventory at dollar-value LIFO retail cost			$18,345

PART D

Change in Inventory Method and Inventory Errors

Change in Inventory Method

● LO9–6

Accounting principles should be applied consistently from period to period to allow for comparability of operating results. However, changes within a company as well as changes in the external economic environment may require a company to change an accounting method. As we mentioned in Chapter 8, in the past, high inflation periods motivated many companies to switch to LIFO for the tax benefit.

Specific accounting treatment and disclosures are prescribed for companies that change accounting principles. Chapter 4 introduced the subject of accounting changes and Chapter 20 provides in-depth coverage of the topic. Here we provide an overview of how changes in inventory methods are reported.

Most Inventory Changes

Changes in inventory methods, other than a change to LIFO, are accounted for retrospectively.

Recall from our brief discussion in Chapter 4 that most voluntary changes in accounting principles are reported retrospectively. This means reporting all previous periods' financial statements as if the new method had been used in all prior periods. Changes in inventory methods, other than a change to LIFO, are treated this way. We discuss the *change to LIFO* exception in the next section. In Chapter 4, we briefly discussed the steps a company undertakes to account for a change in accounting principle. We demonstrate those steps in Illustration 9–16.

Illustration 9–16

Change in Inventory Method

> Autogeek, Inc., a wholesale distributor of auto parts, began business in 2018. Inventory reported in the 2020 year-end balance sheet, determined using the average cost method, was $123,000. In 2021, the company decided to change its inventory method to FIFO. If the company had used the FIFO method in 2020, ending inventory would have been $146,000. What steps should Autogeek take to report this change?

Step 1: Revise comparative financial statements.

The first step is to revise prior years' financial statements. That is, for each year reported in the comparative statements, Autogeek makes those statements appear as if the newly adopted inventory method, FIFO, had been applied all along. In its balance sheets, assuming that the company presents balance sheets for two years for comparative purposes, the company would report 2021 inventory by its newly adopted method, FIFO, and also would revise the amounts it reported last year for its 2020 inventory. In its 2021 and prior year income statements, cost of goods sold would also reflect the new method.

In its statements of shareholders' equity, Autogeek would report retained earnings each year as if it had used FIFO all along. And, for the earliest year reported, the company would revise beginning retained earnings that year to reflect the cumulative income effect of the difference in inventory methods for all prior years. You will see this step illustrated in Chapter 20 after you have studied the statement of shareholders' equity in more depth.

Autogeek also would record a journal entry to adjust the book balances from their current amounts to what those balances would have been using FIFO. Because differences in cost of goods sold and income are reflected in retained earnings, as are the income tax effects, the journal entry updates inventory, retained earnings, and the appropriate income tax account. We ignore the income tax effects here but include those effects in an illustration in Chapter 20. The journal entry below, *ignoring income taxes,* increases the 2021 beginning inventory to the FIFO basis amount of $146,000 and increases retained earnings by the same amount, because that's what the increase in prior years' income would have been had FIFO been used.

Step 2: The affected accounts are adjusted.

Inventory ($146,000 − $123,000)	23,000	
Retained earnings		23,000

Autogeek must provide in a disclosure note clear explanation of why the change to FIFO is preferable. The note also would indicate the effects of the change on (a) income from continuing operations, (b) net income, (c) each line-item affected, (d) earnings per share, and (e) the cumulative effect of the change on retained earnings or other components of equity as of the beginning of the earliest period presented.

Step 3: A disclosure note provides additional information.

We see in Illustration 9–17 an example of such a note in a recent annual report of **CVS Health Corporation** when it changed its inventory method for retail/LTC inventories to the average cost method.

Inventory (in part)

Effective January 1, 2015, the Company changed its methods of accounting for "front store" inventories in the Retail/LTC Segment. Prior to 2015, the Company valued front store inventories at the lower of cost or market on a first-in, first-out ("FIFO") basis in retail stores using the retail inventory method and in distribution centers using the FIFO cost method. Effective January 1, 2015, all front store inventories in the Retail/LTC Segment have been valued at the lower of cost or market using the weighted average cost method.

   These changes were made primarily to provide the Company with better information to manage its retail front store operations and to bring all of the Company's inventories to a common inventory valuation methodology. The Company believes the weighted average cost method is preferable to the retail inventory method and the FIFO cost method because it results in greater precision in the determination of cost of revenues and inventories at the stock keeping unit ("SKU") level and results in a consistent inventory valuation method for all of the Company's inventories as all of the Company's remaining inventories, which consist of prescription drugs, were already being valued using the weighted average cost method.

   The Company recorded the cumulative effect of these changes in accounting principle as of January 1, 2015. The effect of these changes in accounting principle as of January 1, 2015, was a decrease in inventories of $7 million, an increase in current deferred income tax assets of $3 million and a decrease in retained earnings of $4 million.

Source: CVS Health Corporation

Illustration 9–17

Disclosure of Change in Inventory Method—CVS Health Corporation

Real World Financials

Change to the LIFO Method

When a company changes *to the LIFO inventory method* from any other method, it usually is impossible to calculate the income effect on prior years. To do so would require assumptions as to when specific LIFO inventory layers were created in years prior to the change.

Accounting records usually are inadequate for a company changing to *LIFO* to report the change retrospectively.

As a result, a company changing to LIFO usually does not report the change retrospectively. Instead, the LIFO method simply is used from that point on. The base year inventory for all future LIFO determinations is the beginning inventory in the year the LIFO method is adopted.[12]

A disclosure note is needed to explain (a) the nature of and justification for the change, (b) the effect of the change on current year's income and earnings per share, and (c) why retrospective application was impracticable. When **Seneca Foods Corporation** adopted the LIFO inventory method, it reported the change in the note shown in Illustration 9–18.

Illustration 9–18

Change in Inventory Method Disclosure— Seneca Foods Corporation

Real World Financials

> **10. Inventories (in part)**
>
> The Company decided to change its inventory valuation method from the FIFO method to the LIFO method. In the high inflation environment that the Company is experiencing, the Company believes that the LIFO inventory method is preferable over the FIFO method because it better compares the cost of current production to current revenue. Selling prices are established to reflect current market activity, which recognizes the increasing costs. Under FIFO, revenue and costs are not aligned. Under LIFO, the current cost of sales is matched to the current revenue.
>
> The Company determined that retrospective application of LIFO for periods prior to the current fiscal year was impracticable because the period-specific information necessary to analyze inventories, including inventories acquired as part of the prior fiscal year's Signature acquisition, were not readily available and could not be precisely determined at the appropriate level of detail, including the commodity, size and item code information necessary to perform the detailed calculations required to retrospectively compute the internal LIFO indices applicable to prior fiscal years. The effect of this change was to reduce net earnings by $37,917,000 and $18,307,000 in the current and prior fiscal year, respectively, below that which would have been reported using the Company's previous inventory method. The reduction in earnings per share was $3.12 ($3.09 diluted) and $1.50 per share ($1.49 diluted) in the current and prior fiscal year, respectively.
>
> Source: Seneca Foods Corporation

As we discussed in Chapter 8, an important motivation for using LIFO in periods of rising costs is that it produces higher cost of goods sold and lowers net income and income taxes. Notice in the Seneca Foods disclosure note that the switch to LIFO did cause a decrease in net income and therefore income taxes in the year of the switch indicating an environment of increasing costs.

Additional Consideration

> When changing from one generally accepted accounting principle to another, a company must justify that the change results in financial information that more properly portrays operating results and financial position. For income tax purposes, a company generally must obtain consent from the Internal Revenue Service before changing an accounting method. A special form also must be filed with the IRS when a company intends to adopt the LIFO inventory method. When a company changes from LIFO for tax purposes, it can't change back to LIFO until five tax returns have been filed using the non-LIFO method.

Inventory Errors

● LO9–7

Accounting errors must be corrected when they are discovered. In Chapter 4, we briefly discussed the correction of accounting errors, and Chapter 20 provides in-depth coverage. Here we provide an overview of the accounting treatment and disclosures in the context of inventory errors. Inventory errors include the over- or understatement of ending inventory

---

[12]A change to LIFO is handled the same way for income tax purposes.

due to a mistake in physical count or a mistake in pricing inventory quantities. Also, errors include the over- or understatement of purchases which could be caused by the cutoff errors described in Chapter 8.

If an inventory error is discovered in the same accounting period it occurred, the original erroneous entry should simply be reversed and the appropriate entry recorded. This situation presents no particular reporting problem.

If a *material* inventory error is discovered in an accounting period subsequent to the period in which the error was made, any previous years' financial statements that were incorrect as a result of the error are retrospectively restated to reflect the correction.[13] And, of course, any account balances that are incorrect as a result of the error are corrected by journal entry. If, due to an error affecting net income, retained earnings is one of the incorrect accounts, the correction is reported as a prior period adjustment to the beginning balance on the statement of shareholders' equity.[14] In addition, a disclosure note is needed to describe the nature of the error and the impact of its correction on net income, each line-item affected, and earnings per share.

When analyzing inventory errors, it's helpful to visualize the way cost of goods sold, net income, and retained earnings are determined (see Illustration 9–19). Beginning inventory and net purchases are *added* in the calculation of cost of goods sold. If either of these is overstated (understated), then cost of goods sold would be overstated (understated). On the other hand, ending inventory is *deducted* in the calculation of cost of goods sold, so if ending inventory is overstated (understated), then cost of goods sold is understated (overstated). Of course, errors that affect income also will affect income taxes. In the illustration that follows, we ignore the tax effects of the errors and focus on the errors themselves rather than their tax aspects.

For material errors, previous years' financial statements are retrospectively restated.

Incorrect balances are corrected.

A correction of retained earnings is reported as a prior period adjustment.

A disclosure note describes the nature and the impact of the error.

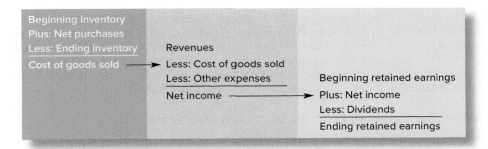

Illustration 9–19

Visualizing the Effect of Inventory Errors

Illustration 9-20 provides a numerical example of how an inventory error affects reported amounts in both the current year and the following year.

When the Inventory Error Is Discovered the Following Year

Now, let's assume the error in Illustration 9-20 is discovered in 2021. The 2020 financial statements that were incorrect as a result of the error are retrospectively restated to reflect the correct inventory amount, cost of goods sold, net income, and retained earnings when those statements are reported again for comparative purposes in the 2021 annual report. The following journal entry, *ignoring income taxes,* is needed in 2021 to correct the error in the company's records.

Previous years' financial statements are retrospectively restated.

Retained earnings	800,000	
Inventory		800,000

A journal entry corrects any incorrect account balance.

---

[13]If the effect of the error is not material, it is simply corrected in the year of discovery.

[14]The prior period adjustment is applied to beginning retained earnings for the year following the error, or for the earliest year being reported in the comparative financial statements when the error occurs prior to the earliest year presented. The retained earnings balances in years after the first year also are adjusted to what those balances would be if the error had not occurred, but a company may choose not to explicitly report those adjustments as separate line items.

Illustration 9–20

Inventory Error Correction

> The Barton Company uses a periodic inventory system. At the end of 2020, a mathematical error caused an $800,000 overstatement of ending inventory. Ending inventories for 2021 and 2022 are correctly determined.
>   The way we correct this error depends on when the error is discovered. Assuming that the error is not discovered until after 2021, the 2020 and 2021 effects of the error, ignoring income tax effects, are shown below. The overstated and understated amounts are $800,000 in each instance.
>
> **Analysis: U = Understated   O = Overstated**
>
> | 2020 | | 2021 | |
> |---|---|---|---|
> | Beginning inventory | | Beginning inventory | O – 800,000 |
> | Plus: Net purchases | | Plus: Net purchases | |
> | Less: Ending inventory | O – 800,000 | Less: Ending inventory | |
> | Cost of goods sold | U – 800,000 | Cost of goods sold | O – 800,000 |
> | | | | |
> | Revenues | | Revenues | |
> | Less: Cost of goods sold | U – 800,000 | Less: Cost of goods sold | O – 800,000 |
> | Less: Other expenses | | Less: Other expenses | |
> | Net income | O – 800,000 | Net income | U – 800,000 |
> | ↓ | | ↓ | |
> | Retained earnings | O – 800,000 | Retained earnings | *corrected* |

When retained earnings requires correction, a *prior period adjustment* is made on the statement of shareholders' equity.

We debit retained earnings in 2021 to correct its balance. Net income in 2020 was overstated by the amount of the inventory error, and this caused retained earnings to be overstated. The correction to retained earnings is reported as a *prior period adjustment* to the 2021 beginning retained earnings balance in Barton's statement of shareholders' equity. Prior period adjustments do not flow through the income statement but directly adjust retained earnings. This adjustment is illustrated in Chapter 20.

When the Inventory Error Is Discovered Two Years Later

If the error in 2020 isn't discovered until 2022, the 2021 financial statements also are retrospectively restated to reflect the correct cost of goods sold and net income even though no correcting entry would be needed at that point. Inventory and retained earnings in 2022 would not require adjustment. The error has self-corrected and no prior period adjustment is needed.

A disclosure note describes the nature of the error and the impact of the correction on income.

Also, a disclosure note in Barton's annual report should describe the nature of the error and the impact of its correction on each year's net income (overstated by $800,000 in 2020; understated by $800,000 in 2021), the line items affected, and earnings per share.

Concept Review Exercise

INVENTORY ERRORS

In 2021, the controller of the Fleischman Wholesale Beverage Company discovered the following material errors related to the 2019 and 2020 financial statements:

a. Inventory at the end of 2019 was understated by $50,000.

b. Late in 2020, a $3,000 purchase was incorrectly recorded as a $33,000 purchase. The invoice has not yet been paid.

c. Inventory at the end of 2020 was overstated by $20,000.

The company uses a periodic inventory system.

Required:

1. Assuming that the errors were discovered after the 2020 financial statements were issued, analyze the effect of the errors on 2019 and 2020 cost of goods sold, net income, and retained earnings. Ignore income taxes.
2. Prepare a journal entry in 2021 to correct the errors.

Solution:

1.

Analysis: U = Understated   O = Overstated

2019			2020	
Beginning inventory			Beginning inventory	U – 50,000
Plus: Net purchases			Plus: Net purchases	O – 30,000
Less: Ending inventory	U – 50,000		Less: Ending inventory	O – 20,000
Cost of goods sold	O – 50,000		Cost of goods sold	U – 40,000
Revenues			Revenues	
Less: Cost of goods sold	O – 50,000		Less: Cost of goods sold	U – 40,000
Less: Other expenses			Less: Other expenses	
Net income	U – 50,000		Net income	O – 40,000
↓			↓	
Retained earnings	U – 50,000		Retained earnings	U – 10,000

2. Prepare a journal entry in 2021 to correct the errors.

Accounts payable..	30,000	
Inventory..		20,000
Retained earnings		10,000

Earnings Quality

A change in the accounting method a company uses to value inventory is one way managers can artificially manipulate income. However, this method of income manipulation is transparent. As we learned in a previous section, the effect on income of switching from one inventory method to another must be disclosed. That disclosure restores comparability between periods and enhances earnings quality.

On the other hand, inventory write-downs are included in the broader category of "big bath" accounting techniques some companies use to manipulate earnings. By overstating the write-down, profits are increased in future periods as the inventory is used or sold. When the demand for many high-technology products decreased significantly in late 2000 and early 2001, several companies, including Sycamore Networks, Cisco Systems, Lucent Technologies, and JDS Uniphase, recorded large inventory write-offs, some in the billions of dollars. Certainly, these write-offs reflected the existing economic environment. However, some analysts questioned the size of some of the write-offs. For example, William Schaff, an investment officer at Bay Isle Financial, noted that Cisco's $2 billion write-off was approximately equal to the balance of inventory on hand at the end of the previous quarter and about equal to the cost of goods actually sold during the quarter.

Inventory write-downs often are cited as a method used to shift income between periods.

A financial analyst must carefully consider the effect of any significant asset write-down on the assessment of a company's permanent earnings.

486   SECTION 2   Assets

Financial Reporting Case Solution

©QualityHD/Shutterstock.com

1. **How does Dollar General avoid counting all its inventory every time it produces financial statements?** *(p. 477)*   Dollar General uses the dollar-value LIFO retail inventory method. The retail inventory estimation technique avoids the counting of ending inventory by keeping track of goods available for sale not only at cost but also at retail prices. Each period's sales, at sales prices, are deducted from the retail amount of goods available for sale to arrive at ending inventory at retail. This amount is then converted to cost using a cost-to-retail percentage.

2. **What is the index formulation used for?** *(p. 477)*   The dollar-value LIFO retail method uses a price index to first convert ending inventory at retail to base year prices. Yearly LIFO layers are then determined, and each layer is converted to that year's current year retail prices using the year's price index and then to cost using the layer's cost-to-retail percentage. ●

The Bottom Line

● **LO9–1**   Companies that use FIFO, average cost, or any other method besides LIFO or the retail inventory method report inventory at the lower of cost or net realizable value (NRV). Net realizable value is selling price less costs to sell. Companies that use LIFO or the retail inventory method report inventory at the lower of cost or market. Market equals replacement cost, except that market should not (a) be greater than NRV (ceiling) or (b) be less than NRV minus an approximately normal profit margin (floor). *(p. 459)*

● **LO9–2**   The gross profit method estimates cost of goods sold which is then subtracted from cost of goods available for sale to estimate ending inventory. The estimate of cost of goods sold is determined by subtracting an estimate of gross profit from net sales. The estimate of gross profit is determined by multiplying the historical gross profit ratio times net sales. *(p. 467)*

● **LO9–3**   The retail inventory method determines the amount of ending inventory at retail by subtracting sales for the period from goods available for sale at retail. Ending inventory at retail is then converted to *cost* by multiplying it by the cost-to-retail percentage, which is based on a current relationship between cost and selling price. *(p. 469)*

● **LO9–4**   By the conventional retail method, we estimate average cost at lower of cost or market. Average cost is estimated by including beginning inventory in the calculation of the cost-to-retail percentage. The lower of average cost or market is estimated by excluding markdowns from the calculation. Markdowns are subtracted in the retail column after the percentage is calculated. *(p. 472)*

● **LO9–5**   By the LIFO retail method, ending inventory includes the beginning inventory plus the current year's layer. To determine layers, we compare ending inventory at retail to beginning inventory at retail and assume that no more than one inventory layer is added if inventory increases. Each layer carries its own cost-to-retail percentage which is used to convert each layer from retail to cost. The dollar-value LIFO retail inventory method combines the LIFO retail method and the dollar-value LIFO method (Chapter 8) to estimate LIFO from retail prices when the price level has changed. *(p. 477)*

● **LO9–6**   Most changes in inventory methods are reported retrospectively. This means revising all previous periods' financial statements to appear as if the newly adopted inventory method had been applied all along. An exception is a change to the LIFO method. In this case, it usually is impossible to calculate the income effect on prior years. To do so would require assumptions as to when specific LIFO inventory layers were created in years prior to the change. As a result, a company changing to LIFO usually does not report the change retrospectively. Instead, the LIFO method simply is used from that point on. *(p. 480)*

● **LO9–7**   If a material inventory error is discovered in an accounting period subsequent to the period in which the error is made, previous years' financial statements that were incorrect as a result of the error are retrospectively restated to reflect the correction. Account balances are corrected by journal entry. A correction of retained earnings is reported as a prior period adjustment to the beginning balance in the statement of shareholders' equity. In addition, a disclosure note is needed to describe the nature of the error and the impact of its correction on continuing operations, net income, and earnings per share. *(p. 482)*

● **LO9–8**   *IAS No. 2* specifies that if circumstances reveal that an inventory write-down is no longer appropriate, it must be reversed. Reversals are not permitted under U.S. GAAP. Under U.S. GAAP, the lower of cost or net realizable value rule can be applied to individual items, inventory categories, or the entire inventory. Using the international standard, the assessment usually is applied to individual items, although using inventory categories is allowed under certain circumstances. (*p. 463*) ●

Purchase Commitments

APPENDIX 9

Purchase commitments are contracts that obligate a company to purchase a specified amount of merchandise or raw materials at specified prices on or before specified dates. Companies enter into these agreements to make sure they will be able to obtain important inventory as well as to protect against increases in purchase price. However, if the purchase price decreases before the agreement is exercised, the commitment has the disadvantage of requiring the company to purchase inventory at a higher than market price. If this happens, a loss on the purchase commitment is recorded.

Purchase commitments protect the buyer against price increases and provide a supply of product.

Because purchase commitments create the possibility of this kind of loss, the loss occurs when the market price falls below the commitment price rather than when the inventory eventually is sold. This means recording the loss when the product is purchased or, if the commitment is still outstanding, at the end of the reporting period. In other words, purchases are recorded at market price when that price is lower than the contract price, and a loss is recognized for the difference. Also, losses are recognized for any purchase commitments outstanding at the end of a reporting period when market price is less than contract price. This is best understood by the example in Illustration 9A–1.

Purchases made pursuant to a purchase commitment are recorded at the lower of contract price or market price on the date the contract is executed.

Illustration 9A–1
Purchase Commitments

> In July 2021, the Lassiter Company signed two purchase commitments. The first requires Lassiter to purchase inventory for $500,000 by November 15, 2021. The second requires Lassiter to purchase inventory for $600,000 by February 15, 2022. Lassiter's fiscal year-end is December 31. The company uses a perpetual inventory system.

Contract Period within Fiscal Year

The contract period for the first commitment is contained within a single fiscal year. Lassiter would record the purchase at the contract price if the market price of inventory at date of acquisition is *equal to or greater than* the contract price of $500,000.[15]

Inventory (contract price)	500,000	
Cash (or accounts payable)		500,000

Purchase inventory at the contract price.

If the market price of inventory at acquisition is *less* than the contract price, inventory is recorded at the market price and a loss is recognized.[16] For example, if the market price is $425,000 at the time of acquisition, Lassiter must still pay $500,000 (contract price) and would record the following entry:

Inventory (market price)	425,000	
Loss on purchase commitment	75,000	
Cash (or accounts payable)		500,000

If market price is less than the contract price at acquisition, a loss is recorded.

[15]In each of the following situations, if a periodic inventory system is used, purchases is debited instead of inventory.
[16]Recall from the chapter that one method of recording losses from inventory write-downs is to report the loss as a line item in the income statement.

The objective of this treatment is to associate the loss with the period in which the price declines rather than with the period in which the company eventually sells the inventory. This is consistent with recording inventory at the lower of cost or market, as you studied in the chapter.

Contract Period Extends beyond Fiscal Year

Now let's consider Lassiter's second purchase commitment that is outstanding at the end of the fiscal year 2021 (that is, the purchases have not yet been made). If the market price of inventory at the end of the year is *equal to or greater than* the contract price of $600,000, no entry is recorded. However, if the market price at year-end is *less* than the contract price, a loss must be recognized. The objective is to associate the loss with the period in which the price declines rather than with the period in which the company eventually sells the inventory. Let's say the year-end market price of the inventory for Lassiter's second purchase commitment is $540,000. The following adjusting entry is recorded:

> If the market price at year-end is less than the contract price, a loss is recorded for the difference.

December 31, 2021

Estimated loss on purchase commitment ($600,000 − $540,000).......	60,000	
Estimated liability on purchase commitment		60,000

> A liability is credited for estimated losses on purchase commitments.

At this point, the loss is an *estimated* loss. The actual loss, if any, will not be known until the inventory actually is purchased. The best estimate of the market price on date of purchase is the current market price, in this case $540,000. Because no inventory has been acquired, we can't credit inventory for the loss. Instead, a liability is credited because, in a sense, the loss represents an obligation to purchase inventory above market price.

The entry to record the actual purchase on or before February 15, 2022, will vary depending on the market price of the inventory at date of purchase. If the market price is unchanged or has increased from the year-end price, the following entry is made:

> If market price on purchase date has not declined from year-end price, the purchase is recorded at the year-end market price.

Inventory (accounting cost)	540,000	
Estimated liability on purchase commitment...	60,000	
Cash (or accounts payable)		600,000

Even if the market price of the inventory increases, there is no recovery of the $60,000 loss recognized in 2021. Similar to the method of recording inventory at the lower of cost or market, the reduced inventory value, in this case the reduced value of purchases, is considered to be the new cost and any recovery of value is ignored.

If the market price declines even further from year-end levels, an additional loss is recognized. For example, if the market price of the inventory covered by the commitment declines to $510,000, the following entry is recorded:

> If market price declines further from year-end, an additional loss is recorded at acquisition.

Inventory (market price)...	510,000	
Loss on purchase commitment ($540,000 − $510,000)..........................	30,000	
Estimated liability on purchase commitment...	60,000	
Cash (or accounts payable)		600,000

The total loss on this purchase commitment of $90,000 is thus allocated between 2021 and 2022 according to when the decline in value of the inventory covered by the commitment occurred.

If there are material amounts of purchase commitments outstanding at the end of a reporting period, the contract details are disclosed in a note. This disclosure is required even if no loss estimate has been recorded. ●

Questions For Review of Key Topics

Q 9–1   Explain the (a) lower of cost or net realizable value (LCNRV) approach and the (b) lower of cost or market (LCM) approach to valuing inventory.

Q 9–2   What are the various levels of aggregation to which the LCNRV and LCM approaches can be applied?

Q 9–3   Describe the typical approach for recording inventory write-downs.

Q 9–4   Explain the gross profit method of estimating ending inventory.

Q 9–5   The Rider Company uses the gross profit method to estimate ending inventory and cost of goods sold. The cost percentage is determined based on historical data. What factors could cause the estimate of ending inventory to be overstated?

Q 9–6   Explain the retail inventory method of estimating ending inventory.

Q 9–7   Both the gross profit method and the retail inventory method provide a way to estimate ending inventory. What is the main difference between the two estimation techniques?

Q 9–8   Define each of the following retail terms: initial markup, additional markup, markup cancellation, markdown, markdown cancellation.

Q 9–9   Explain how to estimate the average cost of inventory when using the retail inventory method.

Q 9–10   What is the conventional retail method?

Q 9–11   Explain the LIFO retail inventory method.

Q 9–12   Discuss the treatment of freight-in, purchase returns, purchase discounts, normal spoilage, sales returns, sales discounts, and employee discounts in the application of the retail inventory method.

Q 9–13   Explain the difference between the retail inventory method using LIFO and the dollar-value LIFO retail method.

Q 9–14   Describe the accounting treatment for a change in inventory method other than to LIFO.

Q 9–15   When a company changes its inventory method to LIFO, an exception is made for the way accounting changes usually are reported. Explain the difference in the accounting treatment of a change *to* the LIFO inventory method from other inventory method changes.

Q 9–16   Explain the accounting treatment of material inventory errors discovered in an accounting period subsequent to the period in which the error is made.

Q 9–17   It is discovered in 2021 that ending inventory in 2019 was understated. What is the effect of the understatement on the following:

2019:	Cost of goods sold
	Net income
	Ending retained earnings
2020:	Net purchases
	Cost of goods sold
	Net income
	Ending retained earnings

IFRS   **Q 9–18**   Identify any differences between U.S. GAAP and IFRS when applying the lower of cost or net realizable value rule to inventory valuation.

Q 9–19   (Based on Appendix 9) Define purchase commitments. What is the advantage(s) of these agreements to buyers?

Q 9–20   (Based on Appendix 9) Explain how purchase commitments are recorded for the lower of contract price or market price.

Brief Exercises

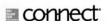

BE 9–1
Lower of cost or net realizable value
● LO9–1

Ross Electronics has one product in its ending inventory. Per unit data consist of the following: cost, $20; selling price, $30; selling costs, $4. What unit value should Ross use when applying the lower of cost or net realizable value rule to ending inventory?

BE 9–2
Lower of cost or net realizable value
● LO9–1

SLR Corporation has 1,000 units of each of its two products in its year-end inventory. Per unit data for each of the products are as follows:

	Product 1	Product 2
Cost	$50	$34
Selling price	70	36
Costs to sell	6	4

490   SECTION 2   Assets

Determine the carrying value of SLR's inventory assuming that the lower of cost or net realizable value (LCNRV) rule is applied to individual products. What is the before-tax income effect of the LCNRV adjustment?

BE 9–3
Lower of cost or market
● LO9–1

[This is a variation of BE 9–1, modified to focus on the lower of cost or market.] Ross Electronics has one product in its ending inventory. Per unit data consist of the following: cost, $20; replacement cost, $18; selling price, $30; selling costs, $4. The normal profit is 30% of selling price. What unit value should Ross use when applying the lower of cost or market (LCM) rule to ending inventory?

BE 9–4
Lower of cost or market
● LO9–1

[This is a variation of BE 9–2, modified to focus on the lower of cost or market.] SLR Corporation has 1,000 units of each of its two products in its year-end inventory. Per unit data for each of the products are as follows:

	Product 1	Product 2
Cost	$50	$34
Replacement cost	48	26
Selling price	70	36
Selling costs	6	4
Normal profit	10	8

Determine the carrying value of SLR's inventory assuming that the lower of cost or market (LCM) rule is applied to individual products. What is the before-tax income effect of the LCM adjustment?

BE 9–5
Gross profit method
● LO9–2

On February 26, a hurricane destroyed the entire inventory stored in a warehouse owned by the Rockford Corporation. The following information is available from the records of the company's periodic inventory system: beginning inventory, $220,000; purchases and net sales from the beginning of the year through February 26, $400,000 and $600,000, respectively; gross profit ratio, 30%. Estimate the cost of the inventory destroyed by the hurricane using the gross profit method.

BE 9–6
Gross profit method; solving for unknown
● LO9–2

Adams Corporation estimates that it lost $75,000 in inventory from a recent flood. The following information is available from the records of the company's periodic inventory system: beginning inventory, $150,000; purchases and net sales from the beginning of the year through the date of the flood, $450,000 and $700,000, respectively. What is the company's gross profit ratio?

BE 9–7
Retail inventory method; average cost
● LO9–3

Kiddie World uses a periodic inventory system and the retail inventory method to estimate ending inventory and cost of goods sold. The following data are available for the quarter ending September 30, 2021:

	Cost	Retail
Beginning inventory	$300,000	$ 450,000
Net purchases	861,000	1,210,000
Freight-in	22,000	
Net markups		48,000
Net markdowns		18,000
Net sales		1,200,000

Estimate ending inventory and cost of goods sold (average cost) using the information provided.

BE 9–8
Retail inventory method; LIFO
● LO9–3

Refer to the situation described in BE 9–7. Estimate ending inventory and cost of goods sold (LIFO) using the information provided.

BE 9–9
Conventional retail method
● LO9–4

Refer to the situation described in BE 9–7. Estimate ending inventory and cost of goods sold using the conventional method and the information provided.

BE 9–10
Conventional retail method
● LO9–4

Roberson Corporation uses a periodic inventory system and the retail inventory method. Accounting records provided the following information for the 2021 fiscal year:

	Cost	Retail
Beginning inventory	$220,000	$ 400,000
Net purchases	640,000	1,180,000
Freight-in	17,800	
Net markups		16,000
Net markdowns		6,000
Normal spoilage		3,000
Sales		1,300,000

The company records sales to employees net of discounts. These discounts totaled $15,000 for the year. Estimate ending inventory and cost of goods sold using the conventional method and the information provided.

BE 9–11
Dollar-value LIFO retail
● LO9–5

On January 1, 2021, Sanderson Variety Store adopted the dollar-value LIFO retail inventory method. Accounting records provided the following information:

	Cost	Retail
Beginning inventory	$ 40,800	$ 68,000
Net purchases	155,440	270,000
Net markups		6,000
Net markdowns		8,000
Net sales		250,000
Retail price index, end of year		1.02

Estimate ending inventory using the dollar-value LIFO retail method and the information provided.

BE 9–12
Dollar-value LIFO retail
● LO9–5

This exercise is a continuation of BE 9–11. During 2022, purchases at cost and retail were $168,000 and $301,000, respectively. Net markups, net markdowns, and net sales for the year were $3,000, $4,000, and $280,000, respectively. The retail price index at the end of 2022 was 1.06. Estimate ending inventory in 2022 using the dollar-value LIFO retail method and the information provided.

BE 9–13
Change in inventory costing methods
● LO9–6

In 2021, Hopyard Lumber changed its inventory method from LIFO to FIFO. Inventory at the end of 2020 of $127,000 would have been $145,000 if FIFO had been used. Inventory at the end of 2021 is $162,000 using the new FIFO method but would have been $151,000 if the company had continued to use LIFO. Describe the steps Hopyard should take to report this change. What is the effect of the change on 2021 cost of goods sold?

BE 9–14
Change in inventory costing methods
● LO9–6

In 2021, Wade Window and Glass changed its inventory method from FIFO to LIFO. Inventory at the end of 2020 is $150,000. Describe the steps Wade Window and Glass should take to report this change.

BE 9–15
Inventory error
● LO9–7

In 2021, Winslow International, Inc.'s controller discovered that ending inventories for 2019 and 2020 were overstated by $200,000 and $500,000, respectively. Determine the effect of the errors on retained earnings at January 1, 2021. (Ignore income taxes.)

BE 9–16
Inventory error
● LO9–7

Refer to the situation described in BE 9–15. What steps would be taken to report the error in the 2021 financial statements?

Exercises

E 9–1
Lower of cost or net realizable value
● LO9–1

Herman Company has three products in its ending inventory. Specific per unit data at the end of the year for each of the products are as follows:

	Product 1	Product 2	Product 3
Cost	$20	$ 90	$50
Selling price	40	120	70
Costs to sell	6	40	10

Required:
What unit values should Herman use for each of its products when applying the lower of cost or net realizable value (LCNRV) rule to ending inventory?

E 9–2
Lower of cost or net realizable value
● LO9–1

The inventory of Royal Decking consisted of five products. Information about the December 31, 2021, inventory is as follows:

Product	Per Unit Cost	Per Unit Selling Price
A	$ 40	$ 60
B	80	100
C	40	80
D	100	130
E	20	30

Costs to sell consist of a sales commission equal to 10% of selling price and shipping costs equal to 5% of cost.

Required:
What unit value should Royal Decking use for each of its products when applying the lower of cost or net realizable value (LCNRV) rule to units of ending inventory?

E 9–3
Lower of cost or net realizable value
● LO9–1

Tatum Company has four products in its inventory. Information about the December 31, 2021, inventory is as follows:

Product	Total Cost	Total Net Realizable Value
101	$120,000	$100,000
102	90,000	110,000
103	60,000	50,000
104	30,000	50,000

Required:
1. Determine the carrying value of inventory at December 31, 2021, assuming the lower of cost or net realizable value (LCNRV) rule is applied to individual products.
2. Assuming that inventory write-downs are common for Tatum Company, record any necessary year-end adjusting entry.

E 9–4
Lower of cost or market
● LO9–1

[This is a variation of E 9-1, modified to focus on the lower of cost or market.] Herman Company has three products in its ending inventory. Specific per unit data at the end of the year for each of the products are as follows:

	Product 1	Product 2	Product 3
Cost	$20	$ 90	$50
Replacement cost	18	85	40
Selling price	40	120	70
Selling costs	6	40	10
Normal profit	5	30	12

Required:
What unit values should Herman use for each of its products when applying the lower of cost or market (LCM) rule to ending inventory?

E 9–5
Lower of cost or market
● LO9–1

[This is a variation of E 9-2, modified to focus on the lower of cost or market.] The inventory of Royal Decking consisted of five products. Information about the December 31, 2021, inventory is as follows:

Product	Per Unit Cost	Per Unit Replacement Cost	Per Unit Selling Price
A	$ 40	$35	$ 60
B	80	70	100
C	40	55	80
D	100	70	130
E	20	28	30

Selling costs consist of a sales commission equal to 10% of selling price and shipping costs equal to 5% of cost. The normal profit is 30% of selling price.

Required:
What unit value should Royal Decking use for each of its products when applying the lower of cost or market (LCM) rule to units of ending inventory?

E 9–6
Lower of cost or market
● LO9–1

[This is a variation of E 9-3, modified to focus on the lower of cost or market.] Tatum Company has four products in its inventory. Information about the December 31, 2021, inventory is as follows:

Product	Total Cost	Total Replacement Cost	Total Net Realizable Value
101	$120,000	$100,000	$100,000
102	90,000	85,000	110,000
103	60,000	40,000	50,000
104	30,000	28,000	50,000

The normal profit is 25% of *total cost.*

Required:

1. Determine the carrying value of inventory at December 31, 2021, assuming the lower of cost or market (LCM) rule is applied to individual products.
2. Assuming that inventory write-downs are common for Tatum Company, record any necessary year-end adjusting entry.

E 9–7
FASB codification research
● LO9–3, LO9–6, LO9–7

Access the *FASB Accounting Standards Codification* at the FASB website (www.fasb.org). Determine each of the following:

1. The specific seven-digit Codification citation (XXX-XX-XX) that contains discussion of the measurement of ending inventory using the lower of cost or net realizable value (LCNRV) rule and the lower of cost or market (LCM) rule.
2. The specific eight-digit Codification citation (XXX-XX-XX-X) that describes the measurement of the ceiling using the lower of cost or market (LCM) rule.
3. The specific eight-digit Codification citation (XXX-XX-XX-X) that describes the measurement of the floor using the lower of cost or market (LCM) rule.

E 9–8
Gross profit method
● LO9–2

On September 22, 2021, a flood destroyed the entire merchandise inventory on hand in a warehouse owned by the Rocklin Sporting Goods Company. The following information is available from the records of the company's periodic inventory system:

Inventory, January 1, 2021	$140,000
Net purchases, January 1 through September 22	370,000
Net sales, January 1 through September 22	550,000
Gross profit ratio	25%

Required:
Estimate the cost of inventory destroyed in the flood using the gross profit method.

E 9–9
Gross profit method
● LO9–2

On November 21, 2021, a fire at Hodge Company's warehouse caused severe damage to its entire inventory of Product Tex. Hodge estimates that all usable damaged goods can be sold for $12,000. The following information was available from the records of Hodge's periodic inventory system:

Inventory, November 1	$100,000
Net purchases from November 1, to the date of the fire	140,000
Net sales from November 1, to the date of the fire	220,000

Based on recent history, Hodge's gross profit ratio on Product Tex is 35% of net sales.

Required:
Calculate the estimated loss on the inventory from the fire, using the gross profit method.

(AICPA adapted)

E 9–10
Gross profit method
● LO9–2

A fire destroyed a warehouse of the Goren Group, Inc., on May 4, 2021. Accounting records on that date indicated the following:

Merchandise inventory, January 1, 2021	$1,900,000
Purchases to date	5,800,000
Freight-in	400,000
Sales to date	8,200,000

The gross profit ratio has averaged 20% of sales for the past four years.

Required:
Use the gross profit method to estimate the cost of the inventory destroyed in the fire.

494 SECTION 2 Assets

E 9–11
Gross profit method
● LO9–2

Royal Gorge Company uses the gross profit method to estimate ending inventory and cost of goods sold when preparing monthly financial statements required by its bank. Inventory on hand at the end of October was $58,500. The following information for the month of November was available from company records:

Purchases	$110,000
Freight-in	3,000
Sales	180,000
Sales returns	5,000
Purchases returns	4,000

In addition, the controller is aware of $8,000 of inventory that was stolen during November from one of the company's warehouses.

Required:
1. Calculate the estimated inventory at the end of November, assuming a gross profit ratio of 40%.
2. Calculate the estimated inventory at the end of November, assuming a markup on cost of 60%.

E 9–12
Gross profit method; solving for unknown cost percentage
● LO9–2

National Distributing Company uses a periodic inventory system to track its merchandise inventory and the gross profit method to estimate ending inventory and cost of goods sold for interim periods. Net purchases for the month of August were $31,000. The July 31 and August 31, 2021, financial statements contained the following information:

Income Statements		
For the Months Ending		
	August 31, 2021	**July 31, 2021**
Net sales	$50,000	$40,000
Balance Sheets at		
	August 31, 2021	**July 31, 2021**
Assets:		
Merchandise inventory	$28,000	$27,000

Required:
Determine the company's cost percentage.

E 9–13
Retail inventory method; average cost
● LO9–3

San Lorenzo General Store uses a periodic inventory system and the retail inventory method to estimate ending inventory and cost of goods sold. The following data are available for the month of October 2021:

	Cost	Retail
Beginning inventory	$35,000	$50,000
Net purchases	19,120	31,600
Net markups		1,200
Net markdowns		800
Net sales		32,000

Required:
Estimate the average cost of ending inventory and cost of goods sold for October using the information provided.

E 9–14
Conventional retail method
● LO9–3

Campbell Corporation uses the retail method to value its inventory. The following information is available for the year 2021:

	Cost	Retail
Merchandise inventory, January 1, 2021	$190,000	$280,000
Purchases	600,000	840,000
Freight-in	8,000	
Net markups		20,000
Net markdowns		4,000
Net sales		800,000

Required:
Determine the December 31, 2021, inventory by applying the conventional retail method using the information provided.

E 9–15
Retail inventory method; LIFO
● LO9–3

Crosby Company owns a chain of hardware stores throughout the state. The company uses a periodic inventory system and the retail inventory method to estimate ending inventory and cost of goods sold. The following data are available for the three months ending March 31, 2021:

	Cost	Retail
Beginning inventory	$160,000	$280,000
Net purchases	607,760	840,000
Net markups		20,000
Net markdowns		4,000
Net sales		800,000

Required:
Estimate the LIFO cost of ending inventory and cost of goods sold for the three months ending March 31, 2021, using the information provided. Assume stable retail prices during the period.

E 9–16
Conventional retail method; normal spoilage
● LO9–4

Almaden Valley Variety Store uses the retail inventory method to estimate ending inventory and cost of goods sold. Data for 2021 are as follows:

	Cost	Retail
Beginning inventory	$ 12,000	$ 20,000
Purchases	102,600	165,000
Freight-in	3,480	
Purchase returns	4,000	7,000
Net markups		6,000
Net markdowns		3,000
Normal spoilage		4,200
Net sales		152,000

Required:
Estimate the ending inventory and cost of goods sold for 2021, applying the conventional retail method using the information provided.

E 9–17
Conventional and average cost retail methods; employee discounts
● LO9–3, LO9–4

LeMay Department Store uses the retail inventory method to estimate ending inventory for its monthly financial statements. The following data pertain to one of its largest departments for the month of March 2021:

	Cost	Retail
Beginning inventory	$ 40,000	$ 60,000
Purchases	207,000	400,000
Freight-in	14,488	
Purchase returns	4,000	6,000
Net markups		5,800
Net markdowns		3,500
Normal breakage		6,000
Net sales		280,000
Employee discounts		1,800

Sales are recorded net of employee discounts.

Required:
1. Compute estimated ending inventory and cost of goods sold for March applying the conventional retail method.
2. Recompute the cost-to-retail percentage using the average cost method.

E 9–18
Retail inventory method; solving for unknowns
● LO9–3

Adams Corporation uses a periodic inventory system and the retail inventory method to estimate ending inventory and cost of goods sold. The following data are available for the month of September 2021:

	Cost	Retail
Beginning inventory	$21,000	$35,000
Net purchases	10,500	?
Net markups		4,000
Net markdowns		1,000
Net sales		?

The company used the average cost flow method and estimated inventory at the end of September to be $17,437.50. If the company had used the LIFO cost flow method, the cost-to-retail percentage would have been 50%.

Required:
Compute net purchases at retail and net sales for the month of September using the information provided.

496   SECTION 2   Assets

E 9–19
Dollar-value LIFO retail
● LO9–5

On January 1, 2021, the Brunswick Hat Company adopted the dollar-value LIFO retail method. The following data are available for 2021:

	Cost	Retail
Beginning inventory	$ 71,280	$ 132,000
Net purchases	112,500	255,000
Net markups		6,000
Net markdowns		11,000
Net sales		232,000
Retail price index, 12/31/2021		1.04

Required:
Calculate the estimated ending inventory and cost of goods sold for 2021 using the information provided.

E 9–20
Dollar-value LIFO retail
● LO9–5

Canova Corporation adopted the dollar-value LIFO retail method on January 1, 2021. On that date, the cost of the inventory on hand was $15,000 and its retail value was $18,750. Information for 2021 and 2022 is as follows:

Date	Ending Inventory at Retail	Retail Price Index	Cost-to-Retail Percentage
12/31/2021	$25,000	1.25	82%
12/31/2022	28,600	1.30	85

Required:
1. What is the cost-to-retail percentage for the inventory on hand at 1/1/2021?
2. Calculate the inventory value at the end of 2021 and 2022 using the dollar-value LIFO retail method.

E 9–21
Dollar-value LIFO retail
● LO9–5

Lance-Hefner Specialty Shoppes decided to use the dollar-value LIFO retail method to value its inventory. Accounting records provide the following information:

	Cost	Retail
Merchandise inventory, January 1, 2021	$160,000	$250,000
Net purchases	350,200	510,000
Net markups		7,000
Net markdowns		2,000
Net sales		380,000

Related retail price indexes are as follows:

January 1, 2021	1.00
December 31, 2021	1.10

Required:
Determine ending inventory and cost of goods sold using the information provided.

E 9–22
Dollar-value LIFO retail; solving for unknowns
● LO9–5

Bosco Company adopted the dollar-value LIFO retail method at the beginning of 2021. Information for 2021 and 2022 is as follows, with certain data intentionally omitted:

	Inventory		Retail Price Index	Cost-to-Retail Percentage
Date	Cost	Retail		
Inventory, 1/1/2021	$21,000	$28,000	1.00	?
Inventory, 12/31/2021	22,792	33,600	1.12	?
2022 net purchases	60,000	88,400		
2022 net sales		80,000		
Inventory, 12/31/2022	?	?	1.20	

Required:
Determine the missing data.

E 9–23
Change in inventory costing methods
● LO9–6

In 2021, CPS Company changed its method of valuing inventory from the FIFO method to the average cost method. At December 31, 2020, CPS's inventories were $32 million (FIFO). CPS's records indicated that the inventories would have totaled $23.8 million at December 31, 2020, if determined on an average cost basis.

Required:
1. Prepare the journal entry to record the adjustment. (Ignore income taxes.)
2. Briefly describe other steps CPS should take to report the change.

E 9–24
Change in
inventory costing
methods
● LO9–6

Goddard Company has used the FIFO method of inventory valuation since it began operations in 2018. Goddard decided to change to the average cost method for determining inventory costs at the beginning of 2021. The following schedule shows year-end inventory balances under the FIFO and average cost methods:

Year	FIFO	Average Cost
2018	$45,000	$54,000
2019	78,000	71,000
2020	83,000	78,000

Required:
1. Ignoring income taxes, prepare the 2021 journal entry to adjust the accounts to reflect the average cost method.
2. How much higher or lower would cost of goods sold be in the 2020 revised income statement?

E 9–25
Error correction;
inventory error
● LO9–7

During 2021, WMC Corporation discovered that its ending inventories reported in its financial statements were misstated by the following material amounts:

2019	understated by	$120,000
2020	overstated by	150,000

WMC uses a periodic inventory system and the FIFO cost method.

Required:
1. Determine the effect of these errors on retained earnings at January 1, 2021, before any adjustments. Explain your answer. (Ignore income taxes.)
2. Prepare a journal entry to correct the errors.
3. What other step(s) would be taken in connection with the correction of the errors?

E 9–26
Inventory errors
● LO9–7

For each of the following inventory errors occurring in 2021, determine the effect of the error on 2021's cost of goods sold, net income, and retained earnings. Assume that the error is not discovered until 2022 and that a periodic inventory system is used. Ignore income taxes.

U = understated   O = overstated   NE = no effect

	Cost of Goods Sold	Net Income	Retained Earnings
1. Overstatement of ending inventory	U	O	O
2. Overstatement of purchases			
3. Understatement of beginning inventory			
4. Freight-in charges are understated			
5. Understatement of ending inventory			
6. Understatement of purchases			
7. Overstatement of beginning inventory			
8. Understatement of purchases plus understatement of ending inventory by the same amount			

E 9–27
Inventory error
● LO9–7

In 2021, the internal auditors of Development Technologies, Inc., discovered that a $4 million purchase of merchandise in 2021 was recorded in 2020 instead. The physical inventory count at the end of 2020 was correct.

Required:
Prepare the journal entry needed in 2021 to correct the error. Also, briefly describe any other measures Development Technologies would take in connection with correcting the error. (Ignore income taxes.)

E 9–28
Inventory errors
● LO9–7

In 2021, the controller of Sytec Corporation discovered that $42,000 of inventory purchases were incorrectly charged to advertising expense in 2020. In addition, the 2020 year-end inventory count failed to include $30,000 of company merchandise held on consignment by Erin Brothers. Sytec uses a periodic inventory system. Other than the omission of the merchandise on consignment, the year-end inventory count was correct. The amounts of the errors are deemed to be material.

Required:

1. Determine the effect of the errors on retained earnings at January 1, 2021. Explain your answer. (Ignore income taxes.)
2. Prepare a journal entry to correct the errors.
3. What other step(s) would be taken in connection with the correction of the errors?

E 9–29
Concepts; terminology
● LO9–1 through LO9–7

Listed below are several terms and phrases associated with inventory measurement. Pair each item from List A with the item from List B (by letter) that is most appropriately associated with it.

List A	List B
_____ 1. Gross profit ratio	a. Reduction in selling price below the original selling price
_____ 2. Cost-to-retail percentage	b. Beginning inventory is not included in the calculation of the cost-to-retail percentage
_____ 3. Additional markup	c. Deducted in the retail column after the calculation of the cost-to-retail percentage
_____ 4. Markdown	d. Requires base year retail to be converted to layer year retail and then to cost
_____ 5. Net markup	e. Gross profit divided by net sales
_____ 6. Retail method, FIFO and LIFO	f. Material inventory error discovered in a subsequent year
_____ 7. Conventional retail method	g. Must be added to sales if sales are recorded net of discounts
_____ 8. Change from LIFO	h. Deducted in the retail column to arrive at goods available for sale at retail
_____ 9. Dollar-value LIFO retail	i. Divide cost of goods available for sale by goods available at retail
_____ 10. Normal spoilage	j. Average cost, lower of cost or market
_____ 11. Requires retrospective restatement	k. Added to the retail column to arrive at goods available for sale
_____ 12. Employee discounts	l. Increase in selling price subsequent to initial markup
_____ 13. Net markdowns	m. Selling price less estimated selling costs
_____ 14. Net realizable value	n. Accounting change requiring retrospective treatment

E 9–30
Purchase commitments
● Appendix

On October 6, 2021, the Elgin Corporation signed a purchase commitment to purchase inventory for $60,000 on or before March 31, 2022. The company's fiscal year-end is December 31. The contract was exercised on March 21, 2022, and the inventory was purchased for cash at the contract price. On the purchase date of March 21, the market price of the inventory was $54,000. The market price of the inventory on December 31, 2021, was $56,000. The company uses a perpetual inventory system.

Required:

1. Prepare the necessary adjusting journal entry (if any is required) on December 31, 2021.
2. Prepare the journal entry to record the purchase on March 21, 2022.

E 9–31
Purchase commitments
● Appendix

In March 2021, the Phillips Tool Company signed two purchase commitments. The first commitment requires Phillips to purchase inventory for $100,000 by June 15, 2021. The second commitment requires the company to purchase inventory for $150,000 by August 20, 2021. The company's fiscal year-end is June 30. Phillips uses a periodic inventory system.

The first commitment is exercised on June 15, 2021, when the market price of the inventory purchased was $85,000. The second commitment was exercised on August 20, 2021, when the market price of the inventory purchased was $120,000.

Required:

Prepare the journal entries required on June 15, June 30, and August 20, 2021, to account for the two purchase commitments. Assume that the market price of the inventory related to the outstanding purchase commitment was $140,000 at June 30.

E 9–32
General ledger exercise; inventory transactions
● Chapter 8 and LO9–1

On January 1, 2021, the general ledger of Big Blast Fireworks included the following account balances:

Account Title	Debits	Credits
Cash	$ 21,900	
Accounts receivable	36,500	
Allowance for uncollectible accounts		$ 3,100
Inventory	30,000	
Land	61,600	
Accounts payable		32,400
Notes payable (8%, due in 3 years)		30,000
Common stock		56,000
Retained earnings		28,500
Totals	$150,000	$150,000

The $30,000 beginning balance of inventory consists of 300 units, each costing $100. During January 2021, Big Blast Fireworks had the following inventory transactions:

Jan. 3	Purchased 1,200 units for $126,000 on account ($105 each).
8	Purchased 1,300 units for $143,000 on account ($110 each).
12	Purchased 1,400 units for $161,000 on account ($115 each).
15	Returned 100 of the units purchased on January 12 because of defects.
19	Sold 4,000 units on account for $600,000. The cost of the units sold is determined using a FIFO perpetual inventory system.
22	Received $580,000 from customers on accounts receivable.
24	Paid $410,000 to inventory suppliers on accounts payable.
27	Wrote off accounts receivable as uncollectible, $2,500.
31	Paid cash for salaries during January, $128,000.

Required:
1. Record each of the transactions listed above in the 'General Journal' tab (these are shown as items 1-13) assuming a perpetual FIFO inventory system. Review the 'General Ledger' and the 'Trial Balance' tabs to see the effect of the transactions on the account balances.
2. Record adjusting entries on January 31 in the 'General Journal' tab (these are shown as items 14-18):
   a. At the end of January, the company estimates that the remaining units of inventory are expected to sell in February for only $100 each.
   b. At the end of January, $4,000 of accounts receivable are past due, and the company estimates that 40% of these accounts will not be collected. Of the remaining accounts receivable, the company estimates that 4% will not be collected.
   c. Accrued interest expense on notes payable for January. Interest is expected to be paid each December 31.
   d. Accrued income taxes at the end of January are $12,300.
3. Review the adjusted 'Trial Balance' as of January 31, 2021, in the 'Trial Balance' tab.
4. Prepare a multiple-step income statement for the period ended January 31, 2021, in the 'Income Statement' tab.
5. Prepare a classified balance sheet as of January 31, 2021, in the 'Balance Sheet' tab.
6. Record closing entries in the 'General Journal' tab (these are shown as items 19-21).
7. Using the information from the requirements above, complete the 'Analysis' tab.
   a. Calculate the inventory turnover ratio for the month of January. If the industry average of the inventory turnover ratio for the month of January is 18.5 times, is the company managing its inventory *more* or *less* efficiently than other companies in the same industry?
   b. Calculate the gross profit ratio for the month of January. If the industry average gross profit ratio is 33%, is the company *more* or *less* profitable per dollar of sales than other companies in the same industry?
   c. Used together, what might the inventory turnover ratio and gross profit ratio suggest about Big Blast Fireworks' business strategy? Is the company's strategy to sell a *higher volume of less expensive* items or does the company appear to be selling a *lower volume of more expensive* items?

Problems

P 9–1
Lower of cost or net realizable value; by product and by total inventory
● LO9–1

Decker Company has five products in its inventory. Information about the December 31, 2021, inventory follows.

Product	Quantity	Unit Cost	Unit Selling Price
A	1,000	$10	$16
B	800	15	18
C	600	3	8
D	200	7	6
E	600	14	13

The cost to sell for each product consists of a 15 percent sales commission.

Required:
1. Determine the carrying value of inventory at December 31, 2021, assuming the lower of cost or net realizable value (LCNRV) rule is applied to individual products.

500   SECTION 2   Assets

2. Determine the carrying value of inventory at December 31, 2021, assuming the LCNRV rule is applied to the entire inventory.

3. Assuming inventory write-downs are common for Decker, record any necessary year-end adjusting entry based on the amount calculated in requirement 2.

P 9–2
Lower of cost or net realizable value; by product, category, and total inventory
● LO9–1

Almaden Hardware Store sells two product categories, tools and paint products. Information pertaining to its 2021 year-end inventory is as follows:

Inventory, by Product Category	Quantity	Per Unit Cost	Net Realizable Value
Tools:			
Hammers	100	$ 5.00	$5.50
Saws	200	10.00	9.00
Screwdrivers	300	2.00	2.60
Paint products:			
1-gallon cans	500	6.00	5.00
Paint brushes	100	4.00	4.50

Required:

1. Determine the carrying value of inventory at year-end, assuming the lower of cost or net realizable value (LCNRV) rule is applied to (a) individual products, (b) product categories, and (c) total inventory.

2. Assuming inventory write-downs are common for Almaden, record any necessary year-end adjusting entry for each of the LCNRV applications in requirement 1.

P 9–3
Lower of cost or market; by product and by total inventory
● LO9–1

Forester Company has five products in its inventory. Information about the December 31, 2021, inventory follows.

Product	Quantity	Unit Cost	Unit Replacement Cost	Unit Selling Price
A	1,000	$10	$12	$16
B	800	15	11	18
C	600	3	2	8
D	200	7	4	6
E	600	14	12	13

The cost to sell for each product consists of a 15 percent sales commission. The normal profit for each product is 40 percent of the selling price.

Required:

1. Determine the carrying value of inventory at December 31, 2021, assuming the lower of cost or market (LCM) rule is applied to individual products.

2. Determine the carrying value of inventory at December 31, 2021, assuming the LCM rule is applied to the entire inventory.

3. Assuming inventory write-downs are common for Forester, record any necessary year-end adjusting entry based on the amount calculated in requirement 2.

P 9–4
Lower of cost or market; by product, category, and total inventory
● LO9–1

Home Stop sells two product categories, furniture and accessories. Information pertaining to its 2021 year-end inventory is as follows:

Inventory, by Product Category	Quantity	Per Unit Cost	Market
Furniture:			
Chairs	50	$25	$31
Desks	10	73	58
Tables	20	84	92
Accessories:			
Rugs	40	60	48
Lamps	30	22	18

Required:

1. Determine the carrying value of inventory at year-end, assuming the lower of cost or market (LCM) rule is applied to (a) individual products, (b) product categories, and (c) total inventory.

2. Assuming inventory write-downs are common for Home Stop, record any necessary year-end adjusting entry for each of the LCM applications in requirement 1.

P 9–5
Gross profit
method
● LO9–2

Smith Distributors, Inc., supplies ice cream shops with various toppings for making sundaes. On November 17, 2021, a fire resulted in the loss of all of the toppings stored in one section of the warehouse. The company must provide its insurance company with an estimate of the amount of inventory lost. The following information is available from the company's accounting records:

	Fruit Toppings	Marshmallow Toppings	Chocolate Toppings
Inventory, January 1, 2021	$ 20,000	$ 7,000	$ 3,000
Net purchases through Nov. 17	150,000	36,000	12,000
Net sales through Nov. 17	200,000	55,000	20,000
Historical gross profit ratio	20%	30%	35%

Required:
1. Calculate the estimated cost of each of the toppings lost in the fire.
2. What factors could cause the estimates to be over- or understated?

P 9–6
Retail inventory
method; average
cost and
conventional
● LO9–3, LO9–4

Sparrow Company uses the retail inventory method to estimate ending inventory and cost of goods sold. Data for 2021 are as follows:

	Cost	Retail
Beginning inventory	· $ 90,000	$180,000
Purchases	355,000	580,000
Freight-in	9,000	
Purchase returns	· 7,000	11,000
Net markups		16,000
Net markdowns		12,000
Normal spoilage		3,000
Abnormal spoilage	4,800	8,000
Sales		540,000
Sales returns		10,000

The company records sales net of employee discounts. Employee discounts for 2021 totaled $4,000.

Required:
Estimate Sparrow's ending inventory and cost of goods sold for the year using the retail inventory method and the following applications:
1. Average cost
2. Conventional

P 9–7
Retail inventory
method;
conventional and
LIFO
● LO9–3, LO9–4

Alquist Company uses the retail method to estimate its ending inventory. Selected information about its year 2021 operations is as follows:
a. January 1, 2021, beginning inventory had a cost of $100,000 and a retail value of $150,000.
b. Purchases during 2021 cost $1,387,500 with an original retail value of $2,000,000.
c. Freight costs were $10,000 for incoming merchandise.
d. Net additional markups were $300,000 and net markdowns were $150,000.
e. Based on prior experience, shrinkage due to shoplifting was estimated to be $15,000 of retail value.
f. Merchandise is sold to employees at a 20% of selling price discount. Employee sales are recorded in a separate account at the net selling price. The balance in this account at the end of 2021 is $250,000.
g. Sales to customers totaled $1,750,000 for the year.

Required:
1. Estimate ending inventory and cost of goods sold using the conventional retail method.
2. Estimate ending inventory and cost of goods sold using the LIFO retail method. (Assume stable prices.)

P 9–8
Retail inventory
method;
conventional
● LO9–4

Grand Department Store, Inc., uses the retail inventory method to estimate ending inventory for its monthly financial statements. The following data pertain to a single department for the month of October 2021:

Inventory, October 1, 2021:	
At cost	$ 20,000
At retail	30,000
Purchases (exclusive of freight and returns):	
At cost	100,151
At retail	146,495
Freight-in	5,100

(continued)

Purchase returns:	
At cost	2,100
At retail	2,800
Additional markups	2,500
Markup cancellations	265
Markdowns (net)	800
Normal spoilage and breakage	4,500
Sales	140,000
Sales returns	4,270

Required:

1. Using the conventional retail method, prepare a schedule computing estimated lower of cost or market (LCM) inventory for October 31, 2021.

2. A department store using the conventional retail inventory method estimates the cost of its ending inventory as $29,000. An accurate physical count reveals only $22,000 of inventory at lower of cost or market. List the factors that may have caused the difference between computed inventory and the physical count.

(AICPA adapted)

P 9–9
Retail method—
average cost and
conventional
● LO9–3, LO9–4

Smith-Kline Company maintains inventory records at selling prices as well as at cost. For 2021, the records indicate the following data:

	($ in thousands)	
	Cost	**Retail**
Beginning inventory	$ 80	$ 125
Purchases	671	1,006
Freight-in on purchases	30	
Purchase returns	1	2
Net markups		4
Net markdowns		8
Net sales		916

Required:
Use the retail method to approximate cost of ending inventory in each of the following ways:
1. Average cost
2. Conventional

P 9–10
Dollar-value LIFO
retail method
● LO9–5

[This is a variation of P 9–9, modified to focus on the dollar-value LIFO retail method.] Smith-Kline Company maintains inventory records at selling prices as well as at cost. For 2021, the records indicate the following data:

	($ in thousands)	
	Cost	**Retail**
Beginning inventory	$ 80	$ 125
Purchases	671	1,006
Freight-in on purchases	30	
Purchase returns	1	2
Net markups		4
Net markdowns		8
Net sales		916

Required:
Assuming the price level increased from 1.00 at January 1 to 1.10 at December 31, 2021, use the dollar-value LIFO retail method to approximate cost of ending inventory and cost of goods sold.

P 9–11
Dollar-value LIFO
retail
● LO9–5

On January 1, 2021, HGC Camera Store adopted the dollar-value LIFO retail inventory method. Inventory transactions at both cost and retail, and cost indexes for 2021 and 2022 are as follows:

	2021		2022	
	Cost	**Retail**	**Cost**	**Retail**
Beginning inventory	$28,000	$ 40,000		
Net purchases	85,000	108,000	$90,000	$114,000
Freight-in	2,000		2,500	
Net markups		10,000		8,000
Net markdowns		2,000		2,200
Net sales to customers		100,000		104,000
Sales to employees (net of 20% discount)		2,400		4,000
Price Index:				
January 1, 2021				1.00
December 31, 2021				1.06
December 31, 2022				1.10

Required:
Estimate the 2021 and 2022 ending inventory and cost of goods sold using the dollar-value LIFO retail inventory method.

P 9–12
Retail inventory
method; various
applications
● LO9–3 through
LO9–5

Raleigh Department Store uses the conventional retail method for the year ended December 31, 2019. Available information follows:

a. The inventory at January 1, 2019, had a retail value of $45,000 and a cost of $27,500 based on the conventional retail method.

b. Transactions during 2019 were as follows:

	Cost	Retail
Gross purchases	$282,000	$490,000
Purchase returns	6,500	10,000
Purchase discounts	5,000	
Sales		492,000
Sales returns		5,000
Employee discounts		3,000
Freight-in	26,500	
Net markups		25,000
Net markdowns		10,000

Sales to employees are recorded net of discounts.

c. The retail value of the December 31, 2020, inventory was $56,100, the cost-to-retail percentage for 2020 under the LIFO retail method was 62%, and the appropriate price index was 102% of the January 1, 2020, price level.

d. The retail value of the December 31, 2021, inventory was $48,300, the cost-to-retail percentage for 2021 under the LIFO retail method was 61%, and the appropriate price index was 105% of the January 1, 2020, price level.

Required:
1. Estimate ending inventory for 2019 using the conventional retail method.
2. Estimate ending inventory for 2019 assuming Raleigh Department Store used the LIFO retail method.
3. Assume Raleigh Department Store adopts the dollar-value LIFO retail method on January 1, 2020. Estimate ending inventory for 2020 and 2021.

(AICPA adapted)

P 9–13
Retail inventory
method; various
applications
● LO9–3 through
LO9–5

On January 1, 2021, Pet Friendly Stores adopted the retail inventory method. Inventory transactions at both cost and retail, and cost indexes for 2021 and 2022 are as follows:

	2021		2022	
	Cost	Retail	Cost	Retail
Beginning inventory	$ 90,000	$150,000		
Purchases	478,000	730,000	$511,000	$760,000
Purchase returns	2,500	3,500	2,200	4,000
Freight-in	6,960		8,000	
Net markups		8,500		10,000
Net markdowns		4,000		6,000
Net sales to customers		650,000		680,000
Sales to employees (net of 30% discount)		14,000		17,500
Normal spoilage		5,000		6,600
Price Index:				
January 1, 2021	1.00			
December 31, 2021	1.03			
December 31, 2022	1.06			

Required:
1. Estimate the 2021 and 2022 ending inventory and cost of goods sold using the dollar-value LIFO retail method.
2. Estimate the 2021 ending inventory and cost of goods sold using the average cost retail method.
3. Estimate the 2021 ending inventory and cost of goods sold using the conventional retail method.

P 9–14
Change in
methods
● LO9–6

Rockwell Corporation uses a periodic inventory system and has used the FIFO cost method since inception of the company in 1979. In 2021, the company decided to switch to the average cost method. Data for 2021 are as follows:

Beginning inventory, FIFO (5,000 units @ $30)		$150,000
Purchases:		
5,000 units @ $36	$180,000	
5,000 units @ $40	200,000	380,000
Cost of goods available for sale		$530,000
Sales for 2021 (8,000 units @ $70)		$560,000

Additional Information:

a. The company's effective income tax rate is 40% for all years.

b. If the company had used the average cost method prior to 2021, ending inventory for 2020 would have been $130,000.

c. 7,000 units remained in inventory at the end of 2021.

Required:

1. Ignoring income taxes, prepare the 2021 journal entry to adjust the accounts to reflect the average cost method.

2. What is the effect of the change in methods on 2021 net income?

P 9–15
Inventory errors
● LO9–7

You have been hired as the new controller for the Ralston Company. Shortly after joining the company in 2021, you discover the following errors related to the 2019 and 2020 financial statements:

a. Inventory at December 31, 2019, was understated by $6,000.

b. Inventory at December 31, 2020, was overstated by $9,000.

c. On December 31, 2020, inventory was purchased for $3,000. The company did not record the purchase until the inventory was paid for early in 2021. At that time, the purchase was recorded by a debit to purchases and a credit to cash.

The company uses a periodic inventory system.

Required:

1. Assuming that the errors were discovered after the 2020 financial statements were issued, analyze the effect of the errors on 2020 and 2019 cost of goods sold, net income, and retained earnings. (Ignore income taxes.)

2. Prepare a journal entry to correct the errors.

3. What other step(s) would be taken in connection with the errors?

P 9–16
Inventory errors
● LO9–7

The December 31, 2021, inventory of Tog Company, based on a physical count, was determined to be $450,000. Included in that count was a shipment of goods received from a supplier at the end of the month that cost $50,000. The purchase was recorded and paid for in 2022. Another supplier shipment costing $20,000 was correctly recorded as a purchase in 2021. However, the merchandise, shipped FOB shipping point, was not received until 2022 and was incorrectly omitted from the physical count. A third purchase, shipped from a supplier FOB shipping point on December 28, 2021, did not arrive until January 3, 2022. The merchandise, which cost $80,000, was not included in the physical count and the purchase has not yet been recorded.

The company uses a periodic inventory system.

Required:

1. Determine the correct December 31, 2021, inventory balance and, assuming that the errors were discovered after the 2021 financial statements were issued, analyze the effect of the errors on 2021 cost of goods sold, net income, and retained earnings. (Ignore income taxes.)

2. Prepare a journal entry to correct the errors.

P 9–17
Integrating
problem;
Chapters 8 and 9;
inventory errors
● LO9–7
☆

Capwell Corporation uses a periodic inventory system. The company's ending inventory on December 31, 2021, its fiscal-year end, based on a physical count, was determined to be $326,000. Capwell's unadjusted trial balance also showed the following account balances: Purchases, $620,000; Accounts payable; $210,000; Accounts receivable, $225,000; Sales revenue, $840,000.

The internal audit department discovered the following items:

1. Goods valued at $32,000 held on consignment from Dix Company were included in the physical count but not recorded as a purchase.

2. Purchases from Xavier Corporation were incorrectly recorded at $41,000 instead of the correct amount of $14,000. The correct amount was included in the ending inventory.

3. Goods that cost $25,000 were shipped from a vendor on December 28, 2021, terms FOB destination. The merchandise arrived on January 3, 2022. The purchase and related accounts payable were recorded in 2021.

4. One inventory item was incorrectly included in ending inventory as 100 units, instead of the correct amount of 1,000 units. This item cost $40 per unit.

5. The 2020 balance sheet reported inventory of $352,000. The internal auditors discovered that a mathematical error caused this inventory to be understated by $62,000. This amount is considered to be material. Comparative financial statements will be issued.

6. Goods shipped to a customer FOB destination on December 25, 2021, were received by the customer on January 4, 2022. The sales price was $40,000 and the merchandise cost $22,000. The sale and corresponding accounts receivable were recorded in 2021.

7. Goods shipped from a vendor FOB shipping point on December 27, 2021, were received on January 3, 2022. The merchandise cost $18,000. The purchase was not recorded until 2022.

Required:

1. Determine the correct amounts for 2021 purchases, accounts payable, sales revenue, and accounts receivable.

2. Calculate ending inventory and cost of goods sold for 2021.

3. Describe the steps Capwell would undertake to correct the error in the 2020 ending inventory. What was the effect of the error on 2020 before-tax income?

P 9–18
Purchase
commitments
● Appendix

In November 2021, the Brunswick Company signed two purchase commitments. The first commitment requires Brunswick to purchase 10,000 units of inventory at $10 per unit by December 15, 2021. The second commitment requires the company to purchase 20,000 units of inventory at $11 per unit by March 15, 2022. Brunswick's fiscal year-end is December 31. The company uses a periodic inventory system. Both contracts were exercised on their expiration date.

Required:

1. Prepare the journal entry to record the December 15 purchase for cash assuming the following alternative unit market prices on that date:
   a. $10.50
   b. $ 9.50

2. Prepare any necessary adjusting entry at December 31, 2021, for the second purchase commitment assuming the following alternative unit market prices on that date:
   a. $12.50
   b. $10.30

3. Assuming that the unit market price on December 31, 2021, was $10.30, prepare the journal entry to record the purchase on March 15, 2022, assuming the following alternative unit market prices on that date:
   a. $11.50
   b. $10.00

Decision Maker's Perspective

Apply your critical-thinking ability to the knowledge you've gained. These cases will provide you an opportunity to develop your research, analysis, judgment, and communication skills. You also will work with other students, integrate what you've learned, apply it in real-world situations, and consider its global and ethical ramifications. This practice will broaden your knowledge and further develop your decision-making abilities.

©ImageGap/Getty Images

**Judgment
Case 9–1**
Inventoriable
costs; lower of
cost or market;
retail inventory
method
● LO9–1, LO9–3,
  LO9–4

Hudson Company, which is both a wholesaler and a retailer, purchases its inventories from various suppliers. Additional facts for Hudson's wholesale operations are as follows:

a. Hudson incurs substantial warehousing costs.

b. Hudson values inventory at the lower of cost or market. Market is below cost of the inventories.

Additional facts for Hudson's retail operations are as follows:

a. Hudson determines the estimated cost of its ending inventories held for sale at retail using the conventional retail inventory method, which approximates lower of average cost or market.

b. Hudson incurs substantial freight-in costs.

c. Hudson has net markups and net markdowns.

Required:

1. Conceptually, in which account should Hudson report the warehousing costs related to its wholesale inventories? Why?

2. a. Inventory valued at the lower of cost or market is an example of which principle in accounting?

   b. At which amount should Hudson's wholesale inventories be reported in the balance sheet?

3. In the calculation of the cost-to-retail percentage used to determine the estimated cost of its ending retail inventories, how should Hudson treat:

   a. Freight-in costs?

   b. Net markups?

   c. Net markdowns?

4. How does Hudson's treatment of net markdowns affect the cost-to-retail percentage?

(AICPA adapted)

Communication Case 9–2
Lower of cost or net realizable value
● LO9–1

The lower of cost or net realizable value (LCNRV) approach to valuing inventory is a departure from the accounting principle of reporting assets at their historical costs. There are those who believe that inventory, as well as other assets, should be valued at NRV, regardless of whether NRV is above or below cost.

The focus of this case is the justification for the LCNRV rule for valuing inventories. Your instructor will divide the class into two to six groups depending on the size of the class. The mission of your group is to defend the LCNRV approach against the alternatives of valuing inventory at either historical cost or NRV.

Required:

1. Each group member should consider the situation independently and draft a tentative argument prior to the class session for which the case is assigned.

2. In class, each group will meet for 10 to 15 minutes in different areas of the classroom. During that meeting, group members will take turns sharing their suggestions for the purpose of arriving at a single group argument.

3. After the allotted time, a spokesperson for each group (selected during the group meetings) will share the group's solution with the class. The goal of the class is to incorporate the views of each group into a consensus approach to the situation.

Integrating Case 9–3
FIFO and lower of cost or net realizable value
● LO9–1

York Co. sells one product, which it purchases from various suppliers. York's trial balance at December 31, 2021, included the following accounts:

Sales (33,000 units @ $16)	$528,000
Sales discounts	7,500
Purchases	380,600
Purchase discounts	18,000
Freight-in	5,000
Freight-out	11,000

York Co.'s inventory purchases during 2021 were as follows:

	Units	Cost per Unit	Total Cost
Beginning inventory	7,000	$7.70	$ 53,900
Purchases, quarter ended March 31	13,000	7.50	97,500
Purchases, quarter ended June 30	15,000	7.90	118,500
Purchases, quarter ended September 30	12,000	8.25	99,000
Purchases, quarter ended December 31	8,000	8.20	65,600
	55,000		$434,500

Additional Information:

a. York's accounting policy is to report inventory in its financial statements at the lower of cost or net realizable value, applied to total inventory. Cost is determined under the first-in, first-out (FIFO) method.

b. York has determined that, at December 31, 2021, the net realizable value was $8.00 per unit.

Required:

1. Prepare York's schedule of cost of goods sold, with a supporting schedule of ending inventory. York includes inventory write-down losses in cost of goods sold.

2. Determine whether inventory should be reported at cost or net realizable value.

(AICPA adapted)

Judgment Case 9–4
The dollar-value LIFO method; the retail inventory method
● LO9–3, LO9–4

Huddell Company, which is both a wholesaler and retailer, purchases merchandise from various suppliers. The dollar-value LIFO method is used for the wholesale inventories.

Huddell determines the estimated cost of its retail ending inventories using the conventional retail inventory method, which approximates lower of average cost or market.

Required:

1. a. What are the advantages of using the dollar-value LIFO method as opposed to the traditional LIFO method?
   b. How does the application of the dollar-value LIFO method differ from the application of the traditional LIFO method?
2. a. In the calculation of the cost-to-retail percentage used to determine the estimated cost of its ending inventories, how should Huddell use
   - Net markups?
   - Net markdowns?
   b. Why does Huddell's retail inventory method approximate lower of average cost or market?

(AICPA adapted)

Communication Case 9–5
Retail inventory method
● LO9–3, LO9–4

The Brenly Paint Company, your client, manufactures paint. The company's president, Mr. Brenly, decided to open a retail store to sell paint as well as wallpaper and other items that would be purchased from other suppliers. He has asked you for information about the retail method of estimating inventories at the retail store.

Required:

Prepare a report to the president explaining the retail method of estimating inventories.

Analysis Case 9–6
Change in inventory method
● LO9–6

Generally accepted accounting principles should be applied consistently from period to period. However, changes within a company, as well as changes in the external economic environment, may force a company to change an accounting method. The specific reporting requirements when a company changes from one generally accepted inventory method to another depend on the methods involved.

Required:

Explain the accounting treatment for a change in inventory method (a) not involving LIFO, (b) from the LIFO method, and (c) to the LIFO method. Explain the logic underlying those treatments. Also, describe how disclosure requirements are designed to address the departure from consistency and comparability of changes in accounting principle.

Real World Case 9–7
Change in inventory method; Abercrombie & Fitch Co.
● LO9–6
Real World Financials

Abercrombie & Fitch Co. (A&F) is a specialty retail company operating over 1,000 stores globally. The following disclosure note was included in recent financial statements:

4. Change in Accounting Principle

The Company elected to change its method of accounting for inventory from the retail method to the weighted average cost method effective February 2, 2013. In accordance with generally accepted accounting principles, all periods have been retroactively adjusted to reflect the period-specific effects of the change to the weighted average cost method. The Company believes that accounting under the weighted average cost method is preferable as it better aligns with the Company's focus on realized selling margin and improves the comparability of the Company's financial results with those of its competitors. Additionally, it will improve the matching of cost of goods sold with the related net sales and reflect the acquisition cost of inventory outstanding at each balance sheet date. The cumulative adjustment as of January 30, 2010, was an increase in its inventory of $73.6 million and an increase in retained earnings of $47.3 million.

Required:

1. What approach should A&F take to account for its change in inventory accounting (retrospective, modified retrospective, or prospective)?
2. Will A&F need to restate financial statements prior to the year of the accounting change (yes/no)?
3. Which enhancing qualitative characteristic of accounting best describes the reason for A&F's approach to accounting for its change in inventory method?

Real World Case 9–8
Various inventory issues; Chapters 8 and 9; Fred's Inc.

● LO9–1, LO9–5, LO9–6

Real World Financials

Fred's Inc. operates general merchandise retail discount stores and full-service pharmacies in the Southeastern United States. Access the company's 10-K for the fiscal year ended January 28, 2017. You can find the 10-K by using EDGAR at www.sec.gov (Hint: do not use the apostrophe in the company name when doing an Edgar search.) Answer the following questions.

Required:

1. What inventory methods does Fred's use to value its inventory?
2. Which price index does the company use in applying the retail inventory method?
3. A company that uses LIFO is allowed to provide supplemental disclosures reporting the effect of using another inventory method rather than LIFO. Using the supplemental LIFO disclosures provided by Fred's, determine the pretax income effect of using LIFO versus another method for the current fiscal year.
4. Calculate the company's inventory turnover ratio for the fiscal year ended January 28, 2017.
5. Assume that in the next fiscal year the company decides to switch to the average cost method. What approach would Fred's take to account for this change (retrospective, modified retrospective, or prospective)?

Communication Case 9–9
Change in inventory method; disclosure note

● LO9–6

Mayfair Department Stores, Inc., operates over 30 retail stores in the Pacific Northwest. Prior to 2021, the company used the FIFO method to value its inventory. In 2021, Mayfair decided to switch to the dollar-value LIFO retail inventory method. One of your responsibilities as assistant controller is to prepare the disclosure note describing the change in method that will be included in the company's 2021 financial statements. Kenneth Meier, the controller, provided the following information:

a. Internally developed retail price indexes are used to adjust for the effects of changing prices.
b. If the change had not been made, cost of goods sold for the year would have been $22 million lower. The company's income tax rate is 40% and there were 100 million shares of common stock outstanding during 2021.
c. The cumulative effect of the change on prior years' income is not determinable.
d. The reasons for the change were (a) to provide a more consistent matching of merchandise costs with sales revenue, and (b) the new method provides a more comparable basis of accounting with competitors that also use the LIFO method.

Required:

1. Prepare for Kenneth Meier the disclosure note that will be included in the 2021 financial statements.
2. Explain why the "cumulative effect of the change on prior years' income is not determinable."

Judgment Case 9–10
Inventory errors

● LO9–7

Some inventory errors are said to be self-correcting in that the error has the opposite financial statement effect in the period following the error, thereby correcting the original account balance errors.

Required:

Despite this self-correcting feature, discuss why these errors should not be ignored and describe the steps required to account for the error correction.

Ethics Case 9–11
Overstatement of ending inventory

● LO9–7

Danville Bottlers is a wholesale beverage company. Danville uses the FIFO inventory method to determine the cost of its ending inventory. Ending inventory quantities are determined by a physical count. For the accounting year-end December 31, 2021, ending inventory was originally determined to be $3,265,000. However, on January 17, 2022, John Howard, the company's controller, discovered an error in the ending inventory count. He determined that the correct ending inventory amount should be $2,600,000.

Danville is a privately owned corporation with significant financing provided by a local bank. The bank requires annual audited financial statements as a condition of the loan. By January 17, the auditors had completed their review of the financial statements which are scheduled to be issued on January 25. They did not discover the inventory error.

John's first reaction was to communicate his finding to the auditors and to revise the financial statements before they are issued. However, he knows that his and his fellow workers' profit-sharing plans are based on annual pretax earnings, and he is uncertain what effect the error correction would have on pretax earnings.

Required:

1. What is the effect of the inventory error on pretax earnings?
2. How would correcting the error affect employee bonuses?
3. If the error is not corrected in the current year and is discovered by the auditors during the following year's audit, how will it be reported in the company's financial statements?
4. Discuss the ethical dilemma John Howard faces.

Analysis Case 9–12
Purchase commitments

● Appendix

The management of the Esquire Oil Company believes that the wholesale price of heating oil that they sell to homeowners will increase again as the result of increased political problems in the Middle East. The company is currently paying $0.80 a gallon. If they are willing to enter an agreement in November 2021 to purchase a million gallons of heating oil during the winter of 2022, their supplier will guarantee the price at $0.80 per gallon. However, if the winter is a mild one, Esquire would not be able to sell a million gallons unless they reduced their retail price and thereby increase the risk of a loss for the year. On the other hand, if the wholesale price did increase substantially, they would be in a favorable position with respect to their competitors. The company's fiscal year-end is December 31.

Required:

Discuss the accounting issues related to the purchase commitment that Esquire is considering.

Data Analytics   connect

Data analytics is the process of examining data sets in order to draw conclusions about the information they contain. If you have not completed any of the prior data analytics cases, follow the instructions listed in the Chapter 1 Data Analytics case to get set up. You will need to watch the videos referred to in the Chapters 1 - 3 Data Analytics cases. No additional videos are required for this case. All short training videos can be found here: https://www.tableau.com/learn/training#getting-started.

In this case you are seeking to gain insight into the relative demand for the company's products in various regions of the country and various states in which it sells. Your focus is on assessing the company's inventory management relative to regional and local demand.

Data Analytics Case
Inventory Management
● LO9–3

Required:

Use Tableau to calculate (a) additional markup percentage and (b) markdown percentage ratios for the company in each of the five regions of the country designated in the company's data base and in each of the states in which the company sells products. Calculate the ratios as the additional markup or markdown amounts as a percentage of sales. (A more precise measure that would produce similar results would replace sales in the ratio denominator with the original selling price of both sales and unsold inventory.) Based upon what you find, answer the following questions:

1. Which of the five regions' operations has the *most* favorable inventory management relative to demand as measured by the *additional markup* percentage ratio and what is that ratio (to the nearest one-tenth of a percent)?
2. Which of the five regions' operations has the *least* favorable inventory management relative to demand as measured by *markdown* percentage ratio and what is that ratio (to the nearest one-tenth of a percent)?

To view the state inventory management results more clearly, highlight the column "Additional Markup %" in the "Inventory Management by State" column and sort from largest to smallest. You can answer problem 4 below by following the same procedure for the "Markdown %" column.

3. Which state's operations has the *most* favorable inventory management relative to demand as measured by *additional markup* percentage ratio and what is that ratio (to the nearest one-tenth of a percent)?
4. Which state's operations has the *least* favorable inventory management relative to demand as measured by *markdown* percentage ratio and what is that ratio (to the nearest one-tenth of a percent)?

Resources:

You have available to you an extensive data set that includes detailed financial data for the company's inventory sales. The data set is in the form of four Excel files available to download from Connect, or under Student Resources within the Library tab. Download the file "Inventory.xlsx" to the computer, save it, and open it in Tableau.

For this case, you will create several calculations to produce a bar chart and a text chart to allow you to compare and contrast a company's inventory management.

After you view the training videos and review instructions in Chapters 1-3, follow these steps to create the charts you'll use for this case:

- Click on the "Sheet 1" tab at the bottom of the canvas, to the right of the Data Source at the bottom of the screen. Drag "Region" under Dimensions to the Columns shelf.
- Drag "Status" under Dimensions to the Filters card. When the Filter window opens, click the "S" so only the sold items will be viewed. Click ok.
- Under the Analysis tab, select Create Calculated Field and label it "Total Sales." Drag "Number" under "Dimensions" to the Calculation Editor window. Type an asterisk sign for multiplication, then drag "Selling Price" under "Dimensions" next to the asterisk. Make sure the window says that the calculation is valid and click OK.
- Repeat the process by creating a calculated field "Total Markups" that consists of "Number" times "Net Markups." Make sure the window says that the calculation is valid and click OK.
- Repeat the process by creating a calculated field "Total Markdowns" that consists of "Number" times "Net Markdowns." Make sure the window says that the calculation is valid and click OK.
- Drag "Total Sales," "Total Markups," and "Total Markdowns" to the Rows shelf.
- Create a calculated field named "Additional Markup %" by dragging "Total Markups" from the Rows shelf into the Calculation Editor window, typing the division sign, and dragging "Total Sales" from the Rows shelf into the window next to it. Make sure the window says that the calculation is valid and click OK.

510   SECTION 2   Assets

- Repeat the process one more time by creating a calculated field "Markdown %" by dragging "Total Markdowns" from the Rows shelf into the Calculation Editor window, typing the division sign, and dragging "Total Sales" from the Rows shelf into the window next to it.
- Drag "Total Sales," "Total Markups" and "Total Markdowns" from the Rows shelf back under Dimensions so they no longer show on the canvas.
- Drag "Additional Markup %" and "Markdown %," to the Rows shelf.
- Click the "Show Me" box on right side of the toolbar and select the "side-by-side bars."
- Show the labels by clicking on Label in the "Marks" card and checking "Show mark labels."
- Change the title of the sheet to be "Inventory Management by Region" by right-clicking and selecting "Edit title." Format the title to Times New Roman, bold, black and 15-point font. Change the title of "Sheet 1" to match the sheet title by right-clicking, selecting "Rename" and typing in the new title.
- Format all the labels on the sheet to Times New Roman, 10-point font, and black. You can also change the color variation by clicking "Color" on the "Marks" card and editing the color.
- Click on the New Worksheet tab on the lower right ("Sheet 2" should open) and drag "State" to the Rows shelf. Select the drop-down arrow on "State" to format the state names to Times New Roman, 10-point font, bold and blue (the format screen will open to the left).
- Double click "Additional Markup %" and "Markdown %." Right click on the drop-down menu of one of them and select "Format." Format to Times New Roman, bold, black, 10-point font, and center alignment (center alignment will be in the drop-down box beside alignment).
- Right click on one of the numbers and select "Format." Click on "Fields" in the upper-right corner of the Format window, select "Measure values," and format the numbers to "Percentage with two decimal places." Note that you can click on the right-side of each of the headings ("Additional Markup %" and "Markdown %") to sort from highest to lowest or lowest to highest. This may help you answer some of the questions.
- Change the title of the sheet to be "Inventory Management by State" by right-clicking and selecting "Edit title." Format the title to Times New Roman, bold, black and 15-point font. Change the title of "Sheet 2" to match the sheet title by right-clicking, selecting "Rename" and typing in the new title.
- Once complete, save the file as "DA9_Your initials.twbx."

Continuing Cases

Target Case

 LO9–3, LO9–4, LO9–5

Target Corporation prepares its financial statements according to U.S. GAAP. Target's financial statements and disclosure notes for the year ended February 3, 2018, are available in Connect. This material is also available under the Investor Relations link at the company's website (www.target.com).

Required:

1. What retail indices (internally measured or externally measured) does Target use to measure the LIFO provision?
2. Does Target adjust the retail value of inventory for permanent markups or permanent markdowns to effectively report inventory at the lower of cost or market?
3. Target has agreements with certain vendors whereby Target does not purchase or pay for merchandise until the merchandise is ultimately sold to a customer. Are sales and cost of sales of this inventory included in Target's income statement? Is unsold inventory at the end of the year included as part of ending inventory in the balance sheet?

Air France–KLM Case

● LO9–8

 IFRS

Air France–KLM (AF), a Franco-Dutch company, prepares its financial statements according to International Financial Reporting Standards. AF's financial statements and disclosure notes for the year ended December 31, 2017, are available in Connect. This material is also available under the Finance link at the company's website (www.airfranceklm.com).

Required:

AF's inventories are valued at the lower of cost or net realizable value. Does this approach differ from U.S. GAAP?

CPA Exam Questions and Simulations

ROGER *CPA Review*

Sample CPA Exam questions from Roger CPA Review are available in Connect as support for the topics in this chapter. These multiple-choice questions and task-based simulations include expert-written explanations and solutions, and provide a starting point for students to become familiar with the content and functionality of the actual CPA Exam.

CHAPTER

10 Property, Plant, and Equipment and Intangible Assets: Acquisition

OVERVIEW — This chapter and the one that follows address the measurement and reporting issues involving property, plant, and equipment and intangible assets. These are the long-lived assets used in the production of goods and services. This chapter covers the valuation at date of acquisition. In Chapter 11, we discuss the allocation of the cost of property, plant, and equipment and intangible assets to the periods benefited by their use, the treatment of expenditures made over the life of these assets to maintain and improve them, impairment, and disposition.

LEARNING OBJECTIVES

After studying this chapter, you should be able to:

- **LO10–1** Identify the various costs included in the initial cost of property, plant, and equipment, natural resources, and intangible assets. (p. 516)
- **LO10–2** Determine the initial cost of individual property, plant, and equipment and intangible assets acquired as a group for a lump-sum purchase price. (p. 525)
- **LO10–3** Determine the initial cost of property, plant, and equipment and intangible assets acquired in exchange for a deferred payment contract. (p. 526)
- **LO10–4** Determine the initial cost of property, plant, and equipment and intangible assets acquired in exchange for equity securities or through donation. (p. 528)
- **LO10–5** Calculate the fixed-asset turnover ratio used by analysts to measure how effectively managers use property, plant, and equipment. (p. 530)
- **LO10–6** Determine the initial cost of property, plant, and equipment and intangible assets acquired in exchange for other nonmonetary assets. (p. 531)
- **LO10–7** Identify the items included in the cost of a self-constructed asset and determine the amount of capitalized interest. (p. 535)
- **LO10–8** Explain the difference in the accounting treatment of costs incurred to purchase intangible assets versus the costs incurred to internally develop intangible assets. (p. 541)
- **LO10–9** Discuss the primary differences between U.S. GAAP and IFRS with respect to the acquisition of property, plant, and equipment and intangible assets. (p. 529, 543)

©Idealphotographer/123RF

FINANCIAL REPORTING CASE

A Disney Adventure

"Now I'm really confused," confessed Stan, your study partner, staring blankly at The Walt Disney Company balance sheet that your professor handed out last week. "I thought that interest is always expensed in the income statement. Now I see that Disney is capitalizing interest. I'm not even sure what *capitalize* means! And what about this other account called *goodwill?* What's that all about?" You respond, "We talked about these topics in our accounting class today. Let's take a look at the Disney financial statements and the disclosure note on capitalized interest and I'll try to explain it all to you."

Borrowings (in part):

The Company capitalizes interest on assets constructed for its parks and resorts and on certain film and television productions. In fiscal years 2017, 2016 and 2015, total interest capitalized was $87 million, $139 million, and $110 million, respectively.

By the time you finish this chapter, you should be able to respond appropriately to the questions posed in this case. Compare your response to the solution provided at the end of the chapter.

QUESTIONS

1. Describe to Stan what it means to capitalize an expenditure. What is the general rule for determining which costs are capitalized when property, plant, and equipment or an intangible asset is acquired? (*p. 516*)

2. Which costs might be included in the initial cost of equipment? (*p. 516*)

3. What is goodwill and how is it measured? (*p. 523*)

4. In what situations is interest capitalized rather than expensed? (*p. 536*)

5. What is the three-step process used to determine the amount of interest capitalized? (*p. 537*)

General Motors Corporation has significant investments in the production facilities it uses to manufacture the automobiles it sells. On the other hand, the principal revenue-producing assets of Microsoft Corporation are the copyrights on its computer software that permit it the exclusive rights to earn profits from those products. Timber reserves provide major revenues to International Paper Company. From a reporting perspective, we classify GM's production facilities as property, plant, and equipment; Microsoft's copyrights as intangible assets; and International Paper's timber reserves as natural resources.[1] Together, these three noncurrent assets constitute the *long-lived, revenue-producing assets* of a company. Unlike manufacturers, many service firms and merchandising companies rely primarily on people or investments in inventories rather than on property, plant, and equipment and intangible assets to generate revenues. Even nonmanufacturing firms, though, typically have at least modest investments in buildings and equipment.

The measurement and reporting issues pertaining to this group of assets include valuation at date of acquisition, disposition, the treatment of expenditures made over the life of these assets to maintain and improve them, the allocation of cost to reporting periods that benefit from their use, and impairment. We focus on initial valuation in this chapter. In Chapter 11, we examine subsequent expenditures, cost allocation, impairment, and disposition.

---

[1]These are sometimes called *plant assets* or *fixed assets.*

PART A

Valuation at Acquisition

Types of Assets

For financial reporting purposes, long-lived, revenue-producing assets typically are classified in two categories.

1. Property, plant, and equipment. Assets in this category include land, land improvements, buildings, machinery used in manufacturing, computers and other office equipment, vehicles, furniture, and fixtures. Natural resources such as oil and gas deposits, timber tracts, and mineral deposits also are included.

2. Intangible assets. Unlike property, plant, and equipment and natural resources, intangible assets lack physical substance, and the extent and timing of their future benefits typically are uncertain. They include items such as patents, copyrights, trademarks, franchises, and goodwill.

Of course, every company maintains its own unique mix of these assets. The way these assets are classified and combined for reporting purposes also varies from company to company. As an example, a recent balance sheet of Semtech Corporation, a leading supplier of semiconductor products, reported net property, plant, and equipment of $124,586 thousand and $108,910 thousand at the end of fiscal years 2018 and 2017, respectively. A disclosure note, shown in Illustration 10–1, provides the details.

Illustration 10–1

Property, Plant, and Equipment—Semtech Corporation

Real World Financials

Note 7. Property, Plant, and Equipment (in part):		
The following is a summary of property and equipment, at cost less accumulated depreciation:		
($ in thousands)	January 28, 2018	January 29, 2017
Property	$ 11,314	$ 11,314
Buildings	32,244	30,294
Leasehold improvements	10,050	9,566
Machinery and equipment	171,731	150,276
Enterprise resource planning systems	32,673	28,166
Furniture and office equipment	39,027	35,025
Construction in progress	7,151	5,505
Property, plant, and equipment, gross	304,190	270,146
Less: accumulated depreciation and amortization	(179,604)	(161,236)
Property, plant, and equipment, net	$124,586	$108,910

Source: Semtech Corporation

In practice, some companies report intangibles as part of property, plant, and equipment, and others show intangibles as a separate balance sheet category. For example, The Walt Disney Company reported goodwill of $31,426 million and other intangible assets of $6,995 million and $6,949 million at the end of fiscal years 2017 and 2016, respectively, as shown in Illustration 10–2.

In this chapter, we'll first discuss how to record the acquisition cost of several types of property, plant, and equipment, and then we'll discuss the acquisition cost of intangible assets. You should find it helpful to study the overview of typical acquisition costs for each type of asset in Illustration 10–3. In Part B of this chapter, we examine how to record the acquisition of these assets when no cash is involved. Self-constructed assets and special issues related to research and development costs are addressed in Part C of the chapter. In the next chapter, we'll see how asset acquisition costs are expensed over time in a process called *depreciation* for plant and equipment, *depletion* for natural resources, and *amortization* for intangibles.

Illustration 10–2

Other Intangible Assets—
The Walt Disney Company

Real World Financials

($ in millions)	2017	2016
Character/franchise intangibles and copyrights	$ 5,829	$ 5,829
Other amortizable intangible assets	1,154	893
Accumulated amortization	(1,828)	(1,635)
Net amortizable intangible assets	5,155	5,087
FCC licenses	602	624
Trademarks	1,218	1,218
Other indefinite lived intangible assets	20	20
	$6,995	$6,949

Source: The Walt Disney Company

Illustration 10–3 Property, Plant, and Equipment and Intangible Assets and Their Acquisition Costs

Asset	Description	Typical Acquisition Costs
Property, plant, and equipment	Productive assets that derive their value from long-term use in operations rather than from resale.	All expenditures necessary to get the asset in condition and location for its intended use.
Equipment	Broad term that includes machinery, computers and other office equipment, vehicles, furniture, and fixtures.	Purchase price (less discounts), taxes, transportation, installation, testing, trial runs, and reconditioning.
Land	Real property used in operations (land held for speculative investment or future use is reported as investments or other assets).	Purchase price, attorney's fees, title, recording fees, commissions, back taxes, mortgages, liens, clearing, filling, draining, and removing old buildings.
Land improvements	Enhancements to property such as parking lots, driveways, private roads, fences, landscaping, and sprinkler systems.	Separately identifiable costs.
Buildings	Structures that include warehouses, plant facilities, and office buildings.	Purchase price, attorney's fees, commissions, and reconditioning.
Natural resources	Productive assets that are physically consumed in operations such as timber, mineral deposits, and oil and gas reserves.	Acquisition, exploration, development, and restoration costs.
Intangible Assets	Productive assets that lack physical substance and have long-term but typically uncertain benefits.	All expenditures necessary to get the asset in condition and location for its intended use.
Patents	Exclusive 20-year right to manufacture a product or use a process.	Purchase price, legal fees, filing fees, not including internal R&D.
Copyrights	Exclusive right to benefit from a creative work such as a song, film, painting, photograph, or book.	Purchase price, legal fees, filing fees, not including internal R&D.
Trademarks (tradenames)	Exclusive right to display a word, a slogan, a symbol, or an emblem that distinctively identifies a company, product, or a service.	Purchase price, legal fees, filing fees, not including internal R&D.
Franchises	A contractual arrangement under which a franchisor grants the franchisee the exclusive right to use the franchisor's trademark or tradename and certain product rights.	Franchise fee plus any legal fees.
Goodwill	The unique value of the company as a whole over and above all identifiable assets.	Excess of the fair value of the consideration given for a company over the fair value of the identifiable net assets acquired.

Costs to be Capitalized

Property, plant, and equipment and intangible assets can be acquired through purchase, exchange, lease, donation, self-construction, or a business combination. We address acquisitions through leasing in Chapter 15.

The initial valuation of property, plant, and equipment and intangible assets usually is quite simple. We know from prior study that assets are valued on the basis of their original costs. In Chapter 8 we introduced the concept of condition and location in determining the cost of inventory. For example, if Thompson Company purchased inventory for $40,000 and incurred $1,000 in freight costs to have the inventory shipped to its location, the initial cost of the inventory is $41,000. This concept applies to the valuation of property, plant, and equipment and intangible assets as well. The initial cost of these assets includes the purchase price and all expenditures necessary to bring the asset to its desired condition and location for use. We discuss these additional expenditures in the next section.

Our objective in identifying the costs of an asset is to distinguish the expenditures that produce future benefits from those that produce benefits only in the current period. The costs in the second group are recorded as expenses, but those in the first group are *capitalized;* that is, they are recorded initially as an asset and then expensed in future periods.[2] For example, the cost of a major improvement to a delivery truck that extends its useful life generally would be capitalized. On the other hand, the cost of an engine tune-up for the delivery truck simply allows the truck to continue its productive activity but does not increase future benefits. These maintenance costs would be expensed. Subsequent expenditures for these assets are discussed in Chapter 11.

The distinction is not trivial. This point was unmistakably emphasized in the summer of 2002 when WorldCom, Inc., disclosed that it had improperly capitalized nearly $4 billion in expenditures related to the company's telecom network. This massive fraud resulted in one of the largest financial statement restatements in history and triggered the collapse of the once powerful corporation. Capitalizing rather than expensing these expenditures caused a substantial understatement of expenses and overstatement of reported income for 2001 and the first quarter of 2002. If the deception had not been discovered, not only would income for 2001 and 2002 have been overstated but also income for many years into the future would have been understated as the fraudulent capitalized assets were depreciated. Of course, the balance sheet also would have overstated the assets and equity of the company.

Property, Plant, and Equipment

COST OF EQUIPMENT   Equipment is a broad term that encompasses machinery used in manufacturing, computers and other office equipment, vehicles, furniture, and fixtures. The cost of equipment includes the purchase price plus any sales tax (less any discounts received from the seller), transportation costs paid by the buyer to transport the asset to the location in which it will be used, expenditures for installation, testing, legal fees to establish title, and any other costs of bringing the asset to its condition and location for use. To the extent that these costs can be identified and measured, they should be included in the asset's initial valuation rather than expensed currently.

Although most costs can be identified easily, others are more difficult. For example, the costs of training personnel to operate machinery could be considered a cost necessary to make the asset ready for use. However, because it is difficult to measure the amount of training costs associated with specific assets, these costs usually are expensed. Consider Illustration 10–4.

---

[2]Exceptions are land and certain intangible assets that have indefinite useful lives. Costs to acquire these assets also produce future benefits and therefore are capitalized, but unlike other property, plant, and equipment and intangible assets, their costs are not systematically expensed in future periods as depreciation or amortization.

Central Machine Tools purchased industrial equipment to be used in its manufacturing process. The purchase price was $62,000. Central paid a freight company $1,000 to transport the equipment to its plant location plus $300 shipping insurance. In addition, the equipment had to be installed and mounted on a special platform built specifically for the equipment at a cost of $1,200. After installation, several trial runs were made to ensure proper operation. The cost of these trials including wasted materials was $600. At what amount should Central capitalize the equipment?

Purchase price	$62,000
Freight and handling	1,000
Insurance during shipping	300
Special platform	1,200
Trial runs	600
Capitalized cost of equipment	$65,100

Each of the expenditures described was necessary to bring the equipment to its condition and location for use and should be capitalized. These costs will be expensed in the future periods in which the equipment is used.

Illustration 10–4

Initial Cost of Equipment

COST OF LAND The cost of land also should include expenditures needed to get the land ready for its intended use. These include the purchase price plus closing costs such as fees for the attorney, real estate agent commissions, title and title search, and recording. If the property is subject to back taxes, liens, mortgages, or other obligations, these amounts are included also. In addition, any expenditures such as clearing, filling, draining, and even removing (razing) old buildings that are needed to prepare the land for its intended use are part of the land's cost. Proceeds from the sale of salvaged materials from old buildings torn down after purchase reduce the cost of land. Illustration 10–5 provides an example.

The Byers Structural Metal Company purchased a six-acre tract of land and an existing building for $500,000. The company plans to remove the old building and construct a new office building on the site. In addition to the purchase price, the company made the following expenditures at closing of the purchase:

Title insurance	$ 3,000
Commissions	16,000
Property taxes	6,000*

*The $6,000 in property taxes included $4,000 of delinquent taxes paid by Byers on behalf of the seller as well as $2,000 attributable to the portion of the current fiscal year that remains *after the purchase date.*

  In addition, shortly after closing, Byers paid a contractor $10,000 to tear down the old building and remove it from the site. An additional $5,000 was paid to grade the land. What should be the capitalized cost of the land?

Purchase price of land (and old building)	$500,000
Title insurance	3,000
Commissions	16,000
Delinquent property taxes	4,000
Cost of removing old building	10,000
Cost of grading	5,000
Capitalized cost of land	$538,000

  Property taxes of $2,000 were not included. These relate only to the current operating period and should be expensed separately as property tax expense. Other costs were necessary to acquire the land and are capitalized.

Illustration 10–5

Initial Cost of Land

LAND IMPROVEMENTS   It's important to distinguish between the cost of land and the cost of land improvements because land has an indefinite life and land improvements usually have useful lives that are estimable. Examples of land improvements include the costs of establishing parking lots, driveways, and private roads and the costs of fences and lawn and garden sprinkler systems. Costs of these assets are separately identified and capitalized. We depreciate their cost over periods benefited by their use.

COST OF BUILDINGS   The cost of acquiring a building usually includes realtor commissions and legal fees in addition to the purchase price. Quite often a building must be refurbished, remodeled, or otherwise modified to suit the needs of the new owner. These reconditioning costs are part of the building's acquisition cost. When a building is constructed rather than purchased, unique accounting issues are raised. We discuss these in Part C in the "Self-Constructed Assets" section.

COST OF NATURAL RESOURCES   Natural resources that provide long-term benefits are reported as property, plant, and equipment. These include timber tracts, mineral deposits, and oil and gas deposits. They can be distinguished from other assets by the fact that their benefits are derived from their physical consumption. For example, mineral deposits are physically diminishing as the minerals are extracted from the ground and either sold or used in the production process.[3] On the contrary, equipment, land, and buildings produce benefits for a company through their *use* in the production of goods and services. Unlike those of natural resources, their physical characteristics usually remain unchanged during their useful lives.

Sometimes a company buys natural resources from another company. In that case, initial valuation is simply the purchase price plus any other costs necessary to bring the asset to condition and location for use. More frequently, though, the company will develop these assets. In this situation, the initial valuation can include (a) acquisition costs, (b) exploration costs, (c) development costs, and (d) restoration costs.

> The cost of a natural resource includes the *acquisition costs* for the use of land, the *exploration* and *development costs* incurred before production begins, and *restoration costs* incurred during or at the end of extraction.

Acquisition costs are the amounts paid to acquire the rights to explore for undiscovered natural resources or to extract proven natural resources. Exploration costs are expenditures such as drilling a well, or excavating a mine, or any other costs of searching for natural resources. Development costs are incurred after the resource has been discovered but before production begins. They include a variety of costs such as expenditures for tunnels, wells, and shafts. Restoration costs include costs to restore land or other property to its original condition after extraction of the natural resource ends. Because restoration expenditures occur later—after production begins—they initially represent an obligation incurred in conjunction with an asset retirement. Restoration costs are one example of *asset retirement obligations,* the topic of the next subsection.

On the other hand, the costs of heavy equipment and other assets a company uses during drilling or excavation usually are not considered part of the cost of the natural resource itself. Instead, they are considered depreciable plant and equipment. However, if an asset used in the development of a natural resource cannot be moved and has no alternative use, its depreciable life is limited by the useful life of the natural resource.

ASSET RETIREMENT OBLIGATIONS   Sometimes a company incurs obligations associated with the disposition of property, plant, and equipment and natural resources, often as a result of acquiring those assets. For example, an oil and gas exploration company might be required to restore land to its original condition after extraction is completed. Accounting guidelines were needed because there was considerable diversity in the ways companies accounted for these obligations. Some companies recognized these asset retirement obligations (AROs) gradually over the life of the asset while others did not recognize the obligations until the asset was retired or sold.

> An asset retirement obligation (ARO) is measured at fair value and is recognized as a liability and corresponding increase in asset valuation.

Generally accepted accounting principles require that an existing legal obligation associated with the retirement of a tangible, long-lived asset be recognized as a liability and

---

[3]Because of this characteristic, natural resources sometimes are called *wasting assets.*

measured at fair value, if value can be reasonably estimated. When the liability is credited, the offsetting debit is to the related asset.[4] These retirement obligations could arise in connection with several types of assets. We introduce the topic here because it often arises with natural resources. Let's consider some of the provisions of the standard that addresses these obligations.

Scope.   AROs arise only from *legal* obligations associated with the retirement of a tangible long-lived asset that result from the acquisition, construction, or development and (or) normal operation of a long-lived asset.

Recognition.   A retirement obligation might arise at the inception of an asset's life or during its operating life. For instance, an offshore oil-and-gas production facility typically incurs its removal obligation when it begins operating. On the other hand, a landfill or a mining operation might incur a reclamation obligation gradually over the life of the asset as space is consumed with waste or as the mine is excavated.

Measurement.   A company recognizes the fair value of an ARO in the period it's incurred. The amount of the liability increases the valuation of the related asset. Usually, the fair value is estimated by calculating the present value of estimated future cash outflows.

Present value calculations.   Traditionally, the way uncertainty has been considered in present value calculations has been by discounting the "best estimate" of future cash flows applying a discount rate that has been adjusted to reflect the uncertainty or risk of those cash flows. That's not the approach we take here. Instead, we follow the approach described in the FASB's *Concept Statement No. 7*, which is to adjust the cash flows, not the discount rate, for the uncertainty or risk of those cash flows.[5] This expected cash flow approach incorporates specific probabilities of cash flows into the analysis. We use a discount rate equal to the *credit-adjusted risk free rate.* The higher a company's credit risk, the higher will be the discount rate. All other uncertainties or risks are incorporated into the cash flow probabilities. Illustration 10–6 demonstrates the approach in connection with the acquisition of a natural resource.

Illustration 10–6

Cost of Natural Resources

The Jackson Mining Company paid $1,000,000 for the right to explore for a coal deposit on 500 acres of land in Pennsylvania. Costs of exploring for the coal deposit totaled $800,000 and intangible development costs incurred in digging and erecting the mine shaft were $500,000. In addition, Jackson purchased new excavation equipment for the project at a cost of $600,000. After the coal is removed from the site, the equipment will be sold.

Jackson is required by its contract to restore the land to a condition suitable for recreational use after it extracts the coal. The company has provided the following three cash flow possibilities (A, B, and C) for the restoration costs to be paid in three years, after extraction is completed:

	Cash Outflow	Probability
A	$500,000	30%
B	600,000	50%
C	700,000	20%

(Continued)

---

[4]FASB ASC 410–20–25: Asset Retirement and Environmental Obligations—Asset Retirement Obligations—Recognition.
[5]"Using Cash Flow Information and Present Value in Accounting Measurements," *Statement of Financial Accounting Concepts No. 7* (Norwalk, Conn.: FASB, 2000).

520 SECTION 2 Assets

Illustration 10–6
(*Concluded*)

The company's credit-adjusted risk free interest rate is 8%. What should be the capitalized cost of the coal deposit?

Purchase of rights to explore	$1,000,000
Exploration costs	800,000
Development costs	500,000
Restoration costs	468,360*
Capitalized cost of the coal deposit	$2,768,360

*Present value of expected cash outflow for restoration costs (asset retirement obligation):

$500,000 × 30% = $150,000
  600,000 × 50% = 300,000
  700,000 × 20% = 140,000

$590,000 × 0.79383 = $468,360
(0.79383 Is the present value of $1, n = 3, i = 8%)

Journal Entries

Coal mine (determined above)	2,768,360	
Cash ($1,000,000 + $800,000 + $500,000)		2,300,000
Asset retirement liability (determined above)		468,360
Excavation equipment	600,000	
Cash (cost)		600,000

As we discuss in Chapter 11, the cost of the coal mine is allocated to future periods as *depletion* using a depletion rate based on the estimated amount of coal discovered. The $600,000 cost of the excavation equipment, less any anticipated residual value, is allocated to future periods as *depreciation*.

Additionally, the difference between the asset retirement liability of $468,360 and the probability-weighted expected cash outflow of $590,000 is recognized as accretion expense, an additional expense that accrues as an operating expense, over the three-year excavation period. This process increases the liability to $590,000 by the end of the excavation period.

Year	Accretion Expense	Increase in Balance	Asset Retirement Obligation
			468,360
1	8% (468,360) = 37,469	37,469	505,829
2	8% (505,829) = 40,466	40,466	546,295
3	8% (546,295) = 43,705*	43,705	590,000

*Rounded

The journal entry to record accretion expense for the first year is as follows:

Accretion expense	37,469	
Asset retirement liability		37,469

If the actual restoration costs are more (less) than the $590,000, we recognize a loss (gain) on retirement of the obligation for the difference. For example, if the actual restoration costs were $625,000, we would record the transaction as follows:

Asset retirement liability	590,000	
Loss ($625,000 − $590,000)	35,000	
Cash		625,000

Asset retirement obligations could result from the acquisition of many different types of tangible assets, not just natural resources.

SM Energy Company is engaged in the exploration, development, acquisition, and production of natural gas and crude oil. For the year ended December 31, 2017, SM reported $114.4 million in asset retirement obligations in its balance sheet. A disclosure note included in a recent annual report shown in Illustration 10–7 describes the company's policy and provides a summary of disclosure requirements.

Illustration 10–7

Disclosure of Asset
Retirement Obligations—
SM Energy Company

Real World Financials

Note 1—Asset Retirement Obligations

The Company recognizes an estimated liability for future costs associated with the abandonment of its oil and gas properties, including facilities requiring decommissioning. A liability for the fair value of an asset retirement obligation and corresponding increase to the carrying value of the related long-lived asset are recorded at the time a well is drilled or acquired and a facility is constructed. The increase in carrying value is included in proved oil and gas properties in the accompanying balance sheets. The Company depletes the amount added to proved oil and gas property costs and recognizes expense in connection with the accretion of the discounted liability over the remaining estimated economic lives of the respective oil and gas properties. Cash paid to settle asset retirement obligations is included in the operating section of the Company's accompanying statements of cash flows.

The Company's estimated asset retirement obligation liability is based on historical experience in plugging and abandoning wells, estimated economic lives, estimated plugging and abandonment cost, and federal and state regulatory requirements. The liability is discounted using the credit-adjusted risk-free rate estimated at the time the liability is incurred or revised. The credit-adjusted risk-free rates used to discount the Company's plugging and abandonment liabilities range from 5.5 percent to 12 percent. In periods subsequent to initial measurement of the liability, the Company must recognize period-to-period changes in the liability resulting from the passage of time, revisions to either the amount of the original estimate of undiscounted cash flows or changes in inflation factors or the Company's credit-adjusted risk-free rate as market conditions warrant. Please refer to Note 9 – Asset Retirement Obligations for a reconciliation of the Company's total asset retirement obligation liability as of December 31, 2017, and 2016.

Source: SM Energy Company

It is important to understand that asset retirement obligations could result from the acquisition of many different types of tangible assets, not just natural resources. For example, Dow Chemical Company reported a $96 million asset retirement liability in its 2016 balance sheet related to anticipated demolition and remediation activities at its manufacturing sites in the United States, Canada, Brazil, China, Argentina, Australia, and Europe; and capping activities at landfill sites in the United States, Canada, Brazil, and Italy.

Sometimes, after exploration or development, it becomes apparent that continuing the project is economically infeasible. If that happens, any costs incurred are expensed rather than capitalized. An exception is in the oil and gas industry, where we have two generally accepted accounting alternatives for accounting for projects that prove unsuccessful. We discuss these alternatives in Appendix 10.

Intangible Assets

Intangible assets are assets, other than financial assets, that lack physical substance. They include such items as patents, copyrights, trademarks, franchises, and goodwill. Despite their lack of physical substance, these assets can be extremely valuable resources for a company. For example, Interbrand Sampson, the world's leading branding consulting company, recently estimated the value of the Coca-Cola trademark to be $70 billion.[6] In general, intangible assets refer to the ownership of exclusive rights that provide benefits to the owner in the production of goods and services.

The issues involved in accounting for intangible assets are similar to those of property, plant, and equipment. One key difference, though, is that the future benefits that we attribute to intangible assets usually are much less certain than those attributed to tangible assets. For example, will the new toy for which a company acquires a patent be accepted by the market? If so, will it be a blockbuster like Silly Bandz or Rubik's Cube, or will it be only a moderate success? Will it have lasting appeal like Barbie dolls, or will it be a short-term fad? In short, it's often very difficult to anticipate the timing, and even the existence, of future benefits attributable to many intangible assets. In fact, this uncertainty is a discriminating

Intangible assets generally represent exclusive rights that provide benefits to the owner.

---

[6]This $70 billion represents an estimate of the fair value to the company at the time the estimate was made, not the historical cost valuation that appears in the balance sheet of Coca-Cola.

522   SECTION 2   Assets

characteristic of intangible assets that perhaps better distinguishes them from tangible assets than their lack of physical substance. After all, other assets, too, do not exist physically but are not considered intangible assets. Accounts receivable and prepaid expenses, for example, have no physical substance and yet are reported among tangible assets.

Companies acquire intangible assets in two ways:

1. They *purchase* intangible assets like patents, copyrights, trademarks, or franchise rights from other companies.
2. They *develop* intangible assets internally, for instance, by developing a new product or process and obtaining a protective patent.

Purchased intangible assets are valued at their original cost plus other necessary costs.

The reporting rules for intangible assets vary depending on whether the company purchased the asset or developed it internally. Reporting purchased intangibles is similar to reporting purchased property, plant, and equipment. We record purchased intangible assets at their original cost plus all other costs, such as legal fees, necessary to get the asset ready for use. For example, if a company purchases a patent from another entity, it might pay legal fees and filing fees in addition to the purchase price. We value intangible assets acquired in exchange for stock, or for other nonmonetary assets, or with deferred payment contracts exactly as we do property, plant, and equipment.

The cost of an intangible asset is amortized over its useful life unless it has an indefinite useful life.[7] Also, just like property, plant, and equipment, intangibles are subject to asset impairment rules. We discuss amortization and impairment in Chapter 11.

Internally-developed intangible assets typically are expensed.

Reporting intangible assets that are developed internally is quite different. Rather than reporting these in the balance sheet as assets, we typically expense them in the income statement in the period we incur those internal development costs. For example, the research and development (R&D) costs incurred in developing a new product or process are not recorded as an intangible asset in the balance sheet. Instead, they are expensed directly in the income statement as incurred. The reason we expense all R&D costs is the difficulty in determining the portion of R&D that benefits future periods. Conceptually, we should record as an intangible asset the portion that benefits future periods. Due to the difficulties in arriving at this estimate, current U.S. accounting rules require firms to expense all R&D costs as incurred.

Let's look in detail at some specific types of intangible assets.

PATENTS   A patent is an exclusive right to manufacture a product or to use a process. The U.S. Patent and Trademark Office grants this right for a period of 20 years. In essence, the holder of a patent has a monopoly on the use, manufacture, or sale of the product or process. If a patent is purchased from an inventor or another individual or company, the amount paid is its initial valuation. The cost might also include such other costs as legal and filing fees to secure the patent. Holders of patents often need to defend a patent in court against infringement. Any attorney fees and other costs of successfully defending a patent are added to the patent account.

In contrast, when a firm engages in its own research activities to develop a new product or process, it expenses those costs as it incurs them. For example, major pharmaceutical companies like Amgen and Gilead Sciences spend over a billion dollars each year developing new drugs. Most of these research and development costs are recorded as operating expenses in the income statement. An exception to this rule is legal fees. The firm will record in the Patent asset account the legal and filing fees to secure a patent, even if it developed the patented item or process internally. We discuss research and development in more detail in a later section.

COPYRIGHTS   A copyright is an exclusive right of protection given by the U.S. Copyright Office to the creator of a published work such as a song, film, painting, photograph, book, or computer software. Copyrights give the creator/owner the exclusive right to reproduce and sell the artistic or published work for the life of the creator plus 70 years.

---

[7]FASB ASC 350–30–35–1: Intangibles—Goodwill and Other—General Intangibles Other Than Goodwill—Subsequent Measurement, and FASB ASC 350–20–35–1: Intangibles—Goodwill and Other—Goodwill—Subsequent Measurement (previously "Goodwill and Other Intangible Assets," *Statement of Financial Accounting Standards No. 142* (Norwalk, Conn.: FASB, 2001)).

A copyright also allows the holder to pursue legal action against anyone who attempts to infringe the copyright. Accounting for the costs of copyrights is virtually identical to that of patents.

TRADEMARKS   A trademark, also called tradename, is a word, slogan, or symbol that distinctively identifies a company, product, or service. The firm can register its trademark with the U.S. Patent and Trademark Office to protect it from use by others for a period of 10 years. The registration can be renewed for an indefinite number of 10-year periods, so a trademark is an example of an intangible asset whose useful life can be indefinite.

Trademarks or tradenames often are considered to have indefinite useful lives.

Trademarks or tradenames often are acquired through a business combination. As an example, in 2002, Hewlett-Packard Company (HP) acquired all of the outstanding stock of Compaq Computer Corporation for $24 billion. Of that amount, $1.4 billion was assigned to the Compaq tradename. HP stated in a disclosure note that this ". . . intangible asset will not be amortized because it has an indefinite remaining useful life based on many factors and considerations, including the length of time that the Compaq name has been in use, the Compaq brand awareness and market position and the plans for continued use of the Compaq brand within a portion of HP's overall product portfolio."

Trademarks or tradenames can be very valuable. The estimated value of $70 billion for the Coca-Cola trademark mentioned previously is a good example. Note that the cost of the trademark reported in the balance sheet is far less than the estimate of its worth to the company. The Coca-Cola Company's balance sheet at December 31, 2017, disclosed all trademarks at a cost of only $7 billion.

FRANCHISES   A franchise is a contractual arrangement under which the franchisor grants the franchisee the exclusive right to use the franchisor's trademark or tradename, as well as possibly product and formula rights, to operate a business within a geographical area and usually for a specified period of time. Many popular retail businesses such as fast-food outlets, automobile dealerships, and motels are franchises. For example, the last time you ordered a hamburger at McDonald's, you were probably dealing with a franchise.

Franchise operations are among the most common ways of doing business.

The owner of that McDonald's outlet paid McDonald's Corporation a fee in exchange for the exclusive right to use the McDonald's name and to sell its products within a specified geographical area. In addition, many franchisors provide other benefits to the franchisee, such as participating in the construction of the retail outlet, training of employees, and national advertising.

Payments to the franchisor usually include an initial payment plus periodic payments over the life of the franchise agreement. The franchisee capitalizes as an intangible asset the initial franchise fee plus any legal costs associated with the contract agreement. The franchise asset is then amortized over the life of the franchise agreement. The periodic payments usually relate to services provided by the franchisor on a continuing basis and are expensed as incurred.

Most purchased intangibles are *specifically identifiable*. That is, cost can be directly associated with a specific intangible right. An exception is goodwill, which we discuss next.

GOODWILL   Goodwill is a unique intangible asset in that its cost can't be directly associated with any specific identifiable right and it is not separable from the company itself. It represents the unique value of a company as a whole over and above its identifiable tangible and intangible assets. Goodwill can emerge from a company's clientele and reputation, its trained employees and management team, its favorable business location, and any other unique features of the company that can't be associated with a specific asset.

Goodwill can only be purchased through the acquisition of another company.

FINANCIAL Reporting Case

Q3, p. 3

Because goodwill can't be separated from a company, it's not possible for a buyer to acquire it without also acquiring the whole company or a portion of it. Goodwill will appear as an asset in a balance sheet only when it was purchased in connection with the acquisition of control over another company. In that case, the capitalized cost of goodwill equals the fair value of the consideration given in exchange for the company (the acquisition price) less the fair value of the identifiable net assets acquired. The fair value of the identifiable net assets equals the fair value of all identifiable tangible and intangible assets less the fair value of any liabilities of the selling company assumed by the buyer. Goodwill is a residual asset; it's the amount left after other assets are identified and valued. Consider Illustration 10–8.

Goodwill is the excess of the fair value of the consideration given over the fair value of the identifiable net assets acquired.

Illustration 10–8

Goodwill

The Smithson Corporation acquired all of the outstanding common stock of the Rider Corporation in exchange for $180 million cash.* Smithson assumed all of Rider's long-term liabilities, which have a fair value of $120 million at the date of acquisition. The fair values of all identifiable assets of Rider are as follows ($ in millions):

Receivables	$ 50
Inventory	70
Property, plant, and equipment	90
Patent	40
Fair value of identifiable assets acquired	$250

The cost of the goodwill resulting from the acquisition is $50 million:

Fair value of consideration given (cash)		$180
Less: Fair value of identifiable net assets acquired		
Fair value of identifiable assets acquired	$250	
Less: Fair value of liabilities assumed	(120)	(130)
Goodwill		$ 50

The following journal entry captures the effect of the acquisition on Smithson's assets and liabilities:

Receivables (fair value)	50	
Inventory (fair value)	70	
Property, plant, and equipment (fair value)	90	
Patent (fair value)	40	
Goodwill (difference)	50	
Liabilities (fair value)		120
Cash (acquisition price)		180

*Determining the amount an acquirer is willing to pay for a company in excess of the identifiable net assets is a question of determining the value of a company as a whole. This question is addressed in most introductory and advanced finance textbooks.

Of course, a company can develop its own goodwill through advertising, training employees, and other efforts. In fact, most do. However, a company must expense all such costs incurred in the internal generation of goodwill. By not capitalizing these items, accountants realize that this results in an understatement of real assets because many of these expenditures do result in significant future benefits. Also, it's difficult to compare two companies when one has acquired goodwill and the other has not. But imagine how difficult it would be to associate these expenditures with any objective measure of goodwill. In essence, we have a situation where the characteristic of faithful representation overshadows relevance.

Goodwill, along with other intangible assets with indefinite useful lives, is not amortized.

Just like for other intangible assets that have indefinite useful lives, *we do not amortize goodwill.* This makes it imperative that companies make every effort to identify specific intangibles other than goodwill that they acquire in a business combination since goodwill is the amount left after other assets are identified.

Additional Consideration

It's possible for the consideration given to be *less than* the fair value of the identifiable net assets. This "bargain purchase" situation could result from an acquisition involving a "forced sale" in which the seller is acting under duress. The FASB previously required this bargain purchase to be allocated as a pro rata reduction of the amounts that otherwise would have been assigned to particular assets acquired. The allocation of a negative amount to assets then resulted in recording assets acquired at less than their fair values. However, current GAAP makes it mandatory that assets and liabilities acquired in a business combination be valued at their fair values.[8] Any bargain purchase is reported as a gain in the year of the acquisition.

---

[8]FASB ASC 805: Business Combinations.

In keeping with that goal, GAAP provides guidelines for determining which intangibles should be separately recognized and valued. Specifically, an intangible should be recognized as an asset apart from goodwill if it arises from contractual or other legal rights or is capable of being separated from the acquired entity. Possibilities are patents, trademarks, copyrights, and franchise agreements, and such items as customer lists, license agreements, order backlogs, employment contracts, and noncompetition agreements.[9] In past years, some of these intangibles, if present in a business combination, often were included in the cost of goodwill.[10]

> In a business combination, an intangible asset must be recognized as an asset apart from goodwill if it arises from contractual or other legal rights or is separable.

Additional Consideration

Contract Acquisition Costs. Chapter 6 introduced you to the new guidance on revenue recognition. Under the new standard, sellers of goods and services are required to capitalize, as an intangible asset, the incremental costs of obtaining and fulfilling a long-term (longer than one year) contract. A sales commission is an example of a contract acquisition cost that could be capitalized, rather than expensed, under this new guidance.

If capitalized, the cost of the resulting intangible asset is amortized on a systematic basis that is consistent with the pattern of transfer of the goods or services to which the asset relates. The intangible asset also is evaluated for impairment using the same approach used for other intangible assets. We discuss amortization and impairment testing of intangible assets in Chapter 11.

Lump-Sum Purchases

It's not unusual for a group of assets to be acquired for a single sum. If these assets are indistinguishable, for example 10 identical delivery trucks purchased for a lump-sum price of $150,000, valuation is obvious. Each of the trucks would be valued at $15,000 ($150,000 ÷ 10). However, if the lump-sum purchase involves different assets, it's necessary to allocate the lump-sum acquisition price among the separate items. The assets acquired may have different characteristics and different useful lives. For example, the acquisition of a factory may include assets that are significantly different such as land, building, and equipment.

> ● LO10–2

The allocation is made in proportion to the individual assets' relative fair values. This process is best explained by an example in Illustration 10–9.

The relative fair value percentages are multiplied by the lump-sum purchase price to determine the initial valuation of each of the separate assets. Notice that the lump-sum purchase includes inventories. The procedure used here to allocate the purchase price in a lump-sum acquisition pertains to any type of asset mix, not just to property, plant, and equipment and intangible assets.

Ethical Dilemma

Grandma's Cookie Company purchased a factory building. The company controller, Don Nelson, is in the process of allocating the lump-sum purchase price between land and building. Don suggests to the company's chief financial officer, Judith Prince, that they fudge a little by allocating a disproportionately higher share of the price to land. Don reasons that this will reduce depreciation expense, boost income, increase their profit-sharing bonus, and hopefully, increase the price of the company's stock. Judith has some reservations about this because the higher reported income will also cause income taxes to be higher than they would be if a correct allocation of the purchase price is made.

What are the ethical issues? What stakeholders' interests are in conflict?

---

[9]Ibid.

[10]An assembled workforce is an example of an intangible asset that is not recognized as a separate asset. A workforce does not represent a contractual or legal right, nor is it separable from the company as a whole.

526 SECTION 2 Assets

Illustration 10–9

Lump-Sum Purchase

The Smyrna Hand & Edge Tools Company purchased an existing factory for a single sum of $2,000,000. The price included title to the land, the factory building, the manufacturing equipment in the building, a patent on a process the equipment uses, and inventories of raw materials. An independent appraisal estimated the fair values of the assets (if purchased separately) as follows:

	Fair Values	
Land	$ 330,000	15%
Building	550,000	25%
Equipment	660,000	30%
Patent	440,000	20%
Inventories	220,000	10%
Total	$2,200,000	100%

Because the $2,200,000 fair value of the assets is greater than the $2,000,000 purchase price, the purchase price is allocated to the separate assets as follows:

Land	(15% × $2,000,000)	300,000	
Building	(25% × $2,000,000)	500,000	
Equipment	(30% × $2,000,000)	600,000	
Patent	(20% × $2,000,000)	400,000	
Inventories	(10% × $2,000,000)	200,000	
Cash			2,000,000

The total purchase price is allocated in proportion to the relative fair values of the assets acquired.

PART B

Noncash Acquisitions

Companies sometimes acquire assets without paying cash at the time of the purchase. In Part B, we examine four situations where this occurs.

1. Deferred payments (notes payable)
2. Issuance of equity securities
3. Donated assets
4. Exchanges of nonmonetary assets for other assets

Assets acquired in noncash transactions are valued at the fair value of the assets given or the fair value of the assets received, whichever is more clearly evident.

   The controlling principle in each of these situations is that in any noncash transaction, the asset acquired is recorded at its fair value. The first indicator of fair value is the fair value of the assets, debt, or equity securities given. Sometimes the fair value of the assets received is used when their fair value is more clearly evident than the fair value of the assets given.

Deferred Payments

● LO10–3

A company can acquire an asset by giving the seller a promise to pay cash in the future and thus creating a liability, usually a note payable. The initial valuation of the asset is, again, quite simple as long as the note payable explicitly requires the payment of interest at a realistic interest rate. For example, suppose a machine is acquired for $15,000 and the buyer signs a note requiring the payment of $15,000 sometime in the future *plus* interest in the meantime at a realistic interest rate. The machine would be valued at $15,000 and the transaction recorded as follows:

Machine	15,000	
Notes payable		15,000

   We know from our discussion of the time value of money in Chapter 5 that most liabilities are valued at the present value of future cash payments, reflecting an appropriate time value of money. As long as the note payable explicitly contains a realistic interest rate, the present value will equal the face value of the note, $15,000 in our previous example. This also should be equal to the fair value of the machine purchased. On the other hand, when an interest rate is not specified or is unrealistic, determining the cost of the asset is less straight-forward. In that case, the accountant should look beyond the form of the transaction and record its substance. Consider Illustration 10–10.

> On January 2, 2021, the Midwestern Steam Gas Corporation purchased industrial equipment. In payment, Midwestern signed a noninterest-bearing note requiring $50,000 to be paid on December 31, 2022 (two years later). If Midwestern had borrowed cash to buy the equipment, the bank would have required an interest rate of 10%.

Illustration 10–10
Asset Acquired with Debt—Present Value of Note Indicative of Fair Value

On the surface, it might appear that Midwestern is paying $50,000 for the equipment, the eventual cash payment. However, when you recognize that the agreement specifies no interest even though the payment won't be made for two years, it becomes obvious that a portion of the $50,000 payment is not actually payment for the equipment, but instead is interest on the note. At what amount should Midwestern value the equipment and the related note payable?

Some portion of the payment(s) required by a noninterest-bearing note in reality is interest.

The answer is fair value, as it is for any noncash transaction. This might be the fair value of the equipment or the fair value of the note. Let's say, in this situation, that the equipment is custom-built, so its cash price is unavailable. But Midwestern can determine the fair value of the note payable by computing the present value of the cash payments at the appropriate interest rate of 10%. The amount actually paid for the equipment, then, is the present value of the cash flows called for by the loan agreement, discounted at the market rate—10% in this case.

Noncash transactions are recorded at the fair value of the items exchanged.

$$PV = \$50,000 \ (0.82645^*) = \$41,323$$
*Present value of $1: $n = 2$, $i = 10\%$ (from Table 2).

So the equipment should be recorded at its *real* cost, $41,323, as follows:[11]

The economic essence of a transaction should prevail over its outward appearance.

Equipment (determined above)	41,323	
Discount on notes payable (difference)	8,677	
Notes payable (face amount)		50,000

Notice that the note also is recorded at $41,323, its present value, but this is accomplished by using a contra account, called *discount on notes payable,* for the difference between the face amount of the note ($50,000) and its present value ($41,323). The difference of $8,677 is the portion of the eventual $50,000 payment that represents interest and is recognized as interest expense over the life of the note.

Assuming that Midwestern's fiscal year-end is December 31 and that adjusting entries are recorded only at the end of each year, the company would record the following entries at the end of 2021 and 2022 to accrue interest and the payment of the note:

December 31, 2021

Interest expense ($41,323 × 10%)	4,132	
Discount on notes payable		4,132

December 31, 2022

Interest expense [($41,323 + 4,132)* × 10%]	4,545	
Discount on notes payable		4,545
Notes payable (face amount)	50,000	
Cash		50,000

*The 2021 unpaid interest increases the amount owed by $4,132.

Discount on notes payable

8,677	Jan. 1, 2021
Dec. 31, 2021 4,132	
Dec. 31, 2022 4,545	
0	Dec. 31, 2022

Interest expense

4,132	Dec. 31, 2021
4,545	Dec. 31, 2022

---

[11]The entry shown assumes the note is recorded using the gross method. By the net method, a discount account is not used and the note is simply recorded at present value.

Equipment	41,323	
Notes payable		41,323

528   SECTION 2   Assets

Sometimes, the fair value of an asset acquired in a noncash transaction is readily available from price lists, previous purchases, or otherwise. In that case, this fair value may be more clearly evident than the fair value of the note, and the fair value of the asset would serve as the best evidence of the exchange value of the transaction. As an example, let's consider Illustration 10–11.

Illustration 10–11

Noninterest-Bearing Note—Fair Value of Asset Is Known

> On January 2, 2021, Dennison, Inc., purchased a machine and signed a noninterest-bearing note in payment. The note requires the company to pay $100,000 on December 31, 2023 (three years later). Dennison is not sure what interest rate appropriately reflects the time value of money. However, price lists indicate the machine could have been purchased for cash at a price of $79,383.
>
> Dennison records both the asset and liability at $79,383 on January 2 as shown:
>
> | | | |
> |---|---|---|
> | Machine (cash price) | 79,383 | |
> | Discount on notes payable (difference) | 20,617 | |
> | Notes payable (face amount) | | 100,000 |

In this situation, we infer the present value of the note from the fair value of the asset. Again, the difference between the note's $79,383 present value and the cash payment of $100,000 represents interest. We can determine the interest rate that is implicit in the agreement as follows:

$$\$79,383 \text{ (present value)} = \$100,000 \text{ (face amount)} \times \text{PV factor}$$
$$\$79,383 \div \$100,000 = 0.79383$$

*Present value of $1: $n = 3$, $i = ?$ (from Table 2, $i = 8\%$).

We refer to the 8% rate as the *implicit rate of interest*. Dennison records interest each year at 8% in the same manner as demonstrated in Illustration 10–10 and discussed in greater depth in Chapter 14.

We now turn our attention to the acquisition of assets acquired in exchange for equity securities and through donation.

Issuance of Equity Securities

● LO10–4

The most common situation in which equity securities are issued for property, plant, and equipment and intangible assets occurs when small companies incorporate and the owner or owners contribute assets to the new corporation in exchange for ownership securities, usually common stock. Because the common shares are not publicly traded, it's difficult to determine their fair value. In that case, the fair value of the assets received by the corporation is probably the better indicator of the transaction's exchange value. In other situations, particularly those involving corporations whose stock is actively traded, the market value of the shares is the best indication of fair value. Consider Illustration 10–12.

Illustration 10–12

Asset Acquired by Issuing Equity Securities

Assets acquired by issuing common stock are valued at the fair value of the securities or the fair value of the assets, whichever is more clearly evident.

> On March 31, 2021, the Elcorn Company issued 10,000 shares of its no-par common stock in exchange for land. On the date of the transaction, the fair value of the common stock, evidenced by its market price, was $20 per share. The journal entry to record this transaction is shown below:
>
> | | | |
> |---|---|---|
> | Land | 200,000 | |
> | Common stock (10,000 shares × $20) | | 200,000 |

If the fair value of the common stock had not been reliably determinable, the value of the land as determined through an independent appraisal would be used as the cost of the land and the value of the common stock.

Donated Assets

Donated assets are recorded at their fair values.

On occasion, companies acquire assets through donation. The donation usually is an enticement to do something that benefits the donor. For example, the developer of an industrial park might pay some of the costs of building a manufacturing facility to entice a company to locate in its park. Companies record assets donated by unrelated parties at their fair values based on either an available market price or an appraisal value. This should not be considered a departure from historical cost valuation. Instead, it is equivalent to the donor contributing cash to the company and the company using the cash to acquire the asset.

As the recipient records the asset at its fair value, what account receives the offsetting credit? Over the years, there has been disagreement over this question. Should the recipient increase its paid-in capital—the part of shareholders' equity representing investments in the firm? Or, should the donated asset be considered revenue? GAAP requires that donated assets be recorded as *revenue*.[12] Recall that revenues generally are inflows of assets from delivering or producing goods, rendering services, or from other activities that constitute the entity's ongoing major or central operations. The rationale is that the company receiving the donation is performing a service for the donor in exchange for the asset donated.

> Revenue is credited for the amount paid by an unrelated party.

Corporations occasionally receive incentives from governmental units. A local governmental unit might provide land or pay all or some of the cost of a new office building or manufacturing plant to entice a company to locate within its geographical boundaries. For example, the city of San Jose, California, paid a significant portion of the cost of a new office building for **IBM Corporation**. The new office building, located in downtown San Jose, brought jobs to a revitalized downtown area and increased revenues to the city. The City of San Jose did not receive an equity interest in IBM through its donation, but significantly benefited nevertheless. Illustration 10–13 provides an example.

Illustration 10–13
Asset Donation

Elcorn Enterprises decided to relocate its office headquarters to the city of Westmont. The city agreed to pay 20% of the $20 million cost of building the headquarters in order to entice Elcorn to relocate. The building was completed on May 3, 2021. Elcorn paid its portion of the cost of the building in cash. Elcorn records the transaction as follows:

Building	20,000,000	
Cash		16,000,000
Revenue—donation of asset (20% × $20 million)		4,000,000

International Financial Reporting Standards

Government Grants. Both U.S. GAAP and IFRS require that companies value donated assets at their fair values. For government grants, though, the way that value is recorded is different under the two sets of standards. Unlike U.S. GAAP, donated assets are not recorded as revenue under IFRS. *IAS No. 20* requires that government grants be recognized in income over the periods necessary to match them on a systematic basis with the related costs that they are intended to compensate. So, for example, *IAS No. 20* allows two alternatives for grants related to assets.[13]

● **LO10–9**

> IFRS requires government grants to be recognized in income over the periods necessary to match them on a systematic basis with the related costs that they are intended to compensate.

1. Deduct the amount of the grant in determining the initial cost of the asset.
2. Record the grant as a liability, deferred income, in the balance sheet and recognize it in the income statement systematically over the asset's useful life.

In Illustration 10–13, if a company chose the first option, the building would be recorded at $16 million. If instead the company chose the second option, the building would be recorded at $20 million, but rather than recognizing $4 million in revenue as with U.S. GAAP, a $4 million credit to deferred income would be recorded and recognized as income over the life of the building.

Siemens, a global electronics and electrical engineering company based in Germany, prepares its financial statements according to IFRS, and sometimes receives government grants for the purchase or production of fixed assets. The following disclosure note included with recent financial statements indicates that Siemens uses the first option, deducting the amount of the grant from the initial cost of the asset.

Government Grants (in part)
Grants awarded for the purchase or the production of fixed assets (grants related to assets) are generally offset against the acquisition or production costs of the respective assets and reduce future depreciations accordingly.

---

[12]FASB ASC 958–605–15–2 and FASB ASC 958–605–25–2: Not-for-Profit Entities—Revenue Recognition—Scope and Scope Exceptions—Contributions Received.
[13]"Government Grants," *International Accounting Standard No. 20* (IASCF), as amended effective January 1, 2018.

530   SECTION 2   Assets

Property, plant, and equipment and intangible assets also can be acquired in an exchange. Because an exchange transaction inherently involves a disposition of one asset as it is given up in exchange for another, we cover these transactions next under Exchanges.

Decision Makers' Perspective

The property, plant, and equipment and intangible asset acquisition decision is among the most significant decisions that management must make. A decision to acquire a new fleet of airplanes or to build or purchase a new office building or manufacturing plant could influence a company's performance for many years.

These decisions, often referred to as capital budgeting decisions, require management to forecast all future net cash flows (cash inflows minus cash outflows) generated by the asset(s). These cash flows are then used in a model to determine if the future cash flows are sufficient to warrant the capital expenditure. One such model, the net present value model, compares the present value of future net cash flows with the required initial acquisition cost of the asset(s). If the present value is higher than the acquisition cost, the asset is acquired. You have studied or will study capital budgeting in considerable depth in a financial management course. The introduction to the time value of money concept in Chapter 5 provided you with important tools necessary to evaluate capital budgeting decisions.

● LO10–5

A key to profitability is how well a company manages and utilizes its assets. Financial analysts often use activity, or turnover, ratios to evaluate a company's effectiveness in managing assets. This concept was illustrated with receivables and inventory in previous chapters. Property, plant, and equipment (PP&E) usually are a company's primary revenue-generating assets. Their efficient use is critical to generating a satisfactory return to owners. One ratio analysts often use to measure how effectively managers use PP&E is the fixed-asset turnover ratio. This ratio is calculated as follows:

The *fixed-asset turnover ratio* measures a company's effectiveness in managing property, plant, and equipment.

$$\text{Fixed-asset turnover ratio} = \frac{\text{Net sales}}{\text{Average fixed assets}}$$

The ratio indicates the level of sales generated by the company's investment in fixed assets. The denominator usually is the book value, sometimes called carrying value or carrying amount (cost less accumulated depreciation and depletion) of property, plant, and equipment.[14]

As with other turnover ratios, we can compare a company's fixed-asset turnover with that of its competitors, with an industry average, or with the same company's ratio over time. Let's compare the fixed-asset turnover ratios for The Gap, Inc., and Ross Stores, Inc., two companies in the retail apparel industry.

	($ in millions)			
	Gap		**Ross Stores**	
	2018	**2017**	**2018**	**2017**
Property, plant, and equipment (net)	$2,805	$2,616	$2,382	$2,328
Net sales—2018	$15,855		$14,135	

The 2018 fixed-asset turnover for Gap is 5.85 ($15,855 ÷ [($2,616 + 2,805) ÷ 2]) compared to the turnover for Ross Stores of 6.00 ($14,135 ÷ [($2,328 + 2,382) ÷ 2]). Ross Stores is able to generate $0.15 more in sales dollars than Gap for each dollar invested in fixed assets. ●

---

[14]If intangible assets are significant, their book value could be added to the denominator to produce a turnover that reflects all long-revenue-producing assets. The use of book value provides an approximation of the company's current investment in these assets.

Exchanges

Sometimes a company will acquire a new asset by giving up an existing asset. For example, a company might purchase a new delivery truck by trading-in its old delivery truck. This is referred to as a *nonmonetary asset exchange.*[15] If the values of those nonmonetary assets are not equal to one another, cash will be received or paid to equalize those values. When a company trades its old delievery truck for a new one, its likely that the fair value of the new delivery truck is higher, so the company trading-in the old delivery truck will pay cash to make up the difference.

> An asset received in an exchange of nonmonetary assets generally is valued at fair value.
>
> ● LO10–6

The basic steps in recording nonmonetary asset exchanges follow:

Step 1: **Record the new asset at fair value.** Fair value is determined based on the fair value of the asset(s) given up or the fair value of the asset received. In a normal exchange, we expect those two fair values to equal.

Step 2: **Remove the book value of the nonmonetary asset given.** Book value equals the recorded cost of the old asset minus its accumulated depreciation.

Step 3: **Record any cash received or paid.** Cash is used to equalize the fair values of the nonmonetary assets in the exchange.

Step 4: **Record any gain or loss.** The gain or loss on the exchange equals the difference between fair value and book value of the asset given up in step 2. If fair value is greater, then a gain is recorded. If book value is greater, then a loss is recorded. The gain or loss also can be viewed as the "plug" that balances debits and credits in the journal entry.

To see an example, look at Illustration 10–14A.

Illustration 10–14A
Nonmonetary Asset Exchange—Gain

The Elcorn Company traded its old laser equipment for the newer air-cooled ion laser equipment manufactured by American Laser Corporation. The old equipment had a book value of $100,000 (cost of $500,000 less accumulated depreciation of $400,000) and a **fair value of $150,000.** Elcorn also paid American Laser **$430,000 in cash** as part of the exchange. The following journal entry records the transaction:

Equipment—new (fair value, determined below)	580,000	
Accumulated depreciation—old (account balance)	400,000	
Equipment—old (account balance)		500,000
Cash (amount paid)		430,000
Gain on exchange of assets (fair value − book value)		50,000

Assets given:	Fair value	Book value
Old equipment	$ 150,000	$100,000
Cash paid	430,000	430,000
Total	$580,000	$530,000

Step 1: Record the new equipment for $580,000. This is the fair value of the assets given.
Step 2: Remove the book value of the old equipment with a credit to Equipment for $500,000 and a debit to Accumulated Depreciation for $400,000.
Step 3: Record the amount paid with a credit to Cash for $430,000.
Step 4: Record a gain of $50,000. The gain is computed as the fair value of the old equipment minus the book value of the old equipment ($150,000 − $100,000). Alternatively, the gain can be computed at the total fair value of the assets given minus their total book value ($580,000 − $530,000).

> A gain is recognized when the fair value of an asset given is more than its book value.

In Illustration 10–14A, the $150,000 fair value of the old asset was known. However, in a trade-in, quite often the fair value of the new asset is more clearly evident than the second-hand value of the asset traded in. For example, if it was known that the fair value of

---

[15]Monetary items are assets and liabilities whose *amounts are fixed* , by contract or otherwise, in terms of a specific number of dollars. Other assets are considered nonmonetary.

532   SECTION 2   Assets

the new asset was $580,000, then the $150,000 fair value of the old asset could have been determined by subtracting the cash paid ($580,000 − $430,000).

Let's modify the illustration slightly by assuming that the fair value of the old equipment is $75,000 instead of $150,000. Illustration 10–14B shows the journal entry to record the transaction.

Illustration 10–14B

Nonmonetary Asset Exchange—Loss

The Elcorn Company traded its old laser equipment for the newer air-cooled ion laser equipment manufactured by American Laser Corporation. The old equipment had a book value of $100,000 (cost of $500,000 less accumulated depreciation of $400,000) and a **fair value of $75,000.** Elcorn also paid American Laser **$430,000 in cash** as part of the exchange. The following journal entry records the transaction:

Equipment—new (fair value determined below)	505,000	
Accumulated depreciation—old (account balance)	400,000	
Loss on exchange of assets (fair value − book value)	25,000	
Equipment—old (account balance)		500,000
Cash (amount paid)		430,000

Assets given:	Fair value	Book value
Old equipment	$ 75,000	$100,000
Cash paid	430,000	430,000
Total	$505,000	$530,000

The new equipment is recorded at $505,000, which is the fair value of the old equipment plus the cash paid ($75,000 + $430,000). Elcorn recognizes a loss of $25,000, the amount by which the fair value of the asset given ($75,000) is less than its book value ($100,000).

A loss is recognized when the fair value of an asset given is less than its book value.

Until 2005, the accounting treatment of nonmonetary asset exchanges depended on a number of factors including (1) whether the assets exchanged were similar or dissimilar, (2) whether a gain or loss was indicated in the exchange, and (3) whether cash was given or received. Then a new accounting standard[16] simplified accounting for exchanges by requiring the use of fair value except in rare situations in which the fair value can't be determined or the exchange lacks commercial substance.[17]

Let's discuss these two rare situations.

Fair Value Not Determinable

It would be unusual for a company to be unable to reasonably determine fair value of either asset in an exchange. Nevertheless, if the situation does occur, we modify step 1 above and use the *book value* of the assets given up to record the asset acquired. For example, if fair value had not been determinable in Illustration 10–14A, Elcorn would have recorded the exchange as follows:

If we can't determine the fair value of either asset in the exchange, the asset received is valued at the book value of the asset given.

Equipment—new (book value + cash: $100,000 + $430,000)	530,000	
Accumulated depreciation—old (account balance)	400,000	
Equipment—old (account balance)		500,000
Cash (amount paid)		430,000

The new equipment is recorded at the book value of the old equipment ($100,000) plus the cash given ($430,000). No gain or loss is recognized on an exchange when fair value is not determinable.

Lack of Commercial Substance

If we record an exchange at fair value, we recognize a gain or loss for the difference between the fair value and book value of the asset given up. To prevent a company from exchanging an asset whose fair value is greater than book value for the sole purpose of recognizing a gain, fair value can be used only in gain situations that have *commercial substance.*

---

[16]FASB ASC 845: Nonmonetary Transactions.

[17]There is a third situation which precludes the use of fair value in a nonmonetary exchange. The transaction is an exchange of inventories to facilitate sales to customers other than the parties to the exchange.

A nonmonetary exchange is considered to have commercial substance if future cash flows will change as a result of the exchange. Most exchanges are for business reasons and would not be transacted if there were no anticipated change in future cash flows. For example, newer models of equipment can increase production or improve manufacturing efficiency, causing an increase in revenue or a decrease in operating costs with a corresponding increase in future cash flows. The exchange of old laser equipment for the *newer* model in Illustration 10–14A is an example of an exchange transacted for business reasons.

> Commercial substance occurs when future cash flows change as a result of the exchange.

GAIN SITUATION   Suppose a company owned a tract of land that had a book value of $1 million and a fair value of $5 million. The only ways to recognize the $4 million difference as a gain are to either sell the land or to exchange the land for another nonmonetary asset for a legitimate business purpose. For example, if the land were exchanged for a different type of asset, say an office building, then future cash flows most likely will change. This exchange has commercial substance, and the $4 million gain can be recognized. On the other hand, if the land were exchanged for a tract of land that has the identical characteristics as the land given, then it is unlikely that future cash flows would change. This exchange lacks commercial substance, and the gain of $4 million cannot be recognized on the exchange. The new land is recorded at the book value of the old land plus any cash paid. Illustration 10–15 provides an example.

The Elcorn Company traded a tract of land to Sanchez Development for a similar tract of land. The old land had a book value of $2,500,000 and a fair value of $4,500,000. Elcorn also paid Sanchez $500,000 in cash. The following journal entry records the transaction, *assuming that the exchange lacks commercial substance:*

Land—new (book value + cash: $2,500,000 + $500,000)	3,000,000	
Land—old (account balance)		2,500,000
Cash (amount paid)		500,000

The new land is recorded at $3,000,000, the book value of the old land plus the cash given ($2,500,000 + $500,000). No gain is recognized because the exchange does not have commercial substance.

Illustration 10–15

Nonmonetary Asset Exchange—Exchange Lacks Commercial Substance

The FASB's intent in including the commercial substance requirement for the use of fair value was to avoid companies' trading property for no business reason other than to recognize the gain.

Additional Consideration

In Illustration 10–15, cash was *given*. What if cash was *received*? Suppose that $450,000 cash was received instead of the $500,000 given. The fair value of the old land was $4,500,000, which means that the fair value of the land received is $4,050,000 ($4,500,000 – $450,000). In that case, a portion of the transaction is considered monetary and we would recognize that portion of the $2,000,000 gain ($4,500,000 fair value – $2,500,000 book value). The amount of gain recognized is equal to the portion of cash received relative to the total received.[18]

$$\frac{\$450,000}{\$450,000 + 4,050,000} = 10\%$$

Elcorn would recognize a $200,000 gain ($2,000,000 × 10%) and would record the land received at $2,250,000, the book value of the land given plus the gain recognized less the cash received ($2,500,000 + $200,000 – $450,000). The following journal entry records the transaction:

Land—new ($2,500,000 + $200,000 – $450,000)	2,250,000	
Cash	450,000	
Land—old		2,500,000
Gain on exchange of assets		200,000

---

[18]If the amount of monetary consideration received is deemed significant, the transaction is considered to be monetary and the entire gain is recognized. In other words, the transaction is accounted for as if it had commercial substance. GAAP defines "significance" in this situation as 25% or more of the fair value of the exchange. FASB ASC 845–10–25–6: Nonmonetary transactions–Overall–Recognition.

When the fair value of the asset given is less than its book value, we always use fair value to record the exchange.

LOSS SITUATION   In Illustration 10–15, what if the fair value of the land given was less than its book value? It's unlikely that a company would enter into this type of transaction unless there was a good reason. When a loss is indicated in a nonmonetary exchange, it's okay to record the loss and we use fair value to record the asset acquired.

Illustration 10–16 summarizes the treatment of gains and losses, as well as the amount to record for the asset received, for each type of exchange discussed above.

Illustration 10–16 Exchanges

	Type of Exchange		
	Fair value Determinable and Commercial Substance	**Fair Value Not Determinable**	**Lack of Commercial Substance**
Step 1: Record new asset	FV given + cash paid (or − cash received).†	BV given + cash paid (or − cash received).	If gain, BV given + cash paid (or − cash received) + gain recognized.* If loss, FV given + cash paid (or − cash received).
Step 2: Remove old asset	BV of cost minus accumulated depreciation.	Same	Same
Step 3: Record cash	Amount paid or received.	Same	Same
Step 4: Record gain or loss	FV given − BV given (Gain if FV > BV; Loss if FV < BV).	No gain or loss recognized.	Calculate gain to be recognized.* Recognize entire loss.

†FV = fair value; BV = book value. All references to FV and BV relate to the asset being given in the exchange.
*A gain situation occurs when FV of the assets given is greater than the BV of those assets. If no cash is received, no gain is recognized. If some cash is received, the amount of the gain recognized = (FV given − BV given) × (cash received ÷ total FV received). If cash constitutes at least 25% of the fair value received, the entire gain is recognized = FV given − BV given.

When fair value is determinable and commercial substance exists, we record the asset received at total fair value. Gains and losses are recorded for the difference between the fair value and book value of the asset given, depending on which is higher.

When fair value is not determinable, fair value cannot be used to record the asset being received, and therefore we don't record a gain or loss on the asset being given. The asset received is simply recorded for the book value of the asset given, adjusted for the effects of any cash exchanged.

The rules for exchanges that lack commercial substance reflect a bias toward preventing gains from being recognized unless some cash is received so that a portion of the transaction represents a monetary exchange. Losses in exchanges that lack commercial substance are fully recognized regardless of cash received or paid, just like losses when fair value is determinable.

Concept Review Exercise

EXCHANGES

The MD Corporation recently acquired new equipment to be used in its production process. In exchange, the company traded in an existing asset that had an original cost of $60,000 and accumulated depreciation on the date of the exchange of $45,000. The fair value of the old equipment is $17,000. In addition, MD paid $40,000 cash to the equipment manufacturer.

Required:

1. Prepare the journal entry MD would use to record the exchange transaction assuming that the transaction has commercial substance.

2. Prepare the journal entry MD would use to record the exchange transaction assuming that the transaction does *not* have commercial substance.

3. Prepare the journal entry MD would use to record the exchange transaction assuming that the fair value of the old equipment is only $10,000.

Solution:

1. Prepare the journal entry MD would use to record the exchange transaction assuming that the transaction has commercial substance.

Equipment—new ($17,000 + $40,000)	57,000	
Accumulated depreciation—old (account balance)	45,000	
Equipment—old (account balance)		60,000
Cash (amount paid)		40,000
Gain on exchange of assets ($17,000 FV − $15,000 BV)		2,000

2. Prepare the journal entry MD would use to record the exchange transaction assuming that the transaction does not have commercial substance.

Equipment—new ($15,000 + $40,000)	55,000	
Accumulated depreciation—old (account balance)	45,000	
Equipment—old (account balance)		60,000
Cash (amount paid)		40,000

3. Prepare the journal entry MD would use to record the exchange transaction assuming that the fair value of the old equipment is only $10,000.

Equipment—new ($10,000 + $40,000)	50,000	
Accumulated depreciation—old (account balance)	45,000	
Loss on exchange of assets ($10,000 FV − $15,000 BV)	5,000	
Equipment—old (account balance)		60,000
Cash (amount paid)		40,000

Self-Constructed Assets and Research and Development

PART C

Two types of expenditures relating to property, plant, and equipment and intangible assets whose accounting treatment has generated considerable controversy are interest costs pertaining to self-constructed assets and amounts spent for research and development. We now consider those expenditures and why those controversies have developed.

Self-Constructed Assets

A company might decide to construct an asset for its own use rather than buy an existing one. For example, a retailer like Nordstrom might decide to build its own store rather than purchase an existing building. A manufacturing company like Intel could construct its own manufacturing facility. In fact, Nordstrom and Intel are just two of the many companies that self-construct assets. Other recognizable examples include Walt Disney, Sears, and Caterpillar. Quite often these companies act as the main contractor and then subcontract most of the actual construction work.

● LO10–7

The critical accounting issue in these instances is identifying the cost of the self-constructed asset. The task is more difficult than for purchased assets because there is no external transaction to establish an exchange price. Actually, two difficulties arise in connection with assigning costs to self-constructed assets: (1) determining the amount of the company's indirect manufacturing costs (overhead) to be allocated to the construction and (2) deciding on the proper treatment of interest (actual or implicit) incurred during construction.

> The cost of a self-constructed asset includes identifiable materials and labor and a portion of the company's manufacturing overhead costs.

Overhead Allocation

One difficulty of associating costs with self-constructed assets is the same difficulty encountered when determining cost of goods manufactured for sale. The costs of material and direct labor usually are easily identified with a particular construction project and are included in cost. However, the treatment of manufacturing overhead cost and its allocation between construction projects and normal production is a controversial issue.

Some accountants advocate the inclusion of only the *incremental* overhead costs in the total cost of construction. That is, the asset's cost would include only those additional costs that are incurred because of the decision to construct the asset. This would exclude such indirect costs as depreciation and the salaries of supervisors that would be incurred whether or not the construction project is undertaken. If, however, a new construction supervisor was hired specifically to work on the project, then that salary would be included in asset cost.

Others advocate assigning overhead on the same basis that is used for a regular manufacturing process. That is, all overhead costs are allocated both to production and to self-constructed assets based on the relative amount of a chosen cost driver (for example, labor hours) incurred. This is known as the *full-cost approach* and is the generally accepted method used to determine the cost of a self-constructed asset.

Interest Capitalization

FINANCIAL Reporting Case

Q4, p. 3

To reiterate, the cost of an asset includes all costs necessary to get the asset ready for its intended use. Unlike one purchased from another company, a self-constructed asset requires time to create it. During this construction period, the project must be financed in some way. This suggests the question as to whether interest costs during the construction period are one of the costs of acquiring the asset itself or simply costs of financing the asset.

On the one hand, we might point to interest charges to finance inventories during their period of manufacture or to finance the purchase of plant assets from others and argue that construction period interest charges are merely costs of financing the asset that should be expensed as incurred like all other interest costs.

On the other hand, we might argue that self-constructed assets are different in that during the construction period, they are not yet ready for their intended use for producing revenues. And, so, in keeping with the historical cost principle, all costs during this period, including interest, should be capitalized. Those costs are then allocated as depreciation during later periods when the assets are providing benefits.

Only assets that are constructed as discrete projects qualify for interest capitalization.

QUALIFYING ASSETS Generally accepted accounting principles are consistent with the second argument. Specifically, interest is capitalized during the construction period for (a) assets built for a company's own use as well as for (b) assets constructed *as discrete projects* for sale or lease (a ship or a real estate development, for example). This excludes from interest capitalization consideration inventories that are routinely manufactured in large quantities on a repetitive basis and assets that already are in use or are ready for their intended use.[19] Interest costs incurred during the productive life of the asset are expensed as incurred.

The interest capitalization period begins when construction begins and the first expenditure is made as long as interest costs are actually being incurred.

PERIOD OF CAPITALIZATION The capitalization period for a self-constructed asset starts with the first expenditure (materials, labor, or overhead) and ends either when the asset is substantially complete and ready for use or when interest costs no longer are being incurred. Interest costs incurred can pertain to borrowings other than those obtained specifically for the construction project. However, interest costs can't be imputed; actual interest costs must be incurred.

Average accumulated expenditures approximates the average debt necessary for construction.

AVERAGE ACCUMULATED EXPENDITURES Because we consider interest to be a necessary cost of getting a self-constructed asset ready for use, the amount capitalized is only that portion of interest cost incurred during the construction period that *could have been avoided* if expenditures for the asset had not been made. In other words, if construction had not been undertaken, debt incurred for the project would not have been necessary and/or other interest-bearing debt could have been liquidated or employed elsewhere.

As a result, interest should be determined for only the construction expenditures *actually incurred* during the capitalization period. And unless all expenditures are made at the outset of the period, it's necessary to determine the *average* amount outstanding during the period. This is the amount of debt that would be required to finance the expenditures and thus the

---

[19]FASB ASC 835–20–25: Interest—Capitalization of Interest—Recognition.

amount on which interest would accrue. For instance, if a company accumulated $1,500,000 of construction expenditures fairly evenly throughout the construction period, the average expenditures would be

Total accumulated expenditures incurred evenly throughout the period	$1,500,000
	÷2
Average accumulated expenditures	$ 750,000

At the beginning of the period, no expenditures have accumulated, so no interest has accrued (on the equivalent amount of debt). But, by the end of the period interest is accruing on the total amount, $1,500,000. On average, then, interest accrues on half the total or $750,000.

If expenditures are not incurred evenly throughout the period, a simple average is insufficient. In that case, a *weighted average* is determined by time-weighting individual expenditures or groups of expenditures by the number of months from their incurrence to the end of the construction period.

Let's use the expenditures and loan information in Illustration 10–17 to demonstrate the calculation of interest capitalization. This calculation will involve three steps: (1) determine the weighted-average accumulated expenditures, (2) calculate the amount of interest to be capitalized, and (3) compare calculated interest with actual interest incurred.

> On January 1, 2021, the Mills Conveying Equipment Company began construction of a building to be used as its office headquarters. The building was completed on June 30, 2022. Expenditures on the project, mainly payments to subcontractors, were as follows:
>
> | | |
> |---|---|
> | January 1, 2021 | $ 500,000 |
> | March 31, 2021 | 400,000 |
> | September 30, 2021 | 600,000 |
> | Accumulated expenditures at December 31, 2021 (before interest capitalization) | $1,500,000 |
> | January 31, 2022 | 600,000 |
> | April 30, 2022 | 300,000 |
>
> On January 1, 2021, the company obtained a $1 million construction loan with an 8% interest rate. The loan was outstanding during the entire construction period. The company's other interest-bearing debt included two long-term notes of $2,000,000 and $4,000,000 with interest rates of 6% and 12%, respectively. Both notes were outstanding during the entire construction period.

Average accumulated expenditures is determined by time-weighting individual expenditures made during the construction period.

Illustration 10–17

Expenditures and Loan Information for Interest Capitalization

The weighted-average accumulated expenditures by the end of 2021 are shown below:

	Actual Expenditures		Portion of Year Outstanding		Time-Weighted Expenditures
January 1, 2021	$ 500,000	×	¹²⁄₁₂	=	$ 500,000
March 31, 2021	400,000	×	⁹⁄₁₂	=	300,000
September 30, 2021	600,000	×	³⁄₁₂	=	150,000
	$1,500,000				$950,000

FINANCIAL Reporting Case

Q5, p. 3

Notice that the weighted-average accumulated expenditures are less than the actual accumulated expenditures of $1,500,000. If Mills had borrowed exactly the amount necessary to finance the project, it would not have incurred interest on a loan of $1,500,000 for the whole year but only on an average loan of $950,000. The next step is to determine the interest to be capitalized for the weighted-average accumulated expenditures.

STEP 1: Determine the weighted-average accumulated expenditures.

INTEREST RATES   In this situation, debt financing was obtained specifically for the construction project, and the amount borrowed is sufficient to cover the average accumulated expenditures. To determine the interest capitalized, then, we simply multiply the construction loan rate of 8% by the weighted-average accumulated expenditures.

STEP 2: Calculate the amount of interest to be capitalized.

Interest capitalized for 2021 = $950,000 × 8% = $76,000

Notice that this is the same answer we would get by assuming separate 8% construction loans were made for each expenditure at the time each expenditure was made.

Actual Expenditures		Annual Rate		Portion of Year Outstanding		Calculated Interest
$500,000	×	8%	×	$^{12}/_{12}$	=	$ 40,000
400,000	×	8%	×	$^{9}/_{12}$	=	24,000
600,000	×	8%	×	$^{3}/_{12}$	=	12,000
Interest capitalized for 2021						$76,000

The interest of $76,000 is added to the cost of the building, bringing accumulated expenditures at December 31, 2021, to $1,576,000 ($1,500,000 + $76,000). The remaining interest cost incurred but not capitalized is expensed.

It should be emphasized that interest capitalization does not require that funds actually be borrowed for this specific purpose, only that the company does have outstanding debt. The presumption is that even if the company doesn't borrow specifically for the project, funds from other borrowings must be diverted to finance the construction. Either way—directly or indirectly—interest costs are incurred. In our illustration, for instance, even without the construction loan, interest would be capitalized because other debt was outstanding. The capitalized interest would be the average accumulated expenditures multiplied by the weighted-average rate on these other loans. The weighted-average interest rate on all debt other than the construction loan would be 10%, calculated as follows:[20]

Loans		Annual Rate		Interest
$2,000,000	×	6%	=	$120,000
4,000,000	×	12%	=	480,000
$6,000,000				$600,000

$$\text{Weighted-average rate:} \frac{\$600,000}{\$6,000,000} = 10\%$$

This is a weighted average because total interest is $600,000 on total debt of $6,000,000. Therefore, in our illustration, without any specific construction loan, interest capitalized for 2021 would have been $95,000 ($950,000 × 10%).

Additional Consideration

The weighted-average rate isn't used for 2021 in our illustration because the specific construction loan is sufficient to cover the average accumulated expenditures. If the specific construction loan had been insufficient to cover the average accumulated expenditures, its 8% interest rate would be applied to the average accumulated expenditures up to the amount of the specific borrowing, and any remaining average accumulated expenditures in excess of specific borrowings would be multiplied by the weighted-average rate on all other outstanding interest-bearing debt. Suppose, for illustration, that the 8% construction loan had been only $500,000 rather than $1,000,000. We would calculate capitalized interest using both the specific rate and the weighted-average rate:

	Time-Weighted Expenditures		Annual Rate		Calculated Interest
Total	$950,000				
Specific borrowing	500,000	×	8%	=	$40,000
Excess	$450,000	×	10%	=	45,000
Capitalized interest					$85,000

In our illustration, it's necessary to use this approach in 2022.

---

[20]The same result can be obtained simply by multiplying the individual debt interest rates by the relative amount of debt at each rate. In this case, one-third of total debt is at 6% and two-thirds of the total debt is at 12% [(1/3 × 6%) + (2/3 × 12%) = 10%].

It's possible that the amount of interest calculated to be capitalized exceeds the amount of interest actually incurred. If that's the case, we limit the interest capitalized to the actual interest incurred. In our illustration, total interest cost incurred during 2021 far exceeds the $76,000 of capitalized interest calculated, so it's not necessary to limit the capitalized amount.

Interest capitalized is limited to interest incurred.

Loans		Annual Rate		Actual Interest		Calculated Interest
$1,000,000	×	8%	=	$ 80,000		
2,000,000	×	6%	=	120,000		
4,000,000	×	12%	=	480,000		
				$680,000		$76,000

STEP 3: Compare calculated interest with actual interest incurred.

↑ Use lower amount

Continuing the example based on the information in Illustration 10–17, let's determine the amount of interest capitalized during 2022 for the building. The total accumulated expenditures by the end of the project follow:

Accumulated expenditures at the beginning of 2022 (including interest capitalization)	$1,576,000
January 31, 2022 expenditures	600,000
April 30, 2022 expenditures	300,000
Accumulated expenditures at June 30, 2022 (before 2022 interest capitalization)	$2,476,000

The weighted-average accumulated expenditures by the end of the project are as follows:

STEP 1: Determine the weighted-average accumulated expenditures.

	Actual Expenditures		Portion of Year by End of Project		Time-Weighted Expenditures
January 1, 2022	$1,576,000	×	6/6	=	$ 1,576,000
January 31, 2022	600,000	×	5/6	=	500,000
April 30, 2022	300,000	×	2/6	=	100,000
Weighted-average accumulated expenditures for 2022					$2,176,000

Notice that the 2022 expenditures are weighted relative to the construction period of six months because the project was finished on June 30, 2022. Interest capitalized for 2022 would be $98,800, calculated as follows:

STEP 2: Calculate the amount of interest to be capitalized.

	Time-Weighted Expenditures		Annual Rate		Portion of Year Outstanding		Calculated Interest
Total	$2,176,000						
Specific borrowing	1,000,000	×	8%	×	6/12	=	$ 40,000
Excess	$1,176,000	×	10%	×	6/12	=	58,800
Interest capitalized for 2022							$98,800

Multiplying by six-twelfths reflects the fact that the interest rates are annual rates (12-month rates) and the construction period is only 6 months. Next, we compare the calculated interest with the actual interest incurred.

STEP 3: Compare calculated interest with actual interest incurred.

Loans		Annual Rate		Portion of Year Outstanding		Actual Interest		Calculated Interest
$1,000,000	×	8%	×	6/12	=	$ 40,000		
2,000,000	×	6%	×	6/12	=	60,000		
4,000,000	×	12%	×	6/12	=	240,000		
						$340,000		$98,800

↑ Use lower amount

540 SECTION 2 Assets

For the first six months of 2022, $98,800 of interest would be capitalized, bringing the total capitalized cost of the building to $2,574,800 ($2,476,000 + $98,800), and $241,200 in interest would be expensed ($340,000 − $98,800).

Additional Consideration

To illustrate how the actual interest limitation might come into play, let's assume the nonspecific borrowings in our illustration were $200,000 and $400,000 (instead of $2,000,000 and $4,000,000). Our comparison would change as follows:

Loans		Annual Rate		Portion of Year Oustanding		Actual Interest	Calculated Interest
$1,000,000	×	8%	×	½	=	$40,000	
200,000	×	6%	×	½	=	6,000	
400,000	×	12%	×	½	=	24,000	
						$70,000	$98,800

Use lower amount

The method of determining interest to capitalize that we've discussed is called the **specific interest method** because we use rates from specific construction loans to the extent of specific borrowings before using the average rate of other debt. Sometimes, though, it's difficult to associate specific borrowings with projects. In these situations, it's acceptable to just use the weighted-average rate on all interest-bearing debt, including all construction loans. This is known as the **weighted-average method**. In our illustration, for example, if the $1,000,000, 8% loan had not been specifically related to construction, we would calculate a single weighted-average rate as shown below.

Weighted-average method

Loans		Annual Rate		Interest
$1,000,000	×	8%	=	$ 80,000
2,000,000	×	6%	=	120,000
4,000,000	×	12%	=	480,000
$7,000,000				$680,000

$$\text{Weighted-average rate: } \frac{\$680,000}{\$7,000,000} = 9.7\%$$

If we were using the weighted-average method rather than the specific interest method, we would simply multiply this single rate times the average accumulated expenditures to determine capitalizable interest.

If material, the amount of interest capitalized during the period must be disclosed.

DISCLOSURE For an accounting period in which interest costs are capitalized, the total amount of interest costs capitalized, if the amount is material, should be disclosed. Illustration 10–18 shows an interest capitalization disclosure note that was included in a recent annual report of **Walmart Stores Inc.**, the world's largest retailer.

Illustration 10–18

Capitalized Interest Disclosure—Walmart Stores Inc.

Real World Financials

Property and equipment (in part)

Interest costs capitalized on construction projects were $36 million, $39 million, and $59 million in fiscal 2017, 2016, and 2015, respectively.

Source: Wal-Mart Stores, Inc.

Research and Development (R&D)

"Innovation" is a word commonly used in the marketing and production departments of most companies. Companies compete fiercely to dream up the next top-selling product or service. In 2015, Volkswagen spent more than $15 billion to research new technology for its hybrid vehicles and improve CO_2 emissions. Microsoft spent $11.4 billion on discovering new technology products. Of the 118,000 people employed by Miscrosoft, 39,000 are in product research and development. Alphabet (Google) spent $9.8 billion on futuristic ideas such as self-driving cars and computer eyewear. Merck invested $7.2 billion to test new drugs related to oncology, infectious diseases, vaccines, and diabetes.

● LO10–8

Companies are willing to spend huge amounts on R&D because they believe the project will eventually provide benefits that exceed the current expenditures. Unfortunately, though, it's difficult to predict which individual research and development projects will ultimately provide benefits. Will Google's expenditures on self-driving cars ever generate enough revenue to cover its costs? Moreover, even for those projects that pan out, a direct relationship between research and development costs and specific future revenue is difficult to establish. In other words, even if R&D costs do lead to future benefits, it's difficult to objectively determine the size of the benefits and in which periods the costs should be expensed if they are capitalized. For these reasons, *the FASB takes a conservative approach and requires R&D costs to be expensed immediately.*[21]

R&D costs entail a high degree of uncertainty of future benefits and are difficult to match with future revenues.

R&D costs are expensed in the periods incurred.

The FASB's decision is controversial. Many companies would prefer to delay the recognition of these expenses until later years when presumably the expenditures bear fruit. In other words, many companies would prefer to record R&D expenditures initially as an asset, because at least some of the R&D expenditures will likely produce future benefits. The requirement to expense R&D immediately leads to assets being understated and expenses being overstated in the current period.

Determining R&D Costs

GAAP distinguishes research and development as follows:

- **Research** is planned search or critical investigation aimed at discovery of new knowledge with the hope that such knowledge will be useful in developing a new product or service or a new process or technique or in bringing about a significant improvement to an existing product or process.

- **Development** is the translation of research findings or other knowledge into a plan or design for a new product or process or for a significant improvement to an existing product or process whether intended for sale or use.[22]

R&D costs include salaries, wages, and other labor costs of personnel engaged in R&D activities, the costs of materials consumed, equipment, facilities, and intangibles used in R&D projects, the costs of services performed by others in connection with R&D activities, and a reasonable allocation of indirect costs related to those activities. General and administrative costs should not be included unless they are clearly related to the R&D activity.

If an asset is purchased specifically for a single R&D project, its cost is considered R&D and expensed immediately even though the asset's useful life extends beyond the current year. However, the cost of an asset that has an alternative future use beyond the current R&D project is *not* a current R&D expense. For example, a small building might be purchased to conduct R&D projects but will then be used for general storage once the projects are complete. The depreciation or amortization of these alternative-use assets is included as R&D expenses only in the periods the assets are used for R&D activities.

R&D expense includes the depreciation and amortization of assets used in R&D activities.

In general, R&D costs pertain to activities that occur prior to the start of commercial production. Commercial production most often refers to the point in time where the company has no other plans to materially change the product prior to beginning production for intended sales to customers.

Costs incurred *before* the start of commercial production are expensed as R&D.

---

[21]FASB ASC 730–10–25–1: Research and Development—Overall—Recognition.
[22]Ibid., section 730–10–20.

542   SECTION 2   Assets

Costs incurred *after* commercial production begins would be either expensed or included in the cost of inventory.

Any costs incurred after the start of commercial production are not classified as R&D costs. These costs would be either expensed or treated as manufacturing overhead and included in the cost of inventory.

Illustration 10–19 captures this concept with a time line beginning with the start of an R&D project and ending with the ultimate sale of a developed product or the use of a developed process. The illustration also provides examples of activities typically included as R&D and examples of activities typically excluded from R&D.[23]

Illustration 10–19

Research and Development Expenditures

| Start of R&D Activity | Start of Commercial Production | Sale of Product or Process |

Examples of R&D Costs:

- Laboratory research aimed at discovery of new knowledge

- Searching for applications of new research findings or other knowledge

- Design, construction, and testing of preproduction prototypes and models

- Modification of the formulation or design of a product or process

Examples of Non-R&D Costs:

- Engineering follow-through in an early phase of commercial production

- Quality control during commercial production including routine testing of products

- Routine ongoing efforts to refine, enrich, or otherwise improve on the qualities of an existing product

- Adaptation of an existing capability to a particular requirement or customer's need as a part of a continuing commercial activity

Let's look at an example in Illustration 10–20.

Illustration 10–20

Research and Development Costs

The Askew Company made the following cash expenditures during 2021 related to the development of a new industrial plastic:

R&D salaries and wages	$ 10,000,000
R&D supplies consumed during 2021	3,000,000
Purchase of R&D equipment	5,000,000
Patent filing and legal costs	100,000
Payments to others for services in connection with R&D activities	1,200,000
Total	$19,300,000

The project resulted in a new product to be manufactured in 2022 (next year). A patent was filed with the U.S. Patent Office. Amortization of the patent's filing and legal costs will begin in 2022. The equipment purchased will be employed in other projects. Depreciation on the equipment for 2021 was $500,000.

Filing and legal costs for patents, copyrights, and other developed intangibles are capitalized and amortized in future periods.

The salaries and wages, supplies consumed, and payments to others for R&D services are expensed in 2021 as R&D. The equipment is capitalized and the 2021 depreciation is expensed as R&D. Even though the costs to develop the patented product are expensed, the filing and legal costs for the patent are capitalized and amortized in future periods, just as similar costs are capitalized for purchased intangibles. Amortization of the patent is discussed in Chapter 11.

[23]Ibid., section 730–10–55.

The various expenditures would be recorded as follows:

R&D expense ($10,000,000 + $3,000,000 + $1,200,000)	14,200,000	
Cash		14,200,000
To record R&D expenses.		
Equipment	5,000,000	
Cash		5,000,000
To record the purchase of equipment.		
R&D expense	500,000	
Accumulated depreciation—equipment		500,000
To record R&D depreciation.		
Patent	100,000	
Cash		100,000
To capitalize the patent filing and legal costs.		

Expenditures reconciliation:	
Recorded as R&D expense	$ 14,200,000
Capitalized as equipment*	5,000,000
Capitalized as patent	100,000
Total expenditures	$19,300,000

* $500,000 of the initial capitalized amount will be depreciated as R&D expense in the first year.

GAAP requires that total R&D expense incurred must be disclosed either as a line item in the income statement or in a disclosure note. In our illustration, total R&D expense disclosed in 2021 would be $14,700,000 ($14,200,000 in expenditures and $500,000 in depreciation). Note that if Askew later sells this patent to another company for, say, $15 million, the buyer would capitalize the entire purchase price rather than only the filing and legal costs. Once again, the reason for the apparent inconsistency in accounting treatment of internally generated intangibles and externally purchased intangibles is the difficulty of associating costs and benefits.

GAAP requires disclosure of total R&D expense incurred during the period.

International Financial Reporting Standards

IAS No. 38 draws a distinction between research activities and development activities.[24] Research expenditures are *expensed* in the period incurred. However, development expenditures that meet specified criteria are *capitalized* as an intangible asset. Under both U.S. GAAP and IFRS, any direct costs to secure a patent, such as legal and filing fees, are capitalized.

Heineken, a company based in Amsterdam, prepares its financial statements according to IFRS. The following disclosure note describes the company's adherence to *IAS No. 38*.

IFRS requires companies to capitalize development expenditures that meet specified criteria.

● LO10–9

Software, Research and Development and Other Intangible Assets (in part)

Expenditures on research activities, undertaken with the prospect of gaining new technical knowledge and understanding, are recognized in the income statement when incurred. Development activities involve a plan or design for the production of new or substantially improved products and processes. Development expenditures are capitalized only if development costs can be measured reliably, the product or process is technically and commercially feasible, future economic benefits are probable, and Heineken intends to, and has sufficient resources to, complete development and to use or sell the asset. The expenditures capitalized include the cost of materials, direct labor and overhead costs that are directly attributable to preparing the asset for its intended use, and capitalized borrowing costs.

Amortization of capitalized development costs begins when development is complete and the asset is available for use. Heineken disclosed that it amortizes its capitalized development costs using the straight-line method over an estimated three-year useful life.

Source: Heineken

---

[24]"Intangible Assets," *International Accounting Standard No. 38* (IASCF), as amended effective January 1, 2018.

We've just discussed that U.S. GAAP requires R&D costs to be expensed immediately. There are three types of costs related to R&D, however, that are capitalized (recorded as an asset). These exceptions are shown below:

1. Development costs for software that has reached the point of technological feasibility
2. R&D performed by the company for sale to others
3. R&D purchased in a business acquisition

Software Development Costs

The computer software industry has become a large and important U.S. business over the last two decades. Companies in this multibillion dollar industry include **Microsoft**, **Oracle**, **IBM**, **Adobe Systems**, and **Intuit**. A significant expenditure for these companies is the cost of developing software. In the early years of the software industry, some software companies were capitalizing software development costs and expensing them in future periods and others were expensing these costs in the period incurred.

Now GAAP establishes a timeline for purposes of accounting for software development costs. Any software costs incurred from initial development activity until **technological feasibility** of the software are treated like all other R&D costs (expensed as incurred). Technological feasibility refers to the point in time "when the enterprise has completed all planning, designing, coding, and testing activities that are necessary to establish that the product can be produced to meet its design specifications including functions, features, and technical performance requirements."[25]

Costs incurred after technological feasibility but before product release are capitalized.

Costs incurred after technological feasibility but before the software is available for general release to customers are capitalized as an intangible asset. These costs include items such as further coding and testing and the production of product masters. Any costs incurred after the software release date generally are expensed but not as part of R&D.

Illustration 10–21 shows the R&D time line introduced earlier in the chapter modified to include the point at which technological feasibility is established. Only the costs incurred between technological feasibility and the software release date are capitalized.

Illustration 10–21

Research and Development Expenditures—Computer Software

Illustration 10–22 shows the software disclosure included in a recent annual report of **CA, Inc.** The note provides a good summary of the accounting treatment of software development costs.

Why do generally accepted accounting principles allow this exception to the general rule of expensing all R&D? We could attribute it to the political process. Software is a very important industry to our economy and perhaps its lobbying efforts resulted in the standard allowing software companies to capitalize certain R&D costs.

We could also attribute the exception to the nature of the software business. Recall that R&D costs in general are expensed in the period incurred for two reasons: (1) they entail a high degree of uncertainty of future benefits, and (2) they are difficult to match with future benefits. With software, there is an important identifiable engineering milestone, technological feasibility. When this milestone is attained, the probability of the software product's

---

[25]FASB ASC 985–20–25–2: Software—Costs of Software to be Sold, Leased, or Marketed—Recognition.

Illustration 10–22

Software Disclosure—
CA, Inc.

Real World Financials

> **Internally Developed Software Products**
> Internally developed software products, which are included in "Capitalized software and other intangible assets, net" in the Consolidated Balance Sheets, consist of capitalized costs associated with the development of computer software to be sold, leased or otherwise marketed. Software development costs associated with new products and significant enhancements to existing software products are expensed as incurred until technological feasibility, as defined in FASB ASC Topic 985-20, has been established. Costs incurred thereafter are capitalized until the product is made generally available. The stage during the Company's development process for a new product or new release at which technological feasibility requirements are established affects the amount of costs capitalized.
>
> Source: CA, Inc.

success increases significantly. And because the useful life of software is fairly short (one to five years in most cases), it is much easier to determine the periods of increased revenues than for R&D projects in other industries. Compare this situation with, say, the development of a new drug. Even after the drug has been developed, it must go through extensive testing to meet approval by the Food and Drug Administration (FDA), which may never be attained. If attained, the useful life of the drug could be anywhere from a few months to many years.

The discussion above relates to costs incurred to develop or purchase computer software to be sold, leased, or otherwise marketed (that is, *for external purposes*).[26] We account for the costs incurred to develop computer software *to be used internally* in a similar manner. Costs incurred during the preliminary project stage are expensed as R&D. After the application development stage is reached (for example, at the coding stage or installation stage), we capitalize any further costs.[27] If, instead, we *purchase* computer software for internal use, those costs generally are capitalized.

Cloud computing arrangements.   Cloud computing arrangements are becoming increasingly popular as a way for companies to utilize software without having to maintain the software and related hardware. These arrangements involve a company using software by accessing (via the Internet or dedicated line) a vendor's or a third party's hardware. The costs of cloud computing arrangements are treated as the purchase of intangible assets if both:

1. The customer has a contractual right to take possession of the software without significant penalty, and
2. The customer could run the software on its own or with an unrelated vendor.

If either of these criteria is not met, the arrangement is treated as a service contract, and costs are expensed as incurred.

Any implementation costs incurred during the application development phase (integration with the company's own software, coding, and configuration or customization) are capitalized. Interestingly, even if the arrangement itself does not qualify for capitalization as an intangible asset (because one of the two criteria above is not met), implementation costs still can be capitalized. Any costs related to preliminary planning or the post-implementation operation, however, would be expensed as incurred.

R&D Performed for Others

The principle requiring the immediate expensing of R&D does not apply to companies that perform R&D for other companies under contract. In these situations, the R&D costs are capitalized as inventory and carried forward into future years until the project is completed. Of course, justification is that the benefits of these expenditures are the contract revenues that will eventually be recognized. Revenue from these contracts can be recognized over time or at a point in time, depending on the specifics of the contract. We discussed these alternatives in Chapter 6.

---

[26]FASB ASC 985–20–25–1: Software—Costs of Software to be Sold, Leased, or Marketed—Recognition.
[27]FASB ASC 350–40–25: Intangibles—Goodwill and Other—Internal-Use Software—Recognition.

R&D Purchased in Business Acquisitions

It's not unusual for one company to buy another company in order to obtain technology that the acquired company has developed or is in the process of developing. Any time a company buys another, it values the tangible and intangible assets acquired at fair value. When part of the acquisition price involves technology, we distinguish between

1. Developed technology.
2. In-process research and development.

In business acquisitions, the fair value of developed technology is capitalized as an finite-life intangible asset.

In business acquisitions, the fair value of in-process research and development is capitalized as an indefinite-life intangible asset.

To distinguish these two types of technology acquired, we borrow a criterion used in accounting for software development costs, and determine whether *technological feasibility* has been achieved. If it has, the technology is considered "developed," and we capitalize its fair value (record it as an asset) and amortize that amount over its useful life just like any other *finite-life* intangible asset.

For in-process R&D (technology that has not reached the feasibility stage), GAAP also requires capitalization of its fair value. However, unlike developed technology, we view in-process R&D as an *indefinite-life* intangible asset.[28] As you will learn in Chapter 11, we don't amortize indefinite-life intangibles. Instead, we monitor these assets and test them for impairment when required by GAAP.

If the acquired R&D project is completed successfully, we switch to the way we account for developed technology and amortize the capitalized amount over the estimated period the product or process developed will provide benefits. If the project instead is abandoned, we expense the entire balance immediately.

R&D costs incurred after the acquisition to complete the project are expensed as incurred, consistent with the treatment of usual R&D expenditures. Similarly, the purchase of R&D from third parties not associated with a business combination is expensed as incurred, just as if the company had performed the R&D activity itself. An exception is when the purchased R&D has an alternative use beyond a specific project.

As an example of R&D associated with a business acquisition, in 2015 AbbVie Inc., a global research-based biopharmaceutical company, acquired Pharmacyclics Inc. for approximately $20.8 billion. The fair values assigned included finite-life intangible assets of $11.4 billion, in-process R&D of $7.2 billion, and goodwill of $7.6 billion (as well as other identifiable assets of $1.7 billion and liabilities of $7.1 billion). As shown in Illustration 10-23, AbbVie classified projects acquired that have not yet received regulatory approval as in-process R&D.

Illustration 10–23

Acquired In-Process Research and Development—AbbVie, Inc.

Real World Financials

Acquired In-Process Research and Development

The initial costs of rights to IPR&D projects acquired in an asset acquisition are expensed as IPR&D in the consolidated statements of earnings unless the project has an alternative future use. These costs include initial payments incurred prior to regulatory approval in connection with research and development collaboration agreements that provide rights to develop, manufacture, market and/or sell pharmaceutical products. The fair value of IPR&D projects acquired in a business combination are capitalized and accounted for as indefinite-lived intangible assets until the underlying project receives regulatory approval, at which point the intangible asset will be accounted for as a definite-lived intangible asset, or discontinuation, at which point the intangible asset will be written off. Development costs incurred after the acquisition are expensed as incurred. Indefinite- and definite-lived assets are subject to impairment reviews as discussed previously.

Source: AbbVie, Inc.

Start-up costs are expensed in the period incurred.

Start-Up Costs

Whenever a company introduces a new product or service, or commences business in a new territory or with a new customer, it incurs start-up costs. Start-up costs also include organization costs related to organizing a new entity, such as legal fees and state filing fees to incorporate. As with R&D expenditures, companies are required to expense all the costs

---

[28]FASB ASC 805: Business Combinations.

related to a company's start-up and organization activities in the period incurred, rather than capitalize those costs as an asset.[29]

For the year ended December 31, 2017, Chipotle Mexican Grill, Inc., opened 240 new restaurants. The company incurred a variety of one-time preopening costs for wages, benefits and travel for the training and opening teams, food, and other restaurant operating costs totaling $17 million. These costs were expensed immediately.

Financial Reporting Case Solution

©Idealphotographer/123RF

1. **Describe to Stan what it means to capitalize an expenditure. What is the general rule for determining which costs are capitalized when property, plant, and equipment or an intangible asset is acquired?** *(p. 516)*   To capitalize an expenditure simply means to record it as an asset. All expenditures other than payments to shareholders and debt repayments are either expensed as incurred or capitalized. In general, the choice is determined by whether the expenditure benefits more than just the current period. Exceptions to this general principle are discussed in the chapter. The initial cost of an asset includes all expenditures necessary to bring the asset to its desired condition and location for use.

2. **Which costs might be included in the initial cost of equipment?** *(p. 516)*   In addition to the purchase price, the cost of equipment might include the cost of transportation, installation, testing, and legal fees to establish title.

3. **What is goodwill and how is it measured?** *(p. 523)*   Goodwill represents the unique value of a company as a whole over and above its identifiable tangible and intangible assets. Because goodwill can't be separated from a company, it's not possible for a buyer to acquire it without also acquiring the whole company or a controlling portion of it. Goodwill will appear as an asset in a balance sheet only when it was purchased in connection with the acquisition of another company. In that case, the capitalized cost of goodwill equals the fair value of the consideration exchanged for the company less the fair value of the net assets acquired. Goodwill is a residual asset; it's the amount left after other assets are identified and valued. Just like for other intangible assets that have indefinite useful lives, we do not amortize goodwill.

4. **In what situations is interest capitalized rather than expensed?** *(p. 536)*   Interest is capitalized only for assets constructed for a company's own use or for assets constructed as discrete products for sale or lease. For example, Walt Disney capitalizes interest on assets constructed for its theme parks, resorts, and other property, and on theatrical and television productions. During the construction period, interest is considered a cost necessary to get the asset ready for its intended use.

5. **What is the three-step process used to determine the amount of interest capitalized?** *(p. 537)*   The first step is to determine the average accumulated expenditures for the period. The second step is to multiply the average accumulated expenditures by an appropriate interest rate or rates to determine the amount of interest capitalized. A final step compares the interest determined in step two with actual interest incurred. Interest capitalized is the lower of the two. ●

The Bottom Line

● **LO10–1**   The initial cost of property, plant, and equipment and intangible assets acquired in an exchange transaction includes the purchase price and all expenditures necessary to bring the asset to its desired condition and location for use. The cost of a natural resource includes the acquisition costs for the use of land, the exploration and development costs incurred before production begins, and restoration costs incurred during or at the end of extraction. Purchased intangible assets are valued at their original cost to include the purchase price and legal and filing fees. *(p. 516)*

---

[29] FASB ASC 720–15–25–1: Other Expenses—Start-Up Costs—Recognition.

548   SECTION 2   Assets

● **LO10–2** If a lump-sum purchase involves different assets, it is necessary to allocate the lump-sum acquisition price among the separate items according to some logical allocation method. A widely used allocation method is to divide the lump-sum purchase price according to the individual asset's relative fair values. (*p. 525*)

● **LO10–3** Assets acquired in exchange for deferred payment contracts are valued at their fair value or the present value of payments using a realistic interest rate. (*p. 526*)

● **LO10–4** Assets acquired through the issuance of equity securities are valued at the fair value of the securities if known; if not known, the fair value of the assets received is used. Donated assets are valued at their fair value. (*p. 528*)

● **LO10–5** A key to profitability is how well a company manages and utilizes its assets. Financial analysts often use activity, or turnover, ratios to evaluate a company's effectiveness in managing its assets. Property, plant, and equipment (PP&E) usually are a company's primary revenue-generating assets. Their efficient use is critical to generating a satisfactory return to owners. One ratio that analysts often use to measure how effectively managers use PP&E is the fixed-asset turnover ratio. This ratio is calculated by dividing net sales by average fixed assets. (*p. 530*)

● **LO10–6** The basic principle used for nonmonetary exchanges is to value the asset(s) received based on the fair value of the asset(s) given up. In certain situations, the valuation of the asset(s) received is based on the book value of the asset(s) given up. (*p. 531*)

● **LO10–7** The cost of a self-constructed asset includes identifiable materials and labor and a portion of the company's manufacturing overhead costs. In addition, GAAP provides for the capitalization of interest incurred during construction. The amount of interest capitalized is equal to the average accumulated expenditures for the period multiplied by the appropriate interest rates, not to exceed actual interest incurred. (*p. 535*)

● **LO10–8** Research and development costs incurred to internally develop an intangible asset are expensed in the period incurred. Filing and legal costs for developed intangibles are capitalized. (*p. 541*)

● **LO10–9** *IAS No. 20* requires that government grants be recognized in income over the periods necessary to match them on a systematic basis with the related costs that they are intended to compensate. Other than software development costs incurred after technological feasibility has been established, U.S. GAAP requires all research and development expenditures to be expensed in the period incurred. *IAS No. 38* draws a distinction between research activities and development activities. Research expenditures are expensed in the period incurred. However, development expenditures that meet specified criteria are capitalized as an intangible asset. (*pp. 529 and 543*) ●

APPENDIX 10 | Oil And Gas Accounting

There are two generally accepted methods that companies can use to account for oil and gas exploration costs. The successful efforts method requires that exploration costs that are known *not* to have resulted in the discovery of oil or gas (sometimes referred to as *dry holes*) be included as expenses in the period the expenditures are made. The alternative, the full-cost method, allows costs incurred in searching for oil and gas within a large geographical area to be capitalized as assets and expensed in the future as oil and gas from the successful wells are removed from that area. Both of these methods are widely used. Illustration 10A–1 compares the two alternatives.

Illustration 10A–1

Oil and Gas Accounting

The Shannon Oil Company incurred $2,000,000 in exploration costs for each of 10 oil wells drilled in 2021 in west Texas. Eight of the 10 wells were dry holes.

The accounting treatment of the $20 million in total exploration costs will vary significantly depending on the accounting method used. The summary journal entries using each of the alternative methods are as follows:

Successful Efforts		Full Cost	
Oil Deposit 4,000,000		Oil Deposit 20,000,000	
Exploration Expense..... 16,000,000		Cash...............	20,000,000
Cash............................	20,000,000		

Using the full-cost method, Shannon would capitalize the entire $20 million which is expensed as oil from the two successful wells is depleted. On the other hand, using the successful efforts method, the cost of the unsuccessful wells is expensed in 2021, and only the $4 million cost related to the successful wells is capitalized and expensed in future periods as the oil is depleted.

Chapter 1 characterized the establishment of accounting and reporting standards as a political process. Standards, particularly changes in standards, can have significant differential effects on companies, investors and creditors, and other interest groups. The FASB must consider potential economic consequences of a change in an accounting standard or the introduction of a new standard. The history of oil and gas accounting provides a good example of this political process and the effect of possible adverse economic consequences on the standard-setting process.

In 1977 the FASB attempted to establish uniformity in the accounting treatment of oil and gas exploration costs. An accounting standard was issued requiring all companies to use the successful efforts method.[30]

This standard met with criticism from the oil and gas companies that were required to switch from full cost to successful efforts accounting. These companies felt that the switch would seriously depress their reported income over time. As a result, they argued, their ability to raise capital in the securities markets would be inhibited, which would result in a cutback of new exploration. The fear that the Standard would cause domestic companies to significantly reduce oil and gas exploration and thus increase our dependence on foreign oil was compelling to Congress, the SEC, and the U.S. Department of Energy.

Extensive pressure from Congress, the SEC, and affected companies forced the FASB to rescind the Standard. Presently, oil and gas companies can use either the successful efforts or full-cost method to account for oil and gas exploration costs. Of course, the method used must be disclosed. For example, Illustration 10A–2 shows how **Chevron Corp.** disclosed its use of the successful efforts method in its summary of significant accounting policies. ●

> Many feared that the requirement to switch to successful efforts accounting would cause a significant cutback in the exploration for new oil and gas in the United States.

Properties, Plant, and Equipment (in part)

The successful efforts method is used for crude oil and natural gas exploration and production activities.

Source: Chevron Corp.

Illustration 10A–2

Oil and Gas Accounting
Disclosure—Chevron Corp.

Real World Financials

Questions For Review of Key Topics

Q 10–1   Explain the difference between tangible and intangible long-lived, revenue-producing assets.

Q 10–2   What is included in the original cost of property, plant, and equipment and intangible assets acquired in an exchange transaction?

Q 10–3   Identify the costs associated with the initial valuation of a developed natural resource.

Q 10–4   Briefly summarize the accounting treatment for intangible assets, explaining the difference between purchased and internally developed intangible assets.

Q 10–5   What is goodwill and how is it measured?

Q 10–6   Explain the method generally used to allocate the cost of a lump-sum purchase to the individual assets acquired.

Q 10–7   When an asset is acquired and a note payable is assumed, explain how acquisition cost of the asset is determined when the interest rate for the note is less than the current market rate for similar notes.

Q 10–8   Explain how assets acquired in exchange for equity securities are valued.

Q 10–9   Explain how property, plant, and equipment and intangible assets acquired through donation are valued.

Q 10–10   What account is credited when a company receives donated assets? What is the rationale for this choice?

---

[30]The rescinded standard was "Financial Accounting and Reporting by Oil and Gas Producing Companies," *Statement of Financial Accounting Standards No. 19* (Stamford, Conn.: FASB, 1977). Authoritative guidance on this topic can now be found at FASB ASC 932: Extractive Activities—Oil and Gas.

Q 10–11 What is the basic principle for valuing property, plant, and equipment and intangible assets acquired in exchange for other nonmonetary assets?

Q 10–12 Identify the two exceptions to valuing property, plant, and equipment and intangible assets acquired in nonmonetary exchanges at the fair value of the asset(s) given up.

Q 10–13 In what situations is interest capitalized?

Q 10–14 Define average accumulated expenditures and explain how the amount is computed.

Q 10–15 Explain the difference between the specific interest method and the weighted-average method in determining the amount of interest to be capitalized.

Q 10–16 Define R&D according to U.S. GAAP.

Q 10–17 Explain the accounting treatment of equipment acquired for use in R&D projects.

Q 10–18 Explain the accounting treatment of costs incurred to develop computer software.

Q 10–19 Explain the difference in the accounting treatment of the cost of developed technology and the cost of in-process R&D in an acquisition.

IFRS **Q 10–20** Identify any differences between U.S. GAAP and International Financial Reporting Standards in accounting for government grants received.

IFRS **Q 10–21** Identify any differences between U.S. GAAP and International Financial Reporting Standards in the treatment of research and development expenditures.

IFRS **Q 10–22** Identify any differences between U.S. GAAP and International Financial Reporting Standards in the treatment of software development costs.

Q 10–23 (Based on Appendix 10) Explain the difference between the successful efforts and the full-cost methods of accounting for oil and gas exploration costs.

Brief Exercises

BE 10–1
Acquisition cost; equipment
● LO10–1

Beaverton Lumber purchased milling equipment for $35,000. In addition to the purchase price, Beaverton made the following expenditures: freight, $1,500; installation, $3,000; testing, $2,000; personal property tax on the equipment for the first year, $500. What is the initial cost of the equipment?

BE 10–2
Acquisition cost; land and building
● LO10–1

Fullerton Waste Management purchased land and a warehouse for $600,000. In addition to the purchase price, Fullerton made the following expenditures related to the acquisition: broker's commission, $30,000; title insurance, $3,000; miscellaneous closing costs, $6,000. The warehouse was immediately demolished at a cost of $18,000 in anticipation of the building of a new warehouse. Determine the amounts Fullerton should capitalize as the cost of the land and the building.

BE 10–3
Lump-sum acquisition
● LO10–2

Refer to the situation described in BE 10–2. Assume that Fullerton decides to use the warehouse rather than demolish it. An independent appraisal estimates the fair values of the land and warehouse at $420,000 and $280,000, respectively. Determine the amounts Fullerton should capitalize as the cost of the land and the building.

BE 10–4
Cost of a natural resource; asset retirement obligation
● LO10–1

Smithson Mining operates a silver mine in Nevada. Acquisition, exploration, and development costs totaled $5.6 million. After the silver is extracted in approximately five years, Smithson is obligated to restore the land to its original condition, including constructing a wildlife preserve. The company's controller has provided the following three cash flow possibilities for the restoration costs: (1) $500,000, 20% probability; (2) $550,000, 45% probability; and (3) $650,000, 35% probability. The company's credit-adjusted, risk-free rate of interest is 6%. What is the initial cost of the silver mine?

BE 10–5
Asset retirement obligation
● LO10–1

Refer to the situation described in BE 10–4. What is the book value of the asset retirement liability at the end of one year? Assuming that the actual restoration costs incurred after extraction is completed are $596,000, what amount of gain or loss will Smithson recognize on retirement of the liability?

BE 10–6
Goodwill
● LO10–1

Pro-tech Software acquired all of the outstanding stock of Reliable Software for $14 million. The book value of Reliable's net assets (assets minus liabilities) was $8.3 million. The fair values of Reliable's assets and liabilities equaled their book values with the exception of certain intangible assets whose fair values exceeded book values by $2.5 million. Calculate the amount paid for goodwill.

BE 10–7
Acquisition cost;
noninterest-
bearing note
● LO10–3

On June 30, 2021, Kimberly Farms purchased custom-made harvesting equipment from a local producer. In payment, Kimberly signed a noninterest-bearing note requiring the payment of $60,000 in two years. The fair value of the equipment is not known, but an 8% interest rate properly reflects the time value of money for this type of loan agreement. At what amount will Kimberly initially value the equipment? How much interest expense will Kimberly recognize in its income statement for this note for the year ended December 31, 2021?

BE 10–8
Acquisition cost;
issuance of equity
securities
● LO10–4

Shackelford Corporation acquired a patent from its founder, Jim Shackelford, in exchange for 50,000 shares of the company's no-par common stock. On the date of the exchange, the common stock had a fair value of $22 per share. Determine the cost of the patent.

BE 10–9
Fixed-asset
turnover ratio
● LO10–5

Huebert Corporation and Winslow Corporation reported the following information:

	($ in millions)			
	Huebert		Winslow	
	2021	**2020**	**2021**	**2020**
Property, plant, and equipment (net)	$210	$220	$680	$650
Net sales—2021	$1,850		$5,120	

Calculate each companies fixed-asset turnover ratio and determine which company utilizes its fixed assets most efficiently to generate sales.

BE 10–10
Fixed-asset
turnover ratio;
solve for
unknown
● LO10–5

The balance sheets of Pinewood Resorts reported net fixed assets of $740,000 and $940,000 at the end of 2020 and 2021, respectively. The fixed-asset turnover ratio for 2021 was 3.25. Calculate Pinewood's net sales for 2021.

BE 10–11
Nonmonetary
exchange
● LO10–6

Calaveras Tire exchanged equipment for two pickup trucks. The book value and fair value of the equipment given up were $20,000 (original cost of $65,000 less accumulated depreciation of $45,000) and $17,000, respectively. Assume Calaveras paid $8,000 in cash and the exchange has commercial substance. (1) At what amount will Calaveras value the pickup trucks? (2) How much gain or loss will the company recognize on the exchange?

BE 10–12
Nonmonetary
exchange
● LO10–6

Refer to the situation described in BE 10–11. Answer the questions assuming that the fair value of the equipment was $24,000, instead of $17,000.

BE 10–13
Nonmonetary
exchange
● LO10–6

Refer to the situation described in BE 10–12. Answer the questions assuming that the exchange lacks commercial substance.

BE 10–14
Interest
capitalization
● LO10–7

A company constructs a building for its own use. Construction began on January 1 and ended on December 30. The expenditures for construction were as follows: January 1, $500,000; March 31, $600,000; June 30, $400,000; October 30, $600,000. To help finance construction, the company arranged a 7% construction loan on January 1 for $700,000. The company's other borrowings, outstanding for the whole year, consisted of a $3 million loan and a $5 million note with interest rates of 8% and 6%, respectively. Assuming the company uses the *specific interest method,* calculate the amount of interest capitalized for the year.

BE 10–15
Interest
capitalization
● LO10–7

Refer to the situation described in BE 10–14. Assuming the company uses the *weighted-average method,* calculate the amount of interest capitalized for the year.

BE 10–16
Research and
development
● LO10–8

Maxtor Technology incurred the following costs during the year related to the creation of a new type of personal computer monitor:

Salaries	$220,000
Depreciation on R&D facilities and equipment	125,000
Utilities and other direct costs incurred for the R&D facilities	66,000
Patent filing and related legal costs	22,000
Payment to another company for performing a portion of the development work	120,000
Costs of adapting the new monitor for the specific needs of a customer	80,000

What amount should Maxtor report as research and development expense in its income statement?

BE 10–17
Software development costs; external purposes
● LO10–8

In February 2021, Culverson Company began developing a new software package to be sold to customers. The software allows people to enter health information and daily eating and exercise habits to track their health status. The project was completed in November 2021 at a cost of $800,000. Of this amount, $300,000 was spent before technological feasibility was established. Culverson expects a useful life of two years for the new product and total revenues of $1,500,000. Determine the amount that Culverson should capitalize as software development costs in 2021.

BE 10–18
Software development costs; internal purposes
● LO10–8

In March 2021, Price Company began developing a new software system to be used internally for managing its inventory. The software integrates customer orders with inventory on hand to automatically place orders for additional inventory when needed. The software then automatically records inventory as the shipment is received and read by scanners. The software development was completed in October 2021 at a cost of $150,000. Of this amount, $25,000 was spent before the application development stage was established. Price expects to use the software for at least five years. Determine the initial amount that Price should capitalize as software development costs.

BE 10–19
Software development costs; cloud computing arrangements
● LO10–8

Garrett Corporation began operations in 2021. To maintain its accounting records, Garrett entered into a two-year agreement with Accurite Company. The agreement specifies that Garrett will pay $35,000 to Accurite immediately, and in return, Accurite will make its accounting software accessible via the Internet to Garrett and maintain all infrastructure necessary to run the software and store records. At any time, Garrett Corporation can freely remove its records and run the software on its own hardware or that of another accounting services company. In addition to the cost of the agreement, Garrett incurred $5,000 early in the year devising a plan for its accounting software needs, $15,000 for customizing its own computers for integration with Accurite's software, and $10,000 after the software was implemented to train its employees. Determine the initial amount that Garrett should capitalize related to the software development costs.

BE 10–20
Research and development; various types
● LO10–8

Maltese Laboratories incurred the following research and developments costs related to its pharmaceutical business:

Internal projects (salaries, supplies, overhead for R&D facilities)	$620,000
Payment to acquire R&D from a third party related to a specific project	75,000
Costs of an R&D project to be sold under contract to Libo Pharmacy, a third party	82,000
In-process R&D associated with the acquisition of Curatics, an independent research company.	148,000

What amount should Maltese report as research and development expense in its income statement?

BE 10–21
Start-up costs
● LO10–8

In the current year, Big Burgers, Inc., expanded its fast-food operations by opening several new stores in Texas. The company incurred the following costs in the current year: market appraisal ($50,000), consulting fees ($72,000), advertising ($47,000), and traveling to train employees ($31,000). The company is willing to incur these costs because it foresees strong customer demand in Texas for the next several years. What amount should Big Burgers report as an expense in its income statement associated with these costs?

Exercises   ■ connect

E 10–1
Acquisition costs; land and building
● LO10–1

On March 1, 2021, Beldon Corporation purchased land as a factory site for $60,000. An old building on the property was demolished, and construction began on a new building that was completed on December 15, 2021. Costs incurred during this period are listed below:

Demolition of old building	$ 4,000
Architect's fees (for new building)	12,000
Legal fees for title investigation of land	2,000
Property taxes on land (for period beginning March 1, 2021)	3,000
Construction costs	500,000
Interest on construction loan	5,000

Salvaged materials resulting from the demolition of the old building were sold for $2,000.

Required:

Determine the amounts that Beldon should capitalize as the cost of the land and the new building.

E 10–2
Acquisition cost;
equipment
● LO10–1

Oaktree Company purchased new equipment and made the following expenditures:

Purchase price	$45,000
Sales tax	2,200
Freight charges for shipment of equipment	700
Insurance on the equipment for the first year	900
Installation of equipment	1,000

The equipment, including sales tax, was purchased on open account, with payment due in 30 days. The other expenditures listed above were paid in cash.

Required:

Prepare the necessary journal entries to record the above expenditures.

E 10–3
Acquisition
costs; lump-sum
acquisition
● LO10–1, LO10–2

Samtech Manufacturing purchased land and building for $4 million. In addition to the purchase price, Samtech made the following expenditures in connection with the purchase of the land and building:

Title insurance	$16,000
Legal fees for drawing the contract	5,000
Pro-rated property taxes for the period after acquisition	36,000
State transfer fees	4,000

An independent appraisal estimated the fair values of the land and building, if purchased separately, at $3.3 and $1.1 million, respectively. Shortly after acquisition, Samtech spent $82,000 to construct a parking lot and $40,000 for landscaping.

Required:

1. Determine the initial valuation of each asset Samtech acquired in these transactions.
2. Repeat requirement 1, assuming that immediately after acquisition, Samtech demolished the building. Demolition costs were $250,000 and the salvaged materials were sold for $6,000. In addition, Samtech spent $86,000 clearing and grading the land in preparation for the construction of a new building.

E 10–4
Cost of a natural
resource; asset
retirement
obligation
● LO10–1

Jackpot Mining Company operates a copper mine in central Montana. The company paid $1,000,000 in 2021 for the mining site and spent an additional $600,000 to prepare the mine for extraction of the copper. After the copper is extracted in approximately four years, the company is required to restore the land to its original condition, including repaving of roads and replacing a greenbelt. The company has provided the following three cash flow possibilities for the restoration costs:

	Cash Outflow	Probability
1	$300,000	25%
2	400,000	40%
3	600,000	35%

To aid extraction, Jackpot purchased some new equipment on July 1, 2021, for $120,000. After the copper is removed from this mine, the equipment will be sold. The credit-adjusted, risk-free rate of interest is 10%.

Required:

1. Determine the cost of the copper mine.
2. Prepare the journal entries to record the acquisition costs of the mine and the purchase of equipment.

E 10–5
Intangibles
● LO10–1

In 2021, Bratten Fitness Company made the following cash purchases:

1. The exclusive right to manufacture and sell the X-Core workout equipment from Symmetry Corporation for $200,000. Symmetry created the unique design for the equipment. Bratten also paid an additional $10,000 in legal and filing fees to attorneys to complete the transaction.
2. An initial fee of $300,000 for a three-year agreement with Silver's Gym to use its name for a new facility in the local area. Silver's Gym has locations throughout the country. Bratten is required to pay an additional fee of $5,000 for each month it operates under the Silver's Gym name, with payments beginning in March 2021. Bratten also purchased $400,000 of exercise equipment to be placed in the new facility.
3. The exclusive right to sell *Healthy Choice,* a book authored by Kent Patterson, for $25,000. The book includes healthy recipes, recommendations for dietary supplements, and natural remedies. Bratten plans to display the book at the check-in counter at its new facility, as well as make it available online.

554 SECTION 2 Assets

Required:
Prepare a summary journal entry to record expenditures related to initial acquisitions.

E 10–6
Goodwill
● LO10–1

On March 31, 2021, Wolfson Corporation acquired all of the outstanding common stock of Barney Corporation for $17,000,000 in cash. The book values and fair values of Barney's assets and liabilities were as follows:

	Book Value	Fair Value
Current assets	$ 6,000,000	$ 7,500,000
Property, plant, and equipment	11,000,000	14,000,000
Other assets	1,000,000	1,500,000
Current liabilities	4,000,000	4,000,000
Long-term liabilities	6,000,000	5,500,000

Required:
Calculate the amount paid for goodwill.

E 10–7
Goodwill
● LO10–1

Johnson Corporation acquired all of the outstanding common stock of Smith Corporation for $11,000,000 in cash. The book value of Smith's net assets (assets minus liabilities) was $7,800,000. The fair values of all of Smith's assets and liabilities were equal to their book values with the following exceptions:

	Book Value	Fair Value
Receivables	$1,300,000	$1,100,000
Property, plant, and equipment	8,000,000	9,400,000
Intangible assets	200,000	1,200,000

Required:
Calculate the amount paid for goodwill.

E 10–8
Lump-sum
acquisition
● LO10–2

Pinewood Company purchased two buildings on four acres of land. The lump-sum purchase price was $900,000. According to independent appraisals, the fair values were $450,000 (building A) and $250,000 (building B) for the buildings and $300,000 for the land.

Required:
Determine the initial valuation of the buildings and the land.

E 10–9
Acquisition cost;
noninterest-
bearing note
● LO10–3

On January 1, 2021, Byner Company purchased a used tractor. Byner paid $5,000 down and signed a noninterest-bearing note requiring $25,000 to be paid on December 31, 2023. The fair value of the tractor is not determinable. An interest rate of 10% properly reflects the time value of money for this type of loan agreement. The company's fiscal year-end is December 31.

Required:
1. Prepare the journal entry to record the acquisition of the tractor. Round computations to the nearest dollar.
2. How much interest expense will the company include in its 2021 and 2022 income statements for this note?
3. What is the amount of the liability the company will report in its 2021 and 2022 balance sheets for this note?

E 10–10
Acquisition costs;
noninterest-
bearing note
● LO10–1, LO10–3

Teradene Corporation purchased land as a factory site and contracted with Maxtor Construction to construct a factory. Teradene made the following expenditures related to the acquisition of the land, building, and equipment for the factory:

Purchase price of the land	$1,200,000
Demolition and removal of old building	80,000
Clearing and grading the land before construction	150,000
Various closing costs in connection with acquiring the land	42,000
Architect's fee for the plans for the new building	50,000
Payments to Maxtor for building construction	3,250,000
Equipment purchased	860,000
Freight charges on equipment	32,000
Trees, plants, and other landscaping	45,000
Installation of a sprinkler system for the landscaping	5,000
Cost to build special platforms and install wiring for the equipment	12,000
Cost of trial runs to ensure proper installation of the equipment	7,000
Fire and theft insurance on the factory for the first year of use	24,000

CHAPTER 10   Property, Plant, and Equipment and Intangible Assets: Acquisition   **555**

In addition to the above expenditures, Teradene purchased four forklifts from Caterpillar. In payment, Teradene paid $16,000 cash and signed a noninterest-bearing note requiring the payment of $70,000 in one year. An interest rate of 7% properly reflects the time value of money for this type of loan.

Required:
Determine the initial valuation of each of the assets Teradene acquired in the above transactions.

E 10–11
IFRS; acquisition cost; issuance of equity securities and donation
● LO10–4, LO10–9
 IFRS

On February 1, 2021, the Xilon Corporation issued 50,000 shares of its no-par common stock in exchange for five acres of land located in the city of Monrovia. On the date of the acquisition, Xilon's common stock had a fair value of $18 per share. An office building was constructed on the site by an independent contractor. The building was completed on November 2, 2021, at a cost of $6,000,000. Xilon paid $4,000,000 in cash and the remainder was paid by the city of Monrovia.

Required:
1. Prepare the journal entries to record the acquisition of the land and the building.
2. Assuming that Xilon prepares its financial statements according to International Financial Reporting Standards, explain the alternatives the company has for recording the acquisition of the office building.

E 10–12
IFRS; acquisition cost; acquisition by donation; government grant
● LO10–9
IFRS

Cranston LTD. prepares its financial statements according to International Financial Reporting Standards. In October 2021, the company received a $2 million government grant. The grant represents 20% of the total cost of equipment that will be used to improve the roads in the local area. Cranston recorded the grant and the purchase of the equipment as follows:

Cash	2,000,000	
Revenue		2,000,000
Equipment	10,000,000	
Cash		10,000,000

Required:
1. Explain the alternative accounting treatments available to Cranston for accounting for this government grant.
2. Prepare any necessary correcting entries under each of the alternatives described in requirement 1.

E 10–13
Fixed-asset turnover ratio; Nvidia
● LO10–5
Real World Financials

Nvidia Corporation, a global technology company located in Santa Clara, California, reported the following information in its 2017 financial statements ($ in millions):

	2017	2016
Balance sheets		
Property, plant, and equipment (net)	$ 521	$ 466
Income statement		
Net sales for 2017	$6,910	

Required:
1. Calculate the company's 2017 fixed-asset turnover ratio.
2. How would you interpret this ratio?

E 10–14
Nonmonetary exchange
● LO10–6

Cedric Company recently traded in an older model of equipment for a new model. The old model's book value was $180,000 (original cost of $400,000 less $220,000 in accumulated depreciation) and its fair value was $200,000. Cedric paid $60,000 to complete the exchange which has commercial substance.

Required:
Prepare the journal entry to record the exchange.

E 10–15
Nonmonetary exchange
● LO10–6

[This is a variation of the previous exercise.]

Required:
Assume the same facts as in Exercise 10–14, except that the fair value of the old equipment is $170,000. Prepare the journal entry to record the exchange.

E 10–16
Nonmonetary exchange
● LO10–6

The Bronco Corporation exchanged land for equipment. The land had a book value of $120,000 and a fair value of $150,000. Bronco paid the owner of the equipment $10,000 to complete the exchange which has commercial substance.

Required:
1. What is the fair value of the equipment?
2. Prepare the journal entry to record the exchange.

556   SECTION 2   Assets

E 10–17
Nonmonetary exchange
● LO10–6

[This is a variation of the previous exercise.]

Required:

Assume the same facts as in Exercise 10–16 except that Bronco *received* $10,000 from the owner of the equipment to complete the exchange.

1. What is the fair value of the equipment?
2. Prepare the journal entry to record the exchange.

E 10–18
Nonmonetary exchange
● LO10–6

The Tinsley Company exchanged land that it had been holding for future plant expansion for a more suitable parcel located farther from residential areas. Tinsley carried the land at its original cost of $30,000. According to an independent appraisal, the land currently is worth $72,000. Tinsley paid $14,000 in cash to complete the transaction.

Required:

1. What is the fair value of the new parcel of land received by Tinsley?
2. Prepare the journal entry to record the exchange assuming the exchange has commercial substance.
3. Prepare the journal entry to record the exchange assuming the exchange lacks commercial substance.
4. Prepare the journal entry to record the exchange except that Tinsley *received* $9,000 in the exchange, and the exchange lacks commercial substance.

E 10–19
Acquisition cost; multiple methods
● LO10–1, LO10–3, LO10–4, LO10–6

Connors Corporation acquired manufacturing equipment for use in its assembly line. Below are four *independent* situations relating to the acquisition of the equipment.

1. The equipment was purchased on account for $25,000. Credit terms were 2/10, n/30. Payment was made within the discount period and the company records the purchases of equipment net of discounts.
2. Connors gave the seller a noninterest-bearing note. The note required payment of $27,000 one year from date of purchase. The fair value of the equipment is not determinable. An interest rate of 10% properly reflects the time value of money in this situation.
3. Connors traded in old equipment that had a book value of $6,000 (original cost of $14,000 and accumulated depreciation of $8,000) and paid cash of $22,000. The old equipment had a fair value of $2,500 on the date of the exchange. The exchange has commercial substance.
4. Connors issued 1,000 shares of its no-par common stock in exchange for the equipment. The market value of the common stock was not determinable. The equipment could have been purchased for $24,000 in cash.

Required:

For each of the above situations, prepare the journal entry required to record the acquisition of the equipment. Round computations to the nearest dollar.

E 10–20
FASB codification research
● LO10–6

CODE

Access the *FASB Accounting Standards Codification* at the FASB website (www.fasb.org). Determine the specific eight-digit Codification citation (XXX-XX-XX-X) that describes each of the following items:

1. The basic principle for recording nonmonetary transactions at fair value.
2. Modifications of the basic principle for recording nonmonetary transactions when fair value is not determinable or the exchange lacks commercial substance.
3. The concept of commercial substance.
4. The required disclosures for nonmonetary transactions.

E 10–21
FASB codification research
● LO10–1, LO10–6, LO10–7, LO10–8

CODE

Access the *FASB Accounting Standards Codification* at the FASB website (www.fasb.org). Determine the specific eight-digit Codification citation (XXX-XX-XX-X) that describes each of the following items:

1. The disclosure requirements in the notes to the financial statements for depreciation on property, plant, and equipment.
2. The criteria for determining commercial substance in a nonmonetary exchange.
3. The disclosure requirements for interest capitalization.
4. The elements of costs to be included as R&D activities.

E 10–22
Interest capitalization
● LO10–7

On January 1, 2021, the Marjlee Company began construction of an office building to be used as its corporate headquarters. The building was completed early in 2022. Construction expenditures for 2021, which were incurred evenly throughout the year, totaled $6,000,000. Marjlee had the following debt obligations which were outstanding during all of 2021:

Construction loan, 10%	$1,500,000
Long-term note, 9%	2,000,000
Long-term note, 6%	4,000,000

Required:
Calculate the amount of interest capitalized in 2021 for the building using the specific interest method.

E 10–23
Interest
capitalization
● LO10–7

On January 1, 2021, the Shagri Company began construction on a new manufacturing facility for its own use. The building was completed in 2022. The only interest-bearing debt the company had outstanding during 2021 was long-term bonds with a book value of $10,000,000 and an effective interest rate of 8%. Construction expenditures incurred during 2021 were as follows:

January 1	$500,000
March 1	600,000
July 31	480,000
September 30	600,000
December 31	300,000

Required:
Calculate the amount of interest capitalized for 2021.

E 10–24
Interest
capitalization
● LO10–7

On January 1, 2021, the Highlands Company began construction on a new manufacturing facility for its own use. The building was completed in 2022. The company borrowed $1,500,000 at 8% on January 1 to help finance the construction. In addition to the construction loan, Highlands had the following debt outstanding throughout 2021:

$5,000,000, 12% bonds
$3,000,000, 8% long-term note

Construction expenditures incurred during 2021 were as follows:

January 1	$ 600,000
March 31	1,200,000
June 30	800,000
September 30	600,000
December 31	400,000

Required:
Calculate the amount of interest capitalized for 2021 using the specific interest method.

E 10–25
Interest
capitalization;
multiple periods
● LO10–7

Thornton Industries began construction of a warehouse on July 1, 2021. The project was completed on March 31, 2022. No new loans were required to fund construction. Thornton does have the following two interest-bearing liabilities that were outstanding throughout the construction period:

$2,000,000, 8% note
$8,000,000, 4% bonds

Construction expenditures incurred were as follows:

July 1, 2021	$400,000
September 30, 2021	600,000
November 30, 2021	600,000
January 30, 2022	540,000

The company's fiscal year-end is December 31.

Required:
Calculate the amount of interest capitalized for 2021 and 2022.

E 10–26
Research and
development
● LO10–8

In 2021, Space Technology Company modified its model Z2 satellite to incorporate a new communication device. The company made the following expenditures:

Basic research to develop the technology	$2,000,000
Engineering design work	680,000
Development of a prototype device	300,000
Acquisition of equipment	60,000
Testing and modification of the prototype	200,000
Legal and other fees for patent application on the new communication system	40,000
Legal fees for successful defense of the new patent	20,000
Total	$3,300,000

The equipment will be used on this and other research projects. Depreciation on the equipment for 2021 is $10,000.

558   SECTION 2   Assets

During your year-end review of the accounts related to intangibles, you discover that the company has capitalized all of the above as costs of the patent. Management contends that the device simply represents an improvement of the existing communication system of the satellite and, therefore, should be capitalized.

Required:
Prepare correcting entries that reflect the appropriate treatment of the expenditures.

E 10–27
Research and development
● **LO10–8**

Delaware Company incurred the following research and development costs during 2021:

Salaries and wages for lab research	$ 400,000
Materials used in R&D projects	200,000
Purchase of equipment	900,000
Fees paid to third parties for R&D projects	320,000
Patent filing and legal costs for a developed product	65,000
Salaries, wages, and supplies for R&D work performed for another company under a contract	350,000
Total	$2,235,000

The equipment has a seven-year life and will be used for a number of research projects. Depreciation for 2021 is $120,000.

Required:
Calculate the amount of research and development expense that Delaware should report in its 2021 income statement.

E 10–28
IFRS; research and development
● **LO10–8, LO10–9**

Janson Pharmaceuticals incurred the following costs in 2021 related to a new cancer drug:

Research for new formulas	$2,425,000
Development of a new formula	1,600,000
Legal and filing fees for a patent for the new formula	60,000
Total	$4,085,000

The development costs were incurred after technological and commercial feasibility was established and after the future economic benefits were deemed probable. The project was successfully completed and the new drug was patented before the end of the 2021 fiscal year.

Required:
1. Calculate the amount of research and development expense Janson should report in its 2021 income statement related to this project.
2. Repeat requirement 1 assuming that Janson prepares its financial statements according to International Financial Reporting Standards.

E 10–29
IFRS; research and development
● **LO10–9**

 IFRS

NXS Semiconductor prepares its financial statements according to International Financial Reporting Standards. The company incurred the following expenditures during 2021 related to the development of a chip to be used in mobile devices:

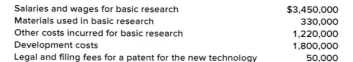

Salaries and wages for basic research	$3,450,000
Materials used in basic research	330,000
Other costs incurred for basic research	1,220,000
Development costs	1,800,000
Legal and filing fees for a patent for the new technology	50,000

The development costs were incurred after NXS established technological and commercial feasibility and after NXS deemed the future economic benefits to be probable. The project was successfully completed, and the new chip was patented near the end of the 2021 fiscal year.

Required:
1. Which of the expenditures should NXS expense in its 2021 income statement?
2. Explain the accounting treatment of the remaining expenditures.

E 10–30
Concepts; terminology
● **LO10–1, LO10–4,**
LO10–6, LO10–7

Listed below are several terms and phrases associated with property, plant, and equipment and intangible assets. Pair each item from List A with the item from List B (by letter) that is most appropriately associated with it.

List A	List B
_____ 1. Property, plant, and equipment	a. Exclusive right to display a word, a symbol, or an emblem.
_____ 2. Land improvements	b. Exclusive right to benefit from a creative work.
_____ 3. Capitalize	c. Assets that represent rights.
_____ 4. Average accumulated expenditures	d. Costs of establishing parking lots, driveways, and private roads.
_____ 5. Revenue	e. Purchase price less fair value of net identifiable assets.
_____ 6. Nonmonetary exchange	f. Assets such as land, buildings, and machinery.
_____ 7. Natural resources	g. Approximation of average amount of debt if all construction funds were borrowed.
_____ 8. Intangible assets	h. Account credited when assets are donated to a corporation.
_____ 9. Copyright	i. Term meaning to record the cost as an asset.
_____ 10. Trademark	j. Basic principle is to value assets acquired using fair value of assets given other than cash.
_____ 11. Goodwill	k. Assets such as timber tracks and mineral deposits.

E 10–31
Software development costs
● LO10–8

Early in 2021, the Excalibur Company began developing a new software package to be marketed. The project was completed in December 2021 at a cost of $6 million. Of this amount, $4 million was spent before technological feasibility was established. Excalibur expects a useful life of five years for the new product with total revenues of $10 million. During 2022, revenue of $3 million was recognized.

Required:
Prepare a journal entry to record the 2021 development costs.

E 10–32
Software development costs
● LO10–8

On September 30, 2021, Athens Software began developing a software program to shield personal computers from malware and spyware. Technological feasibility was established on February 28, 2022, and the program was available for release on April 30, 2022. Development costs were incurred as follows:

September 30 through December 31, 2021	$2,200,000
January 1 through February 28, 2022	800,000
March 1 through April 30, 2022	400,000

Athens expects a useful life of four years for the software and total revenues of $5,000,000 during that time. During 2022, revenue of $1,000,000 was recognized.

Required:
Prepare a journal entry in each year to record development costs for 2021 and 2022.

E 10–33
Intangibles; start-up costs
● LO10–1, LO10–8

Freitas Corporation was organized early in 2021. The following expenditures were made during the first few months of the year:

Attorneys' fees in connection with the organization of the corporation	$ 12,000
State filing fees and other incorporation costs	3,000
Purchase of a patent	20,000
Legal and other fees for transfer of the patent	2,000
Purchase of equipment	30,000
Preopening salaries and employee training	40,000
Total	$107,000

Required:
Prepare a summary journal entry to record the $107,000 in cash expenditures.

E 10–34
Full-cost and successful efforts methods compared
● Appendix

The Manguino Oil Company incurred exploration costs in 2021 searching and drilling for oil as follows:

Well 101	$ 50,000
Well 102	60,000
Well 103	80,000
Wells 104–108	260,000
Total	$450,000

It was determined that Wells 104–108 were dry holes and were abandoned. Wells 101, 102, and 103 were determined to have sufficient oil reserves to be commercially successful.

Required:
1. Prepare a summary journal entry to record the indicated costs assuming that the company uses the full-cost method of accounting for exploration costs. All of the exploration costs were paid in cash.
2. Prepare a summary journal entry to record the indicated costs assuming that the company uses the successful efforts method of accounting for exploration costs. All of the exploration costs were paid in cash.

560   SECTION 2   Assets

Problems

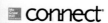

P 10–1
Acquisition costs
● LO10–1 through
LO10–4

Tristar Production Company began operations on September 1, 2021. Listed below are a number of transactions that occurred during its first four months of operations.

1. On September 1, the company acquired five acres of land with a building that will be used as a warehouse. Tristar paid $100,000 in cash for the property. According to appraisals, the land had a fair value of $75,000 and the building had a fair value of $45,000.

2. On September 1, Tristar signed a $40,000 noninterest-bearing note to purchase equipment. The $40,000 payment is due on September 1, 2022. Assume that 8% is a reasonable interest rate.

3. On September 15, a truck was donated to the corporation. Similar trucks were selling for $2,500.

4. On September 18, the company paid its lawyer $3,000 for organizing the corporation.

5. On October 10, Tristar purchased maintenance equipment for cash. The purchase price was $15,000 and $500 in freight charges also were paid.

6. On December 2, Tristar acquired various items of office equipment. The company was short of cash and could not pay the $5,500 normal cash price. The supplier agreed to accept 200 shares of the company's no-par common stock in exchange for the equipment. The fair value of the stock is not readily determinable.

7. On December 10, the company acquired a tract of land at a cost of $20,000. It paid $2,000 down and signed a 10% note with both principal and interest due in one year. Ten percent is an appropriate rate of interest for this note.

Required:
Prepare journal entries to record each of the above transactions.

P 10–2
Acquisition costs;
land and building
● LO10–1, LO10–2,
LO10–7

On January 1, 2021, the Blackstone Corporation purchased a tract of land (site number 11) with a building for $600,000. Additionally, Blackstone paid a real estate broker's commission of $36,000, legal fees of $6,000, and title insurance of $18,000. The closing statement indicated that the land value was $500,000 and the building value was $100,000. Shortly after acquisition, the building was razed at a cost of $75,000.

Blackstone entered into a $3,000,000 fixed-price contract with Barnett Builders, Inc., on March 1, 2021, for the construction of an office building on land site 11. The building was completed and occupied on September 30, 2022. Additional construction costs were incurred as follows:

Plans, specifications, and blueprints	$12,000
Architects' fees for design and supervision	95,000

To finance the construction cost, Blackstone borrowed $3,000,000 on March 1, 2021. The loan is payable in 10 annual installments of $300,000 plus interest at the rate of 14%. Blackstone's average amounts of accumulated building construction expenditures were as follows:

For the period March 1 to December 31, 2021	$ 900,000
For the period January 1 to September 30, 2022	2,300,000

Required:
1. Prepare a schedule that discloses the individual costs making up the balance in the land account in respect of land site 11 as of September 30, 2022.

2. Prepare a schedule that discloses the individual costs that should be capitalized in the office building account as of September 30, 2022.

Source: AICPA adapted

P 10–3
Acquisition costs
● LO10–1, LO10–4,
LO10–6

The plant asset and accumulated depreciation accounts of Pell Corporation had the following balances at December 31, 2020:

	Plant Asset	Accumulated Depreciation
Land	$ 350,000	$ —
Land improvements	180,000	45,000
Building	1,500,000	350,000
Equipment	1,158,000	405,000
Automobiles	150,000	112,000

Transactions during 2021 were as follows:

a. On January 2, 2021, equipment were purchased at a total invoice cost of $260,000, which included a $5,500 charge for freight. Installation costs of $27,000 were incurred.

CHAPTER 10   Property, Plant, and Equipment and Intangible Assets: Acquisition   **561**

b. On March 31, 2021, a small storage building was donated to the company. The person donating the building originally purchased it three years ago for $25,000. The fair value of the building on the day of the donation was $17,000.

c. On May 1, 2021, expenditures of $50,000 were made to repave parking lots at Pell's plant location. The work was necessitated by damage caused by severe winter weather. The repair doesn't provide future benefits beyond those originally anticipated.

d. On November 1, 2021, Pell acquired a tract of land with an existing building in exchange for 10,000 shares of Pell's common stock that had a market price of $38 per share. Pell paid legal fees and title insurance totaling $23,000. Shortly after acquisition, the building was razed at a cost of $35,000 in anticipation of new building construction in 2022.

e. On December 31, 2021, Pell purchased a small storage building by giving $15,250 cash and an old automobile purchased for $18,000 in 2014. Depreciation on the old automobile recorded through December 31, 2021, totaled $13,500. The fair value of the old automobile was $3,750.

Required:

Prepare a schedule analyzing the changes in each of the plant assets during 2021, with detailed supporting computations.

(AICPA adapted)

P 10–4
Intangibles
● LO10–1, LO10–8

The Horstmeyer Corporation commenced operations early in 2021. A number of expenditures were made during 2021 that were debited to one account called *intangible asset*. A recap of the $144,000 balance in this account at the end of 2021 is as follows:

Date		Transaction	Amount
February	3	State incorporation fees and legal costs related to organizing the corporation	$ 7,000
March	1	Fire insurance premium for three-year period	6,000
March	15	Purchased a copyright	20,000
April	30	Research and development costs	40,000
June	15	Legal fees for filing a patent on a new product resulting from an R&D project	3,000
September	30	Legal fee for successful defense of patent developed above	12,000
October	13	Entered into a 10-year franchise agreement with franchisor	40,000
Various		Advertising costs	16,000
		Total	$144,000

Required:

Prepare the necessary journal entry to clear the intangible asset account and to set up accounts for separate intangible assets, other types of assets, and expenses indicated by the transactions.

P 10–5
Acquisition costs;
journal entries
● LO10–1, LO10–3,
LO10–6, LO10–8

Consider each of the transactions below. All of the expenditures were made in cash.

1. The Edison Company spent $12,000 during the year for experimental purposes in connection with the development of a new product.

2. In April, the Marshall Company lost a patent infringement suit and paid the plaintiff $7,500.

3. In March, the Cleanway Laundromat bought equipment. Cleanway paid $6,000 down and signed a noninterest-bearing note requiring the payment of $18,000 in nine months. The cash price for this equipment was $23,000.

4. On June 1, the Jamsen Corporation installed a sprinkler system throughout the building at a cost of $28,000.

5. The Mayer Company, plaintiff, paid $12,000 in legal fees in November, in connection with a successful infringement suit on its patent.

6. The Johnson Company traded its old equipment for new equipment. The new equipment has a fair value of $10,000. The old equipment had an original cost of $7,400 and a book value of $3,000 at the time of the trade. Johnson also paid cash of $8,000 as part of the trade. The exchange has commercial substance.

Required:

Prepare journal entries to record each of the above transactions.

P 10–6
Nonmonetary
exchange
● LO10–6

Southern Company owns a building that it leases to others. The building's fair value is $1,400,000 and its book value is $800,000 (original cost of $2,000,000 less accumulated depreciation of $1,200,000). Southern exchanges this for a building owned by the Eastern Company. The building's book value on Eastern's books is $950,000 (original cost of $1,600,000 less accumulated depreciation of $650,000). Eastern also gives Southern $140,000 to complete the exchange. The exchange has commercial substance for both companies.

Required:

Prepare the journal entries to record the exchange on the books of both Southern and Eastern.

562   SECTION 2   Assets

P 10–7
Nonmonetary
exchange
● LO10–6

On September 3, 2021, the Robers Company exchanged equipment with Phifer Corporation. The facts of the exchange are as follows:

	Robers' Asset	Phifer's Asset
Original cost	$120,000	$140,000
Accumulated depreciation	55,000	63,000
Fair value	75,000	70,000

To equalize the exchange, Phifer paid Robers $5,000 in cash.

Required:
Record the exchange for both Robers and Phifer. The exchange has commercial substance for both companies.

P 10–8
Nonmonetary
exchange
● LO10–6

Case A. Kapono Farms exchanged an old tractor for a newer model. The old tractor had a book value of $12,000 (original cost of $28,000 less accumulated depreciation of $16,000) and a fair value of $9,000. Kapono paid $20,000 cash to complete the exchange. The exchange has commercial substance.

Required:
1. What is the amount of gain or loss that Kapono would recognize on the exchange? What is the initial value of the new tractor?
2. Repeat requirement 1 assuming that the fair value of the old tractor is $14,000 instead of $9,000.

Case B. Kapono Farms exchanged 100 acres of farmland for similar land. The farmland given had a book value of $500,000 and a fair value of $700,000. Kapono paid $50,000 cash to complete the exchange. The exchange has commercial substance.

Required:
1. What is the amount of gain or loss that Kapono would recognize on the exchange? What is the initial value of the new land?
2. Repeat requirement 1 assuming that the fair value of the farmland given is $400,000 instead of $700,000.
3. Repeat requirement 1 assuming that the exchange lacked commercial substance.

P 10–9
Interest
capitalization;
specific interest
method
● LO10–7

On January 1, 2021, the Mason Manufacturing Company began construction of a building to be used as its office headquarters. The building was completed on September 30, 2022. Expenditures on the project were as follows:

January 1, 2021	$1,000,000
March 1, 2021	600,000
June 30, 2021	800,000
October 1, 2021	600,000
January 31, 2022	270,000
April 30, 2022	585,000
August 31, 2022	900,000

On January 1, 2021, the company obtained a $3 million construction loan with a 10% interest rate. The loan was outstanding all of 2021 and 2022. The company's other interest-bearing debt included two long-term notes of $4,000,000 and $6,000,000 with interest rates of 6% and 8%, respectively. Both notes were outstanding during all of 2021 and 2022. Interest is paid annually on all debt. The company's fiscal year-end is December 31.

Required:
1. Calculate the amount of interest that Mason should capitalize in 2021 and 2022 using the specific interest method.
2. What is the total cost of the building?
3. Calculate the amount of interest expense that will appear in the 2021 and 2022 income statements.

P 10–10
Interest
capitalization;
weighted-average
method
● LO10–7

[This is a variation of the previous problem, modified to focus on the weighted-average interest method.]

Required:
Refer to the facts in Problem 10–9 but now assume the $3 million loan is not specifically tied to construction of the building. Answer the following questions:
1. Calculate the amount of interest that Mason should capitalize in 2021 and 2022 using the weighted-average method.
2. What is the total cost of the building?
3. Calculate the amount of interest expense that will appear in the 2021 and 2022 income statements.

P 10–11
Research and development
● LO10–8

In 2021, Starsearch Corporation began work on three research and development projects. One of the projects was completed and commercial production of the developed product began in December. The company's fiscal year-end is December 31. All of the following 2021 expenditures were included in the R&D expense account:

Salaries and wages for:	
Lab research	$ 300,000
Design and construction of preproduction prototype	160,000
Quality control during commercial production	20,000
Materials and supplies consumed for:	
Lab research	60,000
Construction of preproduction prototype	30,000
Purchase of equipment	600,000
Patent filing and legal fees for completed project	40,000
Payments to others for research	120,000
Total	$1,330,000

$200,000 of equipment was purchased solely for use in one of the projects. After the project is completed, the equipment will be abandoned. The remaining $400,000 in equipment will be used on future R&D projects. The useful life of equipment is five years. Assume that all of the equipment was acquired at the beginning of the year.

Required:
Prepare journal entries, reclassifying amounts in R&D expense, to reflect the appropriate treatment of the expenditures.

P 10–12
Acquisition costs; lump-sum acquisition; noninterest-bearing note; interest capitalization
● LO10–1, LO10–2, LO10–3, LO10–7

Early in its fiscal year ending December 31, 2021, San Antonio Outfitters finalized plans to expand operations. The first stage was completed on March 28 with the purchase of a tract of land on the outskirts of the city. The land and existing building were purchased by paying $200,000 immediately and signing a noninterest-bearing note requiring the company to pay $600,000 on March 28, 2023. An interest rate of 8% properly reflects the time value of money for this type of loan agreement. Title search, insurance, and other closing costs totaling $20,000 were paid at closing.

At the end of April, the old building was demolished at a cost of $70,000, and an additional $50,000 was paid to clear and grade the land. Construction of a new building began on May 1 and was completed on October 29. Construction expenditures were as follows:

May 1	$1,200,000
July 30	1,500,000
September 1	900,000
October 1	1,800,000

San Antonio borrowed $3,000,000 at 8% on May 1 to help finance construction. This loan, plus interest, will be paid in 2022. The company also had a $5,250,000, 8% long-term note payable outstanding throughout 2021.

In November, the company purchased 10 identical pieces of equipment and office furniture and fixtures for a lump-sum price of $600,000. The fair values of the equipment and the furniture and fixtures were $455,000 and $245,000, respectively. In December, San Antonio paid a contractor $285,000 for the construction of parking lots and for landscaping.

Required:
1. Determine the initial values of the various assets that San Antonio acquired or constructed during 2021. The company uses the specific interest method to determine the amount of interest capitalized on the building construction.
2. How much interest expense will San Antonio report in its 2021 income statement?

Decision Maker's Perspective

©ImageGap/Getty Images

Apply your critical-thinking ability to the knowledge you've gained. These cases will provide you an opportunity to develop your research, analysis, judgment, and communication skills. You also will work with other students, integrate what you've learned, apply it in real-world situations, and consider its global and ethical ramifications. This practice will broaden your knowledge and further develop your decision-making abilities.

Judgment Case 10–1
Acquisition costs
● LO10–1, LO10–3, LO10–6

A company may acquire property, plant, and equipment and intangible assets for cash, in exchange for a deferred payment contract, by exchanging other assets, or by a combination of these methods.

564   SECTION 2   Assets

Required:

1. Identify six types of costs that should be capitalized as the cost of a parcel of land. For your answer, assume that the land has an existing building that is to be removed in the immediate future in order that a new building can be constructed on the site.

2. At what amount should a company record an asset acquired in exchange for a deferred payment contract?

3. In general, at what amount should assets received in exchange for other nonmonetary assets be valued? Specifically, at what amount should a company value new equipment acquired by exchanging older, similar equipment and paying cash?

(AICPA adapted)

Research Case 10–2
FASB codification; locate and extract relevant information and cite authoritative support for a financial reporting issue; restoration costs; asset retirement obligation

● LO10–1

Your client, Hazelton Mining, recently entered into an agreement to obtain the rights to operate a coal mine in West Virginia for $15 million. Hazelton incurred development costs of $6 million in preparing the mine for extraction, which began on July 1, 2021. The contract requires Hazelton to restore the land and surrounding area to its original condition after extraction is complete in three years.

The company controller, Alice Cushing, is not sure how to account for the restoration costs and has asked your advice. Alice is aware of an accounting standard addressing this issue, but is not sure of its provisions. She has narrowed down the possible cash outflows for the restoration costs to four possibilities.

Cash Outflow	Probability
$3 million	20%
4 million	30%
5 million	25%
6 million	25%

Alice also informs you that the company's credit-adjusted risk-free interest rate is 9%. Before responding to Alice, you need to research the issue.

Required:

1. Access the *FASB Accounting Standards Codification* at the FASB website (www.fasb.org). Determine the specific Codification citation for each of the following, based on the format indicated: (a) accounting for asset retirement obligations (XXX-XX), (b) recognition criteria related to asset retirement obligations (XXX-XX-XX), (c) the requirement to recognize the fair value of the asset retirement obligation as a liability (XXX-XX-XX-X), and (d) how to treat the capitalized cost of the asset retirement obligation for the related tangible long-lived asset (XXX-XX-XX-X).

2. Determine the capitalized cost of the coal mine.

3. Prepare a summary journal entry to record the acquisition costs of the mine.

4. How much accretion expense will the company record in its income statement for the 2021 fiscal year, related to this transaction? Determine the specific Codification citation for each of the following, based on the format indicated: (a) the calculation of accretion expense (XXX-XX-XX-X) and (b) the classification of accretion expense in the income statement (XXX-XX-XX-X).

5. Explain to Alice how Hazelton would account for the restoration if the restoration costs differed from the recorded liability in three years. By way of explanation, prepare the journal entry to record the payment of the retirement obligation in three years assuming that the actual restoration costs were $4.7 million.

6. Describe to Alice the necessary disclosure requirements for the obligation. What specific Codification citation contains these disclosure requirements (XXX-XX-XX-X)?

Judgment Case 10–3
Self-constructed assets

● LO10–7

Chilton Peripherals manufactures printers, scanners, and other computer peripheral equipment. In the past, the company purchased equipment used in manufacturing from an outside vendor. In March 2021, Chilton decided to design and build equipment to replace some obsolete equipment. A section of the manufacturing plant was set aside to develop and produce the equipment. Additional personnel were hired for the project. The equipment was completed and ready for use in September.

Required:

1. In general, what costs should be capitalized for a self-constructed asset?

2. Discuss two alternatives for the inclusion of overhead costs in the cost of the equipment constructed by Chilton. Which alternative is generally accepted for financial reporting purposes?

3. Under what circumstance(s) would interest be included in the cost of the equipment?

Judgment Case 10–4
Interest capitalization

● LO10–7

GAAP provides guidelines for the inclusion of interest in the initial cost of a self-constructed asset.

Required:

1. What assets qualify for interest capitalization? What assets do not qualify for interest capitalization?

2. Over what period should interest be capitalized?

3. Explain average accumulated expenditures.

4. Explain the two methods that could be used to determine the appropriate interest rate(s) to be used in capitalizing interest.
5. Describe the three steps used to determine the amount of interest capitalized during a reporting period.

**Research
Case 10–5**
Goodwill
● LO10–1

Accounting for acquired goodwill has been a controversial issue for many years. In the United States, the amount of acquired goodwill is capitalized and not amortized. Globally, the treatment of goodwill varies significantly, with some countries not recognizing goodwill as an asset. Professors Johnson and Petrone, in "Is Goodwill an Asset?" discuss this issue.

Required:
1. In your library or from some other source, locate the indicated article in *Accounting Horizons,* September 1998.
2. Does goodwill meet the FASB's definition of an asset?
3. What are the key concerns of those that believe goodwill is not an asset?

**Real World
Case 10–6**
Property, plant,
and equipment;
Norfolk Southern
Corporation
● LO10–1

Real World Financials

Norfolk Southern Corporation, one of the nation's premier transportation companies, reported the following amounts in the asset section of its balance sheets for the years ended December 31, 2016 and 2015:

	($ in millions)	
	December 31, 2016	**December 31, 2015**
Property and equipment, net	$29,751	$28,992

In addition, information from the 2016 statement of cash flows and related notes reported the following items ($ in millions):

Depreciation	$1,030
Additions to property and equipment	1,887
Sales price of property and equipment	130

Required:
What is the gain on the sale of property and equipment for the year ended December 31, 2016?

**Judgment
Case 10–7**
Goodwill
● LO10–1

Athena Paper Corporation acquired for cash 100% of the outstanding common stock of Georgia, Inc., a supplier of wood pulp. The $4,500,000 amount paid was significantly higher than the book value of Georgia's net assets (assets less liabilities) of $2,800,000. The Athena controller recorded the difference of $1,700,000 as an asset, goodwill.

Required:
1. Discuss the meaning of the term goodwill.
2. In what situation would the Athena controller be correct in her valuation of goodwill?

**Judgment
Case 10–8**
Research and
development
● LO10–8

Prior to 1974, accepted practice was for companies to either expense or capitalize R&D costs. In 1974, the FASB issued a Standard that requires all research and development costs to be charged to expense when incurred. This was a controversial standard, opposed by many companies who preferred delaying the recognition of these expenses until later years when presumably the expenditures bear fruit.

Several research studies have been conducted to determine if the Standard had any impact on the behavior of companies. One interesting finding was that, prior to 1974, companies that expensed R&D costs were significantly larger than those companies that capitalized R&D costs.

Required:
1. Explain the FASB's logic in deciding to require all companies to expense R&D costs in the period incurred.
2. Identify possible reasons to explain why, prior to 1974, companies that expensed R&D costs were significantly larger than those companies that capitalized R&D costs.

**Judgment
Case 10–9**
Research and
development
● LO10–8

Clonal, Inc., a biotechnology company, developed and patented a diagnostic product called Trouver. Clonal purchased some research equipment to be used for Trouver and subsequent research projects. Clonal defeated a legal challenge to its Trouver patent, and began production and marketing operations for the project.

Corporate headquarters' costs were allocated to Clonal's research division as a percentage of the division's salaries.

Required:

1. How should the equipment purchased for Trouver be reported in Clonal's income statement and balance sheet?
2. a. Describe the accounting treatment of research and development costs.

   b. What is the justification for the accounting treatment of research and development costs?
3. How should corporate headquarters' costs allocated to the research division be classified in Clonal's income statements? Why?
4. How should the legal expenses incurred in defending Trouver's patent be reported in Clonal's financial statements?

(AICPA adapted)

Communication Case 10–10
Research and development
● LO10–8

The focus of this case is the situation described in Case 10–9. What is the appropriate accounting for R&D costs? Do you believe that (1) capitalization is the correct treatment of R&D costs, (2) expensing is the correct treatment of R&D costs, or (3) that companies should be allowed to choose between expensing and capitalizing R&D costs?

Required:

1. Develop a list of arguments in support of your view prior to the class session for which the case is assigned. Do not be influenced by the method required by the FASB. Base your opinion on the conceptual merit of the options.
2. In class, your instructor will pair you (and everyone else) with a classmate who also has independently developed a position.

   a. You will be given three minutes to argue your view to your partner. Your partner likewise will be given three minutes to argue his or her view to you. During these three-minute presentations, the listening partner is not permitted to speak.

   b. Then after each person has had a turn attempting to convince his or her partner, the two partners will have a three-minute discussion in which they will decide which alternative is more convincing and arguments will be merged into a single view for each pair.
3. After the allotted time, a spokesperson for each of the three alternatives will be selected by the instructor. Each spokesperson will field arguments from the class as to the appropriate alternative. The class will then discuss the merits of the alternatives and attempt to reach a consensus view, though a consensus is not necessary.

Communication Case 10–11
Research and development
● LO10–8

Thomas Plastics is in the process of developing a revolutionary new plastic valve. A new division of the company was formed to develop, manufacture, and market this new product. As of year-end (December 31, 2021), the new product has not been manufactured for sale; however, prototype units were built and are in operation.

Throughout 2021, the new division incurred a variety of costs. These costs included expenses (including salaries of administrative personnel) and market research costs. In addition, approximately $500,000 in equipment (estimated useful life of 10 years) was purchased for use in developing and manufacturing the new valve. Approximately $200,000 of this equipment was built specifically for developing the design of the new product; the remaining $300,000 of the equipment was used to manufacture the preproduction prototypes and will be used to manufacture the new product once it is in commercial production.

The president of the company, Sally Rogers, has been told that research and development costs must be expensed as incurred, but she does not understand this treatment. She believes the research will lead to a profitable product and to increased future revenues. Also, she wonders how to account for the $500,000 of equipment purchased by the new division. "I thought I understood accounting," she growled. "Explain to me why expenditures that benefit our future revenues are expensed rather than capitalized!"

Required:

Write a one-to two-page report to Sally Rogers explaining the generally accepted accounting principles relevant to this issue. The report also should address the treatment of the equipment purchases.

(AICPA adapted)

Ethics Case 10–12
Research and development
● LO10–8

Mayer Biotechnical, Inc., develops, manufactures, and sells pharmaceuticals. Significant research and development (R&D) expenditures are made for the development of new drugs and the improvement of existing drugs. During 2021, $220 million was spent on R&D. Of this amount, $30 million was spent on the purchase of equipment to be used in a research project involving the development of a new antibiotic.

The controller, Alice Cooper, is considering capitalizing the equipment and depreciating it over the five-year useful life of the equipment at $6 million per year, even though the equipment likely will be used on only one project. The company president has asked Alice to make every effort to increase 2021 earnings because in 2022 the company will be seeking significant new financing from both debt and equity sources. "I guess we might use the equipment in other projects later," Alice wondered to herself.

Required:

1. Assuming that the equipment was purchased at the beginning of 2021, by how much would Alice's treatment of the equipment increase before tax earnings as opposed to expensing the equipment cost?

2. Discuss the ethical dilemma Alice faces in determining the treatment of the $30 million equipment purchase.

IFRS Case 10–13
Research and development; comparison of U.S. GAAP and IFRS; Siemens AG
● LO10–8, LO10–9

Siemens AG, a German company, is Europe's largest engineering and electronics company. The company prepares its financial statements according to IFRS.

Required:

1. Use the Internet to locate the most recent financial report for Siemens. The address is www.siemens.com. Locate the significant accounting policies disclosure note.

2. How does the company account for research and development expenditures? Does this policy differ from U.S. GAAP?

Analysis Case 10–14
Fixed-asset turnover ratio; Pier 1 Imports, Inc.
● LO10–5

Real World Financials

Pier 1 Imports, Inc., is a leading retailer of domestic merchandise and home furnishings. The company's 2017 fixed-asset turnover ratio, using the average book value of property, plant, and equipment (PP&E) as the denominator, was approximately 9.16. Additional information taken from the company's 2017 annual report is as follows:

	($ in thousands)
Book value of PP&E—beginning of 2017	$207,633
Net purchases of PP&E during 2017*	44,347
Depreciation of PP&E for 2017	60,504

*Net purchases include book value of equipment purchased minus book value of equipment sold.

Required:

1. How is the fixed-asset turnover ratio computed? How would you interpret Pier 1's ratio of 9.16?

2. Use the data to determine Pier 1's net sales for 2017.

3. Obtain annual reports from three corporations in the same primary industry as Pier 1 Imports, Inc. (Bed, Bath & Beyond and Williams-Sonoma, Inc., are two well-known companies in the same industry) and compare the management of each company's investment in property, plant, and equipment.

Note: You can obtain copies of annual reports from your library, from friends who are shareholders, from the investor relations department of the corporations, from a friendly stockbroker, or from EDGAR (Electronic Data Gathering, Analysis, and Retrieval) on the Internet (www.sec.gov).

Judgment Case 10–15
Computer software costs
● LO10–8

The Elegant Software Company recently completed the development and testing of a new software program that provides the ability to transfer data from among a variety of operating systems. The company believes this product will be quite successful and capitalized all of the costs of designing, developing, coding, and testing the software. These costs will be amortized over the expected useful life of the software on a straight-line basis.

Required:

1. Was Elegant correct in its treatment of the software development costs? Why?

2. Explain the appropriate method for determining the amount of periodic amortization for any capitalized software development costs.

Real World Case 10–16
Property, plant, and equipment; Home Depot
● LO10–1, LO10–7

Real World Financials

EDGAR, the Electronic Data Gathering, Analysis, and Retrieval system, performs automated collection, validation, indexing, and forwarding of submissions by companies and others who are required by law to file forms with the U.S. Securities and Exchange Commission (SEC). All publicly traded domestic companies use EDGAR to make the majority of their filings. (Some foreign companies file voluntarily.) Form 10-K, which includes the annual report, is required to be filed on EDGAR. The SEC makes this information available on the Internet.

Required:

1. Access EDGAR on the Internet. The web address is www.sec.gov.

2. Search for Home Depot, Inc. Access the 10-K filing for the most recent fiscal year. Search or scroll to find the financial statements and related notes.

3. Answer the following questions related to the company's property, plant, and equipment:

   a. Name the different types of assets the company lists in its balance sheet under property, plant, and equipment.

   b. How much cash was used for the acquisition of property, plant, and equipment during the year?

   c. What was the amount of interest capitalized during the year?

   d. Compute the fixed-asset turnover ratio for the fiscal year.

Data Analytics

Data analytics is the process of examining data sets in order to draw conclusions about the information they contain. If you haven't completed any of the prior data analytics cases, follow the instructions listed in the Chapter 1 Data Analytics case to get set up. You will need to watch the videos referred to in the Chapters 1 - 3 Data Analytics cases. No additional videos are required for this case. All short training videos can be found here: https://www.tableau.com/learn/training#getting-started.

Data Analytics Case

Asset Turnover

● LO10–5

In the Chapter 3 Data Analytics Case, you applied Tableau to examine a data set and create calculations to compare two companies' profitability. For the case in this chapter, you continue in your role as an analyst conducting introductory research into the relative merits of investing in one or both of these companies. This time you assess the companies' fixed asset turnover ratios to determine which company utilizes its fixed assets most efficiently to generate sales. The fixed-asset turnover ratio is calculated as net sales divided by average fixed assets.

Required:

Use Tableau to calculate each company's fixed-asset turnover ratio in each year from 2012 to 2021. Based upon what you find, answer the following questions:

1. What is the fixed-asset turnover ratio for Big Store (a) in 2012 and (b) in 2021?
2. What is the fixed-asset turnover ratio for Discount Goods (a) in 2012 and (b) in 2021?
3. Comparing the two companies' fixed-asset turnover ratios over the ten-year period, which company exhibits the most favorable fixed asset turnover?
4. Comparing Big Store's fixed-asset turnover ratios over the ten-year period, is the company's turnover (a) generally increasing, (b) roughly the same, or (c) generally decreasing from year to year?

Resources:

You have available to you an extensive data set that includes detailed financial data for 2012–2021 for both Discount Goods and Big Store. The data set is in the form of four Excel files available to download from Connect, or under Student Resources within the Library tab. The file for use in this chapter is named "Discount_Goods_Big_Store_Financials.xlsx." Download this file and save it to the computer on which you will be using Tableau.

For this case, you will create a calculation to produce a bar chart of the fixed-asset turnover ratio that allows you to compare and contrast the two companies.

After you view the training videos, follow these steps to create the charts you'll use for this case:

· Open Tableau and connect to the Excel spreadsheet you downloaded.
· Click on the Sheet 1 tab, at the bottom of the canvas, to the right of the Data Source at the bottom of the screen. Drag "Company" and "Year" under Dimensions to the Rows shelf. Change "Year" to *discrete* by right-clicking and selecting "discrete."
· Drag the "Net sales" and "Average Fixed Assets" under Measures to the Rows shelf. Change each to *discrete*. Note: You must drag accounts into the Rows shelf if you are going to use them in calculated fields and need an *aggregated* sum. If this is not done first, your answer will not match the solutions.
· Under the Analysis tab, select Create Calculated Field. Create a measure named "Fixed Asset Turnover" by dragging "Net sales" from the Rows shelf to the Calculation Editor window, typing a division sign for division, and then dragging "Average Fixed Assets" from the Rows shelf beside it. Make sure the window says that the calculation is valid and click OK.
· Drag the newly created "Fixed Asset Turnover" to the Rows shelf.
· Right click the "Net sales" and "Average Fixed Assets" on the Rows shelf and unclick "Show header." This will hide these items from view but still allow them to be used in the formulas.
· Click on the "Show Me" tab in the upper right corner and select "side-by-side bars." Add labels to the bars by clicking on "Label" under the "Marks" card and clicking the box "Show mark label." Format the labels to Times New Roman, bold, black and 9-point font.
· Change the title of the sheet to be "Fixed Asset Turnover Ratio Bar Chart" by right-clicking and selecting "Edit title." Format the title to Times New Roman, bold, black and 15-point font. Change the title of "Sheet 1" to match the sheet title by right-clicking, selecting "Rename" and typing in the new title.
· Format the labels on the left of the sheet ("Fixed Asset Turnover") to Times New Roman, 9-point font, bold, and black.
· Format all other labels to be Times New Roman, bold, black and 10-point font.
· Once complete, save the file as "*DA10_Your initials*.twbx."

Continuing Cases

Target Case

● LO10–1, LO10–5

Target Corporation prepares its financial statements according to U.S. GAAP. Target's financial statements and disclosure notes for the year ended February 3, 2018, are available in Connect. This material is also available under the Investor Relations link at the company's website (www.target.com).

Required:

1. What amount ($ in millions) does Target report for net property and equipment for the year ended February 3, 2018? What is the largest category of property and equipment reported on the face of the balance sheet?

2. What amount ($ in millions) of cash was used in the fiscal year ended February 3, 2018, to purchase property and equipment? Is this an increase or decrease compared to the previous year?

3. Do you think a company like Target would have more research and development costs or more advertising costs? Explain.

4. What is Target's fixed-asset turnover ratio for the fiscal year ended February 3, 2018? What is the ratio intended to measure?

5. Does Target include any intangible assets in total assets (yes/no)? Hint: see Notes 15 and 16.

Air France–KLM Case

● LO10–9

 IFRS

Air France–KLM (AF), a Franco-Dutch company, prepares its financial statements according to International Financial Reporting Standards. AF's financial statements and disclosure notes for the year ended December 31, 2017, are available in Connect. This material is also available under the Finance link at the company's website (www.airfranceklm.com).

Required:

1. What method does Air France–KLM use to amortize the cost of computer software development costs? How does this approach differ from U.S. GAAP?

2. AF does not report any research and development expenditures. If it did, its approach to accounting for research and development would be significantly different from U.S. GAAP. Describe the differences between IFRS and U.S. GAAP in accounting for research and development expenditures.

3. AF does not report the receipt of any governments grants. If it did, its approach to accounting for government grants would be significantly different from U.S. GAAP. Describe the differences between IFRS and U.S. GAAP in accounting for government grants. If AF received a grant for the purchase of assets, what alternative accounting treatments are available under IFRS?

CPA Exam Questions and Simulations

ROGER CPA Review

Sample CPA Exam questions from Roger CPA Review are available in Connect as support for the topics in this chapter. These multiple-choice questions and task-based simulations include expert-written explanations and solutions, and provide a starting point for students to become familiar with the content and functionality of the actual CPA Exam.

CHAPTER

11

Property, Plant, and Equipment and Intangible Assets: Utilization and Disposition

OVERVIEW

This chapter completes our discussion of accounting for property, plant, and equipment and intangible assets. We address the allocation of the cost of these assets to the periods benefited by their use.

The usefulness of most of these assets is consumed as the assets are applied to the production of goods or services. Cost allocation corresponding to this consumption of usefulness is known as *depreciation* for plant and equipment, *depletion* for natural resources, and *amortization* for intangibles.

We also consider other issues until final disposal such as impairment of these assets and the treatment of expenditures subsequent to acquisition.

LEARNING OBJECTIVES

After studying this chapter, you should be able to:

- **LO11–1** Explain the concept of cost allocation as it pertains to property, plant, and equipment and intangible assets. (p. 571)
- **LO11–2** Determine periodic depreciation using both time-based and activity-based methods and account for dispositions. (p. 574)
- **LO11–3** Calculate the periodic depletion of a natural resource. (p. 589)
- **LO11–4** Calculate the periodic amortization of an intangible asset. (p. 591)
- **LO11–5** Explain the appropriate accounting treatment required when a change is made in the service life or residual value of property, plant, and equipment and intangible assets. (p. 596)
- **LO11–6** Explain the appropriate accounting treatment required when a change in depreciation, amortization, or depletion method is made. (p. 597)
- **LO11–7** Explain the appropriate treatment required when an error in accounting for property, plant, and equipment and intangible assets is discovered. (p. 598)
- **LO11–8** Identify situations that involve a significant impairment of the value of property, plant, and equipment and intangible assets and describe the required accounting procedures. (p. 600)
- **LO11–9** Discuss the accounting treatment of repairs and maintenance, additions, improvements, and rearrangements to property, plant, and equipment and intangible assets. (p. 593)
- **LO11–10** Discuss the primary differences between U.S. GAAP and IFRS with respect to the utilization and impairment of property, plant, and equipment and intangible assets. (pp. 580, 587, 590, 594, 603, 605, 607, and 614)

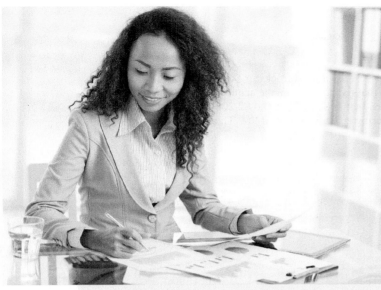

©Dragon Images/Shutterstock

FINANCIAL REPORTING CASE

What's in a Name?

"I don't understand this at all," your friend Penny Lane moaned. "Depreciation, depletion, amortization; what's the difference? Aren't they all the same thing?" Penny and you are part of a class team working on a case involving Weyerhaeuser Company, a large forest products company. Part of the project involves comparing reporting methods over a three-year period. "Look at these disclosure notes from last year's annual report. Besides mentioning those three terms, they also talk about asset impairment. How is that different?" Penny showed you the disclosure notes.

Property and Equipment and Timber and Timberlands (in part)

Depreciation is calculated using a straight-line method at rates based on estimated service lives. Logging roads are generally amortized—as timber is harvested—at rates based on the volume of timber estimated to be removed. We carry timber and timberlands at cost less depletion.

Depletion (in part)

To determine depletion rates, we divide the net carrying value by the related volume of timber estimated to be available over the growth cycle.

Impairment of Long-Lived Assets (in part)

We review long-lived assets—including certain identifiable intangibles—for impairment whenever events or changes in circumstances indicate that the carrying amount of the assets may not be recoverable.

By the time you finish this chapter, you should be able to respond appropriately to the questions posed in this case. Compare your response to the solution provided at the end of the chapter.

QUESTIONS

1. Is Penny correct? Do the terms *depreciation, depletion,* and *amortization* all mean the same thing? (*p. 572*)

2. Weyerhaeuser determines depletion based on the "volume of timber estimated to be available." Explain this approach. (*p. 577*)

3. Explain how asset impairment differs from depreciation, depletion, and amortization. How do companies measure impairment losses for property, plant, and equipment and intangible assets with finite useful lives? (*p. 600*)

Depreciation, Depletion, and Amortization

Cost Allocation—an Overview

PART A

Property, plant, and equipment and intangible assets are purchased with the expectation that they will provide future benefits. Specifically, they are acquired to be used as part of the revenue-generating operations, usually for several years. Logically, then, the cost of these acquisitions initially should be recorded as assets (as we saw in Chapter 10), and then these costs should be allocated to expense over the reporting periods benefited by their use. That is, their costs are reported with the revenues they help generate.

● LO11–1

Let's suppose that a company purchases a used truck for $8,200 to deliver products to customers. The company estimates that five years from the acquisition date the truck will be sold for $2,200. It is estimated, then, that $6,000 ($8,200 – $2,200) of the truck's purchase cost will be used up (consumed) during a five-year useful life. The situation is portrayed in Illustration 11–1.

Illustration 11–1

Cost Allocation

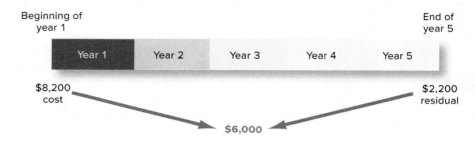

Because the truck will help to produce revenues over the next five years, an asset of $8,200 is recorded at the time of acquisition. Over the subsequent five years, $6,000 of the truck's costs is expected to be consumed and, conceptually, should be allocated to expense in those years in direct proportion to the role the asset played in revenue production. However, very seldom is there a clear-cut relationship between the use of the asset and revenue production. In other words, we can't tell precisely the portion of the total benefits of the asset that was consumed in any particular period. As a consequence, we must resort to arbitrary allocation methods to approximate the portion of the asset's cost used each period. Contrast this situation with the $24,000 prepayment of one year's rent on an office building at $2,000 per month. In that case, we know precisely that the benefits of the asset (prepaid rent) are consumed at a rate of $2,000 per month. That's why we allocate $2,000 of prepaid rent to rent expense for each month that passes.

The process of allocating the cost of plant and equipment over the periods they are used to produce revenues is known as depreciation. The process of depreciation often is confused with measuring a decline in fair value of an asset. For example, let's say our delivery truck purchased for $8,200 can be sold for $5,000 at the end of one year but we intend to keep it for the full five-year estimated life. It has experienced a decline in value of $3,200 ($8,200 – $5,000). However, *depreciation is a process of cost allocation, not valuation.* We would not record depreciation expense of $3,200 for year one of the truck's life. Instead, we would distribute the cost of the asset, less any anticipated residual value, over the estimated useful life in a systematic and rational manner that attempts to associate revenues with the *use* of the asset, not the decline in its value. After all, the truck is purchased to be used in operations, not to be sold.

FINANCIAL Reporting Case

Q1, p. 571

Depreciation, depletion, and amortization are processes that allocate an asset's cost to periods of benefit.

For natural resources, we refer to cost allocation as depletion, and for intangible assets, we refer to it as amortization. While the terms *depreciation, depletion,* and *amortization* differ across types of assets, they conceptually refer to the same idea—the process of allocating an asset's cost over the periods it is used to produce revenues.

For assets used in the manufacture of a product, depreciation, depletion, or amortization is considered a product cost to be included as part of the cost of inventory. Eventually, when the product is sold, it becomes part of the cost of goods sold. For assets *not* used in production, primarily plant and equipment and certain intangibles used in the selling and administrative functions of the company, depreciation and amortization are reported as period expenses in the income statement. You might recognize this distinction between a product cost and a period cost. A product cost is reported as an expense (cost of goods sold) when the related product is sold; a period cost is reported as an expense in the reporting period in which it is incurred.

Measuring Cost Allocation

The process of cost allocation requires that three factors be established at the time the asset is put into use. These factors are

1. Service life—The estimated use that the company expects to receive from the asset.

2. Allocation base—The cost of the asset expected to be consumed during its service life.
3. Allocation method—The pattern in which the allocation base is expected to be consumed.

Let's consider these one at a time.

Service Life

The service life, or useful life, is the amount of use that the company expects to obtain from the asset before disposing of it. This use can be expressed in units of time or in units of activity. For example, the estimated service life of a delivery truck could be expressed in terms of years or in terms of the number of miles that the company expects the truck to be driven before disposition. We use the terms service life and useful life interchangeably throughout the chapter.

> The *service life*, or *useful life*, can be expressed in units of time or in units of activity.

Physical life provides the upper bound for service life of tangible, long-lived assets. Physical life will vary according to the purpose for which the asset is acquired and the environment in which it is operated. For example, a diesel powered electric generator may last for many years if it is used only as an emergency backup or for only a few years if it is used regularly.

The service life of a tangible asset may be less than physical life for a variety of reasons. For example, the expected rate of technological change may shorten service life. If suppliers are expected to develop new technologies that are more efficient, the company may keep an asset for a period of time much shorter than physical life. Likewise, if the company sells its product in a market that frequently demands new products, the machinery and equipment used to produce products may be useful only for as long as its output can be sold. Similarly, a mineral deposit might be projected to contain 4 million tons of a mineral, but it may be economically feasible with existing extraction methods to mine only 2 million tons.

> Expected obsolescence can shorten service life below physical life.

For intangible assets, legal or contractual life often is a limiting factor. For instance, a patent might be capable of providing enhanced profitability for 50 years, but the legal life of a patent is only 20 years.

Management intent also may shorten the period of an asset's usefulness below its physical, legal, or contractual life. For example, a company may have a policy of using its delivery trucks for a three-year period and then trading the trucks for new models.

Companies quite often disclose the range of service lives for different categories of assets. For example, Illustration 11–2 shows how IBM Corporation disclosed its service lives in a note accompanying recent financial statements.

Summary of Significant Accounting Policies (in part)
Depreciation and Amortization
The estimated useful lives of certain depreciable assets are as follows: buildings, 30 to 50 years; building equipment, 10 to 20 years; land improvements, 20 years; plant, laboratory, and office equipment, 2 to 20 years; and computer equipment, 1.5 to 5 years.

Source: International Business Machines Corporation

Illustration 11–2

Service Life Disclosure—International Business Machines Corporation

Real World Financials

Allocation Base

The allocation base is the amount of cost to be allocated over an asset's service life. The amount is the difference between the asset's capitalized cost at the date placed in service and the asset's estimated residual value. Residual value (sometimes called *salvage value*) is the amount the company expects to receive for the asset at the end of its service life, less any anticipated disposal costs.

> *Allocation base* is the difference between the cost of the asset and its estimated *residual value.*

For plant and equipment, we commonly refer to the allocation base as the *depreciable base*. In our delivery truck example above, the depreciable base is $6,000 ($8,200 cost less $2,200 estimated residual value). We will allocate a portion of the $6,000 to each year of the truck's service life. For the depletion of natural resources, we refer to the allocation base as the *depletion base*. For amortization of an intangible asset, we refer to the allocation base as the *amortization base*.

In certain situations, residual value can be estimated by referring to a company's prior experience or to publicly available information concerning resale values of various types of assets. For example, if a company intends to trade its delivery truck in three years for the new model, approximations of the three-year residual value for that type of truck can be obtained from used truck values.

However, estimating residual value for many assets can be very difficult due to the uncertainty about the future. For this reason, along with the fact that residual values often are immaterial, many companies simply assume a residual value of zero. Companies usually do not disclose estimated residual values.

Allocation Method

The allocation method used should be systematic and rational and correspond to the pattern of asset use.

In determining how much cost to allocate to periods of an asset's use, a method should be selected that corresponds to the pattern of benefits received from the asset's use. Generally accepted accounting principles state that the chosen method should allocate the asset's cost "as equitably as possible to the periods during which services are obtained from [its] use." GAAP further specifies that the method should produce a cost allocation in a "systematic and rational manner."[1] The objective is to try to allocate cost to the period in an amount that is proportional to the amount of benefits generated by the asset during the period relative to the total benefits provided by the asset during its life.

In practice, there are two general approaches that attempt to obtain this systematic and rational allocation. The first approach allocates the cost base according to the *passage of time*. Methods following this approach are referred to as time-based methods. The second approach allocates an asset's cost base using a measure of the asset's *input* or *output*. This is an activity-based method. We compare these approaches first in the context of depreciation. Later we see that depletion of natural resources typically follows an activity-based approach, while the amortization of intangibles typically follows a time-based approach.

Depreciation

● LO11–2

To demonstrate and compare the most common depreciation methods, we refer to the situation described in Illustration 11–3.

Illustration 11–3
Depreciation Methods

At the beginning of Year 1, Hogan Manufacturing Company purchased a machine for $250,000 and made the following estimates at that time:

- Estimated residual value of $40,000.
- Estimated service life of 5 years.
- Estimated production of 140,000 units.

Actual production during the five years of the asset's life was as follows:

Year	Units Produced
1	20,000
2	32,000
3	44,000
4	28,000
5	26,000
Total	150,000

Time-Based Depreciation Methods

The straight-line method depreciates an equal amount of the depreciable base to each year of the asset's service life.

STRAIGHT-LINE METHOD   By far the most easily understood and widely used technique for calculating depreciation is the straight-line method. In this approach, an equal amount of the depreciable base (or allocation base) is allocated to each year of the asset's service life. The depreciable base is simply divided by the number of years in the asset's life to

[1]Source: FASB ASC 360-10-35-4: Property, Plant, and Equipment-Overall-Subsequent Measurement (previously "Restatement and Revision of Accounting Research Bulletins," *Accounting Research Bulletin* No. 43 (New York: AICPA, 1953), Ch.9).

determine annual depreciation. Using the information given in Illustration 11–3, straight-line depreciation expense in each year is $42,000, calculated as follows:

$$\frac{\$250{,}000 - \$40{,}000}{5 \text{ years}} = \$42{,}000 \text{ per year}$$

The calculation of depreciation over the entire five-year life is demonstrated in detail in Illustration 11–3A. Notice the last three columns. **Depreciation expense** is the portion of the asset's cost that is allocated to an expense *in the current year*. **Accumulated depreciation** (a contra-asset account) represents the cumulative amount of the asset's cost that has been depreciated *in all prior years including the current year*. This amount represents the reduction in the asset's cost reported in the balance sheet. The asset is reported in the balance sheet at its **book value,** which is the asset's cost minus accumulated depreciation. Book value is sometimes called *carrying value* or carrying amount. The residual value ($40,000 in this example) does not affect the calculation of book value, but the residual value does set a limit on which book value cannot go below.

Illustration 11–3A Straight-Line Depreciation

Using the information given in Illustration 11–3:

Year	Depreciable Base ($250,000 – $40,000)	×	Depreciation Rate per Year	=	Depreciation Expense	Accumulated Depreciation	Book Value End of Year ($250,000 less Accum. Depreciation)
1	$210,000		⅕*		$ 42,000	$ 42,000	$208,000
2	210,000		⅕		42,000	84,000	166,000
3	210,000		⅕		42,000	126,000	124,000
4	210,000		⅕		42,000	168,000	82,000
5	210,000		⅕		42,000	210,000	40,000
Totals					$210,000		

*The rate equals 1 divided by the asset's 5-year estimated service life (⅕ = 20%).

The entry to record depreciation at the end of each year using the straight-line method would be:

Depreciation expense	42,000*	
Accumulated depreciation		42,000

*$42,000 = ($250,000 – $40,000) ÷ 5 years.

ACCELERATED METHODS   Using the straight-line method implicitly assumes that the benefits derived from the use of the asset are the same each year. In some situations it might be more appropriate to assume that the asset will provide greater benefits in the early years of its life than in the later years. In these cases, a more appropriate matching of depreciation with revenues is achieved with a declining pattern of depreciation, with higher depreciation in the early years of the asset's life and lower depreciation in later years.

Accelerated depreciation methods report higher depreciation in earlier years.

An accelerated depreciation method also would be appropriate when benefits derived from the asset are approximately equal over the asset's life, but repair and maintenance costs increase significantly in later years. The early years incur higher depreciation and lower repairs and maintenance expense, while the later years have lower depreciation and higher repairs and maintenance. One way to achieve such a declining pattern of depreciation is a declining-balance method, which we discuss next.

Declining-balance depreciation methods multiply beginning-of-year book value, not depreciable base, by an annual rate that is a multiple of the straight-line rate.

Declining-balance methods.   One way to calculate higher depreciation in the early years of the asset's life is to multiply the asset's book value (cost less accumulated depreciation) at the beginning of the year by a constant percentage rate. Annual depreciation reduces book value each year. Therefore, multiplying a declining book value by a constant rate results in declining depreciation expense in each successive year.

Perhaps the most common declining-balance method is known as the **double-declining-balance (DDB) method**. Under this method, we multiply the asset's beginning-of-year book value by *double* (or 200%) the straight-line rate. For example, in our previous example using a five-year asset, the straight-line rate was 20% (= $1/_5$). For the double-declining-balance method, we double that rate and use 40%. Various other multiples are used in practice, such as 125% or 150% of the straight-line rate.

Depreciation using the double-declining-balance method is calculated in Illustration 11–3B for the five years of the machine's life. Notice that book value at the beginning of the year, rather than the depreciable base, is used as the starting point. As book value decreases each year, so does depreciation. Further, notice that in year 4 we did not multiply $54,000 by 40%. If we had, annual depreciation would have been $21,600. This amount would have resulted in accumulated depreciation by the end of year 4 of $217,600 and book value of $32,400, which is below the asset's expected residual value of $40,000. Therefore, we instead use a plug amount that reduces book value to the expected residual value (book value beginning of year, $54,000, minus expected residual value, $40,000 = **$14,000**). This also means there is no depreciation in year 5 since book value has already been reduced to the expected residual value. Declining balance methods often allocate the asset's depreciable base over fewer years than the expected service life.

Illustration 11–3B   Double-Declining-Balance Depreciation

Using the information given in Illustration 11–3:

Year	Book Value Beginning of Year	×	Depreciation Rate per Year	=	Depreciation Expense	Accumulated Depreciation	Book Value End of Year ($250,000 less Accum. Depreciation)
1	$250,000		40%*		$100,000	$100,000	$150,000
2	150,000		40%		60,000	160,000	90,000
3	90,000		40%		36,000	196,000	54,000
4	54,000				14,000†	210,000	40,000
5	40,000				0	210,000	40,000
Total					$210,000		

*Double the straight-line rate of 20%. The straight-line rate is 1 divided by the asset's 5-year estimated service life ($1/_5$ = 20%).
†Amount necessary to reduce book value to residual value.

Sum-of-the-years'-digits method. Another accelerated depreciation pattern can be achieved by multiplying the depreciable base by a declining fraction. One such method is the **sum-of-the-years'-digits (SYD) method**. This method is seldom used in practice. The denominator of the fraction remains constant and is the *sum of the digits* from one to *n*, where *n* is the number of years in the asset's service life. For example, if there are five years in the service life, the denominator is the sum of 1, 2, 3, 4, and 5, which equals 15.[2] The numerator decreases each year; it begins with the value of *n* in the first year and decreases by one each year until it equals one in the final year of the asset's estimated service life. The annual fractions for an asset with a five-year life are: $5/_{15}$, $4/_{15}$, $3/_{15}$, $2/_{15}$, and $1/_{15}$. We calculate depreciation for the five years of the machine's life using the sum-of-the-years'-digits method in Illustration 11–3C.

Notice that total depreciation ($210,000) is the same for accelerated methods like DDB and SYD as it is for the straight-line method, as shown in Illustration 11–3A. The difference is the pattern in which this total cost is allocated to each year of the asset's service life.

---

[2] A formula useful when calculating the denominator is n (n + 1)/2.

Illustration 11–3C Sum-of-the-Years'-Digits Depreciation

Using the information given in Illustration 11–3:

Year	Depreciable Base ($250,000 – $40,000)	×	Depreciation Rate per Year	=	Depreciation Expense	Accumulated Depreciation	Book Value End of Year ($250,000 less Accum. Depreciation)
1	$210,000		$\frac{5}{15}$*		$ 70,000	$ 70,000	$180,000
2	210,000		$\frac{4}{15}$		56,000	126,000	124,000
3	210,000		$\frac{3}{15}$		42,000	168,000	82,000
4	210,000		$\frac{2}{15}$		28,000	196,000	54,000
5	210,000		$\frac{1}{15}$		14,000	210,000	40,000
Totals			$\frac{15}{15}$		$210,000		

$$*\frac{n(n+1)}{2} = \frac{5(5+1)}{2} = 15$$

SWITCH FROM ACCELERATED TO STRAIGHT-LINE   As a planned approach to depreciation, many companies have a formal policy to use accelerated depreciation for approximately the first half of an asset's service life and then switch to the straight-line method for the remaining life of the asset.

In Illustration 11–3B, the company would switch to the straight-line method in either year 3 or year 4. Assuming the switch is made at the beginning of year 4, and the book value at the beginning of that year is $54,000, an additional $14,000 ($54,000 – $40,000 in residual value) of depreciation must be recorded over the remaining life of the asset. Applying the straight-line concept, $7,000 ($14,000 divided by two remaining years) in depreciation is recorded in both year 4 and year 5.

It should be noted that this switch to straight-line is not a change in depreciation method. The switch is part of the company's planned depreciation approach. However, as you will learn later in the chapter, the accounting treatment is the same as a change in depreciation method.

Activity-Based Depreciation Methods

The most logical way to allocate an asset's cost to periods of an asset's use is to measure the usefulness of the asset in terms of its productivity. For example, we could measure the service life of a machine in terms of its *output* (such as the estimated number of units it will produce) or in terms of its *input* (such as the number of hours it will operate). We have already mentioned that one way to measure the service life of a vehicle is to estimate the number of miles it will be driven. The most common activity-based method is called the units-of-production method.

The measure of output used is the estimated number of units (pounds, items, barrels, etc.) to be produced by the machine. By the units-of-production method, we first compute the average depreciation rate per unit by dividing the depreciable base by the number of units expected to be produced. This per unit rate is then multiplied by the actual number of units produced each period. In our illustration, the depreciation rate per unit is $1.50, computed as follows:

$$\frac{\$250,000 - \$40,000}{140,000 \text{ units}} = \$1.50 \text{ per unit}$$

Each unit produced will require $1.50 of depreciation to be recorded. In other words, each unit produced is assigned $1.50 of the asset's cost.

Illustration 11–3D shows that depreciation each year is the actual units produced multiplied by the depreciation rate per unit. This means that the amount of depreciation each year varies proportionately with the number of units being produced, with one exception. Notice

Activity-based depreciation methods estimate service life in terms of some measure of productivity.

FINANCIAL Reporting Case

Q2, p. 571

The *units-of-production method* computes a depreciation rate per measure of activity and then multiplies this rate by actual activity to determine periodic depreciation.

that the asset produced 26,000 units in year 5, causing total production over the life of the asset (150,000 units) to exceed its estimated production (140,000 units). In this case, we cannot record depreciation for the final 10,000 units produced. Depreciation in year five is limited to the amount that brings the book value of the asset down to its residual value (book value beginning of year, $64,000, minus expected residual value, $40,000, equals $24,000).

Illustration 11–3D

Units-of-Production Depreciation

Using the information given in Illustration 11–3:

Year	Units Produced	×	Depreciation Rate per Unit	=	Depreciation Expense	Accumulated Depreciation	Book Value End of Year ($250,000 less Accum. Depreciation)
1	20,000		$1.50*		$ 30,000	$ 30,000	$220,000
2	32,000		1.50		48,000	78,000	172,000
3	44,000		1.50		66,000	144,000	106,000
4	28,000		1.50		42,000	186,000	64,000
5	26,000				24,000†	210,000	40,000
Totals	150,000				$210,000		

*($250,000 − $40,000) / 140,000 units = $1.50 per unit.
†Amount necessary to reduce book value to residual value.

The machine may produce *fewer than* 140,000 units by the end of its useful life. For example, suppose production in year 5 had been only 6,000 units, bringing total production to 130,000 units, and management has no future plans to use the machine. We would record depreciation in year 5 for $9,000 (6,000 units × $1.50). If management then develops a formal plan to sell the machine, the machine is classified as "held for sale" (discussed in more detail below) and reported at the lower of its current book value or its fair value less any cost to sell. If management plans to retire the asset without selling it, a loss is recorded for the remaining book value.

Decision Makers' Perspective—Selecting A Depreciation Method

All methods provide the same total depreciation over an asset's life.

Illustration 11–3E compares periodic depreciation calculated using each of the alternatives we discussed and illustrated.

Illustration 11–3E

Comparison of Various Depreciation Methods

Year	Straight-Line	Double-Declining-Balance	Sum-of-the-Years'-Digits	Units of Production
1	$ 42,000	$100,000	$ 70,000	$ 30,000
2	42,000	60,000	56,000	48,000
3	42,000	36,000	42,000	66,000
4	42,000	14,000	28,000	42,000
5	42,000	0	14,000	24,000
Total	$210,000	$210,000	$210,000	$210,000

Activity-based methods are conceptually superior to time-based methods but often are impractical to apply in practice.

Conceptually, using an activity-based depreciation method provides a better matching of the asset's cost to the use of that asset to help produce revenues. Clearly, the productivity of an asset is more closely associated with the benefits provided by that asset than the mere passage of time. Also, these methods allow for patterns of depreciation to correspond with the patterns of asset use.

However, activity-based methods quite often are either infeasible or too costly to use. For example, buildings don't have an identifiable measure of productivity. Even for machinery, there may be an identifiable measure of productivity such as machine hours or units produced, but it frequently is more costly to determine each period than it is to simply measure the passage of time. For these reasons, most companies use time-based depreciation methods.

Illustration 11–4 shows the results of a recent survey of depreciation methods used by large public companies.[3]

Depreciation Method	Number of Companies
Straight-line	490
Declining-balance	9
Sum-of-the-years'-digits	2
Accelerated method—not specified	9
Units of production	12
Group/composite	17

Illustration 11–4

Use of Various Depreciation Methods

Real World Financials

Why do so many companies use the straight-line method as opposed to other time-based methods? Many companies perhaps consider the benefits derived from the majority of depreciable assets to be realized approximately evenly over these assets' useful lives. Certainly a contributing factor is that straight-line is the easiest method to understand and apply.

Another motivation is the positive effect on reported income. Straight-line depreciation produces a higher net income than accelerated methods in the early years of an asset's life. In Chapter 8, we pointed out that reported net income can affect bonuses paid to management or debt agreements with lenders.

Conflicting with the desire to report higher profits is the desire to reduce taxes by reducing taxable income. An accelerated method serves this objective by reducing taxable income more in the early years of an asset's life than straight-line. You probably recall a similar discussion from Chapter 8 in which the benefits of using the LIFO inventory method during periods of increasing costs were described. However, remember that the LIFO conformity rule requires companies using LIFO for income tax reporting to also use LIFO for financial reporting. *No such conformity rule exists for depreciation methods.* Income tax regulations allow firms to use different approaches to computing depreciation in their tax returns and in their financial statements. The method used for tax purposes is therefore not a constraint in the choice of depreciation methods for financial reporting. As a result, most companies use the straight-line method for financial reporting and an accelerated method for tax reporting (discussed in Appendix 11A). For example, Illustration 11–5 shows Merck & Co.'s depreciation policy as reported in a disclosure note accompanying recent financial statements.

A company does not have to use the same depreciation method for both financial reporting and income tax purposes.

Summary of Accounting Policies (in part):
Depreciation
Depreciation is provided over the estimated useful lives of the assets, principally using the straight-line method. For tax purposes, accelerated methods are used.

Source: Merck & Co.

Illustration 11–5

Depreciation Method Disclosure—Merck & Co.

Real World Financials

It is not unusual for a company to use different depreciation methods for different classes of assets. For example, Illustration 11–6 illustrates the International Paper Company depreciation policy disclosure contained in a note accompanying recent financial statements.

Summary of Accounting Policies (in part):
Plants, Properties, and Equipment
Plants, properties, and equipment are stated at cost, less accumulated depreciation. The units-of-production method of depreciation is used for major pulp and paper mills and the straight-line method is used for other plants and equipment.

Source: International Paper Company

Illustration 11–6

Depreciation Method Disclosure—International Paper Company

Real World Financials

---

[3]*U.S. GAAP Financial Statements—Best Practices in Presentation and Disclosure—2013* (New York: AICPA, 2013).

580   SECTION 2   Assets

International Financial Reporting Standards

● LO11–10

Depreciation. *IAS No. 16* requires that each component of an item of property, plant, and equipment must be depreciated separately if its cost is significant in relation to the total cost of the item.[4] In the United States, component depreciation is allowed but is not often used in practice.
Consider the following illustration:

Cavandish LTD. purchased a delivery truck for $62,000. The truck is expected to have a service life of six years and a residual value of $12,000. At the end of three years, the oversized tires, which have a cost of $6,000 (included in the $62,000 purchase price), will be replaced.

Under U.S. GAAP, the typical accounting treatment is to depreciate the $50,000 ($62,000 – $12,000) depreciable base of the truck over its six-year useful life. Using IFRS, the depreciable base of the truck is $44,000 ($62,000 – $12,000 – $6,000) and is depreciated over the truck's six-year useful life, and the $6,000 cost of the tires is depreciated separately over a three-year useful life.

U.S. GAAP and IFRS determine depreciable base in the same way, by subtracting estimated residual value from cost. However, IFRS requires a review of residual values at least annually.

Sanofi-Aventis, a French pharmaceutical company, prepares its financial statements using IFRS. In its property, plant, and equipment note, the company discloses its use of the component-based approach to accounting for depreciation.

Property, plant, and equipment (in part)

The component-based approach to accounting for property, plant, and equipment is applied. Under this approach, each component of an item of property, plant, and equipment with a cost which is significant in relation to the total cost of the item and which has a different useful life from the other components must be depreciated separately.

Depreciation Methods. *IAS No. 16* specifically mentions three depreciation methods: straight-line, units-of-production, and the diminishing balance method. The diminishing balance method is similar to the declining balance method sometimes used by U.S. companies. As in the United States, the straight-line method is used by most companies. A recent survey of large companies that prepare their financial statement according to IFRS reports 93% of the surveyed companies used the straight-line method.[5]

Concept Review Exercise

DEPRECIATION METHODS

The Sprague Company purchased a fabricating machine on January 1, 2021, at a net cost of $130,000. At the end of its four-year useful life, the company estimates that the machine will be worth $30,000. Sprague also estimates that the machine will run for 25,000 hours during its four-year life. The company's fiscal year ends on December 31.

Required:
Compute depreciation expense for 2021 through 2024 using each of the following methods:
1. Straight-line
2. Double-declining-balance
3. Sum-of-the-years'-digits
4. Units of production (using machine hours); actual production was as follows:

Year	Machine Hours
2021	6,000
2022	8,000
2023	5,000
2024	7,000

---

[4]"Property, Plant and Equipment," *International Accounting Standard No. 16* (IASCF), par. 42, as amended effective January 1, 2018.
[5]" *IFRS Accounting Trends and Techniques*" (New York, AICPA, 2011), p. 328.

Solution:

1. Straight-line:

$$\frac{\$130,000 - \$30,000}{4 \text{ years}} = \$25,000 \text{ per year}$$

2. Double-declining balance:

Year	Book Value Beginning of Year	×	Depreciation Rate per Year	=	Depreciation Expense	Book Value End of Year
2021	$130,000		50%*		$ 65,000	$65,000
2022	65,000		50%		32,500	32,500
2023	32,500				2,500†	30,000
2024	30,000				0	30,000
Total					$ 100,000	

*Double the straight-line rate of 25%. The straight-line rate is 1 divided by the asset's 4-year estimated service life (¼ = 25%).
†Amount necessary to reduce book value to residual value.

3. Sum-of-the-years'-digits:

Year	Depreciable Base	×	Depreciation Rate per Year	=	Depreciation Expense
2021	$ 100,000		4/10		$ 40,000
2022	100,000		3/10		30,000
2023	100,000		2/10		20,000
2024	100,000		1/10		10,000
Total					$100,000

4. Units of production (using machine hours):

Year	Machine Hours	×	Depreciation Rate per Hour	=	Depreciation Expense	Book Value End of Year
2021	6,000		$4*		$ 24,000	$106,000
2022	8,000		4		32,000	74,000
2023	5,000		4		20,000	54,000
2024	7,000				24,000†	30,000
Total					$ 100,000	

*($130,000 − $30,000)/25,000 hours = $4 per hour.
†Amount necessary to reduce book value to residual value.

Partial Period Depreciation

When acquisition and disposal of property, plant, and equipment occur at times other than the very beginning or very end of a company's fiscal year, a company theoretically must determine how much depreciation to record for the part of the year that each asset actually is used.

Let's repeat the Hogan Manufacturing Company illustration used earlier in Illustration 11–3 but modify it in Illustration 11–7 to assume that the asset was acquired *during* the company's fiscal year.

On April 1, 2021, Hogan Manufacturing Company purchased a machine for $250,000 and made the following estimates at that time:

- Estimated residual value of $40,000.
- Estimated service life of five years.
- Estimated production of 140,000 units.

(continued)

Illustration 11–7
Depreciation Methods—
Partial Year

582   SECTION 2   Assets

Illustration 11–7
(Concluded)

The company has a December 31 year-end. Actual production during the five years of the asset's life was as follows:

Year	Units Produced*
2021 (beginning April 1)	16,000
2022	30,000
2023	40,000
2024	32,000
2025	24,000
2026 (ending April 1)	8,000
Total	150,000

*The units produced in each year do not correspond to Years 1-5 in Illustration 11–3 because the asset was not purchased at the beginning of the first year. In both illustrations, total production occurs over five years for the same total amount of 150,000 units.

Depreciation per year of the asset's life calculated earlier in Illustration 11–3A, Illustration 11–3B, and Illustration 11–3D is summarized in Illustration 11–7A.

Illustration 11–7A
Yearly Depreciation

Year	Straight-Line	Double-Declining-Balance	Units-of-Production
1	$ 42,000	$ 100,000	$ 30,000
2	42,000	60,000	48,000
3	42,000	36,000	66,000
4	42,000	14,000	42,000
5	42,000	0	24,000
Total	**$210,000**	**$210,000**	**$210,000**

Illustration 11–7B shows how Hogan would depreciate the machinery by these three methods assuming an April 1 acquisition date.

Illustration 11–7B   Partial-Year Depreciation

Year	Straight-Line		Double-Declining-Balance		Units-of-Production	
2021	$42,000 × ¾ = $	31,500	$250,000 × ⅖ × ¾ = $	75,000	16,000 units × $1.50^ = $	24,000
2022		42,000	$175,000 × ⅖ =	70,000*		45,000
2023		42,000	$105,000 × ⅖ =	42,000		60,000
2024		42,000		23,000†		48,000
2025		42,000		0		33,000†
2026	$42,000 × ¼ =	10,500		0		0
Totals		**$210,000**		**$210,000**		**$210,000**

*Book value at the beginning of the year times double the straight-line rate: ($250,000 − $75,000) × ²/₅ = $70,000.
^($250,000 − $40,000) / 140,000 units = $1.50 per unit. Depreciation each year equals actual units produced times $1.50.
†Amount necessary to reduce book value to residual value.

The first thing to notice is that even with partial-year depreciation, the total depreciation over the asset's total life ($210,000) is the same whether the asset is purchased at the beginning of a year or during the year. For straight-line, depreciation is ¾ of a full year's depreciation for the first year of the asset's life, because the asset was used only nine months, or ¾ of the year. The asset is depreciated for one full year in the following four years, and then the remaining ¼ of the asset's five-year useful life is depreciated in the final year.

For double-declining-balance, recall that depreciation equals the asset's book value at the beginning of the year times double the straight-line rate. In the first year, depreciation is ¾ of the full year's depreciation. After that, we calculate depreciation for a full year using the updated beginning-of-year book value. We continue each year until a final plug amount is needed to reduce book value to residual value. That final plug was reached in 2024 so no further depreciation is recorded over the remaining life of the asset (2025 and 2026).

For units-of-production, depreciation is not calculated based on time, so the portion of the year the asset is in operation does not matter. Instead, depreciation is calculated as the estimated depreciation rate per unit of output multiplied by the actual output for the year. Once the full allocation base has been depreciated, no further depreciation is recorded. For the example in Illustration 11–7B, the full allocation based was reached in 2025 (when actual production reached 140,000 units), so any further production does not affect depreciation.

Sometimes companies adopt a simplifying assumption, or convention, for computing partial year's depreciation and use it consistently. A common convention is to record one-half of a full year's depreciation in the year of acquisition and another half year in the year of disposal. This is known as the **half-year convention**.[6]

Dispositions

After using property, plant, and equipment, companies will sell or retire those assets. When selling property, plant, and equipment for monetary consideration (cash or a receivable), the seller recognizes a **gain** or **loss** for the difference between the consideration received and the book value of the asset sold.

> A gain or loss is recognized for the difference between the consideration received and the asset's book value.

Selling price (consideration received)		$ xxx
Less: Book value of asset sold		
Original cost	$ xxx	
Accumulated depreciation	(xxx)	(xxx)
Gain/loss on sale of asset		$ xxx

We'll demonstrate this calculation next in Illustration 11–7C by modifying our earlier straight-line method example of Hogan Manufacturing Company in Illustration 11–3A. In Illustration 11–7C, Hogan sells a machine before the end of its service life and receives more cash than the asset's book value (cost minus accumulated depreciation) at the time of the sale. This causes a gain to be recognized.

Illustration 11–7C

Sale of Property, Plant, and Equipment

On January 1, 2021, Hogan Manufacturing Company purchased a machine for $250,000. The company expects the service life of the machine to be five years. The estimated residual value is $40,000. Hogan uses the straight-line depreciation method for machines recorded in the equipment account.

Suppose Hogan decides not to hold the machine for the expected five years but instead sells it on December 31, 2023 (three years later), for $140,000. We first need to update depreciation to the date of sale. Since depreciation for 2021 and 2022 has already been recorded in those years, we need to update depreciation only for the current year, 2023.

The entry to update depreciation for 2023:

Depreciation expense	42,000*	
Accumulated depreciation		42,000

*$42,000 = ($250,000 − $40,000) ÷ 5 years. See also Illustration 11–3A.

The balance of accumulated depreciation equals depreciation that has already been recorded in 2021 and 2022 ($42,000 + $42,000) plus the depreciation recorded above in 2023 ($42,000).

Accumulated Depreciation	
42,000	2021
42,000	2022
42,000	2023
126,000	

(continued)

---

[6]Another common method is the modified half-year convention. This method records a full year's depreciation when the asset is acquired in the first half of the year or sold in the second half. No depreciation is recorded if the asset is acquired in the second half of the year or sold in the first half. These half-year conventions are simple and, in most cases, will not result in material differences from a more precise calculation.

584   **SECTION 2**   Assets

Illustration 11–7C
(Concluded)

We can now calculate the gain or loss on the sale as the difference between the selling price and the asset's book value. In this example, the amount of cash received is greater than the asset's book value, so a gain is recognized.

Selling price (cash received)		$ 140,000
Less: Book value of asset sold		
Original cost	$ 250,000	
Accumulated depreciation	(126,000)	(124,000)
Gain on sale of equipment (machine)		$ 16,000

Finally, the sale of the equipment requires that we do the following:

1. Record the cash received.
2. Remove the book value of the asset sold with a credit to the asset account and a debit to its accumulated depreciation.
3. Record the gain or loss.

The entry to record the sale on December 31, 2023, for $140,000:

Cash	140,000	
Accumulated depreciation (account balance)	126,000	
Equipment (account balance)		250,000
Gain on sale of equipment (selling price − book value)		16,000

The balances of the equipment account and the accumulated depreciation account for the machine will be $0 after this entry. The gain on the sale normally is reported in the income statement as a separate component of operating income.

Now, assume that Hogan sold the machine on December 31, 2023, for only $110,000. This amount is less than book value by $14,000 and a loss on the sale would be recorded.

Selling price (cash received)		$ 110,000
Less: Book value of asset sold		
Original cost	$ 250,000	
Accumulated depreciation	(126,000)	(124,000)
Loss on sale of equipment (machine)		$ (14,000)

The entry to record the sale on December 31, 2023, for $110,000:

Cash	110,000	
Accumulated depreciation (account balance)...................................	126,000	
Loss on sale of equipment (selling price − book value)..................	14,000	
Equipment (account balance)...		250,000

Notice that the amounts of the equipment and accumulated depreciation removed from the books upon sale of the asset do not depend on whether a gain or loss is recorded; the asset's book value is written off completely. It's the amount of cash received relative to the asset's book value that determines the amount of the gain or loss.

Decision Makers' Perspective—Understanding gains and losses

It's tempting to think of a "gain" and "loss" on the sale of a depreciable asset as "good" and "bad" news. For example, we commonly use the term "gain" in everyday language to mean we sold something for more than we bought it. Gain could also be misinterpreted to mean the asset was sold for more than its fair value (we got a "good deal"). However, neither of these represents the meaning of a gain on the sale of assets. Refer back to our example in Illustration 11–7C. The sale of the machine resulted in a gain, but the machine was sold for *less than* its original cost, and there is no indication that Hogan sold the machine for more than its fair value.

A gain on the sale of a depreciable asset simply means the asset was sold for more than its book value. In other words, the asset being received and recorded (such as cash) is greater than the recorded book value of the asset being sold and written off. The net increase in the book value of total assets is an accounting gain (not an economic gain).

The same is true for losses. A loss signifies that the cash received is less than the book value of the asset being sold; there is a net decrease in the book value of total assets. ●

ASSETS HELD FOR SALE   Sometimes management plans to sell property, plant, and equipment or an intangible asset but that sale hasn't yet happened. In this case, the asset is classified as "held for sale" in the period in which all of the following criteria are met:[7]

1. Management commits to a plan to sell the asset.
2. The asset is available for immediate sale in its present condition.
3. An active plan to locate a buyer and sell the asset has been initiated.
4. The completed sale of the asset is probable and typically expected to occur within one year.
5. The asset is being offered for sale at a reasonable price relative to its current fair value.
6. Management's actions indicate the plan is unlikely to change significantly or be withdrawn.

An asset that is classified as held for sale is no longer depreciated or amortized. *An asset classified as held for sale is reported at the lower of its current book value or its fair value less any cost to sell.* If the fair value less cost to sell is below book value, we recognize a loss in the current period. If financial statements are again prepared prior to the sale, we reassess the asset's fair value less selling costs. If a further decline has occurred, we recognize another loss. If the fair value less selling costs has increased since the previous measurement, we recognize a gain, but limited to the cumulative amount of any previous losses.

> Property, plant, and equipment or an intangible asset to be disposed of by sale is classified as held for sale and measured at the lower of the asset's book value or the asset's fair value less cost to sell.

RETIREMENTS   Sometimes instead of selling a used asset, a company will retire (or abandon) the asset. Retirements are treated similarly to selling for monetary consideration. At the time of retirement, the asset account and the corresponding accumulated deprecation account are removed from the books and a loss equal to the remaining book value of the asset is recorded because there will be no monetary consideration received. When there is a formal plan to retire an asset, but before the actual retirement, there may be some revision in depreciation due to a change in the estimated service life or residual value.

Group and Composite Depreciation Methods

As you might imagine, depreciation records could become quite cumbersome and costly if a company has hundreds, or maybe thousands, of depreciable assets. However, the burden can be lessened if the company uses the group or composite method to depreciate assets collectively rather than individually. The two methods are the same except for the way the collection of assets is aggregated for depreciation. The group depreciation method defines the collection as depreciable assets that share similar service lives and other attributes. For example, group depreciation could be used for fleets of vehicles or collections of machinery. The composite depreciation method is used when assets are physically dissimilar but are aggregated anyway to gain the convenience of a collective depreciation calculation. For instance, composite depreciation can be used for all of the depreciable assets in one manufacturing plant, even though individual assets in the composite may have widely diverse service lives.

> Group and composite depreciation methods aggregate assets to reduce the recordkeeping costs of determining periodic depreciation.

Both approaches are similar in that they involve applying a single straight-line rate based on the average service lives of the assets in the group or composite.[8] The process is demonstrated using Illustration 11–8.

---

[7]Source: FASB ASC 360–10–45–9: Property, Plant, and Equipment–Overall–Other Presentation Matters–Impairment or Disposal of Long-Lived Assets.
[8]A declining balance method could also be used with either the group or composite method by applying a multiple (e.g., 200%) to the straight-line group or composite rate.

Illustration 11–8
Group Depreciation

The Express Delivery Company began operations in 2021. It will depreciate its fleet of delivery vehicles using the group method. The cost of vehicles purchased early in 2021, along with residual values, estimated lives, and straight-line depreciation per year by type of vehicle, are as follows:

Asset	Cost	Residual Value	Depreciable Base	Estimated Life (years)	Depreciation per Year (straight line)
Vans	$150,000	$ 30,000	$120,000	6	$ 20,000
Trucks	120,000	16,000	104,000	5	20,800
Wagons	60,000	12,000	48,000	4	12,000
Totals	$330,000	$ 58,000	$272,000		$52,800

The *group depreciation* rate is determined by dividing the depreciation per year by the total cost. The group's *average service* life is calculated by dividing the depreciable base by the depreciation per year:

$$\text{Group depreciation rate} = \frac{\$52,800}{\$330,000} = 16\%$$

$$\text{Average service life} = \frac{\$272,000}{\$52,800} = 5.15 \text{ years (rounded)}$$

The depreciation rate is applied to the total cost of the group or composite for the period.

If there are no changes in the assets contained in the group, depreciation of $52,800 per year ($330,000 × 16%) will be recorded for 5.15 years. This means the depreciation in the sixth year will be $7,920 (0.15 of a full year's depreciation = 15% × $52,800), which depreciates the cost of the group down to its estimated residual value. In other words, the group will be depreciated over the average service life of the assets in the group.

In practice, there very likely will be changes in the assets constituting the group as new assets are added and others are retired or sold. Additions are recorded by increasing the group asset account for the cost of the addition. Depreciation is determined by multiplying the group rate by the total cost of assets in the group for that period. Once the group or composite rate and the average service life are determined, they normally are continued despite the addition and disposition of individual assets. This implicitly assumes that the service lives of new assets approximate those of individual assets they replace.

No gain or loss is recorded when a group or composite asset is retired or sold.

Because depreciation records are not kept on an individual asset basis, dispositions are recorded under the assumption that the book value of the disposed item exactly equals any proceeds received and no gain or loss is recorded. For example, if a delivery truck in the above illustration that cost $15,000 is sold for $3,000 in the year 2024, the following journal entry is recorded:

Cash	3,000	
Accumulated depreciation (difference)	12,000	
Vehicles		15,000

Any actual gain or loss is included in the accumulated depreciation account. This practice generally will not distort income as the unrecorded gains tend to offset unrecorded losses.

The group and composite methods simplify the recordkeeping of depreciable assets. This simplification justifies any immaterial errors in income determination. Illustration 11–9 shows a disclosure note accompanying recent financial statements of the El Paso Natural Gas Company (EPNG) describing the use of the group depreciation method for its property that is regulated by federal statutes.

Summary of Significant Accounting Policies (in part)
Property, Plant, and Equipment (in part)
We use the group method to depreciate property, plant, and equipment. Under this method, assets with similar lives and characteristics are grouped and depreciated as one asset. We apply the depreciation rate approved in our rate settlements to the total cost of the group until its net book value equals its salvage value. The majority of our property, plant, and equipment are on our El Paso Natural Gas Company (EPNG) system, which has depreciation rates ranging from one percent to 50 percent.
When we retire property, plant, and equipment, we charge accumulated depreciation and amortization for the original cost of the assets in addition to the cost to remove, sell, or dispose of the assets, less their salvage value. We do not recognize a gain or loss unless we sell an entire operating unit.

Source: El Paso Natural Gas Company

Illustration 11–9

Disclosure of Depreciation Method—El Paso Natural Gas Company

Real World Financials

Additional group-based depreciation methods, the retirement and replacement methods, are discussed in Appendix 11B.

International Financial Reporting Standards

Valuation of Property, Plant, and Equipment. As we've discussed, under U.S. GAAP a company reports property, plant, and equipment (PP&E) in the balance sheet at cost less accumulated depreciation (book value). *IAS No. 16* allows a company to report property, plant, and equipment at that amount or, alternatively, at its fair value (revaluation).[9] If a company chooses revaluation, all assets within a class of PP&E must be revalued on a regular basis. U.S. GAAP prohibits revaluation.

● LO11–10

If the revaluation option is chosen, the way the company reports the difference between fair value and book value depends on which amount is higher:

- If fair value is higher than book value, the difference is reported as *other comprehensive income (OCI),* which then accumulates in a "revaluation surplus" (sometimes called revaluation reserve) account in equity.

- If book value is higher than fair value, the difference is reported as an *expense in the income statement.* An exception is when a revaluation surplus account relating to the same asset has a balance from a previous *increase* in fair value, that balance is eliminated before debiting revaluation expense.

Consider the following illustration:

Candless Corporation prepares its financial statements according to IFRS. At the beginning of its 2021 fiscal year, the company purchased equipment for $100,000. The equipment is expected to have a five-year useful life with no residual value, so depreciation for 2021 is $20,000. At the end of the year, Candless chooses to revalue the equipment as permitted by *IAS No. 16.* Assuming that the fair value of the equipment at year-end is $84,000, Candless records depreciation and the revaluation using the following journal entries:

(a) Depreciation expense ($100,000 ÷ 5 years)	20,000	
Accumulated depreciation		20,000

After this entry, the book value of the equipment is $80,000; the fair value is $84,000. We use the ratio of the two amounts to adjust both the equipment and the accumulated depreciation accounts (and thus the book value) to fair value ($ in thousands):

December 31, 2021	Before Revaluation					After Revaluation
Equipment	$100	×	$84/80$	=		$105
Accumulated depreciation	20	×	$84/80$	=		21
Book value	$ 80	×	$84/80$	=		$ 84

(continued)

---
[9]"Property, Plant and Equipment," *International Accounting Standard No. 16* (IASCF), as amended effective January 1, 2018.

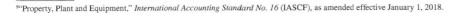

(concluded)

The entries to revalue the equipment and the accumulated depreciation accounts (and thus the book value) are as follows:

To record the revaluation of equipment to its fair value.

(b) Equipment ($105,000 − $100,000)	5,000	
Accumulated depreciation ($21,000 − $20,000)		1,000
Revaluation surplus—OCI ($84,000 − $80,000)		4,000

The new basis for the equipment is its fair value of $84,000 ($105,000 − $21,000), and the following years' depreciation is based on that amount. Thus, 2022 depreciation would be $84,000 divided by the four remaining years, or $21,000:[10]

(a) Depreciation expense ($84,000 ÷ 4 years)	21,000	
Accumulated depreciation		21,000

After this entry, the accumulated depreciation is $42,000 and the book value of the equipment is $63,000. Let's say the fair value now is $57,000. We use the ratio of the two amounts (fair value of $57,000 divided by book value of $63,000) to adjust both the equipment and the accumulated depreciation accounts (and thus the book value) to fair value ($ in thousands):

December 31, 2022	Before Revaluation				After Revaluation
Equipment	$105	×	$57/63$	=	$95
Accumulated depreciation	42	×	$57/63$	=	38
Book value	$63	×	$57/63$	=	$57

The entries to revalue the equipment and the accumulated depreciation accounts (and thus the book value) are as follows:

(b) Revaluation surplus—OCI ($57,000 − $63,000 = $6,000; limit:		
$4,000 balance)	4,000	
Revaluation expense (to balance)...	2,000	
Accumulated depreciation ($38,000 − $42,000)	4,000	
Equipment ($95,000 − $105,000)		10,000

A decrease in fair value, as occurred in 2022, is expensed unless it reverses a revaluation surplus account relating to the same asset, as in this illustration. So, of the $6,000 decrease in value ($63,000 book value less $57,000 fair value), $4,000 is debited to the previously created revaluation surplus and the remaining $2,000 is recorded as revaluation expense in the income statement.

Investcorp, a provider and manager of alternative investment products headquartered in London, prepares its financial statements according to IFRS. The following disclosure note included in a recent annual report discusses the company's method of valuing its building and certain operating assets.

Premises and Equipment (in part)

The Bank carries its building on freehold land and certain operating assets at revalued amounts, being the fair value of the assets at the date of revaluation less any subsequent accumulated depreciation and subsequent accumulated impairment losses. Any revaluation surplus is credited to the asset revaluation reserve included in equity, except to the extent that it reverses a revaluation decrease of the same asset previously recognized in profit and loss, in which case the increase is recognized in profit or loss. A revaluation deficit is recognized directly in profit or loss, except that a deficit directly offsetting a previous surplus on the same asset is directly offset against the surplus in the asset revaluation reserve.

The revaluation alternative is used infrequently. A recent survey of large companies that prepare their financial statements according to IFRS reports that only 10 of the 160 surveyed companies used the revaluation alternative for at least one asset class.[11]

---

[10]*IAS No. 16* allows companies to choose between the method illustrated here and an alternative. The second method eliminates the entire accumulated depreciation account and adjusts the asset account (equipment in this illustration) to fair value. Using either method the revaluation surplus (or expense) would be the same.

[11]" *IFRS Accounting Trends and Techniques*" (New York, AICPA, 2011), p. 171.

Depletion of Natural Resources

Allocation of the cost of natural resources is called depletion. Because the usefulness of natural resources generally is directly related to the amount of the resources extracted, the activity-based units-of-production method is widely used to calculate periodic depletion. Service life is therefore the estimated amount of natural resource to be extracted (for example, tons of mineral or barrels of oil).

The depletion base is cost less any anticipated residual value. Residual value could be significant if cost includes land that has a value after the natural resource has been extracted.

The example in Illustration 11–10 was first introduced in Chapter 10 in Illustration 10–6.

Depletion of the cost of natural resources usually is determined using the units-of-production method.

● LO11–3

In 2021, Jackson Mining Company has the following five costs related to 500 acres of land in Pennsylvania:

1.	Payment for the right to explore for a coal deposit.	$ 1,000,000
2.	Actual exploration costs for a coal deposit.	800,000
3.	Intangible development costs in digging and constructing the mine shaft.	500,000
4.	Expected cost to restore the land after extraction is completed.*	468,360
		$2,768,360
5.	Purchase of excavation equipment for the project.	$ 600,000

* Determined using the expected cash flow approach.

The company's geologist estimates that 1,000,000 tons of coal will be extracted over a three-year period. After the coal is removed from the site, the excavation equipment will be sold for an anticipated residual value of $60,000. During 2021, 300,000 tons were extracted.

Illustration 11–10

Depletion of Natural Resources

The capitalized cost of the coal mine (natural resource), including the expected restoration costs, is $2,768,360. The $600,000 cost for equipment is capitalized separately. Since there is no residual value to the coal mine, the depletion base equals cost and the depletion rate per ton is calculated as follows:

$$\text{Depletion per ton} = \frac{\text{Depletion base}}{\text{Estimated extractable tons}}$$

$$\text{Depletion per ton} = \frac{\$2,768,360}{1,000,000 \text{ tons}} = \$2.76836 \text{ per ton}$$

For each ton of coal extracted, $2.76836 in depletion is recorded. In 2021, the following journal entry records depletion for the 300,000 tons of coal actually extracted.

Depletion ($2.76836 × 300,000 tons)..	830,508	
Coal mine...		830,508

Notice that the credit is to the asset, coal mine, rather than to a contra account, accumulated depletion. Although this approach is traditional, the use of a contra account is acceptable.

Depletion is a product cost and is included in the cost of the inventory of coal, just as the depreciation on manufacturing equipment is included in inventory cost. The depletion is then included in cost of goods sold in the income statement when the coal is sold.

What about depreciation on the $600,000 cost of excavation equipment? If the equipment can be moved from the site and used on future projects, the equipment's depreciable base should be allocated over its useful life. If the asset is not movable, as in our illustration, then it should be depreciated over its useful life or the life of the natural resource, whichever is shorter.

590   SECTION 2   Assets

> The units-of-production method often is used to determine depreciation and amortization on assets used in the extraction of natural resources.

Quite often, companies use the units-of-production method to calculate depreciation and amortization on assets used in the extraction of natural resources. The activity base used is the same as that used to calculate depletion, the estimated recoverable natural resource. In our illustration, the depreciation rate would be $0.54 per ton, calculated as follows.

$$\text{Depreciation per ton} = \$0.54 \text{ per ton} = \frac{\$600,000 - \$60,000}{1,000,000 \text{ tons}}$$

In 2021, depreciation of $162,000 ($0.54 × 300,000 tons) is recorded and also included as part of the cost of the coal inventory.

The summary of significant accounting policies disclosure accompanying recent financial statements of **ConocoPhilips** shown in Illustration 11–11 provides a good summary of depletion, amortization, and depreciation for natural resource properties.

Illustration 11–11

Depletion Method Disclosure—ConocoPhilips

Real World Financials

Summary of Significant Accounting Policies (in part)

Depletion and Amortization—Leasehold costs of producing properties are depleted using the units-of-production method based on estimated proved oil and gas reserves. Amortization of intangible development costs is based on the units-of-production method using estimated proved developed oil and gas reserves.

Depreciation and Amortization—Depreciation and amortization of PP&E on producing hydrocarbon properties and certain pipeline assets (those which are expected to have a declining utilization pattern), are determined by the units-of-production method. Depreciation and amortization of all other PP&E are determined by either the individual-unit-straight-line method or the group-straight-line method (for those individual units that are highly integrated with other units).

Source: ConocoPhilips

Additional Consideration

Percentage Depletion

Depletion of cost less residual value required by GAAP should not be confused with percentage depletion (also called *statutory depletion*) allowable for income tax purposes for oil, gas, and most mineral natural resources. Under these tax provisions, a producer is allowed to deduct the greater of cost-based depletion or a fixed percentage of gross income as depletion expense. Over the life of the asset, depletion could exceed the asset's cost. The percentage allowed for percentage-based depletion varies according to the type of natural resource.

Because percentage depletion usually differs from cost depletion, a difference between taxable income and financial reporting income before tax results. Differences between taxable income and financial reporting income are discussed in Chapter 16.

International Financial Reporting Standards

Biological Assets. Living animals and plants, including the trees in a timber tract or in a fruit orchard, are referred to as *biological assets*. Under U.S. GAAP, a timber tract is valued at cost less accumulated depletion and a fruit orchard at cost less accumulated depreciation. Under IFRS, biological assets are valued at their fair value less estimated costs to sell, with changes in fair value included in the calculation of net income.[12]

● LO11–10

(continued)

---

[12]"Agriculture," *International Accounting Standard No. 41* (IASCF), as amended effective January 1, 2018.

> (concluded)
>
> **Mondi Limited**, an international paper and packing group headquartered in Johannesburg, South Africa, prepares its financial statements according to IFRS. The following disclosure note included in a recent annual report discusses the company's policy for valuing its forestry assets.
>
> **Owned Forestry Assets (in part)**
> Owned forestry assets are measured at fair value, calculated by applying the expected selling price, less costs to harvest and deliver, to the estimated volume of timber on hand at each reporting date.
>
>   Changes in fair value are recognized in the combined and consolidated income statement within other net operating expenses.

Amortization of Intangible Assets

Let's turn now to a third type of long-lived asset—intangible assets. As with other assets we have discussed, we allocate the cost of an intangible asset over its service or useful life. The allocation of intangible asset cost is called amortization. Below we distinguish those intangible assets with *finite* versus *indefinite* useful lives. Intangible assets with finite useful lives will be amortized, and those with indefinite useful lives will not be amortized.

● LO11–4

Intangible Assets Subject to Amortization

Most intangible assets have a finite useful life. This means their estimated useful life is limited in nature. We allocate the capitalized cost less any estimated residual value of an intangible asset to the periods in which the asset is expected to contribute to the company's revenue-generating activities. This requires that we determine the asset's useful life, its amortization base (cost less estimated residual value), and the appropriate allocation method, similar to our depreciating tangible assets.

The cost of an intangible asset with a *finite* useful life is *amortized*.

USEFUL LIFE   Legal, regulatory, or contractual provisions often limit the useful life of an intangible asset. On the other hand, useful life might sometimes be less than the asset's legal or contractual life. For example, the useful life of a patent would be considerably less than its legal life of 20 years if obsolescence were expected to limit the longevity of a protected product.

RESIDUAL VALUE   We discussed the cost of intangible assets in Chapter 10. The expected residual value of an intangible asset usually is zero. This might not be the case, though, if at the end of its useful life to the reporting entity the asset will benefit another entity. For example, if Quadra Corp. has a commitment from another company to purchase one of Quadra's patents at the end of its useful life at a determinable price, we use that price as the patent's residual value.

ALLOCATION METHOD   The method of amortization should reflect the pattern of use of the asset in generating benefits. Most companies use the straight-line method to calculate amortization expense. Intel Corporation reported several intangible assets in a recent balance sheet. A note, shown in Illustration 11–12, disclosed the range of estimated useful lives.

Like depletion, amortization expense traditionally is credited to the asset account itself rather than to accumulated amortization. However, the use of a contra account is acceptable. Many companies choose to report intangible assets for their net amount on the face of the balance sheet and then report the amount of amortization in a disclosure note. Let's look at an example in Illustration 11–13A.

Similar to depreciation, amortization is either a product cost or a period cost depending on the use of the asset. For intangibles used in the manufacture of a product, amortization is a product cost and is included in the cost of inventory (and doesn't become an expense until the inventory is sold). For intangible assets not used in production, such as the franchise cost in our illustration, periodic amortization is expensed in the period incurred.

Illustration 11–12

Intangible Asset Useful
Life Disclosure—Intel
Corporation

Real World Financials

Summary of Significant Accounting Policies (in part)
Identified Intangible Assets (in part)
The estimated useful life ranges for identified intangible assets that are subject to amortization
are as follows:

(in years)	Estimated Useful Life
Acquisition-related developed technology	3 – 9
Acquisition-related customer relationships	5 – 11
Acquisition-related brands	5 – 8
Licensed technology and patents	2 – 17

Source: Intel Corporation

Illustration 11–13A

Amortization of
Intangibles—Franchise and
Patent

Hollins Corporation began operations in 2021. Early in January, the company purchased the
following two intangible assets:

1. A franchise from Ajax Industries for $200,000. The franchise agreement is for a period
   of 10 years.
2. A patent for $50,000. The remaining legal life of the patent is 13 years. However, due
   to expected technological obsolescence, the company estimates that the useful life of
   the patent is only 8 years.

Hollins uses the straight-line amortization method for all intangible assets. The company's
fiscal year-end is December 31.

The journal entries to record a full year of amortization each year for these intangible
assets are as follows:

Amortization expense ($200,000 ÷ 10 years).................	20,000	
Franchise		20,000
To record amortization of franchise.		
Amortization expense ($50,000 ÷ 8 years)	6,250	
Patent..		6,250
To record amortization of patent.		

Hollins decided to sell the patent on December 31, 2025 (five years after acquisition), for
$21,000. Hollins had recorded annual amortization in each of the four prior years (2021-2024).

The journal entries to update amortization of the patent in 2025 and to sell the patent are
as follows:

Amortization expense ($50,000 ÷ 8 years)	6,250	
Patent		6,250
To record amortization of patent in 2025.		
Cash...	21,000	
Patent (account balance)*...		18,750
Gain on sale of patent (selling price – book value)		2,250
To record sale of patent.		

*$50,000 – ($6,250 × 5 years)

In Chapter 10 we discussed that any software development costs incurred after the point
of technological feasibility and before the product is available for sale are capitalized. These
capitalized software development costs are amortized based on whichever of the following
two methods produces a *greater* amount:

1. The ratio of current revenues to current and anticipated revenues (percentage of revenue
   method), or
2. The straight-line method based on the estimated useful life of the asset.

To see an example, let's look at Illustration 11–13B.

The Astro Corporation develops computer software graphics programs for sale. A new development project started in 2020 and reached the point of technological feasibility on June 30, 2021. Costs in 2021 were as follows:

Prior to June 30, 2021... $1,200,000
From June 30 to December 31, 2021 800,000

The software was available for sale on January 1, 2022, and has the following related sales information:

Sales in 2022 .... $ 3,000,000
Estimated sales in 2023–2025.. 7,000,000

Total estimates sales over four years... $10,000,000

In 2021, Astro Corporation would expense the $1,200,000 in costs incurred prior to the establishment of technological feasibility and capitalize the $800,000 in costs incurred between technological feasibility and the product availability date. In 2022, amortization of the intangible asset, software development costs, is calculated as follows:

1. **Percentage-of-revenue method:**

$$\frac{\$3,000,000}{\$3,000,000 + \$7,000,000} = 30\% \times \$800,000 = \$240,000$$

2. **Straight-line method:**

$$\frac{1}{4} \text{ or } 25\% \times \$800,000 = \$200,000.$$

The percentage-of-revenue method is used because it produces the greater amortization, $240,000.

Amortization expense (above) 240,000
   Software development costs 240,000
To record amortization of software development costs in 2022.

Illustration 11–13B

Amortization of Intangibles—Software Development Costs for External Purposes

    The capitalized cost of software developed for internal purposes or as part of cloud computing arrangements is amortized over the software's expected useful life, generally using straight-line amortization.

International Financial Reporting Standards

Software Development Costs. The percentage we use to amortize computer software development costs under U.S. GAAP is the greater of (1) the ratio of current revenues to current and anticipated revenues or (2) the straight-line percentage over the useful life of the software. This approach is allowed under IFRS, but not required. Amortization under IFRS typically occurs over the useful life of the software, based on the pattern of benefits, with straight-line as the default.

● LO11–9

Intangible Assets Not Subject to Amortization

Intangible assets with an indefinite useful life are those with no foreseeable limit on the period of time over which the asset is expected to contribute to the cash flows of the entity.[13] In other words, there are no legal, contractual, or economic factors that are expected to limit their useful life to a company. Because of their indefinite lives, these intangible assets are not subject to periodic amortization.

    For example, suppose Collins Corporation acquired a trademark in conjunction with the acquisition of a tire company. Collins plans to continue to produce the line of tires marketed under the acquired company's trademark. Recall from our discussion in Chapter 10 that

The cost of an intangible asset with an indefinite *useful life is* not *amortized.*

Trademarks or tradenames often are considered to have indefinite useful lives.

---

[13]FASB ASC 350–30–35–4: Intangibles–Goodwill and Other–General Intangibles Other than Goodwill–Subsequent Measurement.

trademarks have a legal life of 10 years, but the registration can be renewed for an indefinite number of 10-year periods. Therefore, the life of the purchased trademark is initially considered to be indefinite and the cost of the trademark is not amortized. However, if after several years management decides to phase out production of the tire line over the next three years, Collins would amortize the remaining book value over a three-year period.

In 2017, Boeing Company reported indefinite-lived intangible assets (other than goodwill) of $490 million. These indefinite-lived intangibles consist of brand and trade names acquired in business combinations. Illustration 11–14 provides another example in a disclosure made by The Estee Lauder Companies Inc., in a recent annual report.

Illustration 11–14

Indefinite-Life Intangibles Disclosure—The Estee Lauder Companies Inc.

Real World Financials

> **Other Intangible Assets**
>
> Indefinite-lived intangible assets (e.g., trademarks) are not subject to amortization and are assessed at least annually for impairment during the fiscal fourth quarter, or more frequently if certain events or circumstances warrant.
>
> Source: The Estee Lauder Companies Inc.

Goodwill is an intangible asset whose cost is *not* expensed through periodic amortization.

Goodwill is the most common intangible asset with an indefinite useful life. Recall that goodwill is measured as the difference between the purchase price of a company and the fair value of all of the identifiable net assets acquired (tangible and intangible assets minus the fair value of liabilities assumed). Does this mean that goodwill and other intangible assets with indefinite useful lives will remain in a company's balance sheet at their original capitalized values indefinitely? Not necessarily. Like other assets, intangibles are subject to the impairment rules we discuss in a subsequent section of this chapter.

International Financial Reporting Standards

● LO11–10

> **Valuation of Intangible Assets.** *IAS No. 38* allows a company to value an intangible asset subsequent to initial valuation at (1) cost less accumulated amortization or (2) fair value, if fair value can be determined by reference to an active market.[14] If revaluation is chosen, all assets within that class of intangibles must be revalued on a regular basis. Goodwill, however, cannot be revalued. U.S. GAAP prohibits revaluation of any intangible asset.
>
> Notice that the revaluation option is possible only if fair value can be determined by reference to an active market, making the option relatively uncommon. However, the option possibly could be used for intangibles such as franchises and certain license agreements.
>
> If the revaluation option is chosen, the accounting treatment is similar to the way we applied the revaluation option for property, plant, and equipment earlier in this chapter. Recall that the way the company reports the difference between fair value and book value depends on which amount is higher. If fair value is higher than book value, the difference is reported as other comprehensive income (OCI) and then accumulates in a revaluation surplus account in equity. On the other hand, if book value is higher than fair value, the difference is expensed after reducing any existing revaluation surplus for that asset.
>
> Consider the following illustration:
>
> Amershan LTD. prepares its financial statements according to IFRS. At the beginning of its 2021 fiscal year, the company purchased a franchise for $500,000. The franchise has a 10-year contractual life and no residual value, so amortization in 2021 is $50,000. The company does not use an accumulated amortization account and credits the franchise account directly when amortization is recorded. At the end of the year, Amershan chooses to revalue the franchise as permitted by *IAS No. 38*. Assuming that the fair value of the
>
> (continued)

---

[14] "Intangible Assets," *International Accounting Standard No. 38* (IASCF), as amended effective January 1, 2018.

(concluded)

franchise at year-end, determined by reference to an active market, is $600,000, Amershan records amortization and the revaluation using the following journal entries:

Amortization expense ($500,000 ÷ 10 years)	50,000	
Franchise		50,000
Franchise ($600,000 − $450,000)	150,000	
Revaluation surplus—OCI		50,000

To record the revaluation of franchise to its fair value.

With the second entry Amershan increases the book value of the franchise from $450,000 ($500,000 − $50,000) to its fair value of $600,000 and records a revaluation surplus for the difference. The new basis for the franchise is its fair value of $600,000, and the following years' amortization is based on that amount. Thus, 2022 amortization would be $600,000 divided by the nine remaining years, or $66,667.

Concept Review Exercise

Part A:

DEPLETION AND AMORTIZATION

On March 29, 2021, the Horizon Energy Corporation purchased the mineral rights to a coal deposit in New Mexico for $2 million. Development costs and the present value of estimated land restoration costs totaled an additional $3.4 million. The company removed 200,000 tons of coal during 2021 and estimated that an additional 1,600,000 tons would be removed over the next 15 months.

Required:
Compute depletion on the mine for 2021.

Solution:

Cost of Coal Mine:	($ in millions)
Purchase price of mineral rights	$2.0
Development and restoration costs	3.4
	$5.4

Depletion:

$$\text{Depletion per ton} = \frac{\$5.4 \text{ million}}{1.8 \text{ million tons}^*} = \$3 \text{ per ton}$$

*200,000 + 1,600,000

$$2021 \text{ depletion} = \$3 \times 200,000 \text{ tons} = \$600,000$$

Part B:

On October 1, 2021, Advanced Micro Circuits, Inc., completed the purchase of Zotec Corporation for $200 million. Included in the allocation of the purchase price were the following identifiable intangible assets ($ in millions), along with the fair values and estimated useful lives:

Intangible Asset	Fair value	Useful Life (in years)
Patent	$10	5
Developed technology	50	4
Customer list	10	2

In addition, the fair value of acquired tangible assets was $100 million. Goodwill was valued at $30 million. Straight-line amortization is used for all purchased intangibles.

During 2021, Advanced finished work on a software development project. Development costs incurred after technological feasibility was achieved and before the product release date totaled $2 million. The software was available for release to the general public on September 29, 2021. At that time, the company estimates that the software will generate total revenue of $40 million over four years. For the final three months of 2021, revenue from the sale of the software was $4 million.

Required:

Compute amortization for purchased intangibles and software development costs for 2021.

Solution:

Amortization of Purchased Intangibles:

Patent	\$10 million / 5 = \$2 million × $^3/_{12}$ year = **\$0.5 million**
Developed technology	\$50 million / 4 = \$12.5 million × $^3/_{12}$ year = **\$3.125 million**
Customer list	\$10 million / 2 = \$5 million × $^3/_{12}$ year = **\$1.25 million**
Goodwill	The cost of goodwill is not amortized.

Amortization of Software Development Costs:

(1) Percentage-of-revenue method:

$$\$2 \text{ million} \times \frac{\$4 \text{ million}}{\$40 \text{ million}} \text{ or } 10\% = \$200,000$$

(2) Straight-line:

$$\$2 \text{ million} \times \frac{3 \text{ months}}{48 \text{ months}} \text{ or } 6.25\% = \$125,000$$

Advanced will use the percentage-of-revenue method since it produces the greater amortization, \$200,000.

PART B

Additional Issues

In this part of the chapter, we discuss the following issues related to cost allocation:

1. Change in estimates
2. Change in method
3. Error correction
4. Impairment of value

Change in Estimates

● LO11–5

The calculation of depreciation, depletion, or amortization requires estimates of both service life and residual value. It's inevitable that at least some estimates will prove incorrect. Chapter 4 briefly introduced the topic of changes in estimates along with coverage of changes in accounting principles and the correction of errors. Here and in subsequent sections of this chapter, we provide overviews of the accounting treatment and disclosures required for these changes and errors when they involve property, plant, and equipment and intangible assets.

> A change in estimate should be reflected in the financial statements of the current period and future periods.

Changes in estimates are accounted for prospectively. When a company revises a previous estimate based on new information, prior financial statements are not restated. Instead, the company merely incorporates the new estimate in any related accounting determinations from then on. So, it usually will affect some aspects of both the balance sheet and the income statement in the current and future periods. Companies typically make these changes at the beginning of the year of the change, but they could be made at other times. A disclosure note should describe the effect of a change in estimate on net income and per share amounts for the current period.

Consider the example in Illustration 11–15.

The asset's book value is depreciated down to the anticipated residual value of \$22,000 at the end of the revised eight-year service life. In addition, a note discloses the effect of the change in estimate on income, if material. The before-tax effect is an increase in income of \$18,000 (depreciation of \$42,000 if the change had not been made, less \$24,000 depreciation after the change).

On January 1, 2019, the Hogan Manufacturing Company purchased a machine for $250,000. At the time of purchase, the company estimated the following:

1. Service life of the machine to be five years.
2. Residual value to be $40,000.

On January 1, 2021 (two years later), the company revised its estimates as follows:

1. Service life from a total of **five to eight years.**
2. Residual value from **$40,000 to $22,000.**

The company's fiscal year-end is December 31 and the straight-line depreciation method is used for all depreciable assets.

Prior to the revision (2019 and 2020), depreciation was $42,000 per year [($250,000 − $40,000) ÷ 5 years] or $84,000 for the two years. The remaining book value at the beginning of 2021 is $166,000 ($250,000 − $84,000). Depreciation for 2021 and subsequent years is determined by allocating the remaining book value less the revised residual value equally over the remaining service life of six years (8 total years − 2 years completed). Depreciation for 2021 and subsequent years is recorded as follows:

Depreciation expense (below)...	24,000	
Accumulated depreciation..		24,000

	$250,000	Cost
$42,000		Previous annual depreciation ($210,000 ÷ 5 years)
× 2 years	(84,000)	Less: Depreciation to date (2019–2020)
	166,000	Book value as of January 1, 2021
	(22,000)	Less: Revised residual value
	144,000	Revised depreciable base
	÷ 6	Estimated remaining life (8 years − 2 years)
	$ 24,000	New annual depreciation

Illustration 11–15

Change in Accounting Estimate

Verizon Communications Inc. recently revised its estimates of the service lives of certain property, plant, and equipment. Illustration 11–16 shows the note that disclosed the change.

Plant and Depreciation (in part)

In connection with our ongoing review of the estimated useful lives of plant, property and equipment during 2016, we determined that the average useful lives of certain leasehold improvements would be increased from 5 to 7 years. This change resulted in a decrease to depreciation expense of $0.2 billion in 2016. We determined that changes were also necessary to the remaining estimated useful lives of certain assets as a result of technology upgrades, enhancements, and planned retirements. These changes resulted in an increase in depreciation expense of $0.3 billion, $0.4 billion and $0.6 billion in 2016, 2015 and 2014, respectively. While the timing and extent of current deployment plans are subject to ongoing analysis and modification, we believe the current estimates of useful lives are reasonable.

Source: Verizon Communications Inc.

Illustration 11–16

Change in Estimate Disclosure—Verizon Communications Inc.

Real World Financials

Change in Depreciation, Amortization, or Depletion Method

Generally accepted accounting principles allow a company to change from one depreciation method to another if the company can justify the change. For example, new information might become available to suggest that a different depreciation method would better represent the pattern of the asset's consumption relative to revenue production.

We account for these changes prospectively, exactly as we would any other change in estimate. One difference is that most changes in estimate do not require a company to justify the change. However, this change in estimate is a result of changing an accounting principle and therefore requires a clear justification as to why the new method is preferable. Consider the example in Illustration 11–17.

Changes in depreciation, amortization, or depletion methods are accounted for the same way as a change in accounting estimate.

● LO11–6

Illustration 11–17

Change in Depreciation Method

On January 1, 2019, the Hogan Manufacturing Company purchased a machine for $250,000. The company expects the service life of the machine to be five years and its anticipated residual value to be $30,000. The company's fiscal year-end is December 31 and the double-declining-balance (DDB) depreciation method is used. During 2021, the company switched from the DDB to the straight-line method. In 2021, the adjusting entry is

| Depreciation expense (below) | 20,000 | |
| Accumulated depreciation | | 20,000 |

DDB depreciation:
2019 $100,000 ($250,000 × 40%*)
2020   60,000 [($250,000 − $100,000) × 40%*]
Total $160,000

*Double the straight-line rate for 5 years [(⅕ = 20%) × 2 = 40%]

$ 250,000	Cost
(160,000)	Less: Depreciation to date, DDB (2019–2020)
90,000	Undepreciated cost as of January 1, 2021
(30,000)	Less: Residual value
60,000	Depreciable base
÷3 yrs.	Remaining life (5 years − 2 years)
$ 20,000	New annual depreciation, straight-line

A disclosure note reports the effect of the change on net income and earnings per share along with clear justification for changing depreciation methods.

Illustration 11–18 shows a disclosure note describing a recent change in depreciation method made by **Agrium Inc.**

Illustration 11–18

Change in Depreciation Method—Agrium Inc.

Real World Financials

Accounting standards and policy changes (in part)

We changed the method of depreciation from the straight-line basis to the units of production basis for our potash facility mining and milling assets beginning January 1, 2015, and our nitrogen and phosphate mining and plant assets beginning October 1, 2015. The change in method of depreciation reflects anticipated changes to our production schedule due to facility expansions, volatility in market conditions, and the frequency and duration of plant turnarounds. The current and expected reduction in depreciation expense is 2015 − $30 million and 2016 − $7 million.

Source: Agrium Inc.

Frequently, when a company changes depreciation method, the change will be effective only for assets placed in service after that date. Of course, that means depreciation schedules do not require revision because the change does not affect assets depreciated in prior periods. A disclosure note still is required to provide justification for the change and to report the effect of the change on the current year's income.

Error Correction

● LO11–7   Errors involving property, plant, and equipment and intangible assets include computational errors in the calculation of depreciation, depletion, or amortization and mistakes made in determining whether expenditures should be capitalized or expensed. These errors can affect many years. For example, let's say a major addition to equipment should be capitalized but incorrectly is expensed. Not only is income in the year of the error understated, but subsequent years' income is overstated because depreciation is omitted.

Recall from our discussion of inventory errors in Chapter 9 that if a material error is discovered in an accounting period subsequent to the period in which the error is made, any previous years' financial statements that were incorrect as a result of the error are retrospectively restated to reflect the correction. Any account balances that are incorrect as a result of the error are corrected by journal entry. If retained earnings is one of the incorrect accounts, the correction is reported as a *prior period adjustment* to the beginning balance in the statement of shareholders' equity.[15] In addition, a disclosure note is needed to describe the nature of the error and the impact of its correction on net income and earnings per share.

Here is a summary of the treatment of material errors occurring in a previous year:

- Previous years' financial statements are retrospectively restated.
- Account balances are corrected.
- If retained earnings requires correction, the correction is reported as a prior period adjustment.
- A note describes the nature of the error and the impact of the correction on income.

Consider Illustration 11–19.

Illustration 11–19
Error Correction

In 2021, the controller of the Hathaway Corporation discovered an error in recording $300,000 in legal fees to successfully defend a patent infringement suit in 2019. The $300,000 was charged to legal fee expense but should have been capitalized and amortized over the five-year remaining life of the patent. Straight-line amortization is used by Hathaway for all intangibles.

Sometimes, the analysis is easier if you re-create the entries actually recorded incorrectly and those that would have been recorded if the error hadn't occurred, and then compare them.

	Correct **(Should Have Been Recorded)**		**Incorrect** **(As Recorded)**	
2019 Patent	300,000		Legal fee expense	300,000	
Cash		300,000	Cash		300,000
2019 Expense	60,000		Amortization entry omitted	
Patent		60,000		
2020 Expense	60,000		Amortization entry omitted	
Patent		60,000		

During the two-year period (2019 and 2020), amortization expense was *understated* by $120,000, but legal fee expenses were *overstated* by $300,000, so net income during the period was *understated* by $180,000 (ignoring income taxes). This means retained earnings by the end of 2020 is *understated* by $180,000. Patent is understated by $180,000. To correct each of these accounts in 2021, we need the following entry:

Patent	180,000	
Retained earnings		180,000
To correct incorrect accounts.		

Because retained earnings is one of the accounts incorrect as a result of the error, a correction to that account of $180,000 is reported as a prior period adjustment to the 2021 beginning retained earnings balance in Hathaway's comparative statements of shareholders' equity. Assuming that 2020 is included with 2021 in the comparative statements, a correction would be made to the 2020 beginning retained earnings balance as well. That prior period adjustment, though, would be for the pre-2020 difference: $300,000 − $60,000 = $240,000.

The 2019 and 2020 balance sheet and income statement that were incorrect as a result of the error are *retrospectively restated* to report the addition to the patent and to reflect the correct amount of amortization expense, assuming both statements are reported again for comparative purposes in the 2021 annual report.

---

[15]The prior period adjustment is applied to beginning retained earnings for the year following the error, or for the earliest year being reported in the comparative financial statements when the error occurs prior to the earliest year presented. The retained earnings balances in years after the first year also are adjusted to what those balances would be if the error had not occurred, but a company may choose not to explicitly report those adjustments as separate line items.

Also, a disclosure note accompanying Hathaway's 2021 financial statements should describe the nature of the error and the impact of its correction on each year's net income (understated by $240,000 in 2019 and overstated by $60,000 in 2020), and earnings per share.

Chapter 20 provides in-depth coverage of changes in estimates and methods, and of accounting errors. We cover the tax effect of these changes and errors in that chapter.

Impairment of Value

Depreciation, depletion, and amortization reflect a gradual consumption of the benefits inherent in property, plant, and equipment and intangible assets. An implicit assumption in allocating the cost of an asset over its useful life is that there has been no significant reduction in the anticipated total benefits or service potential of the asset. Situations can arise, however, that cause a significant decline or impairment of those benefits or service potential. An extreme case would be the destruction of a plant asset—say a building destroyed by fire—before the asset is fully depreciated. The remaining book value of the asset in that case should be written off as a loss. Sometimes, though, the impairment of future value is more subtle.

The way we recognize and measure an impairment loss differs depending on whether the assets are classified as (1) held and used or (2) held for sale. Accounting is different, too, for assets with finite lives and those with indefinite lives. We consider those differences now.

Assets Held and Used

An increasingly common occurrence in practice is the partial write-down of property, plant, and equipment and intangible assets that remain in use. For example, in 2016, Murphy Oil Corporation recorded impairment charges of $95 million. The charges reflect the decline in asset values associated with lower oil and gas prices.

An asset held for use should be written down if there has been a significant impairment of value.

Conceptually, there is considerable merit for a policy requiring the write-down of an asset when there has been a significant decline in value. A write-down can provide important information about the future cash flows that a company can generate from using the asset. However, in practice, this process is very subjective. Even if it appears certain that significant impairment of value has occurred, it often is difficult to measure the amount of the required write-down.

For example, let's say a company purchased $2,000,000 of equipment to be used in the production of a new type of laser printer. Depreciation is determined using the straight-line method over a useful life of six years and the residual value is estimated at $200,000. At the beginning of year 3, the machine's book value has been depreciated to $1,400,000 [$2,000,000 − ($300,000 × 2)]. At that time, new technology is developed causing a significant reduction in the selling price of the new laser printer as well as a reduction in anticipated demand for the product. Management estimates that the equipment will be useful for only two more years and will have no significant residual value.

This situation is not simply a matter of a change in the estimates of useful life and residual value. Management must decide if the events occurring in year 3 warrant a write-down of the asset below $1,400,000. A write-down would be appropriate if the company decided that it would be unable to fully recover this amount through future use.

For assets to be held and used, different guidelines apply to (1) property, plant, and equipment and intangible assets with finite useful lives (subject to depreciation, depletion, or amortization) and (2) intangible assets with indefinite useful lives (not subject to amortization).

PROPERTY, PLANT, AND EQUIPMENT AND FINITE-LIFE INTANGIBLE ASSETS

Generally accepted accounting principles provide guidelines for when to recognize and how to measure impairment losses of long-lived tangible assets and intangible assets with finite useful lives.[16] For purposes of this recognition and measurement, assets are grouped at the

[16]FASB ASC 360–10–35–15 through 25: Property, Plant, and Equipment—Overall—Subsequent Measurement—Impairment or Disposal of Long-Lived Assets.

lowest level for which identifiable cash flows are largely independent of the cash flows of other assets. In simpler terms, assets should not be grouped for determining impairment unless those assets are dependent on one another. Determining which assets can or cannot be grouped requires considerable judgment by management.

When to Test for Impairment.   It would be impractical to test all assets or asset groups for impairment at the end of every reporting period. GAAP requires investigation of possible impairment only *if events or changes in circumstances indicate that the book value of the asset or asset group may not be recoverable.* This might happen from the following:

> *Property, plant, and equipment and finite-life intangible assets are tested for impairment only when events or changes in circumstances indicate book value may not be recoverable.*

   a. A significant decrease in market price.
   b. A significant adverse change in how the asset is being used or in its physical condition.
   c. A significant adverse change in legal factors or in the business climate.
   d. An accumulation of costs significantly higher than the amount originally expected for the acquisition or construction of an asset.
   e. A current-period loss combined with a history of losses or a projection of continuing losses associated with the asset.
   f. A realization that the asset will be disposed of significantly before the end of its esti-mated useful life.[17]

Determining whether an impairment loss has occurred and for how much to record the loss is a two-step process.

Step 1   **Recoverability Test.** An impairment occurs when the undiscounted sum of estimated future cash flows from an asset is less than the asset's book value.
Step 2   **Measurement.** If the recoverability test from step 1 indicates an impairment has occurred, an impairment loss is recorded for the amount by which the asset's fair value is less than its book value.

For step 2, fair value is the amount at which the asset could be bought or sold in a current transaction between willing parties. Quoted market prices could be used if they're available. If fair value is not determinable, it must be estimated.

If an impairment loss is recognized, the written-down book value becomes the new cost base for future cost allocation. Later recovery of an impairment loss is prohibited.

The process is best described by an example. Consider Illustration 11–20.

The Dakota Corporation operates several factories that manufacture medical equipment. Near the end of the company's 2021 fiscal year, a change in business climate related to a competitor's innovative products indicated to management that the $170 million book value (original cost of $300 million less accumulated depreciation of $130 million) of the assets of one of Dakota's factories may not be recoverable.

Management is able to identify cash flows from this factory and estimates that future cash flows over the remaining useful life of the factory will be $150 million. The fair value of the factory's assets is not readily available but is estimated to be $135 million.

Change in circumstances. A change in the business climate related to a competitor's innovative products requires Dakota to investigate for possible impairment.

Step 1. Recoverability Test. Because the undiscounted future cash flows of $150 million are less than book value of $170 million, an impairment loss is indicated.

(continued)

Illustration 11–20

Impairment Loss—Property, Plant, and Equipment

---

[17]FASB ASC 360–10–35–21: Property, Plant, and Equipment—Overall—Subsequent Measurement—Impairment or Disposal of Long-Lived Assets.

(concluded)

Step 2. Measurement of impairment loss. The impairment loss is $35 million, determined as follows:

($ in millions)		
Fair value		$ 135
Less: Book value		
Original cost	$ 300	
Accumulated depreciation	(130)	(170)
Impairment loss		$ (35)

The entry to record the loss is ($ in millions):

Loss on impairment (above)	35	
Accumulated depreciation (reduce to zero)	130	
Factory assets (decrease to fair value; $300 − $135)......................		165

The loss normally is reported in the income statement as a separate component of operating expenses.

In the entry in Illustration 11–20, we reduce accumulated depreciation to zero and decrease the cost base of the assets by $165 million (from book value of $300 million to fair value of $135 million). The new carrying value of $135 million serves as the revised basis for subsequent depreciation over the remaining useful life of the assets, just as if the assets had been acquired on the impairment date for their fair values.

Because the fair value of the factory assets was not readily available to Dakota in Illustration 11–20, the $135 million had to be estimated. One method that can be used to estimate fair value is to compute the discounted present value of future cash flows expected from the asset. Keep in mind that we use *undiscounted* estimates of cash flows in step 1 to determine whether an impairment loss is indicated, but *discounted* estimates of cash flows in step 2 to determine the amount of the loss. In calculating present value, either a traditional approach or an expected cash flow approach can be used. The traditional approach is to incorporate risk and uncertainty into the discount rate. Recall from discussions in previous chapters that the expected cash flow approach incorporates risk and uncertainty instead into a determination of a probability-weighted cash flow expectation, and then discounts this expected cash flow using a risk-free interest rate. We discussed and illustrated the expected cash flow approach in previous chapters.

A disclosure note is needed to describe the impairment loss. The note should include a description of the impaired asset or asset group, the facts and circumstances leading to the impairment, the amount of the loss if not separately disclosed on the face of the income statement, and the method used to determine fair value.

Macy's, Inc., is a department store chain providing brand-name clothing, accessories, home furnishings, and housewares. Illustration 11–21 shows the company's disclosure notes describing recent impairment losses. The notes also provide a summary of the process used to identify and measure impairment losses for property, plant, and equipment and finite-life intangible assets.

The present value of future cash flows often is used as a measure of fair value.

Illustration 11–21

Asset Impairment Disclosure—Macy's, Inc.

Real World Financials

Property and Equipment (in part)

The carrying values of long-lived assets are periodically reviewed by the Company whenever events or changes in circumstances indicate that the carrying value may not be recoverable, such as historical operating losses or plans to close stores before the end of their previously estimated useful lives. Additionally, on an annual basis, the recoverability of the carrying values of individual stores are evaluated. A potential impairment has occurred if projected

(continued)

(concluded)

future undiscounted cash flows are less than the carrying value of the assets. The estimate of cash flows includes management's assumptions of cash inflows and outflows directly resulting from the use of those assets in operations. When a potential impairment has occurred, an impairment write-down is recorded if the carrying value of the long-lived asset exceeds its fair value.

Impairments, Store Closing and Other Costs (in part)

As a result of the Company's projected undiscounted future cash flows related to certain store locations and other assets being less than their carrying value, the Company recorded impairment charges, including properties that were the subject of announced store closings. The fair values of these assets were calculated based on the projected cash flows and an estimated risk-adjusted rate of return that would be used by market participants in valuing these assets or based on prices of similar assets. During 2016, long-lived assets held and used with a carrying value of $405 million were written down to their fair value of $147 million, resulting in asset impairment charges of $258 million.

Source: Macy's, Inc.

International Financial Reporting Standards

Impairment of Value: Property, Plant, and Equipment and Finite-Life Intangible Assets.
Highlighted below are some important differences in accounting for impairment of value for property, plant, and equipment and finite-life intangible assets between U.S. GAAP and *IAS No. 36.*[18]

● LO11–10

	U.S. GAAP	IFRS
When to Test	When events or changes in circumstances indicate that book value may not be recoverable.	Assets must be assessed for indicators of impairment at the end of each reporting period. Indicators of impairment are similar to U.S. GAAP.
Recoverability	An impairment loss is required when the undiscounted sum of estimated future cash flows from an asset is less than the asset's book value.	There is no equivalent recoverability test. An impairment loss is required when the "recoverable amount" (the higher of the asset's value-in-use and fair value less costs to sell) is less than the asset's book value. An asset's value-in-use is calculated as the present value of estimated future cash flows.
Measurement	The impairment loss is the amount by which fair value is less than book value.	The impairment loss is the amount by which the recoverable amount is less than book value.
Subsequent Reversal of Loss	Prohibited.	Required if the circumstances that caused the impairment are resolved.

Let's look at an illustration highlighting the important differences described above. The Jasmine Tea Company has a factory that has significantly decreased in value due to technological innovations in the industry. Below are data related to the factory's assets:

	($ in millions)
Book value	$18.5
Undiscounted sum of estimated future cash flows	19.0
Value-in-use (present value of future cash flows)	16.0
Fair value less cost to sell (determined by appraisal)	15.5

(continued)

---

[18]"Impairment of Assets," *International Accounting Standard No. 36* (IASCF), as amended effective January 1, 2018.

(concluded)

What amount of impairment loss should Jasmine Tea recognize, if any, under U.S. GAAP? Under IFRS?

U.S. GAAP	There is no impairment loss. The sum of undiscounted estimated future cash flows exceeds the book value.
IFRS	Jasmine should recognize an impairment loss of $2.5 million. Indicators of impairment are present and book value exceeds both value-in-use (present value of cash flows) and fair value less costs to sell. The recoverable amount is $16 million, the higher of value-in-use ($16 million) and fair value less costs to sell ($15.5 million). The impairment loss is the difference between book value of $18.5 million and the $16 million recoverable amount.

Nokia, a Finnish company, prepares its financial statements according to IFRS. The following disclosure note describes the company's impairment policy:

Assessment of the Recoverability of Long-Lived Assets, Intangible Assets, and Goodwill (in part)

The carrying value of identifiable intangible assets and long-lived assets is assessed if events or changes in circumstances indicate that such carrying value may not be recoverable. Factors that trigger an impairment review include, but are not limited to, underperformance relative to historical or projected future results, significant changes in the manner of the use of the acquired assets or the strategy for the overall business and significant negative industry or economic trends.

Nokia conducts its impairment testing by determining the recoverable amount for the asset. The recoverable amount of an asset is the higher of its fair value less costs to sell and its value-in-use. The recoverable amount is then compared to the asset's book value and an impairment loss is recognized if the recoverable amount is less than the book value. Impairment losses are recognized immediately in the income statement.

INDEFINITE-LIFE INTANGIBLE ASSETS   Intangible assets with indefinite useful lives should be tested for impairment *annually and more frequently if events or changes in circumstances indicate that it is more likely than not that the asset is impaired.*

A company has the option of first undertaking a qualitative assessment. Companies selecting this option will evaluate relevant events and circumstances to determine whether it is "more likely than not" (a likelihood of more than 50 percent) that the fair value of the asset is less than its book value. Only if that's determined to be the case will the company move forward with measuring the impairment. A list of possible events and circumstances that a company should consider in this qualitative assessment is provided in ASC 350–20–35-3C.

> If fair value is less than book value, an impairment loss is recognized for the difference.

The measurement of an impairment loss for indefinite-life intangible assets is a one-step process. If fair value is less than book value, an impairment loss is recognized for the difference. Notice that we omit the cash flow recoverability test with these assets. Because we anticipate cash flows to continue indefinitely, recoverability is not a good indicator of impairment.[19]

Similar to property, plant, and equipment and finite-life intangible assets, if an impairment loss is recognized, the written-down book value becomes the new cost base for future cost allocation. Recovery of the impairment loss is prohibited. Disclosure requirements also are similar.

---

[19]Until recently, the measurement of impairment for goodwill was a more complicated, two-step process. Step 1 was a recoverability test which involved comparing the fair value of the reporting unit to its book value. If step 1 indicated impairment, step 2 then required calculation of the goodwill's *implied fair value* . The implied fair value was computed as the fair value of the reporting unit minus the fair value of the reporting unit's net assets excluding goodwill. If the implied goodwill was less than the book value of goodwill, an impairment loss was recognized. Accounting Standards Update 2017-04 eliminated step 2 for measurement of impairment for goodwill. Now, the one-step process involves comparing only the fair value of the reporting unit to its book value, as described in the text.

International Financial Reporting Standards

Impairment of Value: Indefinite-Life Intangible Assets. Similar to U.S. GAAP, IFRS requires indefinite-life intangible assets to be tested for impairment at least annually. However, under U.S. GAAP, a company can choose first to provide only a qualitative assessment of the likelihood of impairment to determine if quantitative measurement is then necessary. Also, under U.S. GAAP, the impairment loss is measured as the difference between book value and fair value, while under IFRS the impairment loss is the difference between book value and the recoverable amount. The recoverable amount is the higher of the asset's value-in-use (present value of estimated future cash flows) and fair value less costs to sell.

● LO11–10

IFRS requires the reversal of an impairment loss (other than for goodwill) if the circumstances that caused the impairment are resolved. Reversals are prohibited under U.S. GAAP.

Also, indefinite-life intangible assets may not be combined with other indefinite-life intangible assets for the required annual impairment test. Under U.S. GAAP, though, if certain criteria are met, indefinite-life intangible assets should be combined for the required annual impairment test.

Goodwill.   Recall that goodwill is a unique intangible asset that is recorded only when one company acquires control of another company. Unlike other assets, its cost (a) can't be directly associated with any specific identifiable right and (b) is not separable from the company as a whole. Because of these unique characteristics, we discuss goodwill separately, although conceptually the measurement of impairment for goodwill is the same as for other indefinite-life intangible assets.

For all classifications of assets, we decide whether a write-down due to impairment is required by determining whether the value of an asset has fallen below its book value. However, in this comparison, the value of assets for property, plant, and equipment and finite-life intangible assets is considered to be value-in-use as measured by the sum of undiscounted cash flows expected from the asset. But due to its unique characteristics, the value of goodwill is not associated with any specific cash flows. By its very nature, goodwill is inseparable from a particular *reporting unit.* A reporting unit is an operating segment of a company or a component of an operating segment for which discrete financial information is available and segment management regularly reviews the operating results of that component. So, for purposes of impairment testing, we compare the value of the reporting unit itself with its book value. If the fair value of the reporting unit is less than its book value, an impairment loss is indicated.

A goodwill impairment loss is indicated when the fair value of the reporting unit is less than its book value.

The impairment loss recognized can't exceed the book value of goodwill. In other words, the impairment loss can't reduce the book value of goodwill below zero. Also, if goodwill is tested for impairment at the same time as other assets of the reporting unit, the other assets must be tested first, and any impairment losses and asset write-downs are recorded prior to testing goodwill. Subsequent reversal (recovery) of a previous goodwill impairment loss is not allowed. A goodwill impairment example is provided in Illustration 11–22.

The goodwill impairment loss can't exceed the book value of goodwill.

Illustration 11–22

Impairment Loss—Goodwill

In 2020, the Upjane Corporation acquired Pharmacopia Corporation for $500 million. Upjane recorded $100 million in goodwill related to this acquisition because the fair value of the identifiable net assets of Pharmacopia was $400 million. After the acquisition, Pharmacopia continues to operate as a separate company and is considered a reporting unit.

At the end of 2021, events and circumstances indicated that it is more likely than not that the fair value of Pharmacopia is less than its book value requiring Upjane to perform the goodwill impairment test. The book value of Pharmacopia's net assets at the end of 2021 is $440 million, including the $100 million in goodwill. On that date, the fair value of Pharmacopia is estimated to be $360 million.

(continued)

Illustration 11–22
(concluded)

> **Measurement of the impairment loss:**
>
> | | | |
> |---|---|---|
> | Fair value of Pharmacopia | $360 | million |
> | Book value of the net assets of Pharmacopia | 440 | million |
> | Impairment loss | $ (80) | million |
>
> **The entry to record the loss is** ($ in millions):
>
> | | | |
> |---|---|---|
> | Loss on impairment of goodwill .... | 80 | |
> | Goodwill .... | | 80 |
>
> Recall that Upjane recorded $100 million in goodwill related to the initial acquisition of Pharmacopia. After the impairment loss of $80 million is recorded, the balance of goodwill is reduced to $20 million. If Pharmacopia's fair value was less than its book value by more than $100 million, then the goodwill impairment loss would have been limited to only $100 million to reduce the balance of goodwill to zero. The goodwill impairment loss normally is reported in the income statement as a separate component of operating expenses.
>
> Source: Goodwill

Some examples of multibillion dollar goodwill impairment losses in recent years are shown in Illustration 11–23.

Illustration 11–23

Goodwill Impairment Losses

Real World Financials

> | Company | Goodwill Impairment Loss |
> |---|---|
> | General Motors | $27.1 billion |
> | Hewlett-Packard | 13.7 billion |
> | Microsoft | 11.3 billion |
> | Yahoo | 4.5 billion |
> | Boston Scientific | 4.4 billion |
> | Community Health Systems | 1.4 billion |

Under Armour's disclosure of its goodwill impairment loss is shown in Illustration 11–24.

Illustration 11–24

Goodwill Impairment Disclosure—Under Armour, Inc.

Real World Financials

> **Goodwill Impairment Charge (in part)**
>
> Goodwill and indefinite lived intangible assets are not amortized and are required to be tested for impairment at least annually or sooner whenever events or changes in circumstances indicate that the assets may be impaired. In conducting an annual impairment test, the Company first reviews qualitative factors to determine whether it is more likely than not that the fair value of the reporting unit is less than its carrying amount. If factors indicate that is the case, the Company performs the goodwill impairment test. The Company compares the fair value of the reporting unit with its carrying amount.
>
> During the third quarter of 2017, the Company made the strategic decision to not pursue certain planned future revenue streams in its Connected Fitness business in connection with the 2017 Restructuring Plan. The Company determined sufficient indication existed to trigger the performance of an interim impairment for the Company's Connected Fitness reporting unit resulting in goodwill impairment of $28.6 million, which represents all goodwill allocated to this reporting unit.

Where We're Headed

> In January 2017, the Financial Accounting Standards Board (FASB) completed Phase 1 of its two-phase project on goodwill by issuing ASU 2017-04. This phase involved simplifying the measurement of goodwill impairment, as described in Illustration 11–22.
>
> In Phase 2 of the project (which is not part of the ASU discussed above), the FASB will consider permitting or requiring companies to amortize goodwill and also consider making other changes in the impairment testing methodology.

Additional Consideration

Private Company GAAP—Accounting for Goodwill. The Private Company Council (PCC) sought feedback from private company stakeholders on the issue of goodwill accounting and found that most users of private company financial statements disregard goodwill and goodwill impairment losses. As a result, the PCC concluded that the cost and complexity of goodwill accounting outweigh the benefits for private companies.

In response to the PCC's conclusion, the FASB issued an Accounting Standards Update in 2014 that allows an accounting alternative for the subsequent measurement of goodwill for private companies that calls for goodwill to be amortized and also simplifies the goodwill impairment test.[20]

The main provisions of the alternative are

1. Amortizing goodwill on a straight-line basis over a maximum of 10 years.

2. Testing goodwill for impairment at either the company level or the reporting unit level.

3. Testing goodwill for impairment only when a triggering event occurs indicating that goodwill may be impaired.

4. The option of determining whether a quantitative impairment test is necessary when a triggering event occurs.

5. If a quantitative test is necessary, measuring the goodwill impairment loss as the amount by which fair value of the company (or reporting unit) is less than its book value, not to exceed the book value of goodwill.

The first provision is now being considered for public companies. We discussed this above in the previous "Where We're Headed" box.

International Financial Reporting Standards

Impairment of Value—Goodwill. Highlighted below are some important differences in accounting for the impairment of goodwill between U.S. GAAP and *IAS No. 36*.

● LO11–10

	U.S. GAAP	IFRS
Level of Testing	*Reporting unit*—a segment or a component of an operating segment for which discrete financial information is available.	*Cash-generating unit (CGU)*—the lowest level at which goodwill is monitored by management. A CGU can't be lower than a segment.
Measurement	Compare the fair value of the reporting unit with its book value. A loss is indicated if fair value is less than book value. Other assets must be tested first and any impairment loss and asset write-down is recorded prior to testing goodwill.	Compare the recoverable amount of the CGU to book value. If the recoverable amount is less, reduce goodwill first, then other assets. The recoverable amount is the higher of the asset's value-in-use and fair value less costs to sell. An asset's value-in-use is calculated as the present value of estimated future cash flows.

IAS No. 36 requires goodwill to be tested for impairment at least annually. However, under U.S. GAAP, a company can choose first to provide only a qualitative assessment of the likelihood of goodwill impairment to determine if quantitative measurement is then necessary. Both U.S. GAAP and *IAS No. 36* prohibit the reversal of goodwill impairment losses.

Let's look at an illustration highlighting these differences.

(continued)

---

[20]*Accounting Standards Update No. 2014–02,* "Intangibles—Goodwill and Other (Topic 350): Accounting for Goodwill," (Norwalk, Conn.: FASB, January 2014).

(concluded)

Canterbury LTD. has $38 million of goodwill in its balance sheet from the 2019 acquisition of Denton, Inc. At the end of 2021, Canterbury's management provided the following information for the year-end goodwill impairment test ($ in millions):

Fair value of Denton (determined by appraisal)	$132
Fair value of Denton's net assets (excluding goodwill)	120
Book value of Denton's net assets (including goodwill)	150
Value-in-use (present value of Denton's estimated future cash flows)	135

Assume that Denton is considered a reporting unit under U.S. GAAP and a cash-generating unit under IFRS, and that its fair value approximates fair value less costs to sell. What is the amount of goodwill impairment loss that Canterbury should recognize, if any, under U.S. GAAP? Under IFRS?

U.S. GAAP		
	Fair value of Denton (determined by appraisal)	$ 132
	Book value of Denton's net assets (including goodwill)	150
	Impairment loss	$ (18)

IFRS		
	The recoverable amount is $135 million, the higher of the $135 million value-in-use (present value of estimated future cash flows) and the $132 million fair value less costs to sell.	
	Recoverable amount	$ 135
	Book value of Denton's net assets (including goodwill)	(150)
	Impairment loss	$ (15)

Deutsche Bank is the largest bank in Germany and one of the largest financial institutions in Europe and the world. The company prepares its financial statements according to IFRS. The following disclosures describe the company's goodwill impairment policy as well as goodwill impairment loss:

Impairment of Goodwill (in part)

Goodwill is tested for impairment annually in the fourth quarter by comparing the recoverable amount of each goodwill-carrying cash-generating unit (CGU) with its carrying amount. In addition, in accordance with IAS 36, the Group tests goodwill whenever a triggering event is identified. The recoverable amount is the higher of a CGU's fair value less costs of disposal and its value in use.

Impairment charge during the period (in part)

The goodwill impairment test resulted in goodwill impairments totaling € 4,933 million, consisting of € 2,168 million, and € 2,765 million in the former CGUs, CB&S, and PBC, respectively. The impairment in CB&S was mainly driven by changes to the business mix in light of expected higher regulatory capital requirements, leading to a recoverable amount of approximately € 26.1 billion. The impairment in PBC was, in addition to the changed capital requirements, mainly driven by the disposal expectations regarding Hua Xia Bank Co. Ltd. and Postbank, which resulted in a recoverable amount of approximately € 12.3 billion for the CGU.

Assets Held for Sale

We have been discussing the recognition and measurement for the impairment of value of assets to be held and used. We also test for impairment of assets held for sale. These are assets management has actively committed to immediately sell in their present condition and for which sale is probable.

An asset or group of assets classified as held for sale is measured at the lower of its book value, or fair value minus cost to sell. An impairment loss is recognized for any write-down to fair value minus cost to sell.[21] Except for including the cost to sell, notice the similarity

> For assets held for sale, if fair value minus cost to sell is less than book value, an impairment loss is recognized for the difference.

---

[21]If the asset is unsold at the end of a subsequent reporting period, a gain is recognized for any increase in fair value less cost to sell, but not in excess of the loss previously recognized.

to impairment of assets to be held and used. We don't depreciate or amortize these assets while classified as held for sale and we report them separately in the balance sheet. Recall from our discussion of discontinued operations in Chapter 4 that similar rules apply for a component of an entity that is classified as held for sale.

Illustration 11–25 summarizes the guidelines for the recognition and measurement of impairment losses.

Illustration 11–25

Summary of Asset Impairment Guidelines

Asset Classification	When to Test for Impairment	Impairment Test
Held and Used		
Property, plant, and equipment and finite-life intangible assets	When events or circumstances indicate book value may not be recoverable.	Step 1—An impairment loss is required only when book value is not recoverable (undiscounted sum of estimated future cash flows less than book value).
		Step 2—The impairment loss is the amount by which fair value is less than book value.
Indefinite-life intangible assets (other than goodwill)	At least annually, and more frequently if indicated. Option to first choose qualitative assessment to determine if quantitative measurement is then necessary.	If fair value is less than book value, an impairment loss is recognized for the difference.
Goodwill	At least annually, and more frequently if indicated. Option to first choose qualitative assessment to determine if quantitative measurement is then necessary.	If fair value of the reporting unit is less than its book value, a goodwill impairment loss is recognized for the difference. The impairment loss recognized can't exceed the book value of goodwill.
Held for Sale	At the time of classification as held for sale and thereafter.	If fair value minus cost to sell is less than book value, an impairment loss is recognized for the difference.

Impairment Losses and Earnings Quality

What do losses from the write-down of inventory and restructuring costs have in common? The presence of these items in a corporate income statement presents a challenge to an analyst trying to determine a company's permanent earnings—those likely to continue in the future. We discussed these issues in prior chapters.

We now can add asset impairment losses to the list of "big bath" accounting techniques some companies use to manipulate earnings. By writing off large amounts of assets, companies significantly reduce earnings in the year of the write-off but are able to increase future earnings by lowering future depreciation, depletion, or amortization. Here's how. We measure the impairment loss as the amount by which an asset's fair value is less than its book value. However, in most cases, fair value must be estimated, and the estimation process usually involves a forecast of future net cash flows the company expects to generate from the asset's use. If a company underestimates future net cash flows, fair value is understated. This has two effects: (1) current year's income is unrealistically low due to the impairment loss being overstated and (2) future income is unrealistically high because depreciation, depletion, and amortization are based on understated asset values.

An analyst must decide whether to consider asset impairment losses as temporary in nature or as a part of permanent earnings.

Concept Review Exercise

IMPAIRMENT

Part A:

Illumination Inc. owns a factory in Wisconsin that makes light bulbs. During 2021, due to increased competition from LED light bulb manufacturers, the company determined that an impairment test was appropriate. Management has prepared the following information for the assets of the factory ($ in millions):

Cost	$345
Accumulated depreciation	85
Estimated future undiscounted cash flows to be generated by the factory	230
Estimated fair value of the factory assets	170

Required:

1. Determine the amount of impairment loss Illumination should recognize, if any.
2. If a loss is indicated, prepare the journal entry to record the loss.
3. Repeat requirement 1 assuming that the estimated undiscounted future cash flows are $270 million instead of $230 million.

Solution:

1. Determine the amount of impairment loss Illumination should recognize, if any.

   Recoverability Test: Because the undiscounted future cash flows of $230 million are less than book value of $260 ($345 – $85) million, an impairment loss is indicated.

   Measurement: The impairment loss is $90 million, determined as follows:

	($ in millions)
Fair value	$170
Less: Book value	260
Impairment loss	$ (90)

2. If a loss is indicated, prepare the journal entry to record the loss.

	($ in millions)	
Loss on impairment (determined above)	90	
Accumulated depreciation (balance)	85	
Factory assets ($345 – $170)		175

3. Repeat requirement 1 assuming that the estimated undiscounted future cash flows are $270 million instead of $230 million.

   Because the undiscounted future cash flows of $270 million exceed book value of $260 million, the recoverability test indicates that there is no impairment, so no impairment loss is recorded.

Part B:

In 2019, Illumination Inc. acquired Zapo Lighting Company for $620 million, of which $80 million was allocated to goodwill. After the acquisition, Zapo continues to operate a separate company and is considered a reporting unit. At the end of 2021, management provided the following information for a required goodwill impairment test ($ in millions):

Fair value of Zapo Lighting	$540
Book value of Zapo's net assets (including goodwill)	600

Required:

Determine the amount of goodwill impairment loss that Illumination should recognize at the end of 2021, if any.

Solution:

Measurement of goodwill impairment loss:	($ in millions)
Fair value of Zapo	$540
Book value of Zapo's net assets (including goodwill)	600
Impairment loss	$ (60)

Subsequent Expenditures

Now that we have acquired and measured assets, we can address accounting issues incurred subsequent to their acquisition. This part of the chapter deals with the treatment of expenditures made over the life of these assets to maintain and/or improve them.

Expenditures Subsequent to Acquisition

Many long-lived assets require expenditures to repair, maintain, or improve them after their acquisition. These expenditures can present accounting problems if they are material. In general, a choice must be made between capitalizing the expenditures by either increasing the asset's book value or creating a new asset, or expensing them in the period in which they are incurred. Typically, we capitalize expenditures that are expected to produce benefits beyond the current fiscal year. In contrast, expenditures that simply maintain a given level of benefits are expensed in the period they are incurred.

● LO11–9

Expenditures related to assets can increase future benefits in the following ways:

1. An extension of the *useful life* of the asset.
2. An increase in the *operating efficiency* of the asset resulting in either an increase in the quantity of goods or services produced or a decrease in future operating costs.
3. An increase in the *quality* of the goods or services produced by the asset.

Expenditures that cause any of these results should be capitalized initially and then expensed in future periods through depreciation, depletion, or amortization. Of course, materiality is an important factor in the practical application of this approach.

For convenience, many companies set materiality thresholds for the capitalization of any expenditure. For example, a company might decide to expense all expenditures under $1,000 regardless of whether or not future benefits are increased. Judgment is required to determine the appropriate materiality threshold as well as the appropriate treatment of expenditures over $1,000. There often are practical problems in capitalizing these expenditures. For example, even if future benefits are increased by the expenditure, it may be difficult to determine how long the benefits will last. It's important for a company to establish a policy for treating these expenditures and apply it consistently.

Many companies do not capitalize any expenditure unless it exceeds a predetermined amount that is considered material.

We classify subsequent expenditures as (1) repairs and maintenance, (2) additions, (3) improvements, or (4) rearrangements.

Repairs and Maintenance

These expenditures are made to *maintain* a given level of benefits provided by the asset and do not *increase* future benefits. For example, the cost of an engine tune-up or the repair of an engine part for a delivery truck allows the truck to continue its productive activity. If the maintenance is not performed, the truck will not provide the benefits originally anticipated. In that sense, future benefits are provided; without the repair, the truck will no longer operate. The key, though, is that future benefits are not provided *beyond those originally anticipated.* Expenditures for these activities should be expensed in the period incurred.

Expenditures for repairs and maintenance generally are expensed when incurred.

Additional Consideration

If repairs and maintenance costs are seasonal, interim financial statements may be misstated. For example, suppose annual maintenance is performed on a company's fleet of delivery trucks. The annual income statement correctly includes one year's maintenance expense. However, for interim reporting purposes, if the entire expenditure is made in one quarter, should that quarter's income statement include as expense the entire cost of the annual maintenance? If these expenditures can be anticipated, they should be accrued evenly throughout the year by crediting an allowance account. The allowance account is then debited when the maintenance is performed.

Additions

As the term implies, additions involve adding a new major component to an existing asset and should be capitalized because future benefits are increased. For example, adding a refrigeration unit to a delivery truck increases the capability of the truck, thus increasing its future benefits. Other examples include the construction of a new wing on a building and the addition of a security system to an existing building.

> The costs of *additions* usually are capitalized.

The capitalized cost includes all necessary expenditures to bring the addition to a condition and location for use. For a building addition, this might include the costs of tearing down and removing a wall of the existing building. The capitalized cost of additions is depreciated over the remaining useful life of the original asset or its own useful life, whichever is shorter.

Improvements

> The costs of *improvements* usually are capitalized.

Expenditures classified as improvements involve the replacement of a major component of an asset. The replacement can be a new component with the same characteristics as the old component or a new component with enhanced operating capabilities. For example, an existing refrigeration unit in a delivery truck could be replaced with a new but similar unit or with a new and improved refrigeration unit. In either case, the cost of the improvement usually increases future benefits and should be capitalized by increasing the book value of the related asset (the delivery truck) and depreciated over the useful life of the improved asset. There are three methods used to record the cost of improvements.

1. *Substitution.* The improvement can be recorded as both (1) a disposition of the old component and (2) the acquisition of the new component. This approach is conceptually appealing but it is practical only if the original cost and accumulated depreciation of the old component can be separately identified.
2. *Capitalization of new cost.* Another way to record an improvement is to include the cost of the improvement (net of any consideration received from the disposition of the old component) as a debit to the related asset account, without removing the original cost and accumulated depreciation of the original component. This approach is acceptable only if the book value of the original component has been reduced to an immaterial amount through prior depreciation.
3. *Reduction of accumulated depreciation.* Another way to increase an asset's book value is to leave the asset account unaltered but decrease its related accumulated depreciation. The argument for this method is that many improvements extend the useful life of an asset and are equivalent to a partial recovery of previously recorded depreciation. This approach produces the same book value as the capitalization of cost to the asset account. However, cost and accumulated depreciation amounts will differ under the two methods.

The three methods are compared in Illustration 11–26.

Illustration 11–26

Improvements

> The Palmer Corporation replaced the air conditioning system in one of its office buildings that it leases to tenants. The cost of the old air conditioning system, $200,000, is included in the cost of the building. However, the company has separately depreciated the air conditioning system. Depreciation recorded up to the date of replacement totaled $160,000. The old system was removed and the new system installed at a cost of $230,000, which was paid in cash. Parts from the old system were sold for $12,000.
>
> Accounting for the improvement differs depending on the alternative chosen.
>
> **Alternative 1—Substitution**

> 1. *Substitution* (a)
> Disposition of old component.

Cash..	12,000	
Accumulated depreciation—buildings (remove old).................................	160,000	
Loss on disposal (difference)	28,000	
Buildings (remove old)...		200,000

(continued)

Buildings (add new) 230,000

   Cash 230,000

Alternative 2—Capitalization of new cost

Buildings 218,000

   Cash ($230,000 − $12,000) 218,000

Alternative 3—Reduction of accumulated depreciation

Accumulated depreciation—buildings 218,000

   Cash ($230,000 − $12,000) 218,000

Illustration 11–26
(concluded)

(b) Acquisition of new component.

2. *Capitalization of new cost.*

3. *Reduction of accumulated depreciation.*

Rearrangements

Expenditures made to restructure an asset without addition, replacement, or improvement are termed rearrangements. The objective is to create a new capability for the asset and not necessarily to extend its useful life. Examples include the rearrangement of machinery on the production line to increase operational efficiency and the relocation of a company's operating plant or office building. If these expenditures are material and they clearly increase future benefits, they should be capitalized and expensed in the future periods benefited. If the expenditures are not material or if it's not certain that future benefits have increased, they should be expensed in the period incurred.

Illustration 11–27 provides a summary of the accounting treatment for the various types of expenditures related to property, plant, and equipment.

The costs of material *rearrangements* should be capitalized if they clearly increase future benefits.

Illustration 11–27

Expenditures Subsequent to Acquisition

Type of Expenditure	Definition	Usual Accounting Treatment
Repairs and maintenance	Expenditures to maintain a given level of benefits	Expense in the period incurred
Additions	The addition of a new major component to an existing asset	Capitalize and depreciate over the remaining useful life of the *original asset or its own useful* life, whichever is shorter
Improvements	The replacement of a major component	Capitalize and depreciate over the useful life of the improved asset
Rearrangements	Expenditures to restructure an asset without addition, replacement, or improvement	If expenditures are material and clearly increase future benefits, capitalize and depreciate over the future periods benefited

Costs of Defending Intangible Rights

Repairs, additions, improvements, and rearrangements generally relate to property, plant, and equipment. A possible significant expenditure incurred subsequent to the acquisition of intangible assets is the cost of defending the right that gives the intangible asset its value. If an intangible right is *successfully* defended, the litigation costs should be capitalized and amortized over the remaining useful life of the related intangible. This is the appropriate treatment of these expenditures even if the intangible asset was originally developed internally rather than purchased.

If the defense of an intangible right is *unsuccessful,* then the intangible asset has no future value. In this case, the litigation costs provide no future benefit and should be expensed immediately. In addition, the book value of the intangible asset should be reduced to realizable value. For example, if a company is unsuccessful in defending a patent infringement suit, the patent's value may be eliminated and a loss recorded.

The costs incurred to *successfully* defend an intangible right should be capitalized.

The costs incurred to *unsuccessfully* defend an intangible right should be expensed.

614 SECTION 2 Assets

International Financial Reporting Standards

● LO11–10

> **Costs of Defending Intangible Rights.** Under U.S. GAAP, litigation costs to successfully defend an intangible right are capitalized and amortized over the remaining useful life of the related intangible. Under IFRS, these costs are expensed except in rare situations when an expenditure increases future benefits.[22]

Financial Reporting Case Solution

©Dragon Images/Shutterstock

1. **Is Penny correct? Do the terms *depreciation, depletion,* and *amortization* all mean the same thing?** *(p. 572)*   Penny is correct. Each of these terms refers to the cost allocation of assets over their service lives. The term *depreciation* is used for plant and equipment, *depletion* for natural resources, and *amortization* for intangible assets.

2. **Weyerhaeuser determines depletion based on the "volume of timber estimated to be available." Explain this approach.** *(p. 577)*   Weyerhaeuser is using the units-of-production method to determine depletion. The units-of-production method is an activity-based method that computes a depletion (or depreciation or amortization) rate per measure of activity and then multiplies this rate by actual activity to determine periodic cost allocation. The method is used by Weyerhaeuser to measure depletion of the cost of timber harvested and the amortization of logging roads. Logging roads are intangible assets because the company does not own the roads.

3. **Explain how asset impairment differs from depreciation, depletion, and amortization. How do companies measure impairment losses for property, plant, and equipment and intangible assets with finite useful lives?** *(p. 600)*   Depreciation, depletion, and amortization reflect a gradual consumption of the benefits inherent in a long-lived asset. An implicit assumption in allocating the cost of an asset over its useful life is that there has been no significant reduction in the anticipated total benefits or service potential of the asset. Situations can arise, however, that cause a significant decline or *impairment* of those benefits or service potentials. Determining whether to record an impairment loss for an asset and actually recording the loss is a two-step process. The first step is a recoverability test—an impairment loss is required only when the undiscounted sum of estimated future cash flows from an asset is less than the asset's book value. The measurement of impairment loss—step 2—is the difference between the asset's book value and its fair value. If an impairment loss is recognized, the written-down book value becomes the new cost base for future cost allocation. ●

The Bottom Line

● LO11–1   The use of property, plant, and equipment and intangible assets represents a consumption of benefits, or service potentials, inherent in the assets. The cost of these inherent benefits or service potentials should be recognized as an expense over the periods they help to produce revenues. As there very seldom is a direct relationship between the use of assets and revenue production, accounting resorts to arbitrary methods to allocate these costs over the periods of their use. *(p. 571)*

● LO11–2   The allocation process for plant and equipment is called *depreciation.* Time-based depreciation methods estimate service life in years and then allocate depreciable base, cost less estimated residual value, using either a straight-line or accelerated pattern. Activity-based depreciation methods allocate the depreciable base by estimating service life according to some measure of productivity. When an item of property, plant, and equipment or an intangible asset is sold, a gain or loss is recognized for the difference between the consideration received and the asset's book value. *(p. 574)*

---

[22] "Intangible Assets," *International Accounting Standard No. 38* (IASCF), par. 20, as amended effective January 1, 2018.

● **LO11–3**   The allocation process for natural resources is called *depletion*. The activity-based method called units-of-production usually is employed to determine periodic depletion. (*p. 589*)

● **LO11–4**   The allocation process for intangible assets is called *amortization*. For an intangible asset with a finite useful life, the capitalized cost less any estimated residual value must be allocated to periods in which the asset is expected to contribute to the company's revenue-generating activities. An intangible asset that is determined to have an indefinite useful life is not subject to periodic amortization. Goodwill is perhaps the most typical intangible asset with an indefinite useful life. (*p. 591*)

● **LO11–5**   A change in either the service life or residual value of property, plant, and equipment and intangible assets should be reflected in the financial statements of the current period and future periods by recalculating periodic depreciation, depletion, or amortization. (*p. 596*)

● **LO11–6**   A change in depreciation, depletion, or amortization method is considered a change in accounting estimate that is achieved by a change in accounting principle. We account for these changes prospectively, exactly as we would any other change in estimate. One difference is that most changes in estimate do not require a company to justify the change. However, this change in estimate is a result of changing an accounting principle and therefore requires a clear justification as to why the new method is preferable. (*p. 597*)

● **LO11–7**   A material error in accounting for property, plant, and equipment and intangible assets that is discovered in a year subsequent to the year of the error requires that previous years' financial statements that were incorrect as a result of the error be retrospectively restated to reflect the correction. Any account balances that are incorrect as a result of the error are corrected by journal entry. If retained earnings is one of the incorrect accounts, the correction is reported as a prior period adjustment to the beginning balance in the statement of shareholders' equity. In addition, a disclosure note is needed to describe the nature of the error and the impact of its correction on income. (*p. 598*)

● **LO11–8**   Conceptually, there is considerable merit for a policy requiring the write-down of an asset when there has been a *significant* decline in value below book value. The write-down provides important information about the future cash flows to be generated from the use of the asset. However, in practice this policy is very subjective. GAAP [FASB ASC 360] establishes guidance for when to recognize and how to measure impairment losses of property, plant, and equipment and intangible assets that have finite useful lives. GAAP [FASB ASC 350] also provides guidance for the recognition and measurement of impairment for indefinite-life intangibles and goodwill. (*p. 600*)

● **LO11–9**   Expenditures for repairs and maintenance generally are expensed when incurred. The costs of additions and improvements usually are capitalized. The costs of material rearrangements should be capitalized if they clearly increase future benefits. (*p. 593*)

● **LO11–10**   Among the several differences between U.S. GAAP and IFRS with respect to the utilization and impairment of property, plant, and equipment and intangible assets pertains to reporting assets in the balance sheet. IFRS allows a company to value property, plant, and equipment (PP&E) and intangible assets subsequent to initial valuation at (1) cost less accumulated depreciation/amortization or (2) fair value (revaluation). U.S. GAAP prohibits revaluation. There also are differences in accounting for the impairment of property, plant, and equipment and intangible assets. (*pp. 580, 587, 590, 594, 603, 605, 607, and 614*) ●

Comparison with MACRS (Tax Depreciation)   APPENDIX 11A

Depreciation for financial reporting purposes is an attempt to distribute the cost of the asset, less any anticipated residual value, over the estimated useful life in a systematic and rational manner that attempts to match revenues with the use of the asset. Depreciation for income tax purposes is influenced by the revenue needs of government as well as the desire to influence economic behavior. For example, accelerated depreciation schedules currently allowed are intended to provide incentive for companies to expand and modernize their facilities thus stimulating economic growth.

The federal income tax code allows taxpayers to compute depreciation for their tax returns on assets acquired after 1986 using the modified accelerated cost recovery system (MACRS).[23] Key differences between the calculation of depreciation for financial reporting and the calculation using MACRS are

1. Estimated useful lives and residual values are not used in MACRS.
2. Firms can't choose among various accelerated methods under MACRS.
3. A half-year convention is used in determining the MACRS depreciation amounts.

Under MACRS, each asset generally is placed within a recovery period category. The six categories for personal property are 3, 5, 7, 10, 15, and 20 years. For example, the 5-year category includes automobiles, light trucks, and computers.

Depending on the category, fixed percentage rates are applied to the original cost of the asset. The rates for the 5-year asset category are as follows:

Year	Rate
1	20.00%
2	32.00
3	19.20
4	11.52
5	11.52
6	5.76
Total	100.00%

These rates are equivalent to applying the double-declining-balance (DDB) method with a switch to straight-line in the year straight-line yields an equal or higher deduction than DDB. In most cases, the half-year convention is used regardless of when the asset is placed in service.[24] The first-year rate of 20% for the five-year category is one-half of the DDB rate for an asset with a five-year life ($2 \times 20\%$). The sixth year rate of 5.76% is one-half of the straight-line rate established in year 4, the year straight-line depreciation exceeds DDB depreciation.

Companies have the option to use the straight-line method for the entire tax life of the asset, applying the half-year convention, rather than using MACRS depreciation schedules. Because of the differences discussed above, tax depreciation for a given year will likely be different from GAAP depreciation.

In December 2017, Congress passed the Tax Cuts and Jobs Act that substantially impacts a company's depreciation deduction for tax purposes. Under the new tax law, companies can choose to deduct 100% of the cost of many assets purchased between September 27, 2017, and December 31, 2022. This is called *bonus depreciation,* and for these assets, the MACRS depreciation schedule will not apply because the asset is fully depreciated in the year it is purchased. After 2022 and before 2027, the bonus deduction will still be allowed, but in smaller amounts each year. For qualified assets purchased in 2023, the first-year deduction drops to 80% of the asset's cost. The remaining 20% of the asset's cost would then be depreciated according to MACRS. The first-year deduction drops to 60% in 2024, 40% in 2025, and 20% in 2026. Any assets that do not qualify, or are not chosen, for bonus depreciation under the new tax law will be depreciated using MACRS. Beginning January 1, 2027, the first-year bonus depreciation is no longer available, and qualified assets will be depreciated fully using MACRS. ●

APPENDIX 11B   Retirement and Replacement Methods of Depreciation

Retirement and replacement depreciation methods occasionally are used to depreciate relatively low-valued assets with short service lives. Under either approach, an aggregate asset account that represents a group of similar assets is increased at the time the initial collection is acquired.

---

[23]For assets acquired between 1981 and 1986, tax depreciation is calculated using the accelerated cost recovery system (ACRS), which is similar to MACRS. For assets acquired before 1981, tax depreciation can be calculated using any of the depreciation methods discussed in the chapter. Residual values are used in the calculation of depreciation for pre-1981 assets.
[24]In certain situations, mid-quarter and mid-month conventions are used.

Retirement Method

Using the retirement depreciation method, the asset account also is increased for the cost of subsequent expenditures. When an item is disposed of, the asset account is credited for its cost, and depreciation expense is recorded for the difference between cost and proceeds received, if any. No other entries are made for depreciation. As a consequence, one or more periods may pass without any expense recorded. For example, the following entry records the purchase of 100 handheld calculators at $50 acquisition cost each:

Calculators (100 × $50)	5,000	
Cash		5,000
To record the acquisition of calculators.		

If 20 new calculators are acquired at $45 each, the asset account is increased.

Calculators (20 × $45)	900	
Cash		900
To record additional calculator acquisitions.		

Thirty calculators are disposed of (retired) by selling them secondhand to a bookkeeping firm for $5 each. The following entry reflects the retirement method:

Cash (30 × $5)	150	
Depreciation expense (difference)	1,350	
Calculators (30 × $50)		1,500
To record the sale/depreciation of calculators.		

Notice that the retirement system assumes a FIFO cost flow approach in determining the cost of assets, $50 each, that were disposed.

Replacement Method

By the replacement depreciation method, the initial acquisition of assets is recorded the same way as by the retirement method; that is, the aggregate cost is increased. However, depreciation expense is the amount paid for new or replacement assets. Any proceeds received from asset dispositions reduces depreciation expense. For our example, the acquisition of 20 new calculators at $45 each is recorded as depreciation as follows:

Depreciation expense (20 × $45)	900	
Cash		900
To record the replacement/depreciation of calculators.		

The sale of the old calculators is recorded as a reduction of depreciation:

Cash (30 × $5)	150	
Depreciation expense		150
To record the sale of calculators.		

The asset account balance remains the same throughout the life of the aggregate collection of assets.

Because these methods are likely to produce aggregate expense measurements that differ from individual calculations, retirement and replacement methods are acceptable only in situations where the distortion in depreciation expense does not have a material effect on income. These methods occasionally are encountered in regulated industries such as utilities. ●

The retirement depreciation method records depreciation when assets are disposed of and measures depreciation as the difference between the proceeds received and cost.

By the replacement method, depreciation is recorded when assets are replaced.

Questions For Review of Key Topics

Q 11–1   Explain the similarities in and differences among depreciation, depletion, and amortization.

Q 11–2   Depreciation is a process of cost allocation, not valuation. Explain this statement.

Q 11–3   Identify and define the three characteristics of an asset that must be established to determine periodic depreciation, depletion, or amortization.

Q 11–4   Discuss the factors that influence the estimation of service life for a depreciable asset.

Q 11–5   What is meant by depreciable base? How is it determined?

Q 11–6   Briefly differentiate between activity-based and time-based allocation methods.

Q 11–7   Briefly differentiate between the straight-line depreciation method and accelerated depreciation methods.

Q 11–8   Why are time-based depreciation methods used more frequently than activity-based methods?

Q 11–9   What are some factors that could explain the predominant use of the straight-line depreciation method?

Q 11–10   When an item of property, plant, and equipment is disposed of, how is gain or loss on disposal computed?

Q 11–11   Briefly explain the differences and similarities between the group approach and composite approach to depreciating aggregate assets.

Q 11–12   Define depletion and compare it with depreciation.

Q 11–13   Compare and contrast amortization of intangible assets with depreciation and depletion.

Q 11–14   What are some of the simplifying conventions a company can use to calculate depreciation for partial years?

Q 11–15   Explain the accounting treatment required when a change is made to the estimated service life of equipment.

Q 11–16   Explain the accounting treatment and disclosures required when a change is made in depreciation method.

Q 11–17   Explain the steps required to correct an error in accounting for property, plant, and equipment and intangible assets that is discovered in a year subsequent to the year the error was made.

Q 11–18   Explain what is meant by the impairment of the value of property, plant, and equipment and intangible assets. How should these impairments be accounted for?

Q 11–19   Explain the differences in the accounting treatment of repairs and maintenance, additions, improvements, and rearrangements.

IFRS Q 11–20   Identify any differences between U.S. GAAP and International Financial Reporting Standards in the subsequent valuation of property, plant, and equipment and intangible assets.

IFRS Q 11–21   Briefly explain the difference between U.S. GAAP and IFRS in the *measurement* of an impairment loss for property, plant, and equipment and finite-life intangible assets.

IFRS Q 11–22   Briefly explain the differences between U.S. GAAP and IFRS in the measurement of an impairment loss for goodwill.

IFRS Q 11–23   Under U.S. GAAP, litigation costs to successfully defend an intangible right are capitalized and amortized over the remaining useful life of the related intangible. How are these costs typically accounted for under IFRS?

Brief Exercises

■ connect®

BE 11–1
Cost allocation
● LO11–1

At the beginning of its fiscal year, Koeplin Corporation purchased equipment for $50,000. At the end of the year, the equipment had a fair value of $32,000. Koeplin's controller recorded depreciation of $18,000 for the year, the decline in the equipment's value. Is this the correct approach to measuring periodic depreciation (yes/no)? Discuss.

BE 11–2
Depreciation methods
● LO11–2

On January 1, 2021, Canseco Plumbing Fixtures purchased equipment for $30,000. Residual value at the end of an estimated four-year service life is expected to be $2,000. The company expects the equipment to operate for 10,000 hours. Calculate depreciation expense for 2021 and 2022 using each of the following depreciation methods: (1) straight line, (2) double-declining balance, and (3) units-of-production using hours operated. The equipment operated for 2,200 and 3,000 hours in 2021 and 2022, respectively.

BE 11–3
Depreciation methods; partial periods
● LO11–2

Refer to the situation described in BE 11–2. Assume the equipment was purchased on March 31, 2021, instead of January 1. Calculate depreciation expense for 2021 and 2022 using each of the following depreciation methods: (1) straight line, (2) double-declining balance, and (3) units-of-production using hours operated.

CHAPTER 11   Property, Plant, and Equipment and Intangible Assets: Utilization and Disposition   **619**

BE 11–4
Depreciation
method; Sum-of-
the-years'-digits
● LO11–2

Refer to the situation described in BE 11–2. Calculate depreciation expense for 2021 and 2022 using sum-of-the-years'-digits assuming the equipment was purchased on (1) January 1, 2021, and (2) March 31, 2021.

BE 11–5
Disposal of
property, plant,
and equipment
● LO11–2

Lawler Clothing sold manufacturing equipment for $16,000. Lawler originally purchased the equipment for $80,000, and depreciation through the date of sale totaled $71,000. What was the gain or loss on the sale of the equipment?

BE 11–6
Disposal of
property, plant,
and equipment
● LO11–2

Funseth Farms Inc. purchased a tractor in 2018 at a cost of $30,000. The tractor was sold for $3,000 in 2021. Depreciation recorded through the disposal date totaled $26,000. (1) Prepare the journal entry to record the sale. (2) Now assume the tractor was sold for $10,000; prepare the journal entry to record the sale.

BE 11–7
Disposal of
property, plant,
and equipment
and intangible
assets
● LO11–2

On July 15, 2021, Cottonwood Industries sold a patent and equipment to Roquemore Corporation for $750,000 and $325,000, respectively. On the date of the sale, the book value of the patent was $120,000, and the book value of the equipment was $400,000 (cost of $550,000 less accumulated depreciation of $150,000). Prepare separate journal entries to record (1) the sale of the patent and (2) the sale of the equipment.

BE 11–8
Assets held for
sale
● LO11–2

On December 31, 2021, management of Jines Construction committed to a plan for selling an office building and its related equipment. Both are available for immediate sale. The building has a book value of $800,000 and a fair value of $900,000. The equipment has a book value of $240,000 and a fair value of $200,000. Calculate the amount that each asset will be reported at in the balance sheet and the amount of any gain or loss that will be reported in the income statement for the year ended December 31, 2021. Management expects to sell both assets in 2022.

BE 11–9
Group
depreciation;
disposal
● LO11–2

Mondale Winery depreciates its equipment using the group method. The cost of equipment purchased in 2021 totaled $425,000. The estimated residual value of the equipment was $40,000 and the group depreciation rate was determined to be 18%. (1) What is the annual depreciation for the group? (2) If equipment that cost $42,000 is sold in 2022 for $35,000, what amount of gain or loss will the company recognize for the sale?

BE 11–10
Depletion
● LO11–3

Fitzgerald Oil and Gas incurred costs of $8.25 million for the acquisition and development of a natural gas deposit. The company expects to extract 3 million cubic feet of natural gas during a four-year period. Natural gas extracted during years 1 and 2 were 700,000 and 800,000 cubic feet, respectively. What was the depletion for year 1 and for year 2?

BE 11–11
Amortization;
Partial periods
● LO11–4

On June 28, Lexicon Corporation acquired 100% of the common stock of Gulf & Eastern. The purchase price allocation included the following items: $4 million, patent; $3 million, developed technology; $2 million, indefinite-life trademark; $5 million, goodwill. Lexicon's policy is to amortize intangible assets using the straight-line method, no residual value, and a five-year useful life. What is the total amount of expenses (ignoring taxes) that would appear in Lexicon's income statement for the year ended December 31 related to these items?

BE 11–12
Amortization;
Software
development
costs
● LO11–4

[This is a continuation of Exercise 10–31 in Chapter 10 and includes amortization.]

Early in 2021, the Excalibur Company began developing a new software package to be marketed. The project was completed in December 2021 at a cost of $6 million. Of this amount, $4 million was spent before technological feasibility was established. Excalibur expects a useful life of five years for the new product with total revenues of $10 million. During 2022, revenue of $3 million was recognized.

Required:
(1) Prepare a journal entry to record the 2021 development costs. (2) Calculate the required amortization for 2022, and (3) determine the amount to report for the computer software costs in the December 31, 2022, balance sheet.

620   SECTION 2   Assets

BE 11–13
Amortization;
Software
development
costs
● LO11–4

[This is a continuation of Exercise 10–32 in Chapter 10 and includes amortization.]

On September 30, 2021, Athens Software began developing a software program to shield personal computers from malware and spyware. Technological feasibility was established on February 28, 2022, and the program was available for release on April 30, 2022. Development costs were incurred as follows:

September 30 through December 31, 2021	$ 2,200,000
January 1 through February 28, 2022	800,000
March 1 through April 30, 2022	300,000

Athens expects a useful life of four years for the software and total revenues of $5,000,000 during that time. During 2022, revenue of $1,000,000 was recognized.

Required:

(1) Prepare a journal entry to record the development costs in each year of 2021 and 2022. (2) Calculate the required amortization for 2022.

BE 11–14
Change in
estimate; useful
life of equipment
● LO11–5

At the beginning of 2019, Robotics Inc. acquired a manufacturing facility for $12 million. $9 million of the purchase price was allocated to the building. Depreciation for 2019 and 2020 was calculated using the straight-line method, a 25-year useful life, and a $1 million residual value. In 2021, the estimates of useful life and residual value were changed to 20 total years and $500,000, respectively. What is depreciation on the building for 2021?

BE 11–15
Change in
principle; change
in depreciation
method
● LO11–6

Refer to the situation described in BE 11–14. Assume that instead of changing the useful life and residual value, in 2021 the company switched to the double-declining-balance depreciation method. How should Robotics account for the change? What is depreciation on the building for 2021?

BE 11–16
Error correction
● LO11–7

Refer to the situation described in BE 11–14. Assume that 2019 depreciation was incorrectly recorded as $32,000. This error was discovered in 2021. (1) Record the journal entry needed in 2021 to correct the error. (2) What is depreciation on the building for 2021 assuming no change in estimate of useful life or residual value?

BE 11–17
Impairment;
property, plant,
and equipment
● LO11–8

Collison and Ryder Company (C&R) has been experiencing declining market conditions for its sportswear division. Management decided to test the assets of the division for possible impairment. The test revealed the following: book value of division's assets, $26.5 million; fair value of division's assets, $21 million; undiscounted sum of estimated future cash flows generated from the division's assets, $28 million. What amount of impairment loss should C&R recognize?

BE 11–18
Impairment;
property, plant,
and equipment
● LO11–8

Refer to the situation described in BE 11–17. Assume that the undiscounted sum of estimated future cash flows is $24 million instead of $28 million. What amount of impairment loss should C&R recognize?

BE 11–19
IFRS; impairment;
property, plant,
and equipment
● LO11–8,
LO11–10
● IFRS

Refer to the situation described in BE 11–17. Assume that the present value of the estimated future cash flows generated from the division's assets is $22 million and that their fair value approximates fair value less costs to sell. What amount of impairment loss should C&R recognize if the company prepares its financial statements according to IFRS?

BE 11–20
Impairment;
goodwill
● LO11–8

WebHelper Inc. acquired 100% of the outstanding stock of Silicon Chips Corporation (SCC) for $45 million, of which $15 million was allocated to goodwill. At the end of the current fiscal year, an impairment test revealed the following: fair value of SCC, $40 million; book value of SCC's net assets (including goodwill), $42 million. What amount of impairment loss should WebHelper recognize?

BE 11–21
Impairment;
goodwill
● LO11–8

Refer to the situation described in BE 11–20. Assume that the fair value of SCC is $44 million instead of $40 million. What amount of impairment loss should WebHelper recognize?

BE 11–22
IFRS; impairment;
goodwill
● LO11–10
● IFRS

Refer to the situation described in BE 11–20. Assume that SCC's fair value of $40 million approximates fair value less costs to sell and that the present value of SCC's estimated future cash flows is $41 million. If WebHelper prepares its financial statements according to IFRS and SCC is considered a cash-generating unit, what amount of impairment loss, if any, should WebHelper recognize?

BE 11–23
Subsequent
expenditures
● LO11–9

Demmert Manufacturing incurred the following expenditures during the current fiscal year: annual maintenance on its equipment, $5,400; remodeling of offices, $22,000; rearrangement of the shipping and receiving area resulting in an increase in productivity, $35,000; addition of a security system to the manufacturing facility, $25,000. How should Demmert account for each of these expenditures?

Exercises

E 11–1
Depreciation
methods
● LO11–2

On January 1, 2021, the Excel Delivery Company purchased a delivery van for $33,000. At the end of its five-year service life, it is estimated that the van will be worth $3,000. During the five-year period, the company expects to drive the van 100,000 miles.

Required:
Calculate annual depreciation for the five-year life of the van using each of the following methods. Round all computations to the nearest dollar.
1. Straight line
2. Double-declining balance
3. Units of production using miles driven as a measure of output, and the following actual mileage:

Year	Miles
2021	22,000
2022	24,000
2023	15,000
2024	20,000
2025	21,000

E 11–2
Depreciation
methods
● LO11–2

On January 1, 2021, the Allegheny Corporation purchased equipment for $115,000. The estimated service life of the equipment is 10 years and the estimated residual value is $5,000. The equipment is expected to produce 220,000 units during its life.

Required:
Calculate depreciation for 2021 and 2022 using each of the following methods. Round all computations to the nearest dollar.
1. Straight line
2. Double-declining balance
3. Units of production (units produced in 2021, 30,000; units produced in 2022, 25,000)

E 11–3
Depreciation
methods; partial
periods
● LO11–2

[This is a variation of Exercise 11–2 modified to focus on depreciation for partial years.]
   On October 1, 2021, the Allegheny Corporation purchased equipment for $115,000. The estimated service life of the equipment is 10 years and the estimated residual value is $5,000. The equipment is expected to produce 220,000 units during its life.

Required:
Calculate depreciation for 2021 and 2022 using each of the following methods. Partial-year depreciation is calculated based on the number of months the asset is in service. Round all computations to the nearest dollar.
1. Straight line
2. Double-declining balance
3. Units of production (units produced in 2021, 10,000; units produced in 2022, 25,000)

E 11–4
Other
depreciation
methods
● LO11–2

[This is a variation of Exercise 11–2 modified to focus on other depreciation methods.]
   On January 1, 2021, the Allegheny Corporation purchased equipment for $115,000. The estimated service life of the equipment is 10 years and the estimated residual value is $5,000. The equipment is expected to produce 220,000 units during its life.

Required:
Calculate depreciation for 2021 and 2022 using each of the following methods. Round all computations to the nearest dollar.
1. Sum-of-the-years'-digits
2. One hundred fifty percent declining balance
3. Assume instead the equipment was purchased on October 1, 2021. Calculate depreciation for 2021 and 2022 using each of the two methods. Partial-year depreciation is calculated based on the number of months the asset is in service. Round all computations to the nearest dollar.

622   SECTION 2   Assets

E 11–5
Depreciation methods; asset addition; partial period
● LO11–2, LO11–9

Tristen Company purchased a five-story office building on January 1, 2019, at a cost of $5,000,000. The building has a residual value of $200,000 and a 30-year life. The straight-line depreciation method is used. On June 30, 2021, construction of a sixth floor was completed at a cost of $1,650,000.

Required:
Calculate the depreciation on the building and building addition for 2021 and 2022 assuming that the addition did not change the life or residual value of the building.

E 11–6
Depreciation methods; solving for unknowns
● LO11–2

For each of the following depreciable assets, determine the missing amount (?). Abbreviations for depreciation methods are SL for straight-line and DDB for double-declining-balance.

Asset	Cost	Residual Value	Service Life (Years)	Depreciation Method	Depreciation (Year 2)
A	?	$20,000	5	DDB	$24,000
B	$ 40,000	?	8	SL	4,500
C	65,000	5,000	?	SL	6,000
D	230,000	10,000	10	?	22,000
E	200,000	20,000	8	DDB	?

E 11–7
Depreciation methods; partial periods
● LO11–2

On March 31, 2021, Susquehanna Insurance purchased an office building for $12,000,000. Based on their relative fair values, one-third of the purchase price was allocated to the land and two-thirds to the building. Furniture and fixtures were purchased separately from office equipment on the same date for $1,200,000 and $700,000, respectively. The company uses the straight-line method to depreciate its buildings and the double-declining-balance method to depreciate all other depreciable assets. The estimated useful lives and residual values of these assets are as follows:

	Service Life	Residual Value
Building	30	10% of cost
Furniture and fixtures	10	10% of cost
Office equipment	5	$30,000

Required:
Calculate depreciation for 2021 and 2022.

E 11–8
IFRS; depreciation; partial periods
● LO11–2, LO11–10
 IFRS

On June 30, 2021, Rosetta Granite purchased equipment for $120,000. The estimated useful life of the equipment is eight years and no residual value is anticipated. An important component of the equipment is a specialized high-speed drill that will need to be replaced in four years. The $20,000 cost of the drill is included in the $120,000 cost of the equipment. Rosetta uses the straight-line depreciation method for all equipment.

Required:
1. Calculate depreciation for 2021 and 2022 applying the typical U.S. GAAP treatment.
2. Repeat requirement 1 applying IFRS.

E 11–9
IFRS; revaluation of equipment; depreciation; partial periods
● LO11–10
 IFRS

Dower Corporation prepares its financial statements according to IFRS. On March 31, 2021, the company purchased equipment for $240,000. The equipment is expected to have a six-year useful life with no residual value. Dower uses the straight-line depreciation method for all equipment. On December 31, 2021, the end of the company's fiscal year, Dower chooses to revalue the equipment to its fair value of $220,000.

Required:
1. Calculate depreciation for 2021.
2. Prepare the journal entry to record the revaluation of the equipment.
3. Calculate depreciation for 2022.
4. Repeat requirement 2 assuming that the fair value of the equipment at the end of 2021 is $195,000.

E 11–10
Disposal of property, plant, and equipment
● LO11–2

Mercury Inc. purchased equipment in 2019 at a cost of $400,000. The equipment was expected to produce 700,000 units over the next five years and have a residual value of $50,000. The equipment was sold for $210,000 part way through 2021. Actual production in each year was: 2019 = 100,000 units; 2020 = 160,000 units; 2021 = 80,000 units. Mercury uses units-of-production depreciation, and all depreciation has been recorded through the disposal date.

Required:
1. Calculate the gain or loss on the sale.
2. Prepare the journal entry to record the sale.
3. Assuming that the equipment was instead sold for $245,000, calculate the gain or loss on the sale.
4. Prepare the journal entry to record the sale in requirement 3.

CHAPTER 11 Property, Plant, and Equipment and Intangible Assets: Utilization and Disposition **623**

E 11–11
Disposal of property, plant, and equipment; partial periods
● LO11–2

On July 1, 2016, Farm Fresh Industries purchased a specialized delivery truck for $126,000. At the time, Farm Fresh estimated the truck to have a useful life of eight years and a residual value of $30,000. On March 1, 2021, the truck was sold for $58,000. Farm Fresh uses the straight-line depreciation method for all of its plant and equipment. Partial-year depreciation is calculated based on the number of months the asset is in service.

Required:
1. Prepare the journal entry to update depreciation in 2021.
2. Prepare the journal entry to record the sale of the truck.
3. Assuming that the truck was instead sold for $80,000, prepare the journal entry to record the sale.

E 11–12
Depreciation methods; disposal; partial periods
● LO11–2

Howarth Manufacturing Company purchased equipment on June 30, 2017, at a cost of $800,000. The residual value of the equipment was estimated to be $50,000 at the end of a five-year life. The equipment was sold on March 31, 2021, for $170,000. Howarth uses the straight-line depreciation method for all of its plant and equipment. Partial-year depreciation is calculated based on the number of months the asset is in service.

Required:
1. Prepare the journal entry to record the sale.
2. Assuming that Howarth had instead used the double-declining-balance method, prepare the journal entry to record the sale.

E 11–13
Assets held for sale; partial periods
● LO11–2

On March 31, 2021, management of Quality Appliances committed to a plan to sell equipment. The equipment was available for immediate sale, and an active plan to locate a buyer was initiated. The equipment had been purchased on January 1, 2019, for $260,000. The equipment had an estimated six-year service life and residual value of $20,000. The equipment was being depreciated using the straight-line method. Quality's fiscal year ends on December 31.

Required:
1. Calculate the equipment's book value as of March 31, 2021 (*Hint:* Depreciation for 2021 would include up to March 31).
2. By December 31, 2021, the equipment has not been sold, but management expects that it will be sold in 2022 for $150,000. For what amount is the equipment reported in the December 31, 2021, balance sheet?

E 11–14
Group depreciation
● LO11–2

Highsmith Rental Company purchased an apartment building early in 2021. There are 20 apartments in the building and each is furnished with major kitchen appliances. The company has decided to use the group depreciation method for the appliances. The following data are available:

Appliance	Cost	Residual Value	Service Life (in years)
Stoves	$15,000	$3,000	6
Refrigerators	10,000	1,000	5
Dishwashers	8,000	500	4

In 2024, three new refrigerators costing $2,700 were purchased for cash. In that same year, the old refrigerators, which originally cost $1,500, were sold for $200.

Required:
1. Calculate the group depreciation rate, group life, and depreciation for 2021.
2. Prepare the journal entries to record the purchase of the new refrigerators and the sale of the old refrigerators.

E 11–15
Double-declining-balance method; switch to straight line
● LO11–2, LO11–6

On January 2, 2021, the Jackson Company purchased equipment to be used in its manufacturing process. The equipment has an estimated life of eight years and an estimated residual value of $30,625. The expenditures made to acquire the asset were as follows:

Purchase price	$154,000
Freight charges	2,000
Installation charges	4,000

Jackson's policy is to use the double-declining-balance (DDB) method of depreciation in the early years of the equipment's life and then switch to straight line halfway through the equipment's life.

Required:
1. Calculate depreciation for each year of the asset's eight-year life.
2. Are changes in depreciation methods accounted for retrospectively or prospectively?

624   SECTION 2   Assets

E 11–16
Depletion
● LO11–3

On April 17, 2021, the Loadstone Mining Company purchased the rights to a coal mine. The purchase price plus additional costs necessary to prepare the mine for extraction of the coal totaled $4,500,000. The company expects to extract 900,000 tons of coal during a four-year period. During 2021, 240,000 tons were extracted and sold immediately.

Required:
1. Calculate depletion for 2021.
2. Is depletion considered part of the product cost and included in the cost of inventory (yes/no)? Discuss.

E 11–17
Depreciation and
depletion
● LO11–2, LO11–3

At the beginning of 2021, Terra Lumber Company purchased a timber tract from Boise Cantor for $3,200,000. After the timber is cleared, the land will have a residual value of $600,000. Roads to enable logging operations were constructed and completed on March 30, 2021. The cost of the roads, which have no residual value and no alternative use after the tract is cleared, was $240,000. During 2021, Terra logged 500,000 of the estimated five million board feet of timber.

Required:
Calculate the 2021 depletion of the timber tract and depreciation of the logging roads assuming the units-of-production method is used for both assets.

E 11–18
Cost of a natural
resource;
depletion and
depreciation;
Chapters 10
and 11
● LO11–2, LO11–3

[This exercise is a continuation of Exercise 10–4 in Chapter 10 focusing on depletion and depreciation.]

Jackpot Mining Company operates a copper mine in central Montana. The company paid $1,000,000 in 2021 for the mining site and spent an additional $600,000 to prepare the mine for extraction of the copper. After the copper is extracted in approximately four years, the company is required to restore the land to its original condition, including repaving of roads and replacing a greenbelt. The company has provided the following three cash flow possibilities for the restoration costs:

	Cash Outflow	Probability
1	$300,000	25%
2	400,000	40%
3	600,000	35%

To aid extraction, Jackpot purchased some new equipment on July 1, 2021, for $120,000. After the copper is removed from this mine, the equipment will be sold for an estimated residual amount of $20,000. There will be no residual value for the copper mine. The credit-adjusted risk-free rate of interest is 10%.

The company expects to extract 10 million pounds of copper from the mine. Actual production was 1.6 million pounds in 2021 and 3 million pounds in 2022.

Required:
1. Compute depletion and depreciation on the mine and mining equipment for 2021 and 2022. The units-of-production method is used to calculate depreciation.
2. Discuss the accounting treatment of the depletion and depreciation on the mine and mining equipment.

E 11–19
Amortization
● LO11–4, LO11–5

Janes Company provided the following information on intangible assets:
a. A patent was purchased from the Lou Company for $700,000 on January 1, 2019. Janes estimated the remaining useful life of the patent to be 10 years. The patent was carried on Lou's accounting records at a net book value of $350,000 when Lou sold it to Janes.
b. During 2021, a franchise was purchased from the Rink Company for $500,000. The contractual life of the franchise is 10 years and Janes records a full year of amortization in the year of purchase.
c. Janes incurred research and development costs in 2021 as follows:

Materials and supplies	$140,000
Personnel	180,000
Indirect costs	60,000
Total	$380,000

d. Effective January 1, 2021, based on new events that have occurred, Janes estimates that the remaining life of the patent purchased from Lou is only five more years.

Required:
1. Prepare the entries necessary for years 2019 through 2021 to reflect the above information.
2. Prepare a schedule showing the intangible asset section of Janes's December 31, 2021, balance sheet.

E 11–20
Patent
amortization;
patent defense
● LO11–4, LO11–9

On January 2, 2021, David Corporation purchased a patent for $500,000. The remaining legal life is 12 years, but the company estimated that the patent will be useful only for eight years. In January 2023, the company incurred legal fees of $45,000 in successfully defending a patent infringement suit. The successful defense did not change the company's estimate of useful life.

Required:
Prepare journal entries related to the patent for 2021, 2022, and 2023.

E 11–21
Change in estimate; useful life of patent
● LO11–4, LO11–5

Van Frank Telecommunications has a patent on a cellular transmission process. The company has amortized the patent on a straight-line basis since 2017, when it was acquired at a cost of $9 million at the beginning of that year. Due to rapid technological advances in the industry, management decided that the patent would benefit the company over a total of six years rather than the nine-year life being used to amortize its cost. The decision was made at the beginning of 2021.

Required:
Prepare the year-end journal entry for patent amortization in 2021. No amortization was recorded during the year.

E 11–22
IFRS; revaluation of patent; amortization
● LO11–10

🌐 **IFRS**

Saint John Corporation prepares its financial statements according to IFRS. On June 30, 2021, the company purchased a franchise for $1,200,000. The franchise is expected to have a 10-year useful life with no residual value. Saint John uses the straight-line amortization method for all intangible assets. On December 31, 2021, the end of the company's fiscal year, Saint John chooses to revalue the franchise. There is an active market for this particular franchise and its fair value on December 31, 2021, is $1,180,000.

Required:
1. Calculate amortization for 2021.
2. Prepare the journal entry to record the revaluation of the patent.
3. Calculate amortization for 2022.

E 11–23
Change in estimate; useful life and residual value of equipment
● LO11–2, LO11–5

Wardell Company purchased a minicomputer on January 1, 2019, at a cost of $40,000. The computer was depreciated using the straight-line method over an estimated five-year life with an estimated residual value of $4,000. On January 1, 2021, the estimate of useful life was changed to a total of 10 years, and the estimate of residual value was changed to $900.

Required:
1. Prepare the year-end journal entry for depreciation in 2021. No depreciation was recorded during the year.
2. Repeat requirement 1 assuming that the company uses the sum-of-the-years'-digits method instead of the straight-line method.

E 11–24
Change in principle; change in depreciation methods
● LO11–2, LO11–6

Alteran Corporation purchased office equipment for $1.5 million at the beginning of 2019. The equipment is being depreciated over a 10-year life using the double-declining-balance method. The residual value is expected to be $300,000. At the beginning of 2021 (two years later), Alteran decided to change to the straight-line depreciation method for this equipment.

Required:
Prepare the journal entry to record depreciation for 2021.

E 11–25
Change in principle; change in depreciation methods
● LO11–2, LO11–6

For financial reporting, Clinton Poultry Farms has used the declining-balance method of depreciation for conveyor equipment acquired at the beginning of 2018 for $2,560,000. Its useful life was estimated to be six years, with a $160,000 residual value. At the beginning of 2021, Clinton decides to change to the straight-line method. The effect of this change on depreciation for each year is as follows:

| | ($ in thousands) | | |
Year	Straight Line	Declining Balance	Difference
2018	$ 400	$ 853	$453
2019	400	569	169
2020	400	379	(21)
	$1,200	$1,801	$601

Required:
1. Briefly describe the way Clinton should report this accounting change in the 2019–2021 comparative financial statements.
2. Prepare any 2021 journal entry related to the change.

E 11–26
Error correction
● LO11–2, LO11–7

In 2021, internal auditors discovered that PKE Displays, Inc. had debited an expense account for the $350,000 cost of equipment purchased on January 1, 2018. The equipment's life was expected to be five years with no residual value. Straight-line depreciation is used by PKE.

626 SECTION 2 Assets

Required:

1. Determine the cumulative effect of the error on net income over the three-year period from 2018 through 2020, and on retained earnings by the end of 2020.

2. Prepare the correcting entry assuming the error was discovered in 2021 before the adjusting and closing entries. (Ignore income taxes.)

3. Assume instead that the equipment was disposed of in 2022 and the original error was discovered in 2023 after the 2022 financial statements were issued. Prepare the correcting entry in 2023.

E 11–27
Impairment;
property, plant,
and equipment
● LO11–8

Chadwick Enterprises, Inc., operates several restaurants throughout the Midwest. Three of its restaurants located in the center of a large urban area have experienced declining profits due to declining population. The company's management has decided to test the assets of the restaurants for possible impairment. The relevant information for these assets is presented below.

Book value	$6.5 million
Estimated undiscounted sum of future cash flows	4.0 million
Fair value	3.5 million

Required:

1. Determine the amount of the impairment loss, if any.

2. Repeat requirement 1 assuming that the estimated undiscounted sum of future cash flows is $6.8 million and fair value is $5 million.

E 11–28
IFRS; impairment;
property, plant,
and equipment
● LO11–10

 IFRS

Refer to the situation described in Exercise 11–27.

Required:

How might your solution differ if Chadwick Enterprises, Inc., prepares its financial statements according to International Financial Reporting Standards? Assume that the fair value amount given in the exercise equals both (a) the fair value less costs to sell and (b) the present value of estimated future cash flows.

E 11–29
IFRS; Impairment;
property, plant,
and equipment
● LO11–8,
LO11–10

 IFRS

Collinsworth LTD., a U.K. company, prepares its financial statements according to International Financial Reporting Standards. Late in its 2021 fiscal year, a significant adverse change in business climate indicated to management that the assets of its appliance division may be impaired. The following data relate to the division's assets:

	(£ in millions)
Book value	£220
Undiscounted sum of estimated future cash flows	210
Present value of future cash flows	150
Fair value less cost to sell (determined by appraisal)	145

Required:

1. What amount of impairment loss, if any, should Collinsworth recognize?

2. Assume that Collinsworth prepares its financial statements according to U.S. GAAP and that fair value less cost to sell approximates fair value. What amount of impairment loss, if any, should Collinsworth recognize?

E 11–30
Impairment;
property, plant,
and equipment
● LO11–8

General Optic Corporation operates a manufacturing plant in Arizona. Due to a significant decline in demand for the product manufactured at the Arizona site, an impairment test is deemed appropriate. Management has acquired the following information for the assets at the plant:

Cost	$32,500,000
Accumulated depreciation	14,200,000
General's estimate of the total cash flows to be generated by selling the products manufactured at its Arizona plant, not discounted to present value	15,000,000

The fair value of the Arizona plant is estimated to be $11,000,000.

Required:

1. Determine the amount of impairment loss, if any.

2. If a loss is indicated, prepare the entry to record the loss.

3. Repeat requirement 1 assuming that the estimated undiscounted sum of future cash flows is $12,000,000 instead of $15,000,000.

CHAPTER 11   Property, Plant, and Equipment and Intangible Assets: Utilization and Disposition   **627**

4. Repeat requirement 1 assuming that the estimated undiscounted sum of future cash flows is $19,000,000 instead of $15,000,000

E 11–31
Impairment;
goodwill
● LO11–8

In 2019, Alliant Corporation acquired Centerpoint Inc. for $300 million, of which $50 million was allocated to goodwill. At the end of 2021, management has provided the following information for a required goodwill impairment test:

Fair value of Centerpoint Inc.	$220 million
Book value of Centerpoint's net assets (excluding goodwill)	200 million
Book value of Centerpoint's net assets (including goodwill)	250 million

Required:
1. Determine the amount of the impairment loss.
2. Repeat requirement 1 assuming that the fair value of Centerpoint is $270 million.

E 11–32
IFRS; impairment;
goodwill
● LO11–10

 IFRS

Refer to the situation described in E 11–31, requirement 1. Alliant prepares its financial statements according to IFRS, and Centerpoint is considered a cash-generating unit. Assume that Centerpoint's fair value of $220 million approximates fair value less costs to sell and that the present value of Centerpoint's estimated future cash flows is $225 million.

Required:
Determine the amount of goodwill impairment loss Alliant should recognize.

E 11–33
Goodwill
valuation and
impairment;
Chapters 10
and 11
● LO11–8

On May 28, 2021, Pesky Corporation acquired all of the outstanding common stock of Harman, Inc., for $420 million. The fair value of Harman's identifiable tangible and intangible assets totaled $512 million, and the fair value of liabilities assumed by Pesky was $150 million.

Pesky performed a goodwill impairment test at the end of its fiscal year ended December 31, 2021. Management has provided the following information:

Fair value of Harman, Inc.	$400 million
Fair value of Harman's net assets (excluding goodwill)	370 million
Book value of Harman's net assets (including goodwill)	410 million

Required:
1. Determine the amount of goodwill that resulted from the Harman acquisition.
2. Determine the amount of goodwill impairment loss that Pesky should recognize at the end of 2021, if any.
3. If an impairment loss is required, prepare the journal entry to record the loss.

E 11–34
FASB codification
research
● LO11–8

Access the *FASB Accounting Standards Codification* at the FASB website (www.fasb.org). Determine each of the following:

Required:
1. The topic number (Topic XXX) that provides guidance on accounting for the impairment of long-lived assets.
2. The specific eight-digit Codification citation (XXX-XX-XX-X) that discusses the disclosures required in the notes to the financial statements for the impairment of long-lived assets classified as held and used.
3. Describe the disclosure requirements.

E 11–35
FASB codification
research
● LO11–2,
LO11–1,
LO11–6,
LO11–8

Access the *FASB Accounting Standards Codification* at the FASB website (www.fasb.org). Determine each of the following:
1. The specific eight-digit Codification citation (XXX-XX-XX-X) that discusses depreciation as a systematic and rational allocation of cost rather than a process of valuation.
2. The specific nine-digit Codification citation (XXX-XX-XX-XX) that involves the calculation of an impairment loss for property, plant, and equipment.
3. The specific nine-digit Codification citation (XXX-XX-XX-XX) that provides guidance on accounting for a change in depreciation method.
4. The specific eight-digit Codification citation (XXX-XX-XX-X) that indicates goodwill should not be amortized.

E 11–36
Subsequent
expenditures
● LO11–9

Belltone Company made the following expenditures related to its 10-year-old manufacturing facility:
1. The heating system was replaced at a cost of $250,000. The cost of the old system was not known. The company accounts for improvements as reductions of accumulated depreciation.
2. A new wing was added at a cost of $750,000. The new wing substantially increases the productive capacity of the plant.

628   SECTION 2   Assets

3. Annual building maintenance was performed at a cost of $14,000.

4. All of the equipment on the assembly line in the plant was rearranged at a cost of $50,000. The rearrangement clearly increases the productive capacity of the plant.

Required:
Prepare journal entries to record each of the above expenditures.

E 11–37
IFRS;
amortization;
cost to defend a
patent
● LO11–4,
  LO11–9,
  LO11–10

🌐 **IFRS**

On September 30, 2019, Leeds LTD. acquired a patent in conjunction with the purchase of another company. The patent, valued at $6 million, was estimated to have a 10-year life and no residual value. Leeds uses the straight-line method of amortization for intangible assets. At the beginning of January 2021, Leeds successfully defended its patent against infringement. Litigation costs totaled $500,000.

Required:
1. Calculate amortization of the patent for 2019 and 2020.
2. Prepare the journal entry to record the 2021 litigation costs.
3. Calculate amortization for 2021.
4. Repeat requirements 1–3 assuming that Leeds prepares its financial statements according to IFRS.

E 11–38
Concepts;
terminology
● LO11–1 through
  LO11–6,
  LO11–8

Listed below are several items and phrases associated with depreciation, depletion, and amortization. Pair each item from List A with the item from List B (by letter) that is most appropriately associated with it.

List A	List B
_____ 1. Depreciation	a. Cost allocation for natural resource
_____ 2. Service life	b. Accounted for prospectively
_____ 3. Depreciable base	c. When there has been a significant decline in value
_____ 4. Activity-based methods	d. The amount of use expected from plant and equipment and
_____ 5. Time-based methods	finite-life intangible assets
_____ 6. Double-declining balance	e. Estimates service life in units of output
_____ 7. Group method	f. Cost less residual value
_____ 8. Composite method	g. Cost allocation for plant and equipment
_____ 9. Depletion	h. Does not subtract residual value from cost
_____ 10. Amortization	i. Accounted for in the same way as a change in estimate
_____ 11. Change in useful life	j. Aggregates assets that are similar
_____ 12. Change in depreciation method	k. Aggregates assets that are physically unified
_____ 13. Write-down of asset	l. Cost allocation for an intangible asset
	m. Estimates service life in years

E 11–39
Retirement and
replacement
depreciation
● Appendix B

Cadillac Construction Company uses the retirement method to determine depreciation on its small tools. During 2019, the first year of the company's operations, tools were purchased at a cost of $8,000. In 2021, tools originally costing $2,000 were sold for $250 and replaced with new tools costing $2,500.

Required:
1. Prepare journal entries to record each of the above transactions.
2. Repeat requirement 1 assuming that the company uses the replacement depreciation method instead of the retirement method.

E 11–40
General ledger
exercise;
depreciation
● LO11–2

On January 1, 2021, the general ledger of TNT Fireworks included the following account balances:

Account Title	Debits	Credits
Cash	$ 58,700	
Accounts receivable	25,000	
Allowance for uncollectible accounts		$ 2,200
Inventory	36,300	
Notes receivable (5%, due in 2 years)	12,000	
Land	155,000	
Accounts payable		14,800
Common stock		220,000
Retained earnings		50,000
Totals	$287,000	$287,000

CHAPTER 11   Property, Plant, and Equipment and Intangible Assets: Utilization and Disposition   **629**

During January 2021, the following transactions occurred:

Jan. 1   Purchased equipment for $19,500. The company estimates a residual value of $1,500 and a five-year service life.
4   Paid cash on accounts payable, $9,500.
8   Purchased additional inventory on account, $82,900.
15   Received cash on accounts receivable, $22,000.
19   Paid cash for salaries, $29,800.
28   Paid cash for January utilities, $16,500.
30   Firework sales for January totaled $220,000. All of these sales were on account. The cost of the units sold was $115,000.

Required:

1. Record each of the transactions listed above in the 'General Journal' tab (these are shown as items 1–8) assuming a perpetual FIFO inventory system. Review the 'General Ledger' and the 'Trial Balance' tabs to see the effect of the transactions on the account balances.

2. Record adjusting entries on January 31 in the 'General Journal' tab (these are shown as items 9–13):

   a. Depreciation on the equipment for the month of January is calculated using the straight-line method.

   b. At the end of January, $3,000 of accounts receivable are past due, and the company estimates that 50% of these accounts will not be collected. Of the remaining accounts receivable, the company estimates that 3% will not be collected. The note receivable of $12,000 is considered fully collectible and therefore is not included in the estimate of uncollectible accounts.

   c. Accrued interest revenue on notes receivable for January.

   d. Unpaid salaries at the end of January are $32,600.

   e. Accrued income taxes at the end of January are $9,000.

3. Review the adjusted 'Trial Balance' as of January 31, 2021, in the 'Trial Balance' tab.

4. Prepare a multiple-step income statement for the period ended January 31, 2021, in the 'Income Statement' tab.

5. Prepare a classified balance sheet as of January 31, 2021, in the 'Balance Sheet' tab.

6. Record closing entries in the 'General Journal' tab (these are shown as items 14–15).

7. Using the information from the requirements above, complete the 'Analysis' tab.

   a. Calculate the return on assets ratio for the month of January. If the average return on assets for the industry in January is 2%, is the company *more* or *less* profitable than other companies in the same industry?

   b. Calculate the profit margin for the month of January. If the industry average profit margin is 4%, is the company *more* or *less* efficient at converting sales to profit than other companies in the same industry?

   c. Calculate the asset turnover ratio for the month of January. If the industry average asset turnover is 0.5 times per month, is the company *more* or *less* efficient at producing revenues with its assets than other companies in the same industry?

E 11–41
General ledger exercise; long-term asset transactions
● LO11–2, LO11–4, LO11–8, LO11–9

On January 1, 2021, the general ledger of Parts Unlimited included the following account balances:

Account Title	Debits	Credits
Cash	$162,400	
Accounts receivable	12,400	
Inventory	37,800	
Land	340,000	
Equipment	347,500	
Accumulated depreciation		$172,000
Accounts payable		14,800
Common stock		520,000
Retained earnings		193,300
Totals	$900,100	$900,100

From January 1 to December 31, the following summary transactions occurred:

a. Purchased inventory on account, $325,800.
b. Sold inventory on account, $567,200. The inventory cost $342,600.
c. Received cash from customers on account, $558,700.
d. Paid cash on account, $328,500.
e. Paid cash for salaries, $94,700, and for utilities, $52,700.

630 SECTION 2 Assets

In addition, Parts Unlimited had the following transactions during the year:

April 1	Purchased equipment for $95,000 using a note payable, due in 12 months plus 8% interest. The company also paid cash of $3,200 for freight and $3,800 for installation and testing of the equipment. The equipment has an estimated residual value of $10,000 and a ten-year service life.
June 30	Purchased a patent for $40,000 from a third-party marketing company related to the packaging of the company's products. The patent has a 20-year useful life, after which it is expected to have no value.
October 1	Sold equipment for $30,200. The equipment cost $60,700 and had accumulated depreciation of $37,400 at the beginning of the year. Additional depreciation for 2021 up to the point of the sale is $8,500.
November 15	Several older pieces of equipment were improved by replacing major components at a cost of $54,100. These improvements are expected to enhance the equipment's operating capabilities. [Record this transaction using Alternative 2—capitalization of new cost.]

Required:

1. Record each of the transactions listed above in the 'General Journal' tab (these are shown as items 1–11) assuming a perpetual inventory system. Review the 'General Ledger' and the 'Trial Balance' tabs to see the effect of the transactions on the account balances.

2. Record adjusting entries on December 31 in the 'General Journal' tab (these are shown as items 12–17):

    a. Depreciation on the equipment purchased on April 1, 2021, calculated using the straight-line method.

    b. Depreciation on the remaining equipment, $21,500.

    c. Amortization of the patent purchased on June 30, 2021, using the straight-line method.

    d. Accrued interest payable on the note payable.

    e. Equipment with an original cost of $65,400 had the following related information at the end of the year: accumulated depreciation of $40,300, expected cash flows of $15,700, and a fair value of $10,800.

    f. Accrued income taxes at the end of the year are $12,600.

3. Review the adjusted 'Trial Balance' as of December 31, 2021, in the 'Trial Balance' tab.

4. Prepare a multiple-step income statement for the period ended December 31, 2021, in the 'Income Statement' tab.

5. Prepare a classified balance sheet as of December 31, 2021, in the 'Balance Sheet' tab.

6. Record closing entries in the 'General Journal' tab (these are shown as items 18–19).

7. Using the information from the requirements above, complete the 'Analysis' tab.

    a. Calculate the fixed asset turnover ratio for the year, using the total amount of property, plant, and equipment (net of accumulated deprecation). If the industry average fixed asset turnover is 0.75, is the company *more* or *less* efficient at generating sales with its fixed assets than other companies in the same industry?

    b. Suppose the equipment purchased on April 1, 2021, had been depreciated using the units of production method. At the time of purchase, expected output was 20,000 units, and actual production for 2021 was 2,000 units. Calculate the amount of depreciation expense that would have been recorded and determine the difference in net income and total assets for 2021 (ignoring tax effects).

    c. The transaction on June 30, 2021, shows the company purchased a patent for $40,000 from a third-party marketing company. Suppose the company instead spent $40,000 to internally develop the new packaging technology, which it then patented. Calculate the difference in net income and total assets for 2021 (ignoring tax effects).

Problems ■ connect

P 11–1
Depreciation
methods; change
in methods
● LO11–2, LO11–6

The fact that generally accepted accounting principles allow companies flexibility in choosing between certain allocation methods can make it difficult for a financial analyst to compare periodic performance from firm to firm.

Suppose you were a financial analyst trying to compare the performance of two companies. Company A uses the double-declining-balance depreciation method. Company B uses the straight-line method. You have the following information taken from the 12/31/2021 year-end financial statements for Company B:

Income Statement	
Depreciation expense	$ 10,000

Balance Sheet	
Assets:	
Plant and equipment, at cost	$200,000
Less: Accumulated depreciation	(40,000)
Net	$160,000

You also determine that all of the assets constituting the plant and equipment of Company B were acquired at the same time, and that all of the $200,000 represents depreciable assets. Also, all of the depreciable assets have the same useful life and residual values are zero.

Required:

1. In order to compare performance with Company A, estimate what B's depreciation expense would have been for 2021 if the double-declining-balance depreciation method had been used by Company B since acquisition of the depreciable assets.

2. If Company B decided to switch depreciation methods in 2021 from the straight line to the double-declining-balance method, prepare the 2021 journal entry to record depreciation for the year, assuming no journal entry for depreciation in 2021 has yet been recorded.

P 11–2
Comprehensive problem;
Chapters 10 and 11
● LO11–2, LO11–4

At December 31, 2020, Cord Company's plant asset and accumulated depreciation and amortization accounts had balances as follows:

Category	Plant Asset	Accumulated Depreciation and Amortization
Land	$ 175,000	$ —
Buildings	1,500,000	328,900
Equipment	1,125,000	317,500
Automobiles and trucks	172,000	100,325
Leasehold improvements	216,000	108,000
Land improvements	—	—

Depreciation methods and useful lives:
Buildings—150% declining balance; 25 years.
Equipment—Straight line; 10 years.
Automobiles and trucks—200% declining balance; 5 years, all acquired after 2017.
Leasehold improvements—Straight line.
Land improvements—Straight line.

Depreciation is computed to the nearest month and residual values are immaterial. Transactions during 2021 and other information:

a. On January 6, 2021, a plant facility consisting of land and building was acquired from King Corp. in exchange for 25,000 shares of Cord's common stock. On this date, Cord's stock had a fair value of $50 a share. Current assessed values of land and building for property tax purposes are $187,500 and $562,500, respectively.

b. On March 25, 2021, new parking lots, streets, and sidewalks at the acquired plant facility were completed at a total cost of $192,000. These expenditures had an estimated useful life of 12 years.

c. The leasehold improvements were completed on December 31, 2017, and had an estimated useful life of eight years. The related lease, which would terminate on December 31, 2023, was renewable for an additional four-year term. On April 30, 2021, Cord exercised the renewal option.

d. On July 1, 2021, equipment was purchased at a total invoice cost of $325,000. Additional costs of $10,000 for delivery and $50,000 for installation were incurred.

e. On September 30, 2021, Cord purchased a new automobile for $12,500.

f. On September 30, 2021, a truck with a cost of $24,000 and a book value of $9,100 on date of sale was sold for $11,500. Depreciation for the nine months ended September 30, 2021, was $2,650.

g. On December 20, 2021, equipment with a cost of $17,000 and a book value of $2,975 at date of disposition was scrapped without cash recovery.

632   SECTION 2   Assets

Required:

1. Prepare a schedule analyzing the changes in each of the plant asset accounts during 2021. This schedule should include columns for beginning balance, increase, decrease, and ending balance for each of the plant asset accounts. Do not analyze changes in accumulated depreciation and amortization.

2. For each asset category, prepare a schedule showing depreciation or amortization expense for the year ended December 31, 2021. Round computations to the nearest whole dollar.

(AICPA adapted)

P 11–3
Depreciation methods; partial periods Chapters 10 and 11
● LO11–2

[This problem is a continuation of Problem 10–3 in Chapter 10 focusing on depreciation.]

Required:

For each asset classification, prepare a schedule showing depreciation for the year ended December 31, 2021, using the following depreciation methods and useful lives:

> Land improvements—Straight line; 15 years
> Building—150% declining balance; 20 years
> Equipment—Straight line; 10 years
> Automobiles—Units-of-production; $0.50 per mile

Depreciation is computed to the nearest month and whole dollar amount, and no residual values are used. Automobiles were driven 38,000 miles in 2021.

(AICPA adapted)

P 11–4
Partial-year depreciation; asset addition; increase in useful life
● LO11–2,
   LO11–5,
   LO11–9

On April 1, 2019, the KB Toy Company purchased equipment to be used in its manufacturing process. The equipment cost $48,000, has an eight-year useful life, and has no residual value. The company uses the straight-line depreciation method for all manufacturing equipment.

On January 4, 2021, $12,350 was spent to repair the equipment and to add a feature that increased its operating efficiency. Of the total expenditure, $2,000 represented ordinary repairs and annual maintenance and $10,350 represented the cost of the new feature. In addition to increasing operating efficiency, the total useful life of the equipment was extended to 10 years.

Required:

Prepare journal entries for the following:

1. Depreciation for 2019 and 2020.

2. The 2021 expenditure.

3. Depreciation for 2021.

P 11–5
Property, plant, and equipment and intangible assets; comprehensive
● LO11–2

The Thompson Corporation, a manufacturer of steel products, began operations on October 1, 2019. The accounting department of Thompson has started the fixed-asset and depreciation schedule presented below. You have been asked to assist in completing this schedule. In addition to ascertaining that the data already on the schedule are correct, you have obtained the following information from the company's records and personnel:

a. Depreciation is computed from the first of the month of acquisition to the first of the month of disposition.

b. Land A and Building A were acquired from a predecessor corporation. Thompson paid $812,500 for the land and building together. At the time of acquisition, the land had a fair value of $72,000 and the building had a fair value of $828,000.

c. Land B was acquired on October 2, 2019, in exchange for 3,000 newly issued shares of Thompson's common stock. At the date of acquisition, the stock had a par value of $5 per share and a fair value of $25 per share. During October 2019, Thompson paid $10,400 to demolish an existing building on this land so it could construct a new building.

d. Construction of Building B on the newly acquired land began on October 1, 2020. By September 30, 2021, Thompson had paid $210,000 of the estimated total construction costs of $300,000. Estimated completion and occupancy are July 2022.

e. Certain equipment was donated to the corporation by the city. An independent appraisal of the equipment when donated placed the fair value at $16,000 and the residual value at $2,000.

f. Equipment A's total cost of $110,000 includes installation charges of $550 and normal repairs and maintenance of $11,000. Residual value is estimated at $5,500. Equipment A was sold on February 1, 2021.

g. On October 1, 2020, Equipment B was acquired with a down payment of $4,000 and the remaining payments to be made in 10 annual installments of $4,000 each beginning October 1, 2021. The prevailing interest rate was 8%.

THOMPSON CORPORATION
Fixed Asset and Depreciation Schedule
For Fiscal Years Ended September 30, 2020, and September 30, 2021

Assets	Acquisition Date	Cost	Residual	Depreciation Method	Estimated Life (in years)	Depreciation for Year Ended 9/30 2020	2021
Land A	10/1/2019	$(1)	N/A	N/A	N/A	N/A	N/A
Building A	10/1/2019	(2)	$47,500	SL	(3)	$14,000	$(4)
Land B	10/2/2019	(5)	N/A	N/A	N/A	N/A	N/A
Building B	Under construction	210,000 to date	—	SL	30	—	(6)
Donated Equipment	10/2/2019	(7)	2,000	DDB	10	(8)	(9)
Equipment A	10/2/2019	(10)	5,500	SYD	10	(11)	(12)
Equipment B	10/1/2020	(13)	—	SL	15	—	(14)

N/A = not applicable

Required:

Supply the correct amount for each numbered item on the schedule. For depreciation methods, SL indicates straight-line, DDB indicates double-declining-balance, and SYD indicates sum-of-the-years'-digits. Round each answer to the nearest dollar.

(AICPA adapted)

P 11–6
Depreciation methods; partial-year depreciation; sale of assets
● LO11–2

On March 31, 2021, the Herzog Company purchased a factory complete with vehicles and equipment. The allocation of the total purchase price of $1,000,000 to the various types of assets along with estimated useful lives and residual values are as follows:

Asset	Cost	Estimated Residual Value	Estimated Useful Life (in years)
Land	$ 100,000	N/A	N/A
Building	500,000	none	25
Equipment	240,000	10% of cost	8
Vehicles	160,000	$12,000	8
Total	$1,000,000		

On June 29, 2022, equipment included in the March 31, 2021, purchase that cost $100,000 was sold for $80,000. Herzog uses the straight-line depreciation method for buildings and equipment and the double-declining-balance method for vehicles. Partial-year depreciation is calculated based on the number of months an asset is in service.

Required:

1. Compute depreciation expense on the building, equipment, and vehicles for 2021.
2. Prepare the journal entries for 2022 to record (a) depreciation on the equipment sold on June 29, 2022, and (b) the sale of the equipment. Round to the nearest whole dollar amount.
3. Compute depreciation expense on the building, remaining equipment, and vehicles for 2022.

P 11–7
Depletion; change in estimate
● LO11–3, LO11–5

In 2021, the Marion Company purchased land containing a mineral mine for $1,600,000. Additional costs of $600,000 were incurred to develop the mine. Geologists estimated that 400,000 tons of ore would be extracted. After the ore is removed, the land will have a resale value of $100,000.

To aid in the extraction, Marion built various structures and small storage buildings on the site at a cost of $150,000. These structures have a useful life of 10 years. The structures cannot be moved after the ore has been removed and will be left at the site. In addition, new equipment costing $80,000 was purchased and installed at the site. Marion does not plan to move the equipment to another site, but estimates that it can be sold at auction for $4,000 after the mining project is completed.

In 2021, 50,000 tons of ore were extracted and sold. In 2022, the estimate of total tons of ore in the mine was revised from 400,000 to 487,500. During 2022, 80,000 tons were extracted, of which 60,000 tons were sold.

Required:

1. Compute depletion and depreciation of the mine and the mining facilities and equipment for 2021 and 2022. Marion uses the units-of-production method to determine depreciation on mining facilities and equipment.
2. Compute the book value of the mineral mine, structures, and equipment as of December 31, 2022.
3. Discuss the accounting treatment of the depletion and depreciation on the mine and mining facilities and equipment.

634   **SECTION 2**   Assets

P 11–8
Amortization;
partial period
● LO11–4

The following information concerns the intangible assets of Epstein Corporation:

a. On June 30, 2021, Epstein completed the acquisition of the Johnstone Corporation for $2,000,000 in cash. The fair value of the net identifiable assets of Johnstone was $1,700,000.

b. Included in the assets purchased from Johnstone was a patent that was valued at $80,000. The remaining legal life of the patent was 13 years, but Epstein believes that the patent will only be useful for another eight years.

c. Epstein acquired a franchise on October 1, 2021, by paying an initial franchise fee of $200,000. The contractual life of the franchise is 10 years.

Required:
1. Prepare year-end adjusting journal entries to record amortization expense on the intangibles at December 31, 2021.
2. Prepare the intangible asset section of the December 31, 2021, balance sheet.

P 11–9
Straight-line
depreciation;
disposal; partial
period; change in
estimate
● LO11–2, LO11–5

The property, plant, and equipment section of the Jasper Company's December 31, 2020, balance sheet contained the following:

Property, plant, and equipment:		
Land		$120,000
Building	$ 840,000	
Less: Accumulated depreciation	(200,000)	640,000
Equipment	180,000	
Less: Accumulated depreciation	?	?
Total property, plant, and equipment		?

The land and building were purchased at the beginning of 2016. Straight-line depreciation is used and a residual value of $40,000 for the building is anticipated.

The equipment is comprised of the following three machines:

Machine	Cost	Date Acquired	Residual Value	Life (in years)
101	$70,000	1/1/2018	$7,000	10
102	80,000	6/30/2019	8,000	8
103	30,000	9/1/2020	3,000	9

The straight-line method is used to determine depreciation on the equipment. On March 31, 2021, Machine 102 was sold for $52,500. Early in 2021, the useful life of machine 101 was revised to seven years in total, and the residual value was revised to zero.

Required:
1. Calculate the accumulated depreciation on the equipment at December 31, 2020.
2. Prepare the journal entry to record 2021 depreciation on machine 102 up to the date of sale.
3. Prepare a schedule to calculate the gain or loss on the sale of machine 102.
4. Prepare the journal entry for the sale of machine 102.
5. Prepare the 2021 year-end journal entries to record depreciation on the building and remaining equipment.

P 11–10
Accounting
changes; three
accounting
situations
● LO11–2,
LO11–5,
LO11–6

Described below are three independent and unrelated situations involving accounting changes. Each change occurs during 2021 before any adjusting entries or closing entries are prepared.

a. On December 30, 2017, Rival Industries acquired its office building at a cost of $10,000,000. It has been depreciated on a straight-line basis assuming a useful life of 40 years and no residual value. Early in 2021, the estimate of useful life was revised to 28 years in total with no change in residual value.

b. At the beginning of 2017, the Hoffman Group purchased office equipment at a cost of $330,000. Its useful life was estimated to be 10 years with no residual value. The equipment has been depreciated by the straight-line method. On January 1, 2021, the company changed to the double-declining-balance method.

c. At the beginning of 2021, Jantzen Specialties, which uses the straight-line method, changed to the double-declining-balance method for newly acquired vehicles. The change decreased current year net income by $445,000.

Required:
For each situation:
1. Identify the type of change.
2. Prepare any journal entry necessary as a direct result of the change as well as any adjusting entry for 2021 related to the situation described. (Ignore income tax effects.)
3. Briefly describe any other steps that should be taken to appropriately report the situation.

CHAPTER 11   Property, Plant, and Equipment and Intangible Assets: Utilization and Disposition   **635**

P 11–11
Error correction;
change in
depreciation
method
● LO11–2,
LO11–6,
LO11–7

Collins Corporation purchased office equipment at the beginning of 2019 and capitalized a cost of $2,000,000. This cost figure included the following expenditures:

Purchase price	$1,850,000
Freight charges	30,000
Installation charges	20,000
Annual maintenance charge	100,000
Total	$2,000,000

The company estimated an eight-year useful life for the equipment. No residual value is anticipated. The double-declining-balance method was used to determine depreciation expense for 2019 and 2020.

In 2021, after the 2020 financial statements were issued, the company decided to switch to the straight-line depreciation method for this equipment. At that time, the company's controller discovered that the original cost of the equipment incorrectly included one year of annual maintenance charges for the equipment.

Required:
1. Ignoring income taxes, prepare the appropriate correcting entry for the equipment capitalization error discovered in 2021.

2. Ignoring income taxes, prepare any 2021 journal entry(s) related to the change in depreciation methods.

P 11–12
Depreciation and
amortization;
impairment
● LO11–2,
LO11–4,
LO11–8

At the beginning of 2019, Metatec Inc. acquired Ellison Technology Corporation for $600 million. In addition to cash, receivables, and inventory, the following assets and their fair values were also acquired:

Plant and equipment (depreciable assets)	$150 million
Patent	40 million
Goodwill	100 million

The plant and equipment are depreciated over a 10-year useful life on a straight-line basis. There is no estimated residual value. The patent is estimated to have a 5-year useful life, no residual value, and is amortized using the straight-line method.

At the end of 2021, a change in business climate indicated to management that the assets of Ellison might be impaired. The following amounts have been determined:

Plant and equipment:	
Undiscounted sum of future cash flows	$ 80 million
Fair value	60 million
Patent:	
Undiscounted sum of future cash flows	$ 20 million
Fair value	13 million
Goodwill:	
Fair value of Ellison Technology Corporation	$450 million
Book value of Ellison's net assets (excluding goodwill)	370 million
Book value of Ellison's net assets (including goodwill)	470 million*

*After first recording any impairment losses on plant and equipment and the patent.

Required:
1. Compute the book value of the plant and equipment and patent at the end of 2021.
2. When should the plant and equipment and the patent be tested for impairment?
3. When should goodwill be tested for impairment?
4. Determine the amount of any impairment loss to be recorded, if any, for the three assets.

P 11–13
Depreciation and
depletion; change
in useful life;
asset retirement
obligation;
Chapters 10
and 11
● LO11–2,
LO11–3, LO11–5

On May 1, 2021, Hecala Mining entered into an agreement with the state of New Mexico to obtain the rights to operate a mineral mine in New Mexico for $10 million. Additional costs and purchases included the following:

Development costs in preparing the mine	$3,200,000
Mining equipment	140,000
Construction of various structures on site	68,000

After the minerals are removed from the mine, the equipment will be sold for an estimated residual value of $10,000. The structures will be torn down.

Geologists estimate that 800,000 tons of ore can be extracted from the mine. After the ore is removed the land will revert back to the state of New Mexico.

636   SECTION 2   Assets

The contract with the state requires Hecala to restore the land to its original condition after mining operations are completed in approximately four years. Management has provided the following possible outflows for the restoration costs:

Cash Outflow	Probability
$600,000	30%
700,000	30%
800,000	40%

Hecala's credit-adjusted risk-free interest rate is 8%. During 2021, Hecala extracted 120,000 tons of ore from the mine. The company's fiscal year ends on December 31.

Required:

1. Determine the amount at which Hecala will record the mine.
2. Calculate the depletion of the mine and the depreciation of the mining facilities and equipment for 2021, assuming that Hecala uses the units-of-production method for both depreciation and depletion. Round depletion and depreciation rates to four decimals.
3. How much accretion expense will the company record in its income statement for the 2021 fiscal year?
4. Are depletion of the mine and depreciation of the mining facilities and equipment reported as separate expenses in the income statement? Discuss the accounting treatment of these items in the income statement and balance sheet.
5. During 2022, Hecala changed its estimate of the total amount of ore originally in the mine from 800,000 to 1,000,000 tons. Briefly describe the accounting treatment the company will employ to account for the change *and* calculate the depletion of the mine and depreciation of the mining facilities and equipment for 2022 assuming Hecala extracted 150,000 tons of ore in 2022.

P 11–14
MACRS versus straight-line depreciation

● LO11–2, Appendix 11A

On April 1, 2024, Titan Corporation purchases office equipment for $50,000. For tax reporting, the company uses MACRS and classifies the equipment as 5-year personal property. In 2024, this type of equipment is eligible for 60% first-year bonus depreciation. For financial reporting, the company uses straight-line depreciation. Assume the equipment has no residual value.

Required:

1. Calculate annual depreciation for the five-year life of the equipment according to MACRS. The company uses the half-year convention for tax reporting purposes.
2. Calculate annual depreciation for the five-year life of the equipment according to straight-line depreciation. The company uses partial-year depreciation based on the number of months the asset is in service for financial reporting purposes.
3. In which year(s) is tax depreciation greater than financial reporting depreciation?

Decision Maker's Perspective

©ImageGap/Getty Images

Apply your critical-thinking ability to the knowledge you've gained. These cases will provide you an opportunity to develop your research, analysis, judgment, and communication skills. You also will work with other students, integrate what you've learned, apply it in real-world situations, and consider its global and ethical ramifications. This practice will broaden your knowledge and further develop your decision-making abilities.

Analysis
Case 11–1
Depreciation, depletion, and amortization

● LO11–1

The terms depreciation, depletion, and amortization all refer to the process of allocating the cost of an asset to the periods the asset is used.

Required:

Discuss the differences between depreciation, depletion, and amortization as the terms are used in accounting for property, plant, and equipment and intangible assets.

Communication
Case 11–2
Depreciation

● LO11–1

At a recent luncheon, you were seated next to Mr. Hopkins, the president of a local company that manufactures bicycle parts. He heard that you were a CPA and made the following comments to you:

Why is it that I am forced to recognize depreciation expense in my company's income statement when I know that I could sell many of my assets for more than I paid for them? I thought that the purpose of the balance sheet was to reflect the value of my business and that the purpose of the income statement was to report the net change in value or wealth of a company. It just doesn't make sense to penalize my profits when there hasn't been any loss in value from using the assets.

At the conclusion of the luncheon, you promised to send him a short explanation of the rationale for current depreciation practices.

Required:

Prepare a letter to Mr. Hopkins. Explain the accounting concept of depreciation and include a brief example in your explanation showing that over the life of the asset the change in value approach to depreciation and the allocation of cost approach will result in the same total effect on income.

Judgment Case 11–3
Straight-line method; composite depreciation
● LO11–1, LO11–2

Portland Co. uses the straight-line depreciation method for depreciable assets. All assets are depreciated individually except manufacturing equipment, which is depreciated by the composite method.

Required:

1. What factors should have influenced Portland's selection of the straight-line depreciation method?
2. a. What benefits should derive from using the composite method rather than the individual basis for manufacturing equipment?
   b. How should Portland have calculated the manufacturing equipment's annual depreciation in its first year of operation?

(AICPA adapted)

Judgment Case 11–4
Depreciation
● LO11–1, LO11–2

At the beginning of the year, Patrick Company acquired a computer to be used in its operations. The computer was delivered by the supplier, installed by Patrick, and placed into operation. The estimated useful life of the computer is five years, and its estimated residual value is significant.

Required:

1. a. What costs should Patrick capitalize for the computer?
   b. What is the objective of depreciation accounting?
2. What is the rationale for using accelerated depreciation methods?

(AICPA adapted)

Judgment Case 11–5
Capitalize or expense; materiality
● LO11–9

Redline Publishers, Inc. produces various manuals ranging from computer software instructional booklets to manuals explaining the installation and use of large pieces of industrial equipment. At the end of 2021, the company's balance sheet reported total assets of $62 million and total liabilities of $40 million. The income statement for 2021 reported net income of $1.1 million, which represents an approximate 3% increase from the prior year. The company's effective income tax rate is 30%.

Near the end of 2021, a variety of expenditures were made to overhaul the company's manufacturing equipment. None of these expenditures exceeded $750, the materiality threshold the company has set for the capitalization of any such expenditure. Even though the overhauls extended the service life of the equipment, the expenditures were expensed, not capitalized.

John Henderson, the company's controller, is worried about the treatment of the overhaul expenditures. Even though no individual expenditure exceeded the $750 materiality threshold, total expenditures were $70,000.

Required:

Should the overhaul expenditures be capitalized or expensed?

Communication Case 11–6
Capitalize or expense; materiality
● LO11–9

The focus of the case is the situation described in Judgment Case 11–5. Your instructor will divide the class into two to six groups depending on the size of the class. The mission of your group is to determine the treatment of the overhaul expenditures.

Required:

1. Each group member should deliberate the situation independently and draft a tentative argument prior to the class session for which the case is assigned.
2. In class, each group will meet for 10 to 15 minutes in different areas of the classroom. During the meeting, group members will take turns sharing their suggestions for the purpose of arriving at a single group treatment.
3. After the allotted time, a spokesperson for each group (selected during the group meetings) will share the group's solution with the class. The goal of the class is to incorporate the views of each group into a consensus approach to the situation.

Integrating Case 11–7
Errors; change in estimate; change in principle; inventory, patent, and equipment
● LO11–5 through LO11–7

Whaley Distributors is a wholesale distributor of electronic components. Financial statements for the year ended December 31, 2021, reported the following amounts and subtotals ($ in millions):

	Assets	Liabilities	Shareholders' Equity	Net Income	Expenses
2020	$640	$330	$310	$210	$150
2021	$820	$400	$420	$230	$175

In 2022 the following situations occurred or came to light:

a. Internal auditors discovered that ending inventories reported in the financial statements the two previous years were misstated due to faulty internal controls. The errors were in the following amounts:

2020 inventory	Overstated by $12 million
2021 inventory	Understated by $10 million

b. A patent costing $18 million at the beginning of 2020, expected to benefit operations for a total of six years, has not been amortized since acquired.

c. Whaley's conveyer equipment has been depreciated by the sum-of-the-years'-digits (SYD) method since constructed at the beginning of 2020 at a cost of $30 million. It has an expected useful life of five years and no expected residual value. At the beginning of 2022, Whaley decided to switch to straight-line depreciation.

Required:

For each situation:

1. Prepare any journal entry necessary as a direct result of the change or error correction as well as any adjusting entry for 2022 related to the situation described. (Ignore tax effects.)

2. Determine the amounts to be reported for each of the items shown above from the 2020 and 2021 financial statements when those amounts are reported again in the 2022, 2021, and 2020 comparative financial statements.

Judgment Case 11–8
Accounting changes
● LO11–5, LO11–6

There are various types of accounting changes, each of which is required to be reported differently.

Required:

1. What type of accounting change is a change from the double-declining-balance method of depreciation to the straight-line method for previously recorded assets as a result of new information related to production patterns? Under what circumstances does this type of accounting change occur?

2. What type of accounting change is a change in the expected service life of an asset arising because of more experience with the asset? Under what circumstances does this type of accounting change occur?

(AICPA adapted)

Research Case 11–9
FASB codification; locate and extract relevant information and cite authoritative support for a financial reporting issue; impairment of property, plant, and equipment and intangible assets
● LO11–8

The company controller, Barry Melrose, has asked for your help in interpreting the authoritative accounting literature that addresses the recognition and measurement of impairment losses for property, plant, and equipment and intangible assets. "We have a significant amount of goodwill on our books from last year's acquisition of Churchill Corporation. Also, I think we may have a problem with the assets of some of our factories out West. And one of our divisions is currently considering disposing of a large group of depreciable assets."

Your task as assistant controller is to research the issue. Access the *FASB Accounting Standards Codification* at the FASB website (www.fasb.org). Determine the specific nine-digit Codification citation (XXX-XX-XX-XX) that describes each of the following items:

Required:

1. The measurement of impairment losses for property, plant, and equipment.

2. When to test for impairment of property, plant, and equipment.

3. The new cost basis of impaired property, plant, and equipment and prohibiting later recovery of an impairment loss.

4. The recognition and measurement of impairment losses for intangible assets that are subject to amortization.

5. The requirement that intangible assets not subject to amortization be tested for impairment at least annually.

Ethics Case 11–10
Asset impairment
● LO11–8

At the beginning of 2019, the Healthy Life Food Company purchased equipment for $42 million to be used in the manufacture of a new line of gourmet frozen foods. The equipment was estimated to have a 10-year service life and no residual value. The straight-line depreciation method was used to measure depreciation for 2019 and 2020.

Late in 2021, it became apparent that sales of the new frozen food line were significantly below expectations. The company decided to continue production for two more years (2022 and 2023) and then discontinue the line. At that time, the equipment will be sold for minimal scrap values.

The controller, Heather Meyer, was asked by Harvey Dent, the company's chief executive officer (CEO), to determine the appropriate treatment of the change in service life of the equipment. Heather determined that there has been an impairment of value requiring an immediate write-down of the equipment of $12,900,000. The remaining book value would then be depreciated over the equipment's revised service life.

CHAPTER 11 Property, Plant, and Equipment and Intangible Assets: Utilization and Disposition **639**

The CEO does not like Heather's conclusion because of the effect it would have on 2021 income. "Looks like a simple revision in service life from 10 years to 5 years to me," Dent concluded. "Let's go with it that way, Heather."

Required:

1. What is the difference in before-tax income between the CEO's and Heather's treatment of the situation?

2. Discuss Heather Meyer's ethical dilemma.

Judgment Case 11–11
Earnings management and accounting changes; impairment
● LO11–5, LO11–6, LO11–8

Companies often are under pressure to meet or beat Wall Street earnings projections in order to increase stock prices and also to increase the value of stock options. Some resort to earnings management practices to artificially create desired results.

Required:

1. How can a company manage earnings by changing its depreciation method? Is this an effective technique to manage earnings?

2. How can a company manage earnings by changing the estimated useful lives of depreciable assets? Is this an effective technique to manage earnings?

3. Using a fictitious example and numbers you make up, describe in your own words how asset impairment losses could be used to manage earnings. How might that benefit the company?

Trueblood Accounting Case 11–12
Accounting for impairment losses; property, plant, and equipment
● LO11–8

The following Trueblood case is recommended for use with this chapter. The case provides an excellent opportunity for class discussion, group projects, and writing assignments. The case, along with Professor's Discussion Material, can be obtained from the Deloitte Foundation at its website www.deloitte.com/us/truebloodcases.

Case 12–9: Rough Waters Ahead
This case concerns the impairment test for a cruise ship.

Judgment Case 11–13
Subsequent expenditures
● LO11–9

The Cummings Company charged various expenditures made during 2021 to an account called repairs and maintenance expense. You have been asked by your supervisor in the company's internal audit department to review the expenditures to determine if they were appropriately recorded. The amount of each of the transactions included in the account is considered material.

1. Engine tune-up and oil change on the company's 12 delivery trucks—$1,300.

2. Rearrangement of equipment on the main production line—$5,500. It is not evident that the rearrangement will increase operational efficiency.

3. Installation of aluminum siding on the manufacturing plant—$32,000.

4. Replacement of the old air conditioning system in the manufacturing plant with a new system—$120,000.

5. Replacement of broken parts on three machines—$1,500.

6. Annual painting of the manufacturing plant—$11,000.

7. Purchase of new forklift to move finished product to the loading dock—$6,000.

8. Patching leaks in the roof of the manufacturing plant—$6,500. The repair work did not extend the useful life of the roof.

Required:

For each of the transactions listed above, indicate whether the expenditure is appropriately charged to the repair and maintenance expense account, and if not, indicate the proper account to be charged.

Real World Case 11–14
Disposition and depreciation; Chapters 10 and 11; Amgen
● LO11–1

Real World Financials

Amgen, Inc. is an American multinational biopharmaceutical company headquartered in Thousand Oaks, California. Located in the Conejo Valley, Amgen is the world's largest independent biotechnology firm. Amgen reported the following in a disclosure note accompanying its 2016 financial statements ($ in millions):

	2016	2015
Property and equipment	$12,427	$12,172
Less: Accumulated depreciation	(7,466)	(7,265)
Property, plant, and equipment—Net	$ 4,961	$ 4,907

640   SECTION 2   Assets

Also, the company disclosed that the total cost of property and equipment included $295 and $319 millions in land at the end of 2016 and 2015, respectively. In addition, the statement of cash flows for the year ended December 31, 2016, reported the following as cash flows from investing activities:

	($ in millions)
Purchases of property and equipment	$(738)
Proceeds from the sale of property and equipment	78

The statement of cash flows also reported 2016 depreciation and amortization of $2,105 million (depreciation of $619 and amortization of $1,486).

Required:

1. Assume that all property and equipment acquired during 2016 were purchased for cash. Determine the amount of gain or loss from sale of property and equipment that Amgen recognized during 2016.

2. Assume that Amgen uses the straight-line method to depreciate property and equipment (excluding land). What is the approximate average service life of depreciable assets?

Real World Case 11–15
Depreciation and depletion method; asset impairment; subsequent expenditures; Chevron

● LO11–2, LO11–3, LO11–8, LO11–9

Real World Financials

EDGAR, the Electronic Data Gathering, Analysis, and Retrieval system, performs automated collection, validation, indexing, and forwarding of submissions by companies and others who are required by law to file forms with the U.S. Securities and Exchange Commission (SEC). All publicly traded domestic companies use EDGAR to make the majority of their filings. (Some foreign companies file voluntarily.) Form 10-K, which includes the annual report, is required to be filed on EDGAR. The SEC makes this information available on the Internet.

Required:

1. Access EDGAR on the Internet. The web address is www.sec.gov.

2. Search for Chevron Corporation. Access the 10-K filing for most recent fiscal year. Search or scroll to find the financial statements and related notes.

3. Answer the following questions related to the company's property, plant, and equipment and intangible assets:

    a. Describe the company's depreciation and depletion policies.

    b. Describe the company's policy for subsequent expenditures made for plant and equipment.

IFRS Case 11–16
Subsequent valuation of property, plant, and equipment; comparison of U.S. GAAP and IFRS; GlaxoSmithKline

● LO11–10

Real World Financials

 IFRS

GlaxoSmithKline is a global pharmaceutical and consumer health-related products company located in the United Kingdom. The company prepares its financial statements in accordance with International Financial Reporting Standards.

Required:

1. Use the Internet to locate GlaxoSmithKline's most recent annual report. The address is www.gsk.com/en-gb/investors/. Locate the significant accounting policies disclosure note.

2. How does the company value its property, plant, and equipment? Does the company have any other options under IFRS for valuing these assets? How do these options differ from U.S. GAAP?

3. What are the company's policies for possible reversals of impairment losses for goodwill and for other non-current assets? How do these policies differ from U.S. GAAP?

Data Analytics

Data analytics is the process of examining data sets in order to draw conclusions about the information they contain. If you haven't completed any of the prior data analytics cases, follow the instructions listed in the Chapter 1 Data Analytics case to get set up. You will need to watch the videos referred to in the Chapters 1 - 3 Data Analytics cases. No additional videos are required for this case. All short training videos can be found here: https://www.tableau.com/learn/training#getting-started.

Data Analytics Case
Accumulated Depreciation to Fixed Assets

In the Chapter 10 Data Analytics Case, you used Tableau to examine a data set and create calculations to compare two companies' fixed-asset turnover. In this case you continue in your role as an analyst conducting introductory research into the relative merits of investing in one or both of these companies. This time you assess the companies' accumulated depreciation to fixed assets ratio to determine if new assets are being employed or utilized. The accumulated depreciation to fixed assets ratio = accumulated depreciation / fixed assets.

This ratio allows the investor or analyst to examine factors like the age of the assets and therefore their remaining useful life. A low ratio means that the assets have plenty of life left in them and should be able to be used for years to come. A high ratio means the opposite. Low metrics are not necessarily a good sign though. For example, a company with a very low ratio may be spending huge amounts of money replacing fixed assets too soon. So it's useful to track this metric over time to detect patterns. A continuing increase in the company's accumulated depreciation to fixed assets ratio can indicate that management is struggling to find the cash necessary to acquire new assets.

Required:

Use Tableau to calculate each company's annual accumulated depreciation to fixed assets ratios in each year from 2012 to 2021. Assume both companies use the same depreciation method over the entire period. Based upon what you find, answer the following questions:

1. Comparing the accumulated depreciation to fixed assets ratios over the first five years of the ten-year period, is Big Store's accumulated depreciation to fixed assets ratio (a) generally increasing, (b) roughly the same, or (c) generally decreasing from year to year?

2. Comparing the accumulated depreciation to fixed assets ratios over the second five years of the ten-year period, is Big Store's accumulated depreciation to fixed assets ratio (a) generally increasing, (b) roughly the same, or (c) generally decreasing from year to year?

3. Comparing the accumulated depreciation to fixed assets ratios over the first five years of the ten-year period, is Discount Goods' accumulated depreciation to fixed assets ratio (a) generally increasing, (b) roughly the same, or (c) generally decreasing from year to year?

4. Comparing the accumulated depreciation to fixed assets ratios over the second five years of the ten-year period, is Discount Goods' accumulated depreciation to fixed assets ratio (a) generally increasing, (b) roughly the same, or (c) generally decreasing from year to year?

5. Comparing the accumulated depreciation to fixed assets ratios over the entire ten-year period, which of the two companies appears to maintain fixed assets with longer remaining useful lives?

Resources:

You have available to you an extensive data set that includes detailed financial data for Discount Goods and Big Store and for 2012-2021. The data set is in the form of four Excel files available to download from Connect, or under Student Resources within the Library tab. The file for use in this chapter is named "Discount_Goods_Big_ Store_Financials.xlsx." Download this file and save it to the computer on which you will be using Tableau.

For this case, you will create some calculations to produce a bar chart of the accumulated depreciation to fixed assets ratio to allow you to compare and contrast the two companies.

After you view the training videos, follow these steps to create the charts you'll use for this case:

- Open Tableau and connect to the Excel spreadsheet you downloaded.

- Click on the "Sheet 1" tab at the bottom of the canvas, to the right of the Data Source at the bottom of the screen. Drag "Company" and "Year" under Dimensions to the Rows shelf. Change "Year" to *discrete* by right-clicking and selecting "discrete."

- Drag the "Buildings and Improvements," "Computer hardware and software," "Construction in progress," "Fixtures and Equipment," and "Less accumulated depreciation" under Measures to the Rows shelf. Change each to *discrete*. Right click on the drop-down menu of each of the accounts and uncheck "Show Header" so they are not visible in the field.

- Create a calculated field named "AD to FA ratio" In the Calculation Editor window, from the Rows shelf, drag "Less accumulated depreciation" then type a multiplication sign (*) and a negative 1, followed by a division sign and an open parenthesis, then drag "Buildings and Improvements," type a plus sign, then "Computer hardware and software," plus sign, "Construction in progress," plus sign, "Fixtures and Equipment," then a closed parenthesis. Make sure the window says that the calculation is valid and click OK.

- Drag the newly created "AD to FA ratio" to the Rows shelf.

- Click on the "Show Me" and select "side-by-side bars." Add labels to the bars by clicking on "Label" under the "Marks" card and clicking the box "Show mark labels." Format the labels to Times New Roman, bold, black and 9-point font.

- Change the title of the sheet to be "Accumulated Depreciation to Fixed Assets Ratio Bar Chart" by right-clicking and selecting "Edit title." Format the title to Times New Roman, bold, black and 15-point font. Change the title of "Sheet 1" to match the sheet title by right-clicking, selecting "Rename" and typing in the new title.

- Format the labels on the left of the sheet ("AD to FA ratio") to Times New Roman, 9-point font, bold, and black.

- Format all other labels to be Times New Roman, bold, black and 12-point font.

- Once complete, save the file as "*DA11_Your initials*.twbx."

642   SECTION 2   Assets

Continuing Cases

Target Case

● LO11–2,
   LO11–8, LO11–9

Target Corporation prepares its financial statements according to U.S. GAAP. Target's financial statements and disclosure notes for the year ended February 3, 2018, are available in Connect. This material is also available under the Investor Relations link at the company's website (www.target.com).

Required:

1. Compare the property and equipment listed in the balance sheet with the list in Note 14. What are the estimated useful lives for recording depreciation? Is land listed in Note 14 (yes/no)?

2. In Note 14, which depreciation method does Target use for property and equipment for financial reporting? Which depreciation method is used for tax purposes? Why might these methods be chosen?

3. In Note 14, how does Target record repairs and maintenance expense?

4. In Note 14, does Target report any impairment of property and equipment for the year ended February 3, 2018? If so, what was the amount and what were the reasons for the impairments?

5. From Notes 15 and 16, were any impairments related to intangible assets recorded for the year ended February 3, 2018? If so, what was the amount and what were the reasons for the impairments?

Air France–KLM Case
● LO11–10

IFRS

Air France–KLM (AF), a Franco-Dutch company, prepares its financial statements according to International Financial Reporting Standards. AF's financial statements and disclosure notes for the year ended December 31, 2017, are available in Connect. This material is also available under the Finance link at the company's website (www.airfranceklm.com).

Required:

1. AF's property, plant, and equipment is reported at cost. The company has a policy of not revaluing property, plant, and equipment. Suppose AF decided to revalue its flight equipment on December 31, 2017, and that the fair value of the equipment on that date was €12,000 million. Prepare the journal entry to record the revaluation assuming that the journal entry to record annual depreciation had already been recorded. (*Hint:* you will need to locate the original cost and accumulated depreciation of the equipment at the end of the year in the appropriate disclosure note.)

2. Under U.S. GAAP, what alternatives do companies have to value their property, plant, and equipment?

3. AF calculates depreciation of plant and equipment on a straight-line basis, over the useful life of the asset. Describe any differences between IFRS and U.S. GAAP in the calculation of depreciation.

4. When does AF test for the possible impairment of fixed assets? How does this approach differ from U.S. GAAP?

5. Describe the approach AF uses to determine fixed asset impairment losses. (*Hint:* see Note 4.14) How does this approach differ from U.S. GAAP?

6. The following is included in AF's disclosure note 4.13: "Intangible assets are recorded at initial cost less accumulated amortization and any accumulated impairment losses." Assume that on December 31, 2017, AF decided to revalue its Other intangible assets (see Note 17) and that the fair value on that date was determined to be €500 million. Amortization expense for the year already has been recorded. Prepare the journal entry to record the revaluation.

CPA Exam Questions and Simulations

ROGER *CPA Review*

Sample CPA Exam questions from Roger CPA Review are available in Connect as support for the topics in this chapter. These multiple-choice questions and task-based simulations include expert-written explanations and solutions, and provide a starting point for students to become familiar with the content and functionality of the actual CPA Exam.

CHAPTER

13

Current Liabilities and Contingencies

©Cultura/Image Source

FINANCIAL REPORTING CASE

Debbie's Dad

"My dad is confused," your friend Debbie Hirst proclaimed at the office one morning. "You see, we're competing against each other in that investment game I told you about, and one of his hot investments is Syntel Microsystems. When he got their annual report yesterday afternoon, he started analyzing it, you know, really studying it closely. Then he asked me about the current liability section of the balance sheet and related disclosure note":

SYNTEL MICROSYSTEMS, INC.
Balance Sheet
December 31, 2021 and 2020
($ in millions)

Current Liabilities	2021	2020
Accounts payable	$233.5	$241.6
Short-term borrowings (Note 3)	187.0	176.8
Accrued liabilities	65.3	117.2
Accrued loss contingency	76.9	—
Other current liabilities	34.6	45.2
Current portion of long-term debt	44.1	40.3
Total current liabilities	$641.4	$621.1

Note 3: Short-Term Borrowings (in part)

The components of short-term borrowings and their respective weighted average interest rates at the end of the period are as follows:

($ in millions)	2021		2020	
	Amount	Average Interest Rate	Amount	Average Interest Rate
Commercial paper	$ 34.0	5.2%	$ 27.1	5.3%
Bank loans	218.0	5.5	227.7	5.6
Amount reclassified to long-term liabilities	(65.0)	—	(78.0)	—
Total short-term borrowings	$187.0		$176.8	

The Company maintains bank credit lines sufficient to cover outstanding short-term borrowings. As of December 31, 2021, the Company had $200.0 million fee-paid lines available. At December 31, 2021 and 2020, the Company classified $65.0 million and $78.0 million, respectively, of commercial paper and bank notes as long-term debt. The Company has the intent and ability, through formal renewal agreements, to renew these obligations into future periods.

Note 6: Contingencies (in part)

Between 2019 and 2020, the Company manufactured cable leads that, the Company has learned, contribute to corrosion of linked components with which they are installed. At December 31, 2021, the Company accrued $132.0 million in anticipation of remediation and claims settlement deemed probable, of which $76.9 million is considered a current liability.

"So, what's the problem?" you asked.
"Well, he thinks I'm some sort of financial wizard because I'm in business."
"And because you tell him so all the time," you interrupted.

(continued)

(continued)

"Maybe so, but he's been told that current liabilities are riskier than long-term liabilities, and now he's focusing on that. He can't see why some long-term debt is reported here in the current section. And it also looks like some is reported the other way around; some current liabilities reported as long term. Plus, the contingency amount seems like it's not even a contractual liability. Then he wants to know what some of those terms mean. Lucky for me, I had to leave before I had to admit I didn't know the answers. You're the accountant; help me out."

QUESTIONS ———————— **By the time you finish this chapter, you should be able to respond appropriately to the questions posed in this case. Compare your response to the solution provided at the end of the chapter.**

1. What are accrued liabilities? What is commercial paper? (*p. 723*)

2. Why did Syntel Microsystems include some long-term debt in the current liability section? (*p. 729*)

3. Did they also report some current amounts as long-term debt? Explain. (*p. 730*)

4. Must obligations be known contractual debts in order to be reported as liabilities? (*p. 733*)

5. Is it true that current liabilities are riskier than long-term liabilities? (*p. 745*)

PART A

Liabilities and owners' equity accounts represent specific sources of a company's assets.

Current Liabilities

Before a business can invest in an asset it first must acquire the money to pay for it. This can happen in either of two ways—funds can be provided by owners or the funds must be borrowed. You may recognize this as a description of the basic accounting equation: Assets = Liabilities + Owners' Equity. You studied assets in the chapters leading to this one and you will study owners' equity later. This chapter and the next four describe the various liabilities that constitute creditors' claims on a company's assets.

Characteristics of Liabilities

Most liabilities obligate the debtor to pay cash at specified times and result from legally enforceable agreements.

● LO13–1

Some liabilities are not contractual obligations and may not be payable in cash.

You already know what liabilities are. You encounter them every day. If you are paying for a car or a home with monthly payments, you have a personal liability. Similarly, when businesses issue notes and bonds, their creditors are the banks, individuals, and organizations that exchange cash for those securities. Each of these obligations represents the most common type of liability—one to be paid in cash and for which the amount and timing are specified by a legally enforceable contract.

However, to be reported as a liability, an obligation need not be payable in cash. Instead, it may require the company to transfer other assets or to provide services. A liability doesn't have to be represented by a written agreement nor be legally enforceable. Even the amount and timing of repayment need not be precisely known.

From a financial reporting perspective, a liability has three essential characteristics. Liabilities

1. Are *probable, future* sacrifices of economic benefits.
2. Arise from *present* obligations (to transfer assets or provide services) to other entities.
3. Result from *past* transactions or events.[1]

Notice that the definition of a liability involves the past, the present, and the future. It is a present responsibility to sacrifice assets in the future because of a transaction or other event that happened in the past.

---

[1]"Elements of Financial Statements," *Statement of Financial Accounting Concepts No. 6* (Stamford, Conn.: FASB, 1985), par. 38.

What is a Current Liability?

In a classified balance sheet, we categorize liabilities as either current liabilities or long-term liabilities. We often characterize current liabilities as obligations payable within one year from the balance sheet date or within the firm's operating cycle, whichever is longer. This general definition usually applies. However, a more discriminating definition identifies current liabilities as those expected to be satisfied with *current assets* or by the creation of other *current liabilities*.[2]

Current liabilities are expected to require current assets and usually are payable within one year from the balance sheet date.

Classifying liabilities as either current or long term helps investors and creditors assess the risk that the liabilities will require expenditure of cash or other assets in the near term. Is the due date years in the future, permitting resources to be used for other purposes without risking default? Or, will payment require the use of current assets and reduce the amount of liquid funds available for other uses? If so, are sufficient liquid funds available to make necessary payments of liabilities in addition to meeting current operating needs, or must additional funds be obtained by raising capital? The answers to these questions can have significant implications. For example, a major factor contributing to the collapse of the financial giant Bear Stearns in 2008 was its reliance on short-term liabilities that it couldn't refinance when lenders, clients, and trading partners grew concerned about the quality of Bear's investments.[3]

Classifying liabilities as either current or long term helps investors and creditors assess the relative risk of a business's liabilities.

Conceptually, liabilities should be recorded at their present values. In other words, the amount recorded is the present value of all anticipated future cash payments resulting from the debt (specifically, principal and interest payments).[4] However, in practice, liabilities payable within one year from the balance sheet date ordinarily are recorded instead at their maturity amounts.[5] This inconsistency usually is inconsequential because the relatively short-term maturity of current liabilities makes the interest or time value component immaterial.

Current liabilities ordinarily are reported at their maturity amounts.

The most common obligations reported as current liabilities are accounts payable, notes payable, commercial paper, income tax liability, dividends payable, and accrued liabilities. Liabilities related to income taxes are the subject of Chapter 16. We discuss the others here.

Before we examine specific current liabilities, let's use the current liability section of the balance sheet of General Mills, Inc., and related disclosure notes to provide perspective on some of the liabilities we discuss (Illustration 13–1). General Mills's presentation and supplemental note disclosures are fairly typical.

We'll refer back to portions of Illustration 13–1 as corresponding liabilities are described later in the chapter.

Open Accounts and Notes

Many businesses buy merchandise or supplies on credit. Most also find it desirable to borrow cash from time to time to finance their activities. In this section, we discuss the liabilities these borrowing activities create: trade accounts and trade notes, bank loans, and commercial paper.

Accounts Payable and Trade Notes Payable

Accounts payable are obligations to suppliers of merchandise or of services purchased on *open account*. Most trade credit is offered on open account. This means that the only formal credit instrument is the invoice. Because the time until payment usually is short (often 30, 45, or 60 days), these liabilities typically are noninterest-bearing and are reported at their face amounts. As shown in Illustration 13–1, General Mills's accounts payable in 2017 was $2,120 million. The key accounting considerations relating to accounts payable are determining their existence and ensuring that they are recorded in the appropriate accounting period. You studied these issues and learned how cash discounts are handled during your study of inventories in Chapter 8.

Buying merchandise on account in the ordinary course of business creates *accounts payable*.

---

[2]FASB ASC Master Glossary.
[3]William D. Cohan, *House of Cards: A Tale of Hubris and Wretched Excess on Wall Street* (New York: Doubleday, 2009).
[4]The concepts of the time value of money and the mechanics of present value calculations are covered in Chapter 5.
[5]In fact, those arising in connection with suppliers in the normal course of business and due within a year are specifically exempted from present value reporting by FASB ASC 835–30–15–3: Interest—Imputation of Interest—Scope and Scope Exceptions.

Illustration 13–1

Current Liabilities—General Mills

Real World Financials

GENERAL MILLS, INC.
Excerpt from Consolidated Balance Sheets
May 28, 2017 and May 29, 2016
Liabilities
($ in millions)

Current Liabilities	2017	2016
Accounts payable	$2,119.8	$2,046.5
Current portion of long-term debt	604.7	1,103.4
Notes payable	1,234.1	269.8
Other current liabilities	1,372.2	1,595.0
Total current liabilities	$5,330.8	$5,014.7

Note 8. Debt

Notes Payable The components of notes payable and their respective weighted-average interest rates at the end of the periods were as follows:

	2017		2016	
Dollars in Millions:	Note Payable	Weighted Average Interest Rate	Note Payable	Weighted Average Interest Rate
U.S. commercial paper	$ 954.7	1.1%	$ –	–%
Financial institutions	279.4	7.0	269.8	8.6
Total notes payable	$1,234.1	2.4%	$269.8	8.6%

To ensure availability of funds, we maintain bank credit lines sufficient to cover our outstanding notes payable. Commercial paper is a continuing source of short-term financing. We have commercial paper programs available to us in the United States and Europe. We also have uncommitted and asset-backed credit lines that support our foreign operations. The following table details the fee-paid committed and uncommitted credit lines we had available as of May 28, 2017:

Dollars in Billions:	Facility Amount	Borrowed Amount
Credit facility expiring:		
May 2022	$2.7	$ –
June 2019	0.2	0.1
Total committed credit facilities	2.9	0.1
Uncommitted credit facilities	0.5	0.1
Total committed and uncommitted credit facilities	$3.4	$0.2

Source: General Mills, Inc.

Trade notes payable differ from accounts payable in that they are formally recognized by a written promissory note. Often these are of a somewhat longer term than open accounts and bear interest.

Short-Term Notes Payable

● LO13–2

The most common way for a corporation to obtain temporary financing is to arrange a short-term bank loan. When a company borrows cash from a bank and signs a promissory note (essentially an IOU), the firm's liability is reported as *notes payable* (sometimes *bank loans* or *short-term borrowings*). About two-thirds of bank loans are short term, but because many are routinely renewed, some tend to resemble long-term debt. In fact, in some cases we report them as long-term debt (as you'll see later in the chapter).

Very often, smaller firms are unable to tap into the major sources of long-term financing to the extent necessary to provide for their working capital needs. So they must rely heavily on short-term financing. Even large companies typically utilize short-term debt as a significant and indispensable component of their capital structure. One reason is that short-term funds usually offer lower interest rates than long-term debt. Perhaps most importantly, corporations desire flexibility. Managers want as many financing alternatives as possible.

CREDIT LINES   Usually short-term bank loans are arranged under an existing *line of credit* with a bank or group of banks. A line of credit is an agreement to provide short-term financing, with amounts withdrawn by the borrower only when needed. Even though the loans are short-term, with amounts borrowed and repaid frequently, the agreement to provide a line of credit typically lasts several years. Lines of credit can be noncommitted or committed. A *noncommitted* line of credit is an informal agreement that permits a company to borrow up to a prearranged limit without having to follow formal loan procedures and paperwork. Banks sometimes require the company to maintain a compensating balance on deposit with the bank, say, 5% of the line of credit.[6] A *committed* line of credit is a more formal agreement that usually requires the company to pay a commitment fee to the bank to keep a credit line amount available to the company. A typical annual commitment fee is ¼% of the total committed funds, and may also require a compensating balance. A recent annual report of **IBM Corporation** illustrates noncommitted lines of credit (Illustration 13–2).

A *line of credit* allows a company to borrow cash without having to follow formal loan procedures and paperwork.

Illustration 13–2

Disclosure of Credit Lines— IBM Corporation

Real World Financials

> **Note J. Borrowings (in part)**
>
> **LINES OF CREDIT:** In 2016, the company increased the size of its five-year Credit Agreement (the "Credit Agreement") to $10.25 billion and extended the term by one year to November 10, 2021. The total expense recorded by the company related to this global credit facility was $6.1 million in 2017, $5.5 million in 2016 and $5.3 million in 2015. The Credit Agreement permits the company and its Subsidiary Borrowers to borrow up to $10.25 billion on a revolving basis. Borrowings of the Subsidiary Borrowers will be unconditionally backed by the company. . . . As of December 31, 2017, there were no borrowings by the company, or its subsidiaries, under the Credit Facilities.
>
> Source: IBM Corporation

General Mills's disclosure notes that we looked at in Illustration 13–1 indicate that the company has both noncommitted and committed lines of credit.

INTEREST   When a company borrows money, it pays the lender *interest* in return for using the lender's money during the term of the loan. You might think of the interest as the "rent" paid for using money. Interest is stated in terms of a percentage rate to be applied to the face amount of the loan, which makes this an interest-bearing note. Because the stated rate typically is an annual rate, when calculating interest for a short-term note we must adjust for the fraction of the annual period the loan spans. Interest on notes is calculated as

$$\text{Face amount} \times \text{Annual rate} \times \text{Time to maturity}$$

This is demonstrated in Illustration 13–3.

Illustration 13–3

Interest-Bearing Notes Payable

> On May 1, Affiliated Technologies, Inc., a consumer electronics firm, borrowed $700,000 cash from First BancCorp under a noncommitted short-term line of credit arrangement and issued a *six-month*, 12% promissory note. Interest was payable at maturity.

May 1		
Cash	700,000	
Notes payable		700,000
November 1		
Interest expense ($700,000 × 12% × $^{6}/_{12}$)	42,000	
Notes payable	700,000	
Cash ($700,000 + $42,000)		742,000

---

[6]A compensating balance is a deposit kept by a company in a low-interest or noninterest-bearing account at the bank. The required deposit usually is some percentage of the committed amount or the amount used (say, 2% to 5%). The effect of the compensating balance is to increase the borrower's effective interest rate and the bank's effective rate of return.

Sometimes a note assumes the form of a so-called noninterest-bearing note. Obviously, though, nobody will lend money without interest. Noninterest-bearing loans actually do bear interest, but the interest is deducted (or discounted) from the face amount to determine the cash proceeds made available to the borrower at the outset.

You saw this in Chapter 7 when a company sold a product worth $658,000 and accepted a note receivable from the customer of $700,000 due in six months. While the note had no stated interest rate, implicit in the higher amount of the note is interest of $42,000 ($700,000 − $658,000). We can apply the same concept to our previous example in Illustration 13–3. Suppose Affiliated Technologies bought inventory worth $658,000 by issuing a $700,000 noninterest-bearing note due in six months. The difference of $42,000 is recorded as a discount on notes payable that will be recognized as interest expense over time.[7]

The proceeds of the note are reduced by the interest in a noninterest-bearing note.

May 1

Inventory (difference)	658,000	
Discount on notes payable (to balance)	42,000	
Notes payable (face amount)		700,000

November 1

Interest expense	42,000	
Discount on notes payable		42,000
Notes payable (face amount)	700,000	
Cash		700,000

Sometimes interest in such arrangements is described by referring to a discount rate that is applied to the face amount of the note. In this case, the six-month noninterest-bearing note would be described as "being discounted at issuance at a 12% discount rate," and the amount of interest would be calculated as the face amount times the discount rate times the fraction of the year the note is outstanding ($700,000 × 12% × 6/12 = $42,000). Notice, though, that the amount borrowed under this arrangement is only $658,000. This causes the *effective* interest rate to be higher than the 12% stated rate:

When interest is discounted from the face amount of a note, the effective interest rate is higher than the stated discount rate.

$$\frac{\$42,000 \text{ Interest for 6 months}}{\$658,000 \text{ Amount borrowed}} = 6.38\% \text{ Rate for 6 months}$$

To annualize:

$$6.38\% \times {}^{12}\!/_6 = 12.76\% \text{ Effective interest rate}$$

You can refer back to Chapter 7 and verify that the accounting for a note receivable mirrors what we showed here for a note payable.

Inventory or accounts receivable often are pledged as security for short-term loans.

SECURED LOANS   Sometimes short-term loans are *secured,* meaning a specified asset of the borrower is pledged as collateral or security for the loan. Although many kinds of assets can be pledged, the secured loans most frequently encountered in practice are secured by inventory or accounts receivable. For example, Smithfield Foods, Inc., disclosed the secured notes described in Illustration 13–4.

When accounts receivable serve as collateral, we refer to the arrangement as *pledging* accounts receivable. Sometimes, the receivables actually are sold outright to a finance company as a means of short-term financing. This is called *factoring* receivables.[8]

---

[7]Be sure to understand that we are actually recording the note at 658,000, *not* 700,000, but are recording the interest portion separately in a contra-liability account, *discount on notes payable*. The entries shown reflect the gross method. By the net method, the interest component is netted against the face amount of the note as follows:

May 1

Cash	658,000	
Notes payable		658,000

November 1

Interest expense ($700,000 × 12% × ⁶/12)	42,000	
Notes payable	658,000	
Cash		700,000

[8] Both methods of accounts receivable financing are discussed in Chapter 7, "Cash and Receivables."

Note 7: Debt (in part)

Working Capital Facilities

The obligations under the Inventory Revolver Credit Agreement are guaranteed by substantially all of our subsidiary guarantors' personal property, including accounts receivable (other than those sold and financed pursuant to the Securitization Facility), inventory, cash and cash equivalents, deposit accounts, intercompany notes, intellectual property and certain capital stock and interests pledged by us and our subsidiary guarantors, and all proceeds thereof.

Source: Smithfield Foods, Inc.

Illustration 13–4

Disclosure of Notes Secured by Inventory— Smithfield Foods, Inc.

Real World Financials

Commercial Paper

Some large corporations obtain temporary financing by issuing commercial paper, often purchased by other companies as a short-term investment. Commercial paper refers to unsecured notes sold in minimum denominations of $25,000 with maturities ranging from 1 to 270 days (beyond 270 days the firm would be required to file a registration statement with the SEC). Interest often is discounted at the issuance of the note. Usually commercial paper is issued directly to the buyer (lender) and is backed by a line of credit with a bank. This allows the interest rate to be lower than in a bank loan. Commercial paper has become an increasingly popular way for large companies to raise funds, the total amount having expanded over fivefold in the last decade.

Illustration 13–5 includes a disclosure note from the 2016 annual report of Comcast Corporation that describes Comcast's commercial paper program.

Large, highly rated firms sometimes sell *commercial paper* to borrow funds at a lower rate than through a bank loan.

Note 10: (in part)

Commercial Paper Program

Our commercial paper programs provide a lower-cost source of borrowing to fund our short-term working capital requirements. The maximum borrowing capacity under the Comcast commercial paper program is $6.25 billion. We support this commercial paper program with unused capacity under the Comcast revolving credit facility. The maximum borrowing capacity under the NBCUniversal Enterprise commercial paper program is $1.35 billion. We support this commercial paper program with unused capacity under the NBCUniversal Enterprise revolving credit facility.

Source: Comcast Corporation

Illustration 13–5

Disclosure of Commercial Paper—Comcast Corporation

Real World Financials

The name *commercial paper* refers to the fact that a paper certificate traditionally is issued to the lender to signify the obligation, although there is a trend toward total computerization so that no paper is created. Since commercial paper is a form of notes payable, recording its issuance and payment is exactly the same as our earlier illustration.

In a statement of cash flows, the cash a company receives from using short-term notes to borrow funds as well as the cash it uses to repay the notes are reported among cash flows from financing activities. Most of the other liabilities we study in this chapter, such as accounts payable, interest payable, and bonuses payable, are integrally related to a company's primary operations and thus are part of operating activities. We discuss long-term notes in the next chapter.

FINANCIAL Reporting Case

Q1, p. 718

Accrued Liabilities

Accrued liabilities represent expenses already incurred but not yet paid (accrued expenses). These liabilities are recorded by adjusting entries at the end of the reporting period, prior to preparing financial statements. Common examples are salaries payable, income taxes payable, and interest payable. Although recorded in separate liability accounts, accrued liabilities usually are combined and reported under a single caption or perhaps two accrued liability captions in the balance sheet. General Mills includes accrued liabilities in other current liabilities (totaling $1,372.2 million as of May 28, 2017).

● LO13–3

Liabilities accrue for expenses that are incurred but not yet paid.

Accrued Interest Payable

Accrued interest payable arises in connection with notes payable (as well as other forms of debt). For example, to continue Illustration 13–3, let's assume the fiscal period for Affiliated Technologies ends on June 30, two months after the six-month note is issued. The issuance of the note, intervening adjusting entry, and note payment would be recorded as shown in Illustration 13–6.

Illustration 13–6

Note with Accrued Interest

Issuance of Note on May 1		
Cash..	700,000	
Notes payable..		700,000
Accrual of Interest on June 30		
Interest expense ($700,000 × 12% × 2/12)	14,000	
Interest payable		14,000
Note Payment on November 1		
Interest expense ($700,000 × 12% × 4/12)	28,000	
Interest payable (from June 30 accrual)	14,000	
Notes payable	700,000	
Cash ($700,000 + $42,000)		742,000

At June 30, two months' interest has accrued and is recorded to avoid misstating expenses and liabilities on the June 30 financial statements.

Salaries, Commissions, and Bonuses

Compensation for employee services can be in the form of hourly wages, salary, commissions, bonuses, stock compensation plans, and pensions.[9] Accrued liabilities arise in connection with compensation expense when employees have provided services but will be paid after the financial statement date. These accrued expenses/accrued liabilities are recorded by adjusting entries at the end of the reporting period, prior to preparing financial statements.

VACATIONS, SICK DAYS, AND OTHER PAID FUTURE ABSENCES   Suppose a firm grants two weeks of paid vacation each year to employees. Some employees take their vacations during each period in which the vacations are earned and are compensated then. Some instead accumulate those days and use them in a future period. Should the firm recognize compensation expense during the period for only those employees who actually are paid that period for their absence? When you recall what you've learned about accrual accounting, you probably conclude otherwise.

An employer should accrue an expense and the related liability for employees' compensation for future absences (such as vacation pay) if the obligation meets *all* of the four conditions listed in Illustration 13–7.

Illustration 13–7

Conditions for Accrual of Paid Future Absences

1. The obligation is attributable to employees' services already performed.
2. The paid absence can be taken in a later year—the benefit vests (will be compensated even if employment is terminated) or the benefit can be accumulated over time.
3. Payment is probable.
4. The amount can be reasonably estimated.

If these conditions look familiar, it's because they are simply the characteristics of a liability we discussed earlier, adapted to relate to a potential obligation for future absences of employees. Also, these conditions are consistent with the requirement that we accrue loss contingencies only when the obligation is both (a) probable and (b) can be reasonably estimated, as discussed in Part B of this chapter.

---

[9]We discuss pensions in Chapter 17 and share-based compensation plans in Chapter 19.

The liability for paid absences usually is accrued at the existing wage rate rather than at a rate estimated to be in effect when absences occur.[10] So, if wage rates have risen, the difference between the accrual and the amount paid increases compensation expense that year. This situation is demonstrated in Illustration 13–8, in which vacation time carried over from 2021 is taken in 2022 and the actual amount paid to employees is $5,700,000.

Illustration 13–8
Paid Future Absences

Davidson-Getty Chemicals has 8,000 employees. Each employee earns two weeks of paid vacation per year. Vacation time not taken in the year earned can be carried over to subsequent years. During 2021, 2,500 employees took both weeks' vacation, but at the end of the year, 5,500 employees had vacation time carryovers as follows:

Employees	Vacation Weeks Earned But Not Taken	Total Carryover Weeks
2,500	0	0
2,000	1	2,000
3,500	2	7,000
8,000		9,000

During 2021, compensation averaged $600 a week per employee.

When Vacations Were Taken in 2021

Salaries expense (2,500 × 2 weeks × $600) +		
(2,000 × 1 week × $600)	4,200,000	
Cash (or salaries payable)		4,200,000

December 31, 2021 (adjusting entry)

Salaries expense (9,000 carryover weeks × $600)	5,400,000	
Liability—compensated future absences		5,400,000

When the necessary conditions are met, compensated future absences are accrued in the year the compensation is earned.

Company policy and actual practice should be considered when deciding whether the rights to payment for absences have been earned by services already rendered. For example, scientists in a private laboratory are eligible for paid sabbaticals every seven years. Should a liability be accrued at the end of a scientist's sixth year? No—if sabbatical leave is granted only to perform research beneficial to the employer. Yes—if past practice indicates that sabbatical leave is intended to provide unrestricted compensated absence for past service and other conditions are met.

Customary practice should be considered when deciding whether an obligation exists.

When Year 2021 Vacations Are Taken in 2022

Liability—compensated future absences (account balance)	5,400,000	
Salaries expense (difference)	300,000	
Cash (or salaries payable) (given)...		5,700,000

Custom and practice also influence whether unused rights to paid absences expire or can be carried forward. Obviously, if rights vest (payable even if employment is terminated), they haven't expired. But holiday time, military leave, maternity leave, and jury time typically do not accumulate if unused, so a liability for those benefits usually is not accrued. On the other hand, if it's customary that a particular paid absence, say holiday time, can be carried forward—if employees work on holidays, in this case—a liability is accrued if it's probable that employees will be compensated in a future year.

Interestingly, sick pay quite often meets the conditions for accrual, but accrual is not mandatory because future absence depends on future illness, which usually is not a certainty. Similar to other forms of paid absences, the decision of whether to accrue nonvesting sick pay should be based on actual policy and practice. If company policy or custom is that employees are

Accrual of sick pay is not required, but may be appropriate in some circumstances.

---

[10]Actually, FASB ASC 710–10–25: Compensation—General—Overall—Recognition is silent on how the liability should be measured. In practice, most companies accrue at the current rate because it avoids estimates and usually produces a lower expense and liability. Then, later, they remeasure periodically at updated rates.

paid sick pay even when their absences are not due to illness, it's appropriate to record a liability for unused sick pay. For example, some companies routinely allow unused sick pay benefits to be accumulated and paid at retirement (or to beneficiaries if death comes before retirement). If each condition is met except that the company finds it impractical to reasonably estimate the amount of compensation for future absences, a disclosure note should describe the situation.

> Bonuses sometimes take the place of permanent annual raises.

ANNUAL BONUSES   Sometimes compensation packages include annual bonuses tied to performance objectives designed to provide incentive to executives. The most common performance measures are earnings per share, net income, and operating income, each being used by about a quarter of firms having bonus plans. Nonfinancial performance measures, such as customer satisfaction and product or service quality, also are used.[11] Annual bonuses also are popular, not just for executives, but for nonmanagerial personnel as well. Unfortunately for employees, bonuses often take the place of annual raises. This allows a company to increase employee pay without permanently locking in the increases in salaries. Bonuses are compensation expense of the period in which they are earned, so unpaid bonuses are accrued as a liability at year-end.

Liabilities from Advance Collections

Deposits and advances from customers, as well as collections for third parties, present situations where liabilities are created to either make payments or provide goods or services in the future.

Deposits and Advances from Customers

Collecting cash from a customer as a refundable deposit or as an advance payment for products or services creates a liability to return the deposit or to supply the products or services.[12]

REFUNDABLE DEPOSITS   In some businesses it's typical to require customers to pay cash as a deposit that will be refunded when a specified event occurs. You probably have encountered such situations. When apartments are rented, security or damage deposits often are collected. Utility companies frequently collect deposits when service is begun. Similarly, deposits sometimes are required on returnable containers, to be refunded when the containers are returned. That situation is demonstrated in Illustration 13–9.

Illustration 13–9

Refundable Deposits

Rancor Chemical Company sells combustible chemicals in expensive, reusable containers. Customers are charged a deposit for each container delivered and receive a refund when the container is returned. Deposits collected on containers delivered during the year were $300,000. Deposits are forfeited if containers are not returned within one year. Ninety percent of the containers were returned within the allotted time. Deposits charged are twice the actual cost of containers. The inventory of containers remains on the company's books until deposits are forfeited.

When Deposits Are Collected

Cash	300,000	
Liability—refundable deposits		300,000

When Containers Are Returned*

Liability—refundable deposits	270,000	
Cash		270,000

When Deposits Are Forfeited*

Liability—refundable deposits	30,000	
Revenue—sale of containers		30,000
Cost of goods sold	15,000	
Inventory of containers		15,000

*Of course, not all containers are returned at the same time, nor does the allotted return period expire at the same time for all containers not returned. These entries summarize the several individual returns and forfeitures.

---

[11]C. D. Ittner, D. F. Larcker, and M. V. Rajan, "The Choice of Performance Measures in Annual Bonus Contracts," *The Accounting Review,* Vol. 72, No. 2 (April 1997), pp. 231–255.

[12]*SFAC 6* specifically identifies customer advances and deposits as liabilities under the definition provided in that statement. "Elements of Financial Statements," *Statement of Financial Accounting Concepts No. 6* (Stamford, Conn.: FASB, 1985), par. 197.

ADVANCES FROM CUSTOMERS   At times, businesses require advance payments from customers that will be applied to the purchase price when goods are delivered or services provided. Gift certificates, magazine subscriptions, layaway deposits, special order deposits, and airline tickets are examples. These customer advances, also called *deferred revenue* or *unearned revenue,* represent liabilities until the related product or service is provided. For instance, the New York Times Company reports deferred revenue from unexpired subscriptions of over $75 million in its 2017 balance sheet. Advances are demonstrated in Illustration 13–10.

A customer advance produces an obligation that is satisfied when the product or service is provided.

Illustration 13–10

Customer Advance

> Tomorrow Publications collects magazine subscriptions from customers at the time subscriptions are sold. Subscription revenue is recognized over the term of the subscription. Tomorrow collected $20 million in subscription sales during its first year of operations. At December 31, the average subscription was one-fourth expired.
>
> | | ($ in millions) | |
> |---|---|---|
> | **When Advance Is Collected** | | |
> | Cash | 20 | |
> | Deferred subscription revenue | | 20 |
> | **When Product Is Delivered** | | |
> | Deferred subscription revenue | 5 | |
> | Subscription revenue | | 5 |

This illustration highlights that deferred revenue gets reduced when the revenue associated with the advance has been recognized, either because the seller has delivered the goods or services as promised or because the buyer has forfeited the advance payment (for example, not redeeming a gift certificate before it expires). Less often, deferred revenue is reduced when an advance payment is returned by the seller to the buyer because the seller didn't deliver the goods or services as promised. This should sound familiar—recall from Chapter 6 that revenue recognition must be delayed until the seller has fulfilled its performance obligation. When revenue recognition is delayed, but some advanced payment is received, the seller reports a deferred revenue liability until delivery has occurred.

Additional Consideration

> **Accounting for Interest on Advances from Customers.** Earlier in this chapter you saw that we calculate interest expense on "noninterest-bearing" notes. After all, there is a "time value of money," and nobody is willing to loan money for free. The same reasoning suggests that companies should calculate interest expense when a customer pays far in advance of delivery of a product or service. As indicated in Chapter 6, that's what GAAP for revenue recognition requires.[13]
>
> For example, assume that on January 1, 2021, Lewis Manufacturing Co. enters into a contract to deliver equipment to Williams Surgical Supply, Inc., on December 31, 2022. Williams pays $907 (in thousands) to Lewis at the start of the contract (January 1, 2021). In this arrangement, Williams pays Lewis significantly in advance of delivery, so Williams can be viewed as loaning money to Lewis, and Lewis should recognize interest expense on the loan. Assuming an effective interest rate of 5%, Lewis would recognize interest expense on its deferred revenue liability as follows:
>
> **January 1, 2021**
> ***When prepayment occurs:***
>
> | | | |
> |---|---|---|
> | Cash | 907* | |
> | Deferred revenue | | 907 |
>
> *$907 = $1,000 × 0.90703 (present value of $1, n = 2, I = 5%; from Table 2)
>
> (continued)

---

[13]Source: FASB ASC 606-10-32-16: Revenue from Contracts with Customers-Overall-Measurement-The Existence of a Significant Financing Component in the Contract.

(concluded)

December 31, 2021
Accrual of year 1 interest expense:

Interest expense ($907 × 5%)	45	
Interest payable		45

December 31, 2022
When subsequent delivery occurs:

Interest expense (($907 + $45) × 5%)	48	
Interest payable	45	
Deferred revenue	907	
Sales revenue		1,000

Lewis recognizes revenue of $1,000 rather than $907 because that is the fair value it received from Williams, including the $907 received up front and $45 + $48 = $93 of interest that Williams is allowing Lewis to not pay. Put differently, the equipment must be worth $1,000 for Williams to be willing to accept it in exchange for giving up $907 cash and $93 of interest it is owed by Lewis.

As discussed in Chapter 6, companies can ignore the interest component of advance payments if it is not significant, which is assumed to be the case if the period between payment and delivery is less than one year.

Gift Cards

Gift cards or gift certificates are particularly common forms of advanced payments. As indicated in Chapter 6, when a company sells a gift card, it initially records the cash received as deferred revenue, and then recognizes revenue either when the gift card is redeemed or when the probability of redemption is viewed as remote (called *gift card breakage,* and based on expiration or the company's experience). The amounts involved can be significant. For example, **Best Buy**'s 2017 annual report lists a $472 million liability for unredeemed gift cards and $37 million of income from gift card breakage. Illustration 13–11 shows the journal entries used to account for gift cards.

Illustration 13–11
Accounting for Gift Cards

During May 2021, Great Buy, Inc., sold $2 million of gift cards. Also during May, $1.5 million of gift cards sold in May and in prior periods were redeemed by customers, and $1 million of gift cards sold in prior periods expired and unused. Great Buy would make the following journal entries:

To record sale of gift cards

Cash	2,000,000	
Deferred gift card revenue		2,000,000

To record redemption of gift cards
(ignoring entries to inventory and cost of sales)

Deferred gift card revenue	1,500,000	
Revenue—gift cards		1,500,000

To record expiration of gift cards

Deferred gift card revenue	1,000,000	
Revenue—gift cards		1,000,000

Liabilities for deferred revenue are classified as current or long-term depending on when the obligation is expected to be satisfied.

Collections for Third Parties

Companies often make collections for third parties from customers or from employees and periodically remit these amounts to the appropriate governmental (or other) units. Amounts collected this way represent liabilities until remitted.

Additional Consideration

Escheatment laws specify the rights of a state to claim abandoned property. Unused gift cards are a type of abandoned (or unclaimed) property. While most states exempt gift cards from escheatment laws, some do not. In those states where gift cards are subject to escheatment laws, after a period of three to five years, retailers are required to turn over all or part of the unredeemed value of gift cards to the state. To see how this works, let's modify Illustration 13–11 and assume that Great Buy is subject to an escheatment law that requires payment of 100% of unredeemed gift cards to the state in which Great Buy is incorporated. The third journal entry of Illustration 13–11 would be modified as follows:

To record expiration of gift cards

Deferred gift card revenue (amount of expired gift cards)	1,000,000	
Cash (to balance)		1,000,000

An example is sales taxes. For illustration, assume a state sales tax rate of 4% and local sales tax rate of 3%. Adding the tax to a $100 sale creates a $7 liability until the tax is paid.

Cash (or accounts receivable)	107	
Sales revenue		100
Sales taxes payable [(4% + 3%) × $100]		7

Sales taxes collected from customers represent liabilities until remitted.

Payroll-related deductions such as withholding taxes, Social Security taxes, employee insurance, employee contributions to retirement plans, and union dues also create current liabilities until the amounts collected are paid to appropriate parties. These payroll-related liabilities are discussed further in the appendix to this chapter.

Amounts collected from employees in connection with payroll represent liabilities until remitted.

A Closer Look at the Current and Noncurrent Classification

Given a choice, do you suppose management would prefer to report an obligation as a current liability or as a noncurrent liability? Other things being equal, most would choose the noncurrent classification. The reason is that in most settings outsiders (like banks, bond-holders, and shareholders) consider debt that is payable currently to be riskier than debt that need not be paid for some time, because the current payable requires the company to be able to access the necessary cash relatively soon. Also, the long-term classification enables the company to report higher working capital (current assets minus current liabilities) and a higher current ratio (current assets/current liabilities). Working capital and the current ratio often are explicitly restricted in loan contracts. As you study this section, you should view the classification choice from this perspective. That is, a manager might not so much ask the question "What amount should I report as a current liability?" but rather "What amount can I exclude from classification as a current liability?"

● LO13–4

Current Maturities of Long-Term Debt

Long-term obligations (bonds, notes, lease liabilities, deferred tax liabilities) usually are reclassified and reported as current liabilities when they become payable within the upcoming year (or operating cycle, if longer than a year). For example, a 20-year bond issue is reported as a long-term liability for 19 years but normally is reported as a current liability on the balance sheet prepared during the 20th year of its term to maturity.[14] General Mills reported $604.7 million of its long-term debt as a current liability in 2017 (see Illustration 13–1).

FINANCIAL Reporting Case

Q2, p. 718

Obligations Callable by the Creditor

The requirement to classify currently maturing debt as a current liability includes debt that is *callable* (in other words, due on demand) *by the creditor* in the upcoming year (or

The currently maturing portion of a long-term debt must be reported as a current liability.

---

[14]Debt to be refinanced is an exception we discuss later.

operating cycle, if longer), even if the debt is not expected to be called. The current liability classification also is intended to include situations in which the creditor has the right to demand payment because an *existing violation* of a provision of the debt agreement makes it callable (say, working capital has fallen below a minimum covenant specified by a debt agreement). This also includes situations in which debt is not yet callable but will be callable within the year if an existing violation is not corrected within a specified grace period (unless it's probable the violation will be corrected within the grace period or waived by the creditor).[15]

When Short-Term Obligations Are Expected to Be Refinanced

Reconsider the 20-year bond issue we discussed earlier. Normally we would reclassify it as a current liability on the balance sheet prepared during its 20th year. But suppose a second 20-year bond issue is sold specifically to refund the first issue when it matures. Do we have a long-term liability for 19 years, then a current liability in year 20, and then another long-term liability in years 21 and beyond? Or, do we have a single 40-year, long-term liability? If we look beyond the outward form of the transactions, the substance of the events obviously supports a single, continuing, noncurrent obligation. The concept of substance over form influences the classification of obligations expected to be refinanced.

Short-term obligations (including the callable obligations we discussed in the previous section) that are expected to be refinanced on a long-term basis can be reported as noncurrent, rather than current, liabilities only if two conditions are met:

(1) The company must intend to refinance on a long-term basis, and

(2) the company must actually have demonstrated the ability to refinance on a long-term basis.

Ability to refinance on a long-term basis can be demonstrated by either an existing refinancing agreement or by actual financing prior to the issuance of the financial statements.[16] Illustration 13–12 provides an example.

Illustration 13–12

Short-Term Obligations that Are Expected to Be Refinanced on a Long-Term Basis

Brahm Bros. Ice Cream had $12 million of notes that mature in May 2022 and also had $4 million of bonds issued in 1992 that mature in February 2022. On December 31, 2021, the company's fiscal year-end, management intended to refinance both on a long-term basis.

On February 7, 2022, the company issued $4 million of 20-year bonds, applying the proceeds to repay the bond issue that matured that month. In early March, prior to the actual issuance of the 2021 financial statements, Brahm Bros. negotiated a line of credit with a commercial bank for up to $7 million any time during 2022. Any borrowings will mature two years from the date of borrowing. Interest is at the prime London interbank borrowing rate.*

	December 31, 2021 ($ in thousands)
Classification	
Current Liabilities	
Notes payable	$5,000
Long-Term Liabilities	
Notes payable	$7,000
Bonds payable	4,000

Management's ability to refinance the $4 million of bonds on a long-term basis was demonstrated by actual financing prior to the issuance of the financial statements. Management's ability to refinance $7 million of the $12 million of notes was demonstrated by a refinancing agreement. The remaining $5 million must be reported as a current liability.

*This is a widely available rate often used as a basis for establishing interest rates on lines of credit and often abbreviated as LIBOR.

---

[15]FASB ASC 470–10–45: Debt—Overall—Other Presentation Matters.
[16]FASB ASC 470–10–45–14: Debt—Overall—Other Presentation Matters.

If shares of stock had been issued to refinance the bonds in the illustration, the bonds still would be excluded from classification as a current liability. The specific form of the long-term refinancing (bonds, bank loans, equity securities) is irrelevant when determining the appropriate classification. Requiring companies to actually demonstrate the ability to refinance on a long-term basis in addition to merely intending to do so avoids intentional or unintentional understatements of current liabilities.

It's important to remember that several weeks usually pass between the end of a company's fiscal year and the date the financial statements for that year actually are issued. Events occurring during that period can be used to clarify the nature of financial statement elements at the reporting date. Here we consider refinancing agreements and actual securities transactions to support a company's ability to refinance on a long-term basis. Later in the chapter we use information that becomes available during this period to decide how loss contingencies are reported.

International Financial Reporting Standards

> **Classification of Liabilities to be Refinanced.** Under U.S. GAAP, liabilities payable within the coming year are classified as long-term liabilities if refinancing is completed before the date of issuance of the financial statements. Under IFRS, refinancing must be completed before the balance sheet date.[17]

● LO13–7

Concept Review Exercise

The following selected transactions relate to liabilities of Southern Communications, Inc., for portions of 2021 and 2022. Southern's fiscal year ends on December 31.

CURRENT LIABILITIES

Required:
Prepare the appropriate journal entries for these transactions.

2021

July   1   Arranged an uncommitted short-term line of credit with First City Bank amounting to $25,000,000 at the bank's prime rate (11.5% in July). The company will pay no commitment fees for this arrangement.

Aug.   9   Received a $30,000 refundable deposit from a major customer for copper-lined mailing containers used to transport communications equipment.

Oct.   7   Received most of the mailing containers covered by the refundable deposit and a letter stating that the customer will retain containers represented by $2,000 of the deposit and will forfeit that amount. The cost of the forfeited containers was $1,500.

Nov.   1   Borrowed $7 million cash from First City Bank under the line of credit arranged in July and issued a nine-month promissory note. Interest at the prime rate of 12% was payable at maturity.

Dec. 31   Recorded appropriate adjusting entries for the liabilities described above.

2022

Feb. 12   Using the unused portion of the credit line as support, issued $9 million of commercial paper and issued a six-month promissory note. Interest was discounted at issuance at a 10% discount rate.

Aug.   1   Paid the 12% note at maturity.

        12   Paid the commercial paper at maturity.

2021

> **July 1**
> No entry is made for a line of credit until a loan actually is made. The existence and terms of the line would be described in a disclosure note.
>
> **August 9**
> Cash   30,000
>   Liability—refundable deposits   30,000

---
[17]"Presentation of Financial Statements" *International Accounting Standard No. 1* (IASCF), as amended effective January 1, 2018.

October 7		
Liability—refundable deposits...	30,000	
Cash		28,000
Revenue—sale of containers..		2,000
Cost of goods sold	1,500	
Inventory of containers...		1,500
November 1		
Cash	7,000,000	
Notes payable...		7,000,000
December 31		
Interest expense ($7,000,000 × 12% × $^2/_{12}$)...	140,000	
Interest payable...		140,000

2022

February 12		
Cash [$9,000,000 − ($9,000,000 × 10% × $^5/_{12}$)]...	8,550,000	
Discount on notes payable (difference)	450,000	
Notes payable..		9,000,000
Note that the effective interest rate is [($9,000,000 × 10% × $^5/_{12}$) ÷ $8,550,000] × $^{12}/_6$ = $450,000 ÷ $8,550,000 × 2 = 10.53%.		
August 1		
Interest expense ($7,000,000 × 12% × $^7/_{12}$)...	490,000	
Interest payable (from adjusting entry)...	140,000	
Notes payable (face amount)...	7,000,000	
Cash ($7,000,000 + $630,000)...		7,630,000
August 12		
Interest expense ($9,000,000 × 10% × $^6/_{12}$)...	450,000	
Discount on notes payable		450,000
Notes payable (face amount)...	9,000,000	
Cash ($8,550,000 + $450,000)...		9,000,000

PART B

Contingencies

The feature that distinguishes the loss contingencies we discuss in this part of the chapter from the liabilities we discussed previously is uncertainty as to whether an obligation really exists. The circumstance giving rise to the contingency already has occurred, but there is uncertainty about whether a liability exists that will be resolved only when some future event occurs (or doesn't occur).

Loss Contingencies

● LO13–5   General Motors Company's 2017 financial statements indicate a variety of potential obligations, as shown in Illustration 13–13.

Illustration 13–13

Disclosure of Potential
Contingent Losses—
General Motors Company

Real World Financials

> **17. Commitments and Contingencies (in part)**
>
> Various other legal actions, governmental investigations, claims and proceedings are pending against us or our related companies or joint ventures, including matters arising out of alleged product defects; employment-related matters; governmental regulations relating to product and workplace safety, vehicle emissions, including CO2 and nitrogen oxide, fuel economy, and related governmental regulations; product warranties; financial services; dealer, supplier and other contractual relationships; government regulations relating to
>
> (continued)

(concluded)

payments to foreign companies; government regulations relating to competition issues; tax-related matters not subject to the provision of ASC 740, Income Taxes (indirect tax-related matters); product design, manufacture and performance; consumer protection laws; and environmental protection laws, including laws regulating air emissions, water discharges, waste management and environmental remediation.

These "legal actions, governmental investigations, claims and proceedings" all relate to situations that already have occurred. However, it isn't clear that these situations have given rise to liabilities, because GM doesn't know if it will have to make future payments. How likely is an unfavorable outcome, and how much will GM have to pay if an unfavorable outcome occurs?

A loss contingency is an existing, uncertain situation involving potential loss depending on whether some future event occurs. Whether a contingency is accrued and reported as a liability depends on (a) the likelihood that the confirming event will occur and (b) what can be determined about the amount of loss. For example, consider lawsuits filed against GM by customers who allege they suffered injuries as a result of faulty ignition switches in GM cars that were recalled in 2014. GM's note 17 discloses much information about such claims, including over 100 class-action lawsuits and several hundred personal-injury lawsuits filed against it, as of February 6, 2018. It may take several years for those lawsuits to be settled or litigated. When considering how to account for those lawsuits prior to their resolution, GM must assess the likelihood that it eventually will have to pay damages and, if so, what the amount of those damages will be.

> A *loss contingency* arises when there is uncertainty about whether a past event will result in a future loss. The uncertainty will be resolved only when some future event occurs.

Note that we only account for a loss contingency when the event that gave rise to it occurred before the financial statement date. Otherwise, regardless of the likelihood of the eventual outcome, no liability existed at the statement date. Remember, one of the essential characteristics of a liability is that it results from past transactions or events. In our GM example, GM previously sold the cars to customers, so the event giving rise to potential litigation losses has occurred. The uncertainty relates not to that past event, but to the potential litigation losses that could occur in the future.

Generally accepted accounting principles require that the likelihood that the future event(s) will confirm the incurrence of the liability be (somewhat arbitrarily) categorized as probable, reasonably possible, or remote:[18]

> **FINANCIAL Reporting Case**
>
> Q4, p. 718

Probable	Confirming event is likely to occur.
Reasonably possible	The chance the confirming event will occur is more than remote but less than likely.
Remote	The chance the confirming event will occur is slight.

Also key to reporting a contingent liability is its dollar amount. The amount of the potential loss is classified as either known, reasonably estimable, or not reasonably estimable.

● LO13–6

A liability is accrued if it is both probable that the confirming event will occur and the amount can be at least reasonably estimated. A general depiction of the accrual of a loss contingency is

Loss (or expense)..	x,xxx	
Liability..		x,xxx

If one amount within a range of possible loss appears better than other amounts within the range, that amount is accrued. When no amount within the range appears more likely than others, the minimum amount should be recorded and the possible additional loss should be disclosed.[19]

---

[18]Because FASB ASC 740–10–25: Income Taxes—Overall—Recognition provides guidance on accounting for uncertainty in income taxes, FASB ASC 450–10: Contingencies—Loss Contingencies does not apply to income taxes. GAAP regarding uncertainty in income taxes changes the threshold for recognition of tax positions from the most probable amount to the amount that has a "more likely than not" chance of being sustained upon examination. We discuss accounting for uncertainty in income taxes in Chapter 16.

[19]FASB ASC 450–20–30: Contingencies—Loss Contingencies—Initial Measurement.

As an example, consider the following disclosure note from Merck & Co., Inc.'s 2017 financial statements (Illustration 13–14).

Illustration 13–14

Accrual of a Loss Contingency—Merck & Co., Inc.

Real World Financials

---

11. Contingencies and Environmental Liabilities (in part)

In management's opinion, the liabilities for all environmental matters that are probable and reasonably estimable have been accrued and totaled $82 million and $83 million at December 31, 2017 and 2016, respectively. These liabilities are undiscounted, do not consider potential recoveries from other parties and will be paid out over the periods of remediation for the applicable sites, which are expected to occur primarily over the next 15 years. Although it is not possible to predict with certainty the outcome of these matters, or the ultimate costs of remediation, management does not believe that any reasonably possible expenditures that may be incurred in excess of the liabilities accrued should exceed $63 million in the aggregate. Management also does not believe that these expenditures should result in a material adverse effect on the Company's financial position, results of operations, liquidity or capital resources for any year.

Source: Merck & Co., Inc.

Consistent with GAAP, Merck accrued and disclosed the $82 million loss that is probable and reasonably estimable, and then only disclosed the $63 million estimated range of reasonably possible losses above that amount.

It's important to note that some contingent losses don't involve liabilities at all. Rather, these contingencies, when resolved, cause a noncash asset to be impaired, so accruing the contingency means reducing the related asset rather than recording a liability:

Loss (or expense)	x,xxx	
Asset (or valuation account)..		x,xxx

The most common loss contingency of this type is an uncollectible receivable. You have recorded these before without knowing you were accruing a loss contingency (*Debit:* bad debt expense; *Credit:* allowance for uncollectible accounts).[20]

Not all loss contingencies are accrued. If one or both criteria for accrual are not met, but there is at least a reasonable possibility that a loss will occur, a disclosure note should describe the contingency. It also should provide an estimate of the potential loss or range of loss, if possible. If an estimate cannot be made, a statement to that effect is needed.

As an example of only disclosing a contingent loss, consider a disclosure note accompanying a 2017 annual report of United States Steel Corporation. As shown in Illustration 13–15, U.S. Steel considered it to be impossible to estimate its potential environmental liability associated with previously sold properties and businesses, and so only disclosed that contingent loss.

> A loss contingency is disclosed in notes to the financial statements if there is at least a reasonable possibility that the loss will occur.

Illustration 13–15

Disclosure of Loss Contingency—U. S. Steel

Real World Financials

Note 25: Contingencies and Commitments (in part)

Throughout its history, U.S. Steel has sold numerous properties and businesses and many of these sales included indemnifications and cost sharing agreements related to the assets that were divested. . . . The amount of potential environmental liability associated with these transactions and properties is not estimable due to the nature and extent of the unknown conditions related to the properties divested and deconsolidated.

Source: U.S. Steel

Illustration 13–16 highlights the appropriate accounting treatment for each possible combination of (a) the likelihood of an obligation being confirmed and (b) the determinability of its dollar amount.

---

[20]FASB ASC 310–10–35–7: Receivables—Overall—Subsequent Measurement—Losses from Uncollectible Receivables.

	Dollar Amount of Potential Loss		
Likelihood	**Known**	**Reasonably Estimable**	**Not Reasonably Estimable**
Probable	Liability accrued and disclosure note	Liability accrued and disclosure note	Disclosure note only
Reasonably possible	Disclosure note only	Disclosure note only	Disclosure note only
Remote	No disclosure required*	No disclosure required*	No disclosure required*

*Except for certain guarantees and other specified off-balance-sheet risk situations discussed in the next chapter.

Illustration 13–16
Accounting Treatment of Loss Contingencies

Product Warranties and Guarantees

MANUFACTURER'S QUALITY-ASSURANCE WARRANTY Satisfaction guaranteed! Your money back if not satisfied! If anything goes wrong in the first five years or 100,000 miles . . . ! Three-year guarantee! These and similar promises accompany most consumer goods. In Chapter 6 we called this sort of guarantee a *quality-assurance warranty*. When this type of warranty is included in a contract between a seller and a customer, it isn't a separate performance obligation for the seller. Rather, it is a guarantee by the seller that the customer will be satisfied with the goods or services that the seller provided.

Most consumer products are accompanied by a guarantee.

Why do sellers offer quality-assurance warranties? To boost sales. It follows, then, that any costs of making good on such guarantees should be estimated and recorded as expenses in the same accounting period the products are sold (matching expenses with revenues). Also, it is in the period of sale that the company becomes obligated to eventually make good on a guarantee, so it makes sense that it recognizes a liability in the period of sale. The challenge is that much of the cost of satisfying a guarantee usually occurs later, sometimes years later. So, this is a loss contingency. There may be a future sacrifice of economic benefits (cost of satisfying the guarantee) due to an existing circumstance (the guaranteed products have been sold) that depends on an uncertain future event (customer claim).

The costs of satisfying guarantees should be recorded as expenses in the same accounting period the products are sold.

The criteria for accruing a contingent loss (rather than only disclosing it) almost always are met for product warranties (or product guarantees). While we usually can't predict the liability associated with an individual sale, reasonably accurate estimates of the *total* liability for a period usually are possible, because prior experience makes it possible to predict how many warrantees or guarantees (on average) will need to be satisfied. Illustration 13–17 demonstrates accrual of the contingent liability for warranties in the reporting period in which the product under warranty is sold.

The contingent liability for quality-assurance warranties almost always is accrued.

Illustration 13–17
Product Warranty

Caldor Health, a supplier of in-home health care products, introduced a new therapeutic chair carrying a two-year warranty against defects. Estimates based on industry experience indicate warranty costs of 3% of sales during the first 12 months following the sale and 4% the next 12 months. During December 2021, its first month of availability, Caldor sold $2 million of chairs.

During December

Cash (and accounts receivable)	2,000,000	
Sales revenue		2,000,000

December 31, 2021 (adjusting entry)

Warranty expense [(3% + 4%) × $2,000,000]	140,000	
Warranty liability		140,000

When customer claims are made and costs are incurred to satisfy those claims, the liability is reduced (let's say $61,000 in 2022):

Warranty liability	61,000	
Cash (or salaries payable, parts and supplies, etc.)		61,000

Estimates of warranty costs cannot be expected to be precise. However, if the estimating method is monitored and revised when necessary, overestimates and underestimates should cancel each other over time. The estimated liability may be classified as current or as part current and part long-term, depending on when warranty claims are expected to be satisfied.

SFAC No. 7 provides a framework for using future cash flows in accounting measurements.

EXPECTED CASH FLOW APPROACH   In Chapter 5, you learned of a framework for using future cash flows as the basis for measuring assets and liabilities, introduced by the FASB in 2000 with *Statement of Financial Accounting Concepts No. 7,* "Using Cash Flow Information and Present Value in Accounting Measurements."[21] The approach described in the Concept Statement offers a way to take into account *any uncertainty concerning the amounts and timing of the cash flows.* Although future cash flows in many instances are contractual and certain, the amounts and timing of cash flows are less certain in other situations, such as warranty obligations.

As demonstrated in Illustration 13–17, the traditional way of measuring a warranty obligation is to report the "best estimate" of future cash flows, ignoring the time value of money on the basis of immateriality. However, when the warranty obligation spans more than one year and we can associate probabilities with possible cash flow outcomes, the approach described by *SFAC No. 7* offers a more plausible estimate of the warranty obligation. This "expected cash flow approach" incorporates specific probabilities of cash flows into the analysis. Illustration 13–18 provides an example.

Illustration 13–18

Product Warranty

Probabilities are associated with possible cash outcomes.

Caldor Health, a supplier of in-home health care products, introduced a new therapeutic chair carrying a two-year warranty against defects. During December of 2021, its first month of availability, Caldor sold $2 million of the chairs. Industry experience indicates the following probability distribution for the potential warranty costs:

Warranty Costs	Probability
2022	
$50,000	20%
60,000	50%
70,000	30%
2023	
$70,000	20%
80,000	50%
90,000	30%

An arrangement with a service firm requires that costs for the two-year warranty period be settled at the end of 2022 and 2023. The risk-free rate of interest is 5%. Applying the expected cash flow approach, at the end of the 2021 fiscal year, Caldor would record a warranty liability (and expense) of $131,564, calculated as follows:

The probability-weighted cash outcomes provide the expected cash flows.

2022	$50,000 × 20% =	$10,000
	60,000 × 50% =	30,000
	70,000 × 30% =	21,000
		$61,000
		× 0.95238* $ 58,095

2023	$70,000 × 20% =	$14,000
	80,000 × 50% =	40,000
	90,000 × 30% =	27,000
		$81,000
		× 0.90703† 73,469
		$131,564

The present value of the expected cash flows is the estimated liability.

*Present value of $1, $n = 1$, $i = 5\%$ (from Table 2)
†Present value of $1, $n = 2$, $i = 5\%$ (from Table 2)

December 31, 2021 (adjusting entry)

Warranty expense..	131,564	
Warranty liability (calculated above).....................		131,564

[21]Source: Using Cash Flow Information and Present Value in Accounting Measurements," *Statement of Financial Accounting Concepts No. 7* (Norwalk, Conn.: FASB, 2000). Recall that Concept Statements do not directly prescribe GAAP, but instead provide structure and direction to financial accounting.

EXTENDED WARRANTY CONTRACTS It's difficult these days to buy a computer, a digital camera, a car, or almost any durable consumer product without being asked to buy an extended warranty agreement. An extended warranty provides warranty protection beyond the manufacturer's original warranty. As discussed in Chapter 6, because an extended warranty is priced and sold separately from the warranteed product, it constitutes a separate performance obligation. So, rather than only worrying about how to recognize the contingent liability associated with an extended warranty, we face another accounting question: When should the revenue from the sale of an extended warranty be recognized?

Revenue is recognized when performance obligations are satisfied, not necessarily when cash is received. Because an extended warranty provides coverage over a period of time, these arrangements typically qualify for revenue recognition over the period of coverage. However, cash typically is received up front, when the extended warranty is sold. Similar to other advanced payments for future products and services, revenue from extended warranty contracts is not recognized immediately, but instead is recorded as a deferred revenue liability at the time of sale and recognized as revenue over the contract period, typically on a straight-line basis. We demonstrate accounting for extended warranties in Illustration 13–19.

Illustration 13–19
Extended Warranty

Brand Name Appliances sells major appliances that carry a one-year manufacturer's warranty. Customers are offered the opportunity at the time of purchase to also buy a three-year extended warranty for an additional charge. On January 3, 2021, Brand Name sold a $60 extended warranty, covering years 2022, 2023, and 2024.

January 3, 2021		
Cash (or accounts receivable)	60	
Deferred revenue—extended warranties		60
December 31, 2022, 2023, 2024 (adjusting entries)		
Deferred revenue—extended warranties	20	
Revenue—extended warranties ($60 ÷ 3)		20

The costs incurred to satisfy customer claims under the extended warranties also will be recorded during the same three-year period. That way, net income in each year of the extended warranty will reflect both the warranty revenue recognized and the costs associated with that revenue.

Additional Consideration

Accounting for Rebates, Premiums, and Coupons. Sometimes a company promotes its products in ways that obligate the company to do something in the future. For example, at the time of a sale, customers obtain cash register receipts, bar codes on the product, or other proofs of purchase that later can be mailed to the manufacturer for *cash rebates.* Also, customers sometimes can show proof of purchase to obtain noncash items (called *premiums),* like toys, small appliances, or dishes. Companies may also mail out *coupons,* which entice customers to buy a company's products and services at a discounted price at some point in the future. How should we account for the future obligations created by these promotions?

Until very recently, all of these promotions were viewed as creating a contingent liability. After all, they obligate the seller to transfer some uncertain amount of cash, goods, or services at a future date. However, with recent changes in accounting for revenue recognition, the accounting in this area has changed. Now we view promises to provide rebates and premiums to be part of agreements between sellers and customers. This means we account for them using the revenue recognition process we learned about in Chapter 6.

Cash rebates are an obligation to return cash in the future, so they represent a reduction in the net amount paid by the customer. To record these, we estimate the amount of cash rebates that customers will take and reduce revenue by the amount of that estimate in the period revenue is recognized. We also recognize a liability for the estimated rebate, similar to how we recognize a refundable deposit.

(continued)

(concluded)

Premiums obligate a company to provide noncash items and are treated as separate performance obligations. We allocate a portion of the original sales price to the premiums (based on their relative stand-alone selling prices), record that amount as deferred revenue, and recognize that portion as revenue when premiums are delivered. No contingent liability is recognized because, as with extended warranties, we recognize the cost of premiums in the period in which we deliver them and recognize revenue.

Coupons that aren't offered as part of a sales contract aren't accounted for as part of revenue recognition. Instead, issuing coupons creates a contingent liability that is recognized in the period the coupons are issued. In practice, firms typically either (a) recognize the entire expense associated with estimated coupon redemptions in the period the coupons are issued, or (b) recognize no liability in the period the coupons are issued and instead record the expense when coupons are redeemed. The difference between these approaches typically is not viewed as material.

Litigation Claims

Pending litigation is not unusual. In fact, as you saw for **GM**, the majority of medium and large corporations annually report multiple loss contingencies due to litigation.

In practice, accrual of a loss from pending or ongoing litigation is rare. Can you guess why? Suppose you are chief financial officer of Feinz Foods. Feinz is the defendant in a $44 million class-action suit. The company's legal counsel informally advises you that the chance the company will win the lawsuit is quite doubtful. Counsel feels the company might lose $30 million. Now suppose you decide to accrue a $30 million loss in your financial statements. Later, in the courtroom, your disclosure that Feinz management feels it is probable that the company will lose $30 million would be welcome ammunition for the opposing legal counsel. Understanding this, most companies rely on the knowledge that in today's legal environment the outcome of litigation is highly uncertain, making likelihood predictions difficult.

Therefore, while companies may accrue estimated lawyer fees and other legal costs, they usually do not record a loss until after the ultimate settlement has been reached or negotiations for settlement are substantially completed. While companies should provide extensive disclosure of these contingent liabilities, they do not always do so in practice.[22] In 2010, the SEC began pressuring firms for more complete disclosure of litigation, including better descriptions of the range of losses that are reasonably possible to occur. As an example, Illustration 13–20 provides a few excerpts from the eight pages of litigation note appearing in **JP Morgan Chase & Company**'s 2016 annual report.

Illustration 13–20

Disclosure of Litigation
Contingencies—JP Morgan
Chase & Company

Real World Financials

Note 31: Litigation (in part)

As of December 31, 2016, the Firm and its subsidiaries and affiliates are defendants or putative defendants in numerous legal proceedings, including private, civil litigations and regulatory/government investigations. . . . The Firm believes the estimate of the aggregate range of reasonably possible losses, in excess of reserves established, for its legal proceedings is from $0 to approximately $3.0 billion at December 31, 2016. This estimated aggregate range of reasonably possible losses was based upon currently available information for those proceedings in which the Firm believes that an estimate of reasonably possible loss can be made. For certain matters, the Firm does not believe that such an estimate can be made, as of that date.

Source: JP Morgan Chase & Company

---

[22]For research indicating incomplete disclosure of litigation-related contingent liabilities, see R. Desir, K. Fanning, and R. Pfeiffer, "Are Revisions to SFAS No. 5 Needed?" *Accounting Horizons* 24(4), December 2010, pp. 525–546.

Even after a firm loses in court, it may not make an accrual. As you can see in Illustration 13–21, Ameris Bancorp, in its 2016 annual report, disclosed but did not accrue damages from a lawsuit it lost, because the company was appealing the verdict.

> ### Note 19: Commitments and Contingent Liabilities (in part): Contingencies
>
> As of December 31, 2016, the Company believes that it has valid bases in law and fact to overturn on appeal the verdict. As a result, the Company believes that the likelihood that the amount of the judgment will be affirmed is not probable, and, accordingly, that the amount of any loss cannot be reasonably estimated at this time. Because the Company believes that this potential loss is not probable or estimable, it has not recorded any reserves or contingencies related to this legal matter.
>
> Source: Ameris Bancorp

Illustration 13–21

Disclosure of a Lawsuit—
Ameris Bancorp

Real World Financials

Subsequent Events

Several weeks usually pass between the end of a company's fiscal year and the date the financial statements for that year actually are issued or available to be issued.[23] As shown on the following time line, events occurring during this period can be used to clarify the nature of financial statement elements at the report date.

When the cause of a loss contingency occurs before the year-end, a clarifying event before financial statements are issued can be used to determine how the contingency is reported.

If information becomes available that sheds light on a claim that existed when the fiscal year ended, that information should be used in determining the probability of a loss contingency materializing and in estimating the amount of the loss.

The settlement of a lawsuit after Starbucks' September 29, 2013, fiscal year ended apparently influenced its accrual of a loss contingency (Illustration 13–22).

> ### Note 15: Commitments and Contingencies (in part)
> *Legal Proceedings*
>
> On December 6, 2010, Kraft commenced a federal court action against Starbucks, entitled Kraft Foods Global, Inc. v. Starbucks Corporation, in the U.S. District Court for the Southern District of New York. On November 12, 2013, the arbitrator ordered Starbucks to pay Kraft $2,227.5 million in damages plus prejudgment interest and attorney's fees. We have estimated prejudgment interest, which includes an accrual through the estimated payment date, and attorneys' fees to be approximately $556.6 million. As a result, we recorded a litigation charge of $2,784.1 million in our fiscal 2013 operating results.
>
> Source: Starbucks

Illustration 13–22

Accrual of Litigation
Contingencies—Starbucks

Real World Financials

For a loss contingency to be accrued, the cause of the lawsuit must have occurred before the accounting period ended. It's not necessary that the lawsuit actually was filed during that reporting period.

---

[23]Financial statements are viewed as *issued* if they have been widely distributed to financial statement users in a format consistent with GAAP. Some entities (for example, private companies) do not widely distribute their financial statements to users. For those entities, the key date for subsequent events is not the date of issuance but rather the date upon which the financial statements are *available to be issued,* which occurs when the financial statements are complete, in a format consistent with GAAP, and have obtained the necessary approvals for issuance. Entities must disclose the date through which subsequent events have been evaluated (FASB ASC 855: Subsequent Events).

740   SECTION 3   Liabilities and Shareholders' Equity

Sometimes, the cause of a loss contingency occurs after the end of the year but before the financial statements are issued:

> If an event giving rise to a contingency occurs after the year-end, a liability should not be accrued.

When a contingency comes into existence after the company's fiscal year-end, a liability cannot be accrued because it didn't exist at the end of the year. However, if the failure to disclose the possible loss would cause the financial statements to be misleading, the situation should be described in a disclosure note, including the effect of the possible loss on key accounting numbers affected.[24]

In fact, *any* event occurring after the fiscal year-end but before the financial statements are issued that has a material effect on the company's financial position must be disclosed in a subsequent events disclosure note. Examples are an issuance of debt or equity securities, a business combination, and discontinued operations.

A disclosure note from the Coca-Cola Company's 2016 annual report is shown in Illustration 13–23 and describes events that occurred in the first quarter of 2017.

Illustration 13–23

Subsequent Events—Coca-Cola Company

Real World Financials

> **Note 21: Subsequent events (in part)**
>
> In the first quarter of 2017, additional bottling territories in North America met the criteria to be classified as held for sale. Therefore, we are required to record the related assets and liabilities at the lower of carrying value or fair value less any costs to sell based on the estimated selling prices, which will result in an estimated total loss of $9 million. The Company expects these territories to be refranchised during 2017.
>
> Source: Coca-Cola Company

Additional Consideration

> Contingent liabilities that a company takes on when it acquires another company may be treated differently from those that arise during the normal course of business. If the acquirer can determine the fair value of a contingent liability, the liability is measured at fair value. For example, the acquisition-date fair value of a warranty obligation often can be determined. If the acquirer cannot determine the fair value, then the acquirer uses the normal criteria that apply to contingent liabilities. That is, the contingent liability is accrued if (1) available information indicates that it is probable a liability has been incurred as of the acquisition date, and (2) the amount of the liability can be reasonably estimated.[25] Because some acquired contingencies could be accounted for at fair value, there could be a lack of comparability between contingencies that arise in the normal course of business and those that are obtained as part of an acquisition.

Unasserted Claims and Assessments

> It must be probable that an unasserted claim or assessment will be asserted before considering whether and how to report the possible loss.

Sometimes companies are aware of a potential claim that has not yet been made. Such unasserted claims may require accrual or disclosure of a contingent liability. A two-step process is involved in deciding how the unasserted claim should be reported:

1. Is it probable that a claim will be asserted? If the answer to that question is "no," stop. No accrual or disclosure is necessary. If the answer is "yes," go on to step 2.
2. Treat the claim as if the claim has been asserted. That requires evaluating (a) the likelihood of an unfavorable outcome and (b) whether the dollar amount of loss can be estimated, just as we already have discussed for other loss contingencies for which a claim has already been asserted.

---

[24] FASB ASC 450–20–50v9: Contingencies—Loss Contingencies—Disclosure.
[25] FASB ASC 805-20-25: Business Combinations—Identifiable Assets and Liabilities, and Any Noncontrolling Interest—Recognition.

For example, suppose a trucking company frequently transports hazardous waste materials and is subject to environmental laws and regulations. Management has identified several sites at which it is or may be liable for remediation. For those sites for which no penalties have been asserted, management must assess the likelihood that a claim will be made, and if so, the likelihood that the company actually will be held liable. If management feels an assessment is probable, an estimated loss and contingent liability would be accrued only if an unfavorable outcome is probable and the amount can be reasonably estimated. However, a disclosure note alone would be appropriate if an unfavorable settlement is only reasonably possible or if the settlement is probable but cannot be reasonably estimated. No action is needed if chances of that outcome occurring are remote.

As described in a December 31, 2016, disclosure note (see Illustration 13–24), **Union Pacific** concluded that some unasserted claims met the criteria for accrual under this two-step decision process.

---

15. Commitments and Contingencies (in part)

Asserted and Unasserted Claims—Various claims and lawsuits are pending against us and certain of our subsidiaries. We cannot fully determine the effect of all asserted and unasserted claims on our consolidated results of operations, financial condition, or liquidity. To the extent possible, we have recorded a liability where asserted and unasserted claims are considered probable and where such claims can be reasonably estimated.

Source: Union Pacific Corporation

Illustration 13–24

Unasserted Claims—Union Pacific Corporation

Real World Financials

Notice that the treatment of contingent liabilities is consistent with the accepted definition of liabilities as (a) probable, future sacrifices of economic benefits (b) that arise from present obligations to other entities and (c) that result from past transactions or events.[26] The inherent uncertainty involved with contingent liabilities means additional care is required to determine whether future sacrifices of economic benefits are probable and whether the amount of the sacrifices can be quantified.

International Financial Reporting Standards

Loss Contingencies. Accounting for contingencies is part of a broader international standard, *IAS No. 37*, "Provisions, Contingent Liabilities and Contingent Assets." Overall, accounting for contingent losses under IFRS is quite similar to accounting under U.S. GAAP. A contingent loss is accrued if it's both probable and can be reasonably estimated, and disclosed if it's of at least a remote probability. However, there are some important differences:

● LO13–7

- IFRS refers to accrued liabilities as "provisions," and refers to possible obligations that are not accrued as "contingent liabilities." The term "contingent liabilities" is used for all of these obligations in U.S. GAAP.

- IFRS requires disclosure (but not accrual) of two types of contingent liabilities: (1) possible obligations whose existence will be confirmed by some uncertain future events that the company does not control, and (2) a present obligation for which either it is not probable that a future outflow will occur or the amount of the future outflow cannot be measured with sufficient reliability. U.S. GAAP does not make this distinction but typically would require disclosure of the same contingencies.

- IFRS defines "probable" as "more likely than not" (greater than 50%), which is a lower threshold than typically associated with "probable" in U.S. GAAP.

- If a liability is accrued, IFRS measures the liability as the best estimate of the expenditure required to settle the present obligation. If there is a range of equally likely outcomes, IFRS would use the midpoint of the range, while U.S. GAAP requires use of the low end of the range.

(continued)

---

[26]"Elements of Financial Statements," *Statement of Financial Accounting Concepts No. 6* (Stamford, Conn.: FASB, 1985).

742 SECTION 3 Liabilities and Shareholders' Equity

(concluded)

- If the effect of the time value of money is material, IFRS requires the liability to be stated at present value. U.S. GAAP allows using present values under some circumstances, but liabilities for loss contingencies like litigation typically are not discounted for time value of money.[27]

- IFRS recognizes provisions and contingencies for "onerous" contracts, defined as those in which the unavoidable costs of meeting the obligations exceed the expected benefits.[28] Under U.S. GAAP we generally don't disclose or recognize losses on such money-losing contracts, although there are some exceptions (for example, losses on long-term construction contracts are accrued, as are losses on contracts that have been terminated).

Here's a portion of a note from the 2016 financial statements of Vodafone, which reports under IFRS:

Note 17: Provisions (in part)

Provisions are recognised when the Group has a present obligation (legal or constructive) as a result of a past event, it is probable that the Group will be required to settle that obligation and a reliable estimate can be made of the amount of the obligation. Provisions are measured at the Directors' best estimate of the expenditure required to settle the obligation at the reporting date and are discounted to present value where the effect is material.

Where We're Headed

The controversy over accounting for contingencies and the mixture of approaches is likely to continue. The FASB recently removed from its agenda a project to reconsider the recognition and measurement of contingent losses, and has postponed further work on a project intended to enhance note disclosures of contingent losses. The IASB has a project ongoing, but progress on this project has been slow as the IASB has focused on more pressing projects.

Gain Contingencies

Gain contingencies are not accrued.

● LO13–7

A gain contingency is an uncertain situation that might result in a gain. For example, in a pending lawsuit, one side—the defendant—faces a loss contingency; the other side—the plaintiff—has a gain contingency. As we discussed earlier, loss contingencies are accrued when it's probable that an amount will be paid and the amount can reasonably be estimated. However, gain contingencies are not accrued. The nonparallel treatment of gain contingencies is an example of conservatism, following the reasoning that it's desirable to anticipate losses, but recognizing gains should await their realization.

Though gain contingencies are not recorded in the accounts, material ones are disclosed in notes to the financial statements. Care should be taken that the disclosure note not give "misleading implications as to the likelihood of realization."[29]

International Financial Reporting Standards

Gain Contingencies. Under U.S. GAAP, gain contingencies are never accrued. Under IFRS, gain contingencies are accrued if their future realization is "virtually certain" to occur. Both U.S. GAAP and IFRS *disclose* contingent gains when future realization is probable, but under IFRS "probable" is defined as "more likely than not" (greater than 50%), and so has a lower threshold than it does under U.S. GAAP.

---

[27]See, for example, FASB ASC 410–30–35–12: Asset Retirements and Environmental Obligations—Environmental Obligations—Subsequent Measurement.

[28]Paragraph 10 of "Provisions, Contingent Liabilities and Contingent Assets," *International Accounting Standard 37* (London, UK: IASB, 2008).

[29]Source: FASB ASC 450-30-50: Contingencies-Gain Contingencies-Disclosure.

Additional Consideration

Accounting for contingencies is controversial. Many accountants dislike the idea of only recognizing a liability for a contingent loss when it is probable, and then reporting the liability at the best estimate of the future expenditure. The obvious alternative is fair value, which does not incorporate probability into determining whether to *recognize* a loss but rather considers probability when *measuring* the amount of loss. Recent changes in GAAP have adopted fair value approaches for some types of events that are contingent losses (or appear to be close relatives). Consider the following examples:

- Illustration 13–18 uses a discounted expected cash flow approach to measure the contingent liability associated with a warranty. That approach approximates fair value.
- Recall from Chapter 10 that asset retirement obligations are recorded at fair value when an asset is acquired. The offsetting liability is similar to a contingent liability because it is an uncertain future amount arising from the past purchase of the asset but is recorded at fair value.
- Sometimes a company provides a guarantee that may require it to make payment to another party based on some future event. For example, a company might guarantee the debt of an affiliated company to make it easier for the affiliate to obtain financing. GAAP views this sort of guarantee as having two parts: (1) a certain "stand ready obligation" to meet the terms of the guarantee, and (2) the uncertain contingent obligation to make future payments depending on future events (for example, the affiliate defaulting on their debt). The "stand ready obligation" is recorded initially at fair value, while the contingent obligation is handled as an ordinary contingent loss.[30]

Concept Review Exercise

Hanover Industries manufactures and sells food products and food processing machinery. While preparing the December 31, 2021, financial statements for Hanover, the following information was discovered relating to contingencies and possible adjustments to liabilities. Hanover's 2021 financial statements were issued on April 1, 2022.

CONTINGENCIES

a. On November 12, 2021, a former employee filed a lawsuit against Hanover alleging age discrimination and asking for damages of $750,000. At December 31, 2021, Hanover's attorney indicated that the likelihood of losing the lawsuit was possible but not probable. On March 5, 2022, Hanover agreed to pay the former employee $125,000 in return for withdrawing the lawsuit.

b. Hanover believes there is a possibility a service provider may claim that it has been undercharged for outsourcing a processing service based on verbal indications of the company's interpretation of a negotiated rate. The service provider has not yet made a claim for additional fees as of April 2022, but Hanover thinks it will. Hanover's accountants and legal counsel believe the charges were appropriate but that if an assessment is made, there is a reasonable possibility that subsequent court action would result in an additional tax liability of $55,000.

c. Hanover grants a two-year warranty for each processing machine sold. Past experience indicates that the costs of satisfying warranties are approximately 2% of sales. During 2021, sales of processing machines totaled $21,300,000. 2021 expenditures for warranty repair costs were $178,000 related to 2021 sales and $220,000 related to 2020 sales. The January 1, 2021, balance of the warranty liability account was $250,000.

d. Hanover is the plaintiff in a $600,000 lawsuit filed in 2020 against Ansdale Farms for failing to deliver on contracts for produce. The suit is in final appeal. Legal counsel advises that it is probable that Hanover will prevail and will be awarded $300,000 (considered a material amount).

---

[30]Source: FASB ASC 460-10-25: Guarantees-Overall-Recobnition.

744   SECTION 3   Liabilities and Shareholders' Equity

Required:
1. Determine the appropriate reporting for each situation. Briefly explain your reasoning.
2. Prepare any necessary journal entries and state whether a disclosure note is needed.

Solution:

a. This is a loss contingency. Hanover can use the information occurring after the end of the year in determining appropriate disclosure. The cause for the suit existed at the end of the year. Hanover should accrue the $125,000 loss because an agreement has been reached confirming the loss and the amount is known.

Loss—litigation	125,000	
Liability—litigation		125,000

A disclosure note also is appropriate.

b. At the time financial statements are issued, a claim is as yet unasserted. However, an assessment is probable. Thus, (a) the likelihood of an unfavorable outcome and (b) whether the dollar amount can be estimated are considered. No accrual is necessary because an unfavorable outcome is not probable. But because an unfavorable outcome is reasonably possible, a disclosure note is appropriate.

    Note: If the likelihood of a claim being asserted is not probable, disclosure is not required even if an unfavorable outcome is thought to be probable in the event of an assessment and the amount is estimable.

c. The contingency for warranties should be accrued because it is probable that expenditures will be made and the amount can be estimated from past experience. When customer claims are made and costs are incurred to satisfy those claims the liability is reduced.

Warranty expense (2% × $21,300,000)...	426,000	
Warranty liability...		426,000
Warranty liability ($178,000 + $220,000)..	398,000	
Cash (or salaries payable, parts and supplies, etc.).......................		398,000

The liability at December 31, 2021, would be reported as $278,000:

Warranty Liability
($ in thousands)

		250	Balance, Jan. 1
		426	2021 expense
2021 expenditures	398		
		278	Balance, Dec. 31

A disclosure note explaining the contingency also is appropriate.

d. This is a gain contingency. Gain contingencies cannot be accrued even if the gain is probable and reasonably estimable. The gain should be recognized only when realized. It can be disclosed, but care should be taken to avoid misleading language regarding the realizability of the gain.

Decision Makers' Perspective

Current liabilities impact a company's liquidity. Liquidity refers to a company's cash position and overall ability to obtain cash in the normal course of business. A company is said to be liquid if it has sufficient cash (or other assets convertible to cash in a relatively short time) to pay currently maturing debts. Because the lack of liquidity can cause the demise of an otherwise healthy company, it is critical that managers as well as outside investors and creditors maintain close scrutiny of this aspect of a company's well-being.

    Keeping track of the current ratio is one of the most common ways of doing this. The current ratio is intended as a measure of short-term solvency and is determined by dividing current assets by current liabilities.

A risk analyst should be concerned with a company's ability to meet its short-term obligations.

When we compare liabilities that must be satisfied in the near term with assets that either are cash or will be converted to cash in the near term, we get a useful measure of a company's liquidity. A ratio of 1 to 1 or higher often is considered a rule-of-thumb standard, but like other ratios, acceptability should be evaluated in the context of the industry in which the company operates and other specific circumstances. Keep in mind, though, that industry averages are only one indication of adequacy and that the current ratio is but one indication of liquidity.

We can adjust for the implicit assumption of the current ratio that all current assets are equally liquid. The acid-test, or quick, ratio is similar to the current ratio but is based on a more conservative measure of assets available to pay current liabilities. Specifically, the numerator, quick assets, includes only cash and cash equivalents, short-term investments, and accounts receivable. By eliminating current assets such as inventories and prepaid expenses that are less readily convertible into cash, the acid-test ratio provides a more rigorous indication of a company's short-term solvency than does the current ratio.

If either of these liquidity ratios is less than that of the industry as a whole, does that mean that liquidity is a problem? Not necessarily. It does, though, raise a red flag that suggests caution when assessing other areas. It's important to remember that each ratio is but one piece of the puzzle. For example, profitability is probably the best long-run indication of liquidity. Also, management may be very efficient in managing current assets so that some current assets—receivables or inventory—are converted to cash more quickly than they otherwise would be and are more readily available to satisfy liabilities. The turnover ratios discussed in earlier chapters help measure the efficiency of asset management in this regard.

In fact, some companies view their accounts payable as a free loan from their suppliers, just as they view their accounts receivable as a free loan to their customers. These companies tend to pressure their customers to pay quickly, but try to obtain more extended terms with their suppliers. Although this would produce relatively low current assets and high current liabilities, and therefore a lower current ratio, it could be a very intelligent way to manage cash and decrease the overall amount of capital needed by the company to finance operations.

Given the actual and perceived importance of a company's liquidity in the minds of analysts, it's not difficult to adopt a management perspective and imagine efforts to manipulate the ratios that measure liquidity. For instance, a company might use its economic muscle or persuasive powers to influence the timing of accounts payable recognition by asking suppliers to change their delivery schedules. Because accounts payable is included in the denominator in most measures of liquidity, such as the current ratio, the timing of their recognition could mean the difference between an unacceptable ratio and an acceptable one, or between violating a debt covenant and compliance with the terms of the debt agreement. For example, suppose a company with a current ratio of 1.25 (current assets of $5 million and current liabilities of $4 million) is in violation of a debt covenant requiring a minimum current ratio of 1.3. By delaying the delivery of $1 million of inventory, the ratio would be 1.33 (current assets of $4 million and current liability of $3 million).

It's important for creditors and analysts to be attentive for evidence of activities that would indicate timing strategies, such as unusual variations in accounts payable levels. You might notice that such timing strategies are similar to earnings management techniques we discussed previously—specifically, manipulating the timing of revenue and expense recognition in order to "smooth" income over time.

Finally, all financial statement users need to keep in mind the relation between the recognition of deferred revenue associated with advance payments and the later recognition of revenue. On the one hand, increases in deferred revenue can signal future revenue recognition because the deferred revenue likely will eventually be recognized as revenue. On the other hand, research suggests that some firms that report deferred revenue may manipulate the timing of revenue recognition to manage their earnings.[31]

In the next chapter, we continue our discussion of liabilities. Our focus will shift from current liabilities to long-term liabilities in the form of bonds and long-term notes. ●

FINANCIAL Reporting Case

Q5, p. 718

A manager should actively monitor a company's liquidity.

A liquidity ratio is but one indication of a company's liquidity.

Some companies maintain relatively high current liabilities as part of a cash-management strategy.

Analysts should be alert for efforts to manipulate measures of liquidity.

Changes in deferred revenue provide information about future revenue, and may be used to manipulate it.

---

[31]Marcus Caylor, "Strategic Revenue Recognition to Achieve Earnings Benchmarks," *Journal of Accounting and Public Policy,* January–February 2010, pp. 82–95.

746   SECTION 3   Liabilities and Shareholders' Equity

Financial Reporting Case Solution

©Cultura/Image Source

1. **What are accrued liabilities? What is commercial paper?** *(p. 723)*   Accrued liabilities are reported for expenses already incurred but not yet paid (accrued expenses). These include salaries and wages payable, income taxes payable, and interest payable. Commercial paper is a form of notes payable sometimes used by large corporations to obtain temporary financing. It is sold to other companies as a short-term investment. It represents unsecured notes sold in minimum denominations of $25,000 with maturities ranging from 1 to 270 days. Typically, commercial paper is issued directly to the buyer (lender) and is backed by a line of credit with a bank.

2. **Why did Syntel Microsystems include some long-term debt in the current liability section?** *(p. 729)*   Syntel Microsystems did include some long-term debt in the current liability section. The currently maturing portion of a long-term debt must be reported as a current liability. Amounts are reclassified and reported as current liabilities when they become payable within the upcoming year.

3. **Did they also report some current amounts as long-term debt? Explain.** *(p. 730)*   Yes they did. It is permissible to report short-term obligations as noncurrent liabilities if the company (a) intends to refinance on a long-term basis and (b) demonstrates the ability to do so by a refinancing agreement or by actual financing. As the disclosure note explains, this is the case for a portion of Syntel's currently payable debt.

4. **Must obligations be known contractual debts in order to be reported as liabilities?** *(p. 733)*   No. From an accounting perspective, it is not necessary that obligations be known, legally enforceable debts to be reported as liabilities. They must only be probable and the dollar amount reasonably estimable.

5. **Is it true that current liabilities are riskier than long-term liabilities?** *(p. 745)*   Other things being equal, current liabilities generally are considered riskier than long-term liabilities. For that reason, management usually would rather report a debt as long term. Current debt, though, is not necessarily risky. The liquidity ratios we discussed in the chapter attempt to measure liquidity. Remember, any such measure must be assessed in the context of other factors: industry standards, profitability, turnover ratios, and risk management activities, to name a few. ●

The Bottom Line

● **LO13–1** Liabilities are present obligations to sacrifice assets in the future because of something that already has occurred. Current liabilities are expected to require current assets (or the creation of other current liabilities) and usually are payable within one year. *(p. 718)*

● **LO13–2** Short-term bank loans usually are arranged under an ongoing line of credit with a bank or group of banks. When interest is discounted from the face amount of a note (a type of noninterest-bearing note), the effective interest rate is higher than the stated discount rate. Large, highly rated firms sometimes sell commercial paper directly to the buyer (lender) to borrow funds at a lower rate than through a bank loan. *(p. 720)*

● **LO13–3** Accrued liabilities are recorded by adjusting entries for expenses already incurred, but for which cash has yet to be paid (accrued expenses). Familiar examples are advance collections, salaries payable, income taxes payable, and interest payable *(p. 723)*

● **LO13–4** Short-term obligations can be reported as noncurrent liabilities if the company (a) intends to refinance on a long-term basis and (b) demonstrates the ability to do so by actual financing or a formal agreement to do so. *(p. 729)*

● **LO13–5** A loss contingency is an existing, uncertain situation involving potential loss depending on whether some future event occurs. Whether a contingency is accrued and reported as a liability depends on (a) the likelihood that the confirming event will occur and (b) what can be determined about the amount of loss. It is accrued if it is both probable that the confirming event will occur and the amount can be at least reasonably estimated. *(p. 732)*

● **LO13–6** A clarifying event before financial statements are issued, but after the year-end, can be used to determine how a contingency is reported. An unasserted suit, claim, or assessment warrants accrual or disclosure if it is probable it will be asserted. A gain contingency is a contingency that might result in a gain. A gain contingency is not recognized until it actually is realized. (*p. 733*)

● LO13–7   IFRS and U.S. GAAP are relatively similar with respect to current liabilities and contingencies. Relatively minor differences relate to when financing must be in place for a liability expected to be refinanced to be classified as long term. Also, with respect to contingent losses, IFRS defines "probable" at a lower threshold, requires the accrual of the expected value of loss, and requires the use of present values when measuring amounts to be accrued. Contingent gains are not accrued under U.S. GAAP, but are accrued under IFRS when they are considered to be virtually certain to occur. (*p. 731, 741, and 742*) ●

Payroll-Related Liabilities

APPENDIX 13

All firms incur liabilities in connection with their payrolls. These arise primarily from legal requirements to withhold taxes from employees' paychecks and from payroll taxes on the firms themselves. Some payroll-related liabilities result from voluntary payroll deductions of amounts payable to third parties.

EMPLOYEES' WITHHOLDING TAXES   Employers are required by law to withhold federal (and sometimes state) income taxes and Social Security taxes from employees' paychecks and remit these to the Internal Revenue Service. The amount withheld for federal income taxes is determined by a tax table furnished by the IRS and varies according to the amount earned and the number of exemptions claimed by the employee. Also, the Federal Insurance Contributions Act (FICA) requires employers to withhold a percentage of each employee's earnings up to a specified maximum. Both the percentage and the maximum are changed intermittently. As this text went to print, the deduction for Social Security was 6.2% of the first $128,400 an employee earns, and this ceiling amount changes each year for cost-of-living adjustments. Additionally, a deduction for Medicare tax is 1.45% with no limit on the base amount. The employer also must pay an equal (matching) amount on behalf of the employee. Individuals also must pay additional Medicare tax of 0.9% on wages in excess of $200,000 (there is no employer match against that additional Medicare tax). Self-employed persons must pay both the employer and employee portions (12.4% for Social Security and 2.9% for Medicare).

VOLUNTARY DEDUCTIONS   Besides the required deductions for income taxes and Social Security taxes, employees often authorize their employers to deduct other amounts from their paychecks. These deductions might include union dues, contributions to savings or retirement plans, and insurance premiums. Amounts deducted this way represent liabilities until paid to the appropriate organizations.

EMPLOYERS' PAYROLL TAXES   One payroll tax mentioned previously is the employer's matching amount of FICA taxes. The employer also must pay federal and state unemployment taxes on behalf of its employees. The Federal Unemployment Tax Act (FUTA) requires a tax of 6.0% of the first $7,000 earned by each employee. This amount is reduced by a 5.4% (maximum) credit for contributions to state unemployment programs, so the net federal rate often is 0.6%.[32] The most common state rate is 5.4%, but rates vary between states and also vary within states for different types of employers.

FRINGE BENEFITS   In addition to salaries, withholding taxes, and payroll taxes, many companies provide employees a variety of fringe benefits. Most commonly, employers pay all or part of employees' insurance premiums and/or contributions to retirement income plans.

Representative payroll-related liabilities are presented in Illustration 13A–1. As you study the illustration, you should note the similarity among all payroll-related liabilities. Amounts withheld from paychecks—voluntarily or involuntarily—are liabilities until turned over to appropriate third parties. Payroll taxes and expenses for fringe benefits are incurred as a result of services performed by employees and also are liabilities until paid to appropriate third parties.

---

[32]All states presently have unemployment tax programs.

Illustration 13A–1

Payroll-Related Liabilities

Crescent Lighting and Fixtures' payroll for the second week in January was $100,000. The following deductions, fringe benefits, and taxes apply:

Federal income taxes to be withheld	$20,000
State income taxes to be withheld	3,000
Medical insurance premiums (Blue Cross)—70% paid by employer	1,000
Employee contribution to voluntary retirement plan (Fidelity Investments)—contributions matched by employer	4,000
Union dues (Local No. 222)—paid by employees	100
Life insurance premiums (Prudential Life)—100% paid by employer	200
Social Security tax rate	6.2%
Medicare tax rate	1.45%
Federal unemployment tax rate (after state deduction)	0.60%
State unemployment tax rate	5.40%

Crescent's journal entries to record payroll:

Amounts withheld from paychecks represent liabilities until remitted to third parties.

Salaries expense (total amount earned)	100,000	
Withholding taxes payable (federal income tax)		20,000
Withholding taxes payable (state income tax)		3,000
Social Security taxes payable (employees' portion, 6.2%)		6,200 ◄
Medicare taxes payable (employees' portion, 1.45%)		**1,450** ◄
Payable to Blue Cross (employee's portion of insurance premiums—30%)		300
Payable to Fidelity Investments (employees' investment)		**4,000** ◄
Payable to Local No. 222 (union dues)		100
Salaries payable (net pay)		64,950
Payroll tax expense (total)	13,650	
Social Security taxes payable (employer's matching amount)		6,200 ◄
Medicare taxes payable (employer's matching amount)		**1,450** ◄
FUTA payable (federal unemployment tax: 0.6%)		600
State unemployment tax payable (5.4%)		5,400
Salaries expense (fringe benefits)	4,900	
Payable to Blue Cross (insurance premiums—70%)		700 ◄
Payable to Fidelity Investments (employer's matching amount)		**4,000** ◄
Payable to Prudential life (insurance premiums)		200 ●

The employer's share of FICA and unemployment taxes constitute the employer's payroll tax expense.

Fringe benefits are part of salaries and wages expense and represent liabilities until remitted to third parties.

Questions For Review of Key Topics

Q 13–1   What are the essential characteristics of liabilities for purposes of financial reporting?

Q 13–2   What distinguishes current liabilities from long-term liabilities?

Q 13–3   Bronson Distributors owes a supplier $100,000 on open account. The amount is payable in three months. What is the theoretically correct way to measure the reportable amount for this liability? In practice, how will it likely be reported? Why?

Q 13–4   Bank loans often are arranged under existing lines of credit. What is a line of credit? How does a noncommitted line of credit differ from a committed line?

Q 13–5   Banks sometimes loan cash under noninterest-bearing notes. Is it true that banks lend money without interest?

Q 13–6   How does commercial paper differ from a bank loan? Why is the interest rate often less for commercial paper?

Q 13–7   Salaries of $5,000 have been earned by employees by the end of the period but will not be paid to employees until the following period. How should the expense and related liability be recorded? Why?

Q 13–8   Under what conditions should an employer accrue an expense and the related liability for employees' compensation for future absences? How do company custom and practice affect the accrual decision?

Q 13–9   How are refundable deposits and customer advances similar? How do they differ?

Q 13–10   How do companies account for gift cards?

Q 13–11   Amounts collected for third parties represent liabilities until remitted. Provide several examples of this kind of collection.

Q 13–12   When companies have debt that is not due to be paid for several years but that is callable (due on demand) by the creditor, do they classify the debt as current or as long-term?

Q 13–13   Long-term obligations usually are reclassified and reported as current liabilities when they become payable within the upcoming year (or operating cycle, if longer than a year). So, a 25-year bond issue is reported as a long-term liability for 24 years but normally is reported as a current liability on the balance sheet prepared during the 25th year of its term to maturity. Name a situation in which this would not be the case.

IFRS Q 13–14   How do IFRS and U.S. GAAP differ with respect to the classification of debt that is expected to be refinanced?

Q 13–15   Define a loss contingency. Provide three examples.

Q 13–16   List and briefly describe the three categories of likelihood that a future event(s) will confirm the incurrence of the liability for a loss contingency.

Q 13–17   Under what circumstances should a loss contingency be accrued?

IFRS Q 13–18   What is the difference between the use of the term *contingent liability* in U.S. GAAP and IFRS?

Q 13–19   Suppose the analysis of a loss contingency indicates that an obligation is not probable. What accounting treatment, if any, is warranted?

Q 13–20   Name two loss contingencies that almost always are accrued.

Q 13–21   Distinguish between the accounting treatment of a manufacturer's warranty and an extended warranty. Why the difference?

Q 13–22   At December 31, the end of the reporting period, the analysis of a loss contingency indicates that an obligation is only reasonably possible, though its dollar amount is readily estimable. During February, before the financial statements are issued, new information indicates the loss is probable. What accounting treatment is warranted?

Q 13–23   After the end of the reporting period, a contingency comes into existence. Under what circumstances, if any, should the contingency be reported in the financial statements for the period ended?

IFRS Q 13–24   How do U.S. GAAP and IFRS differ in their treatment of a range of equally likely losses?

IFRS Q 13–25   How do U.S. GAAP and IFRS differ in their use of present values when measuring contingent liabilities?

Q 13–26   Suppose the Environmental Protection Agency is in the process of investigating Ozone Ruination Limited for possible environmental damage but has not proposed a penalty as of December 31, 2020, the company's fiscal year-end. Describe the two-step process involved in deciding how this unasserted assessment should be reported.

Q 13–27   You are the plaintiff in a lawsuit. Your legal counsel advises that your eventual victory is inevitable. "You will be awarded $12 million," your attorney confidently asserts. Describe the appropriate accounting treatment.

IFRS Q 13–28   Answer Q 13–27, but assume that you report under IFRS.

Brief Exercises

BE 13–1
Bank loan;
accrued interest
● LO13–2

On October 1, Eder Fabrication borrowed $60 million and issued a nine-month, 12% promissory note. Interest was payable at maturity. Prepare the journal entry for the issuance of the note and the appropriate adjusting entry for the note at December 31, the end of the reporting period.

BE 13–2
Noninterest-
bearing note;
accrued interest
● LO13–2

On October 1, Eder Fabrication borrowed $60 million and issued a nine-month promissory note. Interest was discounted at issuance at a 12% discount rate. Prepare the journal entry for the issuance of the note and the appropriate adjusting entry for the note at December 31, the end of the reporting period.

BE 13–3
Determining
accrued interest
● LO13–2

On July 1, Orcas Lab issued a $100,000, 12%, eight-month note. Interest is payable at maturity. What is the amount of interest expense that should be recorded in a year-end adjusting entry if the fiscal year-end is (a) December 31? (b) September 30?

BE 13–4
Commercial paper
● LO13–2

Branch Corporation issued $12 million of commercial paper on March 1 on a nine-month note. Interest was discounted at issuance at a 9% discount rate. Prepare the journal entry for the issuance of the commercial paper and its repayment at maturity.

BE 13–5
Noninterest-bearing note; effective interest rate
● LO13–2

Life.com issued $10 million of commercial paper on April 1 on a nine-month note. Interest was discounted at issuance at a 6% discount rate. What is the effective interest rate on the commercial paper?

BE 13–6
Advance collection
● LO13–3

On December 12, 2021, Pace Electronics received $24,000 from a customer toward a cash sale of $240,000 of diodes to be completed on January 16, 2022. What journal entries should Pace record on December 12 and January 16?

BE 13–7
Advance collection
● LO13–3

In Lizzie Shoes' experience, gift cards that have not been redeemed within 12 months are not likely to be redeemed. Lizzie Shoes sold gift cards for $18,000 during August 2021. $4,000 of cards were redeemed in September 2021, $3,000 in October, $2,500 in November, and $2,000 in December 2021. In 2022 an additional $1,000 of cards were redeemed in January and $500 in February. How much gift card revenue associated with the August 2021 gift card sales would Lizzie get to recognize in 2021 and 2022?

BE 13–8
Sales tax
● LO13–3

During December, Rainey Equipment made a $600,000 credit sale. The state sales tax rate is 6% and the local sales tax rate is 1.5%. Prepare the appropriate journal entry.

BE 13–9
Classifying debt
● LO13–4

Consider the following liabilities of Future Brands, Inc., at December 31, 2021, the company's fiscal year-end. Should they be reported as current liabilities or long-term liabilities?
1. $77 million of 8% notes are due on May 31, 2025. The notes are callable by the company's bank, beginning March 1, 2022.
2. $102 million of 8% notes are due on May 31, 2026. A debt covenant requires Future to maintain a current ratio (ratio of current assets to current liabilities) of at least 2 to 1. Future is in violation of this requirement but has obtained a waiver from the bank until May 2022, since both companies feel Future will correct the situation during the first half of 2022.

BE 13–10
Refinancing debt
● LO13–4

Coulson Company is in the process of refinancing some long-term debt. Its fiscal year ends on December 31, 2021, and its financial statements will be issued on March 15, 2022. Under current U.S. GAAP, how would the debt be classified if the refinancing is completed on December 15, 2021? What if instead it is completed on January 15, 2022?

BE 13–11
Refinancing debt
● LO13–4, LO13–7
IFRS

Fleener Company is in the process of refinancing some long-term debt. Its fiscal year ends on December 31, 2021, and its financial statements will be issued on March 15, 2022. Under current IFRS, how would the debt be classified if the refinancing is completed on December 15, 2021? What if instead it is completed on January 15, 2022?

BE 13–12
Warranties
● LO13–5, LO13–6

Right Medical introduced a new implant that carries a five-year warranty against manufacturer's defects. Based on industry experience with similar product introductions, warranty costs are expected to approximate 1% of sales. Sales were $15 million and actual warranty expenditures were $20,000 for the first year of selling the product. What amount (if any) should Right report as a liability at the end of the year?

BE 13–13
Product recall
● LO13–5, LO13–6

Consultants notified management of Goo Goo Baby Products that a crib toy poses a potential health hazard. Counsel indicated that a product recall is probable and is estimated to cost the company $5.5 million. How will this affect the company's income statement and balance sheet this period?

BE 13–14
Contingency
● LO13–5, LO13–6

Skill Hardware is the plaintiff in a $16 million lawsuit filed against a supplier. The litigation is in final appeal and legal counsel advises that it is virtually certain that Skill will win the lawsuit and be awarded $12 million. How should Skill account for this event?

BE 13–15
Contingency
● LO13–5, LO13–6

Bell International estimates that a $10 million loss will occur if a foreign government expropriates some company property. Expropriation is considered reasonably possible. How should Bell report the loss contingency?

BE 13–16
Contingencies
● **LO13–5, LO13–6**

Household Solutions manufactures kitchen storage products. During the year, the company became aware of potential costs due to (1) a recently filed lawsuit for patent infringement for which the probability of loss is remote and damages can be reasonably estimated, (2) another recently filed lawsuit for food contamination by the plastics used in Household Solutions' products for which a loss is probable but the amount of loss cannot be reasonably estimated, and (3) a new product warranty that is probable and can be reasonably estimated. Which, if any, of these costs should be accrued?

BE 13–17
Contingencies
● **LO13–5,**
   LO13–6, LO13–7
 IFRS

Quandary Corporation has a major customer who is alleging a significant product defect. Quandary engineers and attorneys have analyzed the claim and have concluded that there is a 51% chance that the customer would be successful in court and that a successful claim would result in a range of damages from $10 million to $20 million, with each part of the range equally likely to occur. The damages would need to be paid soon enough that time-value-of-money considerations are not material. Would a liability be accrued under U.S. GAAP? Under IFRS? If a liability were accrued, what amount would be accrued under U.S. GAAP? Under IFRS?

BE 13–18
Unasserted
assessment
● **LO13–5, LO13–6**

At March 13, 2022, the Securities Exchange Commission is in the process of investigating a possible securities law violation by Now Chemical. The SEC has not yet proposed a penalty assessment. Now's fiscal year ends on December 31, 2021, and its financial statements are published in March 2022. Management feels an assessment is *reasonably possible,* and if an assessment is made, an unfavorable settlement of $13 million is *probable.* What, if any, action should Now take for its financial statements?

Exercises

E 13–1
Bank loan;
accrued interest
● **LO13–2**

On November 1, 2021, Quantum Technology, a geothermal energy supplier, borrowed $16 million cash to fund a geological survey. The loan was made by Nevada BancCorp under a noncommitted short-term line of credit arrangement. Quantum issued a nine-month, 12% promissory note. Interest was payable at maturity. Quantum's fiscal period is the calendar year.

Required:
1. Prepare the journal entry for the issuance of the note by Quantum Technology.
2. Prepare the appropriate adjusting entry for the note by Quantum on December 31, 2021.
3. Prepare the journal entry for the payment of the note at maturity.

E 13–2
Determining
accrued interest
in various
situations
● **LO13–2**

On July 1, 2021, Ross-Livermore Industries issued nine-month notes in the amount of $400 million. Interest is payable at maturity.

Required:
Determine the amount of interest expense that should be recorded in a year-end adjusting entry under each of the following independent assumptions:

	Interest Rate	Fiscal Year-End
1.	12%	December 31
2.	10%	September 30
3.	9%	October 31
4.	6%	January 31

E 13–3
Short-term notes
● **LO13–2**

The following selected transactions relate to liabilities of United Insulation Corporation. United's fiscal year ends on December 31.

Required:
Prepare the appropriate journal entries through the maturity of each liability.

2021

Jan. 13	Negotiated a revolving credit agreement with Parish Bank that can be renewed annually upon bank approval. The amount available under the line of credit is $20 million at the bank's prime rate.
Feb. 1	Arranged a three-month bank loan of $5 million with Parish Bank under the line of credit agreement. Interest at the prime rate of 10% was payable at maturity.
May 1	Paid the 10% note at maturity.
Dec. 1	Supported by the credit line, issued $10 million of commercial paper on a nine-month note. Interest was discounted at issuance at a 9% discount rate.
31	Recorded any necessary adjusting entry(s).

2022

Sept. 1	Paid the commercial paper at maturity.

752   SECTION 3   Liabilities and Shareholders' Equity

E 13–4
Paid future
absences
● **LO13–3**

JWS Transport Company's employees earn vacation time at the rate of 1 hour per 40-hour work period. The vacation pay vests immediately (that is, an employee is entitled to the pay even if employment terminates). During 2021, total salaries paid to employees equaled $404,000, including $4,000 for vacations actually taken in 2021 but not including vacations related to 2021 that will be taken in 2022. All vacations earned before 2021 were taken before January 1, 2021. No accrual entries have been made for the vacations. No overtime premium and no bonuses were paid during the period.

Required:
Prepare the appropriate adjusting entry for vacations earned but not taken in 2021.

E 13–5
Paid future
absences
● **LO13–3**

On January 1, 2021, Poplar Fabricators Corporation agreed to grant its employees two weeks of vacation each year, with the stipulation that vacations earned each year can be taken the following year. For the year ended December 31, 2021, Poplar Fabricators' employees each earned an average of $900 per week. Seven hundred vacation weeks earned in 2021 were not taken during 2021.

Required:
1. Prepare the appropriate adjusting entry for vacations earned but not taken in 2021.
2. Suppose that, by the time vacations actually are taken in 2022, salary rates for employees have risen by an average of 5 percent from their 2021 level. Also, assume salaries earned in 2022 (including vacations earned and taken in 2022) were $31 million. Prepare a journal entry that summarizes 2022 salaries and the payment for 2021 vacations taken in 2022.

E 13–6
Gift cards; sales
taxes
● **LO13–3**

Bavarian Bar and Grill opened for business in November 2021. During its first two months of operation, the restaurant sold gift cards in various amounts totaling $5,200, mostly as Christmas presents. They are redeemable for meals within two years of the purchase date, although experience within the industry indicates that 80% of gift cards are redeemed within one year. Gift cards totaling $1,300 were presented for redemption during 2021 for meals having a total price of $2,100. The sales tax rate on restaurant sales is 4%, assessed at the time meals (not gift cards) are purchased. Sales taxes will be remitted in January.

Required:
1. Prepare the appropriate journal entries (in summary form) for the gift cards and meals sold during 2021 (keeping in mind that, in actuality, each sale of a gift card or a meal would be recorded individually).
2. Determine the liability for gift cards to be reported on the December 31, 2021, balance sheet.
3. What is the appropriate classification (current or noncurrent) of the liabilities at December 31, 2021? Why?

E 13–7
Customer
deposits
● **LO13–3**

Diversified Semiconductors sells perishable electronic components. Some must be shipped and stored in reusable protective containers. Customers pay a deposit for each container received. The deposit is equal to the container's cost. They receive a refund when the container is returned. During 2021, deposits collected on containers shipped were $850,000.

Deposits are forfeited if containers are not returned within 18 months. Containers held by customers at January 1, 2021, represented deposits of $530,000. In 2021, $790,000 was refunded and deposits forfeited were $35,000.

Required:
1. Prepare the appropriate journal entries for the deposits received, returned, and forfeited during 2021.
2. Determine the liability for refundable deposits to be reported on the December 31, 2021, balance sheet.

E 13–8
Various
transactions
involving advance
collections
● **LO13–3**

The following selected transactions relate to liabilities of Interstate Farm Equipment Company for December 2021. Interstate's fiscal year ends on December 31.

Required:
Prepare the appropriate journal entries for these transactions.
1. On December 15, received $7,500 from Bradley Farms toward the sale by Interstate of a $98,000 tractor to be delivered to Bradley on January 6, 2022.
2. During December, received $25,500 of refundable deposits relating to containers used to transport equipment parts.
3. During December, credit sales totaled $800,000. The state sales tax rate is 5% and the local sales tax rate is 2%. (This is a summary journal entry for the many individual sales transactions for the period).

E 13–9
Gift cards
● **LO13–3**

CircuitTown commenced a gift card program in January 2021 and sold $10,000 of gift cards in January, $15,000 in February, and $16,000 in March 2021 before discontinuing further gift card sales. During 2021, gift card redemptions were $6,000 for the January gift cards sold, $4,500 for the February cards, and $4,000 for the March cards. CircuitTown considers gift cards to be "broken" (not redeemable) 10 months after sale.

Required:
1. How much revenue will CircuitTown recognize with respect to January gift card sales during 2021?
2. Prepare journal entries to record the sale of January gift cards, redemption of gift cards (ignore sales tax), and breakage (expiration) of gift cards.
3. How much revenue will CircuitTown recognize with respect to March gift card sales during 2021?
4. What liability for deferred revenue associated with gift card sales would CircuitTown show as of December 31, 2021?

E 13–10
FASB codification research
● LO13–3,
    LO13–4, LO13–5

Access the *FASB Accounting Standards Codification* at the FASB website (www.fasb.org).

Required:
Determine the specific eight- or nine-digit Codification citation (XXX-XX-XX-XX) that describes the following items:
1. If it is only reasonably possible that a contingent loss will occur, the contingent loss should be disclosed.
2. Criteria allowing short-term liabilities expected to be refinanced to be classified as long-term liabilities.
3. Accounting for the revenue from separately priced extended warranty contracts.
4. The criteria to determine if an employer must accrue a liability for vacation pay.

E 13–11
Current–noncurrent classification of debt; Sprint Corporation
● LO13–1, LO13–4

An annual report of **Sprint Corporation** contained a rather lengthy narrative entitled "Review of Segmental Results of Operation." The narrative noted that short-term notes payable and commercial paper outstanding at the end of the year aggregated $756 million and that during the following year, "This entire balance will be replaced by the issuance of long-term debt or will continue to be refinanced under existing long-term credit facilities."

Required:
How did Sprint report the debt in its balance sheet? Why?

E 13–12
Current–noncurrent classification of debt; Sprint Corporation
● LO13–1, LO13–4,
    LO13–7

 IFRS

Consider the information presented in E 13–11.

Required:
1. How would Sprint report the debt in its balance sheet if it reported under IFRS? Why?
2. Would your answer to requirement 1 change if Sprint obtained its long-term credit facility after the balance sheet date? Why?

E 13–13
Current–noncurrent classification of debt
● LO13–1, LO13–4

At December 31, 2021, Newman Engineering's liabilities include the following:
1. $10 million of 9% bonds were issued for $10 million on May 31, 1999. The bonds mature on May 31, 2029, but bondholders have the option of calling (demanding payment on) the bonds on May 31, 2022. However, the option to call is not expected to be exercised, given prevailing market conditions.
2. $14 million of 8% notes are due on May 31, 2022. A debt covenant requires Newman to maintain current assets at least equal to 175% of its current liabilities. On December 31, 2021, Newman is in violation of this covenant. Newman obtained a waiver from National City Bank until June 2022, having convinced the bank that the company's normal 2 to 1 ratio of current assets to current liabilities will be reestablished during the first half of 2022.
3. $7 million of 11% bonds were issued for $7 million on August 1, 1989. The bonds mature on July 31, 2022. Sufficient cash is expected to be available to retire the bonds at maturity.

Required:
What portion of each liability is reported as a current liability and as a noncurrent liability? Explain.

E 13–14
FASB codification research
● LO13–5

Access the *FASB Accounting Standards Codification* at the FASB website (www.fasb.org).

Required:
1. Obtain the relevant authoritative literature on recognition of contingent losses. What is the specific eight-digit Codification citation (XXX-XX-XX-X) that describes the guidelines for determining when an expense and liability should be accrued for a contingent loss?
2. List the guidelines.

E 13–15
Warranties
● LO13–5, LO13–6

Cupola Awning Corporation introduced a new line of commercial awnings in 2021 that carry a two-year warranty against manufacturer's defects. Based on their experience with previous product introductions, warranty costs are expected to approximate 3% of sales. Sales and actual warranty expenditures for the first year of selling the product were:

Sales	Actual Warranty Expenditures
$5,000,000	$37,500

Required:

1. Does this situation represent a loss contingency? Why or why not? How should Cupola account for it?
2. Prepare journal entries that summarize sales of the awnings (assume all credit sales) and any aspects of the warranty that should be recorded during 2021.
3. What amount should Cupola report as a liability at December 31, 2021?

E 13–16
Extended
warranties
● **LO13–5, LO13–6**

Carnes Electronics sells consumer electronics that carry a 90-day manufacturer's warranty. At the time of purchase, customers are offered the opportunity to also buy a two-year extended warranty for an additional charge. During the year, Carnes received $412,000 for these extended warranties (approximately evenly throughout the year).

Required:

1. Does this situation represent a loss contingency? Why or why not? How should it be accounted for?
2. Prepare journal entries that summarize sales of the extended warranties and any aspects of the warranty that should be recorded during the year.

E 13–17
Contingency;
product recall
● **LO13–5, LO13–6**

Sound Audio manufactures and sells audio equipment for automobiles. Engineers notified management in December 2021 of a circuit flaw in an amplifier that poses a potential fire hazard. An intense investigation indicated that a product recall is virtually certain, estimated to cost the company $2 million. The fiscal year ends on December 31.

Required:

1. Should this loss contingency be accrued, only disclosed, or neither? Explain.
2. What loss, if any, should Sound Audio report in its 2021 income statement?
3. What liability, if any, should Sound Audio report in its 2021 balance sheet?
4. Prepare any journal entry needed.

E 13–18
Impairment
of accounts
receivable
● **LO13–5, LO13–6**

The Manda Panda Company uses the allowance method to account for bad debts. At the beginning of 2021, the allowance account had a credit balance of $75,000. Credit sales for 2021 totaled $2,400,000 and the year-end accounts receivable balance was $490,000. During this year, $73,000 in receivables were determined to be uncollectible. Manda Panda anticipates that 3% of all credit sales will ultimately become uncollectible. The fiscal year ends on December 31.

Required:

1. Does this situation describe a loss contingency? Explain.
2. What is the bad debt expense that Manda Panda should report in its 2021 income statement?
3. Prepare the appropriate journal entry to record the contingency.
4. What is the net accounts receivable value Manda Panda should report in its 2021 balance sheet?

E 13–19
Unasserted
assessment
● **LO13–6**

At April 1, 2022, the Food and Drug Administration is in the process of investigating allegations of false marketing claims by Hulkly Muscle Supplements. The FDA has not yet proposed a penalty assessment. Hulkly's fiscal year ends on December 31, 2021. The company's financial statements are issued in April 2022.

Required:

For each of the following scenarios, determine the appropriate way to report the situation. Explain your reasoning and prepare any necessary journal entry.

1. Management feels an assessment is *reasonably possible,* and if an assessment is made, an unfavorable settlement of $13 million is *reasonably possible.*
2. Management feels an assessment is *reasonably possible,* and if an assessment is made, an unfavorable settlement of $13 million is *probable.*
3. Management feels an assessment is *probable,* and if an assessment is made, an unfavorable settlement of $13 million is *reasonably possible.*
4. Management feels an assessment is *probable,* and if an assessment is made, an unfavorable settlement of $13 million is *probable.*

E 13–20
Various
transactions
involving
contingencies
● **LO13–5, LO13–6**

The following selected transactions relate to contingencies of Classical Tool Makers, Inc., which began operations in July 2021. Classical's fiscal year ends on December 31. Financial statements are issued in April 2022.

Required:

Prepare the year-end entries for any amounts that should be recorded as a result of each of these contingencies and indicate whether a disclosure note is indicated.

1. Classical's products carry a one-year warranty against manufacturer's defects. Based on previous experience, warranty costs are expected to approximate 4% of sales. Sales were $2 million (all credit) for 2021. Actual warranty expenditures were $30,800 and were recorded as warranty expense when incurred.
2. Although no customer accounts have been shown to be uncollectible, Classical estimates that 2% of credit sales will eventually prove uncollectible.

3. In December 2021, the state of Tennessee filed suit against Classical, seeking penalties for violations of clean air laws. On January 23, 2022, Classical reached a settlement with state authorities to pay $1.5 million in penalties.

4. Classical is the plaintiff in a $4 million lawsuit filed against a supplier. The suit is in final appeal and attorneys advise that it is virtually certain that Classical will win the case and be awarded $2.5 million.

5. In November 2021, Classical became aware of a design flaw in an industrial saw that poses a potential electrical hazard. A product recall appears unavoidable. Such an action would likely cost the company $500,000.

6. Classical offered $25 cash rebates on a new model of jigsaw. Customers must mail in a proof-of-purchase seal from the package plus the cash register receipt to receive the rebate. Experience suggests that 60% of the rebates will be claimed. Ten thousand of the jigsaws were sold in 2021. Total rebates to customers in 2021 were $105,000 and were recorded as promotional expense when paid.

E 13–21
Various transactions involving contingencies
● LO13–5, LO13–6

The following selected circumstances relate to pending lawsuits for Erismus, Inc. Erismus's fiscal year ends on December 31. Financial statements are issued in March 2022. Erismus prepares its financial statements according to U.S. GAAP.

Required:
Indicate the amount of asset or liability that Erismus would record, and explain your answer.

1. Erismus is defending against a lawsuit. Erismus's management believes the company has a slightly worse than 50/50 chance of eventually prevailing in court, and that if it loses, the judgment will be $1,000,000.

2. Erismus is defending against a lawsuit. Erismus's management believes it is probable that the company will lose in court. If it loses, management believes that damages could fall anywhere in the range of $2,000,000 to $4,000,000, with any damage in that range equally likely.

3. Erismus is defending against a lawsuit. Erismus's management believes it is probable that the company will lose in court. If it loses, management believes that damages will eventually be $5,000,000, with a present value of $3,500,000.

4. Erismus is a plaintiff in a lawsuit. Erismus's management believes it is probable that the company eventually will prevail in court, and that if it prevails, the judgment will be $1,000,000.

5. Erismus is a plaintiff in a lawsuit. Erismus's management believes it is virtually certain that the company eventually will prevail in court, and that if it prevails, the judgment will be $500,000.

E 13–22
Various transactions involving contingencies; IFRS
● LO13–5, LO13–6, LO13–7
🌐 **IFRS**

[This exercise is a variation of E 13–21 focusing on reporting under IFRS]. Refer to the circumstances listed in E 13–21, but assume that Erismus prepares its financial statements according to International Financial Reporting Standards.

Required:
For each circumstance, indicate the amount of asset or liability that Erismus would record, and explain your answer.

E 13–23
Disclosures of liabilities
● LO13–1 though LO13–6

Indicate (by letter) the way each of the items listed below should be reported in a balance sheet at December 31, 2021.

Item	Reporting Method
____ 1. Commercial paper	N. Not reported
____ 2. Noncommitted line of credit	C. Current liability
____ 3. Customer advances	L. Long-term liability
____ 4. Estimated quality-assurance warranty cost	D. Disclosure note only
____ 5. Accounts payable	A. Asset
____ 6. Long-term bonds that will be callable by the creditor in the upcoming year unless an existing violation is not corrected (there is a reasonable possibility the violation will be corrected within the grace period)	
____ 7. Note due March 3, 2022	
____ 8. Interest accrued on note, December 31, 2021	
____ 9. Short-term bank loan to be paid with proceeds of sale of common stock	
____ 10. A determinable gain that is contingent on a future event that appears extremely likely to occur in three months	
____ 11. Unasserted assessment of taxes owed on prior-year income that probably will be asserted, in which case there would probably be a loss in six months	
____ 12. Unasserted assessment of taxes owed on prior-year income with a reasonable possibility of being asserted, in which case there would probably be a loss in 13 months	
____ 13. A determinable loss from a past event that is contingent on a future event that appears extremely likely to occur in three months	
____ 14. Note payable due April 4, 2024	
____ 15. Long-term bonds callable by the creditor in the upcoming year that are not expected to be called	

756 SECTION 3 Liabilities and Shareholders' Equity

E 13–24
Warranty
expense; change
in estimate
● LO13–5, LO13–6

Woodmier Lawn Products introduced a new line of commercial sprinklers in 2020 that carry a one-year warranty against manufacturer's defects. Because this was the first product for which the company offered a warranty, trade publications were consulted to determine the experience of others in the industry. Based on that experience, warranty costs were expected to approximate 2% of sales. Sales of the sprinklers in 2020 were $2.5 million. Accordingly, the following entries relating to the contingency for warranty costs were recorded during the first year of selling the product:

Accrued liability and expense

Warranty expense (2% × $2,500,000)	50,000	
Warranty liability		50,000

Actual expenditures (summary entry)

Warranty liability	23,000	
Cash		23,000

In late 2021, the company's claims experience was evaluated and it was determined that claims were far more than expected—3% of sales rather than 2%.

Required:

1. Assuming sales of the sprinklers in 2021 were $3.6 million and warranty expenditures in 2021 totaled $88,000, prepare any journal entries related to the warranty.

2. Assuming sales of the sprinklers were discontinued after 2020, prepare any journal entry(s) in 2021 related to the warranty.

E 13–25
Change in
accounting
estimate
● LO13–3

The Commonwealth of Virginia filed suit in October 2019 against Northern Timber Corporation, seeking civil penalties and injunctive relief for violations of environmental laws regulating forest conservation. When the 2020 financial statements were issued in 2021, Northern had not reached a settlement with state authorities, but legal counsel advised Northern Timber that it was probable the ultimate settlement would be $1,000,000 in penalties. The following entry was recorded:

Loss—litigation	1,000,000	
Liability—litigation		1,000,000

Late in 2021, a settlement was reached with state authorities to pay a total of $600,000 to cover the cost of violations.

Required:

1. Prepare any journal entries related to the change.

2. Briefly describe other steps Northern should take to report the change.

E 13–26
Contingency;
DowDuPont Inc.
disclosure
● LO13–5, LO13–6
Real World Financials

DowDuPont Inc. provides chemical, plastic, and agricultural products and services to various consumer markets. The following excerpt is taken from the disclosure notes of DowDuPont's 2017 annual report:

At December 31, 2017, the Company had accrued obligations of $1,311 million for probable environmental remediation and restoration costs, including $219 million for the remediation of Superfund sites. These obligations are included in "Accrued and other current liabilities" and "Other noncurrent obligations" in the consolidated balance sheets. This is management's best estimate of the costs for remediation and restoration with respect to environmental matters for which the Company has accrued liabilities, although it is reasonably possible that the ultimate cost with respect to these particular matters could range up to approximately two times that amount.

Required:

1. Does the excerpt describe a loss contingency?

2. Under what conditions would DowDuPont accrue such a contingency?

3. What journal entry would DowDuPont use to record this amount of provision (loss)?

E 13–27
Payroll-related
liabilities
● Appendix

Lee Financial Services pays employees monthly. Payroll information is listed below for January 2021, the first month of Lee's fiscal year. Assume that none of the employees exceeded any relevant base of pay, such that all benefit percentages apply to the entire $500,000 payroll.

Salaries	$500,000
Federal income taxes to be withheld	$100,000
Federal unemployment tax rate	0.60%
State unemployment tax rate (after SUTA deduction)	5.40%
Social Security tax rate	6.2%
Medicare tax rate	1.45%

Required:
Prepare the appropriate journal entries to record salaries expense and payroll tax expense for the January 2021 pay period.

Problems

P 13–1
Bank loan;
accrued interest
● LO13–2

Blanton Plastics, a household plastic product manufacturer, borrowed $14 million cash on October 1, 2021, to provide working capital for year-end production. Blanton issued a four-month, 12% promissory note to L&T Bank under a prearranged short-term line of credit. Interest on the note was payable at maturity. Each firm's fiscal period is the calendar year.

Required:
1. Prepare the journal entries to record (a) the issuance of the note by Blanton Plastics and (b) L&T Bank's receivable on October 1, 2021.
2. Prepare the journal entries by both firms to record all subsequent events related to the note through January 31, 2022.
3. Suppose the face amount of the note was adjusted to include interest (a noninterest-bearing note) and 12% is the bank's stated discount rate. (a) Prepare the journal entries to record the issuance of the noninterest-bearing note by Blanton Plastics on October 1, 2021, the adjusting entry at December 31, and payment of the note at maturity. (b) What would be the effective interest rate?

P 13–2
Various
transactions
involving liabilities
● LO13–2 through
LO13–4

Camden Biotechnology began operations in September 2021. The following selected transactions relate to liabilities of the company for September 2021 through March 2022. Camden's fiscal year ends on December 31. Its financial statements are issued in April.

2021
a. On September 5, opened checking accounts at Second Commercial Bank and negotiated a short-term line of credit of up to $15,000,000 at the bank's prime rate (10.5% at the time). The company will pay no commitment fees.
b. On October 1, borrowed $12 million cash from Second Commercial Bank under the line of credit and issued a five-month promissory note. Interest at the prime rate of 10% was payable at maturity. Management planned to issue 10-year bonds in February to repay the note.
c. Received $2,600 of refundable deposits in December for reusable containers used to transport and store chemical-based products.
d. For the September–December period, sales on account totaled $4,100,000. The state sales tax rate is 3% and the local sales tax rate is 3%. (This is a summary journal entry for the many individual sales transactions for the period.)
e. Recorded the adjusting entry for accrued interest.

2022
f. In March, paid the entire amount of the note on its March 1 due date, using proceeds from a February issuance of $10 million of 10-year bonds at face value, along with other available cash.
g. The storage containers covered by refundable deposits are expected to be returned during the first nine months of the year. Half of the containers were returned in March 2022.

Required:
1. Prepare the appropriate journal entries for items a–g.
2. Prepare the current and long-term liability sections of the December 31, 2021, balance sheet. Trade accounts payable on that date were $252,000.

758   SECTION 3   Liabilities and Shareholders' Equity

P 13–3
Current–
noncurrent
classification of
debt
● LO13–1, LO13–4

The balance sheet at December 31, 2021, for Nevada Harvester Corporation includes the liabilities listed below:

a. 11% bonds with a face amount of $40 million were issued for $40 million on October 31, 2012. The bonds mature on October 31, 2032. Bondholders have the option of calling (demanding payment on) the bonds on October 31, 2022, at a redemption price of $40 million. Market conditions are such that the call is not expected to be exercised.

b. Management intended to refinance $6 million of its 10% notes that mature in May 2022. In early March, prior to the actual issuance of the 2021 financial statements, Nevada Harvester negotiated a line of credit with a commercial bank for up to $5 million any time during 2022. Any borrowings will mature two years from the date of borrowing.

c. Noncallable 12% bonds with a face amount of $20 million were issued for $20 million on September 30, 2002. The bonds mature on September 30, 2022. Sufficient cash is expected to be available to retire the bonds at maturity.

d. A $12 million 9% bank loan is payable on October 31, 2027. The bank has the right to demand payment after any fiscal year-end in which Nevada Harvester's ratio of current assets to current liabilities falls below a contractual minimum of 1.7 to 1 and remains so for six months. That ratio was 1.45 on December 31, 2021, due primarily to an intentional temporary decline in inventory levels. Normal inventory levels will be reestablished during the first quarter of 2022.

Required:

1. Determine the amount, for each item a through d, that can be reported as a current liability and as a noncurrent liability. Explain the reasoning behind your classifications.

2. Prepare the liability section of a classified balance sheet and any necessary note disclosure for Nevada Harvester at December 31, 2021. Accounts payable and accruals are $22 million.

P 13–4
Various liabilities
● LO13–1 through
LO13–4

The unadjusted trial balance of the Manufacturing Equitable at December 31, 2021, the end of its fiscal year, included the following account balances. Manufacturing's 2021 financial statements were issued on April 1, 2022.

Accounts receivable	$ 92,500
Accounts payable	35,000
10% notes, payable to bank	600,000
Mortgage note payable	1,200,000

Other information:

a. The bank notes, issued August 1, 2021, are due on July 31, 2022, and pay interest at a rate of 10%, payable at maturity.

b. The mortgage note is due on March 1, 2022. Interest at 9% has been paid up to December 31 (assume 9% is a realistic rate). Manufacturing intended at December 31, 2021, to refinance the note on its due date with a new 10-year mortgage note. In fact, on March 1, Manufacturing paid $250,000 in cash on the principal balance and refinanced the remaining $950,000.

c. Included in the accounts receivable balance at December 31, 2021, were two subsidiary accounts that had been overpaid and had credit balances totaling $18,000. The accounts were of two major customers who were expected to order more merchandise from Manufacturing and apply the overpayments to those future purchases.

d. On November 1, 2021, Manufacturing rented a portion of its factory to a tenant for $30,000 per year, payable in advance. The payment for the 12 months ended October 31, 2022, was received as required and was credited to rent revenue.

Required:

1. Prepare any necessary adjusting journal entries at December 31, 2021, pertaining to each item of other information (a–d).

2. Prepare the current and long-term liability sections of the December 31, 2021, balance sheet.

P 13–5
Bonus
compensation;
algebra
● LO13–3

Sometimes compensation packages include bonuses designed to provide performance incentives to employees. The difficulty a bonus can cause accountants is not an accounting problem, but a math problem. The complication is that the bonus formula sometimes specifies that the calculation of the bonus is based in part on the bonus itself. This occurs any time the bonus is a percentage of income because expenses are components of income, and the bonus is an expense.

Regalia Fashions has an incentive compensation plan through which a division manager receives a bonus equal to 10% of the division's net income. Division income in 2021 before the bonus and income tax was $150,000. The tax rate is 30%.

Required:

1. Express the bonus formula as one or more algebraic equation(s).[33]
2. Using these formulas, calculate the amount of the bonus.
3. Prepare the adjusting entry to record the bonus compensation.
4. Bonus arrangements take many forms. Suppose the bonus specifies that the bonus is 10% of the division's income before tax, but after the bonus itself. Calculate the amount of the bonus.

P 13–6
Various contingencies
● LO13–5, LO13–6

Eastern Manufacturing is involved with several situations that possibly involve contingencies. Each is described below. Eastern's fiscal year ends December 31, and the 2021 financial statements are issued on March 15, 2022.

a. Eastern is involved in a lawsuit resulting from a dispute with a supplier. On February 3, 2022, judgment was rendered against Eastern in the amount of $107 million plus interest, a total of $122 million. Eastern plans to appeal the judgment and is unable to predict its outcome though it is not expected to have a material adverse effect on the company.

b. In November 2020, the State of Nevada filed suit against Eastern, seeking civil penalties and injunctive relief for violations of environmental laws regulating hazardous waste. On January 12, 2022, Eastern reached a settlement with state authorities. Based upon discussions with legal counsel, the Company feels it is probable that $140 million will be required to cover the cost of violations. Eastern believes that the ultimate settlement of this claim will not have a material adverse effect on the company.

c. Eastern is the plaintiff in a $200 million lawsuit filed against United Steel for damages due to lost profits from rejected contracts and for unpaid receivables. The case is in final appeal and legal counsel advises that it is probable that Eastern will prevail and be awarded $100 million.

d. At March 15, 2022, Eastern knows a competitor has threatened litigation due to patent infringement. The competitor has not yet filed a lawsuit. Management believes a lawsuit is reasonably possible, and if a lawsuit is filed, management believes damages of up to $33 million are reasonably possible.

Required:
Determine the appropriate way to report each situation, and prepare any necessary journal entries and disclosure notes. Explain your reasoning.

P 13–7
Various liabilities
● LO13–4, LO13–5, LO13–6, LO13–7
🌐 **IFRS**

HolmesWatson (HW) is considering what the effect would be of reporting its liabilities under IFRS rather than U.S. GAAP. The following facts apply:

a. HW is defending against a lawsuit and believes it is virtually certain to lose in court. If it loses the lawsuit, management estimates it will need to pay a range of damages that falls between $5,000,000 and $10,000,000, with each amount in that range equally likely.

b. HW is defending against another lawsuit that is identical to item (a), but the relevant losses will only occur far into the future. The present values of the endpoints of the range are $3,000,000 and $8,000,000, with the timing of cash flow somewhat uncertain. HW considers these effects of the time value of money to be material.

c. HW is defending against another lawsuit for which management believes HW has a slightly worse than 50/50 chance of losing in court. If it loses the lawsuit, management estimates HW will need to pay a range of damages that falls between $3,000,000 and $9,000,000, with each amount in that range equally likely.

d. HW has $10,000,000 of short-term debt that it intends to refinance on a long-term basis. Soon after the balance sheet date, but before issuance of the financial statements, HW obtained the financing necessary to refinance the debt.

Required:

1. For each item, indicate how treatment of the amount would differ between U.S. GAAP and IFRS.
2. Consider the total effect of items a–d. If HW's goal is to show the lowest total liabilities, which set of standards, U.S. GAAP or IFRS, best helps it meet that goal?

P 13–8
Expected cash flow approach; product recall
● LO13–6

The Heinrich Tire Company recalled a tire in its subcompact line in December 2021. Costs associated with the recall were originally thought to approximate $50 million. Now, though, while management feels it is probable the company will incur substantial costs, all discussions indicate that $50 million is an excessive amount. Based on prior recalls in the industry, management has provided the following probability distribution for the potential loss:

Loss Amount	Probability
$40 million	20%
$30 million	50%
$20 million	30%

---

[33] Remember when you were studying algebra and you wondered if you would ever use it?

An arrangement with a consortium of distributors requires that all recall costs be settled at the end of 2022. The risk-free rate of interest is 5%.

Required:

1. By the traditional approach to measuring loss contingencies, what amount would Heinrich record at the end of 2021 for the loss and contingent liability?
2. For the remainder of this problem, apply the expected cash flow approach of *SFAC No. 7*. Estimate Heinrich's liability at the end of the 2021 fiscal year.
3. Prepare the journal entry to record the contingent liability (and loss).
4. Prepare the journal entry to accrue interest on the liability at the end of 2022.
5. Prepare the journal entry to pay the liability at the end of 2022, assuming the actual cost is $31 million. Heinrich records an additional loss if the actual costs are higher or a gain if the costs are lower.

P 13–9
Subsequent events
● LO13–6

Lincoln Chemicals became involved in investigations by the U.S. Environmental Protection Agency in regard to damages connected to waste disposal sites. Below are four possibilities regarding the timing of (A) the alleged damage caused by Lincoln, (B) an investigation by the EPA, (C) the EPA assessment of penalties, and (D) ultimate settlement. In each case, assume that Lincoln is unaware of any problem until an investigation is begun. Also assume that once the EPA investigation begins, it is probable that a damage assessment will ensue and that once an assessment is made by the EPA, it is reasonably possible that a determinable amount will be paid by Lincoln.

Required:

For each case, decide whether (1) a loss should be accrued in the financial statements with an explanatory note, (2) a disclosure note only should be provided, or (3) no disclosure is necessary.

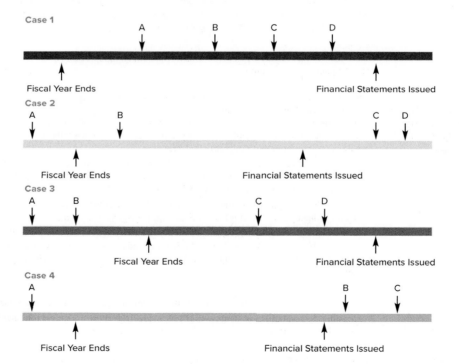

P 13–10
Subsequent events; classification of debt; loss contingency; financial statement effects
● LO13–4, LO13–5

Van Rushing Hunting Goods' fiscal year ends on December 31. At the end of the 2021 fiscal year, the company had notes payable of $12 million due on February 8, 2022. Rushing sold 2 million shares of its $0.25 par, common stock on February 3, 2022, for $9 million. The proceeds from that sale along with $3 million from the maturation of some 3-month CDs were used to pay the notes payable on February 8.

Through his attorney, one of Rushing's construction workers notified management on January 5, 2022, that he planned to sue the company for $1 million related to a work-site injury on December 20, 2021. As of December 31, 2021, management had been unaware of the injury, but reached an agreement on February 23, 2022, to settle the matter by paying the employee's medical bills of $75,000.

Rushing's financial statements were finalized on March 3, 2022.

Required:

1. What amount(s) if any, related to the situations described should Rushing report among current liabilities in its balance sheet at December 31, 2021? Why?

2. What amount(s) if any, related to the situations described should Rushing report among long-term liabilities in its balance sheet at December 31, 2021? Why?

3. How would your answers to requirements 1 and 2 differ if the settlement agreement had occurred on March 15, 2022, instead? Why?

4. How would your answers to requirements 1 and 2 differ if the work-site injury had occurred on January 3, 2022, instead? Why?

P 13–11
Concepts;
terminology

● LO13–1 through
LO13–4

Listed below are several terms and phrases associated with current liabilities. Pair each item from List A (by letter) with the item from List B that is most appropriately associated with it.

List A	List B
_____ 1. Face amount × Interest rate × Time	a. Informal agreement
_____ 2. Payable with current assets	b. Secured loan
_____ 3. Short-term debt to be refinanced with common stock	c. Refinancing prior to the issuance of the financial statements
_____ 4. Present value of interest plus present value of principal	d. Accounts payable
_____ 5. Noninterest-bearing	e. Accrued liabilities
_____ 6. Noncommitted line of credit	f. Commercial paper
_____ 7. Pledged accounts receivable	g. Current liabilities
_____ 8. Reclassification of debt	h. Long-term liability
_____ 9. Purchased by other corporations	i. Usual valuation of liabilities
_____10. Expenses not yet paid	j. Interest on debt
_____11. Liability until refunded	k. Customer advances
_____12. Liability until satisfy performance obligation	l. Customer deposits

P 13–12
Various liabilities;
balance sheet
classification;
prepare liability
section of balance
sheet; write notes

● LO13–4, LO13–5

Transit Airlines provides regional jet service in the Mid-South. The following is information on liabilities of Transit at December 31, 2021. Transit's fiscal year ends on December 31. Its annual financial statements are issued in April.

1. Transit has outstanding 6.5% bonds with a face amount of $90 million. The bonds mature on July 31, 2027. Bondholders have the option of calling (demanding payment on) the bonds on July 31, 2022, at a redemption price of $90 million. Market conditions are such that the call option is not expected to be exercised.

2. A $30 million 8% bank loan is payable on October 31, 2024. The bank has the right to demand payment after any fiscal year-end in which Transit's ratio of current assets to current liabilities falls below a contractual minimum of 1.9 to 1 and remains so for six months. That ratio was 1.75 on December 31, 2021, due primarily to an intentional temporary decline in parts inventories. Normal inventory levels will be reestablished during the sixth week of 2022.

3. Transit management intended to refinance $45 million of 7% notes that mature in May 2022. In late February 2022, prior to the issuance of the 2021 financial statements, Transit negotiated a line of credit with a commercial bank for up to $40 million any time during 2022. Any borrowings will mature two years from the date of borrowing.

4. Transit is involved in a lawsuit resulting from a dispute with a food caterer. On February 13, 2022, judgment was rendered against Transit in the amount of $53 million plus interest, a total of $54 million. Transit plans to appeal the judgment and is unable to predict its outcome though it is not expected to have a material adverse effect on the company.

Required:

1. How should the 6.5% bonds be classified by Transit among liabilities in its balance sheet? Explain.

2. How should the 8% bank loan be classified by Transit among liabilities in its balance sheet? Explain.

3. How should the 7% notes be classified by Transit among liabilities in its balance sheet? Explain.

4. How should the lawsuit be reported by Transit? Explain.

5. Prepare the liability section of a classified balance sheet for Transit Airlines at December 31, 2021. Transit's accounts payable and accruals were $43 million.

6. Draft appropriate note disclosures for Transit's financial statements at December 31, 2021, for each of the five items described.

762   SECTION 3   Liabilities and Shareholders' Equity

P 13–13
Payroll-related
liabilities
● Appendix

Alamar Petroleum Company offers its employees the option of contributing retirement funds up to 5% of their salaries, with the contribution being matched by Alamar. The company also pays 80% of medical and life insurance premiums. Deductions relating to these plans and other payroll information for the first biweekly payroll period of February are listed as follows:

Wages and salaries	$2,000,000
Employee contribution to voluntary retirement plan	84,000
Medical insurance premiums	42,000
Life insurance premiums	9,000
Federal income taxes to be withheld	400,000
Local income taxes to be withheld	53,000
Payroll taxes:	
Federal unemployment tax rate	0.60%
State unemployment tax rate (after SUTA deduction)	5.40%
Social Security tax rate	6.20%
Medicare tax rate	1.45%

Required:

Prepare the appropriate journal entries to record salaries expense and payroll tax expense for the biweekly pay period. Assume that all employees' cumulative wages do not exceed the relevant wage bases for Social Security. Also assume that all employees' cumulative wages do exceed the relevant unemployment wage bases at the end of January.

Decision Maker's Perspective

©ImageGap/Getty Images

Apply your critical-thinking ability to the knowledge you've gained. These cases will provide you an opportunity to develop your research, analysis, judgment, and communication skills. You also will work with other students, integrate what you've learned, apply it in real-world situations, and consider its global and ethical ramifications. This practice will broaden your knowledge and further develop your decision-making abilities.

**Research
Case 13–1**
Bank loan;
accrued interest
● LO13–1, LO13–2

A fellow accountant has solicited your opinion regarding the classification of short-term obligations repaid prior to being replaced by a long-term security. Cheshire Foods, Inc., issued $5,000,000 of short-term commercial paper during 2020 to finance construction of a plant. At September 30, 2021, Cheshire's fiscal year-end, the company intends to refinance the commercial paper by issuing long-term bonds. However, because Cheshire temporarily has excess cash, in November 2021 it liquidates $2,000,000 of the commercial paper as the paper matures. In December 2021, the company completes a $10,000,000 long-term bond issue. Later during December, it issues its September 30, 2021, financial statements. The proceeds of the long-term bond issue are to be used to replenish $2,000,000 in working capital, to pay $3,000,000 of commercial paper as it matures in January 2022, and to pay $5,000,000 of construction costs expected to be incurred later that year to complete the plant.

You initially are hesitant because you don't recall encountering a situation in which short-term obligations were repaid prior to being replaced by a long-term security. However, you are encouraged by a vague memory that this general topic is covered by GAAP literature you came across when reading an Internet article.

Required:

Determine how the $5,000,000 of commercial paper should be classified by citing the specific nine-digit Codification citation (XXX-XX-XX-XX) in the FASB Codification. Before doing so, formulate your own opinion on the proper treatment.

**Real World
Case 13–2**
Returnable
containers
● LO13–1, LO13–3

Real World Financials

The Zoo Doo Compost Company processes a premium organic fertilizer made with the help of the animals at the Memphis Zoo. Zoo Doo is sold in a specially designed plastic pail that may be kept and used for household chores or returned to the seller. The fertilizer is sold for $12.50 per two-gallon pail (including the $1.76 cost of the pail). For each pail returned, Zoo Doo donates $1 to the Memphis Zoo and the pail is used again.[34]

Required:

The founder and president of this start-up firm has asked your opinion on how to account for the donations to be made when fertilizer pails are returned. (Ignore any tax implications.)

---

[34] Case based on Kay McCullen, "Take The Zoo Home With You!" *Head Lions,* July 1991; and a conversation with the Zoo Doo Compost Company president, Pierce Ledbetter.

**Research
Case 13–3**
Relationship of
liabilities to assets
and owners'
equity
● LO13–1

SFAC No. 6, "Elements of Financial Statements," states that "an entity's assets, liabilities, and equity (net assets) all pertain to the same set of probable future economic benefits." Explain this statement.

**Judgment
Case 13–4**
Paid future
absences
● LO13–3

Cates Computing Systems develops and markets commercial software for personal computers and workstations. Three situations involving compensation for possible future absences of Cates's employees are described below.

a. Cates compensates employees at their regular pay rate for time absent for military leave, maternity leave, and jury time. Employees are allowed predetermined absence periods for each type of absence.

b. Members of the new product development team are eligible for three months' paid sabbatical leave every four years. Five members of the team have just completed their fourth year of participation.

c. Company policy permits employees four paid sick days each year. Unused sick days can accumulate and can be carried forward to future years.

Required:

1. What are the conditions that require accrual of an expense and related liability for employees' compensation for future absences?

2. For each of the three situations, indicate the circumstances under which accrual of an expense and related liability is warranted.

Ethics Case 13–5
Outdoors R Us
● LO13–1

Outdoors R Us owns several membership-based campground resorts throughout the Southwest. The company sells campground sites to new members, usually during a get-acquainted visit and tour. The campgrounds offer a wider array of on-site facilities than most. New members sign a multiyear contract, pay a down payment, and make monthly installment payments. Because no credit check is made and many memberships originate on a spur-of-the-moment basis, cancellations are not uncommon.

Business has been brisk during its first three years of operations, and since going public in 2008, the market value of its stock has tripled. The first sign of trouble came in 2021 when new sales dipped sharply.

One afternoon, two weeks before the end of the fiscal year, Diane Rice, CEO, and Gene Sun, controller, were having an active discussion in Sun's office.

Sun: I've thought more about our discussion yesterday. Maybe something can be done about profits.
Rice: I hope so. Our bonuses and stock value are riding on this period's performance.
Sun: We've been recording deferred revenues when new members sign up. Rather than recording liabilities at the time memberships are sold, I think we can justify reporting sales revenue for all memberships sold.
Rice: What will be the effect on profits?
Sun: I haven't run the numbers yet, but let's just say very favorable.

Required:

1. Why do you think liabilities had been recorded previously?

2. Is the proposal ethical?

3. Who would be affected if the proposal is implemented?

**Trueblood
Case 13–6**
Contingencies
● LO13–5

The following Trueblood case is recommended for use with this chapter. The case provides an excellent opportunity for class discussion, group projects, and writing assignments. The case, along with Professor's Discussion Material, can be obtained from the Deloitte Foundation at its website: www.deloitte.com/us/truebloodcases.

Case 13–8: Accounting for a Loss Contingency for a Verdict Overturned on Appeal
This case gives students the opportunity to apply GAAP regarding accrual and disclosure of contingencies with respect to a complex lawsuit. As an addition to the case, students should cite the appropriate location of relevant GAAP in the FASB Codification.

**Communication
Case 13–7**
Exceptions to
the general
classification
guideline; group
interaction
● LO13–4

Domestic Transfer and Storage is a large trucking company headquartered in the Midwest. Rapid expansion in recent years has been financed in large part by debt in a variety of forms. In preparing the financial statements for 2018, questions have arisen regarding the way certain of the liabilities are to be classified in the company's classified balance sheet.

A meeting of several members of the accounting area is scheduled for tomorrow, April 8, 2019. You are confident that that meeting will include the topic of debt classification. You want to appear knowledgeable at the meeting, but realizing it's been a few years since you have dealt with classification issues, you have sought out information you think relevant. Questionable liabilities at the company's fiscal year-end (January 31, 2019) include the following:

a. $15 million of 9% commercial paper is due on July 31, 2019. Management intends to refinance the paper on a long-term basis. In early April 2019, Domestic negotiated a credit agreement with a commercial bank for up to $12 million any time during the next three years, any borrowings from which will mature two years from the date of borrowing.

b. $17 million of 11% notes were issued on June 30, 2016. The notes are due on November 30, 2019. The company has investments of $20 million classified as "available for sale."

c. $25 million of 10% notes were due on February 28, 2019. On February 21, 2019, the company issued 30-year, 9.4% bonds in a private placement to institutional investors.

d. Recently, company management has considered reducing debt in favor of a greater proportion of equity financing. $20 million of 12% bonds mature on July 31, 2019. Discussions with underwriters, which began on January 4, 2019, resulted in a contractual arrangement on March 15 under which new common shares will be sold in July for approximately $20 million.

In order to make notes to yourself in preparation for the meeting concerning the classification of these items, you decide to discuss them with a colleague. Specifically, you want to know what portion of the debt can be excluded from classification as a current liability (that is, reported as a noncurrent liability) and why.

Required:

1. What is the appropriate classification of each liability? Develop a list of arguments in support of your view prior to the class session for which the case is assigned.

2. In class, your instructor will pair you (and everyone else) with a classmate (who also has independently developed a position). You will be given three minutes to argue your view to your partner. Your partner likewise will be given three minutes to argue his or her view to you. During these three-minute presentations, the listening partner is not permitted to speak.

3. Then after each person has had a turn attempting to convince his or her partner, the two partners will have a three-minute discussion to decide which classifications are more convincing. Arguments will be merged into a single view for each pair.

4. After the allotted time, a spokesperson for each of the four liabilities will be selected by the instructor. Each spokesperson will field arguments from the class as to the appropriate classification. The class then will discuss the merits of the classification and attempt to reach a consensus view, though a consensus is not necessary.

Communication Case 13–8
Various contingencies
● LO13–5, LO13–6

"I see an all-nighter coming on," Gayle grumbled. "Why did Mitch just now give us this assignment?" Your client, Western Manufacturing, is involved with several situations that possibly involve contingencies. The assignment Gayle refers to is to draft appropriate accounting treatment for each situation described below in time for tomorrow's meeting of the audit group. Western's fiscal year is the calendar year 2021, and the 2021 financial statements are issued on March 15, 2022.

1. During 2021, Western experienced labor disputes at three of its plants. Management hopes an agreement will soon be reached. However negotiations between the Company and the unions have not produced an acceptable settlement and, as a result, strikes are ongoing at these facilities since March 1, 2022. It is virtually certain that material costs will be incurred but the amount of possible costs cannot be reasonably ascertained.

2. In accordance with a 2019 contractual agreement with A. J. Conner Company, Western is entitled to $37 million for certain fees and expense reimbursements. These were written off as bad debts in 2020. A. J. Conner has filed for bankruptcy. The bankruptcy court on February 4, 2022, ordered A. J. Conner to pay $23 million immediately upon consummation of a proposed merger with Garner Holding Group.

3. Western warrants most products it sells against defects in materials and workmanship for a period of a year. Based on their experience with previous product introductions, warranty costs are expected to approximate 2% of sales. A warranty liability of $39 million was reported at December 31, 2020. Sales of warranted products during 2021 were $2,100 million and actual warranty expenditures were $40 million.

4. Western is involved in a suit filed in January 2022 by Crump Holdings seeking $88 million, as an adjustment to the purchase price in connection with the Company's sale of its textile business in 2021. The suit alleges that Western misstated the assets and liabilities used to calculate the purchase price for the textile division. Legal counsel advises that it is reasonably possible that Western could end up losing an indeterminable amount not expected to have a material adverse effect on the Company's financial position.

Required:

1. Determine the appropriate means of reporting each situation.

2. In a memo to the audit manager, Mitch Riley, explain your reasoning. Include any necessary journal entries and drafts of appropriate disclosure notes.

**Judgment
Case 13–9**
Loss contingency
and full disclosure
● LO13–5, LO13–6

In the March 2022 meeting of Valleck Corporation's board of directors, a question arose as to the way a possible obligation should be disclosed in the forthcoming financial statements for the year ended December 31. A veteran board member brought to the meeting a draft of a disclosure note that had been prepared by the controller's office for inclusion in the annual report. Here is the note:

> On May 9, 2021, the United States Environmental Protection Agency (EPA) issued a Notice of Violation (NOV) to Valleck alleging violations of the Clean Air Act. Subsequently, in June 2021, the EPA commenced a civil action with respect to the foregoing violation seeking civil penalties of approximately $853,000. The EPA alleges that Valleck exceeded applicable volatile organic substance emission limits. The Company estimates that the cost to achieve compliance will be $190,000; in addition the Company expects to settle the EPA lawsuit for a civil penalty of $205,000 which will be paid in 2022.

"Where did we get the $205,000 figure?" he asked. On being informed that this is the amount negotiated last month by company attorneys with the EPA, the director inquires, "Aren't we supposed to report a liability for that in addition to the note?"

Required:
Explain whether Valleck should report a liability in addition to the note. Why or why not? For full disclosure, should anything be added to the disclosure note itself?

**Communication
Case 13–10**
Change in loss
contingency; write
a memo
● LO13–5, LO13–6

Late in 2021, you and two other officers of Curbo Fabrications Corporation just returned from a meeting with officials of the City of Jackson. The meeting was unexpectedly favorable even though it culminated in a settlement with city authorities that required your company pay a total of $475,000 to cover the cost of violations of city construction codes. Jackson had filed suit in November 2019 against Curbo, seeking civil penalties and injunctive relief for violations of city construction codes regulating earthquake damage standards. Alleged violations involved several construction projects completed during the previous three years. When the financial statements were issued in 2020, Curbo had not reached a settlement with state authorities, but legal counsel had advised the Company that it was probable the ultimate settlement would be $750,000 in penalties. The following entry had been recorded:

Loss—litigation	750,000	
Liability—litigation		750,000

The final settlement, therefore, was a pleasant surprise. While returning from the meeting, your conversation turned to reporting the settlement in the 2021 financial statements. You drew the short straw and were selected to write a memo to Janet Zeno, the financial vice president, advising the proper course of action.

Required:
Write the memo. Include descriptions of any journal entries related to the change in amounts. Briefly describe other steps Curbo should take to report the settlement.

**Research
Case 13–11**
Researching
the way
contingencies
are reported;
retrieving
information from
the Internet
● LO13–5, LO13–6

EDGAR (Electronic Data Gathering, Analysis, and Retrieval system) performs automated collection, validation, indexing, acceptance, and forwarding of submissions by companies and others who are required by law to file forms with the U.S. Securities and Exchange Commission (SEC). All publicly traded domestic companies use EDGAR to make the majority of their filings. Form 10-K, which includes the annual report, is required to be filed on EDGAR. The SEC makes this information available on the Internet.

Required:
1. Access the *FASB Accounting Standards Codification* at the FASB website (www.fasb.org). Determine the specific eight-digit Codification citation (XXX-XX-XX-X) that provides guidance on accounting for contingent losses, and indicate the specific eight-digit Codification citation (XXX-XX-XX-X) citation that describes the guidelines for determining when an expense and liability associated with a contingent loss should be accrued versus only disclosed in the notes.
2. Access EDGAR on the Internet at: www.sec.gov.
3. Search for a public company with which you are familiar. Access its most recent 10-K filing. Search or scroll to find the financial statements and related notes.
4. Specifically, look for any contingency(s) reported in the disclosure notes. Identify the nature of the contingency(s) described and explain the reason(s) the loss or losses was or was not accrued.
5. Repeat requirements 2 and 3 for two additional companies.

766   SECTION 3   Liabilities and Shareholders' Equity

Communication Case 13–12
Accounting changes
● LO13–5, LO13–6

Kevin Brantly is a new hire in the controller's office of Fleming Home Products. Two events occurred in late 2021 that the company had not previously encountered. The events appear to affect two of the company's liabilities, but there is some disagreement concerning whether they also affect financial statements of prior years. Each change occurred during 2021 before any adjusting entries or closing entries were prepared. The tax rate for Fleming is 40% in all years.

- Fleming Home Products introduced a new line of commercial awnings in 2020 that carry a one-year warranty against manufacturer's defects. Based on industry experience, warranty costs were expected to approximate 3% of sales. Sales of the awnings in 2020 were $3,500,000. Accordingly, warranty expense and a warranty liability of $105,000 were recorded in 2020. In late 2021, the company's claims experience was evaluated and it was determined that claims were far fewer than expected—2% of sales rather than 3%. Sales of the awnings in 2021 were $4,000,000 and warranty expenditures in 2021 totaled $91,000.

- In November 2019, the State of Minnesota filed suit against the company, seeking penalties for violations of clean air laws. When the financial statements were issued in 2020, Fleming had not reached a settlement with state authorities, but legal counsel advised Fleming that it was probable the company would have to pay $200,000 in penalties. Accordingly, the following entry was recorded:

Loss—litigation	200,000	
Liability—litigation		200,000

Late in 2021, a settlement was reached with state authorities to pay a total of $350,000 in penalties.

Required:
Kevin's supervisor, perhaps unsure of the answer, perhaps wanting to test Kevin's knowledge, e-mails the message, "Kevin, send me a memo on how we should handle our awning warranty and that clean air suit." Wanting to be accurate, Kevin consults his reference materials. What will he find? Prepare the memo requested.

Real World Case 13–13
Lawsuit settlement; Morgan Stanley
● LO13–5, LO13–6

Real World Financials

Morgan Stanley is a leading investment bank founded in 1935. The company's fiscal year ends December 31, 2013, and it filed its financial statements with the SEC on February 25, 2014. On February 5, 2014, *Bloomberg* reported that Morgan Stanley would make a $1.25 billion settlement with the Federal Housing Finance Agency:

> Morgan Stanley said yesterday it reached a $1.25 billion deal to end Federal Housing Finance Agency claims the bank sold faulty mortgage bonds to Fannie Mae (FNMA) and Freddie Mac (FMCC) before the firms' losses pushed them into U.S. conservatorship. . . . Morgan Stanley, which disclosed its settlement in a regulatory filing yesterday, was among 18 banks sued by the FHFA in 2011. Authorities sought to recoup some losses taxpayers covered when the government took control of the failing mortgage-finance companies in 2008.

Required:
1. From an accounting perspective, how should Morgan Stanley have treated the settlement?
2. Relying on the information provided by the news article, re-create the journal entry Morgan Stanley recorded for the settlement. Assume it had not made any prior liability accrual with respect to this litigation.
3. Suppose the settlement had occurred after February 25, 2014. How should Morgan Stanley have treated the settlement?

Ethics Case 13–14
Profits guaranteed
● LO13–5

This was Joel Craig's first visit to the controller's corner office since being recruited for the senior accountant position in May. Because he'd been directed to bring with him his preliminary report on year-end adjustments, Craig presumed he'd done something wrong in preparing the report. That he had not was Craig's first surprise. His second surprise was his boss's request to reconsider one of the estimated expenses.

S & G Fasteners was a new company, specializing in plastic industrial fasteners. All products carry a generous long-term warranty against manufacturer's defects. "Don't you think 4% of sales is a little high for our warranty expense estimate?" his boss wondered. "After all, we're new at this. We have little experience with product introductions. I just got off the phone with Blanchard (the company president). He thinks we'll have trouble renewing our credit line with the profits we're projecting. The pressure's on."

Required:
1. Should Craig follow his boss's suggestion?
2. Does revising the warranty estimate pose an ethical dilemma?
3. Who would be affected if the suggestion is followed?

IFRS Case 13–15
Current
liabilities and
contingencies;
differences
between U.S.
GAAP and IFRS
● LO13–4, LO13–5,
LO13–7

 IFRS

As a second-year financial analyst for A.J. Straub Investments, you are performing an initial analysis on Fizer Pharmaceuticals. A difficulty you've encountered in making comparisons with its chief rival is that Fizer uses U.S. GAAP and the competing company uses International Financial Reporting Standards. Some areas of concern are the following:

1. Fizer has been designated as a potentially responsible party by the United States Environmental Protection Agency with respect to certain waste sites. These claims are in various stages of administrative or judicial proceedings and include demands for recovery of past governmental costs and for future investigations or remedial actions. Fizer accrues costs associated with environmental matters when they become probable and reasonably estimable. Counsel has advised that the likelihood of payments of about $70 million is slightly more than 50%. Accordingly, payment is judged reasonably possible and the contingency was disclosed in a note.

2. Fizer had $10 million of bonds issued in 1992 that mature in February 2022. On December 31, 2021, the company's fiscal year-end, management intended to refinance the bonds on a long-term basis. On February 7, 2022, Fizer issued $10 million of 20-year bonds, applying the proceeds to repay the bond issue that matured that month. The bonds were reported in Fizer's balance sheet as long-term debt.

3. Fizer reported in its 2021 financial statements a long-term contingency at its face amount rather than its present value even though the difference was considered material. The reason the cash flows were not discounted is that their timing is uncertain.

Required:
If Fizer used IFRS as does its competitor, how would the items described be reported differently?

**Analysis
Case 13–16**
Analyzing
financial
statements;
liquidity ratios
● LO13–1

IGF Foods Company is a large, primarily domestic, consumer foods company involved in the manufacture, distribution and sale of a variety of food products. Industry averages are derived from Troy's *The Almanac of Business and Industrial Financial Ratios*. Following are the 2021 and 2020 comparative balance sheets for IGF. (The financial data we use are from actual financial statements of a well-known corporation, but the company name used is fictitious and the numbers and dates have been modified slightly.)

IGF FOODS COMPANY Comparative Balance Sheets Years Ended December 31, 2021 and 2020 ($ in millions)		
	2021	**2020**
Assets		
Current assets:		
Cash	$ 48	$ 142
Accounts receivable	347	320
Marketable securities	358	—
Inventories	914	874
Prepaid expenses	212	154
Total current assets	1,879	1,490
Property, plant, and equipment (net)	2,592	2,291
Intangibles (net)	800	843
Other assets	74	60
Total assets	$5,345	$4,684
Liabilities and Shareholders' Equity		
Current liabilities:		
Accounts payable	$ 254	$ 276
Accrued liabilities	493	496
Notes payable	518	115
Current portion of long-term debt	208	54
Total current liabilities	1,473	941
Long-term debt	534	728
Deferred income taxes	407	344
Total liabilities	2,414	2,013
Shareholders' equity:		
Common stock	180	180
Additional paid-in capital	21	63
Retained earnings	2,730	2,428
Total shareholders' equity	2,931	2,671
Total liabilities and shareholders' equity	$5,345	$4,684

Liquidity refers to a company's cash position and overall ability to obtain cash in the normal course of business. A company is said to be liquid if it has sufficient cash or is capable of converting its other assets to cash in a relatively short period of time so that currently maturing debts can be paid.

Required:

1. Calculate the current ratio for IGF for 2021. The average ratio for the stocks listed on the New York Stock Exchange in a comparable time period was 1.5. What information does your calculation provide an investor?
2. Calculate IGF's acid-test or quick ratio for 2021. The ratio for the stocks listed on the New York Stock Exchange in a comparable time period was .80. What does your calculation indicate about IGF's liquidity?

**Trueblood
Case 13–17**
Accounting
for litigation
contingencies

● LO13–5, LO13–6,
LO13–7

The following Trueblood case is recommended for use with this chapter. The case provides an excellent opportunity for class discussion, group projects, and writing assignments. The case, along with Professor's Discussion Material, can be obtained from the Deloitte Foundation at its website: www.deloitte.com/us/truebloodcases.

Case 14-07: eVade Pays Up
This case gives students an opportunity to consider the difference between a contractual or legal liability and a contingency.

**Real World
Case 13–18**
Contingencies

● LO13–5

Real World Financials

The following is an excerpt from *USAToday.com:*

> Microsoft (MSFT) on Thursday extended the warranty on its Xbox 360 video game console and said it will take a charge of more than $1 billion to pay for "anticipated costs." Under the new warranty, Microsoft will pay for shipping and repairs for three years, worldwide, for consoles afflicted with what gamers call "the red ring of death." Previously, the warranty expired after a year for U.S. customers and two years for Europeans. The charge will be $1.05 billion to $1.15 billion for the quarter ended June 30. Microsoft reports its fourth-quarter results July 19.

Required:

1. Why must Microsoft report this charge of over $1 billion entirely in one quarter, the last quarter of the company's fiscal year?
2. When the announcement was made, analyst Richard Doherty stated that either a high number of Xbox 360s will fail or the company is being overly conservative in its warranty estimate. From an accounting standpoint, what will Microsoft do in the future if the estimate of future repairs is overly conservative (too high)?

**Real World
Case 13–19**
Contingencies

● LO13–5

Real World Financials

 IFRS

Reporting requirements for contingent liabilities under IFRS differ somewhat from those under U.S. GAAP.

Required:

For each of the following, access the online version of the indicated financial report and answer the question. Also compare reporting under IFRS to similar reporting under U.S. GAAP.

1. AU Optronics (Form 20-F, filed 3/21/2016): Where there is a continuous range of possible outcomes, with each point in the range as likely as any other, what amount is accrued as the estimate of the obligation?
2. B Communications LTD (Form 20-F, filed 4/19/2016): With respect to legal claims, at what probability level would B Communications accrue a liability for a possible litigation loss?

**Trueblood
Case 13–20**
Subsequent Events

● LO13–5

The following Trueblood case is recommended for use with this chapter. The case provides an excellent opportunity for class discussion, group projects, and writing assignments. The case, along with Professor's Discussion Material, can be obtained from the Deloitte Foundation at its website: www.deloitte.com/us/truebloodcases.

Case 12-02: To Recognize or Not to Recognize, That is the Question
This case gives students the opportunity to apply GAAP regarding recognition of subsequent events. As an addition to the case, students should cite the appropriate location of relevant GAAP in the FASB Codification.

Data Analytics

Data analytics is the process of examining data sets in order to draw conclusions about the information they contain. If you haven't completed any of the prior data analytics cases, follow the instructions listed in the Chapter 1 Data Analytics case to get set up. You will need to watch the videos referred to in the Chapters 1–3

Data Analytics cases. No additional videos are required for this case. All short training videos can be found here: https://www.tableau.com/learn/training#getting-started.

Data Analytics Case
Ability to Pay Short-Term Debt
● LO13–1

In the Chapter 3 Data Analytics Cases, you used Tableau to examine a data set and create charts to compare our two (hypothetical) publicly traded companies, Discount Goods and Big Store, as to their liquidity - their ability to pay short-term debts as they come due. You did so by comparing current ratios and acid-test ratios. In this case , you will expand your assessment of the companies' liquidity by also evaluating other aspects of liquidity as measured by their cash to current liabilities and current liabilities to net worth ratios.

The cash to current liabilities ratio (also known as the cash ratio) is measured as cash and cash equivalents / total current liabilities and tells us about the ability of a company to settle its current liabilities using only its cash and highly liquid investments.

The current liabilities to net worth ratio is measured as current liabilities / shareholders' equity and tells us about the relationship between capital contributed by current obligation creditors and capital contributed by owners. It indicates the ability of a company to safely meet the obligations of current creditors. The higher the ratio, the less security there is for current obligation creditors.

Required:

Use Tableau to create calculations for the current, acid-test, cash to current liabilities, and current liabilities to net worth ratios for each of the two companies in 2021. Based upon what you find, answer the following questions:

1. Other things being equal, which company appears to have the better liquidity position in terms of their ability to pay short-term debts as they come due as measured by the current ratio?

2. Which company appears to offer the better liquidity position in terms of their ability to pay short-term debts as they come due as measured by the acid-test or quick ratio?

3. Other things being equal, which company appears to have the better liquidity position in terms of ability of the company's current liabilities to be covered using its cash and cash equivalents?

4. Which company appears to offer the better security for its current obligation creditors as measured by the current liabilities to net worth ratio?

Note: As you assess the liquidity aspect of the companies, keep in mind that liquidity ratios should be evaluated in the context of both profitability and efficiency of managing assets and relative to average liquidity ratios of the industry.

Resources:

You have available to you an extensive data set that includes detailed financial data for Discount Goods and Big Store for 2012–2021. The data set is in the form of four Excel files available to download from Connect or under Student Resources within the Library tab.The one for use in this chapter is named "Discount_Goods_Big_Store_Financials.xlsx." Download this file and save it to the computer on which you will be using Tableau. For this case, you will create calculations to produce several liquidity ratios allowing you to compare and contrast the two companies.

After you view the training videos, follow these steps to create the charts you'll use for this case:

● Open Tableau and connect to the Excel spreadsheet you downloaded.

● Click on the "Sheet 1" tab at the bottom of the canvas, to the right of the Data Source at the bottom of the screen. Drag "Company" and "Year" under Dimensions to the Rows shelf. Change "Year" to *discrete* by right-clicking and selecting "Discrete." Select "Show Filter" and uncheck all the years except 2021. Click "Ok."

● Create the "Current Ratio" and "Quick Ratio" by following the steps in the Chapter 3 Data Analytics Case. After creating the two ratios, drag them to the Rows shelf. Change the ratios back to *continuous* by right-clicking and selecting "Continuous."

● Create a calculated field "Cash Ratio" by dragging "Cash and cash equivalents" under Measures into the Calculation Editor window. Type a division sign, then drag the "Total current liabilities" beside it. Make sure the window says that the calculation is valid and click OK. Drag the newly created "Cash Ratio" to the Rows shelf.

● Create a calculated field "Current Liabilities to Net Worth" by dragging "Total current liabilities" from the under Measures into the Calculation Editor window. Type a division sign, then drag the "Total shareholders' equity" beside it. Make sure the window says that the calculation is valid and click OK. Drag the newly created "Current Liabilities to Net Worth" to the Rows shelf.

● Click on the "Show Me" tab in the upper right corner and select "horizontal bars." Add labels to the bars by clicking on "Label" under the "Marks" card and clicking the box "Show mark label." Format the labels to Times New Roman, bold, black and 9-point font.

● Change the title of the sheet to be "Liquidity Ratios" by right-clicking and selecting "Edit title." Format the title to Times New Roman, bold, black and 15-point font. Format all other labels to be Times New Roman, bold, black and 12-point font. Change the title of "Sheet 1" to match the sheet title by right-clicking, selecting "Rename" and typing in the new title. Drag "Company" to the Color card in the "Marks" card to change the bars to two different colors.

● Once complete, save the file as *"DA13_Your initials.twbx."*

Continuing Cases

Target Case

 **LO13–1,
LO13–3, LO13–5**

Target Corporation prepares its financial statements according to U.S. GAAP. Target's financial statements and disclosure notes for the year ended February 3, 2018, are available in Connect. This material also is available under the Investor Relations link at the company's website (www.target.com).

Required:

1. Target's Consolidated Statement of Financial Position (its balance sheet) discloses its current assets and current liabilities.

   a. What are the three components of Target's current liabilities?

   b. Are current assets sufficient to cover current liabilities? What is the current ratio for the year ended February 3, 2018? How does the ratio compare with the prior year?

   c. Why might a company want to avoid having its current ratio be too low? Too high?

2. Disclosure Note 2 discusses Target's accounting for gift card sales. Disclosure Note 18 indicates the amount of gift card liability that is recognized in Target's balance sheet.

   a. By how much did Target's gift card liability change between February 3, 2018, and January 28, 2017?

   b. How would the following affect Target's gift card liability (indicate "increase," "decrease," or "no change" for each):

      i. Sale of a gift card

      ii. Redemption of a gift card (the holder using it to acquire goods or services)

      iii. Increase in breakage estimated for gift cards already sold

3. Disclosure Note 19 discusses Target's accounting for contingencies. What is Target's approach for accruing losses for litigation liabilities? Is their approach appropriate?

Air France–KLM Case

 LO13–7

🌐 **IFRS**

Air France–KLM (AF), a Franco-Dutch company, prepares its financial statements according to International Financial Reporting Standards. AF's financial statements and disclosure notes for the year ended December 31, 2017, are available in Connect. This material is also available under the Finance link at the company's website (www.airfranceklm.com).

Required:

1. Read Notes 4.6 and the Consolidated Balance Sheet. What do you think gave rise to deferred revenue on ticket sales of €2,889 as of the end of fiscal 2017? Would transactions of this type be handled similarly under U.S. GAAP?

2. Is the threshold for recognizing a provision under IFRS different than it is under U.S. GAAP? Explain.

3. Note 31 lists "other provisions."

   a. Do the beginning and ending balances of other provisions shown in Note 31 for fiscal 2017 tie to the balance sheet? By how much has the total amount of the AF's "other provisions" increased or decreased during fiscal 2017?

   b. Prepare journal entries for the following changes in the litigation provision that occurred during fiscal 2017, assuming any amounts recorded on the income statement are recorded as "provision expense," and any use of provision is paid for in cash. In each case, provide a brief explanation of the event your journal entry is capturing.

      i. New provision

      ii. Use of provision

   c. Is AF's treatment of its litigation provision under IFRS similar to how it would be treated under U.S. GAAP?

4. Note 31.2 lists a number of contingent liabilities. Are amounts for those items recognized as a liability on AF's balance sheet? Explain.

CPA Exam Questions and Simulations

 ROGER
CPA Review

Sample CPA Exam questions from Roger CPA Review are available in Connect as support for the topics in this chapter. These multiple-choice questions and task-based simulations include expert-written explanations and solutions, and provide a starting point for students to become familiar with the content and functionality of the actual CPA Exam.

CHAPTER

14

Bonds and Long-Term Notes

OVERVIEW

This chapter continues the presentation of liabilities. While the discussion focuses on the accounting treatment of long-term liabilities, the borrowers' side of the same transactions is presented as well. Long-term notes and bonds are discussed, as well as the extinguishment of debt and debt convertible into stock.

LEARNING OBJECTIVES

After studying this chapter, you should be able to:

- **LO14–1** Identify the underlying characteristics of debt instruments and describe the basic approach to accounting for debt. (p. 773)

- **LO14–2** Account for bonds issued at face value, at a discount, or at a premium, recording interest using the effective interest method or using the straight-line method. (p. 775)

- **LO14–3** Characterize the accounting treatment of notes, including installment notes, issued for cash or for noncash consideration. (p. 786)

- **LO14–4** Describe the disclosures appropriate to long-term debt in its various forms and calculate related financial ratios. (p. 791)

- **LO14–5** Record the early extinguishment of debt, its conversion into equity securities, and bond issues with warrants. (p. 795)

- **LO14–6** Understand the option to report liabilities at their fair values. (p. 801)

- **LO14–7** Discuss the primary differences between U.S. GAAP and IFRS with respect to accounting for bonds and long-term notes. (pp. 797).

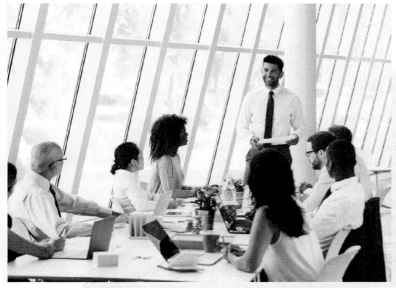

©monkeybusinessimages/Getty Images

FINANCIAL REPORTING CASE

Service Leader, Inc.

The mood is both upbeat and focused on this cool October morning. Executives and board members of Service Leader, Inc., are meeting with underwriters and attorneys to discuss the company's first bond offering in its 20-year history. You are attending in the capacity of company controller and two-year member of the board of directors. The closely held corporation has been financed entirely by equity, internally generated funds, and short-term bank borrowings.

Bank rates of interest, though, have risen recently and the company's unexpectedly rapid, but welcome, growth has prompted the need to look elsewhere for new financing. Under consideration are 15-year, 6.25% first mortgage bonds with a principal amount of $70 million. The bonds would be callable at 103 any time after June 30, 2023, and convertible into Service Leader common stock at the rate of 45 shares per $1,000 bond.

Other financing vehicles have been discussed over the last two months, including the sale of additional stock, nonconvertible bonds, and unsecured notes. This morning *The Wall Street Journal* indicated that market rates of interest for debt similar to the bonds under consideration are about 6.5%.

By the time you finish this chapter, you should be able to respond appropriately to the questions posed in this case. Compare your response to the solution provided at the end of the chapter.

QUESTIONS

1. What does it mean that the bonds are "first mortgage" bonds? What effect does that have on financing? (*p. 774*)
2. From Service Leader's perspective, why are the bonds callable? What does that mean? (*p. 775*)
3. How will it be possible to sell bonds paying investors 6.25% when other, similar investments will provide the investors a return of 6.5%? (*p. 775*)
4. Would accounting differ if the debt were designated as notes rather than bonds? (*p. 786*)
5. Why might the company choose to make the bonds convertible into common stock? (*p. 795*)

The Nature of Long-Term Debt

● LO14–1

A company must raise funds to finance its operations and often the expansion of those operations. Presumably, at least some of the necessary funding can be provided by the company's own operations, though some funds must be provided by external sources. Ordinarily, external financing includes some combination of equity and debt funding. We explore debt financing first.

Liabilities signify borrowers' interests in a company's assets.

In the present chapter, we focus on debt in the form of bonds and notes. The following three chapters deal with liabilities also, namely those arising in connection with leases (Chapter 15), deferred income taxes (Chapter 16), and pensions and employee benefits (Chapter 17). Some employee benefits create equity rather than debt, which are discussed in Chapter 19. In Chapter 18, we examine shareholders' interests arising from external *equity* financing. In Chapter 21, we see that cash flows from both debt and equity financing are reported together in a statement of cash flows as "cash flows from financing activities."

As you read this chapter, you will find the focus to be on the liability side of the transactions we examine. Realize, though, that the mirror image of a liability is an asset (bonds payable/investment in bonds, note payable/note receivable, etc.). So as we discuss accounting for debts from the viewpoint of the issuers of the debt instruments (borrowers), we also will take the opportunity to see how the lender deals with the corresponding asset. Studying the two sides of the same transaction in tandem will emphasize their inherent similarities.

> *A note payable and a note receivable are two sides of the same coin.*

Accounting for a liability is a relatively straightforward concept. This is not to say that all debt instruments are unchallenging, "plain vanilla" loan agreements. Quite the contrary, the financial community continually devises increasingly exotic ways to flavor financial instruments in the attempt to satisfy the diverse and evolving tastes of both debtors and creditors.

> *Periodic interest is the effective interest rate times the amount of the debt outstanding during the interest period.*

Packaging aside, a liability requires the future payment of cash in specified (or estimated) amounts, at specified (or projected) dates. As time passes, interest accrues on debt. As a general rule, the periodic interest is the effective interest rate times the amount of the debt outstanding during the period. This same principle applies regardless of the specific form of the liability—note payable, bonds payable, lease liability, pension obligation, or other debt instruments. Also, as a general rule, long-term liabilities are reported at their present values. The present value of a liability is the present value of its related cash flows (principal and/or interest payments), discounted at the effective rate of interest at issuance.

We begin our study of long-term liabilities by examining accounting for bonds. We follow that section with a discussion of debt in the form of notes in Part B. It's important to note that, although particulars of the two forms of debt differ, the basic approach to accounting for each type is precisely the same. In Part C, we look at various ways bonds and notes are retired or converted into other securities. Finally, in Part D we discuss the option companies have to report liabilities at their fair values.

PART A

Bonds

A company can borrow cash from a bank or other financial institution by signing a promissory note. We discuss notes payable later in the chapter. Medium- and large-sized corporations often choose to borrow cash by issuing bonds to the public. In fact, the most common form of corporate debt is bonds. A bond issue, in effect, breaks down a large debt (large corporations often borrow hundreds of millions of dollars at a time) into manageable parts—usually $1,000 or $5,000 units. This avoids the necessity of finding a single lender who is both willing and able to loan a large amount of money at a reasonable interest rate. So rather than signing a $400 million note to borrow cash from a financial institution, a company may find it more economical to sell 400,000 $1,000 bonds to many lenders—theoretically up to 400,000 lenders.

> *A bond issue divides a large liability into many smaller liabilities.*

Bonds obligate the issuing corporation to repay a stated amount (variously referred to as the *principal, par value, face amount,* or *maturity value*) at a specified *maturity date.* Maturities for bonds typically range from 10 to 40 years. In return for the use of the money borrowed, the company also agrees to pay *interest* to bondholders between the issue date and maturity. The periodic interest is a stated percentage of face amount (variously referred to as the *stated rate, coupon rate,* or *nominal rate*). Ordinarily, interest is paid semiannually on designated interest dates beginning six months after the day the bonds are "dated."

> *Corporations issuing bonds are obligated to repay a stated amount at a specified maturity date and to pay periodic interest between the issue date and maturity.*

The Bond Indenture

The specific promises made to bondholders are described in a document called a bond indenture. Because it would be impractical for the corporation to enter into a direct agreement with each of the many bondholders, the bond indenture is held by a trustee, usually a commercial bank or other financial institution, appointed by the issuing firm to represent the rights of the bondholders. If the company fails to live up to the terms of the bond indenture, the trustee may bring legal action against the company on behalf of the bondholders.

> *A bond indenture describes the specific promises made to bondholders.*

Most corporate bonds are debenture bonds. A debenture bond is backed only by the "full faith and credit" of the issuing corporation. No specific assets are pledged as security. Investors in debentures usually have the same standing as the firm's other general creditors.

> **FINANCIAL Reporting Case**
>
> Q1, p. 773

So in case of bankruptcy, debenture holders won't have priority over other general creditors. An exception is the subordinated debenture, which is not entitled to receive any liquidation payments until the claims of other specified debt issues are satisfied.

A mortgage bond, on the other hand, is backed by a lien on specified real estate owned by the issuer. Because a mortgage bond is considered less risky than debentures, it typically will command a lower interest rate. Alternatively, a bond might be "secured" by non-real estate assets in which case, if in the event the issuer does not pay the holder as promised, the holder has rights to take specified assets belonging to the issuer such as items of property, plant, and equipment.

Today most corporate bonds are registered bonds. Interest checks are mailed directly to the owner of the bond, whose name is registered with the issuing company. Years ago, it was typical for bonds to be structured as coupon bonds (sometimes called *bearer bonds*). The name of the owner of a coupon bond was not registered. Instead, to collect interest on a coupon bond the holder actually clipped an attached coupon and redeemed it in accordance with instructions in the indenture. A carryover effect of this practice is that we still sometimes see the term *coupon rate* in reference to the stated interest rate on bonds.

Most corporate bonds are callable (or redeemable). The call feature allows the issuing company to buy back, or call, outstanding bonds from bondholders before their scheduled maturity date. This feature affords the company some protection against being stuck with relatively high-cost debt in the event interest rates fall during the period before maturity. The call price must be prespecified and often exceeds the bond's face amount (a call premium), sometimes declining as maturity is approached.

**FINANCIAL
Reporting Case**

Q2, p. 773

For example, a 2017 news release of Mueller Industries included this disclosure:

The Debentures will be callable at the option of our company, in whole or in part, at any time or from time to time, subject to declining call premiums during the first five years.

Real World Financials

"No call" provisions usually prohibit calls during the first few years of a bond's life. Very often, calls are mandatory. That is, the corporation may be required to redeem the bonds on a prespecified, year-by-year basis. Bonds requiring such sinking fund redemptions often are labeled *sinking fund debentures*.

Mandatory sinking fund redemptions retire a bond issue gradually over its term to maturity.

Serial bonds provide a more structured (and less popular) way to retire bonds on a piecemeal basis. Serial bonds are retired in installments during all or part of the life of the issue. Each bond has its own specified maturity date. So for a typical 30-year serial issue, 25 to 30 separate maturity dates might be assigned to specific portions of the bond issue.

Convertible bonds are retired as a consequence of bondholders choosing to convert them into shares of stock. We look closer at convertible bonds a little later in the chapter.

Recording Bonds at Issuance

Bonds represent a liability to the corporation that issues the bonds and an asset to an investor who buys the bonds as an investment. Each side of the transaction is the mirror image of the other.[1] This is demonstrated in Illustration 14–1.

● LO14–2

Most bonds these days are issued on the day they are dated (date printed in the indenture contract). On rare occasions, there may be a delay in issuing bonds that causes them to be issued between interest dates, in which case the interest that has accrued since the day they are dated is added to the price of the bonds. We discuss this infrequent event in Appendix 14A to this chapter.

Determining the Selling Price

The price of a bond issue at any particular time is not necessarily equal to its face amount. The $700,000, 12% bond issue in the previous illustration, for example, may sell for more than face amount (at a premium) or less than face amount (at a discount), depending on

**FINANCIAL
Reporting Case**

Q3, p. 773

---

[1]You should recall from Chapter 12 that investments in bonds that are to be held to maturity by the investor are reported at amortized cost, which is the method described here. However, also remember that investments in debt securities *not* to be held to maturity are reported at the fair value of the securities held, as described in Chapter 12, with the interest determined by the effective interest method.

Illustration 14–1

Bonds Sold at Face Amount

On January 1, 2021, Masterwear Industries issued $700,000 of 12% bonds.
- Interest of $42,000 is payable semiannually on June 30 and December 31.
- The bonds mature in three years (an unrealistically short maturity to shorten the illustration).
- The entire bond issue was sold at the face amount.
- United Intergroup, Inc., the sole investor in the bonds, planned to hold the bonds to their maturity.

At Issuance (January 1)

Masterwear (Issuer)

Cash	700,000	
Bonds payable (face amount)		700,000

United (Investor)

Investment in bonds (face amount)	700,000	
Cash		700,000

how the 12% *stated* interest rate compares with the prevailing *market* or *effective rate* of interest (for securities of similar risk and maturity). For instance, if the 12% bonds are competing in a market in which similar bonds are providing a 14% return, the bonds could be sold only at a price less than $700,000. On the other hand, if the market rate is only 10%, the 12% stated rate would seem relatively attractive and the bonds would sell at a premium over face amount. The reason the stated rate often differs from the market rate, resulting in a *discount* or *premium,* is the inevitable delay between the date the terms of the issue are established and the date the issue comes to market.

In addition to the characteristic terms of a bond agreement as specified in the indenture, the market rate for a specific bond issue is influenced by the creditworthiness of the company issuing the bonds. To evaluate the risk and quality of an individual bond issue, investors rely heavily on bond ratings provided by Standard & Poor's Corporation and by Moody's Investors Service, Inc. See the bond ratings in Illustration 14–2.

> Other things being equal, the lower the perceived riskiness of the corporation issuing bonds, the higher the price those bonds will command.

Illustration 14–2

Bond Ratings*

	S&P	Moody's
Investment Grades:		
Highest	AAA	Aaa
High	AA	Aa
Medium	A	A
Minimum investment grade	BBB	Baa
"Junk" Ratings:		
Speculative	BB	Ba
Very speculative	B	B
Default or near default	CCC	Caa
	CC	Ca
	C	C
	D	

*Adapted from Moodys.com and SPRatings.com.

> A bond issue will be priced by the marketplace to yield the market rate of interest for securities of similar risk and maturity.

Forces of supply and demand cause a bond issue to be *priced to yield the market rate.* In other words, an investor paying that price will earn an effective rate of return on the investment equal to the market rate. The price is calculated as the present value of all the cash flows required of the bonds, where the discount rate used in the present value calculation is the market rate. Specifically, the price will be the *present value of the periodic cash interest payments (face amount × stated rate) plus the present value of the principal payable at maturity, both discounted at the market rate.*

Bonds priced at a discount are described in Illustration 14–3.

On January 1, 2021, Masterwear Industries issued $700,000 of 12% bonds, dated January 1.

- Interest of $42,000 is payable semiannually on June 30 and December 31.
- The bonds mature in three years.
- The market yield for bonds of similar risk and maturity is 14%.
- United Intergroup, Inc. purchased the entire bond issue, planning to hold the bonds until maturity.

Calculation of the Price of the Bonds

		Present Values
Interest	$ 42,000 × 4.76654* =	$200,195
Principal (face amount)	$700,000 × 0.66634† =	466,438
Present value (price) of the bonds		$666,633

*Present value of an ordinary annuity of $1: $n = 6$, $i = 7\%$ (Table 4).
†Present value of $1: $n = 6$, $i = 7\%$ (Table 2).
Because interest is paid semiannually, the present value calculations use: (a) one-half the stated rate (6%) to determine cash payments, (b) one-half the market rate (7%) as the discount rate, and (c) six (3 × 2) semiannual periods.
Note: Present value tables are provided at the end of this textbook. If you need to review the concept of the time value of money, refer to the discussions in Chapter 5.
Rounding: Because present value tables truncate decimal places, the solution may be slightly different if you use a calculator or Excel.

Illustration 14–3

Bonds Sold at a Discount

Using a calculator:
Enter: N 6 I 7
PMT – 42000
FV – 700000
Output: PV 666,634

Using Excel, enter:
=PV(.07,6,–42000,
–700000)
Output: 666,634

Bonds Issued at a Discount

The calculation is illustrated in Illustration 14–4.

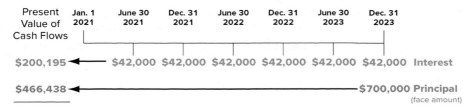

| Present Value of Cash Flows | Jan. 1 2021 | June 30 2021 | Dec. 31 2021 | June 30 2022 | Dec. 31 2022 | June 30 2023 | Dec. 31 2023 |

$200,195 ◄——— $42,000 $42,000 $42,000 $42,000 $42,000 $42,000 Interest

$466,438 ◄————————————————————————————— $700,000 Principal
(face amount)

$666,633 Present value of interest and principal

Illustration 14–4

Cash Flows from a Bond Issue at a Discount

Although the cash flows total $952,000, the present value of those future cash flows as of January 1, 2021, is only $666,633. This is due to the time value of money. These bonds are issued at a discount because the present value of the cash flows is less than the face amount of the bonds.

Masterwear (Issuer)		
Cash (price calculated above)	666,633	
Discount on bonds payable (difference)	33,367	
Bonds payable (face amount)		700,000
United (Investor)		
Investment in bonds (face amount)	700,000	
Discount on investment in bonds (difference)		33,367
Cash (price calculated above)		666,633

Journal Entries at Issuance—Bonds Issued at a Discount

Note: A sometimes-used alternative way to record bonds is the "net method," shown next, in which the discount is included directly in the book value.

Masterwear (Issuer)		
Cash	666,633	
Bonds payable		666,633
United (Investor)		
Investment in bonds	666,633	
Cash		666,633

When bond prices are quoted in financial media, they typically are stated in terms of a percentage of face amounts. Thus, a price quote of 98 means one $1,000 bond will sell for $980; a bond priced at 101 will sell for $1,010.

In one of the largest U.S. corporate bond issuances in history, CVS Health Corporation issued $40,000,000,000 in bonds in 2018. CVS issued the 2.75% bonds to raise funds to pay for its acquisition of Aetna Inc. The bonds were priced at 95.97 to provide an annual yield of 3.75%.

Determining Interest—Effective Interest Method

The *effective interest* on debt is the market rate of interest multiplied by the outstanding balance of the debt.

Interest accrues on an outstanding debt at a constant percentage of the debt each period. Of course, under the concept of accrual accounting, the periodic effective interest is not affected by the time at which the cash interest actually is paid. Recording interest each period as the *effective market rate of interest multiplied by the outstanding balance of the debt* (during the interest period) is referred to as the effective interest method. Although giving this a label—the effective interest method—implies some specialized procedure, this simply is an application of the accrual concept, consistent with accruing all expenses as they are incurred.

Continuing our example, we determined that the amount of debt when the bonds are issued is $666,633. Since the effective interest rate is 14%, interest recorded (as expense to the issuer and revenue to the investor) for the first six-month interest period is $46,664:

$$\underset{\text{Outstanding balance}}{\$666,633} \times \underset{\text{Effective rate}}{(14\% \div 2)} = \underset{\text{Effective interest}}{\$46,664}$$

However, the bond indenture calls for semiannual interest payments of only $42,000—the *stated* rate (6%) times the *face amount* ($700,000). The remainder, $4,664, increases the liability and is reflected as a reduction in the discount (a contra-liability account). This is illustrated in Illustration 14–5.

Illustration 14–5

Change in Debt When Effective Interest Exceeds Cash Paid

The difference between the effective interest and the interest paid increases the existing liability.

| | Outstanding Balance | | Account Balances | | | |
			Bonds Payable (face amount)		Discount on Bonds Payable
January 1	$666,633	=	$700,000	less	$33,367
Interest accrued at 7%	46,664				
Portion of interest paid	(42,000)				(4,664)
June 30	$671,297	=	$700,000	less	$28,703

Interest expense (issuer) and revenue (investor) are calculated on the outstanding debt balance at the effective (or market) rate. Interest *paid* is the amount specified in the bond indenture—the *stated* rate times the face amount. These amounts and the change in the outstanding debt are recorded as follows:

Journal Entries—The Interest Method

The effective interest is calculated each period as the market rate times the outstanding balance of the debt during the interest period.

At the First Interest Date (June 30)

Masterwear (Issuer)

Interest expense (effective rate × outstanding balance)	46,664	
Discount on bonds payable (difference)		4,664
Cash (stated rate × face amount)		42,000
United (Investor)		
Cash (stated rate × face amount)	42,000	
Discount on investment in bonds (difference)	4,664	
Interest revenue (effective rate × outstanding balance)		46,664

In this example and others in the chapter we look at the investor's entries as well as the issuer's to see both sides of the same transactions.

Because the balance of the debt changes each period, the dollar amount of interest (balance × rate) also will change each period. To keep up with the changing amounts, it usually is convenient to prepare a schedule that reflects the changes in the debt over its term to maturity. An amortization schedule for the situation under discussion is shown in Illustration 14–6.

Date	Cash Interest	Effective Interest	Increase in Balance	Outstanding Balance
	(6% × Face amount)	(7% × Outstanding balance)	(Discount reduction)	
1/1/21				666,633
6/30/21	42,000	0.07 (666,633) = 46,664	4,664	671,297
12/31/21	42,000	0.07 (671,297) = 46,991	4,991	676,288
6/30/22	42,000	0.07 (676,288) = 47,340	5,340	681,628
12/31/22	42,000	0.07 (681,628) = 47,714	5,714	687,342
6/30/23	42,000	0.07 (687,342) = 48,114	6,114	693,456
12/31/23	42,000	0.07 (693,456) = 48,544*	6,544	700,000
	252,000		**285,367**	**33,367**

*Rounded

Illustration 14–6
Amortization Schedule—Discount

Amounts for the journal entries each interest date are found in the second, third, and fourth columns of the schedule. The essential point to remember is that the effective interest method is a straightforward application of the accrual concept, whereby interest expense (or revenue) is accrued periodically at the effective rate. We record that amount of interest expense or revenue accrued even though the cash interest is a different amount.

Determining interest in this manner has a convenient side effect. It results in reporting the liability at the present value of future cash payments—the appropriate valuation method for any liability. This is obvious at issuance; we actually calculated the present value to be $666,633. What perhaps is not quite as obvious is that the outstanding amount of debt each subsequent period (shown in the right-hand column of the amortization schedule) is still the present value of the remaining cash flows, discounted at the original rate. The outstanding amount of the debt is its book value, sometimes called carrying value or carrying amount, which is the face amount minus the balance in the discount.

Before moving on, notice some key characteristics of the amortization schedule. As mentioned earlier, the unpaid interest each period ($4,664 the first period) adds to the balance. Since this happens each period, the balance continually increases, eventually becoming the face amount at maturity. Conveniently, that's the amount to be paid at maturity. Also, because the balance increases each period, so does the effective interest. That's because effective interest is the same percentage rate times a higher balance each period.

The balance continually increases, eventually becoming the face amount at maturity.

Now look at the column totals. The total interest expense (from the issuer's perspective) is equal to the sum of the total cash interest plus the total change in the balance (the discount). One way we might view this is to say the total interest paid ($285,367) is the $252,000 cash interest paid during the term to maturity plus the "extra" amount paid at maturity. That $33,367 amount is extra in the sense that, by selling the bonds, we borrow $666,633 but must repay $700,000 at maturity. That's why the effective interest on the bonds is 14% even though the cash interest is only 12% annually; the extra interest at maturity makes up the difference.

Additional Consideration

Although the reported amount each period is the present value of the bonds, at any date after issuance this amount is not necessarily equal to the market value (fair value) of the bonds. This is because the market rate of interest will not necessarily remain the same as the rate implicit in the original issue price (the effective rate). Of course, for negotiable financial instruments, the issue price is the market price at any given time. Differences between market values and present values based on the original rate are holding gains and losses. If we were to use the market rate to revalue bonds on each reporting date—that is, recalculate the present value using the market rate—the reported amount always would be the market value. As we will see later, companies have the option to report their liabilities at fair value.

780   SECTION 3   Liabilities and Shareholders' Equity

Zero-Coupon Bonds

A zero-coupon bond pays no interest. Instead, it offers a return in the form of a "deep discount" from the face amount. For illustration, let's look at the zero-coupon bonds issued by Coca Cola Enterprises. One billion, nine hundred one million dollars face amount of the 25-year securities issued for two hundred forty-one million dollars. As the amortization schedule in Illustration 14–7 demonstrates, they were priced to yield 8.5%.[2]

Illustration 14–7

Zero-Coupon Securities—
Coca Cola Enterprises

Real World Financials

($ in millions)	Cash Interest	Effective Interest		Increase in Balance	Outstanding Balance
	(0% × Face amount)	(8.5% × Outstanding debt)		(Discount reduction)	
					247
1995	0	0.085 (247) =	21	21	268
1996	0	0.085 (268) =	23	23	291
1997	0	0.085 (291) =	25	25	316
◆	◆	◆		◆	◆
◆	◆	◆		◆	◆
◆	◆	◆		◆	◆
2019	0	0.085 (1,614) =	137	137	1,751
2020	0	0.085 (1,751) =	149	149	1,900
			1,653	1,653	

Source: Coca Cola Enterprises.

Zero-coupon bonds provide us with a convenient opportunity to reinforce a key concept we just learned: that we accrue the interest expense (or revenue) each period at the effective rate regardless of how much cash interest actually is paid (zero in this case). An advantage of issuing zero-coupon bonds or notes is that the corporation can deduct for tax purposes the annual interest expense (see schedule) but has no related cash outflow until the bonds mature. However, the reverse is true for investors in "zeros." Investors receive no periodic cash interest, even though annual interest revenue is reportable for tax purposes. So those who invest in zero-coupon bonds usually have tax-deferred or tax-exempt status, such as pension funds, individual retirement accounts (IRAs), and charitable organizations. Zero-coupon bonds and notes have popularity but still constitute a relatively small proportion of corporate debt.

Bonds Issued at a Premium

In Illustration 14–3, Masterwear Industries sold the bonds at a price that would yield an effective rate higher than the stated rate. The result was a discount. On the other hand, if the 12% bonds had been issued when the market yield for bonds of similar risk and maturity was *lower* than the stated rate, say 10%, the issue would have been priced at a *premium*. Because the 12% rate would seem relatively attractive in a 10% market, the bonds would command an issue price of more than $700,000, calculated in Illustration 14–8.

Illustration 14–8

Bonds Sold at a Premium

On January 1, 2021, Masterwear Industries issued $700,000 of 12% bonds, dated January 1.
- Interest of $42,000 is payable semiannually on June 30 and December 31.
- The bonds mature in three years.
- The market yield for bonds of similar risk and maturity is 10%.
- United Intergroup, Inc. purchased the entire bond issue, planning to hold the bonds until maturity.

(continued)

---

[2]The present value of $1.901M, discounted at 8.5% for 25 years, is $247M. The bonds actually were issued in exchange for company warrants valued at $247M.

Illustration 14–8

(concluded)

Calculation of the Price of the Bonds	
	Present Values
Interest	$ 42,000 × 5.07569* = $213,179
Principal	$700,000 × 0.74622† = 522,354
Present value (price) of the bonds	$735,533

*Present value of an ordinary annuity of $1: n = 6, i = 5%.
†Present value of $1: n = 6, i = 5%.

Because interest is paid *semiannually*, the present value calculations use

a. one-half the stated rate (6%),
b. one-half the market rate (5%), and
c. 6 (3 × 2) semiannual periods.

Interest on bonds issued at a premium is determined in precisely the same manner as on bonds issued at a discount. Again, interest is the effective interest rate applied to the debt balance outstanding during each period (balance at the end of the previous interest period), and the cash paid is the stated rate times the face amount, as shown in Illustration 14–9. The difference between the two is the reduction (amortization) of the premium.

Masterwear (Issuer)

Cash (price calculated above)	735,533	
Bonds payable (face amount)		700,000
Premium on bonds payable (difference)		35,533

United (Investor)

Investment in bonds (face amount)	700,000	
Premium on investment in bonds (difference)	35,533	
Cash (price calculated above)		735,533

Journal Entries at Issuance—Bonds Sold at Premium

Illustration 14–9

Amortization Schedule—Premium

Date	Cash Interest	Effective Interest	Decrease in Balance	Outstanding Balance
	(6% × Face amount)	(5% × Outstanding balance)	(Premium reduction)	
1/1/21				735,533
6/30/21	42,000	0.05 (735,533) = 36,777	5,223	730,310
12/31/21	42,000	0.05 (730,310) = 36,516	5,484	724,826
6/30/22	42,000	0.05 (724,826) = 36,241	5,759	719,067
12/31/22	42,000	0.05 (719,067) = 35,953	6,047	713,020
6/30/23	42,000	0.05 (713,020) = 35,651	6,349	706,671
12/31/23	42,000	0.05 (706,671) = 35,329*	6,671	700,000
	252,000	**216,467**	**35,533**	

*Rounded

Since *more* cash is paid each period than the effective interest, the debt outstanding is reduced by the overpayment.

Notice that the debt declines each period. As the premium is reduced by amortization, the book value of the bonds declines toward face value. This is because the effective interest each period is less than the cash interest paid. Remember, this is precisely the opposite of when the bonds are at a discount, when the effective interest each period is more than the cash paid. As the discount is reduced by amortization, the book value of the bonds increases toward face value. This is illustrated in Illustration 14–10.

In practice, corporate bonds rarely are issued at a premium.[3] Because of the delay between the date the terms of the bonds are established and when the bonds are issued, it's difficult to set the stated rate equal to the ever-changing market rate. Knowing that, for marketing reasons, companies deliberately set the terms to more likely create a small discount rather than a premium at the issue date. Some investors are psychologically prone to prefer buying at a discount rather than a premium even if the yield is the same (the market rate).

Whether bonds are issued at a premium or a discount, the outstanding balance becomes the face amount at maturity.

[3]Only about 1% of corporate bonds are issued at a premium. D. Amiram, A. Kalay, and B Ozel, "The Bond Discount Puzzle," *Financial Accounting eJournal,* March 25, 2013.

782   SECTION 3   Liabilities and Shareholders' Equity

Illustration 14–10

Premium and Discount
Amortization Compared

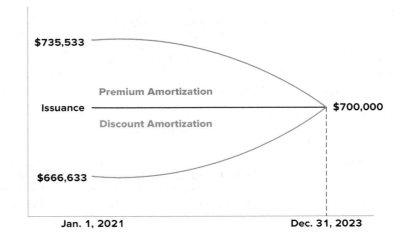

$$\text{\$735,533}$$

Premium Amortization

Issuance ———————————————— **$700,000**

Discount Amortization

$666,633

Jan. 1, 2021   Dec. 31, 2023

Additional Consideration

The preceding illustrations describe bonds sold at a discount and at a premium. The same concepts apply to bonds sold at face amount. But some of the procedures would be unnecessary. For instance, calculating the present value of the interest and the principal always will give us the face amount when the effective rate and the stated rate are the same:

Calculation of the Price of the Bonds

	Present Values
Interest	$ 42,000 × 4.91732* = $206,528
Principal	$700,000 × 0.70496† = 493,472
Present value (price) of the bonds	$700,000

*Present value of an ordinary annuity of $1: $n = 6$, $i = 6\%$.
†Present value of $1: $n = 6$, $i = 6\%$.

When Financial Statements are Prepared between Interest Dates

Any interest that has accrued since the last interest date must be recorded by an adjusting entry prior to preparing financial statements.

When an accounting period ends between interest dates, it is necessary to record interest that has accrued since the last interest date. As an example, refer again to Illustration 14–3. If the fiscal years of Masterwear and United end on October 31 and interest was last paid and recorded on June 30, four months' interest must be accrued in a year-end adjusting entry. Because interest is recorded for only a portion of a semiannual period, amounts recorded are simply the amounts shown in the amortization schedule (Illustration 14–6) times the appropriate fraction of the semiannual period (in this case ⁴⁄₆).

Adjusting Entries—To Accrue Interest

To avoid understating interest in the financial statements, four months' interest is recorded at the end of the reporting period.

At October 31		
Masterwear (Issuer)		
Interest expense (⁴⁄₆ × 46,991)...	31,327	
Discount on bonds payable (⁴⁄₆ × 4,991).............................		3,327
Interest payable (⁴⁄₆ × 42,000)...		28,000
United (Investor)		
Interest receivable (⁴⁄₆ × 42,000).......................................	28,000	
Discount on investment in bonds (⁴⁄₆ × 4,991)	3,327	
Interest revenue (⁴⁄₆ × 46,991)...		31,327

Two months later, when semiannual interest is paid next, the remainder of the interest is allocated to the first two months of the next fiscal year—November and December:

At the December 31 Interest Date		
Masterwear (Issuer)		
Interest expense ($\frac{2}{6}$ × 46,991)	15,664	
Interest payable (from adjusting entry)	28,000	
Discount on bonds payable ($\frac{2}{6}$ × 4,991)		1,664
Cash (stated rate × face amount)		42,000

United (Investor)		
Cash (stated rate × face amount)	42,000	
Discount on investment in bonds ($\frac{2}{6}$ × 4,991)	1,664	
Interest receivable (from adjusting entry)		28,000
Interest revenue ($\frac{2}{6}$ × 46,991)		15,664

Of the six months' interest paid December 31, only the November and December interest is expensed in the new fiscal year.

The Straight-Line Method—A Practical Expediency

In some circumstances, the profession permits an exception to the conceptually appropriate method of determining interest for bond issues. A company is allowed to determine interest indirectly by allocating a discount or a premium equally to each period over the term to maturity—if doing so produces results that are not materially different from the usual (and preferable) interest method. The decision should be guided by whether the straight-line method would tend to mislead investors and creditors in the particular circumstance.

By the straight-line method, the discount in Illustration 14–3 and Illustration 14–6 would be allocated equally to the six semiannual periods (three years):

$$\$33,367 \div 6 \text{ periods} = \$5,561 \text{ per period}$$

At Each of the Six Interest Dates		
Masterwear (Issuer)		
Interest expense (to balance)	47,561	
Discount on bonds payable (discount ÷ 6 periods)		5,561
Cash (stated rate × face amount)		42,000
United (Investor)		
Cash (stated rate × face amount)	42,000	
Discount on bond investment (discount ÷ 6 periods)	5,561	
Interest revenue (to balance)		47,561

Journal Entries—Straight-Line Method

By the straight-line method, interest (expense and revenue) is a plug figure, resulting from calculating the amount of discount reduction.

Allocating the discount or premium equally over the life of the bonds by the straight-line method results in a constant dollar amount of interest each period. An amortization schedule, then, would serve little purpose. For example, if we prepared one for the straight-line method in this situation, it would provide the same amounts each period as shown in Illustration 14–11.

	Cash Interest	**Recorded Interest**	**Increase in Balance**	**Outstanding Balance**
	(6% × Face amount)	(Cash + Discount reduction)	($33,367 ÷ 6)	
1/1/21				666,633
6/30/21	42,000	(42,000 + 5,561) = 47,561	5,561	672,194
12/31/21	42,000	(42,000 + 5,561) = 47,561	5,561	677,755
6/30/22	42,000	(42,000 + 5,561) = 47,561	5,561	683,316
12/31/22	42,000	(42,000 + 5,561) = 47,561	5,561	688,877
6/30/23	42,000	(42,000 + 5,561) = 47,561	5,561	694,438
12/31/23	42,000	(42,000 + 5,561) = 47,561	5,561	700,000*
	252,000	285,366	33,366	

*Rounded

Illustration 14–11

Amortization Schedule—Straight-Line Method

By the straight-line method, the amount of the discount to be reduced periodically is calculated, and the recorded interest is the plug figure.

784   SECTION 3   Liabilities and Shareholders' Equity

Determining interest by allocating the discount (or premium) on a straight-line basis is a practical expediency permitted in some situations by the materiality concept.

Remember, constant dollar amounts are not produced when the effective interest method is used. By that method, the dollar amounts of interest vary over the term to maturity because the percentage rate of interest remains constant but is applied to a changing debt balance.

Also, be sure to realize that the straight-line method is not an alternative method of determining interest in a conceptual sense. Instead, it is an application of the materiality concept, by which an appropriate application of GAAP (e.g., the effective interest method) can be bypassed for reasons of practical expediency in situations when doing so has no material effect on the results. Based on the frequency with which the straight-line method is used in practice, we can infer that managers very frequently conclude that its use has no material impact on investors' decisions.

Concept Review Exercise

ISSUING BONDS AND RECORDING INTEREST

On January 1, 2021, the Meade Group issued $8,000,000 of 11% bonds, dated January 1. Interest is payable semiannually on June 30 and December 31. The bonds mature in four years. The market yield for bonds of similar risk and maturity is 10%.

Required:
1. Determine the price these bonds issued to yield the 10% market rate and record their issuance by the Meade Group.
2. Prepare an amortization schedule that determines interest at the effective rate and record interest on the first interest date, June 30, 2021.

Solution
1. Determine the price these bonds sold for to yield the 10% market rate and record their issuance by the Meade Group.

Calculation of the Price of the Bonds

There are eight semiannual periods and one-half the market rate is 5%.

Interest	$ 440,000 × 6.46321* = $2,843,812
Principal	$ 8,000,000 × 0.67684† = 5,414,720
Present value (price) of the bonds	$8,258,532

*Present value of an ordinary annuity of $1: $n = 8, i = 5\%$.
†Present value of $1: $n = 8, i = 5\%$.

Journal Entries at Issuance

Cash (price calculated above)	8,258,532	
Bonds payable (face amount)		8,000,000
Premium on bonds payable (difference)		258,532

2. Prepare an amortization schedule that determines interest at the effective rate and record interest on the first interest date, June 30, 2021.

Amortization Schedule

Date	Cash Interest (5.5% × Face amount)	Effective Interest (5% × Outstanding balance)	Decrease in Balance (Premium reduction)	Outstanding Balance
1/1/21				8,258,532
6/30/21	440,000	0.05 (8,258,532) = 412,927	27,073	8,231,459
12/31/21	440,000	0.05 (8,231,459) = 411,573	28,427	8,203,032
6/30/22	440,000	0.05 (8,203,032) = 410,152	29,848	8,173,184
12/31/22	440,000	0.05 (8,173,184) = 408,659	31,341	8,141,843
6/30/23	440,000	0.05 (8,141,843) = 407,092	32,908	8,108,935
12/31/23	440,000	0.05 (8,108,935) = 405,447	34,553	8,074,382
6/30/24	440.000	0.05 (8,074,382) = 403,719	36,281	8,038,101
12/31/24	440,000	0.05 (8,038,101) = 401,899*	38,101	8,000,000
	3,520,000	3,261,468	258,532	

More cash is paid each period than the effective interest, so the debt outstanding is reduced by the "overpayment."

*Rounded

Interest expense (5% × $8,258,532)	412,927	
Premium on bonds payable (difference)	27,073	
Cash (5.5% × $8,000,000)		440,000

To record interest for six months.

Debt Issue Costs

Rather than sell bonds directly to the public, corporations usually sell an entire issue to an underwriter who then resells them to other security dealers and the public. By committing to purchase bonds at a set price, investment banks such as JPMorgan Chase and Goldman Sachs are said to underwrite any risks associated with a new issue. The underwriting fee is the spread between the price the underwriter pays and the resale price.

Alternatively, the issuing company may choose to sell the debt securities directly to a single investor (as we assumed in previous illustrations)—often a pension fund or an insurance company. This is referred to as *private placement*. Issue costs are less because privately placed securities are not subject to the costly and lengthy process of registering with the SEC that is required of public offerings. Underwriting fees also are avoided.[4]

When issuing bonds or notes, the issuing company will incur costs, such as legal and accounting fees, printing costs, and registration and underwriting fees. These costs are recorded by combining them with any discount (or subtracting them from any premium) on the debt. The combined valuation account is reported in the balance sheet as a direct deduction from the liability and then amortized over the life of the debt.[5]

> Costs of issuing debt securities are called "debt issue costs" and are accounted for the same way as bond discount.

This approach has the appeal of reflecting the effect that debt issue costs have on the effective interest rate. Debt issue costs reduce the cash proceeds from the issuance of debt, so it makes sense that they should reflect a higher cost of borrowing. By deducting debt issue costs, we lower the carrying amount of the debt, which effectively increases the interest rate on that debt. In other words, with debt issue costs, the net amount borrowed is less, but interest payments are the same, so the effective rate of borrowing is higher.

For example, let's assume that in Illustration 14–11, we had debt issue costs of $14,000. The debt issue costs reduce the net cash the issuing company receives from the issuance of the bonds. The entry for the issuance would reflect the lower net cash proceeds and the higher valuation account for the discount and the debt issue costs:

Masterwear (Issuer)

Cash ($666,633 price minus $14,000 issue costs)	652,633	
Discount and debt issue costs (difference)	47,367	
Bonds payable (face amount)		700,000

> The price discount and the debt issue costs reduce the cash proceeds from the issuance of the bonds.

Interest expense is determined in the usual way; that is, the effective interest rate times the outstanding balance. The outstanding balance is the "net" liability, the face amount reduced by the discount and debt issue costs ($652,633 for the first interest period).[6] The debt issue costs of $14,000 have the effect of increasing the effective rate from 7% semiannually (as in Illustration 14–4) to 7.4389% semiannually (rounded). To see how the effective rate is determined, see the next Additional Consideration box. The first semiannual interest payment would be recorded as follows:

Interest expense ($652,633 × 7.4389%)	48,549	
Discount and debt issue costs (difference)		6,549
Cash ($700,000 × 6% stated rate)		42,000

The corporate bond is the basic long-term debt instrument for most large companies. But for many firms, the debt instrument often used is a *note*. We discuss notes next.

---

[4]Rule 144A of the Securities Act of 1933, as amended, allows for the private resale of unregistered securities to "qualified institutional buyers," which are generally large institutional investors with assets exceeding $100 million.

[5]Accounting Standards Update 2015-03: "Interest—Imputation of Interest (Subtopic 835-30) Simplifying the Presentation of Debt Issuance Costs," FASB, April 2015. This approach is consistent with the treatment of issue costs when equity securities are sold. You will see in Chapter 18 that the effect of share issue costs is to reduce the amount credited to stock accounts. It also is consistent with IFRS.

[6]If we have a premium instead of a discount, the valuation account is the premium reduced by the debt issue costs.

Additional Consideration

One important effect of the debt issue costs is that they reduce the amount of cash Masterwear is borrowing with the bond issuance (from $666,633 to $652,633). A lower (net) amount is borrowed at the same cost, making the *effective* interest rate higher than it would be without the debt issue costs. Previously, in Illustration 14–4 when we had no debt issue costs, the effective (market) rate was 14% (7% semiannually). That was the discount rate that caused the present value of the six interest payments and the maturity amount of $700,000 to be $666,633. Now, though, the effective rate is the one that would cause the present value of the six interest payments and the maturity amount of $700,000 to be $652,633. That annual rate is 14.8778% instead of 14%, and thus is a semiannual rate of 7.4389%, up from 7%. The following amortization schedule demonstrates this:

Cash Payments	Effective Interest		Increase or (decrease) in Balance	Outstanding Balance
6.0%	7.4389% × Balance			
				652,633
42,000	7.4389% × 652,633	= 48,549	6,549	659,182
42,000	7.4389% × 659,182	= 49,036	7,036	666,218
42,000	7.4389% × 666,218	= 49,559	7,559	673,777
42,000	7.4389% × 673,777	= 50,122	8,122	681,898
42,000	7.4389% × 681,898	= 50,726	8,726	690,624
42,000	7.4389% × 690,624	= 51,376	9,376	700,000

You should note that the balance in the last column of the schedule is the amount reported in the balance sheet for the bonds, reduced by both the discount and debt issue costs.

PART B

● LO14–3

FINANCIAL Reporting Case

Q4, p. 773

Long-Term Notes

When a company borrows cash from a bank and signs a promissory note, the firm's loan liability is reported as a *note payable.* Or a note might be issued in exchange for a noncash asset—perhaps to purchase equipment on credit. In concept, notes are accounted for in precisely the same way as bonds. In fact, we could properly substitute notes payable for bonds payable in each of our previous illustrations. For comparison, we continue to also present the lenders' entries (in blue) in the illustrations to follow.

As we discuss accounting for the borrower's notes *payable,* we also will consider the lender's perspective and look at notes *receivable* at the same time. By considering both sides of each transaction at the same time, we will see that the two sides are essentially mirror images of one another. This coverage of long-term notes complements our Chapter 7 discussion of *short-term* notes receivable.

Note Issued for Cash

The interest rate stated in a note is likely to be equal to the market rate because the rate usually is negotiated at the time of the loan. So discounts and premiums are less likely for notes than for bonds. Accounting for a note issued for cash is demonstrated in Illustration 14–12.

Note Exchanged for Assets or Services

Occasionally the *stated* interest rate is not indicative of the *market* rate at the time a note is negotiated. The value of the asset (cash or noncash) or service exchanged for the note establishes the market rate.[7] For example, let's assume Skill Graphics purchased a package-labeling machine from Hughes–Barker Corporation by issuing a 12%, $700,000, three-year note that requires interest to be paid semiannually. Let's also assume that the machine could have been purchased at a cash price of $666,633. You probably recognize this numerical situation as the one used earlier to illustrate bonds sold at a discount (Illustration 14–3).

---

[7]If the debt instrument is negotiable and a dependable exchange price is readily available, the market value of the debt may be better evidence of the value of the transaction than the value of a noncash asset, particularly if it has no established cash selling price. The value of the asset or the debt, whichever is considered more reliable, should be used to record the transaction.

Illustration 14–12
Note Issued for Cash

On January 1, 2021, Skill Graphics, Inc., a product-labeling and graphics firm, borrowed $700,000 cash from First BancCorp and issued a three-year, $700,000 promissory note. Interest of $42,000 was payable semiannually on June 30 and December 31.

At Issuance

Skill Graphics (Borrower)

Cash..	700,000	
Notes payable (face amount)...		700,000

First BancCorp (Lender)

Notes receivable (face amount)..	700,000	
Cash..		700,000

At Each of the Six Interest Dates

Skill Graphics (Borrower)

Interest expense...	42,000	
Cash (stated rate × face amount)		42,000

First BancCorp (Lender)

Cash (stated rate × face amount)...	42,000	
Interest revenue		42,000

At Maturity

Skill Graphics (Borrower)

Notes payable	700,000	
Cash (face amount)...		700,000

First BancCorp (Lender)

Cash (face amount)	700,000	
Notes receivable		700,000

Reference to the earlier example will confirm that exchanging this $700,000 note for a machine with a cash price of $666,633 implies an annual market rate of interest of 14%. That is, 7% is one-half the discount rate that yields a present value of $666,633 for the note's cash flows (interest plus principal):

Present Values

Interest	$ 42,000 × 4.76654* = $200,195
Principal	$700,000 × 0.66634† = 466,438
Present value of the note	$666,633

*Present value of an ordinary annuity of $1: $n = 6$, $i = 7\%$.
†Present value of $1: $n = 6$, $i = 7\%$.

This is referred to as the **implicit rate of interest**—the rate implicit in the agreement. It may be that the implicit rate is not apparent. Sometimes the value of the asset (or service) is not readily determinable, but the interest rate stated in the transaction is unrealistic relative to the rate that would be expected in a similar transaction under similar circumstances. Deciding what the appropriate rate should be is called *imputing* an interest rate.

For example, suppose the machine exchanged for the 12% note is custom-made for Skill Graphics so that no customary cash price is available with which to work backwards to find the implicit rate. In that case, the appropriate rate would have to be found externally. It might be determined, for instance, that a more realistic interest rate for a transaction of this type, at this time, would be 14%. Then it would be apparent that Skill Graphics actually paid less than $700,000 for the machine and that part of the face amount of the note in effect makes up for the lower than normal interest rate. You learned early in your study of accounting that the economic essence of a transaction should prevail over its outward appearance. In keeping with this basic precept, the accountant should look beyond the *form* of this transaction and record its *substance*. The amount actually paid for the machine is the present value of the cash flows called for by the loan agreement, discounted at the market rate—imputed in this case to be 14%. So both the asset acquired and the liability used to purchase it should be recorded at the real cost, $666,633.

A basic concept of accounting is *substance over form.*

Additional Consideration

For another example, let's assume the more realistic interest rate for a transaction of this type is, say, 16%. In that case we would calculate the real cost of the machine by finding the present value of both the interest and the principal, discounted at half the 16% rate (because interest is paid semiannually):

	Present Values
Interest	$ \ 42,000 \times 4.62288^* = \$194,161$
Principal	$\$700,000 \times 0.63017^\dagger = \ \ 441,119$
Present value of the note	$\$635,280$

*Present value of an ordinary annuity of $1: $n = 6$, $i = 8\%$.
†Present value of $1: $n = 6$, $i = 8\%$.

Both the asset acquired and the liability used to purchase it would be recorded at $635,280.

The accounting treatment is the same whether the amount is determined directly from the market value of the machine (and thus the note) or indirectly as the present value of the note (and thus the value of the asset):[8]

Journal Entries at Issuance—Note with Unrealistic Interest Rate

Skill Graphics (Buyer/Issuer)		
Machinery (cash price)	666,633	
Discount on notes payable (difference)	33,367	
Notes payable (face amount)		700,000
Hughes–Barker (Seller/Lender)		
Notes receivable (face amount)	700,000	
Discount on notes receivable (difference)		33,367
Sales revenue (cash price)		666,633

Note: The seller also would debit cost of goods sold and credit inventory for the amount spent to construct the machine.

Likewise, whether the effective interest rate is determined as the rate implicit in the agreement, given the asset's market value, or whether the effective rate is imputed as the appropriate interest rate if the asset's value is unknown, both parties to the transaction should record periodic interest (interest expense to the borrower, interest revenue to the lender) at the effective rate, rather than the stated rate.

Journal Entries—The Interest Method

The effective interest (expense to the issuer; revenue to the investor) is calculated each period as the effective rate times the amount of the debt outstanding during the interest period.

At the First Interest Date (June 30)		
Skill Graphics (Borrower)		
Interest expense (effective rate × outstanding balance)...........................	46,664	
Discount on notes payable (difference)..		4,664
Cash (stated rate × face amount)..		42,000
Hughes–Barker (Seller/Lender)		
Cash (stated rate × face amount)...	42,000	
Discount on notes receivable (difference)..	4,664	
Interest revenue (effective rate × outstanding balance)........................		46,664

---

[8]The method shown is the *gross method*. Alternatively, the *net method* can be used as follows:

Skill Graphics (Buyer/Issuer)		
Machinery (cas price)	666,633	
Notes payable		666,633
Hughes-Barker (Seller/Lender)		
Notes receivable	666,633	
Sales revenue (cash price)		666,633

Under the net method, the note is recorded at the face amount reduced by the discount on notes payable, which is the difference between face value and present value. As cash interest is paid, the note balance increases by the difference between the cash interest payment and the interest revenue (and interest expense). After the last payment, the note account balance will be equal to the face amount of the note.

The interest expense (interest revenue for the lender) varies as the balance of the note changes over time. See the amortization schedule in Illustration 14–13.[9] Be sure to notice that this amortization schedule is identical to the one in Illustration 14–6 for bonds issued at a discount.

Date	Cash Interest	Effective Interest	Increase in Balance	Outstanding Balance
	(6% × Face amount)	(7% × Outstanding balance)	(Discount reduction)	
1/1/21				666,633
6/30/21	42,000	0.07 (666,633) = 46,664	4,664	671,297
12/31/21	42,000	0.07 (671,297) = 46,991	4,991	676,288
6/30/22	42,000	0.07 (676,288) = 47,340	5,340	681,628
12/31/22	42,000	0.07 (681,628) = 47,714	5,714	687,342
6/30/23	42,000	0.07 (687,342) = 48,114	6,114	693,456
12/31/23	42,000	0.07 (693,456) = 48,544*	6,544	700,000
	252,000	285,367	33,367	

*Rounded

Illustration 14–13

Amortization Schedule—Note

Since less cash is paid each period than the effective interest, the unpaid difference (the discount reduction) increases the outstanding balance (book value) of the note.

Installment Notes

You may have recently purchased a car, or maybe a house. If so, unless you paid cash, you signed a note promising to pay a portion of the purchase price over, say, five years for the car, or 30 years for the house. Car and house notes usually call for payment in monthly installments rather than by a single amount at maturity. Corporations, too, often borrow using installment notes. Typically, installment payments are equal amounts each period. Each payment includes both an amount that represents interest and an amount that represents a reduction of the outstanding balance (principal reduction). The periodic reduction of the balance is sufficient that at maturity the note is completely paid. This amount is easily calculated by dividing the amount of the loan by the appropriate discount factor for the present value of an annuity. The installment payment amount that would pay the note described in the previous section is as follows:

$$\underset{\text{Amount of loan}}{\$666,633} \div \underset{\substack{\text{(from Table 4} \\ n = 6, \, i = 7.0\%)}}{4.76654} = \underset{\substack{\text{Installment} \\ \text{payment}}}{\$139,857}$$

Consider Illustration 14–14.

Date	Cash Payment	Effective Interest	Decrease in Balance	Outstanding Balance
		(7% × Outstanding balance)		
1/1/21				666,633
6/30/21	139,857	0.07 (666,633) = 46,664	93,193	573,440
12/31/21	139,857	0.07 (573,440) = 40,141	99,716	473,724
6/30/22	139,857	0.07 (473,724) = 33,161	106,696	367,028
12/31/22	139,857	0.07 (367,028) = 25,692	114,165	252,863
6/30/23	139,857	0.07 (252,863) = 17,700	122,157	130,706
12/31/23	139,857	0.07 (130,706) = 9,151*	130,706	0
	839,142	172,509	666,633	

*Rounded

Illustration 14–14

Amortization Schedule—Installment Note

Each installment payment includes interest on the outstanding debt at the effective rate. The remainder of each payment reduces the outstanding balance.

[9]The creation of amortization schedules is simplified by an electronic spreadsheet such as Microsoft Excel.

For installment notes, the outstanding balance of the note does not eventually become its face amount as it does for notes with designated maturity amounts. Instead, at the maturity date the balance is zero. The procedure is the same as for a note whose principal is paid at maturity, but for an intallment note the periodic cash payments are larger and there is no lump-sum payment at maturity. We calculated the amount of the payments so that after covering the interest on the existing debt each period, the excess would exactly amortize the installment debt balance to zero at maturity (rather than to a designated maturity amount).

Consequently, the significance is lost of maintaining separate balances for the face amount (in a note account) and the discount (or premium). So an installment note typically is recorded at its net book value in a single note payable (or receivable) account:

Journal Entries at Issuance—Installment Note

Skill Graphics (Buyer/Issuer)		
Machinery	666,633	
Notes payable		666,633
Hughes–Barker (Seller/Lender)		
Notes receivable	666,633	
Sales revenue		666,633

At the First Interest Date (June 30)		
Skill Graphics (Borrower)		
Interest expense (effective rate × outstanding balance)	46,664	
Notes payable (difference)	93,193	
Cash (installment payment calculated above)		139,857
Hughes–Barker (Seller/Lender)		
Cash (installment payment calculated above)	139,857	
Notes receivable (difference)		93,193
Interest revenue (effective rate × outstanding balance)		46,664

Each payment includes both an amount that represents interest and an amount that represents a reduction of principal.

Additional Consideration

You will learn in the next chapter that the liability associated with a lease is accounted for the same way as this installment note. In fact, if the asset described above had been leased rather than purchased, the cash payments would be designated lease payments rather than installment loan payments, and a virtually identical amortization schedule would apply.

The reason for the similarity is that we view a finance lease as being, in substance, equivalent to an installment purchase of the right to use an asset. Naturally, then, accounting treatment of the two essentially identical transactions should be consistent. Be sure to notice the parallel treatment as you study leases in the next chapter.

Concept Review Exercise

NOTE WITH AN UNREALISTIC INTEREST RATE

Cameron-Brown, Inc. constructed for Harmon Distributors a warehouse that was completed and ready for occupancy on January 2, 2021.

- Harmon paid for the warehouse by issuing a $900,000, four-year note that required 7% interest to be paid on December 31 of each year.
- The warehouse was custom-built for Harmon, so its cash price was not known.
- By comparison with similar transactions, it was determined that an appropriate interest rate was 10%.

Required:

1. Prepare the journal entry for Harmon's purchase of the warehouse on January 2, 2021.

2. Prepare (a) an amortization schedule for the four-year term of the note and (b) the journal entry for Harmon's first interest payment on December 31, 2021.
3. Suppose Harmon's note had been an installment note to be paid in four equal payments. What would be the amount of each installment if payable (a) at the end of each year, beginning December 31, 2021? or (b) at the beginning of each year, beginning on January 2, 2021?

Solution:

1. Prepare the journal entry for Harmon's purchase of the warehouse on January 2, 2021.

	Present Values	
Interest	\$ 63,000 × 3.16987* =	\$199,702
Principal	\$900,000 × 0.68301' =	614,709
Present value of the note		\$814,411

*Present value of an ordinary annuity of \$1: $n = 4, i = 10\%$.
'Present value of \$1: $n = 4, i = 10\%$.

Warehouse (price determined above)	814,411	
Discount on notes payable (difference)..	85,589	
Notes payable (face amount)..		900,000

2. Prepare (a) an amortization schedule for the four-year term of the note and (b) the journal entry for Harmon's first interest payment on December 31, 2021.

Dec. 31	Cash	Effective Interest	Increase in Balance	Outstanding Balance
	(7% × Face amount)	(10% × Outstanding balance)	(Discount reduction)	
				814,411
2021	63,000	0.10 (814,411) = 81,441	18,441	832,852
2022	63,000	0.10 (832,852) = 83,285	20,285	853,137
2023	63,000	0.10 (853,137) = 85,314	22,314	875,451
2024	63,000	0.10 (875,451) = 87,549*	24,549	900,000
	252,000	337,589	85,589	

*Rounded

Each period the unpaid interest increases the outstanding balance of the debt.

Interest expense (effective rate × outstanding balance)........................	81,441	
Discount on notes payable (difference)...		18,441
Cash (stated rate × face amount)		63,000

The effective interest is the market rate times the amount of the debt outstanding during the year.

3. Suppose Harmon's note had been an installment note to be paid in four equal payments. What would be the amount of each installment if payable (a) at the end of each year, beginning December 31, 2021? or (b) at the beginning of each year, beginning on January 2, 2021?

Because money has a time value, installment payments delayed until the end of each period must be higher than if the payments are made at the beginning of each period.

a. | \$814,411 | ÷ | 3.16987 | = | \$256,923 |
| Amount of loan | | (from Table 4 $n = 4, i = 10\%$) | | Installment payment |

b. | \$814,411 | ÷ | 3.48685 | = | \$233,566 |
| Amount of loan | | (from Table 6 $n = 4, i = 10\%$) | | Installment payment |

Financial Statement Disclosures

In the balance sheet, long-term debt (liability for the debtor; asset for the creditor) typically is reported as a single amount, net of any discount or increased by any premium, rather than at its face amount accompanied by a separate valuation account for the discount or premium. Any portion of the debt to be paid (received) during the upcoming year, or operating cycle if longer, should be reported as a current amount.

● LO14–4

Note disclosure is required of the fair value of bonds, notes, and other financial instruments.

The fair value of financial instruments must be disclosed either in the body of the financial statements or in disclosure notes.[10] These fair values are available for bonds and other securities traded on market exchanges in the form of quoted market prices. On the other hand, financial instruments not traded on market exchanges require other evidence of market value. For example, the market value of a note payable might be approximated by the present value of principal and interest payments using a current discount rate commensurate with the risks involved.

The disclosure note for debt includes the nature of the company's liabilities, interest rates, maturity dates, call provisions, conversion options, restrictions imposed by creditors, and any assets pledged as collateral. For all long-term borrowings, disclosures also should include the aggregate amounts payable for each of the next five years. To comply, **Microsoft**'s annual report for the fiscal year ended June 30, 2017, included the disclosure shown in Illustration 14–15.

Illustration 14–15

Debt Disclosures— Microsoft Corporation

Real World Financials

Maturities of our long-term debt for each of the next five years and thereafter are as follows:

Year Ending June 30,	($ in millions)
2018	$ 2,190
2019	1,698
2020	1,180
2021	1,006
2022	932
Thereafter	3,100
Total	$10,106

Source: Microsoft Corporation

Borrowing is a financing activity; lending is an investing activity.

Paying or receiving interest is an operating activity.

In a statement of cash flows, issuing bonds or notes are reported as cash flows from financing activities by the issuer (borrower) and cash flows from investing activities by the investor (lender). Similarly, as the debt is repaid, the issuer (borrower) reports a financing activity while the investor (lender) reports an investing activity. However, because both interest expense and interest revenue are components of the income statement, both parties to the transaction report interest among operating activities. We discuss the cash flow reporting process in more depth in Chapter 21.

Decision Makers' Perspective

Business decisions involve risk. Failure to properly consider risk in those decisions is one of the most costly, yet one of the most common mistakes investors and creditors can make. Long-term debt is one of the first places decision makers should look when trying to get a handle on risk.

Generally speaking, debt increases risk.

In general, debt increases risk. As an owner, debt would place you in a subordinate position relative to creditors because the claims of creditors must be satisfied first in case of liquidation. In addition, debt requires payment, usually on specific dates. Failure to pay debt interest and principal on a timely basis may result in default and perhaps even bankruptcy. The debt to equity ratio, total liabilities divided by shareholders' equity, often is calculated to measure the degree of risk. Other things being equal, the higher the debt to equity ratio, the higher the risk. The type of risk this ratio measures is called *default risk* because it presumably indicates the likelihood a company will default on its obligations.

To evaluate a firm's risk, you might start by calculating its debt to equity ratio.

Debt also can be an advantage. It can be used to enhance the return to shareholders. This concept, known as leverage, was described and illustrated in Chapter 3. If a company earns a return on borrowed funds in excess of the cost of borrowing the funds, shareholders are provided with a total return greater than what could have been earned with equity funds

---

[10]FASB ASC 825–10–50–10: Financial Instruments—Overall—Disclosure.

alone. This desirable situation is called *favorable financial leverage.* Unfortunately, leverage is not always favorable. Sometimes the cost of borrowing the funds exceeds the returns they generate. This illustrates the typical risk-return trade-off faced by shareholders.

Creditors demand interest payments as compensation for the use of their capital. Failure to pay interest as scheduled may cause several adverse consequences, including bankruptcy. Therefore, another way to measure a company's ability to pay its obligations is by comparing interest payments with income available to pay those charges. The times interest earned ratio does this by dividing income, before subtracting interest expense or income tax expense, by interest expense.

Two points about this ratio are important. First, because interest is deductible for income tax purposes, income before interest and taxes is a better indication of a company's ability to pay interest than is income after interest and taxes (i.e., net income). Second, income before interest and taxes is a rough approximation for cash flow generated from operations. The primary concern of decision makers is, of course, the cash available to make interest payments. In fact, this ratio often is computed by dividing cash flow generated from operations by interest payments.

For illustration, let's compare the ratios for Coca-Cola and PepsiCo. Illustration 14–16 provides condensed financial statements adapted from 2017 annual reports of those companies.

As a manager, you would try to create favorable financial leverage to earn a return on borrowed funds in excess of the cost of borrowing the funds.

As an external analyst or a manager, you are concerned with a company's ability to repay debt.

Illustration 14–16

Condensed Financial Statements—Coca-Cola, PepsiCo

Real World Financials

Balance Sheets	($ in millions)	
	Coca-Cola	**PepsiCo**
Assets		
Current assets	$36,545	$31,027
Property, plant, and equipment (net)	8,203	17,240
Intangibles and other assets	43,148	31,537
Total assets	$87,896	$79,804
Liabilities and Shareholders' Equity		
Current liabilities	$27,194	$20,502
Long-term liabilities	41,725	48,321
Total liabilities	68,919	68,823
Shareholders' equity	18,977	10,981
Total liabilities and shareholders' equity	$87,896	$79,804
Income Statements		
Net sales	$35,410	$63,525
Cost of goods sold	(13,256)	(28,785)
Gross profit	22,154	34,740
Operating and other expenses	(14,423)	(23,987)
Interest expense	(841)	(1,151)
Income before taxes	6,890	9,602
Tax expense	(5,607)	(4,694)
Net income	$ 1,283	$ 4,908

Source: Coca-Cola, PepsiCo

The debt to equity ratio is much higher for PepsiCo:

$$\text{Debt to equity ratio} = \frac{\text{Total liabilities}}{\text{Shareholders' equity}}$$

$$\text{Coca-Cola} = \frac{\$68,919}{\$18,977} = 3.6$$

$$\text{PepsiCo} = \frac{\$68,823}{\$10,981} = 6.3$$

The debt to equity ratio indicates the extent of trading on the equity, or financial leverage.

Remember, that's not necessarily a positive or a negative. Let's look closer. When the return on equity is greater than the return on assets, management is using debt funds to enhance the earnings for shareholders. Both firms do this. We calculate return on assets as follows:

$$\text{Rate of return on assets}^{11} = \frac{\text{Net income}}{\text{Total assets}}$$

$$\text{Coca-Cola} = \frac{\$1,283}{\$87,896} = 1.5\%$$

$$\text{PepsiCo} = \frac{\$4,908}{\$79,804} = 6.2\%$$

> The rate of return on assets indicates profitability without regard to how resources are financed.

The return on assets indicates a company's overall profitability, ignoring specific sources of financing. In this regard, PepsiCo's profitability is significantly higher than Coca-Cola's. That advantage continues when we compare the return to shareholders:

$$\text{Return on equity} = \frac{\text{Net income}}{\text{Shareholder's equity}}$$

$$\text{Coca-Cola} = \frac{\$1,283}{\$18,977} = 6.8\%$$

$$\text{PepsiCo} = \frac{\$4,908}{\$10,981} = 44.7\%$$

> The return on equity indicates the effectiveness of employing resources provided by owners.

PepsiCo's return on assets is four times larger than Coca-Cola's, and its return on equity is six times larger. The reason is that higher leverage has been used by Pepsi to provide a relatively greater return to shareholders. PepsiCo increased its return to shareholders 7.2 times (44.7%/6.2%) the return on assets. Coca-Cola increased its return to shareholders 4.5 times (6.8%/1.5%) the return on assets. Interpret this with caution, though. PepsiCo's higher leverage means higher risk as well. In down times, PepsiCo's return to shareholders will suffer proportionally more than will Coca-Cola's.

From the perspective of a creditor, we might look at which company offers the most comfortable margin of safety in terms of its ability to pay fixed interest charges:

$$\text{Times interest earned ratio} = \frac{\text{Net income plus interest plus taxes}}{\text{Interest}}$$

$$\text{Coca-Cola} = \frac{\$1,283 + \$841 + \$5,607}{\$841} = 9.2 \text{ times}$$

$$\text{PepsiCo} = \frac{\$4,908 + \$1,151 + \$4,694}{\$1,151} = 9.3 \text{ times}$$

> The times interest earned ratio indicates the margin of safety provided to creditors.

In this regard, Coca-Cola provides a much greater margin of safety. And Pepsi has more debt in its capital structure relative to Coca-Cola. However, Pepsi clearly is able to pay the cost of borrowing and provide an impressive return to its shareholders. Both firms, though, trade quite favorably on their leverage.

Liabilities also can have misleading effects on the income statement. Decision makers should look carefully at gains and losses produced by early extinguishment of debt. These have nothing to do with a company's normal operating activities. Unchecked, corporate management can be tempted to schedule debt buybacks to provide discretionary income in down years or even losses in up years to smooth income over time.

> Decision makers should be alert to gains and losses that have nothing to do with a company's normal operating activities.

Alert investors and lenders also look outside the financial statements for risks associated with "off-balance-sheet" financing and other commitments that don't show up on the face of financial statements but nevertheless expose a company to risk. Relatedly, most companies attempt to actively manage the risk associated with these and other obligations. It is important for top management to understand and closely monitor risk management strategies. Some of the financial

> Outside analysts as well as managers should actively monitor risk management activities.

[11]A more accurate way to calculate this ratio is: Rate of return on assets = Net income + Interest expense (1 − tax rate) ÷ Average total assets. The reason for adding back interest expense (net of tax) is that interest represents a return to suppliers of debt capital and should not be deducted in the computation of net income when computing the return on total assets. In other words, the numerator is the total amount of income available to both debt and equity capital.

losses that have grabbed headlines in recent years were permitted by a lack of oversight and scrutiny by senior management of companies involved. It is similarly important for investors and creditors to become informed about risks companies face and how well-equipped those companies are in managing that risk. The supplemental disclosures designed to communicate the degree of risk associated with the financial instruments we discuss in this chapter contribute to that understanding. We examine the significance of lease commitments in the next chapter. ●

Debt Retired Early, Convertible Into Stock, or Providing an Option to Buy Stock

PART C

Early Extinguishment of Debt

● LO14–5

As we saw in the previous section, debt paid in installments is systematically retired over the term to maturity so that at the designated maturity date the outstanding balance is zero. On the other hand, when a maturity amount is specified as in our earlier illustrations, any discount or premium has been systematically reduced to zero as of the maturity date and the debt is retired simply by paying the maturity amount. Sometimes, though, companies choose to retire debt before its scheduled maturity. In that case, a gain or a loss may result.

Earlier we noted that a call feature accompanies most bonds to protect the issuer against declining interest rates. Even when bonds are not callable, the issuing company can retire bonds early by purchasing them on the open market. Regardless of the method, when debt of any type is retired prior to its scheduled maturity date, the transaction is referred to as early extinguishment of debt.

To record the extinguishment, the account balances pertinent to the debt obviously must be removed from the books. Of course cash is credited for the amount paid—the call price or market price. The difference between the book value of the debt and the reacquisition price represents either a gain or a loss on the early extinguishment of debt. When the debt is retired for less than book value, the debtor is in a favorable position and records a gain. The opposite occurs for a loss. Let's continue an earlier example to illustrate the retirement of debt prior to its scheduled maturity (Illustration 14–17).

Any difference between the outstanding debt and the amount paid to retire that debt represents either a gain or a loss.

Illustration 14–17

Early Extinguishment of Debt

On January 1, 2022, Masterwear Industries called its $700,000, 12% bonds when their book value was $676,288.

- The indenture specified a call price of $685,000.
- The bonds were issued previously at a price to yield 14%.

Bonds payable (face amount)	700,000	
Loss on early extinguishment ($685,000 − $676,288)	8,712	
Discount on bonds payable ($700,000 − $676,288)		23,712
Cash (call price)		685,000

For instance, in its 2017 income statement, Waste Management, Inc. reported a $6 million loss on the early extinguishment of debt.

Convertible Bonds

FINANCIAL Reporting Case

Sometimes corporations include a convertible feature as part of a bond offering. Convertible bonds can be converted into (that is, exchanged for) shares of stock at the option of the bondholder. Among the reasons for issuing convertible bonds rather than straight debt are (a) to sell the bonds at a higher price (which means a lower effective interest cost),[12] (b) to use as a medium of exchange in mergers and acquisitions, and (c) to enable smaller firms or debt-heavy companies to obtain access to the bond market. Sometimes convertible bonds

Q5, p. 773

Convertible bonds can be exchanged for shares of stock at the option of the investor.

---

[12]Remember, there is an inverse relationship between bond prices and interest rates. When the price is higher, the rate (yield) is lower, and vice versa.

serve as an indirect way to issue stock when there is shareholder resistance to direct issuance of additional equity.

Convertible bonds have features of both debt and equity.

Central to each of these reasons for issuing convertible debt is that the conversion feature is attractive to investors. This hybrid security has features of both debt and equity. The owner has a fixed-income security that can become common stock if and when the firm's prosperity makes that feasible. This increases the investor's upside potential while limiting the downside risk. The conversion feature has monetary value. Just how valuable it is depends on both the conversion terms and market conditions. But from an accounting perspective the question raised is how to account for its value. To evaluate the question, consider Illustration 14–18.

Illustration 14–18

Convertible Bonds

> On January 1, 2021, HTL Manufacturers issued $100 million of 8% convertible debentures due 2041 at 103 (103% of face value).
> - The bonds are convertible at the option of the holder into no par common stock at a conversion ratio of 40 shares per $1,000 bond.
> - HTL recently issued nonconvertible, 20-year, 8% debentures at 98.

Because of the inseparability of their debt and equity features, the entire issue price of convertible bonds is recorded as debt, as if they are nonconvertible bonds.

It would appear that the conversion feature is valued by the market at $5 million—the difference between the market value of the convertible bonds, $103 million, and the market value of the nonconvertible bonds, $98 million. Some accountants argue that we should record the value of the conversion option in a shareholders' equity account ($5 million in this case) and the debt value in the bond accounts ($100 million bonds payable less $2 million discount). However, counter to that intuitive argument, the currently accepted practice is to record the entire issue price as debt in precisely the same way as for nonconvertible bonds.[13] Treating the features as two inseparable parts of a single security avoids the practical difficulty of trying to measure the separate values of the debt and the conversion option.

Journal Entry at Issuance—Convertible Bonds

	($ in millions)	
Cash (103% × $100 million)	103	
Convertible bonds payable (face amount)		100
Premium on bonds payable (difference)		3

The value of the conversion feature is not separately recorded.

Since we make no provision for the separate value of the conversion option, all subsequent entries, including the periodic reduction of the premium, are exactly the same as if these were nonconvertible bonds. So, the illustrations and examples of bond accounting we discussed earlier would pertain equally to nonconvertible or convertible bonds.

Additional Consideration

> While we normally don't separate the conversion option from the debt for convertible bonds, an exception is when the conversion option is deemed to be a "beneficial conversion feature." That's the case when the conversion option has a positive "intrinsic value" at the time the bonds are issued, meaning the fair value of the stock into which the bonds are convertible exceeds the face amount of the bonds.[14] Suppose, for instance, that HTL's stock in Illustration 14–18 has a fair value of $30 per share when the bonds are issued. This implies an intrinsic value of the conversion feature of $5 per share:
>
> Price per share to convert: $1,000 ÷ 40 shares = $25 per share
>
> | | |
> |---|---|
> | Fair value of stock at issue date | $30 |
> | Conversion price for shares | 25 |
> | Intrinsic value of beneficial conversion option per share | $ 5 |
>
> (continued)

---

[13]FASB ASC 470–20–25: Debt—Debt with Conversion Options—Recognition.

[14] FASB ASC 470–20–25–5: Debt—Debt with Conversion and Other Options—Recognition—Beneficial Conversion Features.

(concluded)

Intrinsic value of beneficial conversion feature:

100,000 bonds × 40 shares = 4,000,000 shares × $5 per share = **$20,000,000**
The intrinsic value of the conversion option is recorded separately:

	($ in millions)	
Cash (103% × $100 million)	103	
Discount on bonds payable (to balance)	17	
Convertible bonds payable (face amount)		100
Equity—conversion option (intrinsic value)		20

Where We're Headed

Accounting for convertible debt is likely to change. In 2017, the FASB added to its agenda a project on distinguishing liabilities from equity, including convertible debt, aiming to reduce complexity in financial statements and improve their understandability. A pre-Codification FASB Staff Position gives us another hint, perhaps, of the direction the project might take. For a limited subset of convertible securities not within the scope of current GAAP—those that could possibly be settled in cash rather than shares—companies must divide the proceeds from convertible securities into its two components and record the fair value of the debt as a liability and the conversion option in an equity account. Lending credence to that projection is the fact that international standards already require that convertible debt be divided into its liability and equity elements, so moving in that direction would be a step closer to convergence of U.S. GAAP and IFRS.

International Financial Reporting Standards

Convertible bonds. Under IFRS, unlike U.S. GAAP, convertible debt is divided into its liability and equity elements. In Illustration 14–18, if HTL prepared its financial statements in accordance with IFRS, it would record the convertible bonds as follows:

	($ in millions)	
Cash (103% × $100 million)	103	
Convertible bonds payable (value of the debt only)		98*
Equity—conversion option (to balance)		5

*Notice that the discount is combined with the face amount of the bonds. This is the "net method". Using the "gross method" we would credit Convertible bonds payable $100 and debit Discount on bonds $2.

In essence, HTL is selling two securities—(1) bonds and (2) an option to convert to stock—for one package price. The bonds represent a liability; the option is shareholders' equity. Compound instruments such as this one are separated into their liability and equity components in accordance with *IAS No. 32*.[15] Because the bonds have a separate fair value of $98 million, we record that amount as the liability and the remaining $5 million (the difference between the fair value of the convertible bonds, $103 million, and the $98 million) as equity. If the fair value of the bonds cannot be determined from an active trading market, that value can be calculated as the present value of the bonds' cash flows, using the market rate of interest.

Journal Entry at Issuance—Convertible Bonds

● LO14–7

The components of compound financial instruments such as convertible bonds are valued and reported separately under IFRS.

When the Conversion Option Is Exercised

If and when the bondholder exercises his or her option to convert the bonds into shares of stock, the bonds are removed from the accounting records and the new shares issued are recorded at the same amount (in other words, at the book value of the bonds). To illustrate,

---

[15]"Financial Statements: Presentation," *International Accounting Standard (IAS) No. 32* (IASCF) as amended effective January 1, 2016.

assume that half the convertible bonds issued by HTL Manufacturers are converted at a time when the remaining unamortized premium is $2 million:

Journal Entry at Conversion

	($ in millions)	
Convertible bonds payable (½ the account balance).................................	50	
Premium on bonds payable (½ the account balance)	1	
Common stock (to balance)...		51

Additional Consideration

The method just described is referred to as the *book value method,* since the new shares are recorded at the book value of the redeemed bonds. It is by far the most popular method in practice. Another acceptable approach, the *market value* method, records the new shares at the market value of the shares themselves or of the bonds, whichever is more determinable. Because the market value most likely will differ from the book value of the bonds, a gain or loss on conversion will result. Assume for illustration that the market value of HTL's stock is $30 per share at the time of the conversion:

	($ in millions)	
Convertible bonds payable (½ the account balance)...	50	
Premium on bonds payable (½ the account balance)	1	
Loss on conversion of bonds (to balance)...	9	
Common stock [(50,000 bonds × 40 shares) × $30]		60

If the 50,000 convertible bonds were held by a single investor, that company would record the conversion as follows:

The 2 million shares issued are recorded at the $51 million book value of the bonds retired.

	($ in millions)	
Investment in common stock	51	
Investment in convertible bonds (account balance)		50
Premium on investment in bonds (account balance)		1

Induced Conversion

Investors often are reluctant to convert bonds to stock, even when share prices have risen significantly since the convertible bonds were purchased. This is because the market price of the convertible bonds will rise along with market prices of the stock. So companies sometimes try to induce conversion. The motivation might be to reduce debt and become a better risk to potential lenders or achieve a lower debt-to-equity ratio.

One way is through the call provision. As we noted earlier, most corporate bonds are callable by the issuing corporation. When the specified call price is less than the conversion value of the bonds (the market value of the shares), calling the convertible bonds provides bondholders with incentive to convert. Bondholders will choose the shares rather than the lower call price.

Any additional consideration provided to induce conversion of convertible debt is recorded as an expense of the period.

Occasionally, corporations may try to encourage voluntary conversion by offering an added inducement in the form of cash, stock warrants, or a more attractive conversion ratio. When additional consideration is provided to induce conversion, the fair value of that consideration is considered an expense incurred to bring about the conversion.[16]

Bonds with Detachable Warrants

Another (less common) way to sweeten a bond issue is to include detachable stock purchase warrants as part of the security issue. A stock warrant gives the investor an option to purchase a stated number of shares of common stock at a specified *option price,* often

---

[16]FASB ASC 470–20–40: Debt—Debt with Conversion Options—Derecognition.

within a given period of time. Like a conversion feature, warrants usually mean a lower interest rate and often enable a company to issue debt when borrowing would not be feasible otherwise.

However, unlike the conversion feature for convertible bonds, warrants can be separated from the bonds. This means they can be exercised independently or traded in the market separately from bonds, having their own market price. In essence, two different securities—the bonds and the warrants—are sold as a package for a single issue price. Accordingly, the issue price is allocated between the two different securities on the basis of their fair values. If the independent market value of only one of the two securities is reliably determinable, that value establishes the allocation. This is demonstrated in Illustration 14–19.

Illustration 14–19

Bonds with Detachable Warrants

On January 1, 2021, HTL Manufacturers issued $100 million of 8% debentures due 2025 at 103 (103% of face value).

- Accompanying each $1,000 bond were 20 warrants.
- Each warrant permitted the holder to buy one share of no par common stock at $25 per share.
- Shortly after issuance, the warrants were listed on the stock exchange at $3 per warrant.

	($ in millions)	
Cash (103% × $100 million)...	103	
Discount on bonds payable (difference)..	3	
Bonds payable (face amount)..		100
Equity—stock warrants* (**100,000** bonds × **20** warrants × **$3**)..................		6

*Reported as part of shareholders' equity rather than as a liability.

The issue price of bonds with detachable warrants is allocated between the two different securities on the basis of their fair values.

Additional Consideration

Market imperfections may cause the separate market values not to sum to the issue price of the package. In this event, allocation is achieved on the basis of the relative market values of the two securities. Let's say the bonds have a separate market price of $940 per bond (priced at 94):

Market Values	Dollars	Percent
	($ in millions)	
Bonds (100,000 bonds × $940)..	$ 94	94%
Warrants (100,000 bonds × 20 warrants × $3)...........................	6	6
Total	$100	100%

Proportion of Issue Price Allocated to Bonds:
$$\$103 \text{ million} \times 94\% = \$96,820,000$$

Proportion of Issue Price Allocated to Warrants:
$$\$103 \text{ million} \times 6\% = \$6,180,000$$

	($ in millions)	
Cash (103% × $100 million)...	103.00	
Discount on bonds payable ($100 million – $96.82 million).........	3.18	
Bonds payable (face amount)...		100.00
Equity—stock warrants ($103 million × 6% = $6,180,000).......		6.18

Notice that this is the same approach we used in Chapter 10 to allocate a single purchase price to two or more assets bought for that single price. We also will allocate the total selling price of two equity securities sold for a single issue in proportion to their relative market values in Chapter 18.

800 SECTION 3 Liabilities and Shareholders' Equity

If one-half of the warrants (1 million) in Illustration 14–19 are exercised when the market value of HTL's common stock is $30 per share, 1 million shares would be issued for one warrant each plus the exercise price of $25 per share.

Journal Entry at Exercise of Detachable Warrants

	($ in millions)	
Cash (1,000,000 warrants × $25)	25	
Equity—stock warrants (1,000,000 warrants × $3)	3	
Common stock (to balance)		28

The $30 market value at the date of exercise is not used in valuing the additional shares issued. The new shares are recorded at the total of the previously measured values of both the warrants and the shares.

Concept Review Exercise

DEBT DISCLOSURES AND EARLY EXTINGUISHMENT OF DEBT

The disclosure notes to the 2021 financial statements of Olswanger Industries included the following:

Note 12: Bonds

On September 15, 2020, the Corporation sold bonds with an aggregate principal amount of $500,000,000 bearing a 14% interest rate. The bonds will mature on September 15, 2030, and are unsecured subordinated obligations of the Corporation. Interest is payable semiannually on March 15 and September 15. The Corporation may redeem the bonds at any time beginning September 15, 2020, as a whole or from time to time in part, through maturity, at specified redemption prices ranging from 112% of principal in declining percentages of principal amount through 2027 when the percentage is set at 100% of principal amount. The cost of issuing the bonds, totaling $11,000,000, and the discount of $5,000,000 are being amortized over the life of the bonds. Amortization of these items for the year ended December 31, 2021, was $1,212,000.

During the year ended December 31, 2021, the Corporation repurchased, in open market transactions, $200,000,000 in face amount of the bonds for $219,333,000. The unamortized cost of issuing these bonds and the unamortized discount, totaling $5,864,000 have been deducted in the current period.

From the information provided by Olswanger in Note 12, you should be able to recreate some of the journal entries the company recorded in connection with this bond issue.

Required:

1. Prepare the journal entry for the issuance of these bonds on September 15, 2020.
2. Prepare the journal entry for the repurchase of these bonds, assuming the date of repurchase was September 15, 2021. The cash paid to repurchase the bonds was $219,333,000.

Solution:

1. Prepare the journal entry for the issuance of these bonds on September 15, 2020.

	($ in thousands)	
Cash (to balance)	484,000	
Discount and debt issue costs (given in note)	16,000	
Bonds payable (face amount—given in note)		500,000

2. Prepare the journal entry for the repurchase of these bonds, assuming the date of repurchase was September 15, 2021.

	($ in thousands)	
Bonds payable (face amount repurchased)	200,000	
Loss on early extinguishment (to balance)	25,197	
Discount and debt issue costs (given in note)		5,864
Cash (given in requirement 2)		219,333

Option to Report Liabilities at Fair Value

Companies are not required to, but have the option to, value some or all of their financial assets and liabilities at fair value.[17] In Chapter 12, we saw examples of the option applied to financial assets—specifically, companies reporting their investments in securities at fair value. Now, we see how liabilities, too, can be reported at fair value.

● LO14–6
A company has the option to value financial assets and liabilities at fair value.

How does a liability's fair value change? Remember that there are two sides to every investment. For example, if a company has an investment in General Motors' bonds, that investment is an asset to the investor, and the same bonds are a liability to GM. So, the same market forces that influence the fair value of an investment in debt securities (interest rates, credit risk, etc.) influence the fair value of liabilities. For bank loans or other debts that aren't traded on a market exchange, the mix of factors will differ, but in any case, changes in the current market rate of interest often are a major contributor to changes in fair value.

Determining Fair Value

For demonstration, we revisit the Masterwear Industries bonds that sold at a discount in Illustration 14–3. Now, suppose it's six months later, the market rate of interest has fallen to 11%, and June 30 is the end of Masterwear's fiscal year. A decline in market interest rates means bond prices rise. Let's say that checking market prices in *The Wall Street Journal* indicates that the fair value of the Masterwear bonds on June 30, 2021, is $714,943. Referring to the amortization schedule, we see that on the same date, with five periods remaining to maturity, the present value of the bonds—their price—would have been $671,297 if the market rate still had been 14% (7% semiannually).

Changes in interest rates cause changes in the fair value of liabilities.

Additional Consideration

If the bonds are not traded on an open-market exchange, their fair value would not be readily observable. In that case, the next most preferable way to determine fair value would be to calculate the fair value as the present value of the remaining cash flows discounted at the current interest rate. If the rate is 11% (5.5% semiannually),[18] as we're assuming now, that present value would be $714,943:

	Present Values
Interest	$ 42,000 × 4.27028* = $179,352
Principal	$700,000 × 0.76513† = 535,591
Present value of the bonds	$714,943

*Present value of an ordinary annuity of $1: $n = 5, i = 5.5\%$.
†Present value of $1: $n = 5, i = 5.5\%$.

When the bonds were issued, Masterwear had a choice—report this liability (a) at its amortized initial measurement throughout the term to maturity or (b) at its current fair value on each reporting date. Had the company not elected the fair value option, on June 30 it would report the $671,297 we calculated earlier for the amortization schedule. On the other hand, if Masterwear had elected the fair value option, it would report the bonds at their current fair value, $714,943.

---

[17]FASB ASC 825–10–25–1: Financial Instruments—Overall—Recognition—Fair Value Option.
[18]The current market rate would consist of the general risk-free rate at the time, increased by a risk premium for the credit risk of the bonds.

Reporting Changes in Fair Value

Electing the FVO means reporting unrealized holding gains and losses in OCI to the extent the change is due to credit risk.

If a company chooses the option to report at fair value, a change in fair value will create a gain or loss. Any portion of that gain or loss that is a result of a change in the "credit risk" of the debt, rather than a change in general interest rates, is reported, not as part of net income, but instead as other comprehensive income (OCI). Credit risk is the risk that the investor in the bonds will not receive the promised interest and maturity amounts at the times they are due. Companies can assume that any change in fair value that exceeds the amount caused by a change in the general (risk-free) interest rate is the result of credit risk changes.

In our example, Masterwear would report the increase in fair value from $666,633 to $714,943, or $48,310. Note, though, that part of the change is due to the unpaid interest we discussed earlier. Here's a recap.

At June 30, 2021, the interest that accrued during the first six months was $46,664, but only $42,000 of that was paid in cash; so the book value increased by the $4,664 unpaid interest. We recorded the following entry:

Interest expense	46,664	
Discount on bonds payable		4,664
Cash		42,000

Amortizing the discount in this entry increased the book value of the liability by $4,664 to $671,297:

Bonds payable
Less: Discount
Book value

January 1 book value and fair value	$666,633
Increase from discount amortization	4,664
June 30 book value (amortized initial amount)	$671,297

FAIR VALUE RISES   Comparing that book value with the fair value of the bonds on that date provides the amount needed to adjust the bonds to their fair value.

June 30 fair value	$714,943
June 30 book value (amortized initial amount)	671,297
Fair value adjustment needed	$ 43,646

Rather than increasing the bonds payable account itself, though, we instead adjust it *indirectly* with a credit to a valuation allowance (or contra) account. If general interest rates have not changed, we assume the change in fair value is due to the credit risk associated with the bonds and report the loss in OCI:

When the fair value option is elected, we report changes in fair value in OCI to the extent caused by changes in credit risk.

Loss on bonds payable (unrealized, OCI)	43,646	
Fair value adjustment ($714,943 – $671,297)		43,646

The *credit* balance in the fair value adjustment *increases* the book value; the discount reduces it.

If any portion of the fair value change is due to a change in general interest rates, that portion would be reported in net income. For instance, if interest rate declines alone would have created a $20,000 increase in fair value, we would report $20,000 of the loss in in the income statement and $23,646 as OCI.

The new book value of the bonds is now the fair value:

Bonds payable	$700,000
Less: Discount ($33,367 – $4,664)	(28,703)
Amortization schedule value	$671,297
Plus: Fair value adjustment	43,646
Book value, June 30	$714,943

FAIR VALUE FALLS   Suppose the fair value at June 30, 2021, had been $650,000 instead of $714,943. In that case, Masterwear would record a *reduction* in the liability from $671,297 to $650,000, or $21,297. Again assuming no change in interest rates, the entry would be as follows:

Fair value adjustment ($671,297 − $650,000)	21,297	
Gain on bonds payable (unrealized, OCI)		21,297

The new book value of the bonds is the fair value:

Bonds payable	$ 700,000
Less: Discount ($33,367 − $4,664)	(28,703)
Amortization schedule value	$ 671,297
Less: Fair value adjustment	(21,297)
Book value, June 30	$650,000

The *debit* balance in the fair value adjustment *reduces* the book value; as does the discount.

The outstanding balance in the last column of the amortization schedule at any date up to and including the balance at maturity will be the bonds payable less the discount (for instance $671,297 at June 30, 2021). But the amount we report in the balance sheet at any reporting date, the fair value, will be that amortized initial amount from the amortization schedule, plus or minus the fair value adjustment. That's the $714,943 or the $650,000 in the two scenarios above.

To understand why we report credit risk-related fair value changes as OCI, it's useful to consider the consequence of reporting them in the income statement, which was the prescribed treatment prior to the FASB mandating their classification as OCI beginning in 2015. Here's one example. As a result of adjusting for fair value changes in its debt, **J.P. Morgan Chase & Co.** reported an impressive $1.9 billion gain in its 2011 third-quarter income statement. This was reason for the company's shareholders and creditors to celebrate, right? Not so fast. It's true that the company followed the proper procedure for recording a decline in the fair value of its debt, which was to record a gain in the income statement. As it turned out, though, the reason the fair value declined was that the company's financial situation had worsened, resulting in increased credit risk, and the increased credit risk caused the fair value of liabilities to decline. This, in fact, is the reason for most if not all of J.P. Morgan's huge gain. Does it make sense to you that worsening credit ratings should result in higher net income? Most observers, including the FASB, saw that as counterintuitive, and as a result, credit risk-related fair value changes are now reported as part of OCI rather as part of net income.

Mix and Match

Remember from our discussions in prior chapters that if a company elects the fair value option, it's not necessary that the company elect the option to report all of its financial instruments at fair value or even all instruments of a particular type at fair value. They can "mix and match" on an instrument-by-instrument basis. So Masterwear, for instance, might choose to report these bonds at fair value but all its other liabilities at their amortized initial measurement. However, the company must make the election when the item originates, in this case when the bonds are issued, and is not allowed to switch methods once a method is chosen.

Companies choose which financial instruments to report at fair value.

Here's an excerpt from the notes to the financial statements of **Citigroup Inc.** describing its fair value option election for some of its liabilities (omitting the portion of the note related to the fair value option election for financial assets):

25. FAIR VALUE ELECTIONS (In part)
The Company may elect to report most financial instruments and certain other items at fair value on an instrument-by-instrument basis. . . . The election is made upon the initial recognition of an eligible financial asset, financial liability or firm commitment or when certain specified reconsideration events occur. The fair value election may not be revoked once made. The changes in fair value are recorded in current earnings, other than DVA [Debit Valuation Adjustments], which from January 1, 2017, is reported in AOCI.

804 SECTION 3 Liabilities and Shareholders' Equity

($ in millions)	Changes in fair value gains (losses) for the years ended December 31	
	2017	**2016**
Liabilities		
Interest-bearing deposits	$ (69)	$ (50)
Federal funds purchased and securities loaned or sold under agreements to repurchase selected portfolios of securities	223	25
Trading account liabilities	70	105
Short-term borrowings	(116)	(61)
Long-term debt	(1,491)	(935)
Total liabilities	$(1,383)	$(896)

Financial Reporting Case Solution

©monkeybusinessimages/Getty Images

1. **What does it mean that the bonds are "first mortgage" bonds? What effect does that have on financing?** *(p. 774)* A mortgage bond is backed by a lien on specified real estate owned by the issuer. This makes it less risky than unsecured debt, so Service Leader can expect to be able to sell the bonds at a higher price (lower interest rate).

2. **From Service Leader's perspective, why are the bonds callable? What does that mean?** *(p. 775)* The call feature gives Service Leader some protection against being stuck with relatively high-cost debt in case interest rates fall during the 15 years to maturity. Service Leader can buy back, or call, the bonds from bondholders before the 15-year maturity date, after June 30, 2020. The call price is prespecified at 103% of the face value— $1,030 per $1,000 bond.

3. **How will it be possible to sell bonds paying investors 6.25% when other, similar investments will provide the investors a return of 6.5%?** *(p. 775)* Service Leader will be able to sell its 6.25% bonds in a 6.5% market only by selling them at a discounted price, below face amount. Bonds are priced by the marketplace to yield the market rate of interest for securities of similar risk and maturity. The price will be the present value of all the periodic cash interest payments (face amount × stated rate) plus the present value of the principal payable at maturity, both discounted at the market rate.

4. **Would accounting differ if the debt were designated as notes rather than bonds?** *(p. 786)* No. Other things being equal, whether they're called bonds, notes, or some other form of debt, the same accounting principles apply. They will be recorded at present value and interest will be recorded at the market rate over the term to maturity.

5. **Why might the company choose to make the bonds convertible into common stock?** *(p. 795)* Convertible bonds can be converted at the option of the bondholders into shares of stock. Sometimes the motivation for issuing convertible bonds rather than straight debt is to use the bonds as a medium of exchange in mergers and acquisitions, as a way for smaller firms or debt-heavy companies to obtain access to the bond market, or as an indirect way to issue stock when there is shareholder resistance to direct issuance of additional equity. None of these seems pertinent to Service Leader. The most likely reason is to sell at a higher price. The conversion feature is attractive to investors. Investors have a fixed-income security that can become common stock if circumstances make that attractive. The investor has additional possibilities for higher returns, with downside risk limited by the underlying debt. ●

The Bottom Line

● **LO14–1** A liability requires the future payment of cash in specified amounts at specified dates. As time passes, interest accrues on debt at the effective interest rate times the amount of the debt outstanding during the period. This same principle applies regardless of the specific form of the liability. *(p. 773)*

- **LO14–2** Forces of supply and demand cause a bond to be priced to yield the market rate, calculated as the present value of all the cash flows required, where the discount rate is the market rate. Interest expense is calculated as the effective market rate of interest multiplied by the outstanding balance (during the interest period). A company is permitted to allocate a discount or a premium equally to each period over the term to maturity if doing so produces results that are not materially different from the interest method. (*p. 775*)

- **LO14–3** In concept, notes are accounted for in precisely the same way as bonds. When a note is issued with an unrealistic interest rate, the effective market rate is used both to determine the amount recorded in the transaction and to record periodic interest thereafter. (*p. 786*)

- **LO14–4** In the balance sheet, disclosure should include, for all long-term borrowings, the aggregate amounts maturing and sinking fund requirements (if any) for each of the next five years. Supplemental disclosures are needed for (a) off-balance-sheet credit or market risk, (b) concentrations of credit risk, and (c) the fair value of financial instruments. (*p. 791*)

- **LO14–5** A gain or loss on early extinguishment of debt should be recorded for the difference between the reacquisition price and the book value of the debt. Convertible bonds are accounted for as straight debt, but the value of the equity feature is recorded separately for bonds issued with detachable warrants. (*p. 795*)

- **LO14–6** Companies are not required to, but have the option to, value some or all of their liabilities at fair value. If the option is elected, an increase (or decrease) in fair value from one balance sheet to the next is reported as a loss (or gain) as other comprehensive income to the extent it's related to credit risk. Otherwise, it's reported in net income. It's a one-time election for each liability when the liability is created. (*p. 801*)

- **LO14–7** U.S. GAAP and IFRS are generally compatible with respect to accounting for bonds and long-term notes. Some differences exist in determining which securities are reported as debt, the way convertible securities are accounted for, and when the fair value option can be elected. (*pp. 797*). ●

Bonds Issued Between Interest Dates

APPENDIX 14A

In Part A of this chapter, we assumed that the bonds were issued on the day they were dated (date printed in the indenture contract). But suppose a weak market caused a delay in selling the bonds until two months after that date (four months before semiannual interest was to be paid). In that case, the buyer would be asked to pay the seller accrued interest for two months in addition to the price of the bonds.

When Bonds Are Issued at Face Amount between Interest Dates

For illustration, assume that in Illustration 14–1, Masterwear was unable to sell the bonds in the previous example until March 1—two months after they are dated. This variation is shown in Illustration 14A–1. United would pay the price of the bonds ($700,000) plus $14,000 accrued interest:

All bonds sell at their price plus any interest that has accrued since the last interest date.

$$\underset{\text{Face amount}}{\$700,000} \times \underset{\text{Annual rate}}{12\%} \times \underset{\text{Fraction of the annual period}}{{}^{2}\!/_{12}} = \underset{\text{Accrued interest}}{\$14,000}$$

Illustration 14A–1

Bonds Sold at Face Amount between Interest Dates

At Issuance (March 1)		
Masterwear (Issuer)		
Cash (price plus accrued interest)	714,000	
Bonds payable (face amount)		700,000
Interest payable (accrued interest determined above)		14,000
United (Investor)		
Investment in bonds (face amount)	700,000	
Interest receivable (accrued interest determined above)	14,000	
Cash (price plus accrued interest)		714,000

806   SECTION 3   Liabilities and Shareholders' Equity

Since the investor will hold the bonds for only four months before receiving six months' interest, two months' accrued interest must be added to the price paid.

When Masterwear pays semiannual interest on June 30, a full six months' interest is paid. But having received two months' accrued interest in advance, Masterwear's net interest expense will be four months' interest, for the four months the bonds have been outstanding at that time. Likewise, when United receives six months' interest—after holding the bonds for only four months—United will net only the four months' interest to which it is entitled:

The issuer incurs interest expense, and the investor recognizes interest revenue, for only the four months the bonds are outstanding.

At the First Interest Date (June 30)

Masterwear (Issuer)

Interest expense (6 mo. − 2 mo. = 4 mo.)	28,000	
Interest payable* (accrued interest determined above)	14,000	
Cash (stated rate × face amount)		42,000

United (Investor)

Cash (stated rate × face amount)	42,000	
Interest receivable (accrued interest determined above)		14,000
Interest revenue (6 mo. − 2 mo. = 4 mo.)		28,000

*Some accountants prefer to credit interest expense, rather than interest payable, when the bonds are sold. When that is done, this entry would require a debit to interest expense and a credit to cash for $42,000. The interest expense account would then reflect the same *net* debit of four months' interest ($42,000 − $14,000).

Interest Expense

	2 months
6 months	
4 months	

Similarly, the investor could debit interest revenue, rather than interest receivable when buying the bonds.

When Bonds Are Issued at a Discount between Interest Dates

All bonds sell at their price plus any interest that has accrued since the last interest date.

Our objective is the same when the bonds are not issued at their face amount. For instance, in Illustration 14–3, the $700,000 of 12% bonds were issued on January 1 when the market rate was 14% and thus were priced at a discount, $666,633. If instead those bonds were issued March 1, two months after they are dated, the price will have increased. That's because the liability will have accrued two months' interest at the effective rate (7% × ⅙ × $666,633, or $15,555). $14,000 of that (6% × ⅙ × $700,000) represents stated interest that will be part of the first interest payment four months later, so the price of the bonds will have increased by the difference, $15,555 − $14,000, or $1,555. We can think of this as the time value of the bonds for 2 months. The cash flows remain the same (six semiannual interest payments plus the face amount at maturity), but because the payments now will be received two months sooner, the *present value* of those payments is greater. The investor would pay the January 1 value of the bonds ($666,633) plus the time value for 2 months ($1,555) plus $14,000 accrued interest (see Illustration 14A–2).

Illustration 14A–2

Bonds Sold at a Discount between Interest Dates

Masterwear (Issuer)

Cash (price plus accrued interest)	682,218*	
Discount on bonds payable (difference)	31,782	
Bonds payable (face amount)		700,000
Interest payable (accrued interest determined above)		14,000

United (Investor)

Investment in bonds (face amount)	700,000	
Interest receivable (accrued interest determined above)	14,000	
Discount on bond investment (difference)		31,782
Cash (price plus accrued interest)		682,218*

*On March 1, the proceeds will be the price of the bonds based on the effective market interest rate on March 1, plus the $14,000 accrued interest. If the price of the bonds was $666,633 on January 1 as we assumed in Illustration 14–3, and the effective market interest rate remained 7% semiannually for the next two months, that price will have increased to $668,218:

$666,663	Balance, Jan. 1
15,555	7% × ⅙ × $666,633 2 mo. *effective* interest
$682,218	Balance, March 1
(14,000)	6% × ⅙ × $700,000 2 mo. *stated* interest
$668,218	Bond price, March 1
14,000	Accrued interest
$682,218	Proceeds: price plus accrued interest

By contract, a full six months' interest is paid on June 30 at the *stated* rate times the face amount. But having received two months' accrued interest in advance, Masterwear's *net* interest expense will be four months' interest, for the four months the bonds have been outstanding at that time. Interest is calculated on the outstanding debt balance at the effective (or market) rate. Interest for the first six months, then, would be $666,633 \times 14\% \times \frac{1}{2} =$ $46,664. But because on June 30 only four months have passed since the date the bonds were issued, only four months' interest, $\frac{4}{6} \times$ $46,664, or $31,109, is recorded as interest expense. Similarly, the reduction of the discount, which for a full six-month interest period would be $46,664 − $42,000, or $4,664, will be only $\frac{4}{6}$ of that amount. These amounts are recorded as follows:

Journal Entries— Interest between Interest Dates

At the First Interest Date (June 30)		
Masterwear (Issuer)		
Interest expense ($\frac{4}{6} \times$ $46,664)	31,109	
Interest payable (accrued interest determined above)	14,000	
Discount on bonds payable ($\frac{4}{6} \times$ $4,664)		3,109
Cash (stated rate × face amount)		42,000
United (Investor)		
Cash (stated rate × face amount)	42,000	
Discount on bond investment ($\frac{4}{6} \times$ $4,664)	3,109	
Interest receivable (accrued interest determined above)		14,000
Interest revenue ($\frac{4}{6} \times$ $46,664)		31,109

Only four months' interest is recorded because the bonds were outstanding only four months.

Troubled Debt Restructuring

APPENDIX 14B

A respected real estate developer, Brillard Properties, was very successful developing and managing a number of properties in the southeastern United States. To finance these investments, the developer had borrowed hundreds of millions of dollars from several regional banks. For years, events occurred as planned. The investments prospered. Cash flow was high. Interest payments on the debt were timely and individual loans were repaid as they matured.

Almost suddenly, however, the real estate climate soured. Investments that had provided handsome profits now did not provide the cash flow necessary to service the debt. Bankers who had loaned substantial funds to Brillard now faced a dilemma. Because contractual interest payments were unpaid, the bankers had the legal right to demand payment, which would force the developer to liquidate all or a major part of the properties to raise the cash. Sound business practice? Not necessarily.

A sharp rise in debt restructurings accompanied the 2008/2009 economic crisis.

If creditors force liquidation, they then must share among themselves the cash raised from selling the properties—at forced sale prices. Believing the developer's financial difficulties were caused by temporary market forces, not by bad management, the bankers felt they could minimize their losses by *restructuring* the debt agreements, rather than by forcing liquidation.

When changing the original terms of a debt agreement is motivated by financial difficulties experienced by the debtor (borrower), the new arrangement is referred to as a troubled debt restructuring. By definition, a troubled debt restructuring involves some concessions on the part of the creditor (lender) that it wouldn't otherwise consider if not for the economic or legal reasons related to the debtor's financial difficulties. In the first half of 2009, the economic crisis prompted nearly 40 companies to negotiate such deals with their creditors, a huge increase over the handful that normally would do so during a six-month period.[19] A troubled debt restructuring may be achieved in either of two ways:

1. The debt may be *settled* at the time of the restructuring.
2. The debt may be *continued*, but with *modified terms*.

---

[19]David Henry, "The Time Bomb in Corporate Debt," *BusinessWeek*, July 15, 2009.

Debt Is Settled

In all areas of accounting, a noncash transaction is recorded at fair value.

In the situation described above, one choice the bankers had was to try to actually settle the debt outright at the time of the troubled debt restructuring. For instance, a bank holding a $30 million note from the developer might agree to accept a property valued at, let's say, $20 million as final settlement of the debt. In that case, the developer has a $10 million gain equal to the difference between the book value of the debt and the fair value of the property transferred. The debtor may need to adjust the book value of an asset to its fair value prior to recording its exchange for a debt. The developer in our example, for instance, would need to change the recorded amount for the property specified in the exchange agreement if it is carried at an amount other than its $20 million fair value. In such an instance, an ordinary gain or loss on disposition of assets should be recorded as shown in Illustration 14B–1.

Illustration 14B–1

Debt Settled

An asset is adjusted to fair value prior to recording its exchange for a debt.

First Prudent Bank agrees to settle Brillard's $30 million debt in exchange for property having a fair value of $20 million. The book value of the property on Brillard's books is $17 million:		
	($ in millions)	
Land ($20 million minus $17 million)	3	
Gain on disposition of assets		3
Notes payable (book value)	30	
Gain on troubled debt restructuring		10
Land (fair value)		20

The payment to settle a debt in a troubled debt restructuring might be cash, or a noncash asset (as in the example here), or even shares of the debtor's stock. An example of shares of stock given in exchange for debt forgiveness is the celebrated reorganization of TWA in 1992 (since acquired by American Airlines), when creditors received a 55% stake in the company's common shares in return for forgiving about $1 billion of the airline's $1.5 billion debt. In any case, the debtor's gain is the difference between the book value of the debt and the fair value of the asset(s) or equity securities transferred.

Debt Is Continued, but with Modified Terms

The book value of a debt is the current balance of the primary debt plus any accrued (unpaid) interest.

We assumed in the previous example that First Prudent Bank agreed to accept property in full settlement of the debt. A more likely occurrence would be that the bank allows the debt to continue, but modifies the terms of the debt agreement to make it easier for the debtor to comply. The bank might agree to reduce or delay the scheduled *interest payments*. Or, it may agree to reduce or delay the *maturity amount*. Often a troubled debt restructuring will call for some combination of these concessions. Distressed by the 2008/2009 economic downturn, amusement park operator **Six Flags** persuaded a group of creditors to trim its debt by 5%, or $130 million, a restructuring designed to give Six Flags a financial cushion going into its busy 2009 summer season and an opportunity to recover its interest-paying ability.

Let's say the stated interest rate on the note in question is 10% and annual interest payments of $3 million (10% × $30 million) are payable in December of each of two remaining years to maturity. Also assume that the developer was unable to pay the $3 million interest payment for the year just ended. This means that the amount owed—the carrying amount (or book value) of the debt—is $33 million ($30 million plus one year's accrued interest).

Two quite different situations are created when the terms of a debt are modified, depending on whether the cash payments are reduced to the extent that interest is eliminated.

The way the debtor accounts for the restructuring depends on the extent of the reduction in cash payments called for by the restructured arrangement. More specifically, the accounting procedure depends on whether, under the new agreement, total cash payments (a) are *less than* the book value of the debt or (b) still *exceed* the book value of the debt.

WHEN TOTAL CASH PAYMENTS ARE LESS THAN THE BOOK VALUE OF THE DEBT By the original agreement, the debtor was to pay at maturity the $30 million loaned, plus enough periodic interest to provide a 10% effective rate of return. If the new agreement calls for less cash than the $33 million now owed, interest is presumed to have been eliminated.

As one of many possibilities, suppose the bank agrees to (1) forgive the interest accrued from last year, (2) reduce the two remaining interest payments from $3 million each to $2 million each, and (3) reduce the face amount from $30 million to $25 million. Clearly, the debtor will pay less by the new agreement than by the original one. In fact, if we add up the total payments called for by the new agreement, the total [($2 million × 2) plus $25 million] is less than the $33 million book value. Because the $29 million does not exceed the amount owed, the restructured debt agreement no longer provides interest on the debt. Actually, the new payments are $4 million short of covering the debt itself. So, after the debt restructuring, no interest expense is recorded. All subsequent cash payments are considered to be payment of the debt itself. Consider Illustration 14B–2.

Illustration 14B–2
Cash Payments Less than the Debt

Brillard Properties owes First Prudent Bank $30 million under a 10% note with two years remaining to maturity. Due to financial difficulties of the developer, the previous year's interest ($3 million) was not paid. First Prudent Bank agrees to:

1. Forgive the interest accrued from last year.
2. Reduce the remaining two interest payments to $2 million each.
3. Reduce the principal to $25 million.

Analysis:	Book value	$30 million + $3 million =	$33 million	
	Future payments	($2 million × 2) + $25 million =	29 million	
	Gain		$ 4 million	

($ in millions)

Interest payable (10% × $30 million)	3	
Notes payable ($30 million − $29 million)	1	
Gain on debt restructuring		4

	Book Value		
	Before Restr.	Adj.	After Restr.
	$30	(1)	$29
	3	(3)	0
	$33	(4)	$29

When the total future cash payments are less than the book value of the debt, the difference is recorded as a gain at the date of restructure. No interest should be recorded thereafter. That is, all subsequent cash payments result in reductions of principal.

After restructuring, no interest expense is recorded. All cash payments are considered to be payment of the note itself.

The $25 million payment at maturity reduces the note to zero.

At Each of the Two Interest Dates	($ in millions)	
Notes payable	2	
Cash (revised "interest" amount)		2
At Maturity		
Notes payable	25	
Cash (revised principal amount)		25

WHEN TOTAL CASH PAYMENTS EXCEED THE BOOK VALUE OF THE DEBT   Let's modify the example in the previous section. Now suppose the bank agrees to delay the due date for all cash payments until maturity and accept $34,333,200 at that time in full settlement of the debt. Rather than just reducing the cash payments as in the previous illustration, the payments are delayed. It is not the nature of the change that creates the need to account differently for this situation, but the amount of the total cash payments under the agreement relative to the book value of the debt. This situation is demonstrated in Illustration 14B–3.

Illustration 14B–3
Cash Payments More than the Debt

Brillard Properties owes First Prudent Bank $30 million under a 10% note with two years remaining to maturity. Due to Brillard's financial difficulties, the previous year's interest ($3 million) was not paid. First Prudent Bank agrees to:

1. Delay the due date for all cash payments until maturity.
2. Accept $34,333,200 at that time in full settlement of the debt.

(continued)

Illustration 14B–3
(concluded)

The discount rate that equates the present value on the debt ($33 million) and its future value ($34,333,200) is the effective rate of interest.

Analysis:	Future payments		$34,333,200
	Book value	$30 million + $3 million =	33,000,000
	Interest		$ 1,333,200

Calculation of the New Effective Interest Rate

- $33,000,000 ÷ $34,333,200 = 0.9612, the Table 2 value for $n = 2$, $i = ?$
- In row 2 of Table 2, the number 0.9612 is in the 2% column. So, this is the new effective interest rate.

As long as cash payments exceed the amount owed there will be interest—although at a lower effective rate.

Now the total payments called for by the new agreement, $34,333,200, exceed the $33 million book value. Because the payments exceed the amount owed, the restructured debt agreement still provides interest on the debt—but less than before the agreement was revised. No longer is the effective rate 10%. The accounting objective now is to determine what the new effective rate is and *record interest for the remaining term of the loan at that new, lower rate,* as shown in Illustration 14B–3.

Unpaid interest is accrued at the effective rate times the book value of the note.

Because the total future cash payments are not less than the book value of the debt, no reduction of the existing debt is necessary and no entry is required at the time of the debt restructuring. Even though no cash is paid until maturity under the restructured debt agreement, interest expense still is recorded annually—but at the new rate.

The book value of the debt is increased by the unpaid interest from the previous year.

The total of the accrued interest account plus the note account is equal to the amount scheduled to be paid at maturity.

At the End of the First Year			
Interest expense [2% × ($30,000,000 + $3,000,000)]		660,000	
Interest payable			660,000
At the End of the Second Year			
Interest expense [2% × ($30,000,000 + $3,660,000)]		673,200	
Interest payable			673,200
At Maturity (End of the Second Year)			
Notes payable		30,000,000	
Interest payable ($3,000,000 + $660,000 + $673,200)		4,333,200	
Cash (required by new agreement)			34,333,200

Additional Consideration

To keep up with the changing amounts, it may be convenient to prepare an amortization schedule for the debt.

Year	Cash Interest	Effective Interest	Increase in Balance	Outstanding Balance
		(2% × Outstanding balance)		
				33,000,000
1	0	0.02 (33,000,000) = 660,000	660,000	33,660,000
2	0	0.02 (33,660,000) = 673,200	673,200	34,333,200
	0	1,333,200	1,333,200	

An amortization schedule is particularly helpful if there are several years remaining to maturity.

In our example, the restructured debt agreement called for a single cash payment at maturity ($34,333,200). If more than one cash payment is required (as in the agreement in our earlier example), calculating the new effective rate is more difficult. The concept would remain straightforward: (1) determine the interest rate that provides a present value of all future cash payments that is equal to the current book value and (2) record the interest at that rate thereafter. Mechanically, though, the computation by hand would be cumbersome, requiring a time-consuming trial-and-error calculation. Since our primary interest is understanding the concepts involved, we will avoid the mathematical complexities of such a situation.

You also should be aware that when a restructuring involves modification of terms, accounting for a liability by the debtor, as described in this section, and accounting for a receivable by the creditor (essentially an impairment of a receivable), which was described in Chapter 7, are inconsistent. You may recall that when a creditor's investment in a receivable becomes impaired, due to a troubled debt restructuring or for any other reason, the receivable is remeasured based on the discounted present value of currently expected cash flows at the loan's *original* effective rate (regardless of the extent to which expected cash receipts have been reduced). For ease of comparison, the example in this chapter (Illustration 14B–3) describes the same situation as the example in Chapter 7 (Illustration 7B–2). There is no conceptual justification for the asymmetry between debtors' and creditors' accounting for troubled debt restructurings. ●

Questions For Review of Key Topics

Q 14–1 How is periodic interest determined for outstanding liabilities? For outstanding receivables? How does the approach compare from one form of debt instrument (say bonds payable) to another (say notes payable)?

Q 14–2 As a general rule, how should long-term liabilities be reported on the debtor's balance sheet?

Q 14–3 How are bonds and notes the same? How do they differ?

Q 14–4 What information is contained in a bond indenture? What purpose does it serve?

Q 14–5 On January 1, 2021, Brandon Electronics issued $85 million of 11.5% bonds, dated January 1. The market yield for bonds of maturity issued by similar firms in terms of riskiness is 12.25%. How can Brandon sell debt paying only 11.5% in a 12.25% market?

Q 14–6 How is the price determined for a bond (or bond issue)?

Q 14–7 A zero-coupon bond pays no interest. Explain.

Q 14–8 When bonds are issued at a premium the debt declines each period. Explain.

Q 14–9 Compare the two commonly used methods of determining interest on bonds.

Q 14–10 What are debt issue costs and how should they be reported?

Q 14–11 When a note's stated rate of interest is unrealistic relative to the market rate, the concept of substance over form should be employed. Explain.

Q 14–12 How does an installment note differ from a note for which the principal is paid as a single amount at maturity?

Q 14–13 Long-term debt can be reported either (a) as a single amount, net of any discount or increased by any premium or (b) at its face amount accompanied by a separate valuation account for the discount or premium. Any portion of the debt to be paid during the upcoming year, or operating cycle if longer, should be reported as a current amount. Regarding amounts to be paid in the future, what additional disclosures should be made in connection with long-term debt?

Q 14–14 Early extinguishment of debt often produces a gain or a loss. How is the gain or loss determined?

Q 14–15 Air Supply issued $6 million of 9%, 10-year convertible bonds at 101. The bonds are convertible into 24,000 shares of common stock. Bonds that are similar in all respects except that they are nonconvertible, currently are selling at 99 (that is, 99% of face amount). What amount should Air Supply record as equity and how much as a liability when the bonds are issued?

Q 14–16 Both convertible bonds and bonds issued with detachable warrants have features of both debt and equity. How does the accounting treatment differ for the two hybrid securities? Why is the accounting treatment different?

Q 14–17 At times, companies try to induce voluntary conversion by offering an added incentive—maybe cash, stock warrants, or a more favorable conversion ratio. How is such an inducement accounted for? How is it measured?

Q 14–18 Cordova Tools has bonds outstanding during a year in which the market rate of interest has risen. If Cordova has elected the fair value option for the bonds, will it report a gain or a loss on the bonds for the year? Explain.

IFRS Q 14–19 If a company prepares its financial statements according to International Financial Reporting Standards, how would it account for convertible bonds it issues for $12.5 million? What is the conceptual justification?

Q 14–20 (Based on Appendix 14A) Why will bonds always sell at their price plus any interest that has accrued since the last interest date?

Q 14–21 (Based on Appendix 14B) When the original terms of a debt agreement are changed because of financial difficulties experienced by the debtor (borrower), the new arrangement is referred to as a *troubled debt restructuring*. Such a restructuring can take a variety of forms. For accounting purposes, these possibilities are categorized. What are the accounting classifications of troubled debt restructurings?

Q 14–22   (Based on Appendix 14B) Pratt Industries owes First National Bank $5 million but, due to financial difficulties, is unable to comply with the original terms of the loan. The bank agrees to settle the debt in exchange for land having a fair value of $3 million. The book value of the property on Pratt's books is $2 million. For the reporting period in which the debt is settled, what amount(s) will Pratt report on its income statement in connection with the troubled debt restructuring?

Q 14–23   (Based on Appendix 14B) The way a debtor accounts for the restructuring depends on the extent of the reduction in cash payments called for by the restructured arrangement. Describe, in general, the accounting procedure for the two basic cases: when, under the new agreement, total cash payments (a) are less than the book value of the debt or (b) still exceed the book value of the debt.

Brief Exercises

BE 14–1
Bond interest
● LO14–1

Holiday Brands issued $30 million of 6%, 30-year bonds for $27.5 million. What is the amount of interest that Holiday will pay semiannually to bondholders?

BE 14–2
Determining the price of bonds
● LO14–2

A company issued 5%, 20-year bonds with a face amount of $80 million. The market yield for bonds of similar risk and maturity is 6%. Interest is paid semiannually. At what price did the bonds sell?

BE 14–3
Determining the price of bonds
● LO14–2

A company issued 6%, 15-year bonds with a face amount of $75 million. The market yield for bonds of similar risk and maturity is 6%. Interest is paid semiannually. At what price did the bonds sell?

BE 14–4
Determining the price of bonds
● LO14–2

A company issued 5%, 20-year bonds with a face amount of $100 million. The market yield for bonds of similar risk and maturity is 4%. Interest is paid semiannually. At what price did the bonds sell?

BE 14–5
Effective interest on bonds
● LO14–2

On January 1, a company issued 7%, 15-year bonds with a face amount of $90 million for $82,218,585 to yield 8%. Interest is paid semiannually. What was interest expense at the effective interest rate on June 30, the first interest date?

BE 14–6
Effective interest on bonds
● LO14–2

On January 1, a company issued 3%, 20-year bonds with a face amount of $80 million for $69,057,808 to yield 4%. Interest is paid semiannually. What was the interest expense at the effective interest rate on the December 31 annual income statement?

BE 14–7
Straight-line interest on bonds
● LO14–2

On January 1, a company issued 3%, 20-year bonds with a face amount of $80 million for $69,033,776 to yield 4%. Interest is paid semiannually. What was the straight-line interest expense on the December 31 annual income statement?

BE 14–8
Investment in bonds
● LO14–2

On January 1, a company purchased 3%, 20-year corporate bonds for $69,033,776 as an investment. The bonds have a face amount of $80 million and are priced to yield 4%. Interest is paid semiannually. Prepare the journal entry to record revenue at the effective interest rate on December 31, the second interest payment date.

BE 14–9
Note issued for cash; borrower and lender
● LO14–3

On January 1, 2021, Nantucket Ferry borrowed $14,000,000 cash from BankOne and issued a four-year, $14,000,000, 6% note. Interest was payable annually on December 31. Prepare the journal entries for both firms to record interest at December 31, 2021.

BE 14–10
Note with unrealistic interest rate
● LO14–3

On January 1, Snipes Construction paid for earth-moving equipment by issuing a $300,000, 3-year note that specified 2% interest to be paid on December 31 of each year. The equipment's retail cash price was unknown, but it was determined that a reasonable interest rate was 5%. At what amount should Snipes record the equipment and the note? What journal entry should it record for the transaction?

BE 14–11
Installment note
● LO14–3

On January 1, a company borrowed cash by issuing a $300,000, 5%, installment note to be paid in three equal payments at the end of each year beginning December 31. What would be the amount of each installment? Prepare the journal entry for the second installment payment.

BE 14–12
Early extinguishment; effective interest
● LO14–5

A company retired $60 million of its 6% bonds at 102 ($61.2 million) before their scheduled maturity. At the time, the bonds had a remaining discount of $2 million. Prepare the journal entry to record the redemption of the bonds.

BE 14–13
Bonds with detachable warrants
● LO14–5

Hoffman Corporation issued $60 million of 5%, 20-year bonds at 102. Each of the 60,000 bonds was issued with 10 detachable stock warrants, each of which entitled the bondholder to purchase, for $20, one share of $1 par common stock. At the time of sale, the market value of the common stock was $25 per share and the market value of each warrant was $5. Prepare the journal entry to record the issuance of the bonds.

BE 14–14
Convertible bonds
● LO14–5

Hoffman Corporation issued $60 million of 5%, 20-year bonds at 102. Each of the 60,000 bonds was convertible into one share of $1 par common stock. Prepare the journal entry to record the issuance of the bonds.

BE 14–15
Reporting bonds at fair value
● LO14–6

AI Tool and Dye issued 8% bonds with a face amount of $160 million on January 1, 2021. The bonds sold for $150 million. For bonds of similar risk and maturity the market yield was 9%. Upon issuance, AI elected the option to report these bonds at their fair value. On June 30, 2021, the fair value of the bonds was $145 million as determined by their market value on the NASDAQ. Will AI report a gain or will it report a loss when adjusting the bonds to fair value? If the change in fair value is attributable to a change in the interest rate, did the rate increase or decrease? Will the gain or loss be reported in net income or as OCI?

Exercises

E 14–1
Bond valuation
● LO14–2

Your investment department has researched possible investments in corporate debt securities. Among the available investments are the following $100 million bond issues, each dated January 1, 2021. Prices were determined by underwriters at different times during the last few weeks.

	Company	Bond Price	Stated Rate
1.	BB Corp.	$109 million	11%
2.	DD Corp.	$100 million	10%
3.	GG Corp.	$ 91 million	9%

Each of the bond issues matures on December 31, 2040, and pays interest semiannually on June 30 and December 31. For bonds of similar risk and maturity, the market yield at January 1, 2021, is 10%.

Required:
Other things being equal, which of the bond issues offers the most attractive investment opportunity if it can be purchased at the prices stated? The least attractive? Why?

E 14–2
Determine the price of bonds in various situations
● LO14–2

Determine the price of a $1 million bond issue under each of the following independent assumptions:

	Maturity	Interest Paid	Stated Rate	Effective (Market) Rate
1.	10 years	annually	10%	12%
2.	10 years	semiannually	10%	12%
3.	10 years	semiannually	12%	10%
4.	20 years	semiannually	12%	10%
5.	20 years	semiannually	12%	12%

E 14–3
Determine the price of bonds; issuance; effective interest
● LO14–2

The Bradford Company issued 10% bonds, dated January 1, with a face amount of $80 million on January 1, 2021. The bonds mature on December 31, 2030 (10 years). For bonds of similar risk and maturity, the market yield is 12%. Interest is paid semiannually on June 30 and December 31.

Required:
1. Determine the price of the bonds at January 1, 2021.
2. Prepare the journal entry to record their issuance by The Bradford Company on January 1, 2021.

814   SECTION 3   Liabilities and Shareholders' Equity

3. Prepare the journal entry to record interest on June 30, 2021 (at the effective rate).

4. Prepare the journal entry to record interest on December 31, 2021 (at the effective rate).

E 14–4
Investor; effective interest
● **LO14–2**

(Note: This is a variation of E 14–3 modified to consider the investor's perspective.) The Bradford Company sold the entire bond issue described in the previous exercise to Saxton-Bose Corporation.

Required:

1. Prepare the journal entry to record the purchase of the bonds by Saxton-Bose on January 1, 2021.

2. Prepare the journal entry to record interest revenue on June 30, 2021 (at the effective rate).

3. Prepare the journal entry to record interest revenue on December 31, 2021 (at the effective rate).

E 14–5
Bonds; issuance; effective interest; financial statement effects
● **LO14–2**

Myriad Solutions, Inc. issued 10% bonds, dated January 1, with a face amount of $320 million on January 1, 2021, for $283,294,720. The bonds mature on December 31, 2030 (10 years). For bonds of similar risk and maturity the market yield is 12%. Interest is paid semiannually on June 30 and December 31.

Required:

1. What would be the net amount of the liability Myriad would report in its balance sheet at December 31, 2021?

2. What would be the amount related to the bonds that Myriad would report in its income statement for the year ended December 31, 2021?

3. What would be the amount(s) related to the bonds that Myriad would report in its statement of cash flows for the year ended December 31, 2021?

E 14–6
Bonds; issuance; effective interest
● **LO14–2**

The Gorman Group issued $900,000 of 13% bonds on June 30, 2021, for $967,707. The bonds were dated on June 30 and mature on June 30, 2041 (20 years). The market yield for bonds of similar risk and maturity is 12%. Interest is paid semiannually on December 31 and June 30.

Required:

1. Prepare the journal entry to record their issuance by The Gorman Group on June 30, 2021.

2. Prepare the journal entry to record interest on December 31, 2021 (at the effective rate).

3. Prepare the journal entry to record interest on June 30, 2022 (at the effective rate).

E 14–7
Determine the price of bonds; issuance; straight-line method
● **LO14–2**

Universal Foods issued 10% bonds, dated January 1, with a face amount of $150 million on January 1, 2021. The bonds mature on December 31, 2035 (15 years). The market rate of interest for similar issues was 12%. Interest is paid semiannually on June 30 and December 31. Universal uses the straight-line method.

Required:

1. Determine the price of the bonds at January 1, 2021.

2. Prepare the journal entry to record their issuance by Universal Foods on January 1, 2021.

3. Prepare the journal entry to record interest on June 30, 2021.

4. Prepare the journal entry to record interest on December 31, 2028.

E 14–8
Investor; straight-line method
● **LO14–2**

(Note: This is a variation of E 14–7 modified to consider the investor's perspective.) Universal Foods sold the entire bond issue described in the previous exercise to Wang Communications.

Required:

1. Prepare the journal entry to record the purchase of the bonds by Wang Communications on January 1, 2021.

2. Prepare the journal entry to record interest revenue on June 30, 2021.

3. Prepare the journal entry to record interest revenue on December 31, 2028.

E 14–9
Issuance of bonds; effective interest; amortization schedule; financial statement effects
● **LO14–2**

When Patey Pontoons issued 6% bonds on January 1, 2021, with a face amount of $600,000, the market yield for bonds of similar risk and maturity was 7%. The bonds mature December 31, 2024 (4 years). Interest is paid semiannually on June 30 and December 31.

Required:

1. Determine the price of the bonds at January 1, 2021.

2. Prepare the journal entry to record their issuance by Patey on January 1, 2021.

3. Prepare an amortization schedule that determines interest at the effective rate each period.

4. Prepare the journal entry to record interest on June 30, 2021.

5. What is the amount(s) related to the bonds that Patey will report in its balance sheet at December 31, 2021?

6. What is the amount(s) related to the bonds that Patey will report in its income statement for the year ended December 31, 2021? (Ignore income taxes.)

7. Prepare the appropriate journal entries at maturity on December 31, 2024.

E 14–10
Issuance of
bonds; effective
interest;
amortization
schedule
● LO14–2

National Orthopedics Co. issued 9% bonds, dated January 1, with a face amount of $500,000 on January 1, 2021. The bonds mature on December 31, 2024 (4 years). For bonds of similar risk and maturity the market yield was 10%. Interest is paid semiannually on June 30 and December 31.

Required:
1. Determine the price of the bonds at January 1, 2021.
2. Prepare the journal entry to record their issuance by National on January 1, 2021.
3. Prepare an amortization schedule that determines interest at the effective rate each period.
4. Prepare the journal entry to record interest on June 30, 2021.
5. Prepare the appropriate journal entries at maturity on December 31, 2024.

E 14–11
Bonds; effective
interest; adjusting
entry
● LO14–2

On February 1, 2021, Strauss-Lombardi issued 9% bonds, dated February 1, with a face amount of $800,000. The bonds sold for $731,364 and mature on January 31, 2041 (20 years). The market yield for bonds of similar risk and maturity was 10%. Interest is paid semiannually on July 31 and January 31. Strauss-Lombardi's fiscal year ends December 31.

Required:
1. Prepare the journal entry to record their issuance by Strauss-Lombardi on February 1, 2021.
2. Prepare the journal entry to record interest on July 31, 2021 (at the effective rate).
3. Prepare the adjusting entry to accrue interest on December 31, 2021.
4. Prepare the journal entry to record interest on January 31, 2022.

E 14–12
Bonds; straight-
line method;
adjusting entry
● LO14–2

On March 1, 2021, Stratford Lighting issued 14% bonds, dated March 1, with a face amount of $300,000. The bonds sold for $294,000 and mature on February 28, 2041 (20 years). Interest is paid semiannually on August 31 and February 28. Stratford uses the straight-line method and its fiscal year ends December 31.

Required:
1. Prepare the journal entry to record the issuance of the bonds by Stratford Lighting on March 1, 2021.
2. Prepare the journal entry to record interest on August 31, 2021.
3. Prepare the journal entry to accrue interest on December 31, 2021.
4. Prepare the journal entry to record interest on February 28, 2022.

E 14–13
Issuance of
bonds; effective
interest
● LO14–2

Federal Semiconductors issued 11% bonds, dated January 1, with a face amount of $800 million on January 1, 2021. The bonds sold for $739,814,813 and mature on December 31, 2040 (20 years). For bonds of similar risk and maturity the market yield was 12%. Interest is paid semiannually on June 30 and December 31.

Required:
1. Prepare the journal entry to record their issuance by Federal on January 1, 2021.
2. Prepare the journal entry to record interest on June 30, 2021 (at the effective rate).
3. Prepare the journal entry to record interest on December 31, 2021 (at the effective rate).
4. At what amount will Federal report the bonds among its liabilities in the December 31, 2021, balance sheet?

E 14–14
New debt
issues; offerings
announcements
● LO14–2

When companies offer new debt security issues, they publicize the offerings in the financial press and on Internet sites. Assume the following were among the debt offerings reported in December 2021:

New Securities Issues
Corporate
National Equipment Transfer Corporation—$200 million bonds via lead managers Second Tennessee Bank N.A. and Morgan, Dunavant & Co., according to a syndicate official. Terms: maturity, Dec. 15, 2030; coupon 7.46%; issue price, par; yield, 7.46%; noncallable; debt ratings: Ba-1 (Moody's Investors Service, Inc.), BBB+ (Standard & Poor's).

IgWig Inc.—$350 million of notes via lead manager Stanley Brothers, Inc., according to a syndicate official. Terms: maturity, Dec. 1, 2032; coupon, 6.46%; Issue price, 99; yield, 6.56%; call date, NC; debt ratings: Baa-1 (Moody's Investors Service, Inc.), A (Standard & Poor's).

Required:
1. Prepare the appropriate journal entries to record the sale of both issues to underwriters. Ignore share issue costs and assume no accrued interest.
2. Prepare the appropriate journal entries to record the first semiannual interest payment for both issues.

E 14–15
Error correction; accrued interest on bonds
● LO14–2

At the end of 2020, Majors Furniture Company failed to accrue $61,000 of interest expense that accrued during the last five months of 2020 on bonds payable. The bonds mature in 2034. The discount on the bonds is amortized by the straight-line method. The following entry was recorded on February 1, 2021, when the semiannual interest was paid:

Interest expense	73,200	
Discount on bonds payable		1,200
Cash		72,000

Required:
Prepare any journal entry necessary to correct the errors as of February 2, 2021, when the errors were discovered. Also, prepare any adjusting entry at December 31, 2021, related to the situation described. (Ignore income taxes.)

E 14–16
Error in amortization schedule
● LO14–3

Wilkins Food Products, Inc., acquired a packaging machine from Lawrence Specialists Corporation. Lawrence completed construction of the machine on January 1, 2019. In payment for the machine Wilkins issued a three-year installment note to be paid in three equal payments at the end of each year. The payments include interest at the rate of 10%.

Lawrence made a conceptual error in preparing the amortization schedule, which Wilkins failed to discover until 2021. The error had caused Wilkins to understate interest expense by $45,000 in 2019 and $40,000 in 2020.

Required:
1. Determine which accounts are incorrect as a result of these errors at January 1, 2021, before any adjustments. Explain your answer. (Ignore income taxes.)
2. Prepare a journal entry to correct the error.
3. What other step(s) would be taken in connection with the error?

E 14–17
Note with unrealistic interest rate; borrower; amortization schedule
● LO14–3

Amber Mining and Milling, Inc., contracted with Truax Corporation to have constructed a custom-made lathe. The machine was completed and ready for use on January 1, 2021. Amber paid for the lathe by issuing a $600,000, three-year note that specified 4% interest, payable annually on December 31 of each year. The cash market price of the lathe was unknown. It was determined by comparison with similar transactions that 12% was a reasonable rate of interest.

Required:
1. Prepare the journal entry on January 1, 2021, for Amber Mining and Milling's purchase of the lathe.
2. Prepare an amortization schedule for the three-year term of the note.
3. Prepare the journal entries to record (a) interest for each of the three years and (b) payment of the note at maturity.

E 14–18
Note with unrealistic interest rate; lender; amortization schedule
● LO14–3

Refer to the situation described in E 14–17.

Required:
1. Prepare the journal entry on January 1, 2021, for Truax Corporation's sale of the lathe. Assume Truax spent $400,000 to construct the lathe.
2. Prepare an amortization schedule for the three-year term of the note.
3. Prepare the journal entries to record (a) interest for each of the three years and (b) payment of the note at maturity for Truax.

E 14–19
Installment note; lender; amortization schedule
● LO14–3

FinanceCo lent $8 million to Corbin Construction on January 1, 2021, to construct a playground. Corbin signed a three-year, 6% installment note to be paid in three equal payments at the end of each year.

Required:
1. Prepare the journal entry for FinanceCo's lending the funds on January 1, 2021.
2. Prepare an amortization schedule for the three-year term of the installment note.
3. Prepare the journal entry for the first installment payment on December 31, 2021.
4. Prepare the journal entry for the third installment payment on December 31, 2023.

E 14–20
Installment note; amortization schedule
● LO14–3

American Food Services, Inc., acquired a packaging machine from Barton and Barton Corporation. Barton and Barton completed construction of the machine on January 1, 2021. In payment for the $4 million machine, American Food Services issued a four-year installment note to be paid in four equal payments at the end of each year. The payments include interest at the rate of 10%.

Required:
1. Prepare the journal entry for American Food Services' purchase of the machine on January 1, 2021.
2. Prepare an amortization schedule for the four-year term of the installment note.
3. Prepare the journal entry for the first installment payment on December 31, 2021.
4. Prepare the journal entry for the third installment payment on December 31, 2023.

E 14–21
Installment note
● LO14–3

LCD Industries purchased a supply of electronic components from Entel Corporation on November 1, 2021. In payment for the $24 million purchase, LCD issued a 1-year installment note to be paid in equal monthly payments at the end of each month. The payments include interest at the rate of 12%.

Required:

1. Prepare the journal entry for LCD's purchase of the components on November 1, 2021.

2. Prepare the journal entry for the first installment payment on November 30, 2021.

3. What is the amount of interest expense that LCD will report in its income statement for the year ended December 31, 2021?

E 14–22
FASB codification research
● LO14–2, LO14–3, LO14–4

Access the *FASB Accounting Standards Codification* at the FASB website (www.fasb.org). Determine the specific eight- or nine-digit Codification citation (XXX-XX-XX-XX) for accounting for each of the following items:

1. Disclosure requirements for maturities of long-term debt.

2. How to estimate the value of a note when a note having no ready market and no interest rate is exchanged for a noncash asset without a readily available fair value.

3. When the straight-line method can be used as an alternative to the interest method of determining interest.

E 14–23
Early extinguishment
● LO14–5

The balance sheet of Indian River Electronics Corporation as of December 31, 2020, included 12.25% bonds having a face amount of $90 million. The bonds had been issued in 2013 and had a remaining discount of $3 million at December 31, 2020. On January 1, 2021, Indian River Electronics called the bonds before their scheduled maturity at the call price of 102.

Required:

Prepare the journal entry by Indian River Electronics to record the redemption of the bonds at January 1, 2021.

E 14–24
Convertible bonds; straight-line interest
● LO14–5

On January 1, 2021, Gless Textiles issued $12 million of 9%, 10-year convertible bonds at 101. The bonds pay interest on June 30 and December 31. Each $1,000 bond is convertible into 40 shares of Gless's no par common stock. Bonds that are similar in all respects, except that they are nonconvertible, currently are selling at 99 (that is, 99% of face amount). Century Services purchased 10% of the issue as an investment.

Required:

1. Prepare the journal entries for the issuance of the bonds by Gless and the purchase of the bond investment by Century.

2. Prepare the journal entries for the June 30, 2025, interest payment by both Gless and Century assuming both use the straight-line method.

3. On July 1, 2026, when Gless's common stock had a market price of $33 per share, Century converted the bonds it held. Prepare the journal entries by both Gless and Century for the conversion of the bonds (book value method).

E 14–25
IFRS; convertible bonds
● LO14–5, LO14–7

Refer to the situation described in E 14–24.

Required:

How might your solution to requirement 1 for the issuer of the bonds differ if Gless Textiles prepares its financial statements according to International Financial Reporting Standards? Include any appropriate journal entry in your response.

E 14–26
Convertible bonds; induced conversion
● LO14–5

On January 1, 2021, Madison Products issued $40 million of 6%, 10-year convertible bonds at a net price of $40.8 million. Madison recently issued similar, but nonconvertible, bonds at 99 (that is, 99% of face amount). The bonds pay interest on June 30 and December 31. Each $1,000 bond is convertible into 30 shares of Madison's no par common stock. Madison records interest by the straight-line method.

On June 1, 2023, Madison notified bondholders of its intent to call the bonds at face value plus a 1% call premium on July 1, 2023. By June 30, all bondholders had chosen to convert their bonds into shares as of the interest payment date. On June 30, Madison paid the semiannual interest and issued the requisite number of shares for the bonds being converted.

Required:

1. Prepare the journal entry for the issuance of the bonds by Madison.

2. Prepare the journal entry for the June 30, 2021, interest payment.

3. Prepare the journal entries for the June 30, 2023, interest payment by Madison and the conversion of the bonds (book value method).

818   SECTION 3   Liabilities and Shareholders' Equity

E 14–27
IFRS; convertible bonds
● **LO14–5, LO14–7**
🌐 **IFRS**

Refer to the situation described in E 14–26.

Required:

How might your solution for the issuer of the bonds differ if Madison Products prepares its financial statements according to International Financial Reporting Standards? Include any appropriate journal entries in your response.

E 14–28
Bonds with detachable warrants
● **LO14–5**

On August 1, 2021, Limbaugh Communications issued $30 million of 10% nonconvertible bonds at 104. The bonds are due on July 31, 2041. Each $1,000 bond was issued with 20 detachable stock warrants, each of which entitled the bondholder to purchase, for $60, one share of Limbaugh Communications' no par common stock. Interstate Containers purchased 20% of the bond issue. On August 1, 2021, the market value of the common stock was $58 per share and the market value of each warrant was $8.

In February 2032, when Limbaugh's common stock had a market price of $72 per share and the unamortized discount balance was $1 million, Interstate Containers exercised the warrants it held.

Required:

1. Prepare the journal entries on August 1, 2021, to record (a) the issuance of the bonds by Limbaugh and (b) the investment by Interstate.

2. Prepare the journal entries for both Limbaugh and Interstate in February 2032, to record the exercise of the warrants.

E 14–29
Reporting bonds at fair value
● **LO14–6**

(Note: This is a variation of E 14–13 modified to consider the fair value option for reporting liabilities.) Federal Semiconductors issued 11% bonds, dated January 1, with a face amount of $800 million on January 1, 2021. The bonds sold for $739,814,813 and mature on December 31, 2040 (20 years). For bonds of similar risk and maturity the market yield was 12%. Interest is paid semiannually on June 30 and December 31. Federal determines interest at the effective rate. Federal elected the option to report these bonds at their fair value. On December 31, 2021, the fair value of the bonds was $730 million as determined by their market value in the over-the-counter market.

Required:

1. Prepare the journal entry to adjust the bonds to their fair value for presentation in the December 31, 2021, balance sheet. Federal determined that none of the change in fair value was due to a decline in general interest rates.

2. Assume the fair value of the bonds on December 31, 2022, had risen to $736 million. Prepare the journal entry to adjust the bonds to their fair value for presentation in the December 31, 2022, balance sheet. Federal determined that one-half of the increase in fair value was due to a decline in general interest rates.

E 14–30
Reporting bonds at fair value
● **LO14–6**

On January 1, 2021, Rapid Airlines issued $200 million of its 8% bonds for $184 million. The bonds were priced to yield 10%. Interest is payable semiannually on June 30 and December 31. Rapid Airlines records interest at the effective rate and elected the option to report these bonds at their fair value. On December 31, 2021, the fair value of the bonds was $188 million as determined by their market value in the over-the-counter market. Rapid determined that $1,000,000 of the increase in fair value was due to a decline in general interest rates.

Required:

1. Prepare the journal entry to record interest on June 30, 2021 (the first interest payment).

2. Prepare the journal entry to record interest on December 31, 2021 (the second interest payment).

3. Prepare the journal entry to adjust the bonds to their fair value for presentation in the December 31, 2021, balance sheet.

E 14–31
Reporting bonds at fair value; calculate fair value
● **LO14–6**

On January 1, 2021, Essence Communications issued $800,000 of its 10-year, 8% bonds for $700,302. The bonds were priced to yield 10%. Interest is payable semiannually on June 30 and December 31. Essence Communications records interest at the effective rate and elected the option to report these bonds at their fair value. On December 31, 2021, the market interest rate for bonds of similar risk and maturity was 9%. The bonds are not traded on an active exchange. The decrease in the market interest rate was due to a 1% decrease in general (risk-free) interest rates.

Required:

1. Using the information provided, estimate the fair value of the bonds at December 31, 2021.

2. Prepare the journal entry to record interest on June 30, 2021 (the first interest payment).

3. Prepare the journal entry to record interest on December 31, 2021 (the second interest payment).

4. Prepare the journal entry to adjust the bonds to their fair value for presentation in the December 31, 2021, balance sheet.

E 14–32
Accrued interest
● **Appendix A**

On March 1, 2021, Brown-Ferring Corporation issued $100 million of 12% bonds, dated January 1, 2021, for $99 million (plus accrued interest). The bonds mature on December 31, 2040, and pay interest semiannually on June 30 and December 31. Brown-Ferring's fiscal period is the calendar year.

Required:

1. Determine the amount of accrued interest that was included in the proceeds received from the bond sale.
2. Prepare the journal entry for the issuance of the bonds by Brown-Ferring.

E 14–33
Troubled debt restructuring; debt settled
● Appendix B

At January 1, 2021, Transit Developments owed First City Bank Group $600,000, under an 11% note with three years remaining to maturity. Due to financial difficulties, Transit was unable to pay the previous year's interest.

First City Bank Group agreed to settle Transit's debt in exchange for land having a fair value of $450,000. Transit purchased the land in 2017 for $325,000.

Required:
Prepare the journal entry(s) to record the restructuring of the debt by Transit Developments.

E 14–34
Troubled debt restructuring; modification of terms
● Appendix B

At January 1, 2021, Brainard Industries, Inc., owed Second BancCorp $12 million under a 10% note due December 31, 2023. Interest was paid last on December 31, 2019. Brainard was experiencing severe financial difficulties and asked Second BancCorp to modify the terms of the debt agreement. After negotiation Second BancCorp agreed to:

a. Forgive the interest accrued for the year just ended.
b. Reduce the remaining two years' interest payments to $1 million each and delay the first payment until December 31, 2022.
c. Reduce the unpaid principal amount to $11 million.

Required:
Prepare the journal entries by Brainard Industries, Inc., necessitated by the restructuring of the debt at (1) January 1, 2021; (2) December 31, 2022; and (3) December 31, 2023.

E 14–35
Troubled debt restructuring; modification of terms; unknown effective rate
● Appendix B

At January 1, 2021, NCI Industries, Inc. was indebted to First Federal Bank under a $240,000, 10% unsecured note. The note was signed January 1, 2014, and was due December 31, 2022. Annual interest was last paid on December 31, 2019. NCI was experiencing severe financial difficulties and negotiated a restructuring of the terms of the debt agreement. First Federal agreed to reduce last year's interest and the remaining two years' interest payments to $11,555 each and delay all payments until December 31, 2022, the maturity date.

Required:
Prepare the journal entries by NCI Industries, Inc., necessitated by the restructuring of the debt at: (1) January 1, 2021; (2) December 31, 2021; and (3) December 31, 2022.

E 14–36
FASB codification research; legal fees in a troubled debt restructuring
● Appendix B

In negotiating and effecting a troubled debt restructuring, the creditor usually incurs various legal costs. The *FASB Accounting Standards Codification* represents the single source of authoritative U.S. generally accepted accounting principles.

Required:
1. Obtain the relevant authoritative literature on the accounting treatment of legal fees incurred by a creditor to effect a troubled debt restructuring using the *FASB Accounting Standards Codification* at the FASB website (www.fasb.org).
2. What is the specific eight-digit Codification citation (XXX-XX-XX-X) that describes the guidelines for reporting legal costs?
3. What is the appropriate accounting treatment?

E 14–37
General ledger exercise; bonds; installment note, early extinguishment
● LO14–2, LO14–3, LO14–5

On January 1, 2021, the general ledger of Freedom Fireworks includes the following account balances:

Accounts	Debit	Credit
Cash	$101,200	
Accounts receivable	34,000	
Inventory	152,000	
Land	67,300	
Buildings	120,000	
Allowance for uncollectible accounts		$ 1,800
Accumulated depreciation		9,600
Accounts payable		17,700
Bonds payable		120,000
Discount on bonds payable	30,000	
Common stock		200,000
Retained earnings		155,400
Totals	$504,500	$504,500

820   SECTION 3   Liabilities and Shareholders' Equity

During January 2021, the following transactions occurred:

January 1	Borrowed $100,000 from Captive Credit Corporation. The installment note bears interest at 7% annually and matures in 5 years. Payments of $1,980 are required at the end of each month for 60 months.
January 1	Called the bonds at the contractual call price of $100,000. The 6% bonds pay interest semiannually each June 30 and December 31.
January 4	Received $31,000 from customers on accounts receivable.
January 10	Paid cash on accounts payable, $11,000.
January 15	Paid cash for salaries, $28,900.
January 30	Firework sales for the month totalled $195,000. Sales included $65,000 for cash and $130,000 on account. The cost of the units sold was $112,500.
January 31	Paid the first monthly installment of $1,980 related to the $100,000 borrowed on January 1. (Round your interest calculation to the nearest dollar.)

The following information is available on January 31, 2021.

1. Depreciation on the building for the month of January is calculated using the straight-line method. At the time the building was purchased, the company estimated a service life of ten years and a residual value of $24,000.

2. At the end of January, $3,000 of accounts receivable are past due, and the company estimates that 50% of these accounts will not be collected. Of the remaining accounts receivable, the company estimates that 2% will not be collected. No accounts were written off as uncollectible in January.

3. Unpaid salaries at the end of January are $26,100.

4. Accrued income taxes at the end of January are $5,000.

Required:

1. Record each of the transactions listed above in the "General Journal" tab (these are shown as items 1–7) assuming a FIFO perpetual inventory system. The transaction on January 30 requires two entries: one to record sales revenue and one to record cost of goods sold. Review the "General Ledger" and the "Trial Balance" tabs to see the effect of the transactions on the account balances.

2. Record adjusting entries on January 31. in the "General Journal" tab (these are shown as items 8–11).

3. Review the adjusted "Trial Balance" as of January 31, 2021, in the "Trial Balance" tab.

4. Prepare an income statement for the period ended January 31, 2021, in the "Income Statement" tab).

5. Prepare a classified balance sheet as of January 31, 2021, in the "Balance Sheet" tab.

6. Record closing entries in the "General Journal" tab (these are shown as items 12 and 13).

7. Using the information from the requirements above, complete the "Analysis" tab.

    a. Calculate the debt to equity ratio. If the average debt to equity ratio for the industry is 1.0, is Freedom Fireworks more or less leveraged than other companies in the same industry?

    b. Calculate the times interest earned ratio. If the average times interest earned ratio for the industry is 20 times, is the company more or less able to meet interest payments than other companies in the same industry?

Problems

P 14–1
Determining the price of bonds; discount and premium; issuer and investor
● LO14–2

On January 1, 2021, Instaform, Inc., issued 10% bonds with a face amount of $50 million, dated January 1. The bonds mature in 2040 (20 years). The market yield for bonds of similar risk and maturity is 12%. Interest is paid semiannually.

Required:

1. Determine the price of the bonds at January 1, 2021, and prepare the journal entry to record their issuance by Instaform.

2. Assume the market rate was 9%. Determine the price of the bonds at January 1, 2021, and prepare the journal entry to record their issuance by Instaform.

3. Assume Broadcourt Electronics purchased the entire issue in a private placement of the bonds. Using the data in requirement 2, prepare the journal entry to record the purchase by Broadcourt.

P 14–2
Effective interest; financial statement effects
● LO14–2

On January 1, 2021, Baddour, Inc., issued 10% bonds with a face amount of $160 million. The bonds were priced at $140 million to yield 12%. Interest is paid semiannually on June 30 and December 31. Baddour's fiscal year ends September 30.

Required:

1. What amount(s) related to the bonds would Baddour report in its balance sheet at September 30, 2021?

2. What amount(s) related to the bonds would Baddour report in its income statement for the year ended September 30, 2021?

3. What amount(s) related to the bonds would Baddour report in its statement of cash flows for the year ended September 30, 2021? In which section(s) should the amount(s) appear?

P 14–3
Straight-line and
effective interest
compared

● LO14–2

On January 1, 2021, Bradley Recreational Products issued $100,000, 9%, four-year bonds. Interest is paid semi-annually on June 30 and December 31. The bonds were issued at $96,768 to yield an annual return of 10%.

Required:
1. Prepare an amortization schedule that determines interest at the effective interest rate.
2. Prepare an amortization schedule by the straight-line method.
3. Prepare the journal entries to record interest expense on June 30, 2023, by each of the two approaches.
4. Explain why the pattern of interest differs between the two methods.
5. Assuming the market rate is still 10%, what price would a second investor pay the first investor on June 30, 2023, for $10,000 of the bonds?

P 14–4
Bond amortization
schedule

● LO14–2

On January 1, 2021, Tennessee Harvester Corporation issued debenture bonds that pay interest semiannually on June 30 and December 31. Portions of the bond amortization schedule appear below:

Payment	Cash Payment	Effective Interest	Increase in Balance	Outstanding Balance
				6,627,273
1	320,000	331,364	11,364	6,638,637
2	320,000	331,932	11,932	6,650,569
3	320,000	332,528	12,528	6,663,097
4	320,000	333,155	13,155	6,676,252
5	320,000	333,813	13,813	6,690,065
6	320,000	334,503	14,503	6,704,568
-	-	-	-	-
-	-	-	-	-
-	-	-	-	-
38	320,000	389,107	69,107	7,851,247
39	320,000	392,562	72,562	7,923,809
40	320,000	396,191	76,191	8,000,000

Required:
1. What is the face amount of the bonds?
2. What is the initial selling price of the bonds?
3. What is the term to maturity in years?
4. Interest is determined by what approach?
5. What is the stated annual interest rate?
6. What is the effective annual interest rate?
7. What is the total cash interest paid over the term to maturity?
8. What is the total effective interest expense recorded over the term to maturity?

P 14–5
Issuer and
investor;
effective interest;
amortization
schedule;
adjusting entries

● LO14–2

On February 1, 2021, Cromley Motor Products issued 9% bonds, dated February 1, with a face amount of $80 million. The bonds mature on January 31, 2025 (4 years). The market yield for bonds of similar risk and maturity was 10%. Interest is paid semiannually on July 31 and January 31. Barnwell Industries acquired $80,000 of the bonds as a long-term investment. The fiscal years of both firms end December 31.

Required:
1. Determine the price of the bonds issued on February 1, 2021.
2. Prepare amortization schedules that indicate (a) Cromley's effective interest expense and (b) Barnwell's effective interest revenue for each interest period during the term to maturity.
3. Prepare the journal entries to record (a) the issuance of the bonds by Cromley and (b) Barnwell's investment on February 1, 2021.
4. Prepare the journal entries by both firms to record all subsequent events related to the bonds through January 31, 2023.

P 14–6
Issuer and
investor; straight-
line method;
adjusting entries

● LO14–2,
   Appendix A

On April 1, 2021, Western Communications, Inc., issued 12% bonds, dated March 1, 2021, with face amount of $30 million. The bonds sold for $29.3 million and mature on February 28, 2024. Interest is paid semiannually on August 31 and February 28. Stillworth Corporation acquired $30,000 of the bonds as a long-term investment. The fiscal years of both firms end December 31, and both firms use the straight-line method.

Required:
1. Prepare the journal entries to record (a) issuance of the bonds by Western and (b) Stillworth's investment on April 1, 2021.
2. Prepare the journal entries by both firms to record all subsequent events related to the bonds through maturity.

822   SECTION 3   Liabilities and Shareholders' Equity

P 14–7
Issuer and
investor; effective
interest
● LO14–2

McWherter Instruments sold $400 million of 8% bonds, dated January 1, on January 1, 2021. The bonds mature on December 31, 2040 (20 years). For bonds of similar risk and maturity, the market yield was 10%. Interest is paid semiannually on June 30 and December 31. Blanton Technologies, Inc., purchased $400,000 of the bonds as a long-term investment.

Required:
1. Determine the price of the bonds issued on January 1, 2021.
2. Prepare the journal entries to record (a) their issuance by McWherter and (b) Blanton's investment on January 1, 2021.
3. Prepare the journal entries by (a) McWherter and (b) Blanton to record interest on June 30, 2021 (at the effective rate).
4. Prepare the journal entries by (a) McWherter and (b) Blanton to record interest on December 31, 2021 (at the effective rate).

P 14–8
Bonds; effective
interest; partial
period interest;
financial
statement effects
● LO14–2

The fiscal year ends December 31 for Lake Hamilton Development. To provide funding for its Moonlight Bay project, LHD issued 5% bonds with a face amount of $500,000 on November 1, 2021. The bonds sold for $442,215, a price to yield the market rate of 6%. The bonds mature October 31, 2041 (20 years). Interest is paid semiannually on April 30 and October 31.

Required:
1. What amount of interest expense related to the bonds will LHD report in its income statement for the year ending December 31, 2021?
2. What amount(s) related to the bonds will LHD report in its balance sheet at December 31, 2021?
3. What amount of interest expense related to the bonds will LHD report in its income statement for the year ending December 31, 2022?
4. What amount(s) related to the bonds will LHD report in its balance sheet at December 31, 2022?

P 14–9
Zero-coupon
bonds
● LO14–2

On January 1, 2021, Darnell Window and Pane issued $18 million of 10-year, zero-coupon bonds for $5,795,518.

Required:
1. Prepare the journal entry to record the bond issue.
2. Determine the effective rate of interest.
3. Prepare the journal entry to record annual interest expense at December 31, 2021.
4. Prepare the journal entry to record annual interest expense at December 31, 2022.
5. Prepare the journal entry to record the extinguishment at maturity.

P 14–10
Notes exchanged
for assets;
unknown
effective rate
● LO14–3

At the beginning of the year, Lambert Motors issued the three notes described below. Interest is paid at year-end.
1. The company issued a two-year, 12%, $600,000 note in exchange for a tract of land. The current market rate of interest is 12%.
2. Lambert acquired some office equipment with a fair value of $94,643 by issuing a one-year, $100,000 note. The stated interest on the note is 6%. The current market rate of interest is 12%.
3. The company purchased a building by issuing a three-year installment note. The note is to be repaid in equal installments of $1 million per year beginning one year hence. The current market rate of interest is 12%.

Required:
Prepare the journal entries to record each of the three transactions and the interest expense at the end of the first year for each.

P 14–11
Note with
unrealistic interest
rate
● LO14–3

At January 1, 2021, Brant Cargo acquired equipment by issuing a five-year, $150,000 (payable at maturity), 4% note. The market rate of interest for notes of similar risk is 10%.

Required:
1. Prepare the journal entry for Brant Cargo to record the purchase of the equipment.
2. Prepare the journal entry for Brant Cargo to record the interest at December 31, 2021.
3. Prepare the journal entry for Brant Cargo to record the interest at December 31, 2022.

P 14–12
Noninterest-
bearing
installment note
● LO14–3

At the beginning of 2021, VHF Industries acquired a machine with a fair value of $6,074,700 by issuing a four-year, noninterest-bearing note in the face amount of $8 million. The note is payable in four annual installments of $2 million at the end of each year.

Required:
1. What is the effective rate of interest implicit in the agreement?
2. Prepare the journal entry to record the purchase of the machine.
3. Prepare the journal entry to record the first installment payment at December 31, 2021.

4. Prepare the journal entry to record the second installment payment at December 31, 2022.

5. Suppose the market value of the machine was unknown at the time of purchase, but the market rate of interest for notes of similar risk was 11%. Prepare the journal entry to record the purchase of the machine.

P 14–13
Note and
installment note
with unrealistic
interest rate
● LO14–3

Braxton Technologies, Inc., constructed a conveyor for A&G Warehousers that was completed and ready for use on January 1, 2021. A&G paid for the conveyor by issuing a $100,000, four-year note that specified 5% interest to be paid on December 31 of each year, and the note is to be repaid at the end of four years. The conveyor was custom-built for A&G, so its cash price was unknown. By comparison with similar transactions it was determined that a reasonable interest rate was 10%.

Required:

1. Prepare the journal entry for A&G's purchase of the conveyor on January 1, 2021.

2. Prepare an amortization schedule for the four-year term of the note.

3. Prepare the journal entry for A&G's third interest payment on December 31, 2023.

4. If A&G's note had been an installment note to be paid in four equal payments at the end of each year beginning December 31, 2021, what would be the amount of each installment?

5. Prepare an amortization schedule for the four-year term of the installment note.

6. Prepare the journal entry for A&G's third installment payment on December 31, 2023.

P 14–14
Early
extinguishment of
debt
● LO14–5

Three years ago American Insulation Corporation issued 10%, $800,000, 10-year bonds for $770,000. American Insulation exercised its call privilege and retired the bonds for $790,000. The corporation uses the straight-line method to determine interest.

Required:

Prepare the journal entry to record the call of the bonds.

P 14–15
Early
extinguishment;
effective interest
● LO14–5

The long-term liability section of Twin Digital Corporation's balance sheet as of December 31, 2020, included 12% bonds having a face amount of $20 million and a remaining discount of $1 million. Disclosure notes indicate the bonds were issued to yield 14%.

   Interest expense is recorded at the effective interest rate and paid on January 1 and July 1 of each year. On July 1, 2021, Twin Digital retired the bonds at 102 ($20.4 million) before their scheduled maturity.

Required:

1. Prepare the journal entry by Twin Digital to record the semiannual interest on July 1, 2021.

2. Prepare the journal entry by Twin Digital to record the redemption of the bonds on July 1, 2021.

P 14–16
Debt issue
costs; issuance;
expensing; early
extinguishment;
straight-line
amortization
● LO14–2, LO14–5

Cupola Fan Corporation issued 10%, $400,000, 10-year bonds for $385,000 on June 30, 2021. Debt issue costs were $1,500. Interest is paid semiannually on December 31 and June 30. One year from the issue date (July 1, 2022), the corporation exercised its call privilege and retired the bonds for $395,000. The corporation uses the straight-line method both to determine interest expense and to amortize debt issue costs.

Required:

1. Prepare the journal entry to record the issuance of the bonds.

2. Prepare the journal entries to record the payment of interest and amortization of debt issue costs on December 31, 2021.

3. Prepare the journal entries to record the payment of interest and amortization of debt issue costs on June 30, 2022.

4. Prepare the journal entry to record the call of the bonds.

P 14–17
IFRS; transaction
costs
● LO14–2, LO14–7

 IFRS

Refer to the situation described in P 14–16.

Required:

How might your solution for the issuer of the bonds differ if Cupola prepares its financial statements according to International Financial Reporting Standards? Include any appropriate journal entries in your response.

P 14–18
Early
extinguishment
● LO14–5

The long-term liability section of Eastern Post Corporation's balance sheet as of December 31, 2020, included 10% bonds having a face amount of $40 million and a remaining premium of $6 million. On January 1, 2021, Eastern Post retired some of the bonds before their scheduled maturity.

Required:

Prepare the journal entry by Eastern Post to record the redemption of the bonds under each of the independent circumstances below:

1. Eastern Post called half the bonds at the call price of 102 (102% of face amount).

2. Eastern Post repurchased $10 million of the bonds on the open market at their market price of $10.5 million.

824   SECTION 3   Liabilities and Shareholders' Equity

P 14–19
Convertible
bonds; induced
conversion; bonds
with detachable
warrants

● LO14–5

Bradley-Link's December 31, 2021, balance sheet included the following items:

Long-Term Liabilities	($ in millions)
9.6% convertible bonds, callable at 101 beginning in 2022, due 2025 (net of unamortized discount of $2) [note 8]	$198
10.4% registered bonds callable at 104 beginning in 2031, due 2035 (net of unamortized discount of $1) [note 8]	49
Shareholders' Equity	
Equity—stock warrants	4

> ### Note 8: Bonds (in part)
> The 9.6% bonds were issued in 2008 at 97.5 to yield 10%. Interest is paid semiannually on June 30 and December 31. Each $1,000 bond is convertible into 40 shares of the Company's no par common stock.
>
> The 10.4% bonds were issued in 2012 at 102 to yield 10%. Interest is paid semiannually on June 30 and December 31. Each $1,000 bond was issued with 40 detachable stock warrants, each of which entitles the holder to purchase one share of the Company's no par common stock for $25, beginning 2022.

On January 3, 2022, when Bradley-Link's common stock had a market price of $32 per share, Bradley-Link called the convertible bonds to force conversion. 90% were converted; the remainder were acquired at the call price. When the common stock price reached an all-time high of $37 in December of 2022, 40% of the warrants were exercised.

Required:

1. Prepare the journal entries that were recorded when each of the two bond issues was originally sold in 2005 and 2012.

2. Prepare the journal entry to record (book value method) the conversion of 90% of the convertible bonds in January 2022 and the retirement of the remainder.

3. Assume Bradley-Link induced conversion by offering $150 cash for each bond converted. Prepare the journal entry to record (book value method) the conversion of 90% of the convertible bonds in January 2022.

4. Assume Bradley-Link induced conversion by modifying the conversion ratio to exchange 45 shares for each bond rather than the 40 shares provided in the contract. Prepare the journal entry to record (book value method) the conversion of 90% of the convertible bonds in January 2022.

5. Prepare the journal entry to record the exercise of the warrants in December 2022.

P 14–20
Convertible
bonds; zero
coupon;
potentially
convertible into
cash; FASB
codification
research

● LO14–5

The 2020 annual report of Mills General Corporation (MGC) included the following disclosure note:

> ### Note 10: Borrowings (in part) Convertible Debt
> On July 1, 2020, we issued $125 million of zero coupon convertible unsecured debt due on July 1, 2022 in a private placement offering, priced to yield 1.85%. Proceeds from the offering were $118.3115 million. Initially, each $1,000 principal amount of bonds was convertible into 30 shares of MGC common stock at a conversion price of $35 per share.
>
> The bonds are convertible at any time. Upon conversion, we will pay cash up to the aggregate principal amount of the bonds and pay or deliver cash, shares of our common stock, or a combination of cash and shares of our common stock, at our election.
>
> Because the convertible debt may be wholly or partially settled in cash, we are required to separately account for the liability and equity components of the bonds in a manner that reflects our nonconvertible debt borrowing rate when interest costs are recognized in subsequent periods. The net proceeds of $118.3 million were allocated between debt for $117.2 million and shareholders' equity for $1.1 million with the portion in shareholders' equity representing the fair value of the option to convert the debt.

Required:

1. Prepare the journal entry that was recorded when the bonds were issued on July 1, 2020.

2. What amount of interest expense, if any, did MGC record the fiscal year ended June 30, 2021?

3. Normally under U.S. GAAP, we record the entire issue price of convertible debt as a liability. However, MGC separately recorded the liability and equity components of the notes. Why?

4. Obtain the relevant authoritative literature on classification of debt expected to be financed using the FASB's Codification Research System. You might gain access from the FASB website (www.fasb.org), from your school library, or some other source. Determine the criteria for reporting debt potentially convertible into cash. What is the specific seven-digit Codification citation (XXX-XX-XX) that MGC would rely on in applying that accounting treatment?

P 14–21
Concepts;
terminology

● LO14–1 through
LO14–5

Listed below are several terms and phrases associated with long-term debt. Pair each item from List A with the item from List B (by letter) that is most appropriately associated with it.

List A	List B
_____ 1. Effective rate times balance	a. Straight-line method
_____ 2. Promises made to bondholders	b. Discount
_____ 3. Present value of interest plus present value of principal	c. Liquidation payments after other claims satisfied
_____ 4. Call feature	d. Name of owner not registered
_____ 5. Debt issue costs	e. Premium
_____ 6. Market rate higher than stated rate	f. Checks are mailed directly
_____ 7. Coupon bonds	g. No specific assets pledged
_____ 8. Convertible bonds	h. Bond indenture
_____ 9. Market rate less than stated rate	i. Backed by a lien
_____ 10. Stated rate times face amount	j. Interest expense
_____ 11. Registered bonds	k. May become stock
_____ 12. Debenture bond	l. Legal, accounting, printing
_____ 13. Mortgage bond	m. Protection against falling rates
_____ 14. Materiality concept	n. Periodic cash payments
_____ 15. Subordinated debenture	o. Bond price

P 14–22
Determine bond
price; record
interest; report
bonds at fair
value

● LO14–6

On January 1, 2021, NFB Visual Aids issued $800,000 of its 20-year, 8% bonds. The bonds were priced to yield 10%. Interest is payable semiannually on June 30 and December 31. NFB Visual Aids records interest expense at the effective rate and elected the option to report these bonds at their fair value. On December 31, 2021, the fair value of the bonds was $668,000 as determined by their market value in the over-the-counter market. General (risk-free) interest rates did not change during 2021.

Required:

1. Determine the price of the bonds at January 1, 2021, and prepare the journal entry to record their issuance.

2. Prepare the journal entry to record interest on June 30, 2021 (the first interest payment).

3. Prepare the journal entry to record interest on December 31, 2021 (the second interest payment).

4. Prepare the journal entry to adjust the bonds to their fair value for presentation in the December 31, 2021, balance sheet.

P 14–23
Report bonds
at fair value;
quarterly
reporting

● LO14–6

Appling Enterprises issued 8% bonds with a face amount of $400,000 on January 1, 2021. The bonds sold for $331,364 and mature in 2040 (20 years). For bonds of similar risk and maturity the market yield was 10%. Interest is paid semiannually on June 30 and December 31. Appling determines interest expense at the effective rate. Appling elected the option to report these bonds at their fair value. The fair values of the bonds at the end of each quarter during 2021 as determined by their market values in the over-the-counter market were the following:

March 31	$350,000
June 30	340,000
September 30	335,000
December 31	342,000

General (risk-free) interest rates did not change during 2021.

Required:

1. By how much will Appling's comprehensive income be increased or decreased by the bonds (ignoring taxes) in the March 31 *quarterly* financial statements?

2. By how much will Appling's comprehensive income be increased or decreased by the bonds (ignoring taxes) in the June 30 *quarterly* financial statements?

3. By how much will Appling's comprehensive income be increased or decreased by the bonds (ignoring taxes) in the September 30 *quarterly* financial statements?

4. By how much will Appling's comprehensive income be increased or decreased by the bonds (ignoring taxes) in the December 31 *annual* financial statements?

826   SECTION 3   Liabilities and Shareholders' Equity

P 14–24
Investments in
bonds; accrued
interest; sale;
straight-line
interest

● LO14–2,
   Appendix A

The following transactions relate to bond investments of Livermore Laboratories. The company's fiscal year ends on December 31. Livermore uses the straight-line method to determine interest.

2021

July	1	Purchased $16 million of Bracecourt Corporation 10% debentures, due in 20 years (June 30, 2041), for $15.7 million. Interest is payable on January 1 and July 1 of each year.
Oct.	1	Purchased $30 million of 12% Framm Pharmaceuticals debentures, due May 31, 2031, for $31,160,000 plus accrued interest. Interest is payable on June 1 and December 1 of each year.
Dec.	1	Received interest on the Framm bonds.
	31	Accrued interest.

2022

Jan.	1	Received interest on the Bracecourt bonds.
June	1	Received interest on the Framm bonds.
July	1	Received interest on the Bracecourt bonds.
Sept.	1	Sold $15 million of the Framm bonds at 101 plus accrued interest.
Dec.	1	Received interest on the remaining Framm bonds.
	31	Accrued interest.

2023

Jan.	1	Received interest on the Bracecourt bonds.
Feb. 28		Sold the remainder of the Framm bonds at 102 plus accrued interest.
Dec. 31		Accrued interest.

Required:
1. Prepare the appropriate journal entries for these long-term bond investments.
2. By how much will Livermore Labs' earnings increase in each of the three years as a result of these investments? (Ignore income taxes.)

P 14–25
Accrued interest;
effective
interest; financial
statement effects

● Appendix A

On March 1, 2021, Baddour, Inc., issued 10% bonds, dated January 1, with a face amount of $160 million. The bonds were priced at $140 million (plus accrued interest) to yield 12%. Interest is paid semiannually on June 30 and December 31. Baddour's fiscal year ends September 30.

Required:
1. What would be the amount(s) related to the bonds Baddour would report in its balance sheet at September 30, 2021?
2. What would be the amount(s) related to the bonds that Baddour would report in its income statement for the year ended September 30, 2021?
3. What would be the amount(s) related to the bonds that Baddour would report in its statement of cash flows for the year ended September 30, 2021?

P 14–26
Troubled debt
restructuring

● Appendix B

At January 1, 2021, Rothschild Chair Company, Inc., was indebted to First Lincoln Bank under a $20 million, 10% unsecured note. The note was signed January 1, 2018, and was due December 31, 2024. Annual interest was last paid on December 31, 2019. Rothschild Chair Company was experiencing severe financial difficulties and negotiated a restructuring of the terms of the debt agreement.

Required:
Prepare all journal entries by Rothschild Chair Company, Inc., to record the restructuring and any remaining transactions relating to the debt under each of the independent circumstances below:
1. First Lincoln Bank agreed to settle the debt in exchange for land having a fair value of $16 million but carried on Rothschild Chair Company's books at $13 million.
2. First Lincoln Bank agreed to (a) forgive the interest accrued from last year, (b) reduce the remaining four interest payments to $1 million each, and (c) reduce the principal to $15 million.
3. First Lincoln Bank agreed to defer all payments (including accrued interest) until the maturity date and accept $27,775,000 at that time in settlement of the debt.

Decision Maker's Perspective

Apply your critical-thinking ability to the knowledge you've gained. These cases will provide you an opportunity to develop your research, analysis, judgment, and communication skills. You also will work with other students, integrate what you've learned, apply it in real-world situations, and consider its global and ethical ramifications. This practice will broaden your knowledge and further develop your decision-making abilities.

Real World Case 14–1
Zero-coupon debt; HP Inc.
● LO14–2

Real World Financials

HP Inc. (formerly Hewlett-Packard Company) issued zero-coupon notes at the end of its 1997 fiscal year that mature at the end of its 2017 fiscal year. One billion, eight hundred million dollars face amount of 20-year debt sold for $968 million, a price to yield 3.149%. In fiscal 2002, HP repurchased $257 million in face value of the notes for a purchase price of $127 million, resulting in a gain on the early extinguishment of debt.

Required:

1. What journal entry did HP Inc. use to record the sale in 1997?

2. Using Excel, prepare an amortization schedule for the notes. Assume interest is calculated annually and use numbers expressed in millions of dollars; that is, the face amount is $1,800.

3. What was the effect on HP's earnings in 1998?

4. From the amortization schedule, determine the book value of the debt at the end of 2002.

5. What journal entry did HP Inc. use to record the early extinguishment of debt in 2002, assuming the purchase was made at the end of the year?

6. If none of the notes is repaid prior to maturity, what entry would HP use to record their repayment at the end of 2017?

Source: Hewlett-Packard Company

Analysis Case 14–2
Issuance of bonds
● LO14–2

The following appeared in the October 15, 2021, issue of the *Financial Smarts Journal:*

> This announcement is not an offer of securities for sale or an offer to buy securities.
> New Issue   October 15, 2021
> ### $750,000,000
> ### CRAFT FOODS, INC.
> ### 7.75% Debentures Due October 1, 2031
> Price 99.57%
> plus accrued interest if any from date of issuance
> Copies of the prospectus and the related prospectus supplement may be obtained from such of the undersigned as may legally offer these securities under applicable securities laws.
> **Keegan Morgan & Co. Inc.**
> **Coldwell Bros. & Co.**
> **Robert Stacks & Co.**
> **Sherwin-William & Co.**

Required:

1 Based on the information provided in the announcement, indicate whether the market rate of interest is higher or lower than 7.75% when the Craft Foods bonds were issued.

2 If debt issue costs were $75,000 and the bonds were issued on an interest payment date, what entry did Craft use to record the sale?

Judgment Case 14–3
Noninterest-bearing debt
● LO14–3

While reading a recent issue of *Health & Fitness,* a trade journal, Brandon Wilde noticed an ad for equipment he had been seeking for use in his business. The ad offered oxygen therapy equipment under the following terms:

> Model BL 44582
> $204,000 zero interest loan
> Quarterly payments of $17,000 for only 3 years

The ad captured Wilde's attention, in part, because he recently had been concerned that the interest charges incurred by his business were getting out of line. The price, though, was somewhat higher than prices for this model he had seen elsewhere.

Required:

You are asked to advise Mr. Wilde on the purchase he is considering.

1. Assume the market rate of interest at the time for this type of transaction is 8%. At what amount should he record the asset purchased and the liability used to purchase it?

2. Assume the market rate of interest is unknown but we know the cash price of the equipment is $185,430. What is the effective rate of interest?

828 SECTION 3 Liabilities and Shareholders' Equity

Judgment Case 14–4
Noninterest-bearing note exchanged for cash and other privileges
● LO14–3

The Jaecke Group, Inc. manufactures various kinds of hydraulic pumps. In June 2021, the company signed a four-year purchase agreement with one of its main parts suppliers, Hydraulics, Inc. Over the four-year period, Jaecke has agreed to purchase 100,000 units of a key component used in the manufacture of its pumps. The agreement allows Jaecke to purchase the component at a price lower than the prevailing market price at the time of purchase. As part of the agreement, Jaecke will lend Hydraulics $200,000 to be repaid after four years with no stated interest (the prevailing market rate of interest for a loan of this type is 10%).

Jaecke's chief accountant has proposed recording the note receivable at $200,000. The parts inventory purchase from Hydraulics over the next four years would then be recorded at the actual prices paid.

Required:

You do not agree with the chief accountant's valuation of the note and his intention to value the parts inventory acquired over the four-year period of the agreement at actual prices paid.

1. What entry would you use to account for the initial transaction?

2. What entry would you use to account for the subsequent purchase of 25,000 units of the component for $650,000 when it's market value is 26.60 per unit?

Judgment Case 14–5
Analyzing financial statements; financial leverage; interest coverage
● LO14–1, LO14–4

AGF Foods Company is a large, primarily domestic, consumer foods company involved in the manufacture, distribution, and sale of a variety of food products. Industry averages are derived from Troy's *The Almanac of Business and Industrial Financial Ratios.* Following are the 2021 and 2020 comparative income statements and balance sheets for AGF. (The financial data we use are from actual financial statements of a well-known corporation, but the company name is fictitious and the numbers and dates have been modified slightly to disguise the company's identity.)

AGF FOODS COMPANY
Years Ended December 31, 2021 and 2020
($ in millions)

Comparative Income Statements	2021	2020
Net sales	$6,440	$5,800
Cost of goods sold	(3,667)	(3,389)
Gross profit	2,773	2,411
Operating expenses	(1,916)	(1,629)
Operating income	857	782
Interest expense	(54)	(53)
Income from operations before tax	803	729
Income taxes	(316)	(287)
Net income	$ 487	$ 442

Comparative Balance Sheets		
Assets		
Total current assets	$1,879	$1,490
Property, plant, and equipment (net)	2,592	2,291
Intangibles (net)	800	843
Other assets	74	60
Total assets	$5,345	$4,684
Liabilities and Shareholders' Equity		
Total current liabilities	$1,473	$ 941
Long-term debt	534	728
Deferred income taxes	407	344
Total liabilities	2,414	2,013
Shareholders' equity:		
Common stock	180	180
Additional paid-in capital	21	63
Retained earnings	2,730	2,428
Total shareholders' equity	2,931	2,671
Total liabilities and shareholders' equity	$5,345	$4,684

Long-term solvency refers to a company's ability to pay its long-term obligations. Financing ratios provide investors and creditors with an indication of this element of risk.

Required:

1. Calculate the debt to equity ratio for AGF for 2021.

2. The average ratio for the stocks listed on the New York Stock Exchange in a comparable time period was 1.0. Other things being equal, does AGF appear to have higher or lower default risk than others in its industry?

3. Is AGF experiencing favorable or unfavorable financial leverage?

4. Calculate AGF's times interest earned ratio for 2021.

5. The coverage for the stocks listed on the New York Stock Exchange in a comparable time period was 5.1. Other things being equal, does AGF appear to have higher or lower interest coverage than others in its industry?

Research Case 14–6
FASB codification research; researching the way long-term debt is reported; Macy's, Inc

● LO14–1 through LO14–4

Real World Financials

EDGAR, the Electronic Data Gathering. Analysis, and Retrieval system, performs automated collection, validation, indexing, acceptance and forwarding of submissions by companies and others who are required by law to file forms with the U.S. Securities and Exchange Commission (SEC). All publicly traded domestic companies use EDGAR to make the majority of their filings. (Some foreign companies do so voluntarily.) Form 10-K, including the annual report, is required to be filed on EDGAR. The SEC makes this information available on the Internet.

Required:

1. Access EDGAR on the Internet at www.sec.gov or from Investor Relations at the Macy's, Inc. (www.macys.com). Search for Macy's. Access its 10-K filing for the year ended January 30, 2017. Search or scroll to find the financial statements and related notes. What is the total debt (including current liabilities and deferred taxes) reported in the balance sheet in the most recent two years?

2. Compare the total liabilities (including current liabilities and deferred taxes) with the shareholders' equity and calculate the debt to equity ratio for the most recent two years.

3. Does Macy's obtain more financing through notes, bonds, or commercial paper? Are required debt payments increasing or decreasing over the next three years?

4. Does Macy's classify any short-term debt as long-term?

5. **Note 6: Financing** includes the following statement: "On November 18, 2014, the Company issued $550 million aggregate principal amount of 4.5% senior notes due 2034. This debt was used to pay for the redemption of the $407 million of 7.875% senior notes due 2015 described above." Under some circumstances, Macy's could have reported the amounts due in 2015 as long-term debt at the end of the previous year even though these amounts were due within the coming year. Obtain the relevant authoritative literature on classification of debt expected to be financed using the *FASB Accounting Standards Codification*. You might gain access from the FASB website (www.fasb.org), from your school library, or some other source. Determine the criteria for reporting currently payable debt as long-term. What is the specific nine-digit Codification citation (XXX-XX-XX-XX) that Macy's would rely on in applying that accounting treatment?

Source: Macy's, Inc.

Analysis Case 14–7
Bonds; conversion; extinguishment
● LO14–5

On August 31, 2018, Chickasaw Industries issued $25 million of its 30-year, 6% convertible bonds dated August 31, priced to yield 5%. The bonds are convertible at the option of the investors into 1,500,000 shares of Chickasaw's common stock. Chickasaw records interest expense at the effective rate. On August 31, 2021, investors in Chickasaw's convertible bonds tendered 20% of the bonds for conversion into common stock that had a market value of $20 per share on the date of the conversion. On January 1, 2020, Chickasaw Industries issued $40 million of its 20-year, 7% bonds dated January 1 at a price to yield 8%. On December 31, 2021, the bonds were extinguished early through acquisition in the open market by Chickasaw for $40.5 million.

Required:

1. Using the book value method, does the conversion of the 6% convertible bonds into common stock result in a gain, a loss, or no gain or loss?

2. Using the market value method, by how much, does the conversion of the 6% convertible bonds into common stock result in a gain, a loss, or no gain or loss?

3. Were the 7% bonds issued at face value, at a discount, or at a premium?

4. In the second year of the term to maturity, will the amount of interest expense for the 7% bonds be higher than, lower than, or the same as in the first year?

5. Does the early extinguishment of the 7% bonds result in a gain, a loss, or no gain or loss?

Communication Case 14–8
Convertible securities and warrants; concepts
● LO14–5

It is not unusual to issue long-term debt in conjunction with an arrangement under which lenders receive an option to buy common stock during all or a portion of the time the debt is outstanding. Sometimes the vehicle is convertible bonds; sometimes warrants to buy stock accompany the bonds and are separable. Interstate Chemical is considering these options in conjunction with a planned debt issue.

"You mean we have to report $7 million more in liabilities if we go with convertible bonds? Makes no sense to me," your CFO said. "Both ways seem pretty much the same transaction. Explain it to me, will you?"

Required:

Write a memo. Include in your explanation each of the following:

1. The differences in accounting for proceeds from the issuance of convertible bonds and of debt instruments with separate warrants to purchase common stock.

2. The underlying rationale for the differences.

3. Arguments that could be presented for the alternative accounting treatment.

Communication Case 14–9
Is convertible debt a liability or is it shareholders' equity? Group Interaction

● LO14–5

Some financial instruments can be considered compound instruments in that they have features of both debt and shareholders' equity. The most common example encountered in practice is convertible debt—bonds or notes convertible by the investor into common stock. A topic of debate for several years has been whether:

- **View 1:** Issuers should account for an instrument with both liability and equity characteristics entirely as a liability or entirely as an equity instrument depending on which characteristic governs.
- **View 2:** Issuers should account for an instrument as consisting of a liability component and an equity component that should be accounted for separately.

In considering this question, you should disregard what you know about the current position of the FASB on the issue. Instead, focus on conceptual issues regarding the practicable and theoretically appropriate treatment, unconstrained by GAAP. Also, focus your deliberations on convertible bonds as the instrument with both liability and equity characteristics.

Required:

1. Which view do you favor? Develop a list of arguments in support of your view prior to the class session for which the case is assigned.

2. In class, your instructor will pair you (and everyone else) with a classmate (who also has independently developed an argument).

   a. You will be given three minutes to argue your view to your partner. Your partner likewise will be given three minutes to argue his or her view to you. During these three-minute presentations, the listening partner is not permitted to speak.

   b. After each person has had a turn attempting to convince his or her partner, the two partners will have a three-minute discussion in which they will decide which view is more convincing. Arguments will be merged into a single view for each pair.

3. After the allotted time, a spokesperson for each of the two views will be selected by the instructor. Each spokesperson will field arguments from the class in support of that view's position and list the arguments on the board. The class then will discuss the merits of the two lists of arguments and attempt to reach a consensus view, though a consensus is not necessary.

Communication Case 14–10
Note receivable exchanged for cash and other services

● LO14–3

The Pastel Paint Company recently loaned $300,000 to KIX 96, a local radio station. The radio station signed a noninterest-bearing note requiring the $300,000 to be repaid in three years. As part of the agreement, the radio station will provide Pastel with a specified amount of free radio advertising over the three-year term of the note.

The focus of this case is the valuation of the note receivable by Pastel Paint Company and the treatment of the "free" advertising provided by the radio station. Your instructor will divide the class into two to six groups depending on the size of the class. The mission of your group is to reach consensus on the appropriate note valuation and accounting treatment of the free advertising.

Required:

1. Each group member should deliberate the situation independently and draft a tentative argument prior to the class session for which the case is assigned.

2. In class, each group will meet for 10 to 15 minutes in different areas of the classroom. During that meeting, group members will take turns sharing their suggestions for the purpose of arriving at a single group treatment.

3. After the allotted time, a spokesperson for each group (selected during the group meetings) will share the group's solution with the class. The goal of the class is to incorporate the views of each group into a consensus approach to the situation.

Ethics Case 14–11
Debt for equity swaps; have your cake and eat it too

● LO14–5

The cloudy afternoon mirrored the mood of the conference of division managers. Claude Meyer, assistant to the controller for Hunt Manufacturing, wore one of the gloomy faces that were just emerging from the conference room. "Wow, I knew it was bad, but not that bad," Claude thought to himself. "I don't look forward to sharing those numbers with shareholders."

The numbers he discussed with himself were fourth-quarter losses which more than offset the profits of the first three quarters. Everyone had known for some time that poor sales forecasts and production delays had wreaked havoc on the bottom line, but most were caught off guard by the severity of damage.

Later that night he sat alone in his office, scanning and rescanning the preliminary financial statements on his computer monitor. Suddenly his mood brightened. "This may work," he said aloud, though no one could hear. Fifteen minutes later he congratulated himself, "Yes!"

The next day he eagerly explained his plan to Susan Barr, controller of Hunt for the last six years. The plan involved $300 million in convertible bonds issued three years earlier.

- *Meyer:* By swapping stock for the bonds, we can eliminate a substantial liability from the balance sheet, wipe out most of our interest expense, and reduce our loss. In fact, the book value of the bonds is significantly more than the market value of the stock we'd issue. I think we can produce a profit.
- *Barr:* But Claude, our bondholders are not inclined to convert the bonds.
- *Meyer:* Right. But, the bonds are callable. As of this year, we can call the bonds at a call premium of 1%. Given the choice of accepting that redemption price or converting to stock, they'll all convert. We won't have to pay a cent. And, since no cash will be paid, we won't pay taxes either.

Required:

Do you perceive an ethical dilemma? What would be the impact of following up on Claude's plan? Who would benefit? Who would be injured?

Data Analytics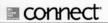

Data analytics is the process of examining data sets in order to draw conclusions about the information they contain. If you haven't completed any of the prior data analytics cases, follow the instructions listed in the Chapter 1 Data Analytics case to get set up. You will need to watch the videos referred to in the Chapters 1 - 3 Data Analytics cases. No additional videos are required for this case. All short training videos can be found here: https://www.tableau.com/learn/training#getting-started.

Data Analytics Case
Long-term Solvency
● LO14–4

In the Chapter 13 Data Analytics Cases, you used Tableau to examine a data set and create charts to compare our two (hypothetical) publicly traded companies: Discount Goods and Big Store as to their liquidity - their ability to pay short-term debts as they come due. In this case, you examine the companies' ability to pay their long-term obligations as measured by their debt to equity and times interest earned ratios.

The debt to equity ratio is measured as total liabilities / shareholder's equity and provides us an indication of the likelihood a company will default on its obligations. Other things being equal, the higher the debt to equity ratio, the higher the risk.

The times interest earned ratio compares interest payments with income available to pay those charges. It is calculated by adding interest plus taxes to net income and dividing by interest expense. The higher the ratio, the greater the margin of safety provided to creditors.

Required:

Use Tableau to calculate and display the trends for the debt to equity and times interest earned ratios for each of the two companies in the period 2018-2021. the average debt to equity ratio and times interest earned ratio for companies in the General Retailers industry sector in a comparable time period are 1.92 and 10.6, respectively. Based upon what you find, answer the following questions:

1. Other things being equal, do both companies appear to have the ability to meet their obligations as measured by the debt to equity ratio?
2. Based solely on the times interest earned ratios, do you reach the same conclusion as in Requirement 1?
3. Is the margin of safety provided to creditors by Discount Goods improving or declining in recent years as measured by the average times interest earned ratio?

Resources:

You have available to you an extensive data set that includes detailed financial data for Discount Goods and Big Store for 2012–2021. The data set is in the form of four Excel files available to download from Connect or under Student Resources within the Library tab. The one for use in this chapter is named "Discount_Goods_Big_Store_Financials.xlsx." Download this file and save it to the computer on which you will be using Tableau.

For this case, you will create several calculations to produce several long-term solvency ratios to allow you to compare and contrast the two companies.

After you view the training videos, follow these steps to create the charts you'll use for this case:

- Open Tableau and connect to the Excel spreadsheet you downloaded.
- Click on the "Sheet 1" tab at the bottom of the canvas, to the right of the Data Source at the bottom of the screen. Drag "Company" and "Year" under Dimensions to the Rows shelf. Change "Year" to *discrete* by right-clicking and selecting "Discrete." Select "Show Filter" and uncheck all the years except 2018–2021. Click OK.
- Drag "Total liabilities" under Measures to the Rows shelf. Change to "Discrete" data following the same instructions.
- Drag "Total shareholders' equity" under Measures to the Rows shelf and change to discrete data.

- Create a calculated field by clicking the "Analysis" tab at the top of the screen and selecting "Create Calculated field." Name the calculation "Debt to Equity Ratio." In the Calculation Editor window drag "Total liabilities" from the Rows shelf, type a division sign (/), and then drag "Total shareholders' equity" from the Rows shelf to the right of the division sign. Make sure the window says that the calculation is valid and click OK.
- Drag the newly created "Debt to Equity Ratio" to the Rows shelf. Click on the "Show Me" and select "side-by-side bars." Add labels to the bars by clicking on "Label" under the "Marks" card and clicking the box "Show marks label." Format the labels to Times New Roman, bold, black and 9-point font. Edit the color on the "Marks" card if desired.
- Change the title of the sheet to be "Long-Term Solvency: Debt to Equity Ratio" by right-clicking and selecting "Edit title." Format the title to Times New Roman, bold, black and 15-point font. Change the title of "Sheet 1" to match the sheet title by right-clicking, selecting "Rename" and typing in the new title.
- Format all other labels to be Times New Roman, bold, black and 12-point font.
- On the Sheet 2 tab, follow the procedure above for the company and year.
- Drag "Net income / (loss)", "Interest expense, and "Provision for income taxes" under Measures into the Rows shelf. Change each to "Discrete" data. Create a calculated field "Times Interest Earned Ratio" following the same process above. In the Calculation Editor window, type an open parenthesis, then drag "Net income / (loss)" from the Rows shelf, type an addition sign (+), drag "Interest expense" from the Rows shelf, type an addition sign, and then drag "Provision for income taxes" from the Rows shelf and close the parenthesis. Next to the closed parenthesis, type a division sign (/) and drag "Interest expense" from the Rows shelf next to the right of the division sign. Make sure the window says that the calculation is valid and click OK.
- Right-click "Net income / loss," "Interest expense," and "Provision for income taxes" and uncheck "Show in Header" so they no longer show on the canvas.
- Drag the newly created "Times Interest Earned Ratio" into the Rows shelf. Click on the "Show Me" and select "side-by-side bars." Add labels to the bars by clicking on "Label" under the "Marks" card and clicking the box "Show mark labels." Format the labels to Times New Roman, bold, black and 10-point font. Edit the color on the Color marks card if desired.
- Change the title of the sheet to be "Long-Term Solvency: Times Interest Earned Ratio" by right-clicking and selecting "Edit title." Format the title to Times New Roman, bold, black and 15-point font. Change the title of "Sheet 2" to match the sheet title by right-clicking, selecting "Rename" and typing in the new title.
- Format all other labels to be Times New Roman, bold, black and 12-point font.
- Once complete, save the file as "*DA14_Your initials.twbx.*"

Continuing Cases

Target Case
● LO14–4

Target Corporation prepares its financial statements according to U.S. GAAP. Target's financial statements and disclosure notes for the year ended February 3, 2018, are available in Connect. This material is also available under the Investor Relations link at the company's website (www.target.com).

Long-term solvency refers to a company's ability to pay its long-term obligations. Financing ratios provide investors and creditors with an indication of this element of risk.

Required:

1. Calculate the debt to equity ratio for Target at February 3, 2018. The average ratio for companies in the Discount Retailers industry sector in a comparable time period was 2.0.

2. Calculate Target's times interest earned ratio for the year ended February 3, 2018. The coverage for companies in the Discount Retailers industry sector in a comparable time period was 6.9.

Air France–KLM Case
● LO14–7
 IFRS

Air France–KLM (AF), a Franco-Dutch company, prepares its financial statements according to International Financial Reporting Standards. AF's financial statements and disclosure notes for the year ended December 31, 2017, are available in Connect. This material also is available under the Finance link at the company's website (www.airfranceklm-finance.com.)

Required:

1. Examine the long-term borrowings in AF's balance sheet and the related note (32.2.2). Note that AF has convertible bonds outstanding that it issued in 2013. Prepare the journal entry AF would use to record the issue of convertible bonds.

2. Prepare the journal entry AF would use to record the issue of the convertible bonds if AF used U.S. GAAP.

3. AF does not elect the fair value option (FVO) to report its financial liabilities. Examine Note 35.3 "Market value of financial instruments." If the company had elected the FVO for all of its debt measured at amortized cost, what would be the balance at December 31, 2017, in the fair value adjustment account?

CPA Exam Questions and Simulations

Sample CPA Exam questions from Roger CPA Review are available in Connect as support for the topics in this chapter. These multiple-choice questions and task-based simulations include expert-written explanations and solutions, and provide a starting point for students to become familiar with the content and functionality of the actual CPA Exam.

CHAPTER

18

Shareholders' Equity

©Peathegee Inc/Blend Images

FINANCIAL REPORTING CASE

Nike, Inc.

Finally, you have some uninterrupted time to get back on the net. Earlier today you noticed on the Internet that the market price of Nike's common stock was up almost 10%. You've been eager to look into why this happened, but have had one meeting after another all day.

You've been a stockholder of Nike since the beginning of the year when you bought your last pair of running shoes and saw how much they sell for these days. The dividends that you receive quarterly are nice, but that's not why you bought the stock; you were convinced at the time that the stock price was poised to rise rapidly. A few well-placed clicks of the mouse and you come across the following news article:

BEAVERTON, Ore.--(BUSINESS WIRE)—NIKE, Inc. (NYSE: NKE) announced today that its Board of Directors has approved a quarterly cash dividend of $0.20 per share on the company's outstanding Class A and Class B Common Stock. This represents an increase of 11% versus the prior quarterly dividend rate of $0.18 per share. The dividend declared today is payable on January 2, 2018, to shareholders of record at the close of business December 4, 2017.

"This marks NIKE's 16th consecutive year of increasing dividend payouts," said Mark Parker, Chairman, President, and CEO of NIKE, Inc. "Today's announcement, combined with the four-year $12 billion share repurchase program we announced in 2015, demonstrates our continued confidence in generating strong cash flow and returns for shareholders through our new Consumer Direct Offense as we continue to invest in fueling sustainable, long-term growth and profitability."

Nike also distributed a two-for-one split of both NIKE's Class A and Class B Common shares in the form of a 100% stock dividend on December 23, 2015.

By the time you finish this chapter, you should be able to respond appropriately to the questions posed in this case. Compare your response to the solution provided at the end of the chapter.

QUESTIONS

1. Do you think the stock price increase is related to Nike's share repurchase plan? (*p. 1062*)

2. What are Nike's choices in accounting for the share repurchases? (*p. 1063*)

3. What effect does the quarterly cash dividend of 20 cents a share have on Nike's assets? Its liabilities? Its shareholders' equity? (*p. 1069*)

4. What effect does the stock split have on Nike's assets? Its liabilities? Its shareholders' equity? (*p. 1072*)

The Nature of Shareholders' Equity

PART A

● LO18–1

A corporation raises money to fund its business operations by some mix of debt and equity financing. In earlier chapters, we examined debt financing in the form of notes, bonds, leases, and other liabilities. Amounts representing those liabilities denote *creditors' interest* in the company's assets. Now we focus on various forms of *equity* financing. Specifically, in this chapter we consider transactions that affect shareholders' equity—those accounts that represent the *ownership interests* of shareholders.

In principle, shareholders' equity is a relatively straightforward concept. Shareholders' equity is a residual amount—what's left over after creditor claims have been subtracted from assets (in other words, net assets). You probably recall the residual nature of shareholders' equity from the basic accounting equation:

$$\underbrace{\text{Assets} - \text{Liabilities}}_{\text{Net Assets}} = \text{Shareholders' Equity}$$

Net assets equal shareholders' equity.

Shareholders' equity accounts denote the ownership interests of shareholders.

Ownership interests of shareholders arise primarily from two sources: (1) amounts *invested* by shareholders in the corporation and (2) amounts *earned* by the corporation on behalf of its shareholders. These two sources are reported as (1) paid-in capital and (2) retained earnings.

Despite being a seemingly clear-cut concept, shareholders' equity and its component accounts often are misunderstood and misinterpreted. As we explore the transactions that affect shareholders' equity and its component accounts, try not to allow yourself to be overwhelmed by unfamiliar terminology or to be overly concerned with precise account titles. Terminology pertaining to shareholders' equity accounts is notoriously diverse. Every shareholders' equity account has several aliases. Indeed, shareholders' equity itself is often referred to as *stockholders' equity* (Walmart), *shareowners' equity* (General Electric), *shareholders' investment* (Target), *stockholders' investment* (FedEx), *shareholders' equity* (Apple), *equity* (Air France–KLM), and many other similar titles.

Complicating matters, transactions that affect shareholders' equity are influenced by corporation laws of individual states in which companies are located. And, as we see later, generally accepted accounting principles provide companies with considerable latitude when choosing accounting methods in this area.

Legal requirements and disclosure objectives make it preferable to separate a corporation's capital into several separate shareholders' equity accounts.

Keeping this perspective in mind while you study the chapter should aid you in understanding the essential concepts. At a very basic level, each transaction we examine can be viewed simply as an increase or decrease in shareholders' equity, per se, without regard to specific shareholders' equity accounts. In fact, for a business organized as a single proprietorship, all capital changes are recorded in a single owner's equity account. The same concepts apply to a corporation. But for corporations, additional considerations make it desirable to separate owners' equity into several separate shareholders' equity accounts. These additional considerations—legal requirements and disclosure objectives—are discussed in later sections of this chapter. So, as you study the separate effects of transactions on retained earnings and specific paid-in capital accounts, you may find it helpful to ask yourself frequently, "What is the net effect of this transaction on shareholders' equity?" or, equivalently, "By how much are net assets (assets minus liabilities) affected by this transaction?"

Financial Reporting Overview

Before we examine the events that underlie specific shareholders' equity accounts, let's summarize how individual accounts relate to each other. The condensed balance sheet in Illustration 18–1 of Exposition Corporation, a hypothetical company, provides that perspective.

Illustration 18–1 depicts a rather comprehensive situation. It's unlikely that any one company would have shareholders' equity from all of these sources at any one time. Remember that, at this point, our objective is only to get a general perspective of the items constituting shareholders' equity. Although company records would include separate accounts for each of these components of shareholders' equity in the balance sheet, in practice Exposition would report a more condensed version similar to that in Illustration 18–1A and the one we will see later in the chapter when we look at the presentation by Abercrombie & Fitch (in Illustration 18–3).

The four classifications within shareholders' equity are paid-in capital, retained earnings, accumulated other comprehensive income, and treasury stock. We discuss these now in the context of Exposition Corporation.

Paid-in Capital

Paid-in capital consists primarily of amounts invested by shareholders when they purchase shares of stock from the corporation or arise from the company buying back some of those

EXPOSITION CORPORATION

Balance Sheet

December 31, 2021

($ in millions)

Assets

$3,000

Liabilities

$1,000

Shareholders' Equity

Paid-in capital:		
Capital stock (par):		
Preferred stock, 10%, $10 par, cumulative, nonparticipating	$100	
Common stock, $1 par	55	
Common stock dividends distributable	5	
Additional paid-in capital:		
Paid-in capital—excess of par, preferred	50	
Paid-in capital—excess of par, common	260	
Paid-in capital—share repurchase	8	
Paid-in capital—conversion of bonds	7	
Paid-in capital—stock options	9	
Paid-in capital—restricted stock	5	
Paid-in capital—lapse of stock options	1	
Total paid-in capital		$ 500
Retained earnings		1,670
Accumulated other comprehensive income:		
Gain (loss) on AFS investments (unrealized)	(85)	
Net unrecognized gain (loss) on pensions	(75)	
Deferred gain (loss) on derivatives*	(4)	
Adjustments from foreign currency translation**	0	(164)
Treasury stock (at cost)		(6)
Total shareholders' equity		$2,000

*When a derivative designated as a cash flow hedge is adjusted to fair value, the gain or loss is deferred as a component of other comprehensive income and included in earnings later, at the same time as earnings are affected by the hedged transaction (described in Appendix A at the end of this textbook).
**Changes in foreign currency exchange rates are discussed elsewhere in your accounting curriculum. The amount could be an addition to or reduction in shareholders' equity.

Illustration 18–1

Detailed Shareholders' Equity Presentation

Assets *minus* Liabilities equals Shareholders' Equity.

The primary source of paid-in capital is the investment made by shareholders when buying preferred and common stock.

Several other events also affect paid-in capital.

Retained earnings represents earned capital.

Preferred stock, 10%, $10 par, cumulative, nonparticipating	$ 100	
Common stock, $1 par	60	
Additional paid-in capital	340	
Retained earnings	1,670	
Accumulated other comprehensive income:		
Gain (loss) on AFS investments (unrealized)	(85)	
Net unrealized loss on pensions	(75)	
Deferred loss on derivatives	(4)	
Treasury stock	(6)	
Total shareholders' equity	$2,000	

Illustration 18–1A

Typical Shareholders' Equity Presentation

shares or from share-based compensation activities. Later in this chapter and the next, we consider in more detail the events and transactions that affect paid-in capital.

Retained Earnings

Retained earnings is accumulated on behalf of shareholders and reported as a single amount. We discuss retained earnings in Part C of this chapter.

1050 SECTION 3   Liabilities and Shareholders' Equity

Treasury Stock

We discuss the final component of shareholders' equity—treasury stock—later in the chapter. It indicates that some of the shares previously sold were bought back by the corporation from shareholders.

● LO18–2

Accumulated Other Comprehensive Income

Also notice that shareholders' equity of Exposition Corporation is adjusted for three events that are not included in net income and so don't affect retained earnings but are part of "other comprehensive income" and therefore are included as a separate component of shareholders' equity: accumulated comprehensive income.[1] Comprehensive income provides a more expansive view of the change in shareholders' equity than does traditional net income. It's the total *nonowner* change in equity for a reporting period. That is, comprehensive income encompasses all changes in equity other than those from transactions with owners. Transactions between the corporation and its shareholders primarily include dividends and the issuance or purchase of shares of the company's stock. Most nonowner changes are reported in the income statement. So, the nonowner changes other than those that are part of traditional net income are the ones reported as "other comprehensive income."

> Comprehensive income includes net income as well as other gains, losses, and adjustments that change shareholders' equity but are not included in traditional net income.

Comprehensive income extends our view of income beyond net income reported in an income statement to include four types of gains and losses not included in income statements.

1. Net holding gains (losses) on available-for-sale investments in debt securities.
2. Gains (losses) from and amendments to postretirement benefit plans.
3. Deferred gains (losses) on derivatives.
4. Adjustments from foreign currency translation.

The first of these are the gains and losses on some securities that occur when the fair values of these investments increase or decrease. As you learned in Chapters 12 and 14, gains and losses on available-for-sale investments in debt securities aren't included in earnings until they are realized through the sale of the securities but are considered components of *other comprehensive income (OCI)* in the meantime. Similarly, as we discussed in Chapter 17, net gains and losses as well as "prior service cost" on pensions sometimes affect other comprehensive income rather than net income as they occur. You have not yet studied the third and fourth potential components of other comprehensive income. As described in Appendix A, "Derivatives," at the back of this textbook, when a derivative designated as a "*cash flow hedge*" is adjusted to fair value, the gain or loss is deferred as a component of other comprehensive income and included in earnings later, at the same time as earnings are affected by the hedged transaction. Adjustments from changes in foreign currency exchange rates are discussed elsewhere in your accounting curriculum. These, too, are included in other comprehensive income (OCI) but not net income.

> OCI is reported in the statement of comprehensive income.
>
> AOCI is reported in the balance sheet.

OCI shares another trait with net income. Just as net income is reported periodically in the income statement and also on a *cumulative* basis as part of retained earnings, OCI too, is reported periodically in the statement of comprehensive income and also as accumulated other comprehensive income (AOCI) in the balance sheet along with retained earnings. In other words, we report two attributes of OCI: (1) components of comprehensive income *created during the reporting period* and (2) the comprehensive income *accumulated* over the current and prior periods.

The first attribute—components of comprehensive income *created during the reporting period*—can be reported either as (a) an expanded version of the income statement or (b) a separate statement immediately following the income statement. Regardless of the placement a company chooses, the presentation is similar. It will report net income, other components of comprehensive income, and total comprehensive income, similar to the presentation in Illustration 18–2. Note that each component is reported net of its related income tax expense or income tax benefit.[2]

---

[1]Comprehensive income was introduced in Chapter 4 and revisited in Chapters 12 and 17.

[2]This can be accomplished by presenting components of other comprehensive income, either net of related income tax effects (as in this presentation) or before income tax effects with disclosure of the income taxes allocated to each component either in a disclosure note or parenthetically in the statement.

Illustration 18–2

Statement of
Comprehensive Income

	($ in millions)	
Net income		$xxx
Other comprehensive income:		
Gains (loss) on AFS investments (unrealized), (net of tax)*	$x	
Gain (loss) from amendments to postretirement benefit plans		
(net of tax)†	(x)	
Deferred gain (loss) on derivatives (net of tax)‡	(x)	
Adjustments from foreign currency translation (net of tax)§	x	xx
Comprehensive income		$xxx

*Changes in the fair value of some investments in debt securities (described in Chapter 12). An unrealized loss also might occur from recording an "other than temporary" impairment in excess of a credit loss for a debt investment. And, as discussed in Chapter 14, applying the "fair value option" to a liability entails reporting in OCI any part of the change in the liability's fair value that's due to the liability's credit risk.
†Gains and losses due to revising assumptions or market returns differing from expectations and prior service cost from amending the plan (described in Chapter 17).
‡When a derivative designated as a cash flow hedge is adjusted to fair value, the gain or loss is deferred as a component of comprehensive income and included in earnings later, at the same time as earnings are affected by the hedged transaction (described in the Derivatives Appendix to the text).
§Changes in foreign currency exchange rates when translating financial statements of foreign subsidiaries to U.S. dollars. The amount could be an addition to or reduction in shareholders' equity. (This item is discussed elsewhere in your accounting curriculum.)

The second measure—the comprehensive income *accumulated* over the current and prior periods—is reported as a separate component of shareholders' equity following retained earnings, similar to the presentation by Exposition Corporation in Illustration 18–1. Note that amounts reported here—accumulated other comprehensive income (AOCI)—represent the *cumulative* sum of the changes in each component of other comprehensive income created during each reporting period (Illustration 18–2) throughout all prior years.

Reporting Shareholders' Equity

You seldom, if ever, will see the numerous list of items shown in Illustration 18–1 reported in the presentation of paid-in capital. Instead, companies keep track of individual additional paid-in capital accounts in company records but ordinarily report these amounts as a single subtotal: additional paid-in capital. Pertinent rights and privileges of various securities outstanding, such as dividend and liquidation preferences, call and conversion information, and voting rights, are summarized in disclosure notes.[3] The shareholders' equity portion of the balance sheet of Abercrombie & Fitch, shown in Illustration 18–3, is a typical presentation format.

The balance sheet reports annual balances of shareholders' equity accounts. However, companies also should disclose the sources of the changes in those accounts.[4] This is the purpose of the statement of shareholders' equity. To illustrate, Illustration 18–4 shows how Walmart reported the changes in its shareholders' equity balances.

The current year changes that Walmart statements of shareholders' equity reveal are net income, other comprehensive income, the purchase of common stock, and dividends declared.

A statement of shareholders' equity reports the transactions that cause changes in its shareholders' equity account balances.

The Corporate Organization

A company may be organized in any of three ways: (1) a sole proprietorship, (2) a partnership, or (3) a corporation. In your introductory accounting course, you studied each form. In this course, we focus exclusively on the corporate form of organization.

Most well-known companies, such as Microsoft, Amazon, and General Electric, are corporations. Also, many smaller companies—even one-owner businesses—are corporations.

● LO18–3

Corporations are the dominant form of business organization.

---

[3]FASB ACS 505–10–50: Equity—Overall—Disclosure.
[4]FASB ASC 505–10–50–2: Equity—Overall—Disclosure.

Illustration 18–3

Typical Presentation Format—Abercrombie & Fitch

Real World Financials

Details of each class of stock are reported in the balance sheet or in disclosure notes.

ABERCROMBIE & FITCH CO. Consolidated Balance Sheets ($ in thousands, except par value amounts)		
	January 28, 2017	**January 30, 2016**
Stockholders' Equity:		
Class A common stock—$0.01 par value: 150,000 shares authorized and 103,300 shares issued at each of January 28, 2017, and January 30, 2016	1,033	1,033
Paid-in capital	396,590	407,029
Retained earnings	2,474,703	2,530,196
Accumulated other comprehensive (loss), net of tax	(121,302)	(114,619)
Treasury stock, at average cost—35,542 and 35,952 shares at January 28, 2017, and January 30, 2016, respectively	(1,507,589)	(1,532,576)
Total Stockholders' Equity	$1,243,435	$1,291,063

Source: Abercrombie & Fitch

Although fewer in number than sole proprietorships and partnerships, in terms of business volume, corporations are the predominant form of business organization.

Accounting for most transactions is the same regardless of the form of business organization.

In most respects, transactions are accounted for in the same way regardless of the form of business organization. Assets and liabilities are unaffected by the way a company is organized. The exception is the method of accounting for capital, the ownership interest in the company. Rather than recording all changes in ownership interests in a single capital account for each owner, as we do for sole proprietorships and partnerships, we use the several capital accounts described in the previous section to record those changes for a corporation. Before discussing how we account for specific ownership changes, let's look at the characteristics of a corporation that make this form of organization distinctive and require special accounting treatment.

International Financial Reporting Standards

● LO18–9

Use of the term "reserves" and other terminology differences. Shareholders' equity is classified under IFRS into two categories: share capital and "reserves." The term reserves is considered misleading and thus is discouraged under U.S. GAAP. Here are some other differences in equity terminology:

U.S. GAAP	IFRS
Capital stock:	Share capital:
Common stock	Ordinary shares
Preferred stock	Preference shares
Paid-in capital—excess of par, common	Share premium, ordinary shares
Paid-in capital—excess of par, preferred	Share premium, preference shares
Accumulated other comprehensive income:	Reserves:
Net gains (losses) on investments—AOCI	Investment revaluation reserve
Net gains (losses) foreign currency translation—AOCI	Translation reserve
{N/A: adjusting P, P, & E to fair value not permitted}	Revaluation reserve
Retained earnings	Retained earnings
Total shareholders' equity	**Total equity**
Presented after Liabilities	Often presented before Liabilities

Illustration 18–4 Statement of Shareholders' Equity—Walmart

($ in millions)	Common Stock		Capital in Excess of Par Value	Retained Earnings	Accumulated Other Comprehensive Income (Loss)	Total Walmart Share-holders' Equity
	Shares	**Amount**				
Balances, January 31, 2014	3,233	$323	$2,362	$76,566	$(2,996)	$76,255
Consolidated net income	—	—	—	16,363	—	16,363
Other comprehensive loss, net of income taxes	—	—	—	—	(4,172)	(4,172)
Cash dividends declared ($1.92 per share)	—	—	—	(6,185)	—	(6,185)
Purchase of Company stock	(13)	(1)	(29)	(950)	—	(980)
Other	8	1	129	(17)	—	113
Balances, January 31, 2015	3,228	323	2,462	85,777	(7,168)	81,394
Consolidated net income	—	—	—	14,694	—	14,694
Other comprehensive income, net of income taxes	—	—	—	—	(4,429)	(4,429)
Cash dividends declared ($1.96 per share)	—	—	—	(6,294)	—	(6,294)
Purchase of Company stock	(65)	(6)	(102)	(4,148)	—	(4,256)
Cash dividend declared to noncontrolling interest	—	—	—	—	—	—
Other	(1)	—	(555)	(8)	—	(563)
Balances, January 31, 2016	3,162	317	1,805	90,021	(11,597)	80,546
Consolidated net income	—	—	—	13,643	—	13,643
Other comprehensive income, net of income taxes	—	—	—	—	(2,635)	(2,653)
Cash dividends declared ($2.00 per share)	—	—	—	(6,216)	—	(6,216)
Purchase of Company stock	(120)	(12)	(174)	(8,090)	—	(8,276)
Other	6	—	740	(4)	—	736
Balances, January 31, 2017	3,048	$ 305	$ 2,371	$ 89,354	$ (14,232)	$ 77,798

Source: Walmart

Limited Liability

The owners are not personally liable for debts of a corporation. Unlike a proprietorship or a partnership, a corporation is a separate legal entity, responsible for its own debts. Shareholders' liability is limited to the amounts they invest in the company when they purchase shares (unless the shareholder also is an officer of the corporation). The limited liability of shareholders is perhaps the single most important advantage of corporate organization. In other forms of business, creditors may look to the personal assets of owners for satisfaction of business debt.

> A corporation is a separate legal entity—separate and distinct from its owners.

Ease of Raising Capital

A corporation is better suited to raising capital than is a proprietorship or a partnership. All companies can raise funds by operating at a profit or by borrowing. However, attracting equity capital is easier for a corporation. Because corporations sell ownership interest in the form of shares of stock, ownership rights are easily transferred. An investor can sell his/her ownership interest at any time and without affecting the corporation or its operations.

> Ownership interest in a corporation is easily transferred.

From the viewpoint of a potential investor, another favorable aspect of investing in a corporation is the lack of mutual agency. Individual partners in a partnership have the power to bind the business to a contract. Therefore, an investor in a partnership must be careful regarding the character and business savvy of fellow co-owners. On the other hand, shareholders' participation in the affairs of a corporation is limited to voting at shareholders'

> Shareholders do not have a mutual agency relationship.

meetings (unless the shareholder also is a member of management). Consequently, a shareholder needn't exercise the same degree of care that partners must in selecting co-owners.

Obviously, then, a corporation offers advantages over the other forms of organization, particularly in its ability to raise investment capital. As you might guess, though, these benefits do not come without a price.

Disadvantages

Corporations are subject to extensive government regulation.

Paperwork! To protect the rights of those who buy a corporation's stock or who loan money to a corporation, the state in which the company is incorporated and the federal government impose extensive reporting requirements. Primarily, the required paperwork is intended to ensure adequate disclosure of information needed by investors and creditors.

Corporations create double taxation.

You read earlier that corporations are separate legal entities. As such, they also are separate taxable entities. Often this causes what is referred to as *double taxation*. Corporations first pay income taxes on their earnings. Then, when those earnings are distributed as cash dividends, shareholders pay personal income taxes on the previously taxed earnings. Proprietorships and partnerships are not taxed at the business level; each owner's share of profits is taxed only as personal income.

Types of Corporations

When referring to corporations in this text, we are referring to corporations formed by private individuals for the purpose of generating profits. These corporations raise capital by selling stock. There are, however, other types of corporations.

Not-for-profit corporations may be owned:
1. By the public sector.
2. By a governmental unit.

Corporations organized for profit may be:
1. Publicly held and traded:
   a. On an exchange.
   b. Over-the-counter.
2. Privately held.

Some corporations, such as churches, hospitals, universities, and charities do not sell stock and are not organized for profit. Also, some not-for-profit corporations are government-owned—the Federal Deposit Insurance Corporation (FDIC), for instance. Accounting for not-for-profit corporations is discussed elsewhere in the accounting curriculum.

Corporations organized for profit may be publicly held or privately (or closely) held. The stock of publicly held corporations is available for purchase by the general public. You can buy shares of Home Depot, Ford Motor Company, or Walmart through a stockbroker. These shares are traded on the New York Stock Exchange. Other publicly held stock, like Apple and Microsoft, are available through Nasdaq (National Association of Securities Dealers Automated Quotations).

Privately held companies' shares are held by only a few individuals and are not available to the general public.

On the other hand, shares of privately held companies are owned by only a few individuals (perhaps a family) and are not available to the general public. Corporations whose stock is privately held do not need to register those shares with the Securities and Exchange Commission and are spared the voluminous, annual reporting requirements of the SEC. Of course, new sources of equity financing are limited when shares are privately held, as is the market for selling existing shares.

Frequently, companies begin as smaller, privately held corporations. Then as success broadens opportunities for expansion, the corporation goes public. For example, in 2012, the shareholders of Facebook decided to take public the privately held company. The result was the largest initial public offering since Visa in 2008. In 2014, Alibaba's IPO surpassed that of both companies to become the largest in history.

Hybrid Organizations

A corporation can elect to comply with a special set of tax rules and be designated an S corporation. S corporations have characteristics of both regular corporations and partnerships. Owners have the limited liability protection of a corporation, but income and expenses are passed through to the owners as in a partnership, avoiding double taxation.

Two particular business structures have evolved in response to liability issues and tax treatment—limited liability companies and limited liability partnerships.

A limited liability company offers several advantages. Owners are not liable for the debts of the business, except to the extent of their investment. Unlike a limited partnership, all members of a limited liability company can be involved with managing the business without losing liability protection. Like an S corporation, income and expenses are passed through to the owners as in a partnership, avoiding double taxation, but there are no limitations on the number of owners as in an S corporation.

A limited liability partnership is similar to a limited liability company, except it doesn't offer all the liability protection available in the limited liability company structure. Partners are liable for their own actions but not entirely liable for the actions of other partners. Professional firms, such as for law and CPAs, often are formed as LLPs.

The Model Business Corporation Act

Corporations are formed in accordance with the corporation laws of individual states. State laws are not uniform, but share many similarities, thanks to the widespread adoption of the Model Business Corporation Act.[5] This act is designed to serve as a guide to states in the development of their corporation statutes. It presently serves as the model for the majority of states.

The *Model Business Corporation Act* serves as the model for the corporation statutes of most states.

State laws regarding the nature of shares that can be authorized, the issuance and repurchase of those shares, and conditions for distributions to shareholders obviously influence actions of corporations. Naturally, differences among state laws affect how we account for many of the shareholders' equity transactions discussed in this chapter. For that reason, we will focus on the normal case, as described by the Model Business Corporation Act, and note situations where variations in state law might require different accounting. Your goal is not to learn diverse procedures caused by peculiarities of state laws, but to understand the broad concepts of accounting for shareholders' equity that can be applied to any specific circumstance.

Variations among state laws influence GAAP pertaining to shareholders' equity transactions.

The process of incorporating a business is similar in all states. The articles of incorporation (sometimes called the *corporate charter*) describe (a) the nature of the firm's business activities, (b) the shares to be issued, and (c) the composition of the initial board of directors. The board of directors establishes corporate policies and appoints officers who manage the corporation.

The number of shares authorized is the maximum number of shares that a corporation is legally permitted to issue, as specified in its articles of incorporation. The number of authorized shares is determined at the company's creation and can only be increased by a vote of the shareholders. At least some of the shares authorized by the articles of incorporation are sold (issued) at the inception of the corporation. Frequently, the initial shareholders include members of the board of directors or officers (who may be one and the same). Ultimately, it is the corporation's shareholders that control the company. Shareholders are the owners of the corporation. By voting their shares, they determine the makeup of the board of directors—who in turn appoint officers, who in turn manage the company.

Shareholders' investment in a corporation ordinarily is referred to as paid-in capital. In the next section, we examine the methods normally used to maintain records of shareholders' investment and to report such paid-in capital in financial statements.

Paid-in Capital

PART B

Fundamental Share Rights

In reading the previous paragraphs, you noted that corporations raise equity funds by selling shares of the corporation. Shareholders are the owners of a corporation. If a corporation has only one class of shares, no designation of the shares is necessary, but they typically are labeled *common* shares, or shares of *common* stock. Ownership rights held by common shareholders, unless specifically withheld by agreement with the shareholders, are as follows:

1. The right to vote on matters that come before the shareholders, including the election of corporate directors. Each share represents one vote.

---

[5]*Model Business Corporation Act*, the American Bar Association, 2016 Revision.

2. The right to share in profits when dividends are declared. The percentage of shares owned by a shareholder determines his/her share of dividends distributed.
3. The right to share in the distribution of assets if the company is liquidated. The percentage of shares owned by a shareholder determines his/her share of assets after creditors and preferred shareholders are paid.

Another right sometimes given to common shareholders is the right to maintain one's percentage share of ownership when new shares are issued. This is referred to as a *preemptive right*. Each shareholder is offered the opportunity to buy a percentage of any new shares issued equal to the percentage of shares he/she owns at the time. In most states, this right must be specifically granted; in others, it is presumed unless contractually excluded.

However, this right usually is not explicitly stated because of the inconvenience it causes corporations when they issue new shares. The exclusion of the preemptive right ordinarily is inconsequential because few shareholders own enough stock to be concerned about their ownership percentage.

Distinguishing Classes of Shares

It is not uncommon for a firm to have more than one, and perhaps several, classes of shares, each with different rights and limitations. To attract investors, companies have devised quite a variety of ownership securities.

If more than one class of shares is authorized by the articles of incorporation, the specific rights of each (for instance, the right to vote, residual interest in assets, and dividend rights) must be stated. Also, some designation must be given to distinguish each class.

Some of the distinguishing designations often used are these:

> **Terminology varies in the way companies differentiate among share types.**

1. Class A, class B, and so on (Tyson Foods)
2. Preferred stock, common stock, and class B stock (Hershey's)
3. Common and preferred (HP)
4. Common stock and capital stock (Alphabet, Inc.)
5. Common and serial preferred (Smucker's)

In your introductory study of accounting, you probably became most familiar with the common stock–preferred stock distinction. That terminology has deep roots in tradition. Early English corporate charters provided for shares that were preferred over others as to dividends and liquidation rights. These provisions were reflected in early American corporation laws. But as our economy developed, corporations increasingly felt the need for innovative ways of attracting investment capital. The result has been a gradual development of a wide range of share classifications that cannot easily be identified by these historical designations.

> **It often is difficult to predict the rights and privileges of shares on the basis of whether they are labeled *common* or *preferred*.**

To reflect the flexibility that now exists in the creation of equity shares, the Model Business Corporation Act, and thus many state statutes, no longer mention the words common and preferred. But the influence of tradition lingers. Most corporations still designate shares as common or preferred. For consistency with practice, the illustrations you study in this chapter use those designations. As you consider the examples, keep in mind that the same concepts apply regardless of the language used to distinguish shares.

Typical Rights of Preferred Shares

An issue of shares with certain preferences or features that distinguish it from the class of shares customarily called common shares may be assigned any of the several labels mentioned earlier. Very often the distinguishing designation is preferred stock. The special rights of preferred shareholders usually include one or both of the following:

1. Preferred shareholders typically have a preference to a specified amount of dividends (stated dollar amount per share or % of par value per share). That is, if the board of directors declares dividends, preferred shareholders will receive the designated dividend before any dividends are paid to common shareholders.

2. Preferred shareholders customarily have a preference (over common shareholders) as to the distribution of assets in the event the corporation is dissolved.

Preferred shareholders sometimes have the right of conversion, which allows them to exchange shares of preferred stock for common stock at a specified conversion ratio. For instance, in 2018, Wells Fargo had outstanding 12.4 million shares of convertible preferred stock. Alternatively, a redemption privilege might allow preferred shareholders the option, under specified conditions, to return their shares for a predetermined redemption price. Preferred shareholders have preference over common stockholders in dividends and liquidation rights. Each Wells Fargo preferred share is convertible into 32 common shares. Similarly, shares may be redeemable at the option of the issuing corporation (sometimes referred to as *callable*).

> **Shares might be:**
> 1. *Convertible* into a specified number of another class of shares.
> 2. *Redeemable* at the option of:
>   a. Shareholders.
>   b. The corporation.

Preferred shares may be cumulative or noncumulative. Typically, preferred shares are cumulative, which means that if the specified dividend is not paid for a given year, the unpaid dividends (called *dividends* in *arrears*) accumulate and must be made up in a later dividend year before any dividends are paid on common shares. We see this illustrated in Part B of the chapter.

Preferred shares may be participating or nonparticipating. A participating feature allows preferred shareholders to receive additional dividends beyond the stated amount. If the preferred shares are fully participating, the distribution of dividends to common and preferred shareholders is a pro rata allocation based on the relative par amounts of common and preferred stock outstanding. Participating preferred stock, previously quite common, is rare today.

Remember that the designations of common and preferred imply no necessary rights, privileges, or limitations of the shares so designated. Such relative rights must be specified by the contract with shareholders. A corporation can create classes of preferred shares that are indistinguishable from common shares in voting rights and/or the right to participate in assets (distributed as dividends or distributed upon liquidation). Likewise, it is possible to devise classes of common shares that possess preferential rights, superior to those of preferred shares.

Is It Equity or Is It Debt?

You probably also can imagine an issue of preferred shares that is almost indistinguishable from a bond issue. Let's say, for instance, that preferred shares call for annual cash dividends of 10% of the par value, dividends are cumulative, and the shares must be redeemed for cash in 10 years. Although the declaration of dividends rests in the discretion of the board of directors, the contract with preferred shareholders can be worded in such a way that directors are compelled to declare dividends each year the company is profitable. For a profitable company, it would be difficult to draw the line between this issue of preferred shares and a 10%, 10-year bond issue. Even in a more typical situation, preferred shares are somewhat hybrid securities—a cross between equity and debt.

> The line between debt and equity is hard to draw.

Sometimes the similarity to debt is even more obvious. Suppose shares are mandatorily redeemable—the company is obligated to buy back the shares at a specified future date. The fact that the company is obligated to pay cash (or other assets) at a fixed or determinable date in the future makes this financial instrument tantamount to debt. A mandatorily redeemable financial instrument must be reported in the balance sheet as a liability, not as shareholders' equity.[6] Extended Stay America, for instance, reported its mandatorily redeemable preferred shares as a liability in its 2018 balance sheet.

> Mandatorily redeemable shares are classified as liabilities.

The Concept of Par Value

Another prevalent practice (besides labeling shares as common and preferred) that has little significance other than historical is assigning a par value to shares. The concept of par value dates back as far as the concept of owning shares of a business. Par value originally indicated the real value of shares. All shares were issued at that price.

> We have inherited the archaic concept of par value from early corporate law.

During the late 19th and early 20th centuries, many cases of selling shares for less than par value—known as *watered shares*—received a great deal of attention and were the subject of

---

[6]FASB ASC 480–10–25–4: Distinguishing Liabilities from Equity—Overall—Recognition.

1058   SECTION 3   Liabilities and Shareholders' Equity

International Financial Reporting Standards

● LO18–9

Distinction between Debt and Equity for Preferred Stock. Differences in the definitions and requirements can result in the same instrument being classified differently between debt and equity under IFRS and U.S. GAAP. Under U.S. GAAP, preferred stock normally is reported as equity, but is reported as debt with the dividends reported in the income statement as interest expense if it is "mandatorily redeemable" preferred stock. Under IFRS, most non-mandatorily redeemable preferred stock (preference shares) also is reported as debt as well as some preference shares that aren't redeemable. Under IFRS (*IAS No. 32*), the critical feature that distinguishes a liability is if the issuer is or can be required to deliver cash (or another financial instrument) to the holder.[7] Unilever describes such a difference in a disclosure note:

Additional Information for U.S. Investors (in part)

Preference Shares

Under IAS 32, Unilever recognizes preference shares that provide a fixed preference dividend as borrowings with preference dividends recognized in the income statement. Under U.S. GAAP such preference shares are classified in shareholders' equity with dividends treated as a deduction to shareholder's equity.

a number of lawsuits. Investors and creditors contended that they relied on the par value as the permanent investment in the corporation and therefore net assets must always be at least that amount. Not only was par value assumed to be the amount invested by shareholders, but it also was defined by early corporation laws as the amount of net assets not available for distribution to shareholders (as dividends or otherwise).

Shares with nominal par value became common to dodge elaborate statutory rules pertaining to par value shares.

Many companies began turning to par value shares with very low par values—often pennies—to escape the watered shares liability of issuing shares below an arbitrary par value and to limit the restrictions on distributions. This practice is common today.

Accountants and attorneys have been aware for decades that laws pertaining to par value and legal capital not only are bewildering but fail in their intent to safeguard creditors from payments to shareholders. Actually, to the extent that creditors are led to believe that they are afforded protection, they are misled. Like the designations of common and preferred shares, the concepts of par value and legal capital have been eliminated entirely from the Model Business Corporation Act.[8]

Many states already have adopted these provisions of the Model Act. But most established corporations issued shares prior to changes in the state statutes. Consequently, most companies have par value shares outstanding and continue to issue previously authorized par value shares. The evolution will be gradual to the simpler, more meaningful provisions of the Model Act.

Most shares continue to bear arbitrarily designated par values.

In the meantime, accountants must be familiar with the outdated concepts of par value and legal capital in order to properly record and report transactions related to par value shares. For that reason, most of the discussion in this chapter centers on par value shares. Largely, this means only that proceeds from shareholders' investment is allocated between stated capital and additional paid-in capital. Be aware, though, that in the absence of archaic laws that prompted the creation of par value shares, there is no theoretical reason to do so.

Accounting for the Issuance of Shares

Par Value Shares Issued For Cash

● LO18–4

When shares are sold for cash (see Illustration 18–5), the capital stock account (usually common or preferred) is credited for the amount representing stated capital. When shares have a designated par value, that amount denotes stated capital and is credited to the stock

---

[7]"Financial Instruments: Presentation," *International Accounting Standard No. 32* (IASCF), as amended effective January 1, 2016.
[8]American Bar Association, official comment to Section 6.21 of the *Model Business Corporation Act,* 2016 Revision.

account. Proceeds in excess of this amount are credited to paid-in capital—excess of par (also called additional paid-in capital).

Dow Industrial sells 10 million of its common shares, $1 par per share, for $10 per share:

	($ in millions)	
Cash (10 million shares at $10 per share)	100	
Common stock (10 million shares at $1 par per share)		10
Paid-in capital—excess of par (remainder: 10 million shares at $10 − $1 = $9 per share)		90

Illustration 18–5

Shares Sold for Cash

When par value shares are issued, only the par amount is credited to the stock account; the remainder to paid-in capital in excess of par.

No-Par Shares Issued for Cash

In states that allow no-par stock, when no-par shares are sold for cash (see Illustration 18–5A), the entire amount received is credited to the stock account.

Dow Industrial sells 10 million of its no-par common shares for $10 per share:

	($ in millions)	
Cash (10 million shares at $10 per share)	100	
Common stock		100

Illustration 18–5A

No-Par Shares Sold for Cash

The total amount received from the sale of no-par shares is credited to the stock account.

Shares Issued for Noncash Consideration

Occasionally, a company might issue its shares for consideration other than cash. It is not uncommon for a new company, yet to establish a reliable cash flow, to pay for promotional and legal services with shares rather than with cash. Similarly, shares might be given in payment for land, or for equipment, or for some other noncash asset.

Even without a receipt of cash to establish the fair value of the shares at the time of the exchange, the transaction still should be recorded at the grant-date fair value of the shares to be issued. This treatment is consistent with the accounting requirement for employee share-based payment awards we discuss in the next chapter and with the general rule for accounting for noncash transactions.[9]

Illustration 18–6 demonstrates a situation where the quoted market price is the best evidence of fair value.

Shares should be issued at fair value.

DuMont Chemicals issues 1 million of its common shares, $1 par per share, in exchange for a custom-built factory for which no cash price is available. Today's issue of *The Wall Street Journal* lists DuMont's stock at $10 per share:

	($ in millions)	
Property, plant, and equipment (1 million shares at $10 per share)	10	
Common stock (1 million shares at $1 par per share)		1
Paid-in capital—excess of par (remainder)		9

Illustration 18–6

Shares Sold for Noncash Consideration

The quoted market price for the shares issued might be the best evidence of fair value.

More Than One Security Issued for a Single Price

Although uncommon, a company might sell more than one security—perhaps common shares and preferred shares—for a single price. As you might expect, the cash received usually is the sum of the separate market values of the two securities. Of course, each is then recorded at its market value. However, if only one security's value is known, the second security's market value is inferred from the total selling price, as demonstrated in Illustration 18–7.

---

[9]FASB Accounting Standards Update (ASU) No. 2018-07, Compensation—Stock Compensation (Topic 718): Improvements to Nonemployee Share-Based Payment Accounting.

1060   SECTION 3   Liabilities and Shareholders' Equity

Illustration 18–7

More than One Security Sold for a Single Price

When only one security's value is known ($40 million), the second security's market value ($60 million) is assumed from the total selling price ($100 million).

AP&P issues 4 million of its common shares, $1 par per share, and 2 million of its preferred shares, $5 par, for $100 million. Today's issue of *The Wall Street Journal* lists AP&P's common at $10 per share. There is no established market for the preferred shares.

	($ in millions)	
Cash..	100	
Common stock (4 million shares × $1 par)...		4
Paid-in capital—excess of par, common...		36
Preferred stock (2 million shares × $5 par)		10
Paid-in capital—excess of par, preferred...		50

Because the shares sell for a total of $100 million, and the market value of the common shares is known to be $40 million (4 million × $10), the preferred shares are inferred to have a market value of $60 million.

Additional Consideration

In the unlikely event that the total selling price is not equal to the sum of the two market prices (when both market values are known), the total selling price is allocated between the two securities, in proportion to their relative market values. You should note that this is the same approach we use (a) when more than one asset is purchased for a single purchase price to allocate the single price to the various assets acquired, (b) when detachable warrants and bonds are issued for a single price, and (c) in any other situation when more than one item is associated with a single purchase price or selling price.

Share Issue Costs

Share issue costs reduce the net cash proceeds from selling the shares and thus paid-in capital—excess of par.

When a company sells shares, it obtains the legal, promotional, and accounting services necessary to effect the sale. The cost of these services reduces the net proceeds from selling the shares. Since paid-in capital—excess of par is credited for the excess of the proceeds over the par value of the shares sold, the effect of share issue costs is to reduce the amount credited to that account. For example, in 2018, AveXis, Inc., sold 4,509,840 shares of its $0.0001 par common stock at $102 per share. the company received net proceeds from the public offering of $431,857,000, after deducting underwriting discounts and commissions and other offering expenses. AveXis's entry to record the sale was as follows:

The cash proceeds is the net amount received after paying share issue costs.

Cash..	431,857,000	
Common stock (4,509,840 shares at $0.0001 par per share) The cash proceeds is the net amount received after paying share issue costs.		451
Paid-in capital—excess of par (remainder)		431,856,549

Concept Review Exercise

EXPANSION OF CORPORATE CAPITAL

Situation: The shareholders' equity section of the balance sheet of National Foods, Inc., included the following accounts at December 31, 2019:

Shareholders' Equity	($ in millions)
Paid-in capital:	
Common stock, 120 million shares at $1 par	$ 120
Paid-in capital—excess of par	836
Retained earnings	2,449
Total shareholders' equity	$3,405

Required:

1. During 2020, several transactions affected the stock of National Foods. Prepare the appropriate entries for these events.

   a. On March 11, National Foods issued 10 million of its 9.2% preferred shares, $1 par per share, for $44 per share.

   b. On November 22, 1 million common shares, $1 par per share, were issued in exchange for eight labeling machines. Each machine was built to custom specifications so no cash price was available. National Food's stock was listed at $10 per share.

   c. On November 23, 1 million of the common shares and 1 million preferred shares were sold for $60 million. The preferred shares had not traded since March and their market value was uncertain.

2. Prepare the shareholders' equity section of the comparative balance sheets for National Foods at December 31, 2020 and 2019. Assume that net income for 2020 was $400 million and the only other transaction affecting shareholders' equity was the payment of the 9.2% dividend on the 11 million preferred shares ($1 million).

Solution:

1. During 2020 several transactions affected the stock of National Foods. Prepare the appropriate entries for these events.

   a. On March 11, National Foods issued 10 million of its preferred shares, $1 par per share, for $44 per share.

	($ in millions)	
Cash	440	
Preferred stock (10 million shares × $1 par per share)		10
Paid-in capital—excess of par, preferred		430

   b. On November 22, 1 million common shares, $1 par per share, were issued in exchange for eight labeling machines:

	($ in millions)	
Machinery (fair value of shares)	10	
Common stock (1 million shares × $1 par per share)		1
Paid-in capital—excess of par, common (1 million shares × $9)		9

The transaction was recorded at the fair value of the shares exchanged for the machinery.

   c. On November 23, 1 million of the common shares and 1 million preferred shares were sold for $60 million:

	($ in millions)	
Cash	60	
Common stock (1 million shares × $1 par per share)		1
Paid-in capital—excess of par, common		9
Preferred stock (1 million shares × $1 par per share)		1
Paid-in capital—excess of par, preferred (to balance)		49

Since the value of only the common stock was known, the preferred stock's market value ($50 per share) was inferred from the total selling price.

2. Prepare the shareholders' equity section of the comparative balance sheets for National Foods at December 31, 2020 and 2019.

1062   SECTION 3   Liabilities and Shareholders' Equity

<table>
<tr><td colspan="3" align="center">**NATIONAL FOODS, INC.**
Balance Sheet
(Shareholders' Equity Section)</td></tr>
<tr><td>($ in millions)</td><td>**2020**</td><td>**2019**</td></tr>
<tr><td>**Shareholders' Equity**</td><td></td><td></td></tr>
<tr><td>Preferred stock, 9.2%, $1 par (2020: $10 million + $1 million)</td><td>$ 11</td><td>$ —</td></tr>
<tr><td>Common stock, $1 par (2020: $120 million + $1 million + $1 million)</td><td>122</td><td>120</td></tr>
<tr><td>Paid-in capital—excess of par, preferred
(2020: $430 million + $49 million)</td><td>479</td><td>—</td></tr>
<tr><td>Paid-in capital—excess of par, common
(2020: $836 million + $9 million + $9 million)</td><td>854</td><td>836</td></tr>
<tr><td>Retained earnings (2019: $2,449 million + $400 million − $1 million)</td><td>2,848</td><td>2,449</td></tr>
<tr><td>*Total shareholders' equity*</td><td>$ 4,314</td><td>$ 3,405</td></tr>
</table>

Note: This situation is continued in the next Concept Review Exercise.

Share repurchases

● LO18–5

In the previous section we examined various ways stock might be issued. In this section, we look at situations in which companies reacquire shares previously sold. Most medium- and large-size companies buy back their own shares. Many have formal share repurchase plans to buy back stock over a series of years.

Decision Makers' Perspective

When a company's management feels the market price of its stock is undervalued, it may attempt to support the price by decreasing the supply of stock in the marketplace. A Johnson & Johnson announcement that it planned to buy back up to $5 billion of its outstanding shares triggered a buying spree that pushed the stock price up by more than 3%.

Decreasing the supply of shares in the marketplace supports the price of remaining shares.

When announcing plans to expand its stock buyback program to $90 billion, Apple chief executive Tim Cook said it "views its shares as undervalued."[10] Although clearly a company may attempt to increase net assets by buying its shares at a low price and selling them back later at a higher price, that investment is not viewed as an asset. Similarly, increases and decreases in net assets from that activity are not reported as gains and losses in the company's income statement. Instead, buying and selling its shares are transactions between the corporation and its owners, analogous to retiring shares and then selling previously unissued shares. You should note the contrast between a company's purchasing of its own shares and its purchasing of shares in another corporation as an investment.

**FINANCIAL
Reporting Case**

Q1 , p. 1047

Unlike an investment in another firm's shares, the acquisition of a company's own shares does not create an asset.

Buybacks zoomed to record highs when tax cuts freed up massive amounts of cash in 2017-18.

Companies buy back shares to offset the increase in shares issued to employees.

Though not considered an investment, the repurchase of shares often is a judicious use of a company's cash. By increasing per share earnings and supporting share price, shareholders benefit. To the extent this strategy is effective, a share buyback can be viewed as a way to "distribute" company profits without paying dividends. Capital gains from any stock price increase are taxed at lower capital gains tax rates than ordinary income tax rates on dividends.

The Tax Cuts and Jobs Act of 2017 ignited an unprecedented volume of share buybacks, exceeding a trillion dollars in 2017 and 2018. The corporate tax rate was slashed from 35% to 21% and other provisions made it advantageous for companies to bring home from overseas huge sums of accumulated earnings from foreign operations. Suddenly finding themselves in the enviable position of having mountains of excess cash, share buybacks became the obvious choice for how to distribute that surplus to shareholders. Apple, alone, bought back over $23 billion of its own stock in March of 2018, a record amount for any U.S. company.

Perhaps the primary motivation for most stock repurchases is to offset the increase in shares that routinely are issued to employees under stock award and stock option

---

[10]Daisuke Wakabayashi, "Apple Boosts Buyback, Splits Stock to Reward Investors," Dow Jones Business Report, **www.nasdaq.com,** April 23, 2014.

compensation programs. Microsoft reported its stock buyback program designed to offset the effect of its stock option and stock purchase plans, as shown in Illustration 18–8.

> **Note 11: Stockholders' Equity (in part)**
> Our board of directors has approved a program to repurchase shares of our common stock to reduce the dilutive effect of our stock option and stock purchase plans.
> Source: Microsoft

Illustration 18–8

Disclosure of Share Repurchase Program—Microsoft

Real World Financials

Similarly, shares might be reacquired to distribute in a stock dividend, a proposed merger, or as a defense against a hostile takeover.[11]

Whatever the reason shares are repurchased, a company has a choice of how to account for the buyback.

1. The shares can be formally retired.
2. The shares can be called treasury stock.

Unfortunately, the choice is not dictated by the nature of the buyback, but by practical motivations of the company. ●

Shares Formally Retired or Viewed as Treasury Stock

When a corporation retires its own shares, those shares assume the same status as authorized but unissued shares, just the same as if they never had been issued. We saw earlier in the chapter that when shares are sold, both cash (usually) and shareholders' equity are increased, the company becomes larger. Conversely, when cash is paid to retire stock, the effect is to decrease both cash and shareholders' equity; the size of the company literally is reduced.

Out of tradition and for practical reasons, companies usually reacquire shares of previously issued stock without formally retiring them.[12] Shares repurchased and not retired are referred to as treasury stock. Because reacquired shares are essentially the same as shares that never were issued at all, treasury shares have no voting rights nor do they receive cash dividends. As demonstrated in Illustration 18–9, when shares are repurchased as treasury stock, we reduce shareholders' equity with a debit to a negative (or contra) shareholders' equity account labeled treasury stock. That entry is reversed later through a credit to treasury stock when the treasury stock is resold. Like the concepts of par value and legal capital, the concept of treasury shares no longer is recognized in most state statutes.[13] Some companies, in fact, are eliminating treasury shares from their financial statements as corporate statutes are modernized. Microsoft retires the shares it buys back rather than labeling them treasury stock. Still, you will see treasury shares reported in the balance sheets of many companies.

FINANCIAL Reporting Case

Q2, p. 1047

Reacquired shares are equivalent to authorized but unissued shares.

Accounting for Retired Shares

When shares are formally retired, we should reduce precisely the same accounts that previously were increased when the shares were sold, namely, common (or preferred) stock and paid-in capital—excess of par. The first column of Illustration 18–9 demonstrates this. The paid-in capital—excess of par account for American Semiconductor shows a balance of $900 million while the common stock account shows a balance of $100 million. Thus the 100 million outstanding shares were originally sold for an average of $9 per share above

---

[11]A corporate takeover occurs when an individual or group of individuals acquires a majority of a company's outstanding common stock from present shareholders. Corporations that are the object of a hostile takeover attempt—a public bid for control of a company's stock against the company's wishes—often take evasive action involving the reacquisition of shares.

[12]The concept of treasury shares originated long ago when new companies found they could sell shares at an unrealistically low price equal to par value to incorporators, who then donated those shares back to the company. Since these shares already had been issued (though not outstanding), they could be sold at whatever the real market price was without adjusting stated capital. Because treasury shares are already issued, different rules apply to their purchase and resale than to unissued shares. Companies can (1) issue shares without regard to preemptive rights of shareholders, or (2) distribute shares as a dividend to shareholders even without a balance in retained earnings.

[13]*The Revised Model Business Corporation Act* eliminated the concept of treasury shares in 1984, after 1980 revisions had eliminated the concepts of par value and legal capital. Most state laws have since followed suit.

1064   SECTION 3   Liabilities and Shareholders' Equity

American Semiconductor's balance sheet included the following:

Shareholders' Equity	($ in millions)
Common stock, 100 million shares at $1 par	$ 100
Paid-in capital—excess of par	900
Paid-in capital—share repurchase	2
Retained earnings	2,000

Retirement   **Treasury Stock**

Reacquired 1 million of its common shares

Case 1: Shares repurchased at $7 per share

Common stock ($1 par × 1 million shares)	1		Treasury stock (cost)......	7
Paid-in capital—excess of par ($9 per share)	9			
Paid-in capital—share repurchase (difference)		3		
Cash		7	Cash	7

OR

Case 2: Shares repurchased at $13 per share

Common stock ($1 par × 1 million shares)	1		Treasury stock (cost).....	13
Paid-in capital—excess of par ($9 per share)	9			
Paid-in capital—share repurchase	2*			
Retained earnings (difference)	1			
Cash		13	Cash	13

*Because there is a $2 million credit balance.

par, or $10 per share. Consequently, when 1 million shares are retired (regardless of the retirement price), American Semiconductor should reduce its common stock account by $1 per share and its paid-in capital—excess of par by $9 per share. Another way to view the reduction is that because 1% of the shares are retired, both share account balances (common stock and paid-in capital—excess of par) are reduced by 1%.

How we treat the difference between the cash paid to buy the shares and the amount the shares originally sold for (amounts debited to common stock and paid-in capital—excess of par) depends on whether the cash paid is *less* than the original issue price (credit difference) or the cash paid is *more* than the original issue price (debit difference):

1. If a *credit* difference is created (as in Case 1 of Illustration 18–9), we credit paid-in capital—share repurchase.
2. If a *debit* difference is created (as in Case 2 of Illustration 18–9), we debit paid-in capital—share repurchase, but only if that account already has a credit balance. Otherwise, we debit retained earnings. (Reducing paid-in capital beyond its previous balance would create a negative balance, which can never happen.)

Why is paid-in capital credited in Case 1 and retained earnings debited in Case 2? The answer lies in the fact that the payments made by a corporation to repurchase its own shares are a distribution of corporate assets to shareholders.

In Case 1, only $7 million is distributed to shareholders to retire shares that originally provided $10 million of paid-in capital. Thus, some of the original investment ($3 million in this case) remains and is labeled *paid-in capital—share repurchase.*

In Case 2, more cash ($13 million) is distributed to shareholders to retire shares than originally was paid in. The amount paid in comprises the original investment of $10 million for the shares being retired, plus $2 million of paid-in capital created by previous repurchase transactions—$12 million total. Thirteen million is returned to shareholders. The additional $1 million paid is viewed as a dividend on the shareholders' investment, and thus a reduction of retained earnings.[14]

---

[14]In the next section of this chapter, you will be reminded that dividends reduce retained earnings. (You first learned this in your introductory accounting course.)

Additional Consideration

> Some companies choose to debit retained earnings for the entire debit difference between the cash paid to repurchase shares and the par amount of those shares rather than allocate that difference in the prescribed way. Target Corporation is an example of a company that follows this approach. While this method lacks conceptual merit by itself, it's permitted by ASC 505-30-30-8, which states that "a corporation can always capitalize or allocate retained earnings for such purposes."

Accounting for Treasury Stock

We view the purchase of treasury stock as a temporary reduction of shareholders' equity, to be reversed later when the treasury stock is resold. The cost of acquiring the shares is "temporarily" debited to the treasury stock account (second column of Illustration 18–9). At this point, the shares are considered to be *issued, but not outstanding.*

The purchase of treasury stock and its subsequent resale are considered to be a "single transaction." The purchase of treasury stock is perceived as a temporary reduction of shareholders' equity, to be reversed later when the treasury stock is resold. The company "temporarily" debits the treasury stock account when acquiring the shares. The common stock account is not affected. Later, when the shares are resold, the treasury stock account will be credited, and any difference from the cash proceeds upon resale will be allocated to specific shareholders' equity accounts. Effectively, we consider the purchase of treasury stock and its subsequent resale to be a "single transaction."

Additional Consideration

> The approach to accounting for treasury stock we discuss in this chapter is referred to as the "cost method." Another permissible approach is the "par value method." It is essentially identical to formally retiring shares, which is why it sometimes is referred to as the *retirement method of accounting for treasury stock.* In fact, if we substitute Treasury stock for Common stock in each of the journal entries we used to account for retirement of shares in Illustrations 18–9 and 18–11, we have the par value method. Because the method has virtually disappeared from practice, we do not discuss it further in this chapter.

BALANCE SHEET EFFECT   Formally retiring shares restores the balances in both the Common stock account and Paid-in capital—excess of par to what those balances would have been if the shares never had been issued at all. If the amount paid in this subsequent repurchase is *less* than the amount received from the initial sale (credit difference), that net increase in assets (cash) is reflected as Paid-in capital—share repurchase. On the other hand, if the amount paid in this subsequent repurchase is *more* than the amount received from the initial sale plus any paid-in capital created by previous repurchases (debit difference), a net reduction in assets (cash) occurs and that reduction is reflected as a decrease in retained earnings.

In contrast, when a share repurchase is viewed as treasury stock, the cost of the treasury stock is simply reported as a reduction in total shareholders' equity. Reporting under the two approaches is compared in Illustration 18–10, using the situation described above for American Semiconductor after the purchase of treasury stock in Illustration 18–9 (Case 2). Notice that either way total shareholders' equity is the same.

Resale of Shares

After shares are formally retired, any subsequent sale of shares is simply the sale of new, unissued shares and is accounted for accordingly. This is demonstrated in the first column of Illustration 18–11.

1066   SECTION 3   Liabilities and Shareholders' Equity

Illustration 18–10

Reporting Share Buyback
in the Balance Sheet

Retirement reduces
common stock and
associated shareholders'
equity accounts.

($ in millions)	Shares Retired	Treasury Stock
Shareholders' Equity		
Paid-in capital:		
Common stock, 100 million shares at $1 par	$ 99	$ 100
Paid-in capital—excess of par	891	900
Paid-in capital—share repurchase		2
Retained earnings	1,999	2,000
Less: Treasury stock, 1 million shares (at cost)		(13)
Total shareholders' equity	$ 2,989	$ 2,989

Illustration 18–11

Comparison of Share
Retirement and Treasury
Stock Accounting—
Subsequent Sale of Shares

After formally retiring
shares, we record a
subsequent sale of shares
exactly like any sale of
shares.

The resale of treasury
shares is viewed as the
consummation of the
"single transaction" begun
when the treasury shares
were purchased.

American Semiconductor sold 1 million shares after reacquiring shares at $13 per share
(Case 2 in Illustration 18–9).

Retirement			**Treasury Stock**	
Sold 1 million shares				
Case A: Shares sold at $14 per share				
Cash...14			Cash...	14
Common stock (par).............................		1	Treasury stock (cost)......................	13
Paid-in capital—excess of par..............		13	Paid-in capital—share repurchase....	1
Or				
Case B: Shares sold at $10 per share				
Cash...10			Cash...	10
Common stock (par).............................		1	Retained earnings (to balance).........	1
Paid-in capital—excess of par..............		9	Paid-in capital—share repurchase.......	2*
			Treasury stock (cost)......................	13

*Because there is a $2 million credit balance.

Allocating the cost of
treasury shares occurs
when the shares are
resold.

    The resale of treasury shares is viewed as the consummation of the single transaction begun when the treasury shares were repurchased. The effect of the single transaction of purchasing treasury stock and reselling it for more than cost (Case 2 of Illustration 18–9 and Case A of Illustration 18–11) is to *increase* both cash and shareholders' equity (by $1 million). The effect of the single transaction of purchasing treasury stock and reselling it for less than cost (Case 2 of Illustration 18–9 and Case B of Illustration 18–11) is to *decrease* both cash and shareholders' equity (by $3 million).

    Note that retained earnings may be debited in a treasury stock transaction, but not credited. Also notice that transactions involving treasury stock have no impact on the income statement. Both of those statements—no credit (increase) to retained earnings and no impact on the income statement—follow the reasoning that a corporation's buying and selling of its own shares are transactions between the corporation and its owners and not part of the revenue recognition process.

Additional Consideration

Determining the cost of
treasury stock sold is
similar to determining the
cost of goods sold.

Treasury Shares Acquired at Different Costs

Notice that the treasury stock account always is credited for the cost of the reissued shares ($13 million in Illustration 18–11). When shares are reissued, if treasury stock on hand has been purchased at different per share prices, the cost of the shares sold must be determined using a cost flow assumption—FIFO, LIFO, or weighted average—similar to determining the cost of goods sold when inventory items are acquired at different unit costs.

Concept Review Exercise

TREASURY STOCK

Situation: The shareholders' equity section of the balance sheet of National Foods, Inc. included the following accounts at December 31, 2020.

Shareholders' Equity	($ in millions)
Paid-in capital:	
Preferred stock, 11 million shares at $1 par	$ 11
Common stock, 122 million shares at $1 par	122
Paid-in capital—excess of par, preferred	479
Paid-in capital—excess of par, common	854
Retained earnings	2,848
Total shareholders' equity	$4,314

Required:

1. National Foods reacquired common shares during 2021 and sold shares in two separate transactions later that year. Prepare the entries for both the purchase and subsequent sale of shares during 2021, assuming that the shares were (a) retired and (b) considered to be treasury stock.

   a. National Foods purchased 6 million shares at $10 per share.

   b. National Foods sold 2 million shares at $12 per share.

   c. National Foods sold 2 million shares at $7 per share.

2. Prepare the shareholders' equity section of National Foods' balance sheet at December 31, 2021, assuming the shares were both (a) retired and (b) viewed as treasury stock. Net income for 2021 was $400 million, and preferred shareholders were paid $1 million cash dividends.

Solution:

1. National Foods reacquired common shares during 2021 and sold shares in two separate transactions later that year. Prepare the entries for both the purchase and subsequent sale of shares during 2021, assuming that the shares were (a) retired and (b) considered to be treasury stock.

   a. National Foods purchased 6 million shares at $10 per share:

Retirement ($ in millions)			**Treasury Stock ($ in millions)**	
Common stock (6 million shares × $1).....................	6		Treasury stock	
Paid-in capital—excess of par			(6 million shares × $10) 60	
(6 million shares × $7*)	42		Cash	60
Retained earnings (to balance)	12			
Cash		60		

*$854 million ÷ 122 million shares

   b. National Foods sold 2 million shares at $12 per share ($ in millions):

Cash	24		Cash	24	
Common stock			Treasury stock		
(2 million shares × $1)..		2	(2 million shares × $10)		20
Paid-in capital—excess of par.................................		22	Paid-in capital—share repurchase......		4

   c. National Foods sold 2 million shares at $7 per share ($ in millions):

Cash	14		Cash	14	
Common stock			Paid-in capital—share repurchase..........		4
(2 million shares× $1 par).....................................		2	Retained earnings (to balance)		2
Paid-in capital—excess of par.................................		12	Treasury stock		
			(2 million shares × $10)		20

2. Prepare the shareholders' equity section of National Foods's balance sheet at December 31, 2021, assuming the shares were both (a) retired and (b) viewed as treasury stock.

NATIONAL FOODS, INC.
Balance Sheet
(Shareholders' Equity Section)
At December 31, 2021

($ in millions)	Shares Retired	Treasury Stock
Shareholders' Equity		
Preferred stock, 11 million shares at $1 par	$ 11	$ 11
Common stock, 122 million shares at $1 par	120	122
Paid-in capital—excess of par, preferred	479	479
Paid-in capital—excess of par, common	846*	854
Retained earnings	3,235†	3,245‡
Treasury stock, at cost; 2 million common shares	—	(20)
Total shareholders' equity	$4,691	$4,691

Note: This situation is continued in the next Concept Review Exercise.

*$854 − $42 + $22 + $12
†$2,848 − $12 + $400 − $1
‡$2,848 − $2 + $400 − $1

PART C

Retained Earnings

Characteristics of Retained Earnings

● LO18–6

In the previous section we examined *invested* capital. Now we consider *earned* capital, that is, retained earnings. In general, retained earnings represents a corporation's accumulated, undistributed net income (or net loss). A more descriptive title used by some companies is reinvested earnings. A credit balance in this account indicates a dollar amount of assets previously earned by the firm but not distributed as dividends to shareholders. We refer to a debit balance in retained earnings as a deficit. Microsoft reported a deficit for several years until retained earnings grew to a positive balance in 2013.

You saw in the previous section that the buyback of shares (as well as the resale of treasury shares in some cases) can decrease retained earnings. We examine in this section the effect on retained earnings of dividends and stock splits.[15]

Dividends

● LO18–7

Shareholders' initial investments in a corporation are represented by amounts reported as paid-in capital. One way a corporation provides a return to its shareholders on their investments is to pay them a dividend, typically cash.[16]

Dividends are distributions of assets the company has generated on behalf of its shareholders. If dividends are paid that exceed the amount of assets earned by the company, then management is, in effect, returning to shareholders a portion of their investments, rather than providing them a return on that investment. So most companies view retained earnings as the amount available for dividends.[17]

---

[15] Retained earnings also can be affected by some changes in accounting principles and for some corrections of errors, as we will see in Chapter 20. And, too, retained earnings can be affected by the repurchase of shares as we discussed in Part A of this chapter.

[16] Dividends are not the only return shareholders earn; when market prices of their shares rise, shareholders benefit also. Indeed, many companies have adopted policies of never paying dividends but reinvesting all assets they earn. The motivation is to accommodate more rapid expansion and thus, presumably, increases in the market price of the stock.

[17] Ordinarily, this is not the legal limitation. Most states permit a company to pay dividends so long as, after the dividend, its assets would not be "less than the sum of its total liabilities plus the amount that would be needed, if the corporation were to be dissolved at the time of the distribution, to satisfy the preferential rights upon dissolution of shareholders whose preferential rights are superior to those receiving the distribution." (Revised Model Business Corporation Act, American Bar Association, 2016.) Thus, legally, a corporation can distribute amounts equal to total shareholders' equity less dissolution preferences of senior equity securities (usually preferred stock).

Liquidating Dividend

In unusual instances in which a dividend exceeds the balance in retained earnings, the excess is referred to as a liquidating dividend because some of the invested capital is being liquidated. This might occur when a corporation is being dissolved and assets (not subject to a superior claim by creditors) are distributed to shareholders. Any portion of a dividend not representing a distribution of earnings should be debited to additional paid-in capital rather than retained earnings.

> Any dividend not representing a distribution of earnings should be debited to paid-in capital.

Retained Earnings Restrictions

Sometimes the amount available for dividends purposely is reduced by management. A restriction of retained earnings designates a portion of the balance in retained earnings as being *unavailable for dividends*. A company might restrict retained earnings to indicate management's intention to withhold for some specific purpose the assets represented by that portion of the retained earnings balance. For example, management might anticipate the need for a specific amount of assets in upcoming years to repay a maturing debt, to cover a contingent loss, or to finance expansion of the facilities. Be sure to understand that the restriction itself does not set aside cash for the designated event but merely communicates management's intention not to distribute the stated amount as a dividend.

> A restriction of retained earnings communicates management's intention to withhold assets represented by a specified portion of the retained earnings balance.

A restriction of retained earnings normally is indicated by a disclosure note to the financial statements. Although instances are rare, a formal journal entry may be used to reclassify a portion of retained earnings to an "appropriated" retained earnings account.

> Normally a restriction of retained earnings is indicated by a disclosure note.

Cash Dividends

You learned in Chapter 14 that paying interest to creditors is a contractual obligation. No such legal obligation exists for paying dividends to shareholders. A liability is not recorded until a company's board of directors votes to declare a dividend. In practice, though, corporations ordinarily try to maintain a stable dividend pattern over time.

When directors declare a cash dividend, we reduce retained earnings and record a liability. Before the payment actually can be made, a listing must be assembled of shareholders entitled to receive the dividend. A specific date is stated as to when the determination will be made of the recipients of the dividend. This date is called the date of record. Registered owners of shares of stock on this date are entitled to receive the dividend—even if they sell those shares prior to the actual cash payment. To be a registered owner of shares on the date of record, an investor must purchase the shares before the ex-dividend date. This date usually is one business day before the date of record. Shares purchased on or after that date are purchased ex dividend—without the right to receive the declared dividend. As a result, the market price of a share typically will decline by the amount of the dividend, other things being equal, on the ex-dividend date. Consider Illustration 18–12.

> **FINANCIAL Reporting Case**
>
> Q3, p. 1047

Illustration 18–12
Cash Dividends

On June 1, the board of directors of Craft Industries declares a cash dividend of $2 per share on its 100 million shares, payable to shareholders of record June 15, to be paid July 1.

June 1—Declaration Date	($ in millions)	
Retained earnings	200	
Cash dividends payable (100 million shares at $2 per share)		200
June 14—Ex-Dividend Date		
No entry		
June 15—Date of Record		
No entry		
July 1—Payment Date		
Cash dividends payable	200	
Cash		200

> At the declaration date, retained earnings is reduced and a liability is recorded.

> Registered owners of shares on the date of record are entitled to receive the dividend.

A sufficient balance in retained earnings permits a dividend to be declared. Note that retained earnings is a shareholders' equity account representing a dollar claim on assets in general, but not on any specific asset in particular. Sufficient retained earnings does not ensure sufficient cash to make payment. These are two separate accounts having no necessary connection with one another.

DIVIDENDS ON PREFERRED SHARES As mentioned in Part A, preferred shares can be cumulative or noncumulative. Cumulative means that if the specified dividend is not paid for a given year, the unpaid dividends (called *dividends* in *arrears*) accumulate and must be made up in a later dividend year before any dividends are paid on common shares. Illustration 18–13 provides an example.

Illustration 18–13

Distribution of Dividends to Preferred Shareholders

> The shareholders' equity section of Corbin Enterprises includes the items shown below. The board of directors declared cash dividends of $360,000, $500,000, and $700,000 in its first three years of operation—2020, 2021, and 2022, respectively.
>
> | | |
> |---|---:|
> | Common stock | $3,000,000 |
> | Paid-in capital—excess of par, common | 9,800,000 |
> | Preferred stock, 8% | 6,000,000 |
> | Paid-in capital—excess of par, preferred | 780,000 |
>
> The preferred shareholders are entitled to dividends of $480,000 (8% × $6,000,000).
>
> Determine the amount of dividends to be paid to preferred and common shareholders in each of the three years, assuming that the preferred stock is cumulative and nonparticipating.
>
> | | Preferred | Common |
> |---|---|---|
> | 2020 | $ 360,000* | $0 |
> | 2021 | 500,000** | 0 |
> | 2022 | 580,000† | 120,000 (remainder) |
>
> *Only $360,000 dividends are declared in 2020 so dividends in arrears are $120,000.
> **$120,000 dividends in arrears plus $380,000 of the $480,000 current preference.
> †$100,000 dividends in arrears ($480,000 − $380,000) plus the $480,000 current preference

Property Dividends

Because cash is the asset most easily divided and distributed to shareholders, most corporate dividends are cash dividends. In concept, though, any asset can be distributed to shareholders as a dividend. When a noncash asset is distributed, it is referred to as a property dividend (often called a *dividend in kind* or a *nonreciprocal transfer to owners*). Gold Resource Corp., a Colorado gold mining company, announced in 2014 that it would make dividend payments in gold bullion instead of cash.

RFM Corporation conferred a property dividend to its shareholders when it distributed shares of Philipine Townships, Inc., stock that RFM was holding as an investment. Securities held as investments are the assets most often distributed in a property dividend due to the relative ease of dividing these assets among shareholders and determining their fair values.

The *fair value* of the assets to be distributed is the amount recorded for a property dividend.

A property dividend should be recorded at the fair value of the assets to be distributed, measured at the date of declaration. This may require revaluing the asset to fair value prior to recording the dividend. If so, a gain or loss is recognized for the difference between book value and fair value. This is demonstrated in Illustration 18–14.

Stock Dividends and Splits

Stock Dividends

● LO18–8

A stock dividend is the distribution of additional shares of stock to current shareholders of the corporation. Be sure to note the contrast between a stock dividend and either a cash or property dividend. A stock dividend affects neither the assets nor the liabilities of the firm.

On October 1 the board of directors of Craft Industries declares a property dividend of 2 million shares of Beaman Corporation's preferred stock.

- Craft had purchased the Beaman shares in March as an investment (book value: $9 million).
- The investment shares have a fair value of $5 per share, **$10** million.
- The property dividend is payable to shareholders of record October 15, to be distributed November 1.

October 1—Declaration Date	($ in millions)	
Investment in equity securities *	1	
Gain on investments ($10 − $9)...		1
Retained earnings (2 million shares at $5 per share)...	10	
Property dividends payable		10
October 15—Date of Record		
No entry		
November 1—Payment Date		
Property dividends payable	10	
Investment in equity securities...		10

*As an alternative to using a fair value adjustment account, we adjust for fair value directly to the investment account.

Illustration 18–14
Property Dividends

Before recording the property dividend, the asset first must be written up to fair value.

Also, because each shareholder receives the same percentage increase in shares, shareholders' proportional interest in (percentage ownership of) the firm remains unchanged. For example, if a 5% stock dividend is declared, every shareholder will receive additional shares of stock to equal 5% of the shares they currently own.

The prescribed accounting treatment of a stock dividend requires that shareholders' equity items be reclassified by reducing one or more shareholders' equity accounts and simultaneously increasing one or more paid-in capital accounts. The amount reclassified depends on the size of the stock dividend. For a "small" stock dividend, typically less than 25%, the fair value of the additional shares distributed is transferred from retained earnings to paid-in capital, as demonstrated in Illustration 18–15.[18]

Craft declares and distributes a 10% common stock dividend (10 million shares) when the market value of the $1 par common stock is $12 per share.

	($ in millions)	
Retained earnings (10 million shares at $12 per share).....................................	120	
Common stock (10 million shares at $1 par per share)		10
Paid-in capital—excess of par (remainder)..		110

Illustration 18–15
Stock Dividend

A "small" stock dividend requires reclassification to paid-in capital of retained earnings equal to the fair value of the additional shares distributed.

Additional Consideration

The entry above is recorded on the declaration date. Since the additional shares are not yet issued, some accountants would prefer to credit "common stock dividends distributable" at this point, instead of common stock. In that case, when the shares are issued, common stock dividends distributable is debited and common stock credited. The choice really is inconsequential; either way the $10 million amount would be reported as part of paid-in capital on a balance sheet prepared between the declaration and distribution of the shares.

STOCK MARKET REACTION TO STOCK DISTRIBUTIONS As a Craft shareholder owning 10 shares at the time of the 10% stock dividend, you would receive an 11th share. Since each is worth $12, would you benefit by $12 when you receive the additional

---

[18]FASB ASC 505–20: Equity—Stock Dividends and Stock Splits. In this pronouncement, a small stock dividend is defined as one 20% to 25% or less. For filings with that agency, the SEC has refined the definition to comprise stock distributions of less than 25%.

share from Craft? Of course not. If the value of each share were to remain $12 when the 10 million new shares are distributed, the total market value of the company would grow by $120 million (10 million shares × $12 per share).

A corporation cannot increase its market value simply by distributing additional stock certificates. Because all shareholders receive the same percentage increase in their respective holdings, you, and all other shareholders, still would own the same percentage of the company as before the distribution. Accordingly, the per share value of your shares should decline from $12 to $10.91 so that your 11 shares would be worth $120— precisely what your 10 shares were worth prior to the stock dividend. You might compare Craft Industries to a pizza. Cutting the pizza into 16 slices instead of 12 doesn't create more to eat; you still have the same pizza, just a higher number of smaller slices. Any failure of the stock price to actually adjust in proportion to the additional shares issued probably would be due to information other than the distribution reaching shareholders at the same time.

Then, what justification is there for recording the additional shares at market value? In 1941 (and reaffirmed in 1953), accounting rule-makers felt that many shareholders are deceived by small stock dividends, believing they benefit by the market value of their additional shares. Furthermore they erroneously felt that these individual beliefs are collectively reflected in the stock market by per share prices that remain unchanged by stock dividends. Consequently, their prescribed accounting treatment is to reduce retained earnings by the same amount as if cash dividends were paid equal to the market value of the shares issued.[19]

This obsolete reasoning is inconsistent with our earlier conclusion that the market price per share *will* decline in approximate proportion to the increase in the number of shares distributed. Our intuitive conclusion is supported also by formal research.[20]

Besides being based on fallacious reasoning, accounting for stock dividends by artificially reclassifying "earned" capital as "invested" capital conflicts with the reporting objective of reporting shareholders' equity by source. Despite these limitations, this outdated accounting standard still applies.

> The market price per share will decline in proportion to the increase in the number of shares distributed in a stock dividend.

> Early rule-makers felt that per share market prices do not adjust in response to an increase in the number of shares.

> Capitalizing retained earnings for a stock dividend artificially reclassifies earned capital as invested capital.

REASONS FOR STOCK DIVIDENDS   Since neither the corporation nor its shareholders apparently benefits from stock dividends, why do companies declare them?[21] Occasionally, a company tries to give shareholders the illusion that they are receiving a real dividend.

Another reason is merely to enable the corporation to take advantage of the accepted accounting practice of capitalizing retained earnings. Specifically, a company might wish to reduce an existing balance in retained earnings—otherwise available for *cash* dividends— so it can reinvest the assets represented by that balance.

> Companies sometimes declare a stock dividend in lieu of a real dividend.

> Companies sometimes declare a stock dividend so they can capitalize retained earnings.

> **FINANCIAL Reporting Case**
>
> Q4, p. 1047

Stock Splits

A frequent reason for issuing a stock dividend is actually to induce the per share market price decline it causes. For instance, after a company declares a 100% stock dividend on 100 million shares of common stock, with a per share market price of $12, it then has 200 million shares, each with an approximate market value of $6. The motivation for reducing the per share market price is to increase the stock's *marketability* by making it attractive to a larger number of potential investors.

A stock distribution of 25% or higher can be accounted for in one of two ways: (1) as a "large" stock dividend or (2) as a stock split.[22] Thus, a 100% stock dividend could be labeled a 2-for-1 stock split and accounted for as such. Conceptually, the proper accounting treatment of a stock distribution is to make no journal entry. This, in fact, is the prescribed accounting treatment for a stock split.

> A large stock dividend is known as a stock *split*.

---

[19]FASB ASC 505–20–30–3: Equity—Stock Dividends and Stock Splits—Initial Measurement.

[20]Taylor W. Foster III and Don Vickrey, "The Information Content of Stock Dividend Announcements," *Accounting Review* (April 1978); and J. David Spiceland and Alan J. Winters, "The Market Reaction to Stock Distributions: The Effect of Market Anticipation and Cash Returns," *Accounting and Business Research* (Summer 1986).

[21]After hitting a high in the 1940s, the number of stock dividends has declined significantly. Currently, about 3% of companies declare stock dividends in any given year.

[22]FASB ASC 505–20–25–2: Equity—Stock Dividends and Stock Splits—Recognition.

Additional Consideration

No cash dividends are paid on treasury shares. Usually stock dividends aren't paid on treasury shares either. Treasury shares are essentially equivalent to shares that never have been issued. In some circumstances, though, the intended use of the repurchased shares will give reason for the treasury shares to participate in a stock dividend. For instance, if the treasury shares have been specifically designated for issuance to executives in a stock option plan or stock award plan, it would be appropriate to adjust the number of shares by the stock distribution.

Since the same common stock account balance (total par) represents twice as many shares in a 2-for-1 stock split, the par value per share will be reduced by one-half. In the previous example, if the par were $1 per share before the stock distribution, then after the 2-for-1 stock split, the par would be $0.50 per share.

As you might expect, having the par value per share change in this way is cumbersome and expensive. All records, printed or electronic, that refer to the previous amount must be changed to reflect the new amount. The practical solution is to account for the large stock distribution as a stock dividend rather than a stock split.

Stock Splits Effected in the Form of Stock Dividends (Large Stock Dividends)

To avoid changing the par value per share, a company can refer to the stock distribution as a *stock split effected in the form of a stock dividend,* or simply a *stock dividend.* In that case, a journal entry increases the common stock account by the par value of the additional shares. Instead of reducing retained earnings in these instances, most companies reduce (debit) paid-in capital—excess of par to offset the credit to common stock (Illustration 18–16).

Craft declares and distributes a 2-for-1 stock split effected in the form of a 100% stock dividend (100 million shares) when the market value of the $1 par common stock is $12 per share.

	($ in millions)	
Paid-in capital—excess of par	100	
Common stock (100 million shares at $1 par per share)		100

Illustration 18–16

Stock Split Effected in the Form of a Stock Dividend

If a *stock split* is effected in the form of a stock dividend, a journal entry prevents the par per share from changing.

Notice that this entry does not reclassify earned capital as invested capital. Some companies, though, choose to debit retained earnings instead.

	($ in millions)	
Retained earnings	100	
Common stock (100 million shares × $1 par per share)		100

Some companies capitalize retained earnings when recording a stock split effected in the form of a stock dividend.

Netflix described a stock split in its disclosure notes as shown in Illustration 18–17.

Note 8—Stock Split
On June 23, 2015, the Company's Board of Directors declared a seven-for-one stock split in the form of a stock dividend that was paid on July 14, 2015, to all shareholders of record as of July 2, 2015. Outstanding share and per-share amounts disclosed for all periods presented have been retroactively adjusted to reflect the effects of the stock split.

Source: Netflix

Illustration 18–17

Stock Split Disclosure—Netflix

Real World Financials

In 2015, Netflix distributed a rare 7-for-1 stock split that dropped the price of Netflix shares from about $700 all the way down to about $100. Three years later, that stock price was $350 per share. If there had been no split in 2015, the price of one share would have been around $2,450.

Additional Consideration

A company choosing to capitalize retained earnings when recording a stock split effected in the form of a stock dividend may elect to capitalize an amount other than par value. Accounting guidelines are vague in this regard, stating only that legal amounts are minimum requirements and do not prevent the capitalization of a larger amount per share.

Source: FASB ASC 505–20–30–4: Equity–Stock Dividends and Stock Splits–Initial Measurement (previously "Restatement and Revision of Accounting Research Bulletins," *Accounting Research Bulletin* No. 43 (New York: AICPA, 1961), Chap. 7, sec. B, par. 14).

REVERSE STOCK SPLIT   A reverse stock split occurs when a company decreases, rather than increases, its outstanding shares. After a 1-for-4 reverse stock split, for example, 100 million shares, $1 par per share, would become 25 million shares, $4 par per share. No journal entry is necessary. Of course the market price per share theoretically would quadruple, which usually is the motivation for declaring a reverse stock split. Companies that reverse split their shares frequently are struggling companies trying to accomplish with the split what the market has been unwilling to do—increase the stock price. Often this is to prevent the stock's price from becoming so low that it is delisted from a market exchange. Reverse splits are not unusual occurrences, particularly during stock market downturns. In 2017, Xerox Corporation declared a 1-for-4 reverse split.

FRACTIONAL SHARES   Typically, a stock dividend or stock split results in some shareholders being entitled to fractions of whole shares. For example, if a company declares a 25% stock dividend, or equivalently a 5-for-4 stock split, a shareholder owning 10 shares would be entitled to 2 1/2 shares. Another shareholder with 15 shares would be entitled to 3 3/4 shares.

Cash payments usually are made to shareholders for *fractional* shares and are called "cash in lieu of payments." In the situation described above, for instance, if the market price at declaration is $12 per share, the shareholder with 15 shares would receive 3 additional shares and $9 in cash ($12 × 3/4).

Cash payments usually are made when shareholders are entitled to fractions of whole shares.

Decision Maker's Perspective

Profitability is the key to a company's long-run survival. A summary measure of profitability often used by investors and potential investors, particularly common shareholders, is the return on shareholders' equity, or simply return on equity. This ratio measures the ability of company management to generate net income from the resources that owners provide. The ratio is computed by dividing net income by average shareholders' equity. A variation of this ratio often is used when a company has both preferred and common stock outstanding. The return to common shareholders' equity is calculated by subtracting dividends to preferred shareholders from the numerator and using average common shareholders' equity as the denominator. The modified ratio focuses on the profits generated on the assets provided by common shareholders.

The return on equity is a popular measure of profitability.

Although the ratio is useful when evaluating the effectiveness of management in employing resources provided by owners, analysts must be careful not to view it in isolation or without considering how the ratio is derived. Keep in mind that shareholders' equity is a measure of the book value of equity, equivalent to the book value of net assets. Book value measures quickly become out of line with market values. An asset's book value usually equals its market value on the date it's purchased; the two aren't necessarily the same after that. Equivalently, the market value of a share of stock (or of total shareholders' equity) usually is different from its book value. As a result, to supplement the return on equity ratio,

Book value measures have limited use in financial analysis.

analysts often relate earnings to the market value of equity, calculating the earnings-price ratio. This ratio is simply the earnings per share divided by the market price per share.

A variation of this ratio often used by analysts is the price-earnings ratio, which is simply the inverse of the earnings-price ratio: the market price per share divided by the earnings per share.

To better understand the differences between the book value ratio and the market value ratio, let's consider the following condensed information reported by Sharp-Novell Industries for 2021 and 2020:

($ in thousands, except per share amounts)	**2021**	**2020**
Sales	$ 3,500	$ 3,100
Net income	125	114
Current assets	$ 750	$ 720
Property, plant, and equipment (net)	900	850
Total assets	$ 1,650	$ 1,570
Current liabilities	$ 550	$ 530
Long-term liabilities	540	520
Paid-in capital	210	210
Retained earnings	350	310
Liabilities and shareholders' equity	$ 1,650	$ 1,570
Shares outstanding	50,000	50,000
Stock price (average)	$ 42.50	$ 42.50

The 2021 return on shareholders' equity is computed by dividing net income by average shareholders' equity:

$$\$125 \div [(\$560 + \$520) \div 2] = \underline{\underline{23.1\%}}$$

The earnings-price ratio is the earnings per share divided by the market price per share:

$$\text{Earnings per share (2021)} = \$125 \div 50 = \$2.50$$
$$\text{Earnings-price ratio} = \$2.50 \div \$42.50 = \underline{\underline{5.9\%}}$$

A variation of this ratio often used by analysts is the price-earnings ratio, which is simply the inverse of the earnings-price ratio: the market price per share divided by the earnings per share.

Obviously, the return on the market value of equity is much lower than on the book value of equity. This points out the importance of looking at more than a single ratio when making decisions. While 23.1% may seem like a desirable return, 5.9% is not nearly so attractive. Companies often emphasize the return on shareholders' equity in their annual reports. Alert investors should not accept this measure of achievement at face value. For some companies this is a meaningful measure of performance; but for others, the market-based ratio means more, particularly for a mature firm whose book value and market value are more divergent.

Decisions managers make with regard to shareholders' equity transactions can significantly impact the return to shareholders. For example, when a company buys back shares of its own stock, the return on equity goes up. Net income is divided by a smaller amount of shareholders' equity. On the other hand, the share buyback uses assets, reducing the resources available to earn net income in the future. So, managers as well as outside analysts must carefully consider the decision to reacquire shares in light of the current economic environment, the firm's investment opportunities, and cost of capital to decide whether such a transaction is in the long-term best interests of owners. Investors should be wary of buybacks during down times because the resulting decrease in shares and increase in earnings per share can be used to mask a slowdown in earnings growth.

The decision to pay dividends requires similar considerations. When earnings are high, are shareholders better off receiving substantial cash dividends or having management reinvest those funds to finance future growth (and future dividends)? The answer, of course, depends on the particular circumstances involved. Dividend decisions should reflect managerial strategy concerning the mix of internal versus external financing, alternative investment opportunities, and industry conditions. High dividends often are found in mature industries and low dividends in growth industries. ●

Share retirement and treasury stock transactions can affect the return to owners.

Share retirement and treasury stock transactions can affect the return to owners.

Dividend decisions should be evaluated in light of prevailing circumstances.

1076 SECTION 3 Liabilities and Shareholders' Equity

Ethical Dilemma

Interworld Distributors has paid quarterly cash dividends since 1985. The dividends have steadily increased from $.25 per share to the latest dividend declaration of $2.00 per share. The board of directors is eager to continue this trend despite the fact that revenues fell significantly during recent months as a result of worsening economic conditions and increased competition. The company founder and member of the board proposes a solution. He suggests a 5% stock dividend in lieu of a cash dividend to be accompanied by the following press announcement:

"In lieu of our regular $2.00 per share cash dividend, Interworld will distribute a 5% stock dividend on its common shares, currently trading at $40 per share. Changing the form of the dividend will permit the Company to direct available cash resources to the modernization of physical facilities in preparation for competing in the 21st century."

What do you think?

Concept Review Exercise

CHANGES IN RETAINED EARNINGS

Situation: The shareholders' equity section of the balance sheet of National Foods, Inc., included the following accounts at December 31, 2021:

Shareholders' Equity	($ in millions)
Paid-in capital	
Preferred stock, 9.09%, 11 million shares at $1 par	$ 11
Common stock, 122 million shares at $1 par	122
Paid-in capital—excess of par, preferred	479
Paid-in capital—excess of par, common	854
Retained earnings	3,245
Treasury stock, at cost, 2 million common shares	(20)
Total shareholders' equity	$4,691

Required:

1. During 2022, several events and transactions affected the retained earnings of National Foods. Prepare the appropriate entries for these events.

   a. On March 1, the board of directors declared a cash dividend of $1 per share on its 120 million outstanding shares (122 million – 2 million treasury shares), payable on April 3 to shareholders of record March 11.

   b. On March 5, the board of directors declared a property dividend of 120 million shares of Kroger common stock that National Foods had purchased in February as an investment (book value: $900 million). The investment shares had a fair value of $8 per share and were distributed March 30 to shareholders of record March 15.

   c. On April 13, a 3-for-2 stock split was declared and distributed. The stock split was effected in the form of a 50% stock dividend. The market value of the $1 par common stock was $20 per share.

   d. On October 13, a 10% common stock dividend was declared and distributed when the market value of the $1 par common stock was $12 per share. Cash in lieu of payments was distributed for fractional shares equivalent to 1 million whole shares.

   e. On December 1, the board of directors declared the 9.09% cash dividend on the 11 million preferred shares, payable on December 23 to shareholders of record December 11.

2. Prepare a statement of shareholders' equity for National Foods reporting the changes in shareholders' equity accounts for 2020, 2021, and 2022. Refer to the previous two Concept Reviews in this chapter for the 2020 and 2021 changes. For 2021, assume that shares were reacquired as treasury stock. Also, look back to the statement of shareholders' equity in Illustration 18–4 for the format of the statement. Assume that net income for 2022 is $225 million.

Solution:

1. During 2022, several events and transactions affected the retained earnings of National Foods. Prepare the appropriate entries for these events.

a. Cash dividend of $1 per share on its 120 million *outstanding* common shares (122 million − 2 million treasury shares), payable on April 3 to shareholders of record March 11. (Note: Dividends aren't paid on treasury shares.)

March 1—Declaration Date	($ in millions)	
Retained earnings	120	
Cash dividends payable (120 million shares at $1 per share)		120
March 11—Date of Record		
No entry		
April 3—Payment Date		
Cash dividends payable	120	
Cash		120

The declaration of a dividend reduces retained earnings and creates a liability.

b. Property dividend of 120 million shares of Kroger common stock:

March 5—Declaration Date	($ in millions)	
Investment in equity securities	60	
Gain on investments ($960 − $900)		60
Retained earnings (fair value of asset to be distributed)	960	
Property dividends payable		960
March 15—Date of Record		
No entry		
March 30—Payment Date		
Property dividends payable	960	
Investment in equity securities		960

The investment first must be written up to the $960 million fair value ($8 × 120 million shares).

The liability is satisfied when the Kroger shares are distributed to shareholders.

c. 3-for-2 stock split effected in the form of a 50% stock dividend:

April 13	($ in millions)	
Paid-in capital—excess of par*	60	
Common stock (60 million shares at $1 par per share)		60

*Alternatively, retained earnings may be debited.

120 million shares times 50% equals 60 million new shares—recorded at par.

d. 10% common stock dividend—with cash in lieu of payments for shares equivalent to 1 million whole shares:

October 13	($ in millions)	
Retained earnings (18 million shares* at $12 per share)	216	
Common stock (17 million shares at $1 par per share)		17
Paid-in capital—excess of par (17 million shares at $11 per share above par)		187
Cash (1 million equivalent shares at $12 market price per share)		12

*(120 million + 60 million) × 10% = 18 million shares

The stock dividend occurs after the 3-for-2 stock split; thus 18 million shares are distributed.

The $12 fair value of the additional shares is capitalized in this small stock dividend.

e. 9.09% cash dividend on the 11 million preferred shares, payable on December 23 to shareholders of record December 11:

December 1—Declaration Date	($ in millions)	
Retained earnings	1	
Cash dividends payable ($11 million par × 9.09%)		1
December 11—Date of Record		
No entry		
December 23—Payment Date		
Cash dividends payable	1	
Cash		1

f. Prepare a statement of shareholders' equity for National Foods reporting the changes in shareholders' equity accounts for 2020, 2021, and 2022.

NATIONAL FOODS
Statement of Shareholders' Equity
For the Years Ended December 31, 2022, 2021, and 2020
($ in millions)

	Preferred Stock	Common Stock	Additional Paid-In Capital	Retained Earnings	Treasury Stock (at cost)	Total Share-holders' Equity
Balance at January 1, 2020		120	836	2,449		3,405
Sale of preferred shares	10		430			440
Issuance of common shares		1	9			10
Issuance of common and preferred shares	1	1	58			60
Net income				400		400
Cash dividends, preferred				(1)		(1)
Balance at December 31, 2020	11	122	1,333	2,848		4,314
Purchase of treasury shares					(60)	(60)
Sale of treasury shares			4		20	24
Sale of treasury shares			(4)	(2)	20	14
Net income				400		400
Cash dividends, preferred				(1)		(1)
Balance at December 31, 2021	11	122	1,333	3,245	(20)	4,691
Cash dividends, common				(120)		(120)
Property dividends, common				(960)		(960)
3-for-2 split effected in the form of a stock dividend		60	(60)			
10% stock dividend		17	187	(216)		(12)
Cash dividends, preferred				(1)		(1)
Net income				225		225
Balance at December 31, 2022	11	199	1,460	2,173	(20)	3,823

These are the transactions from Concept Review Exercise—Expansion of Corporate Capital.

These are the transactions from Concept Review Exercise—Treasury Stock.

These are the transactions from Concept Review Exercise—Changes in Retained Earnings.

Financial Reporting Case Solution

©Peathegee Inc/Blend Images

1. **Do you think the stock price increase is related to Nike's share repurchase plan?** *(p. 1062)*   The stock price increase probably is related to Nike's buyback plan. The marketplace realizes that decreasing the supply of shares supports the price of remaining shares. However, the repurchase of shares is not necessarily the best use of a company's cash. Whether it is in the shareholders' best interests depends on what other opportunities the company has for the cash available.

2. **What are Nike's choices in accounting for the share repurchases?** *(p. 1063)*   When a corporation reacquires its own shares, those shares assume the same status as authorized but unissued shares, just as if they never had been issued. However, for exactly the same transaction, companies can choose between two accounting alternatives: (a) formally retiring them or (b) accounting for the shares repurchased as treasury stock. In actuality, Nike uses alternative (a).

3. **What effect does the quarterly cash dividend of 20 cents per share have on Nike's assets? Its liabilities? Its shareholders' equity?** *(p. 1069)*   Each quarter, when directors declare a cash dividend, retained earnings are reduced and a liability is recorded. The liability is paid with cash on the payment date. So, the net effect is a decrease in Nike's assets and its shareholders' equity. The effect on liabilities is temporary.

4. **What effect does the stock split have on Nike's assets? Its liabilities? Its shareholders' equity?** *(p. 1072)*   Conceptually, the proper accounting treatment of a stock split is to make no journal entry. However, since Nike refers to the stock distribution as a stock split "in the form of a 100% stock dividend," a journal entry would increase the common stock account by the par value of the additional shares and would reduce paid-in capital—excess of par. This merely moves an amount from one part of shareholders' equity to another. Regardless of the accounting method, there is no change in Nike's assets, liabilities, or total shareholders' equity. ●

The Bottom Line

● **LO18–1**   Shareholders' equity is the owners' residual interest in a corporation's assets. It arises primarily from (1) amounts invested by shareholders and (2) amounts earned by the corporation on behalf of its shareholders. These are reported as (1) paid-in capital and (2) retained earnings in a balance sheet. A statement of shareholders' equity reports the sources of the changes in individual shareholders' equity accounts. *(p. 1047)*

● **LO18–2**   Comprehensive income encompasses all changes in equity except those caused by transactions with owners (like dividends and the sale or purchase of shares). It includes traditional net income as well as "other comprehensive income." *(p. 1050)*

● **LO18–3**   A corporation is a separate legal entity—separate and distinct from its owners. A corporation is well suited to raising capital and has limited liability. However, it gives rise to "double taxation." Common shareholders usually have voting rights; preferred shareholders usually have a preference to a specified amount of dividends and to assets in the event of liquidation. *(p. 1051)*

● **LO18–4**   Shares sold for consideration other than cash (maybe services or a noncash asset) should be recorded at the fair value of the shares or the noncash consideration, whichever seems more clearly evident. *(p. 1058)*

● **LO18–5**   When a corporation retires previously issued shares, those shares assume the same status as authorized but unissued shares—just the same as if they had never been issued. Payments made to retire shares are viewed as a distribution of corporate assets to shareholders. When reacquired shares are viewed as treasury stock, the cost of acquiring the shares is temporarily debited to the treasury stock account. Recording the effects on specific shareholders' equity accounts is delayed until later when the shares are reissued. *(p. 1062)*

● **LO18–6**   Retained earnings represents, in general, a corporation's accumulated, undistributed, or reinvested net income (or net loss). Distributions of assets are dividends. *(p. 1068)*

● **LO18–7**   Most corporate dividends are paid in cash. When a noncash asset is distributed, it is referred to as a property dividend. The fair value of the assets to be distributed is the amount recorded for a property dividend. *(p. 1068)*

● **LO18–8**   A stock dividend is the distribution of additional shares of stock to current shareholders. For a small stock dividend (25% or less), the fair value of the additional shares distributed is transferred from retained earnings to paid-in capital. For a stock distribution of 25% or higher, the par value of the additional shares is reclassified within shareholders' equity if referred to as a stock split effected in the form of a stock dividend, but if referred to merely as a stock split, no journal entry is recorded. *(p. 1070)*

● **LO18–9**   U.S. GAAP and IFRS are generally compatible with respect to accounting for shareholders' equity. Some differences exist in presentation format and terminology. *(pp. 1052 and 1058)* ●

Quasi Reorganizations

APPENDIX 18

A firm undergoing financial difficulties, but with favorable future prospects, may use a quasi reorganization to write down inflated asset values and eliminate an accumulated deficit (debit balance in retained earnings). To effect the reorganization, these procedures are followed:

1. The firm's assets (and perhaps liabilities) are revalued (up or down) to reflect fair values, with corresponding credits or debits to retained earnings. This process typically increases the deficit.

2. The debit balance in retained earnings (deficit) is eliminated against additional paid-in capital. If additional paid-in capital is not sufficient to absorb the entire deficit, a reduction in stock may be necessary (with an appropriate restating of the par amount per share).
3. Retained earnings is dated. That is, disclosure is provided to indicate the date the deficit was eliminated and when the new accumulation of earnings began.

The procedure is demonstrated in Illustration 18A–1. The shareholders approved the quasi reorganization effective January 1, 2021. The plan was to be accomplished by a reduction of inventory by $75 million, a reduction in property, plant, and equipment (net) of $175 million, and appropriate adjustments to shareholders' equity.

Illustration 18A–1

Quasi Reorganization

The Emerson-Walsch Corporation has incurred operating losses for several years. A newly elected board of directors voted to implement a quasi reorganization, subject to shareholder approval. The balance sheet, on December 31, 2020, immediately prior to the restatement, includes the data shown below.

	($ in millions)
Cash	$ 75
Receivables	200
Inventory	375
Property, plant, and equipment (net)	400
	$1,050

When assets are revalued to reflect fair values, the process often increases the deficit.

	($ in millions)
Liabilities	$ 400
Common stock (800 million shares at $1 par)	800
Additional paid-in capital	150
Retained earnings (deficit)	(300)
	$1,050

The deficit, $550 ($300 + $75 + $175), can be only partially absorbed by the balance of additional paid-in capital.

To revalue assets:

Retained earnings...	75	
Inventory		75
Retained earnings...	175	
Property, plant, and equipment...........................		175

To eliminate a portion of the deficit against available additional paid-In capital:

Additional paid-in capital...............................	150	
Retained earnings...		150

The remaining deficit, $400 ($300 + $75 + $175 − $150), must be absorbed by reducing the balance in common stock.

To eliminate the remainder of the deficit against common stock:

Common stock...	400	
Retained earnings...		400

The balance sheet immediately after the restatement would include the following:

Assets and liabilities reflect current values.

	($ in millions)
Cash	$ 75
Receivables	200
Inventory	300
Property, plant, and equipment (net)	225
	$800

Because a reduced balance represents the same 800 million shares, the par amount per share must be reduced.

The deficit is eliminated.

	($ in millions)
Liabilities	$400
Common stock (800 million shares at $0.50 par)	400
Additional paid-in capital	0
Retained earnings (deficit)	0
	$800

Note A: Upon the recommendation of the board of directors and approval by shareholders, a quasi reorganization was implemented January 1, 2021. The plan was accomplished by a reduction of inventory by $75 million, a reduction in property, plant, and equipment (net) of $175 million, and appropriate adjustments to shareholders' equity. The balance in retained earnings reflects the elimination of a $300 million deficit on that date. ●

Questions For Review of Key Topics

Q 18–1 Identify and briefly describe the two primary sources of shareholders' equity.

Q 18–2 Identify the three common forms of business organization and the primary difference between the way they are accounted for.

Q 18–3 Corporations offer the advantage of limited liability. Explain what is meant by that statement.

Q 18–4 Distinguish between not-for-profit and for-profit corporations.

Q 18–5 Distinguish between publicly held and privately (or closely) held corporations.

Q 18–6 How does the Model Business Corporation Act affect the way corporations operate?

Q 18–7 The owners of a corporation are its shareholders. If a corporation has only one class of shares, they typically are labeled common shares. Indicate the ownership rights held by common shareholders, unless specifically withheld by agreement.

Q 18–8 What is meant by a shareholder's preemptive right?

Q 18–9 Terminology varies in the way companies differentiate among share types. But many corporations designate shares as common or preferred. What are the two special rights usually given to preferred shareholders?

Q 18–10 Most preferred shares are cumulative. Explain what this means.

Q 18–11 The par value of shares historically indicated the real value of shares and all shares were issued at that price. The concept has changed with time. Describe the meaning of par value as it has evolved to today.

Q 18–12 What is comprehensive income? How does comprehensive income differ from net income? Where do companies report it in a balance sheet?

Q 18–13 How do we report components of comprehensive income *created during the reporting period?*

Q 18–14 The balance sheet reports the balances of shareholders' equity accounts. What additional information is provided by the statement of shareholders' equity?

Q 18–15 At times, companies issue their shares for consideration other than cash. What is the measurement objective in those cases?

Q 18–16 Companies occasionally sell more than one security for a single price. How is the issue price allocated among the separate securities?

Q 18–17 The costs of legal, promotional, and accounting services necessary to effect the sale of shares are referred to as share issue costs. How are these costs recorded? Compare this approach to the way debt issue costs are recorded.

Q 18–18 When a corporation acquires its own shares, those shares assume the same status as authorized but unissued shares, as if they never had been issued. Explain how this is reflected in the accounting records if the shares are formally retired.

Q 18–19 Discuss the conceptual basis for accounting for a share buyback as treasury stock.

Q 18–20 The prescribed accounting treatment for stock dividends implicitly assumes that shareholders are fooled by small stock dividends and benefit by the market value of their additional shares. Explain this statement. Is it logical?

Q 18–21 Brandon Components declares a 2-for-1 stock split. What will be the effects of the split, and how should it be recorded?

Q 18–22 What is a reverse stock split? What would be the effect of a reverse stock split on one million $1 par shares? On the accounting records?

Q 18–23 Suppose you own 80 shares of Facebook common stock when the company declares a 4% stock dividend. What will you receive as a result?

Q 18–24 (Based on Appendix 18) A quasi reorganization is sometimes employed by a firm undergoing financial difficulties but with favorable future prospects. What are two objectives of this procedure? Briefly describe the procedural steps.

Brief Exercises

BE 18–1
Comprehensive income
● LO18–2

Schaeffer Corporation reports $50 million accumulated other comprehensive income in its balance sheet as a component of shareholders' equity. In a related statement reporting comprehensive income for the year, the company reveals net income of $400 million and other comprehensive income of $15 million. What was the balance in accumulated other comprehensive income in last year's balance sheet?

BE 18–2
Stock issued
● LO18–4

Penne Pharmaceuticals sold 8 million shares of its $1 par common stock to provide funds for research and development. If the issue price is $12 per share, what is the journal entry to record the sale of the shares?

1082 SECTION 3   Liabilities and Shareholders' Equity

BE 18–3
Stock issued
● LO18–4

Lewelling Company issued 100,000 shares of its $1 par common stock to the Michael Morgan law firm as compensation for 4,000 hours of legal services performed. Morgan's usual rate is $240 per hour. By what amount should Lewelling's paid-in capital—excess of par increase as a result of this transaction?

BE 18–4
Stock issued
● LO18–4

Hamilton Boats issued 175,000 shares of its no-par common stock to Sudoku Motors in exchange for 1,000 four-stroke outboard motors that normally sell in quantity for $3,500 each. By what amount should Hamilton's shareholders' equity increase as a result of this transaction?

BE 18–5
Retirement of shares
● LO18–5

Horton Industries' shareholders' equity included 100 million shares of $1 par common stock and a balance in paid-in capital—excess of par of $900 million. Assuming that Horton retires shares it reacquires (restores their status to that of authorized but unissued shares), by what amount will Horton's total paid-in capital decline if it reacquires 2 million shares at $8.50 per share?

BE 18–6
Retirement of shares
● LO18–5

Agee Storage issued 35 million shares of its $1 par common stock at $16 per share several years ago. Last year, for the first time, Agee reacquired 1 million shares at $14 per share. If Agee now *retires* 1 million shares at $19 per share. By what amount will Agee's total paid-in capital decline?

BE 18–7
Treasury stock
● LO18–5

The Jennings Group reacquired 2 million of its shares at $70 per share as treasury stock. Last year, for the first time, Jennings sold 1 million treasury shares at $71 per share. If Jennings now sells the remaining 1 million treasury shares at $67 per share, by what amount will retained earnings decline?

BE 18–8
Treasury stock
● LO18–5

In previous years, Cox Transport reacquired 2 million treasury shares at $20 per share and, later, 1 million treasury shares at $26 per share. If Cox now sells 1 million treasury shares at $29 per share and determines cost as the weighted-average cost of treasury shares, by what amount will Cox's paid-in capital—share repurchase increase?

BE 18–9
Treasury stock
● LO18–5

Refer to the situation described in BE 18–8. By what amount will Cox's paid-in capital—share repurchase increase if it determines the cost of treasury shares by the FIFO method?

BE 18–10
Cash dividend
● LO18–7
Real World Financials

Following is a recent **Microsoft** press release:

REDMOND, Wash. — Nov. 29, 2017 — Microsoft Corp. on Wednesday announced that its board of directors declared a quarterly dividend of $0.42 per share. The dividend is payable March 8, 2018, to shareholders of record on Feb. 15, 2018. The ex-dividend date will be Feb. 14, 2018.

Prepare the journal entries Microsoft used to record the declaration and payment of the cash dividend for its 7,720 million shares.

Source: Microsoft

BE 18–11
Effect of preferred stock on dividends
● LO18–7

The shareholders' equity of MLS Enterprises includes $200 million of no par common stock and $400 million of 6% cumulative preferred stock. The board of directors of MLS declared cash dividends of $50 million in 2021 after paying $20 million cash dividends in both 2020 and 2019. What is the amount of dividends common shareholders will receive in 2021?

BE 18–12
Property dividend
● LO18–7

Adams Moving and Storage, a family-owned corporation, declared a property dividend of 1,000 shares of GE common stock that Adams had purchased in February for $37,000 as an investment. GE's shares had a market value of $35 per share on the declaration date. Prepare the journal entries to record the property dividend on the declaration and payment dates.

BE 18–13
Stock dividend
● LO18–8

On June 13, the board of directors of Siewert Inc. declared a 5% stock dividend on its 60 million, $1 par, common shares, to be distributed on July 1. The market price of Siewert common stock was $25 on June 13. Prepare a journal entry that summarizes the declaration and distribution of the stock dividend.

BE 18–14
Stock split
● LO18–8

Refer to the situation described in BE 18–13, but assume a 2-for-1 stock split instead of the 5% stock dividend. Prepare a journal entry that summarizes the declaration and distribution of the stock split if it is *not* to be effected in the form of a stock dividend. What is the par per share after the split?

BE 18–15
Stock split
● LO18–8

Refer to the situation described in BE 18–13, but assume a 2-for-1 stock split instead of the 5% stock dividend. Prepare a journal entry that summarizes the declaration and distribution of the stock split if it is to be effected in the form of a 100% stock dividend. What is the par per share after the split?

BE 18–16
IFRS; reporting shareholders' equity
● LO18–9

 IFRS

Nestlé S.A., the largest food and beverage company in the world, prepares its financial statements according to International Financial Reporting Standards. Its financial statements include ordinary share capital, translation reserve, and share premium. If Nestlé used U.S. GAAP, what would be the likely account titles for these accounts?

Exercises

E 18–1
Comprehensive income
● LO18–2

The following is from the 2021 annual report of Kaufman Chemicals, Inc.:

Statements of Comprehensive Income	Years Ended December 31		
	2021	2020	2019
Net income	$856	$766	$594
Other comprehensive income:			
Change in net unrealized gains on AFS investments, net of tax of $22, ($14), and $15 in 2021, 2020, and 2019, respectively	34	(21)	23
Other	(2)	(1)	1
Total comprehensive income	$888	$744	$618

Kaufman reports accumulated other comprehensive income in its balance sheet as a component of shareholders' equity as follows:

($ in millions)	2021	2020
Shareholders' equity:		
Common stock	355	355
Additional paid-in capital	8,567	8,567
Retained earnings	6,544	5,988
Accumulated other comprehensive income	107	75
Total shareholders' equity	$15,573	$14,985

Required:
1. What is comprehensive income and how does it differ from net income?
2. How is comprehensive income reported in a balance sheet?
3. Why is Kaufman's 2021 balance sheet amount different from the 2021 amount reported in the disclosure note? Explain.
4. From the information provided, determine how Kaufman calculated the $107 million accumulated other comprehensive income in 2021.

E 18–2
FASB codification research; reporting other comprehensive income in shareholders' equity
● LO18–2

Companies are required to transfer "other comprehensive income" each period to shareholders' equity. The *FASB Accounting Standards Codification* represents the single source of authoritative U.S. generally accepted accounting principles. Obtain the relevant authoritative literature on reporting other comprehensive income in shareholders' equity using the *FASB Accounting Standards Codification* at the FASB website (www.fasb.org).

Required:
1. What is the specific nine-digit Codification citation (XXX-XX-XX-XX) that describes the guidelines for reporting that component of shareholders' equity?
2. What is the specific nine-digit Codification citation (XXX-XX-XX-XX) that describes the guidelines for presenting accumulated other comprehensive income on the statement of shareholders' equity?

1084   SECTION 3   Liabilities and Shareholders' Equity

E 18–3
Earnings or OCI?
● LO18–2

Indicate by letter whether each of the items listed below most likely is reported in the income statement as Net Income (**NI**) or in the statement of comprehensive income as Other Comprehensive Income (**OCI**).

Items

_____ 1. Increase in the fair value of available-for-sale (AFS) debt securities
_____ 2. Gain on sale of land
_____ 3. Loss on pension plan assets (actual return less than expected)
_____ 4. Adjustment for foreign currency translation
_____ 5. Increase in the fair value of investments in common stock securities
_____ 6. Loss from revising an assumption related to a pension plan
_____ 7. Loss on sale of patent
_____ 8. Prior service cost in defined benefit pension plan
_____ 9. Increase in the fair value of bonds outstanding due to change in general interest rates; fair value option
_____ 10. Gain on postretirement plan assets (actual return more than expected)

E 18–4
Stock issued
for cash; Wright
Medical Group
● LO18–4
Real World Financials

The following is a news item reported by Reuters:

WASHINGTON, Jan 29 (Reuters)—Wright Medical Group, a maker of reconstructive implants for knees and hips, on Tuesday filed to sell 3 million shares of common stock.

  In a filing with the U.S. Securities and Exchange Commission, it said it plans to use the proceeds from the offering for general corporate purposes, working capital, research and development, and acquisitions.

  After the sale there will be about 31.5 million shares outstanding in the Arlington, Tennessee-based company, according to the SEC filing.

  Wright shares closed at $17.15 on Nasdaq.

The common stock of Wright Medical Group has a par of $0.01 per share.

Required:
Prepare the journal entry to record the sale of the shares assuming the price existing when the announcement was made and ignoring share issue costs.

Source: Reuters

E 18–5
Issuance of
shares; noncash
consideration
● LO18–4

During its first year of operations, Eastern Data Links Corporation entered into the following transactions relating to shareholders' equity. The articles of incorporation authorized the issue of 8 million common shares, $1 par per share, and 1 million preferred shares, $50 par per share.

Required:
Prepare the appropriate journal entries to record each transaction.

Feb. 12   Sold 2 million common shares, for $9 per share.
     13   Issued 40,000 common shares to attorneys in exchange for legal services.
     13   Sold 80,000 of its common shares and 4,000 preferred shares for a total of $945,000.
Nov. 15   Issued 380,000 of its common shares in exchange for equipment for which the cash price was known to be $3,688,000.

E 18–6
Redeemable
shares
● LO18–4

Williams Industries has outstanding 30 million common shares, 20 million Class A shares, and 20 million Class B shares. Williams has the right but not the obligation to repurchase the Class A shares if a change in ownership of the voting common shares causes J. P. Williams, founder and CEO, to have less than 50% ownership. Williams has the unconditional obligation to repurchase the Class B shares upon the death of J. P. Williams.

Required:
Which, if any, of the shares should be reported in Williams's balance sheet as liabilities? Explain.

E 18–7
Share issue costs;
issuance
● LO18–4

ICOT Industries issued 15 million of its $1 par common shares for $424 million on April 11. Legal, promotional, and accounting services necessary to effect the sale cost $2 million.

Required:
1. Prepare the journal entry to record the issuance of the shares.
2. Explain how recording the share issue costs differs from the way debt issue costs are recorded.

E 18–8
Reporting
preferred shares
● LO18–4, LO18–7

Ozark Distributing Company is primarily engaged in the wholesale distribution of consumer products in the Ozark Mountain regions. The following disclosure note appeared in the company's 2021 annual report:

Note 5. Convertible Preferred Stock (in part):

The Company has the following Convertible Preferred Stock outstanding as of September 2021:

Date of issuance:	June 17, 2018
Optionally redeemable beginning:	June 18, 2020
Par value (gross proceeds):	$2,500,000
Number of shares:	100,000
Liquidation preference per share:	$25.00
Conversion price per share:	$30.31
Number of common shares in which to be converted:	82,481
Dividend rate:	6.785%

The Preferred Stock is convertible at any time by the holders into a number of shares of Ozark's common stock equal to the number of preferred shares being converted times a fraction equal to $25.00 divided by the conversion price. The conversion prices for the Preferred Stock are subject to customary adjustments in the event of stock splits, stock dividends and certain other distributions on the Common Stock. Cumulative dividends for the Preferred Stock are payable in arrears, when, as, and if declared by the Board of Directors, on March 31, June 30, September 30, and December 31 of each year.

The Preferred Stock is optionally redeemable by the Company beginning on various dates, as listed above, at redemption prices equal to 112% of the liquidation preference. The redemption prices decrease 1% annually thereafter until the redemption price equals the liquidation preference, after which date it remains the liquidation preference.

Required:

1. What amount of dividends is paid annually to a preferred shareholder owning 100 shares of the Series A preferred stock?

2. If dividends are not paid in 2022 and 2023, but are paid in 2024, what amount of dividends will the shareholder receive?

3. If the investor chooses to convert the shares in 2022, how many shares of common stock will the investor receive for his/her 100 shares?

4. If Ozark chooses to redeem the shares on June 18, 2022, what amount will the investor be paid for his/her 100 shares?

E 18–9
New equity issues; offerings announcements
● LO18–4

When companies offer new equity security issues, they publicize the offerings in the financial press and on Internet sites. Assume the following were among the equity offerings reported in December 2021:

New Securities Issues

Equity

American Materials Transfer Corporation (AMTC)—7.5 million common shares, $.001 par, priced at $13.546 each through underwriters led by Second Tennessee Bank N.A. and Morgan, Dunavant & Co., according to a syndicate official.

Proactive Solutions Inc. (PSI)—Offering of 9 million common shares, $0.01 par, was priced at $15.20 a share via lead manager Stanley Brothers, Inc., according to a syndicate official.

Required:

Prepare the appropriate journal entries to record the sale of both issues to underwriters. Ignore share issue costs.

E 18–10
Retirement of shares
● LO18–5

Borner Communications' articles of incorporation authorized the issuance of 130 million common shares. The transactions described below effected changes in Borner's outstanding shares. Prior to the transactions, Borner's shareholders' equity included the following:

Shareholders' Equity	($ in millions)
Common stock, 100 million shares at $1 par	$100
Paid-in capital—excess of par	300
Retained earnings	210

1086   SECTION 3   Liabilities and Shareholders' Equity

Required:

Assuming that Borner Communications retires shares it reacquires (restores their status to that of authorized but unissued shares), record the appropriate journal entry for each of the following transactions:

1. On January 7, 2021, Borner reacquired 2 million shares at $5 per share.
2. On August 23, 2021, Borner reacquired 4 million shares at $3.50 per share.
3. On July 25, 2022, Borner sold 3 million common shares at $6 per share.

E 18–11
Retirement of shares
● LO18–5

In 2021, Borland Semiconductors entered into the transactions described below. In 2018, Borland had issued 170 million shares of its $1 par common stock at $34 per share.

Required:

Assuming that Borland retires shares it reacquires, record the appropriate journal entry for each of the following transactions:

1. On January 2, 2021, Borland reacquired 10 million shares at $32.50 per share.
2. On March 3, 2021, Borland reacquired 10 million shares at $36 per share.
3. On August 13, 2021, Borland sold 1 million shares at $42 per share.
4. On December 15, 2021, Borland sold 2 million shares at $36 per share.

E 18–12
Treasury stock
● LO18–5

In 2021, Western Transport Company entered into the treasury stock transactions described below. In 2019, Western Transport had issued 140 million shares of its $1 par common stock at $17 per share.

Required:

Prepare the appropriate journal entry for each of the following transactions:

1. On January 23, 2021, Western Transport reacquired 10 million shares at $20 per share.
2. On September 3, 2021, Western Transport sold 1 million treasury shares at $21 per share.
3. On November 4, 2021, Western Transport sold 1 million treasury shares at $18 per share.

E 18–13
Treasury stock;
weighted-average
and FIFO cost
● LO18–5

At December 31, 2020, the balance sheet of Meca International included the following shareholders' equity accounts:

Shareholders' Equity	($ in millions)
Common stock, 60 million shares at $1 par	$ 60
Paid-in capital—excess of par	300
Retained earnings	410

Required:

Assuming that Meca International views its share buybacks as treasury stock, record the appropriate journal entry for each of the following transactions:

1. On February 12, 2021, Meca reacquired 1 million common shares at $13 per share.
2. On June 9, 2022, Meca reacquired 2 million common shares at $10 per share.
3. On May 25, 2023, Meca sold 2 million treasury shares at $15 per share. Determine cost as the weighted-average cost of treasury shares.
4. For the previous transaction, assume Meca determines the cost of treasury shares by the FIFO method.

E 18–14
Reporting
shareholders'
equity after share
repurchase
● LO18–5

On two previous occasions, the management of Dennison and Company, Inc., repurchased some of its common shares. Between buyback transactions, the corporation issued common shares under its management incentive plan. Shown below is shareholders' equity following these share transactions, as reported by two different methods of accounting for reacquired shares.

($ in millions)	Method A	Method B
Shareholders' equity		
Paid-in capital:		
Preferred stock, $10 par	$ 150	$ 150
Common stock, $1 par	200	197
Additional paid-in capital	1,204	1,201
Retained earnings	2,994	2,979
Less: Treasury stock	(21)	
Total shareholders' equity	$4,527	$4,527

Required:

1. Infer from the presentation which method of accounting for reacquired shares is represented by each of the two columns.

2. Explain why presentation formats are different and why some account balances are different for the two methods.

E 18–15
Change from treasury stock to retired stock
● LO18–5

In keeping with a modernization of corporate statutes in its home state, UMC Corporation decided in 2021 to discontinue accounting for reacquired shares as treasury stock. Instead, shares repurchased will be viewed as having been retired, reassuming the status of unissued shares. As part of the change, treasury shares held were reclassified as retired stock. At December 31, 2020, UMC's balance sheet reported the following shareholders' equity:

	($ in millions)
Common stock, $1 par	$ 200
Paid-in capital—excess of par	800
Retained earnings	956
Treasury stock (4 million shares at cost)	(25)
Total shareholders' equity	$1,931

Required:

Identify the type of accounting change this decision represents, and prepare the journal entry to effect the reclassification of treasury shares as retired shares.

E 18–16
Stock buyback; Ford press announcement
● LO18–5

Real World Financials

The following excerpt is from an article reported in an online issue of Bloomberg.

(Bloomberg) Ford Motor Co. (F) said it will repurchase $1.8 billion of its shares to reduce dilution from recent stock grants to executives.

The par amount per share for Ford's common stock is $0.01. Paid-in capital—excess of par is $5.39 per share on average. The market price was $16.

Required:

1. Suppose Ford reacquires 112 million shares through repurchase on the open market at $16 per share. Prepare the appropriate journal entry to record the purchase. Ford considers the shares it buys back to be treasury stock.

2. Suppose Ford considers the shares it buys back to be retired rather than treated as treasury stock. Prepare the appropriate journal entry to record the purchase.

3. What does the company mean by saying that the buyback will serve "to offset dilution from executive compensation?"

Source: Bloomberg

E 18–17
Transactions affecting retained earnings
● LO18–6, LO18–7

Shown below in T-account format are the changes affecting the retained earnings of Brenner-Jude Corporation during 2021. At January 1, 2021, the corporation had outstanding 105 million common shares, $1 par per share.

Retained Earnings ($ in millions)

		90	Beginning balance
Retirement of 5 million common shares for $22 million	2		
		88	Net income for the year
Declaration and payment of a $0.33 per share cash dividend	33		
Declaration and distribution of a 4% stock dividend	20		
		123	Ending balance

Required:

1. From the information provided by the account changes, you should be able to recreate the transactions that affected Brenner-Jude's retained earnings during 2021. Prepare the journal entries that Brenner-Jude must have recorded during the year for these transactions. (Hint: In lieu of revenues and expenses, use an account titled "Income summary" to close net income or net loss.)

2. Prepare a statement of retained earnings for Brenner-Jude for the year ended 2021.

E 18–18
Effect of cumulative, nonparticipating preferred stock on dividends—3 years
● LO18–7

The shareholders' equity of ILP Industries includes the items shown below. The board of directors of ILP declared cash dividends of $8 million, $20 million, and $150 million in its first three years of operation—2021, 2022, and 2023, respectively.

	($ in millions)
Common stock	$100
Paid-in capital—excess of par, common	980
Preferred stock, 8%	200
Paid-in capital—excess of par, preferred	555

Required:
Determine the amount of dividends to be paid to preferred and common shareholders in each of the three years, assuming that the preferred stock is cumulative and nonparticipating.

	Preferred	Common
2021		
2022		
2023		

E 18–19
Stock dividend
● LO18–8

The shareholders' equity of Core Technologies Company on June 30, 2020, included the following:

Common stock, $1 par; authorized, 8 million shares; issued and outstanding, 3 million shares	$ 3,000,000
Paid-in capital—excess of par	12,000,000
Retained earnings	14,000,000

On April 1, 2021, the board of directors of Core Technologies declared a 10% stock dividend on common shares, to be distributed on June 1. The market price of Core Technologies' common stock was $30 on April 1, 2021, and $40 on June 1, 2021.

Required:
Prepare the journal entry to record the declaration and distribution of the stock dividend.

E 18–20
Stock split;
Hanmi Financial Corporation
● LO18–8
Real World Financials

Hanmi Financial Corporation is the parent company of Hanmi Bank. The company's stock split was announced in the following wire:

LOS ANGELES Jan. 20 *BUSINESS WIRE* —Hanmi Financial Corporation (Nasdaq), announced that the Board of Directors has approved a two-for-one stock split, to be effected in the form of a 100 percent common stock dividend. Hanmi Financial Corporation stockholders of record at the close of business on January 31 will receive one additional share of common stock for every share of common stock then held. Distribution of additional shares issued as a result of the split is expected to occur on or about February 15.

At the time of the stock split, 24.5 million shares of common stock, $.001 par per share, were outstanding.

Required:
1. Prepare the journal entry, if any, that Hanmi recorded at the time of the stock split.
2. What is the probable motivation for declaring the 2-for-1 stock split to be effected by a dividend payable in shares of common stock?
3. If Hanmi's stock price had been $36 at the time of the split, what would be its approximate value after the split (other things equal)?

Source: Business Wire

E 18–21
Cash in lieu of fractional share rights
● LO18–8

Douglas McDonald Company's balance sheet included the following shareholders' equity accounts at December 31, 2020:

	($ in millions)
Paid-in capital:	
Common stock, 900 million shares at $1 par	$ 900
Paid-in capital—excess of par	15,800
Retained earnings	14,888
Total shareholders' equity	$31,588

On March 16, 2021, a 4% common stock dividend was declared and distributed. The market value of the common stock was $21 per share. Fractional share rights represented 2 million equivalent whole shares. Cash was paid in lieu of the fractional share rights.

Required:

1. What is a fractional share right?

2. Prepare the appropriate entries for the declaration and distribution of the stock dividend.

E 18–22
FASB codification research
● LO18–1, LO18–5, LO18–8

Access the *FASB Accounting Standards Codification* at the FASB website (www.fasb.org). Determine the specific eight-digit Codification citation (XXX-XX-XX-X) for accounting for each of the following items:

1. Requirements to disclose within the financial statements the pertinent rights and privileges of the various securities outstanding.

2. Requirement to record a "small" stock dividend at the fair value of the shares issued.

3. Requirement to exclude from the determination of net income gains and losses on transactions in a company's own stock.

E 18–23
Transactions affecting retained earnings
● LO18–6 through LO18–8

The balance sheet of Consolidated Paper, Inc., included the following shareholders' equity accounts at December 31, 2020:

Paid-in capital:	
Preferred stock, 8.8%, 90,000 shares at $1 par	$ 90,000
Common stock, 364,000 shares at $1 par	364,000
Paid-in capital—excess of par, preferred	1,437,000
Paid-in capital—excess of par, common	2,574,000
Retained earnings	9,735,000
Treasury stock, at cost; 4,000 common shares	(44,000)
Total shareholders' equity	**$14,156,000**

During 2021, several events and transactions affected the retained earnings of Consolidated Paper.

Required:

1. Prepare the appropriate entries for these events:

    a. On March 3, the board of directors declared a property dividend of 240,000 shares of Leasco International common stock that Consolidated Paper had purchased in January as an investment (book value: $700,000). The investment shares had a fair value of $3 per share and were distributed March 31 to shareholders of record March 15.

    b. On May 3, a 5-for-4 stock split was declared and distributed. The stock split was effected in the form of a 25% stock dividend. The market value of the $1 par common stock was $11 per share.

    c. On July 5, a 2% common stock dividend was declared and distributed. The market value of the common stock was $11 per share.

    d. On December 1, the board of directors declared the 8.8% cash dividend on the 90,000 preferred shares, payable on December 28 to shareholders of record December 20.

    e. On December 1, the board of directors declared a cash dividend of $0.50 per share on its common shares, payable on December 28 to shareholders of record December 20.

2. Prepare the shareholders' equity section of the balance sheet for Consolidated Paper, Inc., at December 31, 2021. Net income for the year was $810,000.

E 18–24
Profitability ratio
● LO18–1

Comparative balance sheets for Softech Canvas Goods for 2021 and 2020 are shown below. Softech pays no dividends and instead reinvests all earnings for future growth.

Comparative Balance Sheets
($ in thousands)

	December 31	
	2021	**2020**
Assets:		
Cash	$ 50	$ 40
Accounts receivable	100	120
Short-term investments	50	40
Inventory	200	140
Property, plant, and equipment (net)	600	550
	$1,000	$ 890

(continued)

1090   SECTION 3   Liabilities and Shareholders' Equity

(concluded)	Liabilities and Shareholders' Equity:		
Current liabilities	$ 240	$ 210
Bonds payable	160	160
Paid-in capital	400	400
Retained earnings	200	120
	$1,000	$ 890

Required:
1. Determine the return on shareholders' equity for 2021.
2. What does the ratio measure?

E 18–25
IFRS; equity
terminology
● LO18–9

Indicate by letter whether each of the terms or phrases listed below is more associated with financial statements prepared in accordance with U.S. GAAP (**U**) or International Financial Reporting Standards (**I**).

Terms and phrases

_____ 1. Common stock
_____ 2. Preference shares
_____ 3. Liabilities often listed before equity in the balance sheet (statement of financial position)
_____ 4. Asset revaluation reserve
_____ 5. Accumulated other comprehensive income
_____ 6. Share premium
_____ 7. Equity often listed before liabilities in the balance sheet (statement of financial position)
_____ 8. Translation reserve
_____ 9. Ordinary shares
_____ 10. Paid-in capital—excess of par
_____ 11. Net gains (losses) on investments—AOCI
_____ 12. Investment revaluation reserve
_____ 13. Preferred stock

E 18–26
General ledger
exercise; bonds;
installment
note, early
extinguishment
● LO18–4, LO18–5,
LO18–7

On January 1, 2021, the general ledger of Freedom Fireworks includes the following account balances:

Accounts	Debit	Credit
Cash	$ 42,700	
Accounts Receivable	44,500	
Supplies	7,500	
Equipment	64,000	
Accumulated Depreciation		$ 9,000
Accounts Payable		14,600
Common Stock, $1 par value		10,000
Paid-in Capital—Excess of Par		80,000
Retained Earnings		45,100
Totals	$158,700	$158,700

During January 2021, the following transactions occur:

January 2   Issue an additional 2,000 shares of $1 par value common stock for $40,000.
January 9   Provide services to customers on account, $14,300.
January 10   Purchase additional supplies on account, $4,900.
January 12   Repurchase 1,000 shares of treasury stock for $18 per share.
January 15   Pay cash on accounts payable, $16,500.
January 21   Provide services to customers for cash, $49,100.
January 22   Receive cash on accounts receivable, $16,600.
January 29   Declare a cash dividend of $0.30 per share to all shares outstanding on January 29. The dividend
              is payable on February 15.
              (*Hint:* Freedom Fireworks had 10,000 shares outstanding on January 1, 2021, and dividends are
              not paid on treasury stock.)
January 30   Reissue 600 shares of treasury stock for $20 per share.
January 31   Pay cash for salaries during January, $42,000.

The following information is available on January 31, 2021.
1. Unpaid utilities for the month of January are $6,200.
2. Supplies at the end of January total $5,100.

3. Depreciation on the equipment for the month of January is calculated using the straight-line method. At the time the equipment was purchased, the company estimated a service life of three years and a residual value of $10,000.

4. Accrued income taxes at the end of January are $2,000.

Required:

1. Record each of the transactions listed above in the "General Journal" tab (these are shown as items 1–10) assuming a FIFO perpetual inventory system. Review the "General Ledger" and the "Trial Balance" tabs to see the effect of the transactions on the account balances.

2. Record adjusting entries on January 31, in the "General Journal" tab (these are shown as items 11–14).

3. Review the adjusted "Trial Balance" as of January 31, 2021, in the "Trial Balance" tab.

4. Prepare a multiple-step income statement for the period ended January 31, 2021, in the "Income Statement" tab.

5. Prepare a classified balance sheet as of January 31, 2021, in the "Balance Sheet" tab.

6. Record closing entries in the "General Journal" tab (these are shown as items 15 and 16).

7. Using the information from the requirements above, complete the "Analysis" tab.

   a. Calculate the return on equity for the month of January. If the average return on equity for the industry for January is 2.5%, is the company more or less profitable than other companies in the same industry?

   b. How many shares of common stock are outstanding as of January 31, 2021?

   c. Calculate earnings per share for the month of January. (Hint: To calculate average shares of common stock outstanding take the beginning shares outstanding plus the ending shares outstanding and divide the total by 2.) If earnings per share was $3.60 last year (i.e., an average of $0.30 per month), is earnings per share for January 2021 better or worse than last year's average?

Problems

P 18–1
Various stock transactions; correction of journal entries
● LO18–4

Part A

During its first year of operations, the McCollum Corporation entered into the following transactions relating to shareholders' equity. The corporation was authorized to issue 100 million common shares, $1 par per share.

Required:
Prepare the appropriate journal entries to record each transaction.

   Jan. 9   Issued 40 million common shares for $20 per share.
   Mar. 11 Issued 5,000 shares in exchange for custom-made equipment. McCollum's shares have traded recently on the stock exchange at $20 per share.

Part B

A new staff accountant for the McCollum Corporation recorded the following journal entries during the second year of operations. McCollum retires shares that it reacquires (restores their status to that of authorized but unissued shares).

Required:
Prepare the journal entries that should have been recorded for each of the transactions.

		($ in millions)	
Sept. 1	Common stock	2	
	Retained earnings...	48	
	Cash		50
Dec. 1	Cash	26	
	Common stock...		1
	Gain on sale of previously issued shares...		25

P 18–2
Share buyback—comparison of retirement and treasury stock treatment
● LO18–5

The shareholders' equity section of the balance sheet of TNL Systems Inc. included the following accounts at December 31, 2020:

Shareholders' Equity	($ in millions)
Common stock, 240 million shares at $1 par	$ 240
Paid-in capital—excess of par	1,680
Paid-in capital—share repurchase	1
Retained earnings	1,100

Required:

1. During 2021, TNL Systems reacquired shares of its common stock and later sold shares in two separate transactions. Prepare the entries for both the purchase and subsequent resale of the shares assuming the shares are (a) retired and (b) viewed as treasury stock.

   a. On February 5, 2021, TNL Systems purchased 6 million shares at $10 per share.

1092   SECTION 3   Liabilities and Shareholders' Equity

   b. On July 9, 2021, the corporation sold 2 million shares at $12 per share.

   c. On November 14, 2023, the corporation sold 2 million shares at $7 per share.

2. Prepare the shareholders' equity section of TNL Systems' balance sheet at December 31, 2023, comparing the two approaches. Assume all net income earned in 2021–2023 was distributed to shareholders as cash dividends.

P 18–3
Reacquired shares—comparison of retired shares and treasury shares
● LO18–5

National Supply's shareholders' equity included the following accounts at December 31, 2020:

Shareholders' Equity	
Common stock, 6 million shares at $1 par	$ 6,000,000
Paid-in capital—excess of par	30,000,000
Retained earnings	86,500,000

Required:

1. National Supply reacquired shares of its common stock in two separate transactions and later sold shares. Prepare the entries for each of the transactions under each of two separate assumptions: the shares are (a) retired and (b) accounted for as treasury stock.

February 15, 2021	Reacquired 300,000 shares at $8 per share.
February 17, 2022	Reacquired 300,000 shares at $5.50 per share.
November 9, 2023	Sold 200,000 shares at $7 per share (assume FIFO cost).

2. Prepare the shareholders' equity section of National Supply's balance sheet at December 31, 2023, assuming the shares are (a) retired and (b) accounted for as treasury stock. Net income was $14 million in 2021, $15 million in 2022, and $16 million in 2023. No dividends were paid during the three-year period.

P 18–4
Statement of retained earnings
● LO18–5, LO18–7

Comparative statements of retained earnings for Renn-Dever Corporation were reported in its 2021 annual report as follows.

RENN-DEVER CORPORATION
Statements of Retained Earnings
For the Years Ended December 31

	2021	2020	2019
Balance at beginning of year	$6,794,292	$5,464,052	$5,624,552
Net income (loss)	3,308,700	2,240,900	(160,500)
Deductions:			
Stock dividend (34,900 shares)	242,000		
Common shares retired (110,000 shares)		212,660	
Common stock cash dividends	889,950	698,000	0
Balance at end of year	$8,971,042	$6,794,292	$5,464,052

At December 31, 2018, common shares consisted of the following:

Common stock, 1,855,000 shares at $1 par	$1,855,000
Paid-in capital—excess of par	7,420,000

Required:

Infer from the reports the events and transactions that affected Renn-Dever Corporation's retained earnings during 2019, 2020, and 2021. Prepare the journal entries that reflect those events and transactions. (Hint: In lieu of revenues and expenses, use an account titled "Income summary" to close net income or net loss.)

P 18–5
Shareholders' equity transactions; statement of shareholders' equity
● LO18–6 through LO18–8

Listed below are the transactions that affected the shareholders' equity of Branch-Rickie Corporation during the period 2021–2023. At December 31, 2020, the corporation's accounts included:

	($ in thousands)
Common stock, 105 million shares at $1 par	$ 105,000
Paid-in capital—excess of par	630,000
Retained earnings	970,000

a. November 1, 2021, the board of directors declared a cash dividend of $0.80 per share on its common shares, payable to shareholders of record November 15, to be paid December 1.

b. On March 1, 2022, the board of directors declared a property dividend consisting of corporate bonds of Warner Corporation that Branch-Rickie was holding as an investment. The bonds had a fair value of $1.6 million, but were purchased two years previously for $1.3 million. Because they were intended to be held to maturity, the bonds had not been previously written up. The property dividend was payable to shareholders of record March 13, to be distributed April 5.

c. On July 12, 2022, the corporation declared and distributed a 5% common stock dividend (when the market value of the common stock was $21 per share). Cash was paid in lieu of fractional shares representing 250,000 equivalent whole shares.

d. On November 1, 2022, the board of directors declared a cash dividend of $0.80 per share on its common shares, payable to shareholders of record November 15, to be paid December 1.

e. On January 15, 2023, the board of directors declared and distributed a 3-for-2 stock split effected in the form of a 50% stock dividend when the market value of the common stock was $22 per share.

f. On November 1, 2023, the board of directors declared a cash dividend of $0.65 per share on its common shares, payable to shareholders of record November 15, to be paid December 1.

Required:

1. Prepare the journal entries that Branch-Rickie recorded during the three-year period for these transactions.
2. Prepare comparative statements of shareholders' equity for Branch-Rickie for the three-year period ($ in 000s). Net income was $330 million, $395 million, and $455 million for 2021, 2022, and 2023, respectively.

P 18–6
Statement of shareholders' equity
● LO18–1, LO18–3 through LO18–8

Comparative statements of shareholders' equity for Anaconda International Corporation were reported as follows for the fiscal years ending December 31, 2021, 2022, and 2023.

ANACONDA INTERNATIONAL CORPORATION
Statements of Shareholders' Equity
For the Years Ended Dec. 31, 2021, 2022, and 2023
($ in millions)

	Preferred Stock $10 par	Common Stock $1 par	Additional Paid-In Capital	Retained Earnings	Total Shareholders' Equity
Balance at January 1, 2021		55	495	1,878	2,428
Sale of preferred shares	10		470		480
Sale of common shares		7	63		70
Cash dividend, preferred				(1)	(1)
Cash dividend, common				(16)	(16)
Net income				290	290
Balance at December 31, 2021	10	62	1,028	2,151	3,251
Retirement of shares		(3)	(27)	(20)	(50)
Cash dividend, preferred				(1)	(1)
Cash dividend, common				(20)	(20)
3-for-2 split effected in the form of a dividend	5		(5)		
Net income				380	380
Balance at December 31, 2022	15	59	996	2,490	3,560
Common stock dividend		6	59	(65)	
Cash dividend, preferred				(1)	(1)
Cash dividend, common				(22)	(22)
Net income				412	412
Balance at December 31, 2023	15	65	1,055	2,814	3,949

Required:

1. Infer from the statements the events and transactions that affected Anaconda International Corporation's shareholders' equity during 2021, 2022, and 2023. Prepare the journal entries that reflect those events and transactions. (Hint: In lieu of revenues and expenses, use an account titled "Income summary" to close net income or net loss.)
2. Prepare the shareholders' equity section of Anaconda's comparative balance sheets at December 31, 2023 and 2022.

P 18–7
Reporting shareholders' equity; comprehensive income; Cisco Systems
● LO18–1 through LO18–4
Real World Financials

The following is a portion of the Statement of Shareholders' Equity from Cisco Systems' July 29, 2017 annual report.

CISCO SYSTEMS, INC.
Consolidated Statements of Equity (in part)

($ in millions)	Shares of Common Stock	Common Stock and Additional Paid-In Capital	Retained Earnings	Accumulated Other Comprehensive Income	Total Shareholder' Equity
Balance at July 25, 2016	5,029	$44,516	$19,396	$(326)	$63,586
Net income			9,609		9,609
Other comprehensive income (loss)				372	372

(continued)

1094   SECTION 3   Liabilities and Shareholders' Equity

(concluded)

Issuance of common stock	92	708			708
Repurchase of common stock	(118)	(1,050)	(2,656)		(3,706)
Shares repurchased for tax withholdings on vesting of restricted stock units	(20)	(619)			(619)
Cash dividends declared ($1.10 per common share)			(5,511)		(5,511)
Tax effects from employee stock incentive plans		(10)			(10)
Share-based compensation expense		1,540			1,540
Purchase acquisitions		168			168
Balance at July 29, 2017	4,983	$45,253	$20,838	$ 46	$66,137

Required:
1. How does Cisco account for its share buybacks? Treasury stock or retired shares?
2. For its share buybacks in the period shown, was the price Cisco paid for the shares repurchased (a) more or (b) less than the average price at which Cisco had sold the shares previously?
3. Reconstruct the journal entry Cisco used to record the buyback. The par amount of Cisco's shares is $0.001.
4. What two amounts caused the change in Cisco's comprehensive income for the period shown?
5. What was the amount of Accumulated other comprehensive income (loss) that Cisco reported in its July 29, 2017 balance sheet?

Source: Cisco Systems

P 18–8
Share issue costs; issuance; dividends; early retirement
● LO18–3, LO18–4, LO18–7

During its first year of operations, Cupola Fan Corporation issued 30,000 of $1 par Class B shares for $385,000 on June 30, 2021. Share issue costs were $1,500. One year from the issue date (July 1, 2022), the corporation retired 10% of the shares for $39,500.

Required:
1. Prepare the journal entry to record the issuance of the shares.
2. Prepare the journal entry to record the declaration of a $2 per share dividend on December 1, 2021.
3. Prepare the journal entry to record the payment of the dividend on December 31, 2021.
4. Prepare the journal entry to record the retirement of the shares.
(Note: You may wish to compare your solution to this problem with that of P 14–16, which deals with parallel issues of debt issue costs and the retirement of debt.)

P 18–9
Effect of preferred stock characteristics on dividends
● LO18–7

The shareholders' equity of Kramer Industries includes the data shown below. During 2022, cash dividends of $150 million were declared. Dividends were not declared in 2020 or 2021.

	($ in millions)
Common stock	$200
Paid-in capital—excess of par, common	800
Preferred stock, 10%, nonparticipating	100
Paid-in capital—excess of par, preferred	270

Required:
Determine the amount of dividends payable to preferred shareholders and to common shareholders under each of the following two assumptions regarding the characteristics of the preferred stock.

Assumption A —The preferred stock is noncumulative.
Assumption B —The preferred stock is cumulative.

P 18–10
Transactions affecting retained earnings
● LO18–4 through LO18–8

Indicate by letter whether each of the transactions listed below increases (**I**), decreases (**D**), or has no effect (**N**) on retained earnings. Assume the shareholders' equity of the transacting company includes only common stock, paid-in capital—excess of par, and retained earnings at the time of each transaction. (Some transactions have two possible answers. Indicate both.)

Transactions

N   1. Sale of common stock

_____   2. Purchase of treasury stock at a cost *less* than the original issue price

_____   3. Purchase of treasury stock at a cost *greater* than the original issue price

_____   4. Declaration of a property dividend

_____   5. Sale of treasury stock for *more* than cost

_____   6. Sale of treasury stock for *less* than cost

_____   7. Net income for the year

_____   8. Declaration of a cash dividend

_____   9. Payment of a previously declared cash dividend

_____   10. Issuance of convertible bonds for cash

_____   11. Declaration and distribution of a 5% stock dividend

_____   12. Retirement of common stock at a cost *less* than the original issue price

_____   13. Retirement of common stock at a cost *greater* than the original issue price

_____   14. A stock split effected in the form of a stock dividend

_____   15. A stock split in which the par value per share is reduced (not effected in the form of a stock dividend)

_____   16. A net loss for the year

P 18–11
Stock dividends received on investments; integrative problem
● LO18–8

Ellis Transport Company acquired 1.2 million shares of stock in L&K Corporation at $44 per share. They are reported by Ellis at "fair value through net income." Ellis sold 200,000 shares at $46, received a 10% stock dividend, and then later in the year sold another 100,000 shares at $43.

Hint: There is no entry for the stock dividend, but a new investment per share must be calculated for use later when the shares are sold.

Required:
Prepare journal entries to record these transactions.

P 18–12
Various shareholders' equity topics; comprehensive
● LO18–1, LO18–4 through LO18–8

Part A
In late 2020, the Nicklaus Corporation was formed. The corporate charter authorizes the issuance of 5,000,000 shares of common stock carrying a $1 par value, and 1,000,000 shares of $5 par value, noncumulative, nonparticipating preferred stock. On January 2, 2021, 3,000,000 shares of the common stock are issued in exchange for cash at an average price of $10 per share. Also on January 2, all 1,000,000 shares of preferred stock are issued at $20 per share.

Required:
1. Prepare journal entries to record these transactions.
2. Prepare the shareholders' equity section of the Nicklaus balance sheet as of March 31, 2021. (Assume net income for the first quarter 2021 was $1,000,000.)

Part B
During 2021, the Nicklaus Corporation participated in three treasury stock transactions:
a. On June 30, 2021, the corporation reacquires 200,000 shares for the treasury at a price of $12 per share.
b. On July 31, 2021, 50,000 treasury shares are reissued at $15 per share.
c. On September 30, 2021, 50,000 treasury shares are reissued at $10 per share.

Required:
1. Prepare journal entries to record these transactions.
2. Prepare the Nicklaus Corporation shareholders' equity section as it would appear in a balance sheet prepared at September 30, 2021. (Assume net income for the second and third quarter was $3,000,000.)

Part C
On October 1, 2021, Nicklaus Corporation receives permission to replace its $1 par value common stock (5,000,000 shares authorized, 3,000,000 shares issued, and 2,900,000 shares outstanding) with a new common stock issue having a $0.50 par value. Since the new par value is one-half the amount of the old, this represents a 2-for-1 stock split. That is, the shareholders will receive two shares of the $0.50 par stock in exchange for each share of the $1 par stock they own. The $1 par stock will be collected and destroyed by the issuing corporation.

On November 1, 2021, the Nicklaus Corporation declares a $0.05 per share cash dividend on common stock and a $0.25 per share cash dividend on preferred stock. Payment is scheduled for December 1, 2021, to shareholders of record on November 15, 2021.

1096   SECTION 3   Liabilities and Shareholders' Equity

On December 2, 2021, the Nicklaus Corporation declares a 1% stock dividend payable on December 28, 2021, to shareholders of record on December 14. At the date of declaration, the common stock was selling in the open market at $10 per share. The dividend will result in 58,000 (0.01 × 5,800,000) additional shares being issued to shareholders.

Required:

1. Prepare journal entries to record the declaration and payment of these stock and cash dividends.
2. Prepare the December 31, 2021, shareholders' equity section of the balance sheet for the Nicklaus Corporation. (Assume net income for the fourth quarter was $2,500,000.)
3. Prepare a statement of shareholders' equity for Nicklaus Corporation for 2021.

P 18–13
Quasi
reorganization
(based on
Appendix 18)
● Appendix 18

A new CEO was hired to revive the floundering Champion Chemical Corporation. The company had endured operating losses for several years, but confidence was emerging that better times were ahead. The board of directors and shareholders approved a quasi reorganization for the corporation. The reorganization included devaluing inventory for obsolescence by $105 million and increasing land by $5 million. Immediately prior to the restatement, at December 31, 2021, Champion Chemical Corporation's balance sheet appeared as follows (in condensed form):

CHAMPION CHEMICAL CORPORATION
Balance Sheet
At December 31, 2021
($ in millions)

Cash	$ 20
Receivables	40
Inventory	230
Land	40
Buildings and equipment (net)	90
	$420
Liabilities	$240
Common stock (320 million shares at $1 par)	320
Additional paid-in capital	60
Retained earnings (deficit)	(200)
	$420

Required:

1. Prepare the journal entries appropriate to record the quasi reorganization on January 1, 2022.
2. Prepare a balance sheet as it would appear immediately after the restatement.

Decision Makers' Perspective

Apply your critical-thinking ability to the knowledge you've gained. These cases will provide you an opportunity to develop your research, analysis, judgment, and communication skills. You also will work with other students, integrate what you've learned, apply it in real-world situations, and consider its global and ethical ramifications. This practice will broaden your knowledge and further develop your decision-making abilities.

©ImageGap/ Getty Images

**Real World
Case 18–1**
Initial public
offering of
common
stock; Dolby
Laboratories
● LO18–4

Real World Financials

Ray Dolby started Dolby Laboratories and since then has been a leader in the entertainment industry and consumer electronics. Closely held since its founding in 1965, Dolby decided to go public. Here's an AP news report:

DOLBY'S IPO EXPECTED TO PLAY SWEET MUSIC—The initial public offering market is hoping for a big bang this week from Dolby Laboratories Inc. The San Francisco company, whose sound systems and double-D logo are ubiquitous in the movie industry as well as in consumer electronics, plans to sell 27.5 million shares for $13.50 to $15.50 each. Founded by Cambridge-trained scientist Ray Dolby 39 years ago, the company started out manufacturing noise-reduction equipment for the music industry that eliminated the background "hiss" on recordings, and has since expanded to encompass everything from digital audio systems to Dolby Surround sound. The company's IPO, which is lead-managed by underwriters Morgan Stanley and Goldman Sachs Group Inc., is expected to do well not only because of its brand recognition, but also because of its strong financials. *(AP)*

Required:

1. Assuming the shares are issued at the midpoint of the price range indicated, how much capital did the IPO raise for Dolby Laboratories before any underwriting discount and offering expenses?
2. If the par amount is $0.01 per share, what journal entry did Dolby use to record the sale?

Source: Associated Press

Analysis
Case 18–2
Statement of shareholders' equity

● LO18–1, LO18–3, LO18–6, LO18–7

The shareholders' equity portion of the balance sheet of Sessel's Department Stores, Inc., a large regional specialty retailer, is as follows:

SESSEL'S DEPARTMENT STORES, INC.
Comparative Balance Sheets
Shareholders' Equity Section

(values and shares in thousands, except per share amounts)	Dec. 31, 2022	Dec. 31, 2021
Shareholders' Equity		
Preferred stock—$1 par value; 20,000 total shares authorized, Series A—600 shares authorized, issued, and outstanding, $50 per share liquidation preference	$ 57,700	$ —
Series B—33 shares authorized, no shares outstanding		
Common stock—$0.10 par; 200,000 shares authorized, 19,940 and 18,580 shares issued and outstanding at Dec. 31, 2022, and Dec. 31, 2021, respectively	1,994	1,858
Additional paid-in capital	227,992	201,430
Retained income	73,666	44,798
Total shareholders' equity	**$361,352**	**$248,086**

Disclosures elsewhere in Sessel's annual report revealed the following changes in shareholders' equity accounts for 2022, 2021, 2020 (values and shares in whole dollars):

2022:
1. The only changes in retained earnings during 2022 were preferred dividends on preferred stock of $3,388,000 and net income.
2. The preferred stock is convertible. During the year, 6,592 shares were issued. All shares were converted into 320,000 shares of common stock. No gain or loss was recorded on the conversion.
3. Common shares were issued in a public offering and upon the exercise of stock options. On the statement of shareholders' equity, Sessel's reports these two items on a single line entitled: "Issuance of shares."

2021:
1. Net income: $12,126,000.
2. Issuance of common stock: 5,580,000 shares at $112,706,000.

2020:
1. Net income: $13,494,000.
2. Issuance of common stock: 120,000 shares at $826,000.

Required:
From these disclosures, prepare comparative statements of shareholders' equity for 2022, 2021, and 2020.

Communication
Case 18–3
IFRS; Is preferred stock debt or equity? Group interaction

● LO18–1, LO18–9

 IFRS

An unsettled question in accounting for stock is this: Should preferred stock be recognized as a liability, or should it be considered equity? Under International Financial Reporting Standards, preferred stock (preference shares) often is reported as debt with the dividends reported in the income statement as interest expense. Under U.S. GAAP, that is the case only for "mandatorily redeemable" preferred stock.

Two opposing viewpoints are:
  View 1: Preferred stock should be considered equity.
  View 2: Preferred stock should be reported as a liability.
In considering this question, focus on conceptual issues regarding the practicable and theoretically appropriate treatment, unconstrained by GAAP.

Required:
1. Which view do you favor? Develop a list of arguments in support of your view prior to the class session for which the case is assigned.
2. In class, your instructor will pair you (and everyone else) with a classmate (who also has independently developed an argument).
   a. You will be given three minutes to argue your view to your partner. Your partner likewise will be given three minutes to argue his or her view to you. During these three-minute presentations, the listening partner is not permitted to speak.
   b. Then after each person has had a turn attempting to convince his or her partner, the two partners will have a three-minute discussion in which they will decide which view is more convincing and arguments will be merged into a single view for each pair.

1098   SECTION 3   Liabilities and Shareholders' Equity

3. After the allotted time, a spokesperson for each of the two views will be selected by the instructor. Each spokesperson will field arguments from the class in support of that view's position and list the arguments on the board. The class then will discuss the merits of the two lists of arguments and attempt to reach a consensus view, though a consensus is not necessary.

Research Case 18–4
FASB codification; comprehensive income; locate and extract relevant information and authoritative support for a financial reporting issue; integrative; Cisco Systems

● LO18–2

Real World Financials

C⌕DE

Titan Networking became a public company through an IPO (initial public offering) two weeks ago. You are looking forward to the challenges of being assistant controller for a publicly owned corporation. One such challenge came in the form of a memo in this morning's in-box. "We need to start reporting comprehensive income in our financials," the message from your boss said. "Do some research on that, will you? That concept didn't exist when I went to school." In response, you sought out the financial statements of Cisco Systems, the networking industry leader. The following are excerpts from disclosure notes from Cisco's 2017 annual report:

	Years Ended		
	July 29, 2017	**July 30, 2016**	**July 25, 2015**
Net income	$9,609	$10,739	$8,981
Other comprehensive income (loss):			
Available-for-sale investments:			
Change in net unrealized gains, net of tax	(89)	92	(12)
Net (gains) losses reclassified into earnings, net of tax	50	1	(100)
	(39)	93	(112)
Cash flow hedging instruments:			
Change in unrealized gains and losses, net of tax	17	(59)	(140)
Net (gains) losses reclassified into earnings	74	16	136
	91	(43)	(4)
Net change in cumulative translation adjustment and actuarial gains and losses, net of tax	321	(447)	(498)
Other comprehensive income (loss)	373	(397)	(614)
Comprehensive income	$9,982	$10,342	$8,367

Required:
1. Locate the financial statements of Cisco in the Investor Relations section of Cisco's website. Search the 2017 annual report for information about how Cisco accounts for comprehensive income. What does Cisco report in its balance sheet for 2017 Accumulated other comprehensive income?
2. From the information Cisco's financial statements provide, show the calculation of the change in the accumulated other comprehensive income from the end of fiscal 2016 to the end of fiscal 2017. *Hint:* One component of the change is Comprehensive (income) loss attributable to noncontrolling interests.
3. Access the *FASB Accounting Standards Codification* at the FASB website (www.fasb.org). Identify the specific eight-digit Codification citation (XXX-XX-XX-X) from the authoritative literature that describes the two alternative formats for reporting comprehensive income.

Source: Cisco Systems

Real World Case 18–5
Share repurchase; stock split; cash dividends; Nike, Inc.

● LO18–5 through LO18–8

Real World Financials

Nike is the world's leading designer, marketer, and distributor of authentic athletic footwear, apparel, equipment, and accessories. The following is a press release from the company:

NIKE, INC. ANNOUNCES 11 PERCENT INCREASE IN QUARTERLY DIVIDEND

BEAVERTON, Ore.—(BUSINESS WIRE)—NIKE, Inc. (NYSE: NKE) announced today that its Board of Directors has approved a quarterly cash dividend of $0.20 per share. . . . This represents an increase of 11 percent versus the prior quarterly dividend rate of $0.18 per share. The dividend declared today is payable on January 2, 2018, to shareholders of record at the close of business December 4, 2017. "Today's announcement, combined with the four-year $12 billion share repurchase program we announced in 2015, demonstrates our continued confidence in generating strong cash flow and returns for shareholders through our new Consumer Direct Offense as we continue to invest in fueling sustainable, long-term growth and profitability."

When the share repurchase program was announced the company also declared a stock split distributed in the form of a 100% stock dividend. At that time Nike's 1,200 million shares were trading at $130 per share. Nike's shares have a stated value of $0.001 per share.

Required:
1. How did Nike account for the stock split? Prepare the appropriate journal entry.
2. Assume Nike repurchased 50 million shares after the stock split at an average price of $59 per share. The original issue price of the shares, after adjusting for the 6 stock splits since the shares were issued, was

$0.15 per share. What entry would Nike have recorded to account for the repurchase? Nike views the repurchase of stock as a formal retirement of shares.

3. Suppose Nike views the repurchase of stock as an acquisition of treasury stock. What entry would Nike have recorded to account for the repurchase?

4. How should Nike account for the cash dividend announced in the press release? Prepare the entries for the declaration and for the payment of the dividend.

Source: Nike, Inc.

Communication Case 18–6
Issuance of shares; share issue costs; prepare a report
● LO18–4

You are the newest member of the staff of Brinks & Company, a medium-size investment management firm. You are supervised by Les Kramer, an employee of two years. Les has a reputation as being technically sound but has a noticeable gap in his accounting education. Knowing you are knowledgeable about accounting issues, he requested you provide him with a synopsis of accounting for share issue costs.

"I thought the cost of issuing securities is recorded separately and expensed over time," he stated in a handwritten memo. "But I don't see that for IBR's underwriting expenses. What gives?"

He apparently was referring to a disclosure note on a page of a prospective investee's annual report, photocopied and attached to his memo. To raise funds for expansion, the company sold additional shares of its $0.10 par common stock. The following disclosure note appeared in the company's most recent annual report:

NOTES TO CONSOLIDATED FINANCIAL STATEMENTS
Note 10—Stock Transactions (in part)

In February and March, the Company sold 2,395,000 shares of Common Stock at $22.25 per share in a public offering. Net proceeds to the Company were approximately $50.2 million after the underwriting discount and offering expenses.

Required:
Write a formal memo to your supervisor. Briefly explain how share issue costs are accounted for and how that accounting differs from that of debt issue costs. To make sure your explanation is understood in context of the footnote, include in your memo the following:

a. At what total amount did the shares sell to the public? How is the difference between this amount and the $50.2 million net proceeds accounted for?

b. The appropriate journal entry to record the sale of the shares.

Analysis Case 18–7
Analyzing financial statements; price-earnings ratio; dividend payout ratio
● LO18–1

AGF Foods Company is a large, primarily domestic, consumer foods company involved in the manufacture, distribution, and sale of a variety of food products. Industry averages are derived from Troy's *The Almanac of Business and Industrial Financial Ratios* and Dun and Bradstreet's *Industry Norms and Key Business Ratios*. Following are the 2021 and 2020 comparative income statements and balance sheets for AGF. The market price of AGF's common stock is $47 at the end of 2021. (The financial data we use are from actual financial statements of a well-known corporation, but the company name used in our illustration is fictitious and the numbers and dates have been modified slightly to disguise the company's identity.)

Profitability is the key to a company's long-run survival. Profitability measures focus on a company's ability to provide an adequate return relative to resources devoted to company operations.

AGF FOODS COMPANY
Years Ended December 31, 2021 and 2020

($ in millions)	2021	2020
Comparative Income Statements		
Net sales	$ 6,440	$ 5,800
Cost of goods sold	(3,667)	(3,389)
Gross profit	2,773	2,411
Operating expenses	(1,916)	(1,629)
Operating income	857	782
Interest expense	(54)	(53)
Income from operations before tax	803	729
Income taxes	(316)	(287)
Net income	$ 487	$ 442
Average shares outstanding	181 million	181 million

(continued)

1100 SECTION 3   Liabilities and Shareholders' Equity

(concluded)

Comparative Balance Sheets

Assets

Current assets:

Cash	$ 48	$ 142
Accounts receivable	347	320
Marketable securities	358	—
Inventories	914	874
Prepaid expenses	212	154
Total current assets	1,879	1,490
Property, plant, and equipment (net)	2,592	2,291
Intangibles (net)	800	843
Other assets	74	60
Total assets	$ 5,345	$ 4,684

Liabilities and Shareholders' Equity

Current liabilities:

Accounts payable	$ 254	$ 276
Accrued liabilities	493	496
Notes payable	518	115
Current portion of long-term debt	208	54
Total current liabilities	1,473	941
Long-term debt	534	728
Deferred income taxes	407	344
Total liabilities	2,414	2,013
Shareholders' equity:		
Common stock, $1 par	180	180
Additional paid-in capital	21	63
Retained earnings	2,730	2,428
Total shareholders' equity	2,931	2,671
Total liabilities and shareholders' equity	$ 5,345	$ 4,684

Required:

1. Calculate the return on shareholders' equity for AGF. The average return for the stocks listed on the New York Stock Exchange in a comparable period was 18.8%. What information does your calculation provide an investor?

2. Calculate AGF's earnings per share and earnings-price ratio. The average return for the stocks listed on the New York Stock Exchange in a comparable time period was 5.4%. What does your calculation indicate about AGF's earnings?

Ethics Case 18–8
The Swiss label maker; value of shares issued for equipment
● LO18–4

Bricker Graphics is a privately held company specializing in package labels. Representatives of the firm have just returned from Switzerland, where a Swiss firm is manufacturing a custom-made high speed, color labeling machine. Confidence is high that the new machine will help rescue Bricker from sharply declining profitability. Bricker's chief operating officer, Don Benson, has been under fire for not reaching the company's performance goals of achieving a rate of return on assets of at least 12%.

The afternoon of his return from Switzerland, Benson called Susan Sharp into his office. Susan is Bricker's Controller.

Benson: I wish you had been able to go. We have some accounting issues to consider.
Sharp: I wish I'd been there, too. I understand the food was marvelous. What are the accounting issues?
Benson: They discussed accepting our notes at the going rate for a face amount of $12.5 million. We also discussed financing with stock.
Sharp: I thought we agreed; debt is the way to go for us now.
Benson: Yes, but I've been thinking. We can issue shares for a total of $10 million. The labeler is custom made and doesn't have a quoted selling price, but the domestic labelers we considered went for around $10 million. It sure would help our rate of return if we keep the asset base as low as possible.

Required:

1. How will Benson's plan affect the return measure? What accounting issue is involved?
2. Is the proposal ethical?
3. Who would be affected if the proposal is implemented?

Data Analytics

Data analytics is the process of examining data sets in order to draw conclusions about the information they contain. If you haven't completed any of the prior data analytics cases, follow the instructions listed in the Chapter 1 Data Analytics case to get set up. You will need to watch the videos referred to in the Chapters 1 - 3 Data Analytics cases. No additional videos are required for this case. All short training videos can be found here: https://www.tableau.com/learn/training#getting-started.

Data Analytics Case
Rate of Return on Shareholders' Equity
● LO18–7

In the Data Analytics Cases in the previous chapter, you used Tableau to examine two (hypothetical) publicly traded companies: GPS Corporation and Tru, Inc. regarding changes in the funded status of their pension plans during the previous ten years as well as the way components of pension expense are reported in the income statement. This time, you investigate the ability of the two companies to provide a return to the investors who buy the companies' stock.

Required:

For each of the two companies in the most recent five-year period, 2017-2021, use Tableau to calculate and display the trends for (a) the debt to equity ratio, (b) the rate of return on shareholders' equity [Net income/Shareholders' equity], and (c) the rate of return on assets [Net income / Total assets]. Based upon what you find, answer the following questions:

1. Which of the two companies, GPS Corporation or Tru, Inc., finances a higher percentage of its assets by borrowed funds relative to funds invested by shareholders as measured by the debt to equity ratio in 2021?

2. Which of the two companies, GPS Corporation or Tru, Inc., indicates a higher profitability during the period 2017-2021 without regard to the sources of financing as measured by the return on assets ratio?

3. Which of the two companies, GPS Corporation or Tru, Inc., indicates a higher effectiveness of employing resources provided by owners during the period 2017-2021 as measured by the return on shareholders' equity ratio?

4. Management is using its borrowed funds to enhance the earnings for shareholders of (a) GPS Corporation, (b) Tru, Inc., (c) both firms, or (d) neither firm during the period 2017-2021?

Resources:

Download the "GPS_Tru_Financials.xlsx" Excel file available in Connect, or under Additional Student Resources within the Library tab. Save it to the computer on which you will be using Tableau.

For this case, you will create calculations to produce several long-term solvency ratios to allow you to compare and contrast the two companies.

After you view the training videos, follow these steps to create the charts you'll use for this case:

- Open Tableau and connect to the Excel spreadsheet you downloaded.
- Click on the "Sheet 1" tab at the bottom of the canvas, to the right of the Data Source at the bottom of the screen.
- Drag "($ in 000s) Company" and "Year" under Dimensions to the Columns shelf. Change "Year" to *discrete* by right-clicking and selecting "discrete." Select "Show Filter" and uncheck all the years except the last five years (2017 – 2021). Click OK.
- Create a calculated field by clicking the "Analysis" tab at the top of the screen and selecting "Create Calculated field." Name the calculation "Debt to equity ratio." In the Calculation Editor window, from Measures, drag "Total liabilities (Cur + noncur)", type a division sign, and drag "Total shareholders' equity" beside it. Make sure the window says that the calculation is valid and click OK.
- Drag the newly created "Debt to equity ratio" to the Rows shelf. Click on the "Show Me" and select "side-by-side bars." Add labels to the bars by clicking on "Label" under the "Marks" card and clicking the box "Show mark labels." Format the labels to Times New Roman, bold, black and 10-point font. Edit the color on the Color marks card if desired.
- Change the title of the sheet to be "Debt to Equity Ratio Trend" by right-clicking and selecting "Edit title." Format the title to Times New Roman, bold, black and 15-point font. Change the title of "Sheet 1" to match the sheet title by right-clicking, selecting "Rename" and typing in the new title.
- Click on the New Worksheet tab ("Sheet 2" should be open) to the right of the newly named "Debt to Equity Ratio Trend" sheet at the bottom of the screen.
- Follow the procedures above for the company and year.
- Create a calculated field by clicking the "Analysis" tab at the top of the screen and selecting "Create Calculated field." Name the calculation "Rate of return on shareholders' equity." In the Calculation Editor window, from Measures, drag "Net income/(loss)", type a division sign, and then drag "Total shareholders' equity". Make sure the window says that the calculation is valid and click OK.

1102   SECTION 3   Liabilities and Shareholders' Equity

- Create a calculated field by clicking the "Analysis" tab at the top of the screen and selecting "Create Calculated field." Name the calculation "Rate of return on assets." In the Calculation Editor window from Measures, drag "Net income/(loss)", type a division sign, and then drag "Total assets". Make sure the window says that the calculation is valid and click OK.
- Drag the newly created "Rate of return on shareholders' equity" and "Rate of return on assets" to the Rows shelf. Add labels to the bars by clicking on "Label" under the "Marks card" and clicking the box "Show mark label." Format the labels to Times New Roman, bold, black and 10-point font. Select Field in the upper right corner of the "Format Font" box and change to Percentage with one decimal place. Edit the color of the years on the Color marks card if desired.
- Edit the axis to utilize the same scale by right-clicking on the axis and selecting "Edit Axis. . .". Select Fixed and set from 0 to 0.35 for both charts.
- Change the title of the sheet to be "Rate of Return on Shareholders' Equity and Assets Trends" by right-clicking and selecting "Edit title." Format the title to Times New Roman, bold, black and 15-point font. Change the title of "Sheet 2" to match the sheet title by right-clicking, selecting "Rename" and typing in the new title.
- Format all other labels to be Times New Roman, bold, black and 12-point font.
- Once complete, save the file as "DA18_Your initials.twbx."

Continuing Cases

Target Case

 LO18–1, LO18–5

Target Corporation prepares its financial statements according to U.S. GAAP. Target's financial statements and disclosure notes for the year ended February 3, 2018, are available in Connect. This material also is available under the Investor Relations link at the company's website (www.target.com). Target refers to its Shareholders' Equity as Shareholders' Investment.

Required:

1. Refer to Target's Consolidated Statements of Shareholders' Investment. What are the six types of events and transactions that affected one or more of the Shareholders' Investment accounts in the year ended February 3, 2018?
2. Note 25, "Share Repurchase," provides the information we need to reconstruct the journal entry that summarizes Target's share repurchases in the year ended February 3, 2018. Provide that entry (dollars in millions, rounded to the nearest million).
3. Does Target account for share repurchases as (a) treasury stock or (b) retired shares?

Air France–KLM Case

● LO18–9

🌐 IFRS

Air France–KLM (AF), a Franco-Dutch company, prepares its financial statements according to International Financial Reporting Standards. AF's financial statements and disclosure notes for the year ended December 31, 2017, are available in Connect. This material is also available under the Finance link at the company's website (www.airfranceklm.com).

Required:

1. Locate Note 28.5 in AF's financial statements. What items comprise "Reserves and retained earnings" as reported in the balance sheet?
2. In its presentation of the components of the balance sheet, which is listed first, current assets or non-current assets? Does this approach differ from U.S. GAAP?
3. In its presentation of the components of the balance sheet, which is listed first, current liabilities or non-current liabilities? Does this approach differ from U.S. GAAP?
4. In its presentation of the components of the balance sheet, which is listed first, liabilities or shareholders' equity? Does this approach differ from U.S. GAAP?

CPA Exam Questions and Simulations

Sample CPA Exam questions from Roger CPA Review are available in Connect as support for the topics in this chapter. These multiple-choice questions and task-based simulations include expert-written explanations and solutions, and provide a starting point for students to become familiar with the content and functionality of the actual CPA Exam.

CHAPTER

19

Share-Based Compensation and Earnings Per Share

OVERVIEW

We've discussed a variety of employee compensation plans in prior chapters, including pension and other postretirement benefits in Chapter 17. In this chapter, we look at some common forms of compensation in which the amount of the compensation employees receive is tied to the market price of company stock. We will see that these *share-based* compensation plans—restricted stock awards, restricted stock units, stock options, and stock appreciation rights—create shareholders' equity, which was the topic of the previous chapter, and which also often affects the way we calculate earnings per share, the topic of the second part of the current chapter. Specifically, we view these as *potential common shares* along with convertible securities, and we calculate earnings per share as if the securities already had been exercised or converted into additional common shares.

LEARNING OBJECTIVES

After studying this chapter, you should be able to:

- **LO19–1** Explain and implement the accounting for restricted stock plans. (*p. 1106*)
- **LO19–2** Explain and implement the accounting for stock options. (*p. 1108*)
- **LO19–3** Explain and implement the accounting for employee share purchase plans. (*p. 1117*)
- **LO19–4** Distinguish between a simple and a complex capital structure. (*p. 1119*)
- **LO19–5** Describe what is meant by the weighted-average number of common shares. (*p. 1120*)
- **LO19–6** Differentiate the effect on EPS of the sale of new shares, a stock dividend or stock split, and the reacquisition of shares. (*p. 1120*)
- **LO19–7** Describe how preferred dividends affect the calculation of EPS. (*p. 1122*)
- **LO19–8** Describe how options, rights, and warrants are incorporated in the calculation of EPS. (*p. 1123*)
- **LO19–9** Describe how convertible securities are incorporated in the calculation of EPS. (*p. 1126*)
- **LO19–10** Determine whether potential common shares are antidilutive. (*p. 1128*)
- **LO19–11** Describe the two components of the proceeds used in the treasury stock method and how restricted stock is incorporated in the calculation of EPS. (*p. 1133*)
- **LO19–12** Explain the way contingently issuable shares are incorporated in the calculation of EPS. (*p. 1134*)
- **LO19–13** Describe the way EPS information should be reported in an income statement. (*p. 1136*)
- **LO19–14** Discuss the primary differences between U.S. GAAP and IFRS with respect to accounting for share-based compensation and earnings per share. (*pp. 1113, 1115,* and *1119*)

©Fabio Cardoso/Getty Images

FINANCIAL REPORTING CASE

Proper Motivation?

The coffee room discussion Thursday morning was particularly lively. Yesterday's press release describing National Electronic Ventures' choice of Sandra Veres as its president and chief operating officer was today's hot topic in all the company's departments. The press release noted that Ms. Veres's compensation package includes elements beyond salary that are intended to not only motivate her to accept the offer, but also to remain with the company and work to increase shareholder value. Excerpts from the release follow:

National Electronic Ventures, Inc., today announced it had attracted G. Sandra Veres, respected executive from the wireless communications industry, to succeed chairman Walter Kovac. Veres will assume the new role as CEO on Jan. 1, 2021. Ms. Veres will receive a compensation package at NEV of more than $1 million in salary, stock options to buy more than 800,000 shares of NEV stock, and a grant of restricted stock.

By the time you finish this chapter, you should be able to respond appropriately to the questions posed in this case. Compare your response to the solution provided at the end of the chapter.

QUESTIONS

1. How can a compensation package such as this serve as an incentive to Ms. Veres? (*p. 1105*)

2. Ms. Veres received a "grant of restricted stock." How should NEV account for the grant? (*p. 1106*)

3. Included were stock options to buy more than 800,000 shares of NEV stock. How will the options affect NEV's compensation expense? (*p. 1108*)

4. How will the presence of these and other similar stock options affect NEV's earnings per share? (*p. 1124*)

Share-Based Compensation

PART A

Employee compensation plans frequently include share-based awards. These awards are forms of payment whose value is dependent on the value of the company's stock. These may be outright awards of shares, stock options, or cash payments tied to the market price of shares. Sometimes only key executives participate in a stock benefit plan. In fact, CEOs typically get more than half their total compensation from share-based compensation plans. Typically, an executive compensation plan is tied to performance in a strategy that uses compensation to motivate its recipients. Some firms pay their directors entirely in shares. Actual compensation depends on the market value of the shares. Obviously, that's quite an incentive to act in the best interests of shareholders.

Although the variations of share-based compensation plans are seemingly endless, each shares common goals. Whether the plan is a stock award plan, a stock option plan, a stock appreciation rights (SARs) plan, or one of the several similar plans, the goals are to provide compensation to designated employees, while sometimes providing those employees with some sort of performance incentive. Likewise, our goals in accounting for each of these plans are the same for each: (1) to determine the fair value of the compensation and (2) to expense that compensation over the periods in which participants perform services. The issue is not trivial. Salary often is a minor portion of executive pay relative to stock awards and stock options.

FINANCIAL Reporting Case

Q1, p. 1105

The accounting objective is to record compensation expense over the periods in which related services are performed.

Restricted Stock Plans

● LO19–1

Executive compensation sometimes includes a grant of shares of stock or the right to receive shares. Usually, such shares are restricted in such a way as to provide some incentive to the recipient. Typically, restricted stock award plans are tied to continued employment. The two primary types of restricted stock plans are (a) restricted stock awards and (b) restricted stock units. Let's compare the two.

Restricted Stock Awards

Usually, restricted shares are subject to forfeiture if the employee doesn't remain with the company.

In a restricted stock award, shares actually are awarded in the name of the employee, although the company might retain physical possession of the shares. The employee has all rights of a shareholder, subject to certain restrictions or forfeiture. Ordinarily, the shares are subject to forfeiture by the employee if employment is terminated within some specified number of years from the date of grant. The employee usually is not free to sell the shares during the restriction period, and a statement to that effect often is inscribed on the stock certificates. These restrictions give the employee incentive to remain with the company until rights to the shares vest.

The compensation associated with a share of restricted stock is the market price at the grant date of an unrestricted share of the same stock. This amount is accrued as compensation expense with a credit to paid-in capital—restricted stock, over the service period for which participants receive the shares, usually from the date of grant to when restrictions are lifted (the vesting date).[1] Once the shares vest and the restrictions are lifted, paid-in capital—restricted stock is replaced by common stock and paid-in capital—excess of par. Any market price changes that might occur after the grant date don't affect the total compensation. This is essentially the same as accounting for restricted stock units to be settled in shares, as demonstrated in the next section.

FINANCIAL Reporting Case

Q2, p. 1105

Restricted Stock Units

An increasingly popular variation of restricted stock awards is restricted stock units (RSUs). In fact, RSUs have become a much more popular form of compensation than their restricted stock award cousins. A restricted stock unit is a right to receive a specified number of shares of company stock. It could be a performance bonus, a signing bonus, or regular compensation. The employee doesn't receive the stock right away. Instead, the shares are distributed as the recipient of RSUs satisfies the vesting requirement.[2] So, like restricted stock awards, the recipient benefits by the value of the shares at the end of the vesting period. Unlike restricted stock awards, though, the shares are not issued at the time of the grant. Delaying the increase in outstanding shares is more acceptable to other shareholders. As part of its share-based compensation plan, Apple Inc. provides compensation to executives in the form of RSUs as we see in Illustration 19–1.

Illustration 19–1

Restricted Stock Units (RSUs); Apple Inc.

Real World Financials

Share-Based Compensation (in part)
Share-based compensation cost for RSUs is measured based on the closing fair market value of the Company's common stock on the date of grant.... The Company recognizes share-based compensation expense over the award's requisite service period on a straight-line basis.

Source: Apple Inc.

Terms of RSUs vary.[3] Sometimes, the recipient is given the *cash equivalent* of the number of shares used to value the RSUs. Or, the terms might stipulate that either the recipient or the company is allowed to choose whether to settle in stock or cash.

Although RSUs delay the issuance of shares and avoid some administrative complexities of outright awards of restricted stock, accounting for RSUs to be settled in stock is

---

[1]Restricted stock plans usually are designed to comply with Tax Code Section 83 to allow employee compensation to be nontaxable to the employee until the date the shares become substantially vested, which is when the restrictions are lifted. Likewise, the employer gets no tax deduction until the compensation becomes taxable to the employee.

[2]Sometimes, the shares to be issued depend upon achieving specific performance targets.

[3]Typically, but not always, RSUs have no voting privileges and receive no dividends until the shares are issued at vesting. Sometimes, restricted stock does have voting privileges and receives dividends during the vesting period even though recipients are restricted from selling the shares until vesting.

essentially the same as for restricted stock awards. We see accounting for award plans or units of restricted stock demonstrated in Illustration 19–2.

Illustration 19–2

Restricted Stock Award Plans or Restricted Stock Units (RSUs)

Under its restricted stock unit (RSU) plan, Universal Communications grants RSUs representing 5 million of its $1 par common shares to certain key executives at January 1, 2021.

- The shares are subject to forfeiture if employment is terminated within four years.
- Shares have a current market price of $12 per share.

January 1, 2021
No entry

Calculate total compensation expense:

$$\begin{array}{r} \$12 \\ \times \quad 5 \text{ million} \\ \hline = \$60 \text{ million} \end{array}$$

The total compensation is the market value of the shares ($12) times 5 million shares.

The total compensation is to be allocated to expense over the four-year service (vesting) period: 2021–2024.

$60 million ÷ 4 years = $15 million per year

December 31, 2021, 2022, 2023, 2024	($ in millions)	
Compensation expense ($60 million ÷ 4 years)	15	
Paid-in capital—restricted stock		15
December 31, 2024		
Paid-in capital—restricted stock (5 million shares at $12)	60	
Common stock (5 million shares at $1 par)		5
Paid-in capital—excess of par (difference)		55

The $60 million is accrued to compensation expense over the four-year service period.

When restrictions are lifted, paid-in capital—restricted stock, is replaced by common stock and paid-in capital—excess of par.

On the other hand, *if the employee will receive cash* or can elect to receive cash, we consider the award to be a *liability* rather than equity, as is the case in Illustration 19–2. When an RSU is considered to be a liability, we determine its fair value at the grant date and recognize that amount as compensation expense over the requisite service period consistent with the way we account for restricted stock awards, RSUs, and other share-based compensation. However, because these plans are considered to be liabilities payable in cash, the credit portion of the entry as we recognize compensation expense each year is to Liability—restricted stock. And, it's necessary to periodically adjust the liability (and corresponding compensation) based on the change in the stock's fair value until the liability is paid. Note that this is consistent with the way we account for other liabilities. Accounting for share-based compensation that's considered to be a liability is demonstrated in Appendix 19B of the chapter.

If restricted stock shares or RSUs are forfeited because, say, the employee leaves the company, entries previously made related to that specific employee would simply be reversed. This would result in a decrease in compensation expense in the year of forfeiture. The total compensation, adjusted for the forfeited amount, is then allocated over the remaining service period.

Additional Consideration

An alternative way of accomplishing the same result is to debit deferred compensation for the full value of the RSUs ($60 million in the illustration) on the date they are granted.

	($ in millions)	
Deferred compensation (5 million shares at $12)	60	
Common stock (5 million shares at $1 par)		5
Paid-in capital—excess of par (difference)		55

If so, deferred compensation (a term used for delayed recognition of compensation expense) is reported as a reduction in shareholders' equity, resulting in a zero net effect on shareholders' equity. Then, deferred compensation is credited when compensation expense is debited over the service period. Just as in Illustration 19–2, the result is an increase in both compensation expense and paid-in capital each year over the vesting period.

1108 SECTION 4 Additional Financial Reporting Issues

Stock Option Plans

Often, employees aren't actually awarded shares, but rather are given the option to buy shares in the future. In fact, stock options have become an integral part of the total compensation package for key officers of most medium and large companies. As with any compensation plan, the accounting objective is to report compensation expense during the period of service for which the compensation is given.

● LO19–2

Expense—The Great Debate

Stock option plans give employees the option to purchase (a) a specified number of shares of the firm's stock, (b) at a specified price, (c) during a specified period of time. One of the most heated controversies in standard-setting history has been the debate over the amount of compensation to be recognized as expense for stock options. At issue is how the value of stock options is measured, which for most options determines whether any expense at all is recognized.

Historically, options were measured at their intrinsic values—the simple difference between the market price of the shares and the option price at which they can be acquired. For instance, an option that permits an employee to buy a $25-per-share stock for $10 per share has an intrinsic value of $15. However, plans in which the exercise price equals the market value of the underlying stock at the date of grant (which describes most executive stock option plans) have no intrinsic value and therefore result in zero compensation when measured this way, even though the fair value of the options can be quite significant. Facebook CEO Mark Zuckerberg reaped a $3.3 billion gain in 2013 alone by exercising stock options.[4] To many, it seems counterintuitive to not recognize compensation expense for plans that routinely provide executives with a substantial part of their total compensation.

FINANCIAL Reporting Case

Q3, p. 1105

After lengthy debate, the FASB consented to encourage, rather than require, that the fair value of options be recognized as expense.

FAILED ATTEMPT TO REQUIRE EXPENSING This is where the controversy ensues. In 1993, the FASB issued an Exposure Draft of a new standard that would have required companies to measure options at their *fair values* at the time they are granted and to expense that amount over the appropriate service period. To jump straight to the punch line, the FASB bowed to public pressure and agreed to withdraw the requirement before it became a standard. The FASB consented to encourage, rather than require, that fair value compensation be recognized as expense. Companies were permitted to continue accounting under prior GAAP (the intrinsic value method referred to in the previous paragraph).[5] Before we discuss the details of accounting for stock options, it's helpful to look back at what led the FASB to first propose fair value accounting and later rescind that proposal.

As the 1990s began, the public was becoming increasingly aware of the enormity of executive compensation in general and compensation in the form of stock options in particular. The lack of accounting for this compensation was apparent, prompting the SEC to encourage the FASB to move forward on its stock option project. Even Congress got into the fray when, in 1992, a bill was introduced that would require firms to report compensation expense based on the fair value of options. Motivated by this encouragement, the FASB issued its exposure draft in 1993. The real disharmony began then. Opposition to the proposed standard was broad and vehement, and that perhaps is an understatement. Critics based their opposition on one or more of these three objections:

1. *Options with no intrinsic value at issue have zero fair value and should not give rise to expense recognition.* The FASB, and even some critics of the proposal, were adamant that options provide valuable compensation at the grant date to recipients.

2. *It is impossible to measure the fair value of the compensation on the grant date.* The FASB argued vigorously that value can be approximated using one of several option pricing models. These are statistical models that use computers to incorporate

---

[4]*San Jose Mercury News,* April 1, 2014.
[5]"Accounting for Stock Issued to Employees," *Opinions of the Accounting Principles Board No. 25* (New York: AICPA, 1972). This pronouncement is superseded and therefore is not codified in the *FASB Accounting Standards Codification*.

information about a company's stock and the terms of the stock option to estimate the options' fair value. We might say the FASB position is that it's better to be approximately right than precisely wrong.

3. *The proposed standard would have unacceptable economic consequences.* Essentially, this argument asserted that requiring this popular means of compensation to be expensed would cause companies to discontinue the use of options.

The opposition included corporate executives, auditors, members of Congress, and the SEC.[6] Ironically, the very groups that provided the most impetus for the rule change initially—the SEC and Congress—were among the most effective detractors in the end. The only group that offered much support at all was the academic community, and that was by-and-large nonvocal support. In reversing its decision, the FASB was not swayed by any of the specific arguments of any opposition group. Dennis Beresford, chair of the FASB at the time, indicated that it was fear of government control of the standard-setting process that prompted the Board to modify its position. The Board remained steadfast that the proposed change was appropriate.

> There were consistent criticisms of the FASB's requirement to expense option compensation.

VOLUNTARY EXPENSING   Prior to 2002, only two companies—Boeing and Winn-Dixie—reported stock option compensation expense at fair value. However, in 2002, public outrage mounted amid high-profile accounting scandals at Enron, WorldCom, Tyco, and others. Some degree of consensus emerged that greed on the part of some corporate executives contributed to the fraudulent and misleading financial reporting at the time. In fact, many in the media were pointing to the proliferation of stock options as a primary form of compensation as a culprit in fueling that greed. An episode of the PBS series *Frontline* argued that not expensing the value of stock options contributed to the collapse of Enron. For these reasons, renewed interest surfaced in requiring stock option compensation to be reported in income statements.

CURRENT REQUIREMENT TO EXPENSE   Emerging from the rekindled debate was a GAAP revision that now requires fair value accounting for employee stock options, eliminating altogether the intrinsic value approach.[7] As you might expect, the proposal did not come without opposition. Many of the same groups that successfully blocked the FASB from enacting a similar requirement in 1995 led the opposition. Not surprisingly, at the forefront of the resistance were the high-tech companies that extensively use stock options as a primary form of compensating employees and thus are most susceptible to a reduction in reported earnings when that compensation is included in income statements. For example, consider Apple Inc.'s earnings for the 12 months ending March 27, 2004. Reported net income of $179 million would have been only $56 million, or 69% less, if the GAAP revision had been in effect then.[8]

> Current GAAP now requires companies to record the value of options in their income statements.

It's important to note that the way we account for stock options has no effect whatsoever on cash flows, only on whether the value of stock options is included among expenses. This is not to say that companies haven't altered their compensation strategies. Already, we have seen a shift in the way some companies compensate their employees. Partly due to the negative connotation that has become associated with executive stock options, we've seen fewer options and more bonuses and restricted stock awards. Let's examine the way stock options are accounted for now.

> We've witnessed a discernable shift in the way executives are compensated—fewer options, more stock awards and bonuses.

Recognizing the Fair Value of Options

Accounting for stock options parallels the accounting for restricted stock we discussed in the first part of this chapter. That is, we measure compensation as the fair value of the stock options at the grant date and then record that amount as compensation expense over the service period for which employees receive the options. Estimating the fair value requires the

---

[6]All of the then "Big Six" CPA firms lobbied against the proposal. Senator Lieberman of Connecticut introduced a bill in Congress that, if passed, would have forbidden the FASB from passing a requirement to expense stock option compensation.
[7]FASB ASC 718–Compensation.
[8]Alex Salkever, "What Could Crunch Apple Shares," *BusinessWeek,* July 12, 2004, p.11.

The fair value of a stock option can be determined by employing a recognized option pricing model.

use of one of several option pricing models. These mathematical models assimilate a variety of information about a company's stock and the terms of the stock option to estimate the option's fair value. The model should take into account the following:

An option pricing model takes into account several variables.

- Exercise price of the option.
- Expected term of the option.
- Current market price of the stock.
- Expected dividends.
- Expected risk-free rate of return during the term of the option.
- Expected volatility of the stock.

The techniques for estimating fair value have been among the most controversial issues in the debate.

The current GAAP for accounting for employee stock options modified the way companies actually measure fair value. It calls for using models that permit greater flexibility in modeling the ways employees are expected to exercise options and their expected employment termination patterns after options vest.[9] Option-pricing theory, on which the pricing models are based, is a topic explored in depth in finance courses and is subject to active empirical investigation and development. A simplified discussion is provided in Appendix 19A.[10]

The total compensation, as estimated by the options' fair value, is reported as compensation expense over the period of service for which the options are given. Recipients normally are not allowed to exercise their options for a specified number of years. This delay provides added incentive to remain with the company. The time between the date options are granted and the first date they can be exercised is the vesting period and usually is considered to be the service period over which the compensation expense is reported. The process is demonstrated in Illustration 19–3.

Illustration 19–3
Stock Options

At January 1, 2021, Universal Communications grants 10 million options to key executives.
- The options permit recipients to acquire 10 million of the company's $1 par common shares within the next eight years, but not before December 31, 2024 (the vesting date).
- The exercise price is the market price of the shares on the date of grant, $35 per share.
- The fair value of the options, estimated by an appropriate option pricing model, is $8 per option.

January 1, 2021
No entry

Calculate total compensation expense:

$ 8	Estimated fair value per option
× 10 million	Options granted
= $ 80 million	Total compensation

Fair value is estimated at the date of grant.

The total compensation is allocated to expense over the four-year service (vesting) period: 2021–2024.

$80 million ÷ 4 years = $20 million per year

The value of the award is expensed over the service period for which the compensation is provided.

December 31, 2021, 2022, 2023, 2024	($ in millions)
Compensation expense ($80 million ÷ 4 years)	20
Paid-in capital—stock options	20

Option compensation expense is based on the number of options expected to vest.

FORFEITURES If previous experience indicates that a material number of the options will be forfeited before they vest (due to employee turnover or violation of other terms of the options), we adjust the amount of compensation recorded (a) by estimating forfeitures or (b) as forfeitures occur.

---

[9]FASB ASC 718–10–55–30 to 32: Compensation—Stock Compensation—Overall—Implementation and Guidance Illustrations—Selecting or Estimating the Expected Term.
[10]An expanded discussion is provided in FASB ASC 718–10–55: Compensation—Stock Compensation—Overall—Implementation and Guidance Illustrations.

The default approach is to *estimate the percentage* of options that will be forfeited and adjust grant date calculation of the fair value of the options to reflect that expectation. For instance, if a forfeiture rate of 5% is expected, Universal's estimated total compensation would be 95% of $80 million, or $76 million. In that case, the annual compensation expense in Illustration 19–3 would have been **$19** million ($76 ÷ 4) instead of $20 million. We see the effect of that possibility in Illustration 19–3A.

Initial Expectation:		($ in millions)
2021		
Compensation expense ([$80 × 95%] ÷ 4)...	19	
Paid-in capital—stock options		19
2022		
Compensation expense ([$80 × 95%] ÷ 4)...	19	
Paid-in capital—stock options...		19
Estimate Revision after 2 Years:		
2023		
Compensation expense [($80 × 90% × 3/4) − ($19 + $19)]...........................	16	
Paid-in capital—stock options...		16
2024		
Compensation expense [($80 × 90% × 4/4) − ($19 + $19 + $16)]..............	18	
Paid-in capital—stock options...		18

Illustration 19–3A

Default Approach: Forfeiture Estimates with Revisions

The value of the compensation is originally estimated to be $76 million, or $19 million per year.

The expense each year is the current estimate of total compensation that should have been recorded to date less the amount already recorded.

What if that expectation changes later? Universal should adjust the cumulative amount of compensation expense recorded to date in the year the estimate changes. Suppose, for instance, that during the third year, Universal revises its estimate of forfeitures from 5% to 10%. The new estimate of total compensation would then be $80 million × 90%, or $72 million. For the first three years, the portion of the total compensation that should have been reported would be $72 million × ¾, or $54 million, and since $38 million (**$19** × 2) of that was recorded in 2021–2022 before the estimate changed, an additional $16 million would now be recorded in 2023. Then if the estimate isn't changed again, the remaining $18 million ($72 − $54) would be recorded in 2024.

When forfeiture estimates change, the cumulative effect on compensation is reflected in current earnings.

Additional Consideration

Notice that the $18 million in 2024 is the amount that would have been reported in each of the four years if Universal had assumed a 10% forfeiture rate from the beginning. Also be aware that this approach is contrary to the usual way companies account for changes in estimates. For instance, assume a company acquires a four-year depreciable asset having an estimated residual value of 5% of cost. The $76 million depreciable cost would be depreciated straight line at **$19** million over the four-year useful life. If the estimated residual value changes after two years to 10%, the new estimated depreciable cost of $72 would be reduced by the $38 million depreciation recorded the first two years, and the remaining $34 million would be depreciated equally, $17 million per year, over the remaining two years.

In an alternative approach, as a practical expedient, companies can elect to account for forfeitures of stock options (or restricted stock) when forfeitures actually occur, rather than estimate forfeitures that will occur during the vesting period. So rather than recording compensation expense and paid-in capital for the *net* amount of awards expected to vest, companies can choose to initially record compensation based on the total amount and then reduce compensation expense and paid-in capital only if and when forfeitures occur.[11] Once

Companies can elect to account for forfeitures when forfeitures actually occur rather than estimate them.

[11]ASC 718-10-35-3: Compensation—Stock Compensation-Overall-Subsequent Measurement Recognition of Compensation Costs over the Requisite Service Period

a forfeiture occurs, we adjust the cumulative amount of compensation expense recorded to date in the year the forfeiture occurs and thereafter in a manner similar to the way estimates are adjusted as demonstrated in Illustration 19–3A.

This election applies only to forfeitures related to employee turnover. A company must disclose its policy election for forfeitures (estimated or recorded as they occur). To demonstrate the alternative approach, let's say Universal Communications recorded compensation of **$20** million in both 2021 and 2022 based on the $80 million fair value of the stock options issued at the beginning of 2021. Then, in 2023, options with a fair value of $8 million when granted are forfeited due to executive turnover. Universal's journal entries would look like those in Illustration 19–3B.

Illustration 19–3B

Optional Approach: Revisions as Forfeitures Occur

December 31, 2021	($ in millions)	
Compensation expense ($80 million ÷ 4 years)	20	
Paid-in capital—stock options		20
December 31, 2022 ($ in millions)		
Compensation expense ($80 million ÷ 4 years)	20	
Paid-in capital—stock options		20
When Actual Forfeitures Occur in the Third Year:		
December 31, 2023 ($ in millions)		
Compensation expense ([($80 − $8) × ¾] − $20 − $20)	14	
Paid-in capital—stock options		14
December 31, 2024 ($ in millions)		
Compensation expense ([($80 − $8) × ¼] − $20 − $20 − $14)	18	
Paid-in capital—stock options		18

This election applies only to forfeitures related to employee *turnover*. For share-based plans with performance conditions (which we discuss later), companies must assess the probability that such conditions will be achieved. A company must disclose its policy election for forfeitures (estimated, or recorded as they occur).

When Options are Exercised

If half the options in Illustration 19–3 (for 5 million shares) are exercised on July 11, 2027, when the market price is $50 per share, the following journal entry is recorded:

Recording the exercise of options is not affected by the market price on the exercise date.

July 11, 2027	($ in millions)	
Cash ($35 exercise price × 5 million shares)	175	
Paid-in capital—stock options (½ account balance)	40	
Common stock (5 million shares at $1 par per share)		5
Paid-in capital—excess of par (to balance)		210

Notice that the market price at exercise is irrelevant. Changes in the market price of underlying shares do not influence the previously measured fair value of options.

When Unexercised Options Expire

If options that have vested expire without being exercised, the following journal entry is made (assuming the remaining 5 million options in our illustration are allowed to expire):

Paid-in capital—stock options becomes paid-in capital—expiration of stock options when options expire without being exercised.

	($ in millions)	
Paid-in capital—stock options (account balance)	40	
Paid-in capital—expiration of stock options		40

In effect, we rename the paid-in capital attributable to the stock option plan. Compensation expense for the four years' service, as of the measurement date, is not affected.

Additional Consideration

Tax Consequences of Stock-Based Compensation Plans In Illustration 19–3 we ignored the tax effect. To illustrate the effect of taxes, let's assume Universal Communications' income tax rate is 25%.

For tax purposes, plans can either qualify as "incentive stock option plans" under the Tax Code or be "nonqualified plans." Among the requirements of a qualified option plan is that the exercise price be equal to the market price at the grant date. Under a qualified incentive plan, the recipient pays no income tax until any shares acquired from exercise of stock options are subsequently sold. On the other hand, the company gets no tax deduction at all. With a nonqualified plan the employee can't delay paying income tax, but the employer is permitted to deduct the difference between the exercise price and the market price at the exercise date. Let's consider both.

Case 1. With an incentive plan, the employer receives no tax deduction at all. If Universal's plan qualifies as an incentive plan, the company will receive no tax deduction upon exercise of the options and thus no tax consequences.

Case 2. On the other hand, if we assume the plan does not qualify as an incentive plan, Universal will deduct from taxable income the difference between the exercise price and the market price at the exercise date. Recall from Chapter 16 that this creates a temporary difference between accounting income (for which compensation expense is recorded currently) and taxable income (for which the tax deduction is taken later upon the exercise of the options). We assume the temporary difference is the cumulative amount expensed for the options. The following entries would be recorded on the dates shown:

December 31, 2021, 2022, 2023, 2024	($ in millions)	
Compensation expense ($80 million ÷ 4 years)	20	
Paid-in capital—stock options		20
Deferred tax asset (25% × $20 million)	5	
Income tax expense		5

The after-tax effect on earnings is thus $15 million each year ($20 − $5).

If all of the options (for 10 million shares) are exercised on April 4, 2026, when the stock's market price is $50 per share:

Cash ($35 exercise price × 10 million shares)	350	
Paid-in capital—stock options (account balance)	80	
Common stock (10 million shares at $1 par per share)		10
Paid-in capital—excess of par (to balance)		420
Income tax payable [($50 − $35) × 10 million shares × 25%]....................	37.5	
Deferred tax asset (4 years × $5 million)..		20.0
Income tax expense (remainder)		17.5

The tax consequences of all nonqualifying stock options as well as restricted stock plans also are accounted for in the manner demonstrated above.

Tax treatment favors the employer in a nonqualified stock option plan.

Because an incentive plan provides no tax deduction, it has no deferred tax consequences.

The difference between the market price at exercise and the eventual tax savings is recognized in income tax expense.

A deferred tax asset is recognized now for the future tax savings from the tax deduction when the nonqualified stock options are exercised.

International Financial Reporting Standards

Recognition of Deferred Tax Asset for Stock Options. Under U.S. GAAP, a deferred tax asset (DTA) is created for the cumulative amount of the fair value of the options the company has recorded for compensation expense. The DTA is the tax rate times the amount of compensation.

Under IFRS, the deferred tax asset isn't created until the award is "in the money;" that is, it has intrinsic value. When it is in the money, the addition to the DTA is the portion of the intrinsic value earned to date times the tax rate.

● LO19–14

1114   SECTION 4   Additional Financial Reporting Issues

Plans with Graded Vesting

The stock option plans we've discussed so far vest (become exercisable) on one single date (e.g., four years from date of grant). This is referred to as *cliff vesting*. More frequently, though, awards specify that recipients gradually become eligible to exercise their options rather than all at once. This is called *graded vesting*. For instance, a company might award stock options that vest 25% the first year, 25% the second year, and 50% the third year, or maybe 25% each year for four years.

In such a case, the company can choose to account for the options essentially the same as the cliff-vesting plans we've discussed to this point. It can estimate a single fair value for each of the options, even though they vest over different time periods, using a single weighted-average expected life of the options. The company then allocates that total compensation cost (fair value per option times number of options) over the entire vesting period.

Most companies, though, choose a slightly more complex method because it usually results in a lower expense.[12] In this approach, we view each vesting group (or tranche) separately, as if it were a separate award. See Illustration 19–4.

Illustration 19–4   Stock Options; Graded Vesting; Separate Valuation Approach

At January 1, 2021, Taggart Mobility issued 10 million executive stock options permitting executives to buy 10 million shares of stock for $25.
- The vesting schedule is 20% the first year, 30% the second year, and 50% the third year (graded-vesting).
- The value of the options that vest over the 3-year period is estimated at January 1, 2021, by separating the total award into three groups (or tranches) according to the year in which they vest (because the expected life for each group differs).

The fair value of the options as of January 1, 2021, is estimated as follows:

Vesting Date	Amount Vesting	Fair Value per Option
Dec. 31, 2021	20%	$3.50
Dec. 31, 2022	30%	$4.00
Dec. 31, 2023	50%	$6.00

We allocate the compensation cost for each of the three groups (tranches) evenly over its *individual* vesting (service) period:

Shares Vesting at	2021	2022	2023	Total	
Dec. 31, 2021	$ 7			$ 7	(10 M × 20% × $3.50)
Dec. 31, 2022	6	$ 6		12	(10 M × 30% × $4.00)
Dec. 31, 2023	10	10	$10	30	(10 M × 50% × $6.00)
Expensed	$23	$16	$10	= $49	

Compensation Expense in ($ in millions)

At any given date, a company must have recognized at least the amount vested by that date. The allocation in this instance meets that constraint:

- The $23 million recognized in 2021 exceeds the $7 million vested.
- The $39 million ($23 + $16) recognized by 2022 exceeds the $19 million ($7 + $12) vested by the same time.

Companies also can choose to use the straight-line method, which would allocate the $49 million total compensation cost equally to 2021, 2022, and 2023 at $16.333 million per year.

---

[12]The fair value of the options usually is higher when estimated using a single weighted-average expected life of the options rather than when estimated as the total of fair values of the multiple vesting groups.

International Financial Reporting Standards

● LO19–14

> When options have graded vesting, U.S. GAAP permits companies to account for each vesting amount separately, for instance, as if there were three separate awards as in the previous illustration, but also allows companies the option to account for the entire award on a straight-line basis over the entire vesting period. Either way, the company must recognize at least the amount of the award that has vested by that date.
>
> Under IFRS, the straight-line choice is not permitted. Also, there's no requirement that the company must recognize at least the amount of the award that has vested by each reporting date.

Plans with Performance or Market Conditions

Stock option (and other share-based) plans often specify a performance condition or a market condition that must be satisfied before employees are allowed the benefits of the award. The objective is to provide employees with additional incentive for managerial achievement. For instance, an option might not be exercisable until a performance target is met. The target could be divisional revenue, earnings per share, sales growth, or rate of return on assets. The possibilities are limitless. On the other hand, the target might be market-related, perhaps a specified stock price or a stock price change exceeding a particular index. The way we account for such plans depends on whether the condition is performance-based or market-based.

The terms of performance options vary with some measure of performance that ties rewards to productivity.

PLANS WITH PERFORMANCE CONDITIONS   Whether we recognize compensation expense for performance-based options depends (a) initially on whether it's probable[13] that the performance target will be met and (b) ultimately on whether the performance target actually is met. Accounting is as described earlier for other stock options. Initial estimates of compensation cost, as well as subsequent revisions of that estimate, take into account the likelihood of both forfeitures and achieving performance targets. For example, in Illustration 19–3, if the options described also had included a condition that the options would become exercisable only if sales increase by 10% after four years, we would estimate the likelihood of that occurring; specifically, is it probable? Let's say we initially estimate that it is probable that sales will increase by 10% after four years. Then, our initial estimate of the total compensation would have been unchanged at

If compensation from a stock option depends on meeting a performance target, compensation is recorded only if we feel it's probable the target will be met.

$$\underset{\substack{\text{Options} \\ \text{expected} \\ \text{to vest}}}{10 \text{ million}} \times \underset{\substack{\text{Fair value} \\ \text{per option}}}{\$8} = \underset{\substack{\text{Estimated} \\ \text{total} \\ \text{compensation}}}{\$80 \text{ million}}$$

Suppose, though, that after two years, we estimate that it is *not* probable that sales will increase by 10% after four years. Then, our new estimate of the total compensation would change to

$$\underset{\substack{\text{Options} \\ \text{expected} \\ \text{to vest}}}{0} \times \underset{\substack{\text{Fair value} \\ \text{per option}}}{\$8} = \underset{\substack{\text{Estimated} \\ \text{total} \\ \text{compensation}}}{\$0}$$

If it later becomes probable that a performance target will not be met, we reverse any compensation expense already recorded.

In that case, we would reverse the $40 million expensed in 2021–2022. No compensation can be recognized for options that don't vest due to performance targets not being met, and that's our expectation.

Conversely, assume that our initial expectation is that it is *not* probable that sales will increase by 10% after four years and so we record no annual compensation expense. But then, in the third year, we estimate that it *is* probable that sales will increase by 10% after four years. At that point, our revised estimate of the total compensation would change to

When we revise our estimate of total compensation because our expectation of probability changes, we record the effect of the change in the current period.

---

[13]"Probable" means the same as it did in Chapter 13, when we were estimating the likelihood that payment would be made for a loss contingency, and elsewhere when making accounting estimates. Probable is a matter of professional judgement (often 70–75%).

$80 million, and we would reflect the cumulative effect on compensation in 2023 earnings and record compensation thereafter:

2023		
Compensation expense [($80 × ¾) − $0]	60	
Paid-in capital—stock options		60
2024		
Compensation expense [($80 × ¼) − $60]	20	
Paid-in capital—stock options		20

If we had begun with our new estimate of total compensation, $20 million would have been expensed in each of the first three years.

Additional Consideration

> Suppose an executive who is granted some of the performance-based options in this example is eligible to retire on January 1, 2021. So, when the options are granted she would be eligible to receive the options even if the performance target (sales increase by 10%) is met after she retires. In that case, the service period needed to receive compensation effectively is one day. Should compensation for her be measured and expensed over the vesting period as in the example, or should that compensation be measured and recorded all at once (full amount if probable, zero otherwise) on the grant date?
>
> It should be treated the same as the compensation for the other options. It should be treated as a performance condition consistent with those for which the requisite service period is not met prior to the performance target being met. So, we would record no compensation expense until meeting the performance target is probable, even if this is not until *after* the requisite vesting period is completed. An important secondary benefit of this treatment is that the employer doesn't need to assess at the grant date whether certain employees are retirement-eligible or will become retirement-eligible during the performance period in order to value the awards.[14]
>
> This treatment differs from that of International Financial Reporting Standards, which specifies that if the performance target can be met *after* the requisite vesting period is completed, compensation should be measured and recorded all at once (full amount if probable, zero otherwise) on the grant date.

If the target is based on changes in the market rather than on performance, we record compensation as if there were no target.

PLANS WITH MARKET CONDITIONS If the award contains a market condition (e.g., a share option with an exercisability requirement based on the stock price reaching a specified level), then no special accounting is required. The fair value estimate of the share option already implicitly reflects market conditions due to the nature of share option pricing models. So, we recognize compensation expense regardless of when, if ever, the market condition is met.

DECLINE IN POPULARITY OF OPTIONS Recent years have witnessed a steady shift in the way companies compensate their top executives. At their peak in 1999, stock options represented about 78% of the average executive's incentive pay. In 2016, stock options accounted for 15% of S&P 500 executive pay while restricted stock accounted for 47.2%.[15] In the wake of past notorious accounting scandals, the image of stock options was tarnished in the view of many who believed that the potential to garner millions in stock option gains created incentives for executives to boost company stock prices through risky or fraudulent behavior. That image motivated many firms to move away from stock options in favor of other forms of share-based compensation, particularly restricted stock awards and, increasingly, restricted stock units. Also contributing to the rise of restricted stock is the feeling by many that it better aligns pay with performance. From the executive's perspective, restricted stock is a more certain, though potentially less lucrative, form of compensation.

---

[14]FASB Emerging Issues Task Force, *Accounting Standards Update No. 2014-12,* "Compensation—Stock Compensation (Topic 718): Accounting for Share-Based Payments When the Terms of an Award Provide That a Performance Target Could Be Achieved after the Requisite Service Period," June 2014.
[15]Source: Equilar. Copyright 2016.

Employee Share Purchase Plans

Employee share purchase plans often permit all employees to buy shares directly from their company at favorable terms. The primary intent of these plans is to encourage employee ownership of the company's shares. Presumably, loyalty is enhanced among employee-shareholders. The employee also benefits because, typically, these plans allow employees to buy shares from their employer without brokerage fees and, perhaps, at a slight discount. Some companies even encourage participation by matching or partially matching employee purchases.

● LO19–3

Share purchase plans permit employees to buy shares directly from the corporation.

When accounting for employee share purchase plans (ESPPs), we need to determine whether or not they provide compensation to employees. If not, we simply record the sale of new shares as employees buy them and do not record compensation expense. An ESPP is considered noncompensatory as long as

1. substantially all employees can participate,
2. employees have no longer than one month after the price is fixed to decide whether to participate, and
3. the discount is no greater than 5% (or can be justified as reasonable).

If these criteria for the plan being noncompensatory are *not* met, say the discount is 15%, accounting is similar to other share-based plans. The 15% discount to employees, then, is considered to be compensation, and that amount is recorded as expense.[16] Compensation expense replaces the cash debit for any employer-provided portion. Say an employee buys shares (no-par) under the plan for $850 rather than the current market price of $1,000. The $150 discount is recorded as compensation expense.

Cash (discounted price)..	850	
Compensation expense ($1,000 × 15%)..	150	
Common stock (market value)..		1,000

Decision Makers' Perspective

In several previous chapters, we have revisited the concept of "earnings quality" (as first defined in Chapter 4). We also have noted that one rather common practice that negatively influences earnings quality is earnings management, which refers to companies' use of one or more of several techniques designed to artificially increase (or decrease) earnings. A frequent objective of earnings management is to meet analysts' expectations regarding projections of income. The share-based compensation plans we discuss in this chapter suggest another motive managers sometimes have to manipulate income. If a manager's personal compensation includes company stock, stock options, or other compensation based on the value of the firm's stock, it's not hard to imagine an increased desire to ensure that market expectations are met and that reported earnings have a positive effect on stock prices. In fact, as we discussed earlier, that is precisely the reaction these incentive compensation plans are designed to elicit. Investors and creditors, though, should be alert to indications of attempts to artificially manipulate income and realize that the likelihood of earnings management is probably higher for companies with generous share-based compensation plans.

Analysts should be aware of the possibility of earnings management as a way to increase managers' compensation.

One way managers might manipulate numbers is to low-ball the data that go into the option-pricing models. The models used to estimate fair value are built largely around subjective assumptions. That possibility emphasizes the need for investors to look closely at the assumptions reported in the stock option disclosure note, and particularly at how those assumptions change from year to year. ●

---

[16]FASB ASC 718–50–25–1 and 2: Compensation—Stock Compensation—Employee Share Purchase Plans—Recognition.

Concept Review Exercise

SHARE-BASED COMPENSATION PLANS

Listed below are transactions dealing with various stock benefit plans of Fortune-Time Corporation during the period 2021–2023. The market price of the stock is $45 at January 1, 2021.

a. On January 1, 2021, the company issued 10 million common shares to divisional managers under its restricted stock award plan. The shares are subject to forfeiture if employment is terminated within three years.

b. On January 1, 2021, the company granted incentive stock options to its senior management, exercisable for 1.5 million common shares. The options must be exercised within five years, but not before January 1, 2023. The exercise price of the stock options is equal to the fair value of the common stock on the date the options are granted. An option pricing model estimates the fair value of the options to be $4 per option. All recipients are expected to remain employed through the vesting date.

c. Recorded compensation expense on December 31, 2021.

d. A divisional manager holding 1 million of the restricted shares left the company to become CEO of a competitor on September 15, 2022, before the required service period ended.

e. Recorded compensation expense on December 31, 2022.

Required:
Prepare the journal entries that Fortune-Time recorded for each of these transactions. (Ignore any tax effects.)

Solution:

January 1, 2021

Restricted Stock Award Plan
No entry.
Total compensation is measured as 10 million shares × $45 = $450 million.

Stock Options
No entry.
Total compensation is measured as 1.5 million shares × $4 = $6 million.

December 31, 2021

Restricted Stock	($ in millions)	
Compensation expense ($450 million ÷ 3 years)	150	
Paid-in capital—restricted stock		150

Stock Options		
Compensation expense ($6 million ÷ 2 years)...	3	
Paid-in capital—stock options...		3

September 15, 2022

Restricted Stock		
Paid-in capital—restricted stock (10% × $150)	15	
Compensation expense		15

December 31, 2022

Restricted Stock		
Compensation expense [$450 − (10% × $450) − $150 + $15] ÷ 2 years...........	135	
Paid-in capital—restricted stock...		135

Stock Options		
Compensation expense ($6 million ÷ 2 years)...	3	
Paid-in capital—stock options...		3

Earnings Per Share

A typical corporate annual report contains four comparative financial statements, an extensive list of disclosure notes and schedules, and several pages of charts, tables, and textual descriptions. Of these myriad facts and figures, the single accounting number that is reported most frequently in the media and receives by far the most attention by investors and creditors is earnings per share (EPS). The reasons for the considerable attention paid to earnings per share certainly include the desire to find a way to summarize the performance of business enterprises into a single number.

Earnings per share is the single accounting number that receives the most media attention.

Summarizing performance in a way that permits comparisons is difficult because the companies that report the numbers are different from one another. And yet, the desire to condense performance to a single number has created a demand for EPS information. The profession has responded with rules designed to maximize the comparability of EPS numbers by minimizing the inconsistencies in their calculation from one company to the next.[17]

Comparability is an enhancing characteristic of relevant accounting information (Conceptual Framework).

Keep in mind as you study the requirements that a primary goal is comparability. As a result, many of the rules devised to achieve consistency are unavoidably arbitrary, meaning that other choices the FASB might have made in many instances would be equally adequate.

International Financial Reporting Standards

Earnings per Share. The earnings per share requirements of U.S. GAAP, *FASB ASC 260: Earnings per Share,* are a result of the FASB's cooperation with the IASB to narrow the differences between IFRS and U.S. GAAP. A few differences remain. The differences that remain are the result of differences in the application of the treasury stock method, the treatment of contracts that may be settled in shares or cash, and contingently issuable shares.

● LO19–14

Basic Earnings Per Share

A firm is said to have a simple capital structure if it has no outstanding securities that could potentially dilute earnings per share. In this context, to dilute means to *reduce* earnings per share. For instance, if a firm has convertible bonds outstanding and those bonds are converted, the resulting increase in common shares could decrease (or dilute) earnings per share. That is, the new shares replaced by the converted bonds might participate in future earnings. So convertible bonds are referred to as potential common shares. Other potential common shares are convertible preferred stock, stock options, and contingently issuable shares. We will see how the potentially dilutive effects of these securities are included in the calculation of EPS later in this chapter. Now, though, our focus is on the calculation of EPS for a simple capital structure—when no potential common shares are present. In these cases, the calculation is referred to as basic EPS, and is simply earnings available to common shareholders divided by the weighted-average number of common shares outstanding.

A firm has a simple capital structure if it has no potential common shares.

● LO19–4

In the most elemental setting, earnings per share (or net loss per share) is merely a firm's net income (or net loss) divided by the number of shares of common stock outstanding throughout the year. The calculation becomes more demanding (a) when the number of shares has changed during the reporting period, (b) when the earnings available to common shareholders are diminished by dividends to preferred shareholders, or (c) when we attempt to take into account the impending effect of potential common shares (which we do in a later section of the chapter). To illustrate the calculation of EPS in each of its dimensions, we will use only one example in this chapter. We'll start with the most basic situation and then add one new element at a time until we have considered all the principal ways the calculation can be affected. In this way, you can see the effect of each component of earnings per share, not just in isolation, but in relation to the effects of other components as well. The basic calculation is shown in Illustration 19–5.

Basic EPS reflects no dilution, only shares now outstanding.

EPS expresses a firm's profitability on a per share basis.

---

[17]FASB ASC 260: Earnings per Share. The guidance is applicable only for public companies.

1120   SECTION 4   Additional Financial Reporting Issues

Illustration 19–5

Fundamental Calculation

In the most elemental setting, earnings per share is simply a company's earnings divided by the number of shares outstanding.

Sovran Financial Corporation reported net income of $154 million in 2021 (tax rate 25%). Its capital structure consisted of the following:

Common Stock

Jan. 1   60 million common shares were outstanding

                                ($ amounts in millions, except per share amount)

Basic EPS:

$$\frac{\text{Net income} \\ \$154}{60 \\ \text{Shares outstanding}} = \$2.57$$

Issuance of New Shares

Because the shares discussed in Illustration 19–5 remained unchanged throughout the year, the denominator of the EPS calculation is simply the number of shares outstanding. But if the number of shares has changed, it's necessary to find the *weighted average* of the shares outstanding during the period the earnings were generated. For instance, if an additional 12 million shares had been issued on March 1 of the year just ended, we calculate the weighted-average number of shares to be 70 million, as demonstrated in Illustration 19–6.

● LO19–5   Because the new shares were outstanding only 10 months, or $^{10}/_{12}$ of the year, we increase the 60 million shares already outstanding by the additional shares—weighted by the fraction of the year ($^{10}/_{12}$) they were outstanding. The weighted average is $60 + 12\ (^{10}/_{12}) = 60 + 10 = 70$ shares. The reason for time-weighting the shares issued is that the resources the stock sale provides the company are available for generating income only after the date the shares are sold. So, weighting is necessary to make the shares in the fraction's denominator consistent with the income in its numerator (see Illustration 19–6).

Illustration 19–6

Weighted Average

Any new shares issued are time-weighted by the fraction of the period they were outstanding and then added to the number of shares outstanding for the entire period.

Sovran Financial Corporation reported net income of $154 million for 2021 (tax rate 25%). Its capital structure included the following:

Common Stock

Jan. 1   60 million common shares were outstanding

Mar. 1   12 million new shares were sold

                                ($ amounts in millions, except per share amount)

Basic EPS:

$$\frac{\text{Net income} \\ \$154}{\underset{\substack{\text{Shares} \\ \text{at Jan. 1}}}{60} + \underset{\substack{\text{New} \\ \text{shares}}}{12\ (^{10}/_{12})}} = \frac{\$154}{70} = \$2.20$$

Stock Dividends and Stock Splits

● LO19–6   Recall that a stock dividend or a stock split is a distribution of additional shares to existing shareholders. But there's an important and fundamental difference between the increase in shares caused by a stock dividend and an increase from selling new shares. When new shares are sold, both assets and shareholders' equity are increased by an additional investment in the firm by shareholders. On the other hand, a stock dividend or stock split merely increases the number of shares without affecting the firm's assets. In effect, the same pie is divided into more pieces. The result is a larger number of less valuable shares. This fundamental change in the nature of the shares is reflected in a calculation of EPS by simply increasing the number of shares.

In Illustration 19–7, notice that the additional shares created by the stock dividend are *not* weighted for the time period they were outstanding. Instead, the increase is treated as if it occurred at the beginning of the year.

Illustration 19–7

Stock Dividends and Stock Splits

Shares outstanding prior to the stock dividend are retroactively restated to reflect the 10% increase in shares—that is, treated as if the distribution occurred at the beginning of the period.

Sovran Financial Corporation reported net income of $154 million in 2021 (tax rate 25%). Its capital structure included the following:

Common Stock

Jan. 1	60 million common shares were outstanding
Mar. 1	12 million new shares were sold
June 17	A 10% stock dividend was distributed

($ amounts in millions, except per share amount)

Basic EPS:

$$\frac{\overset{\text{Net income}}{\$154}}{\underset{\substack{\text{Shares} \\ \text{at Jan. 1}}}{60}\ (1.10)\ +\ \underset{\substack{\text{New} \\ \text{shares}}}{12\ (^{10}\!/_{12})}\ (1.10)} = \frac{\$154}{77} = \$2.00$$

Stock dividend adjustment

The number of shares outstanding after a 10% stock dividend is **1.10** times higher than before. This multiple is applied to both the beginning shares and the new shares sold before the stock distribution. If this had been a 25% stock dividend, the multiple would have been 1.25; a 2-for-1 stock split means a multiple of 2, and so on.

Notice that EPS without the 10% stock dividend ($2.20) is 10% more than it is with the stock distribution ($2). This is caused by the increase in the number of shares. But, unlike a sale of new shares, this should not be interpreted as a "dilution" of earnings per share. Shareholders' interests in their company's earnings have not been diluted. Instead, each shareholder's interest is represented by more—though less valuable—shares.

A simplistic but convenient way to view the effect is to think of the predistribution shares as having been "blue." After the stock dividend, the more valuable "blue" shares are gone, replaced by a larger number of, let's say, "green" shares. From now on, we compute the earnings per "green" share, whereas we previously calculated earnings per "blue" share. We restate the number of shares retroactively to reflect the stock dividend, as if the shares always had been "green." After all, our intent is to let the calculation reflect the fundamental change in the nature of the shares.

Additional Consideration

When last year's EPS is reported in the current year's comparative income statements, it also should reflect the increased shares from the stock dividend. For instance, suppose EPS was $2.09 for 2020: $115 million net income divided by 55 million weighted-average shares. When reported again for comparison purposes in the 2021 comparative income statements, that figure would be restated to reflect the 10% stock dividend [$115 ÷ (55 × **1.10**) = $1.90], as shown:

Earnings per Share:	**2021**	**2020**
	$2.00	$1.90

The EPS numbers now are comparable—both reflect the stock dividend. Otherwise we would be comparing earnings per "green" share with earnings per "blue" share; this way both are earnings per "green" share.

1122   SECTION 4   Additional Financial Reporting Issues

Reacquired Shares

If shares were reacquired during the period (either retired or as treasury stock), the weighted-average number of shares is reduced. The number of reacquired shares is time-weighted for the *fraction of the year they were **not** outstanding,* prior to being *subtracted* from the number of shares outstanding during the period. Let's modify our continuing illustration to assume 8 million shares were reacquired on October 1 as treasury stock (Illustration 19–8).

Illustration 19–8

Reacquired Shares

Sovran Financial Corporation reported net income of $154 million in 2021 (tax rate 25%). Its capital structure included the following:

Common Stock

Jan. 1	60 million common shares outstanding
Mar. 1	12 million new shares were sold
June 17	A 10% stock dividend was distributed
Oct. 1	8 million shares were reacquired as treasury stock

($ amounts in millions, except per share amounts)

Basic EPS:

$$\frac{\overset{\text{Net income}}{\$154}}{\underset{\substack{\text{Shares} \\ \text{at Jan. 1}}}{60} \quad \underset{\text{New shares}}{(1.10) + 12\,(^{10}\!/_{12})\,(1.10)} - \underset{\substack{\text{Treasury} \\ \text{shares}}}{8\,(^{3}\!/_{12})}} = \frac{\$154}{75} = \$2.05$$

Stock dividend adjustment*

*Not necessary for the treasury shares since they were reacquired after the stock dividend and thus already reflect the adjustment (that is, the shares repurchased are 8 million "new green" shares).

The 8 million shares reacquired as treasury stock are weighted by ($^{3}\!/_{12}$) to reflect the fact they were not outstanding the last three months of the year.

The adjustment for reacquired shares is the same as for new shares sold, except the shares are deducted rather than added.

Any sales or purchases of shares that occur before, but not after, a stock dividend or split are affected by the distribution.

Compare the adjustment for treasury shares with the adjustment for new shares sold. Each is time-weighted for the fraction of the year the shares were or were not outstanding. But also notice two differences. The new shares are added, while the reacquired shares are subtracted. The second difference is that the reacquired shares are not multiplied by 1.10 to adjust for the 10% stock dividend. The reason is the shares were repurchased after the June 17 stock dividend; the reacquired shares are 8 million of the new post-distribution shares. (To use our earlier representation, these are 8 million "green" shares.) To generalize, when a stock distribution occurs during the reporting period, any sales or purchases of shares that occur *before* the distribution are increased by the distribution. But the stock distribution does not increase the number of shares sold or purchased, if any, *after* the distribution.

Earnings Available to Common Shareholders

● LO19–7

The denominator in an EPS calculation is the weighted-average number of common shares outstanding. Logically, the numerator should similarly represent earnings available to common shareholders. This was automatic in our illustrations to this point because the only shares outstanding were common shares. But when a senior class of shareholders (like preferred shareholders) is entitled to a specified allocation of earnings (like preferred dividends), those amounts are subtracted from earnings before calculating earnings per share.[18] This is demonstrated in Illustration 19–9.

Preferred dividends reduce earnings available to common shareholders unless the preferred stock is noncumulative and no dividends were declared that year.

Suppose no dividends were declared for the year. Should we adjust for preferred dividends? Yes, if the preferred stock is cumulative—and most preferred stock is. This means that when dividends are not declared, the unpaid dividends accumulate to be paid in a future year when (if) dividends are subsequently declared. Obviously, the presumption is that although the year's dividend preference isn't distributed this year, it eventually will be paid.

---

[18]You learned in Chapter 18 that when dividends are declared, preferred shareholders have a preference (over common shareholders) to a specified amount.

Illustration 19–9
Preferred Dividends

Sovran Financial Corporation reported net income of $154 million in 2021 (tax rate 25%). Its capital structure included the following:

Common Stock

January 1	60 million common shares were outstanding
March 1	12 million new shares were sold
June 17	A 10% stock dividend was distributed
October 1	8 million shares were reacquired as treasury stock

Preferred Stock, Nonconvertible

January 1–December 31	5 million shares 8%, $10 par

($ amounts in millions, except per share amount)

Basic EPS:

$$\frac{\overset{\text{Net income}}{\$154} \quad \overset{\text{Preferred dividends}}{-\$4^*}}{\underset{\substack{\text{Shares} \\ \text{at Jan. 1}}}{60 \;\; (1.10)} \; + \; \underset{\substack{\text{New} \\ \text{shares}}}{12 \,(^{10}\!/_{12}) \,(1.10)} \; - \; \underset{\substack{\text{Treasury} \\ \text{shares}}}{8 \,(^{3}\!/_{12})}} = \frac{\$150}{75} = \$2.00$$

Stock dividend adjustment

*8% × $10 par × 5 million shares.

Preferred dividends are subtracted from net income so that "earnings available to common shareholders" is divided by the weighted-average number of common shares.

We have encountered no potential common shares to this point in our continuing illustration. As a result, we have what is referred to as a simple capital structure. (Although, at this point, you may question this label.) For a simple capital structure, a single presentation of basic earnings per common share is appropriate. We turn our attention now to situations described as complex capital structures. In these situations, two separate presentations are required: basic EPS and diluted EPS.

Diluted Earnings Per Share

Potential Common Shares

Imagine a situation in which convertible bonds are outstanding that will significantly increase the number of common shares if bondholders exercise their options to exchange their bonds for shares of common stock. Should these potential shares be ignored when earnings per share is calculated? After all, they haven't been converted as yet, so to assume an increase in shares for a conversion that may never occur might mislead investors and creditors. On the other hand, if conversion is imminent, not taking into account the dilutive effect of the share increase might mislead investors and creditors. The profession's solution to the dilemma is to calculate earnings per share twice.

Securities such as these convertible bonds, while not being common stock, may become common stock through their exercise or conversion. Therefore, they may dilute (reduce) earnings per share and are called potential common shares. A firm is said to have a complex capital structure if potential common shares are outstanding. Besides convertible bonds, other potential common shares are convertible preferred stock, stock options, and contingently issuable securities. (We'll discuss each of these shortly.) A firm with a complex capital structure reports two EPS calculations. Basic EPS ignores the dilutive effect of such securities; diluted EPS incorporates the dilutive effect of all potential common shares.

In a complex capital structure, a second EPS computation takes into account the assumed effect of *potential common shares*, essentially a "worst case scenario."

Options, Rights, and Warrants

Stock options, stock rights, and stock warrants are similar. Each gives its holders the right to exercise their option to purchase common stock, usually at a specified exercise price. The dilution that would result from their exercise should be reflected in the calculation of diluted EPS, but not basic EPS.

● LO19–8

1124   SECTION 4   Additional Financial Reporting Issues

Stock options are assumed to have been exercised when calculating diluted EPS.

To include the dilutive effect of a security means to calculate EPS *as if* the potential increase in shares already has occurred (even though it hasn't yet). So, for stock options (or rights, or warrants), we pretend the options have been exercised. In fact, we assume the options were exercised at the beginning of the reporting period, or when the options were issued if that's later. We then assume the cash proceeds from selling the new shares at the exercise price are used to buy back as many shares as possible at the shares' average market price during the year. This is demonstrated in Illustration 19–10.

Illustration 19–10

Stock Options

Sovran Financial Corporation reported net income of $154 million in 2021 (tax rate 25%). Its capital structure included the following:

Common Stock

January 1	60 million common shares outstanding
March 1	12 million new shares were sold
June 17	A 10% stock dividend was distributed
October 1	8 million shares were reacquired as treasury stock

(The average market price of the common shares during 2021 was $25 per share.)

Preferred Stock Nonconvertible

January 1–December 31   5 million shares 8%, $10 par

Incentive Stock Options

Executive stock options granted in 2016, exercisable after 2020 for 15 million common shares* at an exercise price of $20 per share

($ amounts in millions, except per share amounts)

Stock options give their holders (company executives in this case) the right to purchase common stock at a specified exercise price ($20 in this case).

The stock options do not affect the calculation of *basic EPS.*

Basic EPS (unchanged)

The calculation of diluted EPS assumes that the shares specified by stock options were issued at the exercise price and that the proceeds were used to buy back (as treasury stock) as many of those shares as can be purchased at the market price during the period.

Diluted EPS

*Adjusted for the stock dividend. Prior to the stock dividend, the options were exercisable for 13 7/11 million of the "old" shares. Upon the stock dividend, the new equivalent of 13 7/11 became 15 million (13 7/11 × 1.10) of the "new" shares.

†Shares Assumed Reacquired for Diluted EPS
	15	million shares
×	$ 20	(exercise price)
	$300	million
÷	$ 25	(average market price)
	12	million shares reacquired

FINANCIAL Reporting Case

Q4, p. 1105

When we simulate the exercise of the stock options, we calculate EPS as if 15 million shares were sold at the beginning of the year. This obviously increases the number of shares in the denominator by 15 million shares. But it is insufficient to simply add the additional shares without considering the accompanying consequences. Remember, if this hypothetical scenario had occurred, the company would have had $300 million cash proceeds from the exercise of the options (15 million shares × $20 exercise price per share). What would have been the effect on earnings per share? This depends on what the company would have done with the $300 million cash proceeds. Would the proceeds have been used to buy more equipment? Increase the sales force? Expand facilities? Pay dividends?

Obviously, there are literally hundreds of choices, and it's unlikely that any two firms would spend the $300 million exactly the same way. But remember, our objective is to create some degree of uniformity in the way firms determine earnings per share so the resulting numbers are comparable. So, standard-setters decided on a single assumption for all firms to enhance comparability.

For diluted EPS, we assume the proceeds from exercise of the options were used to reacquire shares as treasury stock at the average market price of the common stock during the reporting period. Consequently, the weighted-average number of shares is increased by the difference between the shares assumed issued and those assumed reacquired. In our illustration, 15 million shares issued minus 12 million shares reacquired ($300 million ÷ $25 per share) equals 3 million net increase in shares.

The way we take into account the dilutive effect of stock options is called the *treasury stock method* because of our assumption that treasury shares are purchased with the cash proceeds of the exercise of the options. Besides providing comparability, this assumption actually is plausible because, if the options were exercised, more shares would be needed to issue to option-holders. And, as discussed in the previous chapter, many firms routinely buy back shares either to issue to option-holders or, equivalently, to offset the issuance of new shares.

Additional Consideration

Actual Exercise of Options. What if options are actually exercised during the reporting period? In that case, we include in the denominator of both basic and diluted EPS the actual shares issued upon the exercise of the options, time-weighted for the fraction of the year the new shares actually are outstanding. This is consistent with the way we include new shares sold under any circumstances.

In addition, we include in diluted EPS only the incremental shares that would have been issued prior to the actual exercise of the options if we pretend the options were exercised at the beginning of the period. We time-weight those shares by the fraction of the year the shares would be outstanding prior to the actual exercise of the options.

Let's say the options in our illustration were exercised on September 1 and that the average per-share price of the stock from the beginning of the year until September 1 was $24. In that case, we add 5 million shares to the denominator of both basic and diluted EPS: the 15 million shares actually issued × 4/12 of the year actually outstanding = 5 million shares. Then, for *diluted EPS only,* we add the incremental shares that would have been issued *prior to* the actual exercise of the options if we pretend the options were exercised at the beginning of the period. We assume the proceeds (15 million shares × $20 = $300 million) are used to buy shares back at $24.

$$
\begin{array}{rl}
15 & \text{million shares} \\
\times\ \$\ 20 & \text{(exercise price)} \\
\hline
\$300 & \text{million} \\
\div\ \$\ 24 & \text{(average market price prior to exercise)} \\
\hline
12.5 & \text{million shares}
\end{array}
$$

The incremental number of shares to be included in the computation of diluted EPS, then, is weighted for the period the options were outstanding prior to exercise, the 8 months from January 1 to September 1, or 8/12 of a year.

$$\frac{\text{No adjustment to the numerator}}{+ (15 - 12.5)(^{8}\!/_{12})}$$

1126 SECTION 4 Additional Financial Reporting Issues

Convertible Securities

● LO19–9

Sometimes corporations include a conversion feature as part of a bond offering, a note payable, or an issue of preferred stock. Convertible securities can be converted into (exchanged for) shares of stock at the option of the holder of the security. For that reason, convertible securities are potentially dilutive. EPS will be affected if and when such securities are converted and new shares of common stock are issued. In the previous section you learned that the potentially dilutive effect of stock options is reflected in diluted EPS calculations by assuming the options were exercised. Similarly, the potentially dilutive effect of convertible securities is reflected in diluted EPS calculations by assuming they were converted.

> When we assume conversion, the denominator of the EPS fraction is increased by the additional common shares that would have been issued upon conversion.

By the *if converted method,* as it's called, we assume the conversion into common stock occurred at the beginning of the period (or at the time the convertible security is issued, if that's later). We increase the denominator of the EPS fraction by the additional common shares that would have been issued upon conversion. We increase the numerator by the interest (after-tax) on bonds or other debt or the preferred dividends that would have been avoided if the convertible securities had not been outstanding due to having been converted.

CONVERTIBLE BONDS   Now, let's return to our continuing illustration and modify it to include the existence of convertible bonds (Illustration 19–11).

Illustration 19–11

Convertible Bonds

Sovran Financial Corporation reported net income of $154 million in 2021 (tax rate 25%). Its capital structure included the following:

Common Stock

Jan. 1	60 million common shares were outstanding
Mar. 1	12 million new shares were sold
June 17	A 10% stock dividend was distributed
Oct. 1	8 million shares were reacquired as treasury stock

(The average market price of the common shares during 2021 was $25 per share.)

Preferred Stock, Nonconvertible

January 1–December 31   5 million shares 8%, $10 par

Incentive Stock Options

Executive stock options granted in 2016, exercisable after 2020 for 15 million common shares* at an exercise price of $20 per share

Convertible Bonds

8%, $300 million face amount issued in 2020, convertible into 12 million common shares

($ amounts in millions, except per share amounts)

Basic EPS (unchanged)

> The convertible bonds do not affect the calculation of *basic EPS.*

$$\frac{\overset{\text{Net income}}{\$154} \overset{\text{Preferred dividends}}{-\$4}}{\underset{\text{Shares at Jan. 1}}{60} \ \underset{\text{Stock dividend adjustment}}{(1.10)} + \underset{\text{New shares}}{12 \ (^{10}/_{12}) \ (1.10)} - \underset{\text{Treasury shares}}{8 \ (^{3}/_{12})}} = \frac{\$150}{75} = \$2.00$$

Diluted EPS

> The numerator is increased by the after-tax interest that would have been avoided.

$$\frac{\overset{\text{Net income}}{\$154} \overset{\text{Preferred dividends}}{-\$4} \overset{\text{After-tax interest savings}}{+ \$24 - 25\%(\$24)}}{\underset{\text{Shares at Jan. 1}}{60} \ \underset{\text{Stock dividend adjustment}}{(1.10)} + \underset{\text{New shares}}{12 \ (^{10}/_{12}) \ (1.10)} - \underset{\text{Treasury shares}}{8 \ (^{3}/_{12})} + \underset{\text{Exercise of options}}{(15^* - 12)} \ \underset{\text{Conversion of bonds}}{+12^*}} = \frac{\$168}{90} = \$1.87$$

*Adjusted for the stock dividend. For example, prior to the stock dividend, the bonds were exercisable for $10^{10}/_{11}$ million of the "old" shares, which became 12 million ($10^{10}/_{11} \times 1.10$) of the "new" shares after the stock dividend.

We increase the denominator by the 12 million shares that would have been issued if the bonds had been converted. However, if that hypothetical conversion had occurred, the bonds would not have been outstanding during the year. What effect would the absence of the bonds have had on income? Obviously, the bond interest expense (8% × $300 million = $24 million) would have been saved, causing income to be higher. But saving the interest paid would also have meant losing a $24 million tax deduction on the income tax return. With a 25% tax rate that would mean paying $6 million more income taxes. So, to reflect in earnings the $18 million after-tax interest that would have been avoided in the event of conversion, we add back the $24 million of interest expense, but deduct 25% × $24 million for the higher tax expense.

Additional Consideration

The $300 million of convertible bonds in our illustration were issued at face value. Suppose the bonds had been issued for $282 million. In that case, the adjustment to earnings would be modified to include the amortization of the $18 million bond discount. Assuming straight-line amortization and a 10-year maturity, the adjustment to the diluted EPS calculation would have been

$$\frac{+[\$24 + (\$18 \div 10)] \times (1 - 25\%)^*}{12}$$

to reflect the fact that the interest expense would include the $24 million stated interest plus one-tenth of the bond discount.[19]

*This is an alternative way to represent the after-tax adjustment to interest since subtracting 25% of the interest expense is the same as multiplying interest expense by 75%.

Our illustration describes the treatment of convertible bonds. The same treatment pertains to other debt that is convertible into common shares such as convertible notes payable. Remember from our discussion of debt in earlier chapters that all debt is similar, whether in the form of bonds, notes, or other configurations.

Additional Consideration

Notice that we assumed the bonds were converted at the beginning of the reporting period since they were outstanding all year. However, if the convertible bonds had been issued during the reporting period, we would assume their conversion occurred on the date of issue. It would be illogical to assume they were converted before they were issued. If the convertible bonds in our illustration had been sold on September 1, for instance, the adjustment to the EPS calculation would have been

$$\frac{+[\$24 - 25\% (\$24)] (4/12)}{+12 (4/12)}$$

to reflect the fact that the net increase in shares would have been effective for only four months of the year.

We assume convertible securities were converted (or options exercised) at the beginning of the reporting period or at the time the securities are issued, if later.

CONVERTIBLE PREFERRED STOCK   The potentially dilutive effect of convertible preferred stock is reflected in EPS calculations in much the same way as convertible debt. That is, we calculate EPS as if conversion already had occurred. Specifically, we add shares to the denominator of the EPS fraction. We do not subtract the preferred dividends in the numerator because those dividends would have been avoided if the preferred stock had been converted. In Illustration 19–12, we assume our preferred stock is convertible into 3 million shares of common stock.

---

[19]See Chapter 14 if you need to refresh your memory about bond discount amortization.

Illustration 19–12

Convertible Preferred Stock

Sovran Financial Corporation reported net income of $154 million in 2021 (tax rate 25%). Its capital structure included the following:

Common Stock

Jan. 1	60 million common shares were outstanding
Mar. 1	12 million new shares were sold
June 17	A 10% stock dividend was distributed
Oct. 1	8 million shares were reacquired as treasury stock

(The average market price of the common shares during 2021 was $25 per share.)

Preferred Stock, Convertible into 3 million common shares*

January 1–December 31   5 million shares 8%, $10 par

Incentive Stock Options

Executive stock options granted in 2016, exercisable after 2020 for 15 million common shares* at an exercise price of $20 per share

Convertible Bonds

8%, $300 million face amount issued in 2020, convertible into 12 million common shares

($ amounts in millions, except per share amounts)

Basic EPS

$$\frac{\overset{\text{Net income}}{\$154} \quad \overset{\text{Preferred dividends}}{-\$4}}{\underset{\text{Shares at Jan. 1}}{60} \quad (1.10) \quad + \quad \underset{\text{New shares}}{12 \, (^{10}\!/_{12})} \quad (1.10) \quad - \quad \underset{\text{Treasury shares}}{8 \, (^{3}\!/_{12})}} = \frac{\$150}{75} = \$2.00$$

Stock dividend adjustment

Diluted EPS

$$\frac{\overset{\text{Net income}}{\$154} \quad \overset{\text{Preferred dividends}}{\cancel{-\$4}} \quad \overset{\text{After-tax interest savings}}{+ \, \$24 - 25\% \, (\$24)}}{\underset{\text{Shares at Jan. 1}}{60} \; (1.10) + \underset{\text{New shares}}{12 \, (^{10}\!/_{12})} (1.10) - \underset{\text{Treasury shares}}{8 \, (^{3}\!/_{12})} + \underset{\text{Exercise of options}}{(15 - 12)} \; + \underset{\text{Conversion of bonds}}{12} \; + \underset{\text{Conversion of preferred shares}}{3^*}} = \frac{\$172}{93} = \$1.85$$

Stock dividend adjustment

Since diluted EPS is calculated as if the preferred shares had been converted, there are no dividends.

*Adjusted for the stock dividend. For example, prior to the stock dividend, the preferred shares were convertible into $2^8\!/_{11}$ million of the "old" shares, which became 3 million ($2^8\!/_{11}$ × 1.10) of the "new" shares after the stock dividend.

The adjustment for the conversion of the preferred stock is applied only to diluted EPS computations. Basic EPS is unaffected.

However, when diluted EPS is calculated, we hypothetically assume the convertible preferred stock was *not* outstanding. Accordingly, no preferred dividends on these shares would have been paid.

Antidilutive Securities

At times, the effect of the conversion or exercise of potential common shares would be to increase, rather than decrease, EPS. These we refer to as antidilutive securities. Such securities are ignored when calculating both basic and diluted EPS.

Options, Warrants, Rights

LO19–10   For illustration, recall the way we treated the stock options in our continuing illustration. In applying the treasury stock method, the number of shares assumed repurchased is fewer than the number of shares assumed sold. This is the case any time the buyback (average market) price is higher than the exercise price. Consequently, there will be a net increase in the number of shares, so earnings per share will decline.

On the other hand, when the exercise price is *higher* than the market price, to assume shares are sold at the exercise price and repurchased at the market price would mean buying back *more* shares than were sold. This would produce a net decrease in the number of shares. So EPS would increase, not decrease. These would have an antidilutive effect and would not be considered exercised. In fact, a rational investor would not exercise options at an exercise price higher than the current market price anyway. Let's look at the example provided by Illustration 19–13.

> Antidilutive securities are ignored when calculating both basic and diluted EPS.

Illustration 19–13
Antidilutive Warrants

Sovran Financial Corporation reported net income of $154 million in 2021 (tax rate 25%). Its capital structure included the following:

Common Stock

Jan. 1	60 million common shares were outstanding
Mar. 1	12 million new shares were sold
June 17	A 10% stock dividend was distributed
Oct. 1	8 million shares were reacquired as treasury stock

(The average market price of the common shares during 2021 was $25 per share.)

Preferred Stock, Convertible into 3 million common shares

January 1–December 31   5 million shares 8%, $10 par

Incentive Stock Options

Executive stock options granted in 2016, exercisable after 2020 for 15 million common shares at an exercise price of $20 per share

Convertible Bonds

8%, $300 million face amount issued in 2020, convertible into 12 million common shares

Stock Warrants

Warrants granted in 2020, exercisable for 4 million common shares* at an exercise price of $32.50 per share

> The $32.50 exercise price is higher than the market price, $25, so to assume shares are sold at the exercise price and repurchased at the market price would mean reacquiring more shares than were sold.

Calculations

The calculations of both basic and diluted EPS are unaffected by the warrants because the effect of exercising the warrants would be antidilutive

*Adjusted for the stock dividend. For example, prior to the stock dividend, the warrants were exercisable for $3^7/_{11}$ million of the "old" shares, which became 4 million ($3^7/_{11}$ × 1.10) of the "new" shares after the stock dividend.

To assume 4 million shares were sold at the $32.50 exercise price and repurchased at the lower market price ($25) would mean reacquiring 5.2 million shares. That's *more* shares than were assumed sold. Because the effect would be antidilutive, we would simply ignore the warrants in the calculations.

In our continuing illustration, only the stock warrants were antidilutive. The other potential common shares caused EPS to decline when we considered them exercised or converted. In the case of the executive stock options, it was readily apparent that their effect would be dilutive because the exercise price was less than the market price, indicating that fewer shares could be repurchased (at the average market price) than were assumed issued (at the exercise price). As a result, the denominator increased. When only the denominator of a fraction increases, the fraction itself decreases. On the other hand, in the case of the warrants, it was apparent that their effect would be antidilutive because the exercise price was higher than the market price, which would have decreased the denominator and therefore increased the fraction.

When a company has a *net loss,* rather than net income, it reports a loss per share. In that situation, stock options that otherwise are dilutive will be antidilutive. Here's why. Suppose we have a loss per share of $2.00 calculated as ($150 million) ÷ 75 million shares = ($2.00).

Now suppose stock options are outstanding that, if exercised, will increase the number of shares by 5 million. If that increase is included in the calculation, the loss per share will be $1.88 calculated as ($150 million) ÷ 80 million shares = ($1.88). The *loss* per share *declines.* This represents an *increase* in performance—not a dilution of performance. The options would be considered antidilutive, then, and not included in the calculation of the net loss per share. Any potential common shares not included in dilutive EPS because they are antidilutive should be revealed in the disclosure notes.

Convertible Securities

For convertible securities, though, it's not immediately obvious whether the effect of their conversion would be dilutive or antidilutive because the assumed conversion would affect both the numerator and the denominator of the EPS fraction. We discovered each was dilutive only after including the effect in the calculation and observing the result—a decline in EPS. But there's an easier way.

To determine whether convertible securities are dilutive and should be included in a diluted EPS calculation, we can compare the "incremental effect" of the conversion (expressed as a fraction) with the EPS fraction before the effect of any convertible security is considered. This, of course is our basic EPS. Recall from Illustration 19–12 that basic EPS is $2.00.

For comparison, we determine the "earnings per incremental share" of the two convertible securities.

Conversion of bonds

The incremental effect (of conversion) of the bonds is the after-tax interest saved divided by the additional common shares from conversion.

$$\frac{+\$24 - 25\%\,(\$24)}{+12} = \frac{\$18}{12} = \$1.50$$

Conversion of preferred stock

The incremental effect (of conversion) of the preferred stock is the dividends that wouldn't be paid divided by the additional common shares from conversion.

$$\frac{+\$4}{+3} = \$1.33$$

If the incremental effect of a security is *higher* than basic EPS, it is antidilutive. That's not the case in our illustration.

Order of Entry for Multiple Convertible Securities

A convertible security might seem to be dilutive when looked at individually but, in fact, may be antidilutive when included in combination with other convertible securities. This is because the *order of entry* for including their effects in the EPS calculation determines by how much, or even whether, EPS decreases as a result of their assumed conversion. Because our goal is to reveal the maximum potential dilution that might result, theoretically we should calculate diluted EPS using every possible combination of potential common shares to find the combination that yields the lowest EPS. But that's not necessary.

We can use the earnings per incremental share we calculated to determine the sequence of including securities' effects in the calculation. We include the securities in reverse order, beginning with the lowest incremental effect (that is, most dilutive), followed by the next lowest, and so on. This is, in fact, the order in which we included the securities in our continuing illustration.

Additional Consideration

Actually, the order of inclusion made no difference in our example, but would in many instances. For example, suppose the preferred stock had been convertible into 2.1 million shares, rather than 3 million shares. The incremental effect of its conversion would have been as follows:

Conversion of Preferred Stock

$$\frac{\underset{\text{Preferred dividends}}{+\$4}}{\underset{\substack{\text{Conversion of} \\ \text{preferred shares}}}{+2.1}} = \$1.90$$

On the surface, the effect would seem to be dilutive because $1.90 is less than $2.00, basic EPS. In fact, if this were the only convertible security, it would be dilutive. But, after the convertible bonds are assumed converted first, then the assumed conversion of the preferred stock would be *antidilutive*.

With Conversion of Bonds

> Because the incremental effect of the convertible bonds ($1.50) is lower than the incremental effect of the convertible preferred stock ($1.90), it is included first.

With Conversion of Preferred Stock

> A convertible security might seem to be dilutive when looked at individually but may be antidilutive when included in combination with other convertible securities.

Although the incremental effect of the convertible preferred stock ($1.90) is lower than basic EPS ($2.00), when included in the calculation after the convertible bonds, the effect is antidilutive (EPS increases).

Concept Review Exercise

At December 31, 2021, the financial statements of Clevenger Casting Corporation included the following:

BASIC AND DILUTED EPS

Net income for 2021	$500 million
Common stock, $1 par:	
Shares outstanding on January 1	150 million shares
Shares retired for cash on February 1	24 million shares
Shares sold for cash on September 1	18 million shares
2-for-1 split on July 23	

(continued)

1132   SECTION 4   Additional Financial Reporting Issues

(concluded)

Preferred stock, 10%, $70 par, cumulative, nonconvertible	$ 70 million
Preferred stock, 8%, $50 par, cumulative, convertible into 4 million shares of common stock	$100 million
Incentive stock options outstanding, fully vested, for 4 million shares of common stock; the exercise price is $15	
Bonds payable, 10%, convertible into 20 million shares of common stock	$200 million

Additional data:

The market price of the common stock averaged $20 during 2021.

The convertible preferred stock and the bonds payable had been issued at par in 2019. The tax rate for the year was 25%.

Required:

Compute basic and diluted earnings per share for the year ended December 31, 2021.

(\$ amounts in millions, except per share amounts)

Solution:
Basic EPS

Diluted EPS

ª10% × $70 million = $7 million
ᵇ8% × $100 million = $8 million

ᶜExercise of warrants:

$$\begin{array}{r} 4 \text{ million shares} \\ \times\ \$15 \text{ (exercise price)} \\ \hline \$60 \text{ million} \\ \div\ \$20 \text{ (average market price)} \\ \hline 3 \text{ million shares} \end{array}$$

ᵈ10% × $200 million = $20 million

Dilution:

Conversion of Bonds	Conversion of 8% Preferred Stock
$\dfrac{\text{After-tax interest savings}}{\underset{\text{Conversion of bonds}}{+20}}$ $\dfrac{+\$20 - 25\%\,(\$20)}{+20} = \$0.75$	$\dfrac{\text{Preferred dividends}}{\underset{\text{Conversion of preferred shares}}{+4}}$ $\dfrac{+\$8}{+4} = \$2.00^*$

*Because the incremental effect of conversion of the preferred stock ($2) is higher than EPS without the conversion of the preferred stock, the conversion would be *antidilutive* and is *not* considered in the calculation of diluted EPS.

Additional EPS Issues

Components of the "Proceeds" in the Treasury Stock Method

● LO19–11

In calculating diluted EPS when stock options are outstanding, we assume the options have been exercised. That is, we pretend the company sold the shares specified by the options at the exercise price and that the "proceeds" were used to buy back (as treasury stock) as many shares as can be purchased at the average market price of the stock during the year. The proceeds for the calculation should include the amount received from the hypothetical exercise of the options ($300 million in Illustration 19–10). But that's only the first of two possible components.

> For the treasury stock method, "proceeds" include:
>
> 1. The amount, if any, received from the hypothetical exercise of options or vesting of restricted stock.
>
> 2. The total compensation from the award that's not yet expensed.

The second component of the proceeds is the total compensation from the award that's *not yet expensed*. If the fair value of an option had been $4 at the grant date, the total compensation would have been 15 million shares times $4, or $60 million. In our illustration, though, we assumed the options were fully vested before 2021, so all $60 million already had been expensed and this second component of the proceeds was zero. If the options had been only half vested, half the compensation would have been unexpensed and $30 million would have been added to the $300 million proceeds. This would have been the case, for instance, if our calculation was made after two years of a four-year vesting period.

Why do the proceeds include these two components? We might think of it like this. The "proceeds" include everything the firm will receive from the award: (1) cash, if any, at exercise and (2) services from the recipient (value of award given as compensation). The reason we *exclude the expensed portion* is that, when it's expensed, earnings are reduced, so that portion of the dilution already is reflected in EPS. Excluding that expensed portion from the proceeds avoids the additional dilution that would occur if we included those additional proceeds in our hypothetical buyback of shares. Hence, we avoid double-counting the dilutive effect of the compensation.

Restricted Stock Awards in EPS Calculations

As we discussed earlier, restricted stock awards and their cousins, restricted stock units (RSUs), have replaced stock options as the share-based compensation plan of choice. Like stock options, they represent potential common shares and their dilutive effect is included in diluted EPS. In fact, they too are included using the treasury stock method. That is, the shares are added to the denominator and then reduced by the number of shares that can be bought back with the "proceeds" at the average market price of the company's stock during the year. Unlike stock options, though, the first component of the proceeds usually is absent; employees don't pay to acquire their shares.

Also, only *unvested* restricted stock award shares and RSU shares are included in EPS calculations; fully vested shares are actually distributed and thus outstanding. The proceeds for the EPS calculation include the total compensation from the unvested restricted stock that's not yet expensed, the second component. For an example, refer back to the restricted stock in Illustration 19–2. The total compensation for the award is $60 million ($12 market price per share × 5 million shares). Because the restricted stock vests over four years, it is expensed as $15 million each year for four years. At the end of 2021, the first year, $45 million remains unexpensed, so $45 million would be the assumed proceeds in an EPS calculation. If we assume the average market price that year was, say, $15, the $45 million will buy back 3 million shares and we would add to the denominator of diluted EPS 2 million common shares:

$$\frac{\text{No adjustment to the numerator}}{5 \text{ million} - 3^* \text{ million} = 2 \text{ } million}$$

*Assumed purchase of treasury shares

	$45	million
÷	$15	average market price
	3	million shares

*At the end of 2022, the *second* year, $30 million remains unexpensed, so assuming the average market price that year was, say, $12, we would add to the denominator of diluted EPS 2.5 million common shares:

$$\frac{\text{No adjustment to the numerator}}{5 \text{ million} - 2.5^* \text{ million}} = 2.5 \text{ million}$$

*Assumed purchase of treasury shares

	$30	million
÷	$12	average market price
	2.5	million shares

Contingently Issuable Shares

● LO19–12

Sometimes an agreement specifies that additional shares of common stock will be issued, contingent on the occurrence of some future circumstance. For instance, in the disclosure note reproduced in Illustration 19–14, **Hunt Manufacturing Co.** reported contingent shares in connection with its acquisition of **Feeny Manufacturing Company**.

Illustration 19–14

Contingently Issuable Shares—Hunt Manufacturing Company

Real World Financials

> **Note 12: Acquisitions (in part)**
>
> The Company acquired Feeny Manufacturing Company of Muncie, Indiana, for 135,000 shares of restricted common stock with a value of $7.71 per share. Feeny Manufacturing Company is a manufacturer of kitchen storage products. The purchase agreement calls for the issuance of up to 135,000 additional shares of common stock in the next fiscal year based on the earnings of Feeny Manufacturing Company. . . .
>
> Source: Hunt Manufacturing Company

At times, contingent shares are issuable to shareholders of an acquired company, certain key executives, or others in the event a certain level of performance is achieved. Contingent performance may be a desired level of income, a target stock price, or some other measurable activity level.

Contingently issuable shares are considered outstanding in the computation of diluted EPS.

When calculating EPS, contingently issuable shares are considered to be outstanding in the computation of diluted EPS if the target performance level already is being met (assumed to remain at existing levels until the end of the contingency period). For example, if shares will be issued at a future date if a certain level of income is achieved and that level of income or more was already reported this year, those additional shares are simply added to the denominator of the diluted EPS fraction.[20]

For clarification, refer to our continuing illustration of diluted EPS and assume 3 million additional shares will become issuable to certain executives in the following year (2022) if net income that year is $150 million or more. Recall that net income for Sovran Finanical in 2021 was $154 million, so the additional shares would be considered outstanding in the computation of diluted EPS by simply adding 3 million additional shares to the denominator of the EPS fraction. Obviously, the 2022 condition ($150 million net income or more) has not been met yet since it's only 2021. But because that level of income was achieved in 2021, the presumption is that it's likely to be achieved in 2022 as well.

Assumed Issuance of Contingently Issuable Shares (diluted EPS):

If a level of income must be attained before the shares will be issued, and income already is that amount or more, the additional shares are simply added to the denominator.

$$\frac{\text{No adjustment to the numerator}}{+3}$$
$$\text{Additonal shares}$$

On the other hand, if the target income next year is $160 million, the contingent shares would simply be ignored in our calculation.

---

[20]The shares should be included in both basic and diluted EPS if all conditions have actually been met so that there is no *circumstance* under which those shares would not be issued. In essence, these *are no longer contingent shares.*

Summary of the Effect of Potential Common Shares on Earnings Per Share

You have seen that under certain circumstances, securities that have the potential of reducing earnings per share by becoming common stock are assumed already to have become common stock for the purpose of calculating EPS. The table in Illustration 19–15 summarizes the circumstances under which the dilutive effect of these securities is reflected in the calculation of basic and diluted EPS.

Potential Common Shares	Is the Dilutive Effect Reflected in the Calculation of EPS?*	
	Basic EPS	Diluted EPS
• Stock options (or warrants, rights)	no	yes
• Restricted stock	no	yes
• Convertible securities (bonds, notes, preferred stock)	no	yes
• Contingently issuable shares	no	yes†

*The effect is not included for any security if its effect is antidilutive.
†Unless shares are contingent upon some level of performance not yet achieved.

Illustration 19–15
When Potential Common Shares Are Reflected in EPS

Illustration 19–16 summarizes the specific effects on the diluted EPS fraction when the dilutive effect of a potentially dilutive security is reflected in the calculation.

Potential Common Shares	Modification to the Diluted EPS Fractions	
	Numerator	Denominator
• Stock options (or warrants, rights)	None	Add the shares that would be created by their exercise,* reduced by shares repurchased at the average share price.
• Restricted stock	None	Add shares that would be created by their vesting,* reduced by shares repurchased at the average share price.
• Convertible bonds (or notes)	Add the interest (after-tax) that would have been avoided if the debt had been converted.	Add shares that would be created by the conversion* of the bonds (or notes).
• Convertible preferred stock	Do not deduct the dividends that would have been avoided if the preferred stock had been converted.	Add shares that would have been created by the conversion* of the preferred stock.
• Contingently issuable shares: Issuable when specified conditions are met, and those conditions currently are being met	None	Add shares that are issuable.
• Contingently issuable shares: Issuable when specified conditions are met, and those conditions are not currently being met	None	None

*At the beginning of the year or when potential common shares were issued, whichever is later (time-weight the increase in shares if assumed exercised or converted in midyear).

Illustration 19–16
How Potential Common Shares Are Reflected in a Diluted EPS Calculation

Actual Conversions

When calculating EPS in our example, we "pretended" the convertible bonds had been converted at the beginning of the year. What if they actually had been converted, let's say on November 1? Interestingly, diluted EPS would be precisely the same. Here's why:

1. The actual conversion would cause an actual increase in shares of 12 million on November 1. These would be time-weighted so the denominator would increase by 12 ($^2/_{12}$). Also, the numerator would be higher because net income actually would be increased by the after-tax interest saved on the bonds for the last two months, [$24 − 25% ($24)] × ($^2/_{12}$). Be sure to note that this would not be an adjustment in the EPS calculation. Instead, net income would actually have been higher by [$24 − 25% ($24)] × ($^2/_{12}$) = $3. That is, reported net income would have been $157 rather than $154.

2. We would assume conversion for the period before November 1 because they were potentially dilutive during that period. The 12 million shares assumed outstanding from January 1 to November 1 would be time-weighted for that 10-month period: 12 ($^{10}/_{12}$). Also, the numerator would be increased by the after-tax interest assumed saved on the bonds for the first 10 months, [$24 − 25% ($24)] × ($^{10}/_{12}$).

Notice that the incremental effect on diluted EPS is the same either way.

	Not Actually Converted:		**Converted on November 1:**

EPS would be precisely the same whether convertible securities were actually converted or not.

$$\frac{+\ \$24 - 25\%\ (\$24)}{+12} = \frac{+[\$24 - 25\%\ (\$24)] \times (^2/_{12}) + [\$24 - 25\%\ (\$24)] \times (^{10}/_{12})}{+12\ (^2/_{12}) + 12\ (^{10}/_{12})}$$

Assumed after-tax interest savings	Actual after-tax interest savings	Assumed after-tax interest savings
Assumed conversion of bonds	Actual conversion of bonds	Assumed conversion of bonds

$$\frac{\$18}{12} = \frac{\$3 \quad + \quad \$15}{2 \quad + \quad 10}$$

Illustration 19–17 shows the disclosure note **Clorox Company** reported after the conversion of convertible notes during the year.

Illustration 19–17

Conversion of Notes—The Clorox Company

Real World Financials

> **Note 1: Significant Accounting Policies—Earnings Per Common Share (in part)**
>
> A $9,000,000 note payable to Henkel Corporation was converted into 1,200,000 shares of common stock on August 1. . . . Earnings per common share and weighted-average shares outstanding reflect this conversion as if it were effective during all periods presented.
>
> Source: The Clorox Company

● LO19–13   ## Financial Statement Presentation of Earnings Per Share Data

Recall from Chapter 4 that if a company disposes of a component of its operations, the company will report "discontinued operations" as a separate item within the income statement as follows:

Income from Continuing Operations

Discontinued operations

Net income

When the income statement includes discontinued operations, EPS data (both basic and diluted) must also be reported separately for income from continuing operations and net income. Per share amounts for discontinued operations would be disclosed either on the face of the income statement or in the notes to financial statements. Presentation on the face of the income statement is illustrated by the partial income statements of **H&R Block, Inc.**, from a recent annual report and exhibited in Illustration 19–18.

Basic and diluted EPS data should be reported on the face of the income statement for all reporting periods presented in the comparative statements. Businesses without potential

Consolidated Income Statements (partial)
For the Years Ended April 30, 2017 and 2016

	2017	2016
Net income from continuing operations	$420,917	$383,553
Net loss from discontinued operations	(11,972)	(9,286)
Net income	$408,945	$374,267
Basic Earnings (Loss) Per Share:		
Continuing operations	$ 1.97	$ 1.54
Discontinued operations	(0.05)	(0.04)
Consolidated	$ 1.92	$ 1.50
Diluted Earnings (Loss) Per Share:		
Continuing operations	$ 1.96	$ 1.53
Discontinued operations	(0.05)	(0.04)
Consolidated	$ 1.91	$ 1.49

Source: H&R Block

Illustration 19–18

EPS Disclosure—H&R Block

Real World Financials

common shares present basic EPS only. Disclosure notes should provide additional disclosures including the following:

1. A reconciliation of the numerator and denominator used in the basic EPS computations to the numerator and the denominator used in the diluted EPS computations. An example of this is presented in Illustration 19–19 using the situation described previously inIllustration 19–12.
2. Any adjustments to the numerator for preferred dividends.
3. Any potential common shares that weren't included because they were antidilutive.
4. Any transactions that occurred after the end of the most recent period that would materially affect earnings per share.

Earnings per Share Reconciliation

($ in millions)	Income (Numerator)	Share (Denominator)	Per Share Amount
Net income	$ 154		
Preferred dividends	(4)		
Basic earnings per share	150	75	**$2.00**
Stock options	None	3*	
Convertible debt	18	12	
Convertible preferred stock	4	3	
Diluted earnings per share	**$172**	**93**	**$1.85**

Note: Stock warrants to purchase an additional 4 million shares at $32.50 per share were outstanding throughout the year but were not included in diluted EPS because the warrants' exercise price is greater than the average market price of the common shares.
*15 million − [(15 million × $20) ÷ $25] = 3 million net additional shares.

Illustration 19–19

Reconciliation of Basic EPS Computations to Diluted EPS Computations

Additional Consideration

It's possible that potential common shares would have a dilutive effect on one component of net income but an antidilutive effect on another. When the inclusion of the potential common shares has a dilutive effect on "income from continuing operations," the effect should be included in all calculations of diluted EPS. In other words, the same number of potential common shares used in computing the diluted per-share amount for income from continuing operations is used in computing all other diluted per-share amounts, even when amounts are antidilutive to the individual per-share amounts.

Decision Makers' Perspective

We noted earlier in the chapter that investors and creditors pay a great deal of attention to earnings per share information. Because of the importance analysts attach to earnings announcements, companies are particularly eager to meet earnings expectations. As we first noted in Chapter 4, this desire has contributed to a relatively recent trend, especially among technology firms, to report pro forma earnings per share. What exactly are pro forma earnings? Unfortunately there is no answer to that question. Essentially, pro forma earnings are actual (GAAP) earnings increased due to the reduction of any expenses the reporting company feels are unusual and should be excluded. Always, though, the pro forma results of a company look better than the real results. Broadcom Corporation, a provider of broadband and network products, reported pro forma *earnings* of $0.49 per share. However on a GAAP basis, it actually had a *loss* of $3.29 per share. This is not an isolated example.

Make sure you pay lots of attention to the man behind the curtain. If any earnings figure says pro forma, you should immediately look for a footnote or explanation telling you just what is and is not included in the calculation.

When companies report pro forma results, they argue they are trying to help investors by giving them numbers that more accurately reflect their normal business activities, because they exclude unusual expenses. Analysts should be skeptical, though. Because of the purely discretionary nature of pro forma reporting and several noted instances of abuse, analysts should, at a minimum, find out precisely what expenses are excluded and what the actual GAAP numbers are.

Another way management might enhance the appearance of EPS numbers is by massaging the denominator of the calculation. Reducing the number of shares increases earnings *per share.* Some companies judiciously use share buyback programs to manipulate the number of shares and therefore EPS. There is nothing inherently wrong with share buybacks and, as we noted in Chapter 18, they can benefit shareholders. The motivation for buybacks, though, can sometimes be detected in the year-to-year pattern of net income and EPS. Companies whose growth rates in earnings per share routinely exceed their growth in net income may be using buybacks to artificially increase EPS.

One way analysts use EPS data is in connection with the price-earnings ratio. This ratio is simply the market price per share divided by the earnings per share. It measures the market's perception of the quality of a company's earnings by indicating the price multiple the capital market is willing to pay for the company's earnings. Presumably, this ratio reflects the information provided by all financial information in that the market price reflects analysts' perceptions of the company's growth potential, stability, and relative risk. The price-earnings ratio relates these performance measures with the external judgment of the marketplace concerning the value of the firm.

The ratio measures the quality of earnings in the sense that it represents the market's expectation of future earnings as indicated by current earnings. Caution is called for in comparing price-earnings ratios. For instance, a ratio might be low, not because earnings expectations are low, but because of abnormally elevated current earnings. On the contrary, the ratio might be high, not because earnings expectations are high, but because the company's current earnings are temporarily depressed. Similarly, an analyst should be alert to differences among accounting methods used to measure earnings from company to company when making comparisons.

Another ratio frequently calculated by shareholders and potential shareholders is the dividend payout ratio. This ratio expresses the percentage of earnings that is distributed to shareholders as dividends. The ratio is calculated by dividing dividends per common share by the earnings per share.

This ratio provides an indication of a firm's reinvestment strategy. A low payout ratio suggests that a company is retaining a large portion of earnings for reinvestment for new facilities and other operating needs. Low payouts often are found in growth industries and high payouts in mature industries. Often, though, the ratio is merely a reflection of managerial strategy concerning the mix of internal versus external financing. The ratio also is considered by investors who, for tax or other reasons, prefer current income over market price appreciation, or vice versa. ●

> The price-earnings ratio measures the quality of a company's earnings.

> The dividend payout ratio indicates the percentage of earnings that is distributed to shareholders as dividends.

Concept Review Exercise

At December 31, 2021, the financial statements of Bahnson General, Inc. included the following:

ADDITIONAL EPS ISSUES

Net income for 2021 (including a net-of-tax loss from discontinued operations of $10 million)	$180 million
Common stock, $1 par:	
Shares outstanding on January 1	44 million

The share price was $25 and $28 at the beginning and end of the year, respectively.

Additional data:

- At January 1, 2021, $200 million of 8% convertible notes were outstanding. The notes were converted on April 1 into 16 million shares of common stock.

- An agreement with company executives calls for the issuance of up to 12 million additional shares of common stock in 2022 and 2023 based on Bahnson's net income in those years. Executives will receive 2 million shares at the end of each of those two years if the company's stock price is at least $26 and another 4 million shares each year if the stock price is at least $29.50.

The tax rate is 25%.

Required:

Compute basic and diluted earnings per share for the year ended December 31, 2021.

Solution:

($ amounts in millions, except per share amounts)

Basic EPS

$$\frac{\underset{\substack{\text{Net income}}}{\$180}}{\underset{\substack{\text{Shares} \\ \text{at Jan. 1}}}{44} + \underset{\substack{\text{Actual} \\ \text{conversion} \\ \text{of notes}}}{16\ (9/12)}} = \frac{\$180}{56} = \$3.21$$

Diluted EPS

$$\frac{\underset{\substack{\text{Net income}}}{\$180} + \underset{\substack{\text{Assumed after-tax} \\ \text{interest savings}}}{[\$16 - 25\%\ (\$16)] \times (3/12)}}{\underset{\substack{\text{Shares} \\ \text{at Jan. 1}}}{44} + \underset{\substack{\text{Actual} \\ \text{conversion} \\ \text{of notes}}}{16\ (9/12)} + \underset{\substack{\text{Assumed} \\ \text{conversion} \\ \text{of notes}}}{16\ (3/12)} + \underset{\substack{\text{Contingent} \\ \text{shares}}}{(2 + 2)}} = \frac{\$183}{64} = \$2.86$$

Convertible Notes: Notice that the effect on diluted EPS would be precisely the same whether the convertible notes were actually converted or not.

Converted on April 1:

$$\frac{\underset{\substack{\text{Net income including} \\ \text{actual after-tax} \\ \text{interest savings}}}{\$180} + \underset{\substack{\text{Assumed after-tax} \\ \text{interest savings}}}{[\$16 - 25\%\ (\$16)] \times (3/12)}}{\underset{\substack{\text{Shares} \\ \text{at Jan. 1}}}{44} + \underset{\substack{\text{Actual} \\ \text{conversion} \\ \text{of notes}}}{16\ (9/12)} + \underset{\substack{\text{Assumed} \\ \text{conversion} \\ \text{of notes}}}{16\ (3/12)}} = \frac{\$183}{60}$$

1140   SECTION 4   Additional Financial Reporting Issues

Not Actually Converted:

$$\frac{\overset{\substack{\text{Net income without}\\ \text{actual after-tax}\\ \text{interest savings}}}{\$171^*}}{\underset{\substack{\text{Shares}\\ \text{at Jan. 1}}}{44}} + \frac{\overset{\substack{\text{Assumed after-tax}\\ \text{interest savings}}}{+\,[\$16 - 25\%\,(\$16)]}}{\underset{\substack{\text{Assumed}\\ \text{conversion}\\ \text{of notes}}}{16}} = \frac{\$183}{60}$$

*$180 − {[$16 − 25% ($16] × ($^9/_{12}$)} = $171; after-tax interest from Apr. 1 to Dec. 31.

Contingently Issuable Shares:
Because the conditions are met for issuing 4 million shares (2 million for each of two years), those shares are simply added to the denominator of diluted EPS. The current share price ($28) is projected to remain the same throughout the contingency period, so the other 8 million shares (4 million for each of two years) are excluded.

Income Statement Presentation:
To determine the per share amounts for income before discontinued operations, we substitute that amount for net income in the numerator (in this case, that means adding back the $10 million loss from discontinued operations):

$$\text{Basic: } \frac{\$180 + \$10}{56} = \$3.39 \qquad \text{Diluted: } \frac{\$183 + \$10}{64} = \$3.02$$

Earnings per Share:	Basic*	Diluted
Income before discontinued operations	$3.39	$ 3.02
Loss from discontinued operations	(0.18)	(0.16)
Net income	$ 3.21	$ 2.86

*Only diluted EPS is required on the face of the income statement. Basic EPS is reported in the EPS reconciliation shown in the disclosure note (below).

Disclosure Note:
Earnings per Share Reconciliation:

	Income (Numerator)	Shares (Denominator)	Per Share Amount
Basic Earnings per Share			
Income before discontinued operations	$190	56	$ 3.39
Loss from discontinued operations	(10)	56	(0.18)
Net income	$180	56	$ 3.21
Convertible debt	3	4	
Contingently issuable shares	—	4	
Diluted Earnings per Share			
Income before discontinued operations	$193	64	$ 3.02
Loss from discontinued operations	(10)	64	(0.16)
Net income	$183	64	$2.86

Financial Reporting Case Solution

©Fabio Cardoso/Getty Images

1. How can a compensation package such as this serve as an incentive to Ms. Veres? *(p. 1105)* Stock-based plans like the restricted stock and stock options that Ms. Veres is receiving are designed to motivate recipients. If the shares awarded are restricted so that Ms. Veres is not free to sell the shares during the restriction period, she has an incentive to remain with the company until rights to the shares vest. Likewise, stock options can be made exercisable only after a specified period of employment. An additional incentive of stock-based plans is that the recipient will be motivated to take actions that will maximize the value of the shares.

2. **Ms. Veres received a "grant of restricted stock." How should NEV account for the grant?** *(p. 1106)*   The compensation associated with restricted stock is the market price of unrestricted shares of the same stock. NEV will accrue this amount as compensation expense over the service period from the date of grant to when restrictions are lifted.

3. **Included were stock options to buy more than 800,000 shares of NEV stock. How will the options affect NEV's compensation expense?** *(p. 1108)*   Similar to the method used for restricted stock, the value of the options is recorded as compensation over the service period, usually the vesting period.

4. **How will the presence of these and other similar stock options affect NEV's earnings per share?** *(p. 1124)*   If outstanding stock options were exercised, the resulting increase in shares would reduce or dilute EPS. If we don't take into account the dilutive effect of the share increase, we might mislead investors and creditors. So, in addition to basic EPS, we also calculate diluted EPS to include the dilutive effect of options and other potential common shares. This means calculating EPS as if the potential increase in shares already has occurred (even though it hasn't yet). ●

The Bottom Line

● **LO19–1**   We measure the fair value of stock issued in a restricted stock plan and expense it over the service period, usually from the date of grant to the vesting date. *(p. 1106)*

● **LO19–2**   Similarly, we estimate the fair value of stock options at the grant date and expense it over the service period, usually from the date of grant to the vesting date. Fair value is estimated at the grant date using an option-pricing model that considers the exercise price and expected term of the option, the current market price of the underlying stock and its expected volatility, expected dividends, and the expected risk-free rate of return. *(p. 1108)*

● **LO19–3**   Employee share purchase plans allow employees to buy company stock under convenient or favorable terms. Most such plans are considered compensatory and require any discount to be recorded as compensation expense. *(p. 1117)*

● **LO19–4**   A company has a simple capital structure if it has no outstanding securities that could potentially dilute earnings per share. For such a firm, EPS is simply earnings available to common shareholders divided by the weighted-average number of common shares outstanding. When potential common shares are outstanding, the company is said to have a complex capital structure. In that case, two EPS calculations are reported. Basic EPS assumes no dilution. Diluted EPS assumes maximum potential dilution. *(p. 1119)*

● **LO19–5**   EPS calculations are based on the weighted-average number of shares outstanding during the period. Any new shares issued during the period are time-weighted by the fraction of the period they were outstanding and then added to the number of shares outstanding for the period. *(p. 1120)*

● **LO19–6**   For a stock dividend or stock split, shares outstanding prior to the stock distribution are retroactively restated to reflect the increase in shares. When shares are reacquired, as treasury stock or to be retired, they are time-weighted for the fraction of the period they were not outstanding, prior to being subtracted from the number of shares outstanding during the reporting period. *(p. 1120)*

● **LO19–7**   The numerator in the EPS calculation should reflect earnings available to common shareholders. So, any dividends on preferred stock outstanding should be subtracted from reported net income. This adjustment is made for cumulative preferred stock whether or not dividends are declared that period. *(p. 1122)*

● **LO19–8**   For diluted EPS, it is assumed that stock options, rights, and warrants are exercised at the beginning of the period (or at the time the options are issued, if later) and the cash proceeds received are used to buy back (as treasury stock) as many of those shares as can be acquired at the average market price during the period. *(p. 1123)*

● **LO19–9**   To incorporate convertible securities into the calculation of diluted EPS, the conversion is assumed to have occurred at the beginning of the period (or at the time the convertible security is issued, if later). The denominator of the EPS fraction is adjusted for the additional common shares assumed, and the numerator is increased by the interest (after-tax) on bonds and not reduced by the preferred dividends that would have been avoided in the event of conversion. *(p. 1126)*

● **LO19–10** If including potential common shares in the EPS calculation causes EPS to *increase* rather than decrease, then those potential common shares are considered *antidilutive* and are omitted from the calculation. (*p. 1128*)

● **LO19–11** For the treasury stock method, "proceeds" include (1) the amount, if any, received from the hypothetical exercise of options or vesting of restricted stock and (2) the total compensation from the award that's not yet expensed. (*p. 1133*)

● **LO19–12** Contingently issuable shares are considered outstanding in the computation of diluted EPS when they will later be issued upon the mere passage of time or because of conditions that currently are met. (*p. 1134*)

● **LO19–13** EPS data (both basic and diluted) must be reported for (a) income before any discontinued operations, (b) the discontinued operations, and (c) net income. Disclosures also should include a reconciliation of the numerator and denominator used in the computations. (*p. 1136*)

● **LO19–14** When options have graded vesting, unlike under U.S. GAAP, IFRS does not permit the straight-line method for allocating compensation or require that the company recognize at least the amount of the award that has vested by each reporting date. The earnings per share requirements of IFRS and U.S. GAAP are similar. The few differences that remain are the result of differences in the application of the treasury stock method, the treatment of contracts that may be settled in shares or cash, and contingently issuable shares. (*pp. 1113, 1115,* and *1119*) ●

APPENDIX 19A   Option-Pricing Theory

Option values have two essential components: (1) intrinsic value and (2) time value.

Intrinsic Value

Intrinsic value is the benefit the holder of an option would realize by exercising the option rather than buying the underlying stock directly. An option that permits an employee to buy $25 stock for $10 has an intrinsic value of $15. An option that has an exercise price equal to or exceeding the market price of the underlying stock has zero intrinsic value.

Time Value

In addition to their intrinsic value, options also have a time value due to the fact that (a) the holder of an option does not have to pay the exercise price until the option is exercised and (b) the market price of the underlying stock may yet rise and create additional intrinsic value. All options have time value so long as time remains before expiration. The longer the time until expiration, other things being equal, the greater the time value. For instance, the option described above with an intrinsic value of $15, might have a fair value of, say, $22 if time still remains until the option expires. The $7 difference represents the time value of the option. Time value can be subdivided into two components: (1) the effects of time value of money and (2) volatility value.

TIME VALUE OF MONEY

An option's value is enhanced by the delay in paying cash for the shares.

The time value of money component arises because the holder of an option does not have to pay the exercise price until the option is exercised. Instead, the holder can invest funds elsewhere while waiting to exercise the option. For measurement purposes, the time value of money component is assumed to be the rate of return available on risk-free U.S. Treasury Securities. The higher the time value of money, the higher the value of being able to delay payment of the exercise price.

When the underlying stock pays no dividends, the time value of money component is the difference between the exercise price (a future amount) and its discounted present value. Let's say the exercise price is $30. If the present value (discounted at the risk-free rate) is $24, the time value of money component is $6. On the other hand, if the stock pays a dividend (or is expected to during the life of the option), the time value of money component is lower.

The value of being able to delay payment of the exercise price would be partially offset by the cost of forgoing the dividend in the meantime. For instance, if the stock underlying the options just described were expected to pay dividends and the discounted present value of the expected dividends were $2, the time value of money component in that example would be reduced from $6 to $4.

The time value of money component is the difference between the exercise price and its discounted present value minus the present value of expected dividends.

VOLATILITY VALUE

The volatility value represents the possibility that the option holder might profit from market price appreciation of the underlying stock while being exposed to the loss of only the value of the option, rather than the full market value of the stock. For example, fair value of an option to buy a share at an exercise price of $30 might be measured as $7. The potential profit from market price appreciation is conceptually unlimited. And yet, the potential loss from the stock's value failing to appreciate is only $7.

A stock's volatility is the amount by which its price has fluctuated previously or is expected to fluctuate in the future. The greater a stock's volatility, the greater the potential profit. It usually is measured as one standard deviation of a statistical distribution. Statistically, if the expected annualized volatility is 25%, the probability is approximately 67% that the stock's year-end price will fall within roughly plus or minus 25% of its beginning-of-year price. Stated differently, the probability is approximately 33% that the year-end stock price will fall outside that range.

Volatility enhances the likelihood of stock price appreciation.

Option-pricing models make assumptions about the likelihood of various future stock prices by making assumptions about the statistical distribution of future stock prices that take into account the expected volatility of the stock price. One popular option pricing model, the Black–Scholes model, for instance, assumes a log-normal distribution. This assumption posits that the stock price is as likely to fall by half as it is to double and that large price movements are less likely than small price movements. The higher a stock's volatility, the higher the probability of large increases or decreases in market price. Because the cost of large decreases is limited to the option's current value, but the profitability from large increases is unlimited, an option on a highly volatile stock has a higher probability of a large profit than does an option on a less volatile stock.

Summary

In summary, the fair value of an option is (a) its intrinsic value plus (b) its time value of money component plus (c) its volatility component. The variables that affect an option's fair value and the effect of each are indicated in Illustration 19A–1.

All Other Factors Being Equal, If the	The Option Value Will Be
Exercise price is higher	Lower
Term of the option is longer	Higher
Market price of the stock is higher	Higher
Dividends are higher	Lower
Risk-free rate of return is higher	Higher
Volatility of the stock is higher	Higher

Illustration 19A–1

Effect of Variables on an Option's Fair Value

APPENDIX 19B

Stock Appreciation Rights

Stock appreciation rights (SARs) overcome a major disadvantage of stock option plans that require employees to actually buy shares when the options are exercised. Even though the options' exercise price may be significantly lower than the market value of the shares, the employee still must come up with enough cash to take advantage of the bargain. This can be quite a burden if the award is sizable. In a nonqualified stock option plan, income taxes also would have to be paid when the options are exercised.[21]

SARs offer a solution. Unlike stock options, these awards enable an employee to benefit by the amount that the market price of the company's stock rises without having to buy shares. Instead, the employee is awarded the share appreciation, which is the amount by which the market price on the exercise date exceeds a prespecified price (usually the market price at the date of grant). For instance, if the share price rises from $35 to $50, the employee receives $15 cash for each SAR held. The share appreciation usually is payable in cash or the recipient has the choice between cash and shares. A plan of this type offered by IBM is described in Illustration 19B–1.

> *In an SAR plan, the employer pays compensation equal to the increase in share price from a specified level.*

Illustration 19B–1

Stock Appreciation Rights—IBM Corporation

Real World Financials

> **Long-Term Performance Plan (in part)**
> SARs offer eligible optionees the alternative of electing not to exercise the related stock option, but to receive payment in cash and/or stock, equivalent to the difference between the option price and the average market price of IBM stock on the date of exercising the right.
>
> Source: IBM Corporation

IS IT DEBT OR IS IT EQUITY?

In some plans, the employer chooses whether to issue shares or cash at exercise. In other plans, the choice belongs to the employee.[22] Who has the choice determines the way it's accounted for. More specifically, the accounting treatment depends on whether the award is considered an equity instrument or a liability. If the employer can elect to settle in shares of stock rather than cash, the award is considered to be equity. On the other hand, if the employee will receive cash or can elect to receive cash, the award is considered to be a liability.

> *If an employer can elect to settle in shares of stock rather than cash, the award is considered to be equity.*

The distinction between share-based awards that are considered equity and those that are considered liabilities is based on whether the employer is obligated to transfer assets to the employee. A cash SAR requires the transfer of assets, and therefore is a liability. A stock option, on the other hand, is an equity instrument if it requires only the issuance of stock. This does not mean that a stock option whose issuer may later choose to settle in cash is not an equity instrument. Instead, cash settlement would be considered equivalent to repurchasing an equity instrument for cash.

> *If an employee can elect to receive cash, the award is considered to be a liability.*

SARS PAYABLE IN SHARES (EQUITY)

When a SAR is considered to be equity (because the employer can elect to settle in shares of stock rather than cash), we estimate the fair value of the SARs at the grant date and accrue that compensation to expense over the service period. Normally, the fair value of a SAR is the same as the fair value of a stock option with the same terms. The fair value is determined at the grant date and accrued to compensation expense over the service period the same way as for other share-based compensation plans. The total compensation is not revised for subsequent changes in the price of the underlying stock. This is demonstrated in Case 1 of Illustration 19–B2.

> *The cash settlement of an equity award is considered the repurchase of an equity instrument*

SARS PAYABLE IN CASH (LIABILITY)

When a SAR is considered to be a liability (because the employee can elect to receive cash upon settlement), we estimate the fair value of the SARs and recognize that amount as compensation expense over the requisite service period consistent with the way we account for options and other share-based compensation. However, because these plans are considered to be liabilities, it's necessary to periodically re-estimate the fair value in order to continually adjust the liability (and corresponding compensation) until it is paid. Be sure to note that this is consistent with the way we account for other liabilities. Recall from our discussions in Chapter 16, for instance, that when a tax rate change causes a change in the eventual liability for deferred income taxes, we adjust that liability.

> *Compensation expense reported to date is the estimated total compensation multiplied by the fraction of the service period that has expired.*

---

[21]The tax treatment of share-based plans is discussed an earlier Additional Consideration box.

[22]Many such plans are called tandem plans and award an employee both a cash SAR and an SAR that calls for settlement in an equivalent amount of shares. The exercise of one cancels the other.

The periodic expense (and adjustment to the liability) is the fraction of the total compensation earned to date by recipients of the SARs (based on the elapsed fraction of the service period) reduced by any amounts expensed in prior periods. For example, if the fair value of SARs at the end of a period is $8, the total compensation would be $80 million if 10 million SARs are expected to vest. Let's say two years of a four-year service period have elapsed, and $21 million was expensed the first year. Then, compensation expense the second year would be $19 million, calculated as (¾ **of $80** million) minus $21. An example spanning several years is provided in Illustration 19B–2, Case 2.

> We make up for incorrect previous estimates by adjusting expense in the period the estimate is revised.

Illustration 19B–2
Stock Appreciation Rights
Case 1: Equity

At January 1, 2021, Universal Communications issued 10 million SARs that, upon exercise, entitle key executives to receive compensation equal in value to the excess of the market price at exercise over the share price at the date of grant.

- The SARs vest at the end of 2024 (cannot be exercised until then) and expire at the end of 2028.
- The fair value of the SARs, estimated by an appropriate option pricing model, is $8 per SAR at January 1, 2021.
- The fair value re-estimated at December 31, 2021, 2022, 2023, 2024, and 2025, is $8.40, $8, $6, $4.30, and $5, respectively.

Case 1: SARs considered to be equity because Universal can elect to settle in shares of Universal stock at exercise

January 1, 2021
No entry
Calculate total compensation expense:

$ 8	Estimated fair value per SAR
× 10 million	SARs granted
= $80 million	Total compensation

> Fair value is estimated at the date of grant.

The total compensation is allocated to expense over the four-year service (vesting) period: 2021–2024

$80 million ÷ 4 years = $20 million per year

December 31, 2021, 2022, 2023, 2024   ($ in millions)

Compensation expense ($80 million ÷ 4 years)	20	
Paid-in capital—SAR plan		20

> The value of the compensation is estimated each year at the fair value of the SARs.

Case 2: SARs considered to be a liability because employees can elect to receive cash at exercise

January 1, 2021
No entry

December 31, 2021   ($ in millions)

Compensation expense ($8.40 × 10 million × ¼)	21	
Liability—SAR plan		21

December 31, 2022

Compensation expense [($8 × 10 million × ²⁄₄) − $21]	19	
Liability—SAR plan		19

December 31, 2023

Compensation expense [($6 × 10 million × ³⁄₄) − $21 − $19]	5	
Liability—SAR plan		5

December 31, 2024

Liability—SAR plan	2	
Compensation expense [($4.30 × 10 million × ⁴⁄₄) − $21 − $19 − $5]		2

> The expense each year is the current estimate of total compensation that should have been recorded to date less the amount already recorded.

> If the fair value falls below the amount expensed to date, both the liability and expense are reduced.

Note that the way we treat changes in compensation estimates entails a catch-up adjustment in the period of change, *inconsistent* with the usual treatment of a change in estimate.

1146   SECTION 4   Additional Financial Reporting Issues

Remember that for most changes in estimate, revisions are allocated over remaining periods, rather than all at once in the period of change. The treatment is, however, consistent with the way we treat changes in forfeiture rate estimates, as we discussed earlier in the chapter.

The liability continues to be adjusted after the service period if the rights haven't been exercised yet.

Compensation expense and the liability continue to be adjusted until the SARs expire or are exercised.

December 31, 2025		($ in millions)
Compensation expense [($5 × 10 million × all) − $21 − $19 − $5 + $2]	7	
Liability—SAR plan		7

It's necessary to continue to adjust both compensation expense and the liability until the SARs ultimately either are exercised or lapse.[23] Assume, for example, that the SARs are exercised on October 11, 2026, when their fair value is $4.50, and executives choose to receive the market price appreciation in cash.

Adjustment continues after the service period if the SARs have not yet been exercised.

October 11, 2026		($ in millions)
Liability—SAR plan	5	
Compensation expense [($4.50 × 10 million × all) − $50]		5
Liability—SAR plan (balance)	45	
Cash		45

Let's look at the changes in the liability—SAR plan account during the 2021–2026 period:

The liability is adjusted each period as changes in the fair value estimates cause changes in the liability.

Liability—SAR Plan

		($ in millions)	
		21	2021
		19	2022
		5	2023
2024	2		
		7	2025
2026	5		
2026	45		
		0	Balance after exercise

RESTRICTED STOCK UNITS PAYABLE IN CASH (LIABILITY)

Accounting for RSUs payable in cash is essentially the same as accounting for the SARs payable in cash.

Recall from our discussion in the chapter that restricted stock units (RSUs) give the recipient the right to receive a set number of shares of company stock after the vesting requirement is satisfied. But, sometimes the recipient is given the *cash equivalent* of those shares instead. *If the employee will receive cash* or can elect to receive cash, as in the case of an SAR, we consider the award to be a *liability*. We determine its fair value at the grant date and recognize that amount as compensation expense over the requisite service period and, like SARs payable in cash, we periodically adjust the liability (and corresponding compensation) based on the change in the stock's fair value until the liability is paid. Accounting for RSUs payable in cash (sometimes called phantom shares or phantom performance shares) is quite similar to accounting for the SARs payable in cash in case 2 of Illustration 19B–2. Of course, though, we would label the liability "Liability—restricted stock." And, we would determine the periodic value of the liability (and compensation) as the actual fair value of the shares, rather than an *estimated* fair value as is necessary when valuing SARs. ●

---

[23]Except that the cumulative compensation expense cannot be negative; that is, the liability cannot be reduced below zero.

Questions For Review of Key Topics

Q 19–1   What is restricted stock? How do restricted stock awards differ from restricted stock units (RSUs)? Describe how compensation expense is determined and recorded for a restricted stock award plan.

Q 19–2   Stock option plans provide employees the option to purchase (a) a specified number of shares of the firm's stock, (b) at a specified price, (c) during a specified period of time. One of the most controversial aspects of accounting for stock-based compensation is how the fair value of stock options should be measured. Describe the general approach to measuring fair value.

Q 19–3   The Tax Code differentiates between qualified option plans, including incentive plans, and nonqualified plans. What are the major differences in tax treatment between incentive plans and nonqualified plans?

Q 19–4   Stock option (and other share-based) plans often specify a performance condition or a market condition that must be satisfied before employees are allowed the benefits of the award. Describe the general approach we use to account for performance-based options and options with market-related conditions.

Q 19–5   What is a simple capital structure? How is EPS determined for a company with a simple capital structure?

Q 19–6   When calculating the weighted-average number of common shares, how are stock dividends and stock splits treated? Compare this treatment with that of additional shares sold for cash at midyear.

Q 19–7   Blake Distributors had 100,000 common shares outstanding at the beginning of the year, January 1. On May 13, Blake distributed a 5% stock dividend. Blake retired 1,200 shares on August 1. What is the weighted-average number of shares for calculating EPS?

Q 19–8   Why are preferred dividends deducted from net income when calculating EPS? Are there circumstances when this deduction is not made?

Q 19–9   Distinguish between basic and diluted EPS.

Q 19–10   The treasury stock method is used to incorporate the dilutive effect of stock options, stock warrants, and similar securities. Describe this method as it applies to diluted EPS.

Q 19–11   The potentially dilutive effect of convertible securities is reflected in EPS calculations by the if-converted method. Describe this method as it relates to convertible bonds.

Q 19–12   How is the potentially dilutive effect of convertible preferred stock reflected in EPS calculations by the if-converted method? How is this different from the way convertible bonds are considered?

Q 19–13   A convertible security may appear to be dilutive when looked at individually but might be antidilutive when included in combination with other convertible securities. How should the order be determined for inclusion of convertible securities in an EPS calculation to avoid including an antidilutive security?

Q 19–14   If stock options and restricted stock are outstanding when calculating diluted EPS, what are the components of the "proceeds" available for the repurchase of shares under the treasury stock method?

Q 19–15   Wiseman Electronics has an agreement with certain of its division managers that 50,000 contingently issuable shares will be issued next year in the event operating income exceeds $2.1 million that year. In what way, if any, is the calculation of EPS affected by these contingently issuable shares, assuming this year's operating income was $2.2 million? $2.0 million?

Q 19–16   Diluted EPS would be precisely the same whether convertible securities were actually converted or not. Why?

Q 19–17   When the income statement includes discontinued operations, which amounts require per share presentation?

Q 19–18   In addition to EPS numbers themselves, what additional disclosures should be provided concerning the EPS information?

Q 19–19   (Based on Appendix 19A) The fair value of stock options can be considered to comprise two main components. What are they?

Q 19–20   (Based on Appendix 19B) LTV Corporation grants SARs to key executives. Upon exercise, the SARs entitle executives to receive either cash or stock equal in value to the excess of the market price at exercise over the share price at the date of grant. How should LTV account for the awards?

Brief Exercises

BE 19–1
Restricted stock award
● LO19–1

First Link Services granted 8 million of its $1 par common shares to executives, subject to forfeiture if employment is terminated within three years. The common shares have a market price of $6 per share on the grant date of the restricted stock award. Ignoring taxes, what is the total compensation cost pertaining to the restricted shares? What is the effect on earnings in the year after the shares are granted to executives?

1148 SECTION 4 Additional Financial Reporting Issues

BE 19–2
Restricted stock units
● LO19–1

Second Link Services granted restricted stock units (RSUs) representing 16 million of its $1 par common shares to executives, subject to forfeiture if employment is terminated within four years. After the recipients of the RSUs satisfy the vesting requirement, the company will distribute the shares. The common shares had a market price of $10 per share on the grant date. Ignoring taxes, what is the total compensation cost pertaining to the restricted stock units? What is the effect on earnings in the year after the shares are granted to executives?

BE 19–3
Stock options
● LO19–2

Under its executive stock option plan, National Corporation granted 12 million options on January 1, 2021, that permit executives to purchase 12 million of the company's $1 par common shares within the next six years, but not before December 31, 2023 (the vesting date). The exercise price is the market price of the shares on the date of grant, $17 per share. The fair value of the options, estimated by an appropriate option pricing model, is $5 per option. No forfeitures are anticipated. Ignoring taxes, what is the total compensation cost pertaining to the stock options? What is the effect on earnings in the year after the options are granted to executives?

BE 19–4
Stock options; forfeiture
● LO19–2

Refer to the situation described in BE 19–3. Suppose that unexpected turnover during 2022 caused the forfeiture of 5% of the stock options. What is the effect on earnings in 2022? In 2023?

BE 19–5
Stock options; forfeitures
● LO19–2

On January 1, 2021, Hugh Morris Comedy Club (HMCC) granted 1 million stock options to key executives exercisable for 1 million shares of the company's common stock at $20 per share. The stock options are intended as compensation for the next three years. The options are exercisable within a four-year period beginning January 1, 2024, by the executives still in the employ of the company. No options were terminated during 2021. The market price of the common stock was $25 per share at the date of the grant. HMCC estimated the fair value of the options at $9 each. One percent of the options are forfeited during 2022 due to executive turnover. What amount should HMCC record as compensation expense for the year ended December 31, 2022, assuming HMCC chooses the option to record forfeitures as they actually occur?

BE 19–6
Stock options; exercise
● LO19–2

Refer to the situation described in BE 19–3. Suppose that the options are exercised on April 3, 2024, when the market price is $19 per share. What journal entry will National record?

BE 19–7
Stock options; expiration
● LO19–2

Refer to the situation described in BE 19–3. Suppose that the options expire without being exercised. What journal entry will National record?

BE 19–8
Performance-based options
● LO19–2

On January 1, 2021, Farmer Fabrication issued stock options for 100,000 shares to a division manager. The options have an estimated fair value of $6 each. To provide additional incentive for managerial achievement, the options are not exercisable unless divisional revenue increases by 5% in three years. Farmer initially estimates that it is probable the goal will be achieved. How much compensation will be recorded in 2021, 2022, 2023?

BE 19–9
Performance-based options
● LO19–2

Refer to the situation described in BE 19–8. Suppose that after one year, Farmer estimates that it is *not* probable that divisional revenue will increase by 5% in three years. What journal entry will be needed to account for the options in 2022?

BE 19–10
Performance-based options
● LO19–2

Refer to the situation described in BE 19–8. Suppose that Farmer initially estimates that it is *not* probable the goal will be achieved, but then after one year, Farmer estimates that it *is* probable that divisional revenue will increase by 5% by the end of 2023. What journal entry(s) will Farmer record to account for the options in 2022 and thereafter?

BE 19–11
Options with market-based conditions
● LO19–2

On January 1, 2021, Farmer Fabrication issued stock options for 100,000 shares to a division manager. The options have an estimated fair value of $6 each. To provide additional incentive for managerial achievement, the options are not exercisable unless Farmer Fabrication's stock price increases by 5% in three years. Farmer initially estimates that it is not probable the goal will be achieved. How much compensation will be recorded in 2021, 2022, and 2023?

BE 19–12
EPS; shares issued; shares retired
● LO19–5, LO19–6

McDonnell-Myer Corporation reported net income of $741 million. The company had 544 million common shares outstanding at January 1 and sold 36 million shares on February 28. As part of an annual share repurchase plan, 6 million shares were retired on April 30 for $47 per share. Calculate McDonnell-Myer's earnings per share for the year.

BE 19–13
EPS; nonconvertible preferred shares
● LO19–7

At December 31, 2020 and 2021, Funk & Noble Corporation had outstanding 820 million shares of common stock and 2 million shares of 8%, $100 par value cumulative preferred stock. No dividends were declared on either the preferred or common stock in 2020 or 2021. Net income for 2021 was $426 million. The income tax rate is 25%. Calculate earnings per share for the year ended December 31, 2021.

BE 19–14
EPS; stock options
● LO19–8

Fully vested incentive stock options exercisable at $50 per share to obtain 24,000 shares of common stock were outstanding during a period when the average market price of the common stock was $60 and the ending market price was $60. What will be the net increase in the weighted-average number of shares outstanding due to the assumed exercise of these options when calculating diluted earnings per share?

BE 19–15
EPS; convertible preferred shares
● LO19–9

Ahnberg Corporation had 800,000 shares of common stock issued and outstanding at January 1. No common shares were issued during the year, but on January 1, Ahnberg issued 100,000 shares of convertible preferred stock. The preferred shares are convertible into 200,000 shares of common stock. During the year Ahnberg paid $60,000 cash dividends on the preferred stock. Net income was $1,500,000. What were Ahnberg's basic and diluted earnings per share for the year?

BE 19–16
EPS; restricted stock award
● LO19–11

Niles Company granted 9 million of its no par common shares to executives, subject to forfeiture if employment is terminated within three years. The common shares have a market price of $5 per share on January 1, 2020, the grant date of the restricted stock award. When calculating diluted EPS at December 31, 2021, what will be the net increase in the weighted-average number of shares outstanding if the market price of the common shares averaged $5 per share during 2021?

Exercises

E 19–1
Restricted stock award plan
● LO19–1

Allied Paper Products, Inc., offers a restricted stock award plan to its vice presidents. On January 1, 2021, the company granted 16 million of its $1 par common shares, subject to forfeiture if employment is terminated within two years. The common shares have a market price of $5 per share on the grant date.

Required:
1. Determine the total compensation cost pertaining to the restricted shares.
2. Prepare the appropriate journal entries related to the restricted stock through December 31, 2022.

E 19–2
Restricted stock units
● LO19–1

On January 1, 2021, Tru Fashions Corporation awarded restricted stock units (RSUs) representing 12 million of its $1 par common shares to key personnel, subject to forfeiture if employment is terminated within three years. After the recipients of the RSUs satisfy the vesting requirement, the company will distribute the shares. On the grant date, the shares had a market price of $2.50 per share.

Required:
1. Determine the total compensation cost pertaining to the RSUs.
2. Prepare the appropriate journal entry to record the award of RSUs on January 1, 2021.
3. Prepare the appropriate journal entry to record compensation expense on December 31, 2021.
4. Prepare the appropriate journal entry to record compensation expense on December 31, 2022.
5. Prepare the appropriate journal entry to record compensation expense on December 31, 2023.
6. Prepare the appropriate journal entry to record the lifting of restrictions on the RSUs and issuing shares at December 31, 2023.

E 19–3
Restricted stock
units; Facebook
● LO19–1

Real World Financials

Facebook Inc. included the following disclosure note in an annual report:

> **Share-Based Compensation (in part)**
> . . . compensation expense related to these grants is based on the grant date fair value of the RSUs and is recognized on a straight-line basis over the applicable service period.
>
> **The following table summarizes the activities for our unvested RSUs for the year ended December 31, 2017:**
>
> | | Number of Shares | Weighted Average Grant Date Fair Value |
> |---|---|---|
> | Unvested at December 31, 2016 | 98,586 | $ 82.99 |
> | Granted | 36,741 | 147.28 |
> | Vested | (43,176) | 83.74 |
> | Forfeited | (10,937) | 91.76 |
> | Unvested at December 31, 2017 | 81,214 | $110.49 |

Required:
1. Assuming a four-year vesting period, how much compensation expense did Facebook report in the year ended December 31, 2018, for the restricted stock units granted during the year ended December 31, 2017? (Round dollar amounts to the nearest million.)
2. Based on the information provided in the disclosure note, prepare the journal entry that summarizes the vesting of RSUs during the year ended December 31, 2017. (Facebook's common shares have a par amount per share of $0.000006. Round dollar amounts to the nearest million.)

Source: Facebook

E 19–4
Restricted stock
units; forfeitures
anticipated
● LO19–1

Magnetic-Optical Corporation offers a variety of share-based compensation plans to employees. Under its restricted stock unit plan, the company on January 1, 2021, granted restricted stock units (RSUs) representing 4 million of its $1 par common shares to various division managers. The shares are subject to forfeiture if employment is terminated within three years. The common shares have a market price of $22.50 per share on the grant date. Management's policy is to estimate forfeitures.

Required:
1. Determine the total compensation cost pertaining to the RSUs.
2. Prepare the appropriate journal entry to record the RSUs on January 1, 2021.
3. Prepare the appropriate journal entry to record compensation expense on December 31, 2021.
4. Suppose Magnetic-Optical expected a 10% forfeiture rate on the RSUs prior to vesting. Determine the total compensation cost.

E 19–5
Restricted stock
units; forfeitures
● LO19–1

On January 1, 2021, David Mest Communications granted restricted stock units (RSUs) representing 30 million of its $1 par common shares to executives, subject to forfeiture if employment is terminated within three years. After the recipients of the RSUs satisfy the vesting requirement, the company will distribute the shares. The common shares had a market price of $12 per share on the grant date. At the date of grant, Mest anticipated that 6% of the recipients would leave the firm prior to vesting. On January 1, 2022, 5% of the RSUs are forfeited due to executive turnover. Mest chooses the option to account for forfeitures when they actually occur.

Required:
1. Prepare the appropriate journal entry to record compensation expense on December 31, 2021.
2. Prepare the appropriate journal entry to record compensation expense on December 31, 2022.
3. Prepare the appropriate journal entry to record compensation expense on December 31, 2023.

E 19–6
Stock options
● LO19–2

Heidi Software Corporation provides a variety of share-based compensation plans to its employees. Under its executive stock option plan, the company granted options on January 1, 2021, that permit executives to acquire 4 million of the company's $1 par common shares within the next five years, but not before December 31, 2022 (the vesting date). The exercise price is the market price of the shares on the date of grant, $14 per share. The fair value of the 4 million options, estimated by an appropriate option pricing model, is $3 per option. No forfeitures are anticipated. Ignore taxes.

Required:
1. Determine the total compensation cost pertaining to the options.
2. Prepare the appropriate journal entry to record the award of options on January 1, 2021.

3. Prepare the appropriate journal entry to record compensation expense on December 31, 2021.

4. Prepare the appropriate journal entry to record compensation expense on December 31, 2022.

E 19–7
Stock options;
forfeiture of
options
● LO19–2

On January 1, 2021, Adams-Meneke Corporation granted 25 million incentive stock options to division managers, each permitting holders to purchase one share of the company's $1 par common shares within the next six years, but not before December 31, 2023 (the vesting date). The exercise price is the market price of the shares on the date of grant, currently $10 per share. The fair value of the options, estimated by an appropriate option pricing model, is $3 per option. Management's policy is to estimate forfeitures. No forfeitures are anticipated. Ignore taxes.

Required:

1. Determine the total compensation cost pertaining to the options on January 1, 2021.

2. Prepare the appropriate journal entry to record compensation expense on December 31, 2021.

3. Unexpected turnover during 2022 caused an estimate of the forfeiture of 6% of the stock options. Prepare the appropriate journal entry(s) on December 31, 2022 and 2023 in response to the new estimate.

E 19–8
Stock options
exercise;
expirations
● LO19–2

Walters Audio Visual Inc. offers an incentive stock option plan to its regional managers. On January 1, 2021, options were granted for 40 million $1 par common shares. The exercise price is the market price on the grant date—$8 per share. Options cannot be exercised prior to January 1, 2023, and expire December 31, 2027. The fair value of the 40 million options, estimated by an appropriate option pricing model, is $1 per option.

Required:

1. Determine the total compensation cost pertaining to the incentive stock option plan.

2. Prepare the appropriate journal entry to record compensation expense on December 31, 2021.

3. Prepare the appropriate journal entry to record compensation expense on December 31, 2022.

4. Prepare the appropriate journal entry to record the exercise of 75% of the options on March 12, 2023, when the market price is $9 per share.

5. Prepare the appropriate journal entry on December 31, 2027, when the remaining options that have vested expire without being exercised.

E 19–9
Stock options;
exercise
● LO19–2

SSG Cycles manufactures and distributes motorcycle parts and supplies. Employees are offered a variety of share-based compensation plans. Under its nonqualified stock option plan, SSG granted options to key officers on January 1, 2021. The options permit holders to acquire 12 million of the company's $1 par common shares for $11 within the next six years, but not before January 1, 2024 (the vesting date). The market price of the shares on the date of grant is $13 per share. The fair value of the 12 million options, estimated by an appropriate option pricing model, is $3 per option.

Required:

1. Determine the total compensation cost pertaining to the incentive stock option plan.

2. Prepare the appropriate journal entries to record compensation expense on December 31, 2021, 2022, and 2023.

3. Record the exercise of the options if all of the options are exercised on May 11, 2025, when the market price is $14 per share.

E 19–10
Employee share
purchase plan
● LO19–3

In order to encourage employee ownership of the company's $1 par common shares, Washington Distribution permits any of its employees to buy shares directly from the company through payroll deduction. There are no brokerage fees and shares can be purchased at a 15% discount. During March, employees purchased 50,000 shares at a time when the market price of the shares on the New York Stock Exchange was $12 per share.

Required:

Prepare the appropriate journal entry to record the March purchases of shares under the employee share purchase plan.

E 19–11
Employee share
purchase plan;
Tesla Motors
● LO19–3
Real World Financials

Tesla Motors's disclosure notes for the year ending December 31, 2017, included the following regarding its $0.001 par common stock:

EMPLOYEE STOCK PURCHASE PLAN—Our employees are eligible to purchase our common stock through payroll deductions of up to 15% of their eligible compensation, subject to any plan limitations. The purchase price would be 85% of the lower of the fair market value on the first and last trading days of each six-month offering period. During the years ended December 31, 2017, 2016, and 2015, we issued 370,173, 321,788, and 220,571 shares under the ESPP for $71.0 million, $51.7 million, and $37.5 million, respectively. There were 1,423,978 shares available for issuance under the ESPP as of December 31, 2017.

Required:

Prepare the journal entry that summarizes Tesla's employee share purchases for the year ending December 31, 2017.

Source: Tesla Motors

E 19–12
EPS; shares issued; stock dividend
● LO19–5, LO19–6

For the year ended December 31, 2021, Norstar Industries reported net income of $655,000. At January 1, 2021, the company had 900,000 common shares outstanding. The following changes in the number of shares occurred during 2021:

Apr. 30   Sold 60,000 shares in a public offering
May 24   Declared and distributed a 5% stock dividend
June 1   Issued 72,000 shares as part of the consideration for the purchase of assets from a subsidiary

Required:

Compute Norstar's earnings per share for the year ended December 31, 2021.

E 19–13
EPS; treasury stock; new shares; stock dividends; two years
● LO19–5, LO19–6

The Alford Group had 202,000 shares of common stock outstanding at January 1, 2021. The following activities affected common shares during the year. There are no potential common shares outstanding.

2021
Feb. 28   Purchased 6,000 shares of treasury stock.
Oct. 31   Sold the treasury shares purchased on February 28.
Nov. 30   Issued 24,000 new shares.
Dec. 31   Net income for 2021 is $400,000.

2022
Jan. 15   Declared and issued a 2-for-1 stock split.
Dec. 31   Net income for 2022 is $400,000.

Required:

1. Determine the 2021 EPS.
2. Determine the 2022 EPS.
3. At what amount will the 2021 EPS be presented in the 2022 comparative financial statements?

E 19–14
EPS; stock dividend; nonconvertible preferred stock
● LO19–5, LO19–6, LO19–7

Hardaway Fixtures' balance sheet at December 31, 2020, included the following:

Shares issued and outstanding:	
Common stock, $1 par	$800,000
Nonconvertible preferred stock, $50 par	20,000

On July 21, 2021, Hardaway issued a 25% stock dividend on its common stock. On December 12, it paid $50,000 cash dividends on the preferred stock. Net income for the year ended December 31, 2021, was $2,000,000.

Required:

Compute Hardaway's earnings per share for the year ended December 31, 2021.

E 19–15
EPS; net loss; nonconvertible preferred stock; shares sold
● LO19–5, LO19–6, LO19–7

At December 31, 2020, Albrecht Corporation had outstanding 373,000 shares of common stock and 8,000 shares of 9.5%, $100 par value cumulative, nonconvertible preferred stock. On May 31, 2021, Albrecht sold for cash 12,000 shares of its common stock. No cash dividends were declared for 2021. For the year ended December 31, 2021, Albrecht reported a net loss of $114,000.

Required:

Calculate Albrecht's net loss per share for the year ended December 31, 2021.

E 19–16
EPS; stock dividend; nonconvertible preferred stock; treasury shares; shares sold
● LO19–5, LO19–6, LO19–7

On December 31, 2020, Berclair Inc. had 200 million shares of common stock and 3 million shares of 9%, $100 par value cumulative preferred stock issued and outstanding. On March 1, 2021, Berclair purchased 24 million shares of its common stock as treasury stock. Berclair issued a 5% common stock dividend on July 1, 2021. Four million treasury shares were sold on October 1. Net income for the year ended December 31, 2021, was $150 million.

Required:

Compute Berclair's earnings per share for the year ended December 31, 2021.

E 19–17
EPS; stock dividend; nonconvertible preferred stock; treasury shares; shares sold; stock options
● LO19–5 through LO19–8

(Note: This is a variation of E 19–16, modified to include stock options.) On December 31, 2020, Berclair Inc. had 200 million shares of common stock and 3 million shares of 9%, $100 par value cumulative preferred stock issued and outstanding. On March 1, 2021, Berclair purchased 24 million shares of its common stock as treasury stock. Berclair issued a 5% common stock dividend on July 1, 2021. Four million treasury shares were sold on October 1. Net income for the year ended December 31, 2021, was $150 million.

Also outstanding at December 31 were 30 million incentive stock options granted to key executives on September 13, 2016. The options were exercisable as of September 13, 2020, for 30 million common shares at an exercise price of $56 per share. During 2021, the market price of the common shares averaged $70 per share.

Required:
Compute Berclair's basic and diluted earnings per share for the year ended December 31, 2021.

E 19–18
EPS; stock dividend; nonconvertible preferred stock; treasury shares; shares sold; stock options exercised
● LO19–5 through LO19–8

(Note: This is a variation of E 19–16, modified to include the exercise of stock options.)

On December 31, 2020, Berclair Inc. had 200 million shares of common stock and 3 million shares of 9%, $100 par value cumulative preferred stock issued and outstanding. On March 1, 2021, Berclair purchased 24 million shares of its common stock as treasury stock. Berclair issued a 5% common stock dividend on July 1, 2021. Four million treasury shares were sold on October 1. Net income for the year ended December 31, 2021, was $150 million.

Also outstanding at December 31 were 30 million incentive stock options granted to key executives on September 13, 2016. The options were exercisable as of September 13, 2020, for 30 million common shares at an exercise price of $56 per share. During 2021, the market price of the common shares averaged $70 per share.

The options were exercised on September 1, 2021.

Required:
Compute Berclair's basic and diluted earnings per share for the year ended December 31, 2021.

E 19–19
EPS; stock dividend; nonconvertible preferred stock; treasury shares; shares sold; stock options; convertible bonds
● LO19–5 through LO19–9

(Note: This is a variation of E 19–17 modified to include convertible bonds).

On December 31, 2020, Berclair Inc. had 200 million shares of common stock and 3 million shares of 9%, $100 par value cumulative preferred stock issued and outstanding. On March 1, 2021, Berclair purchased 24 million shares of its common stock as treasury stock. Berclair issued a 5% common stock dividend on July 1, 2021. Four million treasury shares were sold on October 1. Net income for the year ended December 31, 2021, was $150 million. The income tax rate is 25%.

Also outstanding at December 31 were incentive stock options granted to key executives on September 13, 2016. The options are exercisable as of September 13, 2020, for 30 million common shares at an exercise price of $56 per share. During 2021, the market price of the common shares averaged $70 per share.

In 2017, $50 million of 8% bonds, convertible into 6 million common shares, were issued at face value.

Required:
Compute Berclair's basic and diluted earnings per share for the year ended December 31, 2021.

E 19–20
EPS; shares issued; stock options
● LO19–6 through LO19–9

Stanley Department Stores reported net income of $720,000 for the year ended December 31, 2021.

Additional Information:

Common shares outstanding at Jan. 1, 2021	80,000
Incentive stock options (vested in 2020) outstanding throughout 2021	24,000
(Each option is exercisable for one common share at an exercise price of $37.50.)	
During the year, the market price of Stanley's common stock averaged $45 per share.	
On Aug. 30, Stanley sold 15,000 common shares.	
Stanley's only debt consisted of $50,000 of 10% short-term bank notes.	
The company's income tax rate is 25%.	

Required:
Compute Stanley's basic and diluted earnings per share for the year ended December 31, 2021.

E 19–21
EPS; convertible preferred stock; convertible bonds; order of entry
● LO19–7, LO19–9

Information from the financial statements of Ames Fabricators, Inc., included the following:

	December 31	
	2021	**2020**
Common shares	100,000	100,000
Convertible preferred shares (convertible into 32,000 shares of common)	12,000	12,000
8% convertible bonds (convertible into 30,000 shares of common)	$1,000,000	$1,000,000

Ames's net income for the year ended December 31, 2021, is $500,000. The income tax rate is 25%. Ames paid dividends of $5 per share on its preferred stock during 2021.

1154   SECTION 4   Additional Financial Reporting Issues

Compute basic and diluted earnings per share for the year ended December 31, 2021.

E 19–22
EPS; restricted stock
● LO19–11

As part of its executive compensation plan, Vertovec Inc. granted 54,000 of its no-par common shares to executives, subject to forfeiture if employment is terminated within three years. Vertovec's common shares have a market price of $5 per share on January 1, 2020, the grant date of the restricted stock award, as well as on December 31, 2021. 800,000 shares were outstanding at January 1, 2021. Net income for 2021 was $120,000.

Required:
Compute Vertovec's basic and diluted earnings per share for the year ended December 31, 2021.

E 19–23
Record restricted stock; effect on EPS
● LO19–1, LO19–11

PHN Foods granted 18 million of its no-par common shares to executives, subject to forfeiture if employment is terminated within three years. The common shares have a market price of $5 per share on January 1, 2020, the grant date.

Required:
1. What journal entry will PHN Foods prepare to record executive compensation regarding these restricted shares at December 31, 2020 and December 31, 2021?
2. When calculating diluted EPS at December 31, 2021, what will be the net increase in the weighted average number of common shares with regard to the restricted stock shares if the market price of the common shares averages $5 per share during 2021?

E 19–24
New shares; contingently issuable shares
● LO19–6, LO19–12

During 2021, its first year of operations, McCollum Tool Works entered into the following transactions relating to shareholders' equity. The corporation was authorized to issue 100 million common shares, $1 par per share.

Jan.	2	Issued 35 million common shares for cash.
	3	Entered an agreement with the company president to issue up to 2 million additional shares of common stock in 2022 based on the earnings of McCollum in 2022. If net income exceeds $140 million, the president will receive 1 million shares; 2 million shares if net income exceeds $150 million.
Mar.	31	Issued 4 million shares in exchange for plant facilities.

Net income for 2021 was $148 million.

Required:
Compute basic and diluted earnings per share for the year ended December 31, 2021.

E 19–25
EPS; new shares; contingent agreements
● LO19–6, LO19–12

Anderson Steel Company began 2021 with 600,000 shares of common stock outstanding. On March 31, 2021, 100,000 new shares were sold at a price of $45 per share. The market price has risen steadily since that time to a high of $50 per share at December 31. No other changes in shares occurred during 2021, and no securities are outstanding that can become common stock. However, there are two agreements with officers of the company for future issuance of common stock. Both agreements relate to compensation arrangements reached in 2020. The first agreement grants to the company president a right to 10,000 shares of stock each year the closing market price is at least $48. The agreement begins in 2022 and expires in 2025. The second agreement grants to the controller a right to 15,000 shares of stock if she is still with the firm at the end of 2029. Net income for 2021 was $2,000,000.

Required:
Compute Anderson Steel Company's basic and diluted EPS for the year ended December 31, 2021.

E 19–26
EPS; concepts; terminology
● LO19–5 through LO19–13

Listed below are several terms and phrases associated with earnings per share. Pair each item from List A with the item from List B (by letter) that is most appropriately associated with it.

List A	List B
_____ 1. Subtract preferred dividends.	a. Options exercised.
_____ 2. Time-weighted by $^5/_{12}$.	b. Simple capital structure.
_____ 3. Time-weighted shares assumed issued plus time-weighted actual shares.	c. Basic EPS.
	d. Convertible preferred stock.
_____ 4. Midyear event treated as if it occurred at the beginning of the reporting period.	e. Earnings available to common shareholders.
	f. Antidilutive.
_____ 5. Preferred dividends do not reduce earnings.	g. Increased marketability.
_____ 6. Single EPS presentation.	h. Discontinued operations.
_____ 7. Stock split.	i. Stock dividend.
_____ 8. Potential common shares.	j. Add after-tax interest to numerator.
_____ 9. Exercise price exceeds market price.	k. Diluted EPS.
_____ 10. No dilution assumed.	l. Noncumulative, undeclared preferred dividends.

(continued)

(concluded)

List A	List B
_____ 11. Convertible bonds.	m. Common shares retired at the beginning of August.
_____ 12. Contingently issuable shares.	
_____ 13. Maximum potential dilution.	n. Include in diluted EPS when conditions for issuance are met.
_____ 14. Shown between per share amounts for net income and for income from continuing operations.	

E 19–27
FASB codification research

● LO19–2

The *FASB Accounting Standards Codification* represents the single source of authoritative U.S. generally accepted accounting principles. Obtain the relevant authoritative literature on stock compensation using the *FASB Accounting Standards Codification* at the FASB website (www.fasb.org).

Required:

1. What is the specific seven-digit Codification citation (XXX-XX-XX) that describes the information that companies must disclose about the exercise prices for their stock option plans?

2. List the disclosure requirements.

E 19–28
FASB codification research

● LO19–2, LO19–3, LO19–7, LO19–13

Access the *FASB Accounting Standards Codification* at the FASB website (www.fasb.org). Determine the specific seven-, eight-, or nine-digit Codification citation (XXX-XX-XX-X) for accounting for each of the following items:

1. Initial measurement of stock options.

2. The measurement date for share-based payments classified as liabilities.

3. The formula to calculate diluted earnings per share.

4. The way stock dividends or stock splits in the current year affect the presentation of EPS in the income statement.

E 19–29
Stock appreciation rights; settlement in shares

● Appendix 19B

As part of its stock-based compensation package, International Electronics (IE) granted 24 million stock appreciation rights (SARs) to top officers on January 1, 2021. At exercise, holders of the SARs are entitled to receive stock equal in value to the excess of the market price at exercise over the share price at the date of grant. The SARs cannot be exercised until the end of 2024 (vesting date) and expire at the end of 2026. The $1 par common shares have a market price of $46 per share on the grant date. The fair value of the SARs, estimated by an appropriate option pricing model, is $3 per SAR at January 1, 2021. The fair value re-estimated at December 31, 2021, 2022, 2023, 2024, and 2025, is $4, $3, $4, $2.50, and $3, respectively. All recipients are expected to remain employed through the vesting date.

Required:

1. Prepare any appropriate journal entry to record the award of SARs on January 1, 2021. Will the SARs be reported as debt or as equity?

2. Prepare the appropriate journal entries pertaining to the SARs on December 31, 2021–December 31, 2024.

3. The SARs remain unexercised on December 31, 2025. Prepare the appropriate journal entry on that date.

4. The SARs are exercised on June 6, 2026, when the share price is $50. Prepare the appropriate journal entry(s) on that date.

E 19–30
Stock appreciation rights; cash settlement

● Appendix 19B

(Note: This is a variation of E 19–29, modified to allow settlement in cash.)

As part of its stock-based compensation package, International Electronics granted 24 million stock appreciation rights (SARs) to top officers on January 1, 2021. At exercise, holders of the SARs are entitled to receive cash or stock equal in value to the excess of the market price at exercise over the share price at the date of grant. The SARs cannot be exercised until the end of 2024 (vesting date) and expire at the end of 2026. The $1 par common shares have a market price of $46 per share on the grant date. The fair value of the SARs, estimated by an appropriate option pricing model, is $3 per SAR at January 1, 2021. The fair value re-estimated at December 31, 2021, 2022, 2023, 2024, and 2025, is $4, $3, $4, $2.50, and $3, respectively. All recipients are expected to remain employed through the vesting date.

Required:

1. Prepare any appropriate journal entry to record the award of SARs on January 1, 2021.

2. Prepare the appropriate journal entries pertaining to the SARs on December 31, 2021–December 31, 2024.

3. The SARs remain unexercised on December 31, 2025. Prepare the appropriate journal entry on that date.

4. The SARs are exercised on June 6, 2026, when the share price is $50, and executives choose to receive the market price appreciation in cash. Prepare the appropriate journal entry(s) on that date.

1156 SECTION 4   Additional Financial Reporting Issues

E 19–31
Restricted stock units; cash settlement
● Appendix 19B

As part of its stock-based compensation package, on January 1, 2021, International Electronics granted restricted stock units (RSUs) representing 50 million $1 par common shares. At exercise, holders of the RSUs are entitled to receive cash or stock equal in value to the market price of those shares at exercise. The RSUs cannot be exercised until the end of 2024 (vesting date) and expire at the end of 2026. The $1 par common shares have a market price of $6 per share on the grant date. The fair value at December 31, 2021, 2022, 2023, 2024, and 2025, is $8, $6, $8, $5, and $6, respectively. All recipients are expected to remain employed through the vesting date. After the recipients of the RSUs satisfy the vesting requirement, the company will distribute the shares.

Required:
1. Prepare any appropriate journal entry to record the award of RSUs on January 1, 2021.
2. Prepare the appropriate journal entries pertaining to the RSUs on December 31, 2021–December 31, 2024.
3. The RSUs remain unexercised on December 31, 2025. Prepare the appropriate journal entry on that date.
4. The RSUs are exercised on June 6, 2026, when the share price is $6.50, and executives choose to receive cash. Prepare the appropriate journal entry(s) on that date.

Problems

P 19–1
Stock options; forfeiture; exercise
● LO19–2

On October 15, 2020, the board of directors of Ensor Materials Corporation approved a stock option plan for key executives. On January 1, 2021, 20 million stock options were granted, exercisable for 20 million shares of Ensor's $1 par common stock. The options are exercisable between January 1, 2024, and December 31, 2026, at 80% of the quoted market price on January 1, 2021, which was $15. The fair value of the 20 million options, estimated by an appropriate option pricing model, is $6 per option. Ensor chooses the option to recognize forfeitures only when they occur.

Ten percent (2 million) of the options were forfeited when an executive resigned in 2022. All other options were exercised on July 12, 2025, when the stock's price jumped unexpectedly to $19 per share.

Required:
1. When is Ensor's stock option measurement date?
2. Determine the compensation expense for the stock option plan in 2021. (Ignore taxes.)
3. Prepare the journal entries to reflect the effect of forfeiture of the stock options on Ensor's financial statements for 2022 and 2023.
4. Is this effect consistent with the general approach for accounting for changes in estimates? Explain.
5. Prepare the journal entry to account for the exercise of the options in 2025.

P 19–2
Stock options; graded vesting
● LO19–2

Pastner Brands is a calendar-year firm with operations in several countries. As part of its executive compensation plan, at January 1, 2021, the company issued 400,000 executive stock options permitting executives to buy 400,000 shares of Pastner stock for $34 per share. One-fourth of the options vest in each of the next four years beginning at December 31, 2021 (graded vesting). Pastner elects to separate the total award into four groups (or tranches) according to the year in which they vest and measures the compensation cost for each vesting date as a separate award. The fair value of each tranche is estimated at January 1, 2021, as follows:

Vesting Date	Amount Vesting	Fair Value per Option
Dec. 31, 2021	25%	$3.50
Dec. 31, 2022	25%	$4.00
Dec. 31, 2023	25%	$4.50
Dec. 31, 2024	25%	$5.00

Required:
1. Determine the compensation expense related to the options to be recorded each year 2021–2024, assuming Pastner allocates the compensation cost for each of the four groups (tranches) separately.
2. Determine the compensation expense related to the options to be recorded each year 2021–2024, assuming Pastner uses the straight-line method to allocate the total compensation cost.

P 19–3
Stock options; graded vesting; measurement using a single fair value per option
● LO19–2

Refer to the situation described in P 19–2. Assume Pastner measures the fair value of all options on January 1, 2021, to be $4.50 per option using a single weighted-average expected life of the options assumption.

Required:

1. Determine the compensation expense related to the options to be recorded each year 2021–2024, assuming Pastner allocates the compensation cost for each of the four groups (tranches) separately.

2. Determine the compensation expense related to the options to be recorded each year 2021–2024, assuming Pastner uses the straight-line method to allocate the total compensation cost.

P 19–4
Stock options;
graded vesting;
IFRS
● LO19–2, LO19–14

 IFRS

Refer to the situation described in P 19–2. Assume Pastner prepares its financial statements using International Financial Reporting Standards (IFRS).

Required:
Would your responses to *requirement* 1 and *requirement* 2 be the same using IFRS?

P 19–5
Stock option
plan; deferred tax
effect recognized
● LO19–2

Walters Audio Visual, Inc., offers a stock option plan to its regional managers. On January 1, 2021, 40 million options were granted for 40 million $1 par common shares. The exercise price is the market price on the grant date, $8 per share. Options cannot be exercised prior to January 1, 2023, and expire December 31, 2027. The fair value of the options, estimated by an appropriate option pricing model, is $2 per option. Because the plan does not qualify as an incentive plan, Walters will receive a tax deduction upon exercise of the options equal to the excess of the market price at exercise over the exercise price. The income tax rate is 25%.

Required:

1. Determine the total compensation cost pertaining to the stock option plan.

2. Prepare the appropriate journal entries to record compensation expense and its tax effect on December 31, 2021.

3. Prepare the appropriate journal entries to record compensation expense and its tax effect on December 31, 2022.

4. Record the exercise of the options and their tax effect if *all* of the options are exercised on March 20, 2026, when the market price is $12 per share.

5. Assume the option plan qualifies as an incentive plan. Prepare the appropriate journal entries to record compensation expense and its tax effect on December 31, 2021.

6. Assuming the option plan qualifies as an incentive plan, record the exercise of the options and their tax effect if *all* of the options are exercised on March 20, 2026, when the market price is $11 per share.

P 19–6
Stock option
plan; deferred
tax effect of a
nonqualifying
plan
● LO19–2

JBL Aircraft manufactures and distributes aircraft parts and supplies. Employees are offered a variety of share-based compensation plans. Under its nonqualified stock option plan, JBL granted options to key officers on January 1, 2021. The options permit holders to acquire 6 million of the company's $1 par common shares for $22 within the next six years, but not before January 1, 2024 (the vesting date). The market price of the shares on the date of grant is $26 per share. The fair value of the 6 million options, estimated by an appropriate option pricing model, is $6 per option. Because the plan does not qualify as an incentive plan, JBL will receive a tax deduction upon exercise of the options equal to the excess of the market price at exercise over the exercise price. The tax rate is 25%.

Required:

1. Determine the total compensation cost pertaining to the incentive stock option plan.

2. Prepare the appropriate journal entries to record compensation expense and its tax effect on December 31, 2021, 2022, and 2023.

3. Record the exercise of the options and their tax effect if *all* of the options are exercised on August 21, 2025, when the market price is $27 per share.

P 19–7
Performance
option plan
● LO19–2

LCI Cable Company grants 1 million performance stock options to key executives at January 1, 2021. The options entitle executives to receive 1 million of LCI $1 par common shares, subject to the achievement of specific financial goals over the next four years. Attainment of these goals is considered probable initially and throughout the service period. The options have a current fair value of $12 per option.

Required:

1. Prepare the appropriate entry when the options are awarded on January 1, 2021.

2. Prepare the appropriate entries on December 31 of each year 2021–2024.

3. Suppose at the beginning of 2023, LCI decided it is not probable that the performance objectives will be met. Prepare the appropriate entries on December 31 of 2023 and 2024.

1158   SECTION 4   Additional Financial Reporting Issues

P 19–8
Net loss; stock dividend; nonconvertible preferred stock; treasury shares; shares sold; discontinued operations
● LO19–5 through LO19–7, LO19–13

On December 31, 2020, Ainsworth, Inc., had 600 million shares of common stock outstanding. Twenty million shares of 8%, $100 par value cumulative, nonconvertible preferred stock were sold on January 2, 2021. On April 30, 2021, Ainsworth purchased 30 million shares of its common stock as treasury stock. Twelve million treasury shares were sold on August 31. Ainsworth issued a 5% common stock dividend on June 12, 2021. No cash dividends were declared in 2021. For the year ended December 31, 2021, Ainsworth reported a net loss of $140 million, including an after-tax loss from discontinued operations of $400 million.

Required:
1. Determine Ainsworth's net loss per share for the year ended December 31, 2021.
2. Determine the per share amount of income or loss from continuing operations for the year ended December 31, 2021.
3. Prepare an EPS presentation that would be appropriate to appear on Ainsworth's 2021 and 2020 comparative income statements. Assume EPS was reported in 2020 as $0.75, based on net income (no discontinued operations) of $450 million and a weighted-average number of common shares of 600 million.

P 19–9
EPS from statement of retained earnings
● LO19–4 through LO19–6

(Note: This problem is based on the same situation described in P 18–4 in Chapter 18, modified to focus on EPS rather than recording the events that affected retained earnings.)

Comparative Statements of Retained Earnings for Renn-Dever Corporation were reported as follows for the fiscal years ending December 31, 2019, 2020, and 2021.

RENN-DEVER CORPORATION
Statements of Retained Earnings

	For the Years Ended December 31		
	2021	**2020**	**2019**
Balance at beginning of year	$6,794,292	$5,464,052	$5,624,552
Net income (loss)	3,308,700	2,240,900	(160,500)
Deductions:			
Stock dividend (34,900 shares)	242,000		
Common shares retired, September 30 (110,000 shares)		212,660	
Common stock cash dividends	889,950	698,000	0
Balance at end of year	$8,971,042	$6,794,292	$5,464,052

At December 31, 2018, paid-in capital consisted of the following:

Common stock, 1,855,000 shares at $1 par	$1,855,000
Paid in capital—excess of par	7,420,000

No preferred stock or potential common shares were outstanding during any of the periods shown.

Required:
Compute Renn-Dever's earnings per share as it would have appeared in income statements for the years ended December 31, 2019, 2020, and 2021.

P 19–10
EPS from statement of shareholders' equity
● LO19–4 through LO19–6

Comparative Statements of Shareholders' Equity for Locke Intertechnology Corporation were reported as follows for the fiscal years ending December 31, 2019, 2020, and 2021.

LOCKE INTERTECHNOLOGY CORPORATION
Statements of Shareholders' Equity
For the Years Ended Dec. 31, 2019, 2020, and 2021
($ in millions)

	Preferred Stock, $10 par	Common Stock, $1 par	Additional Paid-in Capital	Retained Earnings	Total Shareholders' Equity
Balance at January 1, 2019		$ 55	$ 495	$1,878	$2,428
Sale of preferred shares	10		470		480
Sale of common shares, 7/1		9	81		90
Cash dividend, preferred				(1)	(1)
Cash dividend, common				(16)	(16)
Net income				290	290
Balance at December 31, 2019	10	64	1,046	2,151	3,271
Retirement of common shares, 4/1		(4)	(36)	(20)	(60)

(continued)

(concluded)

LOCKE INTERTECHNOLOGY CORPORATION
Statements of Shareholders' Equity
For the Years Ended Dec. 31, 2019, 2020, and 2021
($ in millions)

	Preferred Stock, $10 par	Common Stock, $1 par	Additional Paid-in Capital	Retained Earnings	Total Shareholders' Equity
Cash dividend, preferred				(1)	(1)
Cash dividend, common				(20)	(20)
3-for-2 split effected in the form of a common stock dividend, 8/12		30	(30)		
Net income				380	380
Balance at December 31, 2020	10	90	980	2,490	3,570
10% common stock dividend, 5/1		9	90	(99)	
Sale of common shares, 9/1		3	31		34
Cash dividend, preferred				(2)	(2)
Cash dividend, common				(22)	(22)
Net income				412	412
Balance at December 31, 2021	$10	$102	$1,101	$2,779	$3,992

Required:
Infer from the statements the events and transactions that affected Locke Intertechnology Corporation's shareholders' equity and compute earnings per share as it would have appeared on the income statements for the years ended December 31, 2019, 2020, and 2021. No potential common shares were outstanding during any of the periods shown.

P 19–11
EPS; nonconvertible preferred stock; treasury shares; shares sold; stock dividend
● LO19–4 through LO19–7

On December 31, 2020, Dow Steel Corporation had 600,000 shares of common stock and 300,000 shares of 8%, noncumulative, nonconvertible preferred stock issued and outstanding. Dow issued a 4% common stock dividend on May 15 and paid cash dividends of $400,000 and $75,000 to common and preferred shareholders, respectively, on December 15, 2021.

On February 28, 2021, Dow sold 60,000 common shares. In keeping with its long-term share repurchase plan, 2,000 shares were retired on July 1. Dow's net income for the year ended December 31, 2021, was $2,100,000. The income tax rate is 25%.

Required:
Compute Dow's earnings per share for the year ended December 31, 2021.

P 19–12
EPS; nonconvertible preferred stock; treasury shares; shares sold; stock dividend; options
● LO19–4 through LO19–8, LO19–10

(Note: This is a variation of P 19–11, modified to include stock options.)

On December 31, 2020, Dow Steel Corporation had 600,000 shares of common stock and 300,000 shares of 8%, noncumulative, nonconvertible preferred stock issued and outstanding. Dow issued a 4% common stock dividend on May 15 and paid cash dividends of $400,000 and $75,000 to common and preferred shareholders, respectively, on December 15, 2021.

On February 28, 2021, Dow sold 60,000 common shares. In keeping with its long-term share repurchase plan, 2,000 shares were retired on July 1. Dow's net income for the year ended December 31, 2021, was $2,100,000. The income tax rate is 25%.

As part of an incentive compensation plan, Dow granted incentive stock options to division managers at December 31 of the current and each of the previous two years. Each option permits its holder to buy one share of common stock at an exercise price equal to market value at the date of grant and can be exercised one year from that date. Information concerning the number of options granted and common share prices follows:

Date Granted	Options Granted	Share Price
	(adjusted for the stock dividend)	
December 31, 2019	8,000	$24
December 31, 2020	3,000	$33
December 31, 2021	6,500	$32

The market price of the common stock averaged $32 per share during 2021.

1160   SECTION 4   Additional Financial Reporting Issues

Compute Dow's earnings per share for the year ended December 31, 2021.

P 19–13
EPS;
nonconvertible
preferred stock;
treasury shares;
shares sold; stock
dividend; options;
convertible
bonds;
contingently
issuable shares

● LO19–4 through
LO19–11

(Note: This is a variation of P 19–12, modified to include convertible bonds and contingently issuable shares.) On December 31, 2020, Dow Steel Corporation had 600,000 shares of common stock and 300,000 shares of 8%, noncumulative, nonconvertible preferred stock issued and outstanding. Dow issued a 4% common stock dividend on May 15 and paid cash dividends of $400,000 and $75,000 to common and preferred shareholders, respectively, on December 15, 2021.

On February 28, 2021, Dow sold 60,000 common shares. In keeping with its long-term share repurchase plan, 2,000 shares were retired on July 1. Dow's net income for the year ended December 31, 2021, was $2,100,000. The income tax rate is 25%. Also, as a part of a 2020 agreement for the acquisition of Merrill Cable Company, another 23,000 shares (already adjusted for the stock dividend) are to be issued to former Merrill shareholders on December 31, 2022, if Merrill's 2022 net income is at least $500,000. In 2021, Merrill's net income was $630,000.

As part of an incentive compensation plan, Dow granted incentive stock options to division managers at December 31 of the current and each of the previous two years. Each option permits its holder to buy one share of common stock at an exercise price equal to market value at the date of grant and can be exercised one year from that date. Information concerning the number of options granted and common share prices follows:

Date Granted	Options Granted	Share Price
	(adjusted for the stock dividend)	
December 31, 2019	8,000	$24
December 31, 2020	3,000	$33
December 31, 2021	6,500	$32

The market price of the common stock averaged $32 per share during 2021.

On July 12, 2019, Dow issued $800,000 of convertible 8% bonds at face value. Each $1,000 bond is convertible into 30 common shares (adjusted for the stock dividend).

Compute Dow's basic and diluted earnings per share for the year ended December 31, 2021.

P 19–14
EPS; convertible
preferred stock;
convertible
bonds; order of
entry

● LO19–7, LO19–9,
LO19–10

Information from the financial statements of Henderson-Niles Industries included the following at December 31, 2021:

Common shares outstanding throughout the year	100 million
Convertible preferred shares (convertible into 32 million shares of common)	60 million
Convertible 8% bonds (convertible into 13.5 million shares of common)	$900 million

Henderson-Niles's net income for the year ended December 31, 2021, is $520 million. The income tax rate is 25%. Henderson-Niles paid dividends of $2 per share on its preferred stock during 2021.

Compute basic and diluted earnings per share for the year ended December 31, 2021.

P 19–15
EPS; antidilution

● LO19–4 through
LO19–10,
LO19–13

Alciatore Company reported a net income of $150,000 in 2021. The weighted-average number of common shares outstanding for 2021 was 40,000. The average stock price for 2021 was $33. Assume an income tax rate of 25%.

For each of the following independent situations, indicate whether the effect of the security is antidilutive for diluted EPS.

1. 10,000 shares of 7.7% of $100 par convertible, cumulative preferred stock. Each share may be converted into two common shares.

2. 6.4% convertible 10-year, $500,000 of bonds, issued at face value. The bonds are convertible to 5,000 shares of common stock.

3. Stock options exercisable at $30 per share after January 1, 2023.

4. Warrants for 1,000 common shares with an exercise price of $35 per share.

5. A contingent agreement to issue 5,000 shares of stock to the company president if net income is at least $125,000 in 2022.

P 19–16
EPS; convertible bonds; treasury shares
● LO19–4 through LO19–6, LO19–9

At December 31, 2021, the financial statements of Hollingsworth Industries included the following:

Net income for 2021	$560 million
Bonds payable, 8%, convertible into 36 million shares of common stock	$300 million
Common stock:	
Shares outstanding on January 1	400 million
Treasury shares purchased for cash on September 1	30 million

Additional data:
The bonds payable were issued at par in 2019. The tax rate for 2021 was 25%.

Required:
Compute basic and diluted EPS for the year ended December 31, 2021.

P 19–17
EPS; options; convertible preferred; additional shares
● LO19–4 through LO19–9

On January 1, 2021, Tonge Industries had outstanding 440,000 common shares ($1 par) that originally sold for $20 per share, and 4,000 shares of 10% cumulative preferred stock ($100 par), convertible into 40,000 common shares.

On October 1, 2021, Tonge sold and issued an additional 16,000 shares of common stock at $33. At December 31, 2021, there were 20,000 incentive stock options outstanding, issued in 2020, and exercisable after one year for 20,000 shares of common stock at an exercise price of $30. The market price of the common stock at year-end was $48. During the year, the price of the common shares had averaged $40.

Net income was $650,000. The tax rate for the year was 25%.

Required:
Compute basic and diluted EPS for the year ended December 31, 2021.

P 19–18
EPS; stock options; nonconvertible preferred; convertible bonds; shares sold
● LO19–4 through LO19–9

At January 1, 2021, Canaday Corporation had outstanding the following securities:

600 million common shares
20 million 6% cumulative preferred shares, $50 par
6.4% convertible bonds, $2,000 million face amount, convertible into 80 million common shares

The following additional information is available:

- On September 1, 2021, Canaday sold 72 million additional shares of common stock.
- Incentive stock options to purchase 60 million shares of common stock after July 1, 2020, at $12 per share, were outstanding at the beginning and end of 2021. The average market price of Canaday's common stock was $18 per share during 2021.
- Canaday's net income for the year ended December 31, 2021, was $1,476 million. The effective income tax rate was 25%.

Required:
1. Calculate basic earnings per common share for the year ended December 31, 2021.
2. Calculate the diluted earnings per common share for the year ended December 31, 2021.

P 19–19
EPS; options; restricted stock; additional components for "proceeds" in treasury stock method
● LO19–1, LO19–2, LO19–4, LO19–8, LO19–11

Witter House is a calendar-year firm with 300 million common shares outstanding throughout 2021 and 2022. As part of its executive compensation plan, at January 1, 2020, the company had issued 30 million executive stock options permitting executives to buy 30 million shares of stock for $10 within the next eight years, but not prior to January 1, 2023. The fair value of the options was estimated on the grant date to be $3 per option.

In 2021, Witter House began granting employees stock awards rather than stock options as part of its equity compensation plans and granted 15 million restricted common shares to senior executives at January 1, 2021. The shares vest four years later. The fair value of the stock was $12 per share on the grant date. The average price of the common shares was $12 and $15 during 2021 and 2022, respectively.

The stock options qualify as an incentive plan. The restricted stock does not. The company's net income was $150 million and $160 million in 2021 and 2022, respectively.

Required:
1. Determine basic and diluted earnings per share for Witter House in 2021.
2. Determine basic and diluted earnings per share for Witter House in 2022.

Decision Makers' Perspective

©ImageGap/Getty Images

Apply your critical-thinking ability to the knowledge you've gained. These cases will provide you an opportunity to develop your research, analysis, judgment, and communication skills. You also will work with other students, integrate what you've learned, apply it in real-world situations, and consider its global and ethical ramifications. This practice will broaden your knowledge and further develop your decision-making abilities.

Real World Case 19–1
Restricted stock awards; Microsoft
● LO19–1

Real World Financials

Microsoft provides compensation to executives in the form of a variety of incentive compensation plans, including restricted stock award grants. The following is an excerpt from a disclosure note from Microsoft's 2017 annual report:

Note 20 Employee Stock and Savings Plans (in part)
Stock awards are grants that entitle the holder to shares of common stock as the award vests. Our stock awards generally vest over a five-year period. . . . During fiscal year 2017, the following activity occurred under our plans:

	Shares ($ in millions)	Weighted Average Grant-Date Fair Value
Stock awards:		
Nonvested balance, beginning of year	194	$36.92
Granted	84	55.64
Assumed in acquisitions	23	59.09
Vested	(80)	37.36
Forfeited	(20)	43.71
Nonvested balance, end of year	201	$46.32

Required:
If all awards are granted, acquired, vested, and forfeited evenly throughout the year, what is the compensation expense in fiscal 2017 pertaining to the previous and current stock awards? Assume forfeited shares were granted evenly throughout the three previous years, and perform all calculations to the nearest one-tenth of $1 million (e.g., $7,162,480 = $7,162.5).

Source: Microsoft

Communication Case 19–2
Stock options; basic concepts; prepare a memo
● LO19–2

You are assistant controller of Stamos & Company, a medium-size manufacturer of machine parts. On October 22, 2020, the board of directors approved a stock option plan for key executives. On January 1, 2021, a specific number of stock options were granted. The options were exercisable between January 1, 2026, and December 31, 2030, at 100% of the quoted market price at the grant date. The service period is for 2021 through 2026.

Your boss, the controller, is one of the executives to receive options. Neither he nor you have had occasion to deal with GAAP on accounting for stock options. He and you are aware of the traditional approach your company used years ago but do not know the newer method. Your boss understands how options might benefit him personally but wants to be aware also of how the options will be reported in the financial statements. He has asked you for a one-page synopsis of accounting for stock options under the fair value approach. He instructed you, "I don't care about the effect on taxes or earnings per share—just the basics, please."

Required:
Prepare such a report that includes the following:
1. At what point should the compensation cost be measured? How should it be measured?
2. How should compensation expense be measured for the stock option plan in 2021 and later?
3. If options are forfeited because an executive resigns before vesting, what is the effect of that forfeiture of the stock options on the financial statements?
4. If options are allowed to lapse after vesting, what is the effect on the financial statements?

Ethics Case 19–3
Stock options
● LO19–2

You are in your second year as an auditor with Dantly and Regis, a regional CPA firm. One of the firm's long-time clients is Mayberry-Cleaver Industries, a national company involved in the manufacturing, marketing, and sales of hydraulic devices used in specialized manufacturing applications. Early in this year's audit, you discover that Mayberry-Cleaver has changed its method of determining inventory from LIFO to FIFO. Your client's explanation is that FIFO is consistent with the method used by some other companies in the industry. Upon further investigation, you discover an executive stock option plan whose terms call for a significant increase in the shares available to executives if net income this year exceeds $44 million. Some quick calculations convince you that without the change in inventory methods, the target will not be reached; with the change, it will.

Required:

Do you perceive an ethical dilemma? What would be the likely impact of following the controller's suggestions? Who would benefit? Who would be injured?

Ethics Case 19–4
International Network Solutions
● LO19–6

International Network Solutions provides products and services related to remote access networking. The company has grown rapidly during its first 10 years of operations. As its segment of the industry has begun to mature, though, the fast growth of previous years has begun to slow. In fact, this year revenues and profits are roughly the same as last year.

One morning, nine weeks before the close of the fiscal year, Rob Mashburn, CFO, and Jessica Lane, controller, were sharing coffee and ideas in Lane's office.

Lane:	About the Board meeting Thursday. You may be right. This may be the time to suggest a share buyback program.
Mashburn:	To begin this year, you mean?
Lane:	Right! I know Barber will be lobbying to use the funds for our European expansion. She's probably right about the best use of our funds, but we can always issue more notes next year. Right now, we need a quick fix for our EPS numbers.
Mashburn:	Our shareholders are accustomed to increases every year.

Required:

1. How will a buyback of shares provide a "quick fix" for EPS?
2. Is the proposal ethical?
3. Who would be affected if the proposal is implemented?

Real World Case 19–5
Per share data; stock options; antidilutive securities; Best Buy Co.
● LO19–8

Real World Financials

The 2018 annual report of Best Buy Co., Inc., reported profitable operations for the most recent six years. However, the company suffered a net loss in 2012. Best Buy reported the following for the twelve months ended March 3, 2012:

Basic (loss) earnings per share:	
Continuing operations	$ (2.89)
Discontinued operations	(0.47)
Basic (loss) earnings per share	$ (3.36)
Diluted (loss) earnings per share:	
Continuing operations	$ (2.89)
Discontinued operations	(0.47)
Diluted (loss) earnings per share	$ (3.36)
Dividends declared per Best Buy Co., Inc., common share	$ 0.62
Weighted average common shares outstanding (in millions)	
Basic	366.3
Diluted	366.3

Note: The calculation of diluted earnings per share assumes the conversion of the company's previously outstanding convertible debentures due in 2027 into 8.8 million shares common stock . . . and adds back the related after-tax interest expense of $1.5. . . . The calculation of diluted (loss) per share for the twelve months ended March 3, 2012, does not include potential dilutive shares of common stock because their inclusion would be antidilutive (i.e., reduce the net loss per share).

Required:

1. The note indicates that "diluted earnings per share assumes the conversion of the company's *previously outstanding* convertible debentures due in 2027 into 8.8 million shares common stock . . . and adds back the related after-tax interest expense of $1.5." Apparently, these bonds were actually converted during the year. By how much would diluted EPS have been different if the bonds had not been converted and were still outstanding?

2. Best Buy does not include potentially dilutive shares when calculating EPS for the twelve months ended March 3, 2012. Assume Best Buy had 40 million common equivalent shares and included them in the calculation, what would have been the amount of diluted loss per share for the twelve months ended March 3, 2012?

Source: Best Buy Co., Inc.

1164 SECTION 4 Additional Financial Reporting Issues

Analysis
Case 19–6
EPS concepts
● LO19–4 through
 LO19–8

The shareholders' equity of Proactive Solutions, Inc., included the following at December 31, 2021:

> Common stock, $1 par
> Paid-in capital—excess of par on common stock
> 7% cumulative convertible preferred stock, $100 par value
> Paid-in capital—excess of par on preferred stock
> Retained earnings

Additional Information:
- Proactive had 7 million shares of preferred stock authorized of which 2 million were outstanding. All 2 million shares outstanding were issued in 2015 for $112 a share. The preferred stock is convertible into common stock on a two-for-one basis until December 31, 2023, after which the preferred stock no longer is convertible. None of the preferred stock has been converted into common stock at December 31, 2021. There were no dividends in arrears.
- Of the 13 million common shares authorized, there were 8 million shares outstanding at January 1, 2021. Proactive also sold 3 million shares at the beginning of September 2021 at a price of $52 a share.
- The company has an employee stock option plan in which certain key employees and officers may purchase shares of common stock at the market price at the date of the option grant. All options are exercisable beginning one year after the date of the grant and expire if not exercised within five years of the grant date. On January 1, 2021, options for 2 million shares were outstanding at prices ranging from $45 to $53 a share. Options for 1 million shares were exercised at $49 a share at the end of June 2021. No options expired during 2021. Additional options for 1.5 million shares were granted at $55 a share during the year. The 2.5 million options outstanding at December 31, 2021, were exercisable at $45 to $55 a share.

The only changes in the shareholders' equity for 2021 were those described above, 2021 net income, and cash dividends paid.

Required:

Explain how each of the following amounts should be determined when computing earnings per share for presentation in the income statements. For each, be specific as to the treatment of each item.
1. Numerator for basic EPS
2. Denominator for basic EPS
3. Numerator for diluted EPS
4. Denominator for diluted EPS

Analysis
Case 19–7
EPS
● LO19–5 through
 LO19–8

"I guess I'll win that bet!" you announced to no one in particular.

"What bet?" Renee asked. Renee Patey was close enough to overhear you.

"When I bought my REC stock last year Randy insisted it was a mistake, that they were going to collapse. I bet him a Coke he was wrong. This press release says they have positive earnings," you bragged. Renee was looking over your shoulder now at the article you were pointing at:

CHICAGO (ACCOUNTING WIRE)—July 1, 2021—Republic Enterprise Companies, Inc. (REC), today reported net income attributable to REC of $3.6 billion for the quarter ended May 31, 2021. . . . Diluted earnings per share attributable to REC were $1.52 for the second quarter of 2021, compared with $1.21 for the second quarter of 2020.

Our Board of Directors . . . authorized the repurchase of shares of REC Common Stock, with an aggregate purchase price of up to $2.0 billion.

"A dollar fifty-two a share, huh?" Renee asked. "How many shares do you have? When do you get the check?"

Required:

1. Renee's questions imply that she thinks you will get cash dividends of $1.52 a share. What does earnings per share really tell you?
2. A previous press release indicated that "Share and per share amounts prior to the second quarter of 2019 have been restated to reflect the 1-for-20 reverse stock split effective June 30, 2019." What does that mean?
3. The press release indicates plans to repurchase shares of its own stock. Would the reduction in shares from a stock repurchase be taken into account when EPS is calculated? How?

Source: ACCOUNTING WIRE

Judgment
Case 19–8
Where are the
profits?
● LO19–4 through
 LO19–7, LO19–9

Del Conte Construction Company has experienced generally steady growth since its inception in 1973. Management is proud of its record of having maintained or increased its earnings per share in each year of its existence.

The economic downturn has led to disturbing dips in revenues the past two years. Despite concerted cost-cutting efforts, profits have declined in each of the two previous years. Net income in 2019, 2020, and 2021 was as follows:

2019	$145 million
2020	$134 million
2021	$ 95 million

A major shareholder has hired you to provide advice on whether to continue her present investment position or to curtail that position. Of particular concern is the declining profitability, despite the fact that earnings per share has continued a pattern of growth:

	Basic	Diluted
2019	$2.15	$1.91
2020	$2.44	$2.12
2021	$2.50	$2.50

She specifically asks you to explain this apparent paradox. During the course of your investigation you discover the following events:

- For the decade ending December 31, 2018, Del Conte had 60 million common shares and 20 million shares of 8%, $10 par nonconvertible preferred stock outstanding. Cash dividends have been paid quarterly on both.
- On July 1, 2020, half the preferred shares were retired in the open market. The remaining shares were retired on December 30, 2020.
- $55 million of 8% nonconvertible bonds were issued at the beginning of 2021, and a portion of the proceeds were used to call and retire $50 million of 8% debentures (outstanding since 2016) that were convertible into 9 million common shares.
- In 2019, management announced a share repurchase plan by which up to 24 million common shares would be retired. 12 million shares were retired on March 1 of both 2020 and 2021.
- Del Conte's income tax rate is 25% and has been for the last several years.

Required:

In preparation for your explanation of the apparent paradox to which your client refers, calculate both basic and diluted earnings per share for each of the three years.

Communication Case 19–9
Dilution
● LO19–9

"I thought I understood earnings per share," lamented Brad Dawson, "but you're telling me we need to pretend our convertible bonds have been converted! Or maybe not?"

Dawson, your boss, is the new manager of the Fabricating division of BVT Corporation. His background is engineering and he has only a basic understanding of earnings per share. Knowing you are an accounting graduate, he asks you to explain the questions he has about the calculation of the company's EPS. His reaction is to your explanation that the company's convertible bonds might be included in this year's calculation.

"Put it in a memo!" he grumbled as he left your office.

Required:

Write a memo to Dawson. Explain the effect on earnings per share of each of the following:

1. Convertible securities.

2. Antidilutive securities.

Analysis Case 19–10
Analyzing financial statements; price-earnings ratio; dividend payout ratio
● LO19–13

IGF Foods Company is a large, primarily domestic, consumer foods company involved in the manufacture, distribution, and sale of a variety of food products. Industry averages are derived from Troy's *The Almanac of Business and Industrial Financial Ratios* and Dun and Bradstreet's *Industry Norms and Key Business Ratios.* Following are the 2021 and 2020 comparative income statements and balance sheets for IGF. The market price of IGF's common stock is $47 during 2021. (The financial data we use are from actual financial statements of a well-known corporation, but the company name used in our illustration is fictitious and the numbers and dates have been modified slightly to disguise the company's identity.)

IGF FOODS COMPANY		
Years Ended December 31, 2021 and 2020		
($ in millions)	**2021**	**2020**
Comparative Income Statements		
Net sales	$6,440	$5,800
Cost of goods sold	(3,667)	(3,389)
Gross profit	2,773	2,411
Operating expenses	(1,916)	(1,629)
Operating income	857	782
Interest expense	(54)	(53)
Income from operations before tax	803	729
Income taxes	(316)	(287)

(continued)

1166 SECTION 4 Additional Financial Reporting Issues

(concluded)

IGF FOODS COMPANY
Years Ended December 31, 2021 and 2020

($ in millions)	2021	2020
Net income	$ 487	$ 442
Net income per share	$ 2.69	$ 2.44
Average shares outstanding	181 million	181 million

($ in millions)	2021	2020
Comparative Balance Sheets		
Assets		
Total current assets	$1,879	$1,490
Property, plant, and equipment (net)	2,592	2,291
Intangibles (net)	800	843
Other assets	74	60
Total assets	$5,345	$4,684
Liabilities and Shareholders' Equity		
Total current liabilities	$1,473	$ 941
Long term debt	534	728
Deferred income taxes	407	344
Total liabilities	2,414	2,013
Shareholders' equity:		
Common stock	180	180
Additional paid-in capital	21	63
Retained earnings	2,730	2,428
Total shareholders' equity	2,931	2,671
Total liabilities and shareholders' equity	$5,345	$4,684

Some ratios express income, dividends, and market prices on a per share basis. As such, these ratios appeal primarily to common shareholders, particularly when weighing investment possibilities. These ratios focus less on the fundamental soundness of a company and more on its investment characteristics.

Required:
1. Calculate 2021 earnings per share for IGF.
2. Calculate IGF's 2021 price-earnings ratio.
3. Calculate IGF's 2021 dividend payout ratio.

Analysis
Case 19–11
Kellogg's EPS; PE
ratio; dividend
payout
● LO19–13

Real World Financials

While eating his Kellogg's Frosted Flakes one January morning, Tony noticed the following article in his local paper:

Kellogg Company Reports Fourth-Quarter 2017 Results and Provides Guidance For 2018 *(in part)*

BATTLE CREEK, Mich., Feb. 8, 2018 /PRNewswire/—Kellogg Company (NYSE: K) Reported full-year 2017 net earnings $1,269 million, or $3.62 per share.

As a shareholder, Tony is well aware that Kellogg pays a regular cash dividend of $0.54 per share quarterly. A quick click on a price quote service indicated that Kellogg's shares closed at $67.98 on December 31.

Required:
1. Using the numbers provided, determine the price-earnings ratio for Kellogg Company for 2017.
2. What is the dividend payout ratio for Kellogg?

Source: Kellogg

Research Case 19–12
FASB codification; locate and extract relevant information and cite authoritative support for a financial reporting issue; change in classification of a share-based compensation instrument

● LO19–13

"Now what do I do?" moaned your colleague Matt. "This is a first for me," he confided. You and Matt are recent hires in the Accounting Division of National Paper. A top executive in the company has been given share-based incentive instruments that permit her to receive shares of National Paper equal in value to the amount the company shares rise above the shares' value two years ago when the instruments were issued to her as compensation. The instruments vest in three years. A clause was included in the compensation agreement that would permit her to receive cash rather than shares upon exercise if sales revenue in her division were to double by that time. Because that contingency was considered unlikely, the instruments have been accounted for as equity, with the grant date fair value being expensed over the five-year vesting period.

Now, though, surging sales of her division indicate that the contingent event has become probable, and the instruments should be accounted for as a liability rather than equity. The fair value of the award was estimated at $5 million on the grant date, but now is $8 million. Matt has asked your help in deciding what to recommend to your controller as the appropriate action to take at this point.

Required:

1. Obtain the relevant authoritative literature on accounting for a change in classification due to a change in probable settlement outcome using the *FASB Accounting Standards Codification* at the FASB website (www.fasb.org). To help explain to Matt the basic treatment of the situation described, determine the specific seven-digit Codification citation (XXX-XX-XX) you would rely on in applying that accounting treatment.

2. Prepare the journal entry to record the change in circumstance.

Data Analytics

Data analytics is the process of examining data sets in order to draw conclusions about the information they contain. If you haven't completed any of the prior data analytics cases, follow the instructions listed in the Chapter 1 Data Analytics case to get set up. You will need to watch the videos referred to in the Chapters 1 - 3 Data Analytics cases. No additional videos are required for this case. All short training videos can be found here: https://www.tableau.com/learn/training#getting-started.

Data Analytics Case
Market Performance

● LO19–13

In the Data Analytics Cases in the previous chapter, you used Tableau to examine two (hypothetical) publicly traded companies: GPS Corporation and Tru, Inc. regarding the return on stockholders' equity. This time, you investigate two aspects of the relative desirability of investing in stock of the two companies.

Required:

For each of the two companies in the most recent five-year period, 2017-2021, use Tableau to calculate and display the trends for (a) the dividend payout ratios [Dividends paid / Income from continuing operations] and (b) the price-earnings ratio [Market price per share / Diluted earnings per share]. The 2021 industry averages for the dividend payout and the price-earnings ratio are 20.2% and 27.9%, respectively. Based upon what you find, answer the following questions:

1. Which of the two companies, GPS Corporation or Tru, Inc., pays investors the greater percentage of its earnings during the period 2017-2021?

2. Is the dividend payout ratio for Tru, Inc. (a) increasing significantly, (b) decreasing significantly, or (c) remaining relatively the same during the period 2017-2021?

3. Is the price-earnings ratio for GPS Corporation (a) increasing significantly, (b) decreasing significantly, or (c) remaining relatively the same during the period 2017-2021?

4. Is the price-earnings ratio for Tru, Inc. (a) increasing significantly, (b) decreasing significantly, or (c) remaining relatively the same during the period 2017-2021?

Resources:
Download the "GPS_Tru_Financials.xlsx" Excel file available in Connect, or under Student Resources within the Library tab. Save it to the computer on which you will be using Tableau.

For this case, you will create several calculations to produce performance ratios to allow you to compare and contrast the two companies.

After you view the training videos, follow these steps to create the charts you'll use for this case:

- Open Tableau and connect to the Excel spreadsheet you downloaded.
- Click on the "Sheet 1" tab at the bottom of the canvas, to the right of the Data Source at the bottom of the screen.

1168   SECTION 4   Additional Financial Reporting Issues

- Drag "($ in 000s) Company" and "Year" under Dimensions to the Columns shelf. Change "Year" to *discrete* by right-clicking and selecting "Discrete." Select "Show Filter" and uncheck all the years except the last five years (2017 – 2021).
- Create a calculated field by clicking the "Analysis" tab at the top of the screen and selecting "Create Calculated Field." Name the calculation "Dividend payout ratio." In the Calculation Editor window, from Measures, drag "Dividends paid", type a division sign, drag "Income from continuing operations" beside it, and then type a multiplication sign and a "−1." Make sure the window says that the calculation is valid and click OK.
- Drag the newly created "Dividend payout ratio" to the Rows shelf. Click on the "Show Me" and select "side-by-side bars." Add labels to the bars by clicking on "Label" under the "Marks" card and clicking the box "Show mark labels." Format the labels to Times New Roman, bold, black and 9-point font. Edit the color on the Color marks card if desired.
- Change the title of the sheet to be "Dividends Payout Ratio Trend" by right-clicking and selecting "Edit title." Format the title to Times New Roman, bold, black and 15-point font. Change the title of "Sheet 1" to match the sheet title by right-clicking, selecting "Rename" and typing in the new title.
- Click on the New Worksheet tab ("Sheet 2" should open). to the right of the newly named "Dividend Payout Ratio Trend" sheet at the bottom of the screen.
- Follow the procedures above for the company and year.
- Create a calculated field by clicking the "Analysis" tab at the top of the screen and selecting "Create Calculated Field." Name the calculation "Price-earnings ratio." In the Calculation Editor window, from Measures, drag "Market price per share", type a division sign, and then drag "Diluted EPS". Make sure the window says that the calculation is valid and click OK.
- Drag the newly created "Price-earnings ratio" to the Rows shelf. Click on the "Show Me" and select "side-by-side bars." Add labels to the bars by clicking on "Label" under the "Marks" card and clicking the box "Show mark labels." Format the labels to Times New Roman, bold, black and 10-point font. Edit the color on the Color marks card if desired.
- Change the title of the sheet to be "Price-Earnings Ratio Trend" by right-clicking and selecting "Edit title." Format the title to Times New Roman, bold, black and 15-point font. Change the title of "Sheet 2" to match the sheet title by right-clicking, selecting "Rename" and typing in the new title.
- Format all other labels to be Times New Roman, bold, black and 12-point font.
- Once complete, save the file as "DA19_Your initials.twbx."

Continuing Cases

Target Case

● 19–1, LO19–2, LO19–8

Target Corporation prepares its financial statements according to U.S. GAAP. Target's financial statements and disclosure notes for the year ended February 3, 2018, are available in Connect. This material is also available under the Investor Relations link at the company's website (www.target.com). Target's share-based compensation includes several long-term incentive plans.

Required:

1. What are the three types of awards described in Note 26: Share-Based Compensation?
2. Based on the fair value of the awards granted, what was Target's primary form of share-based compensation for the year ended February 3, 2018?
3. Projections of future performance should be based primarily on continuing operations. What was diluted EPS for continuing operations in each of the most recent three years?
4. How many shares were included in diluted earnings per share but not basic earnings per share due to share-based compensation awards?

Air France–KLM Case

● LO19–9

🌐 IFRS

 AIRFRANCE ✈ KLM

Air France–KLM (AF), a Franco-Dutch company, prepares its financial statements according to International Financial Reporting Standards. AF's financial statements and disclosure notes for the year ended December 31, 2017, are available in Connect. This material is also available under the Finance link at the company's website (www.airfranceklm-finance.com).

Required:

1. AF provides share-based compensation in the form of PPSs, Phantom Performance Shares. Recipients receive compensation in what form? Are such plans reported in the balance sheet as (a) assets, (b) liabilities, or (c) equity? [*Hint:* See Note 29: "Share-Based Compensation."]
2. Are AF's PPSs cliff vesting or graded vesting?

3. The PPS options are performance-based, which means that under either U.S. GAAP or IFRS the amount expensed depends on whether it's "probable" that the performance target will be met. Does this mean it's equally likely that performance-based PPSs will be expensed at the same amount under U.S. GAAP as under IFRS?

4. What amount(s) of earnings per share did AF report in its income statement for the year ended December 31, 2017? If AF used U.S. GAAP, would it have reported EPS using the same classification?

CPA Exam Questions and Simulations

Sample CPA Exam questions from Roger CPA Review are available in Connect as support for the topics in this chapter. These multiple-choice questions and task-based simulations include expert-written explanations and solutions, and provide a starting point for students to become familiar with the content and functionality of the actual CPA Exam.

APPENDIX

A Derivatives

OVERVIEW

A complex class of financial instruments exists in financial markets in response to the desire of firms to manage risks. In fact, these financial instruments would not exist in their own right, but have been created solely to hedge against risks created by other financial instruments or by transactions that have yet to occur but are anticipated. These financial instruments often are called derivatives because they "derive" their values or contractually required cash flows from some other security or index. Accounting for derivatives is the focus of this Appendix.

LEARNING OBJECTIVES

After studying this Appendix, you should be able to:

- **LOA–1**   Identify the major derivative securities used to hedge against risk. *(p. A-3)*
- **LOA–2**   Understand the way we account for fair value hedges. *(p. A-8)*
- **LOA–3**   Understand the way we account for cash flow hedges. *(p. A-12)*
- **LOA–4**   Understand the way we account for foreign currency hedges. *(p. A-16)*
- **LOA–5**   Describe disclosure requirements for derivatives and risk. *(p. A-18)*
- **LOA–6**   Understand the extended method for interest rate swap accounting. *(p. A-18)*

". . . derivatives are financial weapons of mass destruction . . ."
— Warren Buffett, Berkshire Hathaway CEO

". . . the growing use of complex financial instruments known as derivatives does not pose a threat to the country's financial system . . ."
— Alan Greenspan, Federal Reserve Chairman

"Total world derivatives are $1000 trillion or 19 times the total world GDP of $54 trillion."
— Chuck Burr, *Culture Change*

In today's global economy and evolving financial markets, businesses are increasingly exposed to a variety of risks, which, unmanaged, can have major impacts on earnings or even threaten a company's very existence. Risk management, then, has become critical. Derivative financial instruments have become the key tools of risk management.[1]

---

[1] Almost all financial institutions and over half of all nonfinancial companies use derivatives.

Derivatives are financial instruments that "derive" their values or contractually required cash flows from some other security or index. For instance, a contract allowing a company to buy a particular asset (say steel, gold, or flour) at a designated future date at a *predetermined price* is a financial instrument that derives its value from expected and actual changes in the price of the underlying asset. Financial futures, forward contracts, options, and interest rate swaps are the most frequently used derivatives. We discuss each of these in the paragraphs that follow. Derivatives are valued as tools to manage or hedge companies' increasing exposures to risk, including interest rate risk, price risk, and foreign exchange risk. Companies may enter into derivatives to entirely or partially offset these risk exposures. The variety, complexity, and magnitude of derivatives have grown rapidly in recent years. Accounting standard-setters have scrambled to keep pace.

Derivatives are financial instruments that "derive" their values from some other security or *index*.

A persistent stream of headline stories has alerted us to multimillion-dollar losses by many companies and the financial collapse of Bear Stearns and AIG.[2] Focusing on these headlines, it would be tempting to conclude that derivatives are risky business indeed. Certainly they can be quite risky if misused, but the fact is, these financial instruments exist to lessen, not increase, risk. Properly used, they serve as a form of "insurance" against risk. In fact, if a company is exposed to a substantial risk and does not hedge that risk, it is taking a gamble. On the other hand, if a derivative is used improperly, it can be a huge gamble itself.

Derivatives serve as a form of "insurance" against risk.

The notional amount of the derivatives market vastly exceeds the total value of the assets they are intended to mimic or mirror. This implies that firms are using derivatives for purposes other than risk management. Many observers are fearful that the size of the derivatives market poses significant risk to the economy. Some caution that the vast derivatives market could even cause the entire global financial system to crash. Why? If interest rates rise, then many speculative interest rate swaps would incur losses. But it's the size of the interest rate swap market, and thus the size of the resultant losses, that prompts the anxiety. At the end of June 2017, the over-the-counter derivatives market was $542 trillion. Yes, that's 542 with twelve zeroes ($542,000,000,000,000). And, that's nearly 30 times the U.S. Gross Domestic Product. Seventy-seven percent of those derivatives ($416 trillion) are interest rate swaps.[3] Our focus here, though, is not on the risk posed by the speculative use of derivatives, but instead on the use of derivatives to reduce company risk.

Derivatives Used to Hedge Risk

Hedging means taking an action that is expected to produce exposure to a particular type of risk that is precisely the *opposite* of an actual risk to which the company already is exposed. For instance, the volatility of interest rates creates exposure to interest-rate risk for companies that issue debt—which, of course, includes most companies. So, a company that frequently arranges short-term loans from its bank under notes with floating (variable) interest rates is exposed to the risk that interest rates might increase and adversely affect borrowing costs. Similarly, a company that regularly reissues commercial paper (short-term notes) as it matures faces the possibility that new rates will be higher and cut into forecasted income. When borrowings are large, the potential cost can be substantial. So, the firm might choose to hedge its position by entering into a transaction that would produce a *gain* of roughly the same amount as the potential loss if interest rates do, in fact, increase. A way to do this is to enter into a contract that will exchange (swap) floating rate payments for fixed interest payments, or vice versa, without exchanging the underlying notes.

Hedging means taking a risk position that is opposite to an actual position that is exposed to risk.

● LOA–1

Hedging is used to deal with three areas of risk exposure: fair value risk, cash flow risk, and foreign currency risk. Hedging against *fair value risk* protects the existing financial instrument against changes in its fair value. Hedging against *cash flow risk* protects against market related fluctuations in the cash to be paid or cash to be received for items such as interest receivable and payable. Hedging against *foreign currency risk* protects against exchange rate fluctuations that would change the dollar equivalent that must be repaid or will be received on a contract denominated in a foreign currency. Let's look at some of the more common derivatives.

---

[2]Bear Sterns has since been sold at a bargain basement price to JP Morgan, and AIG has since recovered from its difficulties.
[3]Bank for International Settlements, *BIS Quarterly Review,* March 2018.

A-4   APPENDIX A   Derivatives

A *futures contract* allows a firm to sell (or buy) a commodity or a financial instrument at a designated future date, at today's price.

FUTURES A futures contract is an agreement between a seller and a buyer that requires the seller to deliver a particular *commodity* (a nonfinancial asset such as corn, gold, or pork bellies) at a designated future date, at a *predetermined* price. When the contract involves a *financial instrument,* such as a Treasury bond, Treasury bill, commercial paper, or a certificate of deposit, the agreement is referred to as a *financial futures contract.*[4] These contracts are actively traded on regulated futures exchanges.

To appreciate the way these hedges work, you need to remember that when interest rates *rise,* the market price of interest-bearing securities *goes down.* For instance, if you have an investment in a 10% bond and market interest rates go up to, say, 12%, your 10% bond is less valuable relative to other bonds paying the higher rate. Conversely, when interest rates *decline,* the market price of interest-bearing securities *goes up.* This risk that the investment's value might change is referred to as *fair value risk.* The company that issued the securities is faced with fair value risk also. If interest rates decline, the fair value of that company's debt would rise, a risk the borrower may want to hedge against. Later in this section, we'll look at an illustration of how the borrower would account for and report such a hedge.

Now let's look at the effect on a contract to sell or buy securities (or any asset for that matter) at preset prices. One who is contracted to *sell* securities at a *preset* price after their market price has fallen benefits from the rise in interest rates. Consequently, the value of the contract that gives one the right to sell securities at a preset price goes up as the market price declines. The seller in a futures contract derives a gain (loss) when interest rates rise (decline).[5] Conversely, the one obligated to buy securities at a preset price experiences a loss. This risk of having to pay more cash or receive less cash is referred to as *cash flow risk.*

Another example of cash flow risk would be borrowing money by issuing a variable (floating) rate note. If market interest rates rise, the borrower would have to pay more interest. Similarly, the lender (investor) in the variable (floating) rate note transaction would face cash flow risk that interest rates would decline, resulting in lower cash interest receipts.

The seller in a financial futures contract realizes a gain (loss) when interest rates rise (decline).

Let's look closer at how a financial futures contract can mitigate cash flow risk. Consider a company in April that will replace the $10 million of 5.5% notes it owes to its bank with an issuance of bonds to the public when the notes mature in June. The company is exposed to the risk that interest rates in June will have risen, increasing borrowing costs. To counteract that possibility, the firm might enter a contract in April to deliver (sell) bonds in June at their *current* price.

Here's what happens then. If interest rates rise, borrowing costs will go up for our example company because it will have to sell debt securities (like notes payable or bonds payable) at a higher interest cost (or lower price). But that loss will be offset (approximately) by the gain produced by being in the opposite position on Treasury bond futures. Take note, though, this works both ways. If interest rates go down causing debt security prices to rise, the potential benefit of being able to issue debt at that lower interest rate (higher price) will be offset by a loss on the futures position. Since there are no corporate bond futures contracts, the company buys Treasury bond futures, which will accomplish essentially the same purpose. In essence, the firm agrees to sell Treasury bonds in June at a price established now (April). Let's say it's April 6 and the price of Treasury bond futures on the Chicago Mercantile Exchange is quoted as 142.88.[6] Since the trading unit of Treasury bond futures is a 15-year, $100,000, 6% Treasury bond, the company might sell 70 Treasury bond futures to hedge the June issuance of debt. This would effectively provide a hedge of 70 x $100,000 x 142.88% = $10,001,600.[7]

A very important point about futures contracts is that the seller does not need to have actual possession of the commodity or financial instrument (the Treasury bonds, in this case), nor is the purchaser of the contract required to take possession of the commodity. In

---

[4]Note that a financial futures contract meets the definition of a financial instrument because it entails the exchange of financial instruments (cash for Treasury bonds, for instance). But, a futures contract for the sale or purchase of a nonfinancial commodity like corn or gold does not meet the definition because one of the items to be exchanged is not a financial instrument.

[5]The seller of a futures contract is obligated to sell the bonds at a future date. The buyer of a futures contract is obligated to buy the bonds at a future date. The company in our example, then, is the seller of the futures contract.

[6]Price quotes are expressed as a percentage of par.

[7]This is a simplification of the more sophisticated way financial managers determine the optimal number of futures.

fact, virtually all financial futures contracts are "netted out" before the actual transaction is to take place. This is simply a matter of reversing the original position. A seller closes out his transaction with a purchase. Likewise, a purchaser would close out her transaction with a sale. After all, the objective is not to actually buy or sell Treasury bonds (or whatever the commodity or financial instrument might be), but to incur the financial impact of movements in interest rates as reflected in changes in Treasury bond prices. Specifically, it will buy at the lower price (to reverse the original seller position) at the same time it's selling its new bond issue at that same lower price. The financial futures market is an "artificial" exchange in that its reason for existing is to provide a mechanism to transfer risk from those exposed to it to those willing to accept the risk, not to actually buy and sell the underlying financial instruments.

If the impending debt issue being hedged is a short-term issue, the company may attain a more effective hedge by selling Treasury *bill* futures since Treasury bills are 90-day securities, or maybe certificate of deposit (CD) futures that also are traded in futures markets. The object is to get the closest association between the financial effects of interest rate movements on the actual transaction and the effects on the financial instrument used as a hedge.

> The effectiveness of a hedge is influenced by the closeness of the match between the designated risk being hedged and the financial instrument chosen as a hedge.

FORWARD CONTRACTS A forward contract is similar to a futures contract, but a forward contract calls for delivery on a designated date, whereas a futures contract permits the seller to decide later which specific day within the specified month will be the delivery date (if it gets as far as actual delivery before it is closed out). Also, unlike a futures contract, a forward contract usually is not traded on a market exchange. Instead, a forward contract usually is traded in an over-the-counter market using an "intermediary" that will find a seller for a buyer or a buyer for a seller (and who will customize the contract for the exact day, etc.)

To illustrate a nonfinancial forward contract, let's say a large restaurant chain uses 500,000 pounds of avocados each year during the week of Cinco de Mayo to satisfy demand for its famous guacamole. In recent years, the price of avocados has fluctuated significantly. To reduce the *cash flow risk* associated with price volatility, the restaurant chain enters into a forward contract with an intermediary on October 31 to buy 500,000 pounds of avocados at a set price of $2.80/lb, with delivery in six months (April 30). The *hedged transaction* is the forecasted purchase of avocados from suppliers. The *hedging instrument* is the forward contract arranged with an intermediary, and the *hedged risk* is the change in purchase price.

As we saw with the financial futures contract, the seller and purchaser do not need to exchange possession of the underlying commodity or financial instrument. Rather, the forward contract will settle by an exchange of cash between the restaurant chain and the intermediary based on the current market price for avocados on the date the contract is settled (April 30).

How does this impact the restaurant chain? If avocado prices rise and the restaurant chain pays more to suppliers of avocados, this increased cost will be offset by the gain from being in the opposite position in the forward contract. For example, assume the current market price on April 30 is $3.00/lb. The company would receive cash from the settlement of the forward contract of $100,000 ([$3.00 − $2.80] × 500,000 pounds). At the same time, if avocado prices fall and the restaurant pays less to purchase avocados, this decrease in cost will be offset by the loss on the settlement of the forward position. In either scenario, however, the restaurant chain achieves its goal of reducing the cash flow risk related to price volatility—when considering the purchase of avocados from suppliers and the settlement of the forward contract with the intermediary, the restaurant ends up paying $2.80/lb for avocados on April 30, regardless of the actual price movement.

OPTIONS Options frequently are purchased to hedge exposure to the effects of changing interest rates. Options serve the same purpose as futures in that respect but are fundamentally different. An option on a financial instrument—say a Treasury bill—gives its holder the right either to buy (call option) or to sell (put option) the Treasury bill at a specified price and within a given time period. Importantly, though, the option holder has no obligation to exercise the option. On the other hand, the holder of a futures contract must buy or sell within a specified period unless the contract is closed out before delivery comes due.

To illustrate an option contract, let's reconsider the example of the restaurant chain that wants to protect itself from rising avocado prices. Let's say the restaurant chain is able to enter into a contract that gives it the *option* to purchase 500,000 pounds of avocados in six months at the price of $2.80/lb. Assume this option contract has an initial premium of $0.02 per avocado, or $10,000. That is, the market price of avocados at the inception of the contract is lower than the option price. If the price of avocados increases to $3.00/lb, then the outcome of an option contract will be similar to what we saw with the forward contract: the restaurant chain will exercise its option and receive $100,000 ([$3.00 − $2.80] × 500,000 pounds) upon settlement of the option. Because the restaurant chain paid an initial premium, the net cash effect of the option contract ($90,000 = $100,000 cash settlement − $10,000 premium) would be less than in the forward contract example ($100,000 cash settlement). Unlike the forward contract, however, if avocado prices fall, then the restaurant chain does not have to pay to settle the option contract. Rather, it will let the option expire.

FOREIGN CURRENCY FUTURES Foreign loans frequently are denominated in the currency of the lender (Japanese yen, Swiss franc, Euro, and so on). When loans must be repaid in foreign currencies, a new element of risk is introduced. This is because if exchange rates change, the dollar equivalent of the foreign currency that must be repaid differs from the dollar equivalent of the foreign currency borrowed.

> Foreign exchange risk often is hedged in the same manner as interest rate risk.

To hedge against "foreign exchange risk" exposure, some firms buy or sell foreign currency futures contracts. These are similar to financial futures except specific foreign currencies are specified as the underlying in the futures contracts rather than specific debt instruments. They work the same way to protect against foreign exchange risk as financial futures protect against fair value or cash flow risk.

> *Interest rate swaps* exchange fixed interest payments for floating rate payments, or vice versa, without exchanging the underlying notional (principal) amounts.

INTEREST RATE SWAPS Over 82% of derivatives are interest rate contracts, of which 75% are interest rate swaps. These contracts exchange (swap) fixed interest payments for floating rate payments, or vice versa, without exchanging the underlying debt instruments. For example, suppose you owe $100,000 on a 10% fixed rate home loan. You envy your neighbor who also is paying 10% on her $100,000 mortgage, but hers is a floating rate loan, so if market rates fall, so will her loan rate. To the contrary, she is envious of your fixed rate, fearful that rates will rise, increasing her payments. A solution would be for the two of you to effectively swap interest payments using an interest rate swap agreement. The way a swap works, you both would continue to actually make your own interest payments to your respective lenders, but you would exchange with each other the net cash difference between payments at specified intervals. So, in this case, if market rates (and thus floating payments) increase, you would pay your neighbor; if rates fall, she pays you. The net effect is to exchange the consequences of rate changes. In other words, you have effectively converted your fixed-rate debt to floating-rate debt; your neighbor has done the opposite.

Of course, this technique is not dependent on happening into such a fortuitous pairing of two borrowers with opposite philosophies on interest rate risk. Instead, banks or other intermediaries (such as hedge funds) offer, for a fee, one-sided swap agreements to companies desiring to be either fixed-rate payers or variable-rate payers. Intermediaries usually strive to maintain a balanced portfolio of matched, offsetting swap agreements.

Theoretically, the two parties to such a transaction exchange principal amounts, say the $100,000 amount above, in addition to the interest on those amounts. It makes no practical sense, though, for the companies to send each other $100,000. So, instead, the principal amount is not actually exchanged, but serves merely as the computational base for interest calculations and is called the *notional amount*. Similarly, the fixed-rate loan payer doesn't usually send the entire fixed interest amount (say 10% × $100,000 = $10,000) to the variable-rate payer and receive the entire variable interest amount (say 9% × $100,000 = $9,000). Generally, only the net amount ($1,000 in this case) is exchanged. For example, Company A pays its lender 10% and Company B pays its lender a floating rate that is currently 9%, and the two companies have entered into an interest rate swap as illustrated in Illustration A–1.

Illustration A–1 Interest Rate Swap

Swap of annual payments on $100,000 notional amount; fixed interest rate: 10% ($10,000)

$$\boxed{\text{Company A}} \quad \xrightarrow{\text{Fixed } 10\%} \quad \boxed{\text{Company B}}$$
$$\xleftarrow{\text{Floating } \%}$$

Floating rate: 9% at time of first payment ($9,000); Company B pays Company A $1,000.
The result of the swap:
   Company A: $10,000 to lender − $1,000 cash settlement = $9,000 floating amount.
   Company B: $9,000 to lender + $1,000 cash settlement = $10,000 fixed amount.

From an accounting standpoint, the central issue is not the operational differences among various hedge instruments, but their similarities in functioning as hedges against risk.

Accounting for Derivatives

A key to accounting for derivatives is knowing the purpose for which a company holds them and whether the company is effective in serving that purpose. Derivatives, for instance, may be held for risk management (hedging activities). The desired effect, and often the real effect, is a reduction in risk. On the other hand, derivatives sometimes are held for speculative position taking, hoping for large profits. The effect of this activity usually is to *increase* risk. Perhaps more important, derivatives acquired as hedges and intended to reduce risk may, in fact, unintentionally increase risk instead.

It's important to understand that, serving as investments rather than as hedges, derivatives are extremely speculative. This is due to the high leverage inherent in derivatives. Here's why. The investment outlay usually is negligible, but the potential gain or loss on the investment usually is quite high. A small change in interest rates or another underlying event can trigger a large change in the fair value of the derivative. Because the initial investment was minimal, the change in value relative to the investment itself represents a huge percentage gain or loss. Their extraordinarily risky nature prompted Warren Buffett, one of the country's most celebrated financiers, to refer to derivatives as "financial weapons of mass destruction." Accounting for derivatives is designed to treat differently (a) derivatives designated as hedges and those not designated as hedges as well as (b) intended hedges that are highly effective and those that are not.[8]

> Derivatives not serving as hedges are extremely speculative due to the high leverage inherent in such investments.

The basic approach to accounting for derivatives is fairly straightforward, although implementation can be quite cumbersome. All derivatives, no exceptions, are carried on the balance sheet as either assets or liabilities at fair (or market) value.[9] The reasoning is that (a) derivatives create either rights or obligations that meet the definition of assets or liabilities, and (b) fair value is the most meaningful measurement.

> Each derivative contract has a "fair value," which is an amount that one side owes the other at a particular moment.

Accounting for the gain or loss on a derivative depends on how it is used. Specifically, if the derivative is not designated as a hedging instrument or doesn't qualify as one, any gain or loss from fair value changes is recognized immediately in earnings. On the other hand, if a derivative is used to hedge against exposure to risk, any gain or loss from fair value changes is either (a) recognized immediately in earnings along with an offsetting loss or gain on the item being hedged or (b) deferred in comprehensive income until it can be recognized in earnings at the same time as earnings are affected by a hedged transaction. Which way depends on whether the derivative is designated as a (a) fair value hedge, (b) cash flow hedge, or (c) foreign currency hedge. Let's look now at each of the three hedge designations.

---

[8]Accounting Standards Update No. 2017-12, Derivatives and Hedging (Topic 815): Targeted Improvements to Accounting for Hedging Activities, (Norwalk, Conn.: FASB, January 2017).
[9]FASB ASC 815–10: Derivatives and Hedging—Overall.

A-8   **APPENDIX A**   Derivatives

● LOA–2

A gain or loss from a *fair value hedge* is recognized immediately in earnings, along with the loss or gain from the item being hedged.

The income effects of the hedge instrument and the income effects of the item being hedged should affect earnings at the same time and in the same income statement line item.

FAIR VALUE HEDGES A company can be adversely affected when a change in either prices or interest rates causes a change in the fair value of one of its assets, its liabilities, or a commitment to buy or sell assets or liabilities. If a derivative is used to hedge against the exposure to changes in the fair value of an asset, liability, or a firm commitment, it can be designated as a fair value hedge. In that case, when the derivative is adjusted to reflect changes in fair value, the other side of the entry recognizes a gain or loss to be included *currently* in earnings. At the same time, though, the loss or gain from changes in the fair value (due to the risk being hedged)[10] of the item being hedged also is included currently in earnings. This means that, to the extent the hedge is effective in serving its purpose, the gain or loss on the derivative will be offset by the loss or gain on the item being hedged. In fact, this is precisely the concept behind the procedure, and offsetting effects of the derivative and the hedged item are reported in the same line item in the income statement.

The reasoning is that as interest rates or other underlying events change, a hedge instrument will produce a gain approximately equal to a loss on the item being hedged (or vice versa). These income effects are interrelated and offsetting, so it would be improper to report the income effects in different periods. More critically, the intent and effect of having the hedge instrument is to *lessen* risk. And yet, recognizing gains in one period and counterbalancing losses in another period would tend to cause fluctuations in income that convey an *increase* in risk. However, to the extent that a hedge is not perfectly (but still highly) effective and produces gains or losses different from the losses or gains being hedged, the difference is recognized in earnings immediately.

Some of the more common uses of fair value hedges are:

- An interest rate swap to synthetically convert fixed-rate debt (for which interest rate changes could change the fair value of the debt) into floating-rate debt.
- A futures contract to hedge changes in the fair value (due to price changes) of aluminum, sugar, or some other type of inventory.
- A futures contract to hedge the fair value (due to price changes) of a firm commitment to sell natural gas or some other asset.

ILLUSTRATION OF FAIR VALUE HEDGE Because interest rate swaps comprise the majority of derivatives in use, we will use swaps to illustrate accounting for derivatives. Let's look at the example in Illustration A–2. The shortcut method can be used only for an interest-bearing asset or liability.

Illustration A–2
Interest Rate Swap—
Shortcut Method

Wintel Semiconductors issued $1 million of 18-month, 10% notes payable to Third Bank on January 1, 2021. Wintel is exposed to the risk that general interest rates will decline, causing the fair value of its debt to rise. (If the fair value of Wintel's debt increases, its effective borrowing cost is higher relative to the market.)

- To hedge against this fair value risk, the firm entered into an 18-month interest rate swap agreement on January 1 and designated the swap as a hedge against changes in the fair value of the note.
- Although Wintel still will pay the 10% fixed rate to the bank, the swap calls for the company to *receive payment* from the intermediary based on a 10% fixed interest rate on a notional (principal) amount of $1 million and to *make payment* based on a floating interest rate tied to changes in general rates.* The actual cash settlement on the swap will be a net payment to the appropriate party.

As the Illustration will show, this effectively converts Wintel's fixed-rate debt to floating-rate debt. Cash settlement of the net interest amount is made semiannually at June 30 and December 31 of each year, with the net interest being the difference between the $50,000

(continued)

---

[10]The fair value of a hedged item might also change for reasons other than from effects of the risk being hedged. For instance, the hedged risk may be that a change in interest rates will cause the fair value of a bond to change. The bond price might also change, though, if the market perceives that the bond's default risk has changed.

Illustration A–2
(concluded)

fixed interest [$1 million × (10% × ½)] and the floating interest rate, times $1 million at those dates.

Floating (market) settlement rates were 9% at June 30, 2021, 8% at December 31, 2021, and 9% at June 30, 2022. Net interest receipts can be calculated as shown below. Fair values of both the derivative and the note resulting from those market rate changes are assumed to be quotes obtained from securities dealers.

	1/1/21	6/30/21	12/31/21	6/30/22
Fixed rate	10%	10%	10%	10%
Floating rate	10%	9%	8%	9%
Fixed payments [$1 million × (10% × ½)]		$ 50,000	$ 50,000	$ 50,000
Floating payments ($1 million × ½ floating rate)		45,000	40,000	45,000
Net interest receipts		$ 5,000	$ 10,000	$ 5,000
Fair value of interest rate swap	$0	$ 9,363	$ 9,615	$0
Fair value of note payable	$1,000,000	$1,009,363	$1,009,615	$1,000,000

*A common measure for benchmarking variable interest rates is LIBOR, the London Interbank Offered Rate, a base rate at which large international banks lend funds to each other.

When the floating rate declined from 10% to 9%, the fair values of both the derivative (swap) and the note increased. This created an offsetting gain on the derivative and a holding loss on the note. Both are recognized in earnings at the same time (at June 30, 2021). The changes in fair value (holding gains and losses) are presented in the same line item as the earnings effect of the underlying hedged item (interest expense). So, we record these holding gains and losses as decreases or increases in interest expense.

January 1, 2021		
Cash	1,000,000	
Notes payable		1,000,000
To record the issuance of the note.		
June 30, 2021		
Interest expense (10% × ½ × $1 million)	50,000	
Cash		50,000
To record interest on the note.		
Cash [$50,000 − (9% × ½ × $1 million)]	5,000	
Interest expense		5,000
To record the net cash settlement on the swap.		
Interest rate swap* ($9,363 − $0)	9,363	
interest expense		9,363
To record change in fair value of the derivative.		
Interest expense	9,363	
Note payable ($1,009,363 − $1,000,000)		9,363
To record change in fair value of the note due to interest rate changes.		

*This would be a liability rather than an investment (asset) if the fair value had declined.

The interest rate swap is designated as a fair value hedge on this note at issuance.

The swap settlement is the difference between the fixed interest (5%) and variable interest (4.5%).

The fair value of derivatives is recognized in the balance sheet.

The change in fair value of the derivative and of the hedged liability are reported in the same income statement line item as the earnings effect of the hedged item.

The net interest settlement on June 30, 2021, is $5,000 because the fixed rate is 5% (half of the 10% annual rate) and the floating rate is 4.5% (half of the 9% annual rate).

A-10   APPENDIX A   Derivatives

As with any debt, interest expense is the effective rate times the outstanding balance.

December 31, 2021

Interest expense..	50,000	
Cash (10% × ½ × $1,000,000)...		50,000
To record interest on the note.		

The settlement is the difference between the fixed interest (5%) and variable interest (4%).

Cash [$50,000 – (8% × ½ × $1 million)]...	10,000	
Interest expense...		10,000
To record the net cash settlement on the swap.		

The derivative is increased by the change in fair value. The note is increased by the change in fair value.

Interest rate swap ($9,615 – $9,363)...	252	
Interest expense...		252
To record the change in fair value of the derivative.		

Interest expense..	252	
Note payable ($1,009,615 – $1,009,363)..		252
To record the change in fair value of the note due to interest rate changes.		

The fair value of the swap increased by $252 (from $9,363 to $9,615). Similarly, we adjust the note's book value by the amount necessary to increase it to fair value. This produces a holding loss on the note that exactly offsets the gain on the swap. This result is the hedging effect that motivated Wintel to enter the fair value hedging arrangement in the first place.

At June 30, 2022, Wintel repeats the process of adjusting to fair value both the derivative investment and the note being hedged.

June 30, 2022

Interest expense..	50,000	
Cash (10% × ½ × $1,000,000)...		50,000
To record interest on the note.		

The net interest received is the difference between the fixed interest (5%) and floating interest (4.5%).

Cash [$50,000 – (9% × ½ × $1 million)]...	5,000	
Interest expense...		5,000
To record the change in fair value of the derivative.		

Interest expense..	9,615	
Interest rate swap ($0 – $9,615)...		9,615
To record the change in fair value of the derivative.		

The swap's fair value now is zero.

Note payable ($1,000,000 – $1,009,615)..	9,615	
Interest expense...		9,615
To record the change in fair value of the note due to interest rate changes.		

Note payable	1,000,000	
Cash		1,000,000
To repay the loan.		

The net interest received is the difference between the fixed rate (5%) and floating rate (4.5%) times $1 million. The fair value of the swap decreased by $9,615 (from $9,615 to zero).[11] That decline represents a holding *loss* that we recognize in earnings. Similarly, we record an offsetting holding gain on the note for the change in its fair value.

Now let's see how the book values changed for the swap account and the note:

	Swap		Note	
Jan. 1, 2021				1,000,000
June 30, 2021	9,363			9,363
Dec. 31, 2021	252			252
June 30, 2022		9,615	9,615	
			1,000,000	
	0			0

---

[11]Because there are no future cash receipts from the swap arrangement at this point, the fair value of the swap is zero.

The income statement is affected as follows:

	Income Statement + (−)	
June 30, 2021	(50,000)	Interest expense—fixed payment
	5,000	Interest expense—net cash settlement
	9,363	Interest expense—gain on interest rate swap
	(9,363)	Interest expense—loss on hedged note
	(45,000)	Net effect—same as floating interest payment
Dec. 31, 2021	(50,000)	Interest expense—fixed payment
	10,000	Interest expense—net cash settlement
	252	Interest expense—gain on interest rate swap
	(252)	Interest expense—loss on hedged note
	(40,000)	Net effect—same as floating interest payment
June 30, 2022	(50,000)	Interest expense—fixed payment
	5,000	Interest expense—net cash settlement
	9,615	Interest expense—gain on interest rate swap
	(9,615)	Interest expense—loss on hedged note
	(45,000)	Net effect—same as floating interest payment

As this demonstrates, the swap effectively converts fixed-interest debt to floating-interest debt.

Additional Consideration

Fair Value of the Swap

The fair value of a derivative typically is based on a quote obtained from a derivatives dealer. That fair value will approximate the present value of the expected net interest settlement receipts for the remaining term of the swap. In fact, we can actually calculate the fair value of the swap that we accepted as given in our illustration.

Since the June 30, 2021, floating rate of 9% caused the cash settlement on that date to be $5,000, it's reasonable to look at 9% as the best estimate of future floating rates and therefore assume the remaining two cash settlements also will be $5,000 each. We can then calculate at June 30, 2021, the present value of those expected net interest settlement receipts for the remaining term of the swap.

Fixed interest	10% × ½ × $1 million	$ 50,000
Expected floating interest	9% × ½ × $1 million	45,000
Expected cash receipts for both Dec. 31, 2021 and June 30, 2022		$ 5,000
		× 1.87267*
Present value of expected net interest settlement receipts for the remaining term		$ 9,363

*Present value of an ordinary annuity of $1: $n = 2$, $i = 4.5\%$ (½ of 9%) (from Table 4)

Fair Value of the Notes

The fair value of the note payable will be the present value of principal and remaining interest payments discounted at the market rate. The market rate will vary with the designated floating rate but might differ due to changes in default (credit) risk and the term structure of interest rates. Assuming it's 9% at June 30, 2021, we can calculate the fair value (present value) of the notes.

Interest	$50,000* × 1.87267† =	$ 93,633
Principal	$1,000,000 × 0.91573‡ =	915,730
Present value of remaining principal and interest payments		$1,009,363

*½ of 10% × $1,000,000
†Present value of an ordinary annuity of $1: $n = 2$, $i = 4.5\%$ (from Table 4)
‡Present value of $1: $n = 2$, $i = 4.5\%$ (from Table 2)

(continued)

(concluded)

Note: Often the cash settlement rate is "reset" as of each cash settlement date. Thus, the floating rate actually used at the end of each period to determine the payment is the floating market rate as of the beginning of the same period. In our illustration, for instance, there would have been no cash settlement at June 30, 2021, since we would use the beginning floating rate of 10% to determine payment. Similarly, we would have used the 9% floating rate at June 30, 2021, to determine the cash settlement six months later at December 31. In effect, each cash settlement would be delayed six months. Had this arrangement been in effect in the current illustration, there would have been one fewer cash settlement payment (two rather than three), but would not have affected the fair value calculations above because, either way, our expectation would be cash receipts of $5,000 for both December 31, 2021, and June 30, 2022.

● LOA–3

A gain or loss from a *cash flow hedge* is deferred as other comprehensive income until it can be recognized in earnings along with the earnings effect of the item being hedged.

CASH FLOW HEDGES The risk in some transactions or events is the risk of a change in cash flows, rather than a change in fair values. We noted earlier, for instance, that *fixed-rate* debt subjects a company to the risk that interest rate changes could change the fair value of the debt. On the other hand, if the obligation is *floating-rate* debt, the fair value of the debt will *not* change when interest rates do, but cash flows *will* change. If a derivative is used to hedge against the exposure to changes in cash inflows or cash outflows of an asset or liability or a forecasted transaction (like a future purchase or sale), it can be designated as a cash flow hedge. In that case, when the derivative is adjusted to reflect changes in fair value, the other side of the entry is a gain or loss. That gain or loss is *deferred* as a component of other comprehensive income. It's included in earnings later, at the same time as earnings are affected by the hedged transaction. When it ultimately is reported in the income statement, it's included in the same income statement line item as the effects of the hedged item. For instance, let's say that our inventory of carbon fibers is being hedged against the risk of rising carbon fiber prices. Any effect of such a price increase will affect cost of goods sold when we sell the item produced with the carbon fiber. So, we will defer (with a credit to Other comprehensive income) any increase in the value of the hedging contract. Then, when the item is sold, we *debit* Other comprehensive income and reduce (*credit*) cost of goods sold. Once again, the effect is to match the earnings effect of the derivative (reduce cost of goods sold, increasing earnings) with the earnings effect of the item being hedged (increase cost of goods sold, decreasing earnings), precisely the concept behind hedge accounting. Stated differently, when it's time for income statement recognition of the item being hedged, the accumulated change in the hedging contract that's been reflected in Accumulated other comprehensive income will be reclassified out of that account and into the income statement along with effect of the item being hedged.

To understand the deferral of the gain or loss, we need to revisit the concept of comprehensive income. Comprehensive income, as you may recall from Chapters 4, 12, 17, and 18, is a more expansive view of the change in shareholders' equity than traditional net income. In fact, it encompasses all changes in equity other than from transactions with owners.[12] So, in addition to net income itself, comprehensive income includes up to four other changes in equity that don't (yet) belong in net income, namely, net holding gains (losses) on investments in debt securities (Chapter 12), gains (losses) from, and amendments to, postretirement benefit plans (Chapter 17), gains (losses) from foreign currency translation, and deferred gains (losses) from derivatives designated as cash flow hedges and those designated as qualifying hedging relationships.[13]

---

[12]Transactions with owners primarily include dividends and the sale or purchase of shares of the company's stock.
[13]FASB ASC 220–10–55: Comprehensive Income—Overall—Implementation Guidance and Illustrations and Accounting Standards Update No. 2017-12, Derivatives and Hedging (Topic 815): Targeted Improvements to Accounting for Hedging Activities, (Norwalk, Conn.: FASB, January 2017).

Some of the more commonly used cash flow hedges are

- An interest rate swap to synthetically convert floating rate debt (for which interest rate changes could change the cash interest payments) into fixed rate debt.
- A futures contract to hedge a forecasted sale (for which price changes could change the cash receipts) of natural gas, crude oil, or some other asset.
- A forward contract to hedge a forecasted purchase (for which price changes could change the cash payments) of a commodity.

A company can designate the hedged risk as the overall change in cash flows of a hedged item or the change in cash flows attributed able to a contractually specified component of a forecasted purchase or sale or a contractually specified interest rate in floating rate debt.

ILLUSTRATION OF CASH FLOW HEDGE – INTEREST RATE SWAP Let's assume once again that we have a company that enters into an interest rate swap. However, in Illustration A–3, the company seeks to hedge exposure to cash flow risk from interest rate volatility.

Illustration A–3

Cash Flow Hedge; Interest Rate Swap (Floating Rate to Fixed Rate)—Shortcut Method

On January 1, 2021, Daley Company issues $2 million of floating-rate debt based on LIBOR, with interest paid annually.

- The debt has 3 years to maturity, and the LIBOR rate is 5% at issuance.
- Interest payments on the debt, based on beginning-of-year rates, are due on December 31 of each year, and the variable rate is reset after the payment is made.
- Daley is exposed to the risk that interest rates will rise, which will increase its periodic interest payments.
- To hedge against this cash flow risk, the firm entered into a 3-year interest rate swap agreement on January 1 and designated the swap as a cash flow hedge because it protects Daley from having to make higher cash outflows for interest if interest rates do rise.
- The swap calls for the company to pay a fixed interest rate of 5% and receive LIBOR based on a notional amount of $2 million.
- Settlements on the interest rate swap will be made annually on December 31, with interest rate resets after settlement at beginning-of-year rates.
- Assume that LIBOR rates are reset to 5.5% at December 31, 2021, 6% at December 31, 2022, and 6.5% at December 31, 2023.
- The market value of the note in this case does not change as interest rate fluctuates, because the note carries a variable interest rate.
- Fair values of the interest rate swap at the end of each accounting period are assumed to be quotes by securities dealers.
- Net cash settlements for the swap can be calculated as shown below:

	1/1/21	12/31/21	12/31/22	12/31/23
Floating rate	5%	5.5%	4.75%	n/a
Fixed rate	5%	5%	5%	n/a
Receive floating ($2 million × floating rate)		$100,000	$110,000	$ 95,000
Fixed payments ($2 million × 6%)		100,000	100,000	100,000
Net cash settlement		$ 0	$ 10,000	$ (5,000)
Fair value of swap	$0	$ 18,463	$ (4,773)	$ 0

As the illustration shows, this swap effectively converts Daley's variable-rate debt to fixed-rate debt. Daley applies the shortcut method.

January 1, 2021

Cash	2,000,000	
Notes payable		2,000,000

To record the issuance of the floating-rate debt.

December 31, 2021

Interest expense (5% × $2 million)	100,000	
Cash		100,000
To record interest on the note.		
Interest rate swap	18,463	
Other comprehensive income (OCI)		18,463
To record the change in the fair value of the derivative.		

At December 31, 2021, there is no cash exchanged for settlement of the interest rate swap, because the cash settlement is based on beginning-of-year rates (when both the fixed and floating rates were 5%). Daley does recognize an increase in the fair value of the interest rate swap, related to the rising interest rates in the upcoming year. This increase in fair value is recognized in other comprehensive income.

December 31, 2022

Interest expense (5.5% × $2 million)	110,000	
Cash		110,000
To record interest on the note.		
Cash [(5.5% × $2 million) − $100,000]	10,000	
Interest expense		10,000
To record the net cash settlement on the swap.		
Other comprehensive income (OCI)	23,236	
Interest rate swap		23,236
To record the change in the fair value of the derivative		
from an asset of $18,463 to a liability of $4,773.		

The net interest received is the difference between the floating rate at the beginning of 2022 (5.5%) and the fixed rate (5%) times $2 million notional amount. The effect of the net cash settlement is to reduce total cash outflows related to interest at $100,000, which is equal to paying the fixed rate of 5%. This result is the cash flow hedging effect that motivated Daley to enter the derivative arrangement.

At December 31, 2023, Daley repeats the process of adjusting the derivative to fair value. Because interest rates have decreased and Daley anticipates a future net cash payment, the swap represents a liability to the company.

December 31, 2023

Interest expense (4.75% × $2 million)	95,000	
Cash		95,000
To record interest on the note.		
Interest expense	5,000	
Cash [(4.75% × $2 million) − $100,000]		5,000
To record the net cash settlement on the swap.		
Notes payable	2,000,000	
Cash		2,000,000
To repay the debt.		
Interest rate swap	4,773	
Other comprehensive income		4,773
To close out the swap contract account; the swap contract		
was a liability of $4,773 and now has a fair value of zero.		

The fair value of the interest rate swap has decreased to zero, as there are no additional cash settlements expected as the debt and the swap has now matured. All earnings effects of the hedged item and derivative instrument have been recorded in the income statement in interest expense.

Total cash flows are affected as follows:

December 31, 2021	Payment on floating rate debt (5%)	($100,000)
	Net settlement on interest rate swap	0
	Total cash outflow	($100,000)
December 31, 2022	Payment on floating rate debt (5.5%)	($110,000)
	Net settlement on interest rate swap	10,000
	Total cash outflow	($100,000)
December 31, 2023	Payment on floating rate debt (4.75%)	($ 95,000)
	Net settlement on interest rate swap	(5,000)
	Total cash outflow	($100,000)

A company also can use a forward contract to hedge the risk of change in cash flows attributable to a component of a forecasted purchase of a commodity.

ILLUSTRATION OF CASH FLOW HEDGE – FORWARD CONTRACT Let's assume again that we have a company that seeks to hedge exposure to cash flow risk, this time from a forecasted purchase of a commodity. We see this in Illustration A–4, using the extended method. The shortcut method is not available because that can only be used for an interest-bearing asset or liability. A forecasted transaction of a nonfinancial commodity does not fit that category.

Cavalier Bicycles uses carbon fiber to produce its high-performance road and mountain bikes. Cavalier anticipates it will need to purchase 45,000 pounds of carbon fiber in July 2022 to make enough bikes to meet its fourth quarter sales demand. However, if the price of carbon fiber increases, the cost to produce the bikes will increase and, in turn, lower Cavalier's profit margins.

To hedge against the risk of rising carbon fiber prices, on June 1, 2022, Cavalier enters into a forward contract with a third-party intermediary to buy 45,000 pounds of carbon fiber at the current spot price of $10 per pound. It designates the contract as a cash flow hedge of the anticipated carbon fiber purchase because the hedged risk is attributable to the volatility in carbon fiber prices.

The price in the contract expires on July 31, 2022, and the contract will settle by an exchange of cash with the intermediary based on the spot price on the settlement date. As the illustration will show, Cavalier uses this forward contract to lock in the cost of its inventory at the prevailing market price of $450,000 (45,000 pounds × $10 per pound).

Illustration A–4

Cash Flow Hedge; Forward Contract

June 1, 2022 No entry is required, because the current spot price equals the contract price. Thus, the forward contract has no value.

June 30, 2022

Forward contract [($10.50 – $10.00) × 45,000]	22,500	
Other comprehensive income (OCI)		22,500
To record the change in the fair value of the derivative.		

At June 30, 2022, the spot prices of carbon fiber have increased. Therefore, the value of the forward contract to Cavalier Bicycles has increased, as Cavalier is able to buy carbon fiber at a lower price than current market prices. Thus, Cavalier reports the forward contract in the balance sheet as an asset, with the gain on the derivative as a component of other comprehensive income. Cavalier will recognize this gain in current earnings when the hedged item—in this case the cost of carbon fiber—is recognized in earnings (when the produced inventory is sold).

If Cavalier purchases 45,000 pounds of carbon fiber on July 2, 2022, for $10.50, it would make the following entries to record the purchase of inventory and the settlement of the forward contract:

July 2, 2022

Inventory—Carbon Fiber	472,500	
Cash ($10.50 × 45,000 pounds)		472,500
To record purchase of inventory.		
Cash [($10.50 – $10.00) × 45,000]..	22,500	
Forward contract		22,500
To record settlement of the forward contract.		

The $22,500 forward contract settlement offsets the amount paid to purchase the inventory at the prevailing market price of $472,500. The result is a net cash outflow of $10 per pound, and an effective hedge of the cash flow for the purchase of inventory.

Cavalier defers the income effects of the forward contract in other comprehensive income until the period in which it sells the inventory, affecting earnings through the same line item as the hedged item—cost of goods sold. That is, the effect of the inventory price is reflected in cost of goods sold as the inventory is sold, and effect of the forward contract ($22,500) previously deferred with a credit to Other comprehensive income now is reflected as a $22,500 decrease in cost of goods sold as Cavalier debits Other comprehensive income for that same amount previously deferred.

For example, let's say that Cavalier manufactures the carbon fiber into bicycles. Cavalier sells its bikes during the fourth quarter of 2022 for $1,200,000, and the total value of the inventory, which includes the cost of the carbon fiber purchase made on July 2, 2022, is $650,000. The sale is recorded as follows:

Fourth Quarter 2022

Cash..	1,200,000	
Sales revenue..		1,200,000
To record sales.		
Cost of goods sold...	650,000	
Inventory—Bikes...		650,000
To record cost of goods sold.		
Other comprehensive income (OCI)..	22,500	
Cost of goods sold..		22,500
To match the earnings effect of the hedged item (cost of carbon fiber)		
and the forward contract.		

Because the hedged purchase of carbon fiber has now affected earnings, Cavalier also recognizes the previously deferred gain on the value of the forward contract into earnings.

● LOA–4

The possibility that foreign currency exchange rates might change exposes many companies to foreign currency risk.

FOREIGN CURRENCY HEDGES Today's economy is increasingly a global one. The majority of large "U.S." companies are, in truth, multinational companies that may receive only a fraction of their revenues from U.S. operations. Many operations of those companies are located abroad. Foreign operations often are denominated in the currency of the foreign country (the Euro, Japanese yen, Russian rubles, and so on). Even companies without foreign operations sometimes hold investments, issue debt, or conduct other transactions denominated in foreign currencies. As exchange rates change, the dollar equivalent of the foreign currency changes. The possibility of currency rate changes exposes these companies to the risk that some transactions require settlement in a currency other than the entities' functional currency or that foreign operations will require translation adjustments to reported amounts.

A foreign currency hedge can be a hedge of foreign currency exposure of the following:

- A firm commitment—treated as a fair value hedge.
- An available-for-sale security—treated as a fair value hedge.
- A forecasted transaction—treated as a cash flow hedge.
- A company's net investment in a foreign operation—the gain or loss is reported in *other comprehensive income* as part of unrealized gains and losses from foreign currency translation.[14]

HEDGE EFFECTIVENESS When a company elects to apply hedge accounting, it must establish at the inception of the hedge the method it will use to assess the effectiveness of the hedging derivative.[15] The key criterion for qualifying as a hedge is that the hedging relationship must be "highly effective" in achieving offsetting changes in fair values or cash flows based on the hedging company's specified risk management objective and strategy.

An assessment of this effectiveness must be made at least every three months and whenever financial statements are issued or earnings are reported. There are no precise guidelines for assessing effectiveness, but it generally means a high correlation between changes in the fair value or cash flows of the derivative and of the item being hedged, not necessarily a specific reduction in risk. Initial hedge effectiveness assessments are performed quantitatively and, at hedge inception, the company must elect whether it will perform subsequent assessments qualitatively or quantitatively. Hedge accounting must be terminated for hedging relationships that no longer are highly effective.

In Illustration A–2 (and in Illustration A–3), the loss on the hedged note exactly offset the gain on the swap. This is because the swap in this instance was highly effective in hedging the risk due to interest rate changes. However, the loss and gain would not have exactly offset each other if there were differences in critical terms of the swap and the hedged note. For instance, suppose the swap's term had been different from that of the note (say a three-year swap term compared with the 18-month term of the note) or if the notional amount of the swap differed from that of the note (say $500,000 rather than $1 million). In that case, changes in the fair value of the swap and changes in the fair value of the note would not be the same. The result would be a greater (or lesser) amount recognized in earnings for the swap than for the note. Because there would not be an exact offset, earnings would be affected. That is a desired effect of hedge accounting; to the extent that a hedge is effective, the earnings effect of a derivative cancels out the earnings effect of the item being hedged.

Hedge accounting also allows a company to exclude certain components of the change in the value of the derivative from the calculation of hedge effectiveness, including components of the change in time value, as well as differences in spot and forward or futures prices. The company amortizes the initial value of the excluded component and can either (a) elect to recognize the initial value of the excluded component in earnings immediately or (b) amortize it over the life of the hedging instrument. The difference between the initial value recognized in the income statement and the change in the fair value of the excluded component is reported as an item of Other comprehensive income.

FAIR VALUE CHANGES UNRELATED TO THE RISK BEING HEDGED In Illustration A–2, the fair value of the hedged note and the fair value of the swap changed by the same amounts each year because we assumed the fair values changed only due to interest rate changes. It's also possible, though, that the note's fair value would change by an amount different from that of the swap for reasons unrelated to interest rates. Remember from our earlier discussion that the market's perception of a company's creditworthiness, and thus its ability to pay interest and principal when due, also can affect the value of debt, whether interest rates change or not. In hedge accounting, we ignore those changes. We recognize only the fair value changes in the hedged item that we can attribute to the risk being hedged (interest rate risk in this case). For example, if a changing perception of default risk had caused the note's

> To qualify as a hedge, the hedging relationship must be highly effective in achieving offsetting changes in fair values or cash flows.

> Imperfect hedges result in part of the derivative gain or loss being included in current earnings.

> Fair value changes unrelated to the risk being hedged are ignored.

---

[14]This is the same treatment previously prescribed for these translation adjustments by FASB ASC 830: Foreign Currency Matters.

[15]Remember, if a derivative is not designated as a hedge, any gains or losses from changes in its fair value are recognized immediately in earnings.

fair value to increase by an additional, say $5,000, our journal entries in Illustration A–2 would have been unaffected. Notice, then, that although we always mark a *derivative* to fair value, the reported amount of the *item being hedged* may not be its fair value. We mark a hedged item to fair value only to the extent that its fair value changed due to the risk being hedged.

● LOA–5

Disclosure of Derivatives and Risk

To be adequately informed about the effectiveness of a company's risk management, investors and creditors need information about strategies for holding derivatives and specific hedging activities. Toward that end, extensive disclosure requirements provide information that includes the following:

- Objectives and strategies for holding and issuing derivatives.
- A description of the items for which risks are being hedged.
- The location and fair value amounts of derivative instruments reported in the balance sheet.
- For forecasted transactions: a description, time before the transaction is expected to occur, the gains and losses accumulated in other comprehensive income, and the events that will trigger their recognition in earnings.
- Beginning balance of, changes in, and ending balance of the derivative component of other comprehensive income.
- The location and net amount of gain or loss reported in earnings.
- Qualitative and quantitative information about failed fair value or cash flow hedges: canceled commitments or previously hedged forecasted transactions no longer expected to occur.

The intent is to provide information about the company's success in reducing risks and, consequently, about risks not managed successfully. Ample disclosures about derivatives are essential to maintain awareness of potential opportunities and problems with risk management.

In addition, GAAP requires companies to provide enhanced disclosures indicating (a) how and why the company uses derivative instruments, (b) how the company accounts for derivative instruments and related hedged items, and (c) how derivative instruments and related hedged items affect the company's balance sheet, income statement, and cash flows.[16] The required disclosures include two tables, one that highlights the location and fair values of derivative instruments in the balance sheet, and another that indicates the location and amounts of gains and losses on derivative instruments in the income statement. The two tables distinguish between derivative instruments that are designated as hedging instruments and those that are not. The tables also categorize derivative instruments by each major type—interest rate contracts, foreign exchange contracts, equity contracts, commodity contracts, credit contracts, and other types of contracts and by income and expense line item (if applicable).

Even for some traditional liabilities, the amounts reported on the face of the financial statements provide inadequate disclosure about the degree to which a company is exposed to risk of loss. To provide adequate disclosure about a company's exposure to risk, additional information must be provided about (a) concentrations of credit risk and (b) the fair value of all financial instruments.[17]

● LOA–6

Extended Method for Interest Rate Swap Accounting

A shortcut method for accounting for an interest rate swap is permitted when a hedge meets certain criteria. In general, the criteria are designed to see if the hedge supports the assumption of "no ineffectiveness." Illustration A–2 of a fair value hedge met those criteria, in

---

[16]FASB ASC 815: Derivatives and Hedging.
[17]FASB ASC 825–10–50–1: Financial Instruments—Overall—Disclosure.

particular, (a) the swap's notional amount matches the note's principal amount, (b) the swap's expiration date matches the note's maturity date, (c) the fair value of the swap is zero at inception, and (d) the floating payment is at the market rate.[18] Because Wintel can conclude that the swap will be highly effective in offsetting changes in the fair value of the debt, it can use the changes in the fair value of the swap to measure the offsetting changes in the fair value of the debt. That's the essence of the shortcut method used in Illustration A–2. The extended method required when the criteria are *not* met for the shortcut method is described in this section (Illustration A–5 begins by describing the same scenario as in Illustration A–2). It produces the same effect on earnings and in the balance sheet as does the procedure shown in Illustration A–2. Note that the shortcut method is available only for interest rate swaps; the extended method applies to all other hedge instruments.

Illustration A–5
Interest Rate Swap
(Fixed Rate to Variable
Rate)—Extended Method

Wintel Semiconductors issued $1 million of 18-month, 10% notes payable to Third Bank on January 1, 2021. Wintel is exposed to the risk that general interest rates will decline, causing the fair value of its debt to rise. (If the fair value of Wintel's debt increases, its effective borrowing cost is higher relative to the market.)

- To hedge against this fair value risk, the firm entered into an 18-month interest rate swap agreement through an intermediary on January 1 and designated the swap as a hedge against changes in the fair value of the note.

- Although Wintel still will pay the 10% fixed rate to the bank, the swap calls for the company to *receive payment* from the intermediary based on a 10% fixed interest rate on a notional (principal) amount of $1 million and to *make payment* based on a floating interest rate tied to changes in general rates.

- Cash settlement of the net interest amount is made semiannually at June 30 and December 31 of each year, with the net interest being the difference between the $50,000 fixed interest [$1 million × (10% × ½)] and the floating interest rate, times $1 million at those dates. That is, if the floating rate is less than the fixed rate, Wintel will collect cash. If the floating rate is more than the fixed rate, Wintel will pay cash.

- Floating (market) settlement rates were 9% at June 30, 2021, 8% at December 31, 2021, and 9% at June 30, 2022.

Net interest receipts can be calculated as shown below. Fair values of both the derivative and the note resulting from those market rate changes are assumed to be quotes obtained from securities dealers.

	1/1/21	6/30/21	12/31/21	6/30/22
Fixed rate	10%	10%	10%	10%
Floating rate	10%	9%	8%	9%
Fixed payments				
[$1 million × (10% × ½)]		$ 50,000	$ 50,000	$ 50,000
Floating payments				
($1 million × ½ floating rate)		45,000	40,000	45,000
Net interest receipts		$ 5,000	$ 10,000	$ 5,000
Fair value of interest rate swap	$0	$ 9,363	$ 9,615	$0
Fair value of note payable	$1,000,000	$1,009,363	$1,009,615	$1,000,000

When the floating rate declined in Illustration A–5 from 10% to 9%, the fair values of both the derivative (swap) and the note increased. This created an offsetting gain on the derivative and holding loss on the note. Both are recognized in earnings the same period and in the same income statement line item (June 30, 2021). Because the changes in fair value (holding gains and losses) are presented in the same line item as the earnings effect of

---

[18]There is no precise minimum interval, though it generally is three to six months or less. Other criteria are specified by FASB ASC 815–20–25–104: Derivatives and Hedging—Hedging—General—Recognition—Shortcut Method, *SFAS No. 133* (para. 68), in addition to the key conditions listed here.

the underlying hedged item (interest expense), we record these holding gains and losses as decreases or increases in interest expense.

<table>
<tr><td colspan="3">**January 1, 2021**</td></tr>
<tr><td>Cash...</td><td>1,000,000</td><td></td></tr>
<tr><td>   Notes payable ....</td><td></td><td>1,000,000</td></tr>
<tr><td colspan="3">*To record the issuance of the note.*</td></tr>
<tr><td colspan="3">**June 30, 2021**</td></tr>
<tr><td>Interest expense (10% × ½ × $1 million)......................................</td><td>50,000</td><td></td></tr>
<tr><td>   Cash ....</td><td></td><td>50,000</td></tr>
<tr><td colspan="3">*To record interest to Third Bank.*</td></tr>
<tr><td>Cash [$50,000 – (9% × ½ × $1 million)]..</td><td>5,000</td><td></td></tr>
<tr><td>Interest rate swap ($9,363 – $0)..</td><td>9,363</td><td></td></tr>
<tr><td>   Interest expense (to balance)..</td><td></td><td>14,363</td></tr>
<tr><td colspan="3">*To record the net cash settlement, accrued interest on the swap,*
and change in the fair value of the derivative.</td></tr>
<tr><td>Interest expense...</td><td>9,363</td><td></td></tr>
<tr><td>   Notes payable ($1,009,363 – $1,000,000)................................</td><td></td><td>9,363</td></tr>
<tr><td colspan="3">*To record change in fair value of the note due to interest rate changes.*</td></tr>
</table>

The interest rate swap is designated as a fair value hedge on this note at issuance.

The swap settlement is the difference between the fixed interest (5%) and variable interest (4.5%).

The fair value of derivatives is recognized in the balance sheet. All changes in fair value are presented in the same line item as the earnings effect of the hedged item.

The hedged liability (or asset) is adjusted to fair value as well.

The net interest settlement on June 30, 2021, is $5,000 because the fixed rate is 5% (half of the 10% annual rate) and the floating rate is 4.5% (half of the 9% annual rate). A holding gain ($14,363) is produced by holding the derivative security during a time when an interest rate decline caused an increase in the value of that asset. A portion ($5,000) of the gain was received in cash, and another portion ($9,363) is reflected as an increase in the value of the asset.

We also have a holding loss of the same amount. This is because we also held a liability during the same time period, and the interest rate change caused its fair value to increase as well. The changes in fair value (holding gains and losses) are presented in the same line item as the earnings effect of the underlying hedged item (interest expense). So, we record these holding gains and losses as decreases or increases in interest expense.

<table>
<tr><td colspan="3">**December 31, 2021**</td></tr>
<tr><td>Interest expense (9% × ½ × $1,009,363)......................................</td><td>45,421</td><td></td></tr>
<tr><td>Notes payable (difference)*...</td><td>4,579</td><td></td></tr>
<tr><td>   Cash (10% × ½ × $1,000,000)..</td><td></td><td>50,000</td></tr>
<tr><td colspan="3">*To record interest to Third Bank.*</td></tr>
<tr><td>Cash [$50,000 – (8% × ½ × $1 million)].......................................</td><td>10,000</td><td></td></tr>
<tr><td>Interest rate swap ($9,615 – $9,363)..</td><td>252</td><td></td></tr>
<tr><td>   Interest revenue (9% × ½ × $9,363)..</td><td></td><td>421</td></tr>
<tr><td>   Interest expense (to balance)..</td><td></td><td>9,831</td></tr>
<tr><td colspan="3">*To record the net cash settlement, accrued interest on the swap,*
and change in the fair value of the derivative.</td></tr>
<tr><td>Interest expense...</td><td>4,831</td><td></td></tr>
<tr><td>   Notes payable ($1,009,615 – $1,009,363 + $4,579).................</td><td></td><td>4,831</td></tr>
<tr><td colspan="3">*To record the change in fair value of the note due to interest rate changes.*</td></tr>
</table>

As with any debt, interest expense is the effective rate times the outstanding balance.

The cash settlement is the difference between the fixed interest (5%) and variable interest (4%).

Interest ($421) accrues on the asset.

The note is increased by the change in fair value.

*We could use a premium on the note to adjust its book value.

We determine interest on the note the same way we do for any liability, as you learned earlier—at the effective rate (9% × ½) times the outstanding balance ($1,009,363). This results in reducing the note's book value for the cash interest paid in excess of the interest expense.

The fair value of the swap increased due to the interest rate decline by $252 (from $9,363 to $9,615). The holding gain we recognize in earnings consists of that increase (a) plus the $10,000 cash settlement also created by the interest rate decline and (b) minus the $421 increase that results not from the interest rate decline, but from interest accruing on the asset.[19] Similarly, we adjust the note's book value by the amount necessary to increase it to fair value, allowing for the $4,579 reduction in the note in the earlier entry to record interest. Again, all amounts recognized in earnings are presented as interest expense.

At June 30, 2022, Wintel repeats the process of adjusting to fair value both the derivative investment and the note being hedged.

June 30, 2022

Interest expense (8% × ½ × $1,009,615)	40,385	
Notes payable (difference)	9,615	
Cash (10% × ½ × $1,000,000)		50,000
To record interest to Third Bank.		
Cash [$50,000 − (9% × ½ × $1 million)]	5,000	
Interest expense (to balance)	5,000	
Interest rate swap ($0 − $9,615)		9,615
Interest revenue (8% × ½ × $9,615)		385
To record the net cash settlement, accrued interest on the swap,		
and change in the fair value of the derivative.		
Notes payable ($1,000,000 − $1,009,615 + $9,615)	0	
Interest expense		0
To record the change in fair value of the note due to interest		
rate changes.		
Note payable	1,000,000	
Cash		1,000,000
To repay the loan from Third Bank.		

Margin notes:
- Interest expense is the effective rate times the outstanding balance.
- The net interest received is the difference between the fixed interest (5%) and floating interest (4.5%).
- The swap's fair value now is zero.

The net interest received is the difference between the fixed rate (5%) and floating rate (4.5%), times $1 million. The fair value of the swap decreased by $9,615 (from $9,615 to zero).[20] The holding loss we recognize in earnings consists of that decline (a) minus the $5,000 portion of the decline resulting from it being realized in cash settlement and (b) plus the $385 increase that results not from the interest rate change, but from interest accruing on the asset.

Now let's see how the book values changed for the swap account and the note.

	Swap		Note	
Jan. 1, 2021				1,000,000
June 30, 2021	9,363			9,363
Dec. 31, 2021	252		4,579	4,831
June 30, 2022		9,615	9,615	
			1,000,000	
	0			0

---

[19]The investment in the interest rate swap represents the present value of expected future net interest receipts. As with other such assets, interest accrues at the effective rate times the outstanding balance. You also can think of the accrued interest mathematically as the increase in present value of the future cash flows as we get one period nearer to the dates when the cash will be received.

[20]Because there are no future cash receipts or payments from the swap arrangement at this point, the fair value of the swap is zero.

The income statement is affected as follows:

Income Statement + (—)		
June 30, 2021	(50,000)	Interest expense
	0	Interest expense (no time has passed)
	14,363	Interest expense - interest rate swap
	(9,363)	Interest expense - hedged note
	(45,000)	Net effect—same as floating interest payment
Dec. 31, 2021	(45,421)	Interest expense
	421	Interest expense (passage of time)
	9,831	Interest expense - interest rate swap
	(4,831)	Interest expense - hedged note
	(40,000)	Net effect—same as floating interest payment
June 30, 2022	(40,385)	Interest expense
	385	Interest expense (passage of time)
	(5,000)	Interest expense - interest rate swap
	0	Interest expense - hedged note
	(45,000)	Net effect—same as floating interest payment

As this demonstrates, the swap effectively converts Wintel's fixed-interest debt to floating interest debt.

Additional Consideration

Private Company GAAP—Derivatives and Hedging. The Private Company Council (PCC) sought feedback from private company stakeholders and found that most users of private company financial statements find it difficult to obtain fixed-rate borrowing and often enter into an interest rate swap to economically convert their variable-rate borrowing into a fixed-rate borrowing. However, this arrangement caused significant variability in the income statements. The PCC concluded that the cost and complexity of hedge accounting outweighed the benefits for private companies.

In response to the PCC's conclusion, the FASB issued an Accounting Standards Update in 2014 that allows a simplified approach to make it easier for certain interest rate swaps to qualify for hedge accounting for private companies that is quite different from what is required for public companies.[21] This alternative allows a nonpublic company (that's not a financial institution) to apply hedge accounting to its interest rate swaps as long as the terms of the swap and the related debt are aligned. If the conditions are met, the company can assume the cash flow hedge is fully effective. Those applying the simplified hedge accounting approach will be able to recognize the swap at its settlement value, instead of at its fair value. As a result, the amount of interest expense recorded in the income statement approximates the amount that would have been recognized if the private company had borrowed at a fixed rate.

This alternative should significantly reduce the cost and complexity of accounting for derivatives and hedging transactions of private companies.

---

[21]*Accounting Standards Update No. 2014-03,* "Derivatives and Hedging (Topic 815): Accounting for Certain Receive-Variable, Pay-Fixed Interest Rate Swaps—Simplified Hedge Accounting Approach (a consensus of the Private Comapny Council)," (Norwalk, Conn.: FASB, January 2014).

The Bottom Line

● **LOA–1**   A variety of derivative securities are used to hedge against risk. These include futures contracts, forward contracts, and options.

● **LOA–2**   A fair value hedge is used to hedge against the exposure to changes in the fair value of an asset, liability, or a firm commitment.

● **LOA–3**   A cash flow hedge is used to hedge against the exposure to changes in cash inflows or cash outflows of an asset or liability or a forecasted transaction (like a future purchase or sale).

● **LOA–4**   A foreign currency hedge is used to hedge against the possibility that currency rate changes will cause some transactions that require settlement in a currency other than the entities' functional currency or that foreign operations will require translation adjustments to reported amounts.

● **LOA–5**   Ample disclosures about derivatives are essential to maintain awareness of potential opportunities and problems with risk management.

● **LOA–6**   The extended method produces the same results as the short-cut method and must be used unless (a) the swap's notional amount matches the note's principal amount, (b) the swap's expiration date matches the note's maturity date, (c) the fair value of the swap is zero at inception, and (d) the floating payment is at the market rate. ●

Questions For Review of Key Topics

Q A–1   Some financial instruments are called derivatives. Why?

Q A–2   Should gains and losses on a fair value hedge be recorded as they occur, or should they be recorded to coincide with losses and gains on the item being hedged?

Q A–3   Hines Moving Company held a fixed-rate debt of $2 million. The company wanted to hedge its fair value exposure with an interest rate swap. However, the only notional available at the time, on the type of swap it desired, was $2.5 million. What will be the effect of any gain or loss on the $500,000 notional difference?

Q A–4   What is a futures contract?

Q A–5   What is the effect on interest of an interest rate swap?

Q A–6   How are derivatives reported on the balance sheet? Why?

Q A–7   When is a gain or a loss from a cash flow hedge reported in earnings?

Exercises

≡ connect

E A–1
Derivatives;
hedge
classification
● **LOA–1**

Indicate (by abbreviation) the type of hedge each activity described below would represent.

Hedge Type

FV   Fair value hedge
CF   Cash flow hedge
FC   Foreign currency hedge
N   Would not qualify as a hedge

Activity

_____1. An options contract to hedge possible future price changes of inventory.
_____2. A futures contract to hedge exposure to interest rate changes prior to replacing bank notes when they mature.
_____3. An interest rate swap to synthetically convert floating rate debt into fixed rate debt.
_____4. An interest rate swap to synthetically convert fixed rate debt into floating rate debt.
_____5. A futures contract to hedge possible future price changes of timber covered by a firm commitment to sell.
_____6. A futures contract to hedge possible future price changes of a forecasted sale of aluminum.
_____7. ExxonMobil's net investment in a Kuwait oil field.
_____8. An interest rate swap to synthetically convert floating rate interest on a stock investment into fixed rate interest.
_____9. An interest rate swap to synthetically convert fixed rate interest on a held-to-maturity debt investment into floating rate interest.

(continued)

(concluded)   _____10. An interest rate swap to synthetically convert floating rate interest on a held-to-maturity debt investment into fixed rate interest.

_____11. An interest rate swap to synthetically convert fixed rate interest on a stock investment into floating rate interest.

E A–2
Derivatives;
interest rate
swap; fixed rate
debt
● LOA–2

On January 1, 2021, LLB Industries borrowed $200,000 from Trust Bank by issuing a two-year, 10% note, with interest payable quarterly. LLB entered into a two-year interest rate swap agreement on January 1, 2021, and designated the swap as a fair value hedge. Its intent was to hedge the risk that general interest rates will decline, causing the fair value of its debt to increase. The agreement called for the company to receive payment based on a 10% fixed interest rate on a notional amount of $200,000 and to pay interest based on a floating interest rate. The contract called for cash settlement of the net interest amount quarterly.

Floating (LIBOR) settlement rates were 10% at January 1, 8% at March 31, and 6% June 30, 2021. The fair values of the swap are quotes obtained from a derivatives dealer. Those quotes and the fair values of the note are as indicated below.

	January 1	March 31	June 30
Fair value of interest rate swap	0	$ 6,472	$ 11,394
Fair value of note payable	$200,000	$206,472	$211,394

Required:

1. Calculate the net cash settlement at March 31 and June 30, 2021.

2. Prepare the journal entries through June 30, 2021, to record the issuance of the note, interest, and necessary adjustments for changes in fair value.

E A–3
Derivatives;
interest rate
swap; fixed rate
investment
● LOA–2

(This is a variation of E A–2, modified to consider an investment in debt securities.)

On January 1, 2021, S&S Corporation invested in LLB Industries' negotiable two-year, 10% notes, with interest receivable quarterly. The company classified the investment as available-for-sale. S&S entered into a two-year interest rate swap agreement on January 1, 2021, and designated the swap as a fair value hedge. Its intent was to hedge the risk that general interest rates will decline, causing the fair value of its investment to increase. The agreement called for the company to make payment based on a 10% fixed interest rate on a notional amount of $200,000 and to receive interest based on a floating interest rate. The contract called for cash settlement of the net interest amount quarterly.

Floating (LIBOR) settlement rates were 10% at January 1, 8% at March 31, and 6% June 30, 2021. The fair values of the swap are quotes obtained from a derivatives dealer. Those quotes and the fair values of the investment in notes are as follows:

	January 1	March 31	June 30
Fair value of interest rate swap	0	$ 6,472	$ 11,394
Fair value of the investment in notes	$200,000	$206,472	$211,394

Required:

1. Calculate the net cash settlement at March 31 and June 30, 2021.

2. Prepare the journal entries through June 30, 2021, to record the investment in notes, interest, and necessary adjustments for changes in fair value.

E A–4
Derivatives;
interest rate
swap; fixed rate
debt; fair value
change unrelated
to hedged risk
● LOA–2

(This is a variation of E A–2, modified to consider fair value change unrelated to hedged risk.)

LLB Industries borrowed $200,000 from Trust Bank by issuing a two-year, 10% note, with interest payable quarterly. LLB entered into a two-year interest rate swap agreement on January 1, 2021, and designated the swap as a fair value hedge. Its intent was to hedge the risk that general interest rates will decline, causing the fair value of its debt to increase. The agreement called for the company to receive payment based on a 10% fixed interest rate on a notional amount of $200,000 and to pay interest based on a floating interest rate.

Floating (LIBOR) settlement rates were 10% at January 1, 8% at March 31, and 6% at June 30, 2021. The fair values of the swap are quotes obtained from a derivatives dealer. Those quotes and the fair values of the note are as indicated below. The additional rise in the fair value of the note (higher than that of the swap) on June 30 was due to investors' perceptions that the creditworthiness of LLB was improving.

	January 1	March 31	June 30
Fair value of interest rate swap	0	$ 6,472	$ 11,394
Fair value of note payable	$200,000	$206,472	$220,000

Required:

1. Calculate the net cash settlement at June 30, 2021.

2. Prepare the journal entries on June 30, 2021, to record the interest and necessary adjustments for changes in fair value.

E A–5
Derivatives;
interest rate
swap; fixed rate
debt; extended
method
● LOA–6

(This is a variation of Exercise A–2, modified to consider the extended method.)

On January 1, 2021, LLB Industries borrowed $200,000 from Trust Bank by issuing a two-year, 10% note, with interest payable quarterly. LLB entered into a two-year interest rate swap agreement on January 1, 2021, and designated the swap as a fair value hedge. Its intent was to hedge the risk that general interest rates will decline, causing the fair value of its debt to increase. The agreement called for the company to receive payment based on a 10% fixed interest rate on a notional amount of $200,000 and to pay interest based on a floating interest rate. The contract called for cash settlement of the net interest amount quarterly.

Floating (LIBOR) settlement rates were 10% at January 1, 8% at March 31, and 6% at June 30, 2021. The fair values of the swap are quotes obtained from a derivatives dealer. Those quotes and the fair values of the note are as follows:

	January 1	March 31	June 30
Fair value of interest rate swap	0	$ 6,472	$ 11,394
Fair value of note payable	$200,000	$206,472	$211,394

Required:

Prepare the journal entries through June 30, 2021, to record the issuance of the note, interest, and necessary adjustments for changes in fair value. Use the extended method demonstrated in Illustration A–5.

E A–6
Derivatives;
interest rate
swap; fixed-rate
debt; fair value
change unrelated
to hedged
● LOA–6

(Note: This is a variation of Exercise A–5, modified to consider fair value change unrelated to hedged risk.)

On January 1, 2021, LLB Industries borrowed $200,000 from Trust Bank by issuing a two-year, 10% note, with interest payable quarterly. LLB entered into a two-year interest rate swap agreement on January 1, 2021, and designated the swap as a fair value hedge. Its intent was to hedge the risk that general interest rates will decline, causing the fair value of its debt to increase. The agreement called for the company to receive payment based on a 10% fixed interest rate on a notional amount of $200,000 and to pay interest based on a floating interest rate. The contract called for cash settlement of the net interest amount quarterly.

Floating (LIBOR) settlement rates were 10% at January 1, 8% at March 31, and 6% June 30, 2021. The fair values of the swap are quotes obtained from a derivatives dealer. Those quotes and the fair values of the note are as indicated below. The additional rise in the fair value of the note (higher than that of the swap) on June 30 was due to investors' perceptions that the creditworthiness of LLB was improving.

	January 1	March 31	June 30
Fair value of interest rate swap	0	$ 6,472	$ 11,394
Fair value of note payable	$200,000	206,472	220,000

Required:

1. Calculate the net cash settlement at June 30, 2021.

2. Prepare the journal entries on June 30, 2021, to record the interest and necessary adjustments for changes in fair value. Use the extended method demonstrated in Illustration A–5.

E A–7
Derivatives; fair
value hedge—
futures contract
● LOA–2

Arlington Steel Company is a producer of raw steel and steel-related products. On January 3, 2022, Arlington enters into a firm commitment to purchase 10,000 tons of iron ore pellets from a supplier to satisfy spring production demands. The purchase is to be at a fixed price of $63 per ton on April 30, 2022. To protect against the risk of changes in the fair value of the commitment contract, Arlington enters into a futures contract to sell 10,000 tons of iron ore on April 30 for $63/ton (the current price). The contract calls for net cash settlement, and the company must report changes in the fair values of its hedging instruments each quarter.

Required:

On March 31, the price of iron ore fell to $61/ton, and then to $60/ton on April 30.

1. Calculate the net cash settlement at April 30, 2022.

2. Prepare the journal entries for the period January 3 to April 30, 2022, to record the firm commitment, necessary adjustments for changes in fair value, and settlement of the futures contract.

A-26   APPENDIX A   Derivatives

E A–8
Derivatives;
foreign currency;
cash flow hedge
● LOA–4

Cleveland Company is a U.S. firm with a U.S. dollar functional currency that manufactures copper-related products. It forecasts that it will sell 5,000 feet of copper tubing to one of its largest customers at a price of ¥50,000,000. Although this sale has not been firmly committed, Cleveland expects that the sale will occur in six months on June 30, 2022. Thus, Cleveland is exposed to changes in foreign currency exchange rates. To reduce this exposure, Cleveland enters into a six-month foreign currency exchange forward contract with a third-party dealer on January 1, 2022, to deliver ¥ and receive US$. The foreign exchange contract has the following terms:

Contract amount: ¥50,000,000
Maturity date: June 30, 2022
Forward contract rate: ¥105.00 = US $1.00

Yen / US$ Exchange rates:

Date	Spot rate	Forward rate for June 30
January 1	¥100.00/US $1.00	¥105.00/US $1.00
March 31	¥102.00/US $1.00	¥108.00/US $1.00
June 30	¥110.00/US $1.00	

Cleveland obtains the fair values of the forward exchange contract from the third-party dealer.

	January 1	March 31	June 30
Swap fair value	$0	$12,900	$21,645

Required:
1. Calculate the net settlement on June 30, 2022.
2. Prepare the journal entries for the period January 1 to June 30, 2022, to record the forward contract, necessary adjustments for changes in fair value, and settlement.

E A–9
Derivatives; cash
flow hedge;
interest rate
swap; shortcut
method
● LOA–3

On January 1, 2021, JPS Industries borrowed $300,000 from Austin Bank by issuing a three-year, floating rate note based on LIBOR, with interest payable semi-annually on June 30 and December of each year. JPS entered into a three-year interest rate swap agreement on January 1, 2021, and designated the swap as a cash flow hedge. The intent was to hedge the risk that interest rates will rise, increasing its semi-annual interest payments. The swap agreement called for the company to receive payment based on a floating interest rate on a notional amount of $300,000 and to pay a 6% fixed interest rate. The contract called for cash settlement of the net interest amount semi-annually, and the rate on each reset date (June 30 and December 31) determines the variable interest rate for the following six months.

LIBOR rates in 2021 were 6% at January 1, 5.5% at June 30, and 7% at December 31. The fair values of the swap on those dates, obtained by dealer quotes, were as follows:

	January 1	June 30	December 31
Swap fair value	$0	$(3,100)	$4,000

Required:
1. Calculate the net settlement on June 30, 2021.
2. Prepare journal entries for the period January 1 to December 31, 2021, to record the note payable and hedging instrument, necessary adjustments for changes in fair value, and settlement of the swap contract.

Problems

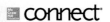

P A–1
Derivatives;
interest rate swap
● LOA–2

On January 1, 2021, Labtech Circuits borrowed $100,000 from First Bank by issuing a three-year, 8% note, payable on December 31, 2023. Labtech wanted to hedge the risk that general interest rates will decline, causing the fair value of its debt to increase. Therefore, Labtech entered into a three-year interest rate swap agreement on January 1, 2021, and designated the swap as a fair value hedge. The agreement called for the company to receive payment based on an 8% fixed interest rate on a notional amount of $100,000 and to pay interest based on a floating interest rate tied to LIBOR. The contract called for cash settlement of the net interest amount on December 31 of each year.

Floating (LIBOR) settlement rates were 8% at inception and 9%, 7%, and 7% at the end of 2021, 2022, and 2023, respectively. The fair values of the swap are quotes obtained from a derivatives dealer. These quotes and the fair values of the note are as follows:

	January 1		December 31	
	2021	**2021**	**2022**	**2023**
Fair value of interest rate swap	0	$ (1,759)	$ 935	0
Fair value of note payable	$100,000	$98,241	$100,935	$100,000

Required:
1. Calculate the net cash settlement at the end of 2021, 2022, and 2023.
2. Prepare the journal entries during 2021 to record the issuance of the note, interest, and necessary adjustments for changes in fair value.
3. Prepare the journal entries during 2022 to record interest, net cash interest settlement for the interest rate swap, and necessary adjustments for changes in fair value.
4. Prepare the journal entries during 2023 to record interest, net cash interest settlement for the interest rate swap, necessary adjustments for changes in fair value, and repayment of the debt.
5. Calculate the book values of both the swap account and the note in each of the three years.
6. Calculate the net effect on earnings of the hedging arrangement in each of the three years. (Ignore income taxes.)
7. Suppose the fair value of the note at December 31, 2021, had been $97,000 rather than $98,241, with the additional decline in fair value due to investors' perceptions that the creditworthiness of Labtech was worsening. How would that affect your entries to record changes in the fair values?

P A–2
Derivatives;
interest rate swap;
comprehensive
● LOA–3

CMOS Chips is hedging a 20-year, $10 million, 7% bond payable with a 20-year interest rate swap and has designated the swap as a fair value hedge. The agreement called for CMOS to receive payment based on a 7% fixed interest rate on a notional amount of $10 million and to pay interest based on a floating interest rate tied to LIBOR. The contract calls for cash settlement of the net interest amount on December 31 of each year.

At December 31, 2021, the fair value of the derivative and of the hedged bonds has increased by $100,000 because interest rates declined during the reporting period.

Required:
1. Does CMOS have an unrealized gain or loss on the derivative for the period? On the bonds? Will earnings increase or decrease due to the hedging arrangement? Why?
2. Suppose interest rates increased, rather than decreased, causing the fair value of both the derivative and of the hedged bonds to decrease by $100,000. Would CMOS have an unrealized gain or loss on the derivative for the period? On the bonds? Would earnings increase or decrease due to the hedging arrangement? Why?
3. Suppose the fair value of the bonds at December 31, 2021, had increased by $110,000 rather than $100,000, with the additional increase in fair value due to investors' perceptions that the creditworthiness of CMOS was improving. Would CMOS have an unrealized gain or loss on the derivative for the period? On the bonds? Would earnings increase or decrease due to the hedging arrangement? Why?
4. Suppose the notional amount of the swap had been $12 million, rather than the $10 million principal amount of the bonds. As a result, at December 31, 2021, the swap's fair value had increased by $120,000 rather than $100,000. Would CMOS have an unrealized gain or loss on the derivative for the period? On the bonds? Would earnings increase or decrease due to the hedging arrangement? Why?
5. Suppose BIOS Corporation is an investor, having purchased all $10 million of the bonds issued by CMOS as described in the original situation above. BIOS is hedging its investment, classified as available-for-sale, with a 20-year interest rate swap and has designated the swap as a fair value hedge. The agreement called for BIOS to make *payment* based on a 7% fixed interest rate on a notional amount of $10 million and to *receive* interest based on a floating interest rate tied to LIBOR. Would BIOS have an unrealized gain or loss on the derivative for the period due to interest rates having declined? On the bonds? Would earnings increase or decrease due to the hedging arrangement? Why?

P A–3
Derivatives;
interest rate
swap; fixed rate
debt; extended
method
● LOA–6

(Note: This is a variation of P A–1, modified to consider the extended method demonstrated in Illustration A–5.)

On January 1, 2021, Labtech Circuits borrowed $100,000 from First Bank by issuing a three-year, 8% note, payable on December 31, 2023. Labtech wanted to hedge the risk that general interest rates will decline, causing the fair value of its debt to increase. Therefore, Labtech entered into a three-year interest rate swap agreement on January 1, 2021, and designated the swap as a fair value hedge. The agreement called for the company to receive payment based on an 8% fixed interest rate on a notional amount of $100,000 and to pay interest based on a floating interest rate tied to LIBOR. The contract called for cash settlement of the net interest amount on December 31 of each year.

Floating (LIBOR) settlement rates were 8% at inception and 9%, 7%, and 7% at the end of 2021, 2022, and 2023, respectively. The fair values of the swap are quotes obtained from a derivatives dealer. Those quotes and the fair values of the note are as follows:

	January 1	December 31		
	2021	2021	2022	2023
Fair value of interest rate swap	0	$ (1,759)	$ 935	0
Fair value of note payable	$100,000	$ 98,241	100,935	$100,000

Required:
Use the extended method demonstrated in Illustration A–5.
1. Calculate the net cash settlement at the end of 2021, 2022, and 2023.
2. Prepare the journal entries during 2021 to record the issuance of the note, interest, and necessary adjustments for changes in fair value.
3. Prepare the journal entries during 2022 to record interest, net cash interest settlement for the interest rate swap, and necessary adjustments for changes in fair value.
4. Prepare the journal entries during 2023 to record interest, net cash interest settlement for the interest rate swap, necessary adjustments for changes in fair value, and repayment of the debt.
5. Calculate the book values of both the swap account and the note in each of the three years.
6. Calculate the net effect on earnings of the hedging arrangement in each of the three years. (Ignore income taxes.)
7. Suppose the fair value of the note at December 31, 2021, had been $97,000 rather than $98,241, with the additional decline in fair value due to investors' perceptions that the creditworthiness of Labtech was worsening. How would that affect your entries to record changes in the fair values?

Decision Makers' Perspective

Apply your critical-thinking ability to the knowledge you've gained. These cases will provide you an opportunity to develop your research, analysis, judgment, and communication skills. You also will work with other students, integrate what you've learned, apply it in real-world situations, and consider its global and ethical ramifications. This practice will broaden your knowledge and further develop your decision-making abilities.

©ImageGap/Getty Images

Real World Case A–1
Derivative losses; recognition in earnings
● LOA–4

The following is an excerpt from a disclosure note of Johnson & Johnson:

6. Fair Value Measurements (in part)
As of December 31, 2017, the balance of deferred net gains on derivatives included in accumulated other comprehensive income was $70 million after-tax. The Company expects that substantially all of the amounts related to forward foreign exchange contracts will be reclassified into earnings over the next 12 months as a result of transactions that are expected to occur over that period.

Required:
1. Johnson & Johnson indicates that it expects that substantially all of the balance of deferred net gains on derivatives will be reclassified into earnings over the next 12 months as a result of transactions that are expected to occur over that period. What is meant by "reclassified into earnings"?
2. What type(s) of hedging transaction might be accounted for in this way?

Communication Case A–2
Derivatives; hedge accounting
● LOA–3

A conceptual question in accounting for derivatives is this: Should gains and losses on a hedge instrument be recorded as they occur, or should they be recorded to coincide (match) with income effects of the item being hedged?

ABI Wholesalers plans to issue long-term notes in May that will replace its $20 million of 9.5% bonds when they mature in July. ABI is exposed to the risk that interest rates in July will have risen, increasing borrowing costs (reducing the selling price of its notes). To hedge that possibility, ABI entered a (Treasury bond) futures contract in May to deliver (sell) bonds in July at their *current* price.

As a result, if interest rates rise, borrowing costs will go up for ABI because it will sell notes at a higher interest cost (or lower price). But that loss will be offset (approximately) by the gain produced by being in the opposite position on Treasury bond futures.

Two opposing viewpoints are:

View 1: Gains and losses on instruments designed to hedge anticipated transactions should be recorded as they occur.

View 2: Gains and losses on instruments designed to hedge anticipated transactions should be recorded to coincide (match) with income effects of the item being hedged.

In considering this question, focus on conceptual issues regarding the practicable and theoretically appropriate treatment, unconstrained by GAAP. Your instructor will divide the class into two to six groups, depending on the size of the class. The mission of your group is to reach consensus on the appropriate accounting for the gains and losses on instruments designed to hedge anticipated transactions.

Required:

1. Each group member should deliberate the situation independently and draft a tentative argument prior to the class session for which the case is assigned.

2. In class, each group will meet for 10 to 15 minutes in different areas of the classroom. During that meeting, group members will take turns sharing their suggestions for the purpose of arriving at a single group treatment.

3. After the allotted time, a spokesperson for each group (selected during the group meetings) will share the group's solution with the class. The goal of the class is to incorporate the views of each group into a consensus approach to the situation.

B GAAP Comprehensive Case

Target Corporation prepares its financial statements according to U.S. GAAP. Target's financial statements and disclosure notes for the year ended February 3, 2018, are available in Connect. This material is also available under the Investor Relations link at the company's website (www.target.com). This case addresses a variety of characteristics of financial statements prepared using U.S. GAAP. Questions are grouped in parts according to various sections of the textbook.

Part A: Financial Statements, Income Measurement, and Current Assets

A1. What amounts did Target report for the following items for the year ended February 3, 2018?
    a. Total revenues
    b. Income from current operations
    c. Net income or net loss
    d. Total assets
    e. Total equity

A2. What was Target's basic earnings per share for the year ended February 3, 2018?

A3. What is Target's fiscal year-end? Why do you think Target chose that year-end?

A4. Regarding Target's audit report:
    a. Who is Target's auditor?
    b. Did Target receive a "clean" (unmodified) audit opinion?

A5. Refer to Target's balance sheet for the years ended February 3, 2018, and January 28, 2017. Based on the amounts reported for accumulated depreciation, and assuming no depreciable assets were sold during the year, prepare an adjusting entry to record Target's depreciation for the year.

A6. Refer to Target's statement of cash flows for the year ended February 3, 2018. Assuming your answer to requirement 1 includes all depreciation expense recognized during the year, how much amortization expense was recognized during the year?

A7. Note 13 provides information on Target's current assets. Assume all prepaid expenses are for prepaid insurance and that insurance expense comprises $50 million of the $14,248 million of selling, general, and administrative expenses reported in the income statement for the year ended February 3, 2018. How much cash did Target pay for insurance coverage during the year? Prepare the adjusting entry Target would make to record all insurance expense for the year. What would be the effect on the income statement and balance sheet if Target didn't record an adjusting entry for prepaid expenses?

A8. By what name does Target label its balance sheet?

A9. What amounts did Target report for the following items on February 3, 2018?
    a. Current assets
    b. Long-term assets
    c. Total assets

    d.　Current liabilities

    e.　Long-term liabilities

    f.　Total liabilities

    g.　Total shareholders' equity

A10.　What was Target's largest current asset? What was its largest current liability?

A11.　Compute Target's current ratio and debt to equity ratio in 2018?

A12.　Assuming Target's industry had an average current ratio of 1.0 and an average debt to equity ratio of 2.5, comment on Target's liquidity and long-term solvency.

A13.　Why do you think Target has chosen to have its fiscal year end on January 30, as opposed to December 31?

A14.　Regarding Target's audit report:

    a.　Who is Target's auditor?

    b.　Did Target receive a "clean" (unqualified) audit opinion?

A15.　By what name does Target label its income statement?

A16.　What amounts did Target report for the following items for the year ended February 3, 2018?

    a.　Sales

    b.　Gross margin

    c.　Earnings from continuing operations before income taxes

    d.　Net earnings from continuing operations

    e.　Net earnings

A17.　What was Target's basic earnings per share for the year ended February 3, 2018?

A18.　Does Target report any items as part of its comprehensive income? If so, what are they.

A19.　Does Target prepare the statement of cash flows using the direct method or the indirect method?

A20.　Which is higher, net earnings or operating cash flows? Which line item is the biggest reason for this difference? Explain why.

A21.　What are the largest investing cash flow and the largest financing cash flow reported by the company for the year ended February 3, 2018?

A22.　On what line of Target's income statement is revenue reported? What was the amount of revenue Target reported for the fiscal year ended February 3, 2018?

A23.　Disclosure Note 2 indicates that Target generally records revenue in retail stores at the point of sale. Does that suggest that Target generally records revenue at a point in time or over a period of time? Explain.

A24.　Disclosure Note 2 indicates that customers ("guests") can return some merchandise within 90 days of purchase and can return other merchandise within a year of purchase. How are Target's revenue and net income affected by returns, given that it does not know at the time a sale is made which items will be returned?

A25.　Disclosure Note 2 indicates that "Commissions earned on sales generated by leased departments are included within sales and were $44 million . . . in 2017 . . ." Do you think it likely that Target is accounting for those sales as a principal or an agent? Explain.

A26.　Disclosure Note 2 discusses Target's accounting for gift card sales. Does Target recognize revenue when it sells a gift card to a customer? If not, when does it recognize revenue? Explain.

A27.　Disclosure Note 4 discussed how Target accounts for consideration received from vendors, which they call "vendor income." Does that consideration produce revenue for Target? Does that consideration produce revenue for Target's vendors? Explain.

A28.　What is Target's policy for designating investments as cash equivalents?

A29.　What is Target's balance of cash equivalents for the fiscal year ended February 3, 2018?

A30. What is Target's policy with respect to accounting for merchandise returns?

A31. Does Target have accounts receivable? Speculate as to why it has the balance that it has. (Hint, see Disclosure Notes 9, 11 and 13.)

A32. Does Target use average cost, FIFO, or LIFO as its inventory cost flow assumption?

A33. In addition to the purchase price, what additional expenditures does the company include in the initial cost of merchandise?

A34. Calculate the gross profit ratio and the inventory turnover ratio for the fiscal year ended February 3, 2018. Compare Target's ratios with the industry averages of 24.5% and 7.1 times. Determine whether Target's ratios indicate the company is more/less profitable and sells its inventory more/less frequently compared to the industry average.

A35. What retail indices (internally measured or externally measured) does Target use to measure the LIFO provision?

A36. Does Target adjust the retail value of inventory for permanent markups or permanent markdowns to effectively report inventory at the lower of cost or market?

A37. Target has agreements with certain vendors whereby Target does not purchase or pay for merchandise until the merchandise is ultimately sold to a customer. Are sales and cost of sales of this inventory included in Target's income statement? Is unsold inventory at the end of the year included as part of ending inventory in the balance sheet?

Part B: Property, Plant, and Equipment and Intangible Assets

B1. What amount ($ in millions) does Target report for net property and equipment for the year ended February 3, 2018? What is the largest category of property and equipment reported on the face of the balance sheet?

B2. What amount ($ in millions) of cash was used in the fiscal year ended February 3, 2018, to purchase property and equipment? Is this an increase or decrease compared to the previous year?

B3. Do you think a company like Target would have more research and development costs or more advertising costs? Explain.

B4. What is Target's fixed-asset turnover ratio for the fiscal year ended February 3, 2018? What is the ratio intended to measure?

B5. Does Target include any intangible assets in total assets (yes/no)? Hint: see Notes 15 and 16.

B6. Compare the property and equipment listed in the balance sheet with the list in Note 14. What are the estimated useful lives for recording depreciation? Is land listed in Note 14 (yes/no)?

B7. In Note 14, which depreciation method does Target use for property and equipment for financial reporting? Which depreciation method is used for tax purposes? Why might these methods be chosen?

B8. In Note 14, how does Target record repairs and maintenance expense?

B9. In Note 14, does Target report any impairment of property and equipment for the year ended February 3, 2018? If so, what was the amount and what were the reasons for the impairments?

B10. From Notes 15 and 16, were any impairments related to intangible assets recorded for the year ended February 3, 2018? If so, what was the amount and what were the reasons for the impairments?

Part C: Investments

Target does not have investments in stock or bonds. However, CVS Health Corp., which purchased Target's pharmacy and clinical business during 2015, does have investments. Access CVS's 2017 10K (issued on February 14, 2018) at investors.cvshealth.com to answer the following questions:

C1. CVS indicates in Note 1 that it has some short-term investments that consist of certificates of deposit (CDs).

   a. How has CVS classified those CDs for accounting purposes?

   b. Per CVS's balance sheet, what was the balance in CVS's short-term investments as of December 31, 2017 and December 31, 2016?

   c. Per CVS's statement of cash flows, what cash transactions affected short-term investments during 2017?

   d. Prepare a T-account that summarizes transactions affecting CVS's short-term investments during 2017. Speculate as to the explanation for any "plug" figure necessary to make the T-account balance.

C2. Per Note 1, CVS has equity-method investments in SureScripts, LLC and in Heartland Healthcare Services. CVS indicates that those investments are immaterial for the year ended December 31, 2017. Assuming that the Heartland investment is material:

   a. How would Heartland's earnings affect CVS's income statement?

   b. How would Heartland's earnings affect CVS's balance sheet?

Part D: Liabilities

D1. Target's Consolidated Statement of Financial Position (its balance sheet) discloses its current assets and current liabilities.

   a. What are the four components of Target's current liabilities?

   b. Are current assets sufficient to cover current liabilities? What is the current ratio for the year ended February 3, 2018? How does the ratio compare with the prior year?

   c. Why might a company want to avoid having its current ratio be too low? Too high?

D2. Disclosure Note 2 discusses Target's accounting for gift card sales. Disclosure Note 18 indicates the amount of gift card liability that is recognized in Target's balance sheet.

   a. By how much did Target's gift card liability change between February 3, 2018 and January 28, 2017?

   b. How would the following affect Target's gift card liability (indicate "increase," "decrease," or "no change" for each):

      i. Sale of a gift card

      ii. Redemption of a gift card (the holder using it to acquire goods or services)

      iii. Increase in breakage estimated for gift cards already sold

D3. Disclosure Note 19 discusses Target's accounting for contingencies.

   a. What is Target's approach for accruing losses for litigation claims associated with the data breach? Is their approach appropriate?

   b. Target experienced a data breach in 2013, when "an intruder stole certain payment card and other guest information from our network." Target recorded a contingent liability for litigation associated with the data breach at that time, and continues to update that liability over time based on new information. Related new expenses for fiscal 2017 totaled $5 million. Prepare a journal entry to record Target's recognition of new expenses associated with the data breach litigation.

D4. Calculate the debt to equity ratio for Target at February 3, 2018. The average ratio for companies in the Discount Retailers industry sector in a comparable time period was 2.0.

D5. Calculate Target's times interest earned ratio for the year ended February 3, 2018. The coverage for companies in the Discount Retailers industry sector in a comparable time period was 6.9.

Part E: Leases, Income Taxes, and Pensions

E1. Refer to disclosure note 22 following Target's financial statements. What is the amount reported for "capital" leases (shown as the present value of minimum lease payments)? What is the total of those lease payments? What accounts for the difference between the two amounts?

E2. What is the total of the operating lease payments?

E3.   New lease accounting guidance (discussed in Chapter 15) will require companies to report a liability for operating leases at present value as well as for capital leases (now called finance leases). If Target had used the new lease accounting guidance in its fiscal 2017 financial statements, what would be the amount reported as a liability for operating leases? Hint: Assume the payments "after 2020" are to be paid evenly over a 16 years period and all payments are at the end of years indicated. Target indicates elsewhere in its financial statements that 6% is an appropriate discount rate for its leases.

E4.   Refer to *Note 22: Leases*. New lease accounting guidance requires companies to record a right-of-use asset and a lease liability for all leases, with the exception of short-term leases, at present value. If Target had used the new lease accounting guidance in its fiscal 2017 (February 3, 2018) financial statements, what would be the amount reported as a liability for its leases, operating and capital (finance) combined [rounded to nearest $ million]?

Hint: Assume the payments "after 2020" are to be paid evenly over a 16-year period and all payments are at the end of years indicated. Target indicates elsewhere in its financial statements that 6% is an appropriate discount rate for its leases.

E5.   From the income statement, determine the income tax expense for the year ended February 3, 2018. Tie that number to the second table in Disclosure Note 23, "Provision for Income Taxes," and prepare a summary journal entry that records Target's tax expense from continuing operations for the year ended February 3, 2018.

E6.   Focusing on the third table in Disclosure Note 23, "Net Deferred Tax Asset/ (Liability)," calculate the change in net deferred tax assets or liability. By how much did that amount change? To what extent did you account for that change in the journal entry you wrote for the first requirement of this case? List possible causes of any difference.

E7.   Target's Note 23 indicates that "In December 2017, the U.S. government enacted the Tax Cuts and Jobs Act tax reform legislation (the Tax Act), which among other matters reduced the U.S. corporate income tax rate from 35 percent to 21 percent effective January 1, 2018. . . . We have recorded a provisional $352 million net tax benefit primarily related to the remeasurement of certain deferred tax assets and liabilities, including $381 million of benefit from the new lower rate, partially offset by $29 million of deferred income tax expense from our foreign operations." What's the effect on net income?

E8.   What is Target's liability for unrecognized tax benefits as of February 3, 2018? If Target were to prevail in court and realize $50 million more in tax savings than it thought more likely than not to occur, what would be the effect on the liability for unrecognized tax benefits and on net income?

E9.   What were the changes in Target's Projected Benefits Obligation in the fiscal years ended February 3, 2018 (fiscal 2017), and January 28, 2017 (fiscal 2016), for its qualified pension plans?

E10. What were the changes in Target's Pension Plan Assets in the fiscal years ended February 3, 2018, and January 28, 2017, for its qualified pension plans?

E11. Were these pension plans overfunded or underfunded for the fiscal years ended February 3, 2018, and January 28, 2017?

E12. What were the components of Target's Pension Expense in the fiscal years 2017, 2016, and 2015?

Part F: Shareholders' Equity and Additional Financial Reporting Issues

F1.   Refer to Target's Consolidated Statements of Shareholders' Investment. What are the six types of events and transactions that affected one or more of the Shareholders' Investment accounts in the year ended February 3, 2018?

F2.   Note 25, "Share Repurchase," provides the information we need to reconstruct the journal entry that summarizes Target's share repurchases in the year ended February 3, 2018. Provide that entry (dollars in millions, rounded to the nearest million).

F3.   Does Target account for share repurchases as (a) treasury stock or (b) retired shares

F4.   What are the three types of awards described in Note 26:Share-Based Compensation?

F5.   Based on the fair value of the awards granted, what was Target's primary form of share-based compensation for the year ended February 3, 2018?

F6.   Projections of future performance should be based primarily on continuing operations. What was diluted EPS for continuing operations in each of the most recent three years?

F7.   How many shares were included in diluted earnings per share but not basic earnings per share due to share-based compensation awards?

F8.   Refer to Target's financial statements for the year ended February 3, 2018. Note 3 provides information on an accounting change Target made in fiscal 2017. Was this a change in estimate, a change in principle, a change in reporting entity, or an error correction?

F9.   Did Target account for and report the change retrospectively or prospectively?

F10. What was the effect of the change on depreciation and amortization in fiscal 2016?

F11. Was the effect of the change on earnings per share in fiscal 2017 an increase, a decrease, or no effect?

F12. Is Target's cash provided by operating activities (a) increasing or (b) decreasing?

F13. Is Target's cash provided by operating activities more or less than net income in fiscal 2017?

F14. Is Target increasing or decreasing its investment in property and equipment?

F15. Is Target increasing or decreasing its long-term debt?

F16. Some transactions that don't increase or decrease cash must be reported in conjunction with a statement of cash flows. What activity of this type did Target report during each of the three years presented?

APPENDIX

C

IFRS Comprehensive Case

Air France–KLM (AF), a Franco-Dutch company, prepares its financial statements according to International Financial Reporting Standards. AF's financial statements and disclosure notes for the year ended December 31, 2017, are available in Connect. This material is also available under the Finance link at the company's website (www.airfranceklm.com). This case addresses a variety of characteristics of financial statements prepared using IFRS, often comparing and contrasting those attributes of statements prepared under U.S. GAAP. Questions are grouped in parts according to various sections of the textbook.

Part A: Financial Statements, Income Measurement, and Current Assets

A1. What amounts did AF report for the following items for the fiscal year ended December 31, 2017?

    a. Total revenues

    b. Income from current operations

    c. Net income or net loss (AF equity holders)

    d. Total assets

    e. Total equity

A2. What was AF's basic earnings or loss per share for the year ended December 31, 2017?

A3. Refer to AF's balance sheet and compare it to the balance sheet presentation in Illustration 2–14. What differences do you see in the format of the two balance sheets?

A4. What differences do you see in the terminology used in the two balance sheets?

A5. Describe the apparent differences in the order of presentation of the components of the balance sheet between IFRS as applied by Air France–KLM (AF) and a typical balance sheet prepared in accordance with U.S. GAAP.

A6. How does AF classify operating expenses in its income statement? How are these expenses typically classified in a U.S. company's income statement?

A7. How does AF classify interest paid, interest received, and dividends received in its statement of cash flows? What other alternatives, if any, does the company have for the classification of these items? How are these items classified under U.S. GAAP?

A8. Refer to AF's Note 30.2 "Description of the actuarial assumptions and related sensitivities."

    a. What are the average discount rates used to measure AF's (a) 10–15 year and (b) 15 year and more pension obligations in the "euro" geographic zone in 2017?

    b. If the rate used had been 1% (100 basis points) higher, what change would have occurred in the pension obligation in 2017? What if the rate had been 1% lower?

A9. In Note 4.6, AF indicates that "Sales related to air transportation are recognized when the transportation service is provided," so passenger and freight tickets are consequently recorded as 'Deferred revenue upon issuance.'"

    a. Examine AF's balance sheet. What is the total amount of deferred revenue on ticket sales as of December 31, 2017?

    b. When transportation services are provided with respect to the deferred revenue on ticket sales, what journal entry would AF make to reduce deferred revenue?

    c. Does AF's treatment of deferred revenue under IFRS appear consistent with how these transactions would be handled under U.S. GAAP? Explain.

A10. AF has a frequent flyer program, "Flying Blue," which allows members to acquire "miles" as they fly on Air France or partner airlines that are redeemable for free flights or other benefits.

    a. How does AF account for these miles?

    b. Does AF report any liability associated with these miles as of December 31, 2017?

    c. Although AF's 2017 annual report was issued prior to the effective date of ASU No. 2014-09, consider whether the manner in which AF accounts for its frequent flier program appears consistent with the revenue recognition guidelines included in the ASU.

A11. In Note 4.11, AF describes how it values trade receivables. How does the approach used by AF compare to U.S. GAAP?

A12. In Note 25, AF reconciles the beginning and ending balances of its valuation allowance for trade accounts receivable. Prepare a T-account for the valuation allowance and include entries for the beginning and ending balances and any reconciling items that affected the account during 2017.

A13. Examine Note 27. Does AF have any bank overdrafts? If so, are the overdrafts shown in the balance sheet the same way they would be shown under U.S. GAAP?

A14. What method does the company use to value its inventory? What other alternatives are available under IFRS? Under U.S. GAAP?

A15. AF's inventories are valued at the lower of cost or net realizable value. Does this approach differ from U.S. GAAP?

Part B: Property, Plant, and Equipment and Intangible Assets

B1. What method does Air France–KLM use to amortize the cost of computer software development costs? How does this approach differ from U.S. GAAP?

B2. AF does not report any research and development expenditures. If it did, its approach to accounting for research and development would be significantly different from U.S. GAAP. Describe the differences between IFRS and U.S. GAAP in accounting for research and development expenditures.

B3. AF does not report the receipt of any governments grants. If it did, its approach to accounting for government grants would be significantly different from U.S. GAAP. Describe the differences between IFRS and U.S. GAAP in accounting for government grants. If AF received a grant for the purchase of assets, what alternative accounting treatments are available under IFRS?

B4. AF's property, plant, and equipment is reported at cost. The company has a policy of not revaluing property, plant, and equipment. Suppose AF decided to revalue its flight equipment on December 31, 2017, and that the fair value of the equipment on that date was €12,000 million. Prepare the journal entry to record the revaluation, assuming that the journal entry to record annual depreciation had already been recorded. (Hint: you will need to locate the original cost and accumulated depreciation of the equipment at the end of the year in the appropriate disclosure note.)

B5. Under U.S. GAAP, what alternatives do companies have to value their property, plant, and equipment?

B6. AF calculates depreciation of plant and equipment on a straight-line basis, over the useful life of the asset. Describe any differences between IFRS and U.S. GAAP in the calculation of depreciation.

B7. When does AF test for the possible impairment of fixed assets? How does this approach differ from U.S. GAAP?

B8.   Describe the approach AF uses to determine fixed asset impairment losses. (Hint: see Note 4.14.) How does this approach differ from U.S. GAAP?

B9.   The following is included in AF's Disclosure Note 4.13: "Intangible assets are recorded at initial cost less accumulated amortization and any accumulated impairment losses." Assume that on December 31, 2017, AF decided to revalue its Other intangible assets (see Note 17), and that the fair value on that date was determined to be €500 million. Amortization expense for the year already has been recorded. Prepare the journal entry to record the revaluation.

Part C: Investments

C1.   Read Notes 23 and 35.4. Focusing on investments accounted for at fair value through profit and loss (FVTPL):

    a.   As of December 31, 2017, what is the total balance of those investments in the balance sheet?

    b.   How much of that balance is classified as current and how much as noncurrent?

    c.   How much of the fair value of those investments is accounted for using level 1, level 2, and level 3 inputs of the fair value hierarchy? Given that information, assess the reliability (representational faithfulness) of this fair value estimate.

C2.   Complete C1 again, but for investments accounted for as available for sale.

C3.   Given your answer to C1c and C2c, which type of investment has more reliable (representational faithful) fair value estimates: FVTPL investments or available for sale investments?

C4.   Read Notes 4.3. and 21.

    a.   When AF can exercise significant influence over an investee, what accounting approach does it use to account for the investment? How does AF determine if it can exercise significant influence?

    b.   If AF is involved in a joint venture, what accounting approach does it use to account for the investment?

    c.   What is the carrying value of AF's equity-method investments in its December 31, 2017, balance sheet?

    d.   How did AF's equity-method investments affect AF's 2017 net income from continuing operations?

Part D: Liabilities

D1.   Read Notes 4.6 and 35. What do you think gave rise to total deferred income of €249 as of the end of fiscal 2017? Would transactions of this type be handled similarly under U.S. GAAP?

D2.   Is the threshold for recognizing a provision under IFRS different than it is under U.S. GAAP? Explain.

D3.   Note 32 lists "other provisions."

    a.   Do the beginning and ending balances of total provisions and retirement benefits shown in Note 32 for fiscal 2017 tie to the balance sheet? By how much has the total amount of AF's "other provisions" increased or decreased during fiscal 2017?

    b.   Write journal entries for the following changes in the litigation provision that occurred during fiscal 2017, assuming any amounts recorded on the income statement are recorded as "provision expense" and any use of provisions is paid for in cash. In each case, provide a brief explanation of the event your journal entry is capturing.

      i.   New provision.

      ii.   Use of provision.

    c.   Is AF's treatment of litigation provision under IFRS similar to how it would be treated under U.S. GAAP?

D4.   Note 32.2 lists a number of contingent liabilities. Are amounts for those items recognized as a liability on AF's balance sheet? Explain.

D5. Examine the long-term borrowings in AF's balance sheet and the related note (33.2.2). Note that AF has convertible bonds outstanding that it issued in 2013. Prepare the journal entry AF would use to record the issue of convertible bonds.

Prepare the journal entry AF would use to record the issue of the convertible bonds if AF used U.S. GAAP.

D6. AF does not elect the fair value option (FVO) to report its financial liabilities. Examine Note 35.3, "Market value of financial instruments." If the company had elected the FVO for all of its debt measured at amortized cost, what would be the balance at December 31, 2017, in the fair value adjustment account?

Part E: Leases, Income Taxes, and Pensions

E1. In Note 4, "Summary of accounting policies," part 4.14, "Leases," AF states that "leases are classified as finance leases when the lease arrangement transfers substantially all the risks and rewards of ownership to the lessee." Is this the policy companies using U.S. GAAP follow?

E2. Is this the policy AF will follow when it begins applying the new lease guidance in the 2015 update to *IFRS 17*? Explain.

E3. What amounts are shown in AF''s December 31, 2017, balance sheet for deferred taxes?

E4. Here's an excerpt from one of AF's notes to its financial statements:

> **Deferred taxes (in part)**
>
> The Group records deferred taxes using the balance sheet liability method, providing for any temporary differences between the carrying amounts of assets and liabilities for financial reporting purposes and the amounts used for taxation purposes, except for exceptions described in IAS 12 "Income taxes." The tax rates used are those enacted or substantively enacted at the balance sheet date.

Is this policy consistent with U.S. GAAP? Explain.

E5. Below is an excerpt from one of AF's notes to its financial statements:

> **Deferred taxes (in part)**
>
> Deferred tax assets related to temporary differences and tax losses carried forward are recognized only to the extent it is probable that a future taxable profit will be available against which the asset can be utilized at the tax entity level.

Is this policy consistent with U.S. GAAP? Explain.

E6. AF reported past service cost (called prior service cost under U.S. GAAP) in its income statement as part of net periodic pension cost. Is that reporting method the same or different from the way we report prior service cost under U.S. GAAP?

E7. Look at Note 30.2, "Retirement Benefits." AF incorporates estimates regarding staff turnover, life expectancy, salary increase, retirement age, and discount rates. How did AF report changes in these assumptions? Is that reporting method the same or different from the way we report changes under U.S. GAAP?

E8. AF does not report remeasurement gains and losses in its income statement. Where did AF report these amounts? Is that reporting method the same or different from the way we report pension expense under U.S. GAAP?

E9. See Note 22. Did AF report Net interest cost or Net interest income in 2017? How is that amount determined?

Part F: Shareholders' Equity and Additional Financial Reporting Issues

F1. Locate Note 28.5 in AF's financial statements. What items comprise "Reserves and retained earnings," as reported in the balance sheet? If Air France–KLM used U.S. GAAP, what would be different for the reporting of these items?

F2. In its presentation of the components of the balance sheet, which is listed first, current assets or non-current assets? Does this approach differ from U.S. GAAP?

F3. In its presentation of the components of the balance sheet, which is listed first, current liabilities or non-current liabilities? Does this approach differ from U.S. GAAP?

F4. In its presentation of the components of the balance sheet, which is listed first, liabilities or shareholders' equity? Does this approach differ from U.S. GAAP?

F5. AF provides share-based compensation in the form of PPSs, Phantom Performance Shares. Recipients receive compensation in what form? Are such plans reported in the balance sheet as (a) assets, (b) liabilities, or (c) equity? [*Hint:* See Note 29: "Share-Based Compensation."]

F6. Are AF's PPSs cliff vesting or graded vesting?

F7. The PPS options are performance-based, which means that under either U.S. GAAP or IFRS the amount expensed depends on whether it's "probable" that the performance target will be met. Does this mean it's equally likely that performance-based PPSs will be expensed at the same amount under U.S. GAAP as under IFRS?

F8. What amount(s) of earnings per share did AF report in its income statement for the year ended December 31, 2017? If AF used U.S. GAAP, would it have reported EPS using the same classification?

F9. Refer to AF's disclosure notes, in particular Note 2, "Restatement of Accounts 2016." Was the change described in the note a change in estimate, a change in principle, a change in reporting entity, or an error correction?

F10. Is this the same approach AF would follow if using U.S. GAAP?

F11. What are the three primary classifications into which AF's cash inflows and cash outflows are separated?

F12. Is this classification the same as or different from cash flow statements prepared in accordance with U.S. GAAP?

F13. In which classification are cash inflows from dividends included in AF's cash flow statements?

F14. Is this classification different from cash flow statements prepared in accordance with U.S. GAAP?

Glossary

Accounting equation Assets = Liabilities + Shareholders' Equity.

Accounting principles board (APB) the second private sector body delegated the task of setting accounting standards.

Accounts storage areas used to keep track of how transactions and events cause increases and decreases in the balances of financial elements.

Accounts payable obligations to suppliers of merchandise or of services purchased on account.

Accounts receivable receivables resulting from the sale of goods or services on account.

Accounts receivable aging schedule calculating the necessary allowance for uncollectible accounts by applying different percentages to accounts receivable balances depending on the length of time outstanding.

Accretion expense the increase in an asset retirement obligation that accrues as an operating expense.

Accrual accounting measures income according to the entity's accomplishments and resource sacrifices during the period from transactions related to providing goods and services to customers, regardless of when cash is received or paid.

Accruals when the cash flow comes after either expense or revenue recognition.

Accrued interest interest that has accrued since the last interest date.

Accrued liabilities expenses already incurred but not yet paid (accrued expenses).

Accrued receivables recognition of revenue earned before cash is received.

Accumulated benefit obligation (ABO) the discounted present value of estimated retirement benefits earned so far by employees, applying the plan's pension formula using existing compensation levels.

Accumulated other comprehensive income (AOCI) a component of stockholders' equity that reports the accumulated amount of other comprehensive income items in the current and prior periods.

Acid-test ratio current assets, excluding inventories and prepaid items, divided by current liabilities.

Acquisition costs the amounts paid to acquire the rights to explore for undiscovered natural resources or to extract proven natural resources.

Activity-based method allocation of an asset's cost base using a measure of the asset's input or output.

Actuary a professional trained in a particular branch of statistics and mathematics to assess the various uncertainties and to estimate the company's obligation to employees in connection with its pension plan.

Additions the adding of a new major component to an existing asset.

Adjusted trial balance trial balance after adjusting entries have been recorded.

Adjusting entries internal transactions recorded at the end of any period when financial statements are prepared.

Advance payment payment made at the beginning of the lease that represents prepaid rent

Agent facilitates transfers of goods and services between sellers and customers.

Allocation base cost of the asset expected to be consumed during its service life.

Allocation method the pattern in which the allocation base is expected to be consumed.

Allowance for uncollectible accounts contra account that reduces accounts receivable to the net amount expected to be collected. Also called the allowance for bad debts, the allowance for doubtful accounts, or the allowance for credit losses.

Allowance method recording bad debt expense and reducing accounts receivable indirectly by crediting the allowance for uncollectible accounts, a contra account to accounts receivable, for an estimate of the amount that eventually will prove uncollectible.

American institute of accountants (AIA)/american institute of certified public accountants (AICPA) national organization of professional public accountants.

Amortization cost allocation for intangibles.

Annual bonuses annual bonuses are one-time payments in addition to normal salary, typically tied to performance of the individual or company during a period

Annuity cash flows received or paid in the same amount each period.

Annuity due cash flows occurring at the beginning of each period.

Antidilutive securities the effect of the conversion or exercise of potential common shares would be to increase, rather than decrease, EPS.

Articles of incorporation statement of the nature of the firm's business activities, the shares to be issued, and the composition of the initial board of directors.

Asset retirement obligations (AROS) obligations associated with the disposition of an operational asset.

Asset turnover ratio measure of a company's efficiency in using assets to generate revenue.

Asset/liability approach recognition and measurement of assets and liabilities drives revenue and expense recognition.

Assigning using receivables as collateral for loans; nonpayment of a debt will require the proceeds from collecting the assigned receivables to go directly toward repayment of the debt.

Auditor's report report issued by CPAs who audit the financial statements that informs users of the audit findings.

Auditors independent professionals who render an opinion about whether the financial statements fairly present the company's financial position, performance, and cash flows in compliance with GAAP.

Average collection period indication of the average age of accounts receivable.

Average cost method assumes cost of goods sold and ending inventory consist of a mixture of all the goods available for sale.

Average days in inventory indicates the average number of days it normally takes to sell inventory.

Balance sheet a financial statement that presents an organized list of assets, liabilities, and equity at a particular point in time.

Balance sheet approach determining an income statement amount by estimating the appropriate carrying value of a balance sheet account and then adjusting the account as necessary to reach that carrying value.

Bank reconciliation comparison of the bank balance with the balance in the company's own records.

Basic EPS computed by dividing income available to common stockholders (net income less any preferred stock dividends) by the weighted-average number of common shares outstanding for the period.

G-2   Glossary

Bill-and-hold occurs when a customer purchases goods but requests that the seller retain physical possession of the goods until a later date.

Billings on construction contract contra account to the asset *construction in progress* recognizing that a customer has been billed for work performed; subtracted from construction in progress to determine balance sheet presentation.

Board of directors establishes corporate policies and appoints officers who manage the corporation.

Bond indenture document that describes specific promises made to bondholders.

Bonds A form of debt consisting of separable units (bonds) that obligates the issuing corporation to repay a stated amount at a specified maturity date and to pay interest to bondholders between the issue date and maturity.

Book value assets minus liabilities as shown in the balance sheet.

Callable allows the issuing company to buy back, or call, outstanding bonds from the bondholders before their scheduled maturity date.

Capital budgeting the process of evaluating the purchase of operational assets.

Capital markets mechanisms that foster the allocation of resources efficiently.

Capital structure the mixture of liabilities and shareholders' equity in a company.

Cash currency and coins, balances in checking accounts, and items acceptable for deposit in these accounts, such as checks and money orders received from customers.

Cash disbursements journal record of cash disbursements.

Cash equivalents short-term investments that have a maturity date no longer than three months from the date of purchase.

Cash flows from financing activities both inflows and outflows of cash resulting from the external financing of a business.

Cash flows from investing activities both outflows and inflows of cash caused by the acquisition and disposition of assets.

Cash flows from operating activities both inflows and outflows of cash that result from activities reported on the income statement.

Cash receipts journal record of cash receipts.

Cash surrender value a determinable amount of money that can be received in exchange for surrendering a life insurance policy while the insured is still alive.

Cash-basis accounting measures income as the difference between cash receipts and cash disbursements during a reporting period from transactions related to providing goods and services to customers.

Certified Public Accountants (CPAS) licensed individuals who can represent that the financial statements have been audited in accordance with generally accepted auditing standards.

Change in accounting estimate a change in an estimate when new information comes to light.

Change in accounting principle switch by a company from one accounting method to another.

Change in reporting entity presentation of consolidated financial statements in place of statements of individual companies, or a change in the specific companies that constitute the group for which consolidated or combined statements are prepared.

Closing process the temporary accounts are reduced to zero balances, and these temporary account balances are closed (transferred) to retained earnings to reflect the changes that have occurred in that account during the period.

Commercial paper unsecured notes sold in minimum denominations of $25,000 with maturities ranging from 30 to 270 days.

Committee on Accounting Procedure (CAP) first private sector body that was delegated the task of setting accounting standards.

Comparability the ability to help users see similarities and differences among events and conditions.

Comparative financial statements corresponding financial statements from the previous years accompanying the issued financial statements.

Compensating balance specified balance (usually some percentage of the committee amount) a borrower of a loan is asked to maintain in a low-interest or noninterest-bearing account at the bank.

Complete depiction is complete if it includes all information necessary for faithful representation.

Complex capital structure potential common shares are outstanding.

Composite depreciation method physically dissimilar assets are aggregated to gain the convenience of group depreciation.

Compound interest interest computed not only on the initial investment but also on the accumulated interest in previous periods.

Comprehensive income change in shareholders' equity for the period from nonowner sources; equal to net income plus other comprehensive income. Traditional net income plus other nonowner changes in equity.

Conceptual framework deals with theoretical and conceptual issues and provides an underlying structure for current and future accounting and reporting standards.

Confirmatory value confirmation of investor expectations about future cash-generating ability.

Conservatism practice followed in an attempt to ensure that uncertainties and risks inherent in business situations are adequately considered.

Consignment a selling arrangement whereby the consignor physically transfers goods to another company ("consignee") to sell, while legal title and risk of ownership of those goods remain with the consignor during the consignment period.

Consistency permits valid comparisons between different periods.

Consolidated financial statements combination of the separate financial statements of the parent and subsidiary each period into a single aggregate set of financial statements, as if there were only one company.

Construction in progress asset account equivalent to the asset work-in-process inventory in a manufacturing company.

Contingently issuable shares additional shares of common stock to be issued, contingent on the occurrence of some future circumstance.

Contract an agreement that creates legally enforceable rights and obligations. Contracts can be explicit or implicit.

Contract asset asset recognizing that a seller has a conditional right to receive payment after satisfying a performance obligation.

Contract liability a label given to deferred revenue or unearned revenue accounts.

Control usually an investor can control the investee if it owns more than 50% of the investee's voting shares.

Conventional retail method application of the retail inventory method that excludes markdowns in the calculation of the cost-to-retail percentage, as a way to approximate the lower of average cost or market.

Convertible bonds bonds for which bondholders have the option to convert the bonds into shares of stock.

Copyright exclusive right of protection given to a creator of a published work, such as a song, painting, photograph, or book.

Corporation dominant form of business organization that acquires capital from investors in exchange for ownership interest and from creditors by borrowing.

Correction of an error an adjustment a company makes due to an error made.

Cost effectiveness the perceived benefit of increased decision usefulness exceeds the anticipated cost of providing that information.

Cost of goods sold cost of the inventory sold during the period.

Cost recovery method deferral of all gross profit recognition until the cost of the item sold has been recovered.

Cost-to-retail percentage ratio found by dividing goods available for sale at cost by goods available for sale at retail.

Coupons bonds name of the owner was not registered; the holder actually clipped an attached coupon and redeemed it in accordance with instructions on the indenture.

Credit losses losses due to failure by customers to pay amounts owed for purchase of goods or services; also called bad debts, impairments of receivables, and uncollectible accounts.

Credits represent the right side of the account.

Cumulative if the specified dividend is not paid in a given year, the unpaid dividends accumulate and must be made up in a later dividend year before any dividends are paid on common shares.

Current assets includes assets that are cash, will be converted into cash, or will be used up within one year from the balance sheet date (or operating cycle, if longer).

Current costs are the costs that would be incurred to purchase or reproduce an asset.

Current expected credit loss (CECL) model a model used to estimate credit losses (bad debts) for receivables as well as those debt investments that are accounted for as held to maturity or as available for sale.

Current liabilities expected to require the use of current assets for payment, and usually are payable within one year from the balance sheet date (or operating cycle, if longer).

Current maturities of long-term debt the portion of long-term notes, loans, mortgages, and bonds payable that is payable within the next year (or operating cycle, if longer), reported as a current liability.

Current ratio current assets divided by current liabilities.

Date of record specific date stated as to when the determination will be made of the recipient of the dividend.

Debenture bond backed only by the "full faith and credit" of the issuing corporation.

Debits represent the left side of the account.

Debt issue costs Costs of issuing debt securities are called *debt issue costs* and are accounted for the same way as bond discount.

Debt to equity ratio compares resources provided by creditors with resources provided by owners.

Decision usefulness the quality of being useful to decision making.

Default risk a company's ability to pay its obligations when they come due.

Deferred annuity first cash flow occurs more than the one period after the date the agreement begins.

Deferred revenues cash received from a customer for goods or services to be provided in a future period.

Deferred tax asset taxes to be saved in the future when future deductible amounts reduce taxable income (when the temporary differences reverse).

Deferred tax liability taxes to be paid in the future when future taxable amounts become taxable (when the temporary differences reverse).

Deficit debit balance in retained earnings.

Defined benefit pension plans fixed retirement benefits defined by a designated formula, based on employees' years of service and annual compensation.

Defined contribution pension plans fixed annual contributions to a pension fund; employees choose where funds are invested—usually stocks or fixed-income securities.

Depletion allocation of the cost of natural resources.

Depreciation cost allocation for plant and equipment.

Derivatives financial instruments usually created to hedge against risks created by other financial instruments or by transactions that have yet to occur but are anticipated and that "derive" their values or contractually required cash flows from some other security or index.

Detachable stock purchase warrants the investor has the option to purchase a stated number of shares of common stock at a specified option price, within a given period of time.

Development costs for natural resources, costs incurred after the resource has been discovered but before production begins.

Diluted EPS incorporates the dilutive effect of all potential common shares in the calculation of EPS.

Direct financing lease lease in which the lessor finances the asset for the lessee and earns interest revenue over the lease term.

Direct method cash effect of each operating activity (i.e., income statement item) is reported directly on the statement of cash flows.

Direct write-off method an allowance for uncollectible accounts is not used; instead bad debts that do arise are written off as bad debt expense.

Disclosure including pertinent information in the financial statements and accompanying notes.

Disclosure notes additional insights about company operations, accounting principles, contractual agreements, and pending litigation written in notes that accompany the financial statements.

Discontinued operations the discontinuance of a component of an entity whose operations and cash flows can be clearly distinguished from the rest of the entity.

Discount arises when bonds are sold for less than face amount.

Discounting the transfer of a note receivable to a financial institution.

Distinct a good or service is *distinct* if it is both *capable of being distinct* and *separately identifiable from other goods or services in the contract*. It is capable of being distinct if the customer could use the good or service on its own or in combination with other goods and services it could obtain elsewhere. It is separately identifiable if the good or service is distinct in the context of the contract because it is not highly interrelated with other goods and services in the contract. Distinct goods and services are accounted for as separate performance obligations.

Dividend distribution to shareholders of a portion of assets earned.

Dollar-value LIFO (DVL) an inventory costing method comprising layers of dollar value from different periods and using cost indexes to adjust for changes in price levels over time.

Dollar-value LIFO retail method LIFO retail method combined with dollar-value LIFO.

Double-declining-balance (DDB) method 200% of the straight-line rate is multiplied by book value.

Double-entry system dual effect that each transaction has on the accounting equation when recorded.

DuPont framework depict return on equity as determined by profit margin (representing profitability), asset turnover (representing efficiency), and the equity multiplier (representing leverage).

Early extinguishment of debt debt is retired prior to its scheduled maturity date.

Earnings per share (EPS) the amount of income earned by a company expressed on a per share basis.

Earnings quality refers to the ability of reported earnings (income) to predict a company's future earnings.

Economic entity assumption presumes that economic events can be identified specifically with an economic entity.

Economic events events that directly affect the financial position of the company.

G-4   Glossary

Effective interest method calculates interest revenue by multiplying the outstanding balance of the investment by the relevant interest rate.

Effective rate the actual rate at which money grows per year.

Effective tax rate equals tax expense divided by pretax accounting income.

Emerging Issues Task Force (EITF) responsible for providing more timely responses to emerging financial reporting issues.

Employee share purchase plans permit all employees to buy shares directly from their company, often at favorable terms.

Equity method used when an investor can't control, but can significantly influence, the investee. Under the equity method, the investor recognizes in its own income statement its proportionate share of the investee's income.

Estimates predictions of future events.

Ethics a code or moral system that provides criteria for evaluating right and wrong.

Ex-dividend date date. usually one business day before the date of record, and is the first day the stock trades without the right to receive the declared dividend.

Expected cash flow approach adjusts the cash flows, not the discount rate, for the uncertainty or risk of those cash flows.

Expected return on plan assets estimated long-term return on invested assets.

Expenses outflows or other using up of assets or incurrences of liabilities from delivering or producing goods, rendering services, or other activities that constitute the entity's ongoing operations.

Exploration costs for natural resources, expenditures such as drilling a well, or excavating a mine, or any other costs of searching for natural resources.

Extended warranties additional, extended service that covers new problems arising after the buyer takes control of the product.

External events exchanges between the company and separate economic entities.

F.O.B. (free on board) destination legal title to the goods does not pass from the seller to the buyer until the goods arrive at their destination (the customer's location); the seller is responsible for shipping costs and transit insurance.

F.O.B. (free on board) shipping point legal title to the goods passes from the seller to the buyer at the point of shipment (when the seller delivers the goods to the common carrier); the buyer is responsible for shipping costs and transit insurance .

Factor financial institution that buys receivables for cash, handles the billing and collection of the receivables, and charges a fee for this service.

Fair value bases measurements on the price that would be received to sell assets or transfer liabilities in an orderly market transaction.

Fair value hedge a derivative is used to hedge against the exposure to changes in the fair value of an asset or liability or a firm commitment.

Fair value option allows companies to report specified financial assets and liabilities at fair value.

Faithful representation exists when there is agreement between a measure or description and the phenomenon it purports to represent.

Finance leases lessee has, in substance, purchased the lease asset; assumed when one of five classification criteria is met.

Financial accounting provides relevant financial information to various external users.

Financial Accounting Foundation (FAF) responsible for selecting the members of the FASB and its Advisory Council, ensuring adequate funding of FASB activities, and exercising general oversight of the FASB's activities.

Financial Accounting Standards Board (FASB) the current private sector body that has been delegated the task of setting accounting standards.

Financial instrument cash; evidence of an ownership interest in an entity; a contract that imposes on one entity an obligation to deliver cash or another financial instrument, and conveys to the second entity a right to receive cash or another financial instrument; and a contract that imposes on one entity an obligation to exchange financial instruments on potentially unfavorable terms and conveys to a second entity a right to exchange other financial instruments on potentially favorable terms.

Financial leverage by earning a return on borrowed funds that exceeds the cost of borrowing the funds, a company can provide its shareholders with a total return higher than it could achieve by employing equity funds alone.

Financial reporting process of providing financial statement information to external users.

Financial statements primary means of communicating financial information to external parties.

Financing activities involve cash inflows and outflows from transactions with creditors (excluding trade creditors) and owners.

Finished goods products that have been completed in the manufacturing process but have not yet been sold.

First-in, first-out (FIFO) method assumes that items sold are those that were acquired first.

Fixed-asset turnover ratio the effectiveness of managers to use fixed assets to generate sales, measured as net sales divided by average fixed assets.

Foreign currency futures contract agreement that requires the seller to deliver a specific foreign currency at a designated future date at a specific price.

Foreign currency hedge if a derivative is used to hedge the risk that some transactions require settlement in a currency other than the entities' functional currency or that foreign operations will require translation adjustments to reported amounts.

Forward contract calls for delivery on a specific date; is not traded on a market exchange; does not call for a daily cash settlement for price changes in the underlying contract.

Franchise contractual arrangement under which the franchisor grants the franchisee the exclusive right to use the franchisor's trademark or tradename within a geographical area, usually for a specified period of time.

Franchisee individual or corporation given the right to operate a business involving the franchisor's products or services and use its name and other symbols for a specific period of time.

Franchisor grants to the franchisee the right to operate a business involving the franchisor's products or services and use its name and other symbols for a specific period of time.

Fraud an intentional act by one or more individuals among management, those charged with governance, employees, or third parties, involving the use of deception that results in a misstatement in the financial statements that are the subject of an audit.

Free from error information is free from error if it contains no errors or omissions.

Freight-in transportation-in; in a periodic system, freight costs generally are added to this temporary account, which is added to purchases in determining net purchases.

Full-cost method allows costs incurred in searching for oil and gas within a large geographical area to be capitalized as assets and expensed in the future as oil and gas from the successful wells are removed from that area.

Full-disclosure principle financial reports should include any information that could affect the decisions made by external users.

Functional intellectual property has significant stand-alone functionality, such that the intellectual property can perform a function or task, be played, or be aired over various types of media; the seller typically recognizes revenue at the point in time the customer can start using functional intellectual property.

Future deductible amounts the future tax consequence of a temporary difference will be to decrease taxable income relative to accounting income.

Future taxable amounts the future tax consequence of temporary difference will be to increase taxable income relative to accounting income.

Future value amount of money that a dollar will grow to at some point in the future.

Gains increases in equity from peripheral, or incidental, transactions of an entity.

General journal used to record any type of transaction.

General ledger collection of accounts that organizes the accounts and allows for keeping track of increases and decreases and resulting balances

Generally Accepted Accounting Principles (GAAP) set of both broad and specific guidelines that companies should follow when measuring and reporting the information in their financial statements and related notes.

Gift card transferable prepayments for a specified dollar value of goods or services to be delivered at a future date. Gift cards give rise to deferred revenue liabilities until they are redeemed or viewed as not going to be redeemed (broken).

Going concern assumption in the absence of information to the contrary, it is anticipated that a business entity will continue to operate indefinitely.

Governmental Accounting Standards Board (GASB) responsible for developing accounting standards for governmental units such as states and cities.

Gross method The buyer views a discount not taken as part of the cost of inventory; the seller views a discount not taken by the customer as part of sales of revenue.

Gross profit method (gross margin method) estimates cost of goods sold, which is then subtracted from cost of goods available for sale to estimate ending inventory.

Gross profit ratio gross profit (net sales minus cost of goods sold) divided by net sales.

Group depreciation method collection of assets defined as depreciable assets that share similar service lives and other attributes.

Half-year convention record one-half of a full year's depreciation in the year of acquisition and another half year in the year of disposal.

Hedging taking an action that is expected to produce exposure to a particular type of risk that is precisely the opposite of an actual risk to which the company already is exposed.

Historical cost original transaction value.

Horizontal analysis comparison by expressing each item as a percentage of that same item in the financial statements of another year (base amount) in order to more easily see year-to-year changes.

Illegal acts violations of the law, such as bribes, kickbacks, and illegal contributions to political candidates.

Implicit rate of interest rate implicit in the agreement.

Improvements replacement of a major component of an operational asset.

Income from continuing operations revenues, expenses (including income taxes), gains, and losses, excluding those related to discontinued operations and extraordinary items.

Income statement statement of operations or statement of earnings that is used to summarize the profit-generating activities that occurred during a particular reporting period.

Income statement approach estimating an income statement amount directly, rather than basing it on the change in a balance sheet account.

Indirect method the net cash increase or decrease from operating activities is derived indirectly by starting with reported net income and working backwards to convert that amount to a cash basis.

Initial direct costs costs incurred by the lessor that are associated directly with originating a lease and are essential to acquire the lease.

Installment sales method recognizes revenue and costs only when cash payments are received.

Institute of Internal Auditors national organization of accountants providing internal auditing services for their own organizations.

Institute of Management Accountants (IMA) primary national organization of accountants working in industry and government.

Intangible assets operational assets that lack physical substance; examples include patents, copyrights, franchises, and goodwill.

Interest "rent" paid for the use of money for some period of time.

Interest cost interest accrued on the projected benefit obligation calculated as the discount rate multiplied by the projected benefit obligation at the beginning of the year.

Interest rate swap agreement to exchange fixed interest payments for floating rate payments, or vice versa, without exchanging the underlying principal amounts.

Interest-bearing note receivable notes that state a principal and interest rate to be paid by a debtor to a creditor.

Internal control a company's plan to encourage adherence to company policies and procedures, promote operational efficiency, minimize errors and theft, and enhance the reliability and accuracy of accounting data.

Internal events events that directly affect the financial position of the company but don't involve an exchange transaction with another entity.

International Accounting Standards Board (IASB) objectives are to develop a single set of high-quality, understandable global accounting standards, to promote the use of those standards, and to bring about the convergence of national accounting standards and International Accounting Standards.

International Accounting Standards Committee (IASC) umbrella organization formed to develop global accounting standards.

International Financial Reporting Standards (IFRS) developed by the IASB and used by more than 100 countries.

Intrinsic value difference between the market price of the shares and the option price at which they can be acquired.

Inventory goods awaiting sale (finished goods), goods in the course of production (work in process), and goods to be consumed directly or indirectly in production (raw materials). Goods acquired, manufactured, or in the process of being manufactured for sale.

Inventory turnover ratio measures a company's efficiency in managing its investment in inventory.

Investing activities involve the acquisition and sale of long-term assets used in the business and nonoperating investment assets.

Journal a chronological record of all economic events affecting financial position.

Journal entry captures the effect of a transaction on financial position in debit/credit form.

Just-in-time (JIT) system a system used by a manufacturer to coordinate production with suppliers so that raw materials or components arrive just as they are needed in the production process.

Land improvements the cost of parking lots, driveways, and private roads and the costs of fences and lawn and garden sprinkler systems.

last-in, first-out (LIFO) method assumes that the last units purchased are the first ones sold.

Lease payments payments the lessee is required to make in connection with the lease.

Leasehold improvement account title when a lessee makes improvements to leased property that reverts back to the lessor at the end of the lease.

Lessee user of a leased asset.

Lessor owner of a leased asset.

Liabilities probable future sacrifices of economic benefits arising from present obligations of a particular entity to transfer assets or provide services to other entities in the future as a result of past transactions or events.

Licenses allow the customer to access the seller's intellectual property.

LIFO conformity rule if a company uses LIFO to measure taxable income, the company also must use LIFO for external financial reporting.

LIFO inventory pools groups of inventory units based on physical similarities of the individual units.

LIFO liquidation the decline in inventory quantity during the period.

LIFO reserve contra account to inventory used to record the difference between the internal method and LIFO.

Limited liability company owners are not liable for the debts of the business, except to the extent of their investment; all members can be involved with managing the business without losing liability protection; no limitations on the number of owners.

Limited liability partnership similar to a limited liability company, except it doesn't offer all the liability protection available in the limited liability company structure.

Line of credit allows a company to borrow cash without having to follow formal loan procedures and paperwork.

Liquidating dividend when a dividend exceeds the balance in retained earnings and returns invested capital to owners

Liquidity the ability of a company to convert its assets to cash to pay its current liabilities.

Long-term solvency an assessment of whether a company will be able to pay all its liabilities, which includes long-term liabilities.

Loss contingency existing, uncertain situation involving potential loss which will be resolved when some future event occurs.

Losses decreases in equity from peripheral, or incidental, transactions of the entity.

Lower of cost or market subsequent measurement of inventory applied by companies that use LIFO or the retail inventory method. This approach requires companies to report ending inventory at the lower of cost or market.

Lower of cost or net realizable value (NRV) subsequent measurement of inventory applied by companies that use FIFO, average cost, or any other method besides LIFO or the retail inventory method. This approach requires companies to report ending inventory at the lower of cost or net realizable value.

Management's discussion and analysis (MDA) provides a biased but informed perspective of a company's operations, liquidity, and capital resources.

Market (for inventory reporting) Current replacement cost of inventory, not to exceed net realizable value (NRV) or to be lower than NRV minus a normal profit margin.

Material has qualitative or quantitative characteristics that make it matter for decision making.

Measurement process of associating numerical amounts with the elements.

Model Business Corporation Act designed to serve as a guide to states in the development of their corporation statutes.

Modified accelerated cost recovery system (MACRS) federal income tax code allows taxpayers to compute depreciation for their tax returns using this method.

Modified retrospective approach accounting change is applied only to the adoption period with adjustment of the balance of retained earnings at the beginning of the adoption period to capture the cumulative effects of prior periods.

Monetary assets money and claims to receive money, the amount of which is fixed or determinable.

Monetary liabilities obligations to pay amounts of cash, the amount of which is fixed or determinable.

Monetary unit assumption states that financial statement elements should be measured in a particular monetary unit (in the United States, the U.S. dollar).

Mortgage bond backed by a lien on specified real estate owned by the issuer.

Multiple-step income statement format that includes a number of intermediate subtotals before arriving at income from continuing operations.

Natural resources oil and gas deposits, timber tracts, and mineral deposits.

Net income Net income is the difference between revenues and expenses.

Net markdown net effect of the change in selling price (increase, decrease, increase).

Net markup net effect of the change in selling price (increase, increase, decrease).

Net method The buyer considers the cost of inventory to include the net, after-discount amount, and any discounts not taken are reported as interest expense; the seller considers sales revenue to be the net amount, after discount, and any discounts not taken by the customer are included in sales revenue.

Net operating cash flow difference between cash receipts and cash disbursements from providing goods and services.

Net operating loss negative taxable income because tax-deductible expenses exceed taxable revenues.

Net operating loss carryforward offsets future taxable income with an NOL to provide a reduction of taxes payable in that future period; therefore, gives rise to a deferred tax asset because it is a future deductible amount.

Net realizable value estimated selling prices in the ordinary course of business, less reasonably predictable costs of completion, disposal, and transportation.

Neutral implies freedom from bias.

Non-gaap earnings actual (GAAP) earnings reduced by any expenses the reporting company feels are unusual and should be excluded.

Noncash investing and financing activities transactions that do not increase or decrease cash but that result in significant investing and financing activities.

Noncumulative if the specified dividend is not declared in any given year, it need never be paid.

Noninterest-bearing note notes for which the interest is deducted from the face amount of the note to determine the cash proceeds made available to the borrower at the outset.

Nonoperating income includes revenues, expenses, gains, and losses related to peripheral or incidental activities of the company.

Nonparticipating preferred shareholder dividends are limited to the stated amount.

Notes payable promissory notes (essentially an IOU) that obligate the issuing corporation to repay a stated amount at or by a specified maturity date and to pay interest to the lender between the issue date and maturity.

Notes receivable receivables supported by a formal agreement or note that specifies payment terms.

Objectives-oriented/principles-based accounting standards approach to standard setting stresses professional judgment, as opposed to following a list of rules.

Operating activities inflows and outflows of cash related to transactions entering into the determination of net income.

Operating cycle period of time necessary to convert cash to raw materials, raw materials to finished product, the finished product to receivables, and then finally receivables back to cash.

Operating income includes revenues, expenses, gains, and losses directly related to the principal revenue-generating activities of the company.

Operating leases fundamental rights and responsibilities of ownership are retained by the lessor and the lessee merely is using the asset temporarily.

Operating segment a component of an enterprise that engages in business activities from which it may earn revenues and incur expenses (including revenues and expenses relating to transactions with other companies of the same enterprise); whose operating results are regularly reviewed by the enterprise's chief operating decision maker to make decisions about resources to be allocated to the segment and assess its performance; for which discrete financial information is available.

Operational risk how adept a company is at withstanding various events and circumstances that might impair its ability to earn profits.

Option gives the holder the right either to buy or sell a financial instrument at a specified price.

Option pricing models statistical models that incorporate information about a company's stock and the terms of the stock option to estimate the option's fair value.

Ordinary annuity cash flows occur at the end of each period.

Organization costs costs related to organizing a new entity, such as legal fees and state filing fees to incorporate.

Other comprehensive income (OCI) changes in stockholders' equity other than transactions with owners and other than items that affect net income.

Paid-in capital invested capital consisting primarily of amounts invested by shareholders when they purchase shares of stock from the corporation.

Parenthetical comments/modifying comments supplemental information disclosed on the face of financial statements.

Participating preferred shareholders are allowed to receive additional dividends beyond the stated amount.

Patent exclusive right to manufacture a product or to use a process.

Pension plan assets employer contributions and accumulated earnings on the investment of those contributions to be used to pay retirement benefits to retired employees.

Performance obligations promises to transfer goods and services to a customer, They are satisfied when the seller transfers *control* of goods or services to the customer.

Periodic inventory system a system of accounting for inventory that involves an adjusting entry at the end of the period to update the balances of the inventory account and the cost of goods sold account for purchases, sales, and returns during the period.

Periodicity assumption allows the life of a company to be divided into artificial time periods to provide timely information.

Permanent accounts represent assets, liabilities, and shareholders' equity at a point in time.

Permanent difference difference between pretax accounting income and taxable income and, consequently, between the reported amount of an asset or liability in the financial statements and its tax basis that will not "reverse" resulting from transactions and events that under existing tax law will never affect taxable income or taxes payable.

Perpetual inventory system a system of accounting for inventory by continuously adjusting the balance of the inventory account for each purchase, sale, or return of inventory; the cost of goods sold account is adjusted for each sale or return of inventory by customers.

Pledging a promise to relinquish control of an asset (or assets) in payment (or partial payment) of an amount due.

Post-closing trial balance verifies that the closing entries were prepared and posted correctly and that the accounts are now ready for next year's transactions.

Posting transferring debits and credits recorded in individual journal entries to the specific accounts affected.

Potential common shares securities that, while not being common stock, may become common stock through their exercise, conversion, or issuance and therefore dilute (reduce) earnings per share.

Predictive value confirmation of investor expectations about future cash-generating ability.

Preferred stock typically has a preference (a) to a specified amount of dividends (stated dollar amount per share or percentage of par value per share) and (b) to distribution of assets in the event the corporation is dissolved.

Premium arises when bonds are sold for more than face amount.

Prepaid expenses costs of assets acquired in one period and expensed in a future period.

Prepayments/deferrals the cash flow precedes either expense or revenue recognition.

Present value Present value is today's equivalent of a particular amount in the future, after backing out the time value of money.

Principal controls goods or services and is responsible for providing them to the customer.

Prior period adjustment addition to or reduction in the beginning retained earnings balance in a statement of shareholders' equity due to a correction of an error.

Prior service cost the cost of credit given for an amendment to a pension plan to employee service rendered in prior years.

Product costs costs associated with products and expensed as cost of goods sold only when the related products are sold.

Profit margin on sales net income divided by net sales; measures the amount of net income achieved per sales dollar.

Projected benefit obligation (PBO) the discounted present value of estimated retirement benefits earned so far by employees, applying the plan's pension formula using projected future compensation levels.

Property dividend when a noncash asset is distributed.

Property, plant, and equipment tangible, long-lived assets used in the operations of the business, such as land, buildings, equipment, machinery, furniture, and vehicles, as well as natural resources, such as mineral mines, timber tracts, and oil wells .

Prospective approach effects of a change are reflected in the financial statements of only the year of the change and future years

Proxy statement contains disclosures on compensation to directors and executives; sent to all shareholders each year.

Purchase commitments contracts that obligate a company to purchase a specified amount of merchandise or raw materials at specified prices on or before specified dates.

Purchase discounts reductions in the amount to be paid if remittance is made within a designated period of time.

Purchase option a provision of some lease contracts that gives the lessee the option of purchasing the leased property during, or at the end of, the lease term at a specified price.

Purchase return a reduction in both inventory and accounts payable (if the account has not yet been paid) at the time of the return.

Purchases journal records the purchase of merchandise on account.

Quality-assurance warranty obligation by the seller to make repairs or replace products that are later demonstrated to be defective for some period of time after the sale.

Quasi reorganization a firm undergoing financial difficulties, but with favorable future prospects, may use a quasi reorganization to write down inflated asset values and eliminate an accumulated deficit.

Rate of return on stock investment
$$\frac{\text{Dividends + Share price appreciation}}{\text{Initial investment}}$$

Ratio analysis comparison of accounting numbers to evaluate the performance and risk of a firm.

Raw materials components purchased from suppliers that will become part of the finished product.

Realization principle realization principle bases revenue recognition on completion of the earnings process and reasonable certainty about collectibility.

Rearrangements expenditures made to restructure an asset without addition, replacement, or improvement.

Receivables a company's claims to the future collection of cash, other assets, or services.

Receivables turnover ratio indicates how quickly a company is able to collect its accounts receivable.

Recognition process of admitting information into the basic financial statements.

Redemption privilege might allow preferred shareholders the option, under specified conditions, to return their shares for a predetermined redemption price.

Refund Liability amount the seller estimates will be refunded to customers who make returns.

Related-party transactions transactions with owners, management, families of owners or management, affiliated companies, and other parties that can significantly influence or be influenced by the company.

Relevance one of the primary decision-specific qualities that make accounting information useful; made up of predictive value and/or feedback value and timeliness.

Replacement depreciation method depreciation is recorded when assets are replaced.

Residual asset carrying amount of a leased asset not transferred to the lessee.

Residual value or salvage value, the amount the company expects to receive for the asset at the end of its service life less any anticipated disposal costs.

Restoration costs costs to restore land or other property to its original condition after extraction of the natural resource ends.

Restricted stock shares issued in the name of the employee, subject to forfeiture by the employee if employment is terminated within some specified number of years from the date of grant.

Restricted stock units right to receive shares, subject to forfeiture by the employee if employment is terminated within some specified number of years from the date of grant.

Restructuring costs costs associated with plans by management to materially change either the scope or manner in which its company's operations are conducted.

Retained earnings amounts earned by the corporation on behalf of its shareholders and not (yet) distributed to them as dividends.

Retired stock shares repurchased and not designated as treasury stock, assuming the same status as authorized but unissued shares, as if never issued

Retirement depreciation method records depreciation when assets are disposed of and measures depreciation as the difference between the proceeds received and cost.

Retrospective approach financial statements issued in previous years are revised to reflect the impact of an accounting change whenever those statements are presented again for comparative purpose.

Return on assets (ROA) a company's profitability in relation to overall resources, measured as net income divided by average total assets.

Return on equity (ROE) amount of profit management can generate from shareholders' equity, measured as net income divided by average shareholders' equity.

Revenue/expense approach recognition and measurement of revenues and expenses are emphasized.

Revenues inflows of assets or settlements of liabilities (or a combination of both) from delivering or producing goods, rendering services, or other activities that constitute the entity's ongoing major or central operations.

Reverse stock split when a company decreases, rather than increases, its outstanding shares.

Reversing entries optional entries that remove the effects of some of the adjusting entries made at the end of the previous reporting period for the sole purpose of simplifying journal entries made during the new period.

Right of conversion shareholders' right to exchange shares of preferred stock for common stock at specified conversion ratio.

Right of return customers' right to return merchandise to retailers if they are not satisfied.

Rules-based accounting standards a list of rules for choosing the appropriate accounting treatment for a transaction.

S corporation has characteristics of both regular corporations and partnerships.

Sale-leaseback transaction the owner of an asset sells it and immediately leases it back from the new owner.

Sales discounts cash discounts; represent reductions not in the selling price of a good or service but in the amount to be received from a credit customer if the amount is paid within a specific period of time.

Sales journal records credit sales.

Sales return the return of merchandise for a refund or for credit to be applied to other purchases.

Sales-type lease lessor transfers control of lease asset to lessee, with or without a selling profit on the sale of the asset.

Securities and Exchange Commission (SEC) has the authority to set accounting standards for companies, but it relies on the private sector to do so.

Securities available-for-sale debt securities the investor acquires for purposes other than active trading or to be held to maturity.

Securities to be held-to-maturity debt securities for which the investor has the "positive intent and ability" to hold the securities to maturity.

Securitization the company creates a special purpose entity (SPE), usually a trust or a subsidiary; the SPE buys a pool of trade receivables, credit card receivables, or loans from the company and then sells related securities.

Selling profit when the fair value of the asset (usually the present value of the lease payments, or "selling price") exceeds the cost or carrying value of the asset sold.

Separation of duties an internal control technique in which various functions are distributed amongst employees to provide cross-checking that encourages accuracy and discourages fraud.

Serial bonds more structured (and less popular) way to retire bonds on a piecemeal basis.

Service cost increase in the projected benefit obligation attributable to employee service performed during the period.

Service life (useful life) the estimated use that the company expects to receive from the asset.

Service method allocation approach that reflects the declining service pattern of the prior service cost.

Short-term investments investments not classified as cash equivalents that the company has the ability and intent to sell within one year (or operating cycle if longer).

Significant influence effective control is absent but the investor is able to affect the operating and financial policies of the investee (usually is the case when investor holds between 20% and 50% of the investee's voting shares).

Simple capital structure a firm that has no potential common shares (outstanding securities that could potentially dilute earnings per share).

Simple interest computed by multiplying an initial investment times both the applicable interest rate and the period of time for which the money is used.

Single-step income statement format that groups all revenues and gains together and all expenses and losses together.

Sinking fund debentures bonds that must be redeemed on a prespecified year-by-year basis; administered by a trustee who repurchases bonds in the open market.

Source documents relay essential information about each transaction to the accountant, e.g., sales invoices, bills from suppliers, cash register tapes.

Special journal record of a repetitive type of transaction, e.g., a sales journal.

Specific identification method each unit sold during the period or each unit on hand at the end of the period is matched with its actual cost.

Specific interest method for interest capitalization, rates from specific construction loans to the extent of specific borrowings are used before using the average rate of other debt.

Stand-alone selling price the amount at which the good or service is sold separately under similar circumstances.

Start-up costs whenever a company introduces a new product or service, or commences business in a new territory or with a new customer, it incurs one-time costs that are expensed in the period incurred.

Statement of cash flows change statement summarizing the transactions that caused cash to change during the period.

Statement of shareholders' equity statement disclosing the source of changes in the shareholders' equity accounts.

Stock appreciation rights (SARS) awards that enable an employee to benefit by the amount that the market price of the company's stock rises above a specified amount, without having to buy shares.

Stock dividend distribution of additional shares of stock to current shareholders of the corporation.

Stock options employees aren't actually awarded shares, but rather are given the option to buy shares at a specified exercise price within some specified number of years from the date of grant.

Stock split stock distribution of 25% or higher, sometimes called a *large* stock dividend.

Straight-line method recording interest each period at the same dollar amount.

Straight-line method allocation of an equal amount to each year. For depreciation of plant and equipment or amortization of intangible assets, an equal amount of the allocation base is allocated to each year of the asset's service life. This method is sometimes used for allocation of other assets, and liabilities, over time.

Subordinated debenture the holder is not entitled to receive any liquidation payments until the claims of other specified debt issues are satisfied.

Subsequent event a significant development that takes place after the company's fiscal year-end but before the financial statements are issued.

Subsidiary ledger record of a group of subsidiary accounts associated with a particular general ledger control account.

Successful efforts method requires that exploration costs that are known not to have resulted in the discovery of oil or gas be included as expense in the period the expenditures are made.

Sum-of-the-years'-digits (SYD) method systematic acceleration of depreciation by multiplying the depreciable base by a fraction that declines each year.

Supplemental schedules and tables reports containing more detailed information than is shown in the primary financial statements.

Symbolic intellectual property has usefulness to the customer that depends on the seller's ongoing activities, so it transfers a right of access; the seller recognizes revenue over the period of time the customer accesses the IP.

T-account account with space at the top for the account title and two sides for recording increases and decreases.

Tax basis of an asset or liability is its original value for tax purposes reduced by any amounts included to date on tax returns.

Technological feasibility established when the enterprise has completed all planning, designing, coding, and testing activities that are necessary to establish that the product can be produced to meet its design specifications including functions, features, and technical performance requirements.

Temporary accounts represent changes in the retained earnings component of shareholders' equity for a corporation caused by revenue, expense, gain, and loss transactions.

Temporary difference difference between pretax accounting income and taxable income and, consequently, between the reported amount of an asset or liability in the financial statements and its tax basis which will "reverse" in later years.

Time value of money money can be invested today to earn interest and grow to a larger dollar amount in the future.

Time-based methods allocates the cost base according to the passage of time.

Timeliness information that is available to users early enough to allow its use in the decision process.

Times interest earned ratio a way to gauge the ability of a company to satisfy its fixed debt obligations by comparing interest charges with the income available to pay those charges.

Trade discounts percentage reduction from the list price.

Trade notes payable formally recognized by a written promissory note.

Trademark (tradename) exclusive right to display a word, a slogan, a symbol, or an emblem that distinctively identifies a company, a product, or a service.

Trading securities debt securities the investor (usually a financial institution) acquires principally for the purpose of selling in the near term.

Transaction analysis process of reviewing the source documents to determine the dual effect on the accounting equation and the specific elements involved.

Transaction price the amount the seller expects to be entitled to receive from the customer in exchange for providing goods and services.

Transactions economic events.

Transportation-in freight-in; in a periodic system, freight costs generally are added to this temporary account, which is added to purchases in determining net purchases.

Treasury stock shares repurchased and not retired.

Troubled debt restructuring the original terms of a debt agreement are changed as a result of financial difficulties experienced by the debtor (borrower).

Trustee person who accepts employer contributions, invests the contributions, accumulates the earnings on the investments, and pays benefits from the plan assets to retired employees or their beneficiaries.

Unadjusted trial balance a list of the general ledger accounts and their balances at a particular date.

Understandability users must understand the information within the context of the decision being made.

Units-of-production method computes a depreciation rate per measure of activity and then multiplies this rate by actual activity to determine periodic depreciation.

Unrealized holding gains and losses gains and losses that arise from holding an investment during a period in which its fair value changes.

Valuation allowance indirect reduction (contra account) in a deferred tax asset when it is more likely than not that some portion or all of the deferred tax asset will not be realized.

Variable consideration transaction price is uncertain because it includes an amount that varies depending on the occurrence or nonoccurrence of a future event.

Verifiability implies a consensus among different measurers.

Vertical analysis expression of each item in the financial statements as a percentage of an appropriate corresponding total, or base amount, but within the same year.

Vested benefits benefits that employees have the right to receive even if their employment were to cease today.

Weighted-average interest method for interest capitalization, weighted-average rate on all interest-bearing debt, including all construction loans, is used.

With recourse the seller retains the risk of uncollectibility.

Without recourse the buyer assumes the risk of bad debts.

Work-in-process inventory products that are not yet complete in the manufacturing process.

Working capital differences between current assets and current liabilities.

Worksheet used to organize the accounting information needed to prepare adjusting and closing entries and the financial statements.

Subject Index

Notes: Page numbers followed by n indicate material in footnotes. General information about standards and standard-setting organizations may be found in this index. Specific standards and pronouncements are listed in the Accounting Standards Index.

Accounting Standards Index

Present and Future Value Tables

This table shows the future value of $1 at various interest rates (i) and time periods (n). It is used to calculate the future value of any single amount.

TABLE 1 Future Value of $1

$$FV = \$1(1 + i)^n$$

n/i	1.0%	1.5%	2.0%	2.5%	3.0%	3.5%	4.0%	4.5%	5.0%	5.5%	6.0%	7.0%	8.0%	9.0%	10.0%	11.0%	12.0%	20.0%
1	1.01000	1.01500	1.02000	1.02500	1.03000	1.03500	1.04000	1.04500	1.05000	1.05500	1.06000	1.07000	1.08000	1.09000	1.10000	1.11000	1.12000	1.20000
2	1.02010	1.03022	1.04040	1.05063	1.06090	1.07123	1.08160	1.09203	1.10250	1.11303	1.12360	1.14490	1.16640	1.18810	1.21000	1.23210	1.25440	1.44000
3	1.03030	1.04568	1.06121	1.07689	1.09273	1.10872	1.12486	1.14117	1.15763	1.17424	1.19102	1.22504	1.25971	1.29503	1.33100	1.36763	1.40493	1.72800
4	1.04060	1.06136	1.08243	1.10381	1.12551	1.14752	1.16986	1.19252	1.21551	1.23882	1.26248	1.31080	1.36049	1.41158	1.46410	1.51807	1.57352	2.07360
5	1.05101	1.07728	1.10408	1.13141	1.15927	1.18769	1.21665	1.24618	1.27628	1.30696	1.33823	1.40255	1.46933	1.53862	1.61051	1.68506	1.76234	2.48832
6	1.06152	1.09344	1.12616	1.15969	1.19405	1.22926	1.26532	1.30226	1.34010	1.37884	1.41852	1.50073	1.58687	1.67710	1.77156	1.87041	1.97382	2.98598
7	1.07214	1.10984	1.14869	1.18869	1.22987	1.27228	1.31593	1.36086	1.40710	1.45468	1.50363	1.60578	1.71382	1.82804	1.94872	2.07616	2.21068	3.58318
8	1.08286	1.12649	1.17166	1.21840	1.26677	1.31681	1.36857	1.42210	1.47746	1.53469	1.59385	1.71819	1.85093	1.99256	2.14359	2.30454	2.47596	4.29982
9	1.09369	1.14339	1.19509	1.24886	1.30477	1.36290	1.42331	1.48610	1.55133	1.61909	1.68948	1.83846	1.99900	2.17189	2.35795	2.55804	2.77308	5.15978
10	1.10462	1.16054	1.21899	1.28008	1.34392	1.41060	1.48024	1.55297	1.62889	1.70814	1.79085	1.96715	2.15892	2.36736	2.59374	2.83942	3.10585	6.19174
11	1.11567	1.17795	1.24337	1.31209	1.38423	1.45997	1.53945	1.62285	1.71034	1.80209	1.89830	2.10485	2.33164	2.58043	2.85312	3.15176	3.47855	7.43008
12	1.12683	1.19562	1.26824	1.34489	1.42576	1.51107	1.60103	1.69588	1.79586	1.90121	2.01220	2.25219	2.51817	2.81266	3.13843	3.49845	3.89598	8.91610
13	1.13809	1.21355	1.29361	1.37851	1.46853	1.56396	1.66507	1.77220	1.88565	2.00577	2.13293	2.40985	2.71962	3.06580	3.45227	3.88328	4.36349	10.69932
14	1.14947	1.23176	1.31948	1.41297	1.51259	1.61869	1.73168	1.85194	1.97993	2.11609	2.26090	2.57853	2.93719	3.34173	3.79750	4.31044	4.88711	12.83918
15	1.16097	1.25023	1.34587	1.44830	1.55797	1.67535	1.80094	1.93528	2.07893	2.23248	2.39656	2.75903	3.17217	3.64248	4.17725	4.78459	5.47357	15.40702
16	1.17258	1.26899	1.37279	1.48451	1.60471	1.73399	1.87298	2.02237	2.18287	2.35526	2.54035	2.95216	3.42594	3.97031	4.59497	5.31089	6.13039	18.48843
17	1.18430	1.28802	1.40024	1.52162	1.65285	1.79468	1.94790	2.11338	2.29202	2.48480	2.69277	3.15882	3.70002	4.32763	5.05447	5.89509	6.86604	22.18611
18	1.19615	1.30734	1.42825	1.55966	1.70243	1.85749	2.02582	2.20848	2.40662	2.62147	2.85434	3.37993	3.99602	4.71712	5.55992	6.54355	7.68997	26.62333
19	1.20811	1.32695	1.45681	1.59865	1.75351	1.92250	2.10685	2.30786	2.52695	2.76565	3.02560	3.61653	4.31570	5.14166	6.11591	7.26334	8.61276	31.94800
20	1.22019	1.34686	1.48595	1.63862	1.80611	1.98979	2.19112	2.41171	2.65330	2.91776	3.20714	3.86968	4.66096	5.60441	6.72750	8.06231	9.64629	38.33760
21	1.23239	1.36706	1.51567	1.67958	1.86029	2.05943	2.27877	2.52024	2.78596	3.07823	3.39956	4.14056	5.03383	6.10881	7.40025	8.94917	10.80385	46.00512
25	1.28243	1.45095	1.64061	1.85394	2.09378	2.36324	2.66584	3.00543	3.38635	3.81339	4.29187	5.42743	6.84848	8.62308	10.83471	13.58546	17.00006	95.39622
30	1.34785	1.56308	1.81136	2.09757	2.42726	2.80679	3.24340	3.74532	4.32194	4.98395	5.74349	7.61226	10.06266	13.26768	17.44940	22.89230	29.95992	237.37631
40	1.48886	1.81402	2.20804	2.68506	3.26204	3.95926	4.80102	5.81636	7.03999	8.51331	10.28572	14.97446	21.72452	31.40942	45.25926	65.00087	93.05097	1469.77160

This table shows the present value of $1 at various interest rates (*i*) and time periods (*n*). It is used to calculate the present value of any single amount.

TABLE 2 Present Value of $1

$$PV = \frac{\$1}{(1+i)^n}$$

n/i	1.0%	1.5%	2.0%	2.5%	3.0%	3.5%	4.0%	4.5%	5.0%	5.5%	6.0%	7.0%	8.0%	9.0%	10.0%	11.0%	12.0%	20.0%
1	0.99010	0.98522	0.98039	0.97561	0.97087	0.96618	0.96154	0.95694	0.95238	0.94787	0.94340	0.93458	0.92593	0.91743	0.90909	0.90090	0.89286	0.83333
2	0.98030	0.97066	0.96117	0.95181	0.94260	0.93351	0.92456	0.91573	0.90703	0.89845	0.89000	0.87344	0.85734	0.84168	0.82645	0.81162	0.79719	0.69444
3	0.97059	0.95632	0.94232	0.92860	0.91514	0.90194	0.88900	0.87630	0.86384	0.85161	0.83962	0.81630	0.79383	0.77218	0.75131	0.73119	0.71178	0.57870
4	0.96098	0.94218	0.92385	0.90595	0.88849	0.87144	0.85480	0.83856	0.82270	0.80722	0.79209	0.76290	0.73503	0.70843	0.68301	0.65873	0.63552	0.48225
5	0.95147	0.92826	0.90573	0.88385	0.86261	0.84197	0.82193	0.80245	0.78353	0.76513	0.74726	0.71299	0.68058	0.64993	0.62092	0.59345	0.56743	0.40188
6	0.94205	0.91454	0.88797	0.86230	0.83748	0.81350	0.79031	0.76790	0.74622	0.72525	0.70496	0.66634	0.63017	0.59627	0.56447	0.53464	0.50663	0.33490
7	0.93272	0.90103	0.87056	0.84127	0.81309	0.78599	0.75992	0.73483	0.71068	0.68744	0.66506	0.62275	0.58349	0.54703	0.51316	0.48166	0.45235	0.27908
8	0.92348	0.88771	0.85349	0.82075	0.78941	0.75941	0.73069	0.70319	0.67684	0.65160	0.62741	0.58201	0.54027	0.50187	0.46651	0.43393	0.40388	0.23257
9	0.91434	0.87459	0.83676	0.80073	0.76642	0.73373	0.70259	0.67290	0.64461	0.61763	0.59190	0.54393	0.50025	0.46043	0.42410	0.39092	0.36061	0.19381
10	0.90529	0.86167	0.82035	0.78120	0.74409	0.70892	0.67556	0.64393	0.61391	0.58543	0.55839	0.50835	0.46319	0.42241	0.38554	0.35218	0.32197	0.16151
11	0.89632	0.84893	0.80426	0.76214	0.72242	0.68495	0.64958	0.61620	0.58468	0.55491	0.52679	0.47509	0.42888	0.38753	0.35049	0.31728	0.28748	0.13459
12	0.88745	0.83639	0.78849	0.74356	0.70138	0.66178	0.62460	0.58966	0.55684	0.52598	0.49697	0.44401	0.39711	0.35553	0.31863	0.28584	0.25668	0.11216
13	0.87866	0.82403	0.77303	0.72542	0.68095	0.63940	0.60057	0.56427	0.53032	0.49856	0.46884	0.41496	0.36770	0.32618	0.28966	0.25751	0.22917	0.09346
14	0.86996	0.81185	0.75788	0.70773	0.66112	0.61778	0.57748	0.53997	0.50507	0.47257	0.44230	0.38782	0.34046	0.29925	0.26333	0.23199	0.20462	0.07789
15	0.86135	0.79985	0.74301	0.69047	0.64186	0.59689	0.55526	0.51672	0.48102	0.44793	0.41727	0.36245	0.31524	0.27454	0.23939	0.20900	0.18270	0.06491
16	0.85282	0.78803	0.72845	0.67362	0.62317	0.57671	0.53391	0.49447	0.45811	0.42458	0.39365	0.33873	0.29189	0.25187	0.21763	0.18829	0.16312	0.05409
17	0.84438	0.77639	0.71416	0.65720	0.60502	0.55720	0.51337	0.47318	0.43630	0.40245	0.37136	0.31657	0.27027	0.23107	0.19784	0.16963	0.14564	0.04507
18	0.83602	0.76491	0.70016	0.64117	0.58739	0.53836	0.49363	0.45280	0.41552	0.38147	0.35034	0.29586	0.25025	0.21199	0.17986	0.15282	0.13004	0.03756
19	0.82774	0.75361	0.68643	0.62553	0.57029	0.52016	0.47464	0.43330	0.39573	0.36158	0.33051	0.27651	0.23171	0.19449	0.16351	0.13768	0.11611	0.03130
20	0.81954	0.74247	0.67297	0.61027	0.55368	0.50257	0.45639	0.41464	0.37689	0.34273	0.31180	0.25842	0.21455	0.17843	0.14864	0.12403	0.10367	0.02608
21	0.81143	0.73150	0.65978	0.59539	0.53755	0.48557	0.43883	0.39679	0.35894	0.32486	0.29416	0.24151	0.19866	0.16370	0.13513	0.11174	0.09256	0.02174
24	0.78757	0.69954	0.62172	0.55288	0.49193	0.43796	0.39012	0.34770	0.31007	0.27666	0.24698	0.19715	0.15770	0.12640	0.10153	0.08170	0.06588	0.01258
25	0.77977	0.68921	0.60953	0.53939	0.47761	0.42315	0.37512	0.33273	0.29530	0.26223	0.23300	0.18425	0.14602	0.11597	0.09230	0.07361	0.05882	0.01048
28	0.75684	0.65910	0.57437	0.50088	0.43708	0.38165	0.33348	0.29157	0.25509	0.22332	0.19563	0.15040	0.11591	0.08955	0.06934	0.05382	0.04187	0.00607
29	0.74934	0.64936	0.56311	0.48866	0.42435	0.36875	0.32065	0.27902	0.24295	0.21168	0.18456	0.14056	0.10733	0.08215	0.06304	0.04849	0.03738	0.00506
30	0.74192	0.63976	0.55207	0.47674	0.41199	0.35628	0.30832	0.26700	0.23138	0.20064	0.17411	0.13137	0.09938	0.07537	0.05731	0.04368	0.03338	0.00421
31	0.73458	0.63031	0.54125	0.46511	0.39999	0.34423	0.29646	0.25550	0.22036	0.19018	0.16425	0.12277	0.09202	0.06915	0.05210	0.03935	0.02980	0.00351
40	0.67165	0.55126	0.45289	0.37243	0.30656	0.25257	0.20829	0.17193	0.14205	0.11746	0.09722	0.06678	0.04603	0.03184	0.02209	0.01538	0.01075	0.00068

This table shows the future value of an ordinary annuity of $1 at various interest rates (i) and time periods (n). It is used to calculate the future value of any series of equal payments made at the *end* of each compounding period.

TABLE 3 Future Value of an Ordinary Annuity of $1

$$FVA = \frac{(1+i)^n - 1}{i}$$

n/i	1.0%	1.5%	2.0%	2.5%	3.0%	3.5%	4.0%	4.5%	5.0%	5.5%	6.0%	7.0%	8.0%	9.0%	10.0%	11.0%	12.0%	20.0%
1	1.0000	1.0000	1.0000	1.0000	1.0000	1.0000	1.0000	1.0000	1.0000	1.0000	1.0000	1.0000	1.0000	1.0000	1.0000	1.0000	1.0000	1.0000
2	2.0100	2.0150	2.0200	2.0250	2.0300	2.0350	2.0400	2.0450	2.0500	2.0550	2.0600	2.0700	2.0800	2.0900	2.1000	2.1100	2.1200	2.2000
3	3.0301	3.0452	3.0604	3.0756	3.0909	3.1062	3.1216	3.1370	3.1525	3.1680	3.1836	3.2149	3.2464	3.2781	3.3100	3.3421	3.3744	3.6400
4	4.0604	4.0909	4.1216	4.1525	4.1836	4.2149	4.2465	4.2782	4.3101	4.3423	4.3746	4.4399	4.5061	4.5731	4.6410	4.7097	4.7793	5.3680
5	5.1010	5.1523	5.2040	5.2563	5.3091	5.3625	5.4163	5.4707	5.5256	5.5811	5.6371	5.7507	5.8666	5.9847	6.1051	6.2278	6.3528	7.4416
6	6.1520	6.2296	6.3081	6.3877	6.4684	6.5502	6.6330	6.7169	6.8019	6.8881	6.9753	7.1533	7.3359	7.5233	7.7156	7.9129	8.1152	9.9299
7	7.2135	7.3230	7.4343	7.5474	7.6625	7.7794	7.8983	8.0192	8.1420	8.2669	8.3938	8.6540	8.9228	9.2004	9.4872	9.7833	10.0890	12.9159
8	8.2857	8.4328	8.5830	8.7361	8.8923	9.0517	9.2142	9.3800	9.5491	9.7216	9.8975	10.2598	10.6366	11.0285	11.4359	11.8594	12.2997	16.4991
9	9.3685	9.5593	9.7546	9.9545	10.1591	10.3685	10.5828	10.8021	11.0266	11.2563	11.4913	11.9780	12.4876	13.0210	13.5795	14.1640	14.7757	20.7989
10	10.4622	10.7027	10.9497	11.2034	11.4639	11.7314	12.0061	12.2882	12.5779	12.8754	13.1808	13.8164	14.4866	15.1929	15.9374	16.7220	17.5487	25.9587
11	11.5668	11.8633	12.1687	12.4835	12.8078	13.1420	13.4864	13.8412	14.2068	14.5835	14.9716	15.7836	16.6455	17.5603	18.5312	19.5614	20.6546	32.1504
12	12.6825	13.0412	13.4121	13.7956	14.1920	14.6020	15.0258	15.4640	15.9171	16.3856	16.8699	17.8885	18.9771	20.1407	21.3843	22.7132	24.1331	39.5805
13	13.8093	14.2368	14.6803	15.1404	15.6178	16.1130	16.6268	17.1599	17.7130	18.2868	18.8821	20.1406	21.4953	22.9534	24.5227	26.2116	28.0291	48.4966
14	14.9474	15.4504	15.9739	16.5190	17.0863	17.6770	18.2919	18.9321	19.5986	20.2926	21.0151	22.5505	24.2149	26.0192	27.9750	30.0949	32.3926	59.1959
15	16.0969	16.6821	17.2934	17.9319	18.5989	19.2957	20.0236	20.7841	21.5786	22.4087	23.2760	25.1290	27.1521	29.3609	31.7725	34.4054	37.2797	72.0351
16	17.2579	17.9324	18.6393	19.3802	20.1569	20.9710	21.8245	22.7193	23.6575	24.6411	25.6725	27.8881	30.3243	33.0034	35.9497	39.1899	42.7533	87.4421
17	18.4304	19.2014	20.0121	20.8647	21.7616	22.7050	23.6975	24.7417	25.8404	26.9964	28.2129	30.8402	33.7502	36.9737	40.5447	44.5008	48.8837	105.9306
18	19.6147	20.4894	21.4123	22.3863	23.4144	24.4997	25.6454	26.8551	28.1324	29.4812	30.9057	33.9990	37.4502	41.3013	45.5992	50.3959	55.7497	128.1167
19	20.8109	21.7967	22.8406	23.9460	25.1169	26.3572	27.6712	29.0636	30.5390	32.1027	33.7600	37.3790	41.4463	46.0185	51.1591	56.9395	63.4397	154.7400
20	22.0190	23.1237	24.2974	25.5447	26.8704	28.2797	29.7781	31.3714	33.0660	34.8683	36.7856	40.9955	45.7620	51.1601	57.2750	64.2028	72.0524	186.6880
21	23.2392	24.4705	25.7833	27.1833	28.6765	30.2695	31.9692	33.7831	35.7193	37.7861	39.9927	44.8652	50.4229	56.7645	64.0025	72.2651	81.6987	225.0256
30	34.7849	37.5387	40.5681	43.9027	47.5754	51.6227	56.0849	61.0071	66.4388	72.4355	79.0582	94.4608	113.2832	136.3075	164.4940	199.0209	241.3327	1181.8816
40	48.8864	54.2679	60.4020	67.4026	75.4013	84.5503	95.0255	107.0303	120.7998	136.6056	154.7620	199.6351	259.0565	337.8824	442.5926	581.8261	767.0914	7343.8578

This table shows the present value of an oridinary annuity due of $1 at various interest rates (i) and time periods (n). It is used to calculate the present value of any series of equal payments made at the *end* of each compounding period.

TABLE 4 Present Value of an Ordinary Annuity of $1

$$PVA = \frac{1 - \frac{1}{(1+i)^n}}{i}$$

n/i	1.0%	1.5%	2.0%	2.5%	3.0%	3.5%	4.0%	4.5%	5.0%	5.5%	6.0%	7.0%	8.0%	9.0%	10.0%	11.0%	12.0%	20.0%
1	0.99010	0.98522	0.98039	0.97561	0.97087	0.96618	0.96154	0.95694	0.95238	0.94787	0.94340	0.93458	0.92593	0.91743	0.90909	0.90090	0.89286	0.83333
2	1.97040	1.95588	1.94156	1.92742	1.91347	1.89969	1.88609	1.87267	1.85941	1.84632	1.83339	1.80802	1.78326	1.75911	1.73554	1.71252	1.69005	1.52778
3	2.94099	2.91220	2.88388	2.85602	2.82861	2.80164	2.77509	2.74896	2.72325	2.69793	2.67301	2.62432	2.57710	2.53129	2.48685	2.44371	2.40183	2.10648
4	3.90197	3.85438	3.80773	3.76197	3.71710	3.67308	3.62990	3.58753	3.54595	3.50515	3.46511	3.38721	3.31213	3.23972	3.16987	3.10245	3.03735	2.58873
5	4.85343	4.78264	4.71346	4.64583	4.57971	4.51505	4.45182	4.38998	4.32948	4.27028	4.21236	4.10020	3.99271	3.88965	3.79079	3.69590	3.60478	2.99061
6	5.79548	5.69719	5.60143	5.50813	5.41719	5.32855	5.24214	5.15787	5.07569	4.99553	4.91732	4.76654	4.62288	4.48592	4.35526	4.23054	4.11141	3.32551
7	6.72819	6.59821	6.47199	6.34939	6.23028	6.11454	6.00205	5.89270	5.78637	5.68297	5.58238	5.38929	5.20637	5.03295	4.86842	4.71220	4.56376	3.60459
8	7.65168	7.48593	7.32548	7.17014	7.01969	6.87396	6.73274	6.59589	6.46321	6.33457	6.20979	5.97130	5.74664	5.53482	5.33493	5.14612	4.96764	3.83716
9	8.56602	8.36052	8.16224	7.97087	7.78611	7.60769	7.43533	7.26879	7.10782	6.95220	6.80169	6.51523	6.24689	5.99525	5.75902	5.53705	5.32825	4.03097
10	9.47130	9.22218	8.98259	8.75206	8.53020	8.31661	8.11090	7.91272	7.72173	7.53763	7.36009	7.02358	6.71008	6.41766	6.14457	5.88923	5.65022	4.19247
11	10.36763	10.07112	9.78685	9.51421	9.25262	9.00155	8.76048	8.52892	8.30641	8.09254	7.88687	7.49867	7.13896	6.80519	6.49506	6.20652	5.93770	4.32706
12	11.25508	10.90751	10.57534	10.25776	9.95400	9.66333	9.38507	9.11858	8.86325	8.61852	8.38384	7.94269	7.53608	7.16073	6.81369	6.49236	6.19437	4.43922
13	12.13374	11.73153	11.34837	10.98319	10.63496	10.30274	9.98565	9.68285	9.39357	9.11708	8.85268	8.35765	7.90378	7.48690	7.10336	6.74987	6.42355	4.53268
14	13.00370	12.54338	12.10625	11.69091	11.29607	10.92052	10.56312	10.22283	9.89864	9.58965	9.29498	8.74547	8.24424	7.78615	7.36669	6.98187	6.62817	4.61057
15	13.86505	13.34323	12.84926	12.38138	11.93794	11.51741	11.11839	10.73955	10.37966	10.03758	9.71225	9.10791	8.55948	8.06069	7.60608	7.19087	6.81086	4.67547
16	14.71787	14.13126	13.57771	13.05500	12.56110	12.09412	11.65230	11.23402	10.83777	10.46216	10.10590	9.44665	8.85137	8.31256	7.82371	7.37916	6.97399	4.72956
17	15.56225	14.90765	14.29187	13.71220	13.16612	12.65132	12.16567	11.70719	11.27407	10.86461	10.47726	9.76322	9.12164	8.54363	8.02155	7.54879	7.11963	4.77463
18	16.39827	15.67256	14.99203	14.35336	13.75351	13.18968	12.65930	12.15999	11.68959	11.24607	10.82760	10.05909	9.37189	8.75563	8.20141	7.70162	7.24967	4.81219
19	17.22601	16.42617	15.67846	14.97889	14.32380	13.70984	13.13394	12.59329	12.08532	11.60765	11.15812	10.33560	9.60360	8.95011	8.36492	7.83929	7.36578	4.84350
20	18.04555	17.16864	16.35143	15.58916	14.87747	14.21240	13.59033	13.00794	12.46221	11.95038	11.46992	10.59401	9.81815	9.12855	8.51356	7.96333	7.46944	4.86958
21	18.85698	17.90014	17.01121	16.18455	15.41502	14.69797	14.02916	13.40472	12.82115	12.27524	11.76408	10.83553	10.01680	9.29224	8.64869	8.07507	7.56200	4.89132
25	22.02316	20.71961	19.52346	18.42438	17.41315	16.48151	15.62208	14.82821	14.09394	13.41393	12.78336	11.65358	10.67478	9.82258	9.07704	8.42174	7.84314	4.94759
30	25.80771	24.01584	22.39646	20.93029	19.60044	18.39205	17.29203	16.28889	15.37245	14.53375	13.76483	12.40904	11.25778	10.27365	9.42691	8.69379	8.05518	4.97894
40	32.83469	29.91585	27.35548	25.10278	23.11477	21.35507	19.79277	18.40158	17.15909	16.04612	15.04630	13.33171	11.92461	10.75736	9.77905	8.95105	8.24378	4.99660

This table shows the future value of an annuity due of $1 at various interest rates (*i*) and time periods (*n*). It is used to calculate the future value of any series of equal payments made at the *beginning* of each compounding period.

TABLE 5 Future Value of an Annuity Due of $1

$$FVAD = \left[\frac{(1+i)^n - 1}{i}\right] \times (1+i)$$

n/i	1.0%	1.5%	2.0%	2.5%	3.0%	3.5%	4.0%	4.5%	5.0%	5.5%	6.0%	7.0%	8.0%	9.0%	10.0%	11.0%	12.0%	20.0%
1	1.0100	1.0150	1.0200	1.0250	1.0300	1.0350	1.0400	1.0450	1.0500	1.0550	1.0600	1.0700	1.0800	1.0900	1.1000	1.1100	1.1200	1.2000
2	2.0301	2.0452	2.0604	2.0756	2.0909	2.1062	2.1216	2.1370	2.1525	2.1680	2.1836	2.2149	2.2464	2.2781	2.3100	2.3421	2.3744	2.6400
3	3.0604	3.0909	3.1216	3.1525	3.1836	3.2149	3.2465	3.2782	3.3101	3.3423	3.3746	3.4399	3.5061	3.5731	3.6410	3.7097	3.7793	4.3680
4	4.1010	4.1523	4.2040	4.2563	4.3091	4.3625	4.4163	4.4707	4.5256	4.5811	4.6371	4.7507	4.8666	4.9847	5.1051	5.2278	5.3528	6.4416
5	5.1520	5.2296	5.3081	5.3877	5.4684	5.5502	5.6330	5.7169	5.8019	5.8881	5.9753	6.1533	6.3359	6.5233	6.7156	6.9129	7.1152	8.9299
6	6.2135	6.3230	6.4343	6.5474	6.6625	6.7794	6.8983	7.0192	7.1420	7.2669	7.3938	7.6540	7.9228	8.2004	8.4872	8.7833	9.0890	11.9159
7	7.2857	7.4328	7.5830	7.7361	7.8923	8.0517	8.2142	8.3800	8.5491	8.7216	8.8975	9.2598	9.6366	10.0285	10.4359	10.8594	11.2997	15.4991
8	8.3685	8.5593	8.7546	8.9545	9.1591	9.3685	9.5828	9.8021	10.0266	10.2563	10.4913	10.9780	11.4876	12.0210	12.5795	13.1640	13.7757	19.7989
9	9.4622	9.7027	9.9497	10.2034	10.4639	10.7314	11.0061	11.2882	11.5779	11.8754	12.1808	12.8164	13.4866	14.1929	14.9374	15.7220	16.5487	24.9587
10	10.5668	10.8633	11.1687	11.4835	11.8078	12.1420	12.4864	12.8412	13.2068	13.5835	13.9716	14.7836	15.6455	16.5603	17.5312	18.5614	19.6546	31.1504
11	11.6825	12.0412	12.4121	12.7956	13.1920	13.6020	14.0258	14.4640	14.9171	15.3856	15.8699	16.8885	17.9771	19.1407	20.3843	21.7132	23.1331	38.5805
12	12.8093	13.2368	13.6803	14.1404	14.6178	15.1130	15.6268	16.1599	16.7130	17.2868	17.8821	19.1406	20.4953	21.9534	23.5227	25.2116	27.0291	47.4966
13	13.9474	14.4504	14.9739	15.5190	16.0863	16.6770	17.2919	17.9321	18.5986	19.2926	20.0151	21.5505	23.2149	25.0192	26.9750	29.0949	31.3926	58.1959
14	15.0969	15.6821	16.2934	16.9319	17.5989	18.2957	19.0236	19.7841	20.5786	21.4087	22.2760	24.1290	26.1521	28.3609	30.7725	33.4054	36.2797	71.0351
15	16.2579	16.9324	17.6393	18.3802	19.1569	19.9710	20.8245	21.7193	22.6575	23.6411	24.6725	26.8881	29.3243	32.0034	34.9497	38.1899	41.7533	86.4421
16	17.4304	18.2014	19.0121	19.8647	20.7616	21.7050	22.6975	23.7417	24.8404	25.9964	27.2129	29.8402	32.7502	35.9737	39.5447	43.5008	47.8837	104.9306
17	18.6147	19.4894	20.4123	21.3863	22.4144	23.4997	24.6454	25.8551	27.1324	28.4812	29.9057	32.9990	36.4502	40.3013	44.5992	49.3959	54.7497	127.1167
18	19.8109	20.7967	21.8406	22.9460	24.1169	25.3572	26.6712	28.0636	29.5390	31.1027	32.7600	36.3790	40.4463	45.0185	50.1591	55.9395	62.4397	153.7400
19	21.0190	22.1237	23.2974	24.5447	25.8704	27.2797	28.7781	30.3714	32.0660	33.8683	35.7856	39.9955	44.7620	50.1601	56.2750	63.2028	71.0524	185.6880
20	22.2392	23.4705	24.7833	26.1833	27.6765	29.2695	30.9692	32.7831	34.7193	36.7861	38.9927	43.8652	49.4229	55.7645	63.0025	71.2651	80.6987	224.0256
21	23.4716	24.8376	26.2990	27.8629	29.5368	31.3289	33.2480	35.3034	37.5052	39.8643	42.3923	48.0057	54.4568	61.8733	70.4027	80.2143	91.5026	270.0307
25	28.5256	30.5140	32.6709	35.0117	37.5530	40.3131	43.3117	46.5706	50.1135	53.9660	58.1564	67.6765	78.9544	92.3240	108.1818	126.9988	149.3339	566.3773
30	35.1327	38.1018	41.3794	45.0003	49.0027	53.4295	58.3283	63.7524	69.7608	76.4194	83.8017	101.0730	122.3459	148.5752	180.9434	220.9132	270.2926	1418.2579
40	49.3752	55.0819	61.6100	69.0876	77.6633	87.5095	98.8265	111.8467	126.8398	144.1189	164.0477	213.6096	279.7810	368.2919	486.8518	645.8269	859.1424	8812.6294

This table shows the present value of an annuity due of $1 at various interest rates (i) and time periods (n). It is used to calculate the present value of any series of equal payments made at the *beginning* of each compounding period.

TABLE 6 Present Value of an Annuity Due of $1

$$PVAD = \left[\frac{1 - \frac{1}{(1+i)^n}}{i} \right] \times (1+i)$$

n/i	1.0%	1.5%	2.0%	2.5%	3.0%	3.5%	4.0%	4.5%	5.0%	5.5%	6.0%	7.0%	8.0%	9.0%	10.0%	11.0%	12.0%	20.0%
1	1.00000	1.00000	1.00000	1.00000	1.00000	1.00000	1.00000	1.00000	1.00000	1.00000	1.00000	1.00000	1.00000	1.00000	1.00000	1.00000	1.00000	1.00000
2	1.99010	1.98522	1.98039	1.97561	1.97087	1.96618	1.96154	1.95694	1.95238	1.94787	1.94340	1.93458	1.92593	1.91743	1.90909	1.90090	1.89286	1.83333
3	2.97040	2.95588	2.94156	2.92742	2.91347	2.89969	2.88609	2.87267	2.85941	2.84632	2.83339	2.80802	2.78326	2.75911	2.73554	2.71252	2.69005	2.52778
4	3.94099	3.91220	3.88388	3.85602	3.82861	3.80164	3.77509	3.74896	3.72325	3.69793	3.67301	3.62432	3.57710	3.53129	3.48685	3.44371	3.40183	3.10648
5	4.90197	4.85438	4.80773	4.76197	4.71710	4.67308	4.62990	4.58753	4.54595	4.50515	4.46511	4.38721	4.31213	4.23972	4.16987	4.10245	4.03735	3.58873
6	5.85343	5.78264	5.71346	5.64583	5.57971	5.51505	5.45182	5.38998	5.32948	5.27028	5.21236	5.10020	4.99271	4.88965	4.79079	4.69590	4.60478	3.99061
7	6.79548	6.69719	6.60143	6.50813	6.41719	6.32855	6.24214	6.15787	6.07569	5.99553	5.91732	5.76654	5.62288	5.48592	5.35526	5.23054	5.11141	4.32551
8	7.72819	7.59821	7.47199	7.34939	7.23028	7.11454	7.00205	6.89270	6.78637	6.68297	6.58238	6.38929	6.20637	6.03295	5.86842	5.71220	5.56376	4.60459
9	8.65168	8.48593	8.32548	8.17014	8.01969	7.87396	7.73274	7.59589	7.46321	7.33457	7.20979	6.97130	6.74664	6.53482	6.33493	6.14612	5.96764	4.83716
10	9.56602	9.36052	9.16224	8.97087	8.78611	8.60769	8.43533	8.26879	8.10782	7.95220	7.80169	7.51523	7.24689	6.99525	6.75902	6.53705	6.32825	5.03097
11	10.47130	10.22218	9.98259	9.75206	9.53020	9.31661	9.11090	8.91272	8.72173	8.53763	8.36009	8.02358	7.71008	7.41766	7.14457	6.88923	6.65022	5.19247
12	11.36763	11.07112	10.78685	10.51421	10.25262	10.00155	9.76048	9.52892	9.30641	9.09254	8.88687	8.49867	8.13896	7.80519	7.49506	7.20652	6.93770	5.32706
13	12.25508	11.90751	11.57534	11.25776	10.95400	10.66333	10.38507	10.11858	9.86325	9.61852	9.38384	8.94269	8.53608	8.16073	7.81369	7.49236	7.19437	5.43922
14	13.13374	12.73153	12.34837	11.98318	11.63496	11.30274	10.98565	10.68285	10.39357	10.11708	9.85268	9.35765	8.90378	8.48690	8.10336	7.74987	7.42355	5.53268
15	14.00370	13.54338	13.10625	12.69091	12.29607	11.92052	11.56312	11.22283	10.89864	10.58965	10.29498	9.74547	9.24424	8.78615	8.36669	7.98187	7.62817	5.61057
16	14.86505	14.34323	13.84926	13.38138	12.93794	12.51741	12.11839	11.73955	11.37966	11.03758	10.71225	10.10791	9.55948	9.06069	8.60608	8.19087	7.81086	5.67547
17	15.71787	15.13126	14.57771	14.05500	13.56110	13.09412	12.65230	12.23402	11.83777	11.46216	11.10590	10.44665	9.85137	9.31256	8.82371	8.37916	7.97399	5.72956
18	16.56225	15.90765	15.29187	14.71220	14.16612	13.65132	13.16567	12.70719	12.27407	11.86461	11.47726	10.76322	10.12164	9.54363	9.02155	8.54879	8.11963	5.77463
19	17.39827	16.67256	15.99203	15.35336	14.75351	14.18968	13.65930	13.15999	12.68959	12.24607	11.82760	11.05909	10.37189	9.75563	9.20141	8.70162	8.24967	5.81219
20	18.22601	17.42617	16.67846	15.97889	15.32380	14.70984	14.13394	13.59329	13.08532	12.60765	12.15812	11.33560	10.60360	9.95011	9.36492	8.83929	8.36578	5.84350
21	19.04555	18.16864	17.35143	16.58916	15.87747	15.21240	14.59033	14.00794	13.46221	12.95038	12.46992	11.59401	10.81815	10.12855	9.51356	8.96333	8.46944	5.86958
25	22.24339	21.03041	19.91393	18.88499	17.93554	17.05837	16.24696	15.49548	14.79864	14.15170	13.55036	12.46933	11.52876	10.70661	9.98474	9.34814	8.78432	5.93710
30	26.06579	24.37608	22.84438	21.45355	20.18845	19.03577	17.98371	17.02189	16.14107	15.33310	14.59072	13.27767	12.15841	11.19828	10.36961	9.65011	9.02181	5.97472
40	33.16303	30.36458	27.90259	25.73034	23.80822	22.10250	20.58448	19.22966	18.01704	16.92866	15.94907	14.26493	12.87858	11.72552	10.75696	9.93567	9.23303	5.99592

Credits